P9-AON-350

Inside Macintosh™
Volumes I, II, and III

Addison-Wesley Publishing Company, Inc.
Reading, Massachusetts   Menlo Park, California   New York
Don Mills, Ontario   Wokingham, England   Amsterdam   Bonn
Sidney   Singapore   Tokyo   Madrid   San Juan   Paris
Seoul   Milan   Mexico City   Taipei

Copyright © 1985 by Apple Computer, Inc.

All rights reserved. No part of this publication may be reproduced, stored in a retrieval system, or transmitted, in any form or by any means, electronic, mechanical, photocopying, recording, or otherwise, without prior written permission of Apple Computer, Inc. Printed in the United States of America.

Apple, the Apple logo, LaserWriter, and Lisa are registered trademarks of Apple Computer, Inc. Macintosh, the Macintosh logo, MacWrite, MacPaint, MacDraw, and MacWorks are trademarks of Apple Computer, Inc.

Simultaneously published in the United States and Canada.

Written by Caroline Rose with Bradley Hacker, Robert Anders, Katie Withey, Mark Metzler, Steve Chernicoff, Chris Espinosa, Andy Averill, Brent Davis, and Brian Howard, assisted by Sandy Tompkins-Leffler and Louella Pizzuti. Special thanks to Cary Clark and Scott Knaster.

This book was produced using the Apple Macintosh computer and the LaserWriter printer.

ISBN 0-201-17737-4

11 12 13 14 15 16 - MU - 94939291
Eleventh printing, June 1991

Inside Macintosh
Volume I

Warranty Information

ALL IMPLIED WARRANTIES ON THIS MANUAL, INCLUDING IMPLIED WARRANTIES OF MERCHANTABILITY AND FITNESS FOR A PARTICULAR PURPOSE, ARE LIMITED IN DURATION TO NINETY (90) DAYS FROM THE DATE OF THE ORIGINAL RETAIL PURCHASE OF THIS PRODUCT.

Even though Apple has reviewed this manual, APPLE MAKES NO WARRANTY OR REPRESENTATION, EITHER EXPRESS OR IMPLIED, WITH RESPECT TO THIS MANUAL, ITS QUALITY, ACCURACY, MERCHANTABILITY, OR FITNESS FOR A PARTICULAR PURPOSE. AS A RESULT, THIS MANUAL IS SOLD "AS IS," AND YOU, THE PURCHASER, ARE ASSUMING THE ENTIRE RISK AS TO ITS QUALITY AND ACCURACY.

IN NO EVENT WILL APPLE BE LIABLE FOR DIRECT, INDIRECT, SPECIAL, INCIDENTAL, OR CONSEQUENTIAL DAMAGES RESULTING FROM ANY DEFECT OR INACCURACY IN THIS MANUAL, even if advised of the possibility of such damages.

THE WARRANTY AND REMEDIES SET FORTH ABOVE ARE EXCLUSIVE AND IN LIEU OF ALL OTHERS, ORAL OR WRITTEN, EXPRESS OR IMPLIED. No Apple dealer, agent, or employee is authorized to make any modification, extension, or addition to this warranty.

Some states do not allow the exclusion or limitation of implied warranties or liability for incidental or consequential damages, so the above limitation or exclusion may not apply to you. This warranty gives you specific legal rights, and you may also have other rights which vary from state to state.

Contents

PREFACE

ABOUT INSIDE MACINTOSH

Inside Macintosh is a three-volume set of manuals that tells you what you need to know to write software for the Apple® Macintosh™ 128K, 512K, or XL (or a Lisa® running MacWorks™ XL). Although directed mainly toward programmers writing standard Macintosh applications, *Inside Macintosh* also contains the information needed to write simple utility programs, desk accessories, device drivers, or any other Macintosh software. It includes:

■ the user interface guidelines for applications on the Macintosh

■ a complete description of the routines available for your program to call (both those built into the Macintosh and others on disk), along with related concepts and background information

■ a description of the Macintosh 128K and 512K hardware

It does *not* include information about:

■ Programming in general.

■ Getting started as a developer. For this, write to:

> Developer Relations
> Mail Stop 27-S
> Apple Computer, Inc.
> 20525 Mariani Avenue
> Cupertino, CA 95014

■ Any specific development system, except where indicated. You'll need to have additional documentation for the development system you're using.

■ The Standard Apple Numeric Environment (SANE), which your program can access to perform extended-precision floating-point arithmetic and transcendental functions. This environment is described in the *Apple Numerics Manual*.

You should already be familiar with the basic information that's in *Macintosh*, the owner's guide, and have some experience using a standard Macintosh application (such as MacWrite™).

The Language

The routines you'll need to call are written in assembly language, but (with a few exceptions) they're also accessible from high-level languages, such as Pascal on the Lisa Workshop development system. *Inside Macintosh* documents the Lisa Pascal interfaces to the routines and the symbolic names defined for assembly-language programmers using the Lisa Workshop; if you're using a different development system, its documentation should tell you how to apply the information presented here to that system.

Inside Macintosh is intended to serve the needs of both high-level language and assembly-language programmers. Every routine is shown in its Pascal form (if it has one), but assembly-language programmers are told how they can access the routines. Information of interest only to assembly-language programmers is isolated and labeled so that other programmers can conveniently skip it.

Familiarity with Lisa Pascal (or a similar high-level language) is recommended for all readers, since it's used for most examples. Lisa Pascal is described in the documentation for the Lisa Pascal Workshop.

What's in Each Volume

Inside Macintosh consists of three volumes. Volume I begins with the following information of general interest:

- a "road map" to the software and the rest of the documentation

- the user interface guidelines

- an introduction to memory management (the least you need to know, with a complete discussion following in Volume II)

- some general information for assembly-language programmers

It then describes the various parts of the **User Interface Toolbox**, the software in ROM that helps you implement the standard Macintosh user interface in your application. This is followed by descriptions of other, RAM-based software that's similar in function to the User Interface Toolbox. (The software overview in the Road Map chapter gives further details.)

Volume II describes the **Operating System**, the software in ROM that does basic tasks such as input and output, memory management, and interrupt handling. As in Volume I, some functionally similar RAM-based software is then described.

Volume III discusses your program's interface with the Finder and then describes the Macintosh 128K and 512K hardware. A comprehensive summary of all the software is provided, followed by some useful appendices and a glossary of all terms defined in *Inside Macintosh*.

Version Numbers

This edition of *Inside Macintosh* describes the following versions of the software:

- version 105 of the ROM in the Macintosh 128K or 512K

- version 112 of the ROM image installed by MacWorks in the Macintosh XL

- version 1.1 of the Lisa Pascal interfaces and the assembly-language definitions

Some of the RAM-based software is read from the file named System (usually kept in the System Folder). This manual describes the software in the System file whose creation date is May 2, 1984.

A HORSE OF A DIFFERENT COLOR

On an innovative system like the Macintosh, programs don't look quite the way they do on other systems. For example, instead of carrying out a sequence of steps in a predetermined order, your program is driven primarily by user actions (such as clicking and typing) whose order cannot be predicted.

You'll probably find that many of your preconceptions about how to write applications don't apply here. Because of this, and because of the sheer volume of information in *Inside Macintosh*, it's essential that you read the Road Map chapter. It will help you get oriented and figure out where to go next.

THE STRUCTURE OF A TYPICAL CHAPTER

Most chapters of *Inside Macintosh* have the same structure, as described below. Reading through this now will save you a lot of time and effort later on. It contains important hints on how to find what you're looking for within this vast amount of technical documentation.

Every chapter begins with a very brief description of its subject and a list of what you should already know before reading that chapter. Then there's a section called, for example, "About the Window Manager", which gives you more information about the subject, telling you what you can do with it in general, elaborating on related user interface guidelines, and introducing terminology that will be used in the chapter. This is followed by a series of sections describing important related concepts and background information; unless they're noted to be for advanced programmers only, you'll have to read them in order to understand how to use the routines described later.

Before the routine descriptions themselves, there's a section called, for example, "Using the Window Manager". It introduces you to the routines, telling you how they fit into the general flow of an application program and, most important, giving you an idea of which ones you'll need to use. Often you'll need only a few routines out of many to do basic operations; by reading this section, you can save yourself the trouble of learning routines you'll never use.

Then, for the details about the routines, read on to the next section. It gives the calling sequence for each routine and describes all the parameters, effects, side effects, and so on.

Following the routine descriptions, there may be some sections that won't be of interest to all readers. Usually these contain information about advanced techniques, or behind the scenes details for the curious.

For review and quick reference, each chapter ends with a summary of the subject matter, including the entire Pascal interface and a separate section for assembly-language programmers.

CONVENTIONS

The following notations are used in *Inside Macintosh* to draw your attention to particular items of information:

Note: A note that may be interesting or useful

Warning: A point you need to be cautious about

Assembly-language note: A note of interest to assembly-language programmers only

[Not in ROM]

Routines marked with this notation are not part of the Macintosh ROM. Depending on how the interfaces have been set up on the development system you're using, these routines may or may not be available. They're available to users of Lisa Pascal; other users should check the documentation for their development system for more information. (For related information of interest to assembly-language programmers, see chapter 4.)

1 A ROAD MAP

ABOUT THIS CHAPTER

This chapter introduces you to the "inside" of Macintosh: the Operating System and User Interface Toolbox routines that your application program will call. It will help you figure out which software you need to learn more about and how to proceed with the rest of the *Inside Macintosh* documentation. To orient you to the software, it presents a simple example program.

OVERVIEW OF THE SOFTWARE

The routines available for use in Macintosh programs are divided according to function, into what are in most cases called "managers" of the feature that they support. As shown in Figure 1, most are part of either the Operating System or the User Interface Toolbox and are in the Macintosh ROM.

The **Operating System** is at the lowest level; it does basic tasks such as input and output, memory management, and interrupt handling. The **User Interface Toolbox** is a level above the Operating System; it helps you implement the standard Macintosh user interface in your application. The Toolbox calls the Operating System to do low-level operations, and you'll also call the Operating System directly yourself.

RAM-based software is available as well. In most cases this software performs specialized operations (such as floating-point arithmetic) that aren't integral to the user interface but may be useful to some applications.

The Toolbox and Other High-Level Software

The Macintosh User Interface Toolbox provides a simple means of constructing application programs that conform to the standard Macintosh user interface. By offering a common set of routines that every application calls to implement the user interface, the Toolbox not only ensures familiarity and consistency for the user but also helps reduce the application's code size and development time. At the same time, it allows a great deal of flexibility: An application can use its own code instead of a Toolbox call wherever appropriate, and can define its own types of windows, menus, controls, and desk accessories.

Figure 2 shows the various parts of the Toolbox in rough order of their relative level. There are many interconnections between these parts; the higher ones often call those at the lower levels. A brief description of each part is given below, to help you figure out which ones you'll need to learn more about. Details are given in the *Inside Macintosh* chapter on that part of the Toolbox. The basic Macintosh terms used below are explained in *Macintosh*, the owner's guide.

To keep the data of an application separate from its code, making the data easier to modify and easier to share among applications, the Toolbox includes the **Resource Manager**. The Resource Manager lets you, for example, store menus separately from your code so that they can be edited or translated without requiring recompilation of the code. It also allows you to get standard data, such as the I-beam pointer for inserting text, from a shared system file. When you call other parts of the Toolbox that need access to the data, they call the Resource Manager. Although most applications never need to call the Resource Manager directly, an understanding of the concepts behind it is essential because they're basic to so many other operations.

```
┌─────────────────────────────────────────────────────────────┐
│            A MACINTOSH APPLICATION PROGRAM                    │
└─────────────────────────────────────────────────────────────┘
                              │
┌─────────────────────────────────────────────────────────────┐
│  ┌──────────────────────────────────┐                        │
│  │  THE USER INTERFACE TOOLBOX      │                        │
│  │         (in ROM)                 │                        │
│  │                                  │                        │
│  │  Resource Manager                │                        │
│  │  QuickDraw                       │  ┌──────────────────────────────┐
│  │  Font Manager                    │  │  OTHER HIGH-LEVEL SOFTWARE   │
│  │  Toolbox Event Manager           │  │         (in RAM)             │
│  │  Window Manager                  │  │                              │
│  │  Control Manager                 │  │  Binary-Decimal Conversion Package │
│  │  Menu Manager                    │  │  International Utilities Package    │
│  │  TextEdit                        │  │  Standard File Package             │
│  │  Dialog Manager                  │  └──────────────────────────────┘
│  │  Desk Manager                    │                        │
│  │  Scrap Manager                   │                        │
│  │  Toolbox Utilities               │                        │
│  │  Package Manager                 │                        │
│  └──────────────────────────────────┘                        │
└─────────────────────────────────────────────────────────────┘
                              │
┌─────────────────────────────────────────────────────────────┐
│  ┌──────────────────────────────────┐                        │
│  │     THE OPERATING SYSTEM         │                        │
│  │         (in ROM)                 │                        │
│  │                                  │                        │
│  │  Memory Manager                  │  ┌──────────────────────────────┐
│  │  Segment Loader                  │  │  OTHER LOW-LEVEL SOFTWARE    │
│  │  Operating System Event Manager  │  │         (in RAM)             │
│  │  File Manager                    │  │                              │
│  │  Device Manager                  │  │  RAM Serial Driver           │
│  │  Disk Driver                     │  │  Printing Manager            │
│  │  Sound Driver                    │  │  Printer Driver              │
│  │  ROM Serial Driver               │  │  AppleTalk Manager           │
│  │  Vertical Retrace Manager        │  │  Disk Initialization Package │
│  │  System Error Handler            │  │  Floating-Point Arithmetic Package │
│  │  Operating System Utilities      │  │  Transcendental Functions Package  │
│  └──────────────────────────────────┘  └──────────────────────────────┘
└─────────────────────────────────────────────────────────────┘
                              │
┌─────────────────────────────────────────────────────────────┐
│              THE MACINTOSH HARDWARE                           │
└─────────────────────────────────────────────────────────────┘
```

Figure 1. Overview

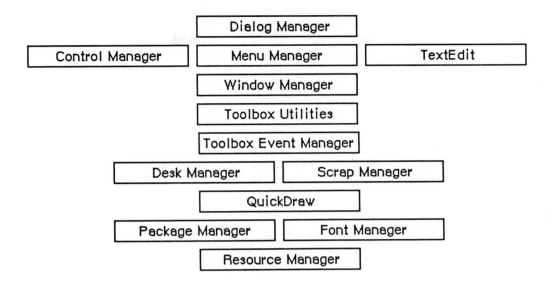

Figure 2. Parts of the Toolbox

Graphics are an important part of every Macintosh application. All graphic operations on the Macintosh are performed by **QuickDraw**. To draw something on the screen, you'll often call one of the other parts of the Toolbox, but it will in turn call QuickDraw. You'll also call QuickDraw directly, usually to draw inside a window, or just to set up constructs like rectangles that you'll need when making other Toolbox calls. QuickDraw's underlying concepts, like those of the Resource Manager, are important for you to understand.

Graphics include text as well as pictures. To draw text, QuickDraw calls the **Font Manager**, which does the background work necessary to make a variety of character fonts available in various sizes and styles. Unless your application includes a font menu, you need to know only a minimal amount about the Font Manager.

An application decides what to do from moment to moment by examining input from the user in the form of mouse and keyboard actions. It learns of such actions by repeatedly calling the **Toolbox Event Manager** (which in turn calls another, lower-level Event Manager in the Operating System). The Toolbox Event Manager also reports occurrences within the application that may require a response, such as when a window that was overlapped becomes exposed and needs to be redrawn.

All information presented by a standard Macintosh application appears in windows. To create windows, activate them, move them, resize them, or close them, you'll call the **Window Manager**. It keeps track of overlapping windows, so you can manipulate windows without concern for how they overlap. For example, the Window Manager tells the Toolbox Event Manager when to inform your application that a window has to be redrawn. Also, when the user presses the mouse button, you call the Window Manager to learn which part of which window it was pressed in, or whether it was pressed in the menu bar or a desk accessory.

Any window may contain controls, such as buttons, check boxes, and scroll bars. You can create and manipulate controls with the **Control Manager**. When you learn from the Window Manager that the user pressed the mouse button inside a window containing controls, you call the Control Manager to find out which control it was pressed in, if any.

A common place for the user to press the mouse button is, of course, in the menu bar. You set up menus in the menu bar by calling the **Menu Manager**. When the user gives a command, either from a menu with the mouse or from the keyboard with the Command key, you call the Menu Manager to find out which command was given.

To accept text typed by the user and allow the standard editing capabilities, including cutting and pasting text within a document via the Clipboard, your application can call **TextEdit**. TextEdit also handles basic formatting such as word wraparound and justification. You can use it just to display text if you like.

When an application needs more information from the user about a command, it presents a dialog box. In case of errors or potentially dangerous situations, it alerts the user with a box containing a message or with sound from the Macintosh's speaker (or both). To create and present dialogs and alerts, and find out the user's responses to them, you call the **Dialog Manager**.

Every Macintosh application should support the use of desk accessories. The user opens desk accessories through the Apple menu, which you set up by calling the Menu Manager. When you learn that the user has pressed the mouse button in a desk accessory, you pass that information on to the accessory by calling the **Desk Manager**. The Desk Manager also includes routines that you must call to ensure that desk accessories work properly.

As mentioned above, you can use TextEdit to implement the standard text editing capability of cutting and pasting via the Clipboard in your application. To allow the use of the Clipboard for cutting and pasting text or graphics between your application and another application or a desk accessory, you need to call the **Scrap Manager**.

Some generally useful operations such as fixed-point arithmetic, string manipulation, and logical operations on bits may be performed with the **Toolbox Utilities**.

The final part of the Toolbox, the **Package Manager**, lets you use RAM-based software called **packages**. The **Standard File Package** will be called by every application whose File menu includes the standard commands for saving and opening documents; it presents the standard user interface for specifying the document. Two of the Macintosh packages can be seen as extensions to the Toolbox Utilities: The **Binary-Decimal Conversion Package** converts integers to decimal strings and vice versa, and the **International Utilities Package** gives you access to country-dependent information such as the formats for numbers, currency, dates, and times.

The Operating System and Other Low-Level Software

The Macintosh Operating System provides the low-level support that applications need in order to use the Macintosh hardware. As the Toolbox is your program's interface to the user, the Operating System is its interface to the Macintosh.

The **Memory Manager** dynamically allocates and releases memory for use by applications and by the other parts of the Operating System. Most of the memory that your program uses is in an area called the **heap**; the code of the program itself occupies space in the heap. Memory space in the heap must be obtained through the Memory Manager.

The **Segment Loader** is the part of the Operating System that loads application code into memory to be executed. Your application can be loaded all at once, or you can divide it up into dynamically loaded segments to economize on memory usage. The Segment Loader also serves as a bridge between the Finder and your application, letting you know whether the application has to open or print a document on the desktop when it starts up.

Low-level, hardware-related events such as mouse-button presses and keystrokes are reported by the **Operating System Event Manager**. (The Toolbox Event Manager then passes them to the application, along with higher-level, software-generated events added at the Toolbox level.) Your program will ordinarily deal only with the Toolbox Event Manager and will rarely call the Operating System Event Manager directly.

File I/O is supported by the **File Manager**, and device I/O by the **Device Manager**. The task of making the various types of devices present the same interface to the application is performed by specialized **device drivers**. The Operating System includes three built-in drivers:

- The **Disk Driver** controls data storage and retrieval on 3 1/2-inch disks.

- The **Sound Driver** controls sound generation, including music composed of up to four simultaneous tones.

- The **Serial Driver** reads and writes asynchronous data through the two serial ports, providing communication between applications and serial peripheral devices such as a modem or printer.

The above drivers are all in ROM; other drivers are RAM-based. There's a Serial Driver in RAM as well as the one in ROM, and there's a **Printer Driver** in RAM that enables applications to print information on any variety of printer via the same interface (called the **Printing Manager**). The **AppleTalk Manager** is an interface to a pair of RAM drivers that enable programs to send and receive information via an AppleTalk network. More RAM drivers can be added independently or built on the existing drivers (by calling the routines in those drivers). For example, the Printer Driver was built on the Serial Driver, and a music driver could be built on the Sound Driver.

The Macintosh video circuitry generates a **vertical retrace interrupt** 60 times a second. An application can schedule routines to be executed at regular intervals based on this "heartbeat" of the system. The **Vertical Retrace Manager** handles the scheduling and execution of tasks during the vertical retrace interrupt.

If a fatal system error occurs while your application is running, the **System Error Handler** assumes control. The System Error Handler displays a box containing an error message and provides a mechanism for the user to start up the system again or resume execution of the application.

The **Operating System Utilities** perform miscellaneous operations such as getting the date and time, finding out the user's preferred speaker volume and other preferences, and doing simple string comparison. (More sophisticated string comparison routines are available in the International Utilities Package.)

Finally, there are three Macintosh packages that perform low-level operations: the **Disk Initialization Package**, which the Standard File Package calls to initialize and name disks; the **Floating-Point Arithmetic Package**, which supports extended-precision arithmetic according to IEEE Standard 754; and the **Transcendental Functions Package**, which contains trigonometric, logarithmic, exponential, and financial functions, as well as a random number generator.

A SIMPLE EXAMPLE PROGRAM

To illustrate various commonly used parts of the software, this section presents an extremely simple example of a Macintosh application program. Though too simple to be practical, this example shows the overall structure that every application program will have, and it does many of the basic things every application will do. By looking it over, you can become more familiar with the software and see how your own program code will be structured.

The example program's source code is shown in Figure 4, which begins at the end of this section. A lot of comments are included so that you can see which part of the Toolbox or Operating System is being called and what operation is being performed. These comments, and those that follow below, may contain terms that are unfamiliar to you, but for now just read along to get the general idea. All the terms are explained at length within *Inside Macintosh*. If you want more information right away, you can look up the terms in the Glossary (Volume III) or the Index.

The application, called Sample, displays a single, fixed-size window in which the user can enter and edit text (see Figure 3). It has three menus: the standard Apple menu, from which desk accessories can be chosen; a File menu, containing only a Quit command; and an Edit menu, containing the standard editing commands Undo, Cut, Copy, Paste, and Clear. The Edit menu also includes the standard keyboard equivalents for Undo, Cut, Copy, and Paste: Command-Z, X, C, and V, respectively. The Backspace key may be used to delete, and Shift-clicking will extend or shorten a selection. The user can move the document window around the desktop by dragging it by its title bar.

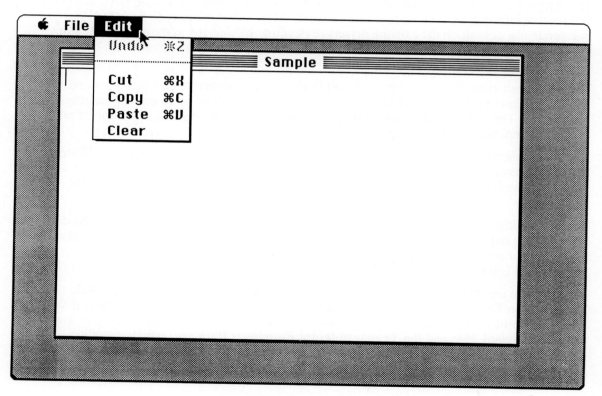

Figure 3. The Sample Application

The Undo command doesn't work in the application's document window, but it and all the other editing commands do work in any desk accessories that allow them (the Note Pad, for example). Some standard features this simple example doesn't support are as follows:

■ Text cannot be cut (or copied) and pasted between the document and a desk accessory.

■ The pointer remains an arrow rather than changing to an I-beam within the document.

■ Except for Undo, editing commands aren't dimmed when they don't apply (for example, Cut or Copy when there's no text selection).

The document window can't be closed, scrolled, or resized. Because the File menu contains only a Quit command, the document can't be saved or printed. Also, the application doesn't have "About Sample..." as the first command in its Apple menu, or a Hide/Show Clipboard command in its Edit menu (for displaying cut or copied text).

In addition to the code shown in Figure 4, the Sample application has a resource file that includes the data listed below. The program uses the numbers in the second column to identify the resources; for example, it makes a Menu Manager call to get menu number 128 from the resource file.

Resource	Resource ID	Description
Menu	128	Menu with the apple symbol as its title and no commands in it
Menu	129	File menu with one command, Quit, with keyboard equivalent Command-Q
Menu	130	Edit menu with the commands Undo (dimmed), Cut, Copy, Paste, and Clear, in that order, with the standard keyboard equivalents and with a dividing line between Undo and Cut
Window template	128	Document window without a size box; top left corner of (50,40) on QuickDraw's coordinate plane, bottom right corner of (300,450); title "Sample"; no close box

Each menu resource also contains a "menu ID" that's used to identify the menu when the user chooses a command from it; for all three menus, this ID is the same as the resource ID.

Note: To create a resource file with the above contents, you can use the Resource Editor or any similar program that may be available on the development system you're using.

The program starts with a USES clause that specifies all the necessary Pascal interface files. (The names shown are for the Lisa Workshop development system, and may be different for other systems.) This is followed by declarations of some useful constants, to make the source code more readable. Then there are a number of variable declarations, some having simple Pascal data types and others with data types defined in the interface files (like Rect and WindowPtr). Variables used in the program that aren't declared here are global variables defined in the interface to QuickDraw.

The variable declarations are followed by two procedure declarations: SetUpMenus and DoCommand. You can understand them better after looking at the main program and seeing where they're called.

The program begins with a standard initialization sequence. Every application will need to do this same initialization (in the order shown), or something close to it.

Additional initialization needed by the program follows. This includes setting up the menus and the menu bar (by calling SetUpMenus) and creating the application's document window (reading its description from the resource file and displaying it on the screen).

The heart of every application program is its **main event loop,** which repeatedly calls the Toolbox Event Manager to get events and then responds to them as appropriate. The most common event is a press of the mouse button; depending on where it was pressed, as reported by the Window Manager, the sample program may execute a command, move the document window, make the window active, or pass the event on to a desk accessory. The DoCommand procedure takes care of executing a command; it looks at information received by the Menu Manager to determine which command to execute.

Besides events resulting directly from user actions such as pressing the mouse button or a key on the keyboard, events are detected by the Window Manager as a side effect of those actions. For example, when a window changes from active to inactive or vice versa, the Window Manager tells the Toolbox Event Manager to report it to the application program. A similar process happens when all or part of a window needs to be updated (redrawn). The internal mechanism in each case is invisible to the program, which simply responds to the event when notified.

The main event loop terminates when the user takes some action to leave the program—in this case, when the Quit command is chosen.

That's it! Of course, the program structure and level of detail will get more complicated as the application becomes more complex, and every actual application will be more complex than this one. But each will be based on the structure illustrated here.

```
PROGRAM Sample;

{ Sample -- A small sample application written by Macintosh User Education }
{ It displays a single, fixed-size window in which the user can enter and edit text. }


{ The following two compiler commands are required for the Lisa Workshop. }
{$X-}  {turn off automatic stack expansion}
{$U-}  {turn off Lisa libraries}


{ The USES clause brings in the units containing the Pascal interfaces. }
{ The $U expression tells the compiler what file to look in for the specified unit. }
USES {$U Obj/MemTypes } MemTypes,    {basic Memory Manager data types}
     {$U Obj/QuickDraw} QuickDraw,   {interface to QuickDraw}
     {$U Obj/OSIntf   } OSIntf,      {interface to the Operating System}
     {$U Obj/ToolIntf } ToolIntf;    {interface to the Toolbox}


CONST appleID = 128;        {resource IDs/menu IDs for Apple, File, and Edit menus}
      fileID  = 129;
      editID  = 130;

      appleM  = 1;          {index for each menu in myMenus (array of menu handles)}
      fileM   = 2;
      editM   = 3;

      menuCount = 3;        {total number of menus}

      windowID = 128;       {resource ID for application's window}

      undoCommand  = 1;     {menu item numbers identifying commands in Edit menu}
      cutCommand   = 3;
      copyCommand  = 4;
      pasteCommand = 5;
      clearCommand = 6;


VAR myMenus: ARRAY[1..menuCount] OF MenuHandle; {array of handles to the menus}
    dragRect: Rect;              {rectangle used to mark boundaries for dragging window}
    txRect: Rect;                {rectangle for text in application window}
    textH: TEHandle;             {handle to information about the text}
    theChar: CHAR;               {character typed on the keyboard or keypad}
    extended: BOOLEAN;           {TRUE if user is Shift-clicking}
    doneFlag: BOOLEAN;           {TRUE if user has chosen Quit command}
    myEvent: EventRecord;        {information about an event}
    wRecord: WindowRecord;       {information about the application window}
    myWindow: WindowPtr;         {pointer to wRecord}
    whichWindow: WindowPtr;      {pointer to window in which mouse button was pressed}


PROCEDURE SetUpMenus;
{ Set up menus and menu bar }

    VAR i: INTEGER;
```

Figure 4. Example Program

```
   BEGIN
   { Read menu descriptions from resource file into memory and store handles }
   { in myMenus array }
   myMenus[appleM] := GetMenu(appleID);   {read Apple menu from resource file}
   AddResMenu(myMenus[appleM],'DRVR');   {add desk accessory names to Apple menu}
   myMenus[fileM] := GetMenu(fileID);     {read File menu from resource file}
   myMenus[editM] := GetMenu(editID);     {read Edit menu from resource file}

   FOR i:=1 TO menuCount DO InsertMenu(myMenus[i],0);   {install menus in menu bar }
   DrawMenuBar;                                          { and draw menu bar}
   END;     {of SetUpMenus}

PROCEDURE DoCommand (mResult: LONGINT);
{ Execute command specified by mResult, the result of MenuSelect }

   VAR theItem: INTEGER;          {menu item number from mResult low-order word}
       theMenu: INTEGER;          {menu number from mResult high-order word}
       name: Str255;              {desk accessory name}
       temp: INTEGER;

 BEGIN
   theItem := LoWord(mResult);                 {call Toolbox Utility routines to set }
   theMenu := HiWord(mResult);                 { menu item number and menu number}

   CASE theMenu OF                             {case on menu ID}

   appleID:
     BEGIN                                     {call Menu Manager to get desk accessory }
     GetItem(myMenus[appleM],theItem,name);   { name, and call Desk Manager to open }
     temp := OpenDeskAcc(name);               { accessory (OpenDeskAcc result not used)}
     SetPort(myWindow);                       {call QuickDraw to restore application }
     END;     {of appleID}                    { window as grafPort to draw in (may have }
                                              { been changed during OpenDeskAcc)}
   fileID:
     doneFlag := TRUE;                        {quit (main loop repeats until doneFlag is TRUE)}

   editID:
     BEGIN                                    {call Desk Manager to handle editing command if }
     IF NOT SystemEdit(theItem-1)             { desk accessory window is the active window}
       THEN                                   {application window is the active window}
         CASE theItem OF                      {case on menu item (command) number}

         cutCommand:    TECut(textH);         {call TextEdit to handle command}
         copyCommand:   TECopy(textH);
         pasteCommand:  TEPaste(textH);
         clearCommand:  TEDelete(textH);

         END;    {of item case}
     END;    {of editID}

   END;    {of menu case}                     {to indicate completion of command, call }
   HiliteMenu(0);                             { Menu Manager to unhighlight menu title }
                                              { (highlighted by MenuSelect)}
   END;    {of DoCommand}
```

Figure 4. Example Program (continued)

```
BEGIN    {main program}
{ Initialization }
InitGraf(@thePort);           {initialize QuickDraw}
InitFonts;                    {initialize Font Manager}
FlushEvents(everyEvent,0);    {call OS Event Manager to discard any previous events}
InitWindows;                  {initialize Window Manager}
InitMenus;                    {initialize Menu Manager}
TEInit;                       {initialize TextEdit}
InitDialogs(NIL);             {initialize Dialog Manager}
InitCursor;                   {call QuickDraw to make cursor (pointer) an arrow}

SetUpMenus;                   {set up menus and menu bar}
WITH screenBits.bounds DO     {call QuickDraw to set dragging boundaries; ensure at }
  SetRect(dragRect,4,24,right-4,bottom-4); { least 4 by 4 pixels will remain visible}
doneFlag := FALSE;            {flag to detect when Quit command is chosen}
myWindow := GetNewWindow(windowID,@wRecord,POINTER(-1)); {put up application window}
SetPort(myWindow);           {call QuickDraw to set current grafPort to this window}
txRect := thePort^.portRect; {rectangle for text in window; call QuickDraw to bring }
InsetRect(txRect,4,0);       { it in 4 pixels from left and right edges of window}
textH := TENew(txRect,txRect);   {call TextEdit to prepare for receiving text}

{ Main event loop }
REPEAT                       {call Desk Manager to perform any periodic }
  SystemTask;                { actions defined for desk accessories}
  TEIdle(textH);            {call TextEdit to make vertical bar blink}

  IF GetNextEvent(everyEvent,myEvent) {call Toolbox Event Manager to get the next }
    THEN                            { event that the application should handle}
      CASE myEvent.what OF          {case on event type}

    mouseDown:               {mouse button down: call Window Manager to learn where}
      CASE FindWindow(myEvent.where,whichWindow) OF

      inSysWindow:           {desk accessory window:  call Desk Manager to handle it}
        SystemClick(myEvent,whichWindow);

      inMenuBar:             {menu bar:  call Menu Manager to learn which command, }
        DoCommand(MenuSelect(myEvent.where)); { then execute it}

      inDrag:                {title bar:  call Window Manager to drag}
        DragWindow(whichWindow,myEvent.where,dragRect);

      inContent:                       {body of application window: }
        BEGIN                          { call Window Manager to check whether }
        IF whichWindow <> FrontWindow  { it's the active window and make it }
          THEN SelectWindow(whichWindow) { active if not}
          ELSE
            BEGIN                       {it's already active:  call QuickDraw to }
            GlobalToLocal(myEvent.where); { convert to window coordinates for }
                                        { TEClick, use Toolbox Utility BitAnd to }
            extended := BitAnd(myEvent.modifiers,shiftKey) <> 0; { test for Shift }
            TEClick(myEvent.where,extended,textH); { key down, and call TextEdit }
            END;                        { to process the event}
        END;    {of inContent}
      END;      {of mouseDown}
```

Figure 4. Example Program (continued)

```
keyDown, autoKey:                          {key pressed once or held down to repeat}
   BEGIN
   theChar := CHR(BitAnd(myEvent.message,charCodeMask));  {get the character}
   IF BitAnd(myEvent.modifiers,cmdKey) <> 0  {if Command key down, call Menu }
      THEN DoCommand(MenuKey(theChar))       { Manager to learn which command,}
      ELSE TEKey(theChar,textH);             { then execute it; else pass }
   END;                                      { character to TextEdit}

activateEvt:
   BEGIN
   IF BitAnd(myEvent.modifiers,activeFlag) <> 0
      THEN                       {application window is becoming active: }
         BEGIN                   { call TextEdit to highlight selection }
         TEActivate(textH);      { or display blinking vertical bar, and call }
         DisableItem(myMenus[editM],undoCommand); { Menu Manager to disable }
         END                     { Undo (since application doesn't support Undo)}
      ELSE
         BEGIN                   {application window is becoming inactive: }
         TEDeactivate(textH);    { unhighlight selection or remove blinking }
         EnableItem(myMenus[editM],undoCommand);  { vertical bar, and enable }
         END;                    { Undo (since desk accessory may support it)}
   END;   {of activateEvt}

updateEvt:                                   {window appearance needs updating}
   BEGIN
   BeginUpdate(WindowPtr(myEvent.message));  {call Window Manager to begin update}
   EraseRect(thePort^.portRect);             {call QuickDraw to erase text area}
   TEUpdate(thePort^.portRect,textH);        {call TextEdit to update the text}
   EndUpdate(WindowPtr(myEvent.message));    {call Window Manager to end update}
   END;     {of updateEvt}

   END;     {of event case}

UNTIL doneFlag;
END.
```

Figure 4. Example Program (continued)

WHERE TO GO FROM HERE

This section contains important directions for every reader of *Inside Macintosh*. It will help you figure out which chapters to read next.

The *Inside Macintosh* chapters are ordered in such a way that you can follow it if you read through it sequentially. Forward references are given wherever necessary to any additional information that you'll need in order to fully understand what's being discussed. Special-purpose information that can possibly be skipped is indicated as such. Most likely you won't need to read everything in each chapter and can even skip entire chapters.

You should begin by reading the following:

1. Chapter 2, The Macintosh User Interface Guidelines. All Macintosh applications should follow these guidelines to ensure that the end user is presented with a consistent, familiar interface.

2. Chapter 3, Macintosh Memory Management: An Introduction.

3. Chapter 4, Using Assembly Language, if you're programming in assembly language. Depending on the debugging tools available on the development system you're using, it may also be helpful or necessary for high-level language programmers to read this chapter. You'll also have to read it if you're creating your own development system and want to know how to write interfaces to the routines.

4. The chapters describing the parts of the Toolbox that deal with the fundamental aspects of the user interface: the Resource Manager, QuickDraw, the Toolbox Event Manager, the Window Manager, and the Menu Manager.

Read the other chapters if you're interested in what they discuss, which you should be able to tell from the overviews in this "road map" and from the introductions to the chapters themselves. Each chapter's introduction will also tell you what you should already know before reading that chapter.

When you're ready to try something out, refer to the appropriate documentation for the development system you'll be using.

2 THE MACINTOSH USER INTERFACE GUIDELINES

ABOUT THIS CHAPTER

This chapter describes the Macintosh user interface, for the benefit of people who want to develop Macintosh applications. More details about many of these features can be found in the "About" sections of the other chapters of *Inside Macintosh* (for example, "About the Window Manager").

Unlike the rest of *Inside Macintosh*, this chapter describes applications from the outside, not the inside. The terminology used is the terminology users are familiar with, which is not necessarily the same as that used elsewhere in *Inside Macintosh*.

The Macintosh user interface consists of those features that are generally applicable to a variety of applications. Not all of the features are found in every application. In fact, some features are hypothetical, and may not be found in any current applications.

The best time to familiarize yourself with the user interface is before beginning to design an application. Good application design on the Macintosh happens when a developer has absorbed the spirit as well as the details of the user interface.

Before reading this chapter, you should have some experience using one or more applications, preferably one each of a word processor, spreadsheet or data base, and graphics application. You should also have read *Macintosh*, the owner's guide, or at least be familiar with the terminology used in that manual.

INTRODUCTION

The Macintosh is designed to appeal to an audience of nonprogrammers, including people who have previously feared and distrusted computers. To achieve this goal, Macintosh applications should be easy to learn and to use. To help people feel more comfortable with the applications, the applications should build on skills that people already have, not force them to learn new ones. The user should feel in control of the computer, not the other way around. This is achieved in applications that embody three qualities: responsiveness, permissiveness, and consistency.

Responsiveness means that the user's actions tend to have direct results. The user should be able to accomplish what needs to be done spontaneously and intuitively, rather than having to think: "Let's see; to do C, first I have to do A and B and then...". For example, with pull-down menus, the user can choose the desired command directly and instantaneously.

Permissiveness means that the application tends to allow the user to do anything reasonable. The user, not the system, decides what to do next. Also, error messages tend to come up infrequently. If the user is constantly subjected to a barrage of error messages, something is wrong somewhere.

The most important way in which an application is permissive is in avoiding modes. This idea is so important that it's dealt with in a separate section, "Avoiding Modes", below.

The third and most important principle is consistency. Since Macintosh users usually divide their time among several applications, they would be confused and irritated if they had to learn a completely new interface for each application. The main purpose of this chapter is to describe the shared interface ideas of Macintosh applications, so that developers of new applications can gain leverage from the time spent developing and testing existing applications.

Consistency is easier to achieve on the Macintosh than on many other computers. This is because many of the routines used to implement the user interface are supplied in the Macintosh Operating System and User Interface Toolbox. However, you should be aware that implementing the user interface guidelines in their full glory often requires writing additional code that isn't supplied.

Of course, you shouldn't feel that you're restricted to using existing features. The Macintosh is a growing system, and new ideas are essential. But the bread-and-butter features, the kind that every application has, should certainly work the same way so that the user can easily move back and forth between applications. The best rule to follow is that if your application has a feature that's described in these guidelines, you should implement the feature exactly as the guidelines describe it. It's better to do something completely different than to half-agree with the guidelines.

Illustrations of most of the features described in this chapter can be found in various existing applications. However, there's probably no one application that illustrates these guidelines in every particular. Although it's useful and important for you to get the feeling of the Macintosh user interface by looking at existing applications, the guidelines in this chapter are the ultimate authority. Wherever an application disagrees with the guidelines, follow the guidelines.

Avoiding Modes

"But, gentlemen, you overdo the mode."

— John Dryden, *The Assignation, or Love in a Nunnery*, 1672

A mode is a part of an application that the user has to formally enter and leave, and that restricts the operations that can be performed while it's in effect. Since people don't usually operate modally in real life, having to deal with modes in computer software reinforces the idea that computers are unnatural and unfriendly.

Modes are most confusing when you're in the wrong one. Being in a mode makes future actions contingent upon past ones, restricts the behavior of familiar objects and commands, and may make habitual actions cause unexpected results.

It's tempting to use modes in a Macintosh application, since most existing software leans on them heavily. If you yield to the temptation too frequently, however, users will consider spending time with your application a chore rather than a satisfying experience.

This is not to say that modes are never used in Macintosh applications. Sometimes a mode is the best way out of a particular problem. Most of these modes fall into one of the following categories:

- Long-term modes with a procedural basis, such as doing word processing as opposed to graphics editing. Each application program is a mode in this sense.

- Short-term "spring-loaded" modes, in which the user is constantly doing something to perpetuate the mode. Holding down the mouse button or a key is the most common example of this kind of mode.

- Alert modes, where the user must rectify an unusual situation before proceeding. These modes should be kept to a minimum.

Other modes are acceptable if they meet one of the following requirements:

- They emulate a familiar real-life model that is itself modal, like picking up different-sized paintbrushes in a graphics editor. MacPaint™ and other palette-based applications are examples of this use of modes.

- They change only the attributes of something, and not its behavior, like the boldface and underline modes of text entry.

- They block most other normal operations of the system to emphasize the modality, as in error conditions incurable through software ("There's no disk in the disk drive", for example).

If an application uses modes, there must be a clear visual indication of the current mode, and the indication should be near the object being most affected by the mode. It should also be very easy to get into or out of the mode (such as by clicking on a palette symbol).

Avoiding Program Dependencies

Another important general concept to keep in mind is that your application program should be as country-independent and hardware-independent as possible.

No words that the user sees should be in the program code itself; storing all these words in resources will make it much easier for the application to be translated to other languages. Similarly, there's a mechanism for reading country-dependent information from resources, such as the currency and date formats, so the application will automatically work right in countries where those resources have been properly set up. You should always use mechanisms like this instead of coding such information directly into your program.

The system software provides many variables and routines whose use will ensure independence from the version of the Macintosh being used—whether a Macintosh 128K, 512K, XL, or even a future version. Though you may know a more direct way of getting the information, or a faster way of doing the operation, it's best to use the system-provided features that will ensure hardware independence. You should, for example, access the variable that gives you the current size of the screen rather than use the numbers that match the screen you're using. You can also write your program so that it will print on any printer, regardless of which type of printer happens to be installed on the Macintosh being used.

TYPES OF APPLICATIONS

Everything on a Macintosh screen is displayed graphically; the Macintosh has no text mode. Nevertheless, it's useful to make a distinction among three types of objects that an application deals with: text, graphics, and arrays. Examples of each of these are shown in Figure 1.

Text can be arranged in a variety of ways on the screen. Some applications, such as word processors, might consist of nothing but text, while others, such as graphics-oriented applications, use text almost incidentally. It's useful to consider all the text appearing together in a particular context as a block of text. The size of the block can range from a single field, as in a dialog box, to the whole document, as in a word processor. Regardless of its size or arrangement, the application sees each block as a one-dimensional string of characters. Text is edited the same way regardless of where it appears.

Graphics are pictures, drawn either by the user or by the application. Graphics in a document tend to consist of discrete objects, which can be selected individually. Graphics are discussed further below, under "Using Graphics".

```
The rest to some faint meaning make pretence
But Shadwell never deviates into sense.
Some beams of wit on other souls may fall,
Strike through and make a lucid interval;
But Shadwell's genuine night admits no ray,
His rising fogs prevail upon the day.

MacFlecknoe                                    Page 1
```

Text

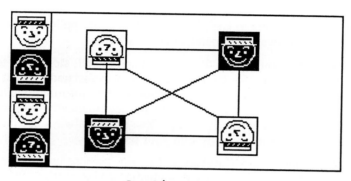

Graphics

Advertising	132.9		
Manufacturing	121.3		
R & D	18.7		
Interest	12.2		
Total	285.1		

Array

Figure 1. Ways of Structuring Information

Arrays are one- or two-dimensional arrangements of fields. If the array is one-dimensional, it's called a form; if it's two-dimensional it's called a table. Each field, in turn, contains a collection of information, usually text, but conceivably graphics. A table can be readily identified on the screen, since it consists of rows and columns of fields (often called cells), separated by horizontal and vertical lines. A form is something you fill out, like a credit-card application. The fields in a form can be arranged in any appropriate way; nevertheless, the application regards the fields as in a definite linear order.

Each of these three ways of presenting information retains its integrity, regardless of the context in which it appears. For example, a field in an array can contain text. When the user is manipulating the field as a whole, the field is treated as part of the array. When the user wants to change the contents of the field, the contents are edited in the same way as any other text.

USING GRAPHICS

A key feature of the Macintosh is its high-resolution graphics screen. To use this screen to its best advantage, Macintosh applications use graphics copiously, even in places where other applications use text. As much as possible, all commands, features, and parameters of an application, and all the user's data, appear as graphic objects on the screen. Figure 2 shows some of the ways that applications can use graphics to communicate with the user.

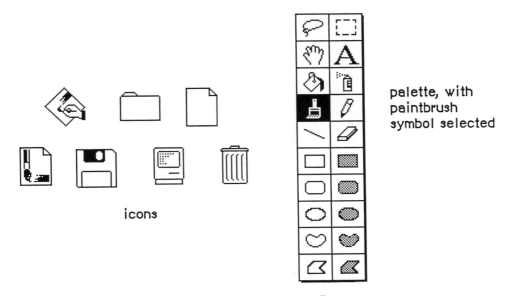

icons

palette, with
paintbrush
symbol selected

Figure 2. Objects on the Screen

Objects, whenever applicable, resemble the familiar material objects whose functions they emulate. Objects that act like pushbuttons "light up" when pressed; the Trash icon looks like a trash can.

Objects are designed to look good on the screen. Predefined graphics patterns can give objects a shape and texture beyond simple line graphics. Placing a drop-shadow slightly below and to the right of an object can give it a three-dimensional appearance.

Generally, when the user clicks on an object, it's **highlighted** to distinguish it from its peers. The most common way to show this highlighting is by inverting the object: changing black to white and vice versa. In some situations, other forms of highlighting may be more appropriate. The important thing is that there should always be some sort of feedback, so that the user knows that the click had an effect.

One special aspect of the appearance of a document on the screen is visual fidelity. This principle is also known as "what you see is what you get". It primarily refers to printing: The version of a document shown on the screen should be as close as possible to its printed version, taking into account inevitable differences due to different media.

Icons

A fundamental object in Macintosh software is the **icon**, a small graphic object that's usually symbolic of an operation or of a larger entity such as a document.

Icons can contribute greatly to the clarity and attractiveness of an application. The use of icons also makes it much easier to translate programs into other languages. Wherever an explanation or label is needed, consider using an icon instead of text.

Palettes

Some applications use **palettes** as a quick way for the user to change from one operation to another. A palette is a collection of small symbols, usually enclosed in rectangles. A symbol can be an icon, a pattern, a character, or just a drawing, that stands for an operation. When the user clicks on one of the symbols (or in its rectangle), it's distinguished from the other symbols, such as by highlighting, and the previous symbol goes back to its normal state.

Typically, the symbol that's selected determines what operations the user can perform. Selecting a palette symbol puts the user into a mode. This use of modes can be justified because changing from one mode to another is almost instantaneous, and the user can always see at a glance which mode is in effect. Like all modal features, palettes should be used only when they're the most natural way to structure an application.

A palette can either be part of a window (as in MacDraw™), or a separate window (as in MacPaint). Each system has its disadvantages. If the palette is part of the window, then parts of the palette might be concealed if the user makes the window smaller. On the other hand, if it's not part of the window, then it takes up extra space on the desktop. If an application supports multiple documents open at the same time, it might be better to put a separate palette in each window, so that a different palette symbol can be in effect in each document.

COMPONENTS OF THE MACINTOSH SYSTEM

This section explains the relationship among the principal large-scale components of the Macintosh system (from an external point of view).

The main vehicle for the interaction of the user and the system is the application. Only one application is active at a time. When an application is active, it's in control of all communications between the user and the system. The application's menus are in the menu bar, and the application is in charge of all windows as well as the desktop.

To the user, the main unit of information is the document. Each document is a unified collection of information—a single business letter or spreadsheet or chart. A complex application, such as a data base, might require several related documents. Some documents can be processed by more than one application, but each document has a principal application, which is usually the one that created it. The other applications that process the document are called secondary applications.

The only way the user can actually see the document (except by printing it) is through a window. The application puts one or more windows on the screen; each window shows a view of a document or of auxiliary information used in processing the document. The part of the screen underlying all the windows is called the **desktop**.

The user returns to the Finder to change applications. When the Finder is active, if the user opens either an application a document belonging to an application, the application becomes active and displays the document window.

Internally, applications and documents are both kept in files. However, the user never sees files as such, so they don't really enter into the user interface.

THE KEYBOARD

The Macintosh keyboard is used primarily for entering text. Since commands are chosen from menus or by clicking somewhere on the screen, the keyboard isn't needed for this function, although it can be used for alternative ways to enter commands.

The keys on the keyboard are arranged in familiar typewriter fashion. The U.S. keyboard on the Macintosh 128K and 512K is shown in Figure 3. The Macintosh XL keyboard looks the same except that the key to the left of the space bar is labeled with an apple symbol.

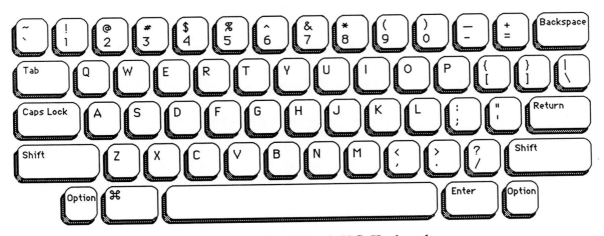

Figure 3. The Macintosh U.S. Keyboard

There are two kinds of keys: **character keys** and **modifier keys**. A character key sends characters to the computer; a modifier key alters the meaning of a character key if it's held down while the character key is pressed.

Character Keys

Character keys include keys for letters, numbers, and symbols, as well as the space bar. If the user presses one of these keys while entering text, the corresponding character is added to the text. Other keys, such as the Enter, Tab, Return, Backspace, and Clear keys, are also considered character keys. However, the result of pressing one of these keys depends on the application and the context.

The Enter key tells the application that the user is through entering information in a particular area of the document, such as a field in an array. Most applications add information to a document as soon as the user types or draws it. However, the application may need to wait until a whole collection of information is available before processing it. In this case, the user presses the Enter key to signal that the information is complete.

The Tab key is a signal to proceed: It signals movement to the next item in a sequence. Tab often implies an Enter operation before the Tab motion is performed.

The Return key is another signal to proceed, but it defines a different type of motion than Tab. A press of the Return key signals movement to the leftmost field one step down (just like a carriage return on a typewriter). Return can also imply an Enter operation before the Return operation.

> **Note:** Return and Enter also dismiss dialog and alert boxes (see "Dialogs and Alerts").

During entry of text into a document, Tab moves to the next tab stop, Return moves to the beginning of the next line, and Enter is ignored.

Backspace is used to delete text or graphics. The exact use of Backspace in text is described in the "Text Editing" section.

The Clear key on the numeric keypad has the same effect as the Clear command in the Edit menu; that is, it removes the selection from the document without putting it in the Clipboard. This is also explained in the "Text Editing" section. Because the keypad is optional equipment on the Macintosh 128K and 512K, no application should ever require use of the Clear key or any other key on the pad.

Modifier Keys: Shift, Caps Lock, Option, and Command

There are six keys on the keyboard that change the interpretation of keystrokes: two Shift keys, two Option keys, one Caps Lock key, and one Command key (the key to the left of the space bar). These keys change the interpretation of keystrokes, and sometimes mouse actions. When one of these keys is held down, the effect of the other keys (or the mouse button) may change.

The Shift and Option keys choose among the characters on each character key. Shift gives the upper character on two-character keys, or the uppercase letter on alphabetic keys. The Shift key is also used in conjunction with the mouse for extending a selection; see "Selecting". Option gives an alternate character set interpretation, including international characters, special symbols, and so on. Shift and Option can be used in combination.

Caps Lock latches in the down position when pressed, and releases when pressed again. When down it gives the uppercase letter on alphabetic keys. The operation of Caps Lock on alphabetic keys is parallel to that of the Shift key, but the Caps Lock key has no effect whatsoever on any of the other keys. Caps Lock and Option can be used in combination on alphabetic keys.

Pressing a character key while holding down the Command key usually tells the application to interpret the key as a command, not as a character (see "Commands").

Typeahead and Auto-Repeat

If the user types when the Macintosh is unable to process the keystrokes immediately, or types more quickly than the Macintosh can handle, the extra keystrokes are queued, to be processed later. This queuing is called typeahead. There's a limit to the number of keystrokes that can be queued, but the limit is usually not a problem unless the user types while the application is performing a lengthy operation.

When a character key is held down for a certain amount of time, it starts repeating automatically. The user can set the delay and the rate of repetition with the Control Panel desk accessory. An application can tell whether a series of n keystrokes was generated by auto-repeat or by pressing the same key n times. It can choose to disregard keystrokes generated by auto-repeat; this is usually a good idea for menu commands chosen with the Command key.

Holding down a modifier key has the same effect as pressing it once. However, if the user holds down a modifier key and a character key at the same time, the effect is the same as if the user held down the modifier key while pressing the character key repeatedly.

Auto-repeat does not function during typeahead; it operates only when the application is ready to accept keyboard input.

Versions of the Keyboard

There are two physical versions of the keyboard: U.S. and international. The international version has one more key than the U.S. version. The standard layout on the international version is designed to conform to the International Standards Organization (ISO) standard; the U.S. key layout mimics that of common American office typewriters. International keyboards have different labels on the keys in different countries, but the overall layout is the same.

Note: An illustration of the international keyboard (with Great Britain key caps) is given in chapter 8.

The Numeric Keypad

An optional numeric keypad can be hooked up between the main unit and the standard keyboard on a Macintosh 128K or 512K; on the Macintosh XL, the numeric keypad is built in, next to the keyboard. Figure 4 shows the U.S. keypad. In other countries, the keys may have different labels.

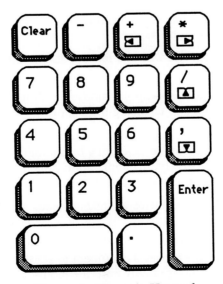

Figure 4. Numeric Keypad

The keypad contains 18 keys, some of which duplicate keys on the main keyboard, and some of which are unique to the keypad. The application can tell whether the keystrokes have come from the main keyboard or the numeric keypad. The keys on the keypad follow the same rules for typeahead and auto-repeat as the keyboard.

Four keys on the keypad are labeled with "field-motion" symbols: small rectangles with arrows pointing in various directions. Some applications may use these keys to select objects in the direction indicated by the key; the most likely use for this feature is in tables. To obtain the characters (+ * / ,) available on these keys, the user must also hold down the Shift key on the keyboard.

Since the numeric keypad is optional equipment on the Macintosh 128K and 512K, no application should require it or any keys available on it in order to perform standard functions. Specifically, since the Clear key isn't available on the main keyboard, a Clear function may be implemented with this key only as the equivalent of the Clear command in the Edit menu.

THE MOUSE

The mouse is a small device the size of a deck of playing cards, connected to the computer by a long, flexible cable. There's a button on the top of the mouse. The user holds the mouse and rolls it on a flat, smooth surface. A pointer on the screen follows the motion of the mouse.

Simply moving the mouse results only in a corresponding movement of the pointer and no other action. Most actions take place when the user positions the "hot spot" of the pointer over an object on the screen and presses and releases the mouse button. The hot spot should be intuitive, like the point of an arrow or the center of a crossbar.

Mouse Actions

The three basic mouse actions are:

- clicking: positioning the pointer with the mouse, and briefly pressing and releasing the mouse button without moving the mouse

- pressing: positioning the pointer with the mouse, and holding down the mouse button without moving the mouse

- dragging: positioning the pointer with the mouse, holding down the mouse button, moving the mouse to a new position, and releasing the button

The system provides "mouse-ahead"; that is, any mouse actions the user performs when the application isn't ready to process them are saved in a buffer and can be processed at the application's convenience. Alternatively, the application can choose to ignore saved-up mouse actions, but should do so only to protect the user from possibly damaging consequences.

Clicking something with the mouse performs an instantaneous action, such as selecting a location within a document or activating an object.

For certain kinds of objects, pressing on the object has the same effect as clicking it repeatedly. For example, clicking a scroll arrow causes a document to scroll one line; pressing on a scroll arrow causes the document to scroll repeatedly until the mouse button is released or the end of the document is reached.

Dragging can have different effects, depending on what's under the pointer when the mouse button is pressed. The uses of dragging include choosing a menu item, selecting a range of objects, moving an object from one place to another, and shrinking or expanding an object.

Some objects, especially graphic objects, can be moved by dragging. In this case, the application attaches a dotted outline of the object to the pointer and moves the outline as the user moves the pointer. When the user releases the mouse button, the application redraws the complete object at the new location.

An object being moved can be restricted to certain boundaries, such as the edges of a window. If the user moves the pointer outside of the boundaries, the application stops drawing the dotted outline of the object. If the user releases the mouse button while the pointer is outside of the boundaries, the object isn't moved. If, on the other hand, the user moves the pointer back within the boundaries again before releasing the mouse button, the outline is drawn again.

In general, moving the mouse changes nothing except the location, and possibly the shape, of the pointer. Pressing the mouse button indicates the intention to do something, and releasing the button completes the action. Pressing by itself should have no effect except in well-defined areas, such as scroll arrows, where it has the same effect as repeated clicking.

Multiple-Clicking

A variant of clicking involves performing a second click shortly after the end of an initial click. If the downstroke of the second click follows the upstroke of the first by a short amount of time (as set by the user in the Control Panel), and if the locations of the two clicks are reasonably close together, the two clicks constitute a double-click. Its most common use is as a faster or easier way to perform an action that can also be performed in another way. For example, clicking twice on an icon is a faster way to open it than selecting it and choosing Open; clicking twice on a word to select it is faster than dragging through it.

To allow the software to distinguish efficiently between single clicks and double-clicks on objects that respond to both, an operation invoked by double-clicking an object must be an enhancement, superset, or extension of the feature invoked by single-clicking that object.

Triple-clicking is also possible; it should similarly represent an extension of a double-click.

Changing Pointer Shapes

The pointer may change shape to give feedback on the range of activities that make sense in a particular area of the screen, in a current mode, or both:

■ The result of any mouse action depends on the item under the pointer when the mouse button is pressed. To emphasize the differences among mouse actions, the pointer may assume different appearances in different areas to indicate the actions possible in each area. This can be distracting, however, and should be kept to a minimum.

■ Where an application uses modes for different functions, the pointer can be a different shape in each mode. For example, in MacPaint, the pointer shape always reflects the active palette symbol.

During a particularly lengthy operation, when the user can do nothing but wait until the operation is completed, the pointer may change to indicate this. The standard pointer used for this purpose is a wristwatch.

Figure 5 shows some examples of pointers and their effect. An application can design additional pointers for other contexts.

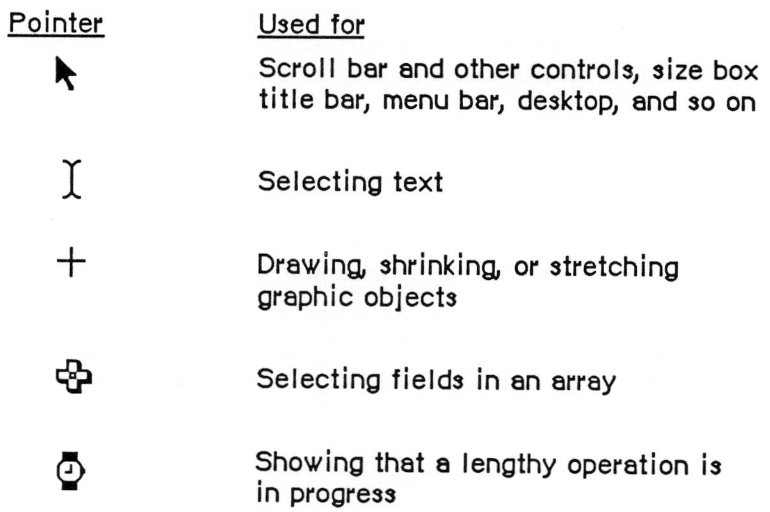

Pointer	Used for
▲	Scroll bar and other controls, size box title bar, menu bar, desktop, and so on
I	Selecting text
+	Drawing, shrinking, or stretching graphic objects
⊕	Selecting fields in an array
⌚	Showing that a lengthy operation is in progress

Figure 5. Pointers

SELECTING

The user selects an object to distinguish it from other objects, just before performing an operation on it. Selecting the object of an operation before identifying the operation is a fundamental characteristic of the Macintosh user interface, since it allows the application to avoid modes.

Selecting an object has no effect on the contents of a document. Making a selection shouldn't commit the user to anything; there should never be a penalty for making an incorrect selection. The user fixes an incorrect selection by making the correct selection.

Although there's a variety of ways to select objects, they fall into easily recognizable groups. Users get used to doing specific things to select objects, and applications that use these methods are therefore easier to learn. Some of these methods apply to every type of application, and some only to particular types of applications.

This section discusses first the general methods, and then the specific methods that apply to text applications, graphics applications, and arrays. Figure 6 shows a comparison of some of the general methods.

Selection by Clicking

The most straightforward method of selecting an object is by clicking on it once. Most things that can be selected in Macintosh applications can be selected this way.

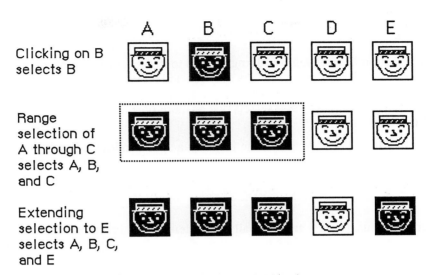

Figure 6. Selection Methods

Some applications support selection by double-clicking and triple-clicking. As always with multiple clicks, the second click extends the effect of the first click, and the third click extends the effect of the second click. In the case of selection, this means that the second click selects the same sort of thing as the first click, only more of them. The same holds true for the third click.

For example, in text, the first click selects an insertion point, whereas the second click selects a whole word. The third click might select a whole block or paragraph of text. In graphics, the first click selects a single object, and double- and triple-clicks might select increasingly larger groups of objects.

Range Selection

The user selects a range of objects by dragging through them. Although the exact meaning of the selection depends on the type of application, the procedure is always the same:

1. The user positions the pointer at one corner of the range and presses the mouse button. This position is called the anchor point of the range.

2. The user moves the pointer in any direction. As the pointer is moved, visual feedback indicates the objects that would be selected if the mouse button were released. For text and arrays, the selected area is continually highlighted. For graphics, a dotted rectangle expands or contracts to show the range that will be selected.

3. When the feedback shows the desired range, the user releases the mouse button. The point at which the button is released is called the endpoint of the range.

Extending a Selection

A user can change the extent of an existing selection by holding down the Shift key and clicking the mouse button. Exactly what happens next depends on the context.

In text or an array, the result of a Shift-click is always a range. The position where the button is clicked becomes the new endpoint or anchor point of the range; the selection can be extended in any direction. If the user clicks within the current range, the new range will be smaller than the old range.

In graphics, a selection is extended by adding objects to it; the added objects do not have to be adjacent to the objects already selected. The user can add either an individual object or a range of objects to the selection by holding down the Shift key before making the additional selection. If the user holds down the Shift key and selects one or more objects that are already highlighted, the objects are deselected.

Extended selections can be made across the panes of a split window. (See "Splitting Windows".)

Making a Discontinuous Selection

In graphics applications, objects aren't usually considered to be in any particular sequence. Therefore, the user can use Shift-click to extend a selection by a single object, even if that object is nowhere near the current selection. When this happens, the objects between the current selection and the new object are not automatically included in the selection. This kind of selection is called a discontinuous selection. In the case of graphics, all selections are discontinuous selections.

This is not the case with arrays and text, however. In these two kinds of applications, an extended selection made by a Shift-click always includes everything between the old selection and the new endpoint. To provide the possibility of a discontinuous selection in these applications, Command-click is included in the user interface.

To make a discontinuous selection in a text or array application, the user selects the first piece in the normal way, then holds down the Command key before selecting the remaining pieces. Each piece is selected in the same way as if it were the whole selection, but because the Command key is held down, the new pieces are added to the existing selection instead of supplanting it.

If one of the pieces selected is already within an existing part of the selection, then instead of being added to the selection it's removed from the selection. Figure 7 shows a sequence in which several pieces are selected and deselected.

Not all applications support discontinuous selections, and those that do might restrict the operations that a user can perform on them. For example, a word processor might allow the user to choose a font after making a discontinuous selection, but not to choose Cut.

Selecting Text

Text is used in most applications; it's selected and edited in a consistent way, regardless of where it appears.

A block of text is a string of characters. A text selection is a substring of this string, which can have any length from zero characters to the whole block. Each of the text selection methods selects a different kind of substring. Figure 8 shows different kinds of text selections.

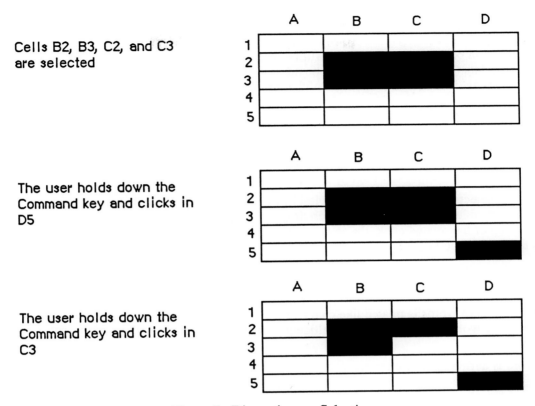

Cells B2, B3, C2, and C3 are selected

The user holds down the Command key and clicks in D5

The user holds down the Command key and clicks in C3

Figure 7. Discontinuous Selection

Insertion point   And|springth the wude nu.

Range of characters   A▮nd spri▮ngth the wude nu.

Word   ▮And▮ springth the wude nu.

Range of words   ▮And springth▮ the wude nu.

Discontinuous selection A▮nd spri▮ngth the ▮wude▮ nu.

Figure 8. Text Selections

Insertion Point

The insertion point is a zero-length text selection. The user establishes the location of the insertion point by clicking between two characters. The insertion point then appears at the nearest character boundary. If the user clicks to the right of the last character on a line, the insertion point appears immediately after the last character. The converse is true if the user clicks to the left of the first character in the line.

The insertion point shows where text will be inserted when the user begins typing, or where cut or copied data (the contents of the Clipboard) will be pasted. After each character is typed, the insertion point is relocated to the right of the insertion.

If, between the mouse-down and the mouse-up, the user moves the pointer more than about half the width of a character, the selection is a range selection rather than an insertion point.

Selecting Words

The user selects a whole word by double-clicking somewhere within that word. If the user begins a double-click sequence, but then drags the mouse between the mouse-down and the mouse-up of the second click, the selection becomes a range of words rather than a single word. As the pointer moves, the application highlights or unhighlights a whole word at a time.

A word, or range of words, can also be selected in the same way as any other range; whether this type of selection is treated as a range of characters or as a range of words depends on the operation. For example, in MacWrite, a range of individual characters that happens to coincide with a range of words is treated like characters for purposes of extending a selection, but is treated like words for purposes of "intelligent" cut and paste (described later in the "Text Editing" section).

A word is defined as any continuous string that contains only the following characters:

- a letter (including letters with diacritical marks)
- a digit
- a nonbreaking space (Option-space)
- a dollar sign, cent sign, English pound symbol, or yen symbol
- a percent sign
- a comma between digits
- a period before a digit
- an apostrophe between letters or digits
- a hyphen, but not a minus sign (Option-hyphen) or a dash (Option-Shift-hyphen)

This is the definition in the United States and Canada; in other countries, it would have to be changed to reflect local formats for numbers, dates, and currency.

If the user double-clicks over any character not on the list above, that character is selected, but it is not considered a word.

Examples of words:

$123,456.78

shouldn't

3 1/2 [with a nonbreaking space]

.5%

Examples of nonwords:

7/10/6

blue cheese   [with a breaking space]

"Yoicks!"   [the quotation marks and exclamation point aren't part of the word]

Selecting a Range of Text

The user selects a range of text by dragging through the range. A range is either a range of words or a range of individual characters, as described under "Selecting Words", above.

If the user extends the range, the way the range is extended depends on what kind of range it is. If it's a range of individual characters, it can be extended one character at a time. If it's a range of words (including a single word), it's extended only by whole words.

Graphics Selections

There are several different ways to select graphic objects and to show selection feedback in existing Macintosh applications. MacDraw, MacPaint, and the Finder all illustrate different possibilities. This section describes the MacDraw paradigm, which is the most extensible to other kinds of applications.

A MacDraw document is a collection of individual graphic objects. To select one of these objects, the user clicks once on the object, which is then shown with knobs. (The knobs are used to stretch or shrink the object, and won't be discussed in these guidelines.) Figure 9 shows some examples of selection in MacDraw.

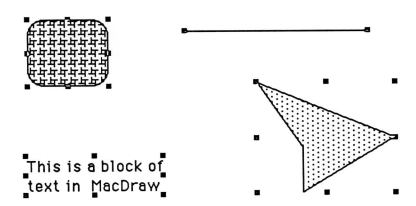

Figure 9. Graphics Selections in MacDraw

To select more than one object, the user can select either a range or a multiple selection. A range selection includes every object completely contained within the dotted rectangle that encloses the range, while an extended selection includes only those objects explicitly selected.

Selections in Arrays

As described above under "Types of Applications", an array is a one- or two-dimensional arrangement of fields. If the array is one-dimensional, it's called a form; if it's two-dimensional, it's called a table. The user can select one or more fields, or part of the contents of a field.

To select a single field, the user clicks in the field. The user can also implicitly select a field by moving into it with the Tab or Return key.

The Tab key cycles through the fields in an order determined by the application. From each field, the Tab key selects the "next" field. Typically, the sequence of fields is first from left to right, and then from top to bottom. When the last field in a form is selected, pressing the Tab key selects the first field in the form. In a form, an application might prefer to select the fields in logical, rather than physical, order.

The Return key selects the first field in the next row. If the idea of rows doesn't make sense in a particular context, then the Return key should have the same effect as the Tab key.

Tables are more likely than forms to support range selections and extended selections. A table can also support selection of rows and columns. The most convenient way for the user to select a column is to click in the column header. To select more than one column, the user drags through several column headers. The same applies to rows.

To select part of the contents of a field, the user must first select the field. The user then clicks again to select the desired part of the field. Since the contents of a field are either text or graphics, this type of selection follows the rules outlined above. Figure 10 shows some selections in an array.

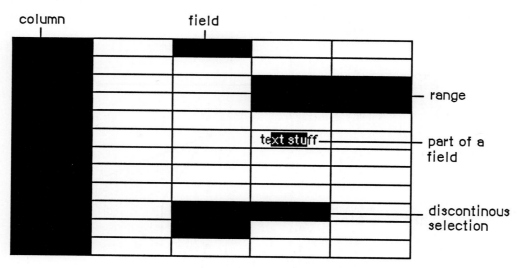

Figure 10. Array Selections

WINDOWS

The rectangles on the desktop that display information are windows. The most commmon types of windows are document windows, desk accessories, dialog boxes, and alert boxes. (Dialog and alert boxes are discussed under "Dialogs and Alerts".) Some of the features described in this section are applicable only to document windows. Figure 11 shows a typical active document window and some of its components.

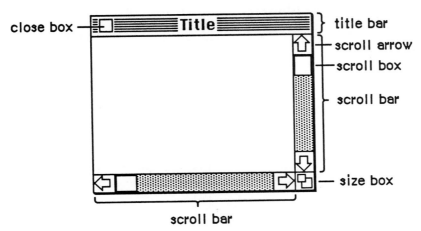

Figure 11. An Active Window

Multiple Windows

Some applications may be able to keep several windows on the desktop at the same time. Each window is in a different plane. Windows can be moved around on the Macintosh's desktop much like pieces of paper can be moved around on a real desktop. Each window can overlap those behind it, and can be overlapped by those in front of it. Even when windows don't overlap, they retain their front-to-back ordering.

Different windows can represent separate documents being viewed or edited simultaneously, or related parts of a logical whole, like the listing, execution, and debugging of a program. Each application may deal with the meaning and creation of multiple windows in its own way.

The advantage of multiple windows is that the user can isolate unrelated chunks of information from each other. The disadvantage is that the desktop can become cluttered, especially if some of the windows can't be moved. Figure 12 shows multiple windows.

Opening and Closing Windows

Windows come up onto the screen in different ways as appropriate to the purpose of the window. The application controls at least the initial size and placement of its windows.

Most windows have a close box that, when clicked, makes the window go away. The application in control of the window determines what's done with the window visually and logically when the close box is clicked. Visually, the window can either shrink to a smaller object such as an icon, or leave no trace behind when it closes. Logically, the information in the window is either retained and then restored when the window is reopened (which is the usual case), or else the window is reinitialized each time it's opened. When a document is closed, the user is given the choice whether to save any changes made to the document since the last time it was saved.

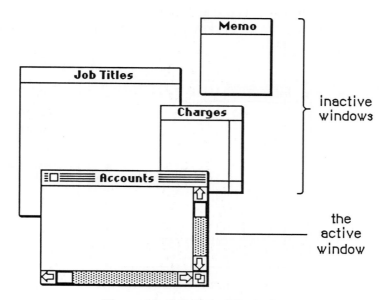

Figure 12. Multiple Windows

If an application doesn't support closing a window with a close box, it shouldn't include a close box on the window.

The Active Window

Of all the windows that are open on the desktop, the user can work in only one window at a time. This window is called the **active** window. All other open windows are **inactive**. To make a window active, the user clicks in it. Making a window active has two immediate consequences:

■ The window changes its appearance: Its title bar is highlighted and the scroll bars and size box are shown. If the window is being reactivated, the selection that was in effect when it was deactivated is rehighlighted.

■ The window is moved to the frontmost plane, so that it's shown in front of any windows that it overlaps.

Clicking in a window does nothing except activate it. To make a selection in the window, the user must click again. When the user clicks in a window that has been deactivated, the window should be reinstated just the way it was when it was deactivated, with the same position of the scroll box, and the same selection highlighted.

When a window becomes inactive, all the visual changes that took place when it was activated are reversed. The title bar becomes unhighlighted, the scroll bars and size box aren't shown, and no selection is shown in the window.

Moving a Window

Each application initially places windows on the screen wherever it wants them. The user can move a window—to make more room on the desktop or to uncover a window it's overlapping

—by dragging it by its title bar. As soon as the user presses in the title bar, that window becomes the active window. A dotted outline of the window follows the pointer until the user releases the mouse button. At the release of the button the full window is drawn in its new location. Moving a window doesn't affect the appearance of the document within the window.

If the user holds down the Command key while moving the window, the window isn't made active; it moves in the same plane.

The application should ensure that a window can never be moved completely off the screen.

Changing the Size of a Window

If a window has a size box in its bottom right corner, where the scroll bars come together, the user can change the size of the window—enlarging or reducing it to the desired size.

Dragging the size box attaches a dotted outline of the window to the pointer. The outline's top left corner stays fixed, while the bottom right corner follows the pointer. When the mouse button is released, the entire window is redrawn in the shape of the dotted outline.

Moving windows and sizing them go hand in hand. If a window can be moved, but not sized, then the user ends up constantly moving windows on and off the screen. The reason for this is that if the user moves the window off the right or bottom edge of the screen, the scroll bars are the first thing to disappear. To scroll the window, the user must move the window back onto the screen again. If, on the other hand, the window can be resized, then the user can change its size instead of moving it off the screen, and will still be able to scroll.

Sizing a window doesn't change the position of the top left corner of the window over the document or the appearance of the part of the view that's still showing; it changes only how much of the view is visible inside the window. One exception to this rule is a command such as Reduce to Fit in MacDraw, which changes the scaling of the view to fit the size of the window. If, after choosing this command, the user resizes the window, the application changes the scaling of the view.

The application can define a minimum window size. Any attempt to shrink the window below this size is ignored.

Scroll Bars

Scroll bars are used to change which part of a document view is shown in a window. Only the active window can be scrolled.

A scroll bar (see Figure 11 above) is a light gray shaft, capped on each end with square boxes labeled with arrows; inside the shaft is a white rectangle. The shaft represents one dimension of the entire document; the white rectangle (called the scroll box) represents the location of the portion of the document currently visible inside the window. As the user moves the document under the window, the position of the rectangle in the scroll bar moves correspondingly. If the document is no larger than the window, the scroll bars are inactive (the scrolling apparatus isn't shown in them). If the document window is inactive, the scroll bars aren't shown at all.

There are three ways to move the document under the window: by sequential scrolling, by "paging" windowful by windowful through the document, and by directly positioning the scroll box.

Clicking a scroll arrow lets the user see more of the document in the direction of the scroll arrow, so it moves the document in the *opposite* direction from the arrow. For example, when the user clicks the top scroll arrow, the document moves down, bringing the view closer to the top of the document. The scroll box moves towards the arrow being clicked.

Each click in a scroll arrow causes movement a distance of one unit in the chosen direction, with the unit of distance being appropriate to the application: one line for a word processor, one row or column for a spreadsheet, and so on. Within a document, units should always be the same size, for smooth scrolling. Pressing the scroll arrow causes continuous movement in its direction.

Clicking the mouse anywhere in the gray area of the scroll bar advances the document by windowfuls. The scroll box, and the document view, move toward the place where the user clicked. Clicking below the scroll box, for example, brings the user the next windowful towards the bottom of the document. Pressing in the gray area keeps windowfuls flipping by until the user releases the mouse button, or until the location of the scroll box catches up to the location of the pointer. Each windowful is the height or width of the window, minus one unit overlap (where a unit is the distance the view scrolls when the scroll arrow is clicked once).

In both the above schemes, the user moves the document incrementally until it's in the proper position under the window; as the document moves, the scroll box moves accordingly. The user can also move the document directly to any position simply by moving the scroll box to the corresponding position in the scroll bar. To move the scroll box, the user drags it along the scroll bar; an outline of the scroll box follows the pointer. When the mouse button is released, the scroll box jumps to the position last held by the outline, and the document jumps to the position corresponding to the new position of the scroll box.

If the user starts dragging the scroll box, and then moves the pointer a certain distance outside the scroll bar, the scroll box detaches itself from the pointer and stops following it; if the user releases the mouse button, the scroll box stays in its original position and the document remains unmoved. But if the user still holds the mouse button and drags the pointer back into the scroll bar, the scroll box reattaches itself to the pointer and can be dragged as usual.

If a document has a fixed size, and the user scrolls to the right or bottom edge of the document, the application displays a gray background between the edge of the document and the window frame.

Automatic Scrolling

There are several instances when the application, rather than the user, scrolls the document. These instances involve some potentially sticky problems about how to position the document within the window after scrolling.

The first case is when the user moves the pointer out of the window while selecting by dragging. The window keeps up with the selection by scrolling automatically in the direction the pointer has been moved. The rate of scrolling is the same as if the user were pressing on the corresponding scroll arrow or arrows.

The second case is when the selection isn't currently showing in the window, and the user performs an operation on it. When this happens, it's usually because the user has scrolled the document after making a selection. In this case, the application scrolls the window so that the selection is showing before performing the operation.

The third case is when the application performs an operation whose side effect is to make a new selection. An example is a search operation, after which the object of the search is selected. If this object isn't showing in the window, the application must scroll the document so as to show it.

The second and third cases present the same problem: Where should the selection be positioned within the window after scrolling? The primary rule is that the application should avoid unnecessary scrolling; users prefer to retain control over the positioning of a document. The following guidelines should be helpful:

- If part of the new selection is already showing in the window, don't scroll at all. An exception to this rule is when the part of the selection that isn't showing is more important than the part that is showing.

- If scrolling in one orientation (horizontal or vertical) is sufficient to reveal the selection, don't scroll in both orientations.

- If the selection is smaller than the window, position the selection so that some of its context is showing on each side. It's better to put the selection somewhere near the middle of the window than right up against the corner.

- Even if the selection is too large to show in the window, it might be preferable to show some context rather than to try to fit as much as possible of the selection in the window.

Splitting a Window

Sometimes it's desirable to be able to see disjoint parts of a document simultaneously. Applications that accommodate such a capability allow the window to be split into independently scrollable **panes**.

Applications that support splitting a window into panes place split bars at the top of the vertical scroll bar and to the left of the horizontal one. Pressing a split bar attaches it to the pointer. Dragging the split bar positions it anywhere along the scroll bar; releasing the mouse button moves the split bar to a new position, splits the window at that location, and divides the appropriate scroll bar into separate scroll bars for each pane. Figure 13 shows the ways a window can be split.

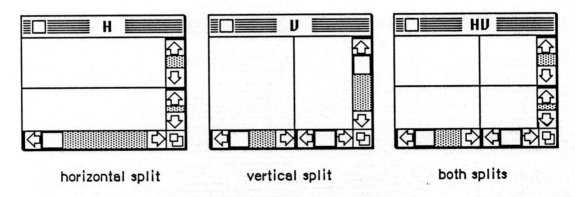

horizontal split   vertical split   both splits

Figure 13. Types of Split Windows

After a split, the document appears the same, except for the split line lying across it. But there are now separate scroll bars for each pane. The panes are still scrolled together in the orientation of the split, but can be scrolled independently in the other orientation. For example, if the split is vertical, then vertical scrolling (using the scroll bar along the right of the window) is still synchronous; horizontal scrolling is controlled separately for each pane, using the two scroll bars along the bottom of the window. This is shown in Figure 14.

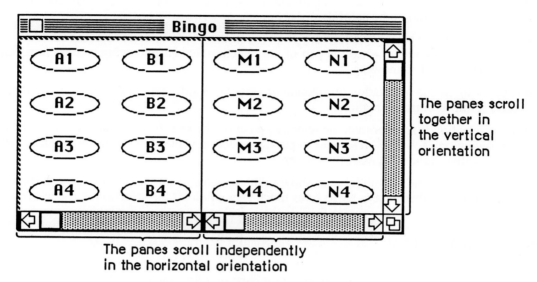

Figure 14. Scrolling a Split Window

To remove a split, the user drags the split bar to either end of the scroll bar.

The number of views in a document doesn't alter the number of selections per document: that is, one. The selection appears highlighted in all views that show it. If the application has to scroll automatically to show the selection, the pane that should be scrolled is the last one that the user clicked in. If the selection is already showing in one of the panes, no automatic scrolling takes place.

Panels

If a document window is more or less permanently divided into different areas, each of which has different content, these areas are called **panels**. Unlike panes, which show different parts of the same document but are functionally identical, panels are functionally different from each other but might show different interpretations of the same part of the document. For example, one panel might show a graphic version of the document while another panel shows a textual version.

Panels can behave much like windows; they can have scroll bars, and can even be split into more than one pane. An example of a panel with scroll bars is the list of files in the Open command's dialog box.

Whether to use panels instead of separate windows is up to the application. Multiple panels in the same window are more compact than separate windows, but they have to be moved, opened, and closed as a unit.

COMMANDS

Once information that's to be operated on has been selected, a command to operate on the information can be chosen from lists of commands called **menus**.

Macintosh's pull-down menus have the advantage that they're not visible until the user wants to see them; at the same time they're easy for the user to see and choose items from.

Most commands either do something, in which case they're verbs or verb phrases, or else they specify an attribute of an object, in which case they're adjectives. They usually apply to the current selection, although some commands apply to the whole document or window.

When you're designing your application, don't assume that everything has to be done through menu commands. Sometimes it's more appropriate for an operation to take place as a result of direct user manipulation of a graphic object on the screen, such as a control or icon. Alternatively, a single command can execute complicated instructions if it brings up a dialog box for the user to fill in.

The Menu Bar

The **menu bar** is displayed at the top of the screen. It contains a number of words and phrases: These are the titles of the menus associated with the current application. Each application has its own menu bar. The names of the menus do not change, except when the user accesses a desk accessory that uses different menus.

Only menu titles appear in the menu bar. If all of the commands in a menu are currently disabled (that is, the user can't choose them), the menu title should be dimmed (drawn in gray). The user can pull down the menu to see the commands, but can't choose any of them.

Choosing a Menu Command

To choose a command, the user positions the pointer over the menu title and presses the mouse button. The application highlights the title and displays the menu, as shown in Figure 15.

While holding down the mouse button, the user moves the pointer down the menu. As the pointer moves to each command, the command is highlighted. The command that's highlighted when the user releases the mouse button is chosen. As soon as the mouse button is released, the command blinks briefly, the menu disappears, and the command is executed. (The user can set the number of times the command blinks in the Control Panel desk accessory.) The menu title in the menu bar remains highlighted until the command has completed execution.

Nothing actually happens until the user chooses the command; the user can look at any of the menus without making a commitment to do anything.

The most frequently used commands should be at the top of a menu; research shows that the easiest item for the user to choose is the second item from the top. The most dangerous commands should be at the bottom of the menu, preferably isolated from the frequently used commands.

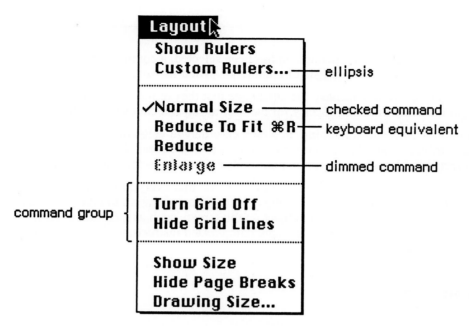

Figure 15. Menu

Appearance of Menu Commands

The commands in a particular menu should be logically related to the title of the menu. In addition to command names, three features of menus help the user understand what each command does: command groups, toggles, and special visual features.

Command Groups

As mentioned above, menu commands can be divided into two kinds: verbs and adjectives, or actions and attributes. An important difference between the two kinds of commands is that an attribute stays in effect until it's canceled, while an action ceases to be relevant after it has been performed. Each of these two kinds can be grouped within a menu. Groups are separated by dotted lines, which are implemented as disabled commands.

The most basic reason to group commands is to break up a menu so it's easier to read. Commands grouped for this reason are logically related, but independent. Commands that are actions are usually grouped this way, such as Cut, Copy, Paste, and Clear in the Edit menu.

Attribute commands that are interdependent are grouped to show this interdependence. Two kinds of attribute command groups are mutually exclusive groups and accumulating groups.

In a mutually exclusive attribute group, only one command in the group is in effect at any time. The command that's in effect is preceded by a check mark. If the user chooses a different command in the group, the check mark is moved to the new command. An example is the Font menu in MacWrite; no more than one font can be in effect at a time.

In an accumulating attribute group, any number of attributes can be in effect at the same time. One special command in the group cancels all the other commands. An example is the Style menu in MacWrite: The user can choose any combination of Bold, Italic, Underline, Outline, or Shadow, but Plain Text cancels all the other commands.

Toggled Commands

Another way to show the presence or absence of an attribute is by a toggled command. In this case, the attribute has two states, and a single command allows the user to toggle between the states. For example, when rulers are showing in MacWrite, a command in the Format menu reads "Hide Rulers". If the user chooses this command, the rulers are hidden, and the command is changed to read "Show Rulers". This kind of group should be used only when the wording of the commands makes it obvious that they're opposites.

Special Visual Features

In addition to the command names and how they're grouped, several other features of commands communicate information to the user:

- A check mark indicates whether an attribute command is currently in effect.

- An ellipsis (...) after a command name means that choosing that command brings up a dialog box. The command isn't actually executed until the user has finished filling in the dialog box and has clicked the OK button or its equivalent.

- The application dims a command when the user can't choose it. If the user moves the pointer over a dimmed item, it isn't highlighted.

- If a command can be chosen from the keyboard, it's followed by the Command key symbol and the character used to choose it. To choose a command this way, the user holds down the Command key and then presses the character key.

Some characters that can be typed along with the Command key are reserved for special purposes, but there are different degrees of stringency. Since almost every application has an Edit menu and a File menu, the keyboard equivalents in those menus are strongly reserved, and should never be used for any other purpose:

Character	Command
C	Copy (Edit menu)
Q	Quit (File menu)
V	Paste (Edit menu)
X	Cut (Edit menu)
Z	Undo (Edit menu)

Note: The keyboard equivalent for the Quit command is useful in case there's a mouse malfunction, so the user will still be able to leave the application in an orderly way (with the opportunity to save any changes to documents that haven't yet been saved).

The keyboard equivalents in the Style menu are conditionally reserved. If an application has this menu, it shouldn't use these characters for any other purpose, but if it doesn't, it can use them however it likes:

Character	Command
B	Bold
I	Italic
O	Outline
P	Plain text
S	Shadow
U	Underline

One keyboard command doesn't have a menu equivalent:

Character	Command
.	Stop current operation

Several other menu features are also supported:

- A command can be shown in Bold, *Italic*, Outline, Underline, or Shadow character style.
- A command can be preceded by an icon.
- The application can draw its own type of menu. An example of this is the Fill menu in MacDraw.

STANDARD MENUS

One of the strongest ways in which Macintosh applications can take advantage of the consistency of the user interface is by using standard menus. The operations controlled by these menus occur so frequently that it saves considerable time for users if they always match exactly. Three of these menus, the Apple, File, and Edit menus, appear in almost every application. The Font, FontSize, and Style menus affect the appearance of text, and appear only in applications where they're relevant.

The Apple Menu

Macintosh doesn't allow two applications to be running at once. Desk accessories, however, are mini-applications that are available while using any application.

At any time the user can issue a command to call up one of several desk accessories; the available accessories are listed in the Apple menu, as shown in Figure 16.

Accessories are disk-based: Only those accessories on an available disk can be used. The list of accessories is expanded or reduced according to what's available. More than one accessory can be on the desktop at a time.

Figure 16. Apple Menu

The Apple menu also contains the "About xxx" menu item, where "xxx" is the name of the application. Choosing this item brings up a dialog box with the name and copyright information for the application, as well as any other information the application wants to display.

The File Menu

The File menu lets the user perform certain simple filing operations without leaving the application and returning to the Finder. It also contains the commands for printing and for leaving the application. The standard File menu includes the commands shown in Figure 17. All of these commands are described below.

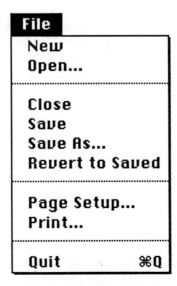

Figure 17. File Menu

New

New opens a new, untitled document. The user names the document the first time it's saved. The New command is disabled when the maximum number of documents allowed by the application is already open; however, an application that allows only one document to be open at a time may make an exception to this, as described below for Open.

Open

Open opens an existing document. To select the document, the user is presented with a dialog box (Figure 18). This dialog box shows a list of all the documents, on the disk whose name is displayed, that can be handled by the current application. The user can scroll this list forward and backward. The dialog box also gives the user the chance to look at documents on another disk, or to eject a disk.

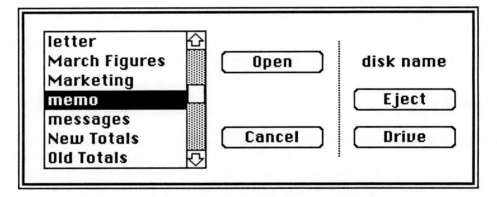

Figure 18. Open Dialog Box

Using the Open command, the user can only open a document that can be processed by the current application. Opening a document that can only be processed by a different application requires leaving the application and returning to the Finder.

The Open command is disabled when the maximum number of documents allowed by the application is already open. An application that allows only one document to be open at a time may make an exception to this, by first closing the open document before opening the new document. In this case, if the user has changed the open document since the last time it was saved, an alert box is presented as when an explicit Close command is given (see below); then the Open dialog box appears. Clicking Cancel in either the Close alert box or the Open dialog box cancels the entire operation.

Close

Close closes the active window, which may be a document window, a desk accessory, or any other type of window. If it's a document window and the user has changed the document since the last time it was saved, the command presents an alert box giving the user the opportunity to save the changes.

Clicking in the close box of a window is the same as choosing Close.

Save

Save makes permanent any changes to the active document since the last time it was saved. It leaves the document open.

If the user chooses Save for a new document that hasn't been named yet, the application presents the Save As dialog box (see below) to name the document, and then continues with the save. The active document remains active.

If there's not enough room on the disk to save the document, the application asks if the user wants to save the document on another disk. If the answer is yes, the application goes through the Save As dialog to find out which disk.

Save As

Save As saves a copy of the active document under a file name provided by the user.

If the document already has a name, Save As closes the old version of the document, creates a copy with the new name, and displays the copy in the window.

If the document is untitled, Save As saves the original document under the specified name. The active document remains active.

Revert to Saved

Revert to Saved returns the active document to the state it was in the last time it was saved. Before doing so, it puts up an alert box to confirm that this is what the user wants.

Page Setup

Page Setup lets the user specify printing parameters such as the paper size and printing orientation. These parameters remain with the document.

Print

Print lets the user specify various parameters such as print quality and number of copies, and then prints the document. The parameters apply only to the current printing operation.

Quit

Quit leaves the application and returns to the Finder. If any open documents have been changed since the last time they were saved, the application presents the same alert box as for Close, once for each document.

The Edit Menu

The Edit menu contains the commands that delete, move, and copy objects, as well as commands such as Undo, Select All, and Show Clipboard. This section also discusses the Clipboard, which is controlled by the Edit menu commands. Text editing methods that don't use menu commands are discussed under "Text Editing".

If the application supports desk accessories, the order of commands in the Edit menu should be exactly as shown here. This is because, by default, the application passes the numbers, not the names, of the menu commands to the desk accessories. (For details, see chapter 14.) In particular, your application must provide an Undo command for the benefit of the desk accessories, even if it doesn't support the command (in which case it can disable the command until a desk accessory is opened).

The standard order of commands in the Edit menu is shown in Figure 19.

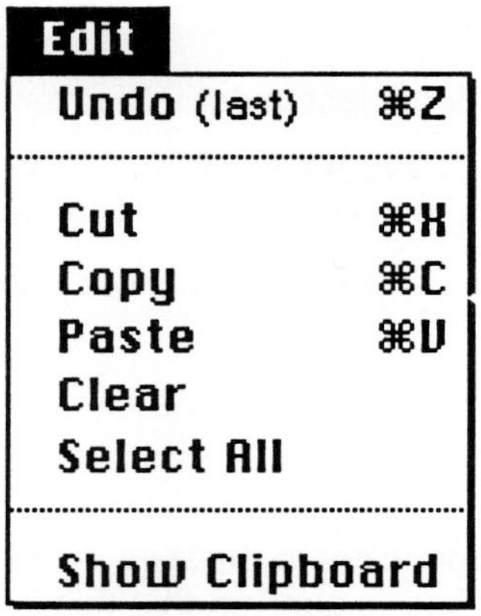

```
┌─────────────────────────┐
│  Edit                   │
├─────────────────────────┤
│  Undo (last)        ⌘Z  │
│ .......................  │
│  Cut                ⌘H  │
│  Copy               ⌘C  │
│  Paste              ⌘U  │
│  Clear                  │
│  Select All             │
│ .......................  │
│  Show Clipboard         │
└─────────────────────────┘
```

Figure 19. Edit Menu

The Clipboard

The Clipboard holds whatever is cut or copied from a document. Its contents stay intact when the user changes documents, opens a desk accessory, or leaves the application. An application can show the contents of the Clipboard in a window, and can choose whether to have the Clipboard window open or closed when the application starts up.

The Clipboard window looks like a document window, with a close box but usually without scroll bars or a size box. The user can see its contents but cannot edit them. In most other ways the Clipboard window behaves just like any other window.

Every time the user performs a Cut or Copy on the current selection, a copy of the selection replaces the previous contents of the Clipboard. The previous contents are kept around in case the user chooses Undo.

There's only one Clipboard, which is present for all applications that support Cut, Copy, and Paste. The user can see the Clipboard window by choosing Show Clipboard from the Edit menu. If the window is already showing, it's hidden by choosing Hide Clipboard. (Show Clipboard and Hide Clipboard are a single toggled command.)

Because the contents of the Clipboard remain unchanged when applications begin and end, or when the user opens a desk accessory, the Clipboard can be used for transferring data among mutually compatible applications and desk accessories.

Undo

Undo reverses the effect of the previous operation. Not all operations can be undone; the definition of an undoable operation is somewhat application-dependent. The general rule is that operations that change the contents of the document are undoable, and operations that don't are not. Most menu items are undoable, and so are typing sequences.

A typing sequence is any sequence of characters typed from the keyboard or numeric keypad, including Backspace, Return, and Tab, but not including keyboard equivalents of commands.

Operations that aren't undoable include selecting, scrolling, and splitting the window or changing its size or location. None of these operations interrupts a typing sequence. For example, if the user types a few characters and then scrolls the document, the Undo command still undoes the typing. Whenever the location affected by the Undo operation isn't currently showing on the screen, the application should scroll the document so the user can see the effect of the Undo.

An application should also allow the user to undo any operations that are initiated directly on the screen, without a menu command. This includes operations controlled by setting dials, clicking check boxes, and so on, as well as drawing graphic objects with the mouse.

The actual wording of the Undo command as it appears in the Edit menu is "Undo xxx", where xxx is the name of the last operation. If the last operation isn't a menu command, use some suitable term after the word Undo. If the last operation can't be undone, the command reads "Undo", but is disabled.

If the last operation was Undo, the menu command is "Redo xxx", where xxx is the operation that was undone. If this command is chosen, the Undo is undone.

Cut

The user chooses Cut either to delete the current selection or to move it. A move is eventually completed by choosing Paste.

When the user chooses Cut, the application removes the current selection from the document and puts it in the Clipboard, replacing the Clipboard's previous contents. The place where the selection used to be becomes the new selection; the visual implications of this vary among applications. For example, in text, the new selection is an insertion point, while in an array, it's an empty but highlighted cell. If the user chooses Paste immediately after choosing Cut, the document should be just as it was before the cut.

Copy

Copy is the first stage of a copy operation. Copy puts a copy of the selection in the Clipboard, but the selection also remains in the document. The user completes the copy operation by choosing Paste.

Paste

Paste is the last stage of a move or copy operation. It pastes the contents of the Clipboard into the document, replacing the current selection. The user can choose Paste several times in a row to paste multiple copies. After a paste, the new selection is the object that was pasted, except in text, where it's an insertion point immediately after the pasted text. The Clipboard remains unchanged.

Clear

When the user chooses Clear, or presses the Clear key on the numeric keypad, the application removes the selection, but doesn't put it in the Clipboard. The new selection is the same as it would be after a Cut.

Select All

Select All selects every object in the document.

Show Clipboard

Show Clipboard is a toggled command. When the Clipboard isn't displayed, the command is "Show Clipboard". If the user chooses this command, the Clipboard is displayed and the command changes to "Hide Clipboard".

Font-Related Menus

Three standard menus affect the appearance of text: Font, which determines the font of a text selection; FontSize, which determines the size of the characters; and Style, which determines aspects of its appearance such as boldface, italics, and so on.

A **font** is a set of typographical characters created with a consistent design. Things that relate characters in a font include the thickness of vertical and horizontal lines, the degree and position of curves and swirls, and the use of serifs. A font has the same general appearance, regardless of the size of the characters. Most Macintosh fonts are proportional rather than fixed-width; an application can't make assumptions about exactly how many characters will fit in a given area when these fonts are used.

Font Menu

The Font menu always lists the fonts that are currently available. Figure 20 shows a Font menu with some of the most common fonts.

Figure 20. Font Menu

FontSize Menu

Font sizes are measured in **points**; a point is about 1/72 of an inch. Each font is available in predefined sizes. The numbers of these sizes for each font are shown outlined in the FontSize menu. The font can also be scaled to other sizes, but it may not look as good. Figure 21 shows a FontSize menu with the standard font sizes.

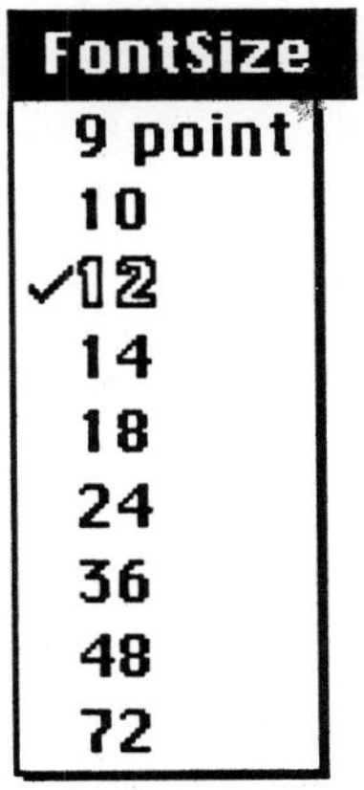

Figure 21. FontSize Menu

If there's insufficient room in the menu bar for the word FontSize, it can be abbreviated to Size. If there's insufficient room for both a Font menu and a Size menu, the sizes can be put at the end of the Font or Style menu.

Style Menu

The commands in the standard Style menu are Plain Text, Bold, Italic, Underline, Outline, and Shadow. All the commands except Plain Text are accumulating attributes; the user can choose any combination. A command that's in effect for the current selection is preceded by a check mark. Plain Text cancels all the other choices. Figure 22 shows these styles.

Figure 22. Style Menu

TEXT EDITING

In addition to the operations described under "The Edit Menu" above, there are other ways to edit text that don't use menu items.

Inserting Text

To insert text, the user selects an insertion point by clicking where the text is to go, and then starts typing it. As the user types, the application continually moves the insertion point to the right of each new character.

Applications with multiline text blocks should support **word wraparound**; that is, no word should be broken between lines. The definition of a word is given under "Selecting Words" above.

Backspace

When the user presses the Backspace key, one of two things happens:

- If the current selection is one or more characters, it's deleted.
- If the current selection is an insertion point, the previous character is deleted.

In either case, the insertion point replaces the deleted characters in the document. The deleted characters don't go into the Clipboard, but the deletion can be undone by immediately choosing Undo.

Replacing Text

If the user starts typing when the selection is one or more characters, the characters that are typed replace the selection. The deleted characters don't go into the Clipboard, but the replacement can be undone by immediately choosing Undo.

Intelligent Cut and Paste

An application that lets the user select a word by double-clicking should also see to it that the user doesn't regret using this feature. The only way to do this is by providing "intelligent" cut and paste.

To understand why this feature is necessary, consider the following sequence of events in an application that doesn't provide it:

1. A sentence in the user's document reads:

   Returns are only accepted if the merchandise is damaged.

   The user wants to change this to:

   Returns are accepted only if the merchandise is damaged.

2. The user selects the word "only" by double-clicking. The letters are highlighted, but not either of the adjacent spaces.

3. The user chooses Cut, clicks just before the word "if", and chooses Paste.

4. The sentence now reads:

   Returns are accepted onlyif the merchandise is damaged.

   To correct the sentence, the user has to remove a space between "are" and "accepted", and add one between "only" and "if". At this point he or she may be wondering why the Macintosh is supposed to be easier to use than other computers.

If an application supports intelligent cut and paste, the rules to follow are:

- If the user selects a word or a range of words, highlight the selection, but not any adjacent spaces.

- When the user chooses Cut, if the character to the left of the selection is a space, discard it. Otherwise, if the character to the right of the selection is a space, discard it.

- When the user chooses Paste, if the character to the left or right of the current selection is part of a word, insert a space before pasting.

If the left or right end of a text selection is a word, follow these rules at that end, regardless of whether there's a word at the other end.

This feature makes more sense if the application supports the full definition of a word (as detailed above under "Selecting Words"), rather than the definition of a word as anything between two spaces.

These rules apply to any selection that's one or more whole words, whether it was chosen with a double click or as a range selection.

Figure 23 shows some examples of intelligent cut and paste.

Editing Fields

If an application isn't primarily a text application, but does use text in fields (such as in a dialog box), it may not be able to provide the full text editing capabilities described so far. It's important, however, that whatever editing capabilities the application provides under these circumstances be upward-compatible with the full text editing capabilities. The following list

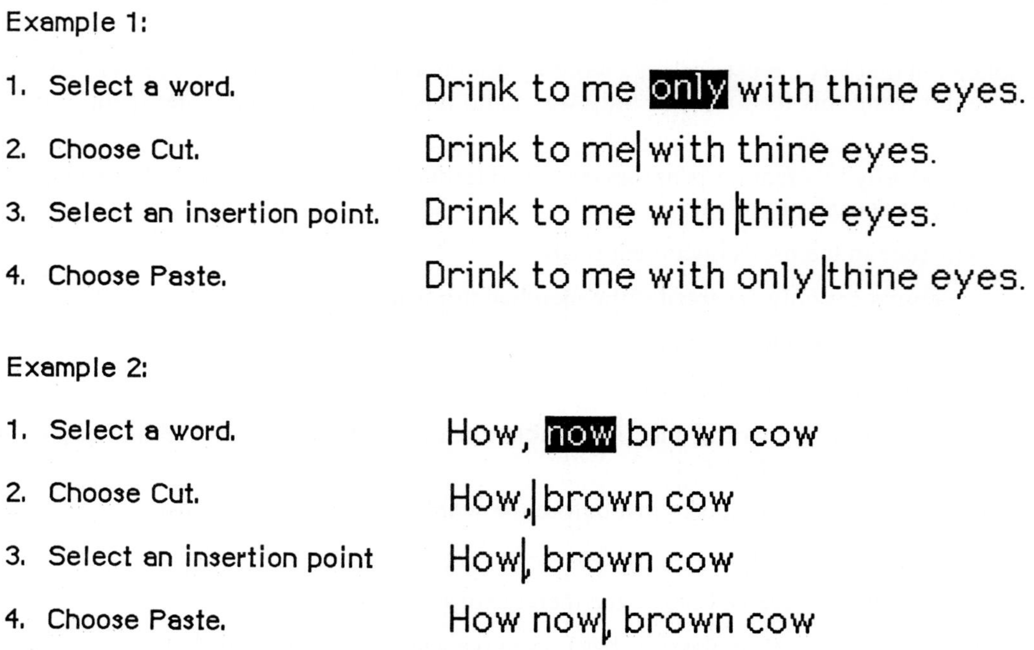

Example 1:

1. Select a word.   Drink to me only with thine eyes.

2. Choose Cut.   Drink to me| with thine eyes.

3. Select an insertion point.   Drink to me with |thine eyes.

4. Choose Paste.   Drink to me with only |thine eyes.

Example 2:

1. Select a word.   How, now brown cow

2. Choose Cut.   How,| brown cow

3. Select an insertion point   How|, brown cow

4. Choose Paste.   How now|, brown cow

Figure 23. Intelligent Cut and Paste

shows the capabilities that can be provided, from the minimal to the most sophisticated:

- The user can select the whole field and type in a new value.
- The user can backspace.
- The user can select a substring of the field and replace it.
- The user can select a word by double-clicking.
- The user can choose Undo, Cut, Copy, Paste, and Clear, as described above under "The Edit Menu". In the most sophisticated version, the application implements intelligent cut and paste.

An application should also perform appropriate edit checks. For example, if the only legitimate value for a field is a string of digits, the application might issue an alert if the user typed any nondigits. Alternatively, the application could wait until the user is through typing before checking the validity of the field's contents. In this case, the appropriate time to check the field is when the user clicks anywhere other than within the field.

DIALOGS AND ALERTS

The "select-then-choose" paradigm is sufficient whenever operations are simple and act on only one object. But occasionally a command will require more than one object, or will need additional parameters before it can be executed. And sometimes a command won't be able to carry out its normal function, or will be unsure of the user's real intent. For these special circumstances the Macintosh user interface includes two additional features:

■ dialogs, to allow the user to provide additional information before a command is executed

■ alerts, to notify the user whenever an unusual situation occurs

Since both of these features lean heavily on controls, controls are described in this section, even though controls are also used in other places.

Controls

Friendly systems act by direct cause-and-effect; they do what they're told. Performing actions on a system in an indirect fashion reduces the sense of direct manipulation. To give Macintosh users the feeling that they're in control of their machines, many of an application's features are implemented with **controls**: graphic objects that, when manipulated with the mouse, cause instant action with visible results. Controls can also change settings to modify future actions.

There are four main types of controls: buttons, check boxes, radio buttons, and dials (see Figure 24). You can also design your own controls, such as a ruler on which tabs can be set.

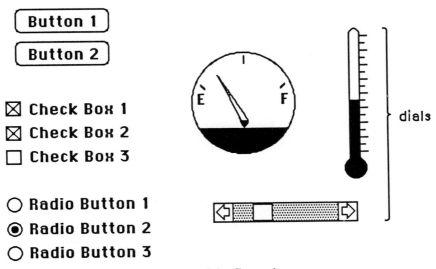

Figure 24. Controls

Buttons

Buttons are small objects labeled with text. Clicking or pressing a button performs the action described by the button's label.

Buttons usually perform instantaneous actions, such as completing operations defined by a dialog box or acknowledging error messages. They can also perform continuous actions, in which case the effect of pressing on the button would be the same as the effect of clicking it repeatedly.

Two particular buttons, OK and Cancel, are especially important in dialogs and alerts; they're discussed under those headings below.

Check Boxes and Radio Buttons

Whereas buttons perform instantaneous or continuous actions, check boxes and radio buttons let the user choose among alternative values for a parameter.

Check boxes act like toggle switches; they're used to indicate the state of a parameter that must be either off or on. The parameter is on if the box is checked, otherwise it's off. The check boxes appearing together in a given context are independent of each other; any number of them can be off or on.

Radio buttons typically occur in groups; they're round and are filled in with a black circle when on. They're called radio buttons because they act like the buttons on a car radio. At any given time, exactly one button in the group is on. Clicking one button in a group turns off the button that's currently on.

Both check boxes and radio buttons are accompanied by text that identifies what each button does.

Dials

Dials display the value, magnitude, or position of something in the application or system, and optionally allow the user to alter that value. Dials are predominantly analog devices, displaying their values graphically and allowing the user to change the value by dragging an **indicator**; dials may also have a digital display.

The most common example of a dial is the scroll bar. The indicator of the scroll bar is the scroll box; it represents the position of the window over the length of the document. The user can drag the scroll box to change that position. (See "Scroll Bars" above.)

Dialogs

Commands in menus normally act on only one object. If a command needs more information before it can be performed, it presents a **dialog box** to gather the additional information from the user. The user can tell which commands bring up dialog boxes because they're followed by an ellipsis (...) in the menu.

A dialog box is a rectangle that may contain text, controls, and icons. There should be some text in the box that indicates which command brought up the dialog box.

The user sets controls and text fields in the dialog box to provide the needed information. When the application puts up the dialog box, it should set the controls to some default setting and fill in the text fields with default values, if possible. One of the text fields (the "first" field) should be highlighted, so that the user can change its value just by typing in the new value. If all the text fields are blank, there should be an insertion point in the first field.

Editing text fields in a dialog box should conform to the guidelines detailed above under "Text Editing".

When the user is through editing an item:

- Pressing Tab accepts the changes made to the item, and selects the next item in sequence.

- Clicking in another item accepts the changes made to the previous item and selects the newly clicked item.

Dialog boxes are either modal or modeless, as described below.

Modal Dialog Boxes

A **modal** dialog box is one that the user must explicitly dismiss before doing anything else, such as making a selection outside the dialog box or choosing a command. Figure 25 shows a modal dialog box.

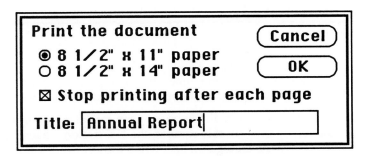

Figure 25. A Modal Dialog Box

Because it restricts the user's freedom of action, this type of dialog box should be used sparingly. In particular, the user can't choose a menu item while a modal dialog box is up, and therefore can only do the simplest kinds of text editing. For these reasons, the main use of a modal dialog box is when it's important for the user to complete an operation before doing anything else.

A modal dialog box usually has at least two buttons: OK and Cancel. OK dismisses the dialog box and performs the original command according to the information provided; it can be given a more descriptive name than "OK". Cancel dismisses the dialog box and cancels the original command; it should always be called "Cancel".

A dialog box can have other kinds of buttons as well; these may or may not dismiss the dialog box. One of the buttons in the dialog box may be outlined boldly. The outlined button is the **default button**; if no button is outlined, then the OK button is the default button. The default button should be the safest button in the current situation. Pressing the Return or Enter key has the same effect as clicking the default button. If there's no default button, Return and Enter have no effect.

A special type of modal dialog box is one with no buttons. This type of box just informs the user of a situation without eliciting any response. Usually, it would describe the progress of an ongoing operation. Since it has no buttons, the user has no way to dismiss it. Therefore, the application must leave it up long enough for the user to read it before taking it down.

Modeless Dialog Boxes

A **modeless** dialog box allows the user to perform other operations without dismissing the dialog box. Figure 26 shows a modeless dialog box.

A modeless dialog box is dismissed by clicking in the close box or by choosing Close when the dialog is active. The dialog box is also dismissed implicitly when the user chooses Quit. It's

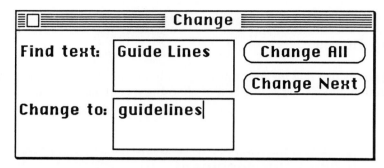

Figure 26. A Modeless Dialog Box

usually a good idea for the application to remember the contents of the dialog box after it's dismissed, so that when it's opened again, it can be restored exactly as it was.

Controls work the same way in modeless dialog boxes as in modal dialog boxes, except that buttons never dismiss the dialog box. In this context, the OK button means "go ahead and perform the operation, but leave the dialog box up", while Cancel usually terminates an ongoing operation.

A modeless dialog box can also have text fields; since the user can choose menu commands, the full range of editing capabilities can be made available.

Alerts

Every user of every application is liable to do something that the application won't understand or can't cope with in a normal manner. **Alerts** give applications a way to respond to errors not only in a consistent manner, but in stages according to the severity of the error, the user's level of expertise, and the particular history of the error. The two kinds of alerts are beeps and alert boxes.

Beeps are used for errors that are both minor and immediately obvious. For example, if the user tries to backspace past the left boundary of a text field, the application could choose to beep instead of putting up an alert box. A beep can also be part of a staged alert, as described below.

An alert box looks like a modal dialog box, except that it's somewhat narrower and appears lower on the screen. An alert box is primarily a one way communication from the system to the user; the only way the user can respond is by clicking buttons. Therefore alert boxes might contain dials and buttons, but usually not text fields, radio buttons, or check boxes. Figure 27 shows a typical alert box.

There are three types of alert boxes:

- Note: A minor mistake that wouldn't have any disastrous consequences if left as is.

- Caution: An operation that may or may not have undesirable results if it's allowed to continue. The user is given the choice whether or not to continue.

- Stop: A serious problem or other situation that requires remedial action by the user.

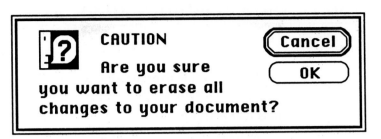

Figure 27. An Alert Box

An application can define different responses for each of several stages of an alert, so that if the user persists in the same mistake, the application can issue increasingly more helpful (or sterner) messages. A typical sequence is for the first two occurrences of the mistake to result in a beep, and for subsequent occurrences to result in an alert box. This type of sequence is especially appropriate when the mistake is one that has a high probability of being accidental (for example, when the user chooses Cut when there's no text selection).

How the buttons in an alert box are labeled depends on the nature of the box. If the box presents the user with a situation in which no alternative actions are available, the box has a single button that's labeled OK. Clicking this button means "I've read the alert." If the user is given alternatives, then typically the alert is phrased as a question that can be answered "yes" or "no". In this case, buttons labeled Yes and No are appropriate, although some variation such as Save and Don't Save is also acceptable. OK and Cancel can be used, as long as their meanings aren't ambiguous.

The preferred (safest) button to use in the current situation is boldly outlined. This is the alert's default button; its effect occurs if the user presses Return or Enter.

It's important to phrase messages in alert boxes so that users aren't left guessing the real meaning. Avoid computer jargon.

Use icons whenever possible. Graphics can better describe some error situations than words, and familiar icons help users distinguish their alternatives better. Icons should be internationally comprehensible; they shouldn't contain any words, or any symbols that are unique to a particular country.

Generally, it's better to be polite than abrupt, even if it means lengthening the message. The role of the alert box is to be helpful and make constructive suggestions, not to give orders. But its focus is to help the user solve the problem, not to give an interesting but academic description of the problem itself.

Under no circumstances should an alert message refer the user to external documentation for further clarification. It should provide an adequate description of the information needed by the user to take appropriate action.

The best way to make an alert message understandable is to think carefully through the error condition itself. Can the application handle this without an error? Is the error specific enough so that the user can fix the situation? What are the recommended solutions? Can the exact item causing the error be displayed in the alert message?

DO'S AND DON'TS OF A FRIENDLY USER INTERFACE

Do:

- Let the user have as much control as possible over the appearance of objects on the screen—their arrangement, size, and visibility.

- Use verbs for menu commands that perform actions.

- Make alert messages self-explanatory.

- Use controls and other graphics instead of just menu commands.

- Take the time to use good graphic design; it really helps.

Don't:

- Overuse modes, including modal dialog boxes.

- Require using the keyboard for an operation that would be easier with the mouse, or require using the mouse for an operation that would be easier with the keyboard.

- Change the way the screen looks unexpectedly, especially by scrolling automatically more than necessary.

- Redraw objects unnecessarily; it causes the screen to flicker annoyingly.

- Make up your own menus and then give them the same names as standard menus.

- Take an old-fashioned prompt-based application originally developed for another machine and pass it off as a Macintosh application.

3 MACINTOSH MEMORY MANAGEMENT: AN INTRODUCTION

ABOUT THIS CHAPTER

This chapter contains the minimum information you'll need about memory management on the Macintosh. Memory management is covered in greater detail in chapter 1 of Volume II.

THE STACK AND THE HEAP

A running program can dynamically **allocate** and **release** memory in two places: the stack or the heap. The **stack** is an area of memory that can grow or shrink at one end while the other end remains fixed, as shown in Figure 1. This means that space on the stack is always allocated and released in LIFO (last-in-first-out) order: The last item allocated is always the first to be released. It also means that the allocated area of the stack is always contiguous. Space is released only at the top of the stack, never in the middle, so there can never be any unallocated "holes" in the stack.

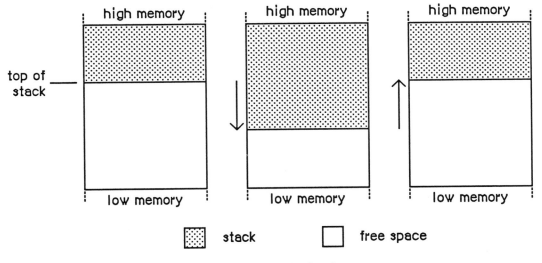

Figure 1. The Stack

By convention, the stack grows from high toward low memory addresses. The end of the stack that grows and shrinks is usually referred to as the "top" of the stack, even though it's actually at the lower end of the stack in memory.

When programs in high-level languages declare static variables (such as with the Pascal VAR declaration), those variables are allocated on the stack.

The other method of dynamic memory allocation is from the **heap**. Heap space is allocated and released only at the program's explicit request, through calls to the Memory Manager.

Space in the heap is allocated in **blocks**, which may be of any size needed for a particular object. The Memory Manager does all the necessary "housekeeping" to keep track of the blocks as they're allocated and released. Because these operations can occur in any order, the heap doesn't grow and shrink in an orderly way like the stack. After a program has been running for a while, the heap tends to become fragmented into a patchwork of allocated and free blocks, as shown in Figure 2.

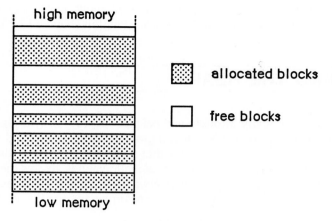

Figure 2. A Fragmented Heap

As a result of heap fragmentation, when the program asks to allocate a new block of a certain size, it may be impossible to satisfy the request even though there's enough free space available, because the space is broken up into blocks smaller than the requested size. When this happens, the Memory Manager will try to create the needed space by **compacting** the heap: moving allocated blocks together in order to collect the free space into a single larger block (see Figure 3).

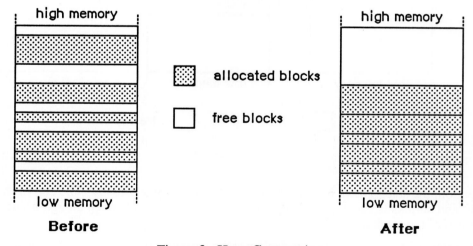

Figure 3. Heap Compaction

There's a **system heap** that's used by the Operating System and an **application heap** that's used by the Toolbox and the application program.

POINTERS AND HANDLES

The Memory Manager contains a few fundamental routines for allocating and releasing heap space. The NewPtr function allocates a block in the heap of a requested size and returns a pointer to the block. You can then make as many copies of the pointer as you need and use them in any way your program requires. When you're finished with the block, you can release the memory it occupies (returning it to available free space) with the DisposPtr procedure.

Once you've called DisposPtr, any pointers you may have to the block become invalid, since the block they're supposed to point to no longer exists. You have to be careful not to use such "dangling" pointers. This type of bug can be very difficult to diagnose and correct, since its effects typically aren't discovered until long after the pointer is left dangling.

Another way a pointer can be left dangling is for its underlying block to be moved to a different location within the heap. To avoid this problem, blocks that are referred to through simple pointers, as in Figure 4, are **nonrelocatable**. The Memory Manager will never move a nonrelocatable block, so you can rely on all pointers to it to remain correct for as long as the block remains allocated.

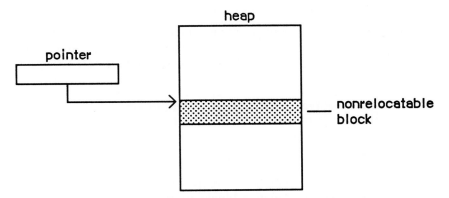

Figure 4. A Pointer to a Nonrelocatable Block

If all blocks in the heap were nonrelocatable, there would be no way to prevent the heap's free space from becoming fragmented. Since the Memory Manager needs to be able to move blocks around in order to compact the heap, it also uses **relocatable** blocks. (All the allocated blocks shown above in Figure 3, the illustration of heap compaction, are relocatable.) To keep from creating dangling pointers, the Memory Manager maintains a single **master pointer** to each relocatable block. Whenever a relocatable block is created, a master pointer is allocated from the heap at the same time and set to point to the block. All references to the block are then made by double indirection, through a pointer to the master pointer, called a **handle** to the block (see Figure 5). If the Memory Manager needs to move the block during compaction, it has only to update the master pointer to point to the block's new location; the master pointer itself is never moved. Since all copies of the handle point to this same master pointer, they can be relied on not to dangle, even after the block has been moved.

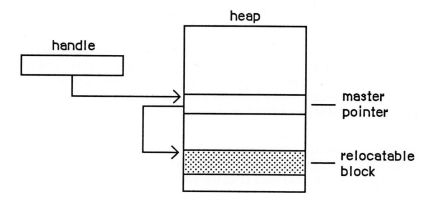

Figure 5. A Handle to a Relocatable Block

Relocatable blocks are moved only by the Memory Manager, and only at well-defined, predictable times. In particular, only the routines listed in Appendix B (Volume III) can cause blocks to move, and these routines can never be called from within an interrupt. If your program doesn't call these routines, you can rely on blocks not being moved.

The NewHandle function allocates a block in the heap of a requested size and returns a handle to the block. You can then make as many copies of the handle as you need and use them in any way your program requires. When you're finished with the block, you can free the space it occupies with the DisposHandle procedure.

> **Note:** Toolbox routines that create new objects of various kinds, such as NewWindow and NewControl, implicitly call the NewPtr and NewHandle routines to allocate the space they need. There are also analogous routines for releasing these objects, such as DisposeWindow and DisposeControl.

If the Memory Manager can't allocate a block of a requested size even after compacting the entire heap, it can try to free some space by **purging** blocks from the heap. Purging a block removes it from the heap and frees the space it occupies. The block's master pointer is set to NIL, but the space occupied by the master pointer itself remains allocated. Any handles to the block now point to a NIL master pointer, and are said to be **empty**. If your program later needs to refer to the purged block, it can detect that the handle has become empty and ask the Memory Manager to **reallocate** the block. This operation updates the original master pointer, so that all handles to the block are left referring correctly to its new location (see Figure 6).

> **Warning:** Reallocating a block recovers only the space it occupies, not its contents. Any information the block contains is lost when the block is purged. It's up to your program to reconstitute the block's contents after reallocating it.

Relocatable and nonrelocatable are permanent properties of a block that can never be changed once the block is allocated. A relocatable block can also be **locked** or **unlocked, purgeable** or **unpurgeable**; your program can set and change these attributes as necessary. Locking a block temporarily prevents it from being moved, even if the heap is compacted. The block can later be unlocked, again allowing the Memory Manager to move it during compaction. A block can be purged only if it's relocatable, unlocked, and purgeable. A newly allocated relocatable block is initially unlocked and unpurgeable.

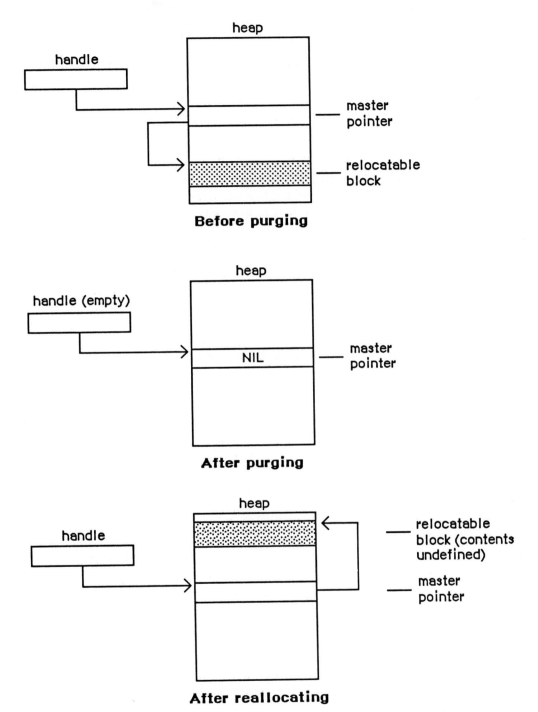

Figure 6. Purging and Reallocating a Block

GENERAL-PURPOSE DATA TYPES

The Memory Manager includes a number of type definitions for general-purpose use. For working with pointers and handles, there are the following definitions:

```
TYPE  SignedByte = -128..127;
      Byte       = 0..255;
      Ptr        = ^SignedByte;
      Handle     = ^Ptr;
```

SignedByte stands for an arbitrary byte in memory, just to give Ptr and Handle something to point to. You can define a buffer of, say, bufSize untyped memory bytes as a PACKED ARRAY[1..bufSize] OF SignedByte. Byte is an alternative definition that treats byte-length data as unsigned rather than signed quantities.

For working with strings, pointers to strings, and handles to strings, the Memory Manager includes the following definitions:

```
TYPE  Str255       = STRING[255];
      StringPtr    = ^Str255;
      StringHandle = ^StringPtr;
```

For treating procedures and functions as data objects, there's the ProcPtr data type:

```
TYPE  ProcPtr = Ptr;
```

For example, after the declarations

```
VAR  aProcPtr: ProcPtr;
       . . .

PROCEDURE MyProc;
   BEGIN
   . . .
   END;
```

you can make aProcPtr point to MyProc by using Lisa Pascal's @ operator, as follows:

```
aProcPtr := @MyProc
```

With the @ operator, you can assign procedures and functions to variables of type ProcPtr, embed them in data structures, and pass them as arguments to other routines. Notice, however, that the data type ProcPtr technically points to an arbitrary byte (SignedByte), not an actual routine. As a result, there's no way in Pascal to access the underlying routine via this pointer in order to call it. Only routines written in assembly language (such as those in the Operating System and the Toolbox) can actually call the routine designated by a pointer of type ProcPtr.

Warning: You can't use the @ operator with procedures or functions whose declarations are nested within other routines.

Finally, for treating long integers as fixed-point numbers, there's the following data type:

```
TYPE Fixed = LONGINT;
```

As illustrated in Figure 7, a **fixed-point number** is a 32-bit signed quantity containing an integer part in the high-order word and a fractional part in the low-order word. Negative numbers are the two's complement; they're formed by treating the fixed-point number as a long integer, inverting each bit, and adding 1 to the least significant bit.

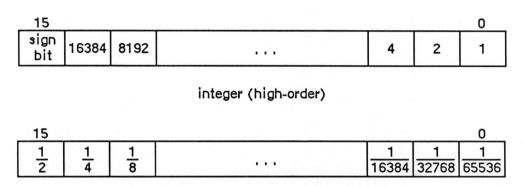

Figure 7. Fixed-Point Number

Type Coercion

Because of Pascal's strong typing rules, you can't directly assign a value of type Ptr to a variable of some other pointer type, or pass it as a parameter of some other pointer type. Instead, you have to coerce the pointer from one type to another. For example, assume the following declarations have been made:

```
TYPE  Thing        =  RECORD
                          . . .
                      END;

      ThingPtr     =  ^Thing;
      ThingHandle  =  ^ThingPtr;

VAR  aPtr: Ptr;
     aThingPtr: ThingPtr;
     aThingHandle: ThingHandle;
```

In the Lisa Pascal statement

```
aThingPtr := ThingPtr(NewPtr(SIZEOF(Thing)))
```

NewPtr allocates heap space for a new record of type Thing and returns a pointer of type Ptr, which is then coerced to type ThingPtr so it can be assigned to aThingPtr. The statement

```
DisposPtr(Ptr(aThingPtr))
```

disposes of the record pointed to by aThingPtr, first coercing the pointer to type Ptr (as required by the DisposPtr procedure). Similar calls to NewHandle and DisposHandle would require coercion between the data types Handle and ThingHandle. Given a pointer aPtr of type Ptr, you can make aThingPtr point to the same object as aPtr with the assignment

```
aThingPtr := ThingPtr(aPtr)
```

or you can refer to a field of a record of type Thing with the expression

```
ThingPtr(aPtr)^.field
```

In fact, you can use this same syntax to equate any two variables of the same length. For example:

```
VAR  aChar: CHAR;
     aByte: Byte;
     . . .

aByte := Byte(aChar)
```

You can also use the Lisa Pascal functions ORD, ORD4, and POINTER, to coerce variables of different length from one type to another. For example:

```
VAR  anInteger: INTEGER;
     aLongInt: LONGINT;
     aPointer: Ptr;
     . . .

anInteger := ORD(aLongInt);      {two low-order bytes only}
anInteger := ORD(aPointer);      {two low-order bytes only}
aLongInt := ORD(anInteger);      {packed into high-order bytes}
aLongInt := ORD4(anInteger);     {packed into low-order bytes}
aLongInt := ORD(aPointer);
aPointer := POINTER(anInteger);
aPointer := POINTER(aLongInt)
```

Assembly-language note: Of course, assembly-language programmers needn't bother with type coercion.

432

SUMMARY

```
TYPE  SignedByte  = -128..127;
      Byte        = 0..255;
      Ptr         = ^SignedByte;
      Handle      = ^Ptr;

      Str255       = STRING[255];
      StringPtr    = ^Str255;
      StringHandle = ^StringPtr;

      ProcPtr  = Ptr;

      Fixed = LONGINT;
```

3 Memory Intro

4 USING ASSEMBLY LANGUAGE

4 Assembly Language

ABOUT THIS CHAPTER

This chapter gives you general information that you'll need to write all or part of your Macintosh application program in assembly language. It assumes you already know how to write assembly-language programs for the Motorola MC68000, the microprocessor in the Macintosh.

DEFINITION FILES

The primary aids to assembly-language programmers are a set of definition files for symbolic names used in assembly-language programs. The definition files include equate files, which equate symbolic names with values, and macro files, which define the macros used to call Toolbox and Operating System routines from assembly language. The equate files define a variety of symbolic names for various purposes, such as:

- useful numeric quantities

- masks and bit numbers

- offsets into data structures

- addresses of global variables (which in turn often contain addresses)

It's a good idea to always use the symbolic names defined in an equate file in place of the corresponding numeric values (even if you know them), since some of these values may change. Note that the names of the offsets for a data structure don't always match the field names in the corresponding Pascal definition. In the documentation, the definitions are normally shown in their Pascal form; the corresponding offset constants for assembly-language use are listed in the summary at the end of each chapter.

Some generally useful global variables defined in the equate files are as follows:

Name	Contents
OneOne	$00010001
MinusOne	$FFFFFFFF
Lo3Bytes	$00FFFFFF
Scratch20	20-byte scratch area
Scratch8	8-byte scratch area
ToolScratch	8-byte scratch area
ApplScratch	12-byte scratch area reserved for use by applications

Scratch20, Scratch8, and ToolScratch will not be preserved across calls to the routines in the Macintosh ROM. ApplScratch will be preserved; it should be used only by application programs and not by desk accessories or other drivers.

Other global variables are described where relevant in *Inside Macintosh*. A list of all the variables described is given in Appendix D (Volume III).

4 Assembly Language

PASCAL DATA TYPES

Pascal's strong typing ability lets Pascal programmers write programs without really considering the size of variables. But assembly-language programmers must keep track of the size of every variable. The sizes of the standard Pascal data types, and some of the basic types defined in the Memory Manager, are listed below. (See the *Apple Numerics Manual* for more information about SINGLE, DOUBLE, EXTENDED, and COMP.)

Type	Size	Contents
INTEGER	2 bytes	Two's complement integer
LONGINT	4 bytes	Two's complement integer
BOOLEAN	1 byte	Boolean value in bit 0
CHAR	2 bytes	Extended ASCII code in low-order byte
SINGLE (or REAL)	4 bytes	IEEE standard single format
DOUBLE	8 bytes	IEEE standard double format
EXTENDED	10 bytes	IEEE standard extended format
COMP (or COMPUTATIONAL)	8 bytes	Two's complement integer with reserved value
STRING[n]	n+1 bytes	Byte containing string length (not counting length byte) followed by bytes containing ASCII codes of characters in string
SignedByte	1 byte	Two's complement integer
Byte	2 bytes	Value in low-order byte
Ptr	4 bytes	Address of data
Handle	4 bytes	Address of master pointer

Other data types are constructed from these. For some commonly used data types, the size in bytes is available as a predefined constant.

Before allocating space for any variable whose size is greater than one byte, Pascal adds "padding" to the next word boundary, if it isn't already at a word boundary. It does this not only when allocating variables declared successively in VAR statements, but also within arrays and records. As you would expect, the size of a Pascal array or record is the sum of the sizes of all its elements or fields (which are stored with the first one at the lowest address). For example, the size of the data type

```
TYPE TestRecord =   RECORD
                    testHandle: Handle;
                    testBoolA:  BOOLEAN;
                    testBoolB:  BOOLEAN;
                    testChar:   CHAR
                END;
```

is eight bytes: four for the handle, one each for the Booleans, and two for the character. If the testBoolB field weren't there, the size would be the same, because of the byte of padding Pascal would add to make the character begin on a word boundary.

In a packed record or array, type BOOLEAN is stored as a bit, and types CHAR and Byte are stored as bytes. The padding rule described above still applies. For example, if the TestRecord data type shown above were declared as PACKED RECORD, it would occupy only six bytes: four for the handle, one for the Booleans (each stored in a bit), and one for the character. If the last field were INTEGER rather than CHAR, padding before the two-byte integer field would cause the size to be eight bytes.

> **Note:** The packing algorithm may not be what you expect. If you need to know exactly how data is packed, or if you have questions about the size of a particular data type, the best thing to do is write a test program in Pascal and look at the results. (You can use the SIZEOF function to get the size.)

THE TRAP DISPATCH TABLE

The Toolbox and Operating System reside in ROM. However, to allow flexibility for future development, application code must be kept free of any specific ROM addresses. So all references to Toolbox and Operating System routines are made indirectly through the **trap dispatch table** in RAM, which contains the addresses of the routines. As long as the location of the trap dispatch table is known, the routines themselves can be moved to different locations in ROM without disturbing the operation of programs that depend on them.

Information about the locations of the various Toolbox and Operating System routines is encoded in compressed form in the ROM itself. When the system starts up, this encoded information is expanded to form the trap dispatch table. Because the trap dispatch table resides in RAM, individual entries can be "patched" to point to addresses other than the original ROM address. This allows changes to be made in the ROM code by loading corrected versions of individual routines into RAM at system startup and patching the trap dispatch table to point to them. It also allows an application program to replace specific Toolbox and Operating System routines with its own "custom" versions. A pair of utility routines for manipulating the trap dispatch table, GetTrapAddress and SetTrapAddress, are described in chapter 13 of Volume II.

For compactness, entries in the trap dispatch table are encoded into one word each, instead of a full long-word address. Since the trap dispatch table is 1024 bytes long, it has room for 512 word-length entries. The high-order bit of each entry tells whether the routine resides in ROM (0) or RAM (1). The remaining 15 bits give the offset of the routine relative to a base address. For routines in ROM, this base address is the beginning of the ROM; for routines in RAM, it's the beginning of the system heap. The two base addresses are kept in a pair of global variables named ROMBase and RAMBase.

The offset in a trap dispatch table entry is expressed in words instead of bytes, taking advantage of the fact that instructions must always fall on word boundaries (even byte addresses). As illustrated in Figure 1, the system does the following to find the absolute address of the routine:

1. checks the high-order bit of the trap dispatch table entry to find out which base address to use

2. doubles the offset to convert it from words to bytes (by left-shifting one bit)

3. adds the result to the designated base address

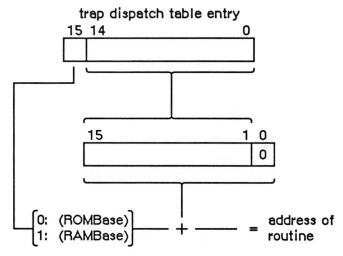

Figure 1. Trap Dispatch Table Entry

Using 15-bit word offsets, the trap dispatch table can address locations within a range of 32K words, or 64K bytes, from the base address. Starting from ROMBase, this range is big enough to cover the entire ROM; but only slightly more than half of the 128K RAM lies within range of RAMBase. RAMBase is set to the beginning of the system heap to maximize the amount of useful space within range; locations below the start of the heap are used to hold global system data and can never contain executable code. If the heap is big enough, however, it's possible for some of the application's code to lie beyond the upper end of the trap dispatch table's range. Any such code is inaccessible through the trap dispatch table.

Note: This problem is particularly acute on the Macintosh 512K and Macintosh XL. To make sure they lie within range of RAMBase, patches to Toolbox and Operating System routines are typically placed in the system heap rather than the application heap.

THE TRAP MECHANISM

Calls to the Toolbox and Operating System via the trap dispatch table are implemented by means of the MC68000's "1010 emulator" trap. To issue such a call in assembly language, you use one of the **trap macros** defined in the macro files. When you assemble your program, the macro generates a **trap word** in the machine-language code. A trap word always begins with the hexadecimal digit $A (binary 1010); the rest of the word identifies the routine you're calling, along with some additional information pertaining to the call.

Note: A list of all Macintosh trap words is given in Appendix C (Volume III).

Instruction words beginning with $A or $F ("A-line" or "F-line" instructions) don't correspond to any valid machine-language instruction, and are known as **unimplemented instructions**. They're used to augment the processor's native instruction set with additional operations that are "emulated" in software instead of being executed directly by the hardware. A-line instructions are reserved for use by Apple; on a Macintosh, they provide access to the Toolbox and Operating System routines. Attempting to execute such an instruction causes a trap to the **trap dispatcher**, which examines the bit pattern of the trap word to determine what operation it stands for, looks up the address of the corresponding routine in the trap dispatch table, and jumps to the routine.

Note: F-line instructions are reserved by Motorola for use in future processors.

Format of Trap Words

As noted above, a trap word always contains $A in bits 12-15. Bit 11 determines how the remainder of the word will be interpreted; usually it's 0 for Operating System calls and 1 for Toolbox calls, though there are some exceptions.

Figure 2 shows the Toolbox trap word format. Bits 0-8 form the **trap number** (an index into the trap dispatch table), identifying the particular routine being called. Bit 9 is reserved for future use. Bit 10 is the "auto-pop" bit; this bit is used by language systems that, rather than directly invoking the trap like Lisa Pascal, do a JSR to the trap word followed immediately by a return to the calling routine. In this case, the return addresses for the both the JSR and the trap get pushed onto the stack, in that order. The auto-pop bit causes the trap dispatcher to pop the trap's return address from the stack and return directly to the calling program.

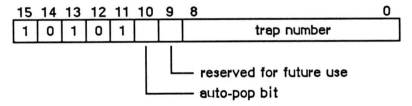

Figure 2. Toolbox Trap Word (Bit 11=1)

For Operating System calls, only the low-order eight bits (bits 0-7) are used for the trap number (see Figure 3). Thus of the 512 entries in the trap dispatch table, only the first 256 can be used for Operating System traps. Bit 8 of an Operating System trap has to do with register usage and is discussed below under "Register-Saving Conventions". Bits 9 and 10 have specialized meanings depending on which routine you're calling, and are covered where relevant in other chapters.

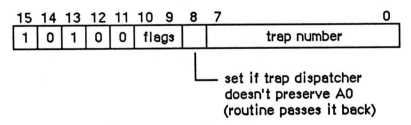

Figure 3. Operating System Trap Word (Bit 11=0)

Trap Macros

The names of all trap macros begin with the underscore character (_), followed by the name of the corresponding routine. As a rule, the macro name is the same as the name used to call the routine from Pascal, as given in the Toolbox and Operating System documentation. For example, to call the Window Manager routine NewWindow, you would use an instruction with the macro name _NewWindow in the opcode field. There are some exceptions, however, in which the spelling of the macro name differs from the name of the Pascal routine itself; these are noted in the documentation for the individual routines.

Note: The reason for the exceptions is that assembler names must be unique to eight characters. Since one character is taken up by the underscore, special macro names must be used for Pascal routines whose names aren't unique to seven characters.

Trap macros for Toolbox calls take no arguments; those for Operating System calls may have as many as three optional arguments. The first argument, if present, is used to load a register with a parameter value for the routine you're calling, and is discussed below under "Register-Based Routines". The remaining arguments control the settings of the various flag bits in the trap word. The form of these arguments varies with the meanings of the flag bits, and is described in the chapters on the relevant parts of the Operating System.

CALLING CONVENTIONS

The calling conventions for Toolbox and Operating System routines fall into two categories: **stack-based** and **register-based**. As the terms imply, stack-based routines communicate via the stack, following the same conventions used by the Pascal Compiler for routines written in Lisa Pascal, while register-based routines receive their parameters and return their results in registers. Before calling any Toolbox or Operating System routine, you have to set up the parameters in the way the routine expects.

Note: As a general rule, Toolbox routines are stack-based and Operating System routines register-based, but there are exceptions on both sides. Throughout *Inside Macintosh*, register-based calling conventions are given for all routines that have them; if none is shown, then the routine is stack-based.

Stack-Based Routines

To call a stack-based routine from assembly language, you have to set up the parameters on the stack in the same way the compiled object code would if your program were written in Pascal. If the routine you're calling is a function, its result is returned on the stack. The number and types of parameters, and the type of result returned by a function, depend on the routine being called. The number of bytes each parameter or result occupies on the stack depends on its type:

Type of parameter or function result	Size	Contents
INTEGER	2 bytes	Two's complement integer
LONGINT	4 bytes	Two's complement integer
BOOLEAN	2 bytes	Boolean value in bit 0 of high-order byte
CHAR	2 bytes	Extended ASCII code in low-order byte
SINGLE (or REAL), DOUBLE, COMP (or COMPUTATIONAL)	4 bytes	Pointer to value converted to EXTENDED
EXTENDED	4 bytes	Pointer to value
STRING[n]	4 bytes	Pointer to string (first byte pointed to is length byte)
SignedByte	2 bytes	Value in low-order byte
Byte	2 bytes	Value in low-order byte
Ptr	4 bytes	Address of data
Handle	4 bytes	Address of master pointer
Record or array	2 or 4 bytes	Contents of structure (padded to word boundary) if <= 4 bytes, otherwise pointer to structure
VAR parameter	4 bytes	Address of variable, regardless of type

The steps to take to call the routine are as follows:

1. If it's a function, reserve space on the stack for the result.

2. Push the parameters onto the stack in the order they occur in the routine's Pascal definition.

3. Call the routine by executing the corresponding trap macro.

The trap pushes the return address onto the stack, along with an extra word of processor status information. The trap dispatcher removes this extra status word, leaving the stack in the state shown in Figure 4 on entry to the routine. The routine itself is responsible for removing its own parameters from the stack before returning. If it's a function, it leaves its result on top of the stack in the space reserved for it; if it's a procedure, it restores the stack to the same state it was in before the call.

For example, the Window Manager function GrowWindow is defined in Pascal as follows:

```
FUNCTION GrowWindow (theWindow: WindowPtr; startPt: Point; sizeRect: Rect)
                    : LONGINT;
```

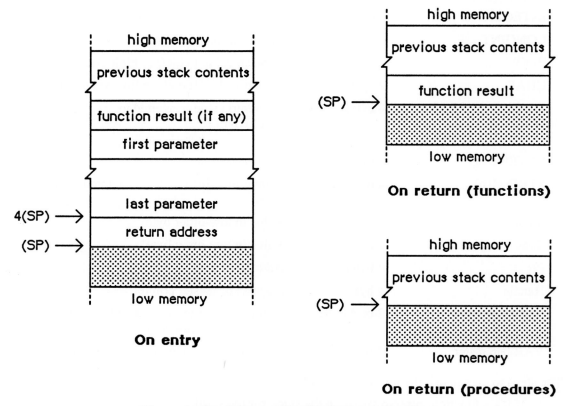

Figure 4. Stack Format for Stack-Based Routines

To call this function from assembly language, you'd write something like the following:

```
SUBQ.L      #4,SP                   ;make room for LONGINT result
MOVE.L      theWindow,-(SP)         ;push window pointer
MOVE.L      startPt,-(SP)           ;a Point is a 4-byte record,
                                    ; so push actual contents
PEA         sizeRect                ;a Rect is an 8-byte record,
                                    ; so push a pointer to it
_GrowWindow                         ;trap to routine
MOVE.L      (SP)+,D3                ;pop result from stack
```

Although the MC68000 hardware provides for separate user and supervisor stacks, each with its own stack pointer, the Macintosh maintains only one stack. All application programs run in supervisor mode and share the same stack with the system; the user stack pointer isn't used.

Warning: For compatibility with future versions of the Macintosh, your program should not rely on capabilities available *only* in supervisor mode (such as the instruction RTE).

Remember that the stack pointer must always be aligned on a word boundary. This is why, for example, a Boolean parameter occupies two bytes; it's actually the Boolean value followed by a byte of padding. Because all Macintosh application code runs in the MC68000's supervisor mode, an odd stack pointer will cause a "double bus fault": an unrecoverable system failure that causes the system to restart.

To keep the stack pointer properly aligned, the MC68000 automatically adjusts the pointer by 2 instead of 1 when you move a byte-length value to or from the stack. This happens only when all of the following three conditions are met:

- A one-byte value is being transferred.

- Either the source or the destination is specified by predecrement or postincrement addressing.

- The register being decremented or incremented is the stack pointer (A7).

An extra, unused byte will automatically be added in the low-order byte to keep the stack pointer even. (Note that if you need to move a character to or from the stack, you must explicitly use a full word of data, with the character in the low-order byte.)

Warning: If you use any other method to manipulate the stack pointer, it's your responsibility to make sure the pointer stays properly aligned.

Note: Some Toolbox and Operating System routines accept the address of one of your own routines as a parameter, and call that routine under certain circumstances. In these cases, you must set up your routine to be stack-based.

Register-Based Routines

By convention, register-based routines normally use register A0 for passing addresses (such as pointers to data objects) and D0 for other data values (such as integers). Depending on the routine, these registers may be used to pass parameters to the routine, result values back to the calling program, or both. For routines that take more than two parameters (one address and one data value), the parameters are normally collected in a **parameter block** in memory and a pointer to the parameter block is passed in A0. However, not all routines obey these conventions; for example, some expect parameters in other registers, such as A1. See the description of each individual routine for details.

Whatever the conventions may be for a particular routine, it's up to you to set up the parameters in the appropriate registers before calling the routine. For instance, the Memory Manager procedure BlockMove, which copies a block of consecutive bytes from one place to another in memory, expects to find the address of the first source byte in register A0, the address of the first destination location in A1, and the number of bytes to be copied in D0. So you might write something like

```
LEA       src(A5),A0      ;source address in A0
LEA       dest(A5),A1     ;destination address in A1
MOVEQ     #20,D0          ;byte count in D0
_BlockMove                ;trap to routine
```

Macro Arguments

The following information applies to the Lisa Workshop Assembler. If you're using some other assembler, you should check its documentation to find out whether this information applies.

Many register-based routines expect to find an address of some sort in register A0. You can specify the contents of that register as an argument to the macro instead of explicitly setting up the register yourself. The first argument you supply to the macro, if any, represents an address to be passed in A0. The macro will load the register with an LEA (Load Effective Address) instruction before trapping to the routine. So, for instance, to perform a Read operation on a file, you could set up the parameter block for the operation and then use the instruction

```
_Read           paramBlock           ;trap to routine with pointer to
                                     ; parameter block in A0
```

This feature is purely a convenience, and is optional: If you don't supply any arguments to a trap macro, or if the first argument is null, the LEA to A0 will be omitted from the macro expansion. Notice that A0 is loaded with the address denoted by the argument, not the contents of that address.

> **Note:** You can use any of the MC68000's addressing modes to specify this address, with one exception: You can't use the two-register indexing mode ("address register indirect with index and displacement"). An instruction such as
>
> ```
> _Read           offset(A3,D5)
> ```

won't work properly, because the comma separating the two registers will be taken as a delimiter marking the end of the macro argument.

Result Codes

Many register-based routines return a result code in the low-order word of register D0 to report successful completion or failure due to some error condition. A result code of 0 indicates that the routine was completed successfully. Just before returning from a register-based call, the trap dispatcher tests the low-order word of D0 with a TST.W instruction to set the processor's condition codes. You can then check for an error by branching directly on the condition codes, without any explicit test of your own. For example:

```
_PurgeMem                            ;trap to routine
BEQ             NoError              ;branch if no error
. . .                                ;handle error
```

> **Warning:** Not all register-based routines return a result code. Some leave the contents of D0 unchanged; others use the full 32 bits of the register to return a long-word result. See the descriptions of individual routines for details.

Register-Saving Conventions

All Toolbox and Operating System routines preserve the contents of all registers except A0, A1, and D0-D2 (and of course A7, which is the stack pointer). In addition, for register-based routines, the trap dispatcher saves registers A1, D1, and D2 before dispatching to the routine and restores them before returning to the calling program. A7 and D0 are never restored; whatever the routine leaves in these registers is passed back unchanged to the calling program, allowing the routine to manipulate the stack pointer as appropriate and to return a result code.

Whether the trap dispatcher preserves register A0 for a register-based trap depends on the setting of bit 8 of the trap word: If this bit is 0, the trap dispatcher saves and restores A0; if it's 1, the routine passes back A0 unchanged. Thus bit 8 of the trap word should be set to 1 only for those routines that return a result in A0, and to 0 for all other routines. The trap macros automatically set this bit correctly for each routine, so you never have to worry about it yourself.

Stack-based traps preserve only registers A2-A6 and D3-D7. If you want to preserve any of the other registers, you have to save them yourself before trapping to the routine—typically on the stack with a MOVEM (Move Multiple) instruction—and restore them afterward.

> **Warning:** When an application starts up, register A5 is set to point to the boundary between the application globals and the application parameters (see the memory map in chapter 1 of Volume II for details). Certain parts of the system rely on finding A5 set up properly (for instance, the first application parameter is a pointer to the first QuickDraw global variable), so you have to be a bit more careful about preserving this register. The safest policy is never to touch A5 at all. If you must use it for your own purposes, just saving its contents at the beginning of a routine and restoring them before returning isn't enough: You have to be sure to restore it before any call that might depend on it. The correct setting of A5 is always available in the global variable CurrentA5.

> **Note:** Any routine in your application that may be called as the result of a Toolbox or Operating System call shouldn't rely on the value of any register except A5, which shouldn't change.

Pascal Interface to the Toolbox and Operating System

When you call a register-based Toolbox or Operating System routine from Pascal, you're actually calling an **interface routine** that fetches the parameters from the stack where the Pascal calling program left them, puts them in the registers where the routine expects them, and then traps to the routine. On return, it moves the routine's result, if any, from a register to the stack and then returns to the calling program. (For routines that return a result code, the interface routine may also move the result code to a global variable, where it can later be accessed.)

For stack-based calls, there's no interface routine; the trap word is inserted directly into the compiled code.

MIXING PASCAL AND ASSEMBLY LANGUAGE

You can mix Pascal and assembly language freely in your own programs, calling routines written in either language from the other. The Pascal and assembly-language portions of the program have to be compiled and assembled separately, then combined with a program such as the Lisa Workshop Linker. For convenience in this discussion, such separately compiled or assembled portions of a program will be called "modules". You can divide a program into any number of modules, each of which may be written in either Pascal or assembly language.

References in one module to routines defined in another are called **external references**, and must be resolved by a program like the Linker that matches them up with their definitions in other modules. You have to identify all the external references in each module so they can be resolved properly. For more information, and for details about the actual process of linking the modules together, see the documentation for the development system you're using.

In addition to being able to call your own Pascal routines from assembly language, you can call certain routines in the Toolbox and Operating System that were created expressly for Lisa Pascal programmers and aren't part of the Macintosh ROM. (These routines may also be available to users of other development systems, depending on how the interfaces have been set up on those systems.) They're marked with the notation

[Not in ROM]

in *Inside Macintosh*. There are no trap macros for these routines (though they may call other routines for which there are trap macros). Some of them were created just to allow Pascal programmers access to assembly-language information, and so won't be useful to assembly-language programmers. Others, however, contain code that's executed before a trap macro is invoked, and you may want to perform the operations they provide.

All calls from one language to the other, in either direction, must obey Pascal's stack-based calling conventions (see "Stack-Based Routines", above). To call your own Pascal routine from assembly language, or one of the Toolbox or Operating System routines that aren't in ROM, push the parameters onto the stack before the call and (if the routine is a function) look for the result on the stack on return. In an assembly-language routine to be called from Pascal, look for the parameters on the stack on entry and leave the result (if any) on the stack before returning.

Under stack-based calling conventions, a convenient way to access a routine's parameters on the stack is with a **frame pointer**, using the MC68000's LINK and UNLK (Unlink) instructions. You can use any address register for the frame pointer (except A7, which is reserved for the stack pointer), but register A6 is conventionally used for this purpose on the Macintosh. The instruction

```
LINK        A6,#-12
```

at the beginning of a routine saves the previous contents of A6 on the stack and sets A6 to point to it. The second operand specifies the number of bytes of stack space to be reserved for the routine's local variables: in this case, 12 bytes. The LINK instruction offsets the stack pointer by this amount after copying it into A6.

> **Warning:** The offset is *added* to the stack pointer, not subtracted from it. So to allocate stack space for local variables, you have to give a *negative* offset; the instruction won't work properly if the offset is positive. Also, to keep the stack pointer correctly aligned, be sure the offset is even. For a routine with no local variables on the stack, use an offset of #0.

Register A6 now points within the routine's **stack frame**; the routine can locate its parameters and local variables by indexing with respect to this register (see Figure 5). The register itself points to its own saved contents, which are often (but needn't necessarily be) the frame pointer of the calling routine. The parameters and return address are found at positive offsets from the frame pointer.

Since the saved contents of the frame pointer register occupy a long word (four bytes) on the stack, the return address is located at 4(A6) and the last parameter at 8(A6). This is followed by the rest of the parameters in reverse order, and finally by the space reserved for the function result, if any. The proper offsets for these remaining parameters and for the function result

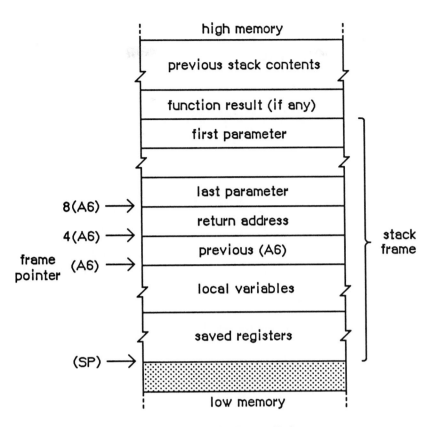

Figure 5. Frame Pointer

depend on the number and types of the parameters, according to the table above under "Stack-Based Routines". If the LINK instruction allocated stack space for any local variables, they can be accessed at negative offsets from the frame pointer, again depending on their number and types.

At the end of the routine, the instruction

```
        UNLK            A6
```

reverses the process: First it releases the local variables by setting the stack pointer equal to the frame pointer (A6), then it pops the saved contents back into register A6. This restores the register to its original state and leaves the stack pointer pointing to the routine's return address.

A routine with no parameters can now just return to the caller with an RTS instruction. But if there are any parameters, it's the routine's responsibility to pop them from the stack before returning. The usual way of doing this is to pop the return address into an address register, increment the stack pointer to remove the parameters, and then exit with an indirect jump through the register.

Remember that any routine called from Pascal must preserve registers A2–A6 and D3–D7. This is usually done by saving the registers that the routine will be using on the stack with a MOVEM instruction, and then restoring them before returning. Any routine you write that will be accessed via the trap mechanism—for instance, your own version of a Toolbox or Operating System routine that you've patched into the trap dispatch table—should observe the same conventions.

Putting all this together, the routine should begin with a sequence like

```
MyRoutine    LINK        A6,#-dd            ;set up frame pointer--
                                            ; dd = number of bytes
                                            ; of local variables

             MOVEM.L     A2-A4/D3-D7,-(SP)  ;...or whatever registers
                                            ; you use
```

and end with something like

```
             MOVEM.L     (SP)+,A2-A4/D3-D7  ;restore registers
             UNLK        A6                 ;restore frame pointer
             MOVE.L      (SP)+,A1           ;save return address in an
                                            ; available register
             ADD.W       #pp,SP             ;pop parameters--
                                            ; pp = number of bytes
                                            ; of parameters
             JMP         (A1)               ;return to caller
```

Notice that A6 doesn't have to be included in the MOVEM instructions, since it's saved and restored by the LINK and UNLK.

SUMMARY

Variables

OneOne	$00010001
MinusOne	$FFFFFFFF
Lo3Bytes	$00FFFFFF
Scratch20	20-byte scratch area
Scratch8	8-byte scratch area
ToolScratch	8-byte scratch area
ApplScratch	12-byte scratch area reserved for use by applications
ROMBase	Base address of ROM
RAMBase	Trap dispatch table's base address for routines in RAM
CurrentA5	Address of boundary between application globals and application parameters

4 Assembly Language

5   THE RESOURCE MANAGER

5 Resource Manager

ABOUT THIS CHAPTER

This chapter describes the Resource Manager, the part of the Toolbox through which an application accesses various resources that it uses, such as menus, fonts, and icons. It discusses resource files, where resources are stored. Resources form the foundation of every Macintosh application; even the application's code is a resource. In a resource file, the resources used by the application are stored separately from the code for flexibility and ease of maintenance.

You can use an existing program for creating and editing resource files, or write one of your own; these programs will call Resource Manager routines. Usually you'll access resources indirectly through other parts of the Toolbox, such as the Menu Manager and the Font Manager, which in turn call the Resource Manager to do the low-level resource operations. In some cases, you may need to call a Resource Manager routine directly.

Familiarity with Macintosh files, as described in chapter 4 of Volume II, is useful if you want a complete understanding of the internal structure of a resource file; however, you don't need it to be able to use the Resource Manager.

If you're going to write your own program to create and edit resource files, you also need to know the exact format of each type of resource. The chapter describing the part of the Toolbox that deals with a particular type of resource will tell you what you need to know for that resource.

ABOUT THE RESOURCE MANAGER

Macintosh applications make use of many **resources**, such as menus, fonts, and icons, which are stored in **resource files**. For example, an icon resides in a resource file as a 32-by-32 bit image, and a font as a large bit image containing the characters of the font. In some cases the resource consists of descriptive information (such as, for a menu, the menu title, the text of each command in the menu, whether the command is checked with a check mark, and so on). The Resource Manager keeps track of resources in resource files and provides routines that allow applications and other parts of the Toolbox to access them.

There's a resource file associated with each application, containing the resources specific to that application; these resources include the application code itself. There's also a **system resource file**, which contains standard resources shared by all applications (called **system resources**).

The resources used by an application are created and changed separately from the application's code. This separation is the main advantage to having resource files. A change in the title of a menu, for example, won't require any recompilation of code, nor will translation to another language.

The Resource Manager is initialized by the system when it starts up, and the system resource file is opened as part of the initialization. Your application's resource file is opened when the application starts up. When instructed to get a certain resource, the Resource Manager normally looks first in the application's resource file and then, if the search isn't successful, in the system resource file. This makes it easy to share resources among applications and also to override a system resource with one of your own (if you want to use something other than a standard icon in an alert box, for example).

Resources are grouped logically by function into **resource types**. You refer to a resource by passing the Resource Manager a **resource specification**, which consists of the resource type

5 Resource Manager

and either an ID number or a name. Any resource type is valid, whether one of those recognized by the Toolbox as referring to standard Macintosh resources (such as menus and fonts), or a type created for use by your application. Given a resource specification, the Resource Manager will read the resource into memory and return a handle to it.

Note: The Resource Manager knows nothing about the formats of the individual types of resources. Only the routines in the other parts of the Toolbox that call the Resource Manager have this knowledge.

While most access to resources is read-only, certain applications may want to modify resources. You can change the content of a resource or its ID number, name, or other attributes— everything except its type. For example, you can designate whether the resource should be kept in memory or whether, as is normal for large resources, it can be removed from memory and read in again when needed. You can change existing resources, remove resources from the resource file altogether, or add new resources to the file.

Resource files aren't limited to applications; anything stored in a file can have its own resources. For instance, an unusual font used in only one document can be included in the resource file for that document rather than in the system resource file.

Note: Although shared resources are usually stored in the system resource file, you can have other resource files that contain resources shared by two or more applications (or documents, or whatever).

A number of resource files may be open at one time; the Resource Manager searches the files in the reverse of the order that they were opened. Since the system resource file is opened when the Resource Manager is initialized, it's always searched last. The search starts with the most recently opened resource file, but you can change it to start with a file that was opened earlier. (See Figure 1.)

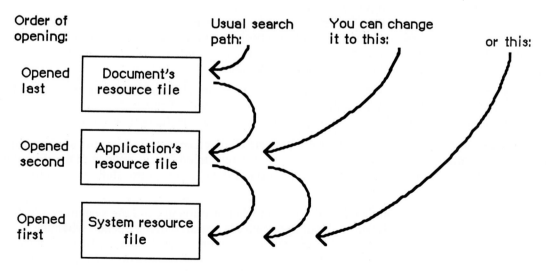

Figure 1. Resource File Searching

OVERVIEW OF RESOURCE FILES

Resources may be put in a resource file with the aid of the Resource Editor, or with whatever tools are provided by the development system you're using.

A resource file is not a file in the strictest sense. Although it's functionally like a file in many ways, it's actually just one of two parts, or **forks**, of a file (see Figure 2). Every file has a **resource fork** and a **data fork** (either of which may be empty). The resource fork of an application file contains not only the resources used by the application but also the application code itself. The code may be divided into different segments, each of which is a resource; this allows various parts of the program to be loaded and purged dynamically. Information is stored in the resource fork via the Resource Manager. The data fork of an application file can contain anything an application wants to store there. Information is stored in the data fork via the File Manager.

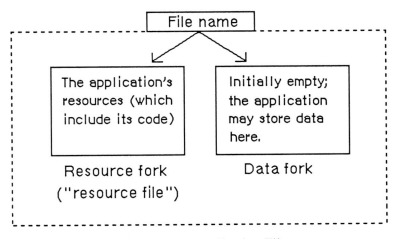

Figure 2. An Application File

As shown in Figure 3, the system resource file has this same structure. The resource fork contains the system resources and the data fork contains "patches" to the routines in the Macintosh ROM. Figure 3 also shows the structure of a file containing a document; the resource fork contains the document's resources and the data fork contains the data that comprises the document.

To open a resource file, the Resource Manager calls the appropriate File Manager routine and returns the **reference number** it gets from the File Manager. This is a number greater than 0 by which you can refer to the file when calling other Resource Manager routines.

Note: This reference number is actually the path reference number, as described in chapter 4 of Volume II.

Most of the Resource Manager routines don't require the resource file's reference number as a parameter. Rather, they assume that the **current resource file** is where they should perform their operation (or begin it, in the case of a search for a resource). The current resource file is the last one that was opened unless you specify otherwise.

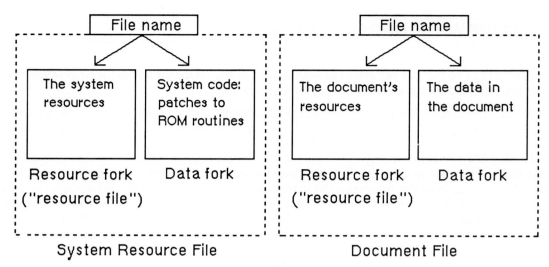

Figure 3. Other Files

A resource file consists primarily of **resource data** and a **resource map**. The resource data consists of the resources themselves (for example, the bit image for an icon or the title and commands for a menu). The resource map contains an entry for each resource that provides the location of its resource data. Each entry in the map either gives the offset of the resource data in the file or contains a handle to the data if it's in memory. The resource map is like the index of a book; the Resource Manager looks in it for the resource you specify and determines where its resource data is located.

The resource map is read into memory when the file is opened and remains there until the file is closed. Although for simplicity we say that the Resource Manager searches resource files, it actually searches the resource maps that were read into memory, and not the resource files on the disk.

Resource data is normally read into memory when needed, though you can specify that it be read in as soon as the resource file is opened. When read in, resource data is stored in a relocatable block in the heap. Resources are designated in the resource map as being either purgeable or unpurgeable; if purgeable, they may be removed from the heap when space is required by the Memory Manager. Resources consisting of a relatively large amount of data are usually designated as purgeable. Before accessing such a resource through its handle, you ask the Resource Manager to read the resource into memory again if it has been purged.

> **Note:** Programmers concerned about the amount of available memory should be aware that there's a 12-byte overhead in the resource map for every resource and an additional 12-byte overhead for memory management if the resource is read into memory.

To modify a resource, you change the resource data or resource map in memory. The change becomes permanent only at your explicit request, and then only when the application terminates or when you call a routine specifically for updating or closing the resource file.

Each resource file also may contain up to 128 bytes of any data the application wants to store there.

RESOURCE SPECIFICATION

In a resource file, every resource is assigned a type, an ID number, and optionally a name. When calling a Resource Manager routine to access a resource, you specify the resource by passing its type and either its ID number or its name. This section gives some general information about resource specification.

Resource Types

The resource type is a sequence of any four characters (printing or nonprinting). Its Pascal data type is:

```
TYPE ResType = PACKED ARRAY[1..4] OF CHAR;
```

The standard Macintosh resource types are as follows:

Resource type	Meaning
'ALRT'	Alert template
'BNDL'	Bundle
'CDEF'	Control definition function
'CNTL'	Control template
'CODE'	Application code segment
'CURS'	Cursor
'DITL'	Item list in a dialog or alert
'DLOG'	Dialog template
'DRVR'	Desk accessory or other device driver
'DSAT'	System startup alert table
'FKEY'	Command-Shift-number routine
'FONT'	Font
'FREF'	File reference
'FRSV'	IDs of fonts reserved for system use
'FWID'	Font widths
'ICN#'	Icon list
'ICON'	Icon
'INIT'	Initialization resource
'INTL'	International resource
'MBAR'	Menu bar
'MDEF'	Menu definition procedure

5 Resource Manager

Resource type	Meaning
'MENU'	Menu
'PACK'	Package
'PAT '	Pattern (The space is required.)
'PAT#'	Pattern list
'PDEF'	Printing code
'PICT'	Picture
'PREC'	Print record
'SERD'	RAM Serial Driver
'STR '	String (The space is required.)
'STR#'	String list
'WDEF'	Window definition function
'WIND'	Window template

Warning: Uppercase and lowercase letters *are* distinguished in resource types. For example, 'Menu' will not be recognized as the resource type for menus.

Notice that some of the resources listed above are "templates". A template is a list of parameters used to build a Toolbox object; it is not the object itself. For example, a window template contains information specifying the size and location of the window, its title, whether it's visible, and so on. After the Window Manager has used this information to build the window in memory, the template isn't needed again until the next window using that template is created.

You can use any four-character sequence (except those listed above) for resource types specific to your application.

Resource ID Numbers

Every resource has an ID number, or **resource ID**. The resource ID should be unique within each resource type, but resources of different types may have the same ID. If you assign the same resource ID to two resources of the same type, the second assignment of the ID will override the first, thereby making the first resource inaccessible by ID.

Warning: Certain resources contain the resource IDs of other resources; for instance, a dialog template contains the resource ID of its item list. In order not to duplicate an existing resource ID, a program that copies resources may need to change the resource ID of a resource; such a program may not, however, change the ID where it is referred to by other resources. For instance, an item list's resource ID contained in a dialog template may not be changed, even though the actual resource ID of the item list was changed to avoid duplication; this would make it impossible for the template to access the item list. Be sure to verify, and if necessary correct, the IDs contained within such resources. (For related information, see the section "Resource IDs of Owned Resources" below.)

By convention, the ID numbers are divided into the following ranges:

Range	Description
–32768 through –16385	Reserved; do not use
–16384 through –1	Used for system resources owned by other system resources (explained below)
0 through 127	Used for other system resources
128 through 32767	Available for your use in whatever way you wish

Note: The chapters that describe the different types of resources in detail give information about resource types that may be more restrictive about the allowable range for their resource IDs. A device driver, for instance, can't have a resource ID greater than 31.

Resource IDs of Owned Resources

This section is intended for advanced programmers who are writing their own desk accessories (or other drivers), or special types of windows, controls, and menus. It's also useful in understanding the way that resource-copying programs recognize resources that are associated with each other.

Certain types of system resources may have resources of their own in the system resource file; the "owning" resource consists of code that reads the "owned" resource into memory. For example, a desk accessory might have its own pattern and string resources. A special numbering convention is used to associate owned system resources with the resources they belong to. This enables resource-copying programs to recognize which additional resources need to be copied along with an owning resource. An owned system resource has the ID illustrated in Figure 4.

15	14	13	11	10		5	4		0
1	1	type bits		ID of owning resource			variable		

Figure 4. Resource ID of an Owned System Resource

Bits 14 and 15 are always 1. Bits 11-13 specify the type of the owning resource, as follows:

Type bits	Type
000	'DRVR'
001	'WDEF'
010	'MDEF'
011	'CDEF'
100	'PDEF'
101	'PACK'
110	Reserved for future use
111	Reserved for future use

Bits 5-10 contain the resource ID of the owning resource (limited to 0 through 63). Bits 0-4 contain any desired value (0 through 31).

Certain types of resources can't be owned, because their IDs don't conform to the special numbering convention described above. For instance, while a resource of type 'WDEF' can own other resources, it cannot itself be owned since its resource ID can't be more than 12 bits long (as described in chapter 9). Fonts are also an exception because their IDs include the font size. The chapters describing the different types of resources provide detailed information about such restrictions.

An owned resource may itself contain the ID of a resource associated with it. For instance, a dialog template owned by a desk accessory contains the resource ID of its item list. Though the item list is associated with the dialog template, it's actually owned (indirectly) by the desk accessory. The resource ID of the item list should conform to the same special convention as the ID of the template. For example, if the resource ID of the desk accessory is 17, the IDs of both the template and the item list should contain the value 17 in bits 5-10.

As mentioned above, a program that copies resources may need to change the resource ID of a resource in order not to duplicate an existing resource ID. Bits 5-10 of resources owned, directly or indirectly, by the copied resource will also be changed when those resources are copied. For instance, in the above example, if the desk accessory must be given a new ID, bits 5-10 of both the template and the item list will also be changed.

> **Warning:** Remember that while the ID of an owned resource may be changed by a resource-copying program, the ID may not be changed where it appears in other resources (such as an item list's ID contained in a dialog template).

Resource Names

A resource may optionally have a **resource name**. Like the resource ID, the resource name should be unique within each type; if you assign the same resource name to two resources of the same type, the second assignment of the name will override the first, thereby making the first resource inaccessible by name. When comparing resource names, the Resource Manager ignores case (but does not ignore diacritical marks).

RESOURCE REFERENCES

The entries in the resource map that identify and locate the resources in a resource file are known as **resource references**. Using the analogy of an index of a book, resource references are like the individual entries in the index (see Figure 5).

Every resource reference includes the type, ID number, and optional name of the resource. Suppose you're accessing a resource for the first time. You pass a resource specification to the Resource Manager, which looks for a match among all the references in the resource map of the current resource file. If none is found, it looks at the references in the resource map of the next resource file to be searched. (Remember, it looks in the resource map in memory, not in the file.) Eventually it finds a reference matching the specification, which tells it where the resource data is in the file. After reading the resource data into memory, the Resource Manager stores a handle to that data in the reference (again, in the resource map in memory) and returns the handle so you can use it to refer to the resource in subsequent routine calls.

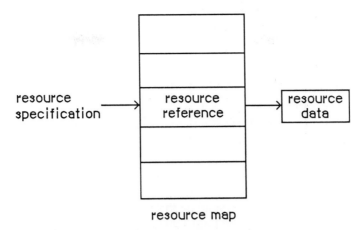

Figure 5. Resource References in Resource Maps

Every resource reference also contains certain **resource attributes** that determine how the resource should be dealt with. In the routine calls for setting or reading them, each attribute is specified by a bit in the low-order byte of a word, as illustrated in Figure 6.

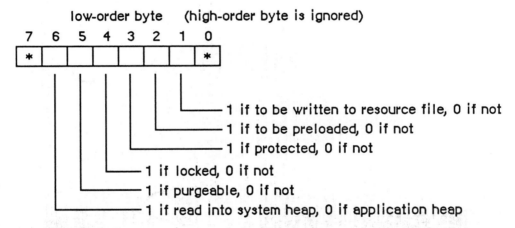

* reserved for use by the Resource Manager

Figure 6. Resource Attributes

The Resource Manager provides a predefined constant for each attribute, in which the bit corresponding to that attribute is set.

```
CONST resSysHeap    = 64;   {set if read into system heap}
      resPurgeable  = 32;   {set if purgeable}
      resLocked     = 16;   {set if locked}
      resProtected  = 8;    {set if protected}
      resPreload    = 4;    {set if to be preloaded}
      resChanged    = 2;    {set if to be written to resource file}
```

Warning: Your application should not change the setting of bit 0 or 7, nor should it set the resChanged attribute directly. (ResChanged is set as a side effect of the procedure you call to tell the Resource Manager that you've changed a resource.)

The resSysHeap attribute should not be set for your application's resources. If a resource with this attribute set is too large for the system heap, the bit will be cleared, and the resource will be read into the application heap.

Since a locked resource is neither relocatable nor purgeable, the resLocked attribute overrides the resPurgeable attribute; when resLocked is set, the resource will not be purgeable regardless of whether resPurgeable is set.

If the resProtected attribute is set, the application can't use Resource Manager routines to change the ID number or name of the resource, modify its contents, or remove the resource from the resource file. The routine that sets the resource attributes may be called, however, to remove the protection or just change some of the other attributes.

The resPreload attribute tells the Resource Manager to read this resource into memory immediately after opening the resource file. This is useful, for example, if you immediately want to draw ten icons stored in the file; rather than read and draw each one individually in turn, you can have all of them read in when the file is opened and just draw all ten.

The resChanged attribute is used only while the resource map is in memory; it must be 0 in the resource file. It tells the Resource Manager whether this resource has been changed.

USING THE RESOURCE MANAGER

The Resource Manager is initialized automatically when the system starts up: The system resource file is opened and its resource map is read into memory. Your application's resource file is opened when the application starts up; you can call CurResFile to get its reference number. You can also call OpenResFile to open any resource file that you specify by name, and CloseResFile to close any resource file. A function named ResError lets you check for errors that may occur during execution of Resource Manager routines.

Note: These are the only routines you need to know about to use the Resource Manager indirectly through other parts of the Toolbox.

Normally when you want to access a resource for the first time, you'll specify it by type and ID number (or type and name) in a call to GetResource (or GetNamedResource). In special situations, you may want to get every resource of each type. There are two routines which, used together, will tell you all the resource types that are in all open resource files: CountTypes and GetIndType. Similarly, CountResources and GetIndResource may be used to get all resources of a particular type.

If you don't specify otherwise, GetResource, GetNamedResource, and GetIndResource read the resource data into memory and return a handle to it. Sometimes, however, you may not need the data to be in memory. You can use a procedure named SetResLoad to tell the Resource Manager not to read the resource data into memory when you get a resource; in this case, the handle returned for the resource will be an empty handle (a pointer to a NIL master pointer). You can pass the empty handle to routines that operate only on the resource map (such as the routine that sets resource attributes), since the handle is enough for the Resource Manager to tell what resource you're referring to. Should you later want to access the resource data, you can read it into memory with the LoadResource procedure. Before calling any of the above routines that read the resource data into memory, it's a good idea to call SizeResource to see how much space is needed.

Normally the Resource Manager starts looking for a resource in the most recently opened resource file, and searches other open resource files in the reverse of the order that they were opened. In some situations, you may want to change which file is searched first. You can do this with the UseResFile procedure. One such situation might be when you want a resource to be read from the same file as another resource; in this case, you can find out which resource file the other resource was read from by calling the HomeResFile function.

Once you have a handle to a resource, you can call GetResInfo or GetResAttrs to get the information that's stored for that resource in the resource map, or you can access the resource data through the handle. (If the resource was designated as purgeable, first call LoadResource to ensure that the data is in memory.)

Usually you'll just read resources from previously created resource files with the routines described above. You may, however, want to modify existing resources or even create your own resource file. To create your own resource file, call CreateResFile (followed by OpenResFile to open it). The AddResource procedure lets you add resources to a resource file; to be sure a new resource won't override an existing one, you can call the UniqueID function to get an ID number for it. To make a copy of an existing resource, call DetachResource followed by AddResource (with a new resource ID). There are a number of procedures for modifying existing resources:

- To remove a resource, call RmveResource.

- If you've changed the resource data for a resource and want the changed data to be written to the resource file, call ChangedResource; it signals the Resource Manager to write the data out when the resource file is later updated.

- To change the information stored for a resource in the resource map, call SetResInfo or SetResAttrs. If you want the change to be written to the resource file, call ChangedResource. (Remember that ChangedResource will also cause the resource data itself to be written out.)

These procedures for adding and modifying resources change only the resource map in memory. The changes are written to the resource file when the application terminates (at which time all resource files other than the system resource file are updated and closed) or when one of the following routines is called:

- CloseResFile, which updates the resource file before closing it

- UpdateResFile, which simply updates the resource file

- WriteResource, which writes the resource data for a specified resource to the resource file

RESOURCE MANAGER ROUTINES

Assembly-language note: Except for LoadResource, all Resource Manager routines preserve all registers except A0 and D0. LoadResource preserves A0 and D0 as well.

Initialization

Although you don't call these initialization routines (because they're executed automatically for you), it's a good idea to familiarize yourself with what they do.

```
FUNCTION InitResources : INTEGER;
```

InitResources is called by the system when it starts up, and should not be called by the application. It initializes the Resource Manager, opens the system resource file, reads the resource map from the file into memory, and returns a reference number for the file.

Assembly-language note: The name of the system resource file is stored in the global variable SysResName; the reference number for the file is stored in the global variable SysMap. A handle to the resource map of the system resource file is stored in the variable SysMapHndl.

Note: The application doesn't need the reference number for the system resource file, because every Resource Manager routine that has a reference number as a parameter interprets 0 to mean the system resource file.

```
PROCEDURE RsrcZoneInit;
```

RsrcZoneInit is called automatically when your application starts up, to initialize the resource map read from the system resource file; normally you'll have no need to call it directly. It "cleans up" after any resource access that may have been done by a previous application. First it closes all open resource files except the system resource file. Then, for every system resource that was read into the application heap (that is, whose resSysHeap attribute is 0), it replaces the handle to that resource in the resource map with NIL. This lets the Resource Manager know that the resource will have to be read in again (since the previous application heap is no longer around).

Opening and Closing Resource Files

When calling the CreateResFile or OpenResFile routine, described below, you specify a resource file by its file name; the routine assumes that the file has a version number of 0 and is on the default volume. (Version numbers and volumes are described in chapter 4 of Volume II.) If you want the routine to apply to a file on another volume, just set the default volume to that volume.

```
PROCEDURE CreateResFile (fileName: Str255);
```

CreateResFile creates a resource file containing no resource data. If there's no file at all with the given name, it also creates an empty data fork for the file. If there's already a resource file with the given name (that is, a resource fork that isn't empty), CreateResFile will do nothing and the ResError function will return an appropriate Operating System result code.

Note: Before you can work with the resource file, you need to open it with OpenResFile.

```
FUNCTION OpenResFile (fileName: Str255) : INTEGER;
```

OpenResFile opens the resource file having the given name and makes it the current resource file. It reads the resource map from the file into memory and returns a reference number for the file. It also reads in every resource whose resPreload attribute is set. If the resource file is already open, it doesn't make it the current resource file; it simply returns the reference number.

Note: You don't have to call OpenResFile to open the system resource file or the application's resource file, because they're opened when the system and the application start up, respectively. To get the reference number of the application's resource file, you can call CurResFile after the application starts up (before you open any other resource file).

If the file can't be opened, OpenResFile will return −1 and the ResError function will return an appropriate Operating System result code. For example, an error occurs if there's no resource file with the given name.

Note: To open a resource file simply for block-level operations such as copying files (without reading the resource map into memory), you can call the File Manager function OpenRF.

Assembly-language note: A handle to the resource map of the most recently opened resource file is stored in the global variable TopMapHndl.

---

5 Resource Manager

```
PROCEDURE CloseResFile (refNum: INTEGER);
```

Given the reference number of a resource file, CloseResFile does the following:

- updates the resource file by calling the UpdateResFile procedure
- for each resource in the resource file, releases the memory it occupies by calling the ReleaseResource procedure
- releases the memory occupied by the resource map
- closes the resource file

If there's no resource file open with the given reference number, CloseResFile will do nothing and the ResError function will return the result code resFNotFound. A refNum of 0 represents the system resource file, but if you ask to close this file, CloseResFile first closes all other open resource files.

A CloseResFile of every open resource file (except the system resource file) is done automatically when the application terminates. So you only need to call CloseResFile if you want to close a resource file before the application terminates.

Checking for Errors

```
FUNCTION ResError : INTEGER;
```

Called after one of the various Resource Manager routines that may result in an error condition, ResError returns a result code identifying the error, if any. If no error occurred, it returns the result code

```
CONST noErr = 0;    {no error}
```

If an error occurred at the Operating System level, it returns an Operating System result code, such as the File Manager "disk I/O" error or the Memory Manager "out of memory" error. (See Appendix A in Volume III for a list of all result codes.) If an error happened at the Resource Manager level, ResError returns one of the following result codes:

```
CONST  resNotFound  = -192;    {resource not found}
       resFNotFound = -193;    {resource file not found}
       addResFailed = -194;    {AddResource failed}
       rmvResFailed = -196;    {RmveResource failed}
```

Each routine description tells which errors may occur for that routine. You can also check for an error after system startup, which calls InitResources, and application startup, which opens the application's resource file.

> **Warning:** In certain cases, the ResError function will return noError even though a Resource Manager routine was unable to perform the requested operation; the routine descriptions give details about the circumstances under which this will happen.

> **Assembly-language note:** The current value of ResError is stored in the global variable ResErr. In addition, you can specify a procedure to be called whenever there's an error by storing the address of the procedure in the global variable ResErrProc (which is normally 0). Before returning a result code other than noErr, the ResError function places that result code in register D0 and calls your procedure.

Setting the Current Resource File

When calling the CurResFile and HomeResFile routines, described below, be aware that for the system resource file the actual reference number is returned. You needn't worry about this number being used (instead of 0) in the routines that require a reference number; those routines recognize both 0 and the actual reference number as referring to the system resource file.

```
FUNCTION CurResFile : INTEGER;
```

CurResFile returns the reference number of the current resource file. You can call it when the application starts up to get the reference number of its resource file.

Assembly-language note: The reference number of the current resource file is stored in the global variable CurMap.

```
FUNCTION HomeResFile (theResource: Handle) : INTEGER;
```

Given a handle to a resource, HomeResFile returns the reference number of the resource file containing that resource. If the given handle isn't a handle to a resource, HomeResFile will return –1 and the ResError function will return the result code resNotFound.

```
PROCEDURE UseResFile (refNum: INTEGER);
```

Given the reference number of a resource file, UseResFile sets the current resource file to that file. If there's no resource file open with the given reference number, UseResFile will do nothing and the ResError function will return the result code resFNotFound. A refNum of 0 represents the system resource file.

Open resource files are arranged as a linked list; the most recently opened file is at the end of the list and is the first one the Resource Manager searches when looking for a resource. UseResFile lets you start the search with a file opened earlier; the file(s) following it in the list are then left out of the search process. Whenever a new resource file is opened, it's added to the end of the list; this overrides any previous calls to UseResFile, causing the entire list of open resource files to be searched. For example, assume there are four open resource files (R0 through R3); the search order is R3, R2, R1, R0. If you call UseResFile(R2), the search order becomes R2, R1, R0; R3 is no longer searched. If you then open a fifth resource file (R4), it's added to the end of the list and the search order becomes R4, R3, R2, R1, R0.

This procedure is useful if you no longer want to override a system resource with one by the same name in your application's resource file. You can call UseResFile(0) to leave the application resource file out of the search, causing only the system resource file to be searched.

Warning: Early versions of some desk accessories may, upon closing, always set the current resource file to the one opened just before the accessory, ignoring any additional resource files that may have been opened while the accessory was open. To be safe, whenever a desk accessory may have been in use, call UseResFile to ensure access to resource files opened while the accessory was open.

Getting Resource Types

```
FUNCTION CountTypes : INTEGER;
```

CountTypes returns the number of resource types in all open resource files.

```
PROCEDURE GetIndType (VAR theType: ResType; index: INTEGER);
```

Given an index ranging from 1 to CountTypes (above), GetIndType returns a resource type in theType. Called repeatedly over the entire range for the index, it returns all the resource types in all open resource files. If the given index isn't in the range from 1 to CountTypes, GetIndType returns four NUL characters (ASCII code 0).

Getting and Disposing of Resources

PROCEDURE SetResLoad (load: BOOLEAN);

Normally, the routines that return handles to resources read the resource data into memory if it's not already in memory. SetResLoad(FALSE) affects all those routines so that they will not read the resource data into memory and will return an empty handle. Furthermore, resources whose resPreload attribute is set will not be read into memory when a resource file is opened.

> **Warning:** If you call SetResLoad(FALSE), be sure to restore the normal state as soon as possible, because other parts of the Toolbox that call the Resource Manager rely on it.

> **Assembly-language note:** The current SetResLoad state is stored in the global variable ResLoad.

FUNCTION CountResources (theType: ResType) : INTEGER;

CountResources returns the total number of resources of the given type in all open resource files.

FUNCTION GetIndResource (theType: ResType; index: INTEGER) :
          Handle;

Given an index ranging from 1 to CountResources(theType), GetIndResource returns a handle to a resource of the given type (see CountResources, above). Called repeatedly over the entire range for the index, it returns handles to all resources of the given type in all open resource files. GetIndResource reads the resource data into memory if it's not already in memory, unless you've called SetResLoad(FALSE).

> **Warning:** The handle returned will be an empty handle if you've called SetResLoad(FALSE) (and the data isn't already in memory). The handle will become empty if the resource data for a purgeable resource is read in but later purged. (You can test for an empty handle with, for example, myHndl^ = NIL.) To read in the data and make the handle no longer be empty, you can call LoadResource.

GetIndResource returns handles for all resources in the most recently opened resource file first, and then for those in the resource files opened before it, in the reverse of the order that they were opened.

> **Note:** The UseResFile procedure affects which file the Resource Manager searches first when looking for a particular resource but not when getting indexed resources with GetIndResource.

If you want to find out how many resources of a given type are in a particular resource file, you can do so as follows: Call GetIndResource repeatedly with the index ranging from 1 to the number of resources of that type (CountResources(theType)). Pass each handle returned by GetIndResource to HomeResFile and count all occurrences where the reference number returned is that of the desired file. Be sure to start the index from 1, and to call SetResLoad(FALSE) so the resources won't be read in.

If the given index is 0 or negative, GetIndResource returns NIL, but the ResError function will return the result code noErr. If the given index is larger than the value CountResources(theType), GetIndResource returns NIL and the ResError function will return the result code resNotFound. GetIndResource also returns NIL if the resource is to be read into memory but won't fit; in this case, ResError will return an appropriate Operating System result code.

```
FUNCTION GetResource (theType: ResType; theID: INTEGER) : Handle;
```

GetResource returns a handle to the resource having the given type and ID number, reading the resource data into memory if it's not already in memory and if you haven't called SetResLoad(FALSE) (see the warning above for GetIndResource). If the resource data is already in memory, GetResource just returns the handle to the resource.

GetResource looks in the current resource file and all resource files opened before it, in the reverse of the order that they were opened; the system resource file is searched last. If it doesn't find the resource, GetResource returns NIL and the ResError function will return the result code resNotFound. GetResource also returns NIL if the resource is to be read into memory but won't fit; in this case, ResError will return an appropriate Operating System result code.

Note: If you call GetResource with a resource type that isn't in any open resource file, it returns NIL but the ResError function will return the result code noErr.

```
FUNCTION GetNamedResource (theType: ResType; name: Str255) :
          Handle;
```

GetNamedResource is the same as GetResource (above) except that you pass a resource name instead of an ID number.

```
PROCEDURE LoadResource (theResource: Handle);
```

Given a handle to a resource (returned by GetIndResource, GetResource, or GetNamedResource), LoadResource reads that resource into memory. It does nothing if the resource is already in memory or if the given handle isn't a handle to a resource; in the latter case, the ResError function will return the result code resNotFound. Call this procedure if you want to access the data for a resource through its handle and either you've called SetResLoad(FALSE) or the resource is purgeable.

If you've changed the resource data for a purgeable resource and the resource is purged before being written to the resource file, the changes will be lost; LoadResource will reread the original resource from the resource file. See the descriptions of ChangedResource and SetResPurge for information about how to ensure that changes made to purgeable resources will be written to the resource file.

Assembly-language note: LoadResource preserves *all* registers.

```
PROCEDURE ReleaseResource (theResource: Handle);
```

Given a handle to a resource, ReleaseResource releases the memory occupied by the resource data, if any, and replaces the handle to that resource in the resource map with NIL (see Figure 7). The given handle will no longer be recognized as a handle to a resource; if the Resource Manager is subsequently called to get the released resource, a new handle will be allocated. Use this procedure only after you're completely through with a resource.

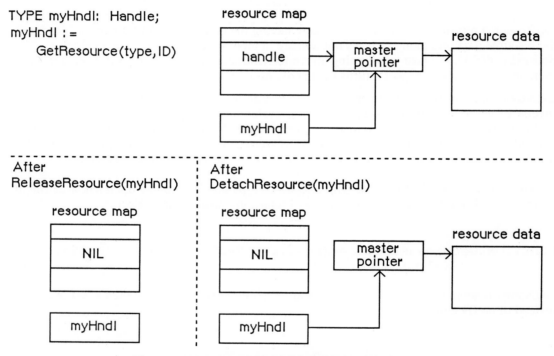

Figure 7. ReleaseResource and DetachResource

If the given handle isn't a handle to a resource, ReleaseResource will do nothing and the ResError function will return the result code resNotFound. ReleaseResource won't let you release a resource whose resChanged attribute has been set; however, ResError will still return noErr.

```
PROCEDURE DetachResource (theResource: Handle);
```

Given a handle to a resource, DetachResource replaces the handle to that resource in the resource map with NIL (see Figure 7 above). The given handle will no longer be recognized as a handle to a resource; if the Resource Manager is subsequently called to get the detached resource, a new handle will be allocated.

DetachResource is useful if you want the resource data to be accessed only by yourself through the given handle and not by the Resource Manager. DetachResource is also useful in the unusual case that you don't want a resource to be released when a resource file is closed. To copy a resource, you can call DetachResource followed by AddResource (with a new resource ID).

If the given handle isn't a handle to a resource, DetachResource will do nothing and the ResError function will return the result code resNotFound. DetachResource won't let you detach a resource whose resChanged attribute has been set; however, ResError will still return noErr.

Getting Resource Information

```
FUNCTION UniqueID (theType: ResType) : INTEGER;
```

UniqueID returns an ID number greater than 0 that isn't currently assigned to any resource of the given type in any open resource file. Using this number when you add a new resource to a resource file ensures that you won't duplicate a resource ID and override an existing resource.

> **Warning:** It's possible that UniqueID will return an ID in the range reserved for system resources (0 to 127). You should check that the ID returned is greater than 127; if it isn't, call UniqueID again.

```
PROCEDURE GetResInfo (theResource: Handle; VAR theID: INTEGER;
        VAR theType: ResType; VAR name: Str255);
```

Given a handle to a resource, GetResInfo returns the ID number, type, and name of the resource. If the given handle isn't a handle to a resource, GetResInfo will do nothing and the ResError function will return the result code resNotFound.

```
FUNCTION GetResAttrs (theResource: Handle) : INTEGER;
```

Given a handle to a resource, GetResAttrs returns the resource attributes for the resource. (Resource attributes are described above under "Resource References".) If the given handle isn't a handle to a resource, GetResAttrs will do nothing and the ResError function will return the result code resNotFound.

```
FUNCTION SizeResource (theResource: Handle) : LONGINT;
```

> **Assembly-language note:** The macro you invoke to call SizeResource from assembly language is named _SizeRsrc.

Given a handle to a resource, SizeResource returns the size in bytes of the resource in the resource file. If the given handle isn't a handle to a resource, SizeResource will return –1 and the ResError function will return the result code resNotFound. It's a good idea to call SizeResource and ensure that sufficient space is available before reading a resource into memory.

Modifying Resources

Except for UpdateResFile and WriteResource, all the routines described below change the resource map in memory and not the resource file itself.

```
PROCEDURE SetResInfo (theResource: Handle; theID: INTEGER; name:
        Str255);
```

Given a handle to a resource, SetResInfo changes the ID number and name of the resource to the given ID number and name.

Assembly-language note: If you pass 0 for the name parameter, the name will not be changed.

Warning: It's a dangerous practice to change the ID number and name of a system resource, because other applications may already access the resource and may no longer work properly.

The change will be written to the resource file when the file is updated if you follow SetResInfo with a call to ChangedResource.

Warning: Even if you don't call ChangedResource for this resource, the change may be written to the resource file when the file is updated. If you've *ever* called ChangedResource for *any* resource in the file, or if you've added or removed a resource, the Resource Manager will write out the entire resource map when it updates the file, so all changes made to resource information in the map will become permanent. If you want any of the changes to be temporary, you'll have to restore the original information before the file is updated.

SetResInfo does nothing in the following cases:

- The given handle isn't a handle to a resource. The ResError function will return the result code resNotFound.

- The resource map becomes too large to fit in memory (which can happen if a name is passed) or the modified resource file can't be written out to the disk. ResError will return an appropriate Operating System result code.

- The resProtected attribute for the resource is set. ResError will, however, return the result code noErr.

```
PROCEDURE SetResAttrs (theResource: Handle; attrs: INTEGER);
```

Given a handle to a resource, SetResAttrs sets the resource attributes for the resource to attrs. (Resource attributes are described above under "Resource References".) The resProtected attribute takes effect immediately; the others take effect the next time the resource is read in.

Warning: Do not use SetResAttrs to set the resChanged attribute; you must call ChangedResource instead. Be sure that the attrs parameter passed to SetResAttrs doesn't change the current setting of this attribute; to determine the current setting, first call GetResAttrs.

The attributes set with SetResAttrs will be written to the resource file when the file is updated if you follow SetResAttrs with a call to ChangedResource. However, even if you don't call ChangedResource for this resource, the change may be written to the resource file when the file is updated. See the last warning for SetResInfo (above).

If the given handle isn't a handle to a resource, SetResAttrs will do nothing and the ResError function will return the result code resNotFound.

```
PROCEDURE ChangedResource (theResource: Handle);
```

Call ChangedResource after changing either the information about a resource in the resource map (as described above under SetResInfo and SetResAttrs) or the resource data for a resource, if you want the change to be permanent. Given a handle to a resource, ChangedResource sets the resChanged attribute for the resource. This attribute tells the Resource Manager to do *both* of the following:

■ write the resource data for the resource to the resource file when the file is updated or when WriteResource is called

■ write the entire resource map to the resource file when the file is updated

Warning: If you change information in the resource map with SetResInfo or SetResAttrs and then call ChangedResource, remember that not only the resource map but also the resource data will be written out when the resource file is updated.

To change the resource data for a purgeable resource and make the change permanent, you have to take special precautions to ensure that the resource won't be purged while you're changing it. You can make the resource temporarily unpurgeable and then write it out with WriteResource before making it purgeable again. You have to use the Memory Manager procedures HNoPurge and HPurge to make the resource unpurgeable and purgeable; SetResAttrs can't be used because it won't take effect immediately. For example:

```
myHndl := GetResource(type,ID);      {or LoadResource(myHndl) if }
                                     { you've gotten it previously}
HNoPurge(myHndl);                    {make it unpurgeable}
. . .                                {make the changes here}
ChangedResource(myHndl);             {mark it changed}
WriteResource(myHndl);               {write it out}
HPurge(myHndl)                       {make it purgeable again}
```

Or, instead of calling WriteResource to write the data out immediately, you can call SetResPurge(TRUE) before making any changes to purgeable resource data.

ChangedResource does nothing in the following cases:

■ The given handle isn't a handle to a resource. The ResError function will return the result code resNotFound.

■ The modified resource file can't be written out to the disk. ResError will return an appropriate Operating System result code.

■ The resProtected attribute for the modified resource is set. ResError will, however, return the result code noErr.

Warning: Be aware that if the modified file can't be written out to the disk, the resChanged attribute won't be set. This means that when WriteResource is called, it won't know that the resource file has been changed; it won't write out the modified file and no error will be returned. For this reason, always check to see that ChangedResource returns noErr.

```
PROCEDURE AddResource (theData: Handle; theType: ResType; theID:
        INTEGER; name: Str255);
```

Given a handle to data in memory (not a handle to an existing resource), AddResource adds to the current resource file a resource reference that points to the data. It sets the resChanged attribute for the resource, so the data will be written to the resource file when the file is updated or when WriteResource is called. If the given handle is empty, zero-length resource data will be written.

Note: To make a copy of an existing resource, call DetachResource before calling AddResource. To add the same data to several different resource files, call the Operating System Utility function HandToHand to duplicate the handle for each resource reference.

AddResource does nothing in the following cases:

■ The given handle is NIL or is already a handle to an existing resource. The ResError function will return the result code addResFailed.

■ The resource map becomes too large to fit in memory or the modified resource file can't be written out to the disk. ResError will return an appropriate Operating System result code. (The warning under ChangedResource above concerning the resChanged attribute also applies to AddResource.)

Warning: AddResource doesn't verify whether the resource ID you pass is already assigned to another resource of the same type; be sure to call UniqueID before adding a resource.

```
PROCEDURE RmveResource (theResource: Handle);
```

Given a handle to a resource in the current resource file, RmveResource removes its resource reference. The resource data will be removed from the resource file when the file is updated.

Note: RmveResource doesn't release the memory occupied by the resource data; to do that, call the Memory Manager procedure DisposHandle after calling RmveResource.

If the resProtected attribute for the resource is set or if the given handle isn't a handle to a resource in the current resource file, RmveResource will do nothing and the ResError function will return the result code rmvResFailed.

```
PROCEDURE UpdateResFile (refNum: INTEGER);
```

Given the reference number of a resource file, UpdateResFile does the following:

- Changes, adds, or removes resource data in the file as appropriate to match the map. Remember that changed resource data is written out only if you called ChangedResource (and the call was successful). UpdateResFile calls WriteResource to write out changed or added resources.

- Compacts the resource file, closing up any empty space created when a resource was removed, made smaller, or made larger. (If the size of a changed resource is greater than its original size in the resource file, it's written at the end of the file rather than at its original location; the space occupied by the original is then compacted.) The actual size of the resource file will be adjusted when a resource is removed or made larger, but not when a resource is made smaller.

- Writes out the resource map of the resource file, if you ever called ChangedResource for any resource in the file or if you added or removed a resource. All changes to resource information in the map will become permanent as a result of this, so if you want any such changes to be temporary, you must restore the original information before calling UpdateResFile.

If there's no open resource file with the given reference number, UpdateResFile will do nothing and the ResError function will return the result code resFNotFound. A refNum of 0 represents the system resource file.

The CloseResFile procedure calls UpdateResFile before it closes the resource file, so you only need to call UpdateResFile yourself if you want to update the file without closing it.

```
PROCEDURE WriteResource (theResource: Handle);
```

Given a handle to a resource, WriteResource checks the resChanged attribute for that resource and, if it's set (which it will be if you called ChangedResource or AddResource successfully), writes its resource data to the resource file and clears its resChanged attribute.

Warning: Be aware that ChangedResource and AddResource determine whether the modified file can be written out to the disk; if it can't, the resChanged attribute won't be set and WriteResource will be unaware of the modifications. For this reason, always verify that ChangedResource and AddResource return noErr.

If the resource is purgeable and has been purged, zero-length resource data will be written. WriteResource does nothing if the resProtected attribute for the resource is set or if the resChanged attribute isn't set; in both cases, however, the ResError function will return the result code noErr. If the given handle isn't a handle to a resource, WriteResource will do nothing and the ResError function will return the result code resNotFound.

Since the resource file is updated when the application terminates or when you call UpdateResFile (or CloseResFile, which calls UpdateResFile), you only need to call WriteResource if you want to write out just one or a few resources immediately.

Warning: The maximum size for a resource to be written to a resource file is 32K bytes.

```
PROCEDURE SetResPurge (install: BOOLEAN);
```

SetResPurge(TRUE) sets a "hook" in the Memory Manager such that before purging data specified by a handle, the Memory Manager will first pass the handle to the Resource Manager. The Resource Manager will determine whether the handle is that of a resource in the application heap and, if so, will call WriteResource to write the resource data for that resource to the resource file if its resChanged attribute is set (see ChangedResource and WriteResource). SetResPurge(FALSE) restores the normal state, clearing the hook so that the Memory Manager will once again purge without checking with the Resource Manager.

SetResPurge(TRUE) is useful in applications that modify purgeable resources. You still have to make the resources temporarily unpurgeable while making the changes, as shown in the description of ChangedResource, but you can set the purge hook instead of writing the data out immediately with WriteResource. Notice that you won't know exactly when the resources are being written out; most applications will want more control than this. If you wish, you can set your own such hook; for details, refer to the section "Memory Manager Data Structures" in chapter 1 of Volume II.

Advanced Routines

The routines described in this section allow advanced programmers to have even greater control over resource file operations. Just as individual resources have attributes, an entire resource file also has attributes, which these routines manipulate. Like the attributes of individual resources, resource file attributes are specified by bits in the low-order byte of a word. The Resource Manager provides the following masks for setting or testing these bits:

```
CONST  mapReadOnly  = 128;      {set if file is read-only}
       mapCompact   = 64;       {set to compact file on update}
       mapChanged   = 32;       {set to write map on update}
```

When the mapReadOnly attribute is set, the Resource Manager will neither write anything to the resource file nor check whether the file can be written out to the disk when the resource map is modified. When this attribute is set, UpdateResFile and WriteResource will do nothing, but the ResError function will return the result code noErr.

> **Warning:** If you set mapReadOnly but then later clear it, the resource file will be written even if there's no room for it on the disk. This would destroy the file.

The mapCompact attribute causes the resource file to be compacted when the file is updated. It's set by the Resource Manager when a resource is removed, or when a resource is made larger and thus has to be written at the end of the resource file. You may want to set mapCompact to force compaction when you've only made resources smaller.

The mapChanged attribute causes the resource map to be written to the resource file when the file is updated. It's set by the Resource Manager when you call ChangedResource or when you add or remove a resource. You can set mapChanged if, for example, you've changed resource attributes only and don't want to call ChangedResource because you don't want the resource data to be written out.

```
FUNCTION GetResFileAttrs (refNum: INTEGER) : INTEGER;
```

Given the reference number of a resource file, GetResFileAttrs returns the resource file attributes for the file. If there's no resource file with the given reference number, GetResFileAttrs will do nothing and the ResError function will return the result code resFNotFound. A refNum of 0 represents the system resource file.

```
PROCEDURE SetResFileAttrs (refNum: INTEGER; attrs: INTEGER);
```

Given the reference number of a resource file, SetResFileAttrs sets the resource file attributes of the file to attrs. If there's no resource file with the given reference number, SetResFileAttrs will do nothing but the ResError function will return the result code noErr. A refNum of 0 represents the system resource file, but you shouldn't change its resource file attributes.

RESOURCES WITHIN RESOURCES

Resources may point to other resources; this section discusses how this is normally done, for programmers who are interested in background information about resources or who are defining their own resource types.

In a resource file, one resource points to another with the ID number of the other resource. For example, the resource data for a menu includes the ID number of the menu's definition procedure (a separate resource that determines how the menu looks and behaves). To work with the resource data in memory, however, it's faster and more convenient to have a handle to the other resource rather than its ID number. Since a handle occupies two words, the ID number in the resource file is followed by a word containing 0; these two words together serve as a placeholder for the handle. Once the other resource has been read into memory, these two words can be replaced by a handle to it. (See Figure 8.)

> **Note:** The practice of using the ID number followed by 0 as a placeholder is simply a convention. If you like, you can set up your own resources to have the ID number followed by a dummy word, or even a word of useful information, or you can put the ID in the second rather than the first word of the placeholder.

In the case of menus, the Menu Manager function GetMenu calls the Resource Manager to read the menu and the menu definition procedure into memory, and then replaces the placeholder in the menu with the handle to the procedure. There may be other cases where you call the Resource Manager directly and store the handle in the placeholder yourself. It might be useful in these cases to call HomeResFile to learn which resource file the original resource is located in, and then, before getting the resource it points to, call UseResFile to set the current resource file to that file. This will ensure that the resource pointed to is read from that same file (rather than one that was opened after it).

> **Warning:** If you modify a resource that points to another resource and you make the change permanent by calling ChangedResource, be sure you reverse the process described here, restoring the other resource's ID number in the placeholder.

5 Resource Manager

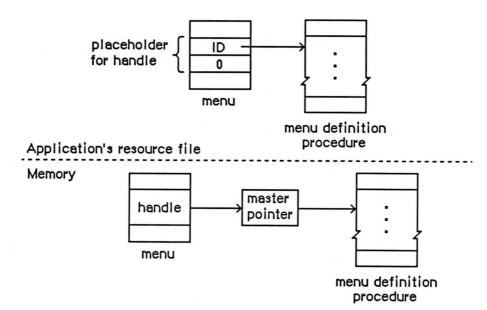

Figure 8. How Resources Point to Resources

FORMAT OF A RESOURCE FILE

You need to know the exact format of a resource file, described below, only if you're writing a program that will create or modify resource files directly; you don't have to know it to be able to use the Resource Manager routines.

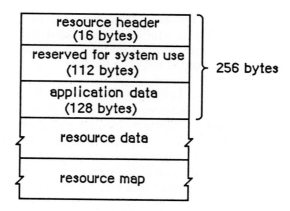

Figure 9. Format of a Resource File

As illustrated in Figure 9, every resource file begins with a **resource header**. The resource header gives the offsets to and lengths of the resource data and resource map parts of the file, as follows:

Number of bytes	Contents
4 bytes	Offset from beginning of resource file to resource data
4 bytes	Offset from beginning of resource file to resource map
4 bytes	Length of resource data
4 bytes	Length of resource map

Note: All offsets and lengths in the resource file are given in bytes.

This is what immediately follows the resource header:

Number of bytes	Contents
112 bytes	Reserved for system use
128 bytes	Available for application data

The application data may be whatever you want.

The resource data follows the space reserved for the application data. It consists of the following for each resource in the file:

Number of bytes	Contents
For each resource:	
4 bytes	Length of following resource data
n bytes	Resource data for this resource

To learn exactly what the resource data is for a standard type of resource, see the chapter describing the part of the Toolbox that deals with that resource type.

After the resource data, the resource map begins as follows:

Number of bytes	Contents
16 bytes	0 (reserved for copy of resource header)
4 bytes	0 (reserved for handle to next resource map to be searched)
2 bytes	0 (reserved for file reference number)
2 bytes	Resource file attributes
2 bytes	Offset from beginning of resource map to type list (see below)
2 bytes	Offset from beginning of resource map to resource name list (see below)

After reading the resource map into memory, the Resource Manager stores the indicated information in the reserved areas at the beginning of the map.

The resource map continues with a type list, reference lists, and a resource name list. The type list contains the following:

5 Resource Manager

Number of bytes	Contents
2 bytes	Number of resource types in the map minus 1
For each type:	
4 bytes	Resource type
2 bytes	Number of resources of this type in the map minus 1
2 bytes	Offset from beginning of type list to reference list for resources of this type

This is followed by the reference list for each type of resource, which contains the resource references for all resources of that type. The reference lists are contiguous and in the same order as the types in the type list. The format of a reference list is as follows:

Number of bytes	Contents
For each reference of this type:	
2 bytes	Resource ID
2 bytes	Offset from beginning of resource name list to length of resource name, or −1 if none
1 byte	Resource attributes
3 bytes	Offset from beginning of resource data to length of data for this resource
4 bytes	0 (reserved for handle to resource)

The resource name list follows the reference list and has this format:

Number of bytes	Contents
For each name:	
1 byte	Length of following resource name
n bytes	Characters of resource name

Figure 10 shows where the various offsets lead to in a resource file, in general and also specifically for a resource reference.

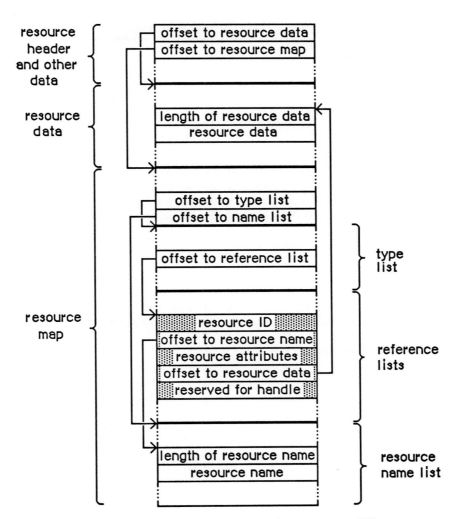

Figure 10. Resource Reference in a Resource File

SUMMARY OF THE RESOURCE MANAGER

Constants

```
CONST  { Masks for resource attributes }

       resSysHeap    = 64;      {set if read into system heap}
       resPurgeable  = 32;      {set if purgeable}
       resLocked     = 16;      {set if locked}
       resProtected  = 8;       {set if protected}
       resPreload    = 4;       {set if to be preloaded}
       resChanged    = 2;       {set if to be written to resource file}

       { Resource Manager result codes }

       resNotFound   = -192;    {resource not found}
       resFNotFound  = -193;    {resource file not found}
       addResFailed  = -194;    {AddResource failed}
       rmvResFailed  = -196;    {RmveResource failed}

       { Masks for resource file attributes }

       mapReadOnly = 128;       {set if file is read-only}
       mapCompact  = 64;        {set to compact file on update}
       mapChanged  = 32;        {set to write map on update}
```

Data Types

```
TYPE ResType = PACKED ARRAY[1..4] OF CHAR;
```

Routines

Initialization

```
FUNCTION  InitResources : INTEGER;
PROCEDURE RsrcZoneInit;
```

Opening and Closing Resource Files

```
PROCEDURE CreateResFile (fileName: Str255);
FUNCTION  OpenResFile   (fileName: Str255) : INTEGER;
PROCEDURE CloseResFile  (refNum: INTEGER);
```

Checking for Errors

```
FUNCTION ResError : INTEGER;
```

Setting the Current Resource File

```
FUNCTION  CurResFile : INTEGER;
FUNCTION  HomeResFile (theResource: Handle) : INTEGER;
PROCEDURE UseResFile  (refNum: INTEGER);
```

Getting Resource Types

```
FUNCTION  CountTypes : INTEGER;
PROCEDURE GetIndType (VAR theType: ResType; index: INTEGER);
```

Getting and Disposing of Resources

```
PROCEDURE SetResLoad       (load: BOOLEAN);
FUNCTION  CountResources   (theType: ResType) : INTEGER;
FUNCTION  GetIndResource   (theType: ResType; index: INTEGER) : Handle;
FUNCTION  GetResource      (theType: ResType; theID: INTEGER) : Handle;
FUNCTION  GetNamedResource (theType: ResType; name: Str255) : Handle;
PROCEDURE LoadResource     (theResource: Handle);
PROCEDURE ReleaseResource  (theResource: Handle);
PROCEDURE DetachResource   (theResource: Handle);
```

Getting Resource Information

```
FUNCTION  UniqueID    (theType: ResType) : INTEGER;
PROCEDURE GetResInfo  (theResource: Handle; VAR theID: INTEGER; VAR
                        theType: ResType; VAR name: Str255);
FUNCTION  GetResAttrs (theResource: Handle) : INTEGER;
FUNCTION  SizeResource (theResource: Handle) : LONGINT;
```

Modifying Resources

```
PROCEDURE SetResInfo       (theResource: Handle; theID: INTEGER; name:
                            Str255);
PROCEDURE SetResAttrs      (theResource: Handle; attrs: INTEGER);
PROCEDURE ChangedResource  (theResource: Handle);
PROCEDURE AddResource      (theData: Handle; theType: ResType; theID:
                            INTEGER; name: Str255);
PROCEDURE RmveResource     (theResource: Handle);
PROCEDURE UpdateResFile    (refNum: INTEGER);
PROCEDURE WriteResource    (theResource: Handle);
PROCEDURE SetResPurge      (install: BOOLEAN);
```

Advanced Routines

```
FUNCTION  GetResFileAttrs (refNum: INTEGER) : INTEGER;
PROCEDURE SetResFileAttrs (refNum: INTEGER; attrs: INTEGER);
```

Assembly-Language Information

Constants

; Resource attributes

```
resSysHeap      .EQU    6     ;set if read into system heap
resPurgeable    .EQU    5     ;set if purgeable
resLocked       .EQU    4     ;set if locked
resProtected    .EQU    3     ;set if protected
resPreload      .EQU    2     ;set if to be preloaded
resChanged      .EQU    1     ;set if to be written to resource file
```

; Resource Manager result codes

```
resNotFound     .EQU    -192    ;resource not found
resFNotFound    .EQU    -193    ;resource file not found
addResFailed    .EQU    -194    ;AddResource failed
rmvResFailed    .EQU    -196    ;RmveResource failed
```

; Resource file attributes

```
mapReadOnly     .EQU    7     ;set if file is read-only
mapCompact      .EQU    6     ;set to compact file on update
mapChanged      .EQU    5     ;set to write map on update
```

Special Macro Names

Pascal name	Macro name
SizeResource	_SizeRsrc

Variables

TopMapHndl	Handle to resource map of most recently opened resource file
SysMapHndl	Handle to map of system resource file
SysMap	Reference number of system resource file (word)
CurMap	Reference number of current resource file (word)
ResLoad	Current SetResLoad state (word)
ResErr	Current value of ResError (word)
ResErrProc	Address of resource error procedure
SysResName	Name of system resource file (length byte followed by up to 19 characters)

6 QUICKDRAW

6 QuickDraw

ABOUT THIS CHAPTER

This chapter describes QuickDraw, the part of the Toolbox that allows Macintosh programmers to perform highly complex graphic operations very easily and very quickly. It describes the data types used by QuickDraw and gives details of the procedures and functions available in QuickDraw.

ABOUT QUICKDRAW

QuickDraw allows you to draw many different things on the Macintosh screen; some of these are illustrated in Figure 1.

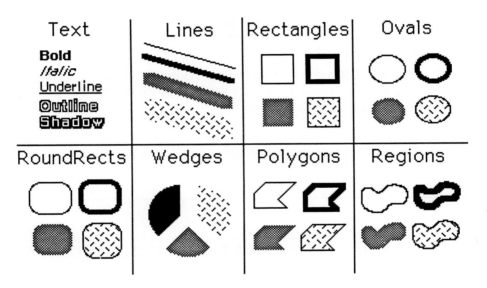

Figure 1. Samples of QuickDraw's Abilities

You can draw:

- text characters in a number of proportionally-spaced fonts, with variations that include boldfacing, italicizing, underlining, and outlining
- straight lines of any length, width, and pattern
- a variety of shapes, including rectangles, rounded-corner rectangles, circles and ovals, and polygons, all either outlined and hollow or filled in with a pattern
- arcs of ovals, or wedge-shaped sections filled in with a pattern
- any other arbitrary shape or collection of shapes
- a picture composed of any combination of the above, drawn with just a single procedure call

QuickDraw also has some other abilities that you won't find in many other graphics packages. These abilities take care of most of the "housekeeping"—the trivial but time-consuming overhead that's necessary to keep things in order. They include:

- The ability to define many distinct "ports" on the screen. Each port has its own complete drawing environment—its own coordinate system, drawing location, character set, location on the screen, and so on. You can easily switch from one drawing port to another.

- Full and complete "clipping" to arbitrary areas, so that drawing will occur only where you want. It's like an electronic coloring book that won't let you color outside the lines. You don't have to worry about accidentally drawing over something else on the screen, or drawing off the screen and destroying memory.

- Off-screen drawing. Anything you can draw on the screen, you can also draw into an off-screen buffer, so you can prepare an image for an output device without disturbing the screen, or you can prepare a picture and move it onto the screen very quickly.

And QuickDraw lives up to its name: It's very fast. The speed and responsiveness of the Macintosh user interface are due primarily to the speed of QuickDraw. You can do good-quality animation, fast interactive graphics, and complex yet speedy text displays using the full features of QuickDraw. This means you don't have to bypass the general-purpose QuickDraw routines by writing a lot of special routines to improve speed.

In addition to its routines and data types, QuickDraw provides global variables that you can use from your Pascal program. For example, there's a variable named thePort that points to the current drawing port.

Assembly-language note: See the discussion of InitGraf in the "QuickDraw Routines" section for details on how to access the QuickDraw global variables from assembly language.

THE MATHEMATICAL FOUNDATION OF QUICKDRAW

To create graphics that are both precise and pretty requires not supercharged features but a firm mathematical foundation for the features you have. If the mathematics that underlie a graphics package are imprecise or fuzzy, the graphics will be, too. QuickDraw defines some clear mathematical constructs that are widely used in its procedures, functions, and data types: the coordinate plane, the point, the rectangle, and the region.

The Coordinate Plane

All information about location or movement is given to QuickDraw in terms of coordinates on a plane. The **coordinate plane** is a two-dimensional grid, as illustrated in Figure 2.

Note the following features of the QuickDraw coordinate plane:

- All grid coordinates are integers (in the range –32767 to 32767).
- All grid lines are infinitely thin.

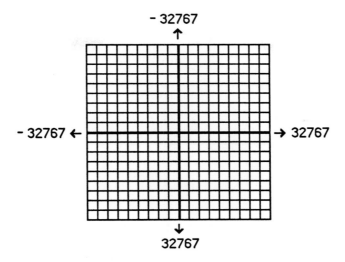

Figure 2. The Coordinate Plane

These concepts are important. First, they mean that the QuickDraw plane is finite, not infinite (although it's very large). Second, they mean that all elements represented on the coordinate plane are mathematically pure. Mathematical calculations using integer arithmetic will produce intuitively correct results. If you keep in mind that grid lines are infinitely thin, you'll never have "endpoint paranoia"—the confusion that results from not knowing whether that last dot is included in the line.

Points

There are 4,294,836,224 unique **points** on the coordinate plane. Each point is at the intersection of a horizontal grid line and a vertical grid line. As the grid lines are infinitely thin, so a point is infinitely small. Of course, there are many more points on this grid than there are dots on the Macintosh screen: When using QuickDraw you associate small parts of the grid with areas on the screen, so that you aren't bound into an arbitrary, limited coordinate system.

The coordinate origin (0,0) is in the middle of the grid. Horizontal coordinates increase as you move from left to right, and vertical coordinates increase as you move from top to bottom. This is the way both a TV screen and a page of English text are scanned: from the top left to the bottom right.

Figure 3 shows the relationship between points, grid lines, and **pixels**, the physical dots on the screen. (Pixels correspond to bits in memory, as described in the next section.)

You can store the coordinates of a point into a Pascal variable of type Point, defined by QuickDraw as a record of two integers:

```
TYPE  VHSelect  =  (v,h);
      Point     =  RECORD CASE INTEGER OF

            0:  (v: INTEGER:       {vertical coordinate}
                 h: INTEGER);      {horizontal coordinate}

            1:  (vh: ARRAY[VHSelect] OF INTEGER)

         END;
```

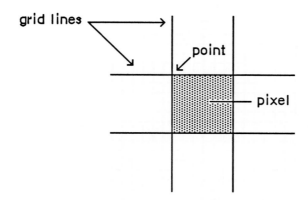

Figure 3. Points and Pixels

The variant part of this record lets you access the vertical and horizontal coordinates of a point either individually or as an array. For example, if the variable goodPt is declared to be of type Point, the following will all refer to the coordinates of the point:

```
goodPt.v          goodPt.h
goodPt.vh[v]      goodPt.vh[h]
```

Rectangles

Any two points can define the top left and bottom right corners of a rectangle. As these points are infinitely small, the borders of the rectangle are infinitely thin (see Figure 4).

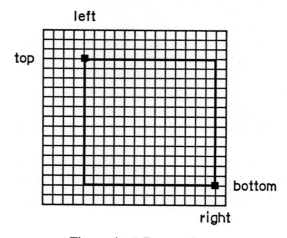

Figure 4. A Rectangle

Rectangles are used to define active areas on the screen, to assign coordinate systems to graphic entities, and to specify the locations and sizes for various drawing commands. QuickDraw also allows you to perform many mathematical calculations on rectangles—changing their sizes, shifting them around, and so on.

Note: Remember that rectangles, like points, are mathematical concepts that have no direct representation on the screen. The association between these conceptual elements and their physical representations is made by the BitMap data type, described in the following section.

The data type for rectangles is called Rect, and consists of four integers or two points:

```
TYPE Rect = RECORD CASE INTEGER OF
          0: (top:      INTEGER;
              left:     INTEGER;
              bottom:   INTEGER;
              right:    INTEGER);
          1: (topLeft:  Point;
              botRight: Point)
        END;
```

Again, the record variant allows you to access a variable of type Rect either as four boundary coordinates or as two diagonally opposite corner points. Combined with the record variant for points, all of the following references to the rectangle named aRect are legal:

```
aRect                                           {type Rect}

aRect.topLeft           aRect.botRight          {type Point}

aRect.top               aRect.left              {type INTEGER}
aRect.topLeft.v         aRect.topLeft.h         {type INTEGER}
aRect.topLeft.vh[v]     aRect.topLeft.vh[h]     {type INTEGER}

aRect.bottom            aRect.right             {type INTEGER}
aRect.botRight.v        aRect.botRight.h        {type INTEGER}
aRect.botRight.vh[v]    aRect.botRight.vh[h]    {type INTEGER}
```

Note: If the bottom coordinate of a rectangle is equal to or less than the top, or the right coordinate is equal to or less than the left, the rectangle is an **empty** rectangle (that is, one that contains no bits).

Regions

Unlike most graphics packages that can manipulate only simple geometric structures (usually rectilinear, at that), QuickDraw has the ability to gather an arbitrary set of spatially coherent points into a structure called a **region**, and perform complex yet rapid manipulations and calculations on such structures. Regions not only make your programs simpler and faster, but will let you perform operations that would otherwise be nearly impossible.

You define a region by calling routines that draw lines and shapes (even other regions). The outline of a region should be one or more closed loops. A region can be concave or convex, can consist of one area or many disjoint areas, and can even have "holes" in the middle. In Figure 5, the region on the left has a hole in the middle, and the region on the right consists of two disjoint areas.

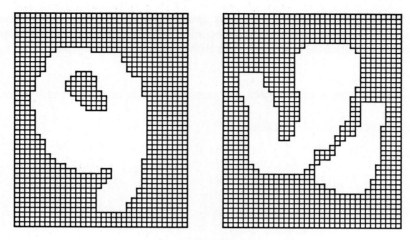

Figure 5. Regions

The data structure for a region consists of two fixed-length fields followed by a variable-length field:

```
TYPE Region =   RECORD
                   rgnSize: INTEGER;    {size in bytes}
                   rgnBBox: Rect;       {enclosing rectangle}
                   {more data if not rectangular}
                END;
```

The rgnSize field contains the size, in bytes, of the region variable. The maximum size of a region is 32K bytes. The rgnBBox field is a rectangle that completely encloses the region.

The simplest region is a rectangle. In this case, the rgnBBox field defines the entire region, and there's no optional region data. For rectangular regions (or empty regions), the rgnSize field contains 10.

The region definition data for nonrectangular regions is stored in a compact way that allows for highly efficient access by QuickDraw routines.

All regions are accessed through handles:

```
TYPE  RgnPtr    = ^Region;
      RgnHandle = ^RgnPtr;
```

Many calculations can be performed on regions. A region can be "expanded" or "shrunk" and, given any two regions, QuickDraw can find their union, intersection, difference, and exclusive-OR; it can also determine whether a given point intersects a region, and so on.

GRAPHIC ENTITIES

Points, rectangles, and regions are all mathematical models rather than actual graphic elements—they're data types that QuickDraw uses for drawing, but they don't actually appear on the screen. Some entities that do have a direct graphic interpretation are the bit image, bit map, pattern, and cursor. This section describes these graphic entities and relates them to the mathematical constructs described above.

Bit Images

A **bit image** is a collection of bits in memory that have a rectilinear representation. Take a collection of words in memory and lay them end to end so that bit 15 of the lowest-numbered word is on the left and bit 0 of the highest-numbered word is on the far right. Then take this array of bits and divide it, on word boundaries, into a number of equal-size rows. Stack these rows vertically so that the first row is on the top and the last row is on the bottom. The result is a matrix like the one shown in Figure 6—rows and columns of bits, with each row containing the same number of bytes. The number of bytes in each row of the bit image is called the **row width** of that image. A bit image can be any length that's a multiple of the row width.

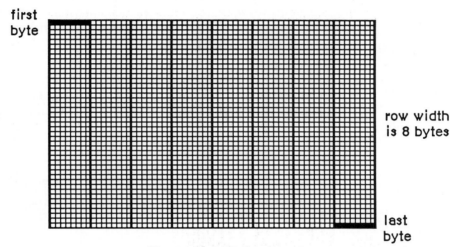

first
byte

row width
is 8 bytes

last
byte

Figure 6. A Bit Image

The screen itself is one large visible bit image. On a Macintosh 128K or 512K, for example, the screen is a 342-by-512 bit image, with a row width of 64 bytes. These 21,888 bytes of memory are displayed as a matrix of 175,104 pixels on the screen, each bit corresponding to one pixel. If a bit's value is 0, its pixel is white; if the bit's value is 1, the pixel is black.

> **Warning:** The numbers given here apply *only* to the Macintosh 128K and 512K systems. To allow for your application running on any version of the Macintosh, you should never use explicit numbers for screen dimensions. The QuickDraw global variable screenBits (a bit map, described below) gives you access to a rectangle whose dimensions are those of the screen, whatever version of the Macintosh is being used.

On a Macintosh 128K or 512K, each pixel on the screen is square, and there are 72 pixels per inch in each direction. On an unmodified Macintosh XL, each pixel is one and a half times taller than it is wide, meaning a rectangle 30 pixels wide by 20 tall looks square; there are 90 pixels per inch horizontally, and 60 per inch vertically. A Macintosh XL may be modified to have square pixels. You can get the the screen resolution by calling the Toolbox Utility procedure ScreenRes.

Note: The values given for pixels per inch may not be exactly the measurement on the screen, but they're the values you should use when calculating the size of printed output.

Note: Since each pixel on the screen represents one bit in a bit image, wherever this chapter says "bit", you can substitute "pixel" if the bit image is the screen. Likewise, this chapter often refers to pixels on the screen where the discussion applies equally to bits in an off-screen bit image.

Bit Maps

A **bit map** in QuickDraw is a data structure that defines a physical bit image in terms of the coordinate plane. A bit map has three parts: a pointer to a bit image, the row width of that image, and a boundary rectangle that gives the bit map both its dimensions and a coordinate system.

There can be several bit maps pointing to the same bit image, each imposing a different coordinate system on it. This important feature is explained in "Coordinates in GrafPorts", below.

As shown in Figure 7, the structure of a bit map is as follows:

```
TYPE BitMap =   RECORD
                    baseAddr:  Ptr;       {pointer to bit image}
                    rowBytes:  INTEGER;   {row width}
                    bounds:    Rect       {boundary rectangle}
                END;
```

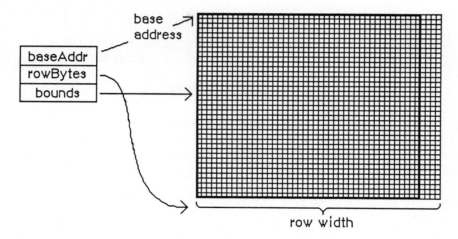

Figure 7. A Bit Map

BaseAddr is a pointer to the beginning of the bit image in memory. RowBytes is the row width in bytes. Both of these must always be even: A bit map must always begin on a word boundary and contain an integral number of words in each row.

The bounds field is the bit map's **boundary rectangle,** which both encloses the active area of the bit image and imposes a coordinate system on it. The top left corner of the boundary rectangle is aligned around the first bit in the bit image.

The relationship between the boundary rectangle and the bit image in a bit map is simple yet very important. First, some general rules:

- Bits in a bit image fall between points on the coordinate plane.

- A rectangle that is H points wide and V points tall encloses exactly (H–1)*(V–1) bits.

The coordinate system assigns integer values to the lines that border and separate bits, not to the bit positions themselves. For example, if a bit map is assigned the boundary rectangle with corners (10,–8) and (34,8), the bottom right bit in the image will be *between* horizontal coordinates 33 and 34, and *between* vertical coordinates 7 and 8 (see Figure 8).

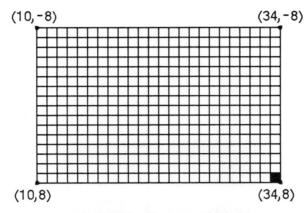

Figure 8. Coordinates and Bit Maps

The width of the boundary rectangle determines how many bits of one row are logically owned by the bit map. This width must not exceed the number of bits in each row of the bit image. The height of the boundary rectangle determines how many rows of the image are logically owned by the bit map. The number of rows enclosed by the boundary rectangle must not exceed the number of rows in the bit image.

Normally, the boundary rectangle completely encloses the bit image. If the rectangle is smaller than the dimensions of the image, the least significant bits in each row, as well as the last rows in the image, aren't affected by any operations on the bit map.

There's a QuickDraw global variable, named screenBits, that contains a bit map corresponding to the screen of the Macintosh being used. Wherever your program needs the exact dimensions of the screen, it should get them from the boundary rectangle of this variable.

Patterns

A **pattern** is a 64-bit image, organized as an 8-by-8-bit square, that's used to define a repeating design (such as stripes) or tone (such as gray). Patterns can be used to draw lines and shapes or to fill areas on the screen.

When a pattern is drawn, it's aligned so that adjacent areas of the same pattern in the same graphics port will blend with it into a continuous, coordinated pattern. QuickDraw provides predefined patterns in global variables named white, black, gray, ltGray, and dkGray. Any other 64-bit variable or constant can also be used as a pattern. The data type definition for a pattern is as follows:

```
TYPE Pattern = PACKED ARRAY[0..7] OF 0..255;
```

The row width of a pattern is one byte.

Cursors

A **cursor** is a small image that appears on the screen and is controlled by the mouse. (It appears only on the screen, and never in an off-screen bit image.)

> **Note:** Macintosh user manuals call this image a "pointer", since it points to a location on the screen. To avoid confusion with other meanings of "pointer" in *Inside Macintosh*, we use the alternate term "cursor".

A cursor is defined as a 256-bit image, a 16-by-16-bit square. The row width of a cursor is two bytes. Figure 9 illustrates four cursors.

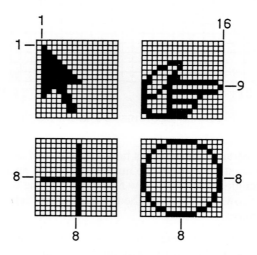

Figure 9. Cursors

A cursor has three fields: a 16-word data field that contains the image itself, a 16-word mask field that contains information about the screen appearance of each bit of the cursor, and a **hotSpot** point that aligns the cursor with the mouse location.

```
TYPE Bits16 = ARRAY[0..15] OF INTEGER;

    Cursor = RECORD
                data:    Bits16; {cursor image}
                mask:    Bits16; {cursor mask}
                hotSpot: Point   {point aligned with mouse}
              END;
```

The data for the cursor must begin on a word boundary.

The cursor appears on the screen as a 16-by-16-bit square. The appearance of each bit of the square is determined by the corresponding bits in the data and mask and, if the mask bit is 0, by the pixel "under" the cursor (the pixel already on the screen in the same position as this bit of the cursor):

Data	Mask	Resulting pixel on screen
0	1	White
1	1	Black
0	0	Same as pixel under cursor
1	0	Inverse of pixel under cursor

Notice that if all mask bits are 0, the cursor is completely transparent, in that the image under the cursor can still be viewed: Pixels under the white part of the cursor appear unchanged, while under the black part of the cursor, black pixels show through as white.

The hotSpot aligns a point (*not* a bit) in the image with the mouse location. Imagine the rectangle with corners (0,0) and (16,16) framing the image, as in each of the examples in Figure 9; the hotSpot is defined in this coordinate system. A hotSpot of (0,0) is at the top left of the image. For the arrow in Figure 9 to point to the mouse location, (1,1) would be its hotSpot. A hotSpot of (8,8) is in the exact center of the image; the center of the plus sign or circle in Figure 9 would coincide with the mouse location if (8,8) were the hotSpot for that cursor. Similarly, the hotSpot for the pointing hand would be (16,9).

Whenever you move the mouse, the low-level interrupt-driven mouse routines move the cursor's hotSpot to be aligned with the new mouse location.

QuickDraw supplies a predefined cursor in the global variable named arrow; this is the standard arrow cursor (illustrated in Figure 9).

Graphic Entities as Resources

You can create cursors and patterns in your program code, but it's usually simpler and more convenient to store them in a resource file and read them in when you need them. Standard cursors and patterns are available not only through the global variables provided by QuickDraw, but also as system resources stored in the system resource file. QuickDraw itself operates independently of the Resource Manager, so it doesn't contain routines for accessing graphics-related resources; instead, these routines are included in the Toolbox Utilities (see chapter 16 for more information).

Besides patterns and cursors, two other graphic entities that may be stored in resource files (and accessed via Toolbox Utility routines) are a QuickDraw picture, described later in this chapter, and an **icon**, a 32-by-32 bit image that's used to graphically represent an object, concept, or message.

THE DRAWING ENVIRONMENT: GRAFPORT

A **grafPort** is a complete drawing environment that defines where and how graphic operations will take place. You can have many grafPorts open at once, and each one will have its own coordinate system, drawing pattern, background pattern, pen size and location, character font and style, and bit map in which drawing takes place. You can instantly switch from one port to another. GrafPorts are the structures upon which a program builds windows, which are fundamental to the Macintosh "overlapping windows" user interface. Besides being used for windows on the screen, grafPorts are used for printing and for off-screen drawing.

A grafPort is defined as follows:

```
TYPE  GrafPtr   =  ^GrafPort;
      GrafPort  =  RECORD
                        device:     INTEGER;    {device-specific information}
                        portBits:   BitMap;     {grafPort's bit map}
                        portRect:   Rect;       {grafPort's rectangle}
                        visRgn:     RgnHandle;  {visible region}
                        clipRgn:    RgnHandle;  {clipping region}
                        bkPat:      Pattern;    {background pattern}
                        fillPat:    Pattern;    {fill pattern}
                        pnLoc:      Point;      {pen location}
                        pnSize:     Point;      {pen size}
                        pnMode:     INTEGER;    {pen's transfer mode}
                        pnPat:      Pattern;    {pen pattern}
                        pnVis:      INTEGER;    {pen visibility}
                        txFont:     INTEGER;    {font number for text}
                        txFace:     Style;      {text's character style}
                        txMode:     INTEGER;    {text's transfer mode}
                        txSize:     INTEGER;    {font size for text}
                        spExtra:    Fixed;      {extra space}
                        fgColor:    LONGINT;    {foreground color}
                        bkColor:    LONGINT;    {background color}
                        colrBit:    INTEGER;    {color bit}
                        patStretch: INTEGER;    {used internally}
                        picSave:    Handle;     {picture being saved}
                        rgnSave:    Handle;     {region being saved}
                        polySave:   Handle;     {polygon being saved}
                        grafProcs:  QDProcsPtr  {low-level drawing routines}
                   END;
```

All QuickDraw operations refer to grafPorts via grafPtrs. (For historical reasons, grafPort is one of the few objects in the Macintosh system software that's referred to by a pointer rather than a handle.)

Warning: You can access all fields and subfields of a grafPort normally, but you should not store new values directly into them. QuickDraw has routines for altering all fields of a grafPort, and using these routines ensures that changing a grafPort produces no unusual side effects.

The device field of a grafPort contains device-specific information that's used by the Font Manager to achieve the best possible results when drawing text in the grafPort. There may be physical differences in the same logical font for different output devices, to ensure the highest-quality printing on the device being used. The default value of the device field is 0, for best results on output to the screen. For more information, see chapter 7.

The portBits field is the bit map that points to the bit image to be used by the grafPort. The default bit map uses the entire screen as its bit image. The bit map may be changed to indicate a different structure in memory: All graphics routines work in exactly the same way regardless of whether their effects are visible on the screen. A program can, for example, prepare an image to be printed on a printer without ever displaying the image on the screen, or develop a picture in an off-screen bit map before transferring it to the screen. The portBits.bounds rectangle determines the coordinate system of the grafPort; all other coordinates in the grafPort are expressed in this system.

The portRect field is a rectangle that defines a subset of the bit map that will be used for drawing: All drawing done by the application occurs inside the portRect. Its coordinates are in the coordinate system defined by the portBits.bounds rectangle. The portRect usually falls within the portBits.bounds rectangle, but it's not required to do so. The portRect usually defines the "writable" interior area of a window, document, or other object on the screen.

The visRgn field is manipulated by the Window Manager; you will normally never change a grafPort's visRgn. It indicates the region of the grafPort that's actually visible on the screen, that is, the part of the window that's not covered by other windows. For example, if you move one window in front of another, the Window Manager logically removes the area of overlap from the visRgn of the window in back. When you draw into the back window, whatever's being drawn is clipped to the visRgn so that it doesn't run over onto the front window. The default visRgn is set to the portRect. The visRgn has no effect on images that aren't displayed on the screen.

The clipRgn is the grafPort's **clipping region**, an arbitrary region that you can use to limit drawing to any region within the portRect. If, for example, you want to draw a half circle on the screen, you can set the clipRgn to half the square that would enclose the whole circle, and then draw the whole circle. Only the half within the clipRgn will actually be drawn in the grafPort. The default clipRgn is set arbitrarily large; you have full control over its setting. Unlike the visRgn, the clipRgn affects the image even if it isn't displayed on the screen.

Figure 10 illustrates a typical bit map (as defined by portBits), portRect, visRgn, and clipRgn.

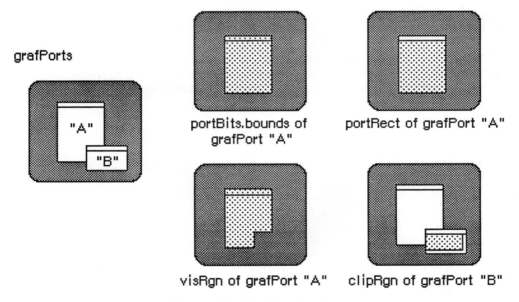

Figure 10. GrafPort Regions

The bkPat and fillPat fields of a grafPort contain patterns used by certain QuickDraw routines. BkPat is the "background" pattern that's used when an area is erased or when bits are scrolled out of it. When asked to fill an area with a specified pattern, QuickDraw stores the given pattern in the fillPat field and then calls a low-level drawing routine that gets the pattern from that field. The various graphic operations are discussed in detail later in the descriptions of individual QuickDraw routines.

Of the next ten fields, the first five determine characteristics of the graphics pen and the last five determine characteristics of any text that may be drawn; these are described in separate sections below.

The fgColor, bkColor, and colrBit fields contain values related to drawing in color. FgColor is the grafPort's foreground color and bkColor is its background color. ColrBit tells the color imaging software which plane of the color picture to draw into. For more information, see "Drawing in Color" in the section "General Discussion of Drawing".

The patStretch field is used during output to a printer to expand patterns if necessary. The application should not change its value.

The picSave, rgnSave, and polySave fields reflect the state of picture, region, and polygon definition, respectively. To define a region, for example, you "open" it, call routines that draw it, and then "close" it. If no region is open, rgnSave contains NIL; otherwise, it contains a handle to information related to the region definition. The application shouldn't be concerned about exactly what information the handle leads to; you may, however, save the current value of rgnSave, set the field to NIL to disable the region definition, and later restore it to the saved value to resume the region definition. The picSave and polySave fields work similarly for pictures and polygons.

Finally, the grafProcs field may point to a special data structure that the application stores into if it wants to customize QuickDraw drawing routines or use QuickDraw in other advanced, highly specialized ways (see "Customizing QuickDraw Operations"). If grafProcs is NIL, QuickDraw responds in the standard ways described in this chapter.

Pen Characteristics

The pnLoc, pnSize, pnMode, pnPat, and pnVis fields of a grafPort deal with the graphics "pen". Each grafPort has one and only one such pen, which is used for drawing lines, shapes, and text. The pen has four characteristics: a location, a size (height and width), a drawing mode, and a drawing pattern (see Figure 11).

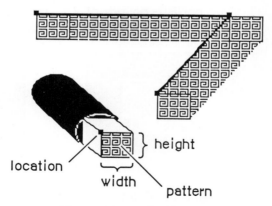

Figure 11. A Graphics Pen

The pnLoc field specifies the point where QuickDraw will begin drawing the next line, shape, or character. It can be anywhere on the coordinate plane: There are no restrictions on the movement or placement of the pen. Remember that the pen location is a point in the grafPort's coordinate system, not a pixel in a bit image. The top left corner of the pen is at the pen location; the pen hangs below and to the right of this point.

The pen is rectangular in shape, and its width and height are specified by pnSize. The default size is a 1-by-1-bit square; the width and height can range from (0,0) to (30000,30000). If either the pen width or the pen height is less than 1, the pen will not draw.

The pnMode and pnPat fields of a grafPort determine how the bits under the pen are affected when lines or shapes are drawn. The pnPat is a pattern that's used like the "ink" in the pen. This pattern, like all other patterns drawn in the grafPort, is always aligned with the port's coordinate system: The top left corner of the pattern is aligned with the top left corner of the portRect, so that adjacent areas of the same pattern will blend into a continuous, coordinated pattern.

The pnMode field determines how the pen pattern is to affect what's already in the bit image when lines or shapes are drawn. When the pen draws, QuickDraw first determines what bits in the bit image will be affected and finds their corresponding bits in the pattern. It then does a bit-by-bit comparison based on the pen mode, which specifies one of eight Boolean operations to perform. The resulting bit is stored into its proper place in the bit image. The pen modes are described under "Transfer Modes" in the section "General Discussion of Drawing".

The pnVis field determines the pen's visibility, that is, whether it draws on the screen. For more information, see the descriptions of HidePen and ShowPen under "Pen and Line-Drawing Routines" in the "QuickDraw Routines" section.

Text Characteristics

The txFont, txFace, txMode, txSize, and spExtra fields of a grafPort determine how text will be drawn—the font, style, and size of characters and how they will be placed in the bit image. QuickDraw can draw characters as quickly and easily as it draws lines and shapes, and in many prepared fonts. **Font** means the complete set of characters of one typeface. The characters may be drawn in any size and **character style** (that is, with stylistic variations such as bold, italic, and underline). Figure 12 shows two characters drawn by QuickDraw and some terms associated with drawing text.

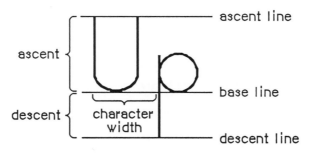

Figure 12. QuickDraw Characters

Text is drawn with the base line positioned at the pen location.

The txFont field is a font number that identifies the character font to be used in the grafPort. The font number 0 represents the system font. For more information about the system font, the other font numbers recognized by the Font Manager, and the construction, layout, and loading of fonts, see chapter 7.

A character font is defined as a collection of images that make up the individual characters of the font. The characters can be of unequal widths, and they're not restricted to their "cells": The lower curl of a lowercase j, for example, can stretch back under the previous character (typographers call this **kerning**). A font can consist of up to 255 distinct characters, yet not all characters need to be defined in a single font. In addition, each font contains a **missing symbol** to be drawn in case of a request to draw a character that's missing from the font.

The txFace field controls the character style of the text with values from the set defined by the Style data type:

```
TYPE  StyleItem  = (bold,italic,underline,outline,shadow,condense,
                    extend);
      Style      = SET OF StyleItem;
```

Assembly-language note: In assembly language, this set is stored as a word whose low-order byte contains bits representing the style. The bit numbers are specified by the following global constants:

```
boldBit      .EQU    0
italicBit    .EQU    1
ulineBit     .EQU    2
outlineBit   .EQU    3
shadowBit    .EQU    5
extendBit    .EQU    6
```

If all bits are 0, it represents the plain character style.

You can apply stylistic variations either alone or in combination; Figure 13 illustrates some as applied to the Geneva font. Most combinations usually look good only for large font sizes.

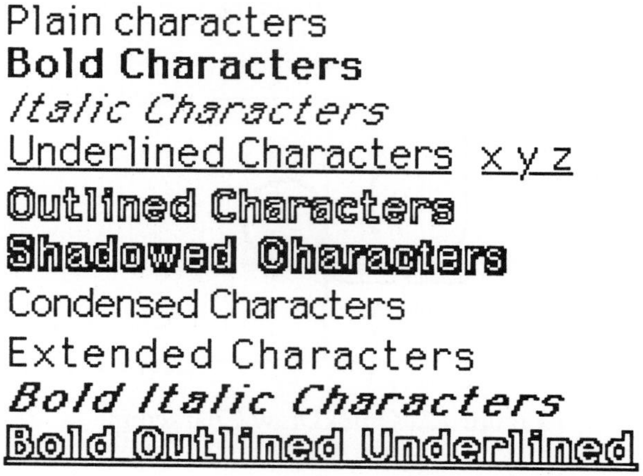

Figure 13. Stylistic Variations

If you specify bold, each character is repeatedly drawn one bit to the right an appropriate number of times for extra thickness.

Italic adds an italic slant to the characters. Character bits above the base line are skewed right; bits below the base line are skewed left.

Underline draws a line below the base line of the characters. If part of a character descends below the base line (as "y" in Figure 13), the underline isn't drawn through the pixel on either side of the descending part.

Outline makes a hollow, outlined character rather than a solid one. Shadow also makes an outlined character, but the outline is thickened below and to the right of the character to achieve the effect of a shadow. If you specify bold along with outline or shadow, the hollow part of the character is widened.

Condense and extend affect the horizontal distance between all characters, including spaces. Condense decreases the distance between characters and extend increases it, by an amount that the Font Manager determines is appropriate.

The txMode field controls the way characters are placed in the bit image. It functions much like a pnMode: When a character is drawn, QuickDraw determines which bits in the bit image will be affected, does a bit-by-bit comparison based on the mode, and stores the resulting bits into the bit image. These modes are described under "Transfer Modes" in the section "General Discussion of Drawing". Only three of them—srcOr, srcXor, and srcBic—should be used for drawing text.

Note: If you use scrCopy, some extra blank space will be appended at the end of the text.

The txSize field specifies the **font size** in points (where "point" is a typographical term meaning approximately 1/72 inch). Any size from 1 to 127 points may be specified. If the Font Manager doesn't have the font in a specified size, it will scale a size it does have as necessary to produce the size desired. A value of 0 in this field represents the system font size (12 points).

Finally, the spExtra field is useful when a line of characters is to be drawn justified such that it's aligned with both a left and a right margin (sometimes called "full justification"). SpExtra contains a fixed-point number equal to the average number of pixels by which each space character should be widened to fill out the line. The Fixed data type is described in chapter 3.

COORDINATES IN GRAFPORTS

Each grafPort has its own **local coordinate system**. All fields in the grafPort are expressed in these coordinates, and all calculations and actions performed in QuickDraw use the local coordinate system of the currently selected port.

Two things are important to remember:

■ Each grafPort maps a portion of the coordinate plane into a similarly-sized portion of a bit image.

■ The portBits.bounds rectangle defines the local coordinates for a grafPort.

The top left corner of portBits.bounds is always aligned around the first bit in the bit image; the coordinates of that corner "anchor" a point on the grid to that bit in the bit image. This forms a common reference point for multiple grafPorts that use the same bit image (such as the screen); given a portBits.bounds rectangle for each port, you know that their top left corners coincide.

The relationship between the portBits.bounds and portRect rectangles is very important: The portBits.bounds rectangle establishes a coordinate system for the port, and the portRect rectangle indicates the section of the coordinate plane (and thus the bit image) that will be used for drawing. The portRect usually falls inside the portBits.bounds rectangle, but it's not required to do so.

When a new grafPort is created, its bit map is set to point to the entire screen, and both the portBits.bounds and the portRect are set to rectangles enclosing the screen. The point (0,0) corresponds to the screen's top left corner.

You can redefine the local coordinates of the top left corner of the grafPort's portRect, using the SetOrigin procedure. This offsets the coordinates of the grafPort's portBits.bounds rectangle, recalculating the coordinates of all points in the grafPort to be relative to the new corner coordinates. For example, consider these procedure calls:

```
SetPort (gamePort);
SetOrigin(90,80)
```

The call to SetPort sets the current grafPort to gamePort; the call to SetOrigin changes the local coordinates of the top left corner of that port's portRect to (90,80) (see Figure 14).

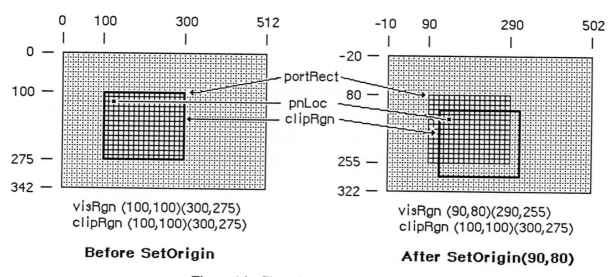

Figure 14. Changing Local Coordinates

This offsets the coordinates of the following elements:

```
gamePort^.portBits.bounds
gamePort^.portRect
gamePort^.visRgn
```

These three elements are always kept "in sync".

Notice that when the local coordinates of a grafPort are offset, the grafPort's clipRgn and pen location are *not* offset. A good way to think of it is that the port's structure "sticks" to the screen, while the document in the grafPort (along with the pen and clipRgn) "sticks" to the coordinate system. For example, in Figure 14, before SetOrigin, the visRgn and clipRgn are the same as the portRect. After the SetOrigin call, the locations of portBits.bounds, portRect, and visRgn do not change on the screen; their coordinates are simply offset. As always, the top left corner of portBits.bounds remains "anchored" around the first bit in the bit image (the first pixel on the screen); the image on the screen doesn't move as a result of SetOrigin. However, the pen location and clipRgn do move on the screen; the top left corner of the clipRgn is still (100,100), but this location has moved down and to the right, and the pen has similarly moved.

If you're moving, comparing, or otherwise dealing with mathematical items in different grafPorts (for example, finding the intersection of two regions in two different grafPorts), you must adjust to a common coordinate system before you perform the operation. A QuickDraw procedure, LocalToGlobal, lets you convert a point's local coordinates to a **global coordinate system** where the top left corner of the bit image is (0,0); by converting the various local coordinates to global coordinates, you can compare and mix them with confidence. For more information, see the description of LocalToGlobal under "Calculations with Points" in the "QuickDraw Routines" section.

GENERAL DISCUSSION OF DRAWING

Drawing occurs:

- always inside a grafPort, in the bit image and coordinate system defined by the grafPort's bit map
- always within the intersection of the grafPort's portBits.bounds and portRect, and clipped to its visRgn and clipRgn
- always at the grafPort's pen location
- usually with the grafPort's pen size, pattern, and mode

With QuickDraw routines, you can draw lines, shapes, and text. Shapes include rectangles, ovals, rounded-corner rectangles, wedge-shaped sections of ovals, regions, and polygons.

Lines are defined by two points: the current pen location and a destination location. When drawing a line, QuickDraw moves the top left corner of the pen along the mathematical trajectory from the current location to the destination. The pen hangs below and to the right of the trajectory (see Figure 15).

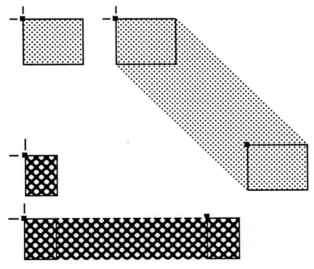

Figure 15. Drawing Lines

Note: No mathematical element (such as the pen location) is ever affected by clipping; clipping only determines what appears where in the bit image. If you draw a line to a location outside the intersection of the portRect, visRgn and clipRgn, the pen location will move there, but only the portion of the line that's inside that area will actually be drawn. This is true for all drawing routines.

Rectangles, ovals, and rounded-corner rectangles are defined by two corner points. The shapes always appear inside the mathematical rectangle defined by the two points. A region is defined in a more complex manner, but also appears only within the rectangle enclosing it. Remember, these enclosing rectangles have infinitely thin borders and are not visible on the screen.

As illustrated in Figure 16, shapes may be drawn either **solid** (filled in with a pattern) or **framed** (outlined and hollow).

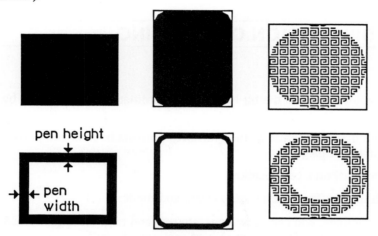

Figure 16. Solid Shapes and Framed Shapes

In the case of framed shapes, the outline appears completely within the enclosing rectangle—with one exception—and the vertical and horizontal thickness of the outline is determined by the pen size. The exception is polygons, as discussed in the section "Pictures and Polygons" below.

The pen pattern is used to fill in the bits that are affected by the drawing operation. The pen mode defines how those bits are to be affected by directing QuickDraw to apply one of eight Boolean operations to the bits in the shape and the corresponding pixels on the screen.

Text drawing doesn't use the pnSize, pnPat, or pnMode, but it does use the pnLoc. QuickDraw starts drawing each character from the current pen location, with the character's base line at the pen location. After a character is drawn, the pen moves to the right to the location where it will draw the next character. No wraparound or carriage return is performed automatically. Clipping of text is performed in exactly the same manner as all other clipping in QuickDraw.

Transfer Modes

When lines or shapes are drawn, the pnMode field of the grafPort determines how the drawing is to appear in the port's bit image; similarly, the txMode field determines how text is to appear. There's also a QuickDraw procedure that transfers a bit image from one bit map to another, and this procedure has a mode parameter that determines the appearance of the result. In all these cases, the mode, called a **transfer mode**, specifies one of eight Boolean operations: For each bit in the item to be drawn, QuickDraw finds the corresponding bit in the destination bit map, performs the Boolean operation on the pair of bits, and stores the resulting bit into the bit image.

There are two types of transfer mode:

- **pattern transfer modes**, for drawing lines or shapes with a pattern
- **source transfer modes**, for drawing text or transferring any bit image between two bit maps

For each type of mode, there are four basic operations—Copy, Or, Xor, and Bic ("bit clear"). The Copy operation simply replaces the pixels in the destination with the pixels in the pattern or source, "painting" over the destination without regard for what's already there. The Or, Xor, and Bic operations leave the destination pixels under the white part of the pattern or source unchanged, and differ in how they affect the pixels under the black part: Or replaces those pixels with black pixels, thus "overlaying" the destination with the black part of the pattern or source; Xor inverts the pixels under the black part; and Bic erases them to white.

Each of the basic operations has a variant in which every pixel in the pattern or source is inverted before the operation is performed, giving eight operations in all. Each mode is defined by name as a constant in QuickDraw (see Figure 17).

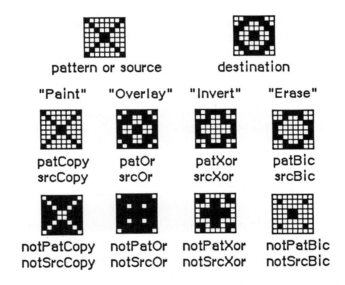

Figure 17. Transfer Modes

Pattern transfer mode	Source transfer mode	Action on each pixel in destination:	
		If black pixel in pattern or source	If white pixel in pattern or source
patCopy	srcCopy	Force black	Force white
patOr	srcOr	Force black	Leave alone
patXor	srcXor	Invert	Leave alone
patBic	srcBic	Force white	Leave alone
notPatCopy	notSrcCopy	Force white	Force black
notPatOr	notSrcOr	Leave alone	Force black
notPatXor	notSrcXor	Leave alone	Invert
notPatBic	notSrcBic	Leave alone	Force white

6 QuickDraw

Drawing in Color

Your application can draw on color output devices by using QuickDraw procedures to set the foreground color and the background color. Eight standard colors may be specified with the following predefined constants:

```
CONST  blackColor    = 33;
       whiteColor    = 30;
       redColor      = 205;
       greenColor    = 341;
       blueColor     = 409;
       cyanColor     = 273;
       magentaColor  = 137;
       yellowColor   = 69;
```

Initially, the foreground color is blackColor and the background color is whiteColor. If you specify a color other than whiteColor, it will appear as black on a black-and-white output device.

To apply the table in the "Transfer Modes" section above to drawing in color, make the following translation: Where the table shows "Force black", read "Force foreground color", and where it shows "Force white", read "Force background color". The effect of inverting a color depends on the device being used.

Note: QuickDraw can support output devices that have up to 32 bits of color information per pixel. A color picture may be thought of, then, as having up to 32 planes. At any one time, QuickDraw draws into only one of these planes. A QuickDraw routine called by the color-imaging software specifies which plane.

PICTURES AND POLYGONS

QuickDraw lets you save a sequence of drawing commands and "play them back" later with a single procedure call. There are two such mechanisms: one for drawing any picture to scale in a destination rectangle that you specify, and another for drawing polygons in all the ways you can draw other shapes in QuickDraw.

Pictures

A **picture** in QuickDraw is a transcript of calls to routines that draw something—anything—in a bit image. Pictures make it easy for one program to draw something defined in another program, with great flexibility and without knowing the details about what's being drawn.

For each picture you define, you specify a rectangle that surrounds it; this rectangle is called the **picture frame**. When you later call the procedure that plays back the saved picture, you supply a destination rectangle, and QuickDraw scales the picture so that its frame is completely aligned with the destination rectangle. Thus, the picture may be expanded or shrunk to fit its destination rectangle. For example, if the picture is a circle inside a square picture frame, and the destination rectangle is not square, the picture will be drawn as an oval.

Since a picture may include any sequence of drawing commands, its data structure is a variable-length entity. It consists of two fixed-length fields followed by a variable-length field:

```
TYPE Picture =  RECORD
                  picSize:  INTEGER;  {size in bytes}
                  picFrame: Rect;     {picture frame}
                  {picture definition data}
                END;
```

The picSize field contains the size, in bytes, of the picture variable. The maximum size of a picture is 32K bytes. The picFrame field is the picture frame that surrounds the picture and gives a frame of reference for scaling when the picture is played back. The rest of the structure contains a compact representation of the drawing commands that define the picture.

All pictures are accessed through handles:

```
TYPE PicPtr    = ^Picture;
     PicHandlle = ^PicPtr;
```

To define a picture, you call a QuickDraw function that returns a picHandle, and then call the drawing routines that define the picture.

QuickDraw also allows you to intersperse **picture comments** with the definition of a picture. These comments, which do not affect the picture's appearance, may be used to provide additional information about the picture when it's played back. This is especially valuable when pictures are transmitted from one application to another. There are two standard types of comments which, like parentheses, serve to group drawing commands together (such as all the commands that draw a particular part of a picture):

```
CONST picLParen = 0;
      picRParen = 1;
```

The application defining the picture can use these standard comments as well as comments of its own design.

Polygons

Polygons are similar to pictures in that you define them by a sequence of calls to QuickDraw routines. They're also similar to other shapes that QuickDraw knows about, since there's a set of procedures for performing graphic operations and calculations on them.

A **polygon** is simply any sequence of connected lines (see Figure 18). You define a polygon by moving to the starting point of the polygon and drawing lines from there to the next point, from that point to the next, and so on.

The data structure for a polygon consists of two fixed-length fields followed by a variable-length array:

```
TYPE Polygon =  RECORD
                  polySize:   INTEGER;  {size in bytes}
                  polyBBox:   Rect;     {enclosing rectangle}
                  polyPoints: ARRAY[0..0] OF Point
                END;
```

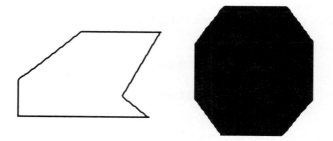

Figure 18. Polygons

The polySize field contains the size, in bytes, of the polygon variable. The maximum size of a polygon is 32K bytes. The polyBBox field is a rectangle that just encloses the entire polygon. The polyPoints array expands as necessary to contain the points of the polygon—the starting point followed by each successive point to which a line is drawn.

Like pictures and regions, polygons are accessed through handles:

```
TYPE  PolyPtr    = ^Polygon;
      PolyHandle = ^PolyPtr;
```

To define a polygon, you call a routine that returns a polyHandle, and then call the line-drawing routines that define the polygon.

Just as for other shapes that QuickDraw knows about, there's a set of graphic operations to draw polygons on the screen. QuickDraw draws a polygon by moving to the starting point and then drawing lines to the remaining points in succession, just as when the routines were called to define the polygon. In this sense it "plays back" those routine calls. As a result, polygons are not treated exactly the same as other QuickDraw shapes. For example, the procedure that frames a polygon draws outside the actual boundary of the polygon, because QuickDraw line-drawing routines draw below and to the right of the pen location. The procedures that fill a polygon with a pattern, however, stay within the boundary of the polygon; if the polygon's ending point isn't the same as its starting point, these procedures add a line between them to complete the shape.

QuickDraw also scales a polygon differently from a similarly-shaped region if it's being drawn as part of a picture: When stretched, a slanted line is drawn more smoothly if it's part of a polygon rather than a region. You may find it helpful to keep in mind the conceptual difference between polygons and regions: A polygon is treated more as a continuous shape, a region more as a set of bits.

USING QUICKDRAW

Call the InitGraf procedure to initialize QuickDraw at the beginning of your program, before initializing any other parts of the Toolbox.

When your application starts up, the cursor will be a wristwatch; the Finder sets it to this to indicate that a lengthy operation is in progress. Call the InitCursor procedure when the application is ready to respond to user input, to change the cursor to the standard arrow. Each time through the main event loop, you should call SetCursor to change the cursor as appropriate for its screen location.

All graphic operations are performed in grafPorts. Before a grafPort can be used, it must be allocated and initialized with the OpenPort procedure. Normally, you don't call OpenPort yourself—in most cases your application will draw into a window you've created with Window Manager routines, and these routines call OpenPort to create the window's grafPort. Likewise, a grafPort's regions are disposed of with ClosePort, and the grafPort itself is disposed of with the Memory Manager procedure DisposPtr—but when you call the Window Manager to close or dispose of a window, it calls these routines for you.

In an application that uses multiple windows, each is a separate grafPort. If your application draws into more than one grafPort, you can call SetPort to set the grafPort that you want to draw in. At times you may need to preserve the current grafPort; you can do this by calling GetPort to save the current port, SetPort to set the port you want to draw in, and then SetPort again when you need to restore the previous port.

Each grafPort has its own local coordinate system. Some Toolbox routines return or expect points that are expressed in a common, global coordinate system, while others use local coordinates. For example, when the Event Manager reports an event, it gives the mouse location in global coordinates; but when you call the Control Manager to find out whether the user clicked in a control in one of your windows, you pass the mouse location in local coordinates. The GlobalToLocal procedure lets you convert global coordinates to local coordinates, and the LocalToGlobal procedure lets you do the reverse.

The SetOrigin procedure will adjust a grafPort's local coordinate system. If your application performs scrolling, you'll use ScrollRect to shift the bits of the image, and then SetOrigin to readjust the coordinate system after this shift.

You can redefine a grafPort's clipping region with the SetClip or ClipRect procedure. Just as GetPort and SetPort are used to preserve the current grafPort, GetClip and SetClip are useful for saving the grafPort's clipRgn while you temporarily perform other clipping functions. This is useful, for example, when you want to reset the clipRgn to redraw the newly displayed portion of a document that's been scrolled.

When drawing text in a grafPort, you can set the font characteristics with TextFont, TextFace, TextMode, and TextSize. CharWidth, StringWidth, or TextWidth will tell you how much horizontal space the text will require, and GetFontInfo will tell you how much vertical space. You can draw text with DrawChar, DrawString, and DrawText.

The LineTo procedure draws a line from the current pen location to a given point, and the Line procedure draws a line between two given points. You can set the pen location with the MoveTo or Move procedure, and set other pen characteristics with PenSize, PenMode, and PenPat.

In addition to drawing text and lines, you can use QuickDraw to draw a variety of shapes. Most of them are defined simply by a rectangle that encloses the shape. Others require you to call a series of routines to define them:

- To define a region, call the NewRgn function to allocate space for it, then call OpenRgn, and then specify the outline of the region by calling routines that draw lines and shapes. End the region definition by calling CloseRgn. When you're completely done with the region, call DisposeRgn to release the memory it occupies.

- To define a polygon, call the OpenPoly function and then form the polygon by calling procedures that draw lines. Call ClosePoly when you're finished defining the polygon, and KillPoly when you're completely done with it.

You can perform the following graphic operations on rectangles, rounded-corner rectangles, ovals, arcs/wedges, regions, and polygons:

- frame, to outline the shape using the current pen pattern and size

- paint, to fill the shape using the current pen pattern

- erase, to paint the shape using the current background pattern

- invert, to invert the pixels in the shape

- fill, to fill the shape with a specified pattern

QuickDraw pictures let you record and play back complex drawing sequences. To define a picture, call the OpenPicture function and then the drawing routines that form the picture. Call ClosePicture when you're finished defining the picture. To draw a picture, call DrawPicture. When you're completely done with a picture, call KillPicture (or the Resource Manager procedure ReleaseResource, if the picture's a resource).

You'll use points, rectangles, and regions not only when drawing with QuickDraw, but also when using other parts of the Toolbox and Operating System. At times, you may find it useful to perform calculations on these entities. You can, for example, add and subtract points, and perform a number of calculations on rectangles and regions, such as offsetting them, rescaling them, calculating their union or intersection, and so on.

Note: When performing a calculation on entities in different grafPorts, you need to adjust to a common coordinate system first, by calling LocalToGlobal to convert to global coordinates.

To transfer a bit image from one bit map to another, you can use the CopyBits procedure. For example, you can call SetPortBits to change the bit map of the current grafPort to an off-screen buffer, draw into that grafPort, and then call CopyBits to transfer the image from the off-screen buffer onto the screen.

QUICKDRAW ROUTINES

GrafPort Routines

```
PROCEDURE InitGraf (globalPtr: Ptr);
```

Call InitGraf once and only once at the beginning of your program to initialize QuickDraw. It initializes the global variables listed below (as well as some private global variables for its own internal use).

Variable	Type	Initial setting
thePort	GrafPtr	NIL
white	Pattern	An all-white pattern
black	Pattern	An all-black pattern
gray	Pattern	A 50% gray pattern
ltGray	Pattern	A 25% gray pattern
dkGray	Pattern	A 75% gray pattern

Variable	Type	Initial setting
arrow	Cursor	The standard arrow cursor
screenBits	BitMap	The entire screen
randSeed	LONGINT	1

You must pass, in the globalPtr parameter, a pointer to the first QuickDraw global variable, thePort. From Pascal programs, you should always pass @thePort for globalPtr.

Assembly-language note: The QuickDraw global variables are stored in reverse order, from high to low memory, and require the number of bytes specified by the global constant grafSize. Most development systems (including the Lisa Workshop) preallocate space for these globals immediately below the location pointed to by register A5. Since thePort is four bytes, you would pass the globalPtr parameter as follows:

```
PEA          -4(A5)
_InitGraf
```

InitGraf stores this pointer to thePort in the location pointed to by A5. This value is used as a base address when accessing the other QuickDraw global variables, which are accessed using negative offsets (the offsets have the same names as the Pascal global variables). For example:

```
MOVE.L  (A5),A0            ;point to first QuickDraw global
MOVE.L  randSeed(A0),A1    ;get global variable randSeed
```

Note: To initialize the cursor, call InitCursor (described under "Cursor-Handling Routines" below).

6 QuickDraw

PROCEDURE OpenPort (port: GrafPtr);

OpenPort allocates space for the given grafPort's visRgn and clipRgn, initializes the fields of the grafPort as indicated below, and makes the grafPort the current port (by calling SetPort). OpenPort is called by the Window Manager when you create a window, and you normally won't call it yourself. If you do call OpenPort, you can create the grafPtr with the Memory Manager procedure NewPtr or reserve the space on the stack (with a variable of type GrafPort).

Field	Type	Initial setting
device	INTEGER	0 (the screen)
portBits	BitMap	screenBits
portRect	Rect	screenBits.bounds
visRgn	RgnHandle	handle to a rectangular region coincident with screenBits.bounds
clipRgn	RgnHandle	handle to the rectangular region (−32767,−32767) (32767,32767)
bkPat	Pattern	white

Field	Type	Initial setting
fillPat	Pattern	black
pnLoc	Point	(0,0)
pnSize	Point	(1,1)
pnMode	INTEGER	patCopy
pnPat	Pattern	black
pnVis	INTEGER	0 (visible)
txFont	INTEGER	0 (system font)
txFace	Style	plain
txMode	INTEGER	srcOr
txSize	INTEGER	0 (system font size)
spExtra	Fixed	0
fgColor	LONGINT	blackColor
bkColor	LONGINT	whiteColor
colrBit	INTEGER	0
patStretch	INTEGER	0
picSave	Handle	NIL
rgnSave	Handle	NIL
polySave	Handle	NIL
grafProcs	QDProcsPtr	NIL

```
PROCEDURE InitPort (port: GrafPtr);
```

Given a pointer to a grafPort that's been opened with OpenPort, InitPort reinitializes the fields of the grafPort and makes it the current port. It's unlikely that you'll ever have a reason to call this procedure.

Note: InitPort does everything OpenPort does except allocate space for the visRgn and clipRgn.

```
PROCEDURE ClosePort (port: GrafPtr);
```

ClosePort releases the memory occupied by the given grafPort's visRgn and clipRgn. When you're completely through with a grafPort, call this procedure and then dispose of the grafPort with the Memory Manager procedure DisposPtr (if it was allocated with NewPtr). This is normally done for you when you call the Window Manager to close or dispose of a window.

Warning: If ClosePort isn't called before a grafPort is disposed of, the memory used by the visRgn and clipRgn will be unrecoverable.

```
PROCEDURE SetPort (port: GrafPtr);
```

SetPort makes the specified grafPort the current port.

> **Note:** Only SetPort (and OpenPort and InitPort, which call it) changes the current port. All the other routines in the Toolbox and Operating System (even those that call SetPort, OpenPort, or InitPort) leave the current port set to what it was when they were called.

The global variable thePort always points to the current port. All QuickDraw drawing routines affect the bit map thePort^.portBits and use the local coordinate system of thePort^.

Each port has its own pen and text characteristics, which remain unchanged when the port isn't selected as the current port.

```
PROCEDURE GetPort (VAR port: GrafPtr);
```

GetPort returns a pointer to the current grafPort. This pointer is also available through the global variable thePort, but you may prefer to use GetPort for better readability of your program text. For example, a procedure could do a GetPort(savePort) before setting its own grafPort and a SetPort(savePort) afterwards to restore the previous port.

```
PROCEDURE GrafDevice (device: INTEGER);
```

GrafDevice sets the device field of the current grafPort to the given value, which consists of device-specific information that's used by the Font Manager to achieve the best possible results when drawing text in the grafPort. The initial value of the device field is 0, for best results on output to the screen. For more information, see chapter 7.

> **Note:** This field is used for communication between QuickDraw and the Font Manager; normally you won't set it yourself.

```
PROCEDURE SetPortBits (bm: BitMap);
```

Assembly-language note: The macro you invoke to call SetPortBits from assembly language is named _SetPBits.

SetPortBits sets the portBits field of the current grafPort to any previously defined bit map. This allows you to perform all normal drawing and calculations on a buffer other than the screen—for example, a small off-screen image for later "stamping" onto the screen (with the CopyBits procedure, described under "Bit Transfer Operations" below).

Remember to prepare all fields of the bit map before you call SetPortBits.

```
PROCEDURE PortSize (width,height: INTEGER);
```

PortSize changes the size of the current grafPort's portRect. This does *not* affect the screen; it merely changes the size of the "active area" of the grafPort.

Note: This procedure is normally called only by the Window Manager.

The top left corner of the portRect remains at its same location; the width and height of the portRect are set to the given width and height. In other words, PortSize moves the bottom right corner of the portRect to a position relative to the top left corner.

PortSize doesn't change the clipRgn or the visRgn, nor does it affect the local coordinate system of the grafPort: It changes only the portRect's width and height. Remember that all drawing occurs only in the intersection of the portBits.bounds and the portRect, clipped to the visRgn and the clipRgn.

```
PROCEDURE MovePortTo (leftGlobal,topGlobal: INTEGER);
```

MovePortTo changes the position of the current grafPort's portRect. This does *not* affect the screen; it merely changes the location at which subsequent drawing inside the port will appear.

Note: This procedure is normally called only by the Window Manager and the System Error Handler.

The leftGlobal and topGlobal parameters set the distance between the top left corner of portBits.bounds and the top left corner of the new portRect.

Like PortSize, MovePortTo doesn't change the clipRgn or the visRgn, nor does it affect the local coordinate system of the grafPort.

```
PROCEDURE SetOrigin (h,v: INTEGER);
```

SetOrigin changes the local coordinate system of the current grafPort. This does *not* affect the screen; it does, however, affect where subsequent drawing inside the port will appear.

The h and v parameters set the coordinates of the top left corner of the portRect. All other coordinates are calculated from this point; SetOrigin also offsets the coordinates of the portBits.bounds rectangle and the visRgn. Relative distances among elements in the port remain the same; only their absolute local coordinates change. All subsequent drawing and calculation routines use the new coordinate system.

Note: SetOrigin does not offset the coordinates of the clipRgn or the pen; the pen and clipRgn "stick" to the coordinate system, and therefore change position on the screen (unlike the portBits.bounds, portRect, and visRgn, which "stick" to the screen, and don't change position). See the "Coordinates in GrafPorts" section for an illustration.

SetOrigin is useful for readjusting the coordinate system after a scrolling operation. (See ScrollRect under "Bit Transfer Operations" below.)

Note: All other routines in the Toolbox and Operating System preserve the local coordinate system of the current grafPort.

```
PROCEDURE SetClip (rgn: RgnHandle);
```

SetClip changes the clipping region of the current grafPort to a region that's equivalent to the given region. Note that this doesn't change the region handle, but affects the clipping region itself. Since SetClip makes a copy of the given region, any subsequent changes you make to that region will not affect the clipping region of the port.

You can set the clipping region to any arbitrary region, to aid you in drawing inside the grafPort. The initial clipRgn is an arbitrarily large rectangle.

>   **Note:** All routines in the Toolbox and Operating System preserve the current clipRgn.

```
PROCEDURE GetClip (rgn: RgnHandle);
```

GetClip changes the given region to a region that's equivalent to the clipping region of the current grafPort. This is the reverse of what SetClip does. Like SetClip, it doesn't change the region handle. GetClip and SetClip are used to preserve the current clipRgn (they're analogous to GetPort and SetPort).

```
PROCEDURE ClipRect (r: Rect);
```

ClipRect changes the clipping region of the current grafPort to a rectangle that's equivalent to the given rectangle. Note that this doesn't change the region handle, but affects the clipping region itself.

```
PROCEDURE BackPat (pat: Pattern);
```

BackPat sets the background pattern of the current grafPort to the given pattern. The background pattern is used in ScrollRect and in all QuickDraw routines that perform an "erase" operation.

Cursor-Handling Routines

```
PROCEDURE InitCursor;
```

InitCursor sets the current cursor to the standard arrow and sets the **cursor level** to 0, making the cursor visible. The cursor level keeps track of the number of times the cursor has been hidden to compensate for nested calls to HideCursor and ShowCursor, explained below.

```
PROCEDURE SetCursor (crsr: Cursor);
```

SetCursor sets the current cursor to the given cursor. If the cursor is hidden, it remains hidden and will attain the new appearance when it's uncovered; if the cursor is already visible, it changes to the new appearance immediately.

The cursor image is initialized by InitCursor to the standard arrow, visible on the screen.

>   **Note:** You'll normally get a cursor from a resource file, by calling the Toolbox Utility function GetCursor, and then doubly dereference the handle it returns.

```
PROCEDURE HideCursor;
```

HideCursor removes the cursor from the screen, restoring the bits under it, and decrements the cursor level (which InitCursor initialized to 0). Every call to HideCursor should be balanced by a subsequent call to ShowCursor.

> **Note:** See also the description of the Toolbox Utility procedure ShieldCursor.

```
PROCEDURE ShowCursor;
```

ShowCursor increments the cursor level, which may have been decremented by HideCursor, and displays the cursor on the screen if the level becomes 0. A call to ShowCursor should balance each previous call to HideCursor. The level isn't incremented beyond 0, so extra calls to ShowCursor have no effect.

The low-level interrupt-driven routines link the cursor with the mouse position, so that if the cursor level is 0 (visible), the cursor automatically follows the mouse. You don't need to do anything but a ShowCursor to have the cursor track the mouse.

If the cursor has been changed (with SetCursor) while hidden, ShowCursor presents the new cursor.

```
PROCEDURE ObscureCursor;
```

ObscureCursor hides the cursor until the next time the mouse is moved. It's normally called when the user begins to type. Unlike HideCursor, it has no effect on the cursor level and must not be balanced by a call to ShowCursor.

Pen and Line-Drawing Routines

The pen and line-drawing routines all depend on the coordinate system of the current grafPort. Remember that each grafPort has its own pen; if you draw in one grafPort, change to another, and return to the first, the pen will remain in the same location.

```
PROCEDURE HidePen;
```

HidePen decrements the current grafPort's pnVis field, which is initialized to 0 by OpenPort; whenever pnVis is negative, the pen doesn't draw on the screen. PnVis keeps track of the number of times the pen has been hidden to compensate for nested calls to HidePen and ShowPen (below). Every call to HidePen should be balanced by a subsequent call to ShowPen. HidePen is called by OpenRgn, OpenPicture, and OpenPoly so that you can define regions, pictures, and polygons without drawing on the screen.

```
PROCEDURE ShowPen;
```

ShowPen increments the current grafPort's pnVis field, which may have been decremented by HidePen; if pnVis becomes 0, QuickDraw resumes drawing on the screen. Extra calls to

ShowPen will increment pnVis beyond 0, so every call to ShowPen should be balanced by a call to HidePen. ShowPen is called by CloseRgn, ClosePicture, and ClosePoly.

```
PROCEDURE GetPen (VAR pt: Point);
```

GetPen returns the current pen location, in the local coordinates of the current grafPort.

```
PROCEDURE GetPenState (VAR pnState: PenState);
```

GetPenState saves the pen location, size, pattern, and mode in pnState, to be restored later with SetPenState. This is useful when calling subroutines that operate in the current port but must change the graphics pen: Each such procedure can save the pen's state when it's called, do whatever it needs to do, and restore the previous pen state immediately before returning. The PenState data type is defined as follows:

```
TYPE PenState = RECORD
                    pnLoc:  Point;    {pen location}
                    pnSize: Point;    {pen size}
                    pnMode: INTEGER;  {pen's transfer mode}
                    pnPat:  Pattern   {pen pattern}
                END;
```

```
PROCEDURE SetPenState (pnState: PenState);
```

SetPenState sets the pen location, size, pattern, and mode in the current grafPort to the values stored in pnState. This is usually called at the end of a procedure that has altered the pen parameters and wants to restore them to their state at the beginning of the procedure. (See GetPenState, above.)

```
PROCEDURE PenSize (width,height: INTEGER);
```

PenSize sets the dimensions of the graphics pen in the current grafPort. All subsequent calls to Line, LineTo, and the procedures that draw framed shapes in the current grafPort will use the new pen dimensions.

The pen dimensions can be accessed in the variable thePort^.pnSize, which is of type Point. If either of the pen dimensions is set to a negative value, the pen assumes the dimensions (0,0) and no drawing is performed. For a discussion of how the pen draws, see the "General Discussion of Drawing" section.

```
PROCEDURE PenMode (mode: INTEGER);
```

PenMode sets the transfer mode through which the pen pattern is transferred onto the bit map when lines or shapes are drawn in the current grafPort. The mode may be any one of the pattern transfer modes:

6 QuickDraw

```
patCopy          notPatCopy
patOr            notPatOr
patXor           notPatXor
patBic           notPatBic
```

If the mode is one of the source transfer modes (or negative), no drawing is performed. The current pen mode can be accessed in the variable thePort^.pnMode. The initial pen mode is patCopy, in which the pen pattern is copied directly to the bit map.

PROCEDURE PenPat (pat: Pattern);

PenPat sets the pattern that's used by the pen in the current grafPort. The standard patterns white, black, gray, ltGray, and dkGray are predefined; the initial pen pattern is black. The current pen pattern can be accessed in the variable thePort^.pnPat, and this value can be assigned to any other variable of type Pattern.

PROCEDURE PenNormal;

PenNormal resets the initial state of the pen in the current grafPort, as follows:

Field	Setting
pnSize	(1,1)
pnMode	patCopy
pnPat	black

The pen location is not changed.

PROCEDURE MoveTo (h,v: INTEGER);

MoveTo moves the pen to location (h,v) in the local coordinates of the current grafPort. No drawing is performed.

PROCEDURE Move (dh,dv: INTEGER);

This procedure moves the pen a distance of dh horizontally and dv vertically from its current location; it calls MoveTo(h+dh,v+dv), where (h,v) is the current location. The positive directions are to the right and down. No drawing is performed.

PROCEDURE LineTo (h,v: INTEGER);

LineTo draws a line from the current pen location to the location specified (in local coordinates) by h and v. The new pen location is (h,v) after the line is drawn. See the "General Discussion of Drawing" section.

If a region or polygon is open and being formed, its outline is infinitely thin and is not affected by the pnSize, pnMode, or pnPat. (See OpenRgn and OpenPoly.)

```
PROCEDURE Line (dh,dv: INTEGER);
```

This procedure draws a line to the location that's a distance of dh horizontally and dv vertically from the current pen location; it calls LineTo(h+dh,v+dv), where (h,v) is the current location. The positive directions are to the right and down. The pen location becomes the coordinates of the end of the line after the line is drawn. See the "General Discussion of Drawing" section.

If a region or polygon is open and being formed, its outline is infinitely thin and is not affected by the pnSize, pnMode, or pnPat. (See OpenRgn and OpenPoly.)

Text-Drawing Routines

Each grafPort has its own text characteristics, and all these procedures deal with those of the current port.

```
PROCEDURE TextFont (font: INTEGER);
```

TextFont sets the current grafPort's font (thePort^.txFont) to the given font number. The initial font number is 0, which represents the system font.

```
PROCEDURE TextFace (face: Style);
```

TextFace sets the current grafPort's character style (thePort^.txFace). The Style data type allows you to specify a set of one or more of the following predefined constants: bold, italic, underline, outline, shadow, condense, and extend. For example:

```
TextFace([bold]);                    {bold}
TextFace([bold,italic]);             {bold and italic}
TextFace(thePort^.txFace+[bold]);    {whatever it was plus bold}
TextFace(thePort^.txFace-[bold]);    {whatever it was but not bold}
TextFace([]);                        {plain text}
```

```
PROCEDURE TextMode (mode: INTEGER);
```

TextMode sets the current grafPort's transfer mode for drawing text (thePort^.txMode). The mode should be srcOr, srcXor, or srcBic. The initial transfer mode for drawing text is srcOr.

```
PROCEDURE TextSize (size: INTEGER);
```

TextSize sets the current grafPort's font size (thePort^.txSize) to the given number of points. Any size may be specified, but the result will look best if the Font Manager has the font in that size (otherwise it will scale a size it does have). The next best result will occur if the given size is an even multiple of a size available for the font. If 0 is specified, the system font size (12 points) will be used. The initial txSize setting is 0.

6 QuickDraw

```
PROCEDURE SpaceExtra (extra: Fixed);
```

SpaceExtra sets the current grafPort's spExtra field, which specifies the average number of pixels by which to widen each space in a line of text. This is useful when text is being fully justified (that is, aligned with both a left and a right margin). The initial spExtra setting is 0.

SpaceExtra will also accept a negative parameter, but be careful not to narrow spaces so much that the text is unreadable.

```
PROCEDURE DrawChar (ch: CHAR);
```

DrawChar places the given character to the right of the pen location, with the left end of its base line at the pen's location, and advances the pen accordingly. If the character isn't in the font, the font's missing symbol is drawn.

Note: If you're drawing a series of characters, it's faster to make one DrawString or DrawText call rather than a series of DrawChar calls.

```
PROCEDURE DrawString (s: Str255);
```

DrawString calls DrawChar for each character in the given string. The string is placed beginning at the current pen location and extending right. No formatting (such as carriage returns and line feeds) is performed by QuickDraw. The pen location ends up to the right of the last character in the string.

Warning: QuickDraw temporarily stores on the stack *all* of the text you ask it to draw, even if the text will be clipped. When drawing large font sizes or complex style variations, it's best to draw only what will be visible on the screen. You can determine how many characters will actually fit on the screen by calling the StringWidth function before calling DrawString.

```
PROCEDURE DrawText (textBuf: Ptr; firstByte,byteCount: INTEGER);
```

DrawText calls DrawChar for each character in the arbitrary structure in memory specified by textBuf, starting firstByte bytes into the structure and continuing for byteCount bytes (firstByte starts at 0). The text is placed beginning at the current pen location and extending right. No formatting (such as carriage returns and line feeds) is performed by QuickDraw. The pen location ends up to the right of the last character in the string.

Warning: Inside a picture definition, DrawText can't have a byteCount greater than 255.

Note: You can determine how many characters will actually fit on the screen by calling the TextWidth function before calling DrawText. (See the warning under DrawString above.)

```
FUNCTION CharWidth (ch: CHAR) : INTEGER;
```

CharWidth returns the character width of the specified character, that is, the value that will be added to the pen horizontal coordinate if the specified character is drawn. CharWidth includes the effects of the stylistic variations set with TextFace; if you change these after determining the character width but before actually drawing the character, the predetermined width may not be correct. If the character is a space, CharWidth also includes the effect of SpaceExtra.

```
FUNCTION StringWidth (s: Str255) : INTEGER;
```

StringWidth returns the width of the given text string, which it calculates by adding the CharWidths of all the characters in the string (see above).

```
FUNCTION TextWidth (textBuf: Ptr; firstByte,byteCount: INTEGER) :
        INTEGER;
```

TextWidth returns the width of the text stored in the arbitrary structure in memory specified by textBuf, starting firstByte bytes into the structure and continuing for byteCount bytes (firstByte starts at 0). TextWidth calculates the width by adding the CharWidths of all the characters in the text. (See CharWidth, above.)

```
PROCEDURE GetFontInfo (VAR info: FontInfo);
```

GetFontInfo returns the following information about the current grafPort's character font, taking into consideration the style and size in which the characters will be drawn: the ascent, descent, maximum character width (the greatest distance the pen will move when a character is drawn), and leading (the vertical distance between the descent line and the ascent line below it), all in pixels. The FontInfo data type is defined as follows:

```
TYPE FontInfo =  RECORD
                    ascent:  INTEGER;   {ascent}
                    descent: INTEGER;   {descent}
                    widMax:  INTEGER;   {maximum character width}
                    leading: INTEGER    {leading}
                END;
```

The line height (in pixels) can be determined by adding the ascent, descent, and leading.

Drawing in Color

These routines enable applications to do color drawing on color output devices. All nonwhite colors will appear as black on black-and-white output devices.

```
PROCEDURE ForeColor (color: LONGINT);
```

ForeColor sets the foreground color for all drawing in the current grafPort (thePort^.fgColor) to the given color. The following standard colors are predefined: blackColor, whiteColor, redColor, greenColor, blueColor, cyanColor, magentaColor, and yellowColor. The initial foreground color is blackColor.

```
PROCEDURE BackColor (color: LONGINT);
```

BackColor sets the background color for all drawing in the current grafPort (thePort^.bkColor) to the given color. Eight standard colors are predefined (see ForeColor above). The initial background color is whiteColor.

```
PROCEDURE ColorBit (whichBit: INTEGER);
```

ColorBit is called by printing software for a color printer, or other color-imaging software, to set the current grafPort's colrBit field to whichBit; this tells QuickDraw which plane of the color picture to draw into. QuickDraw will draw into the plane corresponding to bit number whichBit. Since QuickDraw can support output devices that have up to 32 bits of color information per pixel, the possible range of values for whichBit is 0 through 31. The initial value of the colrBit field is 0.

Calculations with Rectangles

Calculation routines are independent of the current coordinate system; a calculation will operate the same regardless of which grafPort is active.

Remember that if the parameters to a calculation procedure were defined in different grafPorts, you must first adjust them to global coordinates.

```
PROCEDURE SetRect (VAR r: Rect; left,top,right,bottom: INTEGER);
```

SetRect assigns the four boundary coordinates to the given rectangle. The result is a rectangle with coordinates (left,top) (right,bottom).

This procedure is supplied as a utility to help you shorten your program text. If you want a more readable text at the expense of length, you can assign integers (or points) directly into the rectangle's fields. There's no significant code size or execution speed advantage to either method.

```
PROCEDURE OffsetRect (VAR r: Rect; dh,dv: INTEGER);
```

OffsetRect moves the given rectangle by adding dh to each horizontal coordinate and dv to each vertical coordinate. If dh and dv are positive, the movement is to the right and down; if either is negative, the corresponding movement is in the opposite direction. The rectangle retains its shape and size; it's merely moved on the coordinate plane. This doesn't affect the screen unless you subsequently call a routine to draw within the rectangle.

PROCEDURE InsetRect (VAR r: Rect; dh,dv: INTEGER);

InsetRect shrinks or expands the given rectangle. The left and right sides are moved in by the amount specified by dh; the top and bottom are moved toward the center by the amount specified by dv. If dh or dv is negative, the appropriate pair of sides is moved outward instead of inward. The effect is to alter the size by 2*dh horizontally and 2*dv vertically, with the rectangle remaining centered in the same place on the coordinate plane.

If the resulting width or height becomes less than 1, the rectangle is set to the empty rectangle (0,0)(0,0).

FUNCTION SectRect (src1,src2: Rect; VAR dstRect: Rect) : BOOLEAN;

SectRect calculates the rectangle that's the intersection of the two given rectangles, and returns TRUE if they indeed intersect or FALSE if they don't. Rectangles that "touch" at a line or a point are not considered intersecting, because their intersection rectangle (actually, in this case, an intersection line or point) doesn't enclose any bits in the bit image.

If the rectangles don't intersect, the destination rectangle is set to (0,0)(0,0). SectRect works correctly even if one of the source rectangles is also the destination.

PROCEDURE UnionRect (src1,src2: Rect; VAR dstRect: Rect);

UnionRect calculates the smallest rectangle that encloses both of the given rectangles. It works correctly even if one of the source rectangles is also the destination.

FUNCTION PtInRect (pt: Point; r: Rect) : BOOLEAN;

PtInRect determines whether the pixel below and to the right of the given coordinate point is enclosed in the specified rectangle, and returns TRUE if so or FALSE if not.

PROCEDURE Pt2Rect (pt1,pt2: Point; VAR dstRect: Rect);

Pt2Rect returns the smallest rectangle that encloses the two given points.

PROCEDURE PtToAngle (r: Rect; pt: Point; VAR angle: INTEGER);

PtToAngle calculates an integer angle between a line from the center of the rectangle to the given point and a line from the center of the rectangle pointing straight up (12 o'clock high). The angle is in degrees from 0 to 359, measured clockwise from 12 o'clock, with 90 degrees at 3 o'clock, 180 at 6 o'clock, and 270 at 9 o'clock. Other angles are measured relative to the rectangle: If the line to the given point goes through the top right corner of the rectangle, the angle returned is 45 degrees, even if the rectangle isn't square; if it goes through the bottom right corner, the angle is 135 degrees, and so on (see Figure 19).

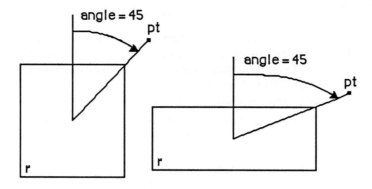

Figure 19. PtToAngle

The angle returned might be used as input to one of the procedures that manipulate arcs and wedges, as described below under "Graphic Operations on Arcs and Wedges".

```
FUNCTION EqualRect (rect1,rect2: Rect) : BOOLEAN;
```

EqualRect compares the two given rectangles and returns TRUE if they're equal or FALSE if not. The two rectangles must have identical boundary coordinates to be considered equal.

```
FUNCTION EmptyRect (r: Rect) : BOOLEAN;
```

EmptyRect returns TRUE if the given rectangle is an empty rectangle or FALSE if not. A rectangle is considered empty if the bottom coordinate is less than or equal to the top or the right coordinate is less than or equal to the left.

Graphic Operations on Rectangles

See also the ScrollRect procedure under "Bit Transfer Operations".

```
PROCEDURE FrameRect (r: Rect);
```

FrameRect draws an outline just inside the specified rectangle, using the current grafPort's pen pattern, mode, and size. The outline is as wide as the pen width and as tall as the pen height. It's drawn with the pnPat, according to the pattern transfer mode specified by pnMode. The pen location is not changed by this procedure.

If a region is open and being formed, the outside outline of the new rectangle is mathematically added to the region's boundary.

```
PROCEDURE PaintRect (r: Rect);
```

PaintRect paints the specified rectangle with the current grafPort's pen pattern and mode. The rectangle is filled with the pnPat, according to the pattern transfer mode specified by pnMode. The pen location is not changed by this procedure.

```
PROCEDURE EraseRect (r: Rect);
```

EraseRect paints the specified rectangle with the current grafPort's background pattern bkPat (in patCopy mode). The grafPort's pnPat and pnMode are ignored; the pen location is not changed.

```
PROCEDURE InvertRect (r: Rect);
```

Assembly-language note: The macro you invoke to call InvertRect from assembly language is named _InverRect.

InvertRect inverts the pixels enclosed by the specified rectangle: Every white pixel becomes black and every black pixel becomes white. The grafPort's pnPat, pnMode, and bkPat are all ignored; the pen location is not changed.

```
PROCEDURE FillRect (r: Rect; pat: Pattern);
```

FillRect fills the specified rectangle with the given pattern (in patCopy mode). The grafPort's pnPat, pnMode, and bkPat are all ignored; the pen location is not changed.

Graphic Operations on Ovals

Ovals are drawn inside rectangles that you specify. If you specify a square rectangle, QuickDraw draws a circle.

```
PROCEDURE FrameOval (r: Rect);
```

FrameOval draws an outline just inside the oval that fits inside the specified rectangle, using the current grafPort's pen pattern, mode, and size. The outline is as wide as the pen width and as tall as the pen height. It's drawn with the pnPat, according to the pattern transfer mode specified by pnMode. The pen location is not changed by this procedure.

If a region is open and being formed, the outside outline of the new oval is mathematically added to the region's boundary.

```
PROCEDURE PaintOval (r: Rect);
```

PaintOval paints an oval just inside the specified rectangle with the current grafPort's pen pattern and mode. The oval is filled with the pnPat, according to the pattern transfer mode specified by pnMode. The pen location is not changed by this procedure.

```
PROCEDURE EraseOval (r: Rect);
```

EraseOval paints an oval just inside the specified rectangle with the current grafPort's background pattern bkPat (in patCopy mode). The grafPort's pnPat and pnMode are ignored; the pen location is not changed.

```
PROCEDURE InvertOval (r: Rect);
```

InvertOval inverts the pixels enclosed by an oval just inside the specified rectangle: Every white pixel becomes black and every black pixel becomes white. The grafPort's pnPat, pnMode, and bkPat are all ignored; the pen location is not changed.

```
PROCEDURE FillOval (r: Rect; pat: Pattern);
```

FillOval fills an oval just inside the specified rectangle with the given pattern (in patCopy mode). The grafPort's pnPat, pnMode, and bkPat are all ignored; the pen location is not changed.

Graphic Operations on Rounded-Corner Rectangles

```
PROCEDURE FrameRoundRect (r: Rect; ovalWidth,ovalHeight:
            INTEGER);
```

FrameRoundRect draws an outline just inside the specified rounded-corner rectangle, using the current grafPort's pen pattern, mode, and size. OvalWidth and ovalHeight specify the diameters of curvature for the corners (see Figure 20). The outline is as wide as the pen width and as tall as the pen height. It's drawn with the pnPat, according to the pattern transfer mode specified by pnMode. The pen location is not changed by this procedure.

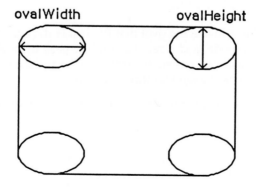

Figure 20. Rounded-Corner Rectangle

If a region is open and being formed, the outside outline of the new rounded-corner rectangle is mathematically added to the region's boundary.

```
PROCEDURE PaintRoundRect (r: Rect; ovalWidth,ovalHeight:
        INTEGER);
```

PaintRoundRect paints the specified rounded-corner rectangle with the current grafPort's pen pattern and mode. OvalWidth and ovalHeight specify the diameters of curvature for the corners.

The rounded-corner rectangle is filled with the pnPat, according to the pattern transfer mode specified by pnMode. The pen location is not changed by this procedure.

```
PROCEDURE EraseRoundRect (r: Rect; ovalWidth,ovalHeight:
        INTEGER);
```

EraseRoundRect paints the specified rounded-corner rectangle with the current grafPort's background pattern bkPat (in patCopy mode).

OvalWidth and ovalHeight specify the diameters of curvature for the corners. The grafPort's pnPat and pnMode are ignored; the pen location is not changed.

```
PROCEDURE InvertRoundRect (r: Rect; ovalWidth,ovalHeight:
        INTEGER);
```

Assembly-language note: The macro you invoke to call InvertRoundRect from assembly language is named _InverRoundRect.

InvertRoundRect inverts the pixels enclosed by the specified rounded-corner rectangle: Every white pixel becomes black and every black pixel becomes white. OvalWidth and ovalHeight specify the diameters of curvature for the corners. The grafPort's pnPat, pnMode, and bkPat are all ignored; the pen location is not changed.

```
PROCEDURE FillRoundRect (r: Rect; ovalWidth,ovalHeight: INTEGER;
        pat: Pattern);
```

FillRoundRect fills the specified rounded-corner rectangle with the given pattern (in patCopy mode). OvalWidth and ovalHeight specify the diameters of curvature for the corners. The grafPort's pnPat, pnMode, and bkPat are all ignored; the pen location is not changed.

Graphic Operations on Arcs and Wedges

These procedures perform graphic operations on arcs and wedge-shaped sections of ovals. See also PtToAngle under "Calculations with Rectangles".

```
PROCEDURE FrameArc (r: Rect; startAngle,arcAngle: INTEGER);
```

FrameArc draws an arc of the oval that fits inside the specified rectangle, using the current grafPort's pen pattern, mode, and size. StartAngle indicates where the arc begins and is treated MOD 360. ArcAngle defines the extent of the arc. The angles are given in positive or negative degrees; a positive angle goes clockwise, while a negative angle goes counterclockwise. Zero degrees is at 12 o'clock high, 90 (or –270) is at 3 o'clock, 180 (or –180) is at 6 o'clock, and 270 (or –90) is at 9 o'clock. Other angles are measured relative to the enclosing rectangle: A line from the center of the rectangle through its top right corner is at 45 degrees, even if the rectangle isn't square; a line through the bottom right corner is at 135 degrees, and so on (see Figure 21).

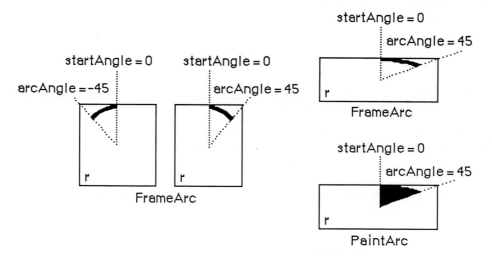

Figure 21. Operations on Arcs and Wedges

The arc is as wide as the pen width and as tall as the pen height. It's drawn with the pnPat, according to the pattern transfer mode specified by pnMode. The pen location is not changed by this procedure.

> **Warning:** FrameArc differs from other QuickDraw routines that frame shapes in that the arc is not mathematically added to the boundary of a region that's open and being formed.

> **Note:** QuickDraw doesn't provide a routine for drawing an outlined wedge of an oval.

```
PROCEDURE PaintArc (r: Rect; startAngle,arcAngle: INTEGER);
```

PaintArc paints a wedge of the oval just inside the specified rectangle with the current grafPort's pen pattern and mode. StartAngle and arcAngle define the arc of the wedge as in FrameArc. The wedge is filled with the pnPat, according to the pattern transfer mode specified by pnMode. The pen location is not changed by this procedure.

```
PROCEDURE EraseArc (r: Rect; startAngle,arcAngle: INTEGER);
```

EraseArc paints a wedge of the oval just inside the specified rectangle with the current grafPort's background pattern bkPat (in patCopy mode). StartAngle and arcAngle define the arc of the wedge as in FrameArc. The grafPort's pnPat and pnMode are ignored; the pen location is not changed.

```
PROCEDURE InvertArc (r: Rect; startAngle,arcAngle: INTEGER);
```

InvertArc inverts the pixels enclosed by a wedge of the oval just inside the specified rectangle: Every white pixel becomes black and every black pixel becomes white. StartAngle and arcAngle define the arc of the wedge as in FrameArc. The grafPort's pnPat, pnMode, and bkPat are all ignored; the pen location is not changed.

```
PROCEDURE FillArc (r: Rect; startAngle,arcAngle: INTEGER; pat:
        Pattern);
```

FillArc fills a wedge of the oval just inside the specified rectangle with the given pattern (in patCopy mode). StartAngle and arcAngle define the arc of the wedge as in FrameArc. The grafPort's pnPat, pnMode, and bkPat are all ignored; the pen location is not changed.

Calculations with Regions

Remember that if the parameters to a calculation procedure were defined in different grafPorts, you must first adjust them to global coordinates.

```
FUNCTION NewRgn : RgnHandle;
```

NewRgn allocates space for a new, variable-size region, initializes it to the empty region defined by the rectangle (0,0)(0,0), and returns a handle to the new region.

> **Warning:** Only this function creates new regions; all other routines just alter the size and shape of existing regions. Before a region's handle can be passed to any drawing or calculation routine, space must already have been allocated for the region.

```
PROCEDURE OpenRgn;
```

OpenRgn tells QuickDraw to allocate temporary space and start saving lines and framed shapes for later processing as a region definition. While a region is open, all calls to Line, LineTo, and the procedures that draw framed shapes (except arcs) affect the outline of the region. Only the line endpoints and shape boundaries affect the region definition; the pen mode, pattern, and size do not affect it. In fact, OpenRgn calls HidePen, so no drawing occurs on the screen while the region is open (unless you called ShowPen just after OpenRgn, or you called ShowPen previously without balancing it by a call to HidePen). Since the pen hangs below and to the right of the pen location, drawing lines with even the smallest pen will change bits that lie outside the region you define.

The outline of a region is mathematically defined and infinitely thin, and separates the bit image into two groups of bits: Those within the region and those outside it. A region should consist of one or more closed loops. Each framed shape itself constitutes a loop. Any lines drawn with Line or LineTo should connect with each other or with a framed shape. Even though the on-screen presentation of a region is clipped, the definition of a region is not; you can define a region anywhere on the coordinate plane with complete disregard for the location of various grafPort entities on that plane.

When a region is open, the current grafPort's rgnSave field contains a handle to information related to the region definition. If you want to temporarily disable the collection of lines and shapes, you can save the current value of this field, set the field to NIL, and later restore the saved value to resume the region definition. Also, calling SetPort while a region is being formed will discontinue formation of the region until another call to SetPort resets the region's original grafPort.

> **Warning:** Do not call OpenRgn while another region or polygon is already open. All open regions but the most recent will behave strangely.

> **Note:** Regions are limited to 32K bytes. You can determine the current size of a region by calling the Memory Manager function GetHandleSize.

```
PROCEDURE CloseRgn (dstRgn: RgnHandle);
```

CloseRgn stops the collection of lines and framed shapes, organizes them into a region definition, and saves the resulting region in the region indicated by dstRgn. CloseRgn does *not* create the destination region; space must already have been allocated for it. You should perform one and only one CloseRgn for every OpenRgn. CloseRgn calls ShowPen, balancing the HidePen call made by OpenRgn.

Here's an example of how to create and open a region, define a barbell shape, close the region, draw it, and dispose of it:

```
barbell := NewRgn;                          {create a new region}
OpenRgn;                                    {begin collecting stuff}
   SetRect(tempRect,20,20,30,50);           {form the left weight}
   FrameOval(tempRect);
   SetRect(tempRect,25,30,85,40);           {form the bar}
   FrameRect(tempRect);
   SetRect(tempRect,80,20,90,50);           {form the right weight}
   FrameOval(tempRect);
CloseRgn(barbell);                          {we're done; save in barbell}
FillRgn(barbell,black);                     {draw it on the screen}
DisposeRgn(barbell)                         {dispose of the region}
```

```
PROCEDURE DisposeRgn (rgn: RgnHandle);
```

> **Assembly-language note:** The macro you invoke to call DisposeRgn from assembly language is named _DisposRgn.

DisposeRgn releases the memory occupied by the given region. Use this only after you're completely through with a temporary region.

PROCEDURE CopyRgn (srcRgn,dstRgn: RgnHandle);

CopyRgn copies the mathematical structure of srcRgn into dstRgn; that is, it makes a duplicate copy of srcRgn. Once this is done, srcRgn may be altered (or even disposed of) without affecting dstRgn. CopyRgn does *not* create the destination region; space must already have been allocated for it.

PROCEDURE SetEmptyRgn (rgn: RgnHandle);

SetEmptyRgn destroys the previous structure of the given region, then sets the new structure to the empty region defined by the rectangle (0,0)(0,0).

PROCEDURE SetRectRgn (rgn: RgnHandle; left,top,right,bottom:
        INTEGER);

Assembly-language note: The macro you invoke to call SetRectRgn from assembly language is named _SetRecRgn.

SetRectRgn destroys the previous structure of the given region, and then sets the new structure to the rectangle specified by left, top, right, and bottom.

If the specified rectangle is empty (that is, right<=left or bottom<=top), the region is set to the empty region defined by the rectangle (0,0)(0,0).

PROCEDURE RectRgn (rgn: RgnHandle; r: Rect);

RectRgn destroys the previous structure of the given region, and then sets the new structure to the rectangle specified by r. This is the same as SetRectRgn, except the given rectangle is defined by a rectangle rather than by four boundary coordinates.

PROCEDURE OffsetRgn (rgn: RgnHandle; dh,dv: INTEGER);

Assembly-language note: The macro you invoke to call OffsetRgn from assembly language is named _OfsetRgn.

OffsetRgn moves the region on the coordinate plane, a distance of dh horizontally and dv vertically. This doesn't affect the screen unless you subsequently call a routine to draw the region. If dh and dv are positive, the movement is to the right and down; if either is negative, the corresponding movement is in the opposite direction. The region retains its size and shape.

Note: OffsetRgn is an especially efficient operation, because most of the data defining a region is stored relative to rgnBBox and so isn't actually changed by OffsetRgn.

```
PROCEDURE InsetRgn (rgn: RgnHandle; dh,dv: INTEGER);
```

InsetRgn shrinks or expands the region. All points on the region boundary are moved inwards a distance of dv vertically and dh horizontally; if dh or dv is negative, the points are moved outwards in that direction. InsetRgn leaves the region "centered" at the same position, but moves the outline in (for positive values of dh and dv) or out (for negative values of dh and dv). InsetRgn of a rectangular region works just like InsetRect.

> **Note:** InsetRgn temporarily uses heap space that's twice the size of the original region.

```
PROCEDURE SectRgn (srcRgnA,srcRgnB,dstRgn: RgnHandle);
```

SectRgn calculates the intersection of two regions and places the intersection in a third region. This does *not* create the destination region; space must already have been allocated for it. The destination region can be one of the source regions, if desired.

If the regions do not intersect, or one of the regions is empty, the destination is set to the empty region defined by the rectangle (0,0)(0,0).

> **Note:** SectRgn may temporarily use heap space that's twice the size of the two input regions.

```
PROCEDURE UnionRgn (srcRgnA,srcRgnB,dstRgn: RgnHandle);
```

UnionRgn calculates the union of two regions and places the union in a third region. This does *not* create the destination region; space must already have been allocated for it. The destination region can be one of the source regions, if desired.

If both regions are empty, the destination is set to the empty region defined by the rectangle (0,0)(0,0).

> **Note:** UnionRgn may temporarily use heap space that's twice the size of the two input regions.

```
PROCEDURE DiffRgn (srcRgnA,srcRgnB,dstRgn: RgnHandle);
```

DiffRgn subtracts srcRgnB from srcRgnA and places the difference in a third region. This does *not* create the destination region; space must already have been allocated for it. The destination region can be one of the source regions, if desired.

If the first source region is empty, the destination is set to the empty region defined by the rectangle (0,0)(0,0).

> **Note:** DiffRgn may temporarily use heap space that's twice the size of the two input regions.

```
PROCEDURE XorRgn (srcRgnA,srcRgnB,dstRgn: RgnHandle);
```

XorRgn calculates the difference between the union and the intersection of srcRgnA and srcRgnB and places the result in dstRgn. This does *not* create the destination region; space must already have been allocated for it. The destination region can be one of the source regions, if desired.

If the regions are coincident, the destination is set to the empty region defined by the rectangle (0,0)(0,0).

Note: XorRgn may temporarily use heap space that's twice the size of the two input regions.

```
FUNCTION PtInRgn (pt: Point; rgn: RgnHandle) : BOOLEAN;
```

PtInRgn checks whether the pixel below and to the right of the given coordinate point is within the specified region, and returns TRUE if so or FALSE if not.

```
FUNCTION RectInRgn (r: Rect; rgn: RgnHandle) : BOOLEAN;
```

RectInRgn checks whether the given rectangle intersects the specified region, and returns TRUE if the intersection encloses at least one bit or FALSE if not.

Note: RectInRgn will sometimes return TRUE when the rectangle merely intersects the region's enclosing rectangle. If you need to know exactly whether a given rectangle intersects the actual region, you can use RectRgn to set the rectangle to a region, and call SectRgn to see whether the two regions intersect: If the result of SectRgn is an empty region, then the rectangle doesn't intersect the region.

```
FUNCTION EqualRgn (rgnA,rgnB: RgnHandle) : BOOLEAN;
```

EqualRgn compares the two given regions and returns TRUE if they're equal or FALSE if not. The two regions must have identical sizes, shapes, and locations to be considered equal. Any two empty regions are always equal.

```
FUNCTION EmptyRgn (rgn: RgnHandle) : BOOLEAN;
```

EmptyRgn returns TRUE if the region is an empty region or FALSE if not. Some of the circumstances in which an empty region can be created are: a NewRgn call; a CopyRgn of an empty region; a SetRectRgn or RectRgn with an empty rectangle as an argument; CloseRgn without a previous OpenRgn or with no drawing after an OpenRgn; OffsetRgn of an empty region; InsetRgn with an empty region or too large an inset; SectRgn of nonintersecting regions; UnionRgn of two empty regions; and DiffRgn or XorRgn of two identical or nonintersecting regions.

6 QuickDraw

Graphic Operations on Regions

These routines all depend on the coordinate system of the current grafPort. If a region is drawn in a different grafPort than the one in which it was defined, it may not appear in the proper position in the port.

> **Warning:** If any horizontal or vertical line drawn through the region would intersect the region's outline more than 50 times, the results of these graphic operations are undefined. The FrameRgn procedure in particular requires that there would be no more than 25 such intersections.

```
PROCEDURE FrameRgn (rgn: RgnHandle);
```

FrameRgn draws an outline just inside the specified region, using the current grafPort's pen pattern, mode, and size. The outline is as wide as the pen width and as tall as the pen height. It's drawn with the pnPat, according to the pattern transfer mode specified by pnMode. The outline will never go outside the region boundary. The pen location is not changed by this procedure.

If a region is open and being formed, the outside outline of the region being framed is mathematically added to that region's boundary.

> **Note:** FrameRgn actually does a CopyRgn, an InsetRgn, and a DiffRgn; it may temporarily use heap space that's three times the size of the original region.

```
PROCEDURE PaintRgn (rgn: RgnHandle);
```

PaintRgn paints the specified region with the current grafPort's pen pattern and pen mode. The region is filled with the pnPat, according to the pattern transfer mode specified by pnMode. The pen location is not changed by this procedure.

```
PROCEDURE EraseRgn (rgn: RgnHandle);
```

EraseRgn paints the specified region with the current grafPort's background pattern bkPat (in patCopy mode). The grafPort's pnPat and pnMode are ignored; the pen location is not changed.

```
PROCEDURE InvertRgn (rgn: RgnHandle);
```

> **Assembly-language note:** The macro you invoke to call InvertRgn from assembly language is named _InverRgn.

InvertRgn inverts the pixels enclosed by the specified region: Every white pixel becomes black and every black pixel becomes white. The grafPort's pnPat, pnMode, and bkPat are all ignored; the pen location is not changed.

```
PROCEDURE FillRgn (rgn: RgnHandle; pat: Pattern);
```

FillRgn fills the specified region with the given pattern (in patCopy mode). The grafPort's pnPat, pnMode, and bkPat are all ignored; the pen location is not changed.

Bit Transfer Operations

```
PROCEDURE ScrollRect (r: Rect; dh,dv: INTEGER; updateRgn:
          RgnHandle);
```

ScrollRect shifts ("scrolls") the bits that are inside the intersection of the specified rectangle and the visRgn, clipRgn, portRect, and portBits.bounds of the current grafPort. No other bits are affected. The bits are shifted a distance of dh horizontally and dv vertically. The positive directions are to the right and down. Bits that are shifted out of the scroll area are lost—they're neither placed outside the area nor saved. The space created by the scroll is filled with the grafPort's background pattern (thePort^.bkPat), and the updateRgn is changed to this filled area (see Figure 22).

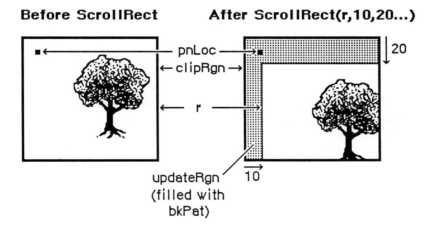

Figure 22. Scrolling

ScrollRect doesn't change the coordinate system of the grafPort, it simply moves the entire document to *different* coordinates. Notice that ScrollRect doesn't move the pen and the clipRgn. However, since the document has moved, they're in a different position relative to the document.

To restore the coordinates of the document to what they were before the ScrollRect, you can use the SetOrigin procedure. In Figure 22, suppose that before the ScrollRect the top left corner of the document was at coordinates (100,100). After ScrollRect(r,10,20...), the coordinates of the document are offset by the specified values. You could call SetOrigin(90,80) to offset the coordinate system to compensate for the scroll (see Figure 14 in the "Coordinates in GrafPorts" section for an illustration). The document itself doesn't move as a result of SetOrigin, but the pen and clipRgn move down and to the right, and are restored to their original position relative to the document. Notice that updateRgn will still need to be redrawn.

```
PROCEDURE CopyBits (srcBits,dstBits: BitMap; srcRect,dstRect:
           Rect; mode: INTEGER; maskRgn: RgnHandle);
```

CopyBits transfers a bit image between any two bit maps and clips the result to the area specified by the maskRgn parameter. The transfer may be performed in any of the eight source transfer modes. The result is always clipped to the maskRgn and the boundary rectangle of the destination bit map; if the destination bit map is the current grafPort's portBits, it's also clipped to the intersection of the grafPort's clipRgn and visRgn. If you don't want to clip to a maskRgn, just pass NIL for the maskRgn parameter. The dstRect and maskRgn coordinates are in terms of the dstBits.bounds coordinate system, and the srcRect coordinates are in terms of the srcBits.bounds coordinates.

> **Warning:** The source bit map must not occupy more memory than half the available stack space. A good rule of thumb is not to copy more than 3K bytes.

> **Warning:** If you perform a CopyBits between two grafPorts that overlap, you must first convert to global coordinates, and then specify screenBits for both srcBits and dstBits.

The bits enclosed by the source rectangle are transferred into the destination rectangle according to the rules of the chosen mode. The source transfer modes are as follows:

srcCopy	notSrcCopy
srcOr	notSrcXor
srcXor	notSrcOr
srcBic	notSrcBic

The source rectangle is completely aligned with the destination rectangle; if the rectangles are of different sizes, the bit image is expanded or shrunk as necessary to fit the destination rectangle. For example, if the bit image is a circle in a square source rectangle, and the destination rectangle is not square, the bit image appears as an oval in the destination (see Figure 23).

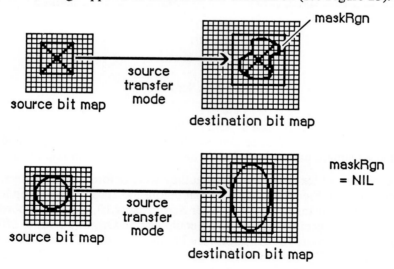

Figure 23. Operation of CopyBits

Pictures

`FUNCTION OpenPicture (picFrame: Rect) : PicHandle;`

OpenPicture returns a handle to a new picture that has the given rectangle as its picture frame, and tells QuickDraw to start saving as the picture definition all calls to drawing routines and all picture comments (if any).

OpenPicture calls HidePen, so no drawing occurs on the screen while the picture is open (unless you call ShowPen just after OpenPicture, or you called ShowPen previously without balancing it by a call to HidePen).

When a picture is open, the current grafPort's picSave field contains a handle to information related to the picture definition. If you want to temporarily disable the collection of routine calls and picture comments, you can save the current value of this field, set the field to NIL, and later restore the saved value to resume the picture definition.

> **Warning:** Do not call OpenPicture while another picture is already open.

> **Warning:** A grafPort's clipRgn is initialized to an arbitrarily large region. You should always change the clipRgn to a smaller region *before* calling OpenPicture, or no drawing may occur when you call DrawPicture.

> **Note:** Pictures are limited to 32K bytes; you can determine the picture size while it's being formed by calling the Memory Manager function GetHandleSize.

`PROCEDURE ClosePicture;`

ClosePicture tells QuickDraw to stop saving routine calls and picture comments as the definition of the currently open picture. You should perform one and only one ClosePicture for every OpenPicture. ClosePicture calls ShowPen, balancing the HidePen call made by OpenPicture.

`PROCEDURE PicComment (kind,dataSize: INTEGER; dataHandle: Handle);`

PicComment inserts the specified comment into the definition of the currently open picture. The kind parameter identifies the type of comment. DataHandle is a handle to additional data if desired, and dataSize is the size of that data in bytes. If there's no additional data for the comment, dataHandle should be NIL and dataSize should be 0. An application that processes the comments must include a procedure to do the processing and store a pointer to it in the data structure pointed to by the grafProcs field of the grafPort (see "Customizing QuickDraw Operations").

> **Note:** The standard low-level procedure for processing picture comments simply ignores all comments.

```
PROCEDURE DrawPicture (myPicture: PicHandle; dstRect: Rect);
```

DrawPicture takes the part of the given picture that's inside the picture frame and draws it in dstRect, expanding or shrinking it as necessary to align the borders of the picture frame with dstRect. DrawPicture passes any picture comments to a low-level procedure accessed indirectly through the grafProcs field of the grafPort (see PicComment above).

Warning: If you call DrawPicture with the initial, arbitrarily large clipRgn and the destination rectangle is offset from the picture frame, you may end up with an empty clipRgn, and no drawing will take place.

Note: Because of a convention not to copy more than 3K bytes with CopyBits, a buffer of approximately 3.5K bytes on the stack should suffice when "playing back" a picture.

```
PROCEDURE KillPicture (myPicture: PicHandle);
```

KillPicture releases the memory occupied by the given picture. Use this only when you're completely through with a picture (unless the picture is a resource, in which case use the Resource Manager procedure ReleaseResource).

Calculations with Polygons

```
FUNCTION OpenPoly : PolyHandle;
```

OpenPoly returns a handle to a new polygon and tells QuickDraw to start saving the polygon definition as specified by calls to line-drawing routines. While a polygon is open, all calls to Line and LineTo affect the outline of the polygon. Only the line endpoints affect the polygon definition; the pen mode, pattern, and size do not affect it. In fact, OpenPoly calls HidePen, so no drawing occurs on the screen while the polygon is open (unless you call ShowPen just after OpenPoly, or you called ShowPen previously without balancing it by a call to HidePen).

A polygon should consist of a sequence of connected lines. Even though the on-screen presentation of a polygon is clipped, the definition of a polygon is not; you can define a polygon anywhere on the coordinate plane.

When a polygon is open, the current grafPort's polySave field contains a handle to information related to the polygon definition. If you want to temporarily disable the polygon definition, you can save the current value of this field, set the field to NIL, and later restore the saved value to resume the polygon definition.

Warning: Do not call OpenPoly while a region or another polygon is already open.

Note: Polygons are limited to 32K bytes; you can determine the polygon size while it's being formed by calling the Memory Manager function GetHandleSize.

```
PROCEDURE ClosePoly;
```

Assembly-language note: The macro you invoke to call ClosePoly from assembly language is named _ClosePgon.

ClosePoly tells QuickDraw to stop saving the definition of the currently open polygon and computes the polyBBox rectangle. You should perform one and only one ClosePoly for every OpenPoly. ClosePoly calls ShowPen, balancing the HidePen call made by OpenPoly.

Here's an example of how to open a polygon, define it as a triangle, close it, and draw it:

```
triPoly := OpenPoly;        {save handle and begin collecting stuff}
   MoveTo(300,100);         {move to first point and  }
   LineTo(400,200);         {               form       }
   LineTo(200,200);         {               the        }
   LineTo(300,100);         {               triangle   }
ClosePoly;                  {stop collecting stuff}
FillPoly(triPoly,gray);     {draw it on the screen}
KillPoly(triPoly)           {we're all done}
```

PROCEDURE KillPoly (poly: PolyHandle);

KillPoly releases the memory occupied by the given polygon. Use this only when you're completely through with a polygon.

PROCEDURE OffsetPoly (poly: PolyHandle; dh,dv: INTEGER);

OffsetPoly moves the polygon on the coordinate plane, a distance of dh horizontally and dv vertically. This doesn't affect the screen unless you subsequently call a routine to draw the polygon. If dh and dv are positive, the movement is to the right and down; if either is negative, the corresponding movement is in the opposite direction. The polygon retains its shape and size.

Note: OffsetPoly is an especially efficient operation, because the data defining a polygon is stored relative to the first point of the polygon and so isn't actually changed by OffsetPoly.

Graphic Operations on Polygons

Four of the operations described here—PaintPoly, ErasePoly, InvertPoly, and FillPoly— temporarily convert the polygon into a region to perform their operations. The amount of memory required for this temporary region may be far greater than the amount required by the polygon alone. You can estimate the size of this region by scaling down the polygon with MapPoly, converting it into a region, checking the region's size with the Memory Manager function GetHandleSize, and multiplying that value by the factor by which you scaled down the polygon.

Warning: If any horizontal or vertical line drawn through the polygon would intersect the polygon's outline more than 50 times, the results of these graphic operations are undefined.

```
PROCEDURE FramePoly (poly: PolyHandle);
```

FramePoly plays back the line-drawing routine calls that define the given polygon, using the current grafPort's pen pattern, mode, and size. The pen will hang below and to the right of each point on the boundary of the polygon; thus, the polygon drawn will extend beyond the right and bottom edges of poly^^.polyBBox by the pen width and pen height, respectively. All other graphic operations occur strictly within the boundary of the polygon, as for other shapes. You can see this difference in Figure 24, where each of the polygons is shown with its polyBBox.

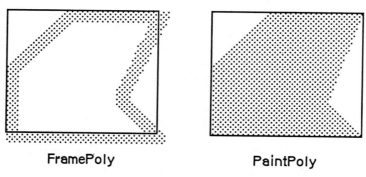

Figure 24. Drawing Polygons

If a polygon is open and being formed, FramePoly affects the outline of the polygon just as if the line-drawing routines themselves had been called. If a region is open and being formed, the outside outline of the polygon being framed is mathematically added to the region's boundary.

```
PROCEDURE PaintPoly (poly: PolyHandle);
```

PaintPoly paints the specified polygon with the current grafPort's pen pattern and pen mode. The polygon is filled with the pnPat, according to the pattern transfer mode specified by pnMode. The pen location is not changed by this procedure.

```
PROCEDURE ErasePoly (poly: PolyHandle);
```

ErasePoly paints the specified polygon with the current grafPort's background pattern bkPat (in patCopy mode). The pnPat and pnMode are ignored; the pen location is not changed.

```
PROCEDURE InvertPoly (poly: PolyHandle);
```

InvertPoly inverts the pixels enclosed by the specified polygon: Every white pixel becomes black and every black pixel becomes white. The grafPort's pnPat, pnMode, and bkPat are all ignored; the pen location is not changed.

```
PROCEDURE FillPoly (poly: PolyHandle; pat: Pattern);
```

FillPoly fills the specified polygon with the given pattern (in patCopy mode). The grafPort's pnPat, pnMode, and bkPat are all ignored; the pen location is not changed.

Calculations with Points

```
PROCEDURE AddPt (srcPt: Point; VAR dstPt: Point);
```

AddPt adds the coordinates of srcPt to the coordinates of dstPt, and returns the result in dstPt.

```
PROCEDURE SubPt (srcPt: Point; VAR dstPt: Point);
```

SubPt subtracts the coordinates of srcPt from the coordinates of dstPt, and returns the result in dstPt.

> **Note:** To get the results of coordinate subtraction returned as a function result, you can use the Toolbox Utility function DeltaPoint.

```
PROCEDURE SetPt (VAR pt: Point; h,v: INTEGER);
```

SetPt assigns the two given coordinates to the point pt.

```
FUNCTION EqualPt (pt1,pt2: Point) : BOOLEAN;
```

EqualPt compares the two given points and returns TRUE if they're equal or FALSE if not.

```
PROCEDURE LocalToGlobal (VAR pt: Point);
```

LocalToGlobal converts the given point from the current grafPort's local coordinate system into a global coordinate system with the origin (0,0) at the top left corner of the port's bit image (such as the screen). This global point can then be compared to other global points, or be changed into the local coordinates of another grafPort.

Since a rectangle is defined by two points, you can convert a rectangle into global coordinates by performing two LocalToGlobal calls. You can also convert a rectangle, region, or polygon into global coordinates by calling OffsetRect, OffsetRgn, or OffsetPoly. For examples, see GlobalToLocal below.

```
PROCEDURE GlobalToLocal (VAR pt: Point);
```

GlobalToLocal takes a point expressed in global coordinates (with the top left corner of the bit image as coordinate (0,0)) and converts it into the local coordinates of the current grafPort. The global point can be obtained with the LocalToGlobal call (see above). For example, suppose a game draws a "ball" within a rectangle named ballRect, defined in the grafPort named gamePort (as illustrated in Figure 25). If you want to draw that ball in the grafPort named selectPort, you can calculate the ball's selectPort coordinates like this:

```
SetPort(gamePort);                    {start in origin port}
selectBall := ballRect;               {make a copy to be moved}
LocalToGlobal(selectBall.topLeft);    {put both corners into }
LocalToGlobal(selectBall.botRight);   { global coordinates}

SetPort(selectPort);                  {switch to destination port}
GlobalToLocal(selectBall.topLeft);    {put both corners into }
GlobalToLocal(selectBall.botRight);   { these local coordinates}
FillOval(selectBall,ballColor)        {draw the ball}
```

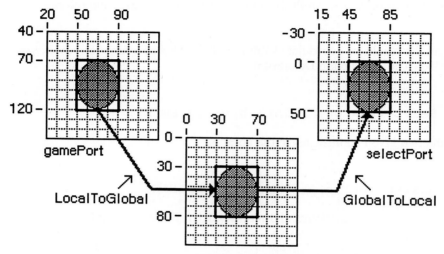

Figure 25. Converting between Coordinate Systems

You can see from Figure 25 that LocalToGlobal and GlobalToLocal simply offset the coordinates of the rectangle by the coordinates of the top left corner of the local grafPort's portBits.bounds rectangle. You could also do this with OffsetRect. In fact, the way to convert regions and polygons from one coordinate system to another is with OffsetRgn or OffsetPoly rather than LocalToGlobal and GlobalToLocal. For example, if myRgn were a region enclosed by a rectangle having the same coordinates as ballRect in gamePort, you could convert the region to global coordinates with

```
OffsetRgn(myRgn,-20,-40)
```

and then convert it to the coordinates of the selectPort grafPort with

```
OffsetRgn(myRgn,15,-30)
```

Miscellaneous Routines

```
FUNCTION Random : INTEGER;
```

This function returns a pseudo-random integer, uniformly distributed in the range –32767 through 32767. The value the sequence starts from depends on the global variable randSeed, which InitGraf initializes to 1. To start the sequence over again from where it began, reset randSeed to 1. To start a new sequence each time, you must reset randSeed to a random number.

Note: You can start a new sequence by storing the current date and time in randSeed; see GetDateTime in chapter 13 of Volume II.

Assembly-language note: From assembly language, it's better to start a new sequence by storing the value of the system global variable RndSeed in randSeed.

```
FUNCTION GetPixel (h,v: INTEGER) : BOOLEAN;
```

GetPixel looks at the pixel associated with the given coordinate point and returns TRUE if it's black or FALSE if it's white. The selected pixel is immediately below and to the right of the point whose coordinates are given in h and v, in the local coordinates of the current grafPort. There's no guarantee that the specified pixel actually belongs to the port, however; it may have been drawn by a port overlapping the current one. To see if the point indeed belongs to the current port, you could call PtInRgn(pt, thePort^.visRgn).

Note: To find out which window's grafPort a point lies in, you call the Window Manager function FindWindow, as described in chapter 9.

```
PROCEDURE StuffHex (thingPtr: Ptr; s: Str255);
```

StuffHex stores bits (expressed as a string of hexadecimal digits) into any data structure. You can easily create a pattern in your program with StuffHex (though more likely, you'll store patterns in a resource file). For example,

```
StuffHex(@stripes,'0102040810204080')
```

places a striped pattern into the pattern variable named stripes.

Warning: There's no range checking on the size of the destination variable. It's easy to overrun the variable and destroy something if you don't know what you're doing.

```
PROCEDURE ScalePt (VAR pt: Point; srcRect,dstRect: Rect);
```

A width and height are passed in pt; the horizontal component of pt is the width, and its vertical component is the height. ScalePt scales these measurements as follows and returns the result in pt: It multiplies the given width by the ratio of dstRect's width to srcRect's width, and multiplies the given height by the ratio of dstRect's height to srcRect's height.

ScalePt can be used, for example, for scaling the pen dimensions. In Figure 26, where dstRect's width is twice srcRect's width and its height is three times srcRect's height, the pen width is scaled from 3 to 6 and the pen height is scaled from 2 to 6.

Note: The minimum value ScalePt will return is (1,1).

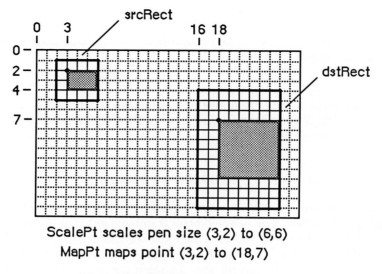

ScalePt scales pen size (3,2) to (6,6)
MapPt maps point (3,2) to (18,7)

Figure 26. ScalePt and MapPt

```
PROCEDURE MapPt (VAR pt: Point; srcRect,dstRect: Rect);
```

Given a point within srcRect, MapPt maps it to a similarly located point within dstRect (that is, to where it would fall if it were part of a drawing being expanded or shrunk to fit dstRect). The result is returned in pt. A corner point of srcRect would be mapped to the corresponding corner point of dstRect, and the center of srcRect to the center of dstRect. In Figure 26, the point (3,2) in srcRect is mapped to (18,7) in dstRect. SrcRect and dstRect may overlap, and pt need not actually be within srcRect.

Note: Remember, if you're going to draw inside the destination rectangle, you'll probably also want to scale the pen size accordingly with ScalePt.

```
PROCEDURE MapRect (VAR r: Rect; srcRect,dstRect: Rect);
```

Given a rectangle within srcRect, MapRect maps it to a similarly located rectangle within dstRect by calling MapPt to map the top left and bottom right corners of the rectangle. The result is returned in r.

```
PROCEDURE MapRgn (rgn: RgnHandle; srcRect,dstRect: Rect);
```

Given a region within srcRect, MapRgn maps it to a similarly located region within dstRect by calling MapPt to map all the points in the region.

Note: MapRgn is useful for determining whether a region operation will exceed available memory: By mapping a large region into a smaller one and performing the operation (without actually drawing), you can estimate how much memory will be required by the anticipated operation.

```
PROCEDURE MapPoly (poly: PolyHandle; srcRect,dstRect: Rect);
```

Given a polygon within srcRect, MapPoly maps it to a similarly located polygon within dstRect by calling MapPt to map all the points that define the polygon.

Note: Like MapRgn, MapPoly is useful for determining whether a polygon operation will succeed.

CUSTOMIZING QUICKDRAW OPERATIONS

For each shape that QuickDraw knows how to draw, there are procedures that perform these basic graphic operations on the shape: frame, paint, erase, invert, and fill. Those procedures in turn call a low-level drawing routine for the shape. For example, the FrameOval, PaintOval, EraseOval, InvertOval, and FillOval procedures all call a low-level routine that draws the oval. For each type of object QuickDraw can draw, including text and lines, there's a pointer to such a routine. By changing these pointers, you can install your own routines, and either completely override the standard ones or call them after your routines have modified parameters as necessary.

Other low-level routines that you can install in this way are:

- The procedure that does bit transfer and is called by CopyBits.
- The function that measures the width of text and is called by CharWidth, StringWidth, and TextWidth.
- The procedure that processes picture comments and is called by DrawPicture. The standard such procedure ignores picture comments.
- The procedure that saves drawing commands as the definition of a picture, and the one that retrieves them. This enables the application to draw on remote devices, print to the disk, get picture input from the disk, and support large pictures.

The grafProcs field of a grafPort determines which low-level routines are called; if it contains NIL, the standard routines are called, so that all operations in that grafPort are done in the standard ways described in this chapter. You can set the grafProcs field to point to a record of pointers to routines. The data type of grafProcs is QDProcsPtr:

```
TYPE QDProcsPtr = ^QDProcs;
     QDProcs    = RECORD
                    textProc:    Ptr;  {text drawing}
                    lineProc:    Ptr;  {line drawing}
                    rectProc:    Ptr;  {rectangle drawing}
                    rRectProc:   Ptr;  {roundRect drawing}
                    ovalProc:    Ptr;  {oval drawing}
                    arcProc:     Ptr;  {arc/wedge drawing}
                    polyProc:    Ptr;  {polygon drawing}
                    rgnProc:     Ptr;  {region drawing}
                    bitsProc:    Ptr;  {bit transfer}
                    commentProc: Ptr;  {picture comment processing}
                    txMeasProc:  Ptr;  {text width measurement}
                    getPicProc:  Ptr;  {picture retrieval}
                    putPicProc:  Ptr   {picture saving}
                  END;
```

To assist you in setting up a QDProcs record, QuickDraw provides the following procedure:

```
PROCEDURE SetStdProcs (VAR procs: QDProcs);
```

This procedure sets all the fields of the given QDProcs record to point to the standard low-level routines. You can then change the ones you wish to point to your own routines. For example, if your procedure that processes picture comments is named MyComments, you'll store @MyComments in the commentProc field of the QDProcs record.

You can either write your own routines to completely replace the standard ones, or do preprocessing and then call the standard routines. The routines you install must of course have the same calling sequences as the standard routines, which are described below.

Note: These low-level routines should be called only from your customized routines.

The standard drawing routines tell which graphic operation to perform from a parameter of type GrafVerb:

```
TYPE GrafVerb = (frame,paint,erase,invert,fill);
```

When the grafVerb is fill, the pattern to use during filling is passed in the fillPat field of the grafPort.

```
PROCEDURE StdText (byteCount: INTEGER; textBuf: Ptr; numer,denom:
            Point);
```

StdText is the standard low-level routine for drawing text. It draws text from the arbitrary structure in memory specified by textBuf, starting from the first byte and continuing for byteCount bytes. Numer and denom specify the scaling factor: numer.v over denom.v gives the vertical scaling, and numer.h over denom.h gives the horizontal scaling.

```
PROCEDURE StdLine (newPt: Point);
```

StdLine is the standard low-level routine for drawing a line. It draws a line from the current pen location to the location specified (in local coordinates) by newPt.

```
PROCEDURE StdRect (verb: GrafVerb; r: Rect);
```

StdRect is the standard low-level routine for drawing a rectangle. It draws the given rectangle according to the specified grafVerb.

```
PROCEDURE StdRRect (verb: GrafVerb; r: Rect; ovalwidth,
            ovalHeight: INTEGER)
```

StdRRect is the standard low-level routine for drawing a rounded-corner rectangle. It draws the given rounded-corner rectangle according to the specified grafVerb. OvalWidth and ovalHeight specify the diameters of curvature for the corners.

```
PROCEDURE StdOval (verb: GrafVerb; r: Rect);
```

StdOval is the standard low-level routine for drawing an oval. It draws an oval inside the given rectangle according to the specified grafVerb.

```
PROCEDURE StdArc (verb: GrafVerb; r: Rect; startAngle,arcAngle:
        INTEGER);
```

StdArc is the standard low-level routine for drawing an arc or a wedge. It draws an arc or wedge of the oval that fits inside the given rectangle, beginning at startAngle and extending to arcAngle. The grafVerb specifies the graphic operation; if it's the frame operation, an arc is drawn; otherwise, a wedge is drawn.

```
PROCEDURE StdPoly (verb: GrafVerb; poly: PolyHandle);
```

StdPoly is the standard low-level routine for drawing a polygon. It draws the given polygon according to the specified grafVerb.

```
PROCEDURE StdRgn (verb: GrafVerb; rgn: RgnHandle);
```

StdRgn is the standard low-level routine for drawing a region. It draws the given region according to the specified grafVerb.

```
PROCEDURE StdBits (VAR srcBits: BitMap; VAR srcRect,dstRect: Rect;
        mode: INTEGER; maskRgn: RgnHandle);
```

StdBits is the standard low-level routine for doing bit transfer. It transfers a bit image between the given bit map and thePort^.portBits, just as if CopyBits were called with the same parameters and with a destination bit map equal to thePort^.portBits.

```
PROCEDURE StdComment (kind,dataSize: INTEGER; dataHandle:
        Handle);
```

StdComment is the standard low-level routine for processing a picture comment. The kind parameter identifies the type of comment. DataHandle is a handle to additional data, and dataSize is the size of that data in bytes. If there's no additional data for the comment, dataHandle will be NIL and dataSize will be 0. StdComment simply ignores the comment.

```
FUNCTION StdTxMeas (byteCount: INTEGER; textAddr: Ptr; VAR numer,
        denom: Point; VAR info: FontInfo) : INTEGER;
```

StdTxMeas is the standard low-level routine for measuring text width. It returns the width of the text stored in the arbitrary structure in memory specified by textAddr, starting with the first byte and continuing for byteCount bytes. Numer and denom specify the scaling as in the StdText procedure; note that StdTxMeas may change them.

```
PROCEDURE StdGetPic (dataPtr: Ptr; byteCount: INTEGER);
```

StdGetPic is the standard low-level routine for retrieving information from the definition of a picture. It retrieves the next byteCount bytes from the definition of the currently open picture and stores them in the data structure pointed to by dataPtr.

```
PROCEDURE StdPutPic (dataPtr: Ptr; byteCount: INTEGER);
```

StdPutPic is the standard low-level routine for saving information as the definition of a picture. It saves as the definition of the currently open picture the drawing commands stored in the data structure pointed to by dataPtr, starting with the first byte and continuing for the next byteCount bytes.

SUMMARY OF QUICKDRAW

Constants

```
CONST  { Source transfer modes }

        srcCopy    = 0;
        srcOr      = 1;
        srcXor     = 2;
        srcBic     = 3;
        notSrcCopy = 4;
        notSrcOr   = 5;
        notSrcXor  = 6;
        notSrcBic  = 7;

        { Pattern transfer modes }

        patCopy    = 8;
        patOr      = 9;
        patXor     = 10;
        patBic     = 11;
        notPatCopy = 12;
        notPatOr   = 13;
        notPatXor  = 14;
        notPatBic  = 15;

        { Standard colors for ForeColor and BackColor }

        blackColor   = 33;
        whiteColor   = 30;
        redColor     = 205;
        greenColor   = 341;
        blueColor    = 409;
        cyanColor    = 273;
        magentaColor = 137;
        yellowColor  = 69;

        { Standard picture comments }

        picLParen = 0;
        picRParen = 1;
```

Data Types

```
TYPE  StyleItem = (bold,italic,underline,outline,shadow,condense,extend);
      Style     = SET OF StyleItem;
```

```
VHSelect = (v,h);
Point    = RECORD CASE INTEGER OF

              0: (v: INTEGER;    {vertical coordinate}
                  h: INTEGER);   {horizontal coordinate}

              1: (vh: ARRAY[VHSelect] OF INTEGER)

           END;


Rect = RECORD CASE INTEGER OF

          0: (top:     INTEGER;
              left:    INTEGER;
              bottom:  INTEGER;
              right:   INTEGER);

          1: (topLeft:  Point;
              botRight: Point)

       END;


RgnHandle = ^RgnPtr;
RgnPtr    = ^Region;
Region    = RECORD
                rgnSize: INTEGER;    {size in bytes}
                rgnBBox: Rect;       {enclosing rectangle}
                {more data if not rectangular}
            END;


BitMap = RECORD
            baseAddr: Ptr;       {pointer to bit image}
            rowBytes: INTEGER;   {row width}
            bounds:   Rect       {boundary rectangle}
         END;


Pattern = PACKED ARRAY[0..7] OF 0..255;


Bits16 = ARRAY[0..15] OF INTEGER;


Cursor = RECORD
            data:    Bits16;   {cursor image}
            mask:    Bits16;   {cursor mask}
            hotSpot: Point     {point aligned with mouse}
         END;
```

```
QDProcsPtr = ^QDProcs;
QDProcs    = RECORD
                 textProc:    Ptr;  {text drawing}
                 lineProc:    Ptr;  {line drawing}
                 rectProc:    Ptr;  {rectangle drawing}
                 rRectProc:   Ptr;  {roundRect drawing}
                 ovalProc:    Ptr;  {oval drawing}
                 arcProc:     Ptr;  {arc/wedge drawing}
                 rgnProc:     Ptr;  {region drawing}
                 bitsProc:    Ptr;  {bit transfer}
                 commentProc: Ptr;  {picture comment processing}
                 txMeasProc:  Ptr;  {text width measurement}
                 getPicProc:  Ptr;  {picture retrieval}
                 putPicProc:  Ptr   {picture saving}
             END;


GrafPtr  = ^GrafPort;
GrafPort = RECORD
                 device:    INTEGER;   {device-specific information}
                 portBits:  BitMap;    {grafPort's bit map}
                 portRect:  Rect;      {grafPort's rectangle}
                 visRgn:    RgnHandle;  {visible region}
                 clipRgn:   RgnHandle;  {clipping region}
                 bkPat:     Pattern;   {background pattern}
                 fillPat:   Pattern;   {fill pattern}
                 pnLoc:     Point;     {pen location}
                 pnSize:    Point;     {pen size}
                 pnMode:    INTEGER;   {pen's transfer mode}
                 pnPat:     Pattern;   {pen pattern}
                 pnVis:     INTEGER;   {pen visibility}
                 txFont:    INTEGER;   {font number for text}
                 txFace:    Style;     {text's character style}
                 txMode:    INTEGER;   {text's transfer mode}
                 txSize:    INTEGER;   {font size for text}
                 spExtra:   Fixed;     {extra space}
                 fgColor:   LONGINT;   {foreground color}
                 bkColor:   LONGINT;   {background color}
                 colrBit:   INTEGER;   {color bit}
                 patStretch: INTEGER;  {used internally}
                 picSave:   Handle;    {picture being saved}
                 rgnSave:   Handle;    {region being saved}
                 polySave:  Handle;    {polygon being saved}
                 grafProcs: QDProcsPtr {low-level drawing routines}
             END;


PicHandle = ^PicPtr;
PicPtr    = ^Picture;
Picture   = RECORD
                 picSize:  INTEGER; {size in bytes}
                 picFrame: Rect;    {picture frame}
                 {picture definition data}
             END;
```

```
PolyHandle = ^PolyPtr;
PolyPtr    = ^Polygon;
Polygon    = RECORD
                 polySize:   INTEGER;   {size in bytes}
                 polyBBox:   Rect;      {enclosing rectangle}
                 polyPoints: ARRAY[0..0] OF Point
             END;

PenState = RECORD
               pnLoc:  Point;    {pen location}
               pnSize: Point;    {pen size}
               pnMode: INTEGER;  {pen's transfer mode}
               pnPat:  Pattern   {pen pattern}
           END;

FontInfo = RECORD
               ascent:  INTEGER;  {ascent}
               descent: INTEGER;  {descent}
               widMax:  INTEGER;  {maximum character width}
               leading: INTEGER   {leading}
           END;

GrafVerb = (frame,paint,erase,invert,fill);
```

Variables

```
VAR thePort:    GrafPtr;   {pointer to current grafPort}
    white:      Pattern;   {all-white pattern}
    black:      Pattern;   {all-black pattern}
    gray:       Pattern;   {50% gray pattern}
    ltGray:     Pattern;   {25% gray pattern}
    dkGray:     Pattern;   {75% gray pattern}
    arrow:      Cursor;    {standard arrow cursor}
    screenBits: BitMap;    {the entire screen}
    randSeed:   LONGINT;   {determines where Random sequence begins}
```

Routines

GrafPort Routines

```
PROCEDURE InitGraf      (globalPtr: Ptr);
PROCEDURE OpenPort      (port: GrafPtr);
PROCEDURE InitPort      (port: GrafPtr);
PROCEDURE ClosePort     (port: GrafPtr);
PROCEDURE SetPort       (port: GrafPtr);
PROCEDURE GetPort       (VAR port: GrafPtr);
PROCEDURE GrafDevice    (device: INTEGER);
PROCEDURE SetPortBits   (bm: BitMap);
PROCEDURE PortSize      (width,height: INTEGER);
```

```
PROCEDURE MovePortTo      (leftGlobal,topGlobal: INTEGER);
PROCEDURE SetOrigin       (h,v: INTEGER);
PROCEDURE SetClip         (rgn: RgnHandle);
PROCEDURE GetClip         (rgn: RgnHandle);
PROCEDURE ClipRect        (r: Rect);
PROCEDURE BackPat         (pat: Pattern);
```

Cursor Handling

```
PROCEDURE InitCursor;
PROCEDURE SetCursor (crsr: Cursor);
PROCEDURE HideCursor;
PROCEDURE ShowCursor;
PROCEDURE ObscureCursor;
```

Pen and Line Drawing

```
PROCEDURE HidePen;
PROCEDURE ShowPen;
PROCEDURE GetPen          (VAR pt: Point);
PROCEDURE GetPenState     (VAR pnState: PenState);
PROCEDURE SetPenState     (pnState: PenState);
PROCEDURE PenSize         (width,height: INTEGER);
PROCEDURE PenMode         (mode: INTEGER);
PROCEDURE PenPat          (pat: Pattern);
PROCEDURE PenNormal;
PROCEDURE MoveTo          (h,v: INTEGER);
PROCEDURE Move            (dh,dv: INTEGER);
PROCEDURE LineTo          (h,v: INTEGER);
PROCEDURE Line            (dh,dv: INTEGER);
```

Text Drawing

```
PROCEDURE TextFont        (font: INTEGER);
PROCEDURE TextFace        (face: Style);
PROCEDURE TextMode        (mode: INTEGER);
PROCEDURE TextSize        (size: INTEGER);
PROCEDURE SpaceExtra      (extra: Fixed);
PROCEDURE DrawChar        (ch: CHAR);
PROCEDURE DrawString      (s: Str255);
PROCEDURE DrawText        (textBuf: Ptr; firstByte,byteCount: INTEGER);
FUNCTION  CharWidth       (ch: CHAR) : INTEGER;
FUNCTION  StringWidth     (s: Str255) : INTEGER;
FUNCTION  TextWidth       (textBuf: Ptr; firstByte,byteCount: INTEGER) :
                           INTEGER;
PROCEDURE GetFontInfo     (VAR info: FontInfo);
```

Drawing in Color

```
PROCEDURE ForeColor  (color: LONGINT);
PROCEDURE BackColor  (color: LONGINT);
PROCEDURE ColorBit   (whichBit: INTEGER);
```

Calculations with Rectangles

```
PROCEDURE SetRect      (VAR r: Rect; left,top,right,bottom: INTEGER);
PROCEDURE OffsetRect   (VAR r: Rect; dh,dv: INTEGER);
PROCEDURE InsetRect    (VAR r: Rect; dh,dv: INTEGER);
FUNCTION  SectRect     (src1,src2: Rect; VAR dstRect: Rect) : BOOLEAN;
PROCEDURE UnionRect    (src1,src2: Rect; VAR dstRect: Rect);
FUNCTION  PtInRect     (pt: Point; r: Rect) : BOOLEAN;
PROCEDURE Pt2Rect      (pt1,pt2: Point; VAR dstRect: Rect);
PROCEDURE PtToAngle    (r: Rect; pt: Point; VAR angle: INTEGER);
FUNCTION  EqualRect    (rect1,rect2: Rect) : BOOLEAN;
FUNCTION  EmptyRect    (r: Rect) : BOOLEAN;
```

Graphic Operations on Rectangles

```
PROCEDURE FrameRect   (r: Rect);
PROCEDURE PaintRect   (r: Rect);
PROCEDURE EraseRect   (r: Rect);
PROCEDURE InvertRect  (r: Rect);
PROCEDURE FillRect    (r: Rect; pat: Pattern);
```

Graphic Operations on Ovals

```
PROCEDURE FrameOval   (r: Rect);
PROCEDURE PaintOval   (r: Rect);
PROCEDURE EraseOval   (r: Rect);
PROCEDURE InvertOval  (r: Rect);
PROCEDURE FillOval    (r: Rect; pat: Pattern);
```

Graphic Operations on Rounded-Corner Rectangles

```
PROCEDURE FrameRoundRect    (r: Rect; ovalWidth,ovalHeight: INTEGER);
PROCEDURE PaintRoundRect    (r: Rect; ovalWidth,ovalHeight: INTEGER);
PROCEDURE EraseRoundRect    (r: Rect; ovalWidth,ovalHeight: INTEGER);
PROCEDURE InvertRoundRect   (r: Rect; ovalWidth,ovalHeight: INTEGER);
PROCEDURE FillRoundRect     (r: Rect; ovalWidth,ovalHeight: INTEGER; pat:
                             Pattern);
```

Graphic Operations on Arcs and Wedges

```
PROCEDURE  FrameArc   (r: Rect; startAngle,arcAngle: INTEGER);
PROCEDURE  PaintArc   (r: Rect; startAngle,arcAngle: INTEGER);
PROCEDURE  EraseArc   (r: Rect; startAngle,arcAngle: INTEGER);
PROCEDURE  InvertArc  (r: Rect; startAngle,arcAngle: INTEGER);
PROCEDURE  FillArc    (r: Rect; startAngle,arcAngle: INTEGER; pat:
                       Pattern);
```

Calculations with Regions

```
FUNCTION   NewRgn :       RgnHandle;
PROCEDURE  OpenRgn;
PROCEDURE  CloseRgn      (dstRgn: RgnHandle);
PROCEDURE  DisposeRgn    (rgn: RgnHandle);
PROCEDURE  CopyRgn       (srcRgn,dstRgn: RgnHandle);
PROCEDURE  SetEmptyRgn   (rgn: RgnHandle);
PROCEDURE  SetRectRgn    (rgn: RgnHandle; left,top,right,bottom: INTEGER);
PROCEDURE  RectRgn       (rgn: RgnHandle; r: Rect);
PROCEDURE  OffsetRgn     (rgn: RgnHandle; dh,dv: INTEGER);
PROCEDURE  InsetRgn      (rgn: RgnHandle; dh,dv: INTEGER);
PROCEDURE  SectRgn       (srcRgnA,srcRgnB,dstRgn: RgnHandle);
PROCEDURE  UnionRgn      (srcRgnA,srcRgnB,dstRgn: RgnHandle);
PROCEDURE  DiffRgn       (srcRgnA,srcRgnB,dstRgn: RgnHandle);
PROCEDURE  XorRgn        (srcRgnA,srcRgnB,dstRgn: RgnHandle);
FUNCTION   PtInRgn       (pt: Point; rgn: RgnHandle) : BOOLEAN;
FUNCTION   RectInRgn     (r: Rect; rgn: RgnHandle) : BOOLEAN;
FUNCTION   EqualRgn      (rgnA,rgnB: RgnHandle) : BOOLEAN;
FUNCTION   EmptyRgn      (rgn: RgnHandle) : BOOLEAN;
```

Graphic Operations on Regions

```
PROCEDURE  FrameRgn    (rgn: RgnHandle);
PROCEDURE  PaintRgn    (rgn: RgnHandle);
PROCEDURE  EraseRgn    (rgn: RgnHandle);
PROCEDURE  InvertRgn   (rgn: RgnHandle);
PROCEDURE  FillRgn     (rgn: RgnHandle; pat: Pattern);
```

Bit Transfer Operations

```
PROCEDURE  ScrollRect  (r: Rect; dh,dv: INTEGER; updateRgn: RgnHandle);
PROCEDURE  CopyBits    (srcBits,dstBits: BitMap; srcRect,dstRect: Rect;
                        mode: INTEGER; maskRgn: RgnHandle);
```

6 QuickDraw

Pictures

```
FUNCTION   OpenPicture    (picFrame: Rect) : PicHandle;
PROCEDURE  PicComment     (kind,dataSize: INTEGER; dataHandle: Handle);
PROCEDURE  ClosePicture;
PROCEDURE  DrawPicture     (myPicture: PicHandle; dstRect: Rect);
PROCEDURE  KillPicture     (myPicture: PicHandle);
```

Calculations with Polygons

```
FUNCTION   OpenPoly :     PolyHandle;
PROCEDURE  ClosePoly;
PROCEDURE  KillPoly       (poly: PolyHandle);
PROCEDURE  OffsetPoly     (poly: PolyHandle; dh,dv: INTEGER);
```

Graphic Operations on Polygons

```
PROCEDURE  FramePoly      (poly: PolyHandle);
PROCEDURE  PaintPoly      (poly: PolyHandle);
PROCEDURE  ErasePoly      (poly: PolyHandle);
PROCEDURE  InvertPoly     (poly: PolyHandle);
PROCEDURE  FillPoly       (poly: PolyHandle; pat: Pattern);
```

Calculations with Points

```
PROCEDURE  AddPt          (srcPt: Point; VAR dstPt: Point);
PROCEDURE  SubPt          (srcPt: Point; VAR dstPt: Point);
PROCEDURE  SetPt          (VAR pt: Point; h,v: INTEGER);
FUNCTION   EqualPt        (pt1,pt2: Point) : BOOLEAN;
PROCEDURE  LocalToGlobal  (VAR pt: Point);
PROCEDURE  GlobalToLocal  (VAR pt: Point);
```

Miscellaneous Routines

```
FUNCTION   Random :    INTEGER;
FUNCTION   GetPixel    (h,v: INTEGER) : BOOLEAN;
PROCEDURE  StuffHex    (thingPtr: Ptr; s: Str255);
PROCEDURE  ScalePt     (VAR pt: Point; srcRect,dstRect: Rect);
PROCEDURE  MapPt       (VAR pt: Point; srcRect,dstRect: Rect);
PROCEDURE  MapRect     (VAR r: Rect; srcRect,dstRect: Rect);
PROCEDURE  MapRgn      (rgn: RgnHandle; srcRect,dstRect: Rect);
PROCEDURE  MapPoly     (poly: PolyHandle; srcRect,dstRect: Rect);
```

Customizing QuickDraw Operations

```
PROCEDURE SetStdProcs    (VAR procs: QDProcs);
PROCEDURE StdText        (byteCount: INTEGER; textBuf: Ptr; numer,denom:
                          Point);
PROCEDURE StdLine        (newPt: Point);
PROCEDURE StdRect        (verb: GrafVerb; r: Rect);
PROCEDURE StdRRect       (verb: GrafVerb; r: Rect; ovalwidth,ovalHeight:
                          INTEGER);
PROCEDURE StdOval        (verb: GrafVerb; r: Rect);
PROCEDURE StdArc         (verb: GrafVerb; r: Rect; startAngle,arcAngle:
                          INTEGER);
PROCEDURE StdPoly        (verb: GrafVerb; poly: PolyHandle);
PROCEDURE StdRgn         (verb: GrafVerb; rgn: RgnHandle);
PROCEDURE StdBits        (VAR srcBits: BitMap; VAR srcRect,dstRect: Rect;
                          mode: INTEGER; maskRgn: RgnHandle);
PROCEDURE StdComment     (kind,dataSize: INTEGER; dataHandle: Handle);
FUNCTION  StdTxMeas      (byteCount: INTEGER; textAddr: Ptr; VAR numer,
                          denom: Point; VAR info: FontInfo) : INTEGER;
PROCEDURE StdGetPic      (dataPtr: Ptr; byteCount: INTEGER);
PROCEDURE StdPutPic      (dataPtr: Ptr; byteCount: INTEGER);
```

Assembly-Language Information

Constants

```
; Size in bytes of QuickDraw global variables

grafSize        .EQU        206

; Source transfer modes

srcCopy         .EQU        0
srcOr           .EQU        1
srcXor          .EQU        2
srcBic          .EQU        3
notSrcCopy      .EQU        4
notSrcOr        .EQU        5
notSrcXor       .EQU        6
notSrcBic       .EQU        7

; Pattern transfer modes

patCopy         .EQU        8
patOr           .EQU        9
patXor          .EQU        10
patBic          .EQU        11
notPatCopy      .EQU        12
notPatOr        .EQU        13
notPatXor       .EQU        14
notPatBic       .EQU        15
```

```
; Standard colors for ForeColor and BackColor

blackColor      .EQU     33
whiteColor      .EQU     30
redColor        .EQU     205
greenColor      .EQU     341
blueColor       .EQU     409
cyanColor       .EQU     273
magentaColor    .EQU     137
yellowColor     .EQU     69

; Standard picture comments

picLParen       .EQU     0
picRParen       .EQU     1

; Character style

boldBit         .EQU     0
italicBit       .EQU     1
ulineBit        .EQU     2
outlineBit      .EQU     3
shadowBit       .EQU     4
condenseBit     .EQU     5
extendBit       .EQU     6

; Graphic operations

frame           .EQU     0
paint           .EQU     1
erase           .EQU     2
invert          .EQU     3
fill            .EQU     4
```

Point Data Structure

v	Vertical coordinate (word)
h	Horizontal coordinate (word)

Rectangle Data Structure

top	Vertical coordinate of top left corner (word)
left	Horizontal coordinate of top left corner (word)
bottom	Vertical coordinate of bottom right corner (word)
right	Horizontal coordinate of bottom right corner (word)
topLeft	Top left corner (point; long)
botRight	Bottom right corner (point; long)

Region Data Structure

rgnSize	Size in bytes (word)
rgnBBox	Enclosing rectangle (8 bytes)
rgnData	More data if not rectangular

Bit Map Data Structure

baseAddr	Pointer to bit image
rowBytes	Row width (word)
bounds	Boundary rectangle (8 bytes)
bitMapRec	Size in bytes of bit map data structure

Cursor Data Structure

data	Cursor image (32 bytes)
mask	Cursor mask (32 bytes)
hotSpot	Point aligned with mouse (long)
cursRec	Size in bytes of cursor data structure

Structure of QDProcs Record

textProc	Address of text-drawing routine
lineProc	Address of line-drawing routine
rectProc	Address of rectangle-drawing routine
rRectProc	Address of roundRect-drawing routine
ovalProc	Address of oval-drawing routine
arcProc	Address of arc/wedge-drawing routine
polyProc	Address of polygon-drawing routine
rgnProc	Address of region-drawing routine
bitsProc	Address of bit-transfer routine
commentProc	Address of routine for processing picture comments
txMeasProc	Address of routine for measuring text width
getPicProc	Address of picture-retrieval routine
putPicProc	Address of picture-saving routine
qdProcsRec	Size in bytes of QDProcs record

GrafPort Data Structure

device	Font-specific information (word)
portBits	GrafPort's bit map (bitMapRec bytes)
portBounds	Boundary rectangle of grafPort's bit map (8 bytes)
portRect	GrafPort's rectangle (8 bytes)
visRgn	Handle to visible region
clipRgn	Handle to clipping region
bkPat	Background pattern (8 bytes)
fillPat	Fill pattern (8 bytes)
pnLoc	Pen location (point; long)

6 QuickDraw

pnSize	Pen size (point; long)
pnMode	Pen's transfer mode (word)
pnPat	Pen pattern (8 bytes)
pnVis	Pen visibility (word)
txFont	Font number for text (word)
txFace	Text's character style (word)
txMode	Text's transfer mode (word)
txSize	Font size for text (word)
spExtra	Extra space (long)
fgColor	Foreground color (long)
bkColor	Background color (long)
colrBit	Color bit (word)
picSave	Handle to picture being saved
rgnSave	Handle to region being saved
polySave	Handle to polygon being saved
grafProcs	Pointer to QDProcs record
portRec	Size in bytes of grafPort

Picture Data Structure

picSize	Size in bytes (word)
picFrame	Picture frame (rectangle; 8 bytes)
picData	Picture definition data

Polygon Data Structure

polySize	Size in bytes (word)
polyBBox	Enclosing rectangle (8 bytes)
polyPoints	Polygon points

Pen State Data Structure

psLoc	Pen location (point; long)
psSize	Pen size (point; long)
psMode	Pen's transfer mode (word)
psPat	Pen pattern (8 bytes)
psRec	Size in bytes of pen state data structure

Font Information Data Structure

ascent	Ascent (word)
descent	Descent (word)
widMax	Maximum character width (word)
leading	Leading (word)

Special Macro Names

Pascal name	Macro name
SetPortBits	_SetPBits
InvertRect	_InverRect
InvertRoundRect	_InverRoundRect
DisposeRgn	_DisposRgn
SetRectRgn	_SetRecRgn
OffsetRgn	_OfSetRgn
InvertRgn	_InverRgn
ClosePoly	_ClosePgon

Variables

RndSeed   Random number seed (long)

7 THE FONT MANAGER

ABOUT THIS CHAPTER

The Font Manager is the part of the Toolbox that supports the use of various character fonts when you draw text with QuickDraw. This chapter introduces you to the Font Manager and describes the routines your application can call to get font information. It also describes the data structures of fonts and discusses how the Font Manager communicates with QuickDraw.

You should already be familiar with:

- the Resource Manager

- the basic concepts and structures behind QuickDraw, particularly bit images and how to draw text

ABOUT THE FONT MANAGER

The main function of the Font Manager is to provide font support for QuickDraw. To the Macintosh user, **font** means the complete set of characters of one typeface; it doesn't include the size of the characters, and usually doesn't include any stylistic variations (such as bold and italic).

> **Note:** Usually fonts are defined in the plain style and stylistic variations are applied to them; for example, the italic style simply slants the plain characters. However, fonts may be designed to include stylistic variations in the first place.

The way you identify a font to QuickDraw or the Font Manager is with a **font number**. Every font also has a name (such as "New York") that's appropriate to include in a menu of available fonts.

The size of the characters, called the **font size**, is given in **points**. Here this term doesn't have the same meaning as the "point" that's an intersection of lines on the QuickDraw coordinate plane, but instead is a typographical term that stands for approximately 1/72 inch. The font size measures the distance between the ascent line of one line of text and the ascent line of the next line of single-spaced text (see Figure 1).

> **Note:** Because measurements cannot be exact on a bit-mapped output device, the actual font size may be slightly different from what it would be in normal typography. Also be aware that two fonts with the same font size may not actually appear to be the same size; the font size is more useful for distinguishing different sizes of the same font (this is true even in typography).

Whenever you call a QuickDraw routine that does anything with text, QuickDraw passes the following information to the Font Manager:

- The font number.

- The character style, which is a set of stylistic variations. The empty set indicates plain text. (See chapter 6 for details.)

- The font size. The size may range from 1 point to 127 points, but for readability should be at least 6 points.

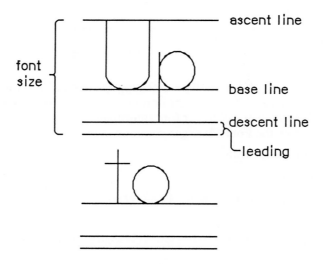

Figure 1. Font Size

- The horizontal and vertical **scaling factors**, each of which is represented by a numerator and a denominator (for example, a numerator of 2 and a denominator of 1 indicates 2-to-1 scaling in that direction).

- A Boolean value indicating whether the characters will actually be drawn or not. They will not be drawn, for example, when the QuickDraw function CharWidth is called (since it only measures characters) or when text is drawn after the pen has been hidden (such as by the HidePen procedure or the OpenPicture function, which calls HidePen).

- Device specific information that enables the Font Manager to achieve the best possible results when drawing text on a particular device. For details, see the section "Communication between QuickDraw and the Font Manager" below.

Given this information, the Font Manager provides QuickDraw with information describing the font and—if the characters will actually be drawn—the bits comprising the characters.

Fonts are stored as resources in resource files; the Font Manager calls the Resource Manager to read them into memory. System-defined fonts are stored in the system resource file. You may define your own fonts and include them in the system resource file so they can be shared among applications. In special cases, you may want to store a font in an application's resource file or even in the resource file for a document. It's also possible to store only the character widths and general font information, and not the bits comprising the characters, for those cases where the characters won't actually be drawn.

A font may be stored in any number of sizes in a resource file. If a size is needed that's not available as a resource, the Font Manager scales an available size.

Fonts occupy a large amount of storage: A 12-point font typically occupies about 3K bytes, and a 24-point font, about 10K bytes; fonts for use on a high resolution output device can take up four times as much space as that (up to 32K bytes). Fonts are normally purgeable, which means they may be removed from the heap when space is required by the Memory Manager. If you wish, you can call a Font Manager routine to make a font temporarily unpurgeable.

There are also routines that provide information about a font. You can find out the name of a font having a particular font number, or the font number for a font having a particular name. You can also learn whether a font is available in a certain size or will have to be scaled to that size.

FONT NUMBERS

The Font Manager includes the following font numbers for identifying system-defined fonts:

```
CONST  systemFont  = 0;     {system font}
       applFont    = 1;     {application font}
       newYork     = 2;
       geneva      = 3;
       monaco      = 4;
       venice      = 5;
       london      = 6;
       athens      = 7;
       sanFran     = 8;
       toronto     = 9;
       cairo       = 11;
       losAngeles  = 12;
       times       = 20;
       helvetica   = 21;
       courier     = 22;
       symbol      = 23;
       taliesin    = 24;
```

The **system font** is so called because it's the font used by the system (for drawing menu titles and commands in menus, for example). The name of the system font is Chicago. The size of text drawn by the system in this font is fixed at 12 points (called the **system font size**).

The **application font** is the font your application will use unless you specify otherwise. Unlike the system font, the application font isn't a separate font, but is essentially a reference to another font—Geneva, by default. (The application font number is determined by a value that you can set in parameter RAM; see chapter 13 in Volume II for more information.)

Assembly-language note: You can get the application font number from the global variable ApFontID.

Font numbers range from 0 to 255. Font numbers 0 through 127 are reserved for fonts provided by Apple. Font numbers 128 through 255 are assigned by Apple to fonts created by software vendors. To obtain a font number for your font and register its name (which must be unique), write to:

Macintosh Technical Support
Mail Stop 3-T
Apple Computer, Inc.
20525 Mariani Avenue
Cupertino, CA 95014

CHARACTERS IN A FONT

A font can consist of up to 255 distinct characters; not all characters need to be defined in a single font. Figure 2 shows the standard printing characters on the Macintosh and their ASCII codes (for example, the ASCII code for "A" is 41 hexadecimal, or 65 decimal).

Note: Codes $00 through $1F and code $7F are normally nonprinting characters (see chapter 8 for details).

The special characters in the system font with codes $11 through $14 can't normally be typed from the keyboard or keypad. The Font Manager defines constants for these characters:

```
CONST   commandMark  = $11;    {Command key symbol}
        checkMark    = $12;    {check mark}
        diamondMark  = $13;    {diamond symbol}
        appleMark    = $14;    {apple symbol}
```

In addition to its maximum of 255 characters, every font contains a **missing symbol** that's drawn in case of a request to draw a character that's missing from the font.

FONT SCALING

The information QuickDraw passes to the Font Manager includes the font size and the scaling factors QuickDraw wants to use. The Font Manager determines the font information it will return to QuickDraw by looking for the exact size needed among the sizes stored for the font. If the exact size requested isn't available, it then looks for a nearby size that it can scale, as follows:

1. It looks first for a font that's twice the size, and scales down that size if there is one.

2. If there's no font that's twice the size, it looks for a font that's half the size, and scales up that size if there is one.

3. If there's no font that's half the size, it looks for a larger size of the font, and scales down the next larger size if there is one.

4. If there's no larger size, it looks for a smaller size of the font, and scales up the closest smaller size if there is one.

5. If the font isn't available in any size at all, it uses the application font instead, scaling the font to the size requested.

6. If the application font isn't available in any size at all, it uses the system font instead, scaling the font to the size requested.

Scaling looks best when the scaled size is an even multiple of an available size.

Second digit ↓ \ First digit	0	1	2	3	4	5	6	7	8	9	A	B	C	D	E	F
0			space	0	@	P	`	p	Ä	ê	†	∞	¿	–		
1		⌘	!	1	A	Q	a	q	Å	ë	°	±	¡	—		
2		✓	"	2	B	R	b	r	Ç	í	¢	≤	¬	“		
3		◆	#	3	C	S	c	s	É	ì	£	≥	√	”		
4			$	4	D	T	d	t	Ñ	î	§	¥	ƒ	‘		
5			%	5	E	U	e	u	Ö	ï	●	µ	≈	’		
6			&	6	F	V	f	v	Ü	ñ	¶	∂	∆	÷		
7			'	7	G	W	g	w	á	ó	ß	∑	«	◊		
8			(	8	H	X	h	x	à	ò	®	∏	»	ÿ		
9			)	9	I	Y	i	y	â	ô	©	π	…			
A			*	:	J	Z	j	z	ä	ö	™	∫	␣			
B			+	;	K	[	k	{	ã	õ	´	ª	À			
C			,	<	L	\	l	|	å	ú	¨	º	Ã			
D			-	=	M	]	m	}	ç	ù	≠	Ω	Õ			
E			.	>	N	^	n	~	é	û	Æ	æ	Œ			
F			/	?	O	_	o		è	ü	Ø	ø	œ			

␣ stands for a nonbreaking space, the same width as a digit.
The first four characters are only in the system font (Chicago).
The shaded characters are not in all fonts.
Codes $D9 through $FF are reserved for future expansion.

Figure 2. Font Characters

Assembly-language note: You can use the global variable FScaleDisable to disable scaling, if desired. Normally, FScaleDisable is 0. If you set it to a nonzero value, the Font Manager will look for the size as described above but will return the font unscaled.

USING THE FONT MANAGER

The InitFonts procedure initializes the Font Manager; you should call it after initializing QuickDraw but before initializing the Window Manager.

You can set up a menu of fonts in your application by using the Menu Manager procedure AddResMenu (see chapter 11 for details). When the user chooses a menu item from the font menu, call the Menu Manager procedure GetItem to get the name of the corresponding font, and then the Font Manager function GetFNum to get the font number. The GetFontName function does the reverse of GetFNum: Given a font number, it returns the font name.

In a menu of font sizes in your application, you may want to let the user know which sizes the current font is available in and therefore will not require scaling (this is usually done by showing those font sizes outlined in the menu). You can call the RealFont function to find out whether a font is available in a given size.

If you know you'll be using a font a lot and don't want it to be purged, you can use the SetFontLock procedure to make the font unpurgeable during that time.

Advanced programmers who want to write their own font editors or otherwise manipulate fonts can access fonts directly with the FMSwapFont function.

FONT MANAGER ROUTINES

Initializing the Font Manager

```
PROCEDURE InitFonts;
```

InitFonts initializes the Font Manager. If the system font isn't already in memory, InitFonts reads it into memory. Call this procedure once before all other Font Manager routines or any Toolbox routine that will call the Font Manager.

Getting Font Information

Warning: Before returning, the routines in this section issue the Resource Manager call SetResLoad(TRUE). If your program previously called SetResLoad(FALSE) and you still want that to be in effect after calling one of these Font Manager routines, you'll have to call SetResLoad(FALSE) again.

```
PROCEDURE GetFontName (fontNum: INTEGER; VAR theName: Str255);
```

Assembly-language note: The macro you invoke to call GetFontName from assembly language is named _GetFName.

GetFontName returns in theName the name of the font having the font number fontNum. If there's no such font, GetFontName returns the empty string.

```
PROCEDURE GetFNum (fontName: Str255; VAR theNum: INTEGER);
```

GetFNum returns in theNum the font number for the font having the given fontName. If there's no such font, GetFNum returns 0.

```
FUNCTION RealFont (fontNum: INTEGER; size: INTEGER) : BOOLEAN;
```

RealFont returns TRUE if the font having the font number fontNum is available in the given size in a resource file, or FALSE if the font has to be scaled to that size.

Note: RealFont will always return FALSE if you pass applFont in fontNum. To find out if the application font is available in a particular size, call GetFontName and then GetFNum to get the actual font number for the application font, and then call RealFont with that number.

Keeping Fonts in Memory

```
PROCEDURE SetFontLock (lockFlag: BOOLEAN);
```

SetFontLock applies to the font in which text was most recently drawn. If lockFlag is TRUE, SetFontLock makes the font unpurgeable (reading it into memory if it isn't already there). If lockFlag is FALSE, it releases the memory occupied by the font (by calling the Resource Manager procedure ReleaseResource). Since fonts are normally purgeable, this procedure is useful for making a font temporarily unpurgeable.

Advanced Routine

The following low-level routine is called by QuickDraw and won't normally be used by an application directly, but it may be of interest to advanced programmers who want to bypass the QuickDraw routines that deal with text.

```
FUNCTION FMSwapFont (inRec: FMInput) : FMOutPtr;
```

FMSwapFont returns a pointer to a font output record containing the size, style, and other information about an adapted version of the font requested in the given font input record. (Font input and output records are explained in the following section.) FMSwapFont is called by QuickDraw every time a QuickDraw routine that does anything with text is used. If you want to call FMSwapFont yourself, you must build a font input record and then use the pointer returned by FMSwapFont to access the resulting font output record.

COMMUNICATION BETWEEN QUICKDRAW AND THE FONT MANAGER

This section describes the data structures that allow QuickDraw and the Font Manager to exchange information. It also discusses the communication that may occur between the Font Manager and the driver of the device on which the characters are being drawn or printed. You can skip this section if you want to change fonts, character style, and font sizes by calling QuickDraw and aren't interested in the lower-level data structures and routines of the Font Manager. To understand this section fully, you'll have to be familiar with device drivers and the Device Manager.

Whenever you call a QuickDraw routine that does anything with text, QuickDraw requests information from the Font Manager about the characters. The Font Manager performs any necessary calculations and returns the requested information to QuickDraw. As illustrated in Figure 3, this information exchange occurs via two data structures, a font input record (type FMInput) and a font output record (type FMOutput).

First, QuickDraw passes the Font Manager a font input record:

```
TYPE FMInput =  PACKED RECORD
                family:   INTEGER;   {font number}
                size:     INTEGER;   {font size}
                face:     Style;     {character style}
                needBits: BOOLEAN;   {TRUE if drawing}
                device:   INTEGER;   {device-specific information}
                numer:    Point;     {numerators of scaling factors}
                denom:    Point      {denominators of scaling factors}
              END;
```

The first three fields contain the font number, size, and character style that QuickDraw wants to use.

The needBits field indicates whether the characters actually will be drawn or not. If the characters are being drawn, all of the information describing the font, including the bit image comprising the characters, will be read into memory. If the characters aren't being drawn and there's a resource consisting of only the character widths and general font information, that resource will be read instead.

The high-order byte of the device field contains a device driver reference number. From the driver reference number, the Font Manager can determine the optimum stylistic variations on the font to produce the highest-quality printing or drawing available on a device (as explained below). The low-order byte of the device field is ignored by the Font Manager but may contain information used by the device driver.

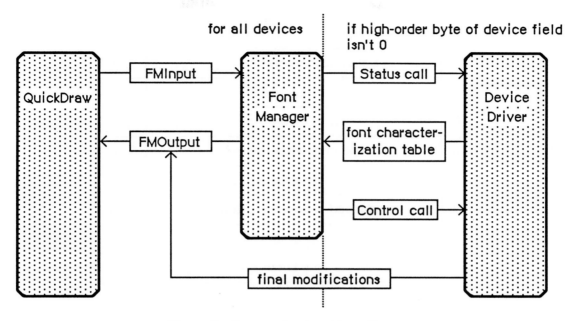

Figure 3. Communication About Fonts

The numer and denom fields contain the scaling factors to be used; numer.v divided by denom.v gives the vertical scaling, and numer.h divided by denom.h gives the horizontal scaling.

The Font Manager takes the font input record and asks the Resource Manager for the font. If the requested size isn't available, the Font Manager scales another size to match (as described under "Font Scaling" above).

Then the Font Manager gets the **font characterization table** via the device field. If the high-order byte of the device field is 0, the Font Manager gets the screen's font characterization table (which is stored in the Font Manager). If the high-order byte of the device field is nonzero, the Font Manager calls the status routine of the device driver having that reference number, and the status routine returns a font characterization table. The status routine may use the value of the low-order byte of the device field to determine the font characterization table it should return.

Note: If you want to make your own calls to the device driver's Status function, the reference number must be the driver reference number from the font input record's device field, csCode must be 8, csParam must be a pointer to where the device driver should put the font characterization table, and csParam+4 must be an integer containing the value of the font input record's device field.

Figure 4 shows the structure of a font characterization table and, on the right, the values it contains for the Macintosh screen.

		screen
byte 0	dots per vertical inch on device	80
2	dots per horizontal inch on device	80
4	bold characteristics	0, 1, 1
7	italic characteristics	1, 8, 0
10	not used	0, 0, 0
13	outline characteristics	5, 1, 1
16	shadow characteristics	5, 2, 2
19	condensed characteristics	0, 0,-1
22	extended characteristics	0, 0, 1
25	underline characteristics	1, 1, 1

Figure 4. Font Characterization Table

The first two words of the font characterization table contain the approximate number of dots per inch on the device. These values are only used for scaling between devices; they don't necessarily correspond to a device's actual resolution.

The remainder of the table consists of three-byte triplets providing information about the different stylistic variations. For all but the triplet defining the underline characteristics:

- The first byte in the triplet indicates which byte beyond the bold field of the font output record (see below) is affected by the triplet.

- The second byte contains the amount to be stored in the affected field.

- The third byte indicates the amount by which the extra field of the font output record is to be incremented (starting from 0).

The triplet defining the underline characteristics indicates the amount by which the font output record's ulOffset, ulShadow, and ulThick fields (respectively) should be incremented.

Based on the information in the font characterization table, the Font Manager determines the optimum ascent, descent, and leading, so that the highest-quality printing or drawing available will be produced. It then stores this information in a font output record:

```
TYPE FMOutput =
        PACKED RECORD
            errNum:      INTEGER;       {not used}
            fontHandle:  Handle;        {handle to font record}
            bold:        Byte;          {bold factor}
            italic:      Byte;          {italic factor}
            ulOffset:    Byte;          {underline offset}
            ulShadow:    Byte;          {underline shadow}
            ulThick:     Byte;          {underline thickness}
            shadow:      Byte;          {shadow factor}
            extra:       SignedByte;    {width of style}
            ascent:      Byte;          {ascent}
            descent:     Byte;          {descent}
            widMax:      Byte;          {maximum character width}
            leading:     SignedByte;    {leading}
            unused:      Byte;          {not used}
            numer:       Point;         {numerators of scaling factors}
            denom:       Point          {denominators of scaling factors}
        END;
```

ErrNum is reserved for future use, and is set to 0. FontHandle is a handle to the font record of the font, as described in the next section. Bold, italic, ulOffset, ulShadow, ulThick, and shadow are all fields that modify the way stylistic variations are done; their values are taken from the font characterization table, and are used by QuickDraw. (You'll need to experiment with these values if you want to determine exactly how they're used.) Extra indicates the number of pixels that each character has been widened by stylistic variation. For example, using the screen values shown in Figure 4, the extra field for bold shadowed characters would be 3. Ascent, descent, widMax, and leading are the same as the fields of the FontInfo record returned by the QuickDraw procedure GetFontInfo. Numer and denom contain the scaling factors.

Just before returning this record to QuickDraw, the Font Manager calls the device driver's control routine to allow the driver to make any final modifications to the record. Finally, the font information is returned to QuickDraw via a pointer to the record, defined as follows:

```
TYPE FMOutPtr = ^FMOutput;
```

Note: If you want to make your own calls to the device driver's Control function, the reference number must be the driver reference number from the font input record's device field, csCode must be 8, csParam must be a pointer to the font output record, and csParam+4 must be the value of the font input record's device field.

FORMAT OF A FONT

This section describes the data structure that defines a font; you need to read it only if you're going to define your own fonts or write your own font editor.

Each character in a font is defined by bits arranged in rows and columns. This bit arrangement is called a **character image**; it's the image inside each of the character rectangles shown in Figure 5.

The **base line** is a horizontal line coincident with the bottom of each character, excluding descenders.

The **character origin** is a point on the base line used as a reference location for drawing the character. Conceptually the base line is the line that the pen is on when it starts drawing a character, and the character origin is the point where the pen starts drawing.

The **character rectangle** is a rectangle enclosing the character image; its sides are defined by the **image width** and the **font height**:

- The image width is simply the width of the character image, which varies among characters in the font. It may or may not include space on either side of the character; to minimize the amount of memory required to store the font, it should not include space.

- The font height is the distance from the ascent line to the descent line (which is the same for all characters in the font).

The image width is different from the **character width**, which is the distance to move the pen from this character's origin to the next character's origin while drawing. The character width may be 0, in which case the following character will be superimposed on this character (useful for accents, underscores, and so on). Characters whose image width is 0 (such as a space) can have a nonzero character width.

Characters in a **proportional font** all have character widths proportional to their image width, whereas characters in a **fixed-width** font all have the same character width.

Characters can **kern**; that is, they can overlap adjacent characters. The first character in Figure 5 below doesn't kern, but the second one kerns left.

In addition to the terms used to describe individual characters, there are terms describing features of the font as a whole (see Figure 6).

The **font rectangle** is related to the character rectangle. Imagine that all the character images in the font are superimposed with their origins coinciding. The smallest rectangle enclosing all the superimposed images is the font rectangle.

The **ascent** is the distance from the base line to the top of the font rectangle, and the **descent** is the distance from the base line to the bottom of the font rectangle.

The height of the font rectangle is the font height, which is the same as the height of each character rectangle. The maximum height is 127 pixels. The maximum width of the font rectangle is 254 pixels.

The **leading** is the amount of blank space to draw between lines of single spaced text—the distance between the descent line of one line of text and the ascent line of the next line of text.

Finally, for each character in a font there's a **character offset**. As illustrated in Figure 7, the character offset is simply the difference in position of the character rectangle for a given character and the font rectangle.

Every font has a bit image that contains a complete sequence of all its character images (see Figure 8). The number of rows in the bit image is equivalent to the font height. The character images in the font are stored in the bit image as though the characters were laid out horizontally (in ASCII order, by convention) along a common base line.

The bit image doesn't have to contain a character image for every character in the font. Instead, any characters marked as being missing from the font are omitted from the bit image. When QuickDraw tries to draw such characters, a missing symbol is drawn instead. The missing symbol is stored in the bit image after all the other character images.

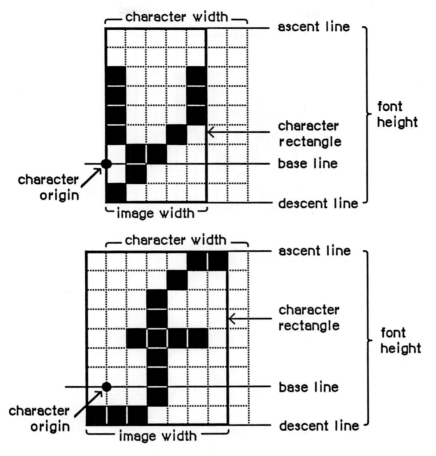

Figure 5. Character Images

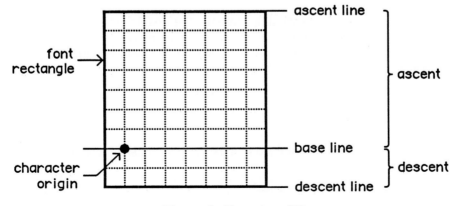

Figure 6. Features of Fonts

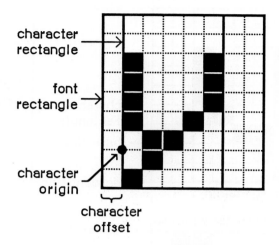

Figure 7. Character Offset

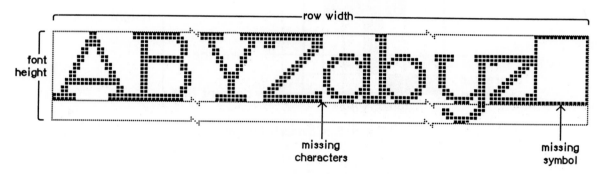

Figure 8. Partial Bit Image for a Font

Warning: Every font *must* have a missing symbol. The characters with ASCII codes 0 (NUL), $09 (horizontal tab), and $0D (Return) must *not* be missing from the font if there's any chance it will ever be used by TextEdit; usually they'll be zero-length, but you may want to store a space for the tab character.

Font Records

The information describing a font is contained in a data structure called a **font record,** which contains the following:

- the font type (fixed-width or proportional)
- the ASCII code of the first character and the last character in the font

■ the maximum character width and maximum amount any character kerns

■ the font height, ascent, descent, and leading

■ the bit image of the font

■ a **location table,** which is an array of words specifying the location of each character image within the bit image

■ an **offset/width table,** which is an array of words specifying the character offset and character width for each character in the font

For every character, the location table contains a word that specifies the bit offset to the location of that character's image in the bit image. The entry for a character missing from the font contains the same value as the entry for the next character. The last word of the table contains the offset to one bit beyond the end of the bit image (that is, beyond the character image for the missing symbol). The image width of each character is determined from the location table by subtracting the bit offset to that character from the bit offset to the next character in the table.

There's also one word in the offset/width table for every character: The high-order byte specifies the character offset and the low order byte specifies the character width. Missing characters are flagged in this table by a word value of −1. The last word is also −1, indicating the end of the table.

Note: The total space occupied by the bit image, location table, and offset/width table cannot exceed 32K bytes. For this reason, the practical font size limit for a full font is about 40 points.

Figure 9 illustrates a sample location table and offset/width table corresponding to the bit image in Figure 8 above.

A font record is referred to by a handle that you can get by calling the FMSwapFont function or the Resource Manager function GetResource. The data type for a font record is as follows:

```
TYPE FontRec =
        RECORD
            fontType:     INTEGER;   {font type}
            firstChar:    INTEGER;   {ASCII code of first character}
            lastChar:     INTEGER;   {ASCII code of last character}
            widMax:       INTEGER;   {maximum character width}
            kernMax:      INTEGER;   {negative of maximum character kern}
            nDescent:     INTEGER;   {negative of descent}
            fRectWidth:   INTEGER;   {width of font rectangle}
            fRectHeight:  INTEGER;   {height of font rectangle}
            owTLoc:       INTEGER;   {offset to offset/width table}
            ascent:       INTEGER;   {ascent}
            descent:      INTEGER;   {descent}
            leading:      INTEGER;   {leading}
            rowWords:     INTEGER;   {row width of bit image / 2}
        { bitImage:     ARRAY[1..rowWords,1..fRectHeight] OF INTEGER; }
                                    {bit image}
        { locTable:     ARRAY[firstChar..lastChar+2] OF INTEGER; }
                                    {location table}
        { owTable:      ARRAY[firstChar..lastChar+2] OF INTEGER; }
                                    {offset/width table}
        END;
```

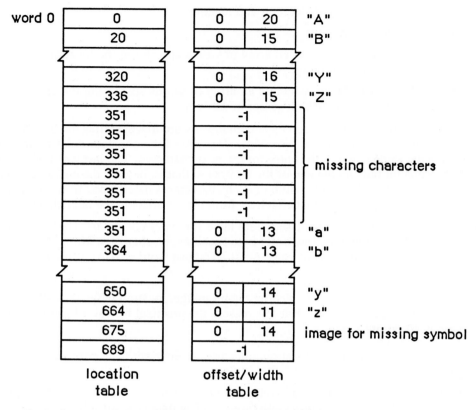

Figure 9. Sample Location Table and Offset/Width Table

Note: The variable-length arrays appear as comments because they're not valid Pascal syntax; they're used only as conceptual aids.

The fontType field must contain one of the following predefined constants:

```
CONST propFont  = $9000;    {proportional font}
      fixedFont = $B000;    {fixed-width font}
```

The values in the widMax, kernMax, nDescent, fRectWidth, fRectHeight, ascent, descent, and leading fields all specify a number of pixels.

KernMax indicates the largest number of pixels any character kerns, that is, the distance from the character origin to the left edge of the font rectangle. It should always be 0 or negative, since the kerned pixels are to the left of the character origin. NDescent is the negative of the descent (the distance from the character origin to the bottom of the font rectangle).

The owTLoc field contains a word offset from itself to the offset/width table; it's equivalent to

4 + (rowWords * fRectHeight) + (lastChar–firstChar+3) + 1

Warning: Remember, the offset and row width in a font record are given in *words*, not bytes.

Assembly-language note: The global variable ROMFont0 contains a handle to the font record for the system font.

Font Widths

A resource can be defined that consists of only the character widths and general font information —everything but the font's bit image and location table. If there is such a resource, it will be read in whenever QuickDraw doesn't need to draw the text, such as when you call one of the routines CharWidth, HidePen, or OpenPicture (which calls HidePen). The FontRec data type described above, minus the rowWords, bitImage, and locTable fields, reflects the structure of this type of resource. The owTLoc field will contain 4, and the fontType field will contain the following predefined constant:

```
CONST fontWid = $ACB0;  {font width data}
```

How QuickDraw Draws Text

This section provides a conceptual discussion of the steps QuickDraw takes to draw characters (without scaling or stylistic variations such as bold and outline). Basically, QuickDraw simply copies the character image onto the drawing area at a specific location.

1. Take the initial pen location as the character origin for the first character.

2. In the offset/width table, check the word for the character to see if it's –1.

   2a. The character exists if the entry in the offset/width table isn't –1. Determine the character offset and character width from this entry. Find the character image at the location in the bit image specified by the location table. Calculate the image width by subtracting this word from the succeeding word in the location table. Determine the number of pixels the character kerns by adding kernMax to the character offset.

   2b. The character is missing if the entry in the offset/width table is –1; information about the missing symbol is needed. Determine the missing symbol's character offset and character width from the next-to-last word in the offset/width table. Find the missing symbol at the location in the bit image specified by the next-to-last word in the location table. Calculate the image width by subtracting the next-to-last word in the location table from the last word in the table. Determine the number of pixels the missing symbol kerns by adding kernMax to the character offset.

3. If the fontType field is fontWid, return to step 2; otherwise, copy each row of the character image onto the drawing area, one row at a time. The number of bits to copy from each word is given by the image width, and the number of words is given by the fRectHeight field.

4. If the fontType field is propFont, move the pen to the right the number of pixels specified by the character width. If fontType is fixedFont, move the pen to the right the number of pixels specified by the widMax field.

5. Return to step 2.

FONTS IN A RESOURCE FILE

Every size of a font is stored as a separate resource. The resource type for a font is 'FONT'. The resource data for a font is simply a font record:

Number of bytes	Contents
2 bytes	FontType field of font record
2 bytes	FirstChar field of font record
2 bytes	LastChar field of font record
2 bytes	WidMax field of font record
2 bytes	KernMax field of font record
2 bytes	NDescent field of font record
2 bytes	FRectWidth field of font record
2 bytes	FRectHeight field of font record
2 bytes	OWTLoc field of font record
2 bytes	Ascent field of font record
2 bytes	Descent field of font record
2 bytes	Leading field of font record
2 bytes	RowWords field of font record
n bytes	Bit image of font n = 2 * rowWords * fRectHeight
m bytes	Location table of font m = 2 * (lastChar–firstChar+3)
m bytes	Offset/width table of font m = 2 * (lastChar–firstChar+3)

The resource type 'FWID' is used to store only the character widths and general information for a font; its resource data is a font record without the rowWords field, bit image, and location table.

As shown in Figure 10, the resource ID of a font has the following format: Bits 0-6 are the font size, bits 7-14 are the font number, and bit 15 is 0. Thus the resource ID corresponding to a given font number and size is

(128 * font number) + font size

Since 0 is not a valid font size, the resource ID having 0 in the size field is used to provide only the name of the font: The name of the resource is the font name. For example, for a font named Griffin and numbered 200, the resource naming the font would have a resource ID of 25600 and the resource name 'Griffin'. Size 10 of that font would be stored in a resource numbered 25610.

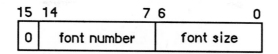

Figure 10. Resource ID for a Font

There's another type of resource related to fonts: 'FRSV', which identifies fonts that are used by the system. Its format is as follows:

Number of bytes	Contents
2 bytes	Number of font resource IDs
n * 2 bytes	n font resource IDs

The Font Mover program looks at the 'FRSV' resource having the resource ID 1, and won't remove the indicated fonts from the system resource file.

SUMMARY OF THE FONT MANAGER

Constants

```
CONST  { Font numbers }

        systemFont  = 0;    {system font}
        applFont    = 1;    {application font}
        newYork     = 2;
        geneva      = 3;
        monaco      = 4;
        venice      = 5;
        london      = 6;
        athens      = 7;
        sanFran     = 8;
        toronto     = 9;
        cairo       = 11;
        losAngeles  = 12;
        times       = 20;
        helvetica   = 21;
        courier     = 22;
        symbol      = 23;
        taliesin    = 24;

        { Special characters }

        commandMark  = $11;   {Command key symbol}
        checkMark    = $12;   {check mark}
        diamondMark  = $13;   {diamond symbol}
        appleMark    = $14;   {apple symbol}

        { Font types }

        propFont   = $9000;   {proportional font}
        fixedFont  = $B000;   {fixed-width font}
        fontWid    = $ACB0;   {font width data}
```

Data Types

```
TYPE FMInput = PACKED RECORD
                family:   INTEGER;   {font number}
                size:     INTEGER;   {font size}
                face:     Style;     {character style}
                needBits: BOOLEAN;   {TRUE if drawing}
                device:   INTEGER;   {device-specific information}
                numer:    Point;     {numerators of scaling factors}
                denom:    Point      {denominators of scaling factors}
              END;
```

```
FMOutPtr = ^FMOutput;
FMOutput =
      PACKED RECORD
          errNum:       INTEGER;       {not used}
          fontHandle:   Handle;        {handle to font record}
          bold:         Byte;          {bold factor}
          italic:       Byte;          {italic factor}
          ulOffset:     Byte;          {underline offset}
          ulShadow:     Byte;          {underline shadow}
          ulThick:      Byte;          {underline thickness}
          shadow:       Byte;          {shadow factor}
          extra:        SignedByte;    {width of style}
          ascent:       Byte;          {ascent}
          descent:      Byte;          {descent}
          widMax:       Byte;          {maximum character width}
          leading:      SignedByte;    {leading}
          unused:       Byte;          {not used}
          numer:        Point;         {numerators of scaling factors}
          denom:        Point          {denominators of scaling factors}
      END;

FontRec =
      RECORD
          fontType:     INTEGER;   {font type}
          firstChar:    INTEGER;   {ASCII code of first character}
          lastChar:     INTEGER;   {ASCII code of last character}
          widMax:       INTEGER;   {maximum character width}
          kernMax:      INTEGER;   {negative of maximum character kern}
          nDescent:     INTEGER;   {negative of descent}
          fRectWidth:   INTEGER;   {width of font rectangle}
          fRectHeight:  INTEGER;   {height of font rectangle}
          owTLoc:       INTEGER;   {offset to offset/width table}
          ascent:       INTEGER;   {ascent}
          descent:      INTEGER;   {descent}
          leading:      INTEGER;   {leading}
          rowWords:     INTEGER;   {row width of bit image / 2}
        { bitImage:     ARRAY[1..rowWords,1..fRectHeight] OF INTEGER; }
                                   {bit image}
        { locTable:     ARRAY[firstChar..lastChar+2] OF INTEGER; }
                                   {location table}
        { owTable:      ARRAY[firstChar..lastChar+2] OF INTEGER; }
                                   {offset/width table}
      END;
```

Routines

Initializing the Font Manager

```
PROCEDURE InitFonts;
```

Getting Font Information

```
PROCEDURE GetFontName (fontNum: INTEGER; VAR theName: Str255);
PROCEDURE GetFNum     (fontName: Str255; VAR theNum: INTEGER);
FUNCTION  RealFont    (fontNum: INTEGER; size: INTEGER) : BOOLEAN;
```

Keeping Fonts in Memory

```
PROCEDURE SetFontLock (lockFlag: BOOLEAN);
```

Advanced Routine

```
FUNCTION FMSwapFont (inRec: FMInput) : FMOutPtr;
```

Assembly-Language Information

Constants

```
; Font numbers

sysFont       .EQU   0        ;system font
applFont      .EQU   1        ;application font
newYork       .EQU   2
geneva        .EQU   3
monaco        .EQU   4
venice        .EQU   5
london        .EQU   6
athens        .EQU   7
sanFran       .EQU   8
toronto       .EQU   9
cairo         .EQU   11
losAngeles    .EQU   12
times         .EQU   20
helvetica     .EQU   21
courier       .EQU   22
symbol        .EQU   23
taliesin      .EQU   24

; Special characters

commandMark   .EQU   $11      ;Command key symbol
checkMark     .EQU   $12      ;check mark
diamondMark   .EQU   $13      ;diamond symbol
appleMark     .EQU   $14      ;apple symbol
```

```
; Font types

propFont       .EQU    $9000   ;proportional font
fixedFont      .EQU    $B000   ;fixed-width font
fontWid        .EQU    $ACB0   ;font width data

; Control and Status call code

fMgrCtl1       .EQU    8       ;code used to get and modify font
                               ; characterization table
```

Font Input Record Data Structure

fmInFamily	Font number (word)
fmInSize	Font size (word)
fmInFace	Character style (word)
fmInNeedBits	Nonzero if drawing (byte)
fmInDevice	Device-specific information (byte)
fmInNumer	Numerators of scaling factors (point; long)
fmInDenom	Denominators of scaling factors (point; long)

Font Output Record Data Structure

fmOutFontH	Handle to font record
fmOutBold	Bold factor (byte)
fmOutItalic	Italic factor (byte)
fmOutUlOffset	Underline offset (byte)
fmOutUlShadow	Underline shadow (byte)
fmOutUlThick	Underline thickness (byte)
fmOutShadow	Shadow factor (byte)
fmOutExtra	Width of style (byte)
fmOutAscent	Ascent (byte)
fmOutDescent	Descent (byte)
fmOutWidMax	Maximum character width (byte)
fmOutLeading	Leading (byte)
fmOutNumer	Numerators of scaling factors (point; long)
fmOutDenom	Denominators of scaling factors (point; long)

Font Record Data Structure

fFontType	Font type (word)
fFirstChar	ASCII code of first character (word)
fLastChar	ASCII code of last character (word)
fWidMax	Maximum character width (word)
fKernMax	Negative of maximum character kern (word)
fNDescent	Negative of descent (word)
fFRectWidth	Width of font rectangle (word)
fFRectHeight	Height of font rectangle (word)
fOWTLoc	Offset to offset/width table (word)

7 Font Manager

fAscent	Ascent (word)
fDescent	Descent (word)
fLeading	Leading (word)
fRowWords	Row width of bit image / 2 (word)

Special Macro Names

Pascal name	Macro name
GetFontName	_GetFName

Variables

ApFontID	Font number of application font (word)
FScaleDisable	Nonzero to disable scaling (byte)
ROMFont0	Handle to font record for system font

8 THE TOOLBOX EVENT MANAGER

ABOUT THIS CHAPTER

This chapter describes the Event Manager, the part of the Toolbox that allows your application to monitor the user's actions, such as those involving the mouse, keyboard, and keypad. The Event Manager is also used by other parts of the Toolbox; for instance, the Window Manager uses events to coordinate the ordering and display of windows on the screen.

There are actually two Event Managers: one in the Operating System and one in the Toolbox. The Toolbox Event Manager calls the Operating System Event Manager and serves as an interface between it and your application; it also adds some features that aren't present at the Operating System level, such as the window management facilities mentioned above. This chapter describes the Toolbox Event Manager, which is the one your application will ordinarily deal with. All references to "the Event Manager" should be understood to refer to the Toolbox Event Manager. For information on the Operating System's Event Manager, see chapter 3 of Volume II.

> **Note:** Most of the constants and data types presented in this chapter are actually defined in the Operating System Event Manager; they're explained here because they're essential to understanding the Toolbox Event Manager.

You should already be familiar with resources and with the basic concepts and structures behind QuickDraw.

ABOUT THE TOOLBOX EVENT MANAGER

The Toolbox Event Manager is your application's link to its user. Whenever the user presses the mouse button, types on the keyboard or keypad, or inserts a disk in a disk drive, your application is notified by means of an **event**. A typical Macintosh application program is event-driven: It decides what to do from moment to moment by asking the Event Manager for events and responding to them one by one in whatever way is appropriate.

Although the Event Manager's primary purpose is to monitor the user's actions and pass them to your application in an orderly way, it also serves as a convenient mechanism for sending signals from one part of your application to another. For instance, the Window Manager uses events to coordinate the ordering and display of windows as the user activates and deactivates them and moves them around on the screen. You can also define your own types of events and use them in any way you wish.

Most events waiting to be processed are kept in the **event queue**, where they're stored (**posted**) by the Operating System Event Manager. The Toolbox Event Manager retrieves events from this queue for your application and also reports other events that aren't kept in the queue, such as those related to windows. In general, events are collected from a variety of sources and reported to your application on demand, one at a time. Events aren't necessarily reported in the order they occurred; some have a higher priority than others.

There are several different types of events. You can restrict some Event Manager routines to apply only to certain event types, in effect disabling the other types.

Other operations your application can perform with Event Manager routines include:

8 Toolbox Event

■ directly reading the current state of the keyboard, keypad, and mouse button

■ monitoring the location of the mouse

■ finding out how much time has elapsed since the system last started up

The Event Manager also provides a **journaling mechanism,** which enables events to be fed to the Event Manager from a source other than the user.

EVENT TYPES

Events are of various types, depending on their origin and meaning. Some report actions by the user; others are generated by the Window Manager, by device drivers, or by your application itself for its own purposes. Some events are handled by the system before your application ever sees them; others are left for your application to handle in its own way.

The most important event types are those that record actions by the user:

■ **Mouse-down** and **mouse-up events** occur when the user presses or releases the mouse button.

■ **Key-down** and **key-up events** occur when the user presses or releases a key on the keyboard or keypad. **Auto-key events** are generated when the user holds down a repeating key. Together, these three event types are called **keyboard events.**

■ **Disk-inserted events** occur when the user inserts a disk into a disk drive or takes any other action that requires a volume to be mounted (as described in chapter 4 in Volume II). For example, a hard disk that contains several volumes may also post a disk-inserted event.

Note: Mere movements of the mouse are not reported as events. If necessary, your application can keep track of them by periodically asking the Event Manager for the current location of the mouse.

The following event types are generated by the Window Manager to coordinate the display of windows on the screen:

■ **Activate events** are generated whenever an inactive window becomes active or an active window becomes inactive. They generally occur in pairs (that is, one window is deactivated and then another is activated).

■ **Update events** occur when all or part of a window's contents need to be drawn or redrawn, usually as a result of the user's opening, closing, activating, or moving a window.

Another event type (**device driver event**) may be generated by device drivers in certain situations; for example, a driver might be set up to report an event when its transmission of data is interrupted. The chapters describing the individual drivers will tell you about any specific device driver events that may occur.

A **network event** may be generated by the AppleTalk Manager. It contains a handle to a parameter block; for details, see chapter 10 of Volume II.

In addition, your application can define as many as four event types of its own and use them for any desired purpose.

Note: You place application-defined events in the event queue with the Operating System Event Manager procedure PostEvent. See chapter 3 of Volume II for details.

One final type of event is the **null event**, which is what the Event Manager returns if it has no other events to report.

PRIORITY OF EVENTS

The event queue is a FIFO (first-in-first-out) list—that is, events are retrieved from the queue in the order they were originally posted. However, the way that various types of events are generated and detected causes some events to have higher priority than others. (Remember, not all events are kept in the event queue.) Furthermore, when you ask the Event Manager for an event, you can specify particular types that are of interest; doing so can cause some events to be passed over in favor of others that were actually posted later. The following discussion is limited to the event types you've specifically requested in your Event Manager call.

The Event Manager always returns the highest-priority event available of the requested types. The priority ranking is as follows:

1. activate (window becoming inactive before window becoming active)

2. mouse-down, mouse-up, key-down, key-up, disk-inserted, network, device driver, application-defined (all in FIFO order)

3. auto-key

4. update (in front-to-back order of windows)

5. null

Activate events take priority over all others; they're detected in a special way, and are never actually placed in the event queue. The Event Manager checks for pending activate events before looking in the event queue, so it will always return such an event if one is available. Because of the special way activate events are detected, there can never be more than two such events pending at the same time; at most there will be one for a window becoming inactive followed by another for a window becoming active.

Category 2 includes most of the event types. Within this category, events are retrieved from the queue in the order they were posted.

If no event is available in categories 1 and 2, the Event Manager reports an auto-key event if the appropriate conditions hold for one. (These conditions are described in detail in the next section.)

Next in priority are update events. Like activate events, these are not placed in the event queue, but are detected in another way. If no higher-priority event is available, the Event Manager checks for windows whose contents need to be drawn. If it finds one, it returns an update event for that window. Windows are checked in the order in which they're displayed on the screen, from front to back, so if two or more windows need to be updated, an update event will be returned for the frontmost such window.

Finally, if no other event is available, the Event Manager returns a null event.

Note: The event queue normally has a capacity of 20 events. If the queue should become full, the Operating System Event Manager will begin discarding old events to make room for new ones as they're posted. The events discarded are always the oldest ones in the queue. The capacity of the event queue is determined by the system startup information stored on a volume; for more information, see the section "Data Organization on Volumes" in chapter 4 of Volume II.

KEYBOARD EVENTS

The **character keys** on the Macintosh keyboard and numeric keypad generate key-down and key-up events when pressed and released; this includes all keys except Shift, Caps Lock, Command, and Option, which are called **modifier keys**. (Modifier keys are treated specially, as described below, and generate no keyboard events of their own.) In addition, an auto-key event is posted whenever all of the following conditions apply:

- Auto-key events haven't been disabled. (This is discussed further under "Event Masks" below.)

- No higher-priority event is available.

- The user is currently holding down a character key.

- The appropriate time interval (see below) has elapsed since the last key-down or auto-key event.

Two different time intervals are associated with auto-key events. The first auto-key event is generated after a certain initial delay has elapsed since the original key-down event (that is, since the key was originally pressed); this is called the **auto-key threshold**. Subsequent auto-key events are then generated each time a certain repeat interval has elapsed since the last such event; this is called the **auto-key rate**. The default values are 16 **ticks** (sixtieths of a second) for the auto-key threshold and four ticks for the auto-key rate. The user can change these values with the Control Panel desk accessory, by adjusting the keyboard touch and the rate of repeating keys.

Assembly-language note: The current values for the auto-key threshold and rate are stored in the global variables KeyThresh and KeyRepThresh, respectively.

When the user presses, holds down, or releases a character key, the character generated by that key is identified internally with a **character code**. Character codes are given in the extended version of ASCII (the American Standard Code for Information Interchange) used by the Macintosh. A table showing the character codes for the standard Macintosh character set appears in Figure 1. All character codes are given in hexadecimal in this table. The first digit of a character's hexadecimal value is shown at the top of the table, the second down the left side. For example, character code $47 stands for "G", which appears in the table at the intersection of column 4 and row 7.

Macintosh, the owner's guide, describes the method of generating the printing characters (codes $20 through $D8) shown in Figure 1. Notice that in addition to the regular space character ($20) there's a **nonbreaking space** ($CA), which is generated by pressing the space bar with the Option key down.

Second digit

First digit

↓	0	1	2	3	4	5	6	7	8	9	A	B	C	D	E	F
0	NUL	DLE	space	0	@	P	`	p	Ä	ê	†	∞	¿	–		
1	SOH	DC1	!	1	A	Q	a	q	Å	ë	°	±	¡	—		
2	STX	DC2	"	2	B	R	b	r	Ç	í	¢	≤	¬	"		
3	ETX	DC3	#	3	C	S	c	s	É	ì	£	≥	√	"		
4	EOT	DC4	$	4	D	T	d	t	Ñ	î	§	¥	ƒ	'		
5	ENQ	NAK	%	5	E	U	e	u	Ö	ï	●	µ	≈	'		
6	ACK	SYN	&	6	F	V	f	v	Ü	ñ	¶	∂	∆	÷		
7	BEL	ETB	'	7	G	W	g	w	á	ó	ß	Σ	«	◊		
8	BS	CAN	(	8	H	X	h	x	à	ò	®	∏	»	ÿ		
9	HT	EM	)	9	I	Y	i	y	â	ô	©	π	…			
A	LF	SUB	*	:	J	Z	j	z	ä	ö	™	∫	␣			
B	VT	ESC	+	;	K	[	k	{	ã	õ	´	ª	À			
C	FF	FS	,	<	L	\	l	|	å	ú	¨	º	Ã			
D	CR	GS	–	=	M	]	m	}	ç	ù	≠	Ω	Õ			
E	SO	RS	.	>	N	^	n	~	é	û	Æ	æ	Œ			
F	SI	US	/	?	O	_	o	DEL	è	ü	Ø	ø	œ			

␣ stands for a nonbreaking space, the same width as a digit.
The shaded characters cannot normally be generated from the Macintosh keyboard or keypad.

Figure 1. Macintosh Character Set

Nonprinting or "control" characters ($00 through $1F, as well as $7F) are identified in the table by their traditional ASCII abbreviations; those that are shaded have no special meaning on the Macintosh and cannot normally be generated from the Macintosh keyboard or keypad. Those that can be generated are listed below along with the method of generating them:

8 Toolbox Event

Code	Abbreviation	Key
$03	ETX	Enter key on keyboard or keypad
$08	BS	Backspace key on keyboard
$09	HT	Tab key on keyboard
$0D	CR	Return key on keyboard
$1B	ESC	Clear key on keypad
$1C	FS	Left arrow key on keypad
$1D	GS	Right arrow key on keypad
$1E	RS	Up arrow key on keypad
$1F	US	Down arrow key on keypad

The association between characters and keys on the keyboard or the keypad is defined by a **keyboard configuration**, which is a resource stored in a resource file. The particular character that's generated by a character key depends on three things:

- the character key being pressed
- which, if any, of the modifier keys were held down when the character key was pressed
- the keyboard configuration currently in effect

The modifier keys, instead of generating keyboard events themselves, modify the meaning of the character keys by changing the character codes that those keys generate. For example, under the standard U.S. keyboard configuration, the "C" key generates any of the following, depending on which modifier keys are held down:

Key(s) pressed	Character generated
"C" by itself	Lowercase c
"C" with Shift or Caps Lock down	Capital C
"C" with Option down	Lowercase c with a cedilla(ç), used in foreign languages
"C" with Option and Shift down, or with Option and Caps Lock down	Capital C with a cedilla (Ç)

The state of each of the modifier keys is also reported in a field of the event record (see next section), where your application can examine it directly.

Note: As described in the owner's guide, some accented characters are generated by pressing Option along with another key for the accent, and then typing the character to be accented. In these cases, a single key-down event occurs for the accented character; there's no event corresponding to the typing of the accent.

Under the standard keyboard configuration, only the Shift, Caps Lock, and Option keys actually modify the character code generated by a character key on the keyboard; the Command key has no effect on the character code generated. Similarly, character codes for the keypad are affected only by the Shift key. To find out whether the Command key was down at the time of an event (or Caps Lock or Option in the case of one generated from the keypad), you have to examine the event record field containing the state of the modifier keys.

EVENT RECORDS

Every event is represented internally by an **event record** containing all pertinent information about that event. The event record includes the following information:

- the type of event

- the time the event was posted (in ticks since system startup)

- the location of the mouse at the time the event was posted (in global coordinates)

- the state of the mouse button and modifier keys at the time the event was posted

- any additional information required for a particular type of event, such as which key the user pressed or which window is being activated

Every event has an event record containing this information—even null events.

Event records are defined as follows:

```
TYPE EventRecord =  RECORD
                    what:       INTEGER;    {event code}
                    message:    LONGINT;    {event message}
                    when:       LONGINT;    {ticks since startup}
                    where:      Point;      {mouse location}
                    modifiers:  INTEGER     {modifier flags}
                END;
```

The when field contains the number of ticks since the system last started up, and the where field gives the location of the mouse, in global coordinates, at the time the event was posted. The other three fields are described below.

Event Code

The what field of an event record contains an **event code** identifying the type of the event. The event codes are available as predefined constants:

```
CONST nullEvent     = 0;     {null}
      mouseDown     = 1;     {mouse-down}
      mouseUp       = 2;     {mouse-up}
      keyDown       = 3;     {key-down}
      keyUp         = 4;     {key-up}
      autoKey       = 5;     {auto-key}
      updateEvt     = 6;     {update}
      diskEvt       = 7;     {disk-inserted}
      activateEvt   = 8;     {activate}
      networkEvt    = 10;    {network}
      driverEvt     = 11;    {device driver}
      app1Evt       = 12;    {application-defined}
      app2Evt       = 13;    {application-defined}
      app3Evt       = 14;    {application-defined}
      app4Evt       = 15;    {application-defined}
```

Event Message

The message field of an event record contains the **event message**, which conveys additional important information about the event. The nature of this information depends on the event type, as summarized in the following table and described below.

Event type	Event message
Keyboard	Character code and key code in low-order word
Activate, update	Pointer to window
Disk-inserted	Drive number in low-order word, File Manager result code in high-order word
Mouse-down, mouse-up, null	Undefined
Network	Handle to parameter block
Device driver	See chapter describing driver
Application-defined	Whatever you wish

For keyboard events, only the low-order word of the event message is used, as shown in Figure 2. The low-order byte of this word contains the ASCII character code generated by the key or combination of keys that was pressed or released; usually this is all you'll need.

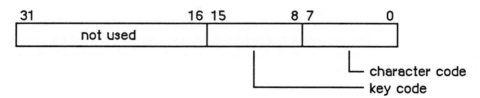

Figure 2. Event Message for Keyboard Events

The **key code** in the event message for a keyboard event represents the character key that was pressed or released; this value is always the same for any given character key, regardless of the modifier keys pressed along with it. Key codes are useful in special cases—in a music generator, for example—where you want to treat the keyboard as a set of keys unrelated to characters. Figure 3 gives the key codes for all the keys on the keyboard and keypad. (Key codes are shown for modifier keys here because they're meaningful in other contexts, as explained later.) Both the U.S. and international keyboards are shown; in some cases the codes are quite different (for example, space and Enter are reversed).

The following predefined constants are available to help you access the character code and key code:

```
CONST  charCodeMask  = $000000FF;   {character code}
       keyCodeMask   = $0000FF00;   {key code}
```

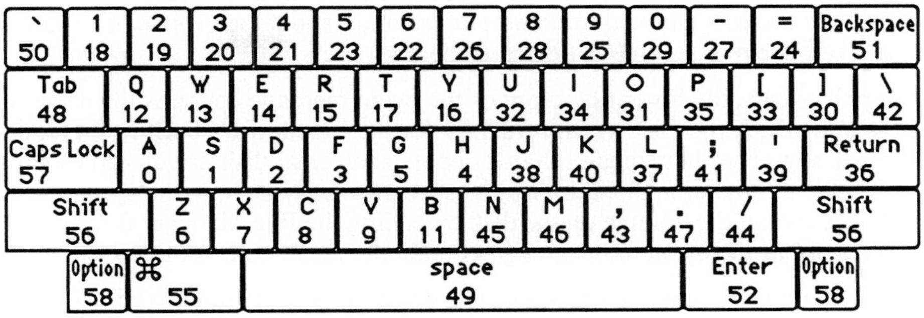

` 50	1 18	2 19	3 20	4 21	5 23	6 22	7 26	8 28	9 25	0 29	- 27	= 24	Backspace 51
Tab 48	Q 12	W 13	E 14	R 15	T 17	Y 16	U 32	I 34	O 31	P 35	[33	] 30	\ 42
Caps Lock 57	A 0	S 1	D 2	F 3	G 5	H 4	J 38	K 40	L 37	; 41	' 39	Return 36	
Shift 56	Z 6	X 7	C 8	V 9	B 11	N 45	M 46	, 43	. 47	/ 44	Shift 56		
Option 58	⌘ 55		space 49							Enter 52	Option 58		

U.S. keyboard

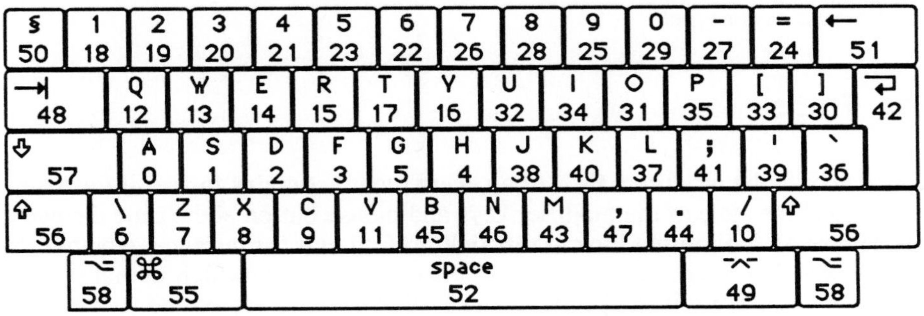

§ 50	1 18	2 19	3 20	4 21	5 23	6 22	7 26	8 28	9 25	0 29	- 27	= 24	← 51
→| 48	Q 12	W 13	E 14	R 15	T 17	Y 16	U 32	I 34	O 31	P 35	[33	] 30	⏎ 42
⇩ 57	A 0	S 1	D 2	F 3	G 5	H 4	J 38	K 40	L 37	; 41	' 39	` 36	
⇧ 56	\ 6	Z 7	X 8	C 9	V 11	B 45	N 46	M 43	, 47	. 44	/ 10	⇧ 56	
⌥ 58	⌘ 55		space 52							⌥ 49	⌥ 58		

International keyboard (Great Britain key caps shown)

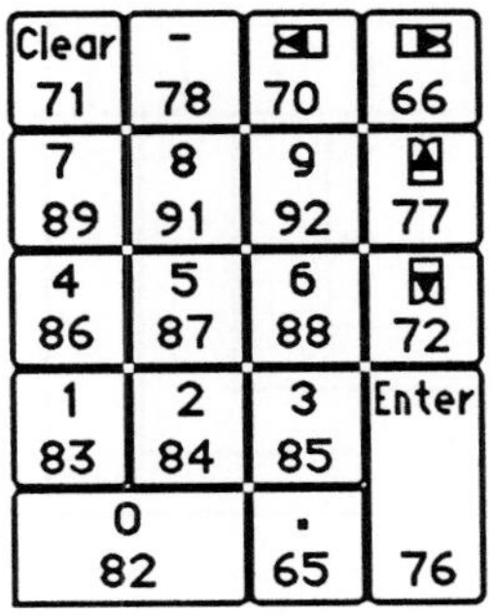

Clear 71	- 78	⌧ 70	⊡ 66
7 89	8 91	9 92	▲ 77
4 86	5 87	6 88	▼ 72
1 83	2 84	3 85	Enter
0 82	. 65		76

Keypad (U.S. key caps shown)

Figure 3. Key Codes

Note: You can use the Toolbox Utility function BitAnd with these constants; for instance, to access the character code, use

```
charCode := BitAnd(myEvent.message,charCodeMask)
```

8 Toolbox Event

For activate and update events, the event message is a pointer to the window affected. (If the event is an activate event, additional important information about the event can be found in the modifiers field of the event record, as described below.)

For disk-inserted events, the low-order word of the event message contains the drive number of the disk drive into which the disk was inserted: 1 for the Macintosh's built-in drive, and 2 for the external drive, if any. Numbers greater than 2 denote additional disk drives connected to the Macintosh. By the time your application receives a disk-inserted event, the system will already have attempted to mount the volume on the disk by calling the File Manager function MountVol; the high-order word of the event message will contain the result code returned by MountVol.

For mouse-down, mouse-up, and null events, the event message is undefined and should be ignored. The event message for a network event contains a handle to a parameter block, as described in chapter 10 of Volume II. For device driver events, the contents of the event message depend on the situation under which the event was generated; the chapters describing those situations will give the details. Finally, you can use the event message however you wish for application-defined event types.

Modifier Flags

As mentioned above, the modifiers field of an event record contains further information about activate events and the state of the modifier keys and mouse button at the time the event was posted (see Figure 4). You might look at this field to find out, for instance, whether the Command key was down when a mouse-down event was posted (which in many applications affects the way objects are selected) or when a key-down event was posted (which could mean the user is choosing a menu item by typing its keyboard equivalent).

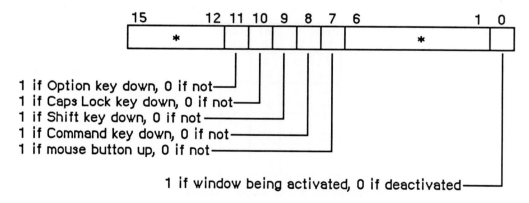

*reserved for future use

Figure 4. Modifier Flags

The following predefined constants are useful as masks for reading the flags in the modifiers field:

```
CONST activeFlag  = 1;     {set if window being activated}
      btnState    = 128;   {set if mouse button up}
      cmdKey      = 256;   {set if Command key down}
      shiftKey    = 512;   {set if Shift key down}
      alphaLock   = 1024;  {set if Caps Lock key down}
      optionKey   = 2048;  {set if Option key down}
```

The activeFlag bit gives further information about activate events; it's set if the window pointed to by the event message is being activated, or 0 if the window is being deactivated. The remaining bits indicate the state of the mouse button and modifier keys. Notice that the btnState bit is set if the mouse button is *up*, whereas the bits for the four modifier keys are set if their corresponding keys are *down*.

EVENT MASKS

Some of the Event Manager routines can be restricted to operate on a specific event type or group of types; in other words, the specified event types are enabled while all others are disabled. For instance, instead of just requesting the next available event, you can specifically ask for the next keyboard event.

You specify which event types a particular Event Manager call applies to by supplying an **event mask** as a parameter. This is an integer in which there's one bit position for each event type, as shown in Figure 5. The bit position representing a given type corresponds to the event code for that type—for example, update events (event code 6) are specified by bit 6 of the mask. A 1 in bit 6 means that this Event Manager call applies to update events; a 0 means that it doesn't.

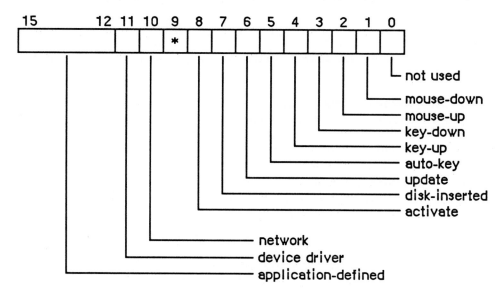

*reserved for future use

Figure 5. Event Mask

Masks for each individual event type are available as predefined constants:

```
CONST  mDownMask    =  2;          {mouse-down}
       mUpMask      =  4;          {mouse-up}
       keyDownMask  =  8;          {key-down}
       keyUpMask    =  16;         {key-up}
       autoKeyMask  =  32;         {auto-key}
       updateMask   =  64;         {update}
       diskMask     =  128;        {disk-inserted}
       activMask    =  256;        {activate}
       networkMask  =  1024;       {network}
       driverMask   =  2048;       {device driver}
       app1Mask     =  4096;       {application-defined}
       app2Mask     =  8192;       {application-defined}
       app3Mask     =  16384;      {application-defined}
       app4Mask     =  -32768;     {application-defined}
```

Note: Null events can't be disabled; a null event will always be reported when none of the enabled types of events are available.

The following predefined mask designates all event types:

```
CONST everyEvent = -1;       {all event types}
```

You can form any mask you need by adding or subtracting these mask constants. For example, to specify every keyboard event, use

```
keyDownMask + keyUpMask + autoKeyMask
```

For every event except an update, use

```
everyEvent - updateMask
```

Note: It's recommended that you always use the event mask everyEvent unless there's a specific reason not to.

There's also a global **system event mask** that controls which event types get posted into the event queue. Only event types corresponding to bits set in the system event mask are posted; all others are ignored. When the system starts up, the system event mask is set to post all except key-up event—that is, it's initialized to

```
everyEvent - keyUpMask
```

Note: Key-up events are meaningless for most applications. Your application will usually want to ignore them; if not, it can set the system event mask with the Operating System Event Manager procedure SetEventMask.

USING THE TOOLBOX EVENT MANAGER

Before using the Event Manager, you should initialize the Window Manager by calling its procedure InitWindows; parts of the Event Manager rely on the Window Manager's data structures and will not work properly unless those structures have been properly initialized. Initializing the Window Manager requires you to have initialized QuickDraw and the Font Manager.

Assembly-language note: If you want to use events but not windows, set the global variable WindowList (a long word) to 0 instead of calling InitWindows.

It's also usually a good idea to issue the Operating System Event Manager call FlushEvents(everyEvent,0) to empty the event queue of any stray events left over from before your application started up (such as keystrokes typed to the Finder). See chapter 3 of Volume II for a description of FlushEvents.

Most Macintosh application programs are event-driven. Such programs have a main loop that repeatedly calls GetNextEvent to retrieve the next available event, and then uses a CASE statement to take whatever action is appropriate for each type of event; some typical responses to commonly occurring events are described below. Your program is expected to respond only to those events that are directly related to its own operations. After calling GetNextEvent, you should test its Boolean result to find out whether your application needs to respond to the event: TRUE means the event may be of interest to your application; FALSE usually means it will not be of interest.

In some cases, you may simply want to look at a pending event while leaving it available for subsequent retrieval by GetNextEvent. You can do this with the EventAvail function.

Responding to Mouse Events

On receiving a mouse-down event, your application should first call the Window Manager function FindWindow to find out where on the screen the mouse button was pressed, and then respond in whatever way is appropriate. Depending on the part of the screen in which the button was pressed, this may involve calls to Toolbox routines such as the Menu Manager function MenuSelect, the Desk Manager procedure SystemClick, the Window Manager routines SelectWindow, DragWindow, GrowWindow, and TrackGoAway, and the Control Manager routines FindControl, TrackControl, and DragControl. See the relevant chapters for details.

If your application attaches some special significance to pressing a modifier key along with the mouse button, you can discover the state of that modifier key while the mouse button is down by examining the appropriate flag in the modifiers field.

If you're using the TextEdit part of the Toolbox to handle text editing, mouse double-clicks will work automatically as a means of selecting a word; to respond to double-clicks in any other context, however, you'll have to detect them yourself. You can do so by comparing the time and location of a mouse-up event with those of the immediately following mouse-down event. You should assume a double-click has occurred if both of the following are true:

- The times of the mouse-up event and the mouse-down event differ by a number of ticks less than or equal to the value returned by the Event Manager function GetDblTime.

- The locations of the two mouse-down events separated by the mouse-up event are sufficiently close to each other. Exactly what this means depends on the particular application. For instance, in a word-processing application, you might consider the two locations essentially the same if they fall on the same character, whereas in a graphics application you might consider them essentially the same if the sum of the horizontal and vertical changes in position is no more than five pixels.

Mouse-up events may be significant in other ways; for example, they might signal the end of dragging to select more than one object. Most simple applications, however, will ignore mouse-up events.

Responding to Keyboard Events

For a key-down event, you should first check the modifiers field to see whether the character was typed with the Command key held down; if so, the user may have been choosing a menu item by typing its keyboard equivalent. To find out, pass the character that was typed to the Menu Manager function MenuKey. (See chapter 11 for details.)

If the key-down event was not a menu command, you should then respond to the event in whatever way is appropriate for your application. For example, if one of your windows is active, you might want to insert the typed character into the active document; if none of your windows is active, you might want to ignore the event.

Usually your application can handle auto-key events the same as key-down events. You may, however, want to ignore auto-key events that invoke commands that shouldn't be continually repeated.

   Note: Remember that most applications will want to ignore key-up events; with the standard system event mask you won't get any.

If you wish to periodically inspect the state of the keyboard or keypad—say, while the mouse button is being held down—use the procedure GetKeys; this procedure is also the only way to tell whether a modifier key is being pressed alone.

Responding to Activate and Update Events

When your application receives an activate event for one of its own windows, the Window Manager will already have done all of the normal "housekeeping" associated with the event, such as highlighting or unhighlighting the window. You can then take any further action that your application may require, such as showing or hiding a scroll bar or highlighting or unhighlighting a selection.

On receiving an update event for one of its own windows, your application should usually call the Window Manager procedure BeginUpdate, draw the window's contents, and then call EndUpdate. See chapter 9 for important additional information on activate and update events.

Responding to Disk-Inserted Events

Most applications will use the Standard File Package, which responds to disk-inserted events for you during standard file saving and opening; you'll usually want to ignore any other disk-inserted events, such as the user's inserting a disk when not expected. If, however, you do want to respond to other disk-inserted events, or if you plan not to use the Standard File Package, then you'll have to handle such events yourself.

When you receive a disk-inserted event, the system will already have attempted to mount the volume on the disk by calling the File Manager function MountVol. You should examine the result code returned by the File Manager in the high-order word of the event message. If the result code indicates that the attempt to mount the volume was unsuccessful, you might want to take some special action, such as calling the Disk Initialization Package function DIBadMount. See chapters 4 and 14 of Volume II for further details.

Other Operations

In addition to receiving the user's mouse and keyboard actions in the form of events, you can directly read the keyboard (and keypad), mouse location, and state of the mouse button by calling GetKeys, GetMouse, and Button, respectively. To follow the mouse when the user moves it with the button down, use StillDown or WaitMouseUp.

The function TickCount returns the number of ticks since the last system startup; you might, for example, compare this value to the when field of an event record to discover the delay since that event was posted.

Finally, the function GetCaretTime returns the number of ticks between blinks of the "caret" (usually a vertical bar) marking the insertion point in editable text. You should call GetCaretTime if you aren't using TextEdit and therefore need to cause the caret to blink yourself. You would check this value each time through your program's main event loop, to ensure a constant frequency of blinking.

TOOLBOX EVENT MANAGER ROUTINES

Accessing Events

```
FUNCTION GetNextEvent (eventMask: INTEGER; VAR theEvent:
        EventRecord) : BOOLEAN;
```

GetNextEvent returns the next available event of a specified type or types and, if the event is in the event queue, removes it from the queue. The event is returned in the parameter theEvent. The eventMask parameter specifies which event types are of interest. GetNextEvent returns the next available event of any type designated by the mask, subject to the priority rules discussed above under "Priority of Events". If no event of any of the designated types is available, GetNextEvent returns a null event.

Note: Events in the queue that aren't designated in the mask are kept in the queue; if you want to remove them, you can do so by calling the Operating System Event Manager procedure FlushEvents.

Before reporting an event to your application, GetNextEvent first calls the Desk Manager function SystemEvent to see whether the system wants to intercept and respond to the event. If so, or if the event being reported is a null event, GetNextEvent returns a function result of FALSE; a function result of TRUE means that your application should handle the event itself. The Desk Manager intercepts the following events:

■ activate and update events directed to a desk accessory

■ mouse-up and keyboard events, if the currently active window belongs to a desk accessory

Note: In each case, the event is intercepted by the Desk Manager only if the desk accessory can handle that type of event; however, as a rule all desk accessories should be set up to handle activate, update, and keyboard events and should not handle mouse-up events.

The Desk Manager also intercepts disk-inserted events: It attempts to mount the volume on the disk by calling the File Manager function MountVol. GetNextEvent will always return TRUE in this case, though, so that your application can take any further appropriate action after examining the result code returned by MountVol in the event message. (See chapter 14 of Volume I and chapter 4 of Volume II for further details.) GetNextEvent returns TRUE for all other non-null events (including all mouse-down events, regardless of which window is active), leaving them for your application to handle.

GetNextEvent also makes the following processing happen, invisible to your program:

■ If the "alarm" is set and the current time is the alarm time, the alarm goes off (a beep followed by blinking the apple symbol in the menu bar). The user can set the alarm with the Alarm Clock desk accessory.

■ If the user holds down the Command and Shift keys while pressing a numeric key that has a special effect, that effect occurs. The standard such keys are 1 and 2 for ejecting the disk in the internal or external drive, and 3 and 4 for writing a snapshot of the screen to a MacPaint document or to the printer.

Note: Advanced programmers can implement their own code to be executed in response to Command-Shift-number combinations (except for Command-Shift-1 and 2, which can't be changed). The code corresponding to a particular number must be a routine having no parameters, stored in a resource whose type is 'FKEY' and whose ID is the number. The system resource file contains code for the numbers 3 and 4.

Assembly-language note: You can disable GetNextEvent's processing of Command-Shift-number combinations by setting the global variable ScrDmpEnb (a byte) to 0.

```
FUNCTION EventAvail (eventMask: INTEGER; VAR theEvent:
        EventRecord) : BOOLEAN;
```

EventAvail works exactly the same as GetNextEvent except that if the event is in the event queue, it's left there.

Note: An event returned by EventAvail will not be accessible later if in the meantime the queue becomes full and the event is discarded from it; since the events discarded are always the oldest ones in the queue, however, this will happen only in an unusually busy environment.

Reading the Mouse

```
PROCEDURE GetMouse (VAR mouseLoc: Point);
```

GetMouse returns the current mouse location in the mouseLoc parameter. The location is given in the local coordinate system of the current grafPort (which might be, for example, the currently active window). Notice that this differs from the mouse location stored in the where field of an event record; that location is always in global coordinates.

```
FUNCTION Button : BOOLEAN;
```

The Button function returns TRUE if the mouse button is currently down, and FALSE if it isn't.

```
FUNCTION StillDown : BOOLEAN;
```

Usually called after a mouse-down event, StillDown tests whether the mouse button is still down. It returns TRUE if the button is currently down and there are no more mouse events pending in the event queue. This is a true test of whether the button is still down from the original press—unlike Button (above), which returns TRUE whenever the button is currently down, even if it has been released and pressed again since the original mouse-down event.

```
FUNCTION WaitMouseUp : BOOLEAN;
```

WaitMouseUp works exactly the same as StillDown (above), except that if the button is not still down from the original press, WaitMouseUp removes the preceding mouse-up event before returning FALSE. If, for instance, your application attaches some special significance both to mouse double-clicks and to mouse-up events, this function would allow your application to recognize a double-click without being confused by the intervening mouse-up.

Reading the Keyboard and Keypad

```
PROCEDURE GetKeys (VAR theKeys: KeyMap);
```

GetKeys reads the current state of the keyboard (and keypad, if any) and returns it in the form of a keyMap:

```
TYPE KeyMap = PACKED ARRAY[0..127] OF BOOLEAN;
```

Each key on the keyboard or keypad corresponds to an element in the keyMap. The index into the keyMap for a particular key is the same as the key code for that key. (The key codes are shown in Figure 3 above.) The keyMap element is TRUE if the corresponding key is down and FALSE if it isn't. The maximum number of keys that can be down simultaneously is two character keys plus any combination of the four modifier keys.

Miscellaneous Routines

```
FUNCTION TickCount : LONGINT;
```

TickCount returns the current number of ticks (sixtieths of a second) since the system last started up.

Warning: Don't rely on the tick count being exact; it will usually be accurate to within one tick, but may be off by more than that. The tick count is incremented during the vertical retrace interrupt, but it's possible for this interrupt to be disabled. Furthermore, don't rely on the tick count being incremented to a certain value, such as testing whether it has become equal to its old value plus 1; check instead for "greater than or equal to" (since an interrupt task may keep control for more than one tick).

Assembly-language note: The value returned by this function is also contained in the global variable Ticks.

```
FUNCTION GetDblTime : LONGINT;    [Not in ROM]
```

GetDblTime returns the suggested maximum difference (in ticks) that should exist between the times of a mouse-up event and a mouse-down event for those two mouse clicks to be considered a double-click. The user can adjust this value by means of the Control Panel desk accessory.

Assembly-language note: This value is available to assembly-language programmers in the global variable DoubleTime.

```
FUNCTION GetCaretTime : LONGINT;    [Not in ROM]
```

GetCaretTime returns the time (in ticks) between blinks of the "caret" (usually a vertical bar) marking the insertion point in editable text. If you aren't using TextEdit, you'll need to cause the caret to blink yourself; on every pass through your program's main event loop, you should check this value against the elapsed time since the last blink of the caret. The user can adjust this value by means of the Control Panel desk accessory.

Assembly-language note: This value is available to assembly-language programmers in the global variable CaretTime.

THE JOURNALING MECHANISM

So far, this chapter has described the Event Manager as responding to events generated by users—keypresses, mouse clicks, disk insertions, and so on. By using the Event Manager's journaling mechanism, though, you can "decouple" the Event Manager from the user and feed it events from some other source. Such a source might be a file into which have been recorded all the events that occurred during some portion of a user's session with the Macintosh. This section briefly describes the journaling mechanism and some examples of its use, and then gives the technical information you'll need if you want to use this mechanism yourself.

> **Note:** The journaling mechanism can be accessed only through assembly language; Pascal programmers may want to skip this discussion.

In the usual sense, "journaling" means the recording of a sequence of user-generated events into a file; specifically, this file is a recording of all calls to the Event Manager routines GetNextEvent, EventAvail, GetMouse, Button, GetKeys, and TickCount. When a journal is being recorded, every call to any of these routines is sent to a journaling device driver, which records the call (and the results of the call) in a file. When the journal is played back, these recorded Event Manager calls are taken from the journal file and sent directly to the Event Manager. The result is that the recorded sequence of user-generated events is reproduced when the journal is played back. The Macintosh Guided Tour is an example of such a journal.

Using the journaling mechanism need not involve a file. Before Macintosh was introduced, Macintosh Software Engineering created a special desk accessory of its own for testing Macintosh software. This desk accessory, which was based on the journaling mechanism, didn't use a file—it generated events randomly, putting Macintosh "through its paces" for long periods of time without requiring a user's attention.

So, the Event Manager's journaling mechanism has a much broader utility than a mechanism simply for "journaling" as it's normally defined. With the journaling mechanism, you can decouple the Event Manager from the user and feed it events from a journaling device driver of your own design. Figure 6 illustrates what happens when the journaling mechanism is off, in recording mode, and in playback mode.

Writing Your Own Journaling Device Driver

If you want to implement journaling in a new way, you'll need to write your own journaling device driver. Details about how to do this are given below; however, you must already have read about writing your own device driver in chapter 6 of Volume II. Furthermore, if you want to implement your journaling device driver as a desk accessory, you'll have to be familiar with details given in chapter 14.

Whenever a call is made to any of the Event Manager routines GetNextEvent, EventAvail, GetMouse, Button, GetKeys, and TickCount, the information returned by the routine is passed to the journaling device driver by means of a Control call. The routine makes the Control call to the journaling device driver with the reference number stored in the global variable JournalRef; the journaling device driver should put its reference number in this variable when it's opened.

You control whether the journaling mechanism is playing or recording by setting the global variable JournalFlag to a negative or positive value. Before the Event Manager routine makes the

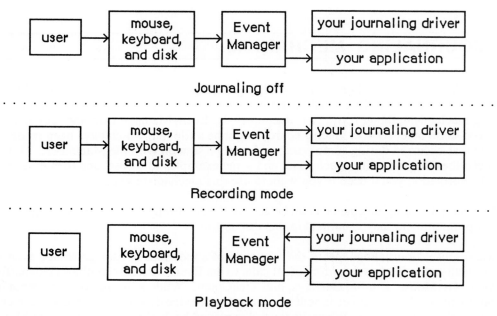

Figure 6. The Journaling Mechanism

Control call, it copies one of the following global constants into the csCode parameter of the Control call, depending on the value of JournalFlag:

JournalFlag	Value of csCode	Meaning
Negative	jPlayCtl .EQU 16	Journal in playback mode
Positive	jRecordCtl .EQU 17	Journal in recording mode

If you set the value of JournalFlag to 0, the Control call won't be made at all.

Before the Event Manager routine makes the Control call, it copies into csParam a pointer to the actual data being polled by the routine (for example, a pointer to a keyMap for GetKeys, or a pointer to an event record for GetNextEvent). It also copies, into csParam+4, a **journal code** designating which routine is making the call:

Control call made during:	csParam contains pointer to:	Journal code at csParam+4:
TickCount	Long word	jcTickCount .EQU 0
GetMouse	Point	jcGetMouse .EQU 1
Button	Boolean	jcButton .EQU 2
GetKeys	KeyMap	jcGetKeys .EQU 3
GetNextEvent	Event record	jcEvent .EQU 4
EventAvail	Event record	jcEvent .EQU 4

SUMMARY OF THE TOOLBOX EVENT MANAGER

Constants

```
CONST { Event codes }

        nullEvent    = 0;      {null}
        mouseDown    = 1;      {mouse-down}
        mouseUp      = 2;      {mouse-up}
        keyDown      = 3;      {key-down}
        keyUp        = 4;      {key-up}
        autoKey      = 5;      {auto-key}
        updateEvt    = 6;      {update}
        diskEvt      = 7;      {disk-inserted}
        activateEvt  = 8;      {activate}
        networkEvt   = 10;     {network}
        driverEvt    = 11;     {device driver}
        app1Evt      = 12;     {application-defined}
        app2Evt      = 13;     {application-defined}
        app3Evt      = 14;     {application-defined}
        app4Evt      = 15;     {application-defined}

        { Masks for keyboard event message }

        charCodeMask = $000000FF;   {character code}
        keyCodeMask  = $0000FF00;   {key code}

        { Masks for forming event mask }

        mDownMask    =  2;      {mouse-down}
        mUpMask      =  4;      {mouse-up}
        keyDownMask  =  8;      {key-down}
        keyUpMask    =  16;     {key-up}
        autoKeyMask  =  32;     {auto-key}
        updateMask   =  64;     {update}
        diskMask     =  128;    {disk-inserted}
        activMask    =  256;    {activate}
        networkMask  =  1024;   {network}
        driverMask   =  2048;   {device driver}
        app1Mask     =  4096;   {application-defined}
        app2Mask     =  8192;   {application-defined}
        app3Mask     =  16384;  {application-defined}
        app4Mask     = -32768;  {application-defined}
        everyEvent   = -1;      {all event types}
```

8 Toolbox Event

```
{ Modifier flags in event record }

activeFlag  = 1;    {set if window being activated}
btnState    = 128;  {set if mouse button up}
cmdKey      = 256;  {set if Command key down}
shiftKey    = 512;  {set if Shift key down}
alphaLock   = 1024; {set if Caps Lock key down}
optionKey   = 2048; {set if Option key down}
```

Data Types

```
TYPE EventRecord = RECORD
                    what:       INTEGER;  {event code}
                    message:    LONGINT;  {event message}
                    when:       LONGINT;  {ticks since startup}
                    where:      Point;    {mouse location}
                    modifiers:  INTEGER   {modifier flags}
                END;

    KeyMap = PACKED ARRAY[0..127] OF BOOLEAN;
```

Routines

Accessing Events

```
FUNCTION GetNextEvent (eventMask: INTEGER; VAR theEvent:
                        EventRecord) : BOOLEAN;
FUNCTION EventAvail   (eventMask: INTEGER; VAR theEvent:
                        EventRecord) : BOOLEAN;
```

Reading the Mouse

```
PROCEDURE  GetMouse      (VAR mouseLoc: Point);
FUNCTION   Button :      BOOLEAN;
FUNCTION   StillDown :   BOOLEAN;
FUNCTION   WaitMouseUp : BOOLEAN;
```

Reading the Keyboard and Keypad

```
PROCEDURE GetKeys (VAR theKeys: KeyMap);
```

Miscellaneous Routines

```
FUNCTION TickCount    : LONGINT;
FUNCTION GetDblTime   : LONGINT;   [Not in ROM]
FUNCTION GetCaretTime : LONGINT;   [Not in ROM]
```

Event Message in Event Record

Event type	Event message
Keyboard	Character code and key code in low-order word
Activate, update	Pointer to window
Disk-inserted	Drive number in low-order word, File Manager result code in high-order word
Mouse-down, mouse-up, null	Undefined
Network	Handle to parameter block
Device driver	See chapter describing driver
Application-defined	Whatever you wish

Assembly-Language Information

Constants

```
; Event codes

nullEvt          .EQU   0    ;null
mButDwnEvt       .EQU   1    ;mouse-down
mButUpEvt        .EQU   2    ;mouse-up
keyDwnEvt        .EQU   3    ;key-down
keyUpEvt         .EQU   4    ;key-up
autoKeyEvt       .EQU   5    ;auto-key
updatEvt         .EQU   6    ;update
diskInsertEvt    .EQU   7    ;disk-inserted
activateEvt      .EQU   8    ;activate
networkEvt       .EQU  10    ;network
ioDrvrEvt        .EQU  11    ;device driver
app1Evt          .EQU  12    ;application-defined
app2Evt          .EQU  13    ;application-defined
app3Evt          .EQU  14    ;application-defined
app4Evt          .EQU  15    ;application-defined

; Modifier flags in event record

activeFlag       .EQU   0    ;set if window being activated
btnState         .EQU   2    ;set if mouse button up
cmdKey           .EQU   3    ;set if Command key down
shiftKey         .EQU   4    ;set if Shift key down
alphaLock        .EQU   5    ;set if Caps Lock key down
optionKey        .EQU   6    ;set if Option key down
```

```
; Journaling mechanism Control call

jPlayCtl        .EQU    16    ;journal in playback mode
jRecordCtl      .EQU    17    ;journal in recording mode
jcTickCount     .EQU    0     ;journal code for TickCount
jcGetMouse      .EQU    1     ;journal code for GetMouse
jcButton        .EQU    2     ;journal code for Button
jcGetKeys       .EQU    3     ;journal code for GetKeys
jcEvent         .EQU    4     ;journal code for GetNextEvent and EventAvail
```

Event Record Data Structure

evtNum	Event code (word)
evtMessage	Event message (long)
evtTicks	Ticks since startup (long)
evtMouse	Mouse location (point; long)
evtMeta	State of modifier keys (byte)
evtMBut	State of mouse button (byte)
evtBlkSize	Size in bytes of event record

Variables

KeyThresh	Auto-key threshold (word)
KeyRepThresh	Auto-key rate (word)
WindowList	0 if using events but not windows (long)
ScrDmpEnb	0 if GetNextEvent shouldn't process Command-Shift-number combinations (byte)
Ticks	Current number of ticks since system startup (long)
DoubleTime	Double-click interval in ticks (long)
CaretTime	Caret-blink interval in ticks (long)
JournalRef	Reference number of journaling device driver (word)
JournalFlag	Journaling mode (word)

9 THE WINDOW MANAGER

ABOUT THIS CHAPTER

The Window Manager is the part of the Toolbox that allows you to create, manipulate, and dispose of windows. This chapter describes the Window Manager in detail.

You should already be familiar with:

■ Resources, as discussed in chapter 5.

■ The basic concepts and structures behind QuickDraw, particularly points, rectangles, regions, grafPorts, and pictures. You don't have to know the QuickDraw routines in order to use the Window Manager, though you'll be using QuickDraw to draw inside a window.

■ The Toolbox Event Manager.

ABOUT THE WINDOW MANAGER

The Window Manager is a tool for dealing with windows on the Macintosh screen. The screen represents a working surface or **desktop**; graphic objects appear on the desktop and can be manipulated with the mouse. A **window** is an object on the desktop that presents information, such as a document or a message. Windows can be any size or shape, and there can be one or many of them, depending on the application.

Some standard types of windows are predefined. One of these is the **document window**, as illustrated in Figure 1. Every document window has a 20-pixel-high title bar containing a title that's centered and in the system font and system font size. In addition, a particular document window may or may not have a close box or a size box; you'll learn in this chapter how to implement them. There may also be scroll bars along the bottom and/or right edge of a document window. Scroll bars are controls, and are supported by the Control Manager.

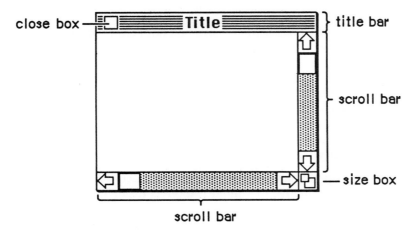

Figure 1. An Active Document Window

Your application can easily create standard types of windows such as document windows, and can also define its own types of windows. Some windows may be created indirectly for you when you use other parts of the Toolbox; an example is the window the Dialog Manager creates to display an alert box. Windows created either directly or indirectly by an application are collectively called **application windows**. There's also a class of windows called **system windows**; these are the windows in which desk accessories are displayed.

The document window shown in Figure 1 is the **active** (frontmost) window, the one that will be acted on when the user types, gives commands, or whatever is appropriate to the application being used. Its title bar is **highlighted**—displayed in a distinctive visual way—so that the window will stand out from other, **inactive** windows that may be on the screen. Since a close box, size box, and scroll bars will have an effect only in an active window, none of them appear in an inactive window (see Figure 2).

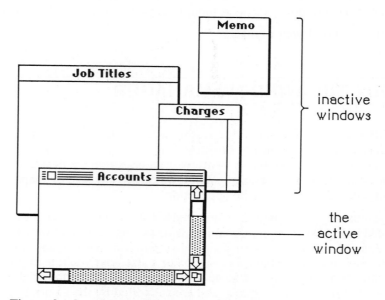

Figure 2. Overlapping Document Windows

Note: If a document window has neither a size box nor scroll bars, the lines delimiting those areas aren't drawn, as in the Memo window in Figure 2.

An important function of the Window Manager is to keep track of overlapping windows. You can draw in any window without running over onto windows in front of it. You can move windows to different places on the screen, change their plane (their front-to-back ordering), or change their size, all without concern for how the various windows overlap. The Window Manager keeps track of any newly exposed areas and provides a convenient mechanism for you to ensure that they're properly redrawn.

Finally, you can easily set up your application so that mouse actions cause these standard responses inside a document window, or similar responses inside other windows:

■ Clicking anywhere in an inactive window makes it the active window by bringing it to the front and highlighting its title bar.

■ Clicking inside the close box of the active window closes the window. Depending on the application, this may mean that the window disappears altogether, or a representation of the window (such as an icon) may be left on the desktop.

■ Dragging anywhere inside the title bar of a window (except in the close box, if any) pulls an outline of the window across the screen, and releasing the mouse button moves the window to the new location. If the window isn't the active window, it becomes the active window unless the Command key was also held down. A window can never be moved completely off the screen; by convention, it can't be moved such that the visible area of the title bar is less than four pixels square.

■ Dragging inside the size box of the active window changes the size of the window.

WINDOWS AND GRAFPORTS

It's easy for applications to use windows: To the application, a window is a grafPort that it can draw into like any other with QuickDraw routines. When you create a window, you specify a rectangle that becomes the portRect of the grafPort in which the window contents will be drawn. The bit map for this grafPort, its pen pattern, and other characteristics are the same as the default values set by QuickDraw, except for the character font, which is set to the application font. These characteristics will apply whenever the application draws in the window, and they can easily be changed with QuickDraw routines (SetPort to make the grafPort the current port, and other routines as appropriate).

There is, however, more to a window than just the grafPort that the application draws in. In a standard document window, for example, the title bar and outline of the window are drawn by the Window Manager, not by the application. The part of a window that the Window Manager draws is called the **window frame**, since it usually surrounds the rest of the window. For drawing window frames, the Window Manager creates a grafPort that has the entire screen as its portRect; this grafPort is called the **Window Manager port**.

WINDOW REGIONS

Every window has the following two regions:

■ the **content region**: the area that your application draws in

■ the **structure region**: the entire window; its complete "structure" (the content region plus the window frame)

The content region is bounded by the rectangle you specify when you create the window (that is, the portRect of the window's grafPort); for a document window, it's the entire portRect. This is where your application presents information and where the size box and scroll bars of a document window are located.

A window may also have any of the regions listed below. Clicking or dragging in one of these regions causes the indicated action.

■ A **go-away region** within the window frame. Clicking in this region of the active window closes the window.

■ A **drag region** within the window frame. Dragging in this region pulls an outline of the window across the screen, moves the window to a new location, and makes it the active window (if it isn't already) unless the Command key was held down.

■ A **grow region**, usually within the content region. Dragging in this region of the active window changes the size of the window. In a document window, the grow region is in the content region, but in windows of your own design it may be in either the content region or the window frame.

Clicking in any region of an inactive window simply makes it the active window.

Note: The results of clicking and dragging that are discussed here don't happen automatically; you have to make the right Window Manager calls to cause them to happen.

Figure 3 illustrates the various regions of a standard document window and its window frame.

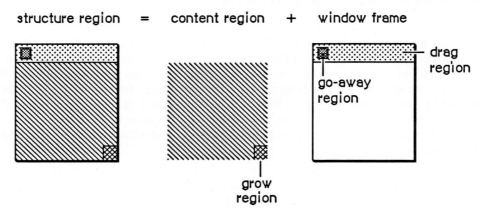

Figure 3. Document Window Regions and Frame

An example of a window that has no drag region is the window that displays an alert box. On the other hand, you could design a window whose drag region is the entire structure region and whose content region is empty; such a window might present a fixed picture rather than information that's to be manipulated.

Another important window region is the **update region**. Unlike the regions described above, the update region is dynamic rather than fixed: The Window Manager keeps track of all areas of the content region that have to be redrawn and accumulates them into the update region. For example, if you bring to the front a window that was overlapped by another window, the Window Manager adds the formerly overlapped (now exposed) area of the front window's content region to its update region. You'll also accumulate areas into the update region yourself; the Window Manager provides update region maintenance routines for this purpose.

WINDOWS AND RESOURCES

The general appearance and behavior of a window is determined by a routine called its **window definition function**, which is stored as a resource in a resource file. The window definition function performs all actions that differ from one window type to another, such as drawing the window frame. The Window Manager calls the window definition function whenever it needs to perform one of these type-dependent actions (passing it a message that tells which action to perform).

The system resource file includes window definition functions for the standard document window and other standard types of windows. If you want to define your own, nonstandard window types, you'll have to write window definition functions for them, as described later in the section "Defining Your Own Windows".

When you create a window, you specify its type with a **window definition ID**, which tells the Window Manager the resource ID of the definition function for that type of window. You can use one of the following constants as a window definition ID to refer to a standard type of window (see Figure 4):

```
CONST  documentProc   = 0;    {standard document window}
       dBoxProc       = 1;    {alert box or modal dialog box}
       plainDBox      = 2;    {plain box}
       altDBoxProc    = 3;    {plain box with shadow}
       noGrowDocProc  = 4;    {document window without size box}
       rDocProc       = 16;   {rounded-corner window}
```

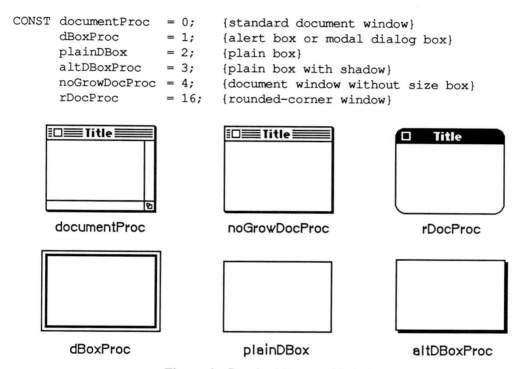

Figure 4. Standard Types of Windows

DocumentProc represents a standard document window that may or may not contain a size box; noGrowDocProc is exactly the same except that the window must *not* contain a size box. If you're working with a number of document windows that need to be treated similarly, but some will have size boxes and some won't, you can use documentProc for all of them. If none of the windows will have size boxes, however, it's more convenient to use noGrowDocProc.

The dBoxProc type of window resembles an alert box or a "modal" dialog box (the kind that requires the user to respond before doing any other work on the desktop). It's a rectangular window with no go-away region, drag region, or grow region and with a two-pixel-thick border two pixels in from the edge. It has no special highlighted state because alerts and modal dialogs are always displayed in the frontmost window. PlainDBox and altDBoxProc are variations of dBoxProc: plainDBox is just a plain box with no inner border, and altDBoxProc has a two-pixel-thick shadow instead of a border.

The rDocProc type of window is like a document window with no grow region, with rounded corners, and with a method of highlighting that inverts the entire title bar (that is, changes white to black and vice versa). It's often used for desk accessories. Rounded-corner windows are drawn by the QuickDraw procedure FrameRoundRect, which requires the diameters of curvature to be passed as parameters. For an rDocProc type of window, the diameters of curvature are both 16. You can add a number from 1 to 7 to rDocProc to get different diameters:

Window definition ID	Diameters of curvature
rDocProc	16, 16
rDocProc + 1	4, 4
rDocProc + 2	6, 6
rDocProc + 3	8, 8
rDocProc + 4	10, 10
rDocProc + 5	12, 12
rDocProc + 6	20, 20
rDocProc + 7	24, 24

To create a window, the Window Manager needs to know not only the window definition ID but also other information specific to this window, such as its title (if any), its location, and its plane. You can supply all the needed information in individual parameters to a Window Manager routine or, better yet, you can store it as a single resource in a resource file and just pass the resource ID. This type of resource is called a **window template**. Using window templates simplifies the process of creating a number of windows of the same type. More important, it allows you to isolate specific window descriptions from your application's code. Translation of window titles to another language, for example, would require only a change to the resource file.

WINDOW RECORDS

The Window Manager keeps all the information it requires for its operations on a particular window in a **window record**. The window record contains the following:

- The grafPort for the window.

- A handle to the window definition function.

- A handle to the window's title, if any.

- The **window class**, which tells whether the window is a system window, a dialog or alert window, or a window created directly by the application.

- A handle to the window's **control list**, which is a list of all the controls, if any, in the window. The Control Manager maintains this list.

- A pointer to the next window in the **window list**, which is a list of all windows on the desktop ordered according to their front-to-back positions.

The window record also contains an indication of whether the window is currently **visible** or **invisible**. These terms refer only to whether the window is drawn in its plane, not necessarily whether you can see it on the screen. If, for example, it's completely overlapped by another window, it's still "visible" even though it can't be seen in its current location.

The 32-bit **reference value** field of the window record is reserved for use by your application. You specify an initial reference value when you create a window, and can then read or change the reference value whenever you wish. For example, it might be a handle to data associated with the window, such as a TextEdit edit record.

Finally, a window record may contain a handle to a QuickDraw picture of the window contents. For a window whose contents never change, the application can simply have the Window Manager redraw this picture instead of using the update event mechanism. For more information, see "How a Window is Drawn".

The data type for a window record is called WindowRecord. A window record is referred to by a pointer, as discussed further under "Window Pointers" below. You can store into and access most of the fields of a window record with Window Manager routines, so normally you don't have to know the exact field names. Occasionally—particularly if you define your own type of window—you may need to know the exact structure; it's given below under "The WindowRecord Data Type".

Window Pointers

There are two types of pointer through which you can access windows: WindowPtr and WindowPeek. Most programmers will only need to use WindowPtr.

The Window Manager defines the following type of window pointer:

```
TYPE WindowPtr = GrafPtr;
```

It can do this because the first field of a window record contains the window's grafPort. This type of pointer can be used to access fields of the grafPort or can be passed to QuickDraw routines that expect pointers to grafPorts as parameters. The application might call such routines to draw into the window, and the Window Manager itself calls them to perform many of its operations. The Window Manager gets the additional information it needs from the rest of the window record beyond the grafPort.

In some cases, however, a more direct way of accessing the window record may be necessary or desirable. For this reason, the Window Manager also defines the following type of window pointer:

```
TYPE WindowPeek = ^WindowRecord;
```

Programmers who want to access WindowRecord fields directly must use this type of pointer (which derives its name from the fact that it lets you "peek" at the additional information about the window). A WindowPeek pointer is also used wherever the Window Manager will not be calling QuickDraw routines and will benefit from a more direct means of getting to the data stored in the window record.

Assembly-language note: From assembly language, of course, there's no type checking on pointers, and the two types of pointer are equal.

The WindowRecord Data Type

The exact data structure of a window record is as follows:

```
TYPE WindowRecord =
        RECORD
            port:           GrafPort;       {window's grafPort}
            windowKind:     INTEGER;        {window class}
            visible:        BOOLEAN;        {TRUE if visible}
            hilited:        BOOLEAN;        {TRUE if highlighted}
            goAwayFlag:     BOOLEAN;        {TRUE if has go-away region}
            spareFlag:      BOOLEAN;        {reserved for future use}
            strucRgn:       RgnHandle;      {structure region}
            contRgn:        RgnHandle;      {content region}
            updateRgn:      RgnHandle;      {update region}
            windowDefProc:  Handle;         {window definition function}
            dataHandle:     Handle;         {data used by windowDefProc}
            titleHandle:    StringHandle;   {window's title}
            titleWidth:     INTEGER;        {width of title in pixels}
            controlList:    ControlHandle;  {window's control list}
            nextWindow:     WindowPeek;     {next window in window list}
            windowPic:      PicHandle;      {picture for drawing window}
            refCon:         LONGINT;        {window's reference value}
        END;
```

The port is the window's grafPort.

WindowKind identifies the window class. If negative, it means the window is a system window (it's the desk accessory's reference number, as described in chapter 14). It may also be one of the following predefined constants:

```
CONST dialogKind = 2;   {dialog or alert window}
      userKind   = 8;   {window created directly by the application}
```

DialogKind is the window class for a dialog or alert window, whether created by the system or indirectly (via the Dialog Manger) by your application. UserKind represents a window created directly by application calls to the Window Manager; for such windows the application can in fact set the window class to any value greater than 8 if desired.

Note: WindowKind values 0, 1, and 3 through 7 are reserved for future use by the system.

When visible is TRUE, the window is currently visible.

Hilited and goAwayFlag are checked by the window definition function when it draws the window frame, to determine whether the window should be highlighted and whether it should have a go-away region. For a document window, this means that if hilited is TRUE, the title bar of the window is highlighted, and if goAwayFlag is also TRUE, a close box appears in the highlighted title bar.

Note: The Window Manager sets the visible and hilited flags to TRUE by storing 255 in them rather than 1. This may cause problems in Lisa Pascal; to be safe, you should check for the truth or falsity of these flags by comparing ORD of the flag to 0. For example, you would check to see if the flag is TRUE with ORD(myWindow^.visible) <> 0.

StrucRgn, contRgn, and updateRgn are region handles, as defined in QuickDraw, to the structure region, content region, and update region of the window. These regions are all in global coordinates.

WindowDefProc is a handle to the window definition function for this type of window. When you create a window, you identify its type with a window definition ID, which is converted into a handle and stored in the windowDefProc field. Thereafter, the Window Manager uses this handle to access the definition function; you should never need to access this field directly.

> **Note:** The high-order byte of the windowDefProc field contains some additional information that the Window Manager gets from the window definition ID; for details, see the section "Defining Your Own Windows".

DataHandle is reserved for use by the window definition function. If the window is one of your own definition, your window definition function may use this field to store and access any desired information. If no more than four bytes of information are needed, the definition function can store the information directly in the dataHandle field rather than use a handle. For example, the definition function for rounded-corner windows uses this field to store the diameters of curvature.

TitleHandle is a string handle to the window's title, if any.

TitleWidth is the width, in pixels, of the window's title in the system font and system font size. This width is determined by the Window Manager and is normally of no concern to the application.

ControlList is a control handle to the window's control list. The ControlHandle data type is defined in the Control Manager.

NextWindow is a pointer to the next window in the window list, that is, the window behind this window. If this window is the farthest back (with no windows between it and the desktop), nextWindow is NIL.

> **Assembly-language note:** The global variable WindowList contains a pointer to the first window in the window list. Remember that any window in the list may be invisible.

WindowPic is a handle to a QuickDraw picture of the window contents, or NIL if the application will draw the window contents in response to an update event, as described below under "How a Window is Drawn".

RefCon is the window's reference value field, which the application may store into and access for any purpose.

> **Note:** Notice that the go-away, drag, and grow regions are not included in the window record. Although these are conceptually regions, they don't necessarily have the formal data structure for regions as defined in QuickDraw. The window definition function determines where these regions are, and it can do so with great flexibility.

HOW A WINDOW IS DRAWN

When a window is drawn or redrawn, the following two-step process usually takes place: The Window Manager draws the window frame, then the application draws the window contents.

To perform the first step of this process, the Window Manager calls the window definition function with a request that the window frame be drawn. It manipulates regions of the Window Manager port as necessary before calling the window definition function, to ensure that only what should and must be drawn is actually drawn on the screen. Depending on a parameter passed to the routine that created the window, the window definition function may or may not draw a go-away region in the window frame (a close box in the title bar, for a document window).

Usually the second step is that the Window Manager generates an **update event** to get the application to draw the window contents. It does this by accumulating in the update region the areas of the window's content region that need updating. The Toolbox Event Manager periodically checks to see if there's any window whose update region is not empty; if it finds one, it reports (via the GetNextEvent function) that an update event has occurred, and passes along the window pointer in the event message. (If it finds more than one such window, it issues an update event for the frontmost one, so that update events are reported in front-to-back order.) The application should respond as follows:

1. Call BeginUpdate. This procedure temporarily replaces the visRgn of the window's grafPort with the intersection of the visRgn and the update region. It then sets the update region to an empty region; this "clears" the update event so it won't be reported again.

2. Draw the window contents, entirely or in part. Normally it's more convenient to draw the entire content region, but it suffices to draw only the visRgn. In either case, since the visRgn is limited to where it intersects the old update region, only the parts of the window that require updating will actually be drawn on the screen.

3. Call EndUpdate, which restores the normal visRgn.

Figure 5 illustrates the effect of BeginUpdate and EndUpdate on the visRgn and update region of a window that's redrawn after being brought to the front.

If you choose to draw only the visRgn in step 2, there are various ways you can check to see whether what you need to draw falls in that region. With the QuickDraw function PtInRgn, you can check whether a point lies in the visRgn. It may be more convenient to look at the visRgn's enclosing rectangle, which is stored in its rgnBBox field. The QuickDraw functions PtInRect and SectRect let you check for intersection with a rectangle.

To be able to respond to update events for one of its windows, the application has to keep track of the window's contents, usually in a data structure. In most cases, it's best *never* to draw immediately into a window; when you need to draw something, just keep track of it and add the area where it should be drawn to the window's update region (by calling one of the Window Manager's update region maintenance routines, InvalRect and InvalRgn). Do the actual drawing only in response to an update event. Usually this will simplify the structure of your application considerably, but be aware of the following possible problems:

■ This method doesn't work if you want to do continuous scrolling while the user presses a scroll arrow; in this case, you would draw directly into the window.

■ This method isn't convenient to apply to areas that aren't easily defined by a rectangle or a region; again, just draw directly into the window.

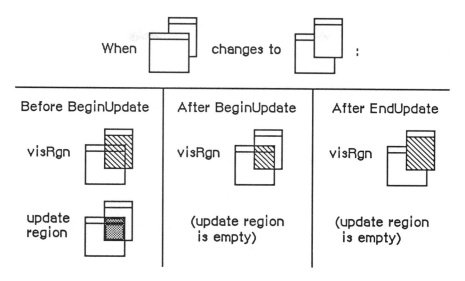

Figure 5. Updating Window Contents

■ If you find that sometimes there's too long a delay before an update event happens, you can get update events first when necessary by calling GetNextEvent with a mask that accepts only that type of event.

The Window Manager allows an alternative to the update event mechanism that may be useful for windows whose contents never change: A handle to a QuickDraw picture may be stored in the window record. If this is done, the Window Manager doesn't generate an update event to get the application to draw the window contents; instead, it calls the QuickDraw procedure DrawPicture to draw the picture whose handle is stored in the window record (and it does all the necessary region manipulation).

MAKING A WINDOW ACTIVE: ACTIVATE EVENTS

A number of Window Manager routines change the state of a window from inactive to active or from active to inactive. For each such change, the Window Manager generates an **activate event**, passing along the window pointer in the event message. The activeFlag bit in the modifiers field of the event record is set if the window has become active, or cleared if it has become inactive.

When the Toolbox Event Manager finds out from the Window Manager that an activate event has been generated, it passes the event on to the application (via the GetNextEvent function). Activate events have the highest priority of any type of event.

Usually when one window becomes active another becomes inactive, and vice versa, so activate events are most commonly generated in pairs. When this happens, the Window Manager generates first the event for the window becoming inactive, and then the event for the window becoming active. Sometimes only a single activate event is generated, such as when there's only one window in the window list, or when the active window is permanently disposed of (since it no longer exists).

Act⁻vate events for dialog and alert windows are handled by the Dialog Manager. In response to activate events for windows created directly by your application, you might take actions such as the following:

- In a document window containing a size box or scroll bars, erase the size box icon or scroll bars when the window becomes inactive and redraw them when it becomes active.

- In a window that contains text being edited, remove the highlighting or blinking vertical bar from the text when the window becomes inactive and restore it when the window becomes active.

- Enable or disable a menu or certain menu items as appropriate to match what the user can do when the window becomes active or inactive.

Assembly-language note: The global variable CurActivate contains a pointer to a window for which an activate event has been generated; the event, however, may not yet have been reported to the application via GetNextEvent, so you may be able to keep the event from happening by clearing CurActivate. Similarly, you may be able to keep a deactivate event from happening by clearing the global variable CurDeactive.

USING THE WINDOW MANAGER

To use the Window Manager, you must have previously called InitGraf to initialize QuickDraw and InitFonts to initialize the Font Manager. The first Window Manager routine to call is the initialization routine InitWindows, which draws the desktop and the (empty) menu bar.

Where appropriate in your program, use NewWindow or GetNewWindow to create any windows you need; these functions return a window pointer, which you can then use to refer to the window. NewWindow takes descriptive information about the window from its parameters, whereas GetNewWindow gets the information from a window template in a resource file. You can supply a pointer to the storage for the window record or let it be allocated by the routine creating the window; when you no longer need a window, call CloseWindow if you supplied the storage, or DisposeWindow if not.

When the Toolbox Event Manager function GetNextEvent reports that an update event has occurred, call BeginUpdate, draw the visRgn or the entire content region, and call EndUpdate (see "How a Window is Drawn"). You can also use InvalRect or InvalRgn to prepare a window for updating, and ValidRect or ValidRgn to protect portions of the window from updating.

When drawing the contents of a window that contains a size box in its content region, you'll draw the size box if the window is active or just the lines delimiting the size box and scroll bar areas if it's inactive. The FrontWindow function tells you which is the active window; the DrawGrowIcon procedure helps you draw the size box or delimiting lines. You'll also call the latter procedure when an activate event occurs that makes the window active or inactive.

Note: Before drawing in a window or making a call that affects the update region, remember to set the window to be the current grafPort with the QuickDraw procedure SetPort.

When GetNextEvent reports a mouse-down event, call the FindWindow function to find out which part of which window the mouse button was pressed in.

- If it was pressed in the content region of an inactive window, make that window the active window by calling SelectWindow.

- If it was pressed in the grow region of the active window, call GrowWindow to pull around an image that shows how the window's size will change, and then SizeWindow to actually change the size.

- If it was pressed in the drag region of any window, call DragWindow, which will pull an outline of the window across the screen, move the window to a new location, and, if the window is inactive, make it the active window (unless the Command key was held down).

- If it was pressed in the go-away region of the active window, call TrackGoAway to handle the highlighting of the go-away region and to determine whether the mouse is inside the region when the button is released. Then do whatever is appropriate as a response to this mouse action in the particular application. For example, call CloseWindow or DisposeWindow if you want the window to go away permanently, or HideWindow if you want it to disappear temporarily.

Note: If the mouse button was pressed in the content region of an active window (but not in the grow region), call the Control Manager function FindControl if the window contains controls. If it was pressed in a system window, call the Desk Manager procedure SystemClick. See chapters 10 and 14 for details.

The MoveWindow procedure simply moves a window without pulling around an outline of it. Note, however, that the application shouldn't surprise the user by moving (or sizing) windows unexpectedly. There are other routines that you normally won't need to use that let you change the title of a window, place one window behind another, make a window visible or invisible, and access miscellaneous fields of the window record. There are also low-level routines that may be of interest to advanced programmers.

WINDOW MANAGER ROUTINES

Initialization and Allocation

```
PROCEDURE InitWindows;
```

InitWindows initializes the Window Manager. It creates the Window Manager port; you can get a pointer to this port with the GetWMgrPort procedure. InitWindows draws the desktop (as a rounded-corner rectangle with diameters of curvature 16,16, in the desktop pattern) and the (empty) menu bar. Call this procedure once before all other Window Manager routines.

Note: The desktop pattern is the pattern whose resource ID is:

```
CONST deskPatID = 16;
```

If you store a pattern with resource ID deskPatID in the application's resource file, that pattern will be used whenever the desktop is drawn.

9 Window Manager

Warning: InitWindows creates the Window Manager port as a nonrelocatable block in the application heap. To prevent heap fragmentation, call InitWindows in the main segment of your program, before any references to routines in other segments.

Assembly-language note: InitWindows initializes the global variable GrayRgn to be a handle to the desktop region (a rounded-corner rectangle occupying the entire screen, minus the menu bar), and draws this region. It initializes the global variable DeskPattern to the pattern whose resource ID is deskPatID, and paints the desktop with this pattern. Any subsequent time that the desktop needs to be drawn, such as when a new area of it is exposed after a window is closed or moved, the Window Manager calls the procedure pointed to by the global variable DeskHook, if any (normally DeskHook is 0). The DeskHook procedure is called with 0 in register D0 to distinguish this use of it from its use in responding to clicks on the desktop (discussed in the description of FindWindow); it should respond by painting thePort^.clipRgn with DeskPattern and then doing anything else it wants.

```
PROCEDURE GetWMgrPort (VAR wPort: GrafPtr);
```

GetWMgrPort returns in wPort a pointer to the Window Manager port.

Warning: Do not change any regions of the Window Manager port, or overlapping windows may not be handled properly.

Assembly-language note: This pointer is stored in the global variable WMgrPort.

```
FUNCTION NewWindow (wStorage: Ptr; boundsRect: Rect; title:
          Str255; visible: BOOLEAN; procID: INTEGER; behind:
          WindowPtr; goAwayFlag: BOOLEAN; refCon: LONGINT) :
          WindowPtr;
```

NewWindow creates a window as specified by its parameters, adds it to the window list, and returns a windowPtr to the new window. It allocates space for the structure and content regions of the window and asks the window definition function to calculate those regions.

WStorage is a pointer to where to store the window record. For example, if you've declared the variable wRecord of type WindowRecord, you can pass @wRecord as the first parameter to NewWindow. If you pass NIL for wStorage, the window record will be allocated as a nonrelocatable object in the heap; in that case, though, you risk ending up with a fragmented heap.

BoundsRect, a rectangle given in global coordinates, determines the window's size and location, and becomes the portRect of the window's grafPort; note, however, that the portRect is in local coordinates. NewWindow sets the top left corner of the portRect to (0,0). For the standard types of windows, the boundsRect defines the content region of the window.

Note: The bit map, pen pattern, and other characteristics of the window's grafPort are the same as the default values set by the OpenPort procedure in QuickDraw, except for the character font, which is set to the application font rather than the system font. (NewWindow actually calls OpenPort to initialize the window's grafPort.) Note, however, that the coordinates of the grafPort's portBits.bounds and visRgn are changed along with its portRect.

The title parameter is the window's title. If the title of a document window is longer than will fit in the title bar, it's truncated in one of two ways: If the window has a close box, the characters that don't fit are truncated from the end of the title; if there's no close box, the title is centered and truncated at both ends.

If the visible parameter is TRUE, NewWindow draws the window. First it calls the window definition function to draw the window frame; if goAwayFlag is also TRUE and the window is frontmost (as specified by the behind parameter, below), it draws a go-away region in the frame. Then it generates an update event for the entire window contents.

ProcID is the window definition ID, which leads to the window definition function for this type of window. The function is read into memory if it's not already in memory. If it can't be read, NewWindow returns NIL. The window definition IDs for the standard types of windows are listed above under "Windows and Resources". Window definition IDs for windows of your own design are discussed later under "Defining Your Own Windows".

The behind parameter determines the window's plane. The new window is inserted in back of the window pointed to by this parameter. To put the new window behind all other windows, use behind=NIL. To place it in front of all other windows, use behind=POINTER(–1); in this case, NewWindow will unhighlight the previously active window, highlight the window being created, and generate appropriate activate events.

RefCon is the window's reference value, set and used only by your application.

NewWindow also sets the window class in the window record to indicate that the window was created directly by the application.

```
FUNCTION GetNewWindow (windowID: INTEGER; wStorage: Ptr; behind:
        WindowPtr) : WindowPtr;
```

Like NewWindow (above), GetNewWindow creates a window as specified by its parameters, adds it to the window list, and returns a windowPtr to the new window. The only difference between the two functions is that instead of having the parameters boundsRect, title, visible, procID, goAwayFlag, and refCon, GetNewWindow has a single windowID parameter, where windowID is the resource ID of a window template that supplies the same information as those parameters. If the window template can't be read from the resource file, GetNewWindow returns NIL. GetNewWindow releases the memory occupied by the resource before returning. The wStorage and behind parameters have the same meaning as in NewWindow.

```
PROCEDURE CloseWindow (theWindow: WindowPtr);
```

CloseWindow removes the given window from the screen and deletes it from the window list. It releases the memory occupied by all data structures associated with the window, but *not* the memory taken up by the window record itself. Call this procedure when you're done with a window if you supplied NewWindow or GetNewWindow a pointer to the window storage (in the wStorage parameter) when you created the window.

Any update events for the window are discarded. If the window was the frontmost window and there was another window behind it, the latter window is highlighted and an appropriate activate event is generated.

> **Warning:** If you allocated memory yourself and stored a handle to it in the refCon field, CloseWindow won't know about it—you must release the memory before calling CloseWindow. Similarly, if you used the windowPic field to access a picture stored as a resource, you must release the memory it occupies; CloseWindow assumes the picture isn't a resource, and calls the QuickDraw procedure KillPicture to delete it.

```
PROCEDURE DisposeWindow (theWindow: WindowPtr);
```

Assembly-language note: The macro you invoke to call DisposeWindow from assembly language is named _DisposWindow.

DisposeWindow calls CloseWindow (above) and then releases the memory occupied by the window record. Call this procedure when you're done with a window if you let the window record be allocated in the heap when you created the window (by passing NIL as the wStorage parameter to NewWindow or GetNewWindow).

Window Display

These procedures affect the appearance or plane of a window but not its size or location.

```
PROCEDURE SetWTitle (theWindow: WindowPtr; title: Str255);
```

SetWTitle sets theWindow's title to the given string, performing any necessary redrawing of the window frame.

```
PROCEDURE GetWTitle (theWindow: WindowPtr; VAR title: Str255);
```

GetWTitle returns theWindow's title as the value of the title parameter.

```
PROCEDURE SelectWindow (theWindow: WindowPtr);
```

SelectWindow makes theWindow the active window as follows: It unhighlights the previously active window, brings theWindow in front of all other windows, highlights theWindow, and generates the appropriate activate events. Call this procedure if there's a mouse-down event in the content region of an inactive window.

```
PROCEDURE HideWindow (theWindow: WindowPtr);
```

HideWindow makes theWindow invisible. If theWindow is the frontmost window and there's a window behind it, HideWindow also unhighlights theWindow, brings the window behind it to the front, highlights that window, and generates appropriate activate events (see Figure 6). If theWindow is already invisible, HideWindow has no effect.

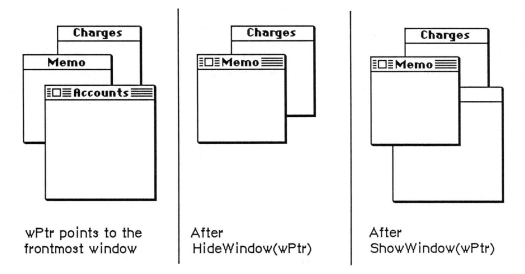

Figure 6. Hiding and Showing Document Windows

```
PROCEDURE ShowWindow (theWindow: WindowPtr);
```

ShowWindow makes theWindow visible. It does not change the front-to-back ordering of the windows. Remember that if you previously hid the frontmost window with HideWindow, HideWindow will have brought the window behind it to the front; so if you then do a ShowWindow of the window you hid, it will no longer be frontmost (see Figure 6). If theWindow is already visible, ShowWindow has no effect.

Note: Although it's inadvisable, you can create a situation where the frontmost window is invisible. If you do a ShowWindow of such a window, it will highlight the window if it's not already highlighted and will generate an activate event to force this window from inactive to active.

```
PROCEDURE ShowHide (theWindow: WindowPtr; showFlag: BOOLEAN);
```

If showFlag is TRUE, ShowHide makes theWindow visible if it's not already visible and has no effect if it is already visible. If showFlag is FALSE, ShowHide makes theWindow invisible if it's not already invisible and has no effect if it is already invisible. Unlike HideWindow and ShowWindow, ShowHide never changes the highlighting or front-to-back ordering of windows or generates activate events.

> **Warning:** Use this procedure carefully, and only in special circumstances where you need more control than allowed by HideWindow and ShowWindow.

```
PROCEDURE HiliteWindow (theWindow: WindowPtr; fHilite: BOOLEAN);
```

If fHilite is TRUE, this procedure highlights theWindow if it's not already highlighted and has no effect if it is highlighted. If fHilite is FALSE, HiliteWindow unhighlights theWindow if it is highlighted and has no effect if it's not highlighted. The exact way a window is highlighted depends on its window definition function.

Normally you won't have to call this procedure, since you should call SelectWindow to make a window active, and SelectWindow takes care of the necessary highlighting changes. Highlighting a window that isn't the active window is contrary to the Macintosh User Interface Guidelines.

```
PROCEDURE BringToFront (theWindow: WindowPtr);
```

BringToFront brings theWindow to the front of all other windows and redraws the window as necessary. Normally you won't have to call this procedure, since you should call SelectWindow to make a window active, and SelectWindow takes care of bringing the window to the front. If you do call BringToFront, however, remember to call HiliteWindow to make the necessary highlighting changes.

```
PROCEDURE SendBehind (theWindow,behindWindow: WindowPtr);
```

SendBehind sends theWindow behind behindWindow, redrawing any exposed windows. If behindWindow is NIL, it sends theWindow behind all other windows. If theWindow is the active window, it unhighlights theWindow, highlights the new active window, and generates the appropriate activate events.

> **Warning:** Do not use SendBehind to deactivate a previously active window. Calling SelectWindow to make a window active takes care of deactivating the previously active window.

> **Note:** If you're moving theWindow closer to the front (that is, if it's initially even farther behind behindWindow), you must make the following calls after calling SendBehind:
>
> ```
> wPeek := POINTER(theWindow);
> PaintOne(wPeek, wPeek^.strucRgn);
> CalcVis(wPeek)
> ```
>
> PaintOne and CalcVis are described under "Low-Level Routines".

```
FUNCTION FrontWindow : WindowPtr;
```

FrontWindow returns a pointer to the first visible window in the window list (that is, the active window). If there are no visible windows, it returns NIL.

Assembly-language note: In the global variable GhostWindow, you can store a pointer to a window that's not to be considered frontmost even if it is (for example, if you want to have a special editing window always present and floating above all the others). If the window pointed to by GhostWindow is the first window in the window list, FrontWindow will return a pointer to the next visible window.

```
PROCEDURE DrawGrowIcon (theWindow: WindowPtr);
```

Call DrawGrowIcon in response to an update or activate event involving a window that contains a size box in its content region. If theWindow is active, DrawGrowIcon draws the size box; otherwise, it draws whatever is appropriate to show that the window temporarily cannot be sized. The exact appearance and location of what's drawn depend on the window definition function. For an active document window, DrawGrowIcon draws the size box icon in the bottom right corner of the portRect of the window's grafPort, along with the lines delimiting the size box and scroll bar areas (15 pixels in from the right edge and bottom of the portRect). It doesn't erase the scroll bar areas, so if the window doesn't contain scroll bars you should erase those areas yourself after the window's size changes. For an inactive document window, DrawGrowIcon draws only the lines delimiting the size box and scroll bar areas, and erases the size box icon.

Mouse Location

```
FUNCTION FindWindow (thePt: Point; VAR whichWindow: WindowPtr) :
         INTEGER;
```

When a mouse-down event occurs, the application should call FindWindow with thePt equal to the point where the mouse button was pressed (in global coordinates, as stored in the where field of the event record). FindWindow tells which part of which window, if any, the mouse button was pressed in. If it was pressed in a window, the whichWindow parameter is set to the window pointer; otherwise, it's set to NIL. The integer returned by FindWindow is one of the following predefined constants:

```
CONST inDesk      = 0;  {none of the following}
      inMenuBar   = 1;  {in menu bar}
      inSysWindow = 2;  {in system window}
      inContent   = 3;  {in content region (except grow, if active)}
      inDrag      = 4;  {in drag region}
      inGrow      = 5;  {in grow region (active window only)}
      inGoAway    = 6;  {in go-away region (active window only)}
```

InDesk usually means that the mouse button was pressed on the desktop, outside the menu bar or any windows; however, it may also mean that the mouse button was pressed inside a window frame but not in the drag region or go-away region of the window. Usually one of the last four values is returned for windows created by the application.

9

Window Manager

Assembly-language note: If you store a pointer to a procedure in the global variable DeskHook, it will be called when the mouse button is pressed on the desktop. The DeskHook procedure will be called with –1 in register D0 to distinguish this use of it from its use in drawing the desktop (discussed in the description of InitWindows). Register A0 will contain a pointer to the event record for the mouse-down event. When you use DeskHook in this way, FindWindow does not return inDesk when the mouse button is pressed on the desktop; it returns inSysWindow, and the Desk Manager procedure SystemClick calls the DeskHook procedure.

If the window is a documentProc type of window that doesn't contain a size box, the application should treat inGrow the same as inContent; if it's a noGrowDocProc type of window, FindWindow will never return inGrow for that window. If the window is a documentProc, noGrowDocProc, or rDocProc type of window with no close box, FindWindow will never return inGoAway for that window.

```
FUNCTION TrackGoAway (theWindow: WindowPtr; thePt: Point) :
          BOOLEAN;
```

When there's a mouse-down event in the go-away region of theWindow, the application should call TrackGoAway with thePt equal to the point where the mouse button was pressed (in global coordinates, as stored in the where field of the event record). TrackGoAway keeps control until the mouse button is released, highlighting the go-away region as long as the mouse location remains inside it, and unhighlighting it when the mouse moves outside it. The exact way a window's go-away region is highlighted depends on its window definition function; the highlighting of a document window's close box is illustrated in Figure 7. When the mouse button is released, TrackGoAway unhighlights the go-away region and returns TRUE if the mouse is inside the go-away region or FALSE if it's outside the region (in which case the application should do nothing).

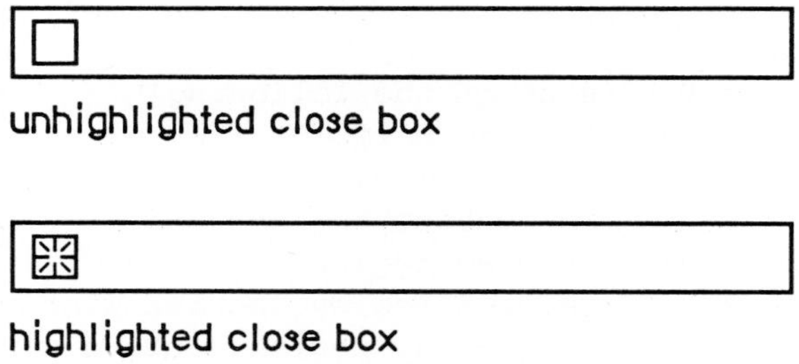

unhighlighted close box

highlighted close box

Figure 7. A Document Window's Close Box

Assembly-language note: If you store a pointer to a procedure in the global variable DragHook, TrackGoAway will call that procedure repeatedly (with no parameters) for as long as the user holds down the mouse button.

Window Movement and Sizing

```
PROCEDURE MoveWindow (theWindow: WindowPtr; hGlobal,vGlobal:
        INTEGER; front: BOOLEAN);
```

MoveWindow moves theWindow to another part of the screen, without affecting its size or plane. The top left corner of the portRect of the window's grafPort is moved to the screen point indicated by the global coordinates hGlobal and vGlobal. The local coordinates of the top left corner remain the same. If the front parameter is TRUE and theWindow isn't the active window, MoveWindow makes it the active window by calling SelectWindow(theWindow).

```
PROCEDURE DragWindow (theWindow: WindowPtr; startPt: Point;
        boundsRect: Rect);
```

When there's a mouse-down event in the drag region of theWindow, the application should call DragWindow with startPt equal to the point where the mouse button was pressed (in global coordinates, as stored in the where field of the event record). DragWindow pulls a dotted outline of theWindow around, following the movements of the mouse until the button is released. When the mouse button is released, DragWindow calls MoveWindow to move theWindow to the location to which it was dragged. If theWindow isn't the active window (and the Command key wasn't being held down), DragWindow makes it the active window by passing TRUE for the front parameter when calling MoveWindow. If the Command key was being held down, the window is moved without being made the active window.

BoundsRect is also given in global coordinates. If the mouse button is released when the mouse location is outside the limits of boundsRect, DragWindow returns without moving theWindow or making it the active window. For a document window, boundsRect typically will be four pixels in from the menu bar and from the other edges of the screen, to ensure that there won't be less than a four-pixel-square area of the title bar visible on the screen.

Assembly-language note: As for TrackGoAway, if you store a pointer to a procedure in the global variable DragHook, that procedure will be called repeatedly while the user holds down the mouse button. (DragWindow calls DragGrayRgn, which calls the DragHook procedure).

```
FUNCTION GrowWindow (theWindow: WindowPtr; startPt: Point;
        sizeRect: Rect) : LONGINT;
```

When there's a mouse-down event in the grow region of theWindow, the application should call GrowWindow with startPt equal to the point where the mouse button was pressed (in global coordinates, as stored in the where field of the event record). GrowWindow pulls a **grow image** of the window around, following the movements of the mouse until the button is released. The grow image for a document window is a dotted outline of the entire window and also the lines delimiting the title bar, size box, and scroll bar areas; Figure 8 illustrates this for a document window containing both scroll bars, but the grow image would be the same even if the window contained one or no scroll bars. In general, the grow image is defined in the window definition function and is whatever is appropriate to show that the window's size will change.

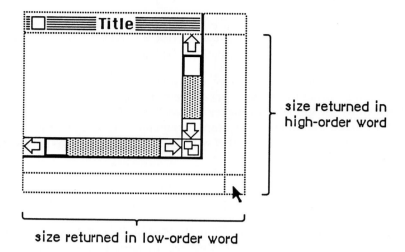

Figure 8. GrowWindow Operation on a Document Window

The application should subsequently call SizeWindow to change the portRect of the window's grafPort to the new one outlined by the grow image. The sizeRect parameter specifies limits, in pixels, on the vertical and horizontal measurements of what will be the new portRect. SizeRect.top is the minimum vertical measurement, sizeRect.left is the minimum horizontal measurement, sizeRect.bottom is the maximum vertical measurement, and sizeRect.right is the maximum horizontal measurement.

GrowWindow returns the actual size for the new portRect as outlined by the grow image when the mouse button is released. The high-order word of the long integer is the vertical measurement in pixels and the low-order word is the horizontal measurement. A return value of 0 indicates that the size is the same as that of the current portRect.

> **Note:** The Toolbox Utility function HiWord takes a long integer as a parameter and returns an integer equal to its high-order word; the function LoWord returns the low-order word.

> **Assembly-language note:** Like TrackGoAway, GrowWindow repeatedly calls the procedure pointed to by the global variable DragHook (if any) as long as the mouse button is held down.

```
PROCEDURE SizeWindow (theWindow: WindowPtr; w,h: INTEGER; fUpdate:
         BOOLEAN);
```

SizeWindow enlarges or shrinks the portRect of theWindow's grafPort to the width and height specified by w and h, or does nothing if w and h are 0. The window's position on the screen does not change. The new window frame is drawn; if the width of a document window changes, the title is again centered in the title bar, or is truncated if it no longer fits. If fUpdate is TRUE, SizeWindow accumulates any newly created area of the content region into the update region (see

Figure 9); normally this is what you'll want. If you pass FALSE for fUpdate, you're responsible for the update region maintenance yourself. For more information, see InvalRect and ValidRect.

After SizeWindow(wPtr, w1, h1, TRUE)

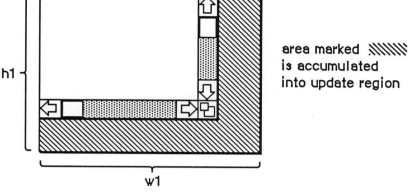

area marked ▧ is accumulated into update region

Figure 9. SizeWindow Operation on a Document Window

Update Region Maintenance

```
PROCEDURE InvalRect (badRect: Rect);
```

InvalRect accumulates the given rectangle into the update region of the window whose grafPort is the current port. This tells the Window Manager that the rectangle has changed and must be updated. The rectangle is given in local coordinates and is clipped to the window's content region.

For example, this procedure is useful when you're calling SizeWindow for a document window that contains a size box or scroll bars. Suppose you're going to call SizeWindow with fUpdate=TRUE. If the window is enlarged as shown in Figure 8, you'll want not only the newly created part of the content region to be updated, but also the two rectangular areas containing the (former) size box and scroll bars; before calling SizeWindow, you can call InvalRect twice to accumulate those areas into the update region. In case the window is made smaller, you'll want the new size box and scroll bar areas to be updated, and so can similarly call InvalRect for those areas after calling SizeWindow. See Figure 10 for an illustration of this type of update region maintenance.

As another example, suppose your application scrolls up text in a document window and wants to show new text added at the bottom of the window. You can cause the added text to be redrawn by accumulating that area into the update region with InvalRect.

```
PROCEDURE InvalRgn (badRgn: RgnHandle);
```

InvalRgn is the same as InvalRect but for a region that has changed rather than a rectangle.

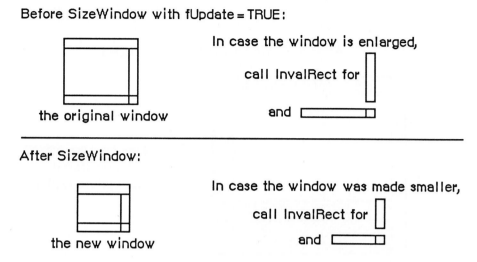

Figure 10. Update Region Maintenance with InvalRect

```
PROCEDURE ValidRect (goodRect: Rect);
```

ValidRect removes goodRect from the update region of the window whose grafPort is the current port. This tells the Window Manager that the application has already drawn the rectangle and to cancel any updates accumulated for that area. The rectangle is clipped to the window's content region and is given in local coordinates. Using ValidRect results in better performance and less redundant redrawing in the window.

For example, suppose you've called SizeWindow with fUpdate=TRUE for a document window that contains a size box or scroll bars. Depending on the dimensions of the newly sized window, the new size box and scroll bar areas may or may not have been accumulated into the window's update region. After calling SizeWindow, you can redraw the size box or scroll bars immediately and then call ValidRect for the areas they occupy in case they were in fact accumulated into the update region; this will avoid redundant drawing.

```
PROCEDURE ValidRgn (goodRgn: RgnHandle);
```

ValidRgn is the same as ValidRect but for a region that has been drawn rather than a rectangle.

```
PROCEDURE BeginUpdate (theWindow: WindowPtr);
```

Call BeginUpdate when an update event occurs for theWindow. BeginUpdate replaces the visRgn of the window's grafPort with the intersection of the visRgn and the update region and then sets the window's update region to an empty region. You would then usually draw the entire content region, though it suffices to draw only the visRgn; in either case, only the parts of the window that require updating will actually be drawn on the screen. Every call to BeginUpdate must be balanced by a call to EndUpdate. (See "How a Window is Drawn".)

Note: In Pascal, BeginUpdate and EndUpdate calls can't be nested (that is, you must call EndUpdate before the next call to BeginUpdate).

Assembly-language note: A handle to a copy of the original visRgn (in global coordinates) is stored in the global variable SaveVisRgn. You can nest BeginUpdate and EndUpdate calls in assembly language if you save and restore this region.

```
PROCEDURE EndUpdate (theWindow: WindowPtr);
```

Call EndUpdate to restore the normal visRgn of theWindow's grafPort, which was changed by BeginUpdate as described above.

Miscellaneous Routines

```
PROCEDURE SetWRefCon (theWindow: WindowPtr; data: LONGINT);
```

SetWRefCon sets theWindow's reference value to the given data.

```
FUNCTION GetWRefCon (theWindow: WindowPtr) : LONGINT;
```

GetWRefCon returns theWindow's current reference value.

```
PROCEDURE SetWindowPic (theWindow: WindowPtr; pic: PicHandle);
```

SetWindowPic stores the given picture handle in the window record for theWindow, so that when theWindow's contents are to be drawn, the Window Manager will draw this picture rather than generate an update event.

```
FUNCTION GetWindowPic (theWindow: WindowPtr) : PicHandle;
```

GetWindowPic returns the handle to the picture that draws theWindow's contents, previously stored with SetWindowPic.

```
FUNCTION PinRect (theRect: Rect; thePt: Point) : LONGINT;
```

PinRect "pins" thePt inside theRect: If thePt is inside theRect, thePt is returned; otherwise, the point associated with the nearest pixel within theRect is returned. (The high-order word of the long integer returned is the vertical coordinate; the low-order word is the horizontal coordinate.) More precisely, for theRect (left,top) (right,bottom) and thePt (h,v), PinRect does the following:

- If h < left, it returns left.
- If v < top, it returns top.
- If h > right, it returns right–1.

■ If v > bottom, it returns bottom–1.

Note: The 1 is subtracted when thePt is below or to the right of theRect so that a pixel drawn at that point will lie within theRect. However, if thePt is exactly on the bottom or right edge of theRect, 1 should be subtracted but isn't.

```
FUNCTION DragGrayRgn (theRgn: RgnHandle; startPt: Point;
          limitRect,slopRect: Rect; axis: INTEGER; actionProc:
          ProcPtr) : LONGINT;
```

Called when the mouse button is down inside theRgn, DragGrayRgn pulls a dotted (gray) outline of the region around, following the movements of the mouse until the button is released. DragWindow calls this function before actually moving the window. You can call it yourself to pull around the outline of any region, and then use the information it returns to determine where to move the region.

Note: DragGrayRgn alters the region; if you don't want the original region changed, pass DragGrayRgn a handle to a copy.

The startPt parameter is assumed to be the point where the mouse button was originally pressed, in the local coordinates of the current grafPort.

LimitRect and slopRect are also in the local coordinates of the current grafPort. To explain these parameters, the concept of "offset point" must be introduced: This is initially the point whose vertical and horizontal offsets from the top left corner of the region's enclosing rectangle are the same as those of startPt. The offset point follows the mouse location, except that DragGrayRgn will never move the offset point outside limitRect; this limits the travel of the region's outline (but not the movements of the mouse). SlopRect, which should completely enclose limitRect, allows the user some "slop" in moving the mouse. DragGrayRgn's behavior while tracking the mouse depends on the location of the mouse with respect to these two rectangles:

■ When the mouse is inside limitRect, the region's outline follows it normally. If the mouse button is released there, the region should be moved to the mouse location.

■ When the mouse is outside limitRect but inside slopRect, DragGrayRgn "pins" the offset point to the edge of limitRect. If the mouse button is released there, the region should be moved to this pinned location.

■ When the mouse is outside slopRect, the outline disappears from the screen, but DragGrayRgn continues to follow the mouse; if it moves back into slopRect, the outline reappears. If the mouse button is released outside slopRect, the region should not be moved from its original position.

Figure 11 illustrates what happens when the mouse is moved outside limitRect but inside slopRect, for a rectangular region. The offset point is pinned as the mouse location moves on.

If the mouse button is released within slopRect, the high-order word of the value returned by DragGrayRgn contains the vertical coordinate of the ending mouse location minus that of startPt and the low-order word contains the difference between the horizontal coordinates. If the mouse button is released outside slopRect, both words contain –32768 ($8000).

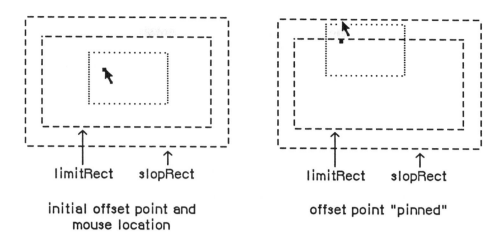

Figure 11. DragGrayRgn Operation on a Rectangular Region

The axis parameter allows you to constrain the region's motion to only one axis. It has one of the following values:

```
CONST noConstraint = 0;    {no constraint}
      hAxisOnly     = 1;    {horizontal axis only}
      vAxisOnly     = 2;    {vertical axis only}
```

If an axis constraint is in effect, the outline will follow the mouse's movements along the specified axis only, ignoring motion along the other axis. With or without an axis constraint, the mouse must still be inside the slop rectangle for the outline to appear at all.

The actionProc parameter is a pointer to a procedure that defines some action to be performed repeatedly for as long as the user holds down the mouse button; the procedure should have no parameters. If actionProc is NIL, DragGrayRgn simply retains control until the mouse button is released.

Assembly-language note: DragGrayRgn calls the procedure pointed to by the global variable DragHook, if any, as long as the mouse button is held down. (If there's an actionProc procedure, the actionProc procedure is called first.)

If you want the region's outline to be drawn in a pattern other than gray, you can store the pattern in the global variable DragPattern and then invoke the macro _DragTheRgn.

Low-Level Routines

These routines are called by higher-level routines; normally you won't need to call them yourself.

```
FUNCTION CheckUpdate (VAR theEvent: EventRecord) : BOOLEAN;
```

CheckUpdate is called by the Toolbox Event Manager. From the front to the back in the window list, it looks for a visible window that needs updating (that is, whose update region is not empty). If it finds one whose window record contains a picture handle, it draws the picture (doing all the necessary region manipulation) and looks for the next visible window that needs updating. If it ever finds one whose window record doesn't contain a picture handle, it stores an update event for that window in theEvent and returns TRUE. If it never finds such a window, it returns FALSE.

```
PROCEDURE ClipAbove (window: WindowPeek);
```

ClipAbove sets the clipRgn of the Window Manager port to be the desktop intersected with the current clipRgn, minus the structure regions of all the windows in front of the given window.

Assembly-language note: ClipAbove gets the desktop region from the global variable GrayRgn.

```
PROCEDURE SaveOld (window: WindowPeek);
```

SaveOld saves the given window's current structure region and content region for the DrawNew operation (see below). It must be balanced by a subsequent call to DrawNew.

```
PROCEDURE DrawNew (window: WindowPeek; update: BOOLEAN);
```

If the update parameter is TRUE, DrawNew updates the area

(OldStructure XOR NewStructure) UNION (OldContent XOR NewContent)

where OldStructure and OldContent are the structure and content regions saved by the SaveOld procedure, and NewStructure and NewContent are the current structure and content regions. It erases the area and adds it to the window's update region. If update is FALSE, it only erases the area.

Warning: In Pascal, SaveOld and DrawNew are *not* nestable.

Assembly-language note: In assembly language, you can nest SaveOld and DrawNew if you save and restore the values of the global variables OldStructure and OldContent.

```
PROCEDURE PaintOne (window: WindowPeek; clobberedRgn: RgnHandle);
```

PaintOne "paints" the given window, clipped to clobberedRgn and all windows above it: It draws the window frame and, if some content is exposed, erases the exposed area (paints it with the background pattern) and adds it to the window's update region. If the window parameter is NIL, the window is the desktop and so is painted with the desktop pattern.

Assembly-language note: The global variables SaveUpdate and PaintWhite are flags used by PaintOne. Normally both flags are set. Clearing SaveUpdate prevents clobberedRgn from being added to the window's update region. Clearing PaintWhite prevents clobberedRgn from being erased before being added to the update region (this is useful, for example, if the background of the window isn't the background pattern). The Window Manager sets both flags periodically, so you should clear the appropriate flag just before each situation you wish it to apply to.

```
PROCEDURE PaintBehind (startWindow: WindowPeek; clobberedRgn:
            RgnHandle);
```

PaintBehind calls PaintOne for startWindow and all the windows behind startWindow, clipped to clobberedRgn.

Assembly-language note: PaintBehind clears the global variable PaintWhite before calling PaintOne, so clobberedRgn isn't erased. (PaintWhite is reset after the call to PaintOne.)

```
PROCEDURE CalcVis (window: WindowPeek);
```

CalcVis calculates the visRgn of the given window by starting with its content region and subtracting the structure region of each window in front of it.

```
PROCEDURE CalcVisBehind (startWindow: WindowPeek; clobberedRgn:
            RgnHandle);
```

Assembly-language note: The macro you invoke to call CalcVisBehind from assembly language is named _CalcVBehind.

CalcVisBehind calculates the visRgns of startWindow and all windows behind startWindow that intersect clobberedRgn. It should be called after PaintBehind.

DEFINING YOUR OWN WINDOWS

Certain types of windows, such as the standard document window, are predefined for you. However, you may want to define your own type of window—maybe a round or hexagonal window, or even a window shaped like an apple. QuickDraw and the Window Manager make it possible for you to do this.

> **Note:** For the convenience of your application's user, remember to conform to the Macintosh User Interface Guidelines for windows as much as possible.

To define your own type of window, you write a window definition function and store it in a resource file. When you create a window, you provide a window definition ID, which leads to the window definition function. The window definition ID is an integer that contains the resource ID of the window definition function in its upper 12 bits and a **variation code** in its lower four bits. Thus, for a given resource ID and variation code, the window definition ID is

16 * resource ID + variation code

The variation code allows a single window definition function to implement several related types of window as "variations on a theme". For example, the dBoxProc type of window is a variation of the standard document window; both use the window definition function whose resource ID is 0, but the document window has a variation code of 0 while the dBoxProc window has a variation code of 1.

The Window Manager calls the Resource Manager to access the window definition function with the given resource ID. The Resource Manager reads the window definition function into memory and returns a handle to it. The Window Manager stores this handle in the windowDefProc field of the window record, along with the variation code in the high-order byte of that field. Later, when it needs to perform a type-dependent action on the window, it calls the window definition function and passes it the variation code as a parameter. Figure 12 illustrates this process.

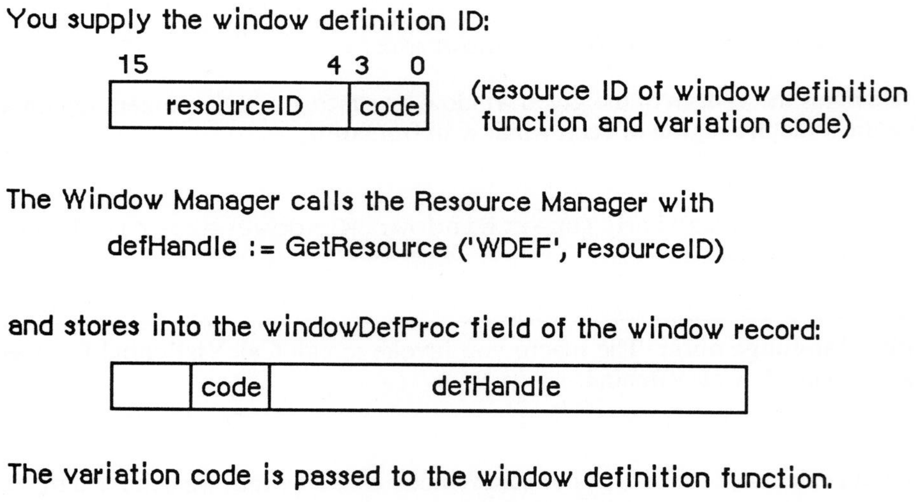

You supply the window definition ID:

```
 15              4 3   0
┌─────────────┬──────┐
│  resourceID │ code │     (resource ID of window definition
└─────────────┴──────┘      function and variation code)
```

The Window Manager calls the Resource Manager with

defHandle := GetResource ('WDEF', resourceID)

and stores into the windowDefProc field of the window record:

```
┌────┬──────┬─────────────────┐
│    │ code │    defHandle    │
└────┴──────┴─────────────────┘
```

The variation code is passed to the window definition function.

Figure 12. Window Definition Handling

The Window Definition Function

The window definition function is usually written in assembly language, but may be written in Pascal.

Assembly-language note: The function's entry point must be at the beginning.

You may choose any name you wish for your window definition function. Here's how you would declare one named MyWindow:

```
FUNCTION MyWindow (varCode: INTEGER; theWindow: WindowPtr; message:
        INTEGER; param: LONGINT) : LONGINT;
```

VarCode is the variation code, as described above.

TheWindow indicates the window that the operation will affect. If the window definition function needs to use a WindowPeek type of pointer more than a WindowPtr, you can simply specify WindowPeek instead of WindowPtr in the function declaration.

The message parameter identifies the desired operation. It has one of the following values:

```
CONST wDraw      = 0;   {draw window frame}
      wHit       = 1;   {tell what region mouse button was pressed in}
      wCalcRgns  = 2;   {calculate strucRgn and contRgn}
      wNew       = 3;   {do any additional window initialization}
      wDispose   = 4;   {take any additional disposal actions}
      wGrow      = 5;   {draw window's grow image}
      wDrawGIcon = 6;   {draw size box in content region}
```

As described below in the discussions of the routines that perform these operations, the value passed for param, the last parameter of the window definition function, depends on the operation. Where it's not mentioned below, this parameter is ignored. Similarly, the window definition function is expected to return a function result only where indicated; in other cases, the function should return 0.

Note: "Routine" here doesn't necessarily mean a procedure or function. While it's a good idea to set these up as subprograms inside the window definition function, you're not required to do so.

The Draw Window Frame Routine

When the window definition function receives a wDraw message, it should draw the window frame in the current grafPort, which will be the Window Manager port. (For details on drawing, see chapter 6.)

This routine should make certain checks to determine exactly what it should do. If the visible field in the window record is FALSE, the routine should do nothing; otherwise, it should examine the value of param received by the window definition function, as described below.

If param is 0, the routine should draw the entire window frame. If the hilited field in the window record is TRUE, the window frame should be highlighted in whatever way is appropriate to show that this is the active window. If goAwayFlag in the window record is also TRUE, the highlighted window frame should include a go-away region; this is useful when you want to define a window such that a particular window of that type may or may not have a go-away region, depending on the situation.

Special action should be taken if the value of param is wInGoAway (a predefined constant, equal to 4, which is one of those returned by the hit routine described below). If param is wInGoAway, the routine should do nothing but "toggle" the state of the window's go-away region from unhighlighted to highlighted or vice versa. The highlighting should be whatever is appropriate to show that the mouse button has been pressed inside the region. Simple inverse highlighting may be used or, as in document windows, the appearance of the region may change considerably. In the latter case, the routine could use a "mask" consisting of the unhighlighted state of the region XORed with its highlighted state (where XOR stands for the logical operation "exclusive or"). When such a mask is itself XORed with either state of the region, the result is the other state; Figure 13 illustrates this for a document window.

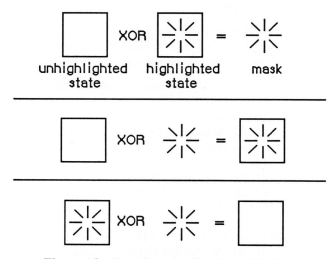

Figure 13. Toggling the Go-Away Region

Typically the window frame will include the window's title, which should be in the system font and system font size. The Window Manager port will already be set to use the system font and system font size.

Note: Nothing drawn outside the window's structure region will be visible.

The Hit Routine

When the window definition function receives a wHit message, it also receives as its param value the point where the mouse button was pressed. This point is given in global coordinates, with the vertical coordinate in the high-order word of the long integer and the horizontal coordinate in the low-order word. The window definition function should determine where the mouse button "hit" and then return one of these predefined constants:

```
CONST wNoHit      = 0;   {none of the following}
      wInContent  = 1;   {in content region (except grow, if active)}
      wInDrag     = 2;   {in drag region}
      wInGrow     = 3;   {in grow region (active window only)}
      wInGoAway   = 4;   {in go-away region (active window only)}
```

Usually, wNoHit means the given point isn't anywhere within the window, but this is not necessarily so. For example, the document window's hit routine returns wNoHit if the point is in the window frame but not in the title bar.

The constants wInGrow and wInGoAway should be returned only if the window is active, since by convention the size box and go-away region won't be drawn if the window is inactive (or, if drawn, won't be operable). In an inactive document window, if the mouse button is pressed in the title bar where the close box would be if the window were active, the hit routine returns wInDrag.

Of the regions that may have been hit, only the content region necessarily has the structure of a region and is included in the window record. The hit routine can determine in any way it likes whether the drag, grow, or go-away "region" has been hit.

The Routine to Calculate Regions

The routine executed in response to a wCalcRgns message should calculate the window's structure region and content region based on the current grafPort's portRect. These regions, whose handles are in the strucRgn and contRgn fields, are in global coordinates. The Window Manager will request this operation only if the window is visible.

> **Warning:** When you calculate regions for your own type of window, do not alter the clipRgn or the visRgn of the window's grafPort. The Window Manager and QuickDraw take care of this for you. Altering the clipRgn or visRgn may result in damage to other windows.

The Initialize Routine

After initializing fields as appropriate when creating a new window, the Window Manager sends the message wNew to the window definition function. This gives the definition function a chance to perform any type-specific initialization it may require. For example, if the content region is unusually shaped, the initialize routine might allocate space for the region and store the region handle in the dataHandle field of the window record. The initialize routine for a standard document window does nothing.

The Dispose Routine

The Window Manager's CloseWindow and DisposeWindow procedures send the message wDispose to the window definition function, telling it to carry out any additional actions required when disposing of the window. The dispose routine might, for example, release space that was allocated by the initialize routine. The dispose routine for a standard document window does nothing.

The Grow Routine

When the window definition function receives a wGrow message, it also receives a pointer to a rectangle as its param value. The rectangle is in global coordinates and is usually aligned at its top left corner with the portRect of the window's grafPort. The grow routine should draw a grow image of the window to fit the given rectangle (that is, whatever is appropriate to show that the window's size will change, such as an outline of the content region). The Window Manager requests this operation repeatedly as the user drags inside the grow region. The grow routine should draw in the current grafPort, which will be the Window Manager port, and should use the grafPort's current pen pattern and pen mode, which are set up (as gray and notPatXor) to conform to the Macintosh User Interface Guidelines.

The grow routine for a standard document window draws a dotted (gray) outline of the window and also the lines delimiting the title bar, size box, and scroll bar areas.

The Draw Size Box Routine

If the window's grow region is in the content region, the wDrawGIcon message tells the window definition function to draw the size box in the grow region if the window is active (highlighted); if the window is inactive it should draw whatever is appropriate to show that the window temporarily can't be sized. For active document windows, this routine draws the size box icon in the bottom right corner of the portRect of the window's grafPort, along with the lines delimiting the size box and scroll bar areas; for inactive windows, it draws just the delimiting lines, and erases the size box icon.

If the grow region is located in the window frame rather than the content region, this routine should do nothing.

FORMATS OF RESOURCES FOR WINDOWS

The Window Manager function GetNewWindow takes the resource ID of a window template as a parameter, and gets from the template the same information that the NewWindow function gets from six of its parameters. The resource type for a window template is 'WIND', and the resource data has the following format:

Number of bytes	Contents
8 bytes	Same as boundsRect parameter to NewWindow
2 bytes	Same as procID parameter to NewWindow
2 bytes	Same as visible parameter to NewWindow
2 bytes	Same as goAwayFlag parameter to NewWindow
4 bytes	Same as refCon parameter to NewWindow
n bytes	Same as title parameter to NewWindow (1-byte length in bytes, followed by the characters of the title)

The resource type for a window definition function is 'WDEF', and the resource data is simply the compiled or assembled code of the function.

SUMMARY OF THE WINDOW MANAGER

Constants

```
CONST  { Window definition IDs }

        documentProc   = 0;     {standard document window}
        dBoxProc       = 1;     {alert box or modal dialog box}
        plainDBox      = 2;     {plain box}
        altDBoxProc    = 3;     {plain box with shadow}
        noGrowDocProc  = 4;     {document window without size box}
        rDocProc       = 16;    {rounded-corner window}

        { Window class, in windowKind field of window record }

        dialogKind  = 2;    {dialog or alert window}
        userKind    = 8;    {window created directly by the application}

        { Values returned by FindWindow }

        inDesk       = 0;    {none of the following}
        inMenuBar    = 1;    {in menu bar}
        inSysWindow  = 2;    {in system window}
        inContent    = 3;    {in content region (except grow, if active)}
        inDrag       = 4;    {in drag region}
        inGrow       = 5;    {in grow region (active window only)}
        inGoAway     = 6;    {in go-away region (active window only)}

        { Axis constraints for DragGrayRgn }

        noConstraint = 0;  {no constraint}
        hAxisOnly    = 1;  {horizontal axis only}
        vAxisOnly    = 2;  {vertical axis only}

        { Messages to window definition function }

        wDraw       = 0;    {draw window frame}
        wHit        = 1;    {tell what region mouse button was pressed in}
        wCalcRgns   = 2;    {calculate strucRgn and contRgn}
        wNew        = 3;    {do any additional window initialization}
        wDispose    = 4;    {take any additional disposal actions}
        wGrow       = 5;    {draw window's grow image}
        wDrawGIcon  = 6;    {draw size box in content region}

        { Values returned by window definition function's hit routine }

        wNoHit      = 0;    {none of the following}
        wInContent  = 1;    {in content region (except grow, if active)}
        wInDrag     = 2;    {in drag region}
        wInGrow     = 3;    {in grow region (active window only)}
        wInGoAway   = 4;    {in go-away region (active window only)}
```

```
{ Resource ID of desktop pattern }

deskPatID  = 16;
```

Data Types

```
TYPE WindowPtr  = GrafPtr;
     WindowPeek = ^WindowRecord;

     WindowRecord =
           RECORD
               port:           GrafPort;       {window's grafPort}
               windowKind:     INTEGER;        {window class}
               visible:        BOOLEAN;        {TRUE if visible}
               hilited:        BOOLEAN;        {TRUE if highlighted}
               goAwayFlag:     BOOLEAN;        {TRUE if has go-away region}
               spareFlag:      BOOLEAN;        {reserved for future use}
               strucRgn:       RgnHandle;      {structure region}
               contRgn:        RgnHandle;      {content region}
               updateRgn:      RgnHandle;      {update region}
               windowDefProc:  Handle;         {window definition function}
               dataHandle:     Handle;         {data used by windowDefProc}
               titleHandle:    StringHandle;   {window's title}
               titleWidth:     INTEGER;        {width of title in pixels}
               controlList:    ControlHandle;  {window's control list}
               nextWindow:     WindowPeek;     {next window in window list}
               windowPic:      PicHandle;      {picture for drawing window}
               refCon:         LONGINT         {window's reference value}
           END;
```

Routines

Initialization and Allocation

```
PROCEDURE  InitWindows;
PROCEDURE  GetWMgrPort     (VAR wPort: GrafPtr);
FUNCTION   NewWindow       (wStorage: Ptr; boundsRect: Rect; title: Str255;
                            visible: BOOLEAN; procID: INTEGER; behind:
                            WindowPtr; goAwayFlag: BOOLEAN; refCon:
                            LONGINT) : WindowPtr;
FUNCTION   GetNewWindow    (windowID: INTEGER; wStorage: Ptr; behind:
                            WindowPtr) : WindowPtr;
PROCEDURE  CloseWindow     (theWindow: WindowPtr);
PROCEDURE  DisposeWindow   (theWindow: WindowPtr);
```

Window Display

```
PROCEDURE  SetWTitle      (theWindow: WindowPtr; title: Str255);
PROCEDURE  GetWTitle      (theWindow: WindowPtr; VAR title: Str255);
PROCEDURE  SelectWindow   (theWindow: WindowPtr);
PROCEDURE  HideWindow     (theWindow: WindowPtr);
PROCEDURE  ShowWindow     (theWindow: WindowPtr);
PROCEDURE  ShowHide       (theWindow: WindowPtr; showFlag: BOOLEAN);
PROCEDURE  HiliteWindow   (theWindow: WindowPtr; fHilite: BOOLEAN);
PROCEDURE  BringToFront   (theWindow: WindowPtr);
PROCEDURE  SendBehind     (theWindow,behindWindow: WindowPtr);
FUNCTION   FrontWindow :  WindowPtr;
PROCEDURE  DrawGrowIcon   (theWindow: WindowPtr);
```

Mouse Location

```
FUNCTION FindWindow   (thePt: Point; VAR whichWindow: WindowPtr) :
                         INTEGER;
FUNCTION TrackGoAway  (theWindow: WindowPtr; thePt: Point) : BOOLEAN;
```

Window Movement and Sizing

```
PROCEDURE MoveWindow  (theWindow: WindowPtr; hGlobal,vGlobal: INTEGER;
                         front: BOOLEAN);
PROCEDURE DragWindow  (theWindow: WindowPtr; startPt: Point; boundsRect:
                         Rect);
FUNCTION  GrowWindow  (theWindow: WindowPtr; startPt: Point; sizeRect:
                         Rect) : LONGINT;
PROCEDURE SizeWindow  (theWindow: WindowPtr; w,h: INTEGER; fUpdate:
                         BOOLEAN);
```

Update Region Maintenance

```
PROCEDURE  InvalRect      (badRect: Rect);
PROCEDURE  InvalRgn       (badRgn: RgnHandle);
PROCEDURE  ValidRect      (goodRect: Rect);
PROCEDURE  ValidRgn       (goodRgn: RgnHandle);
PROCEDURE  BeginUpdate    (theWindow: WindowPtr);
PROCEDURE  EndUpdate      (theWindow: WindowPtr);
```

Miscellaneous Routines

```
PROCEDURE  SetWRefCon     (theWindow: WindowPtr; data: LONGINT);
FUNCTION   GetWRefCon     (theWindow: WindowPtr) : LONGINT;
PROCEDURE  SetWindowPic   (theWindow: WindowPtr; pic: PicHandle);
FUNCTION   GetWindowPic   (theWindow: WindowPtr) : PicHandle;
FUNCTION   PinRect        (theRect: Rect; thePt: Point) : LONGINT;
```

9 Window Manager

```
FUNCTION   DragGrayRgn   (theRgn: RgnHandle; startPt: Point; limitRect,
                          slopRect: Rect; axis: INTEGER; actionProc:
                          ProcPtr) : LONGINT;
```

Low-Level Routines

```
FUNCTION   CheckUpdate    (VAR theEvent: EventRecord) : BOOLEAN;
PROCEDURE  ClipAbove      (window: WindowPeek);
PROCEDURE  SaveOld        (window: WindowPeek);
PROCEDURE  DrawNew        (window: WindowPeek; update: BOOLEAN);
PROCEDURE  PaintOne       (window: WindowPeek; clobberedRgn: RgnHandle);
PROCEDURE  PaintBehind    (startWindow: WindowPeek; clobberedRgn:
                           RgnHandle);
PROCEDURE  CalcVis        (window: WindowPeek);
PROCEDURE  CalcVisBehind  (startWindow: WindowPeek; clobberedRgn:
                           RgnHandle);
```

Diameters of Curvature for Rounded-Corner Windows

Window definition ID	Diameters of curvature
rDocProc	16, 16
rDocProc + 1	4, 4
rDocProc + 2	6, 6
rDocProc + 3	8, 8
rDocProc + 4	10, 10
rDocProc + 5	12, 12
rDocProc + 6	20, 20
rDocProc + 7	24, 24

Window Definition Function

```
FUNCTION MyWindow (varCode: INTEGER; theWindow: WindowPtr; message:
                   INTEGER; param: LONGINT) : LONGINT;
```

Assembly-Language Information

Constants

```
; Window definition IDs

documentProc      .EQU  0   ;standard document window
dBoxProc          .EQU  1   ;alert box or modal dialog box
```

```
plainDBox            .EQU  2   ;plain box
altDBoxProc          .EQU  3   ;plain box with shadow
noGrowDocProc        .EQU  4   ;document window without size box
rDocProc             .EQU  16  ;rounded-corner window
```

; Window class, in windowKind field of window record

```
dialogKind           .EQU  2   ;dialog or alert window
userKind             .EQU  8   ;window created directly by the application
```

; Values returned by FindWindow

```
inDesk               .EQU  0   ;none of the following
inMenuBar            .EQU  1   ;in menu bar
inSysWindow          .EQU  2   ;in system window
inContent            .EQU  3   ;in content region (except grow, if active)
inDrag               .EQU  4   ;in drag region
inGrow               .EQU  5   ;in grow region (active window only)
inGoAway             .EQU  6   ;in go-away region (active window only)
```

; Axis constraints for DragGrayRgn

```
noConstraint         .EQU  0   ;no constraint
hAxisOnly            .EQU  1   ;horizontal axis only
vAxisOnly            .EQU  2   ;vertical axis only
```

; Messages to window definition function

```
wDrawMsg             .EQU  0   ;draw window frame
wHitMsg              .EQU  1   ;tell what region mouse button was pressed in
wCalcRgnMsg          .EQU  2   ;calculate strucRgn and contRgn
wInitMsg             .EQU  3   ;do any additional window initialization
wDisposeMsg          .EQU  4   ;take any additional disposal actions
wGrowMsg             .EQU  5   ;draw window's grow image
wGIconMsg            .EQU  6   ;draw size box in content region
```

; Value returned by window definition function's hit routine

```
wNoHit               .EQU  0   ;none of the following
wInContent           .EQU  1   ;in content region (except grow, if active)
wInDrag              .EQU  2   ;in drag region
wInGrow              .EQU  3   ;in grow region (active window only)
wInGoAway            .EQU  4   ;in go-away region (active window only)
```

; Resource ID of desktop pattern

```
deskPatID            .EQU  16
```

Window Record Data Structure

windowPort	Window's grafPort (portRec bytes)
windowKind	Window class (word)
wVisible	Nonzero if window is visible (byte)

wHilited	Nonzero if window is highlighted (byte)
wGoAway	Nonzero if window has go-away region (byte)
structRgn	Handle to structure region of window
contRgn	Handle to content region of window
updateRgn	Handle to update region of window
windowDef	Handle to window definition function
wDataHandle	Handle to data used by window definition function
wTitleHandle	Handle to window's title (preceded by length byte)
wTitleWidth	Width of title in pixels (word)
wControlList	Handle to window's control list
nextWindow	Pointer to next window in window list
windowPic	Picture handle for drawing window
wRefCon	Window's reference value (long)
windowSize	Size in bytes of window record

Special Macro Names

Pascal name	Macro name
CalcVisBehind	_CalcVBehind
DisposeWindow	_DisposWindow
DragGrayRgn	_DragGrayRgn or, after setting the global variable DragPattern, _DragTheRgn

Variables

WindowList	Pointer to first window in window list
SaveUpdate	Flag for whether to generate update events (word)
PaintWhite	Flag for whether to paint window white before update event (word)
CurActivate	Pointer to window to receive activate event
CurDeactive	Pointer to window to receive deactivate event
GrayRgn	Handle to region drawn as desktop
DeskPattern	Pattern with which desktop is painted (8 bytes)
DeskHook	Address of procedure for painting desktop or responding to clicks on desktop
WMgrPort	Pointer to Window Manager port
GhostWindow	Pointer to window never to be considered frontmost
DragHook	Address of procedure to execute during TrackGoAway, DragWindow, GrowWindow, and DragGrayRgn
DragPattern	Pattern of dragged region's outline (8 bytes)
OldStructure	Handle to saved structure region
OldContent	Handle to saved content region
SaveVisRgn	Handle to saved visRgn

10 THE CONTROL MANAGER

ABOUT THIS CHAPTER

This chapter describes the Control Manager, the part of the Toolbox that deals with controls, such as buttons, check boxes, and scroll bars. Using the Control Manager, your application can create, manipulate, and dispose of controls.

You should already be familiar with:

- resources, as discussed in chapter 5
- the basic concepts and structures behind QuickDraw, particularly points, rectangles, regions, and grafPorts
- the Toolbox Event Manager
- the Window Manager

Note: Except for scroll bars, most controls appear only in dialog or alert boxes. To learn how to implement dialogs and alerts in your application, you'll have to read chapter 13.

ABOUT THE CONTROL MANAGER

The Control Manager is the part of the Toolbox that deals with controls. **A control** is an object on the Macintosh screen with which the user, using the mouse, can cause instant action with visible results or change settings to modify a future action. Using the Control Manager, your application can:

- create and dispose of controls
- display or hide controls
- monitor the user's operation of a control with the mouse and respond accordingly
- read or change the setting or other properties of a control
- change the size, location, or appearance of a control

Your application performs these actions by calling the appropriate Control Manager routines. The Control Manager carries out the actual operations, but it's up to you to decide when, where, and how.

Controls may be of various types (see Figure 1), each with its own characteristic appearance on the screen and responses to the mouse. Each individual control has its own specific properties—such as its location, size, and setting—but controls of the same type behave in the same general way.

Certain standard types of controls are predefined for you. Your application can easily create and use controls of these standard types, and can also define its own "custom" control types. Among the standard control types are the following:

- **Buttons** cause an immediate or continuous action when clicked or pressed with the mouse. They appear on the screen as rounded-corner rectangles with a title centered inside.

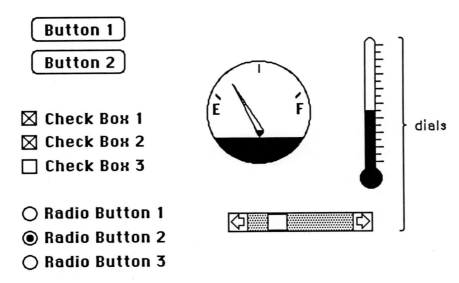

Figure 1. Controls

■ **Check boxes** retain and display a setting, either checked (on) or unchecked (off); clicking with the mouse reverses the setting. On the screen, a check box appears as a small square with a title alongside it; the box is either filled in with an "X" (checked) or empty (unchecked). Check boxes are frequently used to control or modify some future action, instead of causing an immediate action of their own.

■ **Radio buttons** also retain and display an on-or-off setting. They're organized into groups, with the property that only one button in the group can be on at a time: Clicking one button in a group both turns it on and turns off the button that was on, like the buttons on a car radio. Radio buttons are used to offer a choice among several alternatives. On the screen, they look like round check boxes; the radio button that's on is filled in with a small black circle instead of an "X".

Note: The Control Manager doesn't know how radio buttons are grouped, and doesn't automatically turn one off when the user clicks another one on: It's up to your program to handle this.

Another important category of controls is **dials**. These display the value, magnitude, or position of something, typically in some pseudoanalog form such as the position of a sliding switch, the reading on a thermometer scale, or the angle of a needle on a gauge; the setting may be displayed digitally as well. The control's moving part that displays the current setting is called the **indicator**. The user may be able to change a dial's setting by dragging its indicator with the mouse, or the dial may simply display a value not under the user's direct control (such as the amount of free space remaining on a disk).

One type of dial is predefined for you: The standard Macintosh scroll bars. Figure 2 shows the five parts of a scroll bar and the terms used by the Control Manager (and this chapter) to refer to them. Notice that the part of the scroll bar that Macintosh users know as the "scroll box" is called the "thumb" here. Also, for simplicity, the terms "up" and "down" are used even when referring to horizontal scroll bars (in which case "up" really means "left" and "down" means "right").

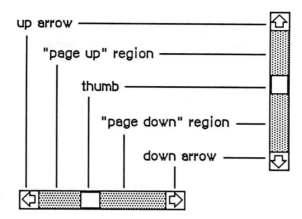

Figure 2. Parts of a Scroll Bar

The up and down arrows scroll the window's contents a line at a time. The two paging regions scroll a "page" (windowful) at a time. The thumb can be dragged to any position in the scroll bar, to scroll to a corresponding position within the document. Although they may seem to behave like individual controls, these are all parts of a single control, the scroll bar type of dial. You can define other dials of any shape or complexity for yourself if your application needs them.

A control may be **active** or **inactive**. Active controls respond to the user's mouse actions; inactive controls don't. When an active control is clicked or pressed, it's usually highlighted (see Figure 3). Standard button controls are inverted, but some control types may use other forms of highlighting, such as making the outline heavier. It's also possible for just a part of a control to be highlighted: For example, when the user presses the mouse button inside a scroll arrow or the thumb in a scroll bar, the arrow or thumb (not the whole scroll bar) becomes highlighted until the button is released.

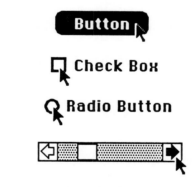

Figure 3. Highlighted Active Controls

A control is made inactive when it has no meaning or effect in the current context, such as an "Open" button when no document has been selected to open, or a scroll bar when there's currently nothing to scroll to. An inactive control remains visible, but is highlighted in some special way, depending on its control type (see Figure 4). For example, the title of an inactive button, check box, or radio button is **dimmed** (drawn in gray rather than black).

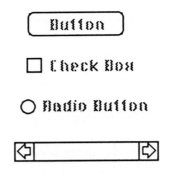

Figure 4. Inactive Controls

CONTROLS AND WINDOWS

Every control "belongs" to a particular window: When displayed, the control appears within that window's content region; when manipulated with the mouse, it acts on that window. All coordinates pertaining to the control (such as those describing its location) are given in its window's local coordinate system.

> **Warning:** In order for the Control Manager to draw a control properly, the control's window must have the top left corner of its grafPort's portRect at coordinates (0,0). If you change a window's local coordinate system for any reason (with the QuickDraw procedure SetOrigin), be sure to change it back—so that the top left corner is again at (0,0)—before drawing any of its controls. Since almost all of the Control Manager routines can (at least potentially) redraw a control, the safest policy is simply to change the coordinate system back before calling *any* Control Manager routine.

Normally you'll include buttons and check boxes in dialog or alert windows only. You create such windows with the Dialog Manager, and the Dialog Manager takes care of drawing the controls and letting you know whether the user clicked one of them. See chapter 13 for details.

CONTROLS AND RESOURCES

The relationship between controls and resources is analogous to the relationship between windows and resources: Just as there are window definition functions and window templates, there are control definition functions and control templates.

Each type of control has a **control definition function** that determines how controls of that type look and behave. The Control Manager calls the control definition function whenever it needs to perform a type-dependent action, such as drawing the control on the screen. Control definition functions are stored as resources and accessed through the Resource Manager. The system resource file includes definition functions for the standard control types (buttons, check boxes, radio buttons, and scroll bars). If you want to define your own, nonstandard control types, you'll have to write control definition functions for them, as described later in the section "Defining Your Own Controls".

When you create a control, you specify its type with a **control definition ID**, which tells the Control Manager the resource ID of the definition function for that control type. The Control Manager provides the following predefined constants for the definition IDs of the standard control types:

```
CONST pushButProc   = 0;    {simple button}
      checkBoxProc  = 1;    {check box}
      radioButProc  = 2;    {radio button}
      scrollBarProc = 16;   {scroll bar}
```

Note: The control definition function for scroll bars figures out whether a scroll bar is vertical or horizontal from a rectangle you specify when you create the control.

The title of a button, check box, or radio button normally appears in the system font, but you can add the following constant to the definition ID to specify that you instead want to use the font currently associated with the window's grafPort:

```
CONST useWFont = 8;   {use window's font}
```

To create a control, the Control Manager needs to know not only the control definition ID but also other information specific to this control, such as its title (if any), the window it belongs to, and its location within the window. You can supply all the needed information in individual parameters to a Control Manager routine, or you can store it in a **control template** in a resource file and just pass the template's resource ID. Using templates is highly recommended, since it simplifies the process of creating controls and isolates the control descriptions from your application's code.

PART CODES

Some controls, such as buttons, are simple and straightforward. Others can be complex objects with many parts: For example, a scroll bar has two scroll arrows, two paging regions, and a thumb (see Figure 2 above). To allow different parts of a control to respond to the mouse in different ways, many of the Control Manager routines accept a **part code** as a parameter or return one as a result.

A part code is an integer between 1 and 253 that stands for a particular part of a control. Each type of control has its own set of part codes, assigned by the control definition function for that type. A simple control such as a button or check box might have just one "part" that encompasses the entire control; a more complex control such as a scroll bar can have as many parts as are needed to define how the control operates.

Note: The values 254 and 255 aren't used for part codes—254 is reserved for future use, and 255 means the entire control is inactive.

The part codes for the standard control types are as follows:

```
CONST inButton      = 10;    {simple button}
      inCheckBox    = 11;    {check box or radio button}
      inUpButton    = 20;    {up arrow of a scroll bar}
      inDownButton  = 21;    {down arrow of a scroll bar}
      inPageUp      = 22;    {"page up" region of a scroll bar}
      inPageDown    = 23;    {"page down" region of a scroll bar}
      inThumb       = 129;   {thumb of a scroll bar}
```

Notice that inCheckBox applies to both check boxes and radio buttons.

Note: For special information about assigning part codes to your own control types, see "Defining Your Own Controls".

CONTROL RECORDS

Every control is represented internally by a **control record** containing all pertinent information about that control. The control record contains the following:

- A pointer to the window the control belongs to.

- A handle to the next control in the window's control list.

- A handle to the control definition function.

- The control's title, if any.

- A rectangle that completely encloses the control, which determines the control's size and location within its window. The entire control, including the title of a check box or radio button, is drawn inside this rectangle.

- An indication of whether the control is currently active and how it's to be highlighted.

- The current setting of the control (if this type of control retains a setting) and the minimum and maximum values the setting can assume. For check boxes and radio buttons, a setting of 0 means the control is off and 1 means it's on.

The control record also contains an indication of whether the control is currently **visible** or **invisible**. These terms refer only to whether the control is drawn in its window, not to whether you can see it on the screen. A control may be "visible" and still not appear on the screen, because it's obscured by overlapping windows or other objects.

There's a field in the control record for a pointer to the control's default **action procedure**. An action procedure defines some action to be performed repeatedly for as long as the user holds down the mouse button inside the control. The default action procedure may be used by the Control Manager function TrackControl if you call it without passing a pointer to an action procedure; this is discussed in detail in the description of TrackControl in the "Control Manager Routines" section.

Finally, the control record includes a 32-bit **reference value** field, which is reserved for use by your application. You specify an initial reference value when you create a control, and can then read or change the reference value whenever you wish.

The data type for a control record is called ControlRecord. A control record is referred to by a handle:

```
TYPE  ControlPtr      = ^ControlRecord;
      ControlHandle   = ^ControlPtr;
```

The Control Manager functions for creating a control return a handle to a newly allocated control record; thereafter, your program should normally refer to the control by this handle. Most of the Control Manager routines expect a control handle as their first parameter.

You can store into and access most of a control record's fields with Control Manager routines, so normally you don't have to know the exact field names. However, if you want more information about the exact structure of a control record—if you're defining your own control types, for instance—it's given below.

The ControlRecord Data Type

The ControlRecord data type is defined as follows:

```
TYPE ControlRecord =
    PACKED RECORD
        nextControl:    ControlHandle;   {next control}
        contrlOwner:    WindowPtr;       {control's window}
        contrlRect:     Rect;            {enclosing rectangle}
        contrlVis:      Byte;            {255 if visible}
        contrlHilite:   Byte;            {highlight state}
        contrlValue:    INTEGER;         {control's current setting}
        contrlMin:      INTEGER;         {control's minimum setting}
        contrlMax:      INTEGER;         {control's maximum setting}
        contrlDefProc:  Handle;          {control definition function}
        contrlData:     Handle;          {data used by contrlDefProc}
        contrlAction:   ProcPtr;         {default action procedure}
        contrlRfCon:    LONGINT;         {control's reference value}
        contrlTitle:    Str255           {control's title}
    END;
```

NextControl is a handle to the next control associated with this control's window. All the controls belonging to a given window are kept in a linked list, beginning in the controlList field of the window record and chained together through the nextControl fields of the individual control records. The end of the list is marked by a NIL value; as new controls are created, they're added to the beginning of the list.

ContrlOwner is a pointer to the window that this control belongs to.

ContrlRect is the rectangle that completely encloses the control, in the local coordinates of the control's window.

When contrlVis is 0, the control is currently invisible; when it's 255, the control is visible.

ContrlHilite specifies whether and how the control is to be highlighted, indicating whether it's active or inactive. The HiliteControl procedure lets you set this field; see the description of HiliteControl for more information about the meaning of the field's value.

ContrlValue is the control's current setting. For check boxes and radio buttons, 0 means the control is off and 1 means it's on. For dials, the fields contrlMin and contrlMax define the range of possible settings; contrlValue may take on any value within that range. Other (custom) control types can use these three fields as they see fit.

ContrlDefProc is a handle to the control definition function for this type of control. When you create a control, you identify its type with a control definition ID, which is converted into a handle to the control definition function and stored in the contrlDefProc field. Thereafter, the Control Manager uses this handle to access the definition function; you should never need to refer to this field directly.

> **Note:** The high-order byte of the contrlDefProc field contains some additional information that the Control Manager gets from the control definition ID; for details, see the section "Defining Your Own Controls".

ContrlData is reserved for use by the control definition function, typically to hold additional information specific to a particular control type. For example, the standard definition function for scroll bars uses this field for a handle to the region containing the scroll bar's thumb. If no more than four bytes of additional information are needed, the definition function can store the information directly in the contrlData field rather than use a handle.

ContrlAction is a pointer to the control's default action procedure, if any. The Control Manager function TrackControl may call this procedure to respond to the user's dragging the mouse inside the control.

ContrlRfCon is the control's reference value field, which the application may store into and access for any purpose.

ContrlTitle is the control's title, if any.

USING THE CONTROL MANAGER

To use the Control Manager, you must have previously called InitGraf to initialize QuickDraw, InitFonts to initialize the Font Manager, and InitWindows to initialize the Window Manager.

> **Note:** For controls in dialogs or alerts, the Dialog Manager makes some of the basic Control Manager calls for you; see chapter 13 for more information.

Where appropriate in your program, use NewControl or GetNewControl to create any controls you need. NewControl takes descriptive information about the new control from its parameters; GetNewControl gets the information from a control template in a resource file. When you no longer need a control, call DisposeControl to remove it from its window's control list and release the memory it occupies. To dispose of all of a given window's controls at once, use KillControls.

> **Note:** The Window Manager procedures DisposeWindow and CloseWindow automatically dispose of all the controls associated with the given window.

When the Toolbox Event Manager function GetNextEvent reports that an update event has occurred for a window, the application should call DrawControls to redraw the window's controls as part of the process of updating the window.

After receiving a mouse-down event from GetNextEvent, do the following:

1. First call FindWindow to determine which part of which window the mouse button was pressed in.

2. If it was in the content region of the active window, call FindControl for that window to find out whether it was in an active control, and if so, in which part of which control.

3. Finally, take whatever action is appropriate when the user presses the mouse button in that part of the control, using routines such as TrackControl (to perform some action repeatedly for as long as the mouse button is down, or to allow the user to drag the control's indicator with the mouse), DragControl (to pull an outline of the control across the screen and move the control to a new location), and HiliteControl (to change the way the control is highlighted).

For the standard control types, step 3 involves calling TrackControl. TrackControl handles the highlighting of the control and determines whether the mouse is still in the control when the mouse button is released. It also handles the dragging of the thumb in a scroll bar and, via your action procedure, the response to presses or clicks in the other parts of a scroll bar. When TrackControl returns the part code for a button, check box, or radio button, the application must do whatever is appropriate as a response to a click of that control. When TrackControl returns the part code for the thumb of a scroll bar, the application must scroll to the corresponding relative position in the document.

The application's exact response to mouse activity in a control that retains a setting will depend on the current setting of the control, which is available from the GetCtlValue function. For controls whose values can be set by the user, the SetCtlValue procedure may be called to change the control's setting and redraw the control accordingly. You'll call SetCtlValue, for example, when a check box or radio button is clicked, to change the setting and draw or clear the mark inside the control.

Wherever needed in your program, you can call HideControl to make a control invisible or ShowControl to make it visible. Similarly, MoveControl, which simply changes a control's location without pulling around an outline of it, can be called at any time, as can SizeControl, which changes its size. For example, when the user changes the size of a document window that contains a scroll bar, you'll call HideControl to remove the old scroll bar, MoveControl and SizeControl to change its location and size, and ShowControl to display it as changed.

Whenever necessary, you can read various attributes of a control with GetCTitle, GetCtlMin, GetCtlMax, GetCRefCon, or GetCtlAction; you can change them with SetCTitle, SetCtlMin, SetCtlMax, SetCRefCon, or SetCtlAction.

CONTROL MANAGER ROUTINES

Initialization and Allocation

```
FUNCTION NewControl (theWindow: WindowPtr; boundsRect: Rect;
        title: Str255; visible: BOOLEAN; value: INTEGER;
        min,max: INTEGER; procID: INTEGER; refCon: LONGINT) :
        ControlHandle;
```

NewControl creates a control, adds it to the beginning of theWindow's control list, and returns a handle to the new control. The values passed as parameters are stored in the corresponding fields of the control record, as described below. The field that determines highlighting is set to 0 (no highlighting) and the pointer to the default action procedure is set to NIL (none).

Note: The control definition function may do additional initialization, including changing any of the fields of the control record. The only standard control for which additional initialization is done is the scroll bar; its control definition function allocates space for a region to hold the thumb and stores the region handle in the contrlData field of the control record.

TheWindow is the window the new control will belong to. All coordinates pertaining to the control will be interpreted in this window's local coordinate system.

BoundsRect, given in theWindow's local coordinates, is the rectangle that encloses the control and thus determines its size and location. Note the following about the enclosing rectangle for the standard controls:

- Simple buttons are drawn to fit the rectangle exactly. (The control definition function calls the QuickDraw procedure FrameRoundRect.) To allow for the tallest characters in the system font, there should be at least a 20-point difference between the top and bottom coordinates of the rectangle.

- For check boxes and radio buttons, there should be at least a 16-point difference between the top and bottom coordinates.

- By convention, scroll bars are 16 pixels wide, so there should be a 16-point difference between the left and right (or top and bottom) coordinates. (If there isn't, the scroll bar will be scaled to fit the rectangle.) A standard scroll bar should be at least 48 pixels long, to allow room for the scroll arrows and thumb.

Title is the control's title, if any (if none, you can just pass the empty string as the title). Be sure the title will fit in the control's enclosing rectangle; if it won't it will be truncated on the right for check boxes and radio buttons, or centered and truncated on both ends for simple buttons.

If the visible parameter is TRUE, NewControl draws the control.

Note: It does *not* use the standard window updating mechanism, but instead draws the control immediately in the window.

The min and max parameters define the control's range of possible settings; the value parameter gives the initial setting. For controls that don't retain a setting, such as buttons, the values you supply for these parameters will be stored in the control record but will never be used. So it doesn't matter what values you give for those controls—0 for all three parameters will do. For controls that just retain an on-or-off setting, such as check boxes or radio buttons, min should be 0 (meaning the control is off) and max should be 1 (meaning it's on). For dials, you can specify whatever values are appropriate for min, max, and value.

ProcID is the control definition ID, which leads to the control definition function for this type of control. (The function is read into memory if it isn't already in memory.) The control definition IDs for the standard control types are listed above under "Controls and Resources". Control definition IDs for custom control types are discussed later under "Defining Your Own Controls".

RefCon is the control's reference value, set and used only by your application.

```
FUNCTION GetNewControl (controlID: INTEGER; theWindow:
          WindowPtr) : ControlHandle;
```

GetNewControl creates a control from a control template stored in a resource file, adds it to the beginning of theWindow's control list, and returns a handle to the new control. ControlID is the resource ID of the template. GetNewControl works exactly the same as NewControl (above), except that it gets the initial values for the new control's fields from the specified control template instead of accepting them as parameters. If the control template can't be read from the resource file, GetNewControl returns NIL. It releases the memory occupied by the resource before returning.

```
PROCEDURE DisposeControl (theControl: ControlHandle);
```

Assembly-language note: The macro you invoke to call DisposeControl from assembly language is named _DisposControl.

DisposeControl removes theControl from the screen, deletes it from its window's control list, and releases the memory occupied by the control record and any data structures associated with the control.

```
PROCEDURE KillControls (theWindow: WindowPtr);
```

KillControls disposes of all controls associated with theWindow by calling DisposeControl (above) for each.

Note: Remember that the Window Manager procedures CloseWindow and DisposeWindow automatically dispose of all controls associated with the given window.

Control Display

These procedures affect the appearance of a control but not its size or location.

```
PROCEDURE SetCTitle (theControl: ControlHandle; title: Str255);
```

SetCTitle sets theControl's title to the given string and redraws the control.

```
PROCEDURE GetCTitle (theControl: ControlHandle; VAR title:
          Str255);
```

GetCTitle returns theControl's title as the value of the title parameter.

```
PROCEDURE HideControl (theControl: ControlHandle);
```

HideControl makes theControl invisible. It fills the region the control occupies within its window with the background pattern of the window's grafPort. It also adds the control's enclosing rectangle to the window's update region, so that anything else that was previously obscured by the control will reappear on the screen. If the control is already invisible, HideControl has no effect.

```
PROCEDURE ShowControl (theControl: ControlHandle);
```

ShowControl makes theControl visible. The control is drawn in its window but may be completely or partially obscured by overlapping windows or other objects. If the control is already visible, ShowControl has no effect.

```
PROCEDURE DrawControls (theWindow: WindowPtr);
```

DrawControls draws all controls currently visible in theWindow. The controls are drawn in reverse order of creation; thus in case of overlap the earliest-created controls appear frontmost in the window.

Note: Window Manager routines such as SelectWindow, ShowWindow, and BringToFront do not automatically call DrawControls to display the window's controls. They just add the appropriate regions to the window's update region, generating an update event. Your program should always call DrawControls explicitly upon receiving an update event for a window that contains controls.

```
PROCEDURE HiliteControl (theControl: ControlHandle; hiliteState:
        INTEGER);
```

HiliteControl changes the way theControl is highlighted. HiliteState has one of the following values:

- The value 0 means no highlighting. (The control is active.)
- A value between 1 and 253 is interpreted as a part code designating the part of the (active) control to be highlighted.
- The value 255 means that the control is to be made inactive and highlighted accordingly.

Note: The value 254 should not be used; this value is reserved for future use.

HiliteControl calls the control definition function to redraw the control with its new highlighting.

Mouse Location

```
FUNCTION FindControl (thePoint: Point; theWindow: WindowPtr; VAR
          whichControl: ControlHandle) : INTEGER;
```

When the Window Manager function FindWindow reports that the mouse button was pressed in the content region of a window, and the window contains controls, the application should call FindControl with theWindow equal to the window pointer and thePoint equal to the point where the mouse button was pressed (in the window's local coordinates). FindControl tells which of the window's controls, if any, the mouse button was pressed in:

- If it was pressed in a visible, active control, FindControl sets the whichControl parameter to the control handle and returns a part code identifying the part of the control that it was pressed in.

- If it was pressed in an invisible or inactive control, or not in any control, FindControl sets whichControl to NIL and returns 0 as its result.

Warning: Notice that FindControl expects the mouse point in the window's local coordinates, whereas FindWindow expects it in global coordinates. Always be sure to convert the point to local coordinates with the QuickDraw procedure GlobalToLocal before calling FindControl.

Note: FindControl also returns NIL for whichControl and 0 as its result if the window is invisible or doesn't contain the given point. In these cases, however, FindWindow wouldn't have returned this window in the first place, so the situation should never arise.

```
FUNCTION TrackControl (theControl: ControlHandle; startPt: Point;
          actionProc: ProcPtr) : INTEGER;
```

When the mouse button is pressed in a visible, active control, the application should call TrackControl with theControl equal to the control handle and startPt equal to the point where the mouse button was pressed (in the local coordinates of the control's window). TrackControl follows the movements of the mouse and responds in whatever way is appropriate until the mouse button is released; the exact response depends on the type of control and the part of the control in which the mouse button was pressed. If highlighting is appropriate, TrackControl does the highlighting, and undoes it before returning. When the mouse button is released, TrackControl returns with the part code if the mouse is in the same part of the control that it was originally in, or with 0 if not (in which case the application should do nothing).

If the mouse button was pressed in an indicator, TrackControl drags a dotted outline of it to follow the mouse. When the mouse button is released, TrackControl calls the control definition function to reposition the control's indicator. The control definition function for scroll bars responds by redrawing the thumb, calculating the control's current setting based on the new relative position of the thumb, and storing the current setting in the control record; for example, if the minimum and maximum settings are 0 and 10, and the thumb is in the middle of the scroll bar, 5 is stored as the current setting. The application must then scroll to the corresponding relative position in the document.

TrackControl may take additional actions beyond highlighting the control or dragging the indicator, depending on the value passed in the actionProc parameter, as described below. The following tells you what to pass for the standard control types; for a custom control, what you pass will depend on how the control is defined.

- If actionProc is NIL, TrackControl performs no additional actions. This is appropriate for simple buttons, check boxes, radio buttons, and the thumb of a scroll bar.

- ActionProc may be a pointer to an action procedure that defines some action to be performed repeatedly for as long as the user holds down the mouse button. (See below for details.)

- If actionProc is POINTER(–1), TrackControl looks in the control record for a pointer to the control's default action procedure. If that field of the control record contains a procedure pointer, TrackControl uses the action procedure it points to; if the field contains POINTER (–1), TrackControl calls the control definition function to perform the necessary action. (If the field contains NIL, TrackControl does nothing.)

The action procedure in the control definition function is described in the section "Defining Your Own Controls". The following paragraphs describe only the action procedure whose pointer is passed in the actionProc parameter or stored in the control record.

If the mouse button was pressed in an indicator, the action procedure (if any) should have no parameters. This procedure must allow for the fact that the mouse may not be inside the original control part.

If the mouse button was pressed in a control part other than an indicator, the action procedure should be of the form

```
PROCEDURE MyAction (theControl: ControlHandle; partCode: INTEGER);
```

In this case, TrackControl passes the control handle and the part code to the action procedure. (It passes 0 in the partCode parameter if the mouse has moved outside the original control part.) As an example of this type of action procedure, consider what should happen when the mouse button is pressed in a scroll arrow or paging region in a scroll bar. For these cases, your action procedure should examine the part code to determine exactly where the mouse button was pressed, scroll up or down a line or page as appropriate, and call SetCtlValue to change the control's setting and redraw the thumb.

Warning: Since it has a different number of parameters depending on whether the mouse button was pressed in an indicator or elsewhere, the action procedure you pass to TrackControl (or whose pointer you store in the control record) can be set up for only one case or the other. If you store a pointer to a default action procedure in a control record, be sure it will be used only when appropriate for that type of action procedure. The only way to specify actions in response to all mouse-down events in a control, regardless of whether they're in an indicator, is via the control definition function.

Assembly-language note: If you store a pointer to a procedure in the global variable DragHook, that procedure will be called repeatedly (with no parameters) for as long as the user holds down the mouse button. TrackControl invokes the Window Manager macro _DragTheRgn, which calls the DragHook procedure. _DragTheRgn uses the pattern stored in the global variable DragPattern for the dragged outline of the indicator.

```
FUNCTION TestControl (theControl: ControlHandle; thePoint: Point)
          : INTEGER;
```

If theControl is visible and active, TestControl tests which part of the control contains thePoint (in the local coordinates of the control's window); it returns the corresponding part code, or 0 if the point is outside the control. If the control is invisible or inactive, TestControl returns 0. TestControl is called by FindControl and TrackControl; normally you won't need to call it yourself.

Control Movement and Sizing

```
PROCEDURE MoveControl (theControl: ControlHandle; h,v: INTEGER);
```

MoveControl moves theControl to a new location within its window. The top left corner of the control's enclosing rectangle is moved to the horizontal and vertical coordinates h and v (given in the local coordinates of the control's window); the bottom right corner is adjusted accordingly, to keep the size of the rectangle the same as before. If the control is currently visible, it's hidden and then redrawn at its new location.

```
PROCEDURE DragControl (theControl: ControlHandle; startPt: Point;
          limitRect,slopRect: Rect; axis: INTEGER);
```

Called with the mouse button down inside theControl, DragControl pulls a dotted outline of the control around the screen, following the movements of the mouse until the button is released. When the mouse button is released, DragControl calls MoveControl to move the control to the location to which it was dragged.

> **Note:** Before beginning to follow the mouse, DragControl calls the control definition function to allow it to do its own "custom dragging" if it chooses. If the definition function doesn't choose to do any custom dragging, DragControl uses the default method of dragging described here.

The startPt, limitRect, slopRect, and axis parameters have the same meaning as for the Window Manager function DragGrayRgn. These parameters are reviewed briefly below; see the description of DragGrayRgn in chapter 9 for more details.

- StartPt is assumed to be the point where the mouse button was originally pressed, in the local coordinates of the control's window.

- LimitRect limits the travel of the control's outline, and should normally coincide with or be contained within the window's content region.

- SlopRect allows the user some "slop" in moving the mouse; it should completely enclose limitRect.

- The axis parameter allows you to constrain the control's motion to only one axis. It has one of the following values:

```
CONST noConstraint = 0;  {no constraint}
      hAxisOnly    = 1;  {horizontal axis only}
      vAxisOnly    = 2;  {vertical axis only}
```

Assembly-language note: Like TrackControl, DragControl invokes the macro
_DragTheRgn, so you can use the global variables DragHook and DragPattern.

```
PROCEDURE SizeControl (theControl: ControlHandle; w,h: INTEGER);
```

SizeControl changes the size of theControl's enclosing rectangle. The bottom right corner of the
rectangle is adjusted to set the rectangle's width and height to the number of pixels specified by w
and h; the position of the top left corner is not changed. If the control is currently visible, it's
hidden and then redrawn in its new size.

Control Setting and Range

```
PROCEDURE SetCtlValue (theControl: ControlHandle; theValue:
           INTEGER);
```

SetCtlValue sets theControl's current setting to theValue and redraws the control to reflect the
new setting. For check boxes and radio buttons, the value 1 fills the control with the appropriate
mark, and 0 clears it. For scroll bars, SetCtlValue redraws the thumb where appropriate.

If the specified value is out of range, it's forced to the nearest endpoint of the current range (that
is, if theValue is less than the minimum setting, SetCtlValue sets the current setting to the
minimum; if theValue is greater than the maximum setting, it sets the current setting to the
maximum).

```
FUNCTION GetCtlValue (theControl: ControlHandle) : INTEGER;
```

GetCtlValue returns theControl's current setting.

```
PROCEDURE SetCtlMin (theControl: ControlHandle; minValue:
           INTEGER);
```

Assembly-language note: The macro you invoke to call SetCtlMin from assembly
language is named _SetMinCtl.

SetCtlMin sets theControl's minimum setting to minValue and redraws the control to reflect the
new range. If the control's current setting is less than minValue, the setting is changed to the
new minimum.

```
FUNCTION GetCtlMin (theControl: ControlHandle) : INTEGER;
```

Assembly-language note: The macro you invoke to call GetCtlMin from assembly language is named _GetMinCtl.

GetCtlMin returns theControl's minimum setting.

```
PROCEDURE SetCtlMax (theControl: ControlHandle; maxValue:
            INTEGER);
```

Assembly-language note: The macro you invoke to call SetCtlMax from assembly language is named _SetMaxCtl.

SetCtlMax sets theControl's maximum setting to maxValue and redraws the control to reflect the new range. If the control's current setting is greater than maxValue, the setting is changed to the new maximum.

Note: If you set the maximum setting of a scroll bar equal to its minimum setting, the control definition function will make the scroll bar inactive.

```
FUNCTION GetCtlMax (theControl: ControlHandle) : INTEGER;
```

Assembly-language note: The macro you invoke to call GetCtlMax from assembly language is named _GetMaxCtl.

GetCtlMax returns theControl's maximum setting.

Miscellaneous Routines

```
PROCEDURE SetCRefCon (theControl: ControlHandle; data: LONGINT);
```

SetCRefCon sets theControl's reference value to the given data.

```
FUNCTION GetCRefCon (theControl: ControlHandle) : LONGINT;
```

GetCRefCon returns theControl's current reference value.

```
PROCEDURE SetCtlAction (theControl: ControlHandle; actionProc:
            ProcPtr);
```

SetCtlAction sets theControl's default action procedure to actionProc.


```
FUNCTION GetCtlAction (theControl: ControlHandle) : ProcPtr;
```

GetCtlAction returns a pointer to theControl's default action procedure, if any. (It returns whatever is in that field of the control record.)

DEFINING YOUR OWN CONTROLS

In addition to the standard, built-in control types (buttons, check boxes, radio buttons, and scroll bars), the Control Manager allows you to define "custom" control types of your own. Maybe you need a three-way selector switch, a memory-space indicator that looks like a thermometer, or a thruster control for a spacecraft simulator—whatever your application calls for. Controls and their indicators may occupy regions of any shape, in the full generality permitted by QuickDraw.

To define your own type of control, you write a control definition function and store it in a resource file. When you create a control, you provide a control definition ID, which leads to the control definition function. The control definition ID is an integer that contains the resource ID of the control definition function in its upper 12 bits and a **variation code** in its lower four bits. Thus, for a given resource ID and variation code, the control definition ID is

16 * resource ID + variation code

For example, buttons, check boxes, and radio buttons all use the standard definition function whose resource ID is 0, but they have variation codes of 0, 1, and 2, respectively.

The Control Manager calls the Resource Manager to access the control definition function with the given resource ID. The Resource Manager reads the control definition function into memory and returns a handle to it. The Control Manager stores this handle in the contrlDefProc field of the control record, along with the variation code in the high-order byte of the field. Later, when it needs to perform a type-dependent action on the control, it calls the control definition function and passes it the variation code as a parameter. Figure 5 illustrates this process.

Keep in mind that the calls your application makes to use a control depend heavily on the control definition function. What you pass to the TrackControl function, for example, depends on whether the definition function contains an action procedure for the control. Just as you need to know how to call TrackControl for the standard controls, each custom control type will have a particular calling protocol that must be followed for the control to work properly.

The Control Definition Function

The control definition function is usually written in assembly language, but may be written in Pascal.

You supply the control definition ID:

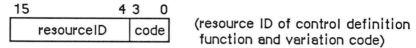

(resource ID of control definition
function and variation code)

The Control Manager calls the Resource Manager with

defHandle := GetResource ('CDEF', resourceID)

and stores into the contrlDefProc field of the control record:

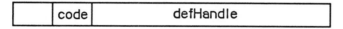

The variation code is passed to the control definition function.

Figure 5. Control Definition Handling

Assembly-language note: The function's entry point must be at the beginning.

You can give your control definition function any name you like. Here's how you would declare one named MyControl:

```
FUNCTION MyControl (varCode: INTEGER; theControl: ControlHandle;
        message: INTEGER; param: LONGINT) : LONGINT;
```

VarCode is the variation code, as described above.

TheControl is a handle to the control that the operation will affect.

The message parameter identifies the desired operation. It has one of the following values:

```
CONST drawCntl  = 0;    {draw the control (or control part)}
      testCntl  = 1;    {test where mouse button was pressed}
      calcCRgns = 2;    {calculate control's region (or indicator's)}
      initCntl  = 3;    {do any additional control initialization}
      dispCntl  = 4;    {take any additional disposal actions}
      posCntl   = 5;    {reposition control's indicator and update it}
      thumbCntl = 6;    {calculate parameters for dragging indicator}
      dragCntl  = 7;    {drag control (or its indicator)}
      autoTrack = 8;    {execute control's action procedure}
```

As described below in the discussions of the routines that perform these operations, the value passed for param, the last parameter of the control definition function, depends on the operation. Where it's not mentioned below, this parameter is ignored. Similarly, the control definition function is expected to return a function result only where indicated; in other cases, the function should return 0.

In some cases, the value of param or the function result is a part code. The part code 128 is reserved for future use and shouldn't be used for parts of your controls. Part codes greater than 128 should be used for indicators; however, 129 has special meaning to the control definition function, as described below.

> **Note:** "Routine" here doesn't necessarily mean a procedure or function. While it's a good idea to set these up as subprograms inside the control definition function, you're not required to do so.

The Draw Routine

The message drawCntl asks the control definition function to draw all or part of the control within its enclosing rectangle. The value of param is a part code specifying which part of the control to draw, or 0 for the entire control. If the control is invisible (that is, if its contrlVis field is 0), there's nothing to do; if it's visible, the definition function should draw it (or the requested part), taking into account the current values of its contrlHilite and contrlValue fields. The control may be either scaled or clipped to the enclosing rectangle.

If param is the part code of the control's indicator, the draw routine can assume that the indicator hasn't moved; it might be called, for example, to highlight the indicator. There's a special case, though, in which the draw routine has to allow for the fact that the indicator may have moved: This happens when the Control Manager procedures SetCtlValue, SetCtlMin, and SetCtlMax call the control definition function to redraw the indicator after changing the control setting. Since they have no way of knowing what part code you chose for your indicator, they all pass 129 to mean the indicator. The draw routine must detect this part code as a special case, and remove the indicator from its former location before drawing it.

> **Note:** If your control has more than one indicator, 129 should be interpreted to mean all indicators.

The Test Routine

The Control Manager function FindControl sends the message testCntl to the control definition function when the mouse button is pressed in a visible control. This message asks in which part of the control, if any, a given point lies. The point is passed as the value of param, in the local coordinates of the control's window; the vertical coordinate is in the high-order word of the long integer and the horizontal coordinate is in the low-order word. The control definition function should return the part code for the part of the control that contains the point; it should return 0 if the point is outside the control or if the control is inactive.

The Routine to Calculate Regions

The control definition function should respond to the message calcCRgns by calculating the region the control occupies within its window. Param is a QuickDraw region handle; the definition function should update this region to the region occupied by the control, expressed in the local coordinate system of its window.

If the high-order bit of param is set, the region requested is that of the control's indicator rather than the control as a whole. The definition function should clear the high *byte* (not just the high bit) of the region handle before attempting to update the region.

The Initialize Routine

After initializing fields as appropriate when creating a new control, the Control Manager sends the message initCntl to the control definition function. This gives the definition function a chance to perform any type-specific initialization it may require. For example, if you implement the control's action procedure in its control definition function, you'll set up the initialize routine to store POINTER(−1) in the contrlAction field; TrackControl calls for this control would pass POINTER(−1) in the actionProc parameter.

The control definition function for scroll bars allocates space for a region to hold the scroll bar's thumb and stores the region handle in the contrlData field of the new control record. The initialize routine for standard buttons, check boxes, and radio buttons does nothing.

The Dispose Routine

The Control Manager's DisposeControl procedure sends the message dispCntl to the control definition function, telling it to carry out any additional actions required when disposing of the control. For example, the standard definition function for scroll bars releases the space occupied by the thumb region, whose handle is kept in the control's contrlData field. The dispose routine for standard buttons, check boxes, and radio buttons does nothing.

The Drag Routine

The message dragCntl asks the control definition function to drag the control or its indicator around on the screen to follow the mouse until the user releases the mouse button. Param specifies whether to drag the indicator or the whole control: 0 means drag the whole control, while a nonzero value means drag only the indicator.

The control definition function need not implement any form of "custom dragging"; if it returns a result of 0, the Control Manager will use its own default method of dragging (calling DragControl to drag the control or the Window Manager function DragGrayRgn to drag its indicator). Conversely, if the control definition function chooses to do its own custom dragging, it should signal the Control Manager not to use the default method by returning a nonzero result.

If the whole control is being dragged, the definition function should call MoveControl to reposition the control to its new location after the user releases the mouse button. If just the indicator is being dragged, the definition function should execute its own position routine (see below) to update the control's setting and redraw it in its window.

The Position Routine

For controls that don't use the Control Manager's default method of dragging the control's indicator (as performed by DragGrayRgn), the control definition function must include a position routine. When the mouse button is released inside the indicator of such a control, TrackControl calls the control definition function with the message posCntl to reposition the indicator and update the control's setting accordingly. The value of param is a point giving the vertical and horizontal offset, in pixels, by which the indicator is to be moved relative to its current position. (Typically, this is the offset between the points where the user pressed and released the mouse button while dragging the indicator.) The vertical offset is given in the high-order word of the long integer and the horizontal offset in the low-order word. The definition function should calculate the control's new setting based on the given offset, update the contrlValue field, and redraw the control within its window to reflect the new setting.

> **Note:** The Control Manager procedures SetCtlValue, SetCtlMin, and SetCtlMax do *not* call the control definition function with this message; instead, they pass the drawCntl message to execute the draw routine (see above).

The Thumb Routine

Like the position routine, the thumb routine is required only for controls that don't use the Control Manager's default method of dragging the control's indicator. The control definition function for such a control should respond to the message thumbCntl by calculating the limiting rectangle, slop rectangle, and axis constraint for dragging the control's indicator. Param is a pointer to the following data structure:

```
RECORD
   limitRect,slopRect: Rect;
   axis: INTEGER
END;
```

On entry, param^.limitRect.topLeft contains the point where the mouse button was first pressed. The definition function should store the appropriate values into the fields of the record pointed to by param; they're analogous to the similarly named parameters to DragGrayRgn.

The Track Routine

You can design a control to have its action procedure in the control definition function. To do this, set up the control's initialize routine to store POINTER(–1) in the contrlAction field of the control record, and pass POINTER(–1) in the actionProc parameter to TrackControl. TrackControl will respond by calling the control definition function with the message autoTrack. The definition function should respond like an action procedure, as discussed in detail in the description of TrackControl. It can tell which part of the control the mouse button was pressed in from param, which contains the part code. The track routine for each of the standard control types does nothing.

FORMATS OF RESOURCES FOR CONTROLS

The GetNewControl function takes the resource ID of a control template as a parameter, and gets from that template the same information that the NewControl function gets from eight of its parameters. The resource type for a control template is 'CNTL', and the resource data has the following format:

Number of bytes	Contents
8 bytes	Same as boundsRect parameter to NewControl
2 bytes	Same as value parameter to NewControl
2 bytes	Same as visible parameter to NewControl
2 bytes	Same as max parameter to NewControl
2 bytes	Same as min parameter to NewControl
2 bytes	Same as procID parameter to NewControl
4 bytes	Same as refCon parameter to NewControl
n bytes	Same as title parameter to NewControl (1-byte length in bytes, followed by the characters of the title)

The resource type for a control definition function is 'CDEF'. The resource data is simply the compiled or assembled code of the function.

SUMMARY OF THE CONTROL MANAGER

Constants

```
CONST  { Control definition IDs }

        pushButProc   = 0;   {simple button}
        checkBoxProc  = 1;   {check box}
        radioButProc  = 2;   {radio button}
        useWFont      = 8;   {add to above to use window's font}
        scrollBarProc = 16;  {scroll bar}

        { Part codes }

        inButton      = 10;  {simple button}
        inCheckBox    = 11;  {check box or radio button}
        inUpButton    = 20;  {up arrow of a scroll bar}
        inDownButton  = 21;  {down arrow of a scroll bar}
        inPageUp      = 22;  {"page up" region of a scroll bar}
        inPageDown    = 23;  {"page down" region of a scroll bar}
        inThumb       = 129; {thumb of a scroll bar}

        { Axis constraints for DragControl }

        noConstraint  = 0;   {no constraint}
        hAxisOnly     = 1;   {horizontal axis only}
        vAxisOnly     = 2;   {vertical axis only}

        { Messages to control definition function }

        drawCntl  = 0;  {draw the control (or control part)}
        testCntl  = 1;  {test where mouse button was pressed}
        calcCRgns = 2;  {calculate control's region (or indicator's)}
        initCntl  = 3;  {do any additional control initialization}
        dispCntl  = 4;  {take any additional disposal actions}
        posCntl   = 5;  {reposition control's indicator and update it}
        thumbCntl = 6;  {calculate parameters for dragging indicator}
        dragCntl  = 7;  {drag control (or its indicator)}
        autoTrack = 8;  {execute control's action procedure}
```

Data Types

```
TYPE ControlHandle = ^ControlPtr;
     ControlPtr    = ^ControlRecord;
```

```
ControlRecord =
    PACKED RECORD
        nextControl:   ControlHandle;    {next control}
        contrlOwner:   WindowPtr;        {control's window}
        contrlRect:    Rect;             {enclosing rectangle}
        contrlVis:     Byte;             {255 if visible}
        contrlHilite:  Byte;             {highlight state}
        contrlValue:   INTEGER;          {control's current setting}
        contrlMin:     INTEGER;          {control's minimum setting}
        contrlMax:     INTEGER;          {control's maximum setting}
        contrlDefProc: Handle;           {control definition function}
        contrlData:    Handle;           {data used by contrlDefProc}
        contrlAction:  ProcPtr;          {default action procedure}
        contrlRfCon:   LONGINT;          {control's reference value}
        contrlTitle:   Str255            {control's title}
    END;
```

Routines

Initialization and Allocation

```
FUNCTION   NewControl      (theWindow: WindowPtr; boundsRect: Rect; title:
                           Str255; visible: BOOLEAN; value: INTEGER;
                           min,max: INTEGER; procID: INTEGER; refCon:
                           LONGINT) : ControlHandle;
FUNCTION   GetNewControl   (controlID: INTEGER; theWindow: WindowPtr) :
                           ControlHandle;
PROCEDURE  DisposeControl  (theControl: ControlHandle);
PROCEDURE  KillControls    (theWindow: WindowPtr);
```

Control Display

```
PROCEDURE  SetCTitle       (theControl: ControlHandle; title: Str255);
PROCEDURE  GetCTitle       (theControl: ControlHandle; VAR title: Str255);
PROCEDURE  HideControl     (theControl: ControlHandle);
PROCEDURE  ShowControl     (theControl: ControlHandle);
PROCEDURE  DrawControls    (theWindow: WindowPtr);
PROCEDURE  HiliteControl   (theControl: ControlHandle; hiliteState:
                           INTEGER);
```

Mouse Location

```
FUNCTION   FindControl     (thePoint: Point; theWindow: WindowPtr; VAR
                           whichControl: ControlHandle) : INTEGER;
FUNCTION   TrackControl    (theControl: ControlHandle; startPt: Point;
                           actionProc: ProcPtr) : INTEGER;
FUNCTION   TestControl     (theControl: ControlHandle; thePoint: Point) :
                           INTEGER;
```

Control Movement and Sizing

```
PROCEDURE MoveControl   (theControl: ControlHandle; h,v: INTEGER);
PROCEDURE DragControl   (theControl: ControlHandle; startPt: Point;
                          limitRect,slopRect: Rect; axis: INTEGER);
PROCEDURE SizeControl   (theControl: ControlHandle; w,h: INTEGER);
```

Control Setting and Range

```
PROCEDURE SetCtlValue   (theControl: ControlHandle; theValue: INTEGER);
FUNCTION  GetCtlValue   (theControl: ControlHandle) : INTEGER;
PROCEDURE SetCtlMin     (theControl: ControlHandle; minValue: INTEGER);
FUNCTION  GetCtlMin     (theControl: ControlHandle) : INTEGER;
PROCEDURE SetCtlMax     (theControl: ControlHandle; maxValue INTEGER);
FUNCTION  GetCtlMax     (theControl: ControlHandle) : INTEGER;
```

Miscellaneous Routines

```
PROCEDURE SetCRefCon    (theControl: ControlHandle; data: LONGINT);
FUNCTION  GetCRefCon    (theControl: ControlHandle) : LONGINT;
PROCEDURE SetCtlAction  (theControl: ControlHandle; actionProc ProcPtr);
FUNCTION  GetCtlAction  (theControl: ControlHandle) : ProcPtr;
```

Action Procedure for TrackControl

```
If an indicator:        PROCEDURE MyAction;
If not an indicator:    PROCEDURE MyAction (theControl: ControlHandle;
                                            partCode: INTEGER);
```

Control Definition Function

```
FUNCTION MyControl  (varCode: INTEGER; theControl: ControlHandle;
                     message: INTEGER; param: LONGINT) : LONGINT;
```

Assembly-Language Information

Constants

```
; Control definition IDs

pushButProc     .EQU   0    ;simple button
checkBoxProc    .EQU   1    ;check box
radioButProc    .EQU   2    ;radio button
useWFont        .EQU   8    ;add to above to use window's font
scrollBarProc   .EQU   16   ;scroll bar
```

```
; Part codes

inButton        .EQU   10    ;simple button
inCheckBox      .EQU   11    ;check box or radio button
inUpButton      .EQU   20    ;up arrow of a scroll bar
inDownButton    .EQU   21    ;down arrow of a scroll bar
inPageUp        .EQU   22    ;"page up" region of a scroll bar
inPageDown      .EQU   23    ;"page down" region of a scroll bar
inThumb         .EQU   129   ;thumb of a scroll bar


; Axis constraints for DragControl

noConstraint    .EQU   0     ;no constraint
hAxisOnly       .EQU   1     ;horizontal axis only
vAxisOnly       .EQU   2     ;vertical axis only


; Messages to control definition function

drawCtlMsg      .EQU   0     ;draw the control (or control part)
hitCtlMsg       .EQU   1     ;test where mouse button was pressed
calcCtlMsg      .EQU   2     ;calculate control's region (or indicator's)
newCtlMsg       .EQU   3     ;do any additional control initialization
dispCtlMsg      .EQU   4     ;take any additional disposal actions
posCtlMsg       .EQU   5     ;reposition control's indicator and update it
thumbCtlMsg     .EQU   6     ;calculate parameters for dragging indicator
dragCtlMsg      .EQU   7     ;drag control (or its indicator)
trackCtlMsg     .EQU   8     ;execute control's action procedure
```

Control Record Data Structure

nextControl	Handle to next control in control list
contrlOwner	Pointer to this control's window
contrlRect	Control's enclosing rectangle (8 bytes)
contrlVis	255 if control is visible (byte)
contrlHilite	Highlight state (byte)
contrlValue	Control's current setting (word)
contrlMin	Control's minimum setting (word)
contrlMax	Control's maximum setting (word)
contrlDefHandle	Handle to control definition function
contrlData	Data used by control definition function (long)
contrlAction	Address of default action procedure
contrlRfCon	Control's reference value (long)
contrlTitle	Handle to control's title (preceded by length byte)
contrlSize	Size in bytes of control record except contrlTitle field

Special Macro Names

Pascal name	Macro name
DisposeControl	_DisposControl
GetCtlMax	_GetMaxCtl
GetCtlMin	_GetMinCtl
SetCtlMax	_SetMaxCtl
SetCtlMin	_SetMinCtl

Variables

DragHook	Address of procedure to execute during TrackControl and DragControl
DragPattern	Pattern of dragged region's outline (8 bytes)

11 THE MENU MANAGER

ABOUT THIS CHAPTER

This chapter describes the Menu Manager, the part of the Toolbox that allows you to create sets of menus, and allows the user to choose from the commands in those menus.

You should already be familiar with:

■ resources, as described in chapter 5

■ the basic concepts and structures behind QuickDraw, particularly points, rectangles, and character style

■ the Toolbox Event Manager

ABOUT THE MENU MANAGER

The Menu Manager supports the use of **menus**, an integral part of the Macintosh user interface. Menus allow users to examine all choices available to them at any time without being forced to choose one of them, and without having to remember command words or special keys. The Macintosh user simply positions the cursor in the **menu bar** and presses the mouse button over a **menu title**. The application then calls the Menu Manager, which highlights that title (by inverting it) and "pulls down" the menu below it. As long as the mouse button is held down, the menu is displayed. Dragging through the menu causes each of the **menu items** (commands) in it to be highlighted in turn. If the mouse button is released over an item, that item is "chosen". The item blinks briefly to confirm the choice, and the menu disappears.

When the user chooses an item, the Menu Manager tells the application which item was chosen, and the application performs the corresponding action. When the application completes the action, it removes the highlighting from the menu title, indicating to the user that the operation is complete.

If the user moves the cursor out of the menu with the mouse button held down, the menu remains visible, though no menu items are highlighted. If the mouse button is released outside the menu, no choice is made: The menu just disappears and the application takes no action. The user can always look at a menu without causing any changes in the document or on the screen.

The Menu Bar

The menu bar always appears at the top of the Macintosh screen; nothing but the cursor ever appears in front of it. The menu bar is white, 20 pixels high, and as wide as the screen, with a 1-pixel black lower border. The menu titles in it are always in the system font and the system font size (see Figure 1).

In applications that support desk accessories, the first menu should be the standard Apple menu (the menu whose title is an apple symbol). The Apple menu contains the names of all available desk accessories. When the user chooses a desk accessory from the menu, the title of a menu belonging to the desk accessory may appear in the menu bar, for as long as the accessory is active, or the entire menu bar may be replaced by menus belonging to the desk accessory. (Desk accessories are discussed in detail in chapter 14.)

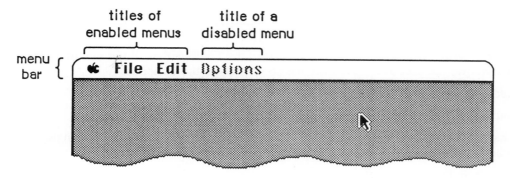

Figure 1. The Menu Bar

A menu may be temporarily **disabled**, so that none of the items in it can be chosen. A disabled menu can still be pulled down, but its title and all the items in it are dimmed.

The maximum number of menu titles in the menu bar is 16; however, ten to twelve titles are usually all that will fit, and you must leave at least enough room in the menu bar for one desk accessory menu. Also keep in mind that if your program is likely to be translated into other languages, the menu titles may take up more space. If you're having trouble fitting your menus into the menu bar, you should review your menu organization and menu titles.

Appearance of Menus

A standard menu consists of a number of menu items listed vertically inside a shadowed rectangle. A menu item may be the text of a command, or just a line dividing groups of choices (see Figure 2). An ellipsis (...) following the text of an item indicates that selecting the item will bring up a dialog box to get further information before the command is executed. Menus always appear in front of everything else (except the cursor); in Figure 2, the menu appears in front of a document window already on the screen.

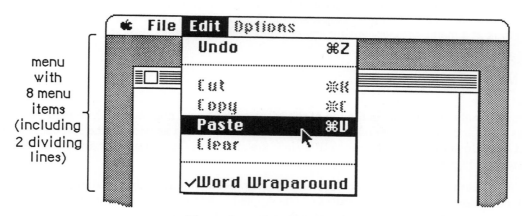

Figure 2. A Standard Menu

The text of a menu item always appears in the system font and the system font size. Each item can have a few visual variations from the standard appearance:

- An icon to the left of the item's text, to give a symbolic representation of the item's meaning or effect.

- A check mark or other character to the left of the item's text (or icon, if any), to denote the status of the item or of the mode it controls.

- The Command key symbol and another character to the right of the item's text, to show that the item may be invoked from the keyboard (that is, it has a **keyboard equivalent**). Pressing this key while holding down the Command key invokes the item just as if it had been chosen from the menu (see "Keyboard Equivalents for Commands" below).

- A character style other than the standard, such as bold, italic, underline, or a combination of these. (Chapter 6 gives a full discussion of character style.)

- A dimmed appearance, to indicate that the item is disabled, and can't be chosen. The Cut, Copy, and Clear commands in Figure 2 are disabled; dividing lines are always disabled.

Note: Special symbols or icons may have an unusual appearance when dimmed; notice the dimmed Command symbol in the Cut and Copy menu items in Figure 2.

The maximum number of menu items that will fit in a standard menu is 20 (less 1 for each item that contains an icon). The fewer menu items you have, the simpler and clearer the menu appears to the user.

If the standard menu doesn't suit your needs—for example, if you want more graphics, or perhaps a nonlinear text arrangement—you can define a custom menu that, although visibly different to the user, responds to your application's Menu Manager calls just like a standard menu.

Keyboard Equivalents for Commands

Your program can set up a keyboard equivalent for any of its menu commands so the command can be invoked from the keyboard with the Command key. The character you specify for a keyboard equivalent will usually be a letter. The user can type the letter in either uppercase or lowercase. For example, typing either "C" or "c" while holding down the Command key invokes the command whose equivalent is "C".

Note: For consistency between applications, you should specify the letter in uppercase in the menu.

You can specify characters other than letters for keyboard equivalents. However, the Shift key will be ignored when the equivalent is typed, so you shouldn't specify shifted characters. For example, when the user types Command-+, the system reads it as Command-=.

Command-Shift-number combinations are *not* keyboard equivalents. They're detected and handled by the Toolbox Event Manager function GetNextEvent, and are never returned to your program. (This is how disk ejection with Command-Shift-1 or 2 is implemented.) Although it's possible to use unshifted Command-number combinations as keyboard equivalents, you shouldn't do so, to avoid confusion.

Warning: You must use the standard keyboard equivalents Z, X, C, and V for the editing commands Undo, Cut, Copy, and Paste, or editing won't work correctly in desk accessories.

MENUS AND RESOURCES

The general appearance and behavior of a menu is determined by a routine called its **menu definition procedure**, which is stored as a resource in a resource file. The menu definition procedure performs all actions that differ from one menu type to another, such as drawing the menu. The Menu Manager calls the menu definition procedure whenever it needs to perform one of these basic actions, passing it a message that tells which action to perform.

The standard menu definition procedure is part of the system resource file. It lists the menu items vertically, and each item may have an icon, a check mark or other symbol, a keyboard equivalent, a different character style, or a dimmed appearance. If you want to define your own, nonstandard menu types, you'll have to write menu definition procedures for them, as described later in the section "Defining Your Own Menus".

You can also use a resource file to store the contents of your application's menus. This allows the menus to be edited or translated to another language without affecting the application's source code. The Menu Manager lets you read complete menu bars as well as individual menus from a resource file.

Warning: Menus in a resource file must not be purgeable.

Even if you don't store entire menus in resource files, it's a good idea to store the text strings they contain as resources; you can call the Resource Manager directly to read them in. Icons in menus are read from resource files; the Menu Manager calls the Resource Manager to read in the icons.

There's a Menu Manager procedure that scans all open resource files for resources of a given type and installs the names of all available resources of that type into a given menu. This is how you fill a menu with the names of all available desk accessories or fonts, for example.

Note: If you use a menu of this type, check to make sure that at least one item is in the menu; if not, you should put a disabled item in it that says "None" (or something else indicating the menu is empty).

MENU RECORDS

The Menu Manager keeps all the information it needs for its operations on a particular menu in a **menu record**. The menu record contains the following:

- The **menu ID**, a number that identifies the menu. The menu ID can be the same number as the menu's resource ID, though it doesn't have to be.

- The menu title.

- The contents of the menu—the text and other parts of each item.

- The horizontal and vertical dimensions of the menu, in pixels. The menu items appear inside the rectangle formed by these dimensions; the black border and shadow of the menu appear outside that rectangle.

- A handle to the menu definition procedure.

■ Flags telling whether each menu item is enabled or disabled, and whether the menu itself is enabled or disabled.

The data type for a menu record is called MenuInfo. A menu record is referred to by a handle:

```
TYPE  MenuPtr     = ^MenuInfo;
      MenuHandle  = ^MenuPtr;
```

You can store into and access all the necessary fields of a menu record with Menu Manager routines, so normally you don't have to know the exact field names. However, if you want more information about the exact structure of a menu record—if you're defining your own menu types, for instance—it's given below.

The MenuInfo Data Type

The type MenuInfo is defined as follows:

```
TYPE MenuInfo =
     RECORD
          menuID:      INTEGER;   {menu ID}
          menuWidth:   INTEGER;   {menu width in pixels}
          menuHeight:  INTEGER;   {menu height in pixels}
          menuProc:    Handle;    {menu definition procedure}
          enableFlags: LONGINT;   {tells if menu or items are enabled}
          menuData:    Str255     {menu title (and other data)}
     END;
```

The menuID field contains the menu ID. MenuWidth and menuHeight are the menu's horizontal and vertical dimensions in pixels. MenuProc is a handle to the menu definition procedure for this type of menu.

Bit 0 of the enableFlags field is 1 if the menu is enabled, or 0 if it's disabled. Bits 1 to 31 similarly tell whether each item in the menu is enabled or disabled.

The menuData field contains the menu title followed by variable-length data that defines the text and other parts of the menu items. The Str255 data type enables you to access the title from Pascal; there's actually additional data beyond the title that's inaccessible from Pascal and is not reflected in the MenuInfo data structure.

Warning: You can read the menu title directly from the menuData field, but do not change the title directly, or the data defining the menu items may be destroyed.

MENU LISTS

A **menu list** contains handles to one or more menus, along with information about the position of each menu in the menu bar. The current menu list contains handles to all the menus currently in the menu bar; the menu bar shows the titles, in order, of all menus in the menu list. When you initialize the Menu Manager, it allocates space for the maximum-size menu list.

The Menu Manager provides all the necessary routines for manipulating the current menu list, so there's no need to access it directly yourself. As a general rule, routines that deal specifically with menus in the menu list use the menu ID to refer to menus; those that deal with any menus, whether in the menu list or not, use the menu handle to refer to menus. Some routines refer to the menu list as a whole, with a handle.

Assembly-language note: The global variable MenuList contains a handle to the current menu list. The menu list has the format shown below.

Number of bytes	Contents
2 bytes	Offset from beginning of menu list to last menu handle (the number of menus in the list times 6)
2 bytes	Horizontal coordinate of right edge of menu title of last menu in list
2 bytes	Not used
For each menu:	
4 bytes	Menu handle
2 bytes	Horizontal coordinate of left edge of menu

CREATING A MENU IN YOUR PROGRAM

The best way to create your application's menus is to set them up as resources and read them in from a resource file. If you want your application to create the menus itself, though, it must call the NewMenu and AppendMenu routines. NewMenu creates a new menu data structure, returning a handle to it. AppendMenu takes a string and a handle to a menu and adds the items in the string to the end of the menu.

The string passed to AppendMenu consists mainly of the text of the menu items. For a dividing line, use one hyphen (–); AppendMenu ignores any following characters, and draws a dotted line across the width of the menu. For a blank item, use one or more spaces. Other characters interspersed in the string have special meaning to the Menu Manager. These "meta-characters" are used in conjunction with text to separate menu items or alter their appearance (for example, you can use one to disable any dividing line or blank item). The meta-characters aren't displayed in the menu.

Meta-character	Meaning
; or Return	Separates items
^	Item has an icon
!	Item has a check or other mark
<	Item has a special character style
/	Item has a keyboard equivalent
(	Item is disabled

None, any, or all of these meta-characters can appear in the AppendMenu string; they're described in detail below. To add one text-only item to a menu would require a simple string without any meta-characters:

```
AppendMenu(thisMenu,'Just Enough')
```

An extreme example could use many meta-characters:

```
AppendMenu(thisMenu,'(Too Much^1<B/T')
```

This example adds to the menu an item whose text is "Too Much", which is disabled, has icon number 1, is boldfaced, and can be invoked by Command-T. Your menu items should be much simpler than this.

> **Note:** If you want any of the meta-characters to appear in the text of a menu item, you can include them by changing the text with the Menu Manager procedure SetItem.

Multiple Items

Each call to AppendMenu can add one or many items to the menu. To add multiple items in the same call, use a semicolon (;) or a Return character to separate the items. The call

```
AppendMenu(thisMenu,'Cut;Copy')
```

has exactly the same effect as the calls

```
AppendMenu(thisMenu,'Cut');
AppendMenu(thisMenu,'Copy')
```

Items with Icons

A circumflex (^) followed by a digit from 1 to 9 indicates that an icon should appear to the left of the text in the menu. The digit, called the **icon number**, yields the resource ID of the icon in the resource file. Icon resource IDs 257 through 511 are reserved for menu icons; thus the Menu Manager adds 256 to the icon number to get the proper resource ID.

> **Note:** The Menu Manager gets the icon number by subtracting 48 from the ASCII code of the character following the "^" (since, for example, the ASCII code of "1" is 49). You can actually follow the "^" with any character that has an ASCII code greater than 48.

You can also use the SetItemIcon procedure to install icons in a menu; it accepts any icon number from 1 to 255.

Marked Items

You can use an exclamation point (!) to cause a check mark or any other character to be placed to the left of the text (or icon, if any). Follow the exclamation point with the character of your choice; note, however, that normally you can't type a check mark from the keyboard. To specify a check mark, you need to take special measures: Declare a string variable to have the length of the desired AppendMenu string, and assign it that string with a space following the exclamation point. Then separately store the check mark in the position of the space.

For example, suppose you want to use AppendMenu to specify a menu item that has the text "Word Wraparound" (15 characters) and a check mark to its left. You can declare the string variable

```
VAR s: STRING[17];
```

and do the following:

```
s := '! Word Wraparound';
s[2] := CHR(checkMark);
AppendMenu(thisMenu,s)
```

The constant checkMark is defined by the Font Manager as the character code for the check mark.

> **Note:** The Font Manager also defines constants for certain other special characters that can't normally be typed from the keyboard: the apple symbol, the Command key symbol, and a diamond symbol. These symbols can be specified in the same way as the check mark.

You can call the SetItemMark or CheckItem procedures to change or clear the mark, and the GetItemMark procedure to find out what mark, if any, is being used.

Character Style of Items

The system font is the only font available for menus; however, you can vary the character style of menu items for clarity and distinction. The meta-character for specifying the character style of an item's text is the less-than symbol (<). With AppendMenu, you can assign one and only one of the stylistic variations listed below.

<B	Bold
<I	Italic
<U	Underline
<O	Outline
<S	Shadow

The SetItemStyle procedure allows you to assign any combination of stylistic variations to an item. For a further discussion of character style, see chapter 6.

Items with Keyboard Equivalents

A slash (/) followed by a character associates that character with the item, allowing the item to be invoked from the keyboard with the Command key. The specified character (preceded by the Command key symbol) appears at the right of the item's text in the menu.

> **Note:** Remember to specify the character in uppercase if it's a letter, and not to specify other shifted characters or numbers.

Given a keyboard equivalent typed by the user, you call the MenuKey function to find out which menu item was invoked.

Disabled Items

The meta-character that disables an item is the left parenthesis, "(". A disabled item cannot be chosen; it appears dimmed in the menu and is not highlighted when the cursor moves over it.

Menu items that are used to separate groups of items (such as a line or a blank item) should always be disabled. For example, the call

```
AppendMenu(thisMenu,'Undo;(-;Cut')
```

adds two enabled menu items, Undo and Cut, with a disabled item consisting of a line between them.

You can change the enabled or disabled state of a menu item with the DisableItem and EnableItem procedures.

USING THE MENU MANAGER

To use the Menu Manager, you must have previously called InitGraf to initialize QuickDraw, InitFonts to initialize the Font Manager, and InitWindows to initialize the Window Manager. The first Menu Manager routine to call is the initialization procedure InitMenus.

Your application can set up the menus it needs in any number of ways:

- Read an entire prepared menu list from a resource file with GetNewMBar, and place it in the menu bar with SetMenuBar.

- Read the menus individually from a resource file using GetMenu, and place them in the menu bar using InsertMenu.

- Allocate the menus with NewMenu, fill them with items using AppendMenu, and place them in the menu bar using InsertMenu.

- Allocate a menu with NewMenu, fill it with items using AddResMenu to get the names of all available resources of a given type, and place the menu in the menu bar using InsertMenu.

You can use AddResMenu or InsertResMenu to add items from resource files to any menu, regardless of how you created the menu or whether it already contains any items.

When you no longer need a menu, call the Resource Manager procedure ReleaseResource if you read the menu from a resource file, or DisposeMenu if you allocated it with NewMenu.

Note: If you want to save changes made to a menu that was read from a resource file, write it back to the resource file before calling ReleaseResource.

If you call NewMenu to allocate a menu, it will store a handle to the standard menu definition procedure in the menu record, so if you want the menu to be one you've designed, you must replace that handle with a handle to your own menu definition procedure. For more information, see "Defining Your Own Menus".

After setting up the menu bar, you need to draw it with the DrawMenuBar procedure.

You can use the SetItem and GetItem procedures to change or examine a menu item's text at any time—for example, to change between the two forms of a toggled command. You can set or examine an item's icon, style, or mark with the procedures SetItemIcon, GetItemIcon, SetItemStyle, GetItemStyle, CheckItem, SetItemMark, and GetItemMark. Individual items or whole menus can be enabled or disabled with the EnableItem and DisableItem procedures. You can change the number of menus in the menu list with InsertMenu or DeleteMenu, remove all the menus with ClearMenuBar, or change the entire menu list with GetNewMBar or GetMenuBar followed by SetMenuBar.

When your application receives a mouse-down event, and the Window Manager's FindWindow function returns the predefined constant inMenuBar, your application should call the Menu Manager's MenuSelect function, supplying it with the point where the mouse button was pressed. MenuSelect will pull down the appropriate menu, and retain control—tracking the mouse, highlighting menu items, and pulling down other menus—until the user releases the mouse button. MenuSelect returns a long integer to the application: The high-order word contains the menu ID of the menu that was chosen, and the low-order word contains the **menu item number** of the item that was chosen. The menu item number is the index, starting from 1, of the item in the menu. If no item was chosen, the high-order word of the long integer is 0, and the low-order word is undefined.

- If the high-order word of the long integer returned is 0, the application should just continue to poll for further events.

- If the high-order word is nonzero, the application should invoke the menu item specified by the low-order word, in the menu specified by the high-order word. Only after the action is completely finished (after all dialogs, alerts, or screen actions have been taken care of) should the application remove the highlighting from the menu bar by calling HiliteMenu(0), signaling the completion of the action.

Note: The Menu Manager automatically saves and restores the bits behind the menu; you don't have to worry about it.

Keyboard equivalents are handled in much the same manner. When your application receives a key-down event with the Command key held down, it should call the MenuKey function, supplying it with the character that was typed. MenuKey will return a long integer with the same format as that of MenuSelect, and the application can handle the long integer in the manner described above. Applications should respond the same way to auto-key events as to key-down events when the Command key is held down if the command being invoked is repeatable.

Note: You can use the Toolbox Utility routines LoWord and HiWord to extract the high-order and low-order words of a given long integer, as described in chapter 16.

There are several miscellaneous Menu Manager routines that you normally won't need to use. CalcMenuSize calculates the dimensions of a menu. CountMItems counts the number of items in a menu. GetMHandle returns the handle of a menu in the menu list. FlashMenuBar inverts the menu bar. SetMenuFlash controls the number of times a menu item blinks when it's chosen.

MENU MANAGER ROUTINES

Initialization and Allocation

```
PROCEDURE InitMenus;
```

InitMenus initializes the Menu Manager. It allocates space for the menu list (a relocatable block in the heap large enough for the maximum-size menu list), and draws the (empty) menu bar. Call InitMenus once before all other Menu Manager routines. An application should never have to call this procedure more than once; to start afresh with all new menus, use ClearMenuBar.

> **Note:** The Window Manager initialization procedure InitWindows has already drawn the empty menu bar; InitMenus redraws it.

```
FUNCTION NewMenu (menuID: INTEGER; menuTitle: Str255) :
        MenuHandle;
```

NewMenu allocates space for a new menu with the given menu ID and title, and returns a handle to it. It sets up the menu to use the standard menu definition procedure. (The menu definition procedure is read into memory if it isn't already in memory.) The new menu (which is created empty) is not installed in the menu list. To use this menu, you must first call AppendMenu or AddResMenu to fill it with items, InsertMenu to place it in the menu list, and DrawMenuBar to update the menu bar to include the new title.

Application menus should always have positive menu IDs. Negative menu IDs are reserved for menus belonging to desk accessories. No menu should ever have a menu ID of 0.

If you want to set up the title of the Apple menu from your program instead of reading it in from a resource file, you can use the constant appleMark (defined by the Font Manager as the character code for the apple symbol). For example, you can declare the string variable

```
VAR myTitle: STRING[1];
```

and do the following:

```
myTitle := ' ';
myTitle[1] := CHR(appleMark)
```

To release the memory occupied by a menu that you created with NewMenu, call DisposeMenu.

```
FUNCTION GetMenu (resourceID: INTEGER) : MenuHandle;
```

> **Assembly-language note:** The macro you invoke to call GetMenu from assembly language is named _GetRMenu.

GetMenu returns a menu handle for the menu having the given resource ID. It calls the Resource Manager to read the menu from the resource file into a menu record in memory. GetMenu stores the handle to the menu definition procedure in the menu record, reading the procedure from the resource file into memory if necessary. If the menu or the menu definition procedure can't be read from the resource file, GetMenu returns NIL. To use the menu, you must call InsertMenu to place it in the menu list and DrawMenuBar to update the menu bar to include the new title.

Warning: Call GetMenu only once for a particular menu. If you need the menu handle to a menu that's already in memory, use the Resource Manager function GetResource.

To release the memory occupied by a menu that you read from a resource file with GetMenu, use the Resource Manager procedure ReleaseResource.

```
PROCEDURE DisposeMenu (theMenu: MenuHandle);
```

Assembly-language note: The macro you invoke to call DisposeMenu from assembly language is named _DisposMenu.

Call DisposeMenu to release the memory occupied by a menu that you allocated with NewMenu. (For menus read from a resource file with GetMenu, use the Resource Manager procedure ReleaseResource instead.) This is useful if you've created temporary menus that you no longer need.

Warning: Make sure you remove the menu from the menu list (with DeleteMenu) before disposing of it.

Forming the Menus

```
PROCEDURE AppendMenu (theMenu: MenuHandle; data: Str255);
```

AppendMenu adds an item or items to the end of the given menu, which must previously have been allocated by NewMenu or read from a resource file by GetMenu. The data string consists of the text of the menu item; it may be blank but should not be the empty string. If it begins with a hyphen (–), the item will be a dividing line across the width of the menu. As described in the section "Creating a Menu in Your Program", the following meta-characters may be embedded in the data string:

Meta-character	Usage
; or Return	Separates multiple items
^	Followed by an icon number, adds that icon to the item
!	Followed by a character, marks the item with that character
<	Followed by B, I, U, O, or S, sets the character style of the item
/	Followed by a character, associates a keyboard equivalent with the item
(	Disables the item

Once items have been appended to a menu, they cannot be removed or rearranged. AppendMenu works properly whether or not the menu is in the menu list.

PROCEDURE AddResMenu (theMenu: MenuHandle; theType: ResType);

AddResMenu searches all open resource files for resources of type theType and appends the names of all resources it finds to the given menu. Each resource name appears in the menu as an enabled item, without an icon or mark, and in the plain character style. The standard Menu Manager calls can be used to get the name or change its appearance, as described in the section "Controlling the Appearance of Items".

> **Note:** So that you can have resources of the given type that won't appear in the menu, any resource names that begin with a period (.) or a percent sign (%) aren't appended by AddResMenu.

Use this procedure to fill a menu with the names of all available fonts or desk accessories. For example, if you declare a variable as

    VAR fontMenu: MenuHandle;

you can set up a menu containing all font names as follows:

    fontMenu := NewMenu(5,'Fonts');
    AddResMenu(fontMenu,'FONT')

> **Warning:** Before returning, AddResMenu issues the Resource Manager call SetResLoad(TRUE). If your program previously called SetResLoad(FALSE) and you still want that to be in effect after calling AddResMenu, you'll have to call it again.

PROCEDURE InsertResMenu (theMenu: MenuHandle; theType: ResType;
        afterItem: INTEGER);

InsertResMenu is the same as AddResMenu (above) except that it inserts the resource names in the menu where specified by the afterItem parameter: If afterItem is 0, the names are inserted before the first menu item; if it's the item number of an item in the menu, they're inserted after that item; if it's equal to or greater than the last item number, they're appended to the menu.

> **Note:** InsertResMenu inserts the names in the reverse of the order that AddResMenu appends them. For consistency between applications in the appearance of menus, use AddResMenu instead of InsertResMenu if possible.

Forming the Menu Bar

PROCEDURE InsertMenu (theMenu: MenuHandle; beforeID: INTEGER);

InsertMenu inserts a menu into the menu list before the menu whose menu ID equals beforeID. If beforeID is 0 (or isn't the ID of any menu in the menu list), the new menu is added after all others. If the menu is already in the menu list or the menu list is already full, InsertMenu does nothing. Be sure to call DrawMenuBar to update the menu bar.

PROCEDURE DrawMenuBar;

DrawMenuBar redraws the menu bar according to the menu list, incorporating any changes since the last call to DrawMenuBar. This procedure should always be called after a sequence of InsertMenu or DeleteMenu calls, and after ClearMenuBar, SetMenuBar, or any other routine that changes the menu list.

Warning: Don't call DrawMenuBar while a menu title is highlighted, or the menu bar may be drawn incorrectly.

PROCEDURE DeleteMenu (menuID: INTEGER);

DeleteMenu deletes a menu from the menu list. If there's no menu with the given menu ID in the menu list, DeleteMenu has no effect. Be sure to call DrawMenuBar to update the menu bar; the menu titles following the deleted menu will move over to fill the vacancy.

Note: DeleteMenu simply removes the menu from the list of currently available menus; it doesn't release the memory occupied by the menu data structure.

PROCEDURE ClearMenuBar;

Call ClearMenuBar to remove all menus from the menu list when you want to start afresh with all new menus. Be sure to call DrawMenuBar to update the menu bar.

Note: ClearMenuBar, like DeleteMenu, doesn't release the memory occupied by the menu data structures; it merely removes them from the menu list.

You don't have to call ClearMenuBar at the beginning of your program, because InitMenus clears the menu list for you.

FUNCTION GetNewMBar (menuBarID: INTEGER) : Handle;

GetNewMBar creates a menu list as defined by the menu bar resource having the given resource ID, and returns a handle to it. If the resource isn't already in memory, GetNewMBar reads it into memory from the resource file. If the resource can't be read, GetNewMBar returns NIL. GetNewMBar calls GetMenu to get each of the individual menus.

To make the menu list created by GetNewMBar the current menu list, call SetMenuBar. To release the memory occupied by the menu list, use the Memory Manager procedure DisposHandle.

Warning: You don't have to know the individual menu IDs to use GetNewMBar, but that doesn't mean you don't have to know them at all: To do anything further with a particular menu, you have to know its ID or its handle (which you can get by passing the ID to GetMHandle, as described in the section "Miscellaneous Routines").

```
FUNCTION GetMenuBar : Handle;
```

GetMenuBar creates a copy of the current menu list and returns a handle to the copy. You can then add or remove menus from the menu list (with InsertMenu, DeleteMenu, or ClearMenuBar), and later restore the saved menu list with SetMenuBar. To release the memory occupied by the saved menu list, use the Memory Manager procedure DisposHandle.

> **Warning:** GetMenuBar doesn't copy the menus themselves, only a list containing their handles. Do not dispose of any menus that might be in a saved menu list.

```
PROCEDURE SetMenuBar (menuList: Handle);
```

SetMenuBar copies the given menu list to the current menu list. You can use this procedure to restore a menu list previously saved by GetMenuBar, or pass it a handle returned by GetNewMBar. Be sure to call DrawMenuBar to update the menu bar.

Choosing From a Menu

```
FUNCTION MenuSelect (startPt: Point) : LONGINT;
```

When there's a mouse-down event in the menu bar, the application should call MenuSelect with startPt equal to the point (in global coordinates) where the mouse button was pressed. MenuSelect keeps control until the mouse button is released, tracking the mouse, pulling down menus as needed, and highlighting enabled menu items under the cursor. When the mouse button is released over an enabled item in an application menu, MenuSelect returns a long integer whose high-order word is the menu ID of the menu, and whose low-order word is the menu item number for the item chosen (see Figure 3). It leaves the selected menu title highlighted. After performing the chosen task, your application should call HiliteMenu(0) to remove the highlighting from the menu title.

If no choice is made, MenuSelect returns 0 in the high-order word of the long integer, and the low-order word is undefined. This includes the case where the mouse button is released over a disabled menu item (such as Cut, Copy, Clear, or one of the dividing lines in Figure 3), over any menu title, or outside the menu.

If the mouse button is released over an enabled item in a menu belonging to a desk accessory, MenuSelect passes the menu ID and item number to the Desk Manager procedure SystemMenu for processing, and returns 0 to your application in the high-order word of the result.

> **Note:** When a menu is pulled down, the bits behind it are stored as a relocatable object in the application heap. If your application has large menus, this can temporarily use up a lot of memory.

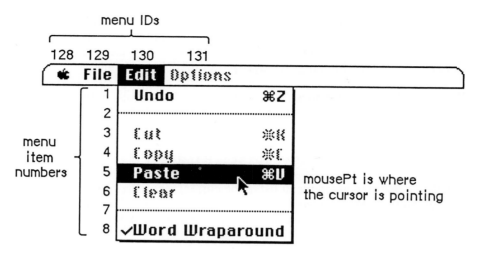

MenuSelect(mousePt) or MenuKey('V') returns:

130	5
high-order word	low-order word

Figure 3. MenuSelect and MenuKey

Assembly-language note: If the global variable MBarEnable is nonzero, MenuSelect knows that every menu currently in the menu bar belongs to a desk accessory. (See chapter 14 for more information.)

You can store in the global variables MenuHook and MBarHook the addresses of routines that will be called during MenuSelect. Both variables are initialized to 0 by InitMenus. The routine whose address is in MenuHook (if any) will be called repeatedly (with no parameters) while the mouse button is down. The routine whose address is in MBarHook (if any) will be called after the title of the menu is highlighted and the menu rectangle is calculated, but before the menu is drawn. (The menu rectangle is the rectangle in which the menu will be drawn, in global coordinates.) The routine is passed a pointer to the menu rectangle on the stack. It should normally return 0 in register D0; returning 1 will abort MenuSelect.

```
FUNCTION MenuKey (ch: CHAR) : LONGINT;
```

MenuKey maps the given character to the associated menu and item for that character. When you get a key-down event with the Command key held down—or an auto-key event, if the command being invoked is repeatable—call MenuKey with the character that was typed. MenuKey highlights the appropriate menu title, and returns a long integer containing the menu ID in its high-order word and the menu item number in its low-order word, just as MenuSelect does (see Figure 3 above). After performing the chosen task, your application should call HiliteMenu(0) to remove the highlighting from the menu title.

If the given character isn't associated with any enabled menu item currently in the menu list, MenuKey returns 0 in the high-order word of the long integer, and the low-order word is undefined.

If the given character invokes a menu item in a menu belonging to a desk accessory, MenuKey (like MenuSelect) passes the menu ID and item number to the Desk Manager procedure SystemMenu for processing, and returns 0 to your application in the high-order word of the result.

> **Note:** There should never be more than one item in the menu list with the same keyboard equivalent, but if there is, MenuKey returns the first such item it encounters, scanning the menus from right to left and their items from top to bottom.

```
PROCEDURE HiliteMenu (menuID: INTEGER);
```

HiliteMenu highlights the title of the given menu, or does nothing if the title is already highlighted. Since only one menu title can be highlighted at a time, it unhighlights any previously highlighted menu title. If menuID is 0 (or isn't the ID of any menu in the menu list), HiliteMenu simply unhighlights whichever menu title is highlighted (if any).

After MenuSelect or MenuKey, your application should perform the chosen task and then call HiliteMenu(0) to unhighlight the chosen menu title.

> **Assembly-language note:** The global variable TheMenu contains the menu ID of the currently highlighted menu.

Controlling the Appearance of Items

```
PROCEDURE SetItem (theMenu: MenuHandle; item: INTEGER; itemString:
          Str255);
```

SetItem changes the text of the given menu item to itemString. It doesn't recognize the metacharacters used in AppendMenu; if you include them in itemString, they will appear in the text of the menu item. The attributes already in effect for this item—its character style, icon, and so on—remain in effect. ItemString may be blank but should not be the empty string.

> **Note:** It's good practice to store the text of itemString in a resource file instead of passing it directly.

Use SetItem to change between the two forms of a toggled command—for example, to change "Show Clipboard" to "Hide Clipboard" when the Clipboard is already showing.

> **Note:** To avoid confusing the user, don't capriciously change the text of menu items.

```
PROCEDURE GetItem (theMenu: MenuHandle; item: INTEGER; VAR
            itemString: Str255);
```

GetItem returns the text of the given menu item in itemString. It doesn't place any meta-characters in the string. This procedure is useful for getting the name of a menu item that was installed with AddResMenu or InsertResMenu.

```
PROCEDURE DisableItem (theMenu: MenuHandle; item: INTEGER);
```

Given a menu item number in the item parameter, DisableItem disables that menu item; given 0 in the item parameter, it disables the entire menu.

Disabled menu items appear dimmed and are not highlighted when the cursor moves over them. MenuSelect and MenuKey return 0 in the high-order word of their result if the user attempts to invoke a disabled item. Use DisableItem to disable all menu choices that aren't appropriate at a given time (such as a Cut command when there's no text selection).

All menu items are initially enabled unless you specify otherwise (such as by using the "(" meta-character in a call to AppendMenu).

When you disable an entire menu, call DrawMenuBar to update the menu bar. The title of a disabled menu and every item in it are dimmed.

```
PROCEDURE EnableItem (theMenu: MenuHandle; item: INTEGER);
```

Given a menu item number in the item parameter, EnableItem enables the item (which may have been disabled with the DisableItem procedure, or with the "(" meta-character in the AppendMenu string).

Given 0 in the item parameter, EnableItem enables the menu as a whole, but any items that were disabled separately (before the entire menu was disabled) remain so. When you enable an entire menu, call DrawMenuBar to update the menu bar.

The item or menu title will no longer appear dimmed and can be chosen like any other enabled item or menu.

```
PROCEDURE CheckItem (theMenu: MenuHandle; item: INTEGER; checked:
            BOOLEAN);
```

CheckItem places or removes a check mark at the left of the given menu item. After you call CheckItem with checked=TRUE, a check mark will appear each subsequent time the menu is pulled down. Calling CheckItem with checked=FALSE removes the check mark from the menu item (or, if it's marked with a different character, removes that mark).

Menu items are initially unmarked unless you specify otherwise (such as with the "!" meta-character in a call to AppendMenu).

```
PROCEDURE SetItemMark (theMenu: MenuHandle; item: INTEGER;
            markChar: CHAR);
```

Assembly-language note: The macro you invoke to call SetItemMark from assembly language is named _SetItmMark.

SetItemMark marks the given menu item in a more general manner than CheckItem. It allows you to place any character in the system font, not just the check mark, to the left of the item. The character is passed in the markChar parameter.

Note: The Font Manager defines constants for the check mark and other special characters that can't normally be typed from the keyboard: the apple symbol, the Command key symbol, and a diamond symbol. See chapter 7 for more information.

To remove an item's mark, you can pass the following predefined constant in the markChar parameter:

```
CONST noMark = 0;
```

```
PROCEDURE GetItemMark (theMenu: MenuHandle; item: INTEGER; VAR
            markChar: CHAR);
```

Assembly-language note: The macro you invoke to call GetItemMark from assembly language is named _GetItmMark.

GetItemMark returns in markChar whatever character the given menu item is marked with, or the predefined constant noMark if no mark is present.

```
PROCEDURE SetItemIcon (theMenu: MenuHandle; item: INTEGER; icon:
            Byte);
```

Assembly-language note: The macro you invoke to call SetItemIcon from assembly language is named _SetItmIcon.

SetItemIcon associates the given menu item with an icon. It sets the item's icon number to the given value (an integer from 1 to 255). The Menu Manager adds 256 to the icon number to get the icon's resource ID, which it passes to the Resource Manager to get the corresponding icon.

Warning: If you call the Resource Manager directly to read or store menu icons, be sure to adjust your icon numbers accordingly.

Menu items initially have no icons unless you specify otherwise (such as with the "^" meta-character in a call to AppendMenu).

```
PROCEDURE GetItemIcon (theMenu: MenuHandle; item: INTEGER; VAR
          icon: Byte);
```

Assembly-language note: The macro you invoke to call GetItemIcon from assembly language is named _GetItmIcon.

GetItemIcon returns the icon number associated with the given menu item, as an integer from 1 to 255, or 0 if the item has not been associated with an icon. The icon number is 256 less than the icon's resource ID.

```
PROCEDURE SetItemStyle (theMenu: MenuHandle; item: INTEGER;
          chStyle: Style);
```

Assembly-language note: The macro you invoke to call SetItemStyle from assembly language is named _SetItmStyle.

SetItemStyle changes the character style of the given menu item to chStyle. For example:

```
SetItemStyle(thisMenu,1,[bold,italic])   {bold and italic}
```

Menu items are initially in the plain character style unless you specify otherwise (such as with the "<" meta-character in a call to AppendMenu).

```
PROCEDURE GetItemStyle (theMenu: MenuHandle; item: INTEGER; VAR
          chStyle: Style);
```

Assembly-language note: The macro you invoke to call GetItemStyle from assembly language is named _GetItmStyle.

GetItemStyle returns the character style of the given menu item in chStyle.

Miscellaneous Routines

PROCEDURE CalcMenuSize (theMenu: MenuHandle);

You can use CalcMenuSize to recalculate the horizontal and vertical dimensions of a menu whose contents have been changed (and store them in the appropriate fields of the menu record). CalcMenuSize is called internally by the Menu Manager after every routine that changes a menu.

FUNCTION CountMItems (theMenu: MenuHandle) : INTEGER;

CountMItems returns the number of menu items in the given menu.

FUNCTION GetMHandle (menuID: INTEGER) : MenuHandle;

Given the menu ID of a menu currently installed in the menu list, GetMHandle returns a handle to that menu; given any other menu ID, it returns NIL.

PROCEDURE FlashMenuBar (menuID: INTEGER);

If menuID is 0 (or isn't the ID of any menu in the menu list), FlashMenuBar inverts the entire menu bar; otherwise, it inverts the title of the given menu. You can call FlashMenuBar(0) twice to blink the menu bar.

PROCEDURE SetMenuFlash (count: INTEGER);

Assembly-language note: The macro you invoke to call SetMenuFlash from assembly language is named _SetMFlash.

When the mouse button is released over an enabled menu item, the item blinks briefly to confirm the choice. Normally, your application shouldn't be concerned with this blinking; the user sets it with the Control Panel desk accessory. If you're writing a desk accessory like the Control Panel, though, SetMenuFlash allows you to control the duration of the blinking. The count parameter is the number of times menu items will blink; it's initially 3 if the user hasn't changed it. A count of 0 disables blinking. Values greater than 3 can be annoyingly slow.

> **Note:** Items in both standard and nonstandard menus blink when chosen. The appearance of the blinking for a nonstandard menu depends on the menu definition procedure, as described in "Defining Your Own Menus".

Assembly-language note: The current count is stored in the global variable MenuFlash.

DEFINING YOUR OWN MENUS

The standard type of Macintosh menu is predefined for you. However, you may want to define your own type of menu—one with more graphics, or perhaps a nonlinear text arrangement. QuickDraw and the Menu Manager make it possible for you to do this.

To define your own type of menu, you write a menu definition procedure and store it in a resource file. The Menu Manager calls the menu definition procedure to perform basic operations such as drawing the menu.

A menu in a resource file contains the resource ID of its menu definition procedure. The routine you use to read in the menu is GetMenu (or GetNewMBar, which calls GetMenu). If you store the resource ID of your own menu definition procedure in a menu in a resource file, GetMenu will take care of reading the procedure into memory and storing a handle to it in the menuProc field of the menu record.

If you create your menus with NewMenu instead of storing them as resources, NewMenu stores a handle to the standard menu definition procedure in the menu record's menuProc field. You must replace this with a handle to your own menu definition procedure, and then call CalcMenuSize. If your menu definition procedure is in a resource file, you get the handle by calling the Resource Manager to read it from the resource file into memory.

The Menu Definition Procedure

The menu definition procedure is usually written in assembly language, but may be written in Pascal.

Assembly-language note: The procedure's entry point must be at the beginning.

You may choose any name you wish for the menu definition procedure. Here's how you would declare one named MyMenu:

```
PROCEDURE MyMenu (message: INTEGER; theMenu: MenuHandle; VAR menuRect:
        Rect; hitPt: Point; VAR whichItem: INTEGER);
```

The message parameter identifies the operation to be performed. It has one of the following values:

```
CONST mDrawMsg   = 0;   {draw the menu}
      mChooseMsg = 1;   {tell which item was chosen and highlight it}
      mSizeMsg   = 2;   {calculate the menu's dimensions}
```

The parameter theMenu indicates the menu that the operation will affect. MenuRect is the rectangle (in global coordinates) in which the menu is located; it's used when the message is mDrawMsg or mChooseMsg.

Note: MenuRect is declared as a VAR parameter not because its value is changed, but because of a Pascal feature that will cause an error when that parameter isn't used.

The message mDrawMsg tells the menu definition procedure to draw the menu inside menuRect. The current grafPort will be the Window Manager port. (For details on drawing, see chapter 6.) The standard menu definition procedure figures out how to draw the menu items by looking in the menu record at the data that defines them; this data is described in detail under "Formats of Resources for Menus" below. For menus of your own definition, you may set up the data defining the menu items any way you like, or even omit it altogether (in which case all the information necessary to draw the menu would be in the menu definition procedure itself). You should also check the enableFlags field of the menu record to see whether the menu is disabled (or whether any of the menu items are disabled, if you're using all the flags), and if so, draw it in gray.

Warning: Don't change the font from the system font for menu text. (The Window Manager port uses the system font.)

When the menu definition procedure receives the message mChooseMsg, the hitPt parameter is the mouse location (in global coordinates), and the whichItem parameter is the item number of the last item that was chosen from this menu (whichItem is initially set to 0). The procedure should determine whether the mouse location is in an enabled menu item, by checking whether hitPt is inside menuRect, whether the menu is enabled, and whether hitPt is in an enabled menu item:

- If the mouse location is in an enabled menu item, unhighlight whichItem and highlight the new item (unless the new item is the same as the whichItem), and return the item number of the new item in whichItem.

- If the mouse location isn't in an enabled item, unhighlight whichItem and return 0.

Note: When the Menu Manager needs to make a chosen menu item blink, it repeatedly calls the menu definition procedure with the message mChooseMsg, causing the item to be alternately highlighted and unhighlighted.

Finally, the message mSizeMsg tells the menu definition procedure to calculate the horizontal and vertical dimensions of the menu and store them in the menuWidth and menuHeight fields of the menu record.

FORMATS OF RESOURCES FOR MENUS

The resource type for a menu definition procedure is 'MDEF'. The resource data is simply the compiled or assembled code of the procedure.

Icons in menus must be stored in a resource file under the resource type 'ICON' with resource IDs from 257 to 511. Strings in resource files have the resource type 'STR'; if you use the SetItem procedure to change a menu item's text, you should store the alternate text as a string resource.

The formats of menus and menu bars in resource files are given below.

Menus in a Resource File

The resource type for a menu is 'MENU'. The resource data for a menu has the format shown below. Once read into memory, this data is stored in a menu record (described earlier in the "Menu Records" section).

Number of bytes	Contents
2 bytes	Menu ID
2 bytes	0; placeholder for menu width
2 bytes	0; placeholder for menu height
2 bytes	Resource ID of menu definition procedure
2 bytes	0 (see comment below)
4 bytes	Same as enableFlags field of menu record
1 byte	Length of following title in bytes
n bytes	Characters of menu title

For each menu item:

1 byte	Length of following text in bytes
m bytes	Text of menu item
1 byte	Icon number, or 0 if no icon
1 byte	Keyboard equivalent, or 0 if none
1 byte	Character marking menu item, or 0 if none
1 byte	Character style of item's text
1 byte	0, indicating end of menu items

The four bytes beginning with the resource ID of the menu definition procedure serve as a placeholder for the handle to the procedure: When GetMenu is called to read the menu from the resource file, it also reads in the menu definition procedure if necessary, and replaces these four bytes with a handle to the procedure. The resource ID of the standard menu definition procedure is

```
CONST textMenuProc = 0;
```

The resource data for a nonstandard menu can define menu items in any way whatsoever, or not at all, depending on the requirements of its menu definition procedure. If the appearance of the items is basically the same as the standard, the resource data might be as shown above, but in fact everything following "For each menu item" can have any desired format or can be omitted altogether. Similarly, bits 1 to 31 of the enableFlags field may be set and used in any way desired by the menu definition procedure; bit 0 applies to the entire menu and must reflect whether it's enabled or disabled.

If your menu definition procedure does use the enableFlags field, menus of that type may contain no more than 31 items (1 per available bit); otherwise, the number of items they may contain is limited only by the amount of room on the screen.

Note: See chapter 6 for the exact format of the character style byte.

Menu Bars in a Resource File

The resource type for the contents of a menu bar is 'MBAR' and the resource data has the following format:

Number of bytes	Contents
2 bytes	Number of menus
For each menu:	
2 bytes	Resource ID of menu

SUMMARY OF THE MENU MANAGER

Constants

```
CONST { Value indicating item has no mark }

    noMark = 0;

    { Messages to menu definition procedure }

    mDrawMsg    = 0;        {draw the menu}
    mChooseMsg  = 1;        {tell which item was chosen and highlight it}
    mSizeMsg    = 2;        {calculate the menu's dimensions}

    { Resource ID of standard menu definition procedure }

    textMenuProc = 0;
```

Data Types

```
TYPE MenuHandle  = ^MenuPtr;
     MenuPtr     = ^MenuInfo;
     MenuInfo    = RECORD
                     menuID:      INTEGER;    {menu ID}
                     menuWidth:   INTEGER;    {menu width in pixels}
                     menuHeight:  INTEGER;    {menu height in pixels}
                     menuProc:    Handle;     {menu definition procedure}
                     enableFlags: LONGINT;    {tells if menu or items are}
                                              {enabled}
                     menuData:    Str255      {menu title (and other data)}
                   END;
```

Routines

Initialization and Allocation

```
PROCEDURE InitMenus;
FUNCTION  NewMenu       (menuID: INTEGER; menuTitle: Str255) : MenuHandle;
FUNCTION  GetMenu       (resourceID: INTEGER) : MenuHandle;
PROCEDURE DisposeMenu   (theMenu: MenuHandle);
```

Forming the Menus

```
PROCEDURE AppendMenu    (theMenu: MenuHandle; data: Str255);
PROCEDURE AddResMenu    (theMenu: MenuHandle; theType: ResType);
PROCEDURE InsertResMenu (theMenu: MenuHandle; theType: ResType;
                          afterItem: INTEGER);
```

Forming the Menu Bar

```
PROCEDURE  InsertMenu      (theMenu: MenuHandle; beforeID: INTEGER);
PROCEDURE  DrawMenuBar;
PROCEDURE  DeleteMenu      (menuID: INTEGER);
PROCEDURE  ClearMenuBar;
FUNCTION   GetNewMBar      (menuBarID: INTEGER) · Handle;
FUNCTION   GetMenuBar  :   Handle;
PROCEDURE  SetMenuBar      (menuList: Handle);
```

Choosing From a Menu

```
FUNCTION   MenuSelect      (startPt: Point) : LONGINT;
FUNCTION   MenuKey         (ch: CHAR) : LONGINT;
PROCEDURE  HiliteMenu      (menuID: INTEGER);
```

Controlling the Appearance of Items

```
PROCEDURE  SetItem         (theMenu: MenuHandle; item: INTEGER; itemString:
                            Str255);
PROCEDURE  GetItem         (theMenu: MenuHandle; item: INTEGER; VAR
                            itemString: Str255);
PROCEDURE  DisableItem     (theMenu: MenuHandle; item: INTEGER);
PROCEDURE  EnableItem      (theMenu: MenuHandle; item: INTEGER);
PROCEDURE  CheckItem       (theMenu: MenuHandle; item: INTEGER; checked:
                            BOOLEAN);
PROCEDURE  SetItemMark     (theMenu: MenuHandle; item: INTEGER; markChar:
                            CHAR);
PROCEDURE  GetItemMark     (theMenu: MenuHandle; item: INTEGER; VAR
                            markChar: CHAR);
PROCEDURE  SetItemIcon     (theMenu: MenuHandle; item: INTEGER; icon: Byte);
PROCEDURE  GetItemIcon     (theMenu: MenuHandle; item: INTEGER; VAR icon:
                            Byte);
PROCEDURE  SetItemStyle    (theMenu: MenuHandle; item: INTEGER; chStyle:
                            Style);
PROCEDURE  GetItemStyle    (theMenu: MenuHandle; item: INTEGER; VAR chStyle:
                            Style);
```

Miscellaneous Routines

```
PROCEDURE  CalcMenuSize    (theMenu: MenuHandle);
FUNCTION   CountMItems     (theMenu: MenuHandle) : INTEGER;
FUNCTION   GetMHandle      (menuID: INTEGER) : MenuHandle;
PROCEDURE  FlashMenuBar    (menuID: INTEGER);
PROCEDURE  SetMenuFlash    (count: INTEGER);
```

Meta-Characters for AppendMenu

Meta-character	Usage
; or Return	Separates multiple items
^	Followed by an icon number, adds that icon to the item
!	Followed by a character, marks the item with that character
<	Followed by B, I, U, O, or S, sets the character style of the item
/	Followed by a character, associates a keyboard equivalent with the item
(	Disables the item

Menu Definition Procedure

```
PROCEDURE MyMenu (message: INTEGER; theMenu: MenuHandle; VAR menuRect:
                  Rect; hitPt: Point; VAR whichItem: INTEGER);
```

Assembly-Language Information

Constants

```
; Value indicating item has no mark

noMark        .EQU      0

; Messages to menu definition procedure

mDrawMsg      .EQU      0      ;draw the menu
mChooseMsg    .EQU      1      ;tell which item was chosen and highlight it
mSizeMsg      .EQU      2      ;calculate the menu's dimensions

; Resource ID of standard menu definition procedure

textMenuProc  .EQU      0
```

Menu Record Data Structure

menuID	Menu ID (word)
menuWidth	Menu width in pixels (word)
menuHeight	Menu height in pixels (word)
menuDefHandle	Handle to menu definition procedure
menuEnable	Enable flags (long)
menuData	Menu title (preceded by length byte) followed by data defining the items
menuBlkSize	Size in bytes of menu record except menuData field

Special Macro Names

Pascal name	Macro name
DisposeMenu	_DisposMenu
GetItemIcon	_GetItmIcon
GetItemMark	_GetItmMark
GetItemStyle	_GetItmStyle
GetMenu	_GetRMenu
SetItemIcon	_SetItmIcon
SetItemMark	_SetItmMark
SetItemStyle	_SetItmStyle
SetMenuFlash	_SetMFlash

Variables

MenuList	Handle to current menu list
MBarEnable	Nonzero if menu bar belongs to a desk accessory (word)
MenuHook	Address of routine called repeatedly during MenuSelect
MBarHook	Address of routine called by MenuSelect before menu is drawn (see below)
TheMenu	Menu ID of currently highlighted menu (word)
MenuFlash	Count for duration of menu item blinking (word)

MBarHook routine

On entry	stack:	pointer to menu rectangle
On exit	D0:	0 to continue MenuSelect
		1 to abort MenuSelect

12   TEXTEDIT

ABOUT THIS CHAPTER

TextEdit is the part of the Toolbox that handles basic text formatting and editing capabilities in a Macintosh application. This chapter describes the TextEdit routines and data types in detail.

You should already be familiar with:

- the basic concepts and structures behind QuickDraw, particularly points, rectangles, grafPorts, fonts, and character style
- the Toolbox Event Manager
- the Window Manager, particularly update and activate events

ABOUT TEXTEDIT

TextEdit is a set of routines and data types that provide the basic text editing and formatting capabilities needed in an application. These capabilities include:

- inserting new text
- deleting characters that are backspaced over
- translating mouse activity into text selection
- scrolling text within a window
- deleting selected text and possibly inserting it elsewhere, or copying text without deleting it

The TextEdit routines follow the Macintosh User Interface Guidelines; using them ensures that your application will present a consistent user interface. The Dialog Manager uses TextEdit for text editing in dialog boxes.

TextEdit supports these standard features:

- Selecting text by clicking and dragging with the mouse, double-clicking to select words. To TextEdit, a **word** is any series of printing characters, excluding spaces (ASCII code $20) but including nonbreaking spaces (ASCII code $CA).
- Extending or shortening the selection by Shift-clicking.
- Inverse highlighting of the current text selection, or display of a blinking vertical bar at the insertion point.
- **Word wraparound**, which prevents a word from being split between lines when text is drawn.
- Cutting (or copying) and pasting within an application via the Clipboard. TextEdit puts text you cut or copy into the **TextEdit scrap**.

Note: The TextEdit scrap is used only by TextEdit; it's not the same as the "desk scrap" used by the Scrap Manager. To support cutting and pasting between applications, or between applications and desk accessories, you must transfer information between the two scraps.

Although TextEdit is useful for many standard text editing operations, there are some additional features that it doesn't support. TextEdit does *not* support:

- the use of more than one font or stylistic variation in a single block of text
- fully justified text (text aligned with both the left and right margins)
- "intelligent" cut and paste (adjusting spaces between words during cutting and pasting)
- tabs

TextEdit also provides "hooks" for implementing some features such as automatic scrolling or a more precise definition of a word.

EDIT RECORDS

To edit text on the screen, TextEdit needs to know where and how to display the text, where to store the text, and other information related to editing. This display, storage, and editing information is contained in an **edit record** that defines the complete editing environment. The data type of an edit record is called TERec.

You prepare to edit text by specifying a **destination rectangle** in which to draw the text and a **view rectangle** in which the text will be visible. TextEdit incorporates the rectangles and the drawing environment of the current grafPort into an edit record, and returns a handle of type TEHandle to the record:

```
TYPE  TEPtr     = ^TERec;
      TEHandle  = ^TEPtr;
```

Most of the text editing routines require you to pass this handle as a parameter.

In addition to the two rectangles and a description of the drawing environment, the edit record also contains:

- a handle to the text to be edited
- a pointer to the grafPort in which the text is displayed
- the current **selection range**, which determines exactly which characters will be affected by the next editing operation
- the **justification** of the text, as left, right, or center

The special terms introduced here are described in detail below.

For most operations, you don't need to know the exact structure of an edit record; TextEdit routines access the record for you. However, to support some operations, such as automatic scrolling, you need to access the fields of the edit record directly. The structure of an edit record is given below.

The Destination and View Rectangles

The destination rectangle is the rectangle in which the text is drawn. The view rectangle is the rectangle within which the text is actually visible. In other words, the view of the text drawn in the destination rectangle is clipped to the view rectangle (see Figure 1).

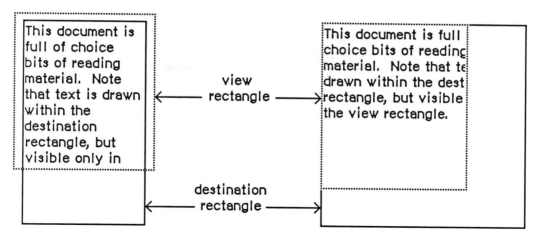

Figure 1. Destination and View Rectangles

You specify both rectangles in the local coordinates of the grafPort. To ensure that the first and last characters in each line are legible in a document window, you may want to inset the destination rectangle at least four pixels from the left and right edges of the grafPort's portRect (20 pixels from the right edge if there's a scroll bar or size box).

Edit operations may of course lengthen or shorten the text. If the text becomes too long to be enclosed by the destination rectangle, it's simply drawn beyond the bottom. In other words, you can think of the destination rectangle as bottomless—its sides determine the beginning and end of each line of text, and its top determines the position of the first line.

Normally, at the right edge of the destination rectangle, the text automatically wraps around to the left edge to begin a new line. A new line also begins where explicitly specified by a Return character in the text. Word wraparound ensures that no word is ever split between lines unless it's too long to fit entirely on one line, in which case it's split at the right edge of the destination rectangle.

The Selection Range

In the text editing environment, a **character position** is an index into the text, with position 0 corresponding to the first character. The edit record includes fields for character positions that specify the beginning and end of the current selection range, which is the series of characters where the next editing operation will occur. For example, the procedures that cut or copy from the text of an edit record do so to the current selection range.

The selection range, which is inversely highlighted when the window is active, extends from the beginning character position to the end character position. Figure 2 shows a selection range between positions 3 and 8, consisting of five characters (the character *at* position 8 isn't included). The end position of a selection range may be 1 greater than the position of the last character of the text, so that the selection range can include the last character.

If the selection range is empty—that is, its beginning and end positions are the same—that position is the text's **insertion point**, the position where characters will be inserted. By default, it's marked with a blinking caret. If, for example, the insertion point is as illustrated in Figure 2 and the inserted characters are "edit ", the text will read "the edit insertion point".

Figure 2. Selection Range and Insertion Point

Note: We use the word **caret** here generically, to mean a symbol indicating where something is to be inserted; the specific symbol is a vertical bar (|).

If you call a procedure to insert characters when there's a selection range of one or more characters rather than an insertion point, the editing procedure automatically deletes the selection range and replaces it with an insertion point before inserting the characters.

Justification

TextEdit allows you to specify the justification of the lines of text, that is, their horizontal placement with respect to the left and right edges of the destination rectangle. The different types of justification supported by TextEdit are illustrated in Figure 3.

■ Left justification aligns the text with the left edge of the destination rectangle. This is the default type of justification.

■ Center justification centers each line of text between the left and right edges of the destination rectangle.

■ Right justification aligns the text with the right edge of the destination rectangle.

```
This is an example      This is an example      This is an example
of left                    of center                   of right
justification. See      justification. See      justification. See
how the text is          how the text is          how the text is
aligned with the       centered between        aligned with the
left edge of the         the edges of the        right edge of the
rectangle.                  rectangle.                   rectangle.
```

Figure 3. Justification

Note: Trailing spaces on a line are ignored for justification. For example, "Fred" and "Fred " will be aligned identically. (Leading spaces are not ignored.)

TextEdit provides three predefined constants for setting the justification:

```
CONST teJustLeft   =  0;
      teJustCenter =  1;
      teJustRight  = -1;
```

The TERec Data Type

The structure of an edit record is given here. Some TextEdit features are available only if you access fields of the edit record directly.

```
TYPE TERec = RECORD
               destRect:    Rect;       {destination rectangle}
               viewRect:    Rect;       {view rectangle}
               selRect:     Rect;       {used from assembly language}
               lineHeight:  INTEGER;    {for line spacing}
               fontAscent:  INTEGER;    {caret/highlighting position}
               selPoint:    Point;      {used from assembly language}
               selStart:    INTEGER;    {start of selection range}
               selEnd:      INTEGER;    {end of selection range}
               active:      INTEGER;    {used internally}
               wordBreak:   ProcPtr;    {for word break routine}
               clikLoop:    ProcPtr;    {for click loop routine}
               clickTime:   LONGINT;    {used internally}
               clickLoc:    INTEGER;    {used internally}
               caretTime:   LONGINT;    {used internally}
               caretState:  INTEGER;    {used internally}
               just:        INTEGER;    {justification of text}
               teLength:    INTEGER;    {length of text}
               hText:       Handle;     {text to be edited}
               recalBack:   INTEGER;    {used internally}
               recalLines:  INTEGER;    {used internally}
               clikStuff:   INTEGER;    {used internally}
               crOnly:      INTEGER;    {if <0, new line at Return only}
               txFont:      INTEGER;    {text font}
               txFace:      Style;      {character style}
               txMode:      INTEGER;    {pen mode}
               txSize:      INTEGER;    {font size}
               inPort:      GrafPtr;    {grafPort}
               highHook:    ProcPtr;    {used from assembly language}
               caretHook:   ProcPtr;    {used from assembly language}
               nLines:      INTEGER;    {number of lines}
               lineStarts:  ARRAY[0..16000] OF INTEGER
                                        {positions of line starts}
             END;
```

Warning: Don't change any of the fields marked "used internally"—these exist solely for internal use among the TextEdit routines.

The destRect and viewRect fields specify the destination and view rectangles.

The lineHeight and fontAscent fields have to do with the vertical spacing of the lines of text, and where the caret or highlighting of the selection range is drawn relative to the text. The fontAscent field specifies how far above the base line the pen is positioned to begin drawing the caret or highlighting. For single-spaced text, this is the ascent of the text in pixels (the height of the tallest characters in the font from the base line). The lineHeight field specifies the vertical distance from the ascent line of one line of text down to the ascent line of the next. For single-spaced text, this is the same as the font size, but in pixels. The values of the lineHeight and fontAscent fields for single-spaced text are shown in Figure 4. For more information on fonts, see chapter 7.

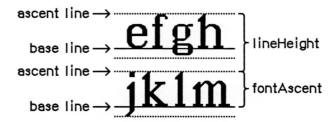

Figure 4. LineHeight and FontAscent

If you want to change the vertical spacing of the text, you should change both the lineHeight and fontAscent fields by the same amount, otherwise the placement of the caret or highlighting of the selection range may not look right. For example, to double the line spacing, add the value of lineHeight to both fields. (This doesn't change the size of the characters; it affects only the spacing between lines.) If you change the size of the text, you should also change these fields; you can get font measurements you'll need with the QuickDraw procedure GetFontInfo.

Assembly-language note: The selPoint field (whose assembly-language offset is named teSelPoint) contains the point selected with the mouse, in the local coordinates of the current grafPort. You'll need this for hit-testing if you use the routine pointed to by the global variable TEDoText (see "Advanced Routines" in the "TextEdit Routines" section).

The selStart and selEnd fields specify the character positions of the beginning and end of the selection range. Remember that character position 0 refers to the first character, and that the end of a selection range can be 1 greater than the position of the last character of the text.

The wordBreak field lets you change TextEdit's definition of a word, and the clikLoop field lets you implement automatic scrolling. These two fields are described in separate sections below.

The just field specifies the justification of the text. (See "Justification", above.)

The teLength field contains the number of characters in the text to be edited (the maximum length is 32K bytes). The hText field is a handle to the text. You can directly change the text of an edit record by changing these two fields.

The crOnly field specifies whether or not text wraps around at the right edge of the destination rectangle, as shown in Figure 5. If crOnly is positive, text does wrap around. If crOnly is negative, text does not wrap around at the edge of the destination rectangle, and new lines are specified explicitly by Return characters only. This is faster than word wraparound, and is useful in an application similar to a programming-language editor, where you may not want a single line of code to be split onto two lines.

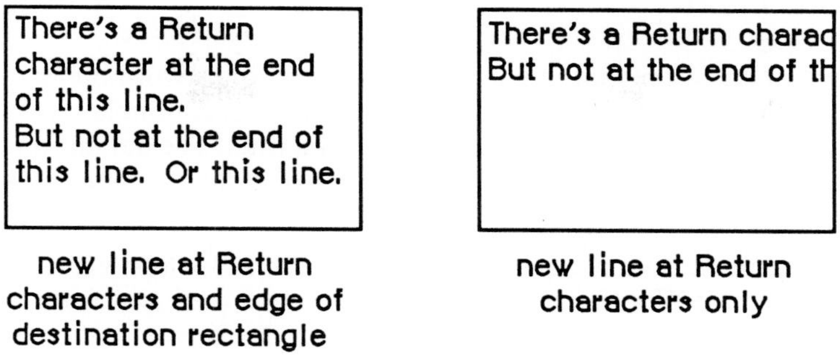

Figure 5. New Lines

The txFont, txFace, txMode, and txSize fields specify the font, character style, pen mode, and font size, respectively, of all the text in the edit record. (See chapter 6 for details about these characteristics.) If you change one of these values, the entire text of this edit record will have the new characteristics when it's redrawn. If you change the txSize field, remember to change the lineHeight and fontAscent fields, too.

The inPort field contains a pointer to the grafPort associated with this edit record.

Assembly-language note: The highHook and caretHook fields—at the offsets teHiHook and teCarHook in assembly language—contain the addresses of routines that deal with text highlighting and the caret. These routines pass parameters in registers; the application must save and restore the registers.

If you store the address of a routine in teHiHook, that routine will be used instead of the QuickDraw procedure InvertRect whenever a selection range is to be highlighted. The routine can destroy the contents of registers A0, A1, D0, D1, and D2. On entry, A3 is a pointer to a locked edit record; the stack contains the rectangle enclosing the text being highlighted. For example, if you store the address of the following routine in teHiHook, selection ranges will be underlined instead of inverted:

```
UnderHigh
    MOVE.L      (SP),A0               ;get address of rectangle to be
                                      ; highlighted
    MOVE        bottom(A0),top(A0)    ;make the top coordinate equal to
    SUBQ        #1,top(A0)            ; the bottom coordinate minus 1
    _InverRect                        ;invert the resulting rectangle
    RTS
```

The routine whose address is stored in teCarHook acts exactly the same way as the teHiHook routine, but on the caret instead of the selection highlighting, allowing you to change the appearance of the caret. The routine is called with the stack containing the rectangle that encloses the caret.

The nLines field contains the number of lines in the text. The lineStarts array contains the character position of the first character in each line. It's declared to have 16001 elements to comply with Pascal range checking; it's actually a dynamic data structure having only as many elements as needed. You shouldn't change the elements of lineStarts.

The WordBreak Field

The wordBreak field of an edit record lets you specify the record's word break routine—the routine that determines the "word" that's highlighted when the user double-clicks in the text, and the position at which text is wrapped around at the end of a line. The default routine breaks words at any character with an ASCII value of $20 or less (the space character or nonprinting control characters).

The word break routine must have two parameters and return a Boolean value. This is how you would declare one named MyWordBreak:

```
FUNCTION MyWordBreak (text: Ptr; charPos: INTEGER) : BOOLEAN;
```

The function should return TRUE to break a word at the character at position charPos in the specified text, or FALSE not to break there. From Pascal, you must call the SetWordBreak procedure to set the wordBreak field so that your routine will be used.

Assembly-language note: You can set this field to point to your own assembly-language word break routine. The registers must contain the following:

On entry	A0:	pointer to text
	D0:	character position (word)
On exit	Z (zero) condition code:	
	0 to break at specified character	
	1 not to break there	

The ClikLoop Field

The clikLoop field of an edit record lets you specify a routine that will be called repeatedly (by the TEClick procedure, described below) as long as the mouse button is held down within the text. You can use this to implement the automatic scrolling of text when the user is making a selection and drags the cursor out of the view rectangle.

The click loop routine has no parameters and returns a Boolean value. You could declare a click loop routine named MyClikLoop like this:

```
FUNCTION MyClikLoop : BOOLEAN;
```

The function should return TRUE. From Pascal, you must call the SetClikLoop procedure to set the clikLoop field so that TextEdit will call your routine.

Warning: Returning FALSE from your click loop routine tells the TEClick procedure that the mouse button has been released, which aborts TEClick.

Assembly-language note: Your routine should set register D0 to 1, and preserve register D2. (Returning 0 in register D0 aborts TEClick.)

An automatic scrolling routine might check the mouse location, and call a scrolling routine if the mouse location is outside the view rectangle. (The scrolling routine can be the same routine that the Control Manager function TrackControl calls.) The handle to the current edit record should be kept as a global variable so the scrolling routine can access it.

USING TEXTEDIT

Before using TextEdit, you must initialize QuickDraw, the Font Manager, and the Window Manager, in that order.

The first TextEdit routine to call is the initialization procedure TEInit. Call TENew to allocate an edit record; it returns a handle to the record. Most of the text editing routines require you to pass this handle as a parameter.

When you've finished working with the text of an edit record, you can get a handle to the text as a packed array of characters with the TEGetText function.

> **Note:** To convert text from an edit record to a Pascal string, you can use the Dialog Manager procedure GetIText, passing it the text handle from the edit record.

When you're completely done with an edit record and want to dispose of it, call TEDispose.

To make a blinking caret appear at the insertion point, call the TEIdle procedure as often as possible (at least once each time through the main event loop); if it's not called often enough, the caret will blink irregularly.

> **Note:** To change the cursor to an I-beam, you can call the Toolbox Utility function GetCursor and the QuickDraw procedure SetCursor. The resource ID for the I-beam cursor is defined in the Toolbox Utilities as the constant iBeamCursor.

When a mouse-down event occurs in the view rectangle (and the window is active) call the TEClick procedure. TEClick controls the placement and highlighting of the selection range, including supporting use of the Shift key to make extended selections.

Key-down, auto-key, and mouse events that pertain to text editing can be handled by several TextEdit procedures:

- TEKey inserts characters and deletes characters backspaced over.

- TECut transfers the selection range to the TextEdit scrap, removing the selection range from the text.

- TEPaste inserts the contents of the TextEdit scrap. By calling TECut, changing the insertion point, and then calling TEPaste, you can perform a "cut and paste" operation, moving text from one place to another.

- TECopy copies the selection range to the TextEdit scrap. By calling TECopy, changing the insertion point, and then calling TEPaste, you can make multiple copies of text.

- TEDelete removes the selection range (without transferring it to the scrap). You can use TEDelete to implement the Clear command.

■ TEInsert inserts specified text. You can use this to combine two or more documents. TEDelete and TEInsert do not modify the scrap, so they're useful for implementing the Undo command.

After each editing procedure, TextEdit redraws the text if necessary from the insertion point to the end of the text. You never have to set the selection range or insertion point yourself; TEClick and the editing procedures leave it where it should be. If you want to modify the selection range directly, however—to highlight an initial default name or value, for example—you can use the TESetSelect procedure.

To implement cutting and pasting of text between different applications, or between applications and desk accessories, you need to transfer the text between the TextEdit scrap (which is a private scrap used only by TextEdit) and the Scrap Manager's desk scrap. You can do this using the functions TEFromScrap and TEToScrap. (See chapter 15 for more information about scrap handling.)

When an update event is reported for a text editing window, call TEUpdate—along with the Window Manager procedures BeginUpdate and EndUpdate—to redraw the text.

Note: After changing any fields of the edit record that affect the appearance of the text, you should call the Window Manager procedure InvalRect(hTE^^.viewRect) so that the text will be updated.

The procedures TEActivate and TEDeactivate must be called each time GetNextEvent reports an activate event for a text editing window. TEActivate simply highlights the selection range or displays a caret at the insertion point; TEDeactivate unhighlights the selection range or removes the caret.

To specify the justification of the text, you can use TESetJust. If you change the justification, be sure to call InvalRect so the text will be updated.

To scroll text within the view rectangle, you can use the TEScroll procedure.

The TESetText procedure lets you change the text being edited. For example, if your application has several separate pieces of text that must be edited one at a time, you don't have to allocate an edit record for each of them. Allocate a single edit record, and then use TESetText to change the text. (This is the method used in dialog boxes.)

Note: TESetText actually makes a copy of the text to be edited. Advanced programmers can save space by storing a handle to the text in the hText field of the edit record itself, then calling TECalText to recalculate the beginning of each line.

If you ever want to draw noneditable text in any given rectangle, you can use the TextBox procedure.

If you've written your own word break or click loop routine in Pascal, you must call the SetWordBreak or SetClikLoop procedure to install your routine so TextEdit will use it.

TEXTEDIT ROUTINES

Initialization and Allocation

```
PROCEDURE TEInit;
```

TEInit initializes TextEdit by allocating a handle for the TextEdit scrap. The scrap is initially empty. Call this procedure once and only once at the beginning of your program.

> **Note:** You should call TEInit even if your application doesn't use TextEdit, so that desk accessories and dialog and alert boxes will work correctly.

```
FUNCTION TENew (destRect,viewRect: Rect) : TEHandle;
```

TENew allocates a handle for text, creates and initializes an edit record, and returns a handle to the new edit record. DestRect and viewRect are the destination and view rectangles, respectively. Both rectangles are specified in the current grafPort's coordinates. The destination rectangle must always be at least as wide as the first character drawn (about 20 pixels is a good minimum width). The view rectangle must not be empty (for example, don't make its right edge less than its left edge if you don't want any text visible—specify a rectangle off the screen instead).

Call TENew once for every edit record you want allocated. The edit record incorporates the drawing environment of the grafPort, and is initialized for left-justified, single-spaced text with an insertion point at character position 0.

> **Note:** The caret won't appear until you call TEActivate.

```
PROCEDURE TEDispose (hTE: TEHandle);
```

TEDispose releases the memory allocated for the edit record and text specified by hTE. Call this procedure when you're completely through with an edit record.

Accessing the Text of an Edit Record

```
PROCEDURE TESetText (text: Ptr; length: LONGINT; hTE: TEHandle);
```

TESetText incorporates a copy of the specified text into the edit record specified by hTE. The text parameter points to the text, and the length parameter indicates the number of characters in the text. The selection range is set to an insertion point at the end of the text. TESetText doesn't affect the text drawn in the destination rectangle, so call InvalRect afterward if necessary. TESetText doesn't dispose of any text currently in the edit record.

```
FUNCTION TEGetText (hTE: TEHandle) : CharsHandle;
```

TEGetText returns a handle to the text of the specified edit record. The result is the same as the handle in the hText field of the edit record, but has the CharsHandle data type, which is defined as:

```
TYPE CharsHandle = ^CharsPtr;
     CharsPtr    = ^Chars;
     Chars       = PACKED ARRAY[0..32000] OF CHAR;
```

You can get the length of the text from the teLength field of the edit record.

Insertion Point and Selection Range

```
PROCEDURE TEIdle (hTE: TEHandle);
```

Call TEIdle repeatedly to make a blinking caret appear at the insertion point (if any) in the text specified by hTE. (The caret appears only when the window containing that text is active, of course.) TextEdit observes a minimum blink interval: No matter how often you call TEIdle, the time between blinks will never be less than the minimum interval.

Note: The initial minimum blink interval setting is 32 ticks. The user can adjust this setting with the Control Panel desk accessory.

To provide a constant frequency of blinking, you should call TEIdle as often as possible—at least once each time through your main event loop. Call it more than once if your application does an unusually large amount of processing each time through the loop.

Note: You actually need to call TEIdle only when the window containing the text is active.

```
PROCEDURE TEClick (pt: Point; extend: BOOLEAN; hTE: TEHandle);
```

TEClick controls the placement and highlighting of the selection range as determined by mouse events. Call TEClick whenever a mouse-down event occurs in the view rectangle of the edit record specified by hTE, and the window associated with that edit record is active. TEClick keeps control until the mouse button is released. Pt is the mouse location (in local coordinates) at the time the button was pressed, obtainable from the event record.

Note: Use the QuickDraw procedure GlobalToLocal to convert the global coordinates of the mouse location given in the event record to the local coordinate system for pt.

Pass TRUE for the extend parameter if the Event Manager indicates that the Shift key was held down at the time of the click (to extend the selection).

TEClick unhighlights the old selection range unless the selection range is being extended. If the mouse moves, meaning that a drag is occurring, TEClick expands or shortens the selection range accordingly. In the case of a double-click, the word under the cursor becomes the selection range; dragging expands or shortens the selection a word at a time.

```
PROCEDURE TESetSelect (selStart,selEnd: LONGINT; hTE: TEHandle);
```

TESetSelect sets the selection range to the text between selStart and selEnd in the text specified by hTE. The old selection range is unhighlighted, and the new one is highlighted. If selStart equals selEnd, the selection range is an insertion point, and a caret is displayed.

SelEnd and selStart can range from 0 to 32767. If selEnd is anywhere beyond the last character of the text, the position just past the last character is used.

```
PROCEDURE TEActivate (hTE: TEHandle);
```

TEActivate highlights the selection range in the view rectangle of the edit record specified by hTE. If the selection range is an insertion point, it displays a caret there. This procedure should be called every time the Toolbox Event Manager function GetNextEvent reports that the window containing the edit record has become active.

```
PROCEDURE TEDeactivate (hTE: TEHandle);
```

TEDeactivate unhighlights the selection range in the view rectangle of the edit record specified by hTE. If the selection range is an insertion point, it removes the caret. This procedure should be called every time the Toolbox Event Manager function GetNextEvent reports that the window containing the edit record has become inactive.

Editing

```
PROCEDURE TEKey (key: CHAR; hTE: TEHandle);
```

TEKey replaces the selection range in the text specified by hTE with the character given by the key parameter, and leaves an insertion point just past the inserted character. If the selection range is an insertion point, TEKey just inserts the character there. If the key parameter contains a Backspace character, the selection range or the character immediately to the left of the insertion point is deleted. TEKey redraws the text as necessary. Call TEKey every time the Toolbox Event Manager function GetNextEvent reports a keyboard event that your application decides should be handled by TextEdit.

> **Note:** TEKey inserts every character passed in the key parameter, so it's up to your application to filter out all characters that aren't actual text (such as keys typed in conjunction with the Command key).

```
PROCEDURE TECut (hTE: TEHandle);
```

TECut removes the selection range from the text specified by hTE and places it in the TextEdit scrap. The text is redrawn as necessary. Anything previously in the scrap is deleted. (See Figure 6.) If the selection range is an insertion point, the scrap is emptied.

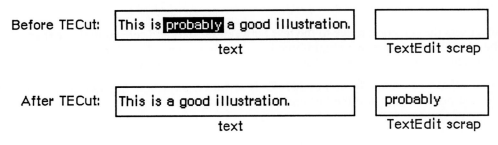

Figure 6. Cutting

```
PROCEDURE TECopy (hTE: TEHandle);
```

TECopy copies the selection range from the text specified by hTE into the TextEdit scrap. Anything previously in the scrap is deleted. The selection range is not deleted. If the selection range is an insertion point, the scrap is emptied.

```
PROCEDURE TEPaste (hTE: TEHandle);
```

TEPaste replaces the selection range in the text specified by hTE with the contents of the TextEdit scrap, and leaves an insertion point just past the inserted text. (See Figure 7.) The text is redrawn as necessary. If the scrap is empty, the selection range is deleted. If the selection range is an insertion point, TEPaste just inserts the scrap there.

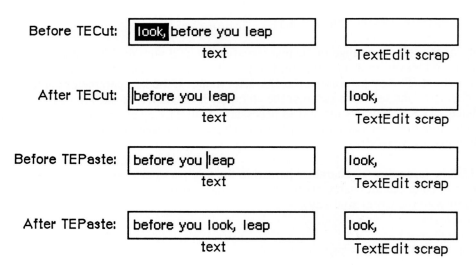

Figure 7. Cutting and Pasting

```
PROCEDURE TEDelete (hTE: TEHandle);
```

TEDelete removes the selection range from the text specified by hTE, and redraws the text as necessary. TEDelete is the same as TECut (above) except that it doesn't transfer the selection range to the scrap. If the selection range is an insertion point, nothing happens.

```
PROCEDURE TEInsert (text: Ptr; length: LONGINT; hTE: TEHandle);
```

TEInsert takes the specified text and inserts it just before the selection range into the text indicated by hTE, redrawing the text as necessary. The text parameter points to the text to be inserted, and the length parameter indicates the number of characters to be inserted. TEInsert doesn't affect either the current selection range or the scrap.

Text Display and Scrolling

```
PROCEDURE TESetJust (just: INTEGER, hTE: TEHandle);
```

TESetJust sets the justification of the text specified by hTE to just. TextEdit provides three predefined constants for setting justification:

```
CONST teJustLeft    =  0;
      teJustCenter  =  1;
      teJustRight   = -1;
```

By default, text is left-justified. If you change the justification, call InvalRect after TESetJust, so the text will be redrawn with the new justification.

```
PROCEDURE TEUpdate (rUpdate: Rect; hTE: TEHandle);
```

TEUpdate draws the text specified by hTE within the rectangle specified by rUpdate (given in the coordinates of the current grafPort). Call TEUpdate every time the Toolbox Event Manager function GetNextEvent reports an update event for a text editing window—after you call the Window Manager procedure BeginUpdate, and before you call EndUpdate.

Normally you'll do the following when an update event occurs:

```
BeginUpdate(myWindow);
EraseRect(myWindow^.portRect);
TEUpdate(myWindow^.portRect,hTE);
EndUpdate(myWindow)
```

If you don't include the EraseRect call, the caret may sometimes remain visible when the window is deactivated.

```
PROCEDURE TextBox (text: Ptr; length: LONGINT; box: Rect; just:
             INTEGER) ;
```

TextBox draws the specified text in the rectangle indicated by the box parameter, with justification just. (See "Justification" under "Edit Records".) The text parameter points to the text, and the length parameter indicates the number of characters to draw. The rectangle is specified in local coordinates, and must be at least as wide as the first character drawn (a good rule of thumb is to make it at least 20 pixels wide). TextBox creates its own edit record, which it deletes when it's finished with it, so the text it draws cannot be edited.

For example:

```
str := 'String in a box';
SetRect(r,100,100,200,200);
TextBox(POINTER(ORD(@str)+1),LENGTH(str),r,teJustCenter);
FrameRect(r)
```

Because Pascal strings start with a length byte, you must advance the pointer one position past the beginning of the string to point to the start of the text.

```
PROCEDURE TEScroll (dh,dv: INTEGER; hTE: TEHandle);
```

TEScroll scrolls the text within the view rectangle of the specified edit record by the number of pixels specified in the dh and dv parameters. The edit record is specified by the hTE parameter. Positive dh and dv values move the text right and down, respectively, and negative values move the text left and up. For example,

```
TEScroll(0,-hTE^^.lineHeight,hTE)
```

scrolls the text up one line. Remember that you scroll text *up* when the user clicks in the scroll arrow pointing *down*. The destination rectangle is offset by the amount you scroll.

Note: To implement automatic scrolling, you store the address of a routine in the clikLoop field of the edit record, as described above under "The TERec Data Type".

Scrap Handling

The TEFromScrap and TEToScrap functions return a result code of type OSErr (defined as INTEGER in the Operating System Utilities) indicating whether an error occurred. If no error occurred, they return the result code

```
CONST noErr = 0;   {no error}
```

Otherwise, they return an Operating System result code indicating an error. (See Appendix A in Volume III for a list of all result codes.)

```
FUNCTION TEFromScrap : OSErr;   [Not in ROM]
```

TEFromScrap copies the desk scrap to the TextEdit scrap. If no error occurs, it returns the result code noErr; otherwise, it returns an appropriate Operating System result code.

Assembly-language note: From assembly language, you can store a handle to the desk scrap in the global variable TEScrpHandle, and the size of the desk scrap in the global variable TEScrpLength; you can get these values with the Scrap Manager function InfoScrap.

```
FUNCTION TEToScrap : OSErr;   [Not in ROM]
```

TEToScrap copies the TextEdit scrap to the desk scrap. If no error occurs, it returns the result code noErr; otherwise, it returns an appropriate Operating System result code.

Warning: You must call the Scrap Manager function ZeroScrap to initialize the desk scrap or clear its previous contents before calling TEToScrap.

Assembly-language note: From assembly language, you can copy the TextEdit scrap to the desk scrap by calling the Scrap Manager function PutScrap; you can get the values you need from the global variables TEScrpHandle and TEScrpLength.

```
FUNCTION TEScrapHandle : Handle;   [Not in ROM]
```

TEScrapHandle returns a handle to the TextEdit scrap.

Assembly-language note: The global variable TEScrpHandle contains a handle to the TextEdit scrap.

```
FUNCTION TEGetScrapLen : LONGINT;   [Not in ROM]
```

TEGetScrapLen returns the size of the TextEdit scrap in bytes.

Assembly-language note: The global variable TEScrpLength contains the size of the TextEdit scrap in bytes.

```
PROCEDURE TESetScrapLen (length: LONGINT);   [Not in ROM]
```

TESetScrapLen sets the size of the TextEdit scrap to the given number of bytes.

Assembly-language note: From assembly language, you can set the global variable TEScrpLength.

Advanced Routines

```
PROCEDURE SetWordBreak (wBrkProc: ProcPtr; hTE: TEHandle);   [Not in
              ROM]
```

SetWordBreak installs in the wordBreak field of the specified edit record a special routine that calls the word break routine pointed to by wBrkProc. The specified word break routine will be called instead of TextEdit's default routine, as described under "The WordBreak Field" in the "Edit Records" section.

Assembly-language note: From assembly language you don't need this procedure; just set the field of the edit record to point to your word break routine.

```
PROCEDURE SetClikLoop (clikProc: ProcPtr; hTE: TEHandle);   [Not in
              ROM]
```

SetClikLoop installs in the clikLoop field of the specified edit record a special routine that calls the click loop routine pointed to by clikProc. The specified click loop routine will be called repeatedly as long as the user holds down the mouse button within the text, as described above under "The ClikLoop Field" in the "Edit Records" section.

Assembly-language note: Like SetWordBreak, this procedure isn't necessary from assembly language; just set the field of the edit record to point to your click loop routine.

```
PROCEDURE TECalText (hTE: TEHandle);
```

TECalText recalculates the beginnings of all lines of text in the edit record specified by hTE, updating elements of the lineStarts array. Call TECalText if you've changed the destination rectangle, the hText field, or any other field that affects the number of characters per line.

Note: There are two ways to specify text to be edited. The easiest method is to use TESetText, which takes an existing edit record, creates a copy of the specified text, and stores a handle to the copy in the edit record. You can instead directly change the hText field of the edit record, and then call TECalText to recalculate the lineStarts array to match the new text. If you have a lot of text, you can use the latter method to save space.

Assembly-language note: The global variable TERecal contains the address of the routine called by TECalText to recalculate the line starts and set the first and last characters that need to be redrawn. The registers contain the following:

On entry	A3:	pointer to the locked edit record
	D7:	change in the length of the record (word)
On exit	D2:	line start of the line containing the first character to be redrawn (word)
	D3:	position of first character to be redrawn (word)
	D4:	position of last character to be redrawn (word)

Assembly-language note: The global variable TEDoText contains the address of a multi-purpose text editing routine that advanced programmers may find useful. It lets you display, highlight, and hit-test characters, and position the pen to draw the caret. "Hit-test" means decide where to place the insertion point when the user clicks the mouse button; the point selected with the mouse is in the teSelPoint field. The registers contain the following:

On entry	A3:	pointer to the locked edit record
	D3:	position of first character to be redrawn (word)
	D4:	position of last character to be redrawn (word)
	D7: (word)	0 to hit-test a character
		1 to highlight the selection range
		−1 to display the text
		−2 to position the pen to draw the caret
On exit	A0:	pointer to current grafPort
	D0:	if hit-testing, character position or −1 for none (word)

SUMMARY OF TEXTEDIT

Constants

```
CONST  { Text justification }

     teJustLeft   =  0;
     teJustCenter =  1;
     teJustRight  = -1;
```

Data Types

```
TYPE TEHandle = ^TEPtr;
     TEPtr    = ^TERec;
     TERec = RECORD
                 destRect:   Rect;     {destination rectangle}
                 viewRect:   Rect;     {view rectangle}
                 selRect:    Rect;     {used from assembly language}
                 lineHeight  INTEGER;  {for line spacing
                 fontAscent: INTEGER;  {caret/highlighting position}
                 selPoint:   Point;    {used from assembly language}
                 selStart:   INTEGER;  {start of selection range}
                 selEnd:     INTEGER;  {end of selection range
                 active:     INTEGER;  {used internally}
                 wordBreak:  ProcPtr;  {for word break routine}
                 clikLoop:   ProcPtr;  {for click loop routine}
                 clickTime:  LONGINT;  {used internally}
                 clickLoc:   INTEGER;  {used internally}
                 caretTime:  LONGINT;  {used internally}
                 caretState: INTEGER;  {used internally}
                 just:       INTEGER;  {justification of text}
                 teLength:   INTEGER;  {length of text}
                 hText:      Handle;   {text to be edited}
                 recalBack:  INTEGER;  {used internally}
                 recalLines: INTEGER;  {used internally}
                 clikStuff:  INTEGER;  {used internally}
                 crOnly:     INTEGER;  {if <0, new line at Return only}
                 txFont:     INTEGER;  {text font}
                 txFace:     Style;    {character style}
                 txMode:     INTEGER;  {pen mode}
                 txSize:     INTEGER;  {font size}
                 inPort:     GrafPtr;  {grafPort}
                 highHook:   ProcPtr;  {used from assembly language}
                 caretHook:  ProcPtr;  {used from assembly language}
                 nLines:     INTEGER;  {number of lines}
                 lineStarts: ARRAY[0..16000] OF INTEGER
                                       {positions of line starts}
             END;
```

```
CharsHandle = ^CharsPtr;
CharsPtr    = ^Chars;
Chars       = PACKED ARRAY[0..32000] OF CHAR;
```

Routines

Initialization and Allocation

```
PROCEDURE TEInit;
FUNCTION  TENew      (destRect,viewRect: Rect) : TEHandle;
PROCEDURE TEDispose (hTE: TEHandle);
```

Accessing the Text of an Edit Record

```
PROCEDURE TESetText (text: Ptr; length: LONGINT; hTE: TEHandle);
FUNCTION  TEGetText (hTE: TEHandle) : CharsHandle;
```

Insertion Point and Selection Range

```
PROCEDURE TEIdle       (hTE: TEHandle);
PROCEDURE TEClick      (pt: Point; extend: BOOLEAN; hTE: TEHandle);
PROCEDURE TESetSelect  (selStart,selEnd: LONGINT; hTE: TEHandle);
PROCEDURE TEActivate   (hTE: TEHandle);
PROCEDURE TEDeactivate (hTE: TEHandle);
```

Editing

```
PROCEDURE TEKey    (key: CHAR; hTE: TEHandle);
PROCEDURE TECut    (hTE: TEHandle);
PROCEDURE TECopy   (hTE: TEHandle);
PROCEDURE TEPaste  (hTE: TEHandle);
PROCEDURE TEDelete (hTE: TEHandle);
PROCEDURE TEInsert (text: Ptr; length: LONGINT; hTE: TEHandle);
```

Text Display and Scrolling

```
PROCEDURE TESetJust (just: INTEGER; hTE: TEHandle);
PROCEDURE TEUpdate  (rUpdate: Rect; hTE: TEHandle);
PROCEDURE TextBox   (text: Ptr; length: LONGINT; box: Rect; just:
                       INTEGER);
PROCEDURE TEScroll  (dh,dv: INTEGER; hTE: TEHandle);
```

Scrap Handling [Not in ROM]

```
FUNCTION    TEFromScrap    :     OSErr;
FUNCTION    TEToScrap      :     OSErr;
FUNCTION    TEScrapHandle  :     Handle;
FUNCTION    TEGetScrapLen  :     LONGINT;
PROCEDURE   TESetScrapLen  :     (length: LONGINT);
```

Advanced Routines

```
PROCEDURE   SetWordBreak  (wBrkProc: ProcPtr; hTE: TEHandle);   [Not in ROM]
PROCEDURE   SetClikLoop   (clikProc: ProcPtr; hTE: TEHandle);   [Not in ROM]
PROCEDURE   TECalText     (hTE: TEHandle);
```

Word Break Routine

```
FUNCTION MyWordBreak (text: Ptr; charPos: INTEGER) : BOOLEAN;
```

Click Loop Routine

```
FUNCTION MyClikLoop : BOOLEAN;
```

Assembly-Language Information

Constants

```
; Text justification

teJustLeft      .EQU     0
teJustCenter    .EQU     1
teJustRight     .EQU    -1
```

Edit Record Data Structure

teDestRect	Destination rectangle (8 bytes)
teViewRect	View rectangle (8 bytes)
teSelRect	Selection rectangle (8 bytes)
teLineHite	For line spacing (word)
teAscent	Caret/highlighting position (word)
teSelPoint	Point selected with mouse (long)
teSelStart	Start of selection range (word)
teSelEnd	End of selection range (word)
teWordBreak	Address of word break routine (see below)
teClikProc	Address of click loop routine (see below)
teJust	Justification of text (word)

teLength	Length of text (word)
teTextH	Handle to text
teCROnly	If <0, new line at Return only (byte)
teFont	Text font (word)
teFace	Character style (word)
teMode	Pen mode (word)
teSize	Font size (word)
teGrafPort	Pointer to grafPort
teHiHook	Address of text highlighting routine (see below)
teCarHook	Address of routine to draw caret (see below)
teNLines	Number of lines (word)
teLines	Positions of line starts (teNLines*2 bytes)
teRecSize	Size in bytes of edit record except teLines field

Word break routine

On entry	A0:	pointer to text
	D0:	character position (word)
On exit	Z condition code:	0 to break at specified character
		1 not to break there

Click loop routine

On exit	D0:	1
	D2:	must be preserved

Text highlighting routine

On entry	A3:	pointer to locked edit record

Caret drawing routine

On entry	A3:	pointer to locked edit record

Variables

TEScrpHandle	Handle to TextEdit scrap
TEScrpLength	Size in bytes of TextEdit scrap (word)
TERecal	Address of routine to recalculate line starts (see below)
TEDoText	Address of multi-purpose routine (see below)

TERecal routine

On entry	A3:	pointer to locked edit record
	D7:	change in length of edit record (word)
On exit	D2:	line start of line containing first character to be redrawn (word)
	D3:	position of first character to be redrawn (word)
	D4:	position of last character to be redrawn (word)

TEDoText routine

On entry   A3:   pointer to locked edit record
             D3:   position of first character to be redrawn (word)
             D4:   position of last character to be redrawn (word)
             D7:   (word)   0 to hit-test a character
                            1 to highlight selection range
                           −1 to display text
                           −2 to position pen to draw caret

On exit   A0:   pointer to current grafPort
             D0:   if hit-testing, character position or −1 for none (word)

13 THE DIALOG MANAGER

ABOUT THIS CHAPTER

This chapter describes the Dialog Manager, the part of the Toolbox that allows you to implement dialog boxes and the alert mechanism, two means of communication between the application and the end user.

You should already be familiar with:

- resources, as discussed in chapter 5
- the basic concepts and structures behind QuickDraw, particularly rectangles, grafPorts, and pictures
- the Toolbox Event Manager, the Window Manager, and the Control Manager
- TextEdit, to understand editing text in dialog boxes

ABOUT THE DIALOG MANAGER

The Dialog Manager is a tool for handling dialogs and alerts in a way that's consistent with the Macintosh User Interface Guidelines.

A **dialog box** appears on the screen when a Macintosh application needs more information to carry out a command. As shown in Figure 1, it typically resembles a form on which the user checks boxes and fills in blanks.

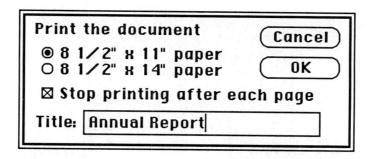

Figure 1. A Typical Dialog Box

By convention, a dialog box comes up slightly below the menu bar, is somewhat narrower than the screen, and is centered between the left and right edges of the screen. It may contain any or all of the following:

- informative or instructional text
- rectangles in which text may be entered (initially blank or containing default text that can be edited)
- controls of any kind
- graphics (icons or QuickDraw pictures)

■ anything else, as defined by the application

The user provides the necessary information in the dialog box, such as by entering text or clicking a check box. There's usually a button labeled "OK" to tell the application to accept the information provided and perform the command, and a button labeled "Cancel" to cancel the command as though it had never been given (retracting all actions since its invocation). Some dialog boxes may use a more descriptive word than "OK"; for simplicity, this chapter will still refer to the button as the "OK button". There may even be more than one button that will perform the command, each in a different way.

Most dialog boxes require the user to respond before doing anything else. Clicking a button to perform or cancel the command makes the box go away; clicking outside the dialog box only causes a beep from the Macintosh's speaker. This type is called a **modal** dialog box because it puts the user in the state or "mode" of being able to work only inside the dialog box. A modal dialog box usually has the same general appearance as shown in Figure 1 above. One of the buttons in the dialog box may be outlined boldly. Pressing the Return key or the Enter key has the same effect as clicking the outlined button or, if none, the OK button; the particular button whose effect occurs is called the dialog's **default button** and is the preferred ("safest") button to use in the current situation. If there's no boldly outlined or OK button, pressing Return or Enter will by convention have no effect.

Other dialog boxes do not require the user to respond before doing anything else; these are called **modeless** dialog boxes (see Figure 2). The user can, for example, do work in document windows on the desktop before clicking a button in the dialog box, and modeless dialog boxes can be set up to respond to the standard editing commands in the Edit menu. Clicking a button in a modeless dialog box will not make the box go away: The box will stay around so that the user can perform the command again. A Cancel button, if present, will simply stop the action currently being performed by the command; this would be useful for long printing or searching operations, for example.

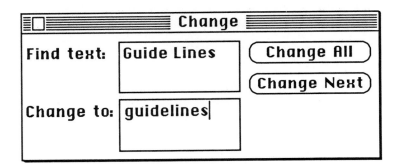

Figure 2. A Modeless Dialog Box

As shown in Figure 2, a modeless dialog box looks like a document window. It can be moved, made inactive and active again, or closed like any document window. When you're done with the command and want the box to go away, you can click its close box or choose Close from the File menu when it's the active window.

Dialog boxes may in fact require no response at all. For example, while an application is performing a time-consuming process, it can display a dialog box that contains only a message telling what it's doing; then, when the process is complete, it can simply remove the dialog box.

The **alert** mechanism provides applications with a means of reporting errors or giving warnings. An **alert box** is similar to a modal dialog box, but it appears only when something has gone wrong or must be brought to the user's attention. Its conventional placement is slightly farther below the menu bar than a dialog box. To assist the user who isn't sure how to proceed when an alert box appears, the preferred button to use in the current situation is outlined boldly so it stands out from the other buttons in the alert box (see Figure 3). The outlined button is also the alert's default button; if the user presses the Return key or the Enter key, the effect is the same as clicking this button.

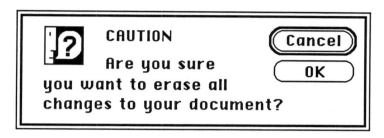

Figure 3. A Typical Alert Box

There are three standard kinds of alerts—Stop, Note, and Caution—each indicated by a particular icon in the top left corner of the alert box. Figure 3 illustrates a Caution alert. The icons identifying Stop and Note alerts are similar; instead of a question mark, they show an exclamation point and an asterisk, respectively. Other alerts can have anything in the the top left corner, including blank space if desired.

The alert mechanism also provides another type of signal: Sound from the Macintosh's speaker. The application can base its response on the number of consecutive times an alert occurs; the first time, it might simply beep, and thereafter it may present an alert box. The sound isn't limited to a single beep but may be any sequence of tones, and may occur either alone or along with an alert box. As an error is repeated, there can also be a change in which button is the default button (perhaps from OK to Cancel). You can specify different responses for up to four occurrences of the same alert.

With Dialog Manager routines, you can create dialog boxes or invoke alerts. The Dialog Manager gets most of the descriptive information about the dialogs and alerts from resources in a resource file. The Dialog Manager calls the Resource Manager to read what it needs from the resource file into memory as necessary. In some cases you can modify the information after it's been read into memory.

DIALOG AND ALERT WINDOWS

A dialog box appears in a **dialog window**. When you call a Dialog Manager routine to create a dialog, you supply the same information as when you create a window with a Window Manager routine. For example, you supply the window definition ID, which determines how the window looks and behaves, and a rectangle that becomes the portRect of the window's grafPort. You specify the window's plane (which, by convention, should initially be the frontmost) and whether the window is visible or invisible. The dialog window is created as specified.

You can manipulate a dialog window just like any other window with Window Manager or QuickDraw routines, showing it, hiding it, moving it, changing its size or plane, or whatever—all, of course, in conformance with the Macintosh User Interface Guidelines. The Dialog Manager observes the clipping region of the dialog window's grafPort, so if you want clipping to occur, you can set this region with a QuickDraw routine.

Similarly, an alert box appears in an **alert window**. You don't have the same flexibility in defining and manipulating an alert window, however. The Dialog Manager chooses the window definition ID, so that all alert windows will have the standard appearance and behavior. The size and location of the box are supplied as part of the definition of the alert and are not easily changed. You don't specify the alert window's plane; it always comes up in front of all other windows. Since an alert box requires the user to respond before doing anything else, and the response makes the box go away, the application doesn't do any manipulation of the alert window.

Figure 4 illustrates a document window, dialog window, and alert window, all overlapping on the desktop.

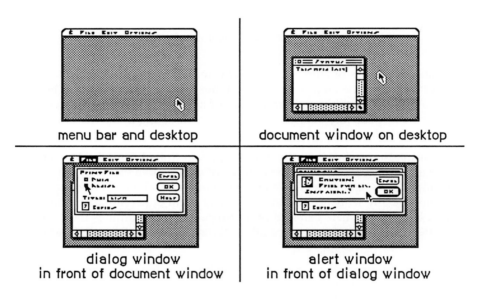

Figure 4. Dialog and Alert Windows

DIALOGS, ALERTS, AND RESOURCES

To create a dialog, the Dialog Manager needs the same information about the dialog window as the Window Manager needs when it creates a new window: The window definition ID along with other information specific to this window. The Dialog Manager also needs to know what items the dialog box contains. You can store the needed information as a resource in a resource file and pass the resource ID to a function that will create the dialog. This type of resource, which is called a **dialog template**, is analogous to a window template, and the function, GetNewDialog, is similar to the Window Manager function GetNewWindow. The Dialog Manager calls the Resource Manager to read the dialog template from the resource file. It then incorporates the information in the template into a dialog data structure in memory, called a **dialog record**.

Similarly, the data that the Dialog Manager needs to create an alert is stored in an **alert template** in a resource file. The various routines for invoking alerts require the resource ID of the alert template as a parameter.

The information about all the **items** (text, controls, or graphics) in a dialog or alert box is stored in an **item list** in a resource file. The resource ID of the item list is included in the dialog or alert template. The item list in turn contains the resource IDs of any icons or QuickDraw pictures in the dialog or alert box, and possibly the resource IDs of control templates for controls in the box. After calling the Resource Manager to read a dialog or alert template into memory, the Dialog Manager calls it again to read in the item list. It then makes a copy of the item list and uses that copy; for this reason, item lists should always be purgeable resources. Finally, the Dialog Manager calls the Resource Manager to read in any individual items as necessary.

If desired, the application can gain some additional flexibility by calling the Resource Manager directly to read templates, item lists, or items from a resource file. For example, you can read in a dialog or alert template directly and modify some of the information in it before calling the routine to create the dialog or alert. Or, as an alternative to using a dialog template, you can read in a dialog's item list directly and then pass a handle to it along with other information to a function that will create the dialog (NewDialog, analogous to the Window Manager function NewWindow).

> **Note:** The use of dialog templates is recommended wherever possible; like window templates, they isolate descriptive information from your application code for ease of modification or translation to other languages.

ITEM LISTS IN MEMORY

This section discusses the contents of an item list once it's been read into memory from a resource file and the Dialog Manager has set it up as necessary to be able to work with it.

An item list in memory contains the following information for each item:

- The type of item. This includes not only whether the item is a control, text, or whatever, but also whether the Dialog Manager should return to the application when the item is clicked.

- A handle to the item or, for special application-defined items, a pointer to a procedure that draws the item.

- A **display rectangle**, which determines the location of the item within the dialog or alert box.

These are discussed below along with **item numbers**, which identify particular items in the item list.

There's a Dialog Manager procedure that, given a pointer to a dialog record and an item number, sets or returns that item's type, handle (or procedure pointer), and display rectangle.

Item Types

The item type is specified by a predefined constant or combination of constants, as listed below. Figure 5 illustrates some of these item types.

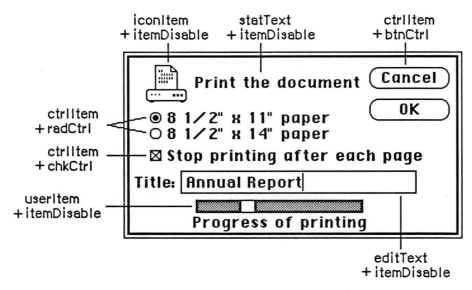

Figure 5. Item Types

Item type	Meaning
ctrlItem+btnCtrl	A standard button control.
ctrlItem+chkCtrl	A standard check box control.
ctrlItem+radCtrl	A standard radio button control.
ctrlItem+resCtrl	A control defined in a control template in a resource file.
statText	Static text; text that cannot be edited.
editText	(Dialogs only) Text that can be edited; the Dialog Manager accepts text typed by the user and allows editing.
iconItem	An icon.
picItem	A QuickDraw picture.
userItem	(Dialogs only) An application-defined item, such as a picture whose appearance changes.
itemDisable+<any of the above>	The item is **disabled** (the Dialog Manager doesn't report events involving this item).

The text of an editText item may initially be either default text or empty. Text entry and editing is handled in the conventional way, as in TextEdit—in fact, the Dialog Manager calls TextEdit to handle it:

- Clicking in the item displays a blinking vertical bar, indicating an insertion point where text may be entered.

- Dragging over text in the item selects that text, and double-clicking selects a word; the selection is highlighted and then replaced by what the user types.

- Clicking or dragging while holding down the Shift key extends or shortens the current selection.

- The Backspace key deletes the current selection or the character preceding the insertion point.

The Tab key advances to the next editText item in the item list, wrapping around to the first if there aren't any more. In an alert box or a modal dialog box (regardless of whether it contains an editText item), the Return key or Enter key has the same effect as clicking the default button; for alerts, the default button is identified in the alert template, whereas for modal dialogs it's always the first item in the item list.

If itemDisable is specified for an item, the Dialog Manager doesn't let the application know about events involving that item. For example, you may not have to be informed every time the user types a character or clicks in an editText item, but may only need to look at the text when the OK button is clicked. In this case, the editText item would be disabled. Standard buttons and check boxes should always be enabled, so your application will know when they've been clicked.

Warning: Don't confuse disabling a control with making one "inactive" with the Control Manager procedure HiliteControl: When you want a control not to respond at all to being clicked, you make it inactive. An inactive control is highlighted to show that it's inactive, while disabling a control doesn't affect its appearance.

Item Handle or Procedure Pointer

The item list contains the following information for the various types of items:

Item type	Contents
any ctrlItem	A control handle
statText	A handle to the text
editText	A handle to the current text
iconItem	A handle to the icon
picItem	A picture handle
userItem	A procedure pointer

The procedure for a userItem draws the item; for example, if the item is a clock, it will draw the clock with the current time displayed. When this procedure is called, the current port will have been set by the Dialog Manager to the dialog window's grafPort. The procedure must have two parameters, a window pointer and an item number. For example, this is how it would be declared if it were named MyItem:

```
PROCEDURE MyItem (theWindow: WindowPtr; itemNo: INTEGER);
```

TheWindow is a pointer to the dialog window; in case the procedure draws in more than one dialog window, this parameter tells it which one to draw in. ItemNo is the item number; in case the procedure draws more than one item, this parameter tells it which one to draw.

Display Rectangle

Each item in the item list is displayed within its display rectangle:

- For controls, the display rectangle becomes the control's enclosing rectangle.

- For an editText item, it becomes TextEdit's destination rectangle and view rectangle. Word wraparound occurs, and the text is clipped if there's more than will fit in the rectangle. In addition, the Dialog Manager uses the QuickDraw procedure FrameRect to draw a rectangle three pixels outside the display rectangle.

- StatText items are displayed in exactly the same way as editText items, except that a rectangle isn't drawn outside the display rectangle.

- Icons and QuickDraw pictures are scaled to fit the display rectangle. For pictures, the Window Manager calls the QuickDraw procedure DrawPicture and passes it the display rectangle.

- If the procedure for a userItem draws outside the item's display rectangle, the drawing is clipped to the display rectangle.

Note: Clicking anywhere within the display rectangle is considered a click in that item. If display rectangles overlap, a click in the overlapping area is considered a click in whichever item comes first in the item list.

By giving an item a display rectangle that's off the screen, you can make the item invisible. This might be useful, for example, if your application needs to display a number of dialog boxes that are similar except that one item is missing or different in some of them. You can use a single dialog box in which the item or items that aren't currently relevant are invisible. To remove an item or make one reappear, you just change its display rectangle (and call the Window Manager procedure InvalRect to accumulate the changed area into the dialog window's update region). The QuickDraw procedure OffsetRect is convenient for moving an item off the screen and then on again later. Note the following, however:

- You shouldn't make an editText item invisible, because it may cause strange things to happen. If one of several editText items is invisible, for example, pressing the Tab key may make the insertion point disappear. However, if you do make this type of item invisible, remember that the changed area includes the rectangle that's three pixels outside the item's display rectangle.

- The rectangle for a statText item must always be at least as wide as the first character of the text; a good rule of thumb is to make it at least 20 pixels wide.

- To change text in a statText item, it's easier to use the Dialog Manager procedure ParamText (as described later in the "Dialog Manager Routines" section).

Item Numbers

Each item in an item list is identified by an item number, which is simply the index of the item in the list (starting from 1). By convention, the first item in an alert's item list should be the OK button (or, if none, then one of the buttons that will perform the command) and the second item should be the Cancel button. The Dialog Manager provides predefined constants equal to the item numbers for OK and Cancel:

```
CONST ok     = 1;
      cancel = 2;
```

In a modal dialog's item list, the first item is assumed to be the dialog's default button; if the user presses the Return key or Enter key, the Dialog Manager normally returns item number 1, just as when that item is actually clicked. To conform to the Macintosh User Interface Guidelines, the application should boldly outline the dialog's default button if it isn't the OK button. The best way to do this is with a userItem. To allow for changes in the default button's size or location, the userItem should identify which button to outline by its item number and then use that number to get the button's display rectangle. The following QuickDraw calls will outline the rectangle in the standard way:

```
PenSize(3,3);
InsetRect(displayRect,-4,-4);
FrameRoundRect(displayRect,16,16)
```

Warning: If the first item in a modal dialog's item list isn't an OK button and you don't boldly outline it, you should set up the dialog to ignore Return and Enter. To learn how to do this, see ModalDialog under "Handling Dialog Events" in the "Dialog Manager Routines" section.

DIALOG RECORDS

To create a dialog, you pass information to the Dialog Manager in a dialog template and in individual parameters, or only in parameters; in either case, the Dialog Manager incorporates the information into a dialog record. The dialog record contains the window record for the dialog window, a handle to the dialog's item list, and some additional fields. The Dialog Manager creates the dialog window by calling the Window Manager function NewWindow and then setting the window class in the window record to indicate that it's a dialog window. The routine that creates the dialog returns a pointer to the dialog record, which you use thereafter to refer to the dialog in Dialog Manager routines or even in Window Manager or QuickDraw routines (see "Dialog Pointers" below). The Dialog Manager provides routines for handling events in the dialog window and disposing of the dialog when you're done.

The data type for a dialog record is called DialogRecord. You can do all the necessary operations on a dialog without accessing the fields of the dialog record directly; for advanced programmers, however, the exact structure of a dialog record is given under "The DialogRecord Data Type" below.

Dialog Pointers

There are two types of dialog pointer, DialogPtr and DialogPeek, analogous to the window pointer types WindowPtr and WindowPeek. Most programmers will only need to use DialogPtr.

The Dialog Manager defines the following type of dialog pointer:

```
TYPE DialogPtr = WindowPtr;
```

It can do this because the first field of a dialog record contains the window record for the dialog window. This type of pointer can be used to access fields of the window record or can be passed to Window Manager routines that expect window pointers as parameters. Since the WindowPtr data type is itself defined as GrafPtr, this type of dialog pointer can also be used to access fields of the dialog window's grafPort or passed to QuickDraw routines that expect pointers to grafPorts as parameters.

For programmers who want to access dialog record fields beyond the window record, the Dialog Manager also defines the following type of dialog pointer:

```
TYPE DialogPeek = ^DialogRecord;
```

Assembly-language note: From assembly language, of course, there's no type checking on pointers, and the two types of pointer are equal.

The DialogRecord Data Type

For those who want to know more about the data structure of a dialog record, the exact structure is given here.

```
TYPE DialogRecord =
          RECORD
              window:    WindowRecord;  {dialog window}
              items:     Handle;        {item list}
              textH:     TEHandle;      {current editText item}
              editField: INTEGER;       {editText item number minus 1}
              editOpen:  INTEGER;       {used internally}
              aDefItem:  INTEGER        {default button item number}
          END;
```

The window field contains the window record for the dialog window. The items field contains a handle to the item list used for the dialog. (Remember that after reading an item list from a resource file, the Dialog Manager makes a copy of it and uses that copy.)

> **Note:** To get or change information about an item in a dialog, you pass the dialog pointer and the item number to a Dialog Manager procedure. You'll never access information directly through the handle to the item list.

The Dialog Manager uses the next three fields when there are one or more editText items in the dialog. If there's more than one such item, these fields apply to the one that currently is selected or displays the insertion point. The textH field contains the handle to the edit record used by TextEdit. EditField is 1 less than the item number of the current editText item, or –1 if there's no editText item in the dialog. The editOpen field is used internally by the Dialog Manager.

> **Note:** Actually, a single edit record is shared by all editText items; any changes you make to it will apply to all such items. See chapter 12 for details about what kinds of changes you can make.

The aDefItem field is used for modal dialogs and alerts, which are treated internally as special modal dialogs. It contains the item number of the default button. The default button for a modal dialog is the first item in the item list, so this field contains 1 for modal dialogs. The default button for an alert is specified in the alert template; see the following section for more information.

ALERTS

When you call a Dialog Manager routine to invoke an alert, you pass it the resource ID of the alert template, which contains the following:

- A rectangle, given in global coordinates, which determines the alert window's size and location. It becomes the portRect of the window's grafPort. To allow for the menu bar and the border around the portRect, the top coordinate of the rectangle should be at least 25 points below the top of the screen.

- The resource ID of the item list for the alert.

- Information about exactly what should happen at each stage of the alert.

Every alert has four **stages**, corresponding to consecutive occurrences of the alert: The first three stages correspond to the first three occurrences, while the fourth stage includes the fourth occurrence and any beyond the fourth. (The Dialog Manager compares the current alert's resource ID to the last alert's resource ID to determine whether it's the same alert.) The actions for each stage are specified by the following three pieces of information:

- which is the default button—the OK button (or, if none, a button that will perform the command) or the Cancel button

- whether the alert box is to be drawn

- which of four sounds should be emitted at this stage of the alert

The alert sounds are determined by a **sound procedure** that emits one of up to four tones or sequences of tones. The sound procedure has one parameter, an integer from 0 to 3; it can emit any sound for each of these numbers, which identify the sounds in the alert template. For example, you might declare a sound procedure named MySound as follows:

```
PROCEDURE MySound (soundNo: INTEGER);
```

If you don't write your own sound procedure, the Dialog Manager uses the standard one: Sound number 0 represents no sound and sound numbers 1 through 3 represent the corresponding number of short beeps, each of the same pitch and duration. The volume of each beep depends on the current speaker volume setting, which the user can adjust with the Control Panel desk accessory. If the user has set the speaker volume to 0, the menu bar will blink in place of each beep.

For example, if the second stage of an alert is to cause a beep and no alert box, you can just specify the following for that stage in the alert template: Don't draw the alert box, and use sound number 1. If instead you want, say, two successive beeps of different pitch, you need to write a procedure that will emit that sound for a particular sound number, and specify that number in the alert template. The Macintosh Operating System includes routines for emitting sound; see chapter 8 of Volume II, and also the simple SysBeep procedure in chapter 13 of Volume II. (The standard sound procedure calls SysBeep.)

Note: When the Dialog Manager detects a click outside an alert box or a modal dialog box, it emits sound number 1; thus, for consistency with the Macintosh User Interface Guidelines, sound number 1 should always be a single beep.

Internally, alerts are treated as special modal dialogs. The alert routine creates the alert window by calling NewDialog. The Dialog Manager works from the dialog record created by NewDialog, just as when it operates on a dialog window, but it disposes of the window before returning to the application. Normally your application won't access the dialog record for an alert; however, there is a way that this can happen: For any alert, you can specify a procedure that will be executed repeatedly during the alert, and this procedure may access the dialog record. For details, see the alert routines under "Invoking Alerts" in the "Dialog Manager Routines" section.

USING THE DIALOG MANAGER

Before using the Dialog Manager, you must initialize QuickDraw, the Font Manager, the Window Manager, the Menu Manager, and TextEdit, in that order. The first Dialog Manager routine to call is InitDialogs, which initializes the Dialog Manager. If you want the font in your dialog and alert windows to be other than the system font, call SetDAFont to change the font.

Where appropriate in your program, call NewDialog or GetNewDialog to create any dialogs you need. Usually you'll call GetNewDialog, which takes descriptive information about the dialog from a dialog template in a resource file. You can instead pass the information in individual parameters to NewDialog. In either case, you can supply a pointer to the storage for the dialog record or let it be allocated by the Dialog Manager. When you no longer need a dialog, you'll usually call CloseDialog if you supplied the storage, or DisposDialog if not.

In most cases, you probably won't have to make any changes to the dialogs from the way they're defined in the resource file. However, if you should want to modify an item in a dialog, you can call GetDItem to get the information about the item and SetDItem to change it. In particular, SetDItem is the routine to use for installing a userItem. In some cases it may be appropriate to call some other Toolbox routine to change the item; for example, to change or move a control in a dialog, you would get its handle from GetDItem and then call the appropriate Control Manager routine. There are also two procedures specifically for accessing or setting the content of a text item in a dialog box: GetIText and SetIText.

To handle events in a modal dialog, just call the ModalDialog procedure after putting up the dialog box. If your application includes any modeless dialog boxes, you'll pass events to IsDialogEvent to learn whether they need to be handled as part of a dialog, and then usually call DialogSelect if so. Before calling DialogSelect, however, you should check whether the user has given the keyboard equivalent of a command, and you may want to check for other special cases, depending on your application. You can support the use of the standard editing commands in a modeless dialog's editText items with DlgCut, DlgCopy, DlgPaste, and DlgDelete.

A dialog box that contains editText items normally comes up with the insertion point in the first such item in its item list. You may instead want to bring up a dialog box with text selected in an editText item, or to cause an insertion point or text selection to reappear after the user has made an error in entering text. For example, the user who accidentally types nonnumeric input when a number is required can be given the opportunity to type the entry again. The SelIText procedure makes this possible.

For alerts, if you want other sounds besides the standard ones (up to three short beeps), write your own sound procedure and call ErrorSound to make it the current sound procedure. To invoke a particular alert, call one of the alert routines: StopAlert, NoteAlert, or CautionAlert for one of the standard kinds of alert, or Alert for an alert defined to have something other than a standard icon (or nothing at all) in its top left corner.

If you're going to invoke a dialog or alert when the resource file might not be accessible, first call CouldDialog or CouldAlert, which will make the dialog or alert template and related resources unpurgeable. You can later make them purgeable again by calling FreeDialog or FreeAlert.

Finally, you can substitute text in statText items with text that you specify in the ParamText procedure. This means, for example, that a document name supplied by the user can appear in an error message.

DIALOG MANAGER ROUTINES

Initialization

```
PROCEDURE InitDialogs (resumeProc: ProcPtr);
```

Call InitDialogs once before all other Dialog Manager routines, to initialize the Dialog Manager. InitDialogs does the following initialization:

- It saves the pointer passed in resumeProc, if any, for access by the System Error Handler in case a fatal system error occurs. ResumeProc can be a pointer to a resume procedure, as described in chapter 12 of Volume II, or NIL if no such procedure is desired.

Assembly-language note: InitDialogs stores the address of the resume procedure in a global variable named ResumeProc.

- It installs the standard sound procedure.
- It passes empty strings to ParamText.

```
PROCEDURE ErrorSound (soundProc: ProcPtr);
```

ErrorSound sets the sound procedure for alerts to the procedure pointed to by soundProc; if you don't call ErrorSound, the Dialog Manager uses the standard sound procedure. (For details, see the "Alerts" section.) If you pass NIL for soundProc, there will be no sound (or menu bar blinking) at all.

Assembly-language note: The address of the sound procedure being used is stored in the global variable DABeeper.

```
PROCEDURE SetDAFont (fontNum: INTEGER);   [Not in ROM]
```

For subsequently created dialogs and alerts, SetDAFont causes the font of the dialog or alert window's grafPort to be set to the font having the specified font number. If you don't call this procedure, the system font is used. SetDAFont affects statText and editText items but not titles of controls, which are always in the system font.

Assembly-language note: Assembly-language programmers can simply set the global variable DlgFont to the desired font number.

Creating and Disposing of Dialogs

```
FUNCTION NewDialog (dStorage: Ptr; boundsRect: Rect; title:
        Str255; visible: BOOLEAN; procID: INTEGER; behind:
        WindowPtr; goAwayFlag: BOOLEAN; refCon: LONGINT; items:
        Handle) : DialogPtr;
```

NewDialog creates a dialog as specified by its parameters and returns a pointer to the new dialog. The first eight parameters (dStorage through refCon) are passed to the Window Manager function NewWindow, which creates the dialog window; the meanings of these parameters are summarized below. The items parameter is a handle to the dialog's item list. You can get the items handle by calling the Resource Manager to read the item list from the resource file into memory.

Note: Advanced programmers can create their own item lists in memory rather than have them read from a resource file. The exact format is given later under "Formats of Resources for Dialogs and Alerts".

DStorage is analogous to the wStorage parameter of NewWindow; it's a pointer to the storage to use for the dialog record. If you pass NIL for dStorage, the dialog record will be allocated in the heap (which, in the case of modeless dialogs, may cause the heap to become fragmented).

BoundsRect, a rectangle given in global coordinates, determines the dialog window's size and location. It becomes the portRect of the window's grafPort. Remember that the top coordinate of this rectangle should be at least 25 points below the top of the screen for a modal dialog, to allow for the menu bar and the border around the portRect, and at least 40 points below the top of the screen for a modeless dialog, to allow for the menu bar and the window's title bar.

Title is the title of a modeless dialog box; pass the empty string for modal dialogs.

If the visible parameter is TRUE, the dialog window is drawn on the screen. If it's FALSE, the window is initially invisible and may later be shown with a call to the Window Manager procedure ShowWindow.

Note: NewDialog generates an update event for the entire window contents, so the items aren't drawn immediately, with the exception of controls. The Dialog Manager calls the Control Manager to draw controls, and the Control Manager draws them immediately rather than via the standard update mechanism. Because of this, the Dialog Manager calls the Window Manager procedure ValidRect for the enclosing rectangle of each control, so the controls won't be drawn twice. If you find that the other items aren't being drawn soon enough after the controls, try making the window invisible initially and then calling ShowWindow to show it.

ProcID is the window definition ID, which leads to the window definition function for this type of window. The window definition IDs for the standard types of dialog window are dBoxProc for the modal type and documentProc for the modeless type.

The behind parameter specifies the window behind which the dialog window is to be placed on the desktop. Pass POINTER(−1) to bring up the dialog window in front of all other windows.

GoAwayFlag applies to modeless dialog boxes; if it's TRUE, the dialog window has a close box in its title bar when the window is active.

RefCon is the dialog window's reference value, which the application may store into and access for any purpose.

NewDialog sets the font of the dialog window's grafPort to the system font or, if you previously called SetDAFont, to the specified font. It also sets the window class in the window record to dialogKind.

```
FUNCTION GetNewDialog (dialogID: INTEGER; dStorage: Ptr; behind:
        WindowPtr) : DialogPtr;
```

Like NewDialog (above), GetNewDialog creates a dialog as specified by its parameters and returns a pointer to the new dialog. Instead of having the parameters boundsRect, title, visible, procID, goAwayFlag, and refCon, GetNewDialog has a single dialogID parameter, where dialogID is the resource ID of a dialog template that supplies the same information as those parameters. The dialog template also contains the resource ID of the dialog's item list. After calling the Resource Manager to read the item list into memory (if it's not already in memory), GetNewDialog makes a copy of the item list and uses that copy; thus you may have multiple independent dialogs whose items have the same types, locations, and initial contents. The dStorage and behind parameters of GetNewDialog have the same meaning as in NewDialog.

Warning: If either the dialog template resource or the item list resource can't be read, the function result is undefined.

Note: GetNewDialog doesn't release the memory occupied by the resources.

```
PROCEDURE CloseDialog (theDialog: DialogPtr);
```

CloseDialog removes theDialog's window from the screen and deletes it from the window list, just as when the Window Manager procedure CloseWindow is called. It releases the memory occupied by the following:

- The data structures associated with the dialog window (such as the window's structure, content, and update regions).

- All the items in the dialog (except for pictures and icons, which might be shared resources), and any data structures associated with them. For example, it would dispose of the region occupied by the thumb of a scroll bar, or a similar region for some other control in the dialog.

CloseDialog does *not* dispose of the dialog record or the item list. Figure 6 illustrates the effect of CloseDialog (and DisposDialog, described below).

CloseDialog releases only the areas marked ▦
DisposDialog releases the areas marked ▦ and ▒

If you created the dialog with NewDialog:

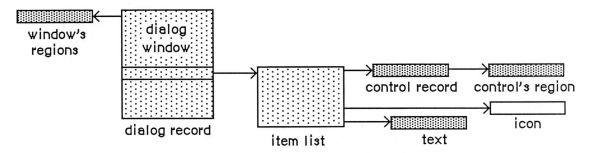

If you created the dialog with GetNewDialog:

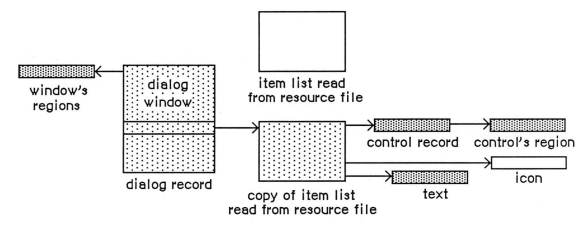

Figure 6. CloseDialog and DisposDialog

Call CloseDialog when you're done with a dialog if you supplied NewDialog or GetNewDialog with a pointer to the dialog storage (in the dStorage parameter) when you created the dialog.

Note: Even if you didn't supply a pointer to the dialog storage, you may want to call CloseDialog if you created the dialog with NewDialog. You would call CloseDialog if you wanted to keep the item list around (since, unlike GetNewDialog, NewDialog does not use a copy of the item list).

```
PROCEDURE DisposDialog (theDialog: DialogPtr);
```

DisposDialog calls CloseDialog (above) and then releases the memory occupied by the dialog's item list and dialog record. Call DisposDialog when you're done with a dialog if you let the dialog record be allocated in the heap when you created the dialog (by passing NIL as the dStorage parameter to NewDialog or GetNewDialog).

```
PROCEDURE CouldDialog (dialogID: INTEGER);
```

CouldDialog makes the dialog template having the given resource ID unpurgeable (reading it into memory if it's not already there). It does the same for the dialog window's definition function, the dialog's item list resource, and any items defined as resources. This is useful if the dialog box may come up when the resource file isn't accessible, such as during a disk copy.

> **Warning:** CouldDialog assumes your dialogs use the system font; if you've changed the font with SetDAFont, calling CouldDialog doesn't make the font unpurgeable.

```
PROCEDURE FreeDialog (dialogID: INTEGER);
```

Given the resource ID of a dialog template previously specified in a call to CouldDialog, FreeDialog undoes the effect of CouldDialog (by making the resources purgeable). It should be called when there's no longer a need to keep the resources in memory.

Handling Dialog Events

```
PROCEDURE ModalDialog (filterProc: ProcPtr; VAR itemHit:
        INTEGER);
```

Call ModalDialog after creating a modal dialog and bringing up its window in the frontmost plane. ModalDialog repeatedly gets and handles events in the dialog's window; after handling an event involving an enabled dialog item, it returns with the item number in itemHit. Normally you'll then do whatever is appropriate as a response to an event in that item.

ModalDialog gets each event by calling the Toolbox Event Manager function GetNextEvent. If the event is a mouse-down event outside the content region of the dialog window, ModalDialog emits sound number 1 (which should be a single beep) and gets the next event; otherwise, it filters and handles the event as described below.

> **Note:** Once before getting each event, ModalDialog calls SystemTask, a Desk Manager procedure that must be called regularly so that desk accessories will work properly.

The filterProc parameter determines how events are filtered. If it's NIL, the standard filterProc function is executed; this causes ModalDialog to return 1 in itemHit if the Return key or Enter key is pressed. If filterProc isn't NIL, ModalDialog filters events by executing the function it points to. Your filterProc function should have three parameters and return a Boolean value. For example, this is how it would be declared if it were named MyFilter:

```
FUNCTION MyFilter (theDialog: DialogPtr; VAR theEvent: EventRecord;
        VAR itemHit: INTEGER) : BOOLEAN;
```

A function result of FALSE tells ModalDialog to go ahead and handle the event, which either can be sent through unchanged or can be changed to simulate a different event. A function result of TRUE tells ModalDialog to return immediately rather than handle the event; in this case, the filterProc function sets itemHit to the item number that ModalDialog should return.

> **Note:** If you want it to be consistent with the standard filterProc function, your function should at least check whether the Return key or Enter key was pressed and, if so, return 1 in itemHit and a function result of TRUE.

You can use the filterProc function, for example, to treat a typed character in a special way (such as ignore it, or make it have the same effect as another character or as clicking a button); in this case, the function would test for a key-down event with that character. As another example, suppose the dialog box contains a userItem whose procedure draws a clock with the current time displayed. The filterProc function can call that procedure and return FALSE without altering the current event.

> **Note:** ModalDialog calls GetNextEvent with a mask that excludes disk-inserted events. To receive disk-inserted events, your filterProc function can call GetNextEvent (or EventAvail) with a mask that accepts only that type of event.

ModalDialog handles the events for which the filterProc function returns FALSE as follows:

- In response to an activate or update event for the dialog window, ModalDialog activates or updates the window.

- If the mouse button is pressed in an editText item, ModalDialog responds to the mouse activity as appropriate (displaying an insertion point or selecting text). If a key-down event occurs and there's an editText item, text entry and editing are handled in the standard way for such items (except that if the Command key is down, ModalDialog responds as though it's not). In either case, ModalDialog returns if the editText item is enabled or does nothing if it's disabled. If a key-down event occurs when there's no editText item, ModalDialog does nothing.

- If the mouse button is pressed in a control, ModalDialog calls the Control Manager function TrackControl. If the mouse button is released inside the control and the control is enabled, ModalDialog returns; otherwise, it does nothing.

- If the mouse button is pressed in any other enabled item in the dialog box, ModalDialog returns. If the mouse button is pressed in any other disabled item or in no item, or if any other event occurs, ModalDialog does nothing.

```
FUNCTION IsDialogEvent (theEvent: EventRecord) : BOOLEAN;
```

If your application includes any modeless dialogs, call IsDialogEvent after calling the Toolbox Event Manager function GetNextEvent.

> **Warning:** If your modeless dialog contains any editText items, you must call IsDialogEvent (and then DialogSelect) even if GetNextEvent returns FALSE; otherwise your dialog won't receive null events and the caret won't blink.

Pass the current event in theEvent. IsDialogEvent determines whether theEvent needs to be handled as part of a dialog. If theEvent is an activate or update event for a dialog window, a mouse-down event in the content region of an active dialog window, or any other type of event when a dialog window is active, IsDialogEvent returns TRUE; otherwise, it returns FALSE.

When FALSE is returned, just handle the event yourself like any other event that's not dialog-related. When TRUE is returned, you'll generally end up passing the event to DialogSelect for it to handle (as described below), but first you should do some additional checking:

- DialogSelect doesn't handle keyboard equivalents of commands. Check whether the event is a key-down event with the Command key held down and, if so, carry out the command if it's one that applies when a dialog window is active. (If the command doesn't so apply, do nothing.)

- In special cases, you may want to bypass DialogSelect or do some preprocessing before calling it. If so, check for those events and respond accordingly. You would need to do this, for example, if the dialog is to respond to disk-inserted events.

For cases other than these, pass the event to DialogSelect for it to handle.

```
FUNCTION DialogSelect (theEvent: EventRecord; VAR theDialog:
        DialogPtr; VAR itemHit: INTEGER) : BOOLEAN;
```

You'll normally call DialogSelect when IsDialogEvent returns TRUE, passing in theEvent an event that needs to be handled as part of a modeless dialog. DialogSelect handles the event as described below. If the event involves an enabled dialog item, DialogSelect returns a function result of TRUE with the dialog pointer in theDialog and the item number in itemHit; otherwise, it returns FALSE with theDialog and itemHit undefined. Normally when DialogSelect returns TRUE, you'll do whatever is appropriate as a response to the event, and when it returns FALSE you'll do nothing.

If the event is an activate or update event for a dialog window, DialogSelect activates or updates the window and returns FALSE.

If the event is a mouse-down event in an editText item, DialogSelect responds as appropriate (displaying a caret at the insertion point or selecting text). If it's a key-down or auto-key event and there's an editText item, text entry and editing are handled in the standard way. In either case, DialogSelect returns TRUE if the editText item is enabled or FALSE if it's disabled. If a key-down or auto-key event is passed when there's no editText item, DialogSelect returns FALSE.

> **Note:** For a keyboard event, DialogSelect doesn't check to see whether the Command key is held down; to handle keyboard equivalents of commands, you have to check for them before calling DialogSelect. Similarly, to treat a typed character in a special way (such as ignore it, or make it have the same effect as another character or as clicking a button), you need to check for a key-down event with that character before calling DialogSelect.

If the event is a mouse-down event in a control, DialogSelect calls the Control Manager function TrackControl. If the mouse button is released inside the control and the control is enabled, DialogSelect returns TRUE; otherwise, it returns FALSE.

If the event is a mouse-down event in any other enabled item, DialogSelect returns TRUE. If it's a mouse-down event in any other disabled item or in no item, or if it's any other event, DialogSelect returns FALSE.

Note: If the event isn't one that DialogSelect specifically checks for (if it's a null event, for example), and there's an editText item in the dialog, DialogSelect calls the TextEdit procedure TEIdle to make the caret blink.

```
PROCEDURE DlgCut (theDialog: DialogPtr);    [Not in ROM]
```

DlgCut checks whether theDialog has any editText items and, if so, applies the TextEdit procedure TECut to the currently selected editText item. (If the dialog record's editField is 0 or greater, DlgCut passes the contents of the textH field to TECut.) You can call DlgCut to handle the editing command Cut when a modeless dialog window is active.

Assembly-language note: Assembly-language programmers can just read the dialog record's fields and call TextEdit directly.

```
PROCEDURE DlgCopy (theDialog: DialogPtr);    [Not in ROM]
```

DlgCopy is the same as DlgCut (above) except that it calls TECopy, for handling the Copy command.

```
PROCEDURE DlgPaste (theDialog: DialogPtr);    [Not in ROM]
```

DlgPaste is the same as DlgCut (above) except that it calls TEPaste, for handling the Paste command.

```
PROCEDURE DlgDelete (theDialog: DialogPtr);    [Not in ROM]
```

DlgDelete is the same as DlgCut (above) except that it calls TEDelete, for handling the Clear command.

```
PROCEDURE DrawDialog (theDialog: DialogPtr);
```

DrawDialog draws the contents of the given dialog box. Since DialogSelect and ModalDialog handle dialog window updating, this procedure is useful only in unusual situations. You would call it, for example, to display a dialog box that doesn't require any response but merely tells the user what's going on during a time-consuming process.

Invoking Alerts

```
FUNCTION Alert (alertID: INTEGER; filterProc: ProcPtr) : INTEGER;
```

This function invokes the alert defined by the alert template that has the given resource ID. It calls the current sound procedure, if any, passing it the sound number specified in the alert template for this stage of the alert. If no alert box is to be drawn at this stage, Alert returns a function result of –1; otherwise, it creates and displays the alert window for this alert and draws the alert box.

Warning: If the alert template resource can't be read, the function result is undefined.

Note: Alert creates the alert window by calling NewDialog, and does the rest of its processing by calling ModalDialog.

Alert repeatedly gets and handles events in the alert window until an enabled item is clicked, at which time it returns the item number. Normally you'll then do whatever is appropriate in response to a click of that item.

Alert gets each event by calling the Toolbox Event Manager function GetNextEvent. If the event is a mouse-down event outside the content region of the alert window, Alert emits sound number 1 (which should be a single beep) and gets the next event; otherwise, it filters and handles the event as described below.

The filterProc parameter has the same meaning as in ModalDialog (see above). If it's NIL, the standard filterProc function is executed, which makes the Return key or the Enter key have the same effect as clicking the default button. If you specify your own filterProc function and want to retain this feature, you must include it in your function. You can find out what the current default button is by looking at the aDefItem field of the dialog record for the alert (via the dialog pointer passed to the function).

Alert handles the events for which the filterProc function returns FALSE as follows:

- If the mouse button is pressed in a control, Alert calls the Control Manager procedure TrackControl. If the mouse button is released inside the control and the control is enabled, Alert returns; otherwise, it does nothing.

- If the mouse button is pressed in any other enabled item, Alert simply returns. If it's pressed in any other disabled item or in no item, or if any other event occurs, Alert does nothing.

Before returning to the application with the item number, Alert removes the alert box from the screen. (It disposes of the alert window and its associated data structures, the item list, and the items.)

Note: When an alert is removed, if it was overlapping the default button of a previous alert, that button's bold outline won't be redrawn.

Note: The Alert function's removal of the alert box would not be the desired result if the user clicked a check box or radio button; however, normally alerts contain only static text, icons, pictures, and buttons that are supposed to make the alert box go away. If your alert contains other items besides these, consider whether it might be more appropriate as a dialog.

```
FUNCTION StopAlert (alertID: INTEGER; filterProc: ProcPtr) :
        INTEGER;
```

StopAlert is the same as the Alert function (above) except that before drawing the items of the alert in the alert box, it draws the Stop icon in the top left corner of the box (within the rectangle (10,20)(42,52)). The Stop icon has the following resource ID:

```
CONST stopIcon = 0;
```

If the application's resource file doesn't include an icon with that ID number, the Dialog Manager uses the standard Stop icon in the system resource file (see Figure 7).

Stop   Note   Caution

Figure 7. Standard Alert Icons

```
FUNCTION NoteAlert (alertID: INTEGER; filterProc: ProcPtr) :
          INTEGER;
```

NoteAlert is like StopAlert except that it draws the Note icon, which has the following resource ID:

```
CONST noteIcon = 1;
```

```
FUNCTION CautionAlert (alertID: INTEGER; filterProc: ProcPtr) :
          INTEGER;
```

CautionAlert is like StopAlert except that it draws the Caution icon, which has the following resource ID:

```
CONST cautionIcon = 2;
```

```
PROCEDURE CouldAlert (alertID: INTEGER);
```

CouldAlert makes the alert template having the given resource ID unpurgeable (reading it into memory if it's not already there). It does the same for the alert window's definition function, the alert's item list resource, and any items defined as resources. This is useful if the alert may occur when the resource file isn't accessible, such as during a disk copy.

> **Warning:** Like CouldDialog, CouldAlert assumes your alerts use the system font; if you've changed the font with SetDAFont, calling CouldAlert doesn't make the font unpurgeable.

```
PROCEDURE FreeAlert (alertID: INTEGER);
```

Given the resource ID of an alert template previously specified in a call to CouldAlert, FreeAlert undoes the effect of CouldAlert (by making the resources purgeable). It should be called when there's no longer a need to keep the resources in memory.

Manipulating Items in Dialogs and Alerts

```
PROCEDURE ParamText (param0,param1,param2,param3: Str255);
```

ParamText provides a means of substituting text in statText items: param0 through param3 will replace the special strings '^0' through '^3' in all statText items in all subsequent dialog or alert boxes. Pass empty strings for parameters not used.

Assembly-language note: Assembly-language programmers may pass NIL for parameters not used or for strings that are not to be changed.

For example, if the text is defined as 'Cannot open document ^0' and docName is a string variable containing a document name that the user typed, you can call ParamText(docName,' ',' ',' ').

Note: All strings that may need to be translated to other languages should be stored in resource files.

Assembly-language note: The Dialog Manager stores handles to the four ParamText parameters in a global array named DAStrings.

```
PROCEDURE GetDItem (theDialog: DialogPtr; itemNo: INTEGER; VAR
            itemType: INTEGER; VAR item: Handle; VAR box: Rect);
```

GetDItem returns in its VAR parameters the following information about the item numbered itemNo in the given dialog's item list: In the itemType parameter, the item type; in the item parameter, a handle to the item (or, for item type userItem, the procedure pointer); and in the box parameter, the display rectangle for the item.

Suppose, for example, that you want to change the title of a control in a dialog box. You can get the item handle with GetDItem, coerce it to type ControlHandle, and call the Control Manager procedure SetCTitle to change the title. Similarly, to move the control or change its size, you would call MoveControl or SizeControl.

Note: To access the text of a statText or editText item, you can pass the handle returned by GetDItem to GetIText or SetIText (see below).

```
PROCEDURE SetDItem (theDialog: DialogPtr; itemNo: INTEGER;
            itemType: INTEGER; item: Handle; box: Rect);
```

SetDItem sets the item numbered itemNo in the given dialog's item list, as specified by the parameters (without drawing the item). The itemType parameter is the item type; the item parameter is a handle to the item (or, for item type userItem, the procedure pointer); and the box parameter is the display rectangle for the item.

Consider, for example, how to install an item of type userItem in a dialog: In the item list in the resource file, define an item in which the type is set to userItem and the display rectangle to

(0,0)(0,0). Specify that the dialog window be invisible (in either the dialog template or the NewDialog call). After creating the dialog, coerce the item's procedure pointer to type Handle; then call SetDItem, passing that handle and the display rectangle for the item. Finally, call the Window Manager procedure ShowWindow to display the dialog window.

Note: Do not use SetDItem to change the text of a statText or editText item or to change or move a control. See the description of GetDItem above for more information.

```
PROCEDURE GetIText (item: Handle; VAR text: Str255);
```

Given a handle to a statText or editText item in a dialog box, as returned by GetDItem, GetIText returns the text of the item in the text parameter. (If the user typed more than 255 characters in an editText item, GetIText returns only the first 255.)

```
PROCEDURE SetIText (item: Handle; text: Str255);
```

Given a handle to a statText or editText item in a dialog box, as returned by GetDItem, SetIText sets the text of the item to the specified text and draws the item. For example, suppose the exact content of a dialog's text item cannot be determined until the application is running, but the display rectangle is defined in the resource file: Call GetDItem to get a handle to the item, and call SetIText with the desired text.

```
PROCEDURE SelIText (theDialog: DialogPtr; itemNo: INTEGER;
          strtSel,endSel: INTEGER);
```

Given a pointer to a dialog and the item number of an editText item in the dialog box, SelIText does the following:

- If the item contains text, SelIText sets the selection range to extend from character position strtSel up to but not including character position endSel. The selection range is inverted unless strtSel equals endSel, in which case a blinking vertical bar is displayed to indicate an insertion point at that position.

- If the item doesn't contain text, SelIText simply displays the insertion point.

For example, if the user makes an unacceptable entry in the editText item, the application can put up an alert box reporting the problem and then select the entire text of the item so it can be replaced by a new entry. (Without this procedure, the user would have to select the item before making the new entry.)

Note: You can select the entire text by specifying 0 for strtSel and 32767 for endSel. For details about selection range and character position, see chapter 12.

```
FUNCTION GetAlrtStage : INTEGER;    [Not in ROM]
```

GetAlrtStage returns the stage of the last occurrence of an alert, as a number from 0 to 3.

> **Assembly-language note:** Assembly-language programmers can get this number by accessing the global variable ACount. In addition, the global variable ANumber contains the resource ID of the alert template of the last alert that occurred.

PROCEDURE ResetAlrtStage;   [Not in ROM]

ResetAlrtStage resets the stage of the last occurrence of an alert so that the next occurrence of that same alert will be treated as its first stage. This is useful, for example, when you've used ParamText to change the text of an alert such that from the user's point of view it's a different alert.

> **Assembly-language note:** Assembly-language programmers can set the global variable ACount to –1 for the same effect.

MODIFYING TEMPLATES IN MEMORY

When you call GetNewDialog or one of the routines that invokes an alert, the Dialog Manager calls the Resource Manager to read the dialog or alert template from the resource file and return a handle to it. If the template is already in memory, the Resource Manager just returns a handle to it. If you want, you can call the Resource Manager yourself to read the template into memory (and make it unpurgeable), and then make changes to it before calling the dialog or alert routine. When called by the Dialog Manager, the Resource Manager will return a handle to the template as you modified it.

To modify a template in memory, you need to know its exact structure and the data type of the handle through which it may be accessed. These are discussed below for dialogs and alerts.

Dialog Templates in Memory

The data structure of a dialog template is as follows:

```
TYPE DialogTemplate =
            RECORD
                boundsRect:   Rect;       {becomes window's portRect}
                procID:       INTEGER;    {window definiton ID}
                visible:      BOOLEAN;    {TRUE if visible}
                filler1:      BOOLEAN;    {not used}
                goAwayFlag:   BOOLEAN;    {TRUE if has go-away region}
                filler2:      BOOLEAN;    {not used}
                refCon:       LONGINT;    {window's reference value}
                itemsID:      INTEGER;    {resource ID of item list}
                title:        Str255      {window's title}
            END;
```

The filler1 and filler2 fields are there because for historical reasons the goAwayFlag and refCon fields have to begin on a word boundary. The itemsID field contains the resource ID of the dialog's item list. The other fields are the same as the parameters of the same name in the NewDialog function; they provide information about the dialog window.

You access the dialog template by converting the handle returned by the Resource Manager to a template handle:

```
TYPE DialogTHndl = ^DialogTPtr;
     DialogTPtr = ^DialogTemplate;
```

Alert Templates in Memory

The data structure of an alert template is as follows:

```
TYPE AlertTemplate =
          RECORD
              boundsRect: Rect;       {becomes window's portRect}
              itemsID:    INTEGER;    {resource ID of item list}
              stages:     StageList   {alert stage information}
          END;
```

BoundsRect is the rectangle that becomes the portRect of the window's grafPort. The itemsID field contains the resource ID of the item list for the alert.

The information in the stages field determines exactly what should happen at each stage of the alert. It's packed into a word that has the following structure:

```
TYPE StageList =
          PACKED RECORD
              boldItm4: 0..1;       {default button item number minus 1}
              boxDrwn4: BOOLEAN;    {TRUE if alert box to be drawn}
              sound4:   0..3        {sound number}
              boldItm3: 0..1;
              boxDrwn3: BOOLEAN;
              sound3:   0..3
              boldItm2: 0..1;
              boxDrwn2: BOOLEAN;
              sound2:   0..3
              boldItm1: 0..1;
              boxDrwn1: BOOLEAN;
              sound1:   0..3
          END;
```

Notice that the information is stored in reverse order—for the fourth stage first, and for the first stage last.

The boldItm field indicates which button should be the default button (and therefore boldly outlined in the alert box). If the first two items in the alert's item list are the OK button and the Cancel button, respectively, 0 will refer to the OK button and 1 to the Cancel button. The reason for this is that the value of boldItm plus 1 is interpreted as an item number, and normally items 1 and 2 are the OK and Cancel buttons, respectively. Whatever the item having the corresponding item number happens to be, a bold rounded-corner rectangle will be drawn outside its display rectangle.

> **Note:** When deciding where to place items in an alert box, be sure to allow room for any bold outlines that may be drawn.

The boxDrwn field is TRUE if the alert box is to be drawn.

The sound field specifies which sound should be emitted at this stage of the alert, with a number from 0 to 3 that's passed to the current sound procedure. You can call ErrorSound to specify your own sound procedure; if you don't, the standard sound procedure will be used (as described earlier in the "Alerts" section).

You access the alert template by converting the handle returned by the Resource Manager to a template handle:

```
TYPE  AlertTHndl = ^AlertTPtr;
      AlertTPtr  = ^AlertTemplate;
```

> **Assembly-language note:** Rather than offsets into the fields of the StageList data structure, there are masks for accessing the information stored for an alert stage in a stages word; they're listed in the summary at the end of this chapter.

FORMATS OF RESOURCES FOR DIALOGS AND ALERTS

Every dialog template, alert template, and item list must be stored in a resource file, as must any icons or QuickDraw pictures in item lists and any control templates for items of type ctrlItem+resCtrl. The exact formats of a dialog template, alert template, and item list in a resource file are given below. For icons and pictures, the resource type is 'ICON' or 'PICT' and the resource data is simply the icon or the picture. The format of a control template is discussed in chapter 10.

Dialog Templates in a Resource File

The resource type for a dialog template is 'DLOG', and the resource data has the same format as a dialog template in memory.

Number of bytes	Contents
8 bytes	Same as boundsRect parameter to NewDialog
2 bytes	Same as procID parameter to NewDialog
1 byte	Same as visible parameter to NewDialog
1 byte	Ignored
1 byte	Same as goAwayFlag parameter to NewDialog
1 byte	Ignored
4 bytes	Same as refCon parameter to NewDialog
2 bytes	Resource ID of item list
n bytes	Same as title parameter to NewDialog (1-byte length in bytes, followed by the characters of the title)

Alert Templates in a Resource File

The resource type for an alert template is 'ALRT', and the resource data has the same format as an alert template in memory.

Number of bytes	Contents
8 bytes	Rectangle enclosing alert window
2 bytes	Resource ID of item list
2 bytes	Four stages

The resource data ends with a word of information about stages. As shown in the example in Figure 8, there are four bits of stage information for each of the four stages, from the four low-order bits for the first stage to the four high-order bits for the fourth stage. Each set of four bits is as follows:

Number of bits	Contents
1 bit	Item number minus 1 of default button; normally 0 is OK and 1 is Cancel
1 bit	1 if alert box is to be drawn, 0 if not
2 bits	Sound number (0 through 3)

Note: So that the disk won't be accessed just for an alert that beeps, you may want to set the resPreload attribute of the alert's template in the resource file. For more information, see chapter 5.

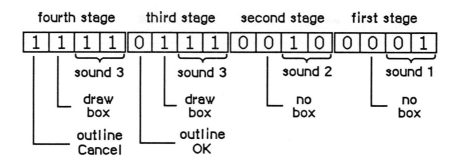

(value: hexadecimal F721)

Figure 8. Sample Stages Word

Item Lists in a Resource File

The resource type for an item list is 'DITL'. The resource data has the following format:

Number of bytes	Contents	
2 bytes	Number of items in list minus 1	
For each item:		
4 bytes	0 (placeholder for handle or procedure pointer)	
8 bytes	Display rectangle (local coordinates)	
1 byte	Item type	
1 byte	Length of following data in bytes	
n bytes	If item type is:	Content is:
(n is even)	ctrlItem+resCtrl	Resource ID (length 2)
	any other ctrlItem	Title of the control
	statText, editText	The text
	iconItem, picItem	Resource ID (length 2)
	userItem	Empty (length 0)

As shown here, the first four bytes for each item serve as a placeholder for the item's handle or, for item type userItem, its procedure pointer; the handle or pointer is stored after the item list is read into memory. After the display rectangle and the item type, there's a byte that gives the length of the data that follows: For a text item, the data is the text itself; for an icon, picture, or control of type ctrlItem+resCtrl, it's the two-byte resource ID for the item; and for any other type of control, it's the title of the control. For userItems, no data is specified. When the data is text or a control title, the number of bytes it occupies must be even to ensure word alignment of the next item.

Note: The text in the item list can't be more than 240 characters long.

Assembly-language note: Offsets into the fields of an item list are available as global constants; they're listed in the summary.

SUMMARY OF THE DIALOG MANAGER

Constants

```
CONST { Item types }

        ctrlItem    = 4;    {add to following four constants}
        btnCtrl     = 0;    {standard button control}
        chkCtrl     = 1;    {standard check box control}
        radCtrl     = 2;    {standard radio button control}
        resCtrl     = 3;    {control defined in control template}
        statText    = 8;    {static text}
        editText    = 16;   {editable text (dialog only)}
        iconItem    = 32;   {icon}
        picItem     = 64;   {QuickDraw picture}
        userItem    = 0;    {application-defined item (dialog only)}
        itemDisable = 128;  {add to any of above to disable}

        { Item numbers of OK and Cancel buttons }

        ok      = 1;
        cancel  = 2;

        { Resource IDs of alert icons }

        stopIcon    = 0;
        noteIcon    = 1;
        cautionIcon = 2;
```

Data Types

```
TYPE DialogPtr  = WindowPtr;
     DialogPeek = ^DialogRecord;

     DialogRecord =
            RECORD
                window:     WindowRecord; {dialog window}
                items:      Handle;       {item list}
                textH:      TEHandle;     {current editText item}
                editField:  INTEGER;      {editText item number minus 1}
                editOpen:   INTEGER;      {used internally}
                aDefItem:   INTEGER       {default button item number}
            END;

     DialogTHndl = ^DialogTPtr;
     DialogTPtr  = ^DialogTemplate;
```

```
DialogTemplate  =
     RECORD
          boundsRect: Rect;        {becomes window's portRect}
          procID:     INTEGER;     {window definition ID}
          visible:    BOOLEAN;     {TRUE if visible}
          filler1:    BOOLEAN;     {not used}
          goAwayFlag: BOOLEAN;     {TRUE if has go-away region}
          filler2:    BOOLEAN;     {not used}
          refCon:     LONGINT;     {window's reference value}
          itemsID:    INTEGER;     {resource ID of item list}
          title:      Str255      {window's title}
     END;

AlertTHndl    = ^AlertTPtr;
AlertTPtr     = ^AlertTemplate;
AlertTemplate = RECORD
                     boundsRect: Rect;        {becomes window's portRect}
                     itemsID:    INTEGER;     {resource ID of item list}
                     stages:     StageList    {alert stage information}
                END:

StageList =  PACKED RECORD
                  boldItm4: 0..1;   {default button item number minus 1}
                  boxDrwn4: BOOLEAN;  {TRUE if alert box to be drawn}
                  sound4:   0..3      {sound number}
                  boldItm3: 0..1;
                  boxDrwn3: BOOLEAN;
                  sound3:   0..3
                  boldItm2: 0..1;
                  boxDrwn2: BOOLEAN;
                  sound2:   0..3
                  boldItm1: 0..1;
                  boxDrwn1: BOOLEAN;
                  sound1:   0..3
             END;
```

Routines

Initialization

```
PROCEDURE  InitDialogs   (resumeProc: ProcPtr);
PROCEDURE  ErrorSound    (soundProc: ProcPtr);
PROCEDURE  SetDAFont     (fontNum: INTEGER);   [Not in ROM]
```

Creating and Disposing of Dialogs

```
FUNCTION   NewDialog     (dStorage: Ptr; boundsRect: Rect; title: Str255;
                          visible: BOOLEAN; procID: INTEGER; behind:
                          WindowPtr; goAwayFlag: BOOLEAN; refCon: LONGINT;
                          items: Handle) : DialogPtr;
```

```
FUNCTION    GetNewDialog  (dialogID: INTEGER; dStorage: Ptr; behind:
                           WindowPtr) : DialogPtr;
PROCEDURE   CloseDialog   (theDialog: DialogPtr);
PROCEDURE   DisposDialog  (theDialog: DialogPtr);
PROCEDURE   CouldDialog   (dialogID: INTEGER);
PROCEDURE   FreeDialog    (dialogID: INTEGER);
```

Handling Dialog Events

```
PROCEDURE   ModalDialog    (filterProc: ProcPtr; VAR itemHit: INTEGER);
FUNCTION    IsDialogEvent  (theEvent: EventRecord) : BOOLEAN;
FUNCTION    DialogSelect   (theEvent: EventRecord; VAR theDialog:
                            DialogPtr; VAR itemHit: INTEGER) : BOOLEAN;
PROCEDURE   DlgCut         (theDialog: DialogPtr);   [Not in ROM]
PROCEDURE   DlgCopy        (theDialog: DialogPtr);   [Not in ROM]
PROCEDURE   DlgPaste       (theDialog: DialogPtr);   [Not in ROM]
PROCEDURE   DlgDelete      (theDialog: DialogPtr);   [Not in ROM]
PROCEDURE   DrawDialog     (theDialog: DialogPtr);
```

Invoking Alerts

```
FUNCTION    Alert         (alertID: INTEGER; filterProc: ProcPtr) : INTEGER;
FUNCTION    StopAlert     (alertID: INTEGER; filterProc: ProcPtr) : INTEGER;
FUNCTION    NoteAlert     (alertID: INTEGER; filterProc: ProcPtr) : INTEGER;
FUNCTION    CautionAlert  (alertID: INTEGER; filterProc: ProcPtr) : INTEGER;
PROCEDURE   CouldAlert    (alertID: INTEGER);
PROCEDURE   FreeAlert     (alertID: INTEGER);
```

Manipulating Items in Dialogs and Alerts

```
PROCEDURE   ParamText       (param0,param1,param2,param3: Str255);
PROCEDURE   GetDItem        (theDialog: DialogPtr; itemNo: INTEGER; VAR
                             itemType: INTEGER; VAR item: Handle; VAR box:
                             Rect);
PROCEDURE   SetDItem        (theDialog: DialogPtr; itemNo: INTEGER;
                             itemType: INTEGER; item: Handle; box: Rect);
PROCEDURE   GetIText        (item: Handle; VAR text: Str255);
PROCEDURE   SetIText        (item: Handle; text: Str255);
PROCEDURE   SelIText        (theDialog: DialogPtr; itemNo: INTEGER;
                             strtSel,endSel: INTEGER);
FUNCTION    GetAlrtStage :  INTEGER;    [Not in ROM]
PROCEDURE   ResetAlrtStage; [Not in ROM]
```

UserItem Procedure

```
PROCEDURE   MyItem (theWindow: WindowPtr; itemNo: INTEGER);
```

Sound Procedure

```
PROCEDURE MySound (soundNo: INTEGER);
```

FilterProc Function for Modal Dialogs and Alerts

```
FUNCTION MyFilter (theDialog: DialogPtr; VAR theEvent: EventRecord;
                   VAR itemHit: INTEGER) : BOOLEAN;
```

Assembly-Language Information

Constants

```
; Item types

ctrlItem      .EQU    4       ;add to following four constants
btnCtrl       .EQU    0       ;standard button control
chkCtrl       .EQU    1       ;standard check box control
radCtrl       .EQU    2       ;standard radio button control
resCtrl       .EQU    3       ;control defined in control template
statText      .EQU    8       ;static text
editText      .EQU    16      ;editable text (dialog only)
iconItem      .EQU    32      ;icon
picItem       .EQU    64      ;QuickDraw picture
userItem      .EQU    0       ;application-defined item (dialog only)
itemDisable   .EQU    128     ;add to any of above to disable

; Item numbers of OK and Cancel buttons

okButton      .EQU    1
cancelButton  .EQU    2

; Resource IDs of alert icons

stopIcon      .EQU    0
noteIcon      .EQU    1
cautionIcon   .EQU    2

; Masks for stages word in alert template

volBits       .EQU    3       ;sound number
alBit         .EQU    4       ;whether to draw box
okDismissal   .EQU    8       ;item number of default button minus 1
```

Dialog Record Data Structure

dWindow	Dialog window
items	Handle to dialog's item list
teHandle	Handle to current editText item
editField	Item number of editText item minus 1 (word)
aDefItem	Item number of default button (word)
dWindLen	Size in bytes of dialog record

Dialog Template Data Structure

dBounds	Rectangle that becomes portRect of dialog window's grafPort (8 bytes)
dWindProc	Window definition ID (word)
dVisible	Nonzero if dialog window is visible (word)
dGoAway	Nonzero if dialog window has a go-away region (word)
dRefCon	Dialog window's reference value (long)
dItems	Resource ID of dialog's item list (word)
dTitle	Dialog window's title (preceded by length byte)

Alert Template Data Structure

aBounds	Rectangle that becomes portRect of alert window's grafPort (8 bytes)
aItems	Resource ID of alert's item list (word)
aStages	Stages word; information for alert stages

Item List Data Structure

dlgMaxIndex	Number of items minus 1 (word)
itmHndl	Handle or procedure pointer for this item
itmRect	Display rectangle for this item (8 bytes)
itmType	Item type for this item (byte)
itmData	Length byte followed by data for this item (data must be even number of bytes)

Variables

ResumeProc	Address of resume procedure
DAStrings	Handles to ParamText strings (16 bytes)
DABeeper	Address of current sound procedure
DlgFont	Font number for dialogs and alerts (word)
ACount	Stage number (0 through 3) of last alert (word)
ANumber	Resource ID of last alert (word)

14 THE DESK MANAGER

14 Desk Manager

ABOUT THIS CHAPTER

This chapter describes the Desk Manager, the part of the Toolbox that supports the use of desk accessories from an application; the Calculator, for example, is a standard desk accessory available to any application. You'll learn how to use the Desk Manager routines and how to write your own accessories.

You should already be familiar with:

- the basic concepts behind the Resource Manager and QuickDraw

- the Toolbox Event Manager, the Window Manager, the Menu Manager, and the Dialog Manager

- device drivers, as discussed in chapter 6 in Volume II, if you want to write your own desk accessories

ABOUT THE DESK MANAGER

The Desk Manager enables your application to support **desk accessories**, which are "mini-applications" that can be run at the same time as a Macintosh application. There are a number of standard desk accessories, such as the Calculator shown in Figure 1. You can also write your own desk accessories if you wish.

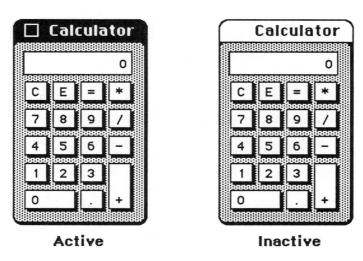

Figure 1. The Calculator Desk Accessory

The Macintosh user opens desk accessories by choosing them from the standard Apple menu (whose title is an apple symbol), which by convention is the first menu in the menu bar. When a desk accessory is chosen from this menu, it's usually displayed in a window on the desktop, and that window becomes the active window (see Figure 2).

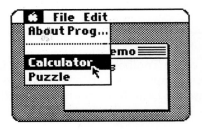
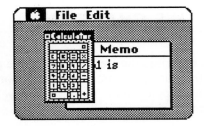

An accessory is chosen
from the Apple menu.

The accessory's window
appears as the active
window.

Figure 2. Opening a Desk Accessory

After being opened, the accessory may be used as long as it's active. The user can activate other windows and then reactivate the desk accessory by clicking inside it. Whenever a standard desk accessory is active, it has a close box in its title bar. Clicking the close box (or choosing Close from the File menu) makes the accessory disappear, and the window that's then frontmost becomes active.

The window associated with a desk accessory is usually a rounded-corner window (as shown in Figure 1) or a standard document window, although it can be any type of window. It may even look and behave like a dialog window; the accessory can call on the Dialog Manager to create the window and then use Dialog Manager routines to operate on it. In any case, the window will be a system window, as indicated by the fact that its windowKind field contains a negative value.

The Desk Manager provides a mechanism that lets standard commands chosen from the Edit menu be applied to a desk accessory when it's active. Even if the commands aren't particularly useful for editing within the accessory, they may be useful for cutting and pasting between the accessory and the application or even another accessory. For example, the result of a calculation made with the Calculator can be copied and pasted into a document prepared in MacWrite.

A desk accessory may also have its own menu. When the accessory becomes active, the title of its menu is added to the menu bar and menu items may be chosen from it. Any of the application's menus or menu items that no longer apply are disabled. A desk accessory can even have an entire menu bar full of its own menus, which will completely replace the menus already in the menu bar. When an accessory that has its own menu or menus becomes inactive, the menu bar is restored to normal.

Although desk accessories are usually displayed in windows (one per accessory); it's possible for an accessory to have only a menu (or menus) and not a window. In this case, the menu includes a command to close the accessory. Also, a desk accessory that's displayed in a window may create any number of additional windows while it's open.

A desk accessory is actually a special type of device driver—special in that it may have its own windows and menus for interacting with the user. The value in the windowKind field of a desk accessory's window is a reference number that uniquely identifies the driver, returned by the Device Manager when the driver was opened. Desk accessories and other RAM drivers used by Macintosh applications are stored in resource files.

USING THE DESK MANAGER

To allow access to desk accessories, your application must do the following:

- Initialize TextEdit and the Dialog Manager, in case any desk accessories are displayed in windows created by the Dialog Manager (which uses TextEdit).

- Set up the Apple menu as the first menu in the menu bar. You can put the names of all currently available desk accessories in a menu by using the Menu Manager procedure AddResMenu.

- Set up an Edit menu that includes the standard commands Undo, Cut, Copy, Paste, and Clear (in that order, with a dividing line between Undo and Cut), even if your application itself doesn't support any of these commands.

Note: Applications should leave enough space in the menu bar for a desk accessory's menu to be added.

When the user chooses a desk accessory from the Apple menu, call the Menu Manager procedure GetItem to get the name of the desk accessory, and then the Desk Manager function OpenDeskAcc to open and display the accessory. When a system window is active and the user chooses Close from the File menu, close the desk accessory with the CloseDeskAcc procedure.

Warning: Most open desk accessories allocate nonrelocatable objects (such as windows) in the heap, resulting in fragmentation of heap space. Before beginning an operation that requires a large amount of memory, your application may want to close all open desk accessories (or allow the user to close some of them).

When the Toolbox Event Manager function GetNextEvent reports that a mouse-down event has occurred, your application should call the Window Manager function FindWindow to find out where the mouse button was pressed. If FindWindow returns the predefined constant inSysWindow, which means that the mouse button was pressed in a system window, call the Desk Manager procedure SystemClick. SystemClick handles mouse-down events in system windows, routing them to desk accessories where appropriate.

Note: The application needn't be concerned with exactly which desk accessories are currently open.

When the active window changes from an application window to a system window, the application should disable any of its menus or menu items that don't apply while an accessory is active, and it should enable the standard editing commands Undo, Cut, Copy, Paste, and Clear, in the Edit menu. An application should disable any editing commands it doesn't support when one of its own windows becomes active.

When a mouse-down event occurs in the menu bar, and the application determines that one of the five standard editing commands has been invoked, it should call SystemEdit. Only if SystemEdit returns FALSE should the application process the editing command itself; if the active window belongs to a desk accessory, SystemEdit passes the editing command on to that accessory and returns TRUE.

Keyboard equivalents of the standard editing commands are passed on to desk accessories by the Desk Manager, not by your application.

14 Desk Manager

Warning: The standard keyboard equivalents for the commands in the Edit menu must not be changed or assigned to other commands; the Desk Manager automatically interprets Command-Z, X, C, and V as Undo, Cut, Copy, and Paste, respectively.

Certain periodic actions may be defined for desk accessories. To see that they're performed, you need to call the SystemTask procedure at least once every time through your main event loop.

The two remaining Desk Manager routines—SystemEvent and SystemMenu—are never called by the application, but are described in this chapter because they reveal inner mechanisms of the Toolbox that may be of interest to advanced programmers.

DESK MANAGER ROUTINES

Opening and Closing Desk Accessories

```
FUNCTION OpenDeskAcc (theAcc: Str255) : INTEGER;
```

OpenDeskAcc opens the desk accessory having the given name and displays its window (if any) as the active window. The name is the accessory's resource name, which you get from the Apple menu by calling the Menu Manager procedure GetItem. OpenDeskAcc calls the Resource Manager to read the desk accessory from the resource file into the application heap.

You should ignore the value returned by OpenDeskAcc. If the desk accessory is successfully opened, the function result is its driver reference number. However, if the desk accessory can't be opened, the function result is undefined; the accessory will have taken care of informing the user of the problem (such as memory full) and won't display itself.

Warning: Early versions of some desk accessories may set the current grafPort to the accessory's port upon return from OpenDeskAcc. To be safe, you should bracket your call to OpenDeskAcc with calls to the QuickDraw procedures GetPort and SetPort, to save and restore the current port.

Note: Programmers concerned about the amount of available memory should be aware that an open desk accessory uses from 1K to 3K bytes of heap space in addition to the space needed for the accessory itself. The desk accessory is responsible for determining whether there is sufficient memory for it to run; this can be done by calling SizeResource followed by ResrvMem.

```
PROCEDURE CloseDeskAcc (refNum: INTEGER);
```

When a system window is active and the user chooses Close from the File menu, call CloseDeskAcc to close the desk accessory. RefNum is the driver reference number for the desk accessory, which you get from the windowKind field of its window.

The Desk Manager automatically closes a desk accessory if the user clicks its close box. Also, since the application heap is released when the application terminates, every desk accessory goes away at that time.

Handling Events in Desk Accessories

```
PROCEDURE SystemClick (theEvent: EventRecord; theWindow:
          WindowPtr);
```

When a mouse-down event occurs and the Window Manager function FindWindow reports that the mouse button was pressed in a system window, the application should call SystemClick with the event record and the window pointer. If the given window belongs to a desk accessory, SystemClick sees that the event gets handled properly.

SystemClick determines which part of the desk accessory's window the mouse button was pressed in, and responds accordingly (similar to the way your application responds to mouse activities in its own windows).

■ If the mouse button was pressed in the content region of the window and the window was active, SystemClick sends the mouse-down event to the desk accessory, which processes it as appropriate.

■ If the mouse button was pressed in the content region and the window was inactive, SystemClick makes it the active window.

■ If the mouse button was pressed in the drag region, SystemClick calls the Window Manager procedure DragWindow to pull an outline of the window across the screen and move the window to a new location. If the window was inactive, DragWindow also makes it the active window (unless the Command key was pressed along with the mouse button).

■ If the mouse button was pressed in the go-away region, SystemClick calls the Window Manager function TrackGoAway to determine whether the mouse is still inside the go-away region when the click is completed: If so, it tells the desk accessory to close itself; otherwise, it does nothing.

```
FUNCTION SystemEdit (editCmd: INTEGER) : BOOLEAN;
```

Assembly-language note: The macro you invoke to call SystemEdit from assembly language is named _SysEdit.

Call SystemEdit when there's a mouse-down event in the menu bar and the user chooses one of the five standard editing commands from the Edit menu. Pass one of the following as the value of the editCmd parameter:

editCmd	Editing command
0	Undo
2	Cut
3	Copy
4	Paste
5	Clear

If your Edit menu contains these five commands in the standard arrangement (the order listed above, with a dividing line between Undo and Cut), you can simply call

```
SystemEdit(menuItem-1)
```

where menuItem is the menu item number.

If the active window doesn't belong to a desk accessory, SystemEdit returns FALSE; the application should then process the editing command as usual. If the active window does belong to a desk accessory, SystemEdit asks that accessory to process the command and returns TRUE; in this case, the application should ignore the command.

> **Note:** It's up to the application to make sure desk accessories get their editing commands that are chosen from the Edit menu. In particular, make sure your application hasn't disabled the Edit menu or any of the five standard commands when a desk accessory is activated.

Performing Periodic Actions

```
PROCEDURE SystemTask;
```

For each open desk accessory (or other device driver performing periodic actions), SystemTask causes the accessory to perform the periodic action defined for it, if any such action has been defined and if the proper time period has passed since the action was last performed. For example, a clock accessory can be defined such that the second hand is to move once every second; the periodic action for the accessory will be to move the second hand to the next position, and SystemTask will alert the accessory every second to perform that action.

You should call SystemTask as often as possible, usually once every time through your main event loop. Call it more than once if your application does an unusually large amount of processing each time through the loop.

> **Note:** SystemTask should be called at least every sixtieth of a second.

Advanced Routines

```
FUNCTION SystemEvent (theEvent: EventRecord) : BOOLEAN;
```

SystemEvent is called only by the Toolbox Event Manager function GetNextEvent when it receives an event, to determine whether the event should be handled by the application or by the system. If the given event should be handled by the application, SystemEvent returns FALSE; otherwise, it calls the appropriate system code to handle the event and returns TRUE.

In the case of a null or mouse-down event, SystemEvent does nothing but return FALSE. Notice that it responds this way to a mouse-down event even though the event may in fact have occurred in a system window (and therefore may have to be handled by the system). The reason for this is that the check for exactly where the event occurred (via the Window Manager function FindWindow) is made later by the application and so would be made twice if SystemEvent were also to do it. To avoid this duplication, SystemEvent passes the event on to the application and lets it make the sole call to FindWindow. Should FindWindow reveal that the mouse-down event did occur in a system window, the application can then call SystemClick, as described above, to get the system to handle it.

If the given event is a mouse-up or any keyboard event (including keyboard equivalents of commands), SystemEvent checks whether the active window belongs to a desk accessory and whether that accessory can handle this type of event. If so, it sends the event to the desk accessory and returns TRUE; otherwise, it returns FALSE.

If SystemEvent is passed an activate or update event, it checks whether the window the event occurred in is a system window belonging to a desk accessory and whether that accessory can handle this type of event. If so, it sends the event to the desk accessory and returns TRUE; otherwise, it returns FALSE.

> **Note:** It's unlikely that a desk accessory would *not* be set up to handle keyboard, activate, and update events, or that it *would* handle mouse-up events.

> If the given event is a disk-inserted event, SystemEvent does some low-level processing (by calling the File Manager function MountVol) but passes the event on to the application by returning FALSE, in case the application wants to do further processing.
> Finally, SystemEvent returns FALSE for network, dvice driver, and application-defined events.

Assembly-language note: Advanced programmers can make SystemEvent always return FALSE by setting the global variable SEvtEnb (a byte) to 0.

```
PROCEDURE SystemMenu (menuResult: LONGINT);
```

SystemMenu is called only by the Menu Manager functions MenuSelect and MenuKey, when an item in a menu belonging to a desk accessory has been chosen. The menuResult parameter has the same format as the value returned by MenuSelect and MenuKey: the menu ID in the high-order word and the menu item number in the low-order word. (The menu ID will be negative.) SystemMenu directs the desk accessory to perform the appropriate action for the given menu item.

WRITING YOUR OWN DESK ACCESSORIES

To write your own desk accessory, you must create it as a device driver and include it in a resource file, as described in chapter 6 of Volume II. Standard or shared desk accessories are stored in the system resource file. Accessories specific to an application are rare; if there are any, they're stored in the application's resource file.

The resource type for a device driver is 'DRVR'. The resource ID for a desk accessory is the driver's unit number and must be between 12 and 31 inclusive.

> **Note:** A desk accessory will often have additional resources (such as pattern and string resources) that are associated with it. These resources *must* observe a special numbering convention, as described in chapter 5.

The resource name should be whatever you want to appear in the Apple menu, but should also include a nonprinting character; by convention, the name should begin with a NUL character (ASCII code 0). The nonprinting character is needed to avoid conflict with file names that are the same as the names of desk accessories.

Device drivers are usually written in assembly language. The structure of a device driver is described in chapter 6 of Volume II. The rest of this section reviews some of that information and presents additional details pertaining specifically to device drivers that are desk accessories.

As shown in Figure 3, a device driver begins with a few words of flags and other data, followed by offsets to the routines that do the work of the driver, an optional title, and finally the routines themselves.

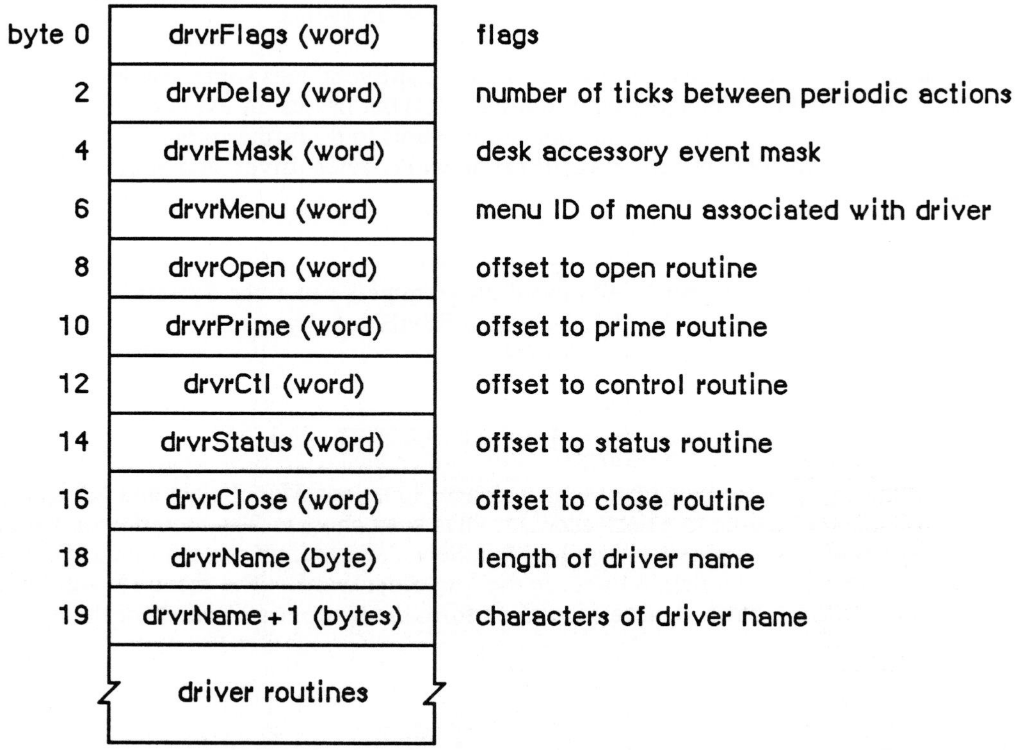

byte 0	drvrFlags (word)	flags
2	drvrDelay (word)	number of ticks between periodic actions
4	drvrEMask (word)	desk accessory event mask
6	drvrMenu (word)	menu ID of menu associated with driver
8	drvrOpen (word)	offset to open routine
10	drvrPrime (word)	offset to prime routine
12	drvrCtl (word)	offset to control routine
14	drvrStatus (word)	offset to status routine
16	drvrClose (word)	offset to close routine
18	drvrName (byte)	length of driver name
19	drvrName + 1 (bytes)	characters of driver name
	driver routines	

Figure 3. Desk Accessory Device Driver

One bit in the high-order byte of the drvrFlags word is frequently used by desk accessories:

```
dNeedTime   .EQU    5       ;set if driver needs time for performing a
                            ; periodic action
```

Desk accessories may need to perform predefined actions periodically. For example, a clock desk accessory may want to change the time it displays every second. If the dNeedTime flag is set, the desk accessory does need to perform a periodic action, and the drvrDelay word contains a tick count indicating how often the periodic action should occur. Whether the action actually occurs as frequently as specified depends on how often the application calls the Desk Manager procedure SystemTask. SystemTask calls the desk accessory's control routine (if the time indicated by drvrDelay has elapsed), and the control routine must perform whatever predefined action is desired.

> **Note:** A desk accessory cannot rely on SystemTask being called regularly or frequently by an application. If it needs precise timing it should install a task to be executed during the vertical retrace interrupt. There are, however, certain restrictions on tasks performed during interrupts, such as not being able to make calls to the Memory Manager. For more information on these restrictions, see chapter 11 of Volume II. Periodic actions performed in response to SystemTask calls are not performed via an interrupt and so don't have these restrictions.

The drvrEMask word contains an event mask specifying which events the desk accessory can handle. If the accessory has a window, the mask should include keyboard, activate, update, and mouse-down events, but must *not* include mouse-up events.

> **Note:** The accessory may not be interested in keyboard input, but it should still respond to key-down and auto-key events, at least with a beep.

When an event occurs, the Toolbox Event Manager calls SystemEvent. SystemEvent checks the drvrEMask word to determine whether the desk accessory can handle the type of event, and if so, calls the desk accessory's control routine. The control routine must perform whatever action is desired.

If the desk accessory has its own menu (or menus), the drvrMenu word contains the menu ID of the menu (or of any one of the menus); otherwise, it contains 0. The menu ID for a desk accessory menu must be negative, and it must be different from the menu ID stored in other desk accessories.

Following these four words are the offsets to the driver routines and, optionally, a title for the desk accessory (preceded by its length in bytes). You can use the title in the driver as the title of the accessory's window, or just as a way of identifying the driver in memory.

> **Note:** A practical size limit for desk accessories is about 8K bytes.

The Driver Routines

Of the five possible driver routines, only three need to exist for desk accessories: the open, close, and control routines. The other routines (prime and status) may be used if desired for a particular accessory.

The open routine opens the desk accessory:

- It creates the window to be displayed when the accessory is opened, if any, specifying that it be invisible (since OpenDeskAcc will display it). The window can be created with the Dialog Manager function GetNewDialog (or NewDialog) if desired; the accessory will look and respond like a dialog box, and subsequent operations may be performed on it with Dialog Manager routines. In any case, the open routine sets the windowKind field of the window record to the driver reference number for the desk accessory, which it gets from the device control entry. (The reference number will be negative.) It also stores the window pointer in the device control entry.

- If the driver has any private storage, it allocates the storage, stores a handle to it in the device control entry, and initializes any local variables. It might, for example, create a menu or menus for the accessory.

If the open routine is unable to complete all of the above tasks (if it runs out of memory, for example), it must do the following:

- Open only the minimum of data structures needed to run the desk accessory.

- Modify the code of every routine (except the close routine) so that the routine just returns (or beeps) when called.

- Modify the code of the close routine so that it disposes of only the minimum data structures that were opened.

- Display an alert indicating failure, such as "The Note Pad is not available".

The close routine closes the desk accessory, disposing of its window (if any) and all the data structures associated with it and replacing the window pointer in the device control entry with NIL. If the driver has any private storage, the close routine also disposes of that storage.

Warning: A driver's private storage shouldn't be in the system heap, because the application heap is reinitialized when an application terminates, and the driver is lost before it can dispose of its storage.

The action taken by the control routine depends on information passed in the parameter block pointed to by register A0. A message is passed in the csCode parameter; this message is simply a number that tells the routine what action to take. There are nine such messages:

```
accEvent     .EQU    64      ;handle a given event
accRun       .EQU    65      ;take the periodic action, if any, for
                             ; this desk accessory
accCursor    .EQU    66      ;change cursor shape if appropriate;
                             ; generate null event if window was
                             ; created by Dialog Manager
accMenu      .EQU    67      ;handle a given menu item
accUndo      .EQU    68      ;handle the Undo command
accCut       .EQU    70      ;handle the Cut command
accCopy      .EQU    71      ;handle the Copy command
accPaste     .EQU    72      ;handle the Paste command
accClear     .EQU    73      ;handle the Clear command
```

Note: As described in chapter 6 of Volume II, the control routine may also receive the message goodBye in the csCode parameter telling it when the heap is about to be reinitialized.

Along with the accEvent message, the control routine receives in the csParam field a pointer to an event record. The control routine must respond by handling the given event in whatever way is appropriate for this desk accessory. SystemClick and SystemEvent call the control routine with this message to send the driver an event that it should handle—for example, an activate event that makes the desk accessory active or inactive. When a desk accessory becomes active, its control routine might install a menu in the menu bar. If the accessory becoming active has more than one menu, the control routine should respond as follows:

- Store the accessory's unique menu ID in the global variable MBarEnable. (This is the negative menu ID in the device driver and the device control entry.)

- Call the Menu Manager routines GetMenuBar to save the current menu list and ClearMenuBar to clear the menu bar.

■ Install the accessory's own menus in the menu bar.

Then, when the desk accessory becomes inactive, the control routine should call SetMenuBar to restore the former menu list, call DrawMenuBar to draw the menu bar, and set MBarEnable to 0.

The accRun message tells the control routine to perform the periodic action for this desk accessory. For every open driver that has the dNeedTime flag set, the SystemTask procedure calls the control routine with this message if the proper time period has passed since the action was last performed.

The accCursor message makes it possible to change the shape of the cursor when it's inside an active desk accessory. SystemTask calls the control routine with this message as long as the desk accessory is active. The control routine should respond by checking whether the mouse location is in the desk accessory's window; if it is, it should set it to the standard arrow cursor (by calling the QuickDraw procedure InitCursor), just in case the application has changed the cursor and failed to reset it. Or, if desired, your accessory may give the cursor a special shape (by calling the QuickDraw procedure SetCursor).

If the desk accessory is displayed in a window created by the Dialog Manager, the control routine should respond to the accCursor message by generating a null event (storing the event code for a null event in an event record) and passing it to DialogSelect. This enables the Dialog Manager to blink the caret in editText items. In assembly language, the code might look like this:

```
CLR.L      -SP       ;event code for null event is 0
PEA        2(SP)     ;pass null event
CLR.L      -SP       ;pass NIL dialog pointer
CLR.L      -SP       ;pass NIL pointer
_DialogSelect        ;invoke DialogSelect
ADDQ.L     #4,SP     ;pop off result and null event
```

When the accMenu message is sent to the control routine, the following information is passed in the parameter block: csParam contains the menu ID of the desk accessory's menu and csParam+2 contains the menu item number. The control routine should take the appropriate action for when the given menu item is chosen from the menu, and then make the Menu Manager call HiliteMenu(0) to remove the highlighting from the menu bar.

Finally, the control routine should respond to one of the last five messages—accUndo through accClear—by processing the corresponding editing command in the desk accessory window if appropriate. SystemEdit calls the control routine with these messages. For information on cutting and pasting between a desk accessory and the application, or between two desk accessories, see chapter 15.

Warning: If the accessory opens a resource file, or otherwise changes which file is the current resource file, it should save and restore the previous current resource file, using the Resource Manager routines CurResFile and UseResFile. Similarly, the accessory should save and restore the port that was the current grafPort, using the QuickDraw routines GetPort and SetPort.

SUMMARY OF THE DESK MANAGER

Routines

Opening and Closing Desk Accessories

```
FUNCTION   OpenDeskAcc  (theAcc: Str255) : INTEGER;
PROCEDURE  CloseDeskAcc (refNum: INTEGER);
```

Handling Events in Desk Accessories

```
PROCEDURE  SystemClick (theEvent: EventRecord; theWindow: WindowPtr);
FUNCTION   SystemEdit  (editCmd: INTEGER) : BOOLEAN;
```

Performing Periodic Actions

```
PROCEDURE  SystemTask;
```

Advanced Routines

```
FUNCTION   SystemEvent (theEvent: EventRecord) : BOOLEAN;
PROCEDURE  SystemMenu  (menuResult: LONGINT);
```

Assembly-Language Information

Constants

```
; Desk accessory flag

dNeedTime      .EQU      5      ;set if driver needs time for performing a
                                ; periodic action

; Control routine messages

accEvent       .EQU      64     ;handle a given event
accRun         .EQU      65     ;take the periodic action, if any, for
                                ; this desk accessory
accCursor      .EQU      66     ;change cursor shape if appropriate;
                                ; generate null event if window was
                                ; created by Dialog Manager
accMenu        .EQU      67     ;handle a given menu item
accUndo        .EQU      68     ;handle the Undo command
```

```
accCut        .EQU      70      ;handle the Cut command
accCopy       .EQU      71      ;handle the Copy command
accPaste      .EQU      72      ;handle the Paste command
accClear      .EQU      73      ;handle the Clear command
```

Special Macro Names

Pascal name	Macro name
SystemEdit	_SysEdit

Variables

MBarEnable	Unique menu ID for active desk accessory, when menu bar belongs to the accessory (word)
SEvtEnb	0 if SystemEvent should return FALSE (byte)

15 THE SCRAP MANAGER

15 Scrap Manager

ABOUT THIS CHAPTER

This chapter describes the Scrap Manager, the part of the Toolbox that supports cutting and pasting among applications and desk accessories.

You should already be familiar with:

- resources, as discussed in chapter 5

- QuickDraw pictures

- the Toolbox Event Manager

ABOUT THE SCRAP MANAGER

The Scrap Manager is a set of routines and data types that let Macintosh applications support cutting and pasting using the **desk scrap**. The desk scrap is the vehicle for transferring data between two applications, between an application and a desk accessory, or between two desk accessories; it can also be used for transferring data that's cut and pasted within an application.

From the user's point of view, all data that's cut or copied resides in the Clipboard. The Cut command deletes data from a document and places it in the Clipboard; the Copy command copies data into the Clipboard without deleting it from the document. The next Paste command—whether applied to the same document or another, in the same application or another—inserts the contents of the Clipboard at a specified place. An application that supports cutting and pasting may also provide a Clipboard window for displaying the current contents of the scrap; it may show the Clipboard window at all times or only when requested via the toggled command Show (or Hide) Clipboard.

> **Note:** The Scrap Manager was designed to transfer *small* amounts of data; attempts to transfer very large amounts of data may fail due to lack of memory.

The nature of the data to be transferred varies according to the application. For example, in a word processor or in the Calculator desk accessory, the data is text; in a graphics application it's a picture. The amount of information retained about the data being transferred also varies. Between two text applications, text can be cut and pasted without any loss of information; however, if the user of a graphics application cuts a picture consisting of text and then pastes it into a word processor document, the text in the picture may not be editable in the word processor, or it may be editable but not look exactly the same as in the graphics application. The Scrap Manager allows for a variety of data types and provides a mechanism whereby applications have some control over how much information is retained when data is transferred.

The desk scrap is usually stored in memory, but can be stored on the disk (in the **scrap file**) if there's not enough room for it in memory. The scrap may remain on the disk throughout the use of the application, but must be read back into memory when the application terminates, since the user may then remove that disk and insert another. The Scrap Manager provides routines for writing the desk scrap to the disk and for reading it back into memory. The routines that access the scrap keep track of whether it's in memory or on the disk.

MEMORY AND THE DESK SCRAP

The desk scrap is initially located in the application heap; a handle to it is stored in low memory. When starting up an application, the Segment Loader temporarily moves the scrap out of the heap into the stack, reinitializes the heap, and puts the scrap back in the heap (see Figure 1). For a short time while it does this, two copies of the scrap exist in the memory allocated for the stack and the heap; for this reason, the desk scrap cannot be bigger than half that amount of memory.

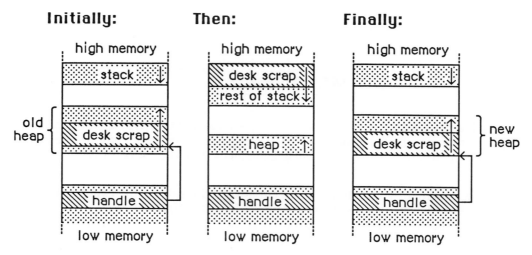

Figure 1. The Desk Scrap at Application Startup

The application can get the size of the desk scrap by calling a Scrap Manager function named InfoScrap. An application concerned about whether there's room for the desk scrap in memory could be set up so that a small initial segment of the application is loaded in just to check the scrap size. After a decision is made about whether to keep the scrap in memory or on the disk, the remaining segments of the application can be loaded in as needed.

There are certain disadvantages to keeping the desk scrap on the disk. The disk may be locked, it may not have enough room for the scrap, or it may be removed during use of the application. If the application can't write the scrap to the disk, it should put up an alert box informing the user, who may want to abort the operation at that point.

DESK SCRAP DATA TYPES

From the user's point of view there can be only one thing in the Clipboard at a time, but the application may store more than one version of the information in the scrap, each representing the same Clipboard contents in a different form. For example, text cut with a word processor may be stored in the desk scrap both as text and as a QuickDraw picture.

Desk scrap data types, like resource types, are a sequence of four characters. As defined in the Resource Manager, their Pascal type is as follows:

```
TYPE ResType = PACKED ARRAY[1..4] OF CHAR;
```

Two standard types of data are defined:

- 'TEXT': a series of ASCII characters

- 'PICT': a QuickDraw picture, which is a saved sequence of drawing commands that can be played back with the DrawPicture command and may include picture comments (see chapter 6 for details)

Applications must write at least one of these standard types of data to the desk scrap and must be able to read *both* types. Most applications will prefer one of these types over the other; for example, a word processor prefers text while a graphics application prefers pictures. An application should write at least its preferred standard type of data to the desk scrap, and may write both types (to pass the most information possible on to the receiving application, which may prefer the other type).

An application reading the desk scrap will look for its preferred data type. If its preferred type isn't there, or if it's there but was written by an application having a different preferred type, the receiving application may or may not be able to convert the data to the type it needs. If not, some information may be lost in the transfer process. For example, a graphics application can easily convert text to a picture, but the reverse isn't true. Figure 2 illustrates the latter case: A picture consisting of text is cut from a graphics application, then pasted into a word processor document.

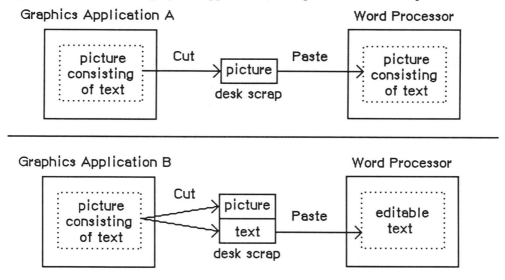

Figure 2. Inter-Application Cutting and Pasting

- If the graphics application writes only its preferred data type (picture) to the desk scrap—like application A in Figure 2—the text in the picture will not be editable in the word processor, because it will be seen as just a series of drawing commands and not as a sequence of characters.

- On the other hand, if the graphics application takes the trouble to recognize which characters have been drawn in the picture, and writes them out to the desk scrap both as a picture and as text—like application B in Figure 2—the word processor will be able to treat them as editable text. In this case, however, any part of the picture that isn't text will be lost.

In addition to the two standard data types, the desk scrap may also contain application-specific types of data. If several applications are to support the transfer of a private type of data, each one will write and read that type, but still must write at least one of the standard types and be able to read both standard types.

The order in which data is written to the desk scrap is important: The application should write out the different types in order of preference. For example, if it's a word processor that has a private type of data as its preferred type, but also can write text and pictures, it should write the data in that order.

Since the size of the desk scrap is limited, it may be too costly to write out both an application-specific data type and one (or both) of the standard types. Instead of creating your own type, if your data is graphic, you may be able to use the standard picture type and encode additional information in picture comments. (As described in chapter 6, picture comments may be stored in the definition of a picture with the QuickDraw procedure PicComment; they're passed by the DrawPicture procedure to a special routine set up by the application for that purpose.) Applications that are to process that information can do so, while others can ignore it.

USING THE SCRAP MANAGER

If you're concerned about memory use, call InfoScrap early in your program to find out the size of the desk scrap and decide whether there will be enough room in the heap for both the desk scrap and the application itself. If there won't be enough room for the scrap, call UnloadScrap to write the scrap from memory onto the disk.

InfoScrap also provides a handle to the desk scrap if it's in memory, its file name on the disk, and a count that changes when the contents of the desk scrap change. If your application supports display of the Clipboard, you can call InfoScrap each time through your main event loop to check this count: If the Clipboard window is visible, it needs to be updated whenever the count changes.

When a Cut or Copy command is given, you need to write the cut or copied data to the desk scrap. First call ZeroScrap to initialize the scrap or clear its previous contents, and then PutScrap to put the data into the scrap. (You can call PutScrap more than once, to put the data in the scrap in different forms.)

Call GetScrap when a Paste command is given, to access data of a particular type in the desk scrap and to get information about the data.

When the user gives a command that terminates the application, call LoadScrap to read the desk scrap back into memory if it's on the disk (in case the user ejects the disk).

> **Note:** ZeroScrap, PutScrap, and GetScrap all keep track of whether the scrap is in memory or on the disk, so you don't have to worry about it.

If your application uses TextEdit and the TextEdit scrap, you'll need to transfer data between the two scraps, as described in the section "Private Scraps", below.

SCRAP MANAGER ROUTINES

Most of these routines return a result code indicating whether an error occurred. If no error occurred, they return the result code

```
CONST noErr = 0;    {no error}
```

If an error occurred at the Operating System level, an Operating System result code is returned; otherwise, a Scrap Manager result code is returned, as indicated in the routine descriptions. (See Appendix A in Volume III for a list of all result codes.)

Getting Desk Scrap Information

```
FUNCTION InfoScrap : PScrapStuff;
```

InfoScrap returns a pointer to information about the desk scrap. The PScrapStuff data type is defined as follows:

```
TYPE  PScrapStuff = ^ScrapStuff;
      ScrapStuff  =
              RECORD
                scrapSize:    LONGINT;    {size of desk scrap}
                scrapHandle:  Handle;     {handle to desk scrap}
                scrapCount:   INTEGER;    {count changed by ZeroScrap}
                scrapState:   INTEGER;    {tells where desk scrap is}
                scrapName:    StringPtr   {scrap file name}
              END;
```

ScrapSize is the size of the desk scrap in bytes. ScrapHandle is a handle to the scrap if it's in memory, or NIL if not.

ScrapCount is a count that changes every time ZeroScrap is called. You can use this count for testing whether the contents of the desk scrap have changed, since if ZeroScrap has been called, presumably PutScrap was also called. This may be useful if your application supports display of the Clipboard or has a private scrap (as described under "Private Scraps", below).

Warning: Just check to see whether the value of the scrapCount field has changed; don't rely on exactly how it has changed.

ScrapState is positive if the desk scrap is in memory, 0 if it's on the disk, or negative if it hasn't been initialized by ZeroScrap.

Note: ScrapState is actually 0 if the scrap *should* be on the disk; for instance, if the user deletes the Clipboard file and then cuts something, the scrap is really in memory, but ScrapState will be 0.

ScrapName is a pointer to the name of the scrap file, usually "Clipboard File".

Note: InfoScrap assumes that the scrap file has a version number of 0 and is on the default volume. (Version numbers and volumes are described in chapter 4 of Volume II.)

Assembly-language note: The scrap information is available in global variables that have the same names as the Pascal fields.

Keeping the Desk Scrap on the Disk

```
FUNCTION UnloadScrap : LONGINT;
```

Assembly-language note: The macro you invoke to call UnloadScrap from assembly language is named _UnlodeScrap.

UnloadScrap writes the desk scrap from memory to the scrap file, and releases the memory it occupied. If the desk scrap is already on the disk, UnloadScrap does nothing. If no error occurs, UnloadScrap returns the result code noErr; otherwise, it returns an Operating System result code indicating an error.

```
FUNCTION LoadScrap : LONGINT;
```

Assembly-language note: The macro you invoke to call LoadScrap from assembly language is named _LodeScrap.

LoadScrap reads the desk scrap from the scrap file into memory. If the desk scrap is already in memory, it does nothing. If no error occurs, LoadScrap returns the result code noErr; otherwise, it returns an Operating System result code indicating an error.

Writing to the Desk Scrap

```
FUNCTION ZeroScrap : LONGINT;
```

If the scrap already exists (in memory or on the disk), ZeroScrap clears its contents; if not, the scrap is initialized in memory. You must call ZeroScrap before the first time you call PutScrap. If no error occurs, ZeroScrap returns the result code noErr; otherwise, it returns an Operating System result code indicating an error.

ZeroScrap also changes the scrapCount field of the record of information provided by InfoScrap.

```
FUNCTION PutScrap (length: LONGINT; theType: ResType; source: Ptr)
          : LONGINT;
```

PutScrap writes the data pointed to by the source parameter to the desk scrap (in memory or on the disk). The length parameter indicates the number of bytes to write, and theType is the data type.

> **Warning:** The specified type must be different from the type of any data already in the desk scrap. If you write data of a type already in the scrap, the new data will be appended to the scrap, and subsequent GetScrap calls will still return the old data.

If no error occurs, PutScrap returns the result code noErr; otherwise, it returns an Operating System result code indicating an error, or the following Scrap Manager result code:

```
CONST noScrapErr = -100;   {desk scrap isn't initialized}
```

> **Warning:** Don't forget to call ZeroScrap to initialize the scrap or clear its previous contents.

> **Note:** To copy the TextEdit scrap to the desk scrap, use the TextEdit function TEToScrap.

Reading from the Desk Scrap

```
FUNCTION GetScrap (hDest: Handle; theType: ResType; VAR offset:
          LONGINT) : LONGINT;
```

Given an existing handle in hDest, GetScrap reads the data of type theType from the desk scrap (whether in memory or on the disk), makes a copy of it in memory, and sets hDest to be a handle to the copy. Usually you'll pass in hDest a handle to a minimum-size block; GetScrap will resize the block and copy the scrap into it. If you pass NIL in hDest, GetScrap will not read in the data. This is useful if you want to be sure the data is there before allocating space for its handle, or if you just want to know the size of the data.

In the offset parameter, GetScrap returns the location of the data as an offset (in bytes) from the beginning of the desk scrap. If no error occurs, the function result is the length of the data in bytes; otherwise, it's either an appropriate Operating System result code (which will be negative) or the following Scrap Manager result code:

```
CONST noTypeErr = -102;   {no data of the requested type}
```

For example, given the declarations

```
VAR pHndl: Handle;     {handle for 'PICT' type}
    tHndl: Handle;     {handle for 'TEXT' type}
    length: LONGINT;
    offset: LONGINT;
    frame: Rect;
```

you can make the following calls:

```
pHndl := NewHandle(0);
length := GetScrap(pHndl,'PICT',offset);
IF length < 0
    THEN
        {error handling}
    ELSE DrawPicture(PicHandle(pHndl),frame)
```

If your application wants data in the form of a picture, and the scrap contains only text, you can convert the text into a picture by doing the following:

```
tHndl := NewHandle(0);
length := GetScrap(tHndl,'TEXT',offset);
IF length < 0
    THEN
        {error handling}
    ELSE
        BEGIN
        HLock(tHndl);
        pHndl := OpenPicture(thePort^.portRect);
        TextBox(tHndl^,length,thePort^.portRect,teJustLeft);
        ClosePicture;
        HUnlock(tHndl);
        END
```

The Memory Manager procedures HLock and HUnlock are used to lock and unlock blocks when handles are dereferenced (see chapter 1 of Volume II).

Note: To copy the desk scrap to the TextEdit scrap, use the TextEdit function TEFromScrap.

Your application should pass its preferred data type to GetScrap. If it doesn't prefer one data type over any other, it should try getting each of the types it can read, and use the type that returns the lowest offset. (A lower offset means that this data type was written before the others, and therefore was preferred by the application that wrote it.)

Note: If you're trying to read in a complicated picture, and there isn't enough room in memory for a copy of it, you can customize QuickDraw's picture retrieval so that DrawPicture will read the picture directly from the scrap file. (QuickDraw also lets you customize how pictures are saved so you can save them in a file; see chapter 6 for details about customizing.)

Note: When reading in a picture from the scrap, allow a buffer of about 3.5K bytes on the stack. (There's a convention that the application defining the picture won't call the QuickDraw procedure CopyBits for more than 3K, so 3.5K bytes should be large enough for any picture.)

PRIVATE SCRAPS

Instead of using the desk scrap for storing data that's cut and pasted within an application, advanced programmers may want to set up a private scrap for this purpose. In applications that use the standard 'TEXT' or 'PICT' data types, it's simpler to use the desk scrap, but if your application defines its own private type of data, or if it's likely that very large amounts of data will be cut and pasted, using a private scrap may result in faster cutting and pasting within the application.

The format of a private scrap can be whatever the application likes, since no other application will use it. For example, an application can simply maintain a pointer to data that's been cut or copied. The application must, however, be able to convert data between the format of its private scrap and the format of the desk scrap.

> **Note:** The TextEdit scrap is a private scrap for applications that use TextEdit. TextEdit provides routines for accessing this scrap; you'll need to transfer data between the TextEdit scrap and the desk scrap.

If you use a private scrap, you must be sure that the right data will always be pasted when the user gives a Paste command (the right data being whatever was most recently cut or copied in any application or desk accessory), and that the Clipboard, if visible, always shows the current data. You should copy the contents of the desk scrap to your private scrap at application startup and whenever a desk accessory is deactivated (call GetScrap to access the desk scrap). When the application is terminated or when a desk accessory is activated, you should copy the contents of the private scrap to the desk scrap: Call ZeroScrap to initialize the desk scrap or clear its previous contents, and PutScrap to write data to the desk scrap.

If transferring data between the two scraps means converting it, and possibly losing information, you can copy the scrap only when you actually need to, at the time something is cut or pasted. The desk scrap needn't be copied to the private scrap unless a Paste command is given before the first Cut or Copy command since the application started up or since a desk accessory that changed the scrap was deactivated. Until that point, you must keep the contents of the desk scrap intact, displaying it instead of the private scrap in the Clipboard window if that window is visible. Thereafter, you can ignore the desk scrap until a desk accessory is activated or the application is terminated; in either of these cases, you must copy the private scrap back to the desk scrap. Thus whatever was last cut or copied within the application will be pasted if a Paste command is given in a desk accessory or in the next application. If no Cut or Copy commands are given within the application, you never have to change the desk scrap.

To find out whether a desk accessory has changed the desk scrap, you can check the scrapCount field of the record returned by InfoScrap. Save the value of this field when one of your application's windows is deactivated and a system window is activated. Check each time through the main event loop to see whether its value has changed; if so, the contents of the desk scrap have changed.

If the application encounters problems in trying to copy one scrap to another, it should alert the user. The desk scrap may be too large to copy to the private scrap, in which case the user may want to leave the application or just proceed with an empty Clipboard. If the private scrap is too large to copy to the desk scrap, either because it's disk-based and too large to copy into memory or because it exceeds the maximum size allowed for the desk scrap, the user may want to stay in the application and cut or copy something smaller.

FORMAT OF THE DESK SCRAP

In general, the desk scrap consists of a series of data items that have the following format:

Number of bytes	Contents
4 bytes	Type (a sequence of four characters)
4 bytes	Length of following data in bytes
n bytes	Data; n must be even (if the above length is odd, add an extra byte)

The standard types are 'TEXT' and 'PICT'. You may use any other four-character sequence for types specific to your application.

The format of the data for the 'TEXT' type is as follows:

Number of bytes	Contents
4 bytes	Number of characters in the text
n bytes	The characters in the text

The data for the 'PICT' type is a QuickDraw picture, which consists of the size of the picture in bytes, the picture frame, and the picture definition data (which may include picture comments). See chapter 6 for details.

SUMMARY OF THE SCRAP MANAGER

Constants

```
CONST { Scrap Manager result codes }

        noScrapErr = -100;   {desk scrap isn't initialized}
        noTypeErr  = -102;   {no data of the requested type}
```

Data Types

```
TYPE PScrapStuff  = ^ScrapStuff;
     ScrapStuff   = RECORD
                        scrapSize:    LONGINT;    {size of desk scrap}
                        scrapHandle:  Handle;     {handle to desk scrap}
                        scrapCount:   INTEGER;    {count changed by ZeroScrap}
                        scrapState:   INTEGER;    {tells where desk scrap is}
                        scrapName:    StringPtr   {scrap file name}
                    END;
```

Routines

Getting Desk Scrap Information

```
FUNCTION InfoScrap : PScrapStuff;
```

Keeping the Desk Scrap on the Disk

```
FUNCTION UnloadScrap : LONGINT;
FUNCTION LoadScrap :   LONGINT;
```

Writing to the Desk Scrap

```
FUNCTION ZeroScrap : LONGINT;
FUNCTION PutScrap    (length: LONGINT; theType: ResType; source: Ptr) :
                    LONGINT;
```

Reading from the Desk Scrap

```
FUNCTION GetScrap (hDest: Handle; theType: ResType; VAR offset: LONGINT)
                : LONGINT;
```

Assembly-Language Information

Constants

```
; Scrap Manager result codes

noScrapErr      .EQU    -100    ;desk scrap isn't initialized
noTypeErr       .EQU    -102    ;no data of the requested type
```

Special Macro Names

Pascal name	Macro name
LoadScrap	_LodeScrap
UnloadScrap	_UnlodeScrap

Variables

ScrapSize	Size in bytes of desk scrap (long)
ScrapHandle	Handle to desk scrap in memory
ScrapCount	Count changed by ZeroScrap (word)
ScrapState	Tells where desk scrap is (word)
ScrapName	Pointer to scrap file name (preceded by length byte)

16 TOOLBOX UTILITIES

16 Toolbox Utilities

ABOUT THIS CHAPTER

This chapter describes the Toolbox Utilities, a set of routines and data types in the Toolbox that perform generally useful operations such as fixed-point arithmetic, string manipulation, and logical operations on bits.

Depending on which Toolbox Utilities you're interested in using, you may need to be familiar with:

- resources, as described in chapter 5
- the basic concepts and structures behind QuickDraw

TOOLBOX UTILITY ROUTINES

Fixed-Point Arithmetic

Fixed-point numbers are described in chapter 3. Note that fixed-point values can be added and subtracted as long integers.

In addition to the following routines, the HiWord and LoWord functions (described under "Other Operations on Long Integers" below) are useful when you're working with fixed-point numbers.

```
FUNCTION FixRatio (numer,denom: INTEGER) : Fixed;
```

FixRatio returns the fixed-point quotient of numer and denom. Numer or denom may be any signed integer. The result is truncated. If denom is 0, FixRatio returns $7FFFFFFF if numer is positive or $80000001 if numer is negative.

```
FUNCTION FixMul (a,b: Fixed) : Fixed;
```

FixMul returns the signed fixed-point product of a and b. The result is computed MOD 65536, truncated, and signed according to the signs of a and b.

```
FUNCTION FixRound (x: Fixed) : INTEGER;
```

Given a positive fixed-point number, FixRound rounds it to the nearest integer and returns the result. If the value is halfway between two integers (.5), it's rounded up.

> **Note:** To round a negative fixed-point number, negate it, round, then negate it again.

String Manipulation

```
FUNCTION NewString (theString: Str255) : StringHandle;
```

NewString allocates the specified string as a relocatable object in the heap and returns a handle to it.

> **Note:** NewString returns a handle to a string whose size is based on its actual length (not necessarily 255); if you're going to use Pascal string functions that could change the length of the string, you may want to call SetString or the Memory Manager procedure SetHandleSize first to set the string to the maximum size.

```
PROCEDURE SetString (h: StringHandle; theString: Str255);
```

SetString sets the string whose handle is passed in h to the string specified by theString.

```
FUNCTION GetString (stringID: INTEGER) : StringHandle;
```

GetString returns a handle to the string having the given resource ID, reading it from the resource file if necessary. It calls the Resource Manager function GetResource('STR ',stringID). If the resource can't be read, GetString returns NIL.

> **Note:** Like NewString, GetString returns a handle to a string whose size is based on its actual length.

> **Note:** If your application uses a large number of strings, storing them in a string list in the resource file will be more efficient. You can access strings in a string list with GetIndString, as described below.

```
PROCEDURE GetIndString (VAR theString: Str255; strListID:
        INTEGER; index: INTEGER);   [Not in ROM]
```

GetIndString returns in theString a string in the string list that has the resource ID strListID. It reads the string list from the resource file if necessary, by calling the Resource Manager function GetResource('STR#',strListID). It returns the string specified by the index parameter, which can range from 1 to the number of strings in the list. If the resource can't be read or the index is out of range, the empty string is returned.

Byte Manipulation

```
FUNCTION Munger (h: Handle; offset: LONGINT; ptr1: Ptr; len1:
        LONGINT; ptr2: Ptr; len2: LONGINT) : LONGINT;
```

Munger (which rhymes with "plunger") lets you manipulate bytes in the string of bytes (the "destination string") to which h is a handle. The operation starts at the specified byte offset in the destination string.

Note: Although the term "string" is used here, Munger does *not* assume it's manipulating a Pascal string; if you pass it a handle to a Pascal string, you must take into account the length byte.

The exact nature of the operation done by Munger depends on the values you pass it in two pointer/length parameter pairs. In general, (ptr1,len1) defines a target string to be replaced by the second string (ptr2,len2). If these four parameters are all positive and nonzero, Munger looks for the target string in the destination string, starting from the given offset and ending at the end of the string; it replaces the first occurrence it finds with the replacement string and returns the offset of the first byte past where the replacement occurred. Figure 1 illustrates this; the bytes represent ASCII characters as shown.

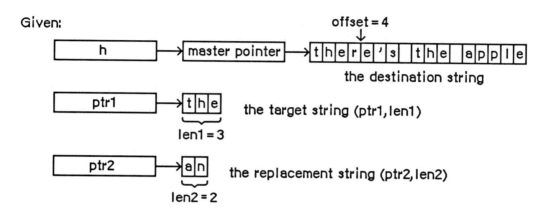

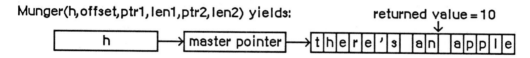

Figure 1. Munger Function

Different operations occur if either pointer is NIL or either length is 0:

- If ptr1 is NIL, the substring of length len1 starting at the given offset is replaced by the replacement string. If len1 is negative, the substring from the given offset to the end of the destination string is replaced by the replacement string. In either case, Munger returns the offset of the first byte past where the replacement occurred.

- If len1 is 0, (ptr2,len2) is simply inserted at the given offset; no text is replaced. Munger returns the offset of the first byte past where the insertion occurred.

- If ptr2 is NIL, Munger returns the offset at which the target string was found. The destination string isn't changed.

- If len2 is 0 (and ptr2 is *not* NIL), the target string is deleted rather than replaced (since the replacement string is empty). Munger returns the offset at which the deletion occurred.

If it can't find the target string in the destination string, Munger returns a negative value.

There's one case in which Munger performs a replacement even if it doesn't find all of the target string. If the substring from the offset to the end of the destination string matches the beginning of the target string, the portion found is replaced with the replacement string.

Warning: Be careful not to specify an offset that's greater than the length of the destination string, or unpredictable results may occur.

Note: The destination string must be in a relocatable block that was allocated by the Memory Manager. Munger accesses the string's length by calling the Memory Manager routines GetHandleSize and SetHandleSize.

```
PROCEDURE PackBits (VAR srcPtr,dstPtr: Ptr;  srcBytes: INTEGER);
```

PackBits compresses srcBytes bytes of data starting at srcPtr and stores the compressed data at dstPtr. The value of srcBytes should not be greater than 127. Bytes are compressed when there are three or more consecutive equal bytes. After the data is compressed, srcPtr is incremented by srcBytes and dstPtr is incremented by the number of bytes that the data was compressed to. In the worst case, the compressed data can be one byte longer than the original data.

PackBits is usually used to compress QuickDraw bit images; in this case, you should call it for one row at a time. (Because of the repeating patterns in QuickDraw images, there are more likely to be consecutive equal bytes there than in other data.) Use UnpackBits (below) to expand data compressed by PackBits.

```
PROCEDURE UnpackBits (VAR srcPtr,dstPtr: Ptr;  dstBytes: INTEGER);
```

Given in srcPtr a pointer to data that was compressed by PackBits, UnpackBits expands the data and stores the result at dstPtr. DstBytes is the length that the expanded data will be; it should be the value that was passed to PackBits in the srcBytes parameter. After the data is expanded, srcPtr is incremented by the number of bytes that were expanded and dstPtr is incremented by dstBytes.

Bit Manipulation

Given a pointer and an offset, these routines can manipulate any specific bit. The pointer can point to an even or odd byte; the offset can be any positive long integer, starting at 0 for the high-order bit of the specified byte (see Figure 2).

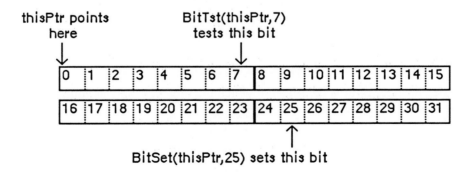

Figure 2. Bit Numbering for Utility Routines

Note: This bit numbering is the opposite of the MC68000 bit numbering to allow for greater generality. For example, you can directly access bit 1000 of a bit image given a pointer to the beginning of the bit image.

```
FUNCTION BitTst (bytePtr: Ptr; bitNum: LONGINT) : BOOLEAN;
```

BitTst tests whether a given bit is set and returns TRUE if so or FALSE if not. The bit is specified by bitNum, an offset from the high-order bit of the byte pointed to by bytePtr.

```
PROCEDURE BitSet (bytePtr: Ptr; bitNum: LONGINT);
```

BitSet sets the bit specified by bitNum, an offset from the high-order bit of the byte pointed to by bytePtr.

```
PROCEDURE BitClr (bytePtr: Ptr; bitNum: LONGINT);
```

BitSet clears the bit specified by bitNum, an offset from the high-order bit of the byte pointed to by bytePtr.

Logical Operations

```
FUNCTION BitAnd (value1,value2: LONGINT) : LONGINT;
```

BitAnd returns the result of the AND logical operation on the bits comprising the given long integers (value1 AND value2).

```
FUNCTION BitOr (value1,value2: LONGINT) : LONGINT;
```

BitOr returns the result of the OR logical operation on the bits comprising given long integers (value1 OR value2).

```
FUNCTION BitXor (value1,value2: LONGINT) : LONGINT;
```

BitXor returns the result of the XOR logical operation on the bits comprising the given long integers (value1 XOR value2).

```
FUNCTION BitNot (value: LONGINT) : LONGINT;
```

BitNot returns the result of the NOT logical operation on the bits comprising the given long integer (NOT value).

```
FUNCTION BitShift (value: LONGINT; count: INTEGER) : LONGINT;
```

BitShift logically shifts the bits of the given long integer. The count parameter specifies the direction and extent of the shift, and is taken MOD 32. If count is positive, BitShift shifts that many positions to the left; if count is negative, it shifts to the right. Zeroes are shifted into empty positions at either end.

Other Operations on Long Integers

```
FUNCTION HiWord (x: LONGINT) : INTEGER;
```

HiWord returns the high-order word of the given long integer. One use of this function is to extract the integer part of a fixed-point number.

```
FUNCTION LoWord (x: LONGINT) : INTEGER;
```

LoWord returns the low-order word of the given long integer. One use of this function is to extract the fractional part of a fixed-point number.

> **Note:** If you're dealing with a long integer that contains two separate integer values, you can define a variant record instead of using HiWord and LoWord. For example, for fixed-point numbers, you could define the following type:

```
TYPE FixedAndInt =  RECORD CASE INTEGER OF
                      1: (fixedView:  Fixed);
                      2: (intView:    RECORD
                                        whole: INTEGER;
                                        part:  INTEGER
                                      END;
                    END;
```

> If you declare x to be of type FixedAndInt, you can access it as a fixed-point value with x.fixedView, or access the integer part with x.intView.whole and the fractional part with x.intView.part.

```
PROCEDURE LongMul (a,b: LONGINT; VAR dest: Int64Bit);
```

LongMul multiplies the given long integers and returns the signed result in dest, which has the following data type:

```
TYPE Int64Bit = RECORD
                  hiLong: LONGINT;
                  loLong: LONGINT
                END;
```

Graphics Utilities

PROCEDURE ScreenRes (VAR scrnHRes,scrnVRes: INTEGER);   [Not in ROM]

ScreenRes returns the resolution of the screen of the Macintosh being used. ScrnHRes and scrnVRes are the number of pixels per inch horizontally and vertically, respectively.

Assembly-language note: The number of pixels per inch horizontally is stored in the global variable ScrHRes, and the number of pixels per inch vertically is stored in ScrVRes.

FUNCTION GetIcon (iconID: INTEGER) : Handle;

GetIcon returns a handle to the icon having the given resource ID, reading it from the resource file if necessary. It calls the Resource Manager function GetResource('ICON',iconID). If the resource can't be read, GetIcon returns NIL.

PROCEDURE PlotIcon (theRect: Rect; theIcon: Handle);

PlotIcon draws the icon whose handle is theIcon in the rectangle theRect, which is in the local coordinates of the current grafPort. It calls the QuickDraw procedure CopyBits and uses the srcCopy transfer mode.

FUNCTION GetPattern (patID: INTEGER) : PatHandle;

GetPattern returns a handle to the pattern having the given resource ID, reading it from the resource file if necessary. It calls the Resource Manager function GetResource('PAT ',patID). If the resource can't be read, GetPattern returns NIL. The PatHandle data type is defined in the Toolbox Utilities as follows:

```
TYPE PatPtr    = ^Pattern;
     PatHandle = ^PatPtr;
```

PROCEDURE GetIndPattern (VAR thePattern: Pattern; patListID:
          INTEGER; index: INTEGER);   [Not in ROM]

GetIndPattern returns in thePattern a pattern in the pattern list that has the resource ID patListID. It reads the pattern list from the resource file if necessary, by calling the Resource Manager function GetResource('PAT#',patListID). It returns the pattern specified by the index parameter, which can range from 1 to the number of patterns in the pattern list.

There's a pattern list in the system resource file that contains the standard Macintosh patterns used by MacPaint (see Figure 3). Its resource ID is:

```
CONST sysPatListID = 0;
```

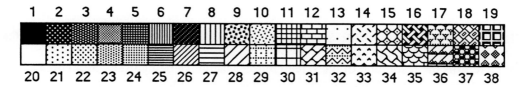

Figure 3. Standard Patterns

```
FUNCTION GetCursor (cursorID: INTEGER) : CursHandle;
```

GetCursor returns a handle to the cursor having the given resource ID, reading
it from the resource file if necessary. It calls the Resource Manager function
GetResource('CURS',cursorID). If the resource can't be read, GetCursor returns NIL.
The CursHandle data type is defined in the Toolbox Utilities as follows:

```
TYPE  CursPtr     = ^Cursor;
      CursHandle  = ^CursPtr;
```

The standard cursors shown in Figure 4 are defined in the system resource file. Their resource
IDs are:

```
CONST  iBeamCursor = 1;   {to select text}
       crossCursor = 2;   {to draw graphics}
       plusCursor  = 3;   {to select cells in structured documents}
       watchCursor = 4;   {to indicate a long wait}
```

I	+	⊕	⌚
iBeamCursor	crossCursor	plusCursor	watchCursor

Figure 4. Standard Cursors

Note: You can set the cursor with the QuickDraw procedure SetCursor. The arrow
cursor is defined in QuickDraw as a global variable named arrow.

```
PROCEDURE ShieldCursor (shieldRect: Rect; offsetPt: Point);
```

If the cursor and the given rectangle intersect, ShieldCursor hides the cursor. If they don't
intersect, the cursor remains visible while the mouse isn't moving, but is hidden when the mouse
moves.

Like the QuickDraw procedure HideCursor, ShieldCursor decrements the cursor level, and
should be balanced by a call to ShowCursor.

The rectangle may be given in global or local coordinates:

- If they're global coordinates, pass (0,0) in offsetPt.

■ If they're a grafPort's local coordinates, pass the top left corner of the grafPort's boundary rectangle in offsetPt. (Like the QuickDraw procedure LocalToGlobal, ShieldCursor will offset the coordinates of the rectangle by the coordinates of this point.)

```
FUNCTION GetPicture (picID: INTEGER) : PicHandle;
```

GetPicture returns a handle to the picture having the given resource ID, reading it from the resource file if necessary. It calls the Resource Manager function GetResource('PICT',picID). If the resource can't be read, GetPicture returns NIL. The PicHandle data type is defined in QuickDraw.

Miscellaneous Utilities

```
FUNCTION DeltaPoint (ptA,ptB: Point) : LONGINT;
```

DeltaPoint subtracts the coordinates of ptB from the coordinates of ptA. The high-order word of the result is the difference of the vertical coordinates and the low-order word is the difference of the horizontal coordinates.

Note: The QuickDraw procedure SubPt also subtracts the coordinates of one point from another, but returns the result in a VAR parameter of type Point.

```
FUNCTION SlopeFromAngle (angle: INTEGER) : Fixed;
```

Given an angle, SlopeFromAngle returns the slope dh/dv of the line forming that angle with the y-axis (dh/dv is the horizontal change divided by the vertical change between any two points on the line). Figure 5 illustrates SlopeFromAngle (and AngleFromSlope, described below, which does the reverse). The angle is treated MOD 180, and is in degrees measured from 12 o'clock; positive degrees are measured clockwise, negative degrees are measured counterclockwise (for example, 90 degrees is at 3 o'clock and –90 degrees is at 9 o'clock). Positive y is down; positive x is to the right.

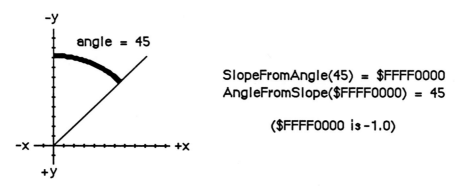

Figure 5. SlopeFromAngle and AngleFromSlope

```
FUNCTION AngleFromSlope (slope: Fixed) : INTEGER;
```

Given the slope dh/dv of a line (see SlopeFromAngle above), AngleFromSlope returns the angle formed by that line and the y-axis. The angle returned is between 1 and 180 (inclusive), in degrees measured clockwise from 12 o'clock.

AngleFromSlope is meant for use when speed is much more important than accuracy—its integer result is guaranteed to be within one degree of the correct answer, but not necessarily within half a degree. However, the equation

AngleFromSlope(SlopeFromAngle(x)) = x

is true for all x except 0 (although its reverse is not).

Note: SlopeFromAngle(0) is 0, and AngleFromSlope(0) is 180.

FORMATS OF MISCELLANEOUS RESOURCES

The following table shows the exact format of various resources. For more information about the contents of the graphics-related resources, see chapter 6.

Resource	Resource type	Number of bytes	Contents
Icon	'ICON'	128 bytes	The icon
Icon list	'ICN#'	n * 128 bytes	n icons
Pattern	'PAT '	8 bytes	The pattern
Pattern list	'PAT#'	2 bytes	Number of patterns
		n * 8 bytes	n patterns
Cursor	'CURS'	32 bytes	The data
		32 bytes	The mask
		4 bytes	The hotSpot
Picture	'PICT'	2 bytes	Picture length (m+10)
		8 bytes	Picture frame
		m bytes	Picture definition data
String	'STR '	m bytes	The string (1-byte length followed by the characters)
String list	'STR#'	2 bytes	Number of strings
		m bytes	The strings

Note: Unlike a pattern list or a string list, an icon list doesn't start with the number of items in the list.

SUMMARY OF THE TOOLBOX UTILITIES

Constants

```
CONST { Resource ID of standard pattern list }

        sysPatListID = 0;

        { Resource IDs of standard cursors }

        iBeamCursor = 1;   {to select text}
        crossCursor = 2;   {to draw graphics}
        plusCursor  = 3;   {to select cells in structured documents}
        watchCursor = 4;   {to indicate a long wait}
```

Data Types

```
TYPE Int64Bit =  RECORD
                     hiLong: LONGINT;
                     loLong: LONGINT
                 END;

    CursPtr    = ^Cursor;
    CursHandle = ^CursPtr;

    PatPtr     = ^Pattern;
    PatHandle  = ^PatPtr;
```

Routines

Fixed-Point Arithmetic

```
FUNCTION FixRatio (numer,denom: INTEGER) : Fixed;
FUNCTION FixMul    (a,b: Fixed) : Fixed;
FUNCTION FixRound (x: Fixed) : INTEGER;
```

String Manipulation

```
FUNCTION  NewString    (theString: Str255) : StringHandle;
PROCEDURE SetString    (h: StringHandle; theString: Str255);
FUNCTION  GetString    (stringID: INTEGER) : StringHandle;
PROCEDURE GetIndString (VAR theString: Str255; strListID: INTEGER;
                           index: INTEGER);   [Not in ROM]
```

Byte Manipulation

```
FUNCTION   Munger      (h: Handle; offset: LONGINT; ptr1: Ptr; len1:
                          LONGINT; ptr2: Ptr; len2: LONGINT) : LONGINT;
PROCEDURE  PackBits    (VAR srcPtr,dstPtr: Ptr; srcBytes: INTEGER);
PROCEDURE  UnpackBits  (VAR srcPtr,dstPtr: Ptr; dstBytes: INTEGER);
```

Bit Manipulation

```
FUNCTION   BitTst (bytePtr: Ptr; bitNum: LONGINT) : BOOLEAN;
PROCEDURE  BitSet (bytePtr: Ptr; bitNum: LONGINT);
PROCEDURE  BitClr (bytePtr: Ptr; bitNum: LONGINT);
```

Logical Operations

```
FUNCTION BitAnd   (value1,value2: LONGINT) : LONGINT;
FUNCTION BitOr    (value1,value2: LONGINT) : LONGINT;
FUNCTION BitXor   (value1,value2: LONGINT) : LONGINT;
FUNCTION BitNot   (value: LONGINT) : LONGINT;
FUNCTION BitShift (value: LONGINT; count: INTEGER) : LONGINT;
```

Other Operations on Long Integers

```
FUNCTION   HiWord  (x: LONGINT) : INTEGER;
FUNCTION   LoWord  (x: LONGINT) : INTEGER;
PROCEDURE  LongMul (a,b: LONGINT; VAR dest: Int64Bit);
```

Graphics Utilities

```
PROCEDURE  ScreenRes     (VAR scrnHRes,scrnVRes: INTEGER);   [Not in ROM]
FUNCTION   GetIcon       (iconID: INTEGER) : Handle;
PROCEDURE  PlotIcon      (theRect: Rect; theIcon: Handle);
FUNCTION   GetPattern    (patID: INTEGER) : PatHandle;
PROCEDURE  GetIndPattern (VAR thePattern: Pattern; patListID: INTEGER;
                            index: INTEGER);   [Not in ROM]
FUNCTION   GetCursor     (cursorID: INTEGER) : CursHandle;
PROCEDURE  ShieldCursor  (shieldRect: Rect; offsetPt: Point);
FUNCTION   GetPicture    (picID: INTEGER) : PicHandle;
```

Miscellaneous Utilities

```
FUNCTION DeltaPoint      (ptA,ptB: Point) : LONGINT;
FUNCTION SlopeFromAngle  (angle: INTEGER) : Fixed;
FUNCTION AngleFromSlope  (slope: Fixed) : INTEGER;
```

Assembly-Language Information

Constants

```
; Resource ID of standard pattern list

sysPatListID    .EQU    0

; Resource IDs of standard cursors

iBeamCursor     .EQU    1       ;to select text
crossCursor     .EQU    2       ;to draw graphics
plusCursor      .EQU    3       ;to select cells in structured documents
watchCursor     .EQU    4       ;to indicate a long wait
```

Variables

ScrVRes   Pixels per inch vertically (word)
ScrHRes   Pixels per inch horizontally (word)

17 THE PACKAGE MANAGER

Contents I-481

ABOUT THIS CHAPTER

This chapter describes the Package Manager, which is the part of the Toolbox that provides access to **packages**. The Macintosh packages include one for presenting the standard user interface when a file is to be saved or opened, and others for doing more specialized operations such as floating-point arithmetic.

You should already be familiar with the Resource Manager.

ABOUT PACKAGES

Packages are sets of data types and routines that are stored as resources and brought into memory only when needed. They serve as extensions to the Toolbox and Operating System, for the most part performing less common operations.

The Macintosh packages, which are stored in the system resource file, include the following:

- The Standard File Package, for presenting the standard user interface when a file is to be saved or opened.

- The Disk Initialization Package, for initializing and naming new disks. This package is called by the Standard File Package; you'll only need to call it in nonstandard situations.

- The International Utilities Package, for accessing country-dependent information such as the formats for numbers, currency, dates, and times.

- The Binary-Decimal Conversion Package, for converting integers to decimal strings and vice versa.

- The Floating-Point Arithmetic Package, which supports extended-precision arithmetic according to IEEE Standard 754.

- The Transcendental Functions Package, which contains trigonometric, logarithmic, exponential, and financial functions, as well as a random number generator.

Packages have the resource type 'PACK' and the following resource IDs:

```
CONST dskInit = 2;     {Disk Initialization}
      stdFile = 3;     {Standard File}
      flPoint = 4;     {Floating-Point Arithmetic}
      trFunc  = 5;     {Transcendental Functions}
      intUtil = 6;     {International Utilities}
      bdConv  = 7;     {Binary-Decimal Conversion}
```

Assembly-language note: Just as for the routines in ROM, you can invoke a package routine with a macro that has the same name as the routine preceded by an underscore. These macros, however, aren't trap macros themselves; instead, they expand to invoke the trap macro _PackN, where N is the resource ID of the package. The package determines which routine to execute from the **routine selector**, an integer that's passed to it in a word on the stack. For example, the routine selector for the Standard File Package procedure SFPutFile is 1, so invoking the macro _SFPutFile pushes 1 onto the stack and

17 Package Manager

invokes _Pack3. The routines in the Floating-Point Arithmetic and Transcendental Functions packages also invoke a trap macro of the form _PackN, but the mechanism through which they're called is somewhat different, as explained in the chapter describing those packages.

PACKAGE MANAGER ROUTINES

There are two Package Manager routines that you can call directly from Pascal: one that lets you access a specified package and one that lets you access all packages. The latter will already have been called when your application starts up, so normally you won't ever have to call the Package Manager yourself. Its procedures are described below for advanced programmers who may want to use them in unusual situations.

```
PROCEDURE InitPack (packID: INTEGER);
```

InitPack enables you to use the package specified by packID, which is the package's resource ID. (It gets a handle that will be used later to read the package into memory.)

```
PROCEDURE InitAllPacks;
```

InitAllPacks enables you to use all Macintosh packages (as though InitPack were called for each one). It will already have been called when your application starts up.

SUMMARY OF THE PACKAGE MANAGER

Constants

```
CONST { Resource IDs for packages }

        dskInit = 2;      {Disk Initialization}
        stdFile = 3;      {Standard File}
        flPoint = 4;      {Floating-Point Arithmetic}
        trFunc  = 5;      {Transcendental Functions}
        intUtil = 6;      {International Utilities}
        bdConv  = 7;      {Binary-Decimal Conversion}
```

Routines

```
PROCEDURE InitPack      (packID: INTEGER);
PROCEDURE InitAllPacks;
```

Assembly-Language Information

Constants

```
; Resource IDs for packages

dskInit    .EQU    2     ;Disk Initialization
stdFile    .EQU    3     ;Standard File
flPoint    .EQU    4     ;Floating-Point Arithmetic
trFunc     .EQU    5     ;Transcendental Functions
intUtil    .EQU    6     ;International Utilities
bdConv     .EQU    7     ;Binary-Decimal Conversion
```

Trap Macros for Packages

Disk Initialization	_Pack2	
Standard File	_Pack3	
Floating-Point Arithmetic	_Pack4	(synonym: _FP68K)
Transcendental Functions	_Pack5	(synonym: _Elems68K)
International Utilities	_Pack6	
Binary-Decimal Conversion	_Pack7	

18 THE BINARY-DECIMAL CONVERSION PACKAGE

18 Binary-Decimal

ABOUT THIS CHAPTER

This chapter describes the Binary-Decimal Conversion Package, which contains only two routines: One converts an integer from its internal (binary) form to a string that represents its decimal (base 10) value; the other converts a decimal string to the corresponding integer.

You should already be familiar with packages in general, as described in chapter 17.

BINARY-DECIMAL CONVERSION PACKAGE ROUTINES

The Binary-Decimal Conversion Package is automatically read into memory when one of its routines is called; it occupies a total of about 200 bytes. The routines are register-based, so the Pascal form of each is followed by a box containing information needed to use the routine from assembly language.

Assembly-language note: The trap macro for the Binary-Decimal Conversion Package is _Pack7. The routine selectors are as follows:

```
numToString    .EQU    0
stringToNum    .EQU    1
```

PROCEDURE NumToString (theNum: LONGINT; VAR theString: Str255);

On entry	A0: pointer to theString (preceded by length byte)
	D0: theNum (long word)
On exit	A0: pointer to theString

NumToString converts theNum to a string that represents its decimal value, and returns the result in theString. If the value is negative, the string begins with a minus sign; otherwise, the sign is omitted. Leading zeroes are suppressed, except that the value 0 produces '0'. For example:

theNum	theString
12	'12'
−23	'−23'
0	'0'

18 Binary-Decimal

```
PROCEDURE StringToNum (theString: Str255; VAR theNum: LONGINT);
```

On entry	A0: pointer to theString (preceded by length byte)
On exit	D0: theNum (long word)

Given a string representing a decimal integer, StringToNum converts it to the corresponding integer and returns the result in theNum. The string may begin with a plus or minus sign. For example:

theString	theNum
'12'	12
'–23'	–23
'–0'	0
'055'	55

The magnitude of the integer is converted modulo 2^{32}, and the 32-bit result is negated if the string begins with a minus sign; integer overflow occurs if the magnitude is greater than $2^{31}-1$. (Negation is done by taking the two's complement—reversing the state of each bit and then adding 1.) For example:

theString	theNum
'2147483648' (magnitude is 2^{31})	–2147483648
'–2147483648'	–2147483648
'4294967295' (magnitude is $2^{32}-1$)	–1
'–4294967295'	1

StringToNum doesn't actually check whether the characters in the string are between '0' and '9'; instead, since the ASCII codes for '0' through '9' are $30 through $39, it just masks off the last four bits and uses them as a digit. For example, '2:' is converted to the number 30 because the ASCII code for ':' is $3A. Spaces are treated as zeroes, since the ASCII code for a space is $20. Given that the ASCII codes for 'C', 'A', and 'T' are $43, $41, and $54, respectively, consider the following examples:

theString	theNum
'CAT'	314
'+CAT'	314
'–CAT'	–314

SUMMARY OF THE BINARY-DECIMAL CONVERSION PACKAGE

Routines

```
PROCEDURE NumToString (theNum: LONGINT; VAR theString: Str255);
PROCEDURE StringToNum (theString: Str255; VAR theNum: LONGINT);
```

Assembly-Language Information

Constants

```
; Routine selectors

numToString     .EQU    0
stringToNum     .EQU    1
```

Routines

Name	On entry	On exit
NumToString	A0: ptr to theString (preceded by length byte) D0: theNum (long)	A0: ptr to theString
StringToNum	A0: ptr to theString (preceded by length byte)	D0: theNum (long)

Trap Macro Name

_Pack7

18 Binary-Decimal

19 THE INTERNATIONAL UTILITIES PACKAGE

19 Int'l Utilities

ABOUT THIS CHAPTER

This chapter describes the International Utilities Package, which enables you to make your Macintosh application country-independent. Routines are provided for formatting dates and times and comparing strings in a way that's appropriate to the country where your application is being used. There's also a routine for testing whether to use the metric system of measurement. These routines access country-dependent information (stored in a resource file) that also tells how to format numbers and currency; you can access this information yourself for your own routines that may require it.

You should already be familiar with:

- resources, as discussed in chapter 5

- packages in general, as described in chapter 17

INTERNATIONAL RESOURCES

Country-dependent information is kept in the system resource file in two resources of type 'INTL', with the resource IDs 0 and 1:

- International resource 0 contains the formats for numbers, currency, and time, a short date format, and an indication of whether to use the metric system.

- International resource 1 contains a longer format for dates (spelling out the month and possibly the day of the week, with or without abbreviation) and a routine for localizing string comparison.

The system resource file released in each country contains the standard international resources for that country. Figure 1 illustrates the standard formats for the United States, Great Britain, Italy, Germany, and France.

The routines in the International Utilities Package use the information in these resources; for example, the routines for formatting dates and times yield strings that look like those shown in Figure 1. Routines in other packages, in desk accessories, and in ROM also access the international resources when necessary, as should your own routines if they need such information.

In some cases it may be appropriate to store either or both of the international resources in the application's or document's resource file, to override those in the system resource file. For example, suppose an application creates documents containing currency amounts and gets the currency format from international resource 0. Documents created by such an application should have their own copy of the international resource 0 that was used to create them, so that the unit of currency will be the same if the document is displayed on a Macintosh configured for another country.

Information about the exact components and structure of each international resource follows here; you can skip this if you intend only to call the formatting routines in the International Utilities Package and won't access the resources directly yourself.

	United States	Great Britain	Italy	Germany	France
Numbers	1,234.56	1,234.56	1.234,56	1.234,56	1 234.56
List separator	;	,	;	;	;
Currency	$0.23	£0.23	L. 0,23	0,23 DM	0,23 F
	($0.45)	(£0.45)	L. -0,45	-0,45 DM	-0,45 F
	$345.00	£345	L. 345	325,00 DM	325 F
Time	9:05 AM	09:05	9:05	9.05 Uhr	9:05
	11:30 AM	11:30	11:30	11.30 Uhr	11:30
	11:20 PM	23:20	23:20	23.20 Uhr	23:20
	11:20:09 PM	23:20:00	23:20:09	23.20.09 Uhr	23:20:09
Short date	12/22/85	22/12/1985	22-12-1985	22.12.1985	22.12.85
	2/1/85	01/02/1985	1-02-1985	1.02.1985	1.02.85

		Unabbreviated	Abbreviated
Long date	United States	Wednesday, February 1, 1985	Wed, Feb 1, 1985
	Great Britain	Wednesday, February 1, 1985	Wed, Feb 1, 1985
	Italy	mercoledì 1 Febbraio 1985	mer 1 Feb 1985
	Germany	Mittwoch, 1. Februar 1985	Mit, 1. Feb 1985
	France	Mercredi 1 fevrier 1985	Mer 1 fev 1985

Figure 1. Standard International Formats

International Resource 0

The International Utilities Package contains the following data types for accessing international resource 0:

```
TYPE Intl0Hndl  = ^Intl0Ptr;
     Intl0Ptr   = ^Intl0Rec;
```

```
Intl0Rec  =
 PACKED RECORD
   decimalPt:     CHAR;     {decimal point character}
   thousSep:      CHAR;     {thousands separator}
   listSep:       CHAR;     {list separator}
   currSym1:      CHAR;     {currency symbol}
   currSym2:      CHAR;
   currSym3:      CHAR;
   currFmt:       Byte;     {currency format}
   dateOrder:     Byte;     {order of short date elements}
   shrtDateFmt:   Byte;     {short date format}
   dateSep:       CHAR;     {date separator}
   timeCycle:     Byte;     {0 if 24-hour cycle, 255 if 12-hour}
   timeFmt:       Byte;     {time format}
   mornStr:       PACKED ARRAY[1..4] OF CHAR;
                            {trailing string for first 12-hour cycle}
   eveStr:        PACKED ARRAY[1..4] OF CHAR;
                            {trailing string for last 12-hour cycle}
   timeSep:       CHAR;     {time separator}
   time1Suff:     CHAR;     {trailing string for 24-hour cycle}
   time2Suff:     CHAR;
   time3Suff:     CHAR;
   time4Suff:     CHAR;
   time5Suff:     CHAR;
   time6Suff:     CHAR;
   time7Suff:     CHAR;
   time8Suff:     CHAR;
   metricSys:     Byte;     {255 if metric, 0 if not}
   intl0Vers:     INTEGER {version information}
 END;
```

Note: A NUL character (ASCII code 0) in a field of type CHAR means there's no such character. The currency symbol and the trailing string for the 24-hour cycle are separated into individual CHAR fields because of Pascal packing conventions. All strings include any required spaces.

The decimalPt, thousSep, and listSep fields define the number format. The **thousands separator** is the character that separates every three digits to the left of the decimal point. The **list separator** is the character that separates numbers, as when a list of numbers is entered by the user; it must be different from the decimal point character. If it's the same as the thousands separator, the user must not include the latter in entered numbers.

CurrSym1 through currSym3 define the currency symbol (only one character for the United States and Great Britain, but two for France and three for Italy and Germany). CurrFmt determines the rest of the currency format, as shown in Figure 2. The decimal point character and thousands separator for currency are the same as in the number format.

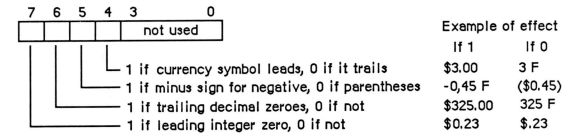

Figure 2. CurrFmt Field

The following predefined constants are masks that can be used to set or test the bits in the currFmt field:

```
CONST currSymLead   = 16;    {set if currency symbol leads}
      currNegSym    = 32;    {set if minus sign for negative}
      currTrailingZ = 64;    {set if trailing decimal zeroes}
      currLeadingZ  = 128;   {set if leading integer zero}
```

Note: You can also apply the currency format's leading- and trailing-zero indicators to the number format if desired.

The dateOrder, shrtDateFmt, and dateSep fields define the short date format. DateOrder indicates the order of the day, month, and year, with one of the following values:

```
CONST mdy = 0;    {month day year}
      dmy = 1;    {day month year}
      ymd = 2;    {year month day}
```

ShrtDateFmt determines whether to show leading zeroes in day and month numbers and whether to show the century, as illustrated in Figure 3. DateSep is the character that separates the different parts of the date.

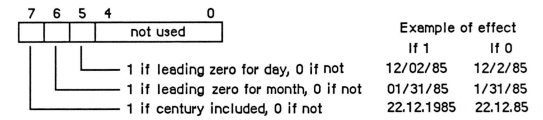

Figure 3. ShrtDateFmt Field

To set or test the bits in the shrtDateFmt field, you can use the following predefined constants as masks:

```
CONST dayLdingZ = 32;    {set if leading zero for day}
      mntLdingZ = 64;    {set if leading zero for month}
      century   = 128;   {set if century included}
```

The next several fields define the time format: the cycle (12 or 24 hours); whether to show leading zeroes (timeFmt, as shown in Figure 4); a string to follow the time (two for 12-hour cycle, one for 24-hour); and the time separator character.

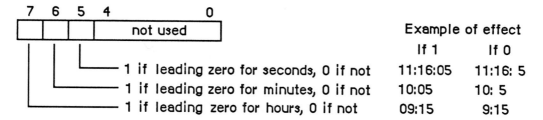

Figure 4. TimeFmt Field

The following masks are available for setting or testing bits in the timeFmt field:

```
CONST secLeadingZ  = 32;   {set if leading zero for seconds}
      minLeadingZ  = 64;   {set if leading zero for minutes}
      hrLeadingZ   = 128;  {set it leading zero for hours}
```

MetricSys indicates whether to use the metric system. The last field, intl0Vers, contains a version number in its low-order byte and one of the following constants in its high-order byte:

```
CONST verUS           = 0;
      verFrance       = 1;
      verBritain      = 2;
      verGermany      = 3;
      verItaly        = 4;
      verNetherlands  = 5;
      verBelgiumLux   = 6;
      verSweden       = 7;
      verSpain        = 8;
      verDenmark      = 9;
      verPortugal     = 10;
      verFrCanada     = 11;
      verNorway       = 12;
      verIsrael       = 13;
      verJapan        = 14;
      verAustralia    = 15;
      verArabia       = 16;
      verFinland      = 17;
      verFrSwiss      = 18;
      verGrSwiss      = 19;
      verGreece       = 20;
      verIceland      = 21;
      verMalta        = 22;
      verCyprus       = 23;
      verTurkey       = 24;
      verYugoslavia   = 25;
```

International Resource 1

The International Utilities Package contains the following data types for accessing international resource 1:

```
TYPE Intl1Hndl = ^Intl1Ptr;
     Intl1Ptr  = ^Intl1Rec;
     Intl1Rec  =
             PACKED RECORD
                days:          ARRAY[1..7] OF STRING[15];  {day names}
                months:        ARRAY[1..12] OF STRING[15]; {month names}
                suppressDay:   Byte;        {0 for day name, 255 for none}
                lngDateFmt:    Byte;        {order of long date elements}
                dayLeading0:   Byte;        {255 for leading 0 in day number}
                abbrLen:       Byte;        {length for abbreviating names}
                st0:           PACKED ARRAY[1..4] OF CHAR; {strings }
                st1:           PACKED ARRAY[1..4] OF CHAR; { for }
                st2:           PACKED ARRAY[1..4] OF CHAR; { long }
                st3:           PACKED ARRAY[1..4] OF CHAR; { date }
                st4:           PACKED ARRAY[1..4] OF CHAR; { format}
                intl1Vers:     INTEGER; {version information}
                localRtn:      INTEGER  {routine for localizing string }
                                        { comparison; actually may be }
                                        { longer than one integer}
             END;
```

All fields except the last two determine the long date format. The day names in the days array are ordered from Sunday to Saturday. (The month names are of course ordered from January to December.) As shown below, the lngDateFmt field determines the order of the various parts of the date. St0 through st4 are strings (usually punctuation) that appear in the date.

lngDateFmt	Long date format								
0	st0	day name	st1	day	st2	month	st3	year	st4
255	st0	day name	st1	month	st2	day	st3	year	st4

See Figure 5 for examples of how the International Utilities Package formats dates based on these fields. The examples assume that the suppressDay and dayLeading0 fields contain 0. A suppressDay value of 255 causes the day name and st1 to be omitted, and a dayLeading value of 255 causes a 0 to appear before day numbers less than 10.

lngDateFmt	st0	st1	st2	st3	st4	Sample result
0	" "	', '	'. '	' '	" "	Mittwoch, 2. Februar 1985
255	" "	', '	' '	', '	" "	Wednesday, February 1, 1985

Figure 5. Long Date Formats

AbbrLen is the number of characters to which month and day names should be abbreviated when abbreviation is desired.

The intl1Vers field contains version information with the same format as the intl0Vers field of international resource 0.

LocalRtn contains a routine that localizes the built-in character ordering (as described below under "International String Comparison").

INTERNATIONAL STRING COMPARISON

The International Utilities Package lets you compare strings in a way that accounts for diacritical marks and other special characters. The sort order built into the package may be localized through a routine stored in international resource 1.

The sort order is determined by a ranking of the entire Macintosh character set. The ranking can be thought of as a two-dimensional table. Each row of the table is a class of characters such as all A's (uppercase and lowercase, with and without diacritical marks). The characters are ordered within each row, but this ordering is secondary to the order of the rows themselves. For example, given that the rows for letters are ordered alphabetically, the following are all true under this scheme:

	'A'	<	'a'
and	'Ab'	<	'ab'
but	'Ac'	>	'ab'

Even though 'A' < 'a' within the A row, 'Ac' > 'ab' because the order 'c' > 'b' takes precedence over the secondary ordering of the 'a' and the 'A'. In effect, the secondary ordering is ignored unless the comparison based on the primary ordering yields equality.

> **Note:** The Pascal relational operators are used here for convenience only. String comparison in Pascal yields very different results, since it simply follows the ordering of the characters' ASCII codes.

When the strings being compared are of different lengths, each character in the longer string that doesn't correspond to a character in the shorter one compares "greater"; thus 'a' < 'ab'. This takes precedence over secondary ordering, so 'a' < 'Ab' even though 'A' < 'a'.

Besides letting you compare strings as described above, the International Utilities Package includes a routine that compares strings for equality without regard for secondary ordering. The effect on comparing letters, for example, is that diacritical marks are ignored and uppercase and lowercase are not distinguished.

Figure 6 shows the two-dimensional ordering of the character set (from least to greatest as you read from top to bottom or left to right). The numbers on the left are ASCII codes corresponding to each row; ellipses (...) designate sequences of rows of just one character. Some codes do not correspond to rows (such as $61 through $7A, because lowercase letters are included in with their uppercase equivalents). See chapter 8 for a table showing all the characters and their ASCII codes.

Characters combining two letters, as in the $AE row, are called **ligatures**. As shown in Figure 7, they're actually expanded to the corresponding two letters, in the following sense:

- Primary ordering: The ligature is equal to the two-character sequence.
- Secondary ordering: The ligature is greater than the two-character sequence.

```
$00     ASCII NUL
...
$1F     ASCII US
$20     space     nonbreaking space
$21     !
$22     "     «   »     "     "
$23     #
$24     $
$25     %
$26     &
$27     '     '   ,
$28     (
...
$40     @     À   Ä   Ã   Å   a   á   à   â   ä   ã   å
$41     A
$42     B   b
$43     C   Ç   c   ç
$45     E   É   e   é   è   ê   ë
$49     I   Í   í   ì   î   ï
$4E     N   Ñ   n   ñ
$4F     O   Ö   Õ   Ø   o   ó   ò   ô   ö   õ   ø
$55     U   Ü   u   ú   ù   û   ü
$59     Y   y   ÿ
$5B     [
$5C     \
$5D     ]
$5E     ^
$5F     _
$60     `
$7B     {
$7C     |
$7D     }
$7E     ~
$7F     ASCII DEL
$A0     †
...
$AD     ≠
$AE     Æ   æ   Œ   œ     (see remarks about ligatures)
$B0     ∞
...
$BD     Ω
$C0     ¿
...
$C9     …
$D0     –
$D1     —
$D6     ÷
$D7     ◊
```

letters not shown
are like "B   b"

Figure 6.   International Character Ordering

Ligatures are ordered somewhat differently in Germany to accommodate umlauted characters (see Figure 7). This is accomplished by means of the routine in international resource 1 for localizing the built-in character ordering. In the system resource file for Germany, this routine expands umlauted characters to the corresponding two letters (for example, "AE" for A-umlaut). The secondary ordering places the umlauted character between the two-character sequence and the ligature, if any. Likewise, the German double-s character expands to "ss".

Built-in ordering:

AE Æ ae æ

OE Œ oe œ

German ordering:

AE Ä Æ ae ä æ

OE Ö Œ oe ö œ

ss ß

UE Ü ue ü

Figure 7. Ordering for Special Characters

In the system resource file for Great Britain, the localization routine in international resource 1 orders the pound currency sign between double quote and the pound weight sign (see Figure 8). For the United States, France, and Italy, the localization routine does nothing.

$22   " « » " "
$A3   £
$23   #

Figure 8. Special Ordering for Great Britain

Assembly-language note: The null localization routine consists of an RTS instruction.

USING THE INTERNATIONAL UTILITIES PACKAGE

The International Utilities Package is automatically read into memory from the system resource file when one of its routines is called. When a routine needs to access an international resource, it asks the Resource Manager to read the resource into memory. Together, the package and its resources occupy about 2K bytes.

As described in chapter 13 of Volume II, you can get the date and time as a long integer from the GetDateTime procedure. If you need a string corresponding to the date or time, you can pass this long integer to the IUDateString or IUTimeString procedure in the International Utilities Package. These procedures determine the local format from the international resources read into memory by the Resource Manager (that is, resource type 'INTL' and resource ID 0 or 1). In some situations, you may need the format information to come instead from an international resource that you specify by its handle; if so, you can use IUDatePString or IUTimePString. This is useful, for example, if you want to use an international resource in a document's resource file after you've closed that file.

Applications that use measurements, such as on a ruler for setting margins and tabs, can call IUMetric to find out whether to use the metric system. This function simply returns the value of the corresponding field in international resource 0. To access any other fields in an international resource—say, the currency format in international resource 0—call IUGetIntl to get a handle to the resource. If you change any of the fields and want to write the changed resource to a resource file, the IUSetIntl procedure lets you do this.

To sort strings, you can use IUCompString or, if you're not dealing with Pascal strings, the more general IUMagString. These routines compare two strings and give their exact relationship, whether equal, less than, or greater than. Subtleties like diacritical marks and case differences are taken into consideration, as described above under "International String Comparison". If you need to know only whether two strings are equal, and want to ignore the subtleties, use IUEqualString (or the more general IUMagIDString) instead.

Note: The Operating System Utility function EqualString also compares two Pascal strings for equality. It's less sophisticated than IUEqualString in that it follows ASCII order more strictly; for details, see chapter 13 of Volume II.

INTERNATIONAL UTILITIES PACKAGE ROUTINES

Assembly-language note: The trap macro for the International Utilities Package is _Pack6. The routine selectors are as follows:

```
iuDateString      .EQU    0
iuTimeString      .EQU    2
iuMetric          .EQU    4
iuGetIntl         .EQU    6
iuSetIntl         .EQU    8
iuMagString       .EQU   10
iuMagIDString     .EQU   12
iuDatePString     .EQU   14
iuTimePString     .EQU   16
```

```
PROCEDURE IUDateString (dateTime: LONGINT; form: DateForm; VAR
                result: Str255);
```

Given a date and time as returned by the Operating System Utility procedure GetDateTime, IUDateString returns in the result parameter a string that represents the corresponding date. The form parameter has the following data type:

```
TYPE DateForm = (shortDate,longDate,abbrevDate);
```

ShortDate requests the short date format, longDate the long date, and abbrevDate the abbreviated long date. IUDateString determines the exact format from international resource 0 for the short date or 1 for the long date. See Figure 1 above for examples of the standard formats.

If the abbreviated long date is requested and the abbreviation length in international resource 1 is greater than the actual length of the name being abbreviated, IUDateString fills the abbreviation with NUL characters (ASCII code 0); the abbreviation length should not be greater than 15, the maximum name length.

```
PROCEDURE IUDatePString (dateTime: LONGINT; form: DateForm; VAR
        result: Str255; intlParam: Handle);
```

IUDatePString is the same as IUDateString except that it determines the exact format of the date from the resource whose handle is passed in intlParam, overriding the resource that would otherwise be used.

```
PROCEDURE IUTimeString (dateTime: LONGINT; wantSeconds: BOOLEAN;
        VAR result: Str255);
```

Given a date and time as returned by the Operating System Utility procedure GetDateTime, IUTimeString returns in the result parameter a string that represents the corresponding time of day. If wantSeconds is TRUE, seconds are included in the time; otherwise, only the hour and minute are included. IUTimeString determines the time format from international resource 0. See Figure 1 for examples of the standard formats.

```
PROCEDURE IUTimePString (dateTime: LONGINT; wantSeconds: BOOLEAN;
        VAR result: Str255; intlParam: Handle);
```

IUTimePString is the same as IUTimeString except that it determines the time format from the resource whose handle is passed in intlParam, overriding the resource that would otherwise be used.

```
FUNCTION IUMetric : BOOLEAN;
```

If international resource 0 specifies that the metric system is to be used, IUMetric returns TRUE; otherwise, it returns FALSE.

```
FUNCTION IUGetIntl (theID: INTEGER) : Handle;
```

IUGetIntl returns a handle to the international resource numbered theID (0 or 1). It calls the Resource Manager function GetResource('INTL',theID). For example, if you want to access individual fields of international resource 0, you can do the following:

```
VAR myHndl: Handle;
    int0: Intl0Hndl;
    . . .
myHndl := IUGetIntl(0);
int0 := Intl0Hndl(myHndl)
```

19 Int'l Utilities

```
PROCEDURE IUSetIntl (refNum: INTEGER; theID: INTEGER; intlParam:
            Handle);
```

In the resource file having the reference number refNum, IUSetIntl sets the international resource numbered theID (0 or 1) to the data specified by intlParam. The data may be either an existing resource or data that hasn't yet been written to a resource file. IUSetIntl adds the resource to the specified file or replaces the resource if it's already there.

```
FUNCTION IUCompString (aStr,bStr: Str255) : INTEGER;    [Not in ROM]
```

IUCompString compares aStr and bStr as described above under "International String Comparison", taking both primary and secondary ordering into consideration. It returns one of the values listed below.

		Example	
Result	Meaning	aStr	bStr
−1	aStr is less than bStr	'Ab'	'ab'
0	aStr equals bStr	'Ab'	'Ab'
1	aStr is greater than bStr	'Ac'	'ab'

Assembly-language note: IUCompString was created for the convenience of Pascal programmers; there's no trap for it. It eventually calls IUMagString, which is what you should use from assembly language.

```
FUNCTION IUMagString (aPtr,bPtr: Ptr; aLen,bLen: INTEGER) :
            INTEGER;
```

IUMagString is the same as IUCompString (above) except that instead of comparing two Pascal strings, it compares the string defined by aPtr and aLen to the string defined by bPtr and bLen. The pointer points to the first character of the string (any byte in memory, not necessarily word-aligned), and the length specifies the number of characters in the string.

```
FUNCTION IUEqualString (aStr,bStr: Str255) : INTEGER;    [Not in ROM]
```

IUEqualString compares aStr and bStr for equality without regard for secondary ordering, as described above under "International String Comparison". If the strings are equal, it returns 0; otherwise, it returns 1. For example, if the strings are 'Rose' and 'rose', IUEqualString considers them equal and returns 0.

Note: See also EqualString in chapter 13 of Volume II.

Assembly-language note: IUEqualString was created for the convenience of Pascal programmers; there's no trap for it. It eventually calls IUMagIDString, which is what you should use from assembly language.

```
FUNCTION IUMagIDString (aPtr,bPtr: Ptr; aLen,bLen: INTEGER) :
        INTEGER;
```

IUMagIDString is the same as IUEqualString (above) except that instead of comparing two Pascal strings, it compares the string defined by aPtr and aLen to the string defined by bPtr and bLen. The pointer points to the first character of the string (any byte in memory, not necessarily word-aligned), and the length specifies the number of characters in the string.

SUMMARY OF THE INTERNATIONAL UTILITIES PACKAGE

Constants

```
CONST { Masks for currency format }

        currSymLead    = 16;   {set if currency symbol leads}
        currNegSym     = 32;   {set if minus sign for negative}
        currTrailingZ  = 64;   {set if trailing decimal zeroes}
        currLeadingZ   = 128;  {set if leading integer zero}

        { Order of short date elements }

        mdy = 0;       {month day year}
        dmy = 1;       {day month year}
        ymd = 2;       {year month day}

        { Masks for short date format }

        dayLdingZ = 32;   {set if leading zero for day}
        mntLdingZ = 64;   {set if leading zero for month}
        century   = 128;  {set if century included}

        { Masks for time format }

        secLeadingZ = 32;   {set if leading zero for seconds}
        minLeadingZ = 64;   {set if leading zero for minutes}
        hrLeadingZ  = 128;  {set if leading zero for hours}

        { High-order byte of version information }

        verUS          = 0;
        verFrance      = 1;
        verBritain     = 2;
        verGermany     = 3;
        verItaly       = 4;
        verNetherlands = 5;
        verBelgiumLux  = 6;
        verSweden      = 7;
        verSpain       = 8;
        verDenmark     = 9;
        verPortugal    = 10;
        verFrCanada    = 11;
        verNorway      = 12;
        verIsrael      = 13;
        verJapan       = 14;
        verAustralia   = 15;
        verArabia      = 16;
        verFinland     = 17;
```

```
verFrSwiss      = 18;
verGrSwiss      = 19;
verGreece       = 20;
verIceland      = 21;
verMalta        = 22;
verCyprus       = 23;
verTurkey       = 24;
verYugoslavia   = 25;
```

Data Types

```
TYPE Intl0Hndl = ^Intl0Ptr;
     Intl0Ptr   = ^Intl0Rec;
     Intl0Rec   =
         PACKED RECORD
            decimalPt:    CHAR;   {decimal point character}
            thousSep:     CHAR;   {thousands separator}
            listSep:      CHAR;   {list separator}
            currSym1:     CHAR;   {currency symbol}
            currSym2:     CHAR;
            currSym3:     CHAR;
            currFmt:      Byte;   {currency format}
            dateOrder:    Byte;   {order of short date elements}
            shrtDateFmt:  Byte;   {short date format}
            dateSep:      CHAR;   {date separator}
            timeCycle:    Byte;   {0 if 24-hour cycle, 255 if 12-hour}
            timeFmt:      Byte;   {time format}
            mornStr:      PACKED ARRAY[1..4] OF CHAR;
                                  {trailing string for first 12-hour cycle}
            eveStr:       PACKED ARRAY[1..4] OF CHAR;
                                  {trailing string for last 12-hour cycle}
            timeSep:      CHAR;   {time separator}
            time1Suff:    CHAR;   {trailing string for 24-hour cycle}
            time2Suff:    CHAR;
            time3Suff:    CHAR;
            time4Suff:    CHAR;
            time5Suff:    CHAR;
            time6Suff:    CHAR;
            time7Suff:    CHAR;
            time8Suff:    CHAR;
            metricSys:    Byte;     {255 if metric, 0 if not}
            intl0Vers:    INTEGER {version information}
         END;
```

19 Int'l Utilities

```
Intl1Hndl = ^Intl1Ptr;
Intl1Ptr  = ^Intl1Rec;
Intl1Rec  =
        PACKED RECORD
          days:        ARRAY[1..7] OF STRING[15];   {day names}
          months:      ARRAY[1..12] OF STRING[15];  {month names}
          suppressDay: Byte; {0 for day name, 255 for none}
          lngDateFmt:  Byte; {order of long date elements}
          dayLeading0: Byte; {255 for leading 0 in day number}
          abbrLen:     Byte; {length for abbreviating names}
          st0:         PACKED ARRAY[1..4] OF CHAR;   {strings }
          st1:         PACKED ARRAY[1..4] OF CHAR;   { for }
          st2:         PACKED ARRAY[1..4] OF CHAR;   { long }
          st3:         PACKED ARRAY[1..4] OF CHAR;   { date }
          st4:         PACKED ARRAY[1..4] OF CHAR;   { format}
          intl1Vers:   INTEGER; {version information}
          localRtn:    INTEGER  {routine for localizing string }
                                { comparison; actually may be }
                                { longer than one integer}
        END;

    DateForm = (shortDate,longDate,abbrevDate);
```

Routines

```
PROCEDURE IUDateString  (dateTime: LONGINT; form: DateForm; VAR result:
                         Str255);
PROCEDURE IUDatePString (dateTime: LONGINT; form: DateForm; VAR result:
                         Str255; intlParam: Handle);
PROCEDURE IUTimeString  (dateTime: LONGINT; wantSeconds: BOOLEAN; VAR
                         result: Str255);
PROCEDURE IUTimePString (dateTime: LONGINT; wantSeconds: BOOLEAN; VAR
                         result: Str255; intlParam: Handle);
FUNCTION  IUMetric :     BOOLEAN;
FUNCTION  IUGetIntl     (theID: INTEGER) : Handle;
PROCEDURE IUSetIntl     (refNum: INTEGER; theID: INTEGER; intlParam:
                         Handle);
FUNCTION  IUCompString  (aStr,bStr: Str255) : INTEGER;   [Not in ROM]
FUNCTION  IUMagString   (aPtr,bPtr: Ptr; aLen,bLen: INTEGER) : INTEGER;
FUNCTION  IUEqualString (aStr,bStr: Str255) : INTEGER;   [Not in ROM]
FUNCTION  IUMagIDString (aPtr,bPtr: Ptr; aLen,bLen: INTEGER) : INTEGER;
```

Assembly-Language Information

Constants

```
; Masks for currency format

currSymLead    .EQU    16      ;set if currency symbol leads
currNegSym     .EQU    32      ;set if minus sign for negative
currTrailingZ  .EQU    64      ;set if trailing decimal zeroes
currLeadingZ   .EQU    128     ;set if leading integer zero

; Order of short date elements

mdy            .EQU    0       ;month day year
dmy            .EQU    1       ;day month year
ymd            .EQU    2       ;year month day

; Masks for short date format

dayLdingZ      .EQU    32      ;set if leading zero for day
mntLdingZ      .EQU    64      ;set if leading zero for month
century        .EQU    128     ;set if century included

; Masks for time format

secLeadingZ    .EQU    32      ;set if leading zero for seconds
minLeadingZ    .EQU    64      ;set if leading zero for minutes
hrLeadingZ     .EQU    128     ;set if leading zero for hours

; High-order byte of version information

verUS          .EQU    0
verFrance      .EQU    1
verBritain     .EQU    2
verGermany     .EQU    3
verItaly       .EQU    4
verNetherlands .EQU    5
verBelgiumLux  .EQU    6
verSweden      .EQU    7
verSpain       .EQU    8
verDenmark     .EQU    9
verPortugal    .EQU    10
verFrCanada    .EQU    11
verNorway      .EQU    12
verIsrael      .EQU    13
verJapan       .EQU    14
verAustralia   .EQU    15
verArabia      .EQU    16
verFinland     .EQU    17
verFrSwiss     .EQU    18
verGrSwiss     .EQU    19
```

```
verGreece        .EQU    20
verIceland       .EQU    21
verMalta         .EQU    22
verCyprus        .EQU    23
verTurkey        .EQU    24
verYugoslavia    .EQU    25


; Date form for IUDateString and IUDatePString

shortDate        .EQU    0      ;short form of date
longDate         .EQU    1      ;long form of date
abbrevDate       .EQU    2      ;abbreviated long form


; Routine selectors

iuDateString     .EQU    0
iuTimeString     .EQU    2
iuMetric         .EQU    4
iuGetIntl        .EQU    6
iuSetIntl        .EQU    8
iuMagString      .EQU    10
iuMagIDString    .EQU    12
iuDatePString    .EQU    14
iuTimePString    .EQU    16
```

International Resource 0 Data Structure

decimalPt	Decimal point character (byte)
thousSep	Thousands separator (byte)
listSep	List separator (byte)
currSym	Currency symbol (3 bytes)
currFmt	Currency format (byte)
dateOrder	Order of short date elements (byte)
shrtDateFmt	Short date format (byte)
dateSep	Date separator (byte)
timeCycle	0 if 24-hour cycle, 255 if 12-hour (byte)
timeFmt	Time format (byte)
mornStr	Trailing string for first 12-hour cycle (long)
eveStr	Trailing string for last 12-hour cycle (long)
timeSep	Time separator (byte)
timeSuff	Trailing string for 24-hour cycle (8 bytes)
metricSys	255 if metric, 0 if not (byte)
intl0Vers	Version information (word)

International Resource 1 Data Structure

days	Day names (112 bytes)
months	Month names (192 bytes)
suppressDay	0 for day name, 255 for none (byte)
lngDateFmt	Order of long date elements (byte)

dayLeading0	255 for leading 0 in day number (byte)
abbrLen	Length for abbreviating names (byte)
st0	Strings for long date format (longs)
st1	
st2	
st3	
st4	
intl1Vers	Version information (word)
localRtn	Comparison localization routine

Trap Macro Name

Pack6

20 THE STANDARD FILE PACKAGE

20 Standard File

ABOUT THIS CHAPTER

This chapter describes the Standard File Package, which provides the standard user interface for specifying a file to be opened or saved. The Standard File Package allows the file to be on a disk in any drive connected to the Macintosh, and lets a currently inserted disk be ejected so that another can be inserted.

You should already be familiar with:

■ the basic concepts and structures behind QuickDraw, particularly points and rectangles

■ the Toolbox Event Manager

■ the Dialog Manager, especially the ModalDialog procedure

■ packages in general, as described in chapter 17

ABOUT THE STANDARD FILE PACKAGE

Standard Macintosh applications should have a File menu from which the user can save and open documents, via the Save, Save As, and Open commands. In response to these commands, the application can call the Standard File Package to find out the document name and let the user switch disks if desired. As described below, a dialog box is presented for this purpose.

When the user chooses Save As, or Save when the document is untitled, the application needs a name for the document. The corresponding dialog box lets the user enter the document name and click a button labeled "Save" (or just click "Cancel" to abort the command). By convention, the dialog box comes up displaying the current document name, if any, so the user can edit it.

In response to an Open command, the application needs to know which document to open. The corresponding dialog box displays the names of all documents that might be opened; the user opens one by clicking it and then clicking a button labeled "Open", or simply by double-clicking on the document name. If there are more names than can be shown at once, the user can scroll through them using a vertical scroll bar, or type a character on the keyboard to cause the list to scroll to the first name beginning with that character.

Both of these dialog boxes let the user:

■ access a disk in an external drive connected to the Macintosh

■ eject a disk from either drive and insert another

■ initialize and name an inserted disk that's uninitialized

■ switch from one drive to another

On the right in the dialog box, separated from the rest of the box by a dotted line, there's a disk name with one or two buttons below it; Figure 1 shows what this looks like when an external drive is connected to the Macintosh but currently has no disk in it. Notice that the Drive button is inactive (dimmed). After the user inserts a disk in the external drive (and, if necessary, initializes and names it), the Drive button becomes active. If there's no external drive, the Drive button isn't displayed at all.

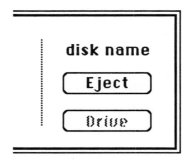

Figure 1. Partial Dialog Box

The disk name displayed in the dialog box is the name of the current disk, initially the disk from which the application was started. The user can click Eject to eject the current disk and insert another, which then becomes the current disk. If there's an external drive, clicking the Drive button changes the current disk from the one in the external drive to the one in the internal drive or vice versa. The Drive button is inactive whenever there's only one disk inserted.

> **Note:** Clicking the Drive button actually cycles through all volumes in drives currently connected to the Macintosh. (Volumes and drives are discussed in chapter 4 of Volume II.)

If an uninitialized or otherwise unreadable disk is inserted, the Standard File Package calls the Disk Initialization Package to provide the standard user interface for initializing and naming a disk.

USING THE STANDARD FILE PACKAGE

The Standard File Package and the resources it uses are automatically read into memory when one of its routines is called. It in turn reads the Disk Initialization Package into memory if a disk is ejected (in case an uninitialized disk is inserted next); together these packages occupy about 8.5K to 10K bytes, depending on the number of files on the disk.

Call SFPutFile when your application is to save to a file and needs to get the name of the file from the user. Standard applications should do this when the user chooses Save As from the File menu, or Save when the document is untitled. SFPutFile displays a dialog box allowing the user to enter a file name.

Similarly, SFGetFile is useful whenever your application is to open a file and needs to know which one, such as when the user chooses the Open command from a standard application's File menu. SFGetFile displays a dialog box with a list of file names to choose from.

You pass these routines a reply record, as shown below, and they fill it with information about the user's reply.

```
TYPE SFReply =    RECORD
                    good:     BOOLEAN;      {FALSE if ignore command}
                    copy:     BOOLEAN;      {not used}
                    fType:    OSType;       {file type or not used}
                    vRefNum:  INTEGER;      {volume reference number}
                    version:  INTEGER;      {file's version number}
                    fName:    STRING[63]    {file name}
                  END;
```

The first field of this record determines whether the file operation should take place or the command should be ignored (because the user clicked the Cancel button in the dialog box). The fType field is used by SFGetFile to store the file's type. The vRefNum, version, and fName fields identify the file chosen by the user; the application passes their values on to the File Manager routine that does the actual file operation. VRefNum contains the volume reference number of the volume containing the file. The version field always contains 0; the use of nonzero version numbers is *not* supported by this package. For more information on files, volumes, and file operations, see chapter 4 of Volume II.

Assembly-language note: Before calling a Standard File Package routine, if you set the global variable SFSaveDisk to the negative of a volume reference number, Standard File will use that volume and display its name in the dialog box. (Note that since the volume reference number is negative, you set SFSaveDisk to a positive value.)

Both SFPutFile and SFGetFile allow you to use a nonstandard dialog box; two additional routines, SFPPutFile and SFPGetFile, provide an even more convenient and powerful way of doing this.

STANDARD FILE PACKAGE ROUTINES

Assembly-language note: The trap macro for the Standard File Package is _Pack3. The routine selectors are as follows:

```
    sfPutFile     .EQU    1
    sfGetFile     .EQU    2
    sfPPutFile    .EQU    3
    sfPGetFile    .EQU    4
```

```
PROCEDURE SFPutFile (where: Point; prompt: Str255; origName:
          Str255; dlgHook: ProcPtr; VAR reply: SFReply);
```

SFPutFile displays a dialog box allowing the user to specify a file to which data will be written (as during a Save or Save As command). It then repeatedly gets and handles events until the user either confirms the command after entering an appropriate file name or aborts the command by clicking Cancel in the dialog. It reports the user's reply by filling the fields of the reply record specified by the reply parameter, as described above; the fType field of this record isn't used.

The general appearance of the standard SFPutFile dialog box is shown in Figure 2. The where parameter specifies the location of the top left corner of the dialog box in global coordinates. The prompt parameter is a line of text to be displayed as a statText item in the dialog box, where shown in Figure 2. The origName parameter contains text that appears as an enabled, selected editText item; for the standard document-saving commands, it should be the current name of the document, or the empty string (to display an insertion point) if the document hasn't been named yet.

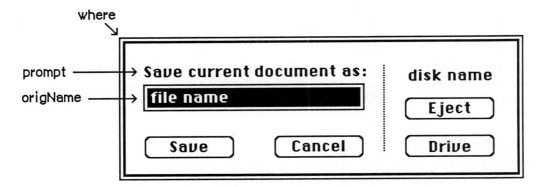

Figure 2. Standard SFPutFile Dialog

If you want to use the standard SFPutFile dialog box, pass NIL for dlgHook; otherwise, see the information for advanced programmers below.

SFPutFile repeatedly calls the Dialog Manager procedure ModalDialog. When an event involving an enabled dialog item occurs, ModalDialog handles the event and returns the item number, and SFPutFile responds as follows:

- If the Eject or Drive button is clicked, or a disk is inserted, SFPutFile responds as described above under "About the Standard File Package".

- Text entered into the editText item is stored in the fName field of the reply record. (SFPutFile keeps track of whether there's currently any text in the item, and makes the Save button inactive if not.)

- If the Save button is clicked, SFPutFile determines whether the file name in the fName field of the reply record is appropriate. If so, it returns control to the application with the first field of the reply record set to TRUE; otherwise, it responds accordingly, as described below.

- If the Cancel button in the dialog is clicked, SFPutFile returns control to the application with the first field of the reply record set to FALSE.

Note: Notice that disk insertion is one of the user actions listed above, even though ModalDialog normally ignores disk-inserted events. The reason this works is that SFPutFile calls ModalDialog with a filterProc function that lets it receive disk-inserted events.

The situations that may cause an entered name to be inappropriate, and SFPutFile's response to each, are as follows:

■ If a file with the specified name already exists on the disk and is different from what was passed in the origName parameter, the alert in Figure 3 is displayed. If the user clicks Yes, the file name is appropriate.

Figure 3. Alert for Existing File

■ If the disk to which the file should be written is locked, the alert in Figure 4 is displayed. If a system error occurs, a similar alert is displayed, with the message "A system error occurred; please try again" (this is unrelated to the fatal system errors reported by the System Error Handler).

Figure 4. Alert for Locked Disk

Note: The user may specify a disk name (preceding the file name and separated from it by a colon). If the disk isn't currently in a drive, an alert similar to the one in Figure 4 is displayed. The ability to specify a disk name is supported for historical reasons only; users should not be encouraged to do it.

After the user clicks No or Cancel in response to one of these alerts, SFPutFile dismisses the alert box and continues handling events (so a different name may be entered).

Advanced programmers: You can create your own dialog box rather than use the standard SFPutFile dialog. However, future compatibility is *not* guaranteed if you don't use the standard SFPutFile dialog. To create a nonstandard dialog, you must provide your own dialog template and store it in your application's resource file with the same resource ID that the standard template has in the system resource file:

```
CONST putDlgID = -3999;   {SFPutFile dialog template ID}
```

Note: The SFPPutFile procedure, described below, lets you use any resource ID for your nonstandard dialog box.

Your dialog template must specify that the dialog window be invisible, and your dialog must contain all the standard items, as listed below. The appearance and location of these items in your dialog may be different. You can make an item "invisible" by giving it a display rectangle that's off the screen. The display rectangle for each item in the standard dialog box is given below. The rectangle for the standard dialog box itself is (0,0)(304,104).

Item number	Item	Standard display rectangle
1	Save button	(12,74)(82,92)
2	Cancel button	(114,74)(184,92)
3	Prompt string (statText)	(12,12)(184,28)
4	UserItem for disk name	(209,16)(295,34)
5	Eject button	(217,43)(287,61)
6	Drive button	(217,74)(287,92)
7	EditText item for file name	(14,34)(182,50)
8	UserItem for dotted line	(200,16)(201,88)

Note: Remember that the display rectangle for any "invisible" text item must be at least about 20 pixels wide.

If your dialog has additional items beyond the standard ones, or if you want to handle any of the standard items in a nonstandard manner, you must write your own dlgHook function and point to it with dlgHook. Your dlgHook function should have two parameters and return an integer value. For example, this is how it would be declared if it were named MyDlg:

```
FUNCTION MyDlg (item: INTEGER; theDialog: DialogPtr) : INTEGER;
```

Immediately after calling ModalDialog, SFPutFile calls your dlgHook function, passing it the item number returned by ModalDialog and a pointer to the dialog record describing your dialog box. Using these two parameters, your dlgHook function should determine how to handle the event. There are predefined constants for the item numbers of standard enabled items, as follows:

```
CONST putSave    = 1;     {Save button}
      putCancel  = 2;     {Cancel button}
      putEject   = 5;     {Eject button}
      putDrive   = 6;     {Drive button}
      putName    = 7;     {editText item for file name}
```

ModalDialog returns the "fake" item number 100 when it receives a null event. Note that since it calls GetNextEvent with a mask that excludes disk-inserted events, ModalDialog sees them as null events, too.

After handling the event (or, perhaps, after ignoring it) the dlgHook function must return an item number to SFPutFile. If the item number is one of those listed above, SFPutFile responds in the standard way; otherwise, it does nothing.

Note: For advanced programmers who want to change the appearance of the alerts displayed when an inappropriate file name is entered, the resource IDs of those alerts in the system resource file are listed below.

Alert	Resource ID
Disk not found	–3994
System error	–3995
Existing file	–3996
Locked disk	–3997

```
PROCEDURE SFPPutFile (where: Point; prompt: Str255; origName:
        Str255; dlgHook: ProcPtr; VAR reply: SFReply; dlgID:
        INTEGER; filterProc: ProcPtr);
```

SFPPutFile is an alternative to SFPutFile for advanced programmers who want to use a nonstandard dialog box. It's the same as SFPutFile except for the two additional parameters dlgID and filterProc.

DlgID is the resource ID of the dialog template to be used instead of the standard one (so you can use whatever ID you wish rather than the same one as the standard).

The filterProc parameter determines how ModalDialog will filter events when called by SFPPutFile. If filterProc is NIL, ModalDialog does the standard filtering that it does when called by SFPutFile; otherwise, filterProc should point to a function for ModalDialog to execute *after* doing the standard filtering. The function must be the same as one you would pass directly to ModalDialog in its filterProc parameter. (See chapter 13 for more information.)

```
PROCEDURE SFGetFile (where: Point; prompt: Str255; fileFilter:
        ProcPtr; numTypes: INTEGER; typeList: SFTypeList;
        dlgHook: ProcPtr; VAR reply: SFReply);
```

SFGetFile displays a dialog box listing the names of a specific group of files from which the user can select one to be opened (as during an Open command). It then repeatedly gets and handles events until the user either confirms the command after choosing a file name or aborts the command by clicking Cancel in the dialog. It reports the user's reply by filling the fields of the reply record specified by the reply parameter, as described above under "Using the Standard File Package".

The general appearance of the standard SFGetFile dialog box is shown in Figure 5. File names are sorted in order of the ASCII codes of their characters, ignoring diacritical marks and mapping lowercase characters to their uppercase equivalents. If there are more file names than can be displayed at one time, the scroll bar is active; otherwise, the scroll bar is inactive.

The where parameter specifies the location of the top left corner of the dialog box in global coordinates. The prompt parameter is ignored; it's there for historical purposes only.

The fileFilter, numTypes, and typeList parameters determine which files appear in the dialog box. SFGetFile first looks at numTypes and typeList to determine what types of files to display, then it executes the function pointed to by fileFilter (if any) to do additional filtering on which files to display. File types are discussed in chapter 1 of Volume III. For example, if the application is concerned only with pictures, you won't want to display the names of any text files.

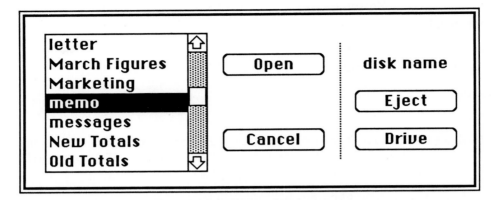

Figure 5. Standard SFGetFile Dialog

Pass –1 for numTypes to display all types of files; otherwise, pass the number of file types (up to 4) that you want to display, and pass the types themselves in typeList. The SFTypeList data type is defined as follows:

```
TYPE SFTypeList = ARRAY[0..3] OF OSType;
```

Assembly-language note: If you need to specify more than four types, pass a pointer to an array with the desired number of entries.

If fileFilter isn't NIL, SFGetFile executes the function it points to for each file, to determine whether the file should be displayed. The fileFilter function has one parameter and returns a Boolean value. For example:

```
FUNCTION MyFileFilter (paramBlock: ParmBlkPtr) : BOOLEAN;
```

SFGetFile passes this function the file information it gets by calling the File Manager procedure GetFileInfo (see chapter 4 of Volume II for details). The function selects which files should appear in the dialog by returning FALSE for every file that should be shown and TRUE for every file that shouldn't be shown.

Note: As described in chapter 4 of Volume II, a flag can be set that tells the Finder not to display a particular file's icon on the desktop; this has no effect on whether SFGetFile will list the file name.

If you want to use the standard SFGetFile dialog box, pass NIL for dlgHook; otherwise, see the information for advanced programmers below.

Like SFPutFile, SFGetFile repeatedly calls the Dialog Manager procedure ModalDialog. When an event involving an enabled dialog item occurs, ModalDialog handles the event and returns the item number, and SFGetFile responds as follows:

■ If the Eject or Drive button is clicked, or a disk is inserted, SFGetFile responds as described above under "About the Standard File Package".

- If clicking or dragging occurs in the scroll bar, the contents of the dialog box are redrawn accordingly.

- If a file name is clicked, it's selected and stored in the fName field of the reply record. (SFGetFile keeps track of whether a file name is currently selected, and makes the Open button inactive if not.)

- If the Open button is clicked, SFGetFile returns control to the application with the first field of the reply record set to TRUE.

- If a file name is double-clicked, SFGetFile responds as if the user clicked the file name and then the Open button.

- If the Cancel button in the dialog is clicked, SFGetFile returns control to the application with the first field of the reply record set to FALSE.

If a character key is pressed, SFGetFile selects the first file name starting with the character typed, scrolling the list of names if necessary to show the selection. If no file name starts with the character, SFGetFile selects the first file name starting with a character whose ASCII code is greater than the character typed.

Advanced programmers: You can create your own dialog box rather than use the standard SFGetFile dialog. However, future compatibility is *not* guaranteed if you don't use the standard SFGetFile dialog. To create a nonstandard dialog, you must provide your own dialog template and store it in your application's resource file with the same resource ID that the standard template has in the system resource file:

```
CONST getDlgID = -4000;   {SFGetFile dialog template ID}
```

Note: The SFPGetFile procedure, described below, lets you use any resource ID for your nonstandard dialog box.

Your dialog template must specify that the dialog window be invisible, and your dialog must contain all the standard items, as listed below. The appearance and location of these items in your dialog may be different. You can make an item "invisible" by giving it a display rectangle that's off the screen. The display rectangle for each item in the standard dialog box is given below. The rectangle for the standard dialog box itself is (0,0)(348,136).

Item number	Item	Standard display rectangle
1	Open button	(152,28)(232,46)
2	Invisible button	(1152,59)(1232,77)
3	Cancel button	(152,90)(232,108)
4	UserItem for disk name	(248,28)(344,46)
5	Eject button	(256,59)(336,77)
6	Drive button	(256,90)(336,108)
7	UserItem for file name list	(12,11)(125,125)
8	UserItem for scroll bar	(124,11)(140,125)
9	UserItem for dotted line	(244,20)(245,116)
10	Invisible text (statText)	(1044,20)(1145,116)

If your dialog has additional items beyond the standard ones, or if you want to handle any of the standard items in a nonstandard manner, you must write your own dlgHook function and point to it with dlgHook. Your dlgHook function should have two parameters and return an integer value. For example, this is how it would be declared if it were named MyDlg:

```
FUNCTION MyDlg (item: INTEGER; theDialog: DialogPtr) : INTEGER;
```

Immediately after calling ModalDialog, SFGetFile calls your dlgHook function, passing it the item number returned by ModalDialog and a pointer to the dialog record describing your dialog box. Using these two parameters, your dlgHook function should determine how to handle the event. There are predefined constants for the item numbers of standard enabled items, as follows:

```
CONST  getOpen    = 1;    {Open button}
       getCancel  = 3;    {Cancel button}
       getEject   = 5;    {Eject button}
       getDrive   = 6;    {Drive button}
       getNmList  = 7;    {userItem for file name list}
       getScroll  = 8;    {userItem for scroll bar}
```

ModalDialog also returns "fake" item numbers in the following situations, which are detected by its filterProc function:

■ When it receives a null event, it returns 100. Note that since it calls GetNextEvent with a mask that excludes disk-inserted events, ModalDialog sees them as null events, too.

■ When a key-down event occurs, it returns 1000 plus the ASCII code of the character.

After handling the event (or, perhaps, after ignoring it) your dlgHook function must return an item number to SFGetFile. If the item number is one of those listed above, SFGetFile responds in the standard way; otherwise, it does nothing.

```
PROCEDURE SFPGetFile (where: Point; prompt: Str255; fileFilter:
        ProcPtr; numTypes: INTEGER; typeList: SFTypeList;
        dlgHook: ProcPtr; VAR reply: SFReply; dlgID: INTEGER;
        filterProc: ProcPtr);
```

SFPGetFile is an alternative to SFGetFile for advanced programmers who want to use a nonstandard dialog box. It's the same as SFGetFile except for the two additional parameters dlgID and filterProc.

DlgID is the resource ID of the dialog template to be used instead of the standard one (so you can use whatever ID you wish rather than the same one as the standard).

The filterProc parameter determines how ModalDialog will filter events when called by SFPGetFile. If filterProc is NIL, ModalDialog does the standard filtering that it does when called by SFGetFile; otherwise, filterProc should point to a function for ModalDialog to execute *after* doing the standard filtering. The function must be the same as one you would pass directly to ModalDialog in its filterProc parameter. (See chapter 13 for more information.) Note that the standard filtering will detect key-down events only if the dialog template ID is the standard one.

SUMMARY OF THE STANDARD FILE PACKAGE

Constants

```
CONST  { SFPutFile dialog template ID }

       putDlgID = -3999;

       { Item numbers of enabled items in SFPutFile dialog }

       putSave   = 1;     {Save button}
       putCancel = 2;     {Cancel button}
       putEject  = 5;     {Eject button}
       putDrive  = 6;     {Drive button}
       putName   = 7;     {editText item for file name}

       { SFGetFile dialog template ID }

       getDlgID = -4000;

       { Item numbers of enabled items in SFGetFile dialog }

       getOpen   = 1;     {Open button}
       getCancel = 3;     {Cancel button}
       getEject  = 5;     {Eject button}
       getDrive  = 6;     {Drive button}
       getNmList = 7;     {userItem for file name list}
       getScroll = 8;     {userItem for scroll bar}
```

Data Types

```
TYPE  SFReply = RECORD
                  good:     BOOLEAN;     {FALSE if ignore command}
                  copy:     BOOLEAN;     {not used}
                  fType:    OSType;      {file type or not used}
                  vRefNum:  INTEGER;     {volume reference number}
                  version:  INTEGER;     {file's version number}
                  fName:    STRING[63]   {file name}
                END;

      SFTypeList = ARRAY[0..3] OF OSType;
```

Routines

```
PROCEDURE SFPutFile      (where: Point; prompt: Str255; origName: Str255;
                          dlgHook: ProcPtr; VAR reply: SFReply);
PROCEDURE SFPPutFile     (where: Point; prompt: Str255; origName: Str255;
                          dlgHook: ProcPtr; VAR reply: SFReply; dlgID:
                          INTEGER; filterProc: ProcPtr);
PROCEDURE SFGetFile      (where: Point; prompt: Str255; fileFilter: ProcPtr;
                          numTypes: INTEGER; typeList: SFTypeList; dlgHook:
                          ProcPtr; VAR reply: SFReply);
PROCEDURE SFPGetFile     (where: Point; prompt: Str255; fileFilter: ProcPtr;
                          numTypes: INTEGER; typeList: SFTypeList; dlgHook:
                          ProcPtr; VAR reply: SFReply; dlgID: INTEGER;
                          filterProc: ProcPtr);
```

DlgHook Function

```
FUNCTION MyDlg (item: INTEGER; theDialog: DialogPtr) : INTEGER;
```

FileFilter Function

```
FUNCTION MyFileFilter (paramBlock: ParmBlkPtr) : BOOLEAN;
```

Standard SFPutFile Items

Item number	Item	Standard display rectangle
1	Save button	(12,74)(82,92)
2	Cancel button	(114,74)(184,92)
3	Prompt string (statText)	(12,12)(184,28)
4	UserItem for disk name	(209,16)(295,34)
5	Eject button	(217,43)(287,61)
6	Drive button	(217,74)(287,92)
7	EditText item for file name	(14,34)(182,50)
8	UserItem for dotted line	(200,16)(201,88)

Resource IDs of SFPutFile Alerts

Alert	Resource ID
Disk not found	–3994
System error	–3995
Existing file	–3996
Locked disk	–3997

Standard SFGetFile Items

Item number	Item	Standard display rectangle
1	Open button	(152,28)(232,46)
2	Invisible button	(1152,59)(1232,77)
3	Cancel button	(152,90)(232,108)
4	UserItem for disk name	(248,28)(344,46)
5	Eject button	(256,59)(336,77)
6	Drive button	(256,90)(336,108)
7	UserItem for file name list	(12,11)(125,125)
8	UserItem for scroll bar	(124,11)(140,125)
9	UserItem for dotted line	(244,20)(245,116)
10	Invisible text (statText)	(1044,20)(1145,116)

Assembly-Language Information

Constants

```
; SFPutFile dialog template ID

putDlgID    .EQU    -3999

; Item numbers of enabled items in SFPutFile dialog

putSave     .EQU    1      ;Save button
putCancel   .EQU    2      ;Cancel button
putEject    .EQU    5      ;Eject button
putDrive    .EQU    6      ;Drive button
putName     .EQU    7      ;editText item for file name

; SFGetFile dialog template ID

getDlgID    .EQU    -4000
```

```
; Item numbers of enabled items in SFGetFile dialog

getOpen      .EQU    1    ;Open button
getCancel    .EQU    3    ;Cancel button
getEject     .EQU    5    ;Eject button
getDrive     .EQU    6    ;Drive button
getNmList    .EQU    7    ;userItem for file name list
getScroll    .EQU    8    ;userItem for scroll bar

; Routine selectors

sfPutFile    .EQU    1
sfGetFile    .EQU    2
sfPPutFile   .EQU    3
sfPGetFile   .EQU    4
```

Reply Record Data Structure

rGood	0 if ignore command (byte)
rType	File type (long)
rVolume	Volume reference number (word)
rVersion	File's version number (word)
rName	File name (length byte followed by up to 63 characters)

Trap Macro Name

_Pack3

Variables

SFSaveDisk	Negative of volume reference number used by Standard File Package (word)

Inside Macintosh
Volume II

Contents

PREFACE

ABOUT INSIDE MACINTOSH

Inside Macintosh is a three-volume set of manuals that tells you what you need to know to write software for the Apple® Macintosh™ 128K, 512K, or XL (or a Lisa® running MacWorks™ XL). Although directed mainly toward programmers writing standard Macintosh applications, *Inside Macintosh* also contains the information needed to write simple utility programs, desk accessories, device drivers, or any other Macintosh software. It includes:

- the user interface guidelines for applications on the Macintosh

- a complete description of the routines available for your program to call (both those built into the Macintosh and others on disk), along with related concepts and background information

- a description of the Macintosh 128K and 512K hardware

It does *not* include information about:

- Programming in general.

- Getting started as a developer. For this, write to:

      Developer Relations
      Mail Stop 27-S
      Apple Computer, Inc.
      20525 Mariani Avenue
      Cupertino, CA 95014

- Any specific development system, except where indicated. You'll need to have additional documentation for the development system you're using.

- The Standard Apple Numeric Environment (SANE), which your program can access to perform extended-precision floating-point arithmetic and transcendental functions. This environment is described in the *Apple Numerics Manual*.

You should already be familiar with the basic information that's in *Macintosh*, the owner's guide, and have some experience using a standard Macintosh application (such as MacWrite™).

The Language

The routines you'll need to call are written in assembly language, but (with a few exceptions) they're also accessible from high-level languages, such as Pascal on the Lisa Workshop development system. *Inside Macintosh* documents the Lisa Pascal interfaces to the routines and the symbolic names defined for assembly-language programmers using the Lisa Workshop; if you're using a different development system, its documentation should tell you how to apply the information presented here to that system.

Inside Macintosh is intended to serve the needs of both high-level language and assembly-language programmers. Every routine is shown in its Pascal form (if it has one), but assembly-language programmers are told how they can access the routines. Information of interest only to assembly-language programmers is isolated and labeled so that other programmers can conveniently skip it.

Familiarity with Lisa Pascal (or a similar high-level language) is recommended for all readers, since it's used for most examples. Lisa Pascal is described in the documentation for the Lisa Pascal Workshop.

What's in Each Volume

Inside Macintosh consists of three volumes. Volume I begins with the following information of general interest:

- a "road map" to the software and the rest of the documentation
- the user interface guidelines
- an introduction to memory management (the least you need to know, with a complete discussion following in Volume II)
- some general information for assembly-language programmers

It then describes the various parts of the **User Interface Toolbox**, the software in ROM that helps you implement the standard Macintosh user interface in your application. This is followed by descriptions of other, RAM-based software that's similar in function to the User Interface Toolbox. (The software overview in the Road Map chapter gives further details.)

Volume II describes the **Operating System**, the software in ROM that does basic tasks such as input and output, memory management, and interrupt handling. As in Volume I, some functionally similar RAM-based software is then described.

Volume III discusses your program's interface with the Finder and then describes the Macintosh 128K and 512K hardware. A comprehensive summary of all the software is provided, followed by some useful appendices and a glossary of all terms defined in *Inside Macintosh*.

Version Numbers

This edition of *Inside Macintosh* describes the following versions of the software:

- version 105 of the ROM in the Macintosh 128K or 512K
- version 112 of the ROM image installed by MacWorks in the Macintosh XL
- version 1.1 of the Lisa Pascal interfaces and the assembly-language definitions

Some of the RAM-based software is read from the file named System (usually kept in the System Folder). This manual describes the software in the System file whose creation date is May 2, 1984.

A HORSE OF A DIFFERENT COLOR

On an innovative system like the Macintosh, programs don't look quite the way they do on other systems. For example, instead of carrying out a sequence of steps in a predetermined order, your program is driven primarily by user actions (such as clicking and typing) whose order cannot be predicted.

You'll probably find that many of your preconceptions about how to write applications don't apply here. Because of this, and because of the sheer volume of information in *Inside Macintosh*, it's essential that you read the Road Map chapter. It will help you get oriented and figure out where to go next.

THE STRUCTURE OF A TYPICAL CHAPTER

Most chapters of *Inside Macintosh* have the same structure, as described below. Reading through this now will save you a lot of time and effort later on. It contains important hints on how to find what you're looking for within this vast amount of technical documentation.

Every chapter begins with a very brief description of its subject and a list of what you should already know before reading that chapter. Then there's a section called, for example, "About the Window Manager", which gives you more information about the subject, telling you what you can do with it in general, elaborating on related user interface guidelines, and introducing terminology that will be used in the chapter. This is followed by a series of sections describing important related concepts and background information; unless they're noted to be for advanced programmers only, you'll have to read them in order to understand how to use the routines described later.

Before the routine descriptions themselves, there's a section called, for example, "Using the Window Manager". It introduces you to the routines, telling you how they fit into the general flow of an application program and, most important, giving you an idea of which ones you'll need to use. Often you'll need only a few routines out of many to do basic operations; by reading this section, you can save yourself the trouble of learning routines you'll never use.

Then, for the details about the routines, read on to the next section. It gives the calling sequence for each routine and describes all the parameters, effects, side effects, and so on.

Following the routine descriptions, there may be some sections that won't be of interest to all readers. Usually these contain information about advanced techniques, or behind the scenes details for the curious.

For review and quick reference, each chapter ends with a summary of the subject matter, including the entire Pascal interface and a separate section for assembly-language programmers.

CONVENTIONS

The following notations are used in *Inside Macintosh* to draw your attention to particular items of information:

Note: A note that may be interesting or useful

Warning: A point you need to be cautious about

Assembly-language note: A note of interest to assembly-language programmers only

---

[Not in ROM]

Routines marked with this notation are not part of the Macintosh ROM. Depending on how the interfaces have been set up on the development system you're using, these routines may or may not be available. They're available to users of Lisa Pascal; other users should check the documentation for their development system for more information. (For related information of interest to assembly-language programmers, see chapter 4 of Volume I.)

1 THE MEMORY MANAGER

ABOUT THIS CHAPTER

This chapter describes the Memory Manager, the part of the Macintosh Operating System that controls the dynamic allocation of memory space in the heap.

ABOUT THE MEMORY MANAGER

Using the Memory Manager, your program can maintain one or more independent areas of heap memory (called **heap zones**) and use them to allocate blocks of memory of any desired size. Unlike stack space, which is always allocated and released in strict LIFO (last-in-first-out) order, blocks in the heap can be allocated and released in any order, according to your program's needs. So instead of growing and shrinking in an orderly way like the stack, the heap tends to become fragmented into a patchwork of allocated and free blocks, as shown in Figure 1. The Memory Manager does all the necessary "housekeeping" to keep track of the blocks as it allocates and releases them.

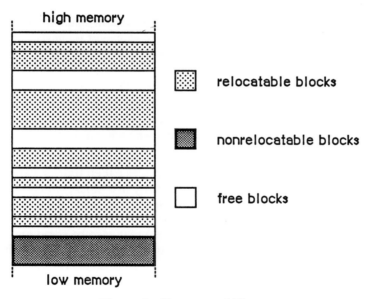

Figure 1. Fragmented Heap

The Memory Manager always maintains at least two heap zones: a **system heap zone** that's used by the Operating System and an **application heap zone** that's used by the Toolbox and your application program. The system heap zone is initialized to a fixed size when the system starts up; typically this size is 16.75K bytes on a Macintosh 128K, and 48K on a Macintosh 512K or XL.

Note: The initial size of the system heap zone is determined by the system startup information stored on a volume; for more information, see the section "Data Organization on Volumes" in chapter 4. The default initial size of this zone depends on the memory size of the machine and may be different in future versions of the Macintosh.

Objects in the system heap zone remain allocated even when one application terminates and another starts up. In contrast, the application heap zone is automatically reinitialized at the start of each new application program, and the contents of any previous application zone are lost.

Assembly-language note: If desired, you can prevent the application heap zone from being reinitialized when an application starts up; see the discussion of the Chain procedure in chapter 2 for details.

The initial size of the application zone is 6K bytes, but it can grow as needed. Your program can create additional heap zones if it chooses, either by subdividing this original application zone or by allocating space on the stack for more heap zones.

Note: In this chapter, unless otherwise stated, the term "application heap zone" (or "application zone") always refers to the original application heap zone provided by the system, before any subdivision.

Your program's code typically resides in the application zone, in space reserved for it at the request of the Segment Loader. Similarly, the Resource Manager requests space in the application zone to hold resources it has read into memory from a resource file. Toolbox routines that create new entities of various kinds, such as NewWindow, NewControl, and NewMenu, also call the Memory Manager to allocate the space they need.

At any given time, there's one **current heap zone**, to which most Memory Manager operations implicitly apply. You can control which heap zone is current by calling a Memory Manager procedure. Whenever the system needs to access its own (system) heap zone, it saves the setting of the current heap zone and restores it later.

Space within a heap zone is divided into contiguous pieces called **blocks**. The blocks in a zone fill it completely: Every byte in the zone is part of exactly one block, which may be either **allocated** (reserved for use) or **free** (available for allocation). Each block has a **block header** for the Memory Manager's own use, followed by the block's **contents**, the area available for use by your application or the system (see Figure 2). There may also be some unused bytes at the end of the block, beyond the end of the contents. A block can be of any size, limited only by the size of the heap zone itself.

Assembly-language note: Blocks are always aligned on even word boundaries, so you can access them with word (.W) and long-word (.L) instructions.

An allocated block may be **relocatable** or **nonrelocatable**. Relocatable blocks can be moved around within the heap zone to create space for other blocks; nonrelocatable blocks can never be moved. These are permanent properties of a block. If relocatable, a block may be **locked** or **unlocked**; if unlocked, it may be **purgeable** or **unpurgeable**. These attributes can be set and changed as necessary. Locking a relocatable block prevents it from being moved. Making a block purgeable allows the Memory Manager to remove it from the heap zone, if necessary, to

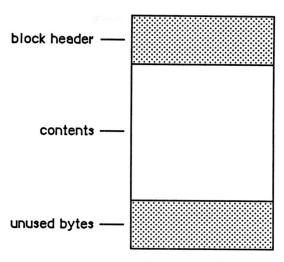

Figure 2. A Block

make room for another block. (Purging of blocks is discussed further below under "How Heap Space Is Allocated".) A newly allocated relocatable block is initially unlocked and unpurgeable.

Relocatable blocks are moved only by the Memory Manager, and only at well-defined, predictable times. In particular, only the routines listed in Appendix B can cause blocks to move, and these routines can never be called from within an interrupt. If your program doesn't call these routines, you can rely on blocks not being moved.

POINTERS AND HANDLES

Relocatable and nonrelocatable blocks are referred to in different ways: nonrelocatable blocks by pointers, relocatable blocks by handles. When the Memory Manager allocates a new block, it returns a pointer or handle to the contents of the block (not to the block's header) depending on whether the block is nonrelocatable (Figure 3) or relocatable (Figure 4).

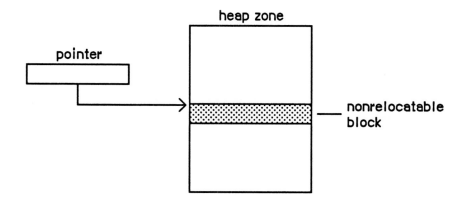

Figure 3. A Pointer to a Nonrelocatable Block

A pointer to a nonrelocatable block never changes, since the block itself can't move. A pointer to a relocatable block can change, however, since the block can move. For this reason, the Memory Manager maintains a single nonrelocatable **master pointer** to each relocatable block. The master pointer is created at the same time as the block and set to point to it. When you allocate a relocatable block, the Memory Manager returns a pointer to the master pointer, called a **handle** to the block (see Figure 4). If the Memory Manager later has to move the block, it has only to update the master pointer to point to the block's new location.

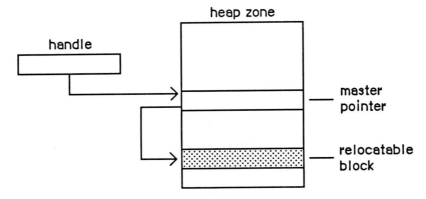

Figure 4. A Handle to a Relocatable Block

HOW HEAP SPACE IS ALLOCATED

The Memory Manager allocates space for relocatable blocks according to a "first fit" strategy. It looks for a free block of at least the requested size, scanning forward from the end of the last block allocated and "wrapping around" from the top of the zone to the bottom if necessary. As soon as it finds a free block big enough, it allocates the requested number of bytes from that block.

If a single free block can't be found that's big enough, the Memory Manager will try to create the needed space by **compacting** the heap zone: moving allocated blocks together in order to collect the free space into a single larger block. Only relocatable, unlocked blocks are moved. The compaction continues until either a free block of at least the requested size has been created or the entire heap zone has been compacted. Figure 5 illustrates what happens when the entire heap must be compacted to create a large enough free block.

Nonrelocatable blocks (and relocatable ones that are temporarily locked) interfere with the compaction process by forming immovable "islands" in the heap. This can prevent free blocks from being collected together and lead to fragmentation of the available free space, as shown in Figure 6. (Notice that the Memory Manager will never move a relocatable block around a nonrelocatable block.) To minimize this problem, the Memory Manager tries to keep all the nonrelocatable blocks together at the bottom of the heap zone. When you allocate a nonrelocatable block, the Memory Manager will try to make room for the new block near the bottom of the zone, by moving other blocks upward, expanding the zone, or purging blocks from it (see below).

Warning: To avoid heap fragmentation, use relocatable instead of nonrelocatable blocks.

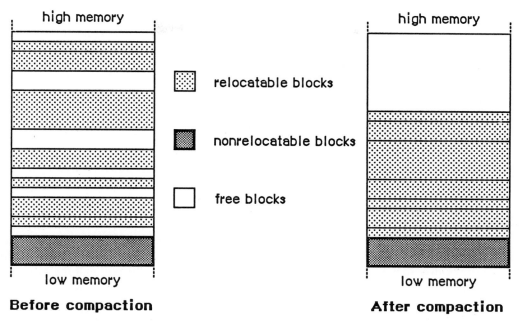

Figure 5. Heap Compaction

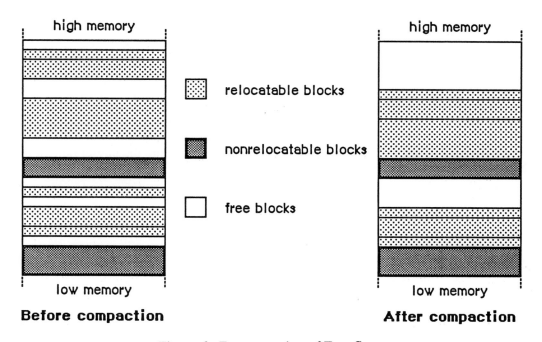

Figure 6. Fragmentation of Free Space

If the Memory Manager can't satisfy the allocation request after compacting the entire heap zone, it next tries expanding the zone by the requested number of bytes (rounded up to the nearest 1K bytes). Only the original application zone can be expanded, and only up to a certain limit (discussed more fully under "The Stack and the Heap"). If any other zone is current, or if the application zone has already reached or exceeded its limit, this step is skipped.

Next the Memory Manager tries to free space by **purging** blocks from the zone. Only relocatable blocks can be purged, and then only if they're explicitly marked as unlocked and purgeable. Purging a block removes it from its heap zone and frees the space it occupies. The space occupied by the block's master pointer itself remains allocated, but the master pointer is set to NIL. Any handles to the block now point to a NIL master pointer, and are said to be **empty**. If your program later needs to refer to the purged block, it must detect that the handle has become empty and ask the Memory Manager to **reallocate** the block. This operation updates the master pointer (see Figure 7).

> **Warning:** Reallocating a block recovers only its space, not its contents (which were lost when the block was purged). It's up to your program to reconstitute the block's contents.

Finally, if all else fails, the Memory Manager calls the **grow zone function**, if any, for the current heap zone. This is an optional routine that an application can provide to take any last-ditch measures to try to "grow" the zone by freeing some space in it. The grow zone function can try to create additional free space by purging blocks that were previously marked unpurgeable, unlocking previously locked blocks, and so on. The Memory Manager will call the grow zone function repeatedly, compacting the heap again after each call, until either it finds the space it's looking for or the grow zone function has exhausted all possibilities. In the latter case, the Memory Manager will finally give up and report that it's unable to satisfy the allocation request.

> **Note:** The Memory Manager moves a block by copying the entire block to a new location; it won't "slide" a block up or down in memory. If there isn't free space at least as large as the block, the block is effectively not relocatable.

Dereferencing a Handle

Accessing a block by double indirection, through its handle instead of through its master pointer, requires an extra memory reference. For efficiency, you may sometimes want to **dereference** the handle—that is, make a copy of the block's master pointer, and then use that pointer to access the block by single indirection. But *be careful!* Any operation that allocates space from the heap may cause the underlying block to be moved or purged. In that event, the master pointer itself will be correctly updated, but your copy of it will be left dangling.

One way to avoid this common type of program bug is to lock the block before dereferencing its handle. For example:

```
VAR  aPointer: Ptr;
     aHandle: Handle;
     . . .

aHandle := NewHandle(...);    {create relocatable block}
. . .
HLock(aHandle);               {lock before dereferencing}
aPointer := aHandle^;         {dereference handle}
WHILE ... DO
  BEGIN
   ...aPointer^...            {use simple pointer}
  END;
HUnlock(aHandle)              {unlock block when finished}
```

1 Memory Manager

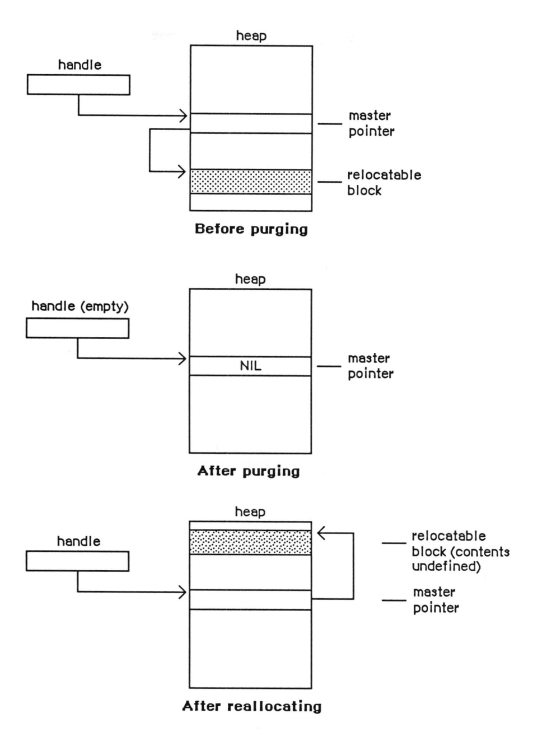

Figure 7. Purging and Reallocating a Block

Assembly-language note: To dereference a handle in assembly language, just copy the master pointer into an address register and use it to access the block by single indirection.

Remember, however, that when you lock a block it becomes an "island" in the heap that may interfere with compaction and cause free space to become fragmented. It's recommended that you use this technique only in parts of your program where efficiency is critical, such as inside tight inner loops that are executed many times (and that don't allocate other blocks).

Warning: Don't forget to unlock the block again when you're through with the dereferenced handle.

Instead of locking the block, you can update your copy of the master pointer after any "dangerous" operation (one that can invalidate the pointer by moving or purging the block it points to). For a complete list of all routines that may move or purge blocks, see Appendix B.

The Lisa Pascal compiler frequently dereferences handles during its normal operation. You should take care to write code that will protect you when the compiler dereferences handles in the following cases:

- Use of the WITH statement with a handle, such as

```
WITH aHandle^^ DO ...
```

- Assigning the result of a function that can move or purge blocks (or of any function in a package or another segment) to a field in a record referred to by a handle, such as

```
aHandle^^.field := NewHandle(...)
```

A problem may arise because the compiler generates code that dereferences the handle before calling NewHandle—and NewHandle may move the block containing the field.

- Passing an argument of more than four bytes referred to by a handle, to a routine that can move or purge a block or to any routine in a package or another segment. For example:

```
TEUpdate(hTE^^.viewRect,hTE)
```

or

```
DrawString(theControl^^.contrlTitle)
```

You can avoid having the compiler generate and use dangling pointers by locking a block before you use its handle in the above situations. Or you can use temporary variables, as in the following:

```
temp := NewHandle(...);
aHandle^^.field := temp
```

THE STACK AND THE HEAP

The LIFO nature of the stack makes it particularly convenient for memory allocation connected with the activation and deactivation of routines (procedures and functions). Each time a routine is called, space is allocated for a **stack frame**. The stack frame holds the routine's parameters, local variables, and return address. Upon exit from the routine, the stack frame is released, restoring the stack to the same state it was in when the routine was called.

In Lisa Pascal, all stack management is done by the compiler. When you call a routine, the compiler generates code to reserve space if necessary for a function result, place the parameter values and return link on the stack, and jump to the routine. The routine can then allocate space on the stack for its own local variables.

Before returning, the routine releases the stack space occupied by its local variables, return link, and parameters. If the routine is a function, it leave its result on the stack for the calling program.

The application heap zone and the stack share the same area in memory, growing toward each other from opposite ends (see Figure 8). Naturally it would be disastrous for either to grow so far that it collides with the other. To help prevent such collisions, the Memory Manager enforces a limit on how far the application heap zone can grow toward the stack. Your program can set this **application heap limit** to control the allotment of available space between the stack and the heap.

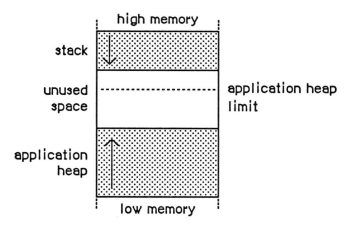

Figure 8. The Stack and the Heap

The application heap limit marks the boundary between the space available for the application heap zone and the space reserved exclusively for the stack. At the start of each application program, the limit is initialized to allow 8K bytes for the stack. Depending on your program's needs, you can adjust the limit to allow more heap space at the expense of the stack or vice versa.

Assembly-language note: The global variables DefltStack and MinStack contain the default and minimum sizes of the stack, respectively.

Notice that the limit applies only to expansion of the *heap*; it has no effect on how far the *stack* can expand. Athough the heap can never expand beyond the limit into space reserved for the stack, there's nothing to prevent the stack from crossing the limit. It's up to you to set the limit low enough to allow for the maximum stack depth your program will ever need.

> **Note:** Regardless of the limit setting, the application zone is never allowed to grow to within 1K of the current end of the stack. This gives a little extra protection in case the stack is approaching the boundary or has crossed over onto the heap's side, and allows some safety margin for the stack to expand even further.

To help detect collisions between the stack and the heap, a "stack sniffer" routine is run sixty times a second, during the Macintosh's vertical retrace interrupt. This routine compares the current ends of the stack and the heap and invokes the System Error Handler in case of a collision.

The stack sniffer can't prevent collisions, it can only detect them after the fact: A lot of computation can take place in a sixtieth of a second. In fact, the stack can easily expand into the heap, overwrite it, and then shrink back again before the next activation of the stack sniffer, escaping detection completely. The stack sniffer is useful mainly during software development; the alert box the System Error Handler displays can be confusing to your program's end user. Its purpose is to warn you, the programmer, that your program's stack and heap are colliding, so that you can adjust the heap limit to correct the problem before the user ever encounters it.

GENERAL-PURPOSE DATA TYPES

The Memory Manager includes a number of type definitions for general-purpose use. The types listed below are explained in chapter 3 of Volume I.

```
TYPE  SignedByte = -128..127;
      Byte       = 0..255;
      Ptr        = ^SignedByte;
      Handle     = ^Ptr;

      Str255       = STRING[255];
      StringPtr    = ^Str255;
      StringHandle = ^StringPtr;

      ProcPtr = Ptr;

      Fixed = LONGINT;
```

For specifying the sizes of blocks in the heap, the Memory Manager defines a special type called Size:

```
TYPE Size = LONGINT;
```

All Memory Manager routines that deal with block sizes expect parameters of type Size or return them as results.

MEMORY ORGANIZATION

This section discusses the organization of memory in the Macintosh 128K, 512K, and XL.

Note: The information presented in this section may be different in future versions of Macintosh system software.

The organization of the Macintosh 128K and 512K RAM is shown in Figure 9. The variable names listed on the right in the figure refer to global variables for use by assembly-language programmers.

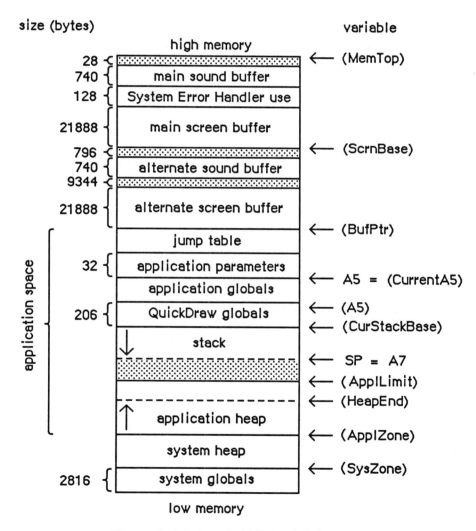

Figure 9. Macintosh 128K and 512K RAM

Assembly-language note: The global variables, shown in parentheses, contain the addresses of the indicated areas. Names identified as marking the end of an area actually refer to the address *following* the last byte in that area.

The lowest 2816 bytes are used for system globals. Immediately following this are the system heap and the **application space**, which is memory available for dynamic allocation by applications. Most of the application space is shared between the stack and the application heap, with the heap growing forward from the bottom of the space and the stack growing backward from the top. The remainder of the application space is occupied by QuickDraw global variables, the application's global variables, the application parameters, and the jump table. The **application parameters** are 32 bytes of memory located above the application globals; they're reserved for use by the system. The first application parameter is the address of the first QuickDraw global variable (thePort). The jump table is explained in chapter 2.

Note: Some development systems may place the QuickDraw global variables in a different location, but the first application parameter will always point to them.

Assembly-language note: The location pointed to by register A5 will always point to the first QuickDraw global variable.

At (almost) the very end of memory are the main sound buffer, used by the Sound Driver to control the sounds emitted by the built-in speaker and by the Disk Driver to control disk motor speed, and the main screen buffer, which holds the bit image to be displayed on the Macintosh screen. The area between the main screen and sound buffers is used by the System Error Handler.

There are alternate screen and sound buffers for special applications. If you use either or both of these, the memory available for use by your application is reduced accordingly. The Segment Loader provides routines for specifying that an alternate screen or sound buffer will be used.

Note: The alternate screen and sound buffers may not be supported in future versions of the Macintosh. The main and alternate sound buffers, as well as the alternate screen buffer, are not supported on the Macintosh XL.

The memory organization of a Macintosh XL is shown in Figure 10.

MEMORY MANAGER DATA STRUCTURES

This section discusses the internal data structures of the Memory Manager. You don't need to know this information if you're just using the Memory Manager routinely to allocate and release blocks of memory from the application heap zone.

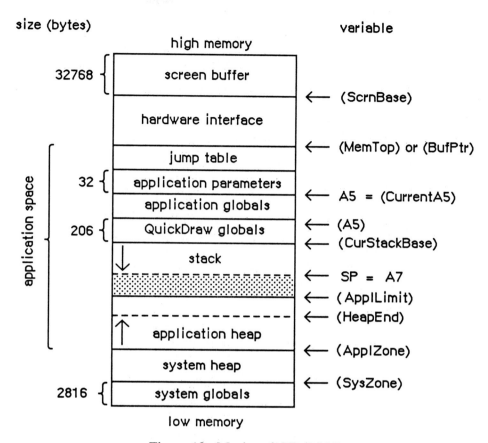

Figure 10. Macintosh XL RAM

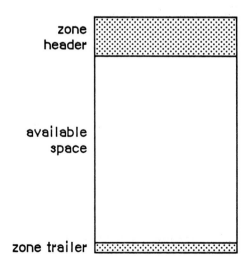

Figure 11. Structure of a Heap Zone

Structure of Heap Zones

Each heap zone begins with a 52-byte **zone header** and ends with a 12-byte **zone trailer** (see Figure 11). The header contains all the information the Memory Manager needs about that heap zone; the trailer is just a minimum-size free block (described in the next section) placed at the end of the zone as a marker. All the remaining space between the header and trailer is available for allocation.

In Pascal, a heap zone is defined as a **zone record** of type Zone. It's always referred to with a **zone pointer** of type THz ("the heap zone"):

```
TYPE  THz  = ^Zone;
      Zone = RECORD
                  bkLim:       Ptr;       {zone trailer block}
                  purgePtr:    Ptr;       {used internally}
                  hFstFree:    Ptr;       {first free master pointer}
                  zcbFree:     LONGINT;   {number of free bytes}
                  gzProc:      ProcPtr;   {grow zone function}
                  moreMast:    INTEGER;   {master pointers to allocate}
                  flags:       INTEGER;   {used internally}
                  cntRel:      INTEGER;   {not used}
                  maxRel:      INTEGER;   {not used}
                  cntNRel:     INTEGER;   {not used}
                  maxNRel:     INTEGER;   {not used}
                  cntEmpty:    INTEGER;   {not used}
                  cntHandles:  INTEGER;   {not used}
                  minCBFree:   LONGINT;   {not used}
                  purgeProc:   ProcPtr;   {purge warning procedure}
                  sparePtr:    Ptr;       {used internally}
                  allocPtr:    Ptr;       {used internally}
                  heapData:    INTEGER    {first usable byte in zone}
              END;
```

> **Warning:** The fields of the zone header are for the Memory Manager's own internal use. You can examine the contents of the zone's fields, but in general it doesn't make sense for your program to try to change them. The few exceptions are noted below in the discussions of the specific fields.

BkLim is a pointer to the zone's trailer block. Since the trailer is the last block in the zone, bkLim is a pointer to the byte *following* the last byte of usable space in the zone.

HFstFree is a pointer to the first free master pointer in the zone. Instead of just allocating space for one master pointer each time a relocatable block is created, the Memory Manager "preallocates" several master pointers at a time; as a group they form a nonrelocatable block. The moreMast field of the zone record tells the Memory Manager how many master pointers at a time to preallocate for this zone.

> **Note:** Master pointers are allocated 32 at a time for the system heap zone and 64 at a time for the application zone; this may be different on future versions of the Macintosh.

All master pointers that are allocated but not currently in use are linked together into a list beginning in the hFstFree field. When you allocate a new relocatable block, the Memory

Manager removes the first available master pointer from this list, sets it to point to the new block, and returns its address to you as a handle to the block. (If the list is empty, it allocates a fresh block of moreMast master pointers.) When you release a relocatable block, its master pointer isn't released, but is linked onto the beginning of the list to be reused. Thus the amount of space devoted to master pointers can increase, but can never decrease until the zone is reinitialized.

The zcbFree field always contains the number of free bytes remaining in the zone. As blocks are allocated and released, the Memory Manager adjusts zcbFree accordingly. This number represents an upper limit on the size of block you can allocate from this heap zone.

> **Warning:** It may not actually be possible to allocate a block as big as zcbFree bytes. Because nonrelocatable and locked blocks can't be moved, it isn't always possible to collect all the free space into a single block by compaction.

The gzProc field is a pointer to the grow zone function. You can supply a pointer to your own grow zone function when you create a new heap zone and can change it at any time.

> **Warning:** Don't store directly into the gzProc field; if you want to supply your own grow zone function, you must do so with a procedure call (InitZone or SetGrowZone).

PurgeProc is a pointer to the zone's **purge warning procedure,** or NIL if there is none. The Memory Manager will call this procedure before it purges a block from the zone.

> **Warning:** Whenever you call the Resource Manager with SetResPurge(TRUE), it installs its own purge warning procedure, overriding any purge warning procedure you've specified to the Memory Manager; for further details, see chapter 5 of Volume I.

The last field of a zone record, heapData, is a dummy field marking the bottom of the zone's usable memory space. HeapData nominally contains an integer, but this integer has no significance in itself—it's just the first two bytes in the block header of the first block in the zone. The purpose of the heapData field is to give you a way of locating the effective bottom of the zone. For example, if myZone is a zone pointer, then

```
@(myZone^.heapData)
```

is a pointer to the first usable byte in the zone, just as

```
myZone^.bkLim
```

is a pointer to the byte following the last usable byte in the zone.

Structure of Blocks

Every block in a heap zone, whether allocated or free, has a block header that the Memory Manager uses to find its way around in the zone. Block headers are completely transparent to your program. All pointers and handles to allocated blocks point to the beginning of the block's contents, following the end of the header. Similarly, all block sizes seen by your program refer to the block's **logical size** (the number of bytes in its contents) rather than its **physical size** (the number of bytes it actually occupies in memory, including the header and any unused bytes at the end of the block).

Since your program shouldn't normally have to deal with block headers directly, there's no Pascal record type defining their structure. A block header consists of eight bytes, as shown in Figure 12.

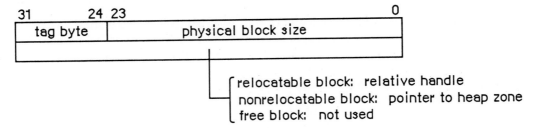

Figure 12. Block Header

The first byte of the block header is the tag byte, discussed below. The next three bytes contain the block's physical size in bytes. Adding this number to the block's address gives the address of the next block in the zone.

The contents of the second long word (four bytes) in the block header depend on the type of block. For relocatable blocks, it contains the block's **relative handle**: a pointer to the block's master pointer, expressed as an offset relative to the start of the heap zone rather than as an absolute memory address. Adding the relative handle to the zone pointer produces a true handle for this block. For nonrelocatable blocks, the second long word of the header is just a pointer to the block's zone. For free blocks, these four bytes are unused.

The structure of a tag byte is shown in Figure 13.

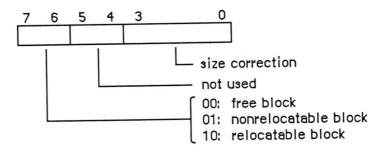

Figure 13. Tag Byte

Assembly-language note: You can use the global constants tyBkFree, tyBkNRel, and tyBkRel to test whether the value of the tag byte indicates a free, nonrelocatable, or relocatable block, respectively.

The "size correction" in the tag byte of a block header is the number of unused bytes at the end of the block, beyond the end of the block's contents. It's equal to the difference between the block's logical and physical sizes, excluding the eight bytes of overhead for the block header:

physicalSize = logicalSize + sizeCorrection + 8

There are two reasons why a block may contain such unused bytes:

- The Memory Manager allocates space only in even numbers of bytes. If the block's logical size is odd, an extra, unused byte is added at the end to keep the physical size even.

- The minimum number of bytes in a block is 12. This minimum applies to all blocks, free as well as allocated. If allocating the required number of bytes from a free block would leave a fragment of fewer than 12 free bytes, the leftover bytes are included unused at the end of the newly allocated block instead of being returned to free storage.

Structure of Master Pointers

The master pointer to a relocatable block has the structure shown in Figure 14. The low-order three bytes of the long word contain the address of the block's contents. The high-order byte contains some flag bits that specify the block's current status. Bit 7 of this byte is the **lock bit** (1 if the block is locked, 0 if it's unlocked); bit 6 is the **purge bit** (1 if the block is purgeable, 0 if it's unpurgeable). Bit 5 is used by the Resource Manager to identify blocks containing resource information; such blocks are marked by a 1 in this bit.

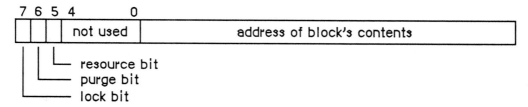

Figure 14. Structure of a Master Pointer

Warning: Note that the flag bits in the high-order byte have numerical significance in any operation performed on a master pointer. For example, the lock bit is also the sign bit.

Assembly-language note: You can use the mask in the global variable Lo3Bytes to determine the value of the low-order three bytes of a master pointer. To determine the value of bits 5, 6, and 7, you can use the global constants resourc, purge, and lock, respectively.

USING THE MEMORY MANAGER

There's ordinarily no need to initialize the Memory Manager before using it. The system heap zone is automatically initialized each time the system starts up, and the application heap zone each time an application program starts up. In the unlikely event that you need to reinitialize the application zone while your program is running, you can call InitApplZone.

When your application starts up, it should allocate the memory it requires in the most space-efficient manner possible, ensuring that most of the nonrelocatable blocks it will need are packed together at the bottom of the heap. The main segment of your program should call the

MaxApplZone procedure, which expands the application heap zone to its limit. Then call the procedure MoreMasters repeatedly to allocate as many blocks of master pointers as your application and any desk accessories will need. Next initialize QuickDraw and the Window Manager (if you're going to use it).

To allocate a new relocatable block, use NewHandle; for a nonrelocatable block, use NewPtr. These functions return a handle or a pointer, as the case may be, to the newly allocated block. To release a block when you're finished with it, use DisposHandle or DisposPtr.

You can also change the size of an already allocated block with SetHandleSize or SetPtrSize, and find out its current size with GetHandleSize or GetPtrSize. Use HLock and HUnlock to lock and unlock relocatable blocks. Before locking a relocatable block, call MoveHHi.

> **Note:** If you lock a relocatable block, unlock it at the earliest possible opportunity. Before allocating a block that you know will be locked for long periods of time, call ResrvMem to make room for the block as near as possible to the bottom of the zone.

In some situations it may be desirable to determine the handle that points to a given master pointer. To do this you can call the RecoverHandle function. For example, a relocatable block of code might want to find out the handle that refers to it, so it can lock itself down in the heap.

Ordinarily, you shouldn't have to worry about compacting the heap or purging blocks from it; the Memory Manager automatically takes care of this for you. You can control which blocks are purgeable with HPurge and HNoPurge. If for some reason you want to compact or purge the heap explicitly, you can do so with CompactMem or PurgeMem. To explicitly purge a specific block, use EmptyHandle.

> **Warning:** Before attempting to access any purgeable block, you must check its handle to make sure the block is still allocated. If the handle is empty, then the block has been purged; before accessing it, you have to reallocate it by calling ReallocHandle, and then recreate its contents. (If it's a resource block, just call the Resource Manager procedure LoadResource; it checks the handle and reads the resource into memory if it's not already in memory.)

You can find out how much free space is left in a heap zone by calling FreeMem (to get the total number of free bytes) or MaxMem (to get the size of the largest single free block and the maximum amount by which the zone can grow). Beware: MaxMem compacts the entire zone and purges all purgeable blocks. To determine the current application heap limit, use GetApplLimit; to limit the growth of the application zone, use SetApplLimit. To install a grow zone function to help the Memory Manager allocate space in a zone, use SetGrowZone.

You can create additional heap zones for your program's own use, either within the original application zone or in the stack, with InitZone. If you do maintain more than one heap zone, you can find out which zone is current at any given time with GetZone and switch from one to another with SetZone. Almost all Memory Manager operations implicitly apply to the current heap zone. To refer to the system heap zone or the (original) application heap zone, use the Memory Manager function SystemZone or ApplicZone. To find out which zone a particular block resides in, use HandleZone (if the block is relocatable) or PtrZone (if it's nonrelocatable).

> **Warning:** Be sure, when calling routines that access blocks, that the zone in which the block is located is the current zone.

Note: Most applications will just use the original application heap zone and never have to worry about which zone is current.

After calling any Memory Manager routine, you can determine whether it was successfully completed or failed, by calling MemError.

Warning: Code that will be executed via an interrupt must not make any calls to the Memory Manager, directly or indirectly, and can't depend on handles to unlocked blocks being valid.

MEMORY MANAGER ROUTINES

In addition to their normal results, many Memory Manager routines yield a result code that you can examine by calling the MemError function. The description of each routine includes a list of all result codes it may yield.

Assembly-language note: When called from assembly language, not all Memory Manager routines return a result code. Those that do always leave it as a word-length quantity in the low-order word of register D0 on return from the trap. However, some routines leave something else there instead; see the descriptions of individual routines for details. Just before returning, the trap dispatcher tests the low-order word of D0 with a TST.W instruction, so that on return from the trap the condition codes reflect the status of the result code, if any.

The stack-based interface routines called from Pascal always yield a result code. If the underlying trap doesn't return one, the interface routine "manufactures" a result code of noErr and stores it where it can later be accessed with MemError.

Assembly-language note: You can specify that some Memory Manager routines apply to the system heap zone instead of the current zone by setting bit 10 of the routine trap word. If you're using the Lisa Workshop Assembler, you do this by supplying the word SYS (uppercase) as the second argument to the routine macro:

```
_FreeMem ,SYS
```

If you want a block of memory to be cleared to zeroes when it's allocated by a NewPtr or NewHandle call, set bit 9 of the routine trap word. You can do this by supplying the word CLEAR (uppercase) as the second argument to the routine macro:

```
_NewHandle ,CLEAR
```

You can combine SYS and CLEAR in the same macro call, but SYS must come first:

```
_NewHandle ,SYS,CLEAR
```

The description of each routine lists whether SYS or CLEAR is applicable. (The syntax shown above and in the routine descriptions applies to the Lisa Workshop Assembler; programmers using another development system should consult its documentation for the proper syntax.)

Initialization and Allocation

PROCEDURE InitApplZone;

Trap macro	_InitApplZone
On exit	D0: result code (word)

InitApplZone initializes the application heap zone and makes it the current zone. The contents of any previous application zone are lost; all previously existing blocks in that zone are discarded. The zone's grow zone function is set to NIL. InitApplZone is called by the Segment Loader when starting up an application; you shouldn't normally need to call it.

Warning: Reinitializing the application zone from within a running program is tricky, since the program's code itself normally resides in the application zone. To do it safely, the code containing the InitApplZone call cannot be in the application zone.

Result codes   noErr   No error

PROCEDURE SetApplBase (startPtr: Ptr);

Trap macro	_SetAppBase
On entry	A0: startPtr (pointer)
On exit	D0: result code (word)

SetApplBase changes the starting address of the application heap zone to the address designated by startPtr, and then calls InitApplZone. SetApplBase is normally called only by the system itself; you should never need to call this procedure.

Since the application heap zone begins immediately following the end of the system zone, changing its starting address has the effect of changing the size of the system zone. The system zone can be made larger, but never smaller; if startPtr points to an address lower than the current end of the system zone, it's ignored and the application zone's starting address is left unchanged.

Warning: Like InitApplZone, SetApplBase is a tricky operation, because the program's code itself normally resides in the application heap zone. To do it safely, the code containing the SetApplBase call cannot be in the application zone.

Result codes   noErr   No error

```
PROCEDURE InitZone (pGrowZone: ProcPtr; cMoreMasters: INTEGER;
         limitPtr,startPtr: Ptr);
```

Trap macro	_InitZone	
On entry	A0: pointer to parameter block	
Parameter block		
0	startPtr	pointer
4	limitPtr	pointer
8	cMoreMasters	word
10	pGrowZone	pointer
On exit	D0: result code (word)	

InitZone creates a new heap zone, initializes its header and trailer, and makes it the current zone. The startPtr parameter is a pointer to the first byte of the new zone; limitPtr points to the first byte beyond the end of the zone. The new zone will occupy memory addresses from ORD(startPtr) through ORD(limitPtr)–1.

CMoreMasters tells how many master pointers should be allocated at a time for the new zone. This number of master pointers are created initially; should more be needed later, they'll be added in increments of this same number.

The pGrowZone parameter is a pointer to the grow zone function for the new zone, if any. If you're not defining a grow zone function for this zone, pass NIL.

The new zone includes a 52-byte header and a 12-byte trailer, so its actual usable space runs from ORD(startPtr)+52 through ORD(limitPtr)–13. In addition, there's an eight-byte header for the master pointer block, as well as four bytes for each master pointer, within this usable area. Thus the total available space in the zone, in bytes, is initially

$$ORD(limitPtr) - ORD(startPtr) - 64 - (8 + (4*cMoreMasters))$$

This number must not be less than 0. Note that the amount of available space in the zone will decrease as more master pointers are allocated.

Result codes	noErr	No error

```
FUNCTION GetApplLimit : Ptr;   [Not in ROM]
```

GetApplLimit returns the current application heap limit. It can be used in conjunction with SetApplLimit, described below, to determine and then change the application heap limit.

Assembly-language note: The global variable ApplLimit contains the current application heap limit.

```
PROCEDURE SetApplLimit (zoneLimit: Ptr);
```

Trap macro	_SetApplLimit
On entry	A0: zoneLimit (pointer)
On exit	D0: result code (word)

SetApplLimit sets the application heap limit, beyond which the application heap can't be expanded. The actual expansion isn't under your program's control, but is done automatically by the Memory Manager when necessary to satisfy allocation requests. Only the original application zone can be expanded.

ZoneLimit is a pointer to a byte in memory beyond which the zone will not be allowed to grow. The zone can grow to include the byte *preceding* zoneLimit in memory, but no farther. If the zone already extends beyond the specified limit it won't be cut back, but it will be prevented from growing any more.

Warning: Notice that zoneLimit is *not* a byte count. To limit the application zone to a particular size (say 8K bytes), you have to write something like

```
SetApplLimit(Ptr(ApplicZone)+8192)
```

The Memory Manager function ApplicZone is explained below.

Assembly-language note: You can just store the new application heap limit in the global variable ApplLimit.

Result codes	noErr	No error
	memFullErr	Not enough room in heap zone

```
PROCEDURE MaxApplZone;    [Not in ROM]
```

MaxApplZone expands the application heap zone to the application heap limit without purging any blocks currently in the zone. If the zone already extends to the limit, it won't be changed.

Assembly-language note: To expand the application heap zone to the application heap limit from assembly language, call this Pascal procedure from your program.

Result codes	noErr	No error

```
PROCEDURE MoreMasters;
```

Trap macro	_MoreMasters

MoreMasters allocates another block of master pointers in the current heap zone. This procedure is usually called very early in an application.

Result codes	noErr	No error
	memFullErr	Not enough room in heap zone

Heap Zone Access

```
FUNCTION GetZone : THz;
```

Trap macro	_GetZone
On exit	A0: function result (pointer)
	D0: result code (word)

GetZone returns a pointer to the current heap zone.

Assembly-language note: The global variable TheZone contains a pointer to the current heap zone.

Result codes	noErr	No error

```
PROCEDURE SetZone (hz: THz);
```

Trap macro	_SetZone
On entry	A0: hz (pointer)
On exit	D0: result code (word)

SetZone sets the current heap zone to the zone pointed to by hz.

Assembly-language note: You can set the current heap zone by storing a pointer to it in the global variable TheZone.

Result codes	noErr	No error

```
FUNCTION SystemZone : THz;   [Not in ROM]
```

SystemZone returns a pointer to the system heap zone.

Assembly-language note: The global variable SysZone contains a pointer to the system heap zone.

```
FUNCTION ApplicZone : THz;   [Not in ROM]
```

ApplicZone returns a pointer to the original application heap zone.

Assembly-language note: The global variable ApplZone contains a pointer to the original application heap zone.

Allocating and Releasing Relocatable Blocks

```
FUNCTION NewHandle (logicalSize: Size) : Handle;
```

Trap macro	_NewHandle	
	_NewHandle ,SYS	(applies to system heap)
	_NewHandle ,CLEAR	(clears allocated block)
	_NewHandle ,SYS,CLEAR	(applies to system heap and clears allocated block)
On entry	D0: logicalSize (long word)	
On exit	A0: function result (handle)	
	D0: result code (word)	

NewHandle attempts to allocate a new relocatable block of logicalSize bytes from the current heap zone and then return a handle to it. The new block will be unlocked and unpurgeable. If logicalSize bytes can't be allocated, NewHandle returns NIL.

NewHandle will pursue all available avenues to create a free block of the requested size, including compacting the heap zone, increasing its size, purging blocks from it, and calling its grow zone function, if any.

Result codes	noErr	No error
	memFullErr	Not enough room in heap zone

```
PROCEDURE DisposHandle (h: Handle);
```

Trap macro	_DisposHandle
On entry	A0: h (handle)
On exit	D0: result code (word)

DisposHandle releases the memory occupied by the relocatable block whose handle is h.

Warning: After a call to DisposHandle, all handles to the released block become invalid and should not be used again. Any subsequent calls to DisposHandle using an invalid handle will damage the master pointer list.

Result codes	noErr	No error
	memWZErr	Attempt to operate on a free block

```
FUNCTION GetHandleSize (h: Handle) : Size;
```

Trap macro	_GetHandleSize
On entry	A0: h (handle)
On exit	D0: if >= 0, function result (long word)
	if < 0, result code (word)

GetHandleSize returns the logical size, in bytes, of the relocatable block whose handle is h. In case of an error, GetHandleSize returns 0.

Assembly-language note: Recall that the trap dispatcher sets the condition codes before returning from a trap by testing the low-order word of register D0 with a TST.W instruction. Since the block size returned in D0 by _GetHandleSize is a full 32-bit long word, the word-length test sets the condition codes incorrectly in this case. To branch on the contents of D0, use your own TST.L instruction on return from the trap to test the full 32 bits of the register.

Result codes	noErr	No error [Pascal only]
	nilHandleErr	NIL master pointer
	memWZErr	Attempt to operate on a free block

```
PROCEDURE SetHandleSize (h: Handle; newSize: Size);
```

Trap macro	_SetHandleSize
On entry	A0: h (handle)
	D0: newSize (long word)
On exit	D0: result code (word)

SetHandleSize changes the logical size of the relocatable block whose handle is h to newSize bytes.

Note: Be prepared for an attempt to increase the size of a locked block to fail, since there may be a block above it that's either nonrelocatable or locked.

Result codes	noErr	No error
	memFullErr	Not enough room in heap zone
	nilHandleErr	NIL master pointer
	memWZErr	Attempt to operate on a free block

```
FUNCTION HandleZone (h: Handle) : THz;
```

Trap macro	_HandleZone
On entry	A0: h (handle)
On exit	A0: function result (pointer)
	D0: result code (word)

HandleZone returns a pointer to the heap zone containing the relocatable block whose handle is h. In case of an error, the result returned by HandleZone is undefined and should be ignored.

Warning: If handle h is empty (points to a NIL master pointer), HandleZone returns a pointer to the current heap zone.

Result codes	noErr	No error
	memWZErr	Attempt to operate on a free block

```
FUNCTION RecoverHandle (p: Ptr) : Handle;
```

Trap macro	_RecoverHandle
	_RecoverHandle ,SYS (applies to system heap)
On entry	A0: p (pointer)
On exit	A0: function result (handle)
	D0: unchanged

RecoverHandle returns a handle to the relocatable block pointed to by p.

Assembly-language note: The trap _RecoverHandle doesn't return a result code in register D0; the previous contents of D0 are preserved unchanged.

| Result codes | noErr | No error [Pascal only] |

```
PROCEDURE ReallocHandle (h: Handle; logicalSize: Size);
```

Trap macro	_ReallocHandle
On entry	A0: h (handle)
	D0: logicalSize (long word)
On exit	D0: result code (word)

ReallocHandle allocates a new relocatable block with a logical size of logicalSize bytes. It then updates handle h by setting its master pointer to point to the new block. The main use of this procedure is to reallocate space for a block that has been purged. Normally h is an empty handle, but it need not be: If it points to an existing block, that block is released before the new block is created.

In case of an error, no new block is allocated and handle h is left unchanged.

Result codes	noErr	No error
	memFullErr	Not enough room in heap zone
	memWZErr	Attempt to operate on a free block
	memPurErr	Attempt to purge a locked block

Allocating and Releasing Nonrelocatable Blocks

```
FUNCTION NewPtr (logicalSize: Size) : Ptr;
```

Trap macro	_NewPtr	
	_NewPtr ,SYS	(applies to system heap)
	_NewPtr ,CLEAR	(clears allocated block)
	_NewPtr ,SYS,CLEAR	(applies to system heap and clears allocated block)
On entry	D0: logicalSize (long word)	
On exit	A0: function result (pointer)	
	D0: result code (word)	

NewPtr attempts to allocate a new nonrelocatable block of logicalSize bytes from the current heap zone and then return a pointer to it. If logicalSize bytes can't be allocated, NewPtr returns NIL.

NewPtr will pursue all available avenues to create a free block of the requested size at the lowest possible location in the heap zone, including compacting the heap zone, increasing its size, purging blocks from it, and calling its grow zone function, if any.

Result codes	noErr	No error
	memFullErr	Not enough room in heap zone

```
PROCEDURE DisposPtr (p: Ptr);
```

Trap macro	_DisposPtr
On entry	A0: p (pointer)
On exit	D0: result code (word)

DisposPtr releases the memory occupied by the nonrelocatable block pointed to by p.

Warning: After a call to DisposPtr, all pointers to the released block become invalid and should not be used again. Any subsequent calls to DisposPtr using an invalid pointer will damage the master pointer list.

Result codes	noErr	No error
	memWZErr	Attempt to operate on a free block

```
FUNCTION GetPtrSize (p: Ptr) : Size;
```

Trap macro	_GetPtrSize
On entry	A0: p (pointer)
On exit	D0: if >= 0, function result (long word)
	if < 0, result code (word)

GetPtrSize returns the logical size, in bytes, of the nonrelocatable block pointed to by p. In case of an error, GetPtrSize returns 0.

Assembly-language note: Recall that the trap dispatcher sets the condition codes before returning from a trap by testing the low-order word of register D0 with a TST.W instruction. Since the block size returned in D0 by _GetPtrSize is a full 32-bit long word, the word-length test sets the condition codes incorrectly in this case. To branch on the contents of D0, use your own TST.L instruction on return from the trap to test the full 32 bits of the register.

Result codes	noErr	No error [Pascal only]
	memWZErr	Attempt to operate on a free block

```
PROCEDURE SetPtrSize (p: Ptr; newSize: Size);
```

Trap macro	_SetPtrSize
On entry	A0: p (pointer)
	D0: newSize (long word)
On exit	D0: result code (word)

SetPtrSize changes the logical size of the nonrelocatable block pointed to by p to newSize bytes.

Result codes	noErr	No error
	memFullErr	Not enough room in heap zone
	memWZErr	Attempt to operate on a free block

```
FUNCTION PtrZone (p: Ptr) : THz;
```

Trap macro	_PtrZone
On entry	A0: p (pointer)
On exit	A0: function result (pointer)
	D0: result code (word)

PtrZone returns a pointer to the heap zone containing the nonrelocatable block pointed to by p. In case of an error, the result returned by PtrZone is undefined and should be ignored.

Result codes	noErr	No error
	memWZErr	Attempt to operate on a free block

Freeing Space in the Heap

```
FUNCTION FreeMem : LONGINT;
```

Trap macro	_FreeMem
	_FreeMem ,SYS (applies to system heap)
On exit	D0: function result (long word)

FreeMem returns the total amount of free space in the current heap zone, in bytes. Note that it usually isn't possible to allocate a block of this size, because of fragmentation due to nonrelocatable or locked blocks.

Result codes	noErr	No error [Pascal only]

```
FUNCTION MaxMem (VAR grow: Size) : Size;
```

Trap macro	_MaxMem
	_MaxMem ,SYS (applies to system heap)
On exit	D0: function result (long word)
	A0: grow (long word)

MaxMem compacts the current heap zone and purges all purgeable blocks from the zone. It returns as its result the size in bytes of the largest contiguous free block in the zone after the compaction. If the current zone is the original application heap zone, the grow parameter is set to the maximum number of bytes by which the zone can grow. For any other heap zone, grow is set to 0. MaxMem doesn't actually expand the zone or call its grow zone function.

Result codes   noErr   No error [Pascal only]

```
FUNCTION CompactMem (cbNeeded: Size) : Size;
```

Trap macro	_CompactMem
	_CompactMem ,SYS (applies to system heap)
On entry	D0: cbNeeded (long word)
On exit	D0: function result (long word)

CompactMem compacts the current heap zone by moving relocatable blocks down and collecting free space together until a contiguous block of at least cbNeeded free bytes is found or the entire zone is compacted; it doesn't purge any purgeable blocks. CompactMem returns the size in bytes of the largest contiguous free block remaining. Note that it doesn't actually allocate the block.

Result codes   noErr   No error [Pascal only]

```
PROCEDURE ResrvMem (cbNeeded: Size);
```

Trap macro	_ResrvMem
	_ResrvMem ,SYS (applies to system heap)
On entry	D0: cbNeeded (long word)
On exit	D0: result code (word)

ResrvMem creates free space for a block of cbNeeded contiguous bytes at the lowest possible position in the current heap zone. It will try every available means to place the block as close as possible to the bottom of the zone, including moving other blocks upward, expanding the zone, or purging blocks from it. Note that ResrvMem doesn't actually allocate the block.

Note: When you allocate a relocatable block that you know will be locked for long periods of time, call ResrvMem first. This reserves space for the block near the bottom of the heap zone, where it will interfere with compaction as little as possible. It isn't necessary to call ResrvMem for a nonrelocatable block; NewPtr calls it automatically. It's also called automatically when locked resources are read into memory.

Result codes	noErr	No error
	memFullErr	Not enough room in heap zone

```
PROCEDURE PurgeMem (cbNeeded: Size);
```

Trap macro	_PurgeMem	
	_PurgeMem ,SYS	(applies to system heap)
On entry	D0: cbNeeded (long word)	
On exit	D0: result code (word)	

PurgeMem sequentially purges blocks from the current heap zone until a contiguous block of at least cbNeeded free bytes is created or the entire zone is purged; it doesn't compact the heap zone. Only relocatable, unlocked, purgeable blocks can be purged. Note that PurgeMem doesn't actually allocate the block.

Result codes	noErr	No error
	memFullErr	Not enough room in heap zone

```
PROCEDURE EmptyHandle (h: Handle);
```

Trap macro	_EmptyHandle
On entry	A0: h (handle)
On exit	A0: h (handle)
	D0: result code (word)

EmptyHandle purges the relocatable block whose handle is h from its heap zone and sets its master pointer to NIL (making it an empty handle). If h is already empty, EmptyHandle does nothing.

Note: Since the space occupied by the block's master pointer itself remains allocated, all handles pointing to it remain valid but empty. When you later reallocate space for the block with ReallocHandle, the master pointer will be updated, causing all existing handles to access the new block correctly.

The block whose handle is h must be unlocked, but need not be purgeable.

Result codes	noErr	No error
	memWZErr	Attempt to operate on a free block
	memPurErr	Attempt to purge a locked block

Properties of Relocatable Blocks

```
PROCEDURE HLock (h: Handle);
```

Trap macro	_HLock
On entry	A0: h (handle)
On exit	D0: result code (word)

HLock locks a relocatable block, preventing it from being moved within its heap zone. If the block is already locked, HLock does nothing.

> **Warning:** To prevent heap fragmentation, you should always call MoveHHi before locking a relocatable block.

Result codes   noErr   No error
                             nilHandleErr   NIL master pointer
                             memWZErr   Attempt to operate on a free block

```
PROCEDURE HUnlock (h: Handle);
```

Trap macro	_HUnlock
On entry	A0: h (handle)
On exit	D0: result code (word)

HUnlock unlocks a relocatable block, allowing it to be moved within its heap zone. If the block is already unlocked, HUnlock does nothing.

Result codes   noErr   No error
                             nilHandleErr   NIL master pointer
                             memWZErr   Attempt to operate on a free block

```
PROCEDURE HPurge (h: Handle);
```

Trap macro	_HPurge
On entry	A0: h (handle)
On exit	D0: result code (word)

HPurge marks a relocatable block as purgeable. If the block is already purgeable, HPurge does nothing.

Note: If you call HPurge on a locked block, it won't unlock the block, but it will mark the block as purgeable. If you later call HUnlock, the block will be subject to purging.

Result codes   noErr   No error
                nilHandleErr   NIL master pointer
                memWZErr   Attempt to operate on a free block

PROCEDURE HNoPurge (h: Handle);

Trap macro	_HNoPurge
On entry	A0: h (handle)
On exit	D0: result code (word)

HNoPurge marks a relocatable block as unpurgeable. If the block is already unpurgeable, HNoPurge does nothing.

Result codes   noErr   No error
                nilHandleErr   NIL master pointer
                memWZErr   Attempt to operate on a free block

Grow Zone Operations

PROCEDURE SetGrowZone (growZone: ProcPtr);

Trap macro	_SetGrowZone
On entry	A0: growZone (pointer)
On exit	D0: result code (word)

SetGrowZone sets the current heap zone's grow zone function as designated by the growZone parameter. A NIL parameter value removes any grow zone function the zone may previously have had.

Note: If your program presses the limits of the available heap space, it's a good idea to have a grow zone function of some sort. At the very least, the grow zone function should take some graceful action—such as displaying an alert box with the message "Out of memory"—instead of just failing unpredictably.

If it has failed to create a block of the needed size after compacting the zone, increasing its size (in the case of the original application zone), and purging blocks from it, the Memory Manager calls the grow zone function as a last resort.

The grow zone function should be of the form

```
FUNCTION MyGrowZone (cbNeeded: Size) : LONGINT;
```

The cbNeeded parameter gives the physical size of the needed block in bytes, *including the block header*. The grow zone function should attempt to create a free block of at least this size. It should return a nonzero number if it's able to allocate some memory, or 0 if it's not able to allocate any.

If the grow zone function returns 0, the Memory Manager will give up trying to allocate the needed block and will signal failure with the result code memFullErr. Otherwise it will compact the heap zone and try again to allocate the block. If still unsuccessful, it will continue to call the grow zone function repeatedly, compacting the zone again after each call, until it either succeeds in allocating the needed block or receives a zero result and gives up.

The usual way for the grow zone function to free more space is to call EmptyHandle to purge blocks that were previously marked unpurgeable. Another possibility is to unlock blocks that were previously locked

> **Note:** Although just unlocking blocks doesn't actually free any additional space in the zone, the grow zone function should still return a nonzero result in this case. This signals the Memory Manager to compact the heap and try again to allocate the needed block.

> **Warning:** Depending on the circumstances in which the grow zone function is called, there may be a particular block within the heap zone that must not be moved. For this reason, it's essential that your grow zone function call the function GZSaveHnd (see below).

> Result codes   noErr   No error

```
FUNCTION GZSaveHnd : Handle;   [Not in ROM]
```

GZSaveHnd returns a handle to a relocatable block that must not be moved by the grow zone function, or NIL if there is no such block. Your grow zone function must be sure to call GZSaveHnd; if a handle is returned, it must ensure that this block is *not* moved.

Assembly-language note: You can find the same handle in the global variable GZRootHnd.

Miscellaneous Routines

PROCEDURE BlockMove (sourcePtr,destPtr: Ptr; byteCount: Size);

Trap macro	_BlockMove
On entry	A0: sourcePtr (pointer)
	A1: destPtr (pointer)
	D0: byteCount (long word)
On exit	D0: result code (word)

BlockMove moves a block of byteCount consecutive bytes from the address designated by sourcePtr to that designated by destPtr. No pointers are updated. BlockMove works correctly even if the source and destination blocks overlap.

　　Result codes　　noErr　　No error

FUNCTION TopMem : Ptr;　　[Not in ROM]

On a Macintosh 128K or 512K, TopMem returns a pointer to the end of RAM; on the Macintosh XL, it returns a pointer to the end of the memory available for use by the application.

Assembly-language note: This value is stored in the global variable MemTop.

PROCEDURE MoveHHi (h: Handle);　　[Not in ROM]

MoveHHi moves the relocatable block whose handle is h toward the top of the current heap zone, until the block hits either a nonrelocatable block, a locked relocatable block, or the last block in the current heap zone. By calling MoveHHi before you lock a relocatable block, you can avoid fragmentation of the heap, as well as make room for future pointers as low in the heap as possible.

Result codes	noErr	No error
	nilHandleErr	NIL master pointer
	memLockedErr	Block is locked

FUNCTION MemError : OSErr;　　[Not in ROM]

MemError returns the result code produced by the last Memory Manager routine called directly by your program. (OSErr is an Operating System Utility data type declared as INTEGER.)

Assemby-language note: To get a routine's result code from assembly language, look in register D0 on return from the routine (except for certain routines as noted).

CREATING A HEAP ZONE ON THE STACK

The following code is an example of how advanced programmers can get the space for a new heap zone from the stack:

```
CONST zoneSize = 2048;
VAR   zoneArea: PACKED ARRAY[1..zoneSize] OF SignedByte;
      stackZone: THz;
      limit: Ptr;
      . . .


stackZone := @zoneArea;
limit := POINTER(ORD(stackZone)+zoneSize);
InitZone(NIL,16,limit,@zoneArea)
```

The heap zone created by this method will be usable until the routine containing this code is completed (because its variables will then be released).

Assembly-language note: Here's how you might do the same thing in assembly language:

```
zoneSize    .EQU    2048
            . . .
            MOVE.L  SP,A2               ;save stack pointer for limit
            SUB.W   #zoneSize,SP        ;make room on stack
            MOVE.L  SP,A1               ;save stack pointer for start
            MOVE.L  A1,stackZone        ;store as zone pointer

            SUB.W   #14,SP                  ;allocate space on stack
            CLR.L   pGrowZone(SP)           ;NIL grow zone function
            MOVE.W  #16,cMoreMasters(SP)    ;16 master pointers
            MOVE.L  A2,limitPtr(SP)         ;pointer to zone trailer
            MOVE.L  A1,startPtr(SP)         ;pointer to first byte
                                            ; of zone

            MOVE.L  SP,A0               ;point to argument block
            _InitZone                   ;create zone 1
            ADD.W   #14,SP              ;pop arguments off stack
            . . .
```

SUMMARY OF THE MEMORY MANAGER

Constants

```
CONST { Result codes }

    memFullErr   = -108;    {not enough room in heap zone}
    memLockedErr = -117;    {block is locked}
    memPurErr    = -112;    {attempt to purge a locked block}
    memWZErr     = -111;    {attempt to operate on a free block}
    nilHandleErr = -109;    {NIL master pointer}
    noErr        =   0;     {no error}
```

Data Types

```
TYPE SignedByte = -128..127;
     Byte       = 0..255;
     Ptr        = ^SignedByte;
     Handle     = ^Ptr;

     Str255       = STRING[255];
     StringPtr    = ^Str255;
     StringHandle = ^StringPtr;

     ProcPtr = Ptr;

     Fixed = LONGINT;

     Size = LONGINT;

     THz = ^Zone;
     Zone = RECORD
                bkLim:       Ptr;        {zone trailer block}
                purgePtr:    Ptr;        {used internally}
                hFstFree:    Ptr;        {first free master pointer}
                zcbFree:     LONGINT;    {number of free bytes}
                gzProc:      ProcPtr;    {grow zone function}
                moreMast:    INTEGER;    {master pointers to allocate}
                flags:       INTEGER;    {used internally}
                cntRel:      INTEGER;    {not used}
                maxRel:      INTEGER;    {not used}
                cntNRel:     INTEGER;    {not used}
                maxNRel:     INTEGER;    {not used}
                cntEmpty:    INTEGER;    {not used}
                cntHandles:  INTEGER;    {not used}
                minCBFree:   LONGINT;    {not used}
                purgeProc:   ProcPtr;    {purge warning procedure}
                sparePtr:    Ptr;        {used internally}
                allocPtr:    Ptr;        {used internally}
                heapData:    INTEGER     {first usable byte in zone}
            END;
```

Routines

Initialization and Allocation

```
PROCEDURE  InitApplZone;
PROCEDURE  SetApplBase      (startPtr: Ptr);
PROCEDURE  InitZone         (pGrowZone: ProcPtr; cMoreMasters: INTEGER;
                             limitPtr,startPtr: Ptr);
FUNCTION   GetApplLimit :  Ptr;   [Not in ROM]
PROCEDURE  SetApplLimit     (zoneLimit: Ptr);
PROCEDURE  MaxApplZone;     [Not in ROM]
PROCEDURE  MoreMasters;
```

Heap Zone Access

```
FUNCTION   GetZone :      THz;
PROCEDURE  SetZone        (hz: THz);
FUNCTION   SystemZone :  THz;   [Not in ROM]
FUNCTION   ApplicZone :  THz;   [Not in ROM]
```

Allocating and Releasing Relocatable Blocks

```
FUNCTION   NewHandle      (logicalSize: Size) : Handle;
PROCEDURE  DisposHandle   (h: Handle);
FUNCTION   GetHandleSize  (h: Handle) : Size;
PROCEDURE  SetHandleSize  (h: Handle; newSize: Size);
FUNCTION   HandleZone     (h: Handle) : THz;
FUNCTION   RecoverHandle  (p: Ptr) : Handle;
PROCEDURE  ReallocHandle  (h: Handle; logicalSize: Size);
```

Allocating and Releasing Nonrelocatable Blocks

```
FUNCTION   NewPtr       (logicalSize: Size) : Ptr;
PROCEDURE  DisposPtr (p: Ptr);
FUNCTION   GetPtrSize (p: Ptr) : Size;
PROCEDURE  SetPtrSize (p: Ptr; newSize: Size);
FUNCTION   PtrZone      (p: Ptr) : THz;
```

Freeing Space in the Heap

```
FUNCTION   FreeMem :     LONGINT;
FUNCTION   MaxMem      (VAR grow: Size) : Size;
FUNCTION   CompactMem (cbNeeded: Size) : Size;
PROCEDURE  ResrvMem    (cbNeeded: Size);
PROCEDURE  PurgeMem    (cbNeeded: Size);
PROCEDURE  EmptyHandle (h: Handle);
```

Properties of Relocatable Blocks

```
PROCEDURE HLock    (h: Handle);
PROCEDURE HUnlock  (h: Handle);
PROCEDURE HPurge   (h: Handle);
PROCEDURE HNoPurge (h: Handle);
```

Grow Zone Operations

```
PROCEDURE SetGrowZone (growZone: ProcPtr);
FUNCTION  GZSaveHnd :  Handle;   [Not in ROM]
```

Miscellaneous Routines

```
PROCEDURE BlockMove  (sourcePtr,destPtr: Ptr; byteCount: Size);
FUNCTION  TopMem :    Ptr;   [Not in ROM]
PROCEDURE MoveHHi    (h: Handle);   [Not in ROM]
FUNCTION  MemError :  OSErr;   [Not in ROM]
```

Grow Zone Function

```
FUNCTION MyGrowZone (cbNeeded: Size) : LONGINT;
```

Assembly-Language Information

Constants

```
; Values for tag byte of a block header

tyBkFree    .EQU   0    ;free block
tyBkNRel    .EQU   1    ;nonrelocatable block
tyBkRel     .EQU   2    ;relocatable block

; Flags for the high-order byte of a master pointer

lock        .EQU   7    ;lock bit
purge       .EQU   6    ;purge bit
resourc     .EQU   5    ;resource bit

; Result codes

memFullErr   .EQU   -108   ;not enough room in heap zone
memLockedErr .EQU   -117   ;block is locked
memPurErr    .EQU   -112   ;attempt to purge a locked block
memWZErr     .EQU   -111   ;attempt to operate on a free block
nilHandleErr .EQU   -109   ;NIL master pointer
noErr        .EQU   0      ;no error
```

Zone Record Data Structure

bkLim	Pointer to zone trailer block
hFstFree	Pointer to first free master pointer
zcbFree	Number of free bytes (long)
gzProc	Address of grow zone function
mAllocCnt	Master pointers to allocate (word)
purgeProc	Address of purge warning procedure
heapData	First usable byte in zone

Block Header Data Structure

tagBC	Tag byte and physical block size (long)
handle	Relocatable block: relative handle
	Nonrelocatable block: zone pointer
blkData	First byte of block contents

Parameter Block Structure for InitZone

startPtr	Pointer to first byte in zone
limitPtr	Pointer to first byte beyond end of zone
cMoreMasters	Number of master pointers for zone (word)
pGrowZone	Address of grow zone function

Routines

Trap macro	On entry	On exit
_InitApplZone		D0: result code (word)
_SetApplBase	A0: startPtr (ptr)	D0: result code (word)

_InitZone	A0: ptr to parameter block
	    0 startPtr (ptr)
	    4 limitPtr (ptr)
	    8 cMoreMasters (word)
	  10 pGrowZone (ptr)
		D0: result code (word)

_SetApplLimit	A0: zoneLimit (ptr)	D0: result code (word)
_MoreMasters		
_GetZone		A0: function result (ptr) D0: result code (word)
_SetZone	A0: hz (ptr)	D0: result code (word)
_NewHandle	D0: logicalSize (long)	A0: function result (handle) D0: result code (word)
_DisposHandle	A0: h (handle)	D0: result code (word)

Trap macro	On entry	On exit
_GetHandleSize	A0: h (handle)	D0: if >=0, function result (long) if <0, result code (word)
_SetHandleSize	A0: h (handle) D0: newSize (long)	D0: result code (word)
_HandleZone	A0: h (handle)	A0: function result (ptr) D0: result code (word)
_RecoverHandle	A0: p (ptr)	A0: function result (handle) D0: unchanged
_ReallocHandle	A0: h (handle) D0: logicalSize (long)	D0: result code (word)
_NewPtr	D0: logicalSize (long)	A0: function result (ptr) D0: result code (word)
_DisposPtr	A0: p (ptr)	D0: result code (word)
_GetPtrSize	A0: p (ptr)	D0: if >=0, function result (long) if <0, result code (word)
_SetPtrSize	A0: p (ptr) D0: newSize (long)	D0: result code (word)
_PtrZone	A0: p (ptr)	A0: function result (ptr) D0: result code (word)
_FreeMem		D0: function result (long)
_MaxMem		D0: function result (long) A0: grow (long)
_CompactMem	D0: cbNeeded (long)	D0: function result (long)
_ResrvMem	D0: cbNeeded (long)	D0: result code (word)
_PurgeMem	D0: cbNeeded (long)	D0: result code (word)
_EmptyHandle	A0: h (handle)	A0: h (handle) D0: result code (word)
_HLock	A0: h (handle)	D0: result code (word)
_HUnlock	A0: h (handle)	D0: result code (word)
_HPurge	A0: h (handle)	D0: result code (word)
_HNoPurge	A0: h (handle)	D0: result code (word)
_SetGrowZone	A0: growZone (ptr)	D0: result code (word)
_BlockMove	A0: sourcePtr (ptr) A1: destPtr (ptr) D0: byteCount (long)	D0: result code (word)

Variables

DefltStack	Default space allotment for stack (long)
MinStack	Minimum space allotment for stack (long)
MemTop	Address of end of RAM (on Macintosh XL, end of RAM available to applications)
ScrnBase	Address of main screen buffer
BufPtr	Address of end of jump table
CurrentA5	Address of boundary between application globals and application parameters
CurStackBase	Address of base of stack; start of application globals
ApplLimit	Application heap limit
HeapEnd	Address of end of application heap zone
ApplZone	Address of application heap zone
SysZone	Address of system heap zone
TheZone	Address of current heap zone
GZRootHnd	Handle to relocatable block not to be moved by grow zone function

2 THE SEGMENT LOADER

2 Segment Loader

ABOUT THIS CHAPTER

This chapter describes the Segment Loader, the part of the Macintosh Operating System that lets you divide your application into several parts and have only some of them in memory at a time. The Segment Loader also provides routines for accessing information about documents that the user has selected to be opened or printed.

You should already be familiar with:

- the basic concepts behind the Resource Manager
- the Memory Manager

ABOUT THE SEGMENT LOADER

The Segment Loader allows you to divide the code of your application into several parts or **segments**. The Finder starts up an application by calling a Segment Loader routine that loads in the **main segment** (the one containing the main program). Other segments are loaded in automatically when they're needed. Your application can call the Segment Loader to have these segments removed from memory when they're no longer needed.

The Segment Loader enables you to have programs larger than 32K bytes, the maximum size of a single segment. Also, any code that isn't executed often (such as code for printing) needn't occupy memory when it isn't being used, but can instead be in a separate segment that's "swapped in" when needed.

This mechanism may remind you of the resources of an application, which the Resource Manager reads into memory when necessary. An application's segments are in fact themselves stored as resources; their resource type is 'CODE'. A "loaded" segment has been read into memory by the Resource Manager and locked (so that it's neither relocatable nor purgeable). When a segment is unloaded, it's made relocatable and purgeable.

Every segment has a name. If you do nothing about dividing your program into segments, it will consist only of the main segment. Dividing your program into segments means specifying in your source file the beginning of each segment by name. The names are for your use only; they're not kept around after linking.

FINDER INFORMATION

When the Finder starts up your application, it passes along a list of documents selected by the user to be printed or opened, if any. This information is called the **Finder information**; its structure is shown in Figure 1.

It's up to your application to access the Finder information and open or print the documents selected by the user.

The message in the first word of the Finder information indicates whether the documents are to be opened (0) or printed (1), and the count following it indicates the number of documents (0 if none). The rest of the Finder information specifies each of the selected documents by volume

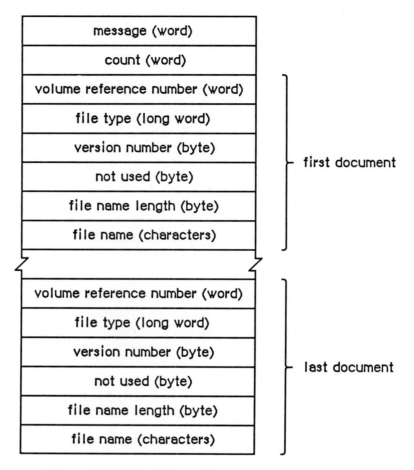

Figure 1. Finder Information

reference number, file type, version number, and file name; these terms are explained in chapter 4 of Volume II and chapter 1 of Volume III. File names are padded to an even number of bytes if necessary.

Your application should start up with an empty untitled document on the desktop if there are no documents listed in the Finder information. If one or more documents are to be opened, your application should go through each document one at a time, and determine whether it can be opened. If it can be opened, you should do so, and then check the next document in the list (unless you've opened your maximum number of documents, in which case you should ignore the rest). If your application doesn't recognize a document's file type (which can happen if the user selected your application along with another application's document), you may want to open the document anyway and check its internal structure to see if it's a compatible type. Display an alert box including the name of each document that can't be opened.

If one or more documents are to be printed, your application should go through each document in the list and determine whether it can be printed. If any documents can be printed, the application should display the standard Print dialog box and then print each document—preferably without doing its entire startup sequence. For example, it may not be necessary to show the menu bar or the document window. If the document can't be printed, ignore it; it may be intended for another application.

USING THE SEGMENT LOADER

When your application starts up, you should determine whether any documents were selected to be printed or opened by it. First call CountAppFiles, which returns the number of selected documents and indicates whether they're to be printed or opened. If the number of selected documents is 0, open an empty untitled document in the normal manner. Otherwise, call GetAppFiles once for each selected document. GetAppFiles returns information about each document, including its file type. Based on the file type, your application can decide how to treat the document, as described in the preceding section. For each document that your application opens or prints, call ClrAppFiles, which indicates to the Finder that you've processed it.

To unload a segment when it's no longer needed, call UnloadSeg. If you don't want to keep track of when each particular segment should be unloaded, you can call UnloadSeg for every segment in your application at the end of your main event loop. This isn't harmful, since the segments aren't purged unless necessary.

Note: The main segment is always loaded and locked.

Warning: A segment should never unload the segment that called it, because the return addresses on the stack would refer to code that may be moved or purged.

Another procedure, GetAppParms, lets you get information about your application such as its name and the reference number for its resource file. The Segment Loader also provides the ExitToShell procedure—a way for an application to quit and return the user to the Finder.

Finally, there are three advanced routines that can be called only from assembly language: Chain, Launch, and LoadSeg. Chain starts up another application without disturbing the application heap. Thus the current application can let another application take over while still keeping its data around in the heap. Launch is called by the Finder to start up an application; it's like Chain but doesn't retain the application heap. LoadSeg is called indirectly (via the jump table, as described later) to load segments when necessary—that is, whenever a routine in an unloaded segment is invoked.

SEGMENT LOADER ROUTINES

Assembly-language note: Instead of using CountAppFiles, GetAppFiles, and ClrAppFiles, assembly-language programmers can access the Finder information via the global variable AppParmHandle, which contains a handle to the Finder information. Parse the Finder information as shown in Figure 1 above. For each document that your application opens or prints, set the file type in the Finder information to 0.

```
PROCEDURE CountAppFiles (VAR message: INTEGER; VAR count:
        INTEGER);   [Not in ROM]
```

CountAppFiles deciphers the Finder information passed to your application, and returns information about the documents that were selected when your application started up. It returns the number of selected documents in the count parameter, and a number in the message parameter that indicates whether the documents are to opened or printed:

```
CONST appOpen  = 0;   {open the document(s)}
      appPrint = 1;   {print the document(s)}
```

PROCEDURE GetAppFiles (index: INTEGER; VAR theFile: AppFile);
          [Not in ROM]

GetAppFiles returns information about a document that was selected when your application started up (as listed in the Finder information). The index parameter indicates the file for which information should be returned; it must be between 1 and the number returned by CountAppFiles, inclusive. The information is returned in the following data structure:

```
TYPE AppFile = RECORD
                   vRefNum: INTEGER;  {volume reference number}
                   fType:   OSType;   {file type}
                   versNum: INTEGER;  {version number}
                   fName:   Str255    {file name}
               END;
```

PROCEDURE ClrAppFiles (index: INTEGER);   [Not in ROM]

ClrAppFiles changes the Finder information passed to your application about the specified file such that the Finder knows you've processed the file. The index parameter must be between 1 and the number returned by CountAppFiles. You should call ClrAppFiles for every document your application opens or prints, so that the information returned by CountAppFiles and GetAppFiles is always correct. (ClrAppFiles sets the file type in the Finder information to 0.)

PROCEDURE GetAppParms (VAR apName: Str255; VAR apRefNum: INTEGER;
          VAR apParam: Handle);

GetAppParms returns information about the current application. It returns the application name in apName and the reference number for the application's resource file in apRefNum. A handle to the Finder information is returned in apParam, but the Finder information is more easily accessed with the GetAppFiles call.

Assembly-language note: Assembly-language programmers can instead get the application name, reference number, and handle to the Finder information directly from the global variables CurApName, CurApRefNum, and AppParmHandle.

Note: If you simply want the application's resource file reference number, you can call the Resource Manager function CurResFile when the application starts up.

```
PROCEDURE UnloadSeg (routineAddr: Ptr);
```

UnloadSeg unloads a segment, making it relocatable and purgeable; routineAddr is the address of any externally referenced routine in the segment. The segment won't actually be purged until the memory it occupies is needed. If the segment is purged, the Segment Loader will reload it the next time one of the routines in it is called.

> **Note:** UnloadSeg will work only if called from outside the segment to be unloaded.

```
PROCEDURE ExitToShell;
```

ExitToShell provides an exit from an application by starting up the Finder (after releasing the entire application heap).

Assembly-language note: ExitToShell actually launches the application whose name is stored in the global variable FinderName.

Advanced Routines

The routines below are provided for advanced programmers; they can be called only from assembly language.

Chain procedure

Trap macro	_Chain
On entry	(A0): pointer to application's file name (preceded by length byte)
	4(A0): configuration of sound and screen buffers (word)

Chain starts up an application without doing anything to the application heap, so the current application can let another application take over while still keeping its data around in the heap.

Chain also configures memory for the sound and screen buffers. The value you pass in 4(A0) determines which sound and screen buffers are allocated:

- If you pass 0 in 4(A0), you get the main sound and screen buffers; in this case, you have the largest amount of memory available to your application.

- Any positive value in 4(A0) causes the alternate sound buffer and main screen buffer to be allocated.

- Any negative value in 4(A0) causes the alternate sound buffer and alternate screen buffer to be allocated.

The memory map in chapter 1 shows the locations of the screen and sound buffers.

Warning: The sound buffers and alternate screen buffer are not supported on the Macintosh XL, and the alternate sound and screen buffers may not be supported in future versions of the Macintosh.

Note: You can get the most recent value passed in 4(A0) to the Chain procedure from the global variable CurPageOption.

Chain closes the resource file for any previous application and opens the resource file for the application being started; call DetachResource for any resources that you still wish to access.

Launch procedure

Trap macro	_Launch
On entry	(A0): pointer to application's file name (preceded by length byte)
	4(A0): configuration of sound and screen buffers (word)

Launch is called by the Finder to start up an application and will rarely need to be called by an application itself. It's the same as the Chain procedure (described above) except that it frees the storage occupied by the application heap and restores the heap to its original size.

Note: Launch preserves a special handle in the application heap which is used for preserving the desk scrap between applications; see chapter 15 of Volume I for details.

LoadSeg procedure

Trap macro	_LoadSeg
On entry	stack: segment number (word)

LoadSeg is called indirectly via the jump table (as described in the following section) when the application calls a routine in an unloaded segment. It loads the segment having the given segment number, which was assigned by the Linker. If the segment isn't in memory, LoadSeg calls the Resource Manager to read it in. It changes the jump table entries for all the routines in the segment from the "unloaded" to the "loaded" state and then invokes the routine that was called.

Note: Since LoadSeg is called via the jump table, there isn't any need for you to call it yourself.

THE JUMP TABLE

This section describes how the Segment Loader works internally, and is included here for advanced programmers; you don't have to know about this to be able to use the common Segment Loader routines.

The loading and unloading of segments is implemented through the application's **jump table**. The jump table contains one eight-byte entry for every externally referenced routine in every segment; all the entries for a particular segment are stored contiguously. The location of the jump table is shown in chapter 1.

When the Linker encounters a call to a routine in another segment, it creates a jump table entry for the routine (see Figure 2). The jump table refers to segments by segment numbers assigned by the Linker. If the segment is loaded, the jump table entry contains code that jumps to the routine. If the segment isn't loaded, the entry contains code that loads the segment.

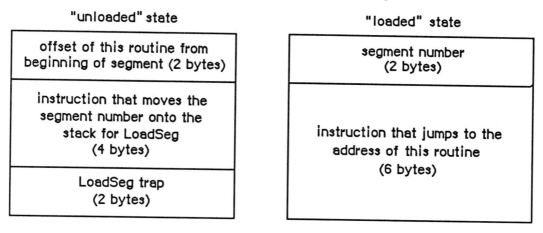

"unloaded" state

| offset of this routine from beginning of segment (2 bytes) |
| instruction that moves the segment number onto the stack for LoadSeg (4 bytes) |
| LoadSeg trap (2 bytes) |

"loaded" state

| segment number (2 bytes) |
| instruction that jumps to the address of this routine (6 bytes) |

Figure 2. Format of a Jump Table Entry

When a segment is unloaded, all its jump table entries are in the "unloaded" state. When a call to a routine in an unloaded segment is made, the code in the last six bytes of its jump table entry is executed. This code calls LoadSeg, which loads the segment into memory, transforms all of its jump table entries to the "loaded" state, and invokes the routine by executing the instruction in the last six bytes of the jump table entry. Subsequent calls to the routine also execute this instruction. If UnloadSeg is called to unload the segment, it restores the jump table entries to their "unloaded" state. Notice that whether the segment is loaded or unloaded, the last six bytes of the jump table entry are executed; the effect depends on the state of the entry at the time.

To be able to set all the jump table entries for a segment to a particular state, LoadSeg and UnloadSeg need to know exactly where in the jump table all the entries are located. They get this information from the segment header, four bytes at the beginning of the segment which contain the following:

Number of bytes	Contents
2 bytes	Offset of the first routine's entry from the beginning of the jump table
2 bytes	Number of entries for this segment

When an application starts up, its jump table is read in from segment 0 (which is the 'CODE' resource with an ID of 0). This is a special segment created by the Linker for every executable file. It contains the following:

Number of bytes	Contents
4 bytes	"Above A5" size; size in bytes from location pointed to by A5 to upper end of application space
4 bytes	"Below A5" size; size in bytes of application globals plus QuickDraw globals
4 bytes	Length of jump table in bytes
4 bytes	Offset to jump table from location pointed to by A5
n bytes	Jump table

Note: For all applications, the offset to the jump table from the location pointed to by A5 is 32, and the "above A5" size is 32 plus the length of the jump table.

The Segment Loader then executes the first entry in the jump table, which loads the main segment ('CODE' resource 1) and starts the application.

Assembly-language note: The offset to the jump table from the location pointed to by A5 is stored in the global variable CurJTOffset.

SUMMARY OF THE SEGMENT LOADER

Constants

```
CONST { Message returned by CountAppleFiles }

    appOpen  = 0;   {open the document(s)}
    appPrint = 1;   {print the document(s)}
```

Data Types

```
TYPE AppFile = RECORD
                vRefNum: INTEGER; {volume reference number}
                fType:   OSType;  {file type}
                versNum: INTEGER; {version number}
                fName:   Str255   {file name}
              END;
```

Routines

```
PROCEDURE CountAppFiles (VAR message: INTEGER; VAR count: INTEGER);   [Not
                        in ROM]
PROCEDURE GetAppFiles   (index: INTEGER; VAR theFile: AppFile);   [Not in
                        ROM]
PROCEDURE ClrAppFiles   (index: INTEGER);   [Not in ROM]
PROCEDURE GetAppParms   (VAR apName: Str255; VAR apRefNum: INTEGER; VAR
                        apParam: Handle);
PROCEDURE UnloadSeg     (routineAddr: Ptr);
PROCEDURE ExitToShell;
```

Assembly-Language Information

Advanced Routines

Trap macro	On entry	
_Chain	(A0):	pointer to application's file name (preceded by length byte)
	4(A0):	configuration of sound and screen buffers (word)
_Launch	(A0):	pointer to application's file name (preceded by length byte)
	4(A0):	configuration of sound and screen buffers (word)
_LoadSeg	stack:	segment number (word)

Variables

AppParmHandle	Handle to Finder information
CurApName	Name of current application (length byte followed by up to 31 characters)
CurApRefNum	Reference number of current application's resource file (word)
CurPageOption	Sound/screen buffer configuration passed to Chain or Launch (word)
CurJTOffset	Offset to jump table from location pointed to by A5 (word)
FinderName	Name of the Finder (length byte followed by up to 15 characters)

3 THE OPERATING SYSTEM EVENT MANAGER

3 OS Event

ABOUT THIS CHAPTER

This chapter describes the Operating System Event Manager, the part of the Operating System that reports low-level user actions such as mouse-button presses and keystrokes. Usually your application will find out about events by calling the Toolbox Event Manager, which calls the Operating System Event Manager for you, but in some situations you'll need to call the Operating System Event Manager directly.

Note: All references to "the Event Manager" in this chapter refer to the Operating System Event Manager.

You should already be familiar with the Toolbox Event Manager.

Note: Constants and data types defined in the Operating System Event Manager are presented in detail in the Toolbox Event Manager chapter (chapter 8 of Volume I), since they're necessary for using that part of the Toolbox. They're also listed in the summary of this chapter.

ABOUT THE OPERATING SYSTEM EVENT MANAGER

The Event Manager is the part of the Operating System that detects low-level, hardware-related events: mouse, keyboard, disk-inserted, device driver, and network events. It stores information about these events in the event queue and provides routines that access the queue (analogous to GetNextEvent and EventAvail in the Toolbox Event Manager). It also allows your application to post its own events into the event queue. Like the Toolbox Event Manager, the Operating System Event Manager returns a null event if it has no other events to report.

The Toolbox Event Manager calls the Operating System Event Manager to retrieve events from the event queue; in addition, it reports activate and update events, which aren't kept in the queue. It's extremely unusual for an application not to have to know about activate and update events, so usually you'll call the Toolbox Event Manager to get events.

The Operating System Event Manager also lets you:

- remove events from the event queue

- set the system event mask, to control which types of events get posted into the queue

USING THE OPERATING SYSTEM EVENT MANAGER

If you're using application-defined events in your program, you'll need to call the Operating System Event Manager function PostEvent to post them into the event queue. This function is sometimes also useful for reposting events that you've removed from the event queue with GetNextEvent.

In some situations you may want to remove from the event queue some or all events of a certain type or types. You can do this with the procedure FlushEvents. A common use of FlushEvents is to get rid of any stray events left over from before your application started up.

You'll probably never call the other Operating System Event Manager routines: GetOSEvent, which gets an event from the event queue, removing it from the queue in the process; OSEventAvail, for looking at an event without dequeueing it; and SetEventMask, which changes the setting of the system event mask.

OPERATING SYSTEM EVENT MANAGER ROUTINES

Posting and Removing Events

```
FUNCTION PostEvent (eventCode: INTEGER; eventMsg: LONGINT) :
          OSErr;
```

Trap macro	_PostEvent
On entry	A0: eventCode (word)
	D0: eventMsg (long word)
On exit	D0: result code (word)

PostEvent places in the event queue an event of the type designated by eventCode, with the event message specified by eventMsg and with the current time, mouse location, and state of the modifier keys and mouse button. It returns a result code (of type OSErr, defined as INTEGER in the Operating System Utilities) equal to one of the following predefined constants:

```
CONST noErr     = 0;   {no error (event posted)}
      evtNotEnb = 1;   {event type not designated in system event mask}
```

Warning: Be very careful when posting any events other than your own application-defined events into the queue; attempting to post an activate or update event, for example, will interfere with the internal operation of the Toolbox Event Manager, since such events aren't normally placed in the queue at all.

Warning: If you use PostEvent to repost an event, remember that the event time, location, and state of the modifier keys and mouse button will all be changed from their values when the event was originally posted, possibly altering the meaning of the event.

```
PROCEDURE FlushEvents (eventMask,stopMask: INTEGER);
```

Trap macro	_FlushEvents
On entry	D0: low-order word: eventMask
	high-order word: stopMask
On exit	D0: 0 or event code (word)

FlushEvents removes events from the event queue as specified by the given event masks. It removes all events of the type or types specified by eventMask, up to but not including the first event of any type specified by stopMask; if the event queue doesn't contain any events of the types specified by eventMask, it does nothing. To remove all events specified by eventMask, use a stopMask value of 0.

At the beginning of your application, it's usually a good idea to call FlushEvents(everyEvent,0) to empty the event queue of any stray events that may have been left lying around, such as unprocessed keystrokes typed to the Finder.

> **Assembly-language note:** On exit from this routine, D0 contains 0 if all events were removed from the queue or, if not, an event code specifying the type of event that caused the removal process to stop.

Accessing Events

```
FUNCTION GetOSEvent (eventMask: INTEGER; VAR theEvent:
        EventRecord) : BOOLEAN;
```

Trap macro	_GetOSEvent
On entry	A0: pointer to event record theEvent
	D0: eventMask (word)
On exit	D0: 0 if non-null event returned, or −1 if null event returned (byte)

GetOSEvent returns the next available event of a specified type or types and removes it from the event queue. The event is returned as the value of the parameter theEvent. The eventMask parameter specifies which event types are of interest. GetOSEvent will return the next available event of any type designated by the mask. If no event of any of the designated types is available, GetOSEvent returns a null event and a function result of FALSE; otherwise it returns TRUE.

> **Note:** Unlike the Toolbox Event Manager function GetNextEvent, GetOSEvent doesn't call the Desk Manager to see whether the system wants to intercept and respond to the event; nor does it perform GetNextEvent's processing of the alarm and Command-Shift-number combinations.

```
FUNCTION OSEventAvail (eventMask: INTEGER; VAR theEvent:
          EventRecord) : BOOLEAN;
```

Trap macro	_OSEventAvail
On entry	A0: pointer to event record theEvent
	D0: eventMask (word)
On exit	D0: 0 if non-null event returned, or –1 if null event returned (byte)

OSEventAvail works exactly the same as GetOSEvent (above) except that it doesn't remove the event from the event queue.

Note: An event returned by OSEventAvail will not be accessible later if in the meantime the queue becomes full and the event is discarded from it; since the events discarded are always the oldest ones in the queue, however, this will happen only in an unusually busy environment.

Setting the System Event Mask

```
PROCEDURE SetEventMask (theMask: INTEGER);    [Not in ROM]
```

SetEventMask sets the system event mask to the specified event mask. The Operating System Event Manager will post only those event types that correspond to bits set in the mask. (As usual, it will not post activate and update events, which are generated by the Window Manager and not stored in the event queue.) The system event mask is initially set to post all except key-up events.

Warning: Because desk accessories may rely on receiving certain types of events, your application shouldn't set the system event mask to prevent any additional types (besides key-up) from being posted. You should use SetEventMask only to enable key-up events in the unusual case that your application needs to respond to them.

Assembly-language note: The system event mask is available to assembly-language programmers in the global variable SysEvtMask.

STRUCTURE OF THE EVENT QUEUE

The event queue is a standard Macintosh Operating System queue, as described in chapter 13. Most programmers will never need to access the event queue directly; some advanced programmers, though, may need to do so for special purposes.

Each entry in the event queue contains information about an event:

```
TYPE EvQEl = RECORD
               qLink:          QElemPtr;    {next queue entry}
               qType:          INTEGER;     {queue type}
               evtQWhat:       INTEGER;     {event code}
               evtQMessage:    LONGINT;     {event message}
               evtQWhen:       LONGINT;     {ticks since startup}
               evtQWhere:      Point;       {mouse location}
               evtQModifiers:  INTEGER      {modifier flags}
             END;
```

QLink points to the next entry in the queue, and qType indicates the queue type, which must be ORD(evType). The remaining five fields of the event queue entry contain exactly the same information about the event as do the fields of the event record for that event; see chapter 8 of Volume I for a detailed description of the contents of these fields.

You can get a pointer to the header of the event queue by calling the Operating System Event Manager function GetEvQHdr.

```
FUNCTION GetEvQHdr : QHdrPtr;   [Not in ROM]
```

GetEvQHdr returns a pointer to the header of the event queue.

Assembly-language note: The global variable EventQueue contains the header of the event queue.

SUMMARY OF THE OPERATING SYSTEM EVENT MANAGER

Constants

```
CONST { Event codes }

        nullEvent     = 0;     {null}
        mouseDown     = 1;     {mouse-down}
        mouseUp       = 2;     {mouse-up}
        keyDown       = 3;     {key-down}
        keyUp         = 4;     {key-up}
        autoKey       = 5;     {auto-key}
        updateEvt     = 6;     {update; Toolbox only}
        diskEvt       = 7;     {disk-inserted}
        activateEvt   = 8;     {activate; Toolbox only}
        networkEvt    = 10;    {network}
        driverEvt     = 11;    {device driver}
        app1Evt       = 12;    {application-defined}
        app2Evt       = 13;    {application-defined}
        app3Evt       = 14;    {application-defined}
        app4Evt       = 15;    {application-defined}

        { Masks for keyboard event message }

        charCodeMask  = $000000FF;    {character code}
        keyCodeMask   = $0000FF00;    {key code}

        { Masks for forming event mask }

        mDownMask     = 2;     {mouse-down}
        mUpMask       = 4;     {mouse-up}
        keyDownMask   = 8;     {key-down}
        keyUpMask     = 16;    {key-up}
        autoKeyMask   = 32;    {auto-key}
        updateMask    = 64;    {update}
        diskMask      = 128;   {disk-inserted}
        activMask     = 256;   {activate}
        networkMask   = 1024;  {network}
        driverMask    = 2048;  {device driver}
        app1Mask      = 4096;  {application-defined}
        app2Mask      = 8192;  {application-defined}
        app3Mask      = 16384; {application-defined}
        app4Mask      = -32768; {application-defined}
        everyEvent    = -1;    {all event types}
```

```
{ Modifier flags in event record }

activeFlag = 1;       {set if window being activated}
btnState   = 128;     {set if mouse button up}
cmdKey     = 256;     {set if Command key down}
shiftKey   = 512;     {set if Shift key down}
alphaLock  = 1024;    {set if Caps Lock key down}
optionKey  = 2048;    {set if Option key down}

{ Result codes returned by PostEvent }

noErr      = 0;  {no error (event posted)}
evtNotEnb  = 1;  {event type not designated in system event mask}
```

Data Types

```
TYPE EventRecord =  RECORD
                      what:      INTEGER;    {event code}
                      message:   LONGINT;    {event message}
                      when:      LONGINT;    {ticks since startup}
                      where:     Point;      {mouse location}
                      modifiers: INTEGER     {modifier flags}
                    END;

     EvQEl = RECORD
               qLink:         QElemPtr;  {next queue entry}
               qType:         INTEGER;   {queue type}
               evtQWhat:      INTEGER;   {event code}
               evtQMessage:   LONGINT;   {event message}
               evtQWhen:      LONGINT;   {ticks since startup}
               evtQWhere:     Point;     {mouse location}
               evtQModifiers: INTEGER    {modifier flags}
             END;
```

Routines

Posting and Removing Events

```
FUNCTION  PostEvent   (eventCode: INTEGER; eventMsg: LONGINT) : OSErr;
PROCEDURE FlushEvents (eventMask,stopMask: INTEGER);
```

Accessing Events

```
FUNCTION GetOSEvent    (eventMask: INTEGER; VAR theEvent: EventRecord) :
                        BOOLEAN;
FUNCTION OSEventAvail  (eventMask: INTEGER; VAR theEvent: EventRecord) :
                        BOOLEAN;
```

Setting the System Event Mask

```
PROCEDURE SetEventMask (theMask: INTEGER);    [Not in ROM]
```

Directly Accessing the Event Queue

```
FUNCTION GetEvQHdr : QHdrPtr;    [Not in ROM]
```

Assembly-Language Information

Constants

```
; Event codes

nullEvt         .EQU    0       ;null
mButDwnEvt      .EQU    1       ;mouse-down
mButUpEvt       .EQU    2       ;mouse-up
keyDwnEvt       .EQU    3       ;key-down
keyUpEvt        .EQU    4       ;key-up
autoKeyEvt      .EQU    5       ;auto-key
updatEvt        .EQU    6       ;update; Toolbox only
diskInsertEvt   .EQU    7       ;disk-inserted
activateEvt     .EQU    8       ;activate; Toolbox only
networkEvt      .EQU    10      ;network
ioDrvrEvt       .EQU    11      ;device driver
app1Evt         .EQU    12      ;application-defined
app2Evt         .EQU    13      ;application-defined
app3Evt         .EQU    14      ;application-defined
app4Evt         .EQU    15      ;application-defined

; Modifier flags in event record

activeFlag      .EQU    0       ;set if window being activated
btnState        .EQU    2       ;set if mouse button up
cmdKey          .EQU    3       ;set if Command key down
shiftKey        .EQU    4       ;set if Shift key down
alphaLock       .EQU    5       ;set if Caps Lock key down
optionKey       .EQU    6       ;set if Option key down

; Result codes returned by PostEvent

noErr           .EQU    0       ;no error (event posted)
evtNotEnb       .EQU    1       ;event type not designated in system
                                ; event mask
```

Event Record Data Structure

evtNum	Event code (word)
evtMessage	Event message (long)
evtTicks	Ticks since startup (long)
evtMouse	Mouse location (point; long)
evtMeta	State of modifier keys (byte)
evtMBut	State of mouse button (byte)
evtBlkSize	Size in bytes of event record

Event Queue Entry Data Structure

qLink	Pointer to next queue entry
qType	Queue type (word)
evtQWhat	Event code (word)
evtQMessage	Event message (long)
evtQWhen	Ticks since startup (long)
evtQWhere	Mouse location (point; long)
evtQMeta	State of modifier keys (byte)
evtQMBut	State of mouse button (byte)
evtQBlkSize	Size in bytes of event queue entry

Routines

Trap macro	On entry	On exit
_PostEvent	A0: eventCode (word) D0: eventMsg (long)	D0: result code (word)
_FlushEvents	D0: low word: eventMask high word: stopMask	D0: 0 or event code (word)
_GetOSEvent and _OSEventAvail	A0: ptr to event record theEvent D0: eventMask (word)	D0: 0 if non-null event, −1 if null event (byte)

Variables

SysEvtMask	System event mask (word)
EventQueue	Event queue header (10 bytes)

4 THE FILE MANAGER

ABOUT THIS CHAPTER

This chapter describes the File Manager, the part of the Operating System that controls the exchange of information between a Macintosh application and files. The File Manager allows you to create and access any number of files containing whatever information you choose.

ABOUT THE FILE MANAGER

The File Manager is the part of the Operating System that handles communication between an application and files on block devices such as disk drives. (Block devices are discussed in chapter 6.) Files are a principal means by which data is stored and transmitted on the Macintosh. A **file** is a named, ordered sequence of bytes. The File Manager contains routines used to read from and write to files.

Volumes

A **volume** is a piece of storage medium, such as a disk, formatted to contain files. A volume can be an entire disk or only part of a disk. The 400K-byte 3 1/2-inch Macintosh disk is one volume.

   Note: Specialized memory devices other than disks can also contain volumes, but the information in this chapter applies only to volumes on disk.

You identify a volume by its **volume name**, which consists of any sequence of 1 to 27 printing characters. When passed to a routine, volume names must always be followed by a colon (:) to distinguish them from other names. You can use uppercase and lowercase letters when naming volumes, but the File Manager ignores case when comparing names (it doesn't ignore diacritical marks).

   Note: The colon after a volume name should be used only when calling File Manager routines; it should never be seen by the user.

A volume contains descriptive information about itself, including its name and a **file directory** that lists information about files contained on the volume; it also contains files. The files are contained in **allocation blocks**, which are areas of volume space occupying multiples of 512 bytes.

A volume can be mounted or unmounted. A volume becomes **mounted** when it's in a disk drive and the File Manager reads descriptive information about the volume into memory. Once mounted, a volume may remain in a drive or be ejected. Only mounted volumes are known to the File Manager, and an application can access information on mounted volumes only. A volume becomes **unmounted** when the File Manager releases the memory used to store the descriptive information. Your application should unmount a volume when it's finished with the volume, or when it needs the memory occupied by the volume.

The File Manager assigns each mounted volume a **volume reference number** that you can use instead of its volume name to refer to it. Every mounted volume is also assigned a **volume buffer**, which is temporary storage space in the heap used when reading or writing information on the volume. The number of volumes that may be mounted at any time is limited only by the number of drives attached and available memory.

A mounted volume can be on-line or off-line. A mounted volume is **on-line** as long as the volume buffer and all the descriptive information read from the volume when it was mounted remain in memory (about 1K to 1.5K bytes); it becomes **off-line** when all but 94 bytes of descriptive information are released. You can access information on on-line volumes immediately, but off-line volumes must be placed on-line before their information can be accessed. An application should place a volume off-line whenever it needs most of the memory the volume occupies. When an application ejects a volume from a drive, the File Manager automatically places the volume off-line.

To prevent unauthorized writing to a volume, volumes can be **locked**. Locking a volume involves either setting a software flag on the volume or changing some part of the volume physically (for example, sliding a tab from one position to another on a disk). Locking a volume ensures that none of the data on the volume can be changed.

Accessing Volumes

You can access a mounted volume via its volume name or volume reference number. On-line volumes in disk drives can also be accessed via the **drive number** of the drive on which the volume is mounted (the internal drive is number 1, the external drive is number 2, and any additional drives connected to the Macintosh will have larger numbers). When accessing a mounted volume, you should always use the volume name or volume reference number, rather than a drive number, because the volume may have been ejected or placed off-line. Whenever possible, use the volume reference number (to avoid confusion between volumes with the same name).

One volume is always the **default volume**. Whenever you call a routine to access a volume but don't specify which volume, the default volume is accessed. Initially, the volume used to start up the application is the default volume, but an application can designate any mounted volume as the default volume.

Whenever the File Manager needs to access a mounted volume that's been ejected from its drive, the dialog box shown in Figure 1 is displayed, and the File Manager waits until the user inserts the disk named volName into a drive.

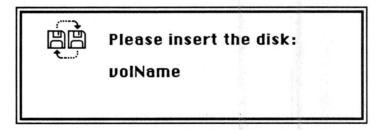

Figure 1. Disk-Switch Dialog

Note: This dialog is actually a system error alert, as described in chapter 12.

Files

A file is a finite sequence of numbered bytes. Any byte or group of bytes in the sequence can be accessed individually. A file is identified by its **file name** and **version number**. A file name consists of any sequence of 1 to 255 printing characters, excluding colons (:). You can use uppercase and lowercase letters when naming files, but the File Manager ignores case when comparing names (it doesn't ignore diacritical marks). The version number is any number from 0 to 255, and is used by the File Manager to distinguish between different files with the same name. A byte within a file is identified by its position within the ordered sequence.

> **Warning:** Your application should constrain file names to fewer than 64 characters, because the Finder will generate an error if given a longer name. You should always assign files a version number of 0, because the Resource Manager, Segment Loader, and Standard File Package won't operate on files with nonzero version numbers, and the Finder ignores version numbers.

There are two parts or **forks** to a file: the **data fork** and the **resource fork**. Normally the resource fork of an application file contains the resources used by the application, such as menus, fonts, and icons, and also the application code itself. The data fork can contain anything an application wants to store there. Information stored in resource forks should always be accessed via the Resource Manager. Information in data forks can only be accessed via the File Manager. For simplicity, "file" will be used instead of "data fork" in this chapter.

The size of a file is limited only by the size of the volume it's on. Each byte is numbered: The first byte is byte 0. You can read bytes from and write bytes to a file either singly or in sequences of unlimited length. Each read or write operation can start anywhere in the file, regardless of where the last operation began or ended. Figure 2 shows the structure of a file.

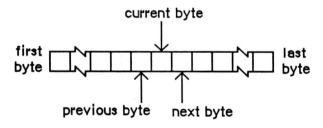

Figure 2. A File

A file's maximum size is defined by its **physical end-of-file**, which is 1 greater than the number of the last byte in its last allocation block (see Figure 3). The physical end-of-file is equivalent to the maximum number of bytes the file can contain. A file's actual size is defined by its **logical end-of-file**, which is 1 greater than the number of the last byte in the file. The logical end-of-file is equivalent to the actual number of bytes in the file, since the first byte is byte number 0. The physical end-of-file is always greater than the logical end-of-file. For example, an empty file (one with 0 bytes) in a 1K-byte allocation block has a logical end-of-file of 0 and a physical end-of-file of 1024. A file with 50 bytes has a logical end-of-file of 50 and a physical end-of-file of 1024.

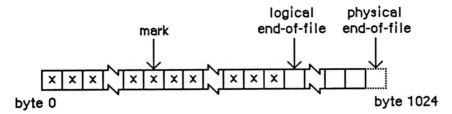

Figure 3. End-of-File and Mark

The current position marker, or **mark**, is the number of the next byte that will be read or written. The value of the mark can't exceed the value of the logical end-of-file. The mark automatically moves forward one byte for every byte read from or written to the file. If, during a write operation, the mark meets the logical end-of-file, both are moved forward one position for every additional byte written to the file. Figure 4 shows the movement of the mark and logical end-of-file.

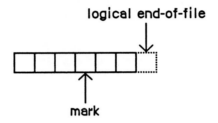

Beginning position

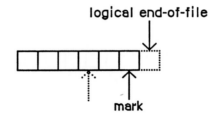

After reading two bytes

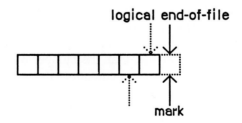

After writing two bytes

Figure 4. Movement of Mark and Logical End-of-File

If, during a write operation, the mark must move past the physical end-of-file, another allocation block is added to the file—the physical end-of-file is placed one byte beyond the end of the new allocation block, and the mark and logical end-of-file are placed at the first byte of the new allocation block.

An application can move the logical end-of-file to anywhere from the beginning of the file to the physical end-of-file (the mark is adjusted accordingly). If the logical end-of-file is moved to a position more than one allocation block short of the current physical end-of-file, the unneeded allocation block will be deleted from the file. The mark can be placed anywhere from the first byte in the file to the logical end-of-file.

Accessing Files

A file can be **open** or **closed**. An application can perform only certain operations, such as reading and writing, on open files; other operations, such as deleting, can be performed only on closed files.

To open a file, you must identify the file and the volume containing it. When a file is opened, the File Manager creates an **access path**, a description of the route to be followed when accessing the file. The access path specifies the volume on which the file is located (by volume reference number, drive number, or volume name) and the location of the file on the volume. Every access path is assigned a unique **path reference number** (a number greater than 0) that's used to refer to it. You should always refer to a file via its path reference number, to avoid confusion between files with the same name.

A file can have one access path open for writing or for both reading and writing, and one or more access paths for reading only; there cannot be more than one access path that writes to a file. Each access path is separate from all other access paths to the file. A maximum of 12 access paths can be open at one time. Each access path can move its own mark and read at the position it indicates. All access paths to the same file share common logical and physical end-of-file markers.

The File Manager reads descriptive information about a newly opened file from its volume and stores it in memory. For example, each file has **open permission** information, which indicates whether data can only be read from it, or both read from and written to it. Each access path contains **read/write permission** information that specifies whether data is allowed to be read from the file, written to the file, both read and written, or whatever the file's open permission allows. If an application wants to write data to a file, both types of permission information must allow writing; if either type allows reading only, then no data can be written.

When an application requests that data be read from a file, the File Manager reads the data from the file and transfers it to the application's **data buffer**. Any part of the data that can be transferred in entire 512-byte blocks is transferred directly. Any part of the data composed of fewer than 512 bytes is also read from the file in one 512-byte block, but placed in temporary storage space in memory. Then, only the bytes containing the requested data are transferred to the application.

When an application writes data to a file, the File Manager transfers the data from the application's data buffer and writes it to the file. Any part of the data that can be transferred in entire 512-byte blocks is written directly. Any part of the data composed of fewer than 512 bytes is placed in temporary storage space in memory until 512 bytes have accumulated; then the entire block is written all at once.

Normally the temporary space in memory used for all reading and writing is the volume buffer, but an application can specify that an **access path buffer** be used instead for a particular access path (see Figure 5).

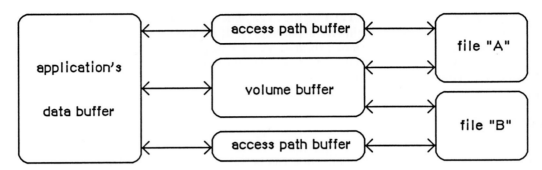

Figure 5. Buffers For Transferring Data

Warning: You must lock any access path buffers of files in relocatable blocks, so their location doesn't change while the file is open.

Your application can **lock** a file to prevent unauthorized writing to it. Locking a file ensures that none of the data in it can be changed. This is distinct from the user-accessible lock maintained by the Finder, which won't let you rename or delete a locked file, but will let you change the data contained in the file.

Note: Advanced programmers: The File Manager can also read a continuous stream of characters or a line of characters. In the first case, you ask the File Manager to read a specific number of bytes: When that many have been read or when the mark has reached the logical end-of-file, the read operation terminates. In the second case, called **newline mode**, the read will terminate when either of the above conditions is met or when a specified character, the **newline character**, is read. The newline character is usually Return (ASCII code $0D), but can be any character. Information about newline mode is associated with each access path to a file, and can differ from one access path to another.

FILE INFORMATION USED BY THE FINDER

A file directory on a volume lists information about all the files on the volume. The information used by the Finder is contained in a data structure of type FInfo:

```
TYPE FInfo = RECORD
            fdType:     OSType;   {file type}
            fdCreator:  OSType;   {file's creator}
            fdFlags:    INTEGER;  {flags}
            fdLocation: Point;    {file's location}
            fdFldr:     INTEGER   {file's window}
        END;
```

Normally an application need only set the file type and creator when a file is created, and the Finder will manipulate the other fields. (File type and creator are discussed in chapter 1 of Volume III.)

FdFlags indicates whether the file's icon is invisible, whether the file has a bundle, and other characteristics used internally by the Finder:

Bit	Meaning
13	Set if file has a bundle
14	Set if file's icon is invisible

Masks for these two bits are available as predefined constants:

```
CONST fHasBundle = 8192;     {set if file has a bundle}
      fInvisible = 16384;    {set if file's icon is invisible}
```

For more information about bundles, see chapter 1 of Volume III.

The last two fields indicate where the file's icon will appear if the icon is visible. FdLocation contains the location of the file's icon in its window, given in the local coordinate system of the window. It's used by the Finder to position the icon; when creating a file you should set it to 0 and let the Finder position the icon for you. FdFldr indicates the window in which the file's icon will appear, and may contain one of the following values:

```
CONST fTrash   = -3;   {file is in Trash window}
      fDesktop = -2;   {file is on desktop}
      fDisk    =  0;   {file is in disk window}
```

If fdFldr contains a positive number, the file's icon will appear in a folder; the numbers that identify folders are assigned by the Finder. You can also get the folder number of an existing file, and place additional files in that same folder.

USING THE FILE MANAGER

You can call File Manager routines via three different methods: high-level Pascal calls, low-level Pascal calls, and assembly language. The high-level Pascal calls are designed for Pascal programmers interested in using the File Manager in a simple manner; they provide adequate file I/O and don't require much special knowledge to use. The low-level Pascal and assembly-language calls are designed for advanced Pascal programmers and assembly-language programmers interested in using the File Manager to its fullest capacity; they require some special knowledge to be used most effectively.

Information for all programmers follows here. The next two sections contain special information for high-level Pascal programmers and for low-level Pascal and assembly-language programmers.

Note: The names used to refer to File Manager routines here are actually the assembly-language macro names for the low-level routines, but the Pascal routine names are very similar.

The File Manager is automatically initialized each time the system starts up.

To create a new, empty file, call Create. Create allows you to set some of the information stored on the volume about the file.

To open a file, call Open. The File Manager creates an access path and returns a path reference number that you'll use every time you want to refer to it. Before you open a file, you may want to call the Standard File Package, which presents the standard interface through which the user can specify the file to be opened. The Standard File Package will return the name of the file, the volume reference number of the volume containing the file, and additional information. (If the user inserts an unmounted volume into a drive, the Standard File Package will automatically call the Disk Initialization Package to attempt to mount it.)

After opening a file, you can transfer data from it to an application's data buffer with Read, and send data from an application's data buffer to the file with Write. You can't use Write on a file whose open permission only allows reading, or on a file on a locked volume.

You can specify the byte position of the mark before calling Read or Write by calling SetFPos. GetFPos returns the byte position of the mark.

Once you've completed whatever reading and writing you want to do, call Close to close the file. Close writes the contents of the file's access path buffer to the volume and deletes the access path. You can remove a closed file (both forks) from a volume by calling Delete.

To protect against power loss or unexpected disk ejection, you should periodically call FlushVol (probably after each time you close a file), which writes the contents of the volume buffer and all access path buffers (if any) to the volume and updates the descriptive information contained on the volume.

Whenever your application is finished with a disk, or the user chooses Eject from a menu, call Eject. Eject calls FlushVol, places the volume off-line, and then physically ejects the volume from its drive.

The preceding paragraphs covered the simplest File Manager routines. The remainder of this section describes the less commonly used routines, some of which are available only to advanced programmers.

Applications will normally use the Resource Manager to open resource forks and change the information contained within, but programmers writing unusual applications (such as a disk-copying utility) might want to use the File Manager to open resource forks. This is done by calling OpenRF. As with Open, the File Manager creates an access path and returns a path reference number that you'll use every time you want to refer to this resource fork.

When the Toolbox Event Manager function GetNextEvent receives a disk-inserted event, it calls the Desk Manager function SystemEvent. SystemEvent calls the File Manager function MountVol, which attempts to mount the volume on the disk. GetNextEvent then returns the disk-inserted event: The low-order word of the event message contains the number of the drive, and the high-order word contains the result code of the attempted mounting. If the result code indicates that an error occurred, you'll need to call the Disk Initialization Package to allow the user to initialize or eject the volume.

Note: Applications that rely on the Operating System Event Manager function GetOSEvent to learn about events (and don't call GetNextEvent) must explicitly call MountVol to mount volumes.

After a volume has been mounted, your application can call GetVolInfo, which will return the name of the volume, the amount of unused space on the volume, and a volume reference number that you can use to refer to that volume.

To minimize the amount of memory used by mounted volumes, an application can unmount or place off-line any volumes that aren't currently being used. To unmount a volume, call UnmountVol, which flushes a volume (by calling FlushVol) and releases all of the memory used for it (about 1 to 1.5K bytes). To place a volume off-line, call OffLine, which flushes a volume and releases all of the memory used for it except for 94 bytes of descriptive information about the volume. Off-line volumes are placed on-line by the File Manager as needed, but your application must remount any unmounted volumes it wants to access. The File Manager itself may place volumes off-line during its normal operation.

If you would like all File Manager calls to apply to one volume, you can specify that volume as the default. You can use SetVol to set the default volume to any mounted volume, and GetVol to learn the name and volume reference number of the default volume.

Normally, volume initialization and naming is handled by the Standard File Package, which calls the Disk Initialization Package. If you want to initialize a volume explicitly or erase all files from a volume, you can call the Disk Initialization Package directly. When you want to change the name of a volume, call the File Manager function Rename.

Whenever a disk has been reconstructed in an attempt to salvage lost files (because its directory or other file-access information has been destroyed), the logical end-of-file of each file will probably be equal to each physical end-of-file, regardless of where the actual logical end-of-file is. The first time an application attempts to read from a file on a reconstructed volume, it will blindly pass the correct logical end-of-file and read misinformation until it reaches the new, incorrect logical end-of-file. To prevent this from happening, an application should always maintain an independent record of the logical end-of-file of each file it uses. To determine the File Manager's conception of the length of a file, or find out how many bytes have yet to be read from it, call GetEOF, which returns the logical end-of-file. You can change the length of a file by calling SetEOF.

Allocation blocks are automatically added to and deleted from a file as necessary. If this happens to a number of files alternately, each of the files will be contained in allocation blocks scattered throughout the volume, which increases the time required to access those files. To prevent such fragmentation of files, you can allocate a number of contiguous allocation blocks to an open file by calling Allocate.

Instead of calling FlushVol, an unusual application might call FlushFile. FlushFile forces the contents of a file's volume buffer and access path buffer (if any) to be written to its volume. FlushFile doesn't update the descriptive information contained on the volume, so the volume information won't be correct until you call FlushVol.

To get information about a file stored on a volume (such as its name and creation date), call GetFileInfo. You can change this information by calling SetFileInfo. Changing the name or version number of a file is accomplished by calling Rename or SetFilType, respectively; they have a similar effect, since both the file name and version number are needed to identify a file. You can lock or unlock a file by calling SetFilLock or RstFilLock, respectively. Given a path reference number, you can get the volume reference number of the volume containing that file by calling GetVRefNum.

4 File Manager

HIGH-LEVEL FILE MANAGER ROUTINES

This section describes all the high-level Pascal routines of the File Manager. For information on calling the low-level Pascal and assembly-language routines, see the next section.

When accessing a volume other than the default volume, you must identify it by its volume name, its volume reference number, or the drive number of its drive. The parameter names used in identifying a volume are volName, vRefNum, and drvNum. VRefNum and drvNum are both integers. VolName is a pointer, of type StringPtr, to a volume name.

> **Note:** VolName is declared as type StringPtr instead of type STRING to allow you to pass NIL in routines where the parameter is optional.

The File Manager determines which volume to access by using one of the following:

1. VolName. (If volName points to a zero-length name, an error is returned.)

2. If volName is NIL or points to an improper volume name, then vRefNum or drvNum (only one is given per routine).

3. If vRefNum or drvNum is 0, the default volume. (If there isn't a default volume, an error is returned.)

> **Warning:** Before you pass a parameter of type StringPtr to a File Manager routine, be sure that memory has been allocated for the variable. For example, the following statements will ensure that memory is allocated for the variable myStr:

```
VAR   myStr: Str255;
      . . .

result := GetVol(@myStr,myRefNum)
```

When accessing a closed file on a volume, you must identify the volume by the method given above, and identify the file by its name in the fileName parameter. (The high-level File Manager routines will work only with files having a version number of 0.) FileName can contain either the file name alone or the file name prefixed by a volume name.

> **Note:** Although fileName can include both the volume name and the file name, applications shouldn't encourage users to prefix a file name with a volume name.

You can't specify an access path buffer when calling high-level Pascal routines. All access paths open on a volume will share the volume buffer, causing a slight increase in the amount of time required to access files.

All high-level File Manager routines return an integer result code of type OSErr as their function result. Each routine description lists all of the applicable result codes, along with a short description of what the result code means. Lengthier explanations of all the result codes can be found in the summary at the end of this chapter.

Accessing Volumes

```
FUNCTION GetVInfo (drvNum: INTEGER; volName: StringPtr; VAR
        vRefNum: INTEGER; VAR freeBytes: LONGINT) : OSErr;
        [Not in ROM]
```

GetVInfo returns the name, reference number, and available space (in bytes), in volName, vRefNum, and freeBytes, for the volume in the drive specified by drvNum.

Result codes	noErr	No error
	nsvErr	No default volume
	paramErr	Bad drive number

```
FUNCTION GetVRefNum (pathRefNum: INTEGER; VAR vRefNum: INTEGER) :
        OSErr;   [Not in ROM]
```

Given a path reference number in pathRefNum, GetVRefNum returns the volume reference number in vRefNum.

Result codes	noErr	No error
	rfNumErr	Bad reference number

```
FUNCTION GetVol (volName: StringPtr; VAR vRefNum: INTEGER) :
        OSErr;   [Not in ROM]
```

GetVol returns the name of the default volume in volName and its volume reference number in vRefNum.

Result codes	noErr	No error
	nsvErr	No such volume

```
FUNCTION SetVol (volName: StringPtr; vRefNum: INTEGER) : OSErr;
        [Not in ROM]
```

SetVol sets the default volume to the mounted volume specified by volName or vRefNum.

Result codes	noErr	No error
	bdNamErr	Bad volume name
	nsvErr	No such volume
	paramErr	No default volume

```
FUNCTION FlushVol (volName: StringPtr; vRefNum: INTEGER) : OSErr;
        [Not in ROM]
```

On the volume specified by volName or vRefNum, FlushVol writes the contents of the associated volume buffer and descriptive information about the volume (if they've changed since the last time FlushVol was called).

Result codes	noErr	No error
	bdNamErr	Bad volume name
	extFSErr	External file system
	ioErr	I/O error
	nsDrvErr	No such drive
	nsvErr	No such volume
	paramErr	No default volume

```
FUNCTION UnmountVol (volName: StringPtr; vRefNum: INTEGER) :
        OSErr;   [Not in ROM]
```

UnmountVol unmounts the volume specified by volName or vRefNum, by calling FlushVol to flush the volume buffer, closing all open files on the volume, and releasing the memory used for the volume.

Warning: Don't unmount the startup volume.

Result codes	noErr	No error
	bdNamErr	Bad volume name
	extFSErr	External file system
	ioErr	I/O error
	nsDrvErr	No such drive
	nsvErr	No such volume
	paramErr	No default volume

```
FUNCTION Eject (volName: StringPtr; vRefNum: INTEGER) : OSErr;
        [Not in ROM]
```

Eject flushes the volume specified by volName or vRefNum, places it off-line, and then ejects the volume.

Result codes	noErr	No error
	bdNamErr	Bad volume name
	extFSErr	External file system
	ioErr	I/O error
	nsDrvErr	No such drive
	nsvErr	No such volume
	paramErr	No default volume

Accessing Files

```
FUNCTION Create (fileName: Str255; vRefNum: INTEGER; creator:
        OSType; fileType: OSType) : OSErr;   [Not in ROM]
```

Create creates a new file (both forks) with the specified name, file type, and creator, on the specified volume. (File type and creator are discussed in chapter 1 of Volume III.) The new file is unlocked and empty. The date and time of its creation and last modification are set to the current date and time.

Result codes	noErr	No error
	bdNamErr	Bad file name
	dupFNErr	Duplicate file name and version
	dirFulErr	File directory full
	extFSErr	External file system
	ioErr	I/O error
	nsvErr	No such volume
	vLckdErr	Software volume lock
	wPrErr	Hardware volume lock

```
FUNCTION FSOpen (fileName: Str255; vRefNum: INTEGER; VAR refNum:
       INTEGER) : OSErr;   [Not in ROM]
```

FSOpen creates an access path to the file having the name fileName on the volume specified by vRefNum. A path reference number is returned in refNum. The access path's read/write permission is set to whatever the file's open permission allows.

Result codes	noErr	No error
	bdNamErr	Bad file name
	extFSErr	External file system
	fnfErr	File not found
	ioErr	I/O error
	nsvErr	No such volume
	opWrErr	File already open for writing
	tmfoErr	Too many files open

```
FUNCTION OpenRF (fileName: Str255; vRefNum: INTEGER; VAR refNum:
       INTEGER) : OSErr;   [Not in ROM]
```

OpenRF is similar to FSOpen; the only difference is that OpenRF opens the resource fork of the specified file rather than the data fork. A path reference number is returned in refNum. The access path's read/write permission is set to whatever the file's open permission allows.

Note: Normally you should access a file's resource fork through the routines of the Resource Manager rather than the File Manager. OpenRF doesn't read the resource map into memory; it's really only useful for block-level operations such as copying files.

Result codes	noErr	No error
	bdNamErr	Bad file name
	extFSErr	External file system
	fnfErr	File not found
	ioErr	I/O error
	nsvErr	No such volume
	opWrErr	File already open for writing
	tmfoErr	Too many files open

4 File Manager

```
FUNCTION FSRead (refNum: INTEGER; VAR count: LONGINT; buffPtr:
        Ptr) : OSErr;   [Not in ROM]
```

FSRead attempts to read the number of bytes specified by the count parameter from the open file whose access path is specified by refNum, and transfer them to the data buffer pointed to by buffPtr. The read operation begins at the current mark, so you might want to precede this with a call to SetFPos. If you try to read past the logical end-of-file, FSRead moves the mark to the end-of-file and returns eofErr as its function result. After the read is completed, the number of bytes actually read is returned in the count parameter.

Result codes		
	noErr	No error
	eofErr	End-of-file
	extFSErr	External file system
	fnOpnErr	File not open
	ioErr	I/O error
	paramErr	Negative count
	rfNumErr	Bad reference number

```
FUNCTION FSWrite (refNum: INTEGER; VAR count: LONGINT; buffPtr:
        Ptr) : OSErr;   [Not in ROM]
```

FSWrite takes the number of bytes specified by the count parameter from the buffer pointed to by buffPtr and attempts to write them to the open file whose access path is specified by refNum. The write operation begins at the current mark, so you might want to precede this with a call to SetFPos. After the write is completed, the number of bytes actually written is returned in the count parameter.

Result codes		
	noErr	No error
	dskFulErr	Disk full
	fLckdErr	File locked
	fnOpnErr	File not open
	ioErr	I/O error
	paramErr	Negative count
	rfNumErr	Bad reference number
	vLckdErr	Software volume lock
	wPrErr	Hardware volume lock
	wrPermErr	Read/write permission doesn't allow writing

```
FUNCTION GetFPos (refNum: INTEGER; VAR filePos: LONGINT) : OSErr;
        [Not in ROM]
```

GetFPos returns, in filePos, the mark of the open file whose access path is specified by refNum.

Result codes		
	noErr	No error
	extFSErr	External file system
	fnOpnErr	File not open
	ioErr	I/O error
	rfNumErr	Bad reference number

```
FUNCTION SetFPos (refNum: INTEGER; posMode: INTEGER; posOff:
          LONGINT) : OSErr;   [Not in ROM]
```

SetFPos sets the mark of the open file whose access path is specified by refNum, to the position specified by posMode and posOff. PosMode indicates how to position the mark; it must contain one of the following values:

```
CONST fsAtMark    = 0;  {at current mark}
      fsFromStart = 1;  {offset relative to beginning of file}
      fsFromLEOF  = 2;  {offset relative to logical end-of-file}
      fsFromMark  = 3;  {offset relative to current mark}
```

PosOff specifies the byte offset (either positive or negative), relative to the position specified by posMode, where the mark should be set (except when posMode is equal to fsAtMark, in which case posOff is ignored). If you try to set the mark past the logical end-of-file, SetFPos moves the mark to the end-of-file and returns eofErr as its function result.

Result codes	noErr	No error
	eofErr	End-of-file
	extFSErr	External file system
	fnOpnErr	File not open
	ioErr	I/O error
	posErr	Attempt to position before start of file
	rfNumErr	Bad reference number

```
FUNCTION GetEOF (refNum: INTEGER; VAR logEOF: LONGINT) : OSErr;
          [Not in ROM]
```

GetEOF returns, in logEOF, the logical end-of-file of the open file whose access path is specified by refNum.

Result codes	noErr	No error
	extFSErr	External file system
	fnOpnErr	File not open
	ioErr	I/O error
	rfNumErr	Bad reference number

```
FUNCTION SetEOF (refNum: INTEGER; logEOF: LONGINT) : OSErr;   [Not in
          ROM]
```

SetEOF sets the logical end-of-file of the open file whose access path is specified by refNum, to the position specified by logEOF. If you attempt to set the logical end-of-file beyond the physical end-of-file, the physical end-of-file is set to one byte beyond the end of the next free allocation block; if there isn't enough space on the volume, no change is made, and SetEOF returns dskFulErr as its function result. If logEOF is 0, all space occupied by the file on the volume is released.

Result codes   noErr   No error
     dskFulErr   Disk full
     extFSErr   External file system
     fLckdErr   File locked
     fnOpnErr   File not open
     ioErr   I/O error
     rfNumErr   Bad reference number
     vLckdErr   Software volume lock
     wPrErr   Hardware volume lock
     wrPermErr   Read/write permission doesn't allow writing

```
FUNCTION Allocate (refNum: INTEGER; VAR count: LONGINT) : OSErr;
        [Not in ROM]
```

Allocate adds the number of bytes specified by the count parameter to the open file whose access path is specified by refNum, and sets the physical end-of-file to one byte beyond the last block allocated. The number of bytes actually allocated is rounded up to the nearest multiple of the allocation block size, and returned in the count parameter. If there isn't enough empty space on the volume to satisfy the allocation request, Allocate allocates the rest of the space on the volume and returns dskFulErr as its function result.

Result codes   noErr   No error
     dskFulErr   Disk full
     fLckdErr   File locked
     fnOpnErr   File not open
     ioErr   I/O error
     rfNumErr   Bad reference number
     vLckdErr   Software volume lock
     wPrErr   Hardware volume lock
     wrPermErr   Read/write permission doesn't allow writing

```
FUNCTION FSClose (refNum: INTEGER) : OSErr;   [Not in ROM]
```

FSClose removes the access path specified by refNum, writes the contents of the volume buffer to the volume, and updates the file's entry in the file directory.

Note: Some information stored on the volume won't be correct until FlushVol is called.

Result codes   noErr   No error
     extFSErr   External file system
     fnfErr   File not found
     fnOpnErr   File not open
     ioErr   I/O error
     nsvErr   No such volume
     rfNumErr   Bad reference number

Changing Information About Files

All of the routines described in this section affect both forks of the file, and don't require the file to be open.

```
FUNCTION GetFInfo (fileName: Str255; vRefNum: INTEGER; VAR
        fndrInfo: FInfo) : OSErr;  [Not in ROM]
```

For the file having the name fileName on the specified volume, GetFInfo returns information used by the Finder in fndrInfo (see the section "File Information Used by the Finder").

Result codes	noErr	No error
	bdNamErr	Bad file name
	extFSErr	External file system
	fnfErr	File not found
	ioErr	I/O error
	nsvErr	No such volume
	paramErr	No default volume

```
FUNCTION SetFInfo (fileName: Str255; vRefNum: INTEGER; fndrInfo:
        FInfo) : OSErr;  [Not in ROM]
```

For the file having the name fileName on the specified volume, SetFInfo sets information used by the Finder to fndrInfo (see the section "File Information Used by the Finder").

Result codes	noErr	No error
	extFSErr	External file system
	fLckd Err	File locked
	fnfErr	File not found
	ioErr	I/O error
	nsvErr	No such volume
	vLckdErr	Software volume lock
	wPrErr	Hardware volume lock

```
FUNCTION SetFLock (fileName: Str255; vRefNum: INTEGER) : OSErr;
        [Not in ROM]
```

SetFLock locks the file having the name fileName on the specified volume. Access paths currently in use aren't affected.

Note: This lock is controlled by your application, and is distinct from the user-accessible lock maintained by the Finder.

Result codes	noErr	No error
	extFSErr	External file system
	fnfErr	File not found
	ioErr	I/O error
	nsvErr	No such volume
	vLckdErr	Software volume lock
	wPrErr	Hardware volume lock

```
FUNCTION RstFLock (fileName: Str255; vRefNum: INTEGER) : OSErr;
         [Not in ROM]
```

RstFLock unlocks the file having the name fileName on the specified volume. Access paths currently in use aren't affected.

Result codes	noErr	No error
	extFSErr	External file system
	fnfErr	File not found
	ioErr	I/O error
	nsvErr	No such volume
	vLckdErr	Software volume lock
	wPrErr	Hardware volume lock

```
FUNCTION Rename (oldName: Str255; vRefNum: INTEGER; newName:
         Str255) : OSErr;   [Not in ROM]
```

Given a file name in oldName, Rename changes the name of the file to newName. Access paths currently in use aren't affected. Given a volume name in oldName or a volume reference number in vRefNum, Rename changes the name of the specified volume to newName.

Warning: If you're renaming a volume, be sure that oldName ends with a colon, or Rename will consider it a file name.

Result codes	noErr	No error
	bdNamErr	Bad file name
	dirFulErr	Directory full
	dupFNErr	Duplicate file name
	extFSErr	External file system
	fLckdErr	File locked
	fnfErr	File not found
	fsRnErr	Problem during rename
	ioErr	I/O error
	nsvErr	No such volume
	paramErr	No default volume
	vLckdErr	Software volume lock
	wPrErr	Hardware volume lock

```
FUNCTION FSDelete (fileName: Str255; vRefNum: INTEGER) : OSErr;
          [Not in ROM]
```

FSDelete removes the closed file having the name fileName from the specified volume.

Note: This function will delete *both* forks of the file.

Result codes		
	noErr	No error
	bdNamErr	Bad file name
	extFSErr	External file system
	fBsyErr	File busy
	fLckdErr	File locked
	fnfErr	File not found
	ioErr	I/O error
	nsvErr	No such volume
	vLckdErr	Software volume lock
	wPrErr	Hardware volume lock

LOW-LEVEL FILE MANAGER ROUTINES

This section contains information for programmers using the low-level Pascal or assembly-language routines of the File Manager, and describes them in detail.

Most low-level File Manager routines can be executed either **synchronously** (meaning that the application can't continue until the routine is completed) or **asynchronously** (meaning that the application is free to perform other tasks while the routine is executing). Some cannot be executed asynchronously, because they use the Memory Manager to allocate and release memory.

When an application calls a File Manager routine asynchronously, an **I/O request** is placed in the **file I/O queue,** and control returns to the calling program—possibly even before the actual I/O is completed. Requests are taken from the queue one at a time, and processed; meanwhile, the calling program is free to work on other things.

The calling program may specify a **completion routine** to be executed at the end of an asynchronous operation.

At any time, you can clear all queued File Manager calls except the current one by using the InitQueue procedure. InitQueue is especially useful when an error occurs and you no longer want queued calls to be executed.

Routine parameters passed by an application to the File Manager and returned by the File Manager to an application are contained in a **parameter block,** which is a data structure in the heap or stack. Most low-level calls to the File Manager are of the form

```
FUNCTION PBCallName (paramBlock: ParmBlkPtr; async: BOOLEAN) : OSErr;
```

PBCallName is the name of the routine. ParamBlock points to the parameter block containing the parameters for the routine. If async is TRUE, the call is executed asynchronously; otherwise the call is executed synchronously. The routine returns an integer result code of type OSErr. Each routine description lists all of the applicable result codes, along with a short description of what the result code means. Lengthier explanations of all the result codes can be found in the summary at the end of this chapter.

Assembly-language note: When you call a File Manager routine, A0 must point to a parameter block containing the parameters for the routine. If you want the routine to be executed asynchronously, set bit 10 of the routine trap word. You can do this by supplying the word ASYNC as the second argument to the routine macro. For example:

```
_Read   ,ASYNC
```

You can set or test bit 10 of a trap word by using the global constant asyncTrpBit. (The syntax shown above applies to the Lisa Workshop Assembler; programmers using another development system should consult its documentation for the proper syntax.)

All routines except InitQueue return a result code in D0.

Routine Parameters

There are three different kinds of parameter blocks you'll pass to File Manager routines. Each kind is used with a particular set of routine calls: I/O routines, file information routines, and volume information routines.

The lengthy, variable-length data structure of a parameter block is given below. The Device Manager and File Manager use this same data structure, but only the parts relevant to the File Manager are discussed here. Each kind of parameter block contains eight fields of standard information and nine to 16 fields of additional information:

```
TYPE ParamBlkType  = (ioParam,fileParam,volumeParam,cntrlParam);

     ParamBlockRec = RECORD
                     qLink:        QElemPtr;    {next queue entry}
                     qType:        INTEGER;     {queue type}
                     ioTrap:       INTEGER;     {routine trap}
                     ioCmdAddr:    Ptr;         {routine address}
                     ioCompletion: ProcPtr;     {completion routine}
                     ioResult:     OSErr;       {result code}
                     ioNamePtr:    StringPtr;   {volume or file name}
                     ioVRefNum:    INTEGER;     {volume reference or }
                                                { drive number}
                     CASE ParamBlkType OF
                      ioParam:
                        . . . {I/O routine parameters}
                      fileParam:
                        . . . {file information routine parameters}
                      volumeParam:
                        . . . {volume information routine parameters}
                      cntrlParam:
                        . . . {used by the Device Manager}
                     END;

     ParmBlkPtr = ^ParamBlockRec;
```

The first four fields in each parameter block are handled entirely by the File Manager, and most programmers needn't be concerned with them; programmers who are interested in them should see the section "Data Structures in Memory".

IOCompletion contains a pointer to a completion routine to be executed at the end of an asynchronous call; it should be NIL for asynchronous calls with no completion routine, and is automatically set to NIL for all synchronous calls.

> **Warning:** Completion routines are executed at the interrupt level and must preserve all registers other than A0, A1, and D0-D2. Your completion routine must not make any calls to the Memory Manager, directly or indirectly, and can't depend on handles to unlocked blocks being valid. If it uses application globals, it must also ensure that register A5 contains the address of the boundary between the application globals and the application parameters; for details, see SetUpA5 and RestoreA5 in chapter 13.

> **Assembly-language note:** When your completion routine is called, register A0 points to the parameter block of the asynchronous call and register D0 contains the result code.

Routines that are executed asynchronously return control to the calling program with the result code noErr as soon as the call is placed in the file I/O queue. This isn't an indication of successful call completion, but simply indicates that the call was successfully queued. To determine when the call is actually completed, you can poll the ioResult field; this field is set to 1 when the call is made, and receives the actual result code upon completion of the call. Completion routines are executed after the result code is placed in ioResult.

IONamePtr points to either a volume name or a file name (which can be prefixed by a volume name).

> **Note:** Although ioNamePtr can include both the volume name and the file name, applications shouldn't encourage users to prefix a file name with a volume name.

IOVRefNum contains either the reference number of a volume or the drive number of a drive containing a volume.

For routines that access volumes, the File Manager determines which volume to access by using one of the following:

1. IONamePtr, a pointer to the volume name (which must be followed by a colon).

2. If ioNamePtr is NIL, or points to an improper volume name, then ioVRefNum. (If ioVRefNum is negative, it's a volume reference number; if positive, it's a drive number.)

3. If ioVRefNum is 0, the default volume. (If there isn't a default volume, an error is returned.)

For routines that access closed files, the File Manager determines which file to access by using ioNamePtr, a pointer to the name of the file (and possibly also of the volume).

- If the string pointed to by ioNamePtr doesn't include the volume name, the File Manager uses steps 2 and 3 above to determine the volume.

- If ioNamePtr is NIL or points to an improper file name, an error is returned.

I/O Parameters

When you call one of the I/O routines, you'll use these nine additional fields after the standard eight fields in the parameter block:

```
ioParam:
  (ioRefNum:    INTEGER;      {path reference number}
   ioVersNum:   SignedByte;   {version number}
   ioPermssn:   SignedByte;   {read/write permission}
   ioMisc:      Ptr;          {miscellaneous}
   ioBuffer:    Ptr;          {data buffer}
   ioReqCount:  LONGINT;      {requested number of bytes}
   ioActCount:  LONGINT;      {actual number of bytes}
   ioPosMode:   INTEGER;      {positioning mode and newline character}
   ioPosOffset: LONGINT);     {positioning offset}
```

For routines that access open files, the File Manager determines which file to access by using the path reference number in ioRefNum. IOVersNum is the file's version number, normally 0. IOPermssn requests permission to read or write via an access path, and must contain one of the following values:

```
CONST fsCurPerm  = 0;  {whatever is currently allowed}
      fsRdPerm   = 1;  {request to read only}
      fsWrPerm   = 2;  {request to write only}
      fsRdWrPerm = 3;  {request to read and write}
```

This request is compared with the open permission of the file. If the open permission doesn't allow I/O as requested, a result code indicating the error is returned.

The content of ioMisc depends on the routine called. It contains either a new logical end-of-file, a new version number, a pointer to an access path buffer, or a pointer to a new volume or file name. Since ioMisc is of type Ptr, you'll need to perform type coercion to correctly interpret the value of ioMisc when it contains an end-of-file (a LONGINT) or version number (a SignedByte).

IOBuffer points to a data buffer into which data is written by Read calls and from which data is read by Write calls. IOReqCount specifies the requested number of bytes to be read, written, or allocated. IOActCount contains the number of bytes actually read, written, or allocated.

IOPosMode and ioPosOffset contain positioning information used for Read, Write, and SetFPos calls. IOPosMode contains the positioning mode; bits 0 and 1 indicate how to position the mark, and you can use the following predefined constants to set or test their value:

```
CONST fsAtMark    = 0;  {at current mark}
      fsFromStart = 1;  {offset relative to beginning of file}
      fsFromLEOF  = 2;  {offset relative to logical end-of-file}
      fsFromMark  = 3;  {offset relative to current mark}
```

IOPosOffset specifies the byte offset (either positive or negative), relative to the position specified by the positioning mode, where the operation will be performed (except when the positioning mode is fsAtMark, in which case ioPosOffset is ignored).

To have the File Manager verify that all data written to a volume exactly matches the data in memory, make a Read call right after the Write call. The parameters for a read-verify operation are the same as for a standard Read call, except that the following constant must be added to the positioning mode:

```
CONST rdVerify = 64;   {read-verify mode}
```

The result code ioErr is returned if any of the data doesn't match.

> **Note:** Advanced programmers: Bit 7 of ioPosMode is the newline flag; it's set if read operations should terminate at a newline character. The ASCII code of the newline character is specified in the high-order byte of ioPosMode. If the newline flag is set, the data will be read one byte at a time until the newline character is encountered, ioReqCount bytes have been read, or the end-of-file is reached. If the newline flag is clear, the data will be read one byte at a time until ioReqCount bytes have been read or the end-of-file is reached.

File Information Parameters

Some File Manager routines, including GetFileInfo and SetFileInfo, use the following 16 additional fields after the standard eight fields in the parameter block:

```
fileParam:
 (ioFRefNum:     INTEGER;      {path reference number}
  ioFVersNum:    SignedByte;   {version number}
  filler1:       SignedByte;   {not used}
  ioFDirIndex:   INTEGER;      {sequence number of file}
  ioFlAttrib:    SignedByte;   {file attributes}
  ioFlVersNum:   SignedByte;   {version number}
  ioFlFndrInfo:  FInfo;        {information used by the Finder}
  ioFlNum:       LONGINT;      {file number}
  ioFlStBlk:     INTEGER;      {first allocation block of data fork}
  ioFlLgLen:     LONGINT;      {logical end-of-file of data fork}
  ioFlPyLen:     LONGINT;      {physical end-of-file of data fork}
  ioFlRStBlk:    INTEGER;      {first allocation block of resource fork}
  ioFlRLgLen:    LONGINT;      {logical end-of-file of resource fork}
  ioFlRPyLen:    LONGINT;      {physical end-of-file of resource fork}
  ioFlCrDat:     LONGINT;      {date and time of creation}
  ioFlMdDat:     LONGINT);     {date and time of last modification}
```

IOFDirIndex contains the sequence number of the file, and can be used as a way of indexing all the files on a volume. IOFlNum is a unique number assigned to a file; most programmers needn't be concerned with file numbers, but those interested can read the section "Data Organization on Volumes".

> **Note:** IOFDirIndex maintains the sequence numbers without gaps, so you can use it as a way of indexing all the files on a volume.

IOFlAttrib contains the following file attributes:

Bit	Meaning
0	Set if file is locked

IOFlStBlk and ioFlRStBlk contain 0 if the file's data or resource fork is empty, respectively. The date and time in the ioFlCrDat and ioFlMdDat fields are specified in seconds since midnight, January 1, 1904.

Volume Information Parameters

When you call GetVolInfo, you'll use the following 14 additional fields:

```
volumeParam:
 (filler2:       LONGINT;      {not used}
  ioVolIndex:    INTEGER;      {volume index}
  ioVCrDate:     LONGINT;      {date and time of initialization}
  ioVLsBkUp:     LONGINT;      {date and time of last backup}
  ioVAtrb:       INTEGER;      {bit 15=1 if volume locked}
  ioVNmFls:      INTEGER;      {number of files in directory}
  ioVDirSt:      INTEGER;      {first block of directory}
  ioVBlLn:       INTEGER;      {length of directory in blocks}
  ioVNmAlBlks:   INTEGER;      {number of allocation blocks}
  ioVAlBlkSiz:   LONGINT;      {size of allocation blocks}
  ioVClpSiz:     LONGINT;      {number of bytes to allocate}
  ioAlBlSt:      INTEGER;      {first block in volume block map}
  ioVNxtFNum:    LONGINT;      {next unused file number}
  ioVFrBlk:      INTEGER);     {number of unused allocation blocks}
```

IOVolIndex contains the **volume index**, another method of referring to a volume; the first volume mounted has an index of 1, and so on.

> **Note:** IOVolIndex maintains the volume numbers sequentially (without gaps), so you can use it as a way of indexing all mounted volumes.

Most programmers needn't be concerned with the parameters providing information about file directories and block maps (such as ioVNmFls), but interested programmers can read the section "Data Organization on Volumes".

Routine Descriptions

This section describes the procedures and functions. Each routine description includes the low-level Pascal form of the call and the routine's assembly-language macro. A list of the fields in the parameter block affected by the call is also given.

Assembly-language note: The field names given in these descriptions are those of the ParamBlockRec data type; see the summary at the end of this chapter for the names of the corresponding assembly-language offsets. (The names for some offsets differ from their Pascal equivalents, and in certain cases more than one name for the same offset is provided.)

The number next to each parameter name indicates the byte offset of the parameter from the start of the parameter block pointed to by register A0; only assembly-language programmers need be concerned with it. An arrow next to each parameter name indicates whether it's an input, output, or input/output parameter:

Arrow   **Meaning**
→   Parameter is passed to the routine

←   Parameter is returned by the routine

↔   Parameter is passed to and returned by the routine

Initializing the File I/O Queue

```
PROCEDURE FInitQueue;
```

Trap macro   _InitQueue

FInitQueue clears all queued File Manager calls except the current one.

Accessing Volumes

To get the volume reference number of a volume, given the path reference number of a file on that volume, both Pascal and assembly-language programmers should call the high-level File Manager function GetVRefNum.

```
FUNCTION PBMountVol (paramBlock: ParmBlkPtr) : OSErr;
```

Trap macro   _MountVol

Parameter block

←	16	ioResult	word
↔	22	ioVRefNum	word

PBMountVol mounts the volume in the drive specified by ioVRefNum, and returns a volume reference number in ioVRefNum. If there are no volumes already mounted, this volume becomes the default volume. PBMountVol is always executed synchronously.

Result codes	noErr	No error
	badMDBErr	Bad master directory block
	extFSErr	External file system
	ioErr	I/O error
	memFullErr	Not enough room in heap zone
	noMacDskErr	Not a Macintosh disk
	nsDrvErr	No such drive
	paramErr	Bad drive number
	volOnLinErr	Volume already on-line

```
FUNCTION PBGetVInfo (paramBlock: ParmBlkPtr; async: BOOLEAN) :
         OSErr;
```

Trap macro   _GetVolInfo

Parameter block

→	12	ioCompletion	pointer
←	16	ioResult	word
↔	18	ioNamePtr	pointer
↔	22	ioVRefNum	word
→	28	ioVolIndex	word
←	30	ioVCrDate	long word
←	34	ioVLsBkUp	long word
←	38	ioVAtrb	word
←	40	ioVNmFls	word
←	42	ioVDirSt	word
←	44	ioVBlLn	word
←	46	ioVNmAlBlks	word
←	48	ioVAlBlkSiz	long word
←	52	ioVClpSiz	long word
←	56	ioAlBlSt	word
←	58	ioVNxtFNum	long word
←	62	ioVFrBlk	word

PBGetVInfo returns information about the specified volume. If ioVolIndex is positive, the File Manager attempts to use it to find the volume; for instance, if ioVolIndex is 2, the File Manager will attempt to access the second mounted volume. If ioVolIndex is negative, the File Manager uses ioNamePtr and ioVRefNum in the standard way to determine which volume. If ioVolIndex is 0, the File Manager attempts to access the volume by using ioVRefNum only. The volume reference number is returned in ioVRefNum, and the volume name is returned in ioNamePtr (unless ioNamePtr is NIL).

Result codes	noErr	No error
	nsvErr	No such volume
	paramErr	No default volume

```
FUNCTION PBGetVol (paramBlock: ParmBlkPtr; async: BOOLEAN) :
         OSErr;
```

Trap macro   _GetVol

Parameter block

→	12	ioCompletion	pointer
←	16	ioResult	word
←	18	ioNamePtr	pointer
←	22	ioVRefNum	word

PBGetVol returns the name of the default volume in ioNamePtr (unless ioNamePtr is NIL) and its volume reference number in ioVRefNum.

Result codes	noErr	No error
	nsvErr	No default volume

```
FUNCTION PBSetVol (paramBlock: ParmBlkPtr; async: BOOLEAN) :
        OSErr;
```

Trap macro   _SetVol

Parameter block

→	12	ioCompletion	pointer
←	16	ioResult	word
→	18	ioNamePtr	pointer
→	22	ioVRefNum	word

PBSetVol sets the default volume to the mounted volume specified by ioNamePtr or ioVRefNum.

Result codes	noErr	No error
	bdNamErr	Bad volume name
	nsvErr	No such volume
	paramErr	No default volume

```
FUNCTION PBFlushVol (paramBlock: ParmBlkPtr; async: BOOLEAN) :
        OSErr;
```

Trap macro   _FlushVol

Parameter block

→	12	ioCompletion	pointer
←	16	ioResult	word
→	18	ioNamePtr	pointer
→	22	ioVRefNum	word

On the volume specified by ioNamePtr or ioVRefNum, PBFlushVol writes descriptive information about the volume, the contents of the associated volume buffer, and all access path buffers for the volume (if they've changed since the last time PBFlushVol was called). The date and time of the last modification to the volume are set to the current date and time.

Result codes	noErr	No error
	bdNamErr	Bad volume name
	extFSErr	External file system
	ioErr	I/O error
	nsDrvErr	No such drive
	nsvErr	No such volume
	paramErr	No default volume

```
FUNCTION PBUnmountVol (paramBlock: ParmBlkPtr) : OSErr;
```

Trap macro   _UnmountVol

Parameter block

←	16	ioResult	word
→	18	ioNamePtr	pointer
→	22	ioVRefNum	word

PBUnmountVol unmounts the volume specified by ioNamePtr or ioVRefNum, by calling PBFlushVol to flush the volume, closing all open files on the volume, and releasing the memory used for the volume. PBUnmountVol is always executed synchronously.

Warning: Don't unmount the startup volume.

Result codes	noErr	No error
	bdNamErr	Bad volume name
	extFSErr	External file system
	ioErr	I/O error
	nsDrvErr	No such drive
	nsvErr	No such volume
	paramErr	No default volume

```
FUNCTION PBOffLine (paramBlock: ParmBlkPtr) : OSErr;
```

Trap macro   _OffLine

Parameter block

→	12	ioCompletion	pointer
←	16	ioResult	word
→	18	ioNamePtr	pointer
→	22	ioVRefNum	word

PBOffLine places off-line the volume specified by ioNamePtr or ioVRefNum, by calling PBFlushVol to flush the volume, and releasing all the memory used for the volume except for 94 bytes of descriptive information. PBOffLine is always executed synchronously.

Result codes	noErr	No error
	bdNamErr	Bad volume name
	extFSErr	External file system
	ioErr	I/O error
	nsDrvErr	No such drive
	nsvErr	No such volume
	paramErr	No default volume

```
FUNCTION PBEject (paramBlock: ParmBlkPtr) : OSErr;
```

Trap macro   _Eject

Parameter block

→	12	ioCompletion	pointer
←	16	ioResult	word
→	18	ioNamePtr	pointer
→	22	ioVRefNum	word

PBEject flushes the volume specified by ioNamePtr or ioVRefNum, places it off-line, and then ejects the volume.

Assembly-language note: You may invoke the macro _Eject asynchronously; the first part of the call is executed synchronously, and the actual ejection is executed asynchronously.

Result codes   noErr   No error
                 bdNamErr   Bad volume name
                 extFSErr   External file system
                 ioErr   I/O error
                 nsDrvErr   No such drive
                 nsvErr   No such volume
                 paramErr   No default volume

Accessing Files

```
FUNCTION PBCreate (paramBlock: ParmBlkPtr; async: BOOLEAN) :
         OSErr;
```

Trap macro   _Create

Parameter block

→	12	ioCompletion	pointer
←	16	ioResult	word
→	18	ioNamePtr	pointer
→	22	ioVRefNum	word
→	26	ioFVersNum	byte

PBCreate creates a new file (both forks) having the name ioNamePtr and the version number ioFVersNum, on the volume specified by ioVRefNum. The new file is unlocked and empty. The date and time of its creation and last modification are set to the current date and time. If the file created isn't temporary (that is, if it will exist after the application terminates), the application should call PBSetFInfo (after PBCreate) to fill in the information needed by the Finder.

Assembly-language note: If a desk accessory creates a file, it should always create it on the system startup volume (and not on the default volume) by passing the reference number of the system startup volume in ioVRefNum. The volume reference number can be obtained by calling the high-level File Manager function GetVRefNum with the reference number of the system resource file, which is stored in the global variable SysMap.

Result codes
noErr	No error
bdNamErr	Bad file name
dupFNErr	Duplicate file name and version
dirFulErr	File directory full
extFSErr	External file system
ioErr	I/O error
nsvErr	No such volume
vLckdErr	Software volume lock
wPrErr	Hardware volume lock

```
FUNCTION PBOpen (paramBlock: ParmBlkPtr; async: BOOLEAN) : OSErr;
```

Trap macro _Open

Parameter block

→	12	ioCompletion	pointer
←	16	ioResult	word
→	18	ioNamePtr	pointer
→	22	ioVRefNum	word
←	24	ioRefNum	word
→	26	ioVersNum	byte
→	27	ioPermssn	byte
→	28	ioMisc	pointer

PBOpen creates an access path to the file having the name ioNamePtr and the version number ioVersNum, on the volume specified by ioVRefNum. A path reference number is returned in ioRefNum.

IOMisc either points to a 524-byte portion of memory to be used as the access path's buffer, or is NIL if you want the volume buffer to be used instead.

Warning: All access paths to a single file that's opened multiple times should share the same buffer so that they will read and write the same data.

IOPermssn specifies the path's read/write permission. A path can be opened for writing even if it accesses a file on a locked volume, and an error won't be returned until a PBWrite, PBSetEOF, or PBAllocate call is made.

If you attempt to open a locked file for writing, PBOpen will return permErr as its function result. If you attempt to open a file for writing and it already has an access path that allows writing, PBOpen will return the reference number of the existing access path in ioRefNum and opWrErr as its function result.

Result codes	noErr	No error
	bdNamErr	Bad file name
	extFSErr	External file system
	fnfErr	File not found
	ioErr	I/O error
	nsvErr	No such volume
	opWrErr	File already open for writing
	permErr	Attempt to open locked file for writing
	tmfoErr	Too many files open

```
FUNCTION PBOpenRF (paramBlock: ParmBlkPtr; async: BOOLEAN) :
         OSErr;
```

Trap macro   _OpenRF

Parameter block

→	12	ioCompletion	pointer
←	16	ioResult	word
→	18	ioNamePtr	pointer
→	22	ioVRefNum	word
←	24	ioRefNum	word
→	26	ioVersNum	byte
→	27	ioPermssn	byte
→	28	ioMisc	pointer

PBOpenRF is identical to PBOpen, except that it opens the file's resource fork instead of its data fork.

Note: Normally you should access a file's resource fork through the routines of the Resource Manager rather than the File Manager. PBOpenRF doesn't read the resource map into memory; it's really only useful for block-level operations such as copying files.

Result codes	noErr	No error
	bdNamErr	Bad file name
	extFSErr	External file system
	fnfErr	File not found
	ioErr	I/O error
	nsvErr	No such volume
	opWrErr	File already open for writing
	permErr	Attempt to open locked file for writing
	tmfoErr	Too many files open

```
FUNCTION PBRead (paramBlock: ParmBlkPtr; async: BOOLEAN) : OSErr;
```

Trap macro   _Read

Parameter block

→	12	ioCompletion	pointer
←	16	ioResult	word
→	24	ioRefNum	word
→	32	ioBuffer	pointer
→	36	ioReqCount	long word
←	40	ioActCount	long word
→	44	ioPosMode	word
↔	46	ioPosOffset	long word

PBRead attempts to read ioReqCount bytes from the open file whose access path is specified by ioRefNum, and transfer them to the data buffer pointed to by ioBuffer. The position of the mark is specified by ioPosMode and ioPosOffset. If you try to read past the logical end-of-file, PBRead moves the mark to the end-of-file and returns eofErr as its function result. After the read is completed, the mark is returned in ioPosOffset and the number of bytes actually read is returned in ioActCount.

Result codes	noErr	No error
	eofErr	End-of-file
	extFSErr	External file system
	fnOpnErr	File not open
	ioErr	I/O error
	paramErr	Negative ioReqCount
	rfNumErr	Bad reference number

```
FUNCTION PBWrite (paramBlock: ParmBlkPtr; async: BOOLEAN) : OSErr;
```

Trap macro   _Write

Parameter block

→	12	ioCompletion	pointer
←	16	ioResult	word
→	24	ioRefNum	word
→	32	ioBuffer	pointer
→	36	ioReqCount	long word
←	40	ioActCount	long word
→	44	ioPosMode	word
↔	46	ioPosOffset	long word

PBWrite takes ioReqCount bytes from the buffer pointed to by ioBuffer and attempts to write them to the open file whose access path is specified by ioRefNum. The position of the mark is specified by ioPosMode and ioPosOffset. After the write is completed, the mark is returned in ioPosOffset and the number of bytes actually written is returned in ioActCount.

Result codes   noErr   No error
                                dskFulErr   Disk full

Result codes	noErr	No error
	dskFulErr	Disk full
	fLckdErr	File locked
	fnOpnErr	File not open
	ioErr	I/O error
	paramErr	Negative ioReqCount
	posErr	Attempt to position before start of file
	rfNumErr	Bad reference number
	vLckdErr	Software volume lock
	wPrErr	Hardware volume lock
	wrPermErr	Read/write permission doesn't allow writing

FUNCTION PBGetFPos (paramBlock: ParmBlkPtr; async: BOOLEAN) : OSErr;

Trap macro   _GetFPos

Parameter block

→	12	ioCompletion	pointer
←	16	ioResult	word
→	24	ioRefNum	word
←	36	ioReqCount	long word
←	40	ioActCount	long word
←	44	ioPosMode	word
←	46	ioPosOffset	long word

PBGetFPos returns, in ioPosOffset, the mark of the open file whose access path is specified by ioRefNum. It sets ioReqCount, ioActCount, and ioPosMode to 0.

Result codes	noErr	No error
	extFSErr	External file system
	fnOpnErr	File not open
	gfpErr	Error during GetFPos
	ioErr	I/O error
	rfNumErr	Bad reference number

FUNCTION PBSetFPos (paramBlock: ParmBlkPtr; async: BOOLEAN) : OSErr;

Trap macro   _SetFPos

Parameter block

→	12	ioCompletion	pointer
←	16	ioResult	word
→	24	ioRefNum	word
→	44	ioPosMode	word
↔	46	ioPosOffset	long word

PBSetFPos sets the mark of the open file whose access path is specified by ioRefNum, to the position specified by ioPosMode and ioPosOffset. The position at which the mark is actually set is returned in ioPosOffset. If you try to set the mark past the logical end-of-file, PBSetFPos moves the mark to the end-of-file and returns eofErr as its function result.

Result codes	noErr	No error
	eofErr	End-of-file
	extFSErr	External file system
	fnOpnErr	File not open
	ioErr	I/O error
	posErr	Attempt to position before start of file
	rfNumErr	Bad reference number

FUNCTION PBGetEOF (paramBlock: ParmBlkPtr; async: BOOLEAN) :
      OSErr;

Trap macro   _GetEOF

Parameter block

→	12	ioCompletion	pointer
←	16	ioResult	word
→	24	ioRefNum	word
←	28	ioMisc	long word

PBGetEOF returns, in ioMisc, the logical end-of-file of the open file whose access path is specified by ioRefNum.

Result codes	noErr	No error
	extFSErr	External file system
	fnOpnErr	File not open
	ioErr	I/O error
	rfNumErr	Bad reference number

FUNCTION PBSetEOF (paramBlock: ParmBlkPtr; async: BOOLEAN) :
      OSErr;

Trap macro   _SetEOF

Parameter block

→	12	ioCompletion	pointer
←	16	ioResult	word
→	24	ioRefNum	word
→	28	ioMisc	long word

PBSetEOF sets the logical end-of-file of the open file whose access path is specified by ioRefNum, to ioMisc. If you attempt to set the logical end-of-file beyond the physical end-of-file, the physical end-of-file is set to one byte beyond the end of the next free allocation block; if there isn't enough space on the volume, no change is made, and PBSetEOF returns dskFulErr as its function result. If ioMisc is 0, all space occupied by the file on the volume is released.

Result codes	noErr	No error
	dskFulErr	Disk full
	extFSErr	External file system
	fLckdErr	File locked
	fnOpnErr	File not open
	ioErr	I/O error
	rfNumErr	Bad reference number
	vLckdErr	Software volume lock
	wPrErr	Hardware volume lock
	wrPermErr	Read/write permission doesn't allow writing

```
FUNCTION PBAllocate (paramBlock: ParmBlkPtr; async: BOOLEAN) :
         OSErr;
```

Trap macro   _Allocate

Parameter block

→	12	ioCompletion	pointer
←	16	ioResult	word
→	24	ioRefNum	word
→	36	ioReqCount	long word
←	40	ioActCount	long word

PBAllocate adds ioReqCount bytes to the open file whose access path is specified by ioRefNum, and sets the physical end-of-file to one byte beyond the last block allocated. The number of bytes actually allocated is rounded up to the nearest multiple of the allocation block size, and returned in ioActCount. If there isn't enough empty space on the volume to satisfy the allocation request, PBAllocate allocates the rest of the space on the volume and returns dskFulErr as its function result.

Result codes	noErr	No error
	dskFulErr	Disk full
	fLckdErr	File locked
	fnOpnErr	File not open
	ioErr	I/O error
	rfNumErr	Bad reference number
	vLckdErr	Software volume lock
	wPrErr	Hardware volume lock
	wrPermErr	Read/write permission doesn't allow writing

```
FUNCTION PBFlushFile (paramBlock: ParmBlkPtr; async: BOOLEAN) :
          OSErr;
```

Trap macro   _FlushFile

Parameter block

→	12	ioCompletion	pointer
←	16	ioResult	word
→	24	ioRefNum	word

PBFlushFile writes the contents of the access path buffer indicated by ioRefNum to the volume, and updates the file's entry in the file directory.

Warning: Some information stored on the volume won't be correct until PBFlushVol is called.

Result codes	noErr	No error
	extFSErr	External file system
	fnfErr	File not found
	fnOpnErr	File not open
	ioErr	I/O error
	nsvErr	No such volume
	rfNumErr	Bad reference number

```
FUNCTION PBClose (paramBlock: ParmBlkPtr; async: BOOLEAN) :
          OSErr;
```

Trap macro   _Close

Parameter block

→	12	ioCompletion	pointer
←	16	ioResult	word
→	24	ioRefNum	word

PBClose writes the contents of the access path buffer specified by ioRefNum to the volume and removes the access path.

Warning: Some information stored on the volume won't be correct until PBFlushVol is called.

Result codes	noErr	No error
	extFSErr	External file system
	fnfErr	File not found
	fnOpnErr	File not open
	ioErr	I/O error
	nsvErr	No such volume
	rfNumErr	Bad reference number

Changing Information About Files

All of the routines described in this section affect both forks of a file, and don't require the file to be open.

```
FUNCTION PBGetFInfo (paramBlock: ParmBlkPtr; async: BOOLEAN) :
        OSErr;
```

Trap macro   _GetFileInfo

Parameter block

→	12	ioCompletion	pointer
←	16	ioResult	word
↔	18	ioNamePtr	pointer
→	22	ioVRefNum	word
←	24	ioFRefNum	word
→	26	ioFVersNum	byte
→	28	ioFDirIndex	word
←	30	ioFlAttrib	byte
←	31	ioFlVersNum	byte
←	32	ioFlFndrInfo	16 bytes
←	48	ioFlNum	long word
←	52	ioFlStBlk	word
←	54	ioFlLgLen	long word
←	58	ioFlPyLen	long word
←	62	ioFlRStBlk	word
←	64	ioFlRLgLen	long word
←	68	ioFlRPyLen	long word
←	72	ioFlCrDat	long word
←	76	ioFlMdDat	long word

PBGetFInfo returns information about the specified file. If ioFDirIndex is positive, the File Manager returns information about the file whose sequence number is ioFDirIndex on the volume specified by ioVRefNum (see the section "Data Organization on Volumes" if you're interested in using this method). If ioFDirIndex is negative or 0, the File Manager returns information about the file having the name ioNamePtr and the version number ioFVersNum, on the volume specified by ioFVRefNum. If the file is open, the reference number of the first access path found is returned in ioFRefNum, and the name of the file is returned in ioNamePtr (unless ioNamePtr is NIL).

Result codes	noErr	No error
	bdNamErr	Bad file name
	extFSErr	External file system
	fnfErr	File not found
	ioErr	I/O error
	nsvErr	No such volume
	paramErr	No default volume

```
FUNCTION PBSetFInfo (paramBlock: ParmBlkPtr; async: BOOLEAN) :
          OSErr;
```

Trap macro   _SetFileInfo

Parameter block

→	12	ioCompletion	pointer
←	16	ioResult	word
→	18	ioNamePtr	pointer
→	22	ioVRefNum	word
→	26	ioFVersNum	byte
→	32	ioFlFndrInfo	16 bytes
→	72	ioFlCrDat	long word
→	76	ioFlMdDat	long word

PBSetFInfo sets information (including the date and time of creation and modification, and information needed by the Finder) about the file having the name ioNamePtr and the version number ioFVersNum, on the volume specified by ioVRefNum. You should call PBGetFInfo just before PBSetFInfo, so the current information is present in the parameter block.

Result codes	noErr	No error
	bdNamErr	Bad file name
	extFSErr	External file system
	fLckdErr	File locked
	fnfErr	File not found
	ioErr	I/O error
	nsvErr	No such volume
	vLckdErr	Software volume lock
	wPrErr	Hardware volume lock

```
FUNCTION PBSetFLock (paramBlock: ParmBlkPtr; async: BOOLEAN) :
          OSErr;
```

Trap macro   _SetFilLock

Parameter block

→	12	ioCompletion	pointer
←	16	ioResult	word
→	18	ioNamePtr	pointer
→	22	ioVRefNum	word
→	26	ioFVersNum	byte

PBSetFLock locks the file having the name ioNamePtr and the version number ioFVersNum on the volume specified by ioVRefNum. Access paths currently in use aren't affected.

Note: This lock is controlled by your application, and is distinct from the user-accessible lock maintained by the Finder.

Result codes	noErr	No error
	extFSErr	External file system
	fnfErr	File not found
	ioErr	I/O error
	nsvErr	No such volume
	vLckdErr	Software volume lock
	wPrErr	Hardware volume lock

```
FUNCTION PBRstFLock (paramBlock: ParmBlkPtr; async: BOOLEAN) :
        OSErr;
```

Trap macro   _RstFilLock

Parameter block

→	12	ioCompletion	pointer
←	16	ioResult	word
→	18	ioNamePtr	pointer
→	22	ioVRefNum	word
→	26	ioFVersNum	byte

PBRstFLock unlocks the file having the name ioNamePtr and the version number ioFVersNum on the volume specified by ioVRefNum. Access paths currently in use aren't affected.

Result codes	noErr	No error
	extFSErr	External file system
	fnfErr	File not found
	ioErr	I/O error
	nsvErr	No such volume
	vLckdErr	Software volume lock
	wPrErr	Hardware volume lock

```
FUNCTION PBSetFVers (paramBlock: ParmBlkPtr; async: BOOLEAN) :
        OSErr;
```

Trap macro   _SetFilType

Parameter block

→	12	ioCompletion	pointer
←	16	ioResult	word
→	18	ioNamePtr	pointer
→	22	ioVRefNum	word
→	26	ioVersNum	byte
→	28	ioMisc	byte

PBSetFVers changes the version number of the file having the name ioNamePtr and version number ioVersNum, on the volume specified by ioVRefNum, to the version number stored in the high-order byte of ioMisc. Access paths currently in use aren't affected.

Warning: The Resource Manager, the Segment Loader, and the Standard File Package operate only on files with version number 0; changing the version number of a file to a nonzero number will prevent them from operating on it.

Result codes		
	noErr	No error
	bdNamErr	Bad file name
	dupFNErr	Duplicate file name and version
	extFSErr	External file system
	fLckdErr	File locked
	fnfErr	File not found
	nsvErr	No such volume
	ioErr	I/O error
	paramErr	No default volume
	vLckdErr	Software volume lock
	wPrErr	Hardware volume lock

```
FUNCTION PBRename (paramBlock: ParmBlkPtr; async: BOOLEAN) :
        OSErr;
```

Trap macro   _Rename

Parameter block

→	12	ioCompletion	pointer
←	16	ioResult	word
→	18	ioNamePtr	pointer
→	22	ioVRefNum	word
→	26	ioVersNum	byte
→	28	ioMisc	pointer

Given a file name in ioNamePtr and a version number in ioVersNum, PBRename changes the name of the file to the name specified by ioMisc. Access paths currently in use aren't affected. Given a volume name in ioNamePtr or a volume reference number in ioVRefNum, it changes the name of the volume to the name specified by ioMisc.

Warning: If you're renaming a volume, be sure that the volume name given in ioNamePtr ends with a colon, or Rename will consider it a file name.

Result codes		
	noErr	No error
	bdNamErr	Bad file name
	dirFulErr	File directory full
	dupFNErr	Duplicate file name and version
	extFSErr	External file system
	fLckdErr	File locked
	fnfErr	File not found
	fsRnErr	Problem during rename
	ioErr	I/O error
	nsvErr	No such volume
	paramErr	No default volume
	vLckdErr	Software volume lock
	wPrErr	Hardware volume lock

```
FUNCTION PBDelete (paramBlock: ParmBlkPtr; async: BOOLEAN) :
        OSErr;
```

Trap macro   _Delete

Parameter block

→	12	ioCompletion	pointer
←	16	ioResult	word
→	18	ioNamePtr	pointer
→	22	ioVRefNum	word
→	26	ioFVersNum	byte

PBDelete removes the closed file having the name ioNamePtr and the version number ioFVersNum, from the volume specified by ioVRefNum.

Note: This function will delete *both* forks of the file.

Result codes		
	noErr	No error
	bdNamErr	Bad file name
	extFSErr	External file system
	fBsyErr	File busy
	fLckdErr	File locked
	fnfErr	File not found
	nsvErr	No such volume
	ioErr	I/O error
	vLckdErr	Software volume lock
	wPrErr	Hardware volume lock

DATA ORGANIZATION ON VOLUMES

This section explains how information is organized on volumes. Most of the information is accessible only through assembly language, but some advanced Pascal programmers may be interested.

The File Manager communicates with device drivers that read and write data via block-level requests to devices containing Macintosh-initialized volumes. (Macintosh-initialized volumes are volumes initialized by the Disk Initialization Package.) The actual type of volume and device is unimportant to the File Manager; the only requirements are that the volume was initialized by the Disk Initialization Package and that the device driver is able to communicate via block-level requests.

The 3 1/2-inch built-in and optional external drives are accessed via the Disk Driver. If you want to use the File Manager to access files on Macintosh-initialized volumes on other types of devices, you must write a device driver that can read and write data via block-level requests to the device on which the volume will be mounted. If you want to access files on volumes not initialized by the Macintosh, you must write your own external file system (see the section "Using an External File System").

The information on all block-formatted volumes is organized in **logical blocks** and allocation blocks. Logical blocks contain a number of bytes of standard information (512 bytes on Macintosh-initialized volumes), and an additional number of bytes of information specific to the

Disk Driver (12 bytes on Macintosh-initialized volumes; for details, see chapter 7). Allocation blocks are composed of any integral number of logical blocks, and are simply a means of grouping logical blocks together in more convenient parcels.

The remainder of this section applies only to Macintosh-initialized volumes; the information may be different in future versions of Macintosh system software. Other volumes must be accessed via an external file system, and the information on them must be organized by an external initializing program.

A Macintosh-initialized volume contains **system startup information** in logical blocks 0 and 1 (see Figure 6) that's read in at system startup. This information consists of certain configurable system parameters, such as the capacity of the event queue, the initial size of the system heap, and the number of open files allowed. The development system you're using may include a utility program for modifying the system startup blocks on a volume.

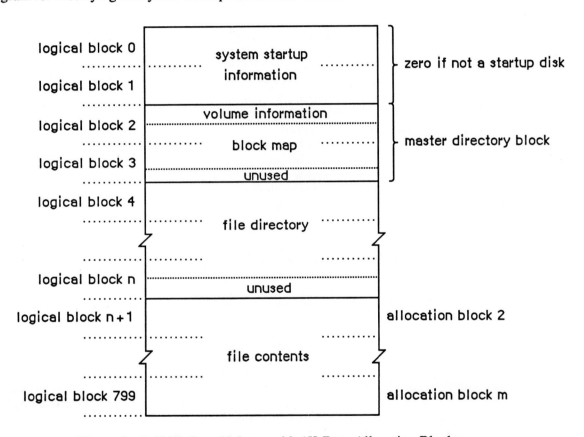

Figure 6. A 400K-Byte Volume with 1K-Byte Allocation Blocks

Logical block 2 of the volume begins the **master directory block**. The master directory block contains **volume information** and the **volume allocation block map**, which records whether each block on the volume is unused or what part of a file it contains data from.

The master directory "block" always occupies two blocks—the Disk Initialization Package varies the allocation block size as necessary to achieve this constraint.

In the next logical block following the block map begins the file directory, which contains descriptions and locations of all the files on the volume. The rest of the logical blocks on the volume contain files or garbage (such as parts of deleted files). The exact format of the volume information, volume allocation block map, and file directory is explained in the following sections.

Volume Information

The volume information is contained in the first 64 bytes of the master directory block (see Figure 7). This information is written on the volume when it's initialized, and modified thereafter by the File Manager.

byte 0	drSigWord (word)	always $D2D7
2	drCrDate (long word)	date and time of initialization
6	drLsBkUp (long word)	date and time of last backup
10	drAtrb (word)	volume attributes
12	drNmFls (word)	number of files in directory
14	drDirSt (word)	first block of directory
16	drBlLen (word)	length of directory in blocks
18	drNmAlBlks (word)	number of allocation blocks on volume
20	drAlBlkSiz (long word)	size of allocation blocks
24	drClpSiz (long word)	number of bytes to allocate
28	drAlBlSt (word)	first allocation block in block map
30	drNxtFNum (long word)	next unused file number
34	drFreeBks (word)	number of unused allocation blocks
36	drVN (byte)	length of volume name
37	drVN + 1 (bytes)	characters of volume name

Figure 7. Volume Information

DrAtrb contains the **volume attributes**, as follows:

Bit	Meaning
7	Set if volume is locked by hardware
15	Set if volume is locked by software

DrClpSiz contains the minimum number of bytes to allocate each time the Allocate function is called, to minimize fragmentation of files; it's always a multiple of the allocation block size. DrNxtFNum contains the next unused file number (see the "File Directory" section below for an explanation of file numbers).

Warning: The format of the volume information may be different in future versions of Macintosh system software.

Volume Allocation Block Map

The volume allocation block map represents every allocation block on the volume with a 12-bit entry indicating whether the block is unused or allocated to a file. It begins in the master directory block at the byte following the volume information, and continues for as many logical blocks as needed.

The first entry in the block map is for block number 2; the block map doesn't contain entries for the system startup blocks. Each entry specifies whether the block is unused, whether it's the last block in the file, or which allocation block is next in the file:

Entry	Meaning
0	Block is unused
1	Block is the last block of the file
2 to 4095	Number of next block in the file

For instance, assume that there's one file on the volume, stored in allocation blocks 8, 11, 12, and 17; the first 16 entries of the block map would read

0 0 0 0 0 0 11 0 0 12 17 0 0 0 0 1

The first allocation block on a volume typically follows the file directory. It's numbered 2 because of the special meaning of numbers 0 and 1.

Note: As explained below, it's possible to begin the allocation blocks immediately following the master directory block and place the file directory somewhere within the allocation blocks. In this case, the allocation blocks occupied by the file directory must be marked with $FFF's in the allocation block map.

File Directory

The file directory contains an entry for each file. Each entry lists information about one file on the volume, including its name and location. Each file is listed by its own unique **file number,** which the File Manager uses to distinguish it from other files on the volume.

A file directory entry contains 51 bytes plus one byte for each character in the file name. If the file names average 20 characters, a directory can hold seven file entries per logical block. Entries are always an integral number of words and don't cross logical block boundaries. The length of a file directory depends on the maximum number of files the volume can contain; for example, on a 400K-byte volume the file directory occupies 12 logical blocks.

The file directory conventionally follows the block map and precedes the allocation blocks, but a volume-initializing program could actually place the file directory anywhere within the allocation blocks as long as the blocks occupied by the file directory are marked with $FFF's in the block map.

The format of a file directory entry is shown in Figure 8.

byte 0	flFlags (byte)	bit 7 = 1 if entry used; bit 0 = 1 if file locked
1	flTyp (byte)	version number
2	flUsrWds (16 bytes)	information used by the Finder
18	flFlNum (long word)	file number
22	flStBlk (word)	first allocation block of data fork
24	flLgLen (long word)	logical end-of-file of data fork
28	flPyLen (long word)	physical end-of-file of data fork
32	flRStBlk (word)	first allocation block of resource fork
34	flRLgLen (long word)	logical end-of-file of resource fork
38	flRPyLen (long word)	physical end-of-file of resource fork
42	flCrDat (long word)	date and time of creation
46	flMdDat (long word)	date and time of last modification
50	flNam (byte)	length of file name
51	flNam + 1 (bytes)	characters of file name

Figure 8. A File Directory Entry

FlStBlk and flRStBlk are 0 if the data or resource fork doesn't exist. FlCrDat and flMdDat are given in seconds since midnight, January 1, 1904.

Each time a new file is created, an entry for the new file is placed in the file directory. Each time a file is deleted, its entry in the file directory is cleared, and all blocks used by that file on the volume are released.

Warning: The format of the file directory may be different in future versions of Macintosh system software.

DATA STRUCTURES IN MEMORY

This section describes the memory data structures used by the File Manager and any external file system that accesses files on Macintosh-initialized volumes. Some of this data is accessible only through assembly language.

The data structures in memory used by the File Manager and all external file systems include:

- the file I/O queue, listing all asynchronous routines awaiting execution (including the currently executing routine, if any)

- the volume-control-block queue, listing information about each mounted volume

- copies of volume allocation block maps (one for each on-line volume)

- the file-control-block buffer, listing information about each access path

- volume buffers (one for each on-line volume)

- optional access path buffers (one for each access path)

- the drive queue, listing information about each drive connected to the Macintosh

The File I/O Queue

The file I/O queue is a standard Operating System queue (described in chapter 13) that contains parameter blocks for all asynchronous routines awaiting execution. Each time a routine is called, an entry is placed in the queue; each time a routine is completed, its entry is removed from the queue.

Each entry in the file I/O queue consists of a parameter block for the routine that was called. Most of the fields of this parameter block contain information needed by the specific File Manager routines; these fields are explained above in the section "Low-Level File Manager Routines". The first four fields of the parameter block, shown below, are used by the File Manager in processing the I/O requests in the queue.

```
TYPE ParamBlockRec =  RECORD
                   qLink:     QElemPtr;   {next queue entry}
                   qType:     INTEGER;    {queue type}
                   ioTrap:    INTEGER;    {routine trap}
                   ioCmdAddr: Ptr;        {routine address}
                     . . .                {rest of block}
              END;
```

QLink points to the next entry in the queue, and qType indicates the queue type, which must always be ORD(ioQType). IOTrap and ioCmdAddr contain the trap word and address of the File Manager routine that was called.

You can get a pointer to the header of the file I/O queue by calling the File Manager function GetFSQHdr.

```
FUNCTION GetFSQHdr : QHdrPtr;    [Not in ROM]
```

GetFSQHdr returns a pointer to the header of the file I/O queue.

Assembly-language note: The global variable FSQHdr contains the header of the file I/O queue.

Volume Control Blocks

Each time a volume is mounted, its volume information is read from it and is used to build a new **volume control block** in the **volume-control-block queue** (unless an ejected or off-line volume is being remounted). A copy of the volume allocation block map is also read from the volume and placed in the system heap, and a volume buffer is created in the system heap.

The volume-control-block queue is a standard Operating System queue that's maintained in the system heap. It contains a volume control block for each mounted volume. A volume control block is a 94-byte nonrelocatable block that contains volume-specific information, including the first 64 bytes of the master directory block (bytes 8-71 of the volume control block match bytes 0-63 of the volume information). It has the following structure:

```
TYPE VCB =
    RECORD
        qLink:      QElemPtr;    {next queue entry}
        qType:      INTEGER;     {queue type}
        vcbFlags:   INTEGER;     {bit 15=1 if dirty}
        vcbSigWord: INTEGER;     {always $D2D7}
        vcbCrDate:  LONGINT;     {date and time of initialization}
        vcbLsBkUp:  LONGINT;     {date and time of last backup}
        vcbAtrb:    INTEGER;     {volume attributes}
        vcbNmFls:   INTEGER;     {number of files in directory}
        vcbDirSt:   INTEGER;     {first block of directory}
        vcbBlLn:    INTEGER;     {length of directory in blocks}
        vcbNmBlks:  INTEGER;     {number of allocation blocks}
        vcbAlBlkSiz: LONGINT;    {size of allocation blocks}
        vcbClpSiz:  LONGINT;     {number of bytes to allocate}
        vcbAlBlSt:  INTEGER;     {first allocation block in block map}
        vcbNxtFNum: LONGINT;     {next unused file number}
        vcbFreeBks: INTEGER;     {number of unused allocation blocks}
        vcbVN:      STRING[27];  {volume name}
        vcbDrvNum:  INTEGER;     {drive number}
        vcbDRefNum: INTEGER;     {driver reference number}
        vcbFSID:    INTEGER;     {file-system identifier}
        vcbVRefNum: INTEGER;     {volume reference number}
        vcbMAdr:    Ptr;         {pointer to block map}
        vcbBufAdr:  Ptr;         {pointer to volume buffer}
        vcbMLen:    INTEGER;     {number of bytes in block map}
        vcbDirIndex: INTEGER;    {used internally}
        vcbDirBlk:  INTEGER      {used internally}
    END;
```

QLink points to the next entry in the queue, and qType indicates the queue type, which must always be ORD(fsQType). Bit 15 of vcbFlags is set if the volume information has been changed by a routine call since the volume was last affected by a FlushVol call. VCBAtrb contains the volume attributes, as follows:

Bit	Meaning
0-2	Set if inconsistencies were found between the volume information and the file directory when the volume was mounted
6	Set if volume is busy (one or more files are open)
7	Set if volume is locked by hardware
15	Set if volume is locked by software

VCBDirSt contains the number of the first logical block of the file directory; vcbNmBlks, the number of allocation blocks on the volume; vcbAlBlSt, the number of the first logical block in the block map; and vcbFreeBks, the number of unused allocation blocks on the volume.

VCBDrvNum contains the drive number of the drive on which the volume is mounted; vcbDRefNum contains the driver reference number of the driver used to access the volume. When a mounted volume is placed off-line, vcbDrvNum is cleared. When a volume is ejected, vcbDrvNum is cleared and vcbDRefNum is set to the negative of vcbDrvNum (becoming a positive number). VCBFSID identifies the file system handling the volume; it's 0 for volumes handled by the File Manager, and nonzero for volumes handled by other file systems.

When a volume is placed off-line, its buffer and block map are released. When a volume is unmounted, its volume control block is removed from the volume-control-block queue.

You can get a pointer to the header of the volume-control-block queue by calling the File Manager function GetVCBQHdr.

```
FUNCTION GetVCBQHdr : QHdrPtr;    [Not in ROM]
```

GetVCBQHdr returns a pointer to the header of the volume-control-block queue.

Assembly-language note: The global variable VCBQHdr contains the header of the volume-control-block queue. The default volume's volume control block is pointed to by the global variable DefVCBPtr.

File Control Blocks

Each time a file is opened, the file's directory entry is used to build a **file control block** in the **file-control-block buffer**, which contains information about all access paths. Each open fork of a file requires one access path. Two access paths are used for the system and application resource files (whose resource forks are always open); this leaves a capacity of up to 10 file control blocks on a Macintosh 128K, and up to 46 file control blocks on the Macintosh 512K and XL.

Note: The size of the file-control-block buffer is determined by the system startup information stored on a volume.

The file-control-block buffer is a nonrelocatable block in the system heap; the first word contains the length of the buffer. You can refer to the file-control-block buffer by using the global variable FCBSPtr, which points to the length word. Each file control block contains 30 bytes of information about an access path (Figure 9).

byte 0	fcbFlNum (long word)	file number
4	fcbMdRByt (byte)	flags
5	fcbTypByt (byte)	version number
6	fcbSBlk (word)	first allocation block of file
8	fcbEOF (long word)	logical end-of-file
12	fcbPLen (long word)	physical end-of-file
16	fcbCrPs (long word)	mark
20	fcbVPtr (pointer)	pointer to volume control block
24	fcbBfAdr (pointer)	pointer to access path buffer
28	fcbFlPos (word)	for internal use of File Manager

Figure 9. A File Control Block

Warning: The size and structure of a file control block may be different in future versions of Macintosh system software.

Bit 7 of fcbMdRByt is set if the file has been changed since it was last flushed; bit 1 is set if the entry describes a resource fork; bit 0 is set if data can be written to the file.

The Drive Queue

Disk drives connected to the Macintosh are opened when the system starts up, and information describing each is placed in the **drive queue**. This is a standard Operating System queue, and each entry in it has the following structure:

```
TYPE DrvQEl = RECORD
            qLink:      QElemPtr;  {next queue entry}
            qType:      INTEGER;   {queue type}
            dQDrive:    INTEGER;   {drive number}
            dQRefNum:   INTEGER;   {driver reference number}
            dQFSID:     INTEGER;   {file-system identifier}
            dQDrvSize:  INTEGER    {number of logical blocks}
         END;
```

QLink points to the next entry in the queue, and qType indicates the queue type, which must always be ORD(drvQType). DQDrive contains the drive number of the drive on which the volume is mounted; dQRefNum contains the driver reference number of the driver controlling the device on which the volume is mounted. DQFSID identifies the file system handling the volume in the drive; it's 0 for volumes handled by the File Manager, and nonzero for volumes handled by other file systems. If the volume isn't a 3 1/2-inch disk, dQDrvSize contains the number of 512-byte blocks on the volume mounted in this drive; if the volume is a 3 1/2-inch disk, this field isn't used. Four bytes of flags precede each drive queue entry; they're accessible only from assembly language.

Assembly-language note: These bytes contain the following:

Byte	Contents
0	Bit 7=1 if volume is locked
1	0 if no disk in drive; 1 or 2 if disk in drive; 8 if nonejectable disk in drive; $FC-$FF if disk was ejected within last 1.5 seconds
2	Used internally during system startup
3	Bit 7=0 if disk is single-sided

You can get a pointer to the header of the drive queue by calling the File Manager function GetDrvQHdr.

```
FUNCTION GetDrvQHdr : QHdrPtr;   [Not in ROM]
```

GetDrvQHdr returns a pointer to the header of the drive queue.

Assembly-language note: The global variable DrvQHdr contains the header of the drive queue.

The drive queue can support any number of drives, limited only by memory space.

USING AN EXTERNAL FILE SYSTEM

The File Manager is used to access files on Macintosh-initialized volumes. If you want to access files on other volumes, you must write your own external file system and volume-initializing program. After the external file system has been written, it must be used in conjunction with the File Manager as described in this section.

Before any File Manager routines are called, you must place the memory location of the external file system in the global variable ToExtFS, and link the drive(s) accessed by your file system into the drive queue. As each volume is mounted, you must create your own volume control block for each mounted volume and link each one into the volume-control-block queue. As each access path is opened, you must create your own file control block and add it to the file-control-block buffer.

All SetVol, GetVol, and GetVolInfo calls then can be handled by the File Manager via the volume-control-block queue and drive queue; external file systems needn't support these calls.

When the application calls any other File Manager routine accessing a volume, the File Manager passes control to the address contained in ToExtFS (if ToExtFS is 0, the File Manager returns directly to the application with the result code extFSErr). The external file system must then use the information in the file I/O queue to handle the call as it wishes, set the result code, and return control to the File Manager. Control is passed to an external file system for the following specific routine calls:

- for MountVol if the drive queue entry for the requested drive has a nonzero file-system identifier

- for Create, Open, OpenRF, GetFileInfo, SetFileInfo, SetFilLock, RstFilLock, SetFilType, Rename, Delete, FlushVol, Eject, OffLine, and UnmountVol, if the volume control block for the requested file or volume has a nonzero file-system identifier

- for Close, Read, Write, Allocate, GetEOF, SetEOF, GetFPos, SetFPos, and FlushFile, if the file control block for the requested file points to a volume control block with a nonzero file-system identifier

---

SUMMARY OF THE FILE MANAGER

Constants

```
CONST { Flags in file information used by the Finder }

        fHasBundle =  8192;   {set if file has a bundle}
        fInvisible = 16384;   {set if file's icon is invisible}
        fTrash     = -3;      {file is in Trash window}
        fDesktop   = -2;      {file is on desktop}
        fDisk      =  0;      {file is in disk window}

        { Values for requesting read/write access }

        fsCurPerm  = 0;   {whatever is currently allowed}
        fsRdPerm   = 1;   {request to read only}
        fsWrPerm   = 2;   {request to write only}
        fsRdWrPerm = 3;   {request to read and write}

        { Positioning modes }

        fsAtMark    = 0;   {at current mark}
        fsFromStart = 1;   {offset relative to beginning of file}
        fsFromLEOF  = 2;   {offset relative to logical end-of-file}
        fsFromMark  = 3;   {offset relative to current mark}
        rdVerify    = 64;  {add to above for read-verify}
```

Data Types

```
TYPE FInfo = RECORD
                fdType:     OSType;  {file type}
                fdCreator:  OSType;  {file's creator}
                fdFlags:    INTEGER; {flags}
                fdLocation: Point;   {file's location}
                fdFldr:     INTEGER  {file's window}
             END;

     ParamBlkType  = (ioParam,fileParam,volumeParam,cntrlParam);

     ParmBlkPtr    = ^ParamBlockRec;
     ParamBlockRec = RECORD
        qLink:        QElemPtr;   {next queue entry}
        qType:        INTEGER;    {queue type}
        ioTrap:       INTEGER;    {routine trap}
        ioCmdAddr:    Ptr;        {routine address}
        ioCompletion: ProcPtr;    {completion routine}
        ioResult:     OSErr;      {result code}
        ioNamePtr:    StringPtr;  {volume or file name}
        ioVRefNum:    INTEGER;    {volume reference or drive number}
```

```
CASE ParamBlkType OF
  ioParam:
    (ioRefNum:       INTEGER;       {path reference number}
     ioVersNum:      SignedByte;    {version number}
     ioPermssn:      SignedByte;    {read/write permission}
     ioMisc:         Ptr;           {miscellaneous}
     ioBuffer:       Ptr;           {data buffer}
     ioReqCount:     LONGINT;       {requested number of bytes}
     ioActCount:     LONGINT;       {actual number of bytes}
     ioPosMode:      INTEGER;       {positioning mode and newline character}
     ioPosOffset:    LONGINT);      {positioning offset}
  fileParam:
    (ioFRefNum:      INTEGER;       {path reference number}
     ioFVersNum:     SignedByte;    {version number}
     filler1:        SignedByte;    {not used}
     ioFDirIndex:    INTEGER;       {sequence number of file}
     ioFlAttrib:     SignedByte;    {file attributes}
     ioFlVersNum:    SignedByte     {version number}
     ioFlFndrInfo:   FInfo;         {information used by the Finder}
     ioFlNum:        LONGINT;       {file number}
     ioFlStBlk:      INTEGER;       {first allocation block of data fork}
     ioFlLgLen:      LONGINT;       {logical end-of-file of data fork}
     ioFlPyLen:      LONGINT;       {physical end-of-file of data fork}
     ioFlRStBlk:     INTEGER;       {first allocation block of resource }
                                    { fork}
     ioFlRLgLen:     LONGINT;       {logical end-of-file of resource fork}
     ioFlRPyLen:     LONGINT;       {physical end-of-file of resource }
                                    { fork}
     ioFlCrDat:      LONGINT;       {date and time of creation}
     ioFlMdDat:      LONGINT);      {date and time of last modification}
  volumeParam:
    (filler2:        LONGINT;       {not used}
     ioVolIndex:     INTEGER;       {volume index}
     ioVCrDate:      LONGINT;       {date and time of initialization}
     ioVLsBkUp:      LONGINT;       {date and time of last backup}
     ioVAtrb:        INTEGER;       {bit 15=1 if volume locked}
     ioVNmFls:       INTEGER;       {number of files in directory}
     ioVDirSt:       INTEGER;       {first block of directory}
     ioVBlLn:        INTEGER;       {length of directory in blocks}
     ioVNmAlBlks:    INTEGER;       {number of allocation blocks}
     ioVAlBlkSiz:    LONGINT;       {size of allocation blocks}
     ioVClpSiz:      LONGINT;       {number of bytes to allocate}
     ioAlBlSt:       INTEGER;       {first allocation block in block map}
     ioVNxtFNum:     LONGINT;       {next unused file number}
     ioVFrBlk:       INTEGER);      {number of unused allocation blocks}
  cntrlParam:
    . . .   {used by Device Manager}
END;
```

```
VCB = RECORD
        qLink:        QElemPtr;   {next queue entry}
        qType:        INTEGER;    {queue type}
        vcbFlags:     INTEGER;    {bit 15=1 if dirty}
        vcbSigWord:   INTEGER;    {always $D2D7}
        vcbCrDate:    LONGINT;    {date and time of initialization}
        vcbLsBkUp:    LONGINT;    {date and time of last backup}
        vcbAtrb:      INTEGER;    {volume attributes}
        vcbNmFls:     INTEGER;    {number of files in directory}
        vcbDirSt:     INTEGER;    {first block of directory}
        vcbBlLn:      INTEGER;    {length of directory in blocks}
        vcbNmBlks:    INTEGER;    {number of allocation blocks}
        vcbAlBlkSiz:  LONGINT;    {size of allocation blocks}
        vcbClpSiz:    LONGINT;    {number of bytes to allocate}
        vcbAlBlSt:    INTEGER;    {first allocation block in block map}
        vcbNxtFNum:   LONGINT;    {next unused file number}
        vcbFreeBks:   INTEGER;    {number of unused allocation blocks}
        vcbVN:        STRING[27]; {volume name}
        vcbDrvNum     INTEGER;    {drive number}
        vcbDRefNum:   INTEGER;    {driver reference number}
        vcbFSID:      INTEGER;    {file-system identifier}
        vcbVRefNum:   INTEGER;    {volume reference number}
        vcbMAdr:      Ptr;        {pointer to block map}
        vcbBufAdr:    Ptr;        {pointer to volume buffer}
        vcbMLen:      INTEGER;    {number of bytes in block map}
        vcbDirIndex:  INTEGER;    {used internally}
        vcbDirBlk:    INTEGER     {used internally}
      END;

DrvQEl = RECORD
        qLink:        QElemPtr;   {next queue entry}
        qType:        INTEGER;    {queue type}
        dQDrive:      INTEGER;    {drive number}
        dQRefNum:     INTEGER;    {driver reference number}
        dQFSID:       INTEGER;    {file-system identifier}
        dQDrvSize:    INTEGER     {number of logical blocks}
      END;
```

High-Level Routines [Not in ROM]

Accessing Volumes

```
FUNCTION GetVInfo      (drvNum: INTEGER; volName: StringPtr; VAR vRefNum:
                         INTEGER; VAR freeBytes: LONGINT) : OSErr;
FUNCTION GetVRefNum    (pathRefNum: INTEGER; VAR vRefNum: INTEGER) : OSErr;
FUNCTION GetVol        (volName: StringPtr; VAR vRefNum: INTEGER) : OSErr;
FUNCTION SetVol        (volName: StringPtr; vRefNum: INTEGER) : OSErr;
FUNCTION FlushVol      (volName: StringPtr; vRefNum: INTEGER) : OSErr;
FUNCTION UnmountVol    (volName: StringPtr; vRefNum: INTEGER) : OSErr;
FUNCTION Eject         (volName: StringPtr; vRefNum: INTEGER) : OSErr;
```

Accessing Files

```
FUNCTION Create      (fileName: Str255; vRefNum: INTEGER; creator: OSType;
                      fileType: OSType) : OSErr;
FUNCTION FSOpen      (fileName: Str255; vRefNum: INTEGER; VAR refNum:
                      INTEGER) : OSErr;
FUNCTION OpenRF      (fileName: Str255; vRefNum: INTEGER; VAR refNum:
                      INTEGER) : OSErr;
FUNCTION FSRead      (refNum: INTEGER; VAR count: LONGINT; buffPtr: Ptr) :
                      OSErr;
FUNCTION FSWrite     (refNum: INTEGER; VAR count: LONGINT; buffPtr: Ptr) :
                      OSErr;
FUNCTION GetFPos     (refNum: INTEGER; VAR filePos: LONGINT) : OSErr;
FUNCTION SetFPos     (refNum: INTEGER; posMode: INTEGER; posOff: LONGINT) :
                      OSErr;
FUNCTION GetEOF      (refNum: INTEGER; VAR logEOF: LONGINT) : OSErr;
FUNCTION SetEOF      (refNum: INTEGER; logEOF: LONGINT) : OSErr;
FUNCTION Allocate    (refNum: INTEGER; VAR count: LONGINT) : OSErr;
FUNCTION FSClose     (refNum: INTEGER) : OSErr;
```

Changing Information About Files

```
FUNCTION GetFInfo (fileName: Str255; vRefNum: INTEGER; VAR fndrInfo:
                   FInfo) : OSErr;
FUNCTION SetFInfo (fileName: Str255; vRefNum: INTEGER; fndrInfo: FInfo):
                   OSErr;
FUNCTION SetFLock (fileName: Str255; vRefNum: INTEGER) : OSErr;
FUNCTION RstFLock (fileName: Str255; vRefNum: INTEGER) : OSErr;
FUNCTION Rename   (oldName: Str255; vRefNum: INTEGER; newName: Str255) :
                   OSErr;
FUNCTION FSDelete (fileName: Str255; vRefNum: INTEGER) : OSErr;
```

Low-Level Routines

Initializing the File I/O Queue

```
PROCEDURE FInitQueue;
```

Accessing Volumes

```
FUNCTION PBMountVol (paramBlock: ParmBlkPtr) : OSErr;
    ←  16    ioResult          word
    ↔  22    ioVRefNum         word
```

```
FUNCTION PBGetVInfo (paramBlock: ParmBlkPtr; async: BOOLEAN) : OSErr;
    →   12      ioCompletion        pointer
    ←   16      ioResult            word
    ↔   18      ioNamePtr           pointer
    ↔   22      ioVRefNum           word
    →   28      ioVolIndex          word
    ←   30      ioVCrDate           long word
    ←   34      ioVLsBkUp           long word
    ←   38      ioVAtrb             word
    ←   40      ioVNmFls            word
    ←   42      ioVDirSt            word
    ←   44      ioVBlLn             word
    ←   46      ioVNmAlBlks         word
    ←   48      ioVAlBlkSiz         long word
    ←   52      ioVClpSiz           long word
    ←   56      ioAlBlSt            word
    ←   58      ioVNxtFNum          long word
    ←   62      ioVFrBlk            word


FUNCTION PBGetVol (paramBlock: ParmBlkPtr; async: BOOLEAN) : OSErr;
    →   12      ioCompletion        pointer
    ←   16      ioResult            word
    ←   18      ioNamePtr           pointer
    ←   22      ioVRefNum           word


FUNCTION PBSetVol (paramBlock: ParmBlkPtr; async: BOOLEAN) : OSErr;
    →   12      ioCompletion        pointer
    ←   16      ioResult            word
    →   18      ioNamePtr           pointer
    →   22      ioVRefNum           word


FUNCTION PBFlushVol (paramBlock: ParmBlkPtr; async: BOOLEAN) : OSErr;
    →   12      ioCompletion        pointer
    ←   16      ioResult            word
    →   18      ioNamePtr           pointer
    →   22      ioVRefNum           word


FUNCTION PBUnmountVol (paramBlock: ParmBlkPtr) : OSErr;
    ←   16      ioResult            word
    →   18      ioNamePtr           pointer
    →   22      ioVRefNum           word


FUNCTION PBOffLine (paramBlock: ParmBlkPtr) : OSErr;
    →   12      ioCompletion        pointer
    ←   16      ioResult            word
    →   18      ioNamePtr           pointer
    →   22      ioVRefNum           word
```

```
FUNCTION PBEject (paramBlock: ParmBlkPtr) : OSErr;
    →   12      ioCompletion        pointer
    ←   16      ioResult            word
    →   18      ioNamePt            pointer
    →   22      ioVRefNum           word
```

Accessing Files

```
FUNCTION PBCreate (paramBlock: ParmBlkPtr; async: BOOLEAN) : OSErr;
    →   12      ioCompletion        pointer
    ←   16      ioResult            word
    →   18      ioNamePtr           pointer
    →   22      ioVRefNum           word
    →   26      ioFVersNum          byte


FUNCTION PBOpen (paramBlock: ParmBlkPtr; async: BOOLEAN) : OSErr;
    →   12      ioCompletion        pointer
    ←   16      ioResult            word
    →   18      ioNamePtr           pointer
    →   22      ioVRefNum           word
    ←   24      ioRefNum            word
    →   26      ioVersNum           byte
    →   27      ioPermssn           byte
    →   28      ioMisc              pointer


FUNCTION PBOpenRF (paramBlock: ParmBlkPtr; async: BOOLEAN) : OSErr;
    →   12      ioCompletion        pointer
    ←   16      ioResult            word
    →   18      ioNamePtr           pointer
    →   22      ioVRefNum           word
    ←   24      ioRefNum            word
    →   26      ioVersNum           byte
    →   27      ioPermssn           byte
    →   28      ioMisc              pointer


FUNCTION PBRead (paramBlock: ParmBlkPtr; async: BOOLEAN) : OSErr;
    →   12      ioCompletion        pointer
    ←   16      ioResult            word
    →   24      ioRefNum            word
    →   32      ioBuffer            pointer
    →   36      ioReqCount          long word
    ←   40      ioActCount          long word
    →   44      ioPosMode           word
    ↔   46      ioPosOffset         long word
```

```
FUNCTION PBWrite (paramBlock: ParmBlkPtr; async: BOOLEAN) : OSErr;
    →   12      ioCompletion        pointer
    ←   16      ioResult            word
    →   24      ioRefNum            word
    →   32      ioBuffer            pointer
    →   36      ioReqCount          long word
    ←   40      ioActCount          long word
    →   44      ioPosMode           word
    ↔   46      ioPosOffset         long word


FUNCTION PBGetFPos (paramBlock: ParmBlkPtr; async: BOOLEAN) : OSErr;
    →   12      ioCompletion        pointer
    ←   16      ioResult            word
    →   24      ioRefNum            word
    ←   36      ioReqCount          long word
    ←   40      ioActCount          long word
    ←   44      ioPosMode           word
    ←   46      ioPosOffset         long word


FUNCTION PBSetFPos (paramBlock: ParmBlkPtr; async: BOOLEAN) : OSErr;
    →   12      ioCompletion        pointer
    ←   16      ioResult            word
    →   24      ioRefNum            word
    →   44      ioPosMode           word
    ↔   46      ioPosOffset         long word


FUNCTION PBGetEOF (paramBlock: ParmBlkPtr; async: BOOLEAN) : OSErr;
    →   12      ioCompletion        pointer
    ←   16      ioResult            word
    →   24      ioRefNum            word
    ←   28      ioMisc              long word


FUNCTION PBSetEOF (paramBlock: ParmBlkPtr; async: BOOLEAN) : OSErr;
    →   12      ioCompletion        pointer
    ←   16      ioResult            word
    →   24      ioRefNum            word
    →   28      ioMisc              long word


FUNCTION PBAllocate (paramBlock: ParmBlkPtr; async: BOOLEAN) : OSErr;
    →   12      ioCompletion        pointer
    ←   16      ioResult            word
    →   24      ioRefNum            word
    →   36      ioReqCount          long word
    ←   40      ioActCount          long word


FUNCTION PBFlushFile (paramBlock: ParmBlkPtr; async: BOOLEAN) : OSErr;
    →   12      ioCompletion        pointer
    ←   16      ioResult            word
    →   24      ioRefNum            word
```

```
FUNCTION PBClose (paramBlock: ParmBlkPtr; async: BOOLEAN) : OSErr;
    →   12      ioCompletion        pointer
    ←   16      ioResult            word
    →   24      ioRefNum            word
```

Changing Information About Files

```
FUNCTION PBGetFInfo (paramBlock: ParmBlkPtr; async: BOOLEAN) : OSErr;
    →   12      ioCompletion        pointer
    ←   16      ioResult            word
    ↔   18      ioNamePtr           pointer
    →   22      ioVRefNum           word
    ←   24      ioFRefNum           word
    →   26      ioFVersNum          byte
    →   28      ioFDirIndex         word
    ←   30      ioFlAttrib          byte
    ←   31      ioFlVersNum         byte
    ←   32      ioFlFndrInfo        16 bytes
    ←   48      ioFlNum             long word
    ←   52      ioFlStBlk           word
    ←   54      ioFlLgLen           long word
    ←   58      ioFlPyLen           long word
    ←   62      ioFlRStBlk          word
    ←   64      ioFlRLgLen          long word
    ←   68      ioFlRPyLen          long word
    ←   72      ioFlCrDat           long word
    ←   76      ioFlMdDat           long word

FUNCTION PBSetFInfo (paramBlock: ParmBlkPtr; async: BOOLEAN) : OSErr;
    →   12      ioCompletion        pointer
    ←   16      ioResult            word
    →   18      ioNamePtr           pointer
    →   22      ioVRefNum           word
    →   26      ioFVersNum          byte
    →   32      ioFlFndrInfo        16 bytes
    →   72      ioFlCrDat           long word
    →   76      ioFlMdDat           long word

FUNCTION PBSetFLock (paramBlock: ParmBlkPtr; async: BOOLEAN) : OSErr;
    →   12      ioCompletion        pointer
    ←   16      ioResult            word
    →   18      ioNamePtr           pointer
    →   22      ioVRefNum           word
    →   26      ioFVersNum          byte

FUNCTION PBRstFLock (paramBlock: ParmBlkPtr; async: BOOLEAN) : OSErr;
    →   12      ioCompletion        pointer
    ←   16      ioResult            word
    →   18      ioNamePtr           pointer
    →   22      ioVRefNum           word
    →   26      ioFVersNum          byte
```

```
FUNCTION PBSetFVers (paramBlock: ParmBlkPtr; async: BOOLEAN) : OSErr;
    →  12    ioCompletion      pointer
    ←  16    ioResult          word
    →  18    ioNamePtr         pointer
    →  22    ioVRefNum         word
    →  26    ioVersNum         byte
    →  28    ioMisc            byte

FUNCTION PBRename (paramBlock: ParmBlkPtr; async: BOOLEAN) : OSErr;
    →  12    ioCompletion      pointer
    ←  16    ioResult          word
    →  18    ioNamePtr         pointer
    →  22    ioVRefNum         word
    →  26    ioVersNum         byte
    →  28    ioMisc            pointer

FUNCTION PBDelete (paramBlock: ParmBlkPtr; async: BOOLEAN) : OSErr;
    →  12    ioCompletion      pointer
    ←  16    ioResult          word
    →  18    ioNamePtr         pointer
    →  22    ioVRefNum         word
    →  26    ioFVersNum        byte
```

Accessing Queues   [Not in ROM]

```
FUNCTION GetFSQHdr  : QHdrPtr;
FUNCTION GetVCBQHdr : QHdrPtr;
FUNCTION GetDrvQHdr : QHdrPtr;
```

Result Codes

Name	Value	Meaning
badMDBErr	−60	Master directory block is bad; must reinitialize volume
bdNamErr	−37	Bad file name or volume name (perhaps zero-length)
dirFulErr	−33	File directory full
dskFulErr	−34	All allocation blocks on the volume are full
dupFNErr	−48	A file with the specified name and version number already exists
eofErr	−39	Logical end-of-file reached during read operation
extFSErr	−58	External file system; file-system identifier is nonzero, or path reference number is greater than 1024
fBsyErr	−47	One or more files are open
fLckdErr	−45	File locked
fnfErr	−43	File not found
fnOpnErr	−38	File not open

Name	Value	Meaning
fsRnErr	−59	Problem during rename
gfpErr	−52	Error during GetFPos
ioErr	−36	I/O error
memFullErr	−108	Not enough room in heap zone
noErr	0	No error
noMacDskErr	−57	Volume lacks Macintosh-format directory
nsDrvErr	−56	Specified drive number doesn't match any number in the drive queue
nsvErr	−35	Specified volume doesn't exist
opWrErr	−49	The read/write permission of only one access path to a file can allow writing
paramErr	−50	Parameters don't specify an existing volume, and there's no default volume
permErr	−54	Attempt to open locked file for writing
posErr	−40	Attempt to position before start of file
rfNumErr	−51	Reference number specifies nonexistent access path
tmfoErr	−42	Too many files open
volOffLinErr	−53	Volume not on-line
volOnLinErr	−55	Specified volume is already mounted and on-line
vLckdErr	−46	Volume is locked by a software flag
wrPermErr	−61	Read/write permission doesn't allow writing
wPrErr	−44	Volume is locked by a hardware setting

Assembly-Language Information

Constants

```
; Flags in file information used by the Finder

fHasBundle      .EQU     13      ;set if file has a bundle
fInvisible      .EQU     14      ;set if file's icon is invisible

; Flags in trap words

asnycTrpBit     .EQU     10      ;set for an asynchronous call
noQueueBit      .EQU      9      ;set for immediate execution
```

```
; Values for requesting read/write access

fsCurPerm       .EQU    0       ;whatever is currently allowed
fsRdPerm        .EQU    1       ;request to read only
fsWrPerm        .EQU    2       ;request to write only
fsRdWrPerm      .EQU    3       ;request to read and write

; Positioning modes

fsAtMark        .EQU    0       ;at current mark
fsFromStart     .EQU    1       ;offset relative to beginning of file
fsFromLEOF      .EQU    2       ;offset relative to logical end-of-file
fsFromMark      .EQU    3       ;offset relative to current mark
rdVerify        .EQU    64      ;add to above for read-verify
```

Structure of File Information Used by the Finder

fdType	File type (long)
fdCreator	File's creator (long)
fdFlags	Flags (word)
fdLocation	File's location (point; long)
fdFldr	File's window (word)

Standard Parameter Block Data Structure

qLink	Pointer to next queue entry
qType	Queue type (word)
ioTrap	Routine trap (word)
ioCmdAddr	Routine address
ioCompletion	Address of completion routine
ioResult	Result code (word)
ioFileName	Pointer to file name (preceded by length byte)
ioVNPtr	Pointer to volume name (preceded by length byte)
ioVRefNum	Volume reference number (word)
ioDrvNum	Drive number (word)

I/O Parameter Block Data Structure

ioRefNum	Path reference number (word)
ioFileType	Version number (byte)
ioPermssn	Read/write permission (byte)
ioNewName	Pointer to new file or volume name for Rename
ioLEOF	Logical end-of-file for SetEOF (long)
ioOwnBuf	Pointer to access path buffer
ioNewType	New version number for SetFilType (byte)
ioBuffer	Pointer to data buffer
ioReqCount	Requested number of bytes (long)
ioActCount	Actual number of bytes (long)
ioPosMode	Positioning mode and newline character (word)

| ioPosOffset | Positioning offset (long) |
| ioQElSize | Size in bytes of I/O parameter block |

Structure of File Information Parameter Block

ioRefNum	Path reference number (word)
ioFileType	Version number (byte)
ioFDirIndex	Sequence number of file (word)
ioFlAttrib	File attributes (byte)
ioFFlType	Version number (byte)
ioFlUsrWds	Information used by the Finder (16 bytes)
ioFFlNum	File number (long)
ioFlStBlk	First allocation block of data fork (word)
ioFlLgLen	Logical end-of-file of data fork (long)
ioFlPyLen	Physical end-of-file of data fork (long)
ioFlRStBlk	First allocation block of resource fork (word)
ioFlRLgLen	Logical end-of-file of resource fork (long)
ioFlRPyLen	Physical end-of-file of resource fork (long)
ioFlCrDat	Date and time of creation (long)
ioFlMdDat	Date and time of last modification (long)
ioFQElSize	Size in bytes of file information parameter block

Structure of Volume Information Parameter Block

ioVolIndex	Volume index (word)
ioVCrDate	Date and time of initialization (long)
ioVLsBkUp	Date and time of last backup (long)
ioVAtrb	Volume attributes (word)
ioVNmFls	Number of files in directory (word)
ioVDirSt	First block of directory (word)
ioVBlLn	Length of directory in blocks (word)
ioVNmAlBlks	Number of allocation blocks on volume (word)
ioVAlBlkSiz	Size of allocation blocks (long)
ioVClpSiz	Number of bytes to allocate (long)
ioAlBlSt	First allocation block in block map (word)
ioVNxtFNum	Next unused file number (long)
ioVFrBlk	Number of unused allocation blocks (word)
ioVQElSize	Size in bytes of volume information parameter block

Volume Information Data Structure

drSigWord	Always $D2D7 (word)
drCrDate	Date and time of initialization (long)
drLsBkUp	Date and time of last backup (long)
drAtrb	Volume attributes (word)
drNmFls	Number of files in directory (word)
drDirSt	First block of directory (word)
drBlLn	Length of directory in blocks (word)
drNmAlBlks	Number of allocation blocks on volume (word)
drAlBlkSiz	Size of allocation blocks (long)

drClpSiz   Number of bytes to allocate (long)
drAlBlSt   First allocation block in block map (word)
drNxtFNum   Next unused file number (long)
drFreeBks   Number of unused allocation blocks (word)
drVN   Volume name preceded by length byte (28 bytes)

File Directory Entry Data Structure

flFlags   Bit 7=1 if entry used; bit 0=1 if file locked (byte)
flTyp   Version number (byte)
flUsrWds   Information used by the Finder (16 bytes)
flFlNum   File number (long)
flStBlk   First allocation block of data fork (word)
flLgLen   Logical end-of-file of data fork (long)
flPyLen   Physical end-of-file of data fork (long)
flRStBlk   First allocation block of resource fork (word)
flRLgLen   Logical end-of-file of resource fork (long)
flRPyLen   Physical end-of-file of resource fork (long)
flCrDat   Date and time file of creation (long)
flMdDat   Date and time of last modification (long)
flNam   File name preceded by length byte

Volume Control Block Data Structure

qLink   Pointer to next queue entry
qType   Queue type (word)
vcbFlags   Bit 15=1 if volume control block is dirty (word)
vcbSigWord   Always $D2D7 (word)
vcbCrDate   Date and time of initialization (word)
vcbLsBkUp   Date and time of last backup (long)
vcbAtrb   Volume attributes (word)
vcbNmFls   Number of files in directory (word)
vcbDirSt   First block of directory (word)
vcbBlLn   Length of directory in blocks (word)
vcbNmBlks   Number of allocation blocks on volume (word)
vcbAlBlkSiz   Size of allocation blocks (long)
vcbClpSiz   Number of bytes to allocate (long)
vcbAlBlSt   First allocation block in block map (word)
vcbNxtFNum   Next unused file number (long)
vcbFreeBks   Number of unused allocation blocks (word)
vcbVN   Volume name preceded by length byte (28 bytes)
vcbDrvNum   Drive number of drive in which volume is mounted (word)
vcbDRefNum   Driver reference number of driver for drive in which volume is mounted (word)
vcbFSID   File-system identifier (word)
vcbVRefNum   Volume reference number (word)
vcbMAdr   Pointer to volume block map
vcbBufAdr   Pointer to volume buffer
vcbMLen   Number of bytes in volume block map (word)

File Control Block Data Structure

fcbFlNum	File number (long)
fcbMdRByt	Flags (byte)
fcbTypByt	Version number (byte)
fcbSBlk	First allocation block of file (word)
fcbEOF	Logical end-of-file (long)
fcbPLen	Physical end-of-file (long)
fcbCrPs	Mark (long)
fcbVPtr	Pointer to volume control block (long)
fcbBfAdr	Pointer to access path buffer (long)

Drive Queue Entry Data Structure

qLink	Pointer to next queue entry
qType	Queue type (word)
dQDrive	Drive number (word)
dQRefNum	Driver reference number (word)
dQFSID	File-system identifier (word)
dQDrvSize	Number of logical blocks (word)

Macro Names

Pascal name	Macro name
FInitQueue	_InitQueue
PBMountVol	_MountVol
PBGetVInfo	_GetVolInfo
PBGetVol	_GetVol
PBSetVol	_SetVol
PBFlushVol	_FlushVol
PBUnmountVol	_UnmountVol
PBOffLine	_OffLine
PBEject	_Eject
PBCreate	_Create
PBOpen	_Open
PBOpenRF	_OpenRF
PBRead	_Read
PBWrite	_Write
PBGetFPos	_GetFPos
PBSetFPos	_SetFPos
PBGetEOF	_GetEOF
PBSetEOF	_SetEOF
PBAllocate	_Allocate
PBFlushFile	_FlushFile
PBClose	_Close
PBGetFInfo	_GetFileInfo
PBSetFInfo	_SetFileInfo
PBSetFLock	_SetFilLock
PBRstFLock	_RstFilLock

PBSetFVers	_SetFilType
PBRename	_Rename
PBDelete	_Delete

Variables

FSQHdr	File I/O queue header (10 bytes)
VCBQHdr	Volume-control-block queue header (10 bytes)
DefVCBPtr	Pointer to default volume control block
FCBSPtr	Pointer to file-control-block buffer
DrvQHdr	Drive queue header (10 bytes)
ToExtFS	Pointer to external file system

5 THE PRINTING MANAGER

ABOUT THIS CHAPTER

The Printing Manager is a set of RAM-based routines and data types that allow you to use standard QuickDraw routines to print text or graphics on a printer. The Printing Manager calls the Printer Driver, a device driver in RAM. It also includes low-level calls to the Printer Driver so that you can implement alternate, low-level printing routines.

You should already be familiar with the following:

- the Resource Manager

- QuickDraw

- dialogs, as described in chapter 13 of Volume I

- the Device Manager, if you're interested in writing your own Printer Driver

ABOUT THE PRINTING MANAGER

The Printing Manager isn't in the Macintosh ROM; to access the Printing Manager routines, you must link with an object file or files provided as part of your development system.

The Macintosh user prints a document by choosing the Print command from the application's File menu; a dialog then requests information such as the print quality and number of copies. The Page Setup command in the File menu lets the user specify formatting information, such as the page size, that rarely needs to be changed and is saved with the document. The Printing Manager provides your application with two standard dialogs for obtaining Page Setup and Print information. The user can also print directly from the Finder by selecting one or more documents and choosing Print from the Finder's File menu; the Print dialog is then applied to all of the documents selected.

The Printing Manager is designed so that your application doesn't have to be concerned with what kind of printer is connected to the Macintosh; you call the same printing routines, regardless of the printer. This printer independence is possible because the actual printing code (which is different for different printers) is contained in a separate **printer resource file** on the user's disk. The printer resource file contains a device driver, called the **Printer Driver**, that communicates between the Printing Manager and the printer.

The user installs a new printer with the Choose Printer desk accessory, which gives the Printing Manager a new printer resource file. This process is transparent to your application, and your application should not make any assumptions about the printer type.

Figure 1 shows the flow of control for printing on the Macintosh.

You define the image to be printed by using a **printing grafPort**, a QuickDraw grafPort with additional fields that customize it for printing:

```
TYPE TPPrPort = ^TPrPort;
     TPrPort   = RECORD
                     gPort: GrafPort;   {grafPort to draw in}
                     {more fields for internal use}
                 END;
```

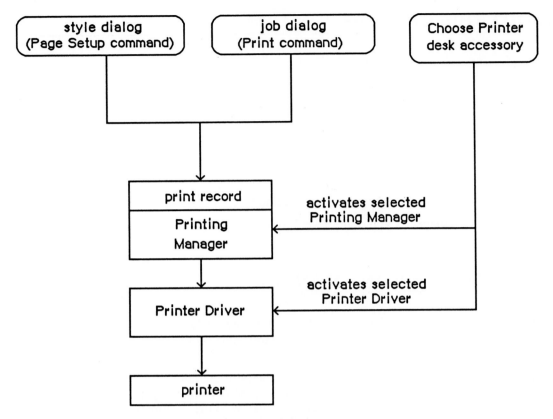

Figure 1. Printing Overview

The Printing Manager gives you a printing grafPort when you open a document for printing. You then print text and graphics by drawing into this port with QuickDraw, just as if you were drawing on the screen. The Printing Manager installs its own versions of QuickDraw's low-level drawing routines in the printing grafPort, causing your higher-level QuickDraw calls to drive the printer instead of drawing on the screen.

Warning: You should not try to do your own customization of QuickDraw routines in the printing grafPort unless you're sure of what you're doing.

PRINT RECORDS AND DIALOGS

To format and print a document, your application must know the following:

- the dimensions of the printable area of the page
- if the application must calculate the margins, the size of the physical sheet of paper and the printer's vertical and horizontal resolution
- which printing method is being used (draft or spool, explained below)

This information is contained in a data structure called a **print record.** The Printing Manager fills in the entire print record for you. Information that the user can specify is set through two standard dialogs.

The **style dialog** should be presented when the user selects the application's Page Setup command from the File menu. It lets the user specify any options that affect the page dimensions, that is, the information you need for formatting the document to match the printer. Figure 2 shows the standard style dialog for the Imagewriter printer.

```
 Paper:      ● US Letter    ○ A4 Letter                  ┌──────────┐
             ○ US Legal     ○ International Fanfold       │    OK    │
                                                          └──────────┘
 Orientation:  ● Tall        ○ Tall Adjusted   ○ Wide    ┌──────────┐
                                                          │  Cancel  │
                                                          └──────────┘
```

Figure 2. The Style Dialog

The **job dialog** should be presented when the user chooses to start printing with the Print command. It requests information about how to print the document *this time,* such as the print quality (for printers that offer a choice of resolutions), the type of paper feed (such as fanfold or cut-sheet), the range of pages to print, and the number of copies. Figure 3 shows the standard job dialog for the Imagewriter.

```
 Quality:       ○ High      ● Standard   ○ Draft        ┌──────────┐
 Page Range:    ● All        ○ From: [   ] To: [     ]   │    OK    │
 Copies:        [1]                                       └──────────┘
 Paper Feed:    ● Continuous  ○ Cut Sheet                ┌──────────┐
                                                          │  Cancel  │
                                                          └──────────┘
```

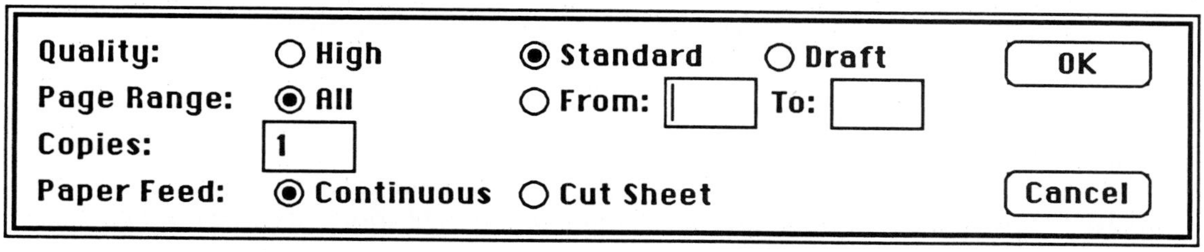

Figure 3. The Job Dialog

Note: The dialogs shown in Figures 2 and 3 are examples only; the actual content of these dialogs is customized for each printer.

Print records are referred to by handles. Their structure is as follows:

```
TYPE THPrint  =  ^TPPrint;
     TPPrint  =  ^TPrint;
     TPrint   =  RECORD
                   iPrVersion: INTEGER;      {Printing Manager version}
                   prInfo:     TPrInfo;      {printer information subrecord}
                   rPaper:     Rect;         {paper rectangle}
                   prStl:      TPrStl;       {additional device information}
                   prInfoPT:   TPrInfo;      {used internally}
                   prXInfo:    TPrXInfo;     {additional device information}
                   prJob:      TPrJob;       {job subrecord}
                   printX:     ARRAY[1..19] OF INTEGER   {not used}
                 END;
```

Warning: Your application should not change the data in the print record—be sure to use the standard dialogs for setting this information. The only fields you'll need to set directly are some containing optional information in the job subrecord (explained below). Attempting to set other values directly in the print record can produce unexpected results.

IPrVersion identifies the version of the Printing Manager that initialized this print record. If you try to use a print record that's invalid for the current version of the Printing Manager or for the currently installed printer, the Printing Manager will correct the record by filling it with default values.

The other fields of the print record are discussed in separate sections below.

Note: Whenever you save a document, you should write an appropriate print record in the document's resource file. This lets the document "remember" its own printing parameters for use the next time it's printed.

The Printer Information Subrecord

The printer information subrecord (field prInfo of the print record) gives you the information needed for page composition. It's defined as follows:

```
TYPE TPrInfo =  RECORD
                   iDev:   INTEGER;   {used internally}
                   iVRes:  INTEGER;   {vertical resolution of printer}
                   iHRes:  INTEGER;   {horizontal resolution of printer}
                   rPage:  Rect       {page rectangle}
                END;
```

RPage is the **page rectangle**, representing the boundaries of the printable page: The printing grafPort's boundary rectangle, portRect, and clipRgn are set to this rectangle. Its top left corner always has coordinates (0,0); the coordinates of the bottom right corner give the maximum page height and width attainable on the given printer, in dots. Typically these are slightly less than the physical dimensions of the paper, because of the printer's mechanical limitations. RPage is set as a result of the style dialog.

The rPage rectangle is inside the **paper rectangle**, specified by the rPaper field of the print record. RPaper gives the physical paper size, defined in the same coordinate system as rPage (see Figure 4). Thus the top left coordinates of the paper rectangle are typically negative and its bottom right coordinates are greater than those of the page rectangle.

IVRes and iHRes give the printer's vertical and horizontal resolution in dots per inch. Thus, if you divide the width of rPage by iHRes, you get the width of the page rectangle in inches.

The Job Subrecord

The job subrecord (field prJob of the print record) contains information about a particular printing job. Its contents are set as a result of the job dialog.

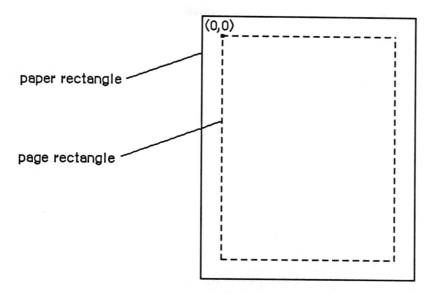

Figure 4. Page and Paper Rectangles

The job subrecord is defined as follows:

```
TYPE TPrJob =
        RECORD
            iFstPage:   INTEGER;        {first page to print}
            iLstPage:   INTEGER;        {last page to print}
            iCopies:    INTEGER;        {number of copies}
            bJDocLoop:  SignedByte;     {printing method}
            fFromUsr:   BOOLEAN;        {used internally}
            pIdleProc:  ProcPtr;        {background procedure}
            pFileName:  StringPtr;      {spool file name}
            iFileVol:   INTEGER;        {spool file volume reference number}
            bFileVers:  SignedByte;     {spool file version number}
            bJobX:      SignedByte      {used internally}
        END;
```

BJDocLoop designates the printing method that the Printing Manager will use. It will be one of the following predefined constants:

```
CONST bDraftLoop = 0;    {draft printing}
      bSpoolLoop = 1;    {spool printing}
```

Draft printing means that the document will be printed immediately. **Spool printing** means that printing may be deferred: The Printing Manager writes out a representation of the document's printed image to a disk file (or possibly to memory); this information is then converted into a bit image and printed. For details about the printing methods, see the "Methods of Printing" section below. The Printing Manager sets the bJDocLoop field; your application should not change it.

IFstPage and iLstPage designate the first and last pages to be printed. These page numbers are relative to the first page counted by the Printing Manager. The Printing Manager knows nothing about any page numbering placed by an application within a document.

ICopies is the number of copies to print. The Printing Manager automatically handles multiple copies for spool printing or for printing on the LaserWriter. Your application only needs this number for draft printing on the Imagewriter.

PIdleProc is a pointer to the background procedure (explained below) for this printing operation. In a newly initialized print record this field is set to NIL, designating the default background procedure, which just polls the keyboard and cancels further printing if the user types Command-period. You can install a background procedure of your own by storing a pointer to your procedure directly into the pIdleProc field.

For spool printing, your application may optionally provide a spool file name, volume reference number, and version number (described in chapter 4):

- PFileName is the name of the spool file. This field is initialized to NIL, and generally not changed by the application. NIL denotes the default file name (normally 'Print File') stored in the printer resource file.

- IFileVol is the volume reference number of the spool file. This field is initialized to 0, representing the default volume. You can use the File Manager function SetVol to change the default volume, or you can override the default setting by storing directly into this field.

- BFileVers is the version number of the spool file, initialized to 0.

Additional Device Information

The prStl and prXInfo fields of the print record provide device information that your application may need to refer to.

The prStl field of the print record is defined as follows:

```
TYPE TPrStl = RECORD
                wDev: INTEGER;    {high byte specifies device}
                {more fields for internal use}
              END;
```

The high-order byte of the wDev field indicates which printer is currently selected:

```
CONST bDevCItoh = 1;   {Imagewriter printer}
      bDevLaser = 3;   {LaserWriter printer}
```

A value of 0 indicates the Macintosh screen; other values are reserved for future use. The low-order byte of wDev is used internally.

The prXInfo field of the print record is defined as follows:

```
TYPE TPrXInfo = RECORD
                  iRowBytes: INTEGER;    {used internally}
                  iBandV:    INTEGER;    {used internally}
                  iBandH:    INTEGER;    {used internally}
                  iDevBytes: INTEGER;    {size of buffer}
                  {more fields for internal use}
                END;
```

lDevBytes is the number of bytes of memory required as a buffer for spool printing. (You need this information only if you choose to allocate your own buffer.)

METHODS OF PRINTING

There are two basic methods of printing documents: draft and spool. The Printing Manager determines which method to use; the two methods are implemented in different ways for different printers.

In draft printing, your QuickDraw calls are converted directly into command codes the printer understands, which are then immediately used to drive the printer:

- On the Imagewriter, draft printing is used for printing quick, low-quality drafts of text documents that are printed straight down the page from top to bottom and left to right.

- On the LaserWriter, draft printing is used to obtain high-quality output. (This typically requires 15K bytes of memory for your data and printing code.)

Spool printing is a two-stage process. First, the Printing Manager writes out ("spools") a representation of your document's printed image to a disk file or to memory. This information is then converted into a bit image and printed. On the Imagewriter, spool printing is used for standard or high-quality printing.

Spooling and printing are two separate stages because of memory considerations: Spooling a document takes only about 3K bytes of memory, but may require large portions of your application's code and data in memory; printing the spooled document typically requires from 20K to 40K for the printing code, buffers, and fonts, but most of your application's code and data are no longer needed. Normally you'll make your printing code a separate program segment, so you can swap the rest of your code and data out of memory during printing and swap it back in after you're finished (see chapter 2).

Note: This chapter frequently refers to spool files, although there may be cases when the document is spooled to memory. This difference will be transparent to the application.

Note: The internal format of spool files is private to the Printing Manager and may vary from one printer to another. This means that spool files destined for one printer can't be printed on another. In spool files for the Imagewriter, each page is stored as a QuickDraw picture. It's envisioned that most other printers will use this same approach, but there may be exceptions. Spool files can be identified by their file type ('PFIL') and creator ('PSYS'). File type and creator are discussed in chapter 1 of Volume III.

BACKGROUND PROCESSING

As mentioned above, the job subrecord includes a pointer, pIdleProc, to an optional **background procedure** to be run whenever the Printing Manager has directed output to the printer and is waiting for the printer to finish. The background procedure takes no parameters and returns no result; the Printing Manager simply runs it at every opportunity.

If you don't designate a background procedure, the Printing Manager uses a default procedure for canceling printing: The default procedure just polls the keyboard and sets a Printing Manager error code if the user types Command-period. If you use this option, you should display a dialog box during printing to inform the user that the Command-period option is available.

Note: If you designate a background procedure, you must set pIdleProc *after* presenting the dialogs, validating the print record, and initializing the printing grafPort: The routines that perform these operations reset pIdleProc to NIL.

Warning: If you write your own background procedure, you must be careful to avoid a number of subtle concurrency problems that can arise. For instance, if the background procedure uses QuickDraw, it must be sure to restore the printing grafPort as the current port before returning. It's particularly important not to attempt any printing from within the background procedure: The Printing Manager is *not* reentrant! If you use a background procedure that runs your application concurrently with printing, it should disable all menu items having to do with printing, such as Page Setup and Print.

USING THE PRINTING MANAGER

To use the Printing Manager, you must first initialize QuickDraw, the Font Manager, the Window Manager, the Menu Manager, TextEdit, and the Dialog Manager. The first Printing Manager routine to call is PrOpen; the last routine to call is PrClose.

Before you can print a document, you need a valid print record. You can either use an existing print record (for instance, one saved with a document), or initialize one by calling PrintDefault or PrValidate. If you use an existing print record, be sure to call PrValidate to make sure it's valid for the current version of the Printing Manager and for the currently installed printer. To create a new print record, you must first create a handle to it with the Memory Manager function NewHandle, as follows:

```
prRecHdl := THPrint(NewHandle(SIZEOF(TPrint)))
```

Print record information is obtained via the style and job dialogs:

- Call PrStlDialog when the user chooses the Page Setup commmand, to get the page dimensions. From the rPage field of the printer information subrecord, you can then determine where page breaks will be in the document. You can show rulers and margins correctly by using the information in the iVRes, iHRes, and rPaper fields.

- Call PrJobDialog when the user chooses the Print commmand, to get the specific information about that printing job, such as the page range and number of copies.

You can apply the results of one job dialog to several documents (when printing from the Finder, for example) by calling PrJobMerge.

After getting the job information, you should immediately print the document.

The Printing Loop

To print a document, you call the following procedures:

1. PrOpenDoc, which returns a printing grafPort that's set up for draft or spool printing (depending on the bJDocLoop field of the job subrecord)

2. PrOpenPage, which starts each new page (reinitializing the grafPort)

3. QuickDraw routines, for drawing the page in the printing grafPort created by PrOpenDoc

4. PrClosePage, which terminates the page

5. PrCloseDoc, at the end of the entire document, to close the printing grafPort

Each page is either printed immediately (draft printing) or written to the disk or to memory (spool printing). You should test to see whether spooling was done, and if so, print the spooled document: First, swap as much of your program out of memory as you can (see chapter 2), and then call PrPicFile.

It's a good idea to call PrError after each Printing Manager call, to check for any errors. To cancel a printing operation in progress, use PrSetError. If an error occurs and you cancel printing (or if the user aborts printing), be sure to exit normally from the printing loop so that all files are closed properly; that is, be sure that every PrOpenPage is matched by a PrClosePage and PrOpenDoc is matched by PrCloseDoc.

To sum up, your application's printing loop will typically use the following basic format for printing:

```
myPrPort := PrOpenDoc(prRecHdl,NIL,NIL); {open printing grafPort}
FOR pg := 1 TO myPgCount DO            {page loop: ALL pages of document}
   IF PrError = noErr
      THEN
        BEGIN
        PrOpenPage(myPrPort,NIL);      {start new page}
        IF PrError = noErr
           THEN MyDrawingProc(pg);     {draw page with QuickDraw}
        PrClosePage(myPrPort);         {end current page}
        END;
PrCloseDoc(myPrPort);                  {close printing grafPort}
IF prRecHdl^^.prJob.bJDocLoop = bSpoolLoop AND PrError = noErr
   THEN
      BEGIN
      MySwapOutProc;        {swap out code and data}
      PrPicFile(prRecHdl,NIL,NIL,NIL,myStRec); {print spooled document}
      END;
IF PrError <> noErr THEN MyPrErrAlertProc   {report any errors}
```

Note an important assumption in this example: The MyDrawingProc procedure must be able to determine the page boundaries without stepping through each page of the document.

Although spool printing may not be supported on all printers, you must be sure to include PrPicFile in your printing code, as shown above. The application should make no assumptions about the printing method.

Note: The maximum number of pages in a spool file is defined by the following constant:

```
CONST iPFMaxPgs = 128;
```

If you need to print more than 128 pages at one time, just repeat the printing loop (*without* calling PrValidate, PrStlDialog, or PrJobDialog).

Printing a Specified Range of Pages

The above example loops through every page of the document, regardless of which pages the user has selected; the Printing Manager draws each page but actually prints only the pages from iFstPage to iLstPage.

If you know the page boundaries in the document, it's much faster to loop through only the specified pages. You can do this by saving the values of iFstPage and iLstPage and then changing these fields in the print record: For example, to print pages 20 to 25, you would set iFstPage to 1 and iLstPage to 6 (or greater) and then begin printing at your page 20. You could implement this for all cases as follows:

```
myFirst := prRecHdl^^.prJob.iFstPage;    {save requested page numbers}
myLast  := prRecHdl^^.prJob.iLstPage;
prRecHdl^^.prJob.iFstPage := 1;          {print "all" pages in loop}
prRecHdl^^.prJob.iLstPage := 999;
FOR pg := myFirst TO myLast DO           {page loop: requested pages only}
   . . .                                 {print as in first example}
```

Remember that iFstPage and iLstPage are relative to the first page counted by the Printing Manager. The Printing Manager counts one page each time PrOpenPage is called; the count begins at 1.

Using QuickDraw for Printing

When drawing to the printing grafPort, you should note the following:

- With each new page, you get a completely reinitialized grafPort, so you'll need to reset font information and other grafPort characteristics as desired.

- Don't make calls that don't do anything on the printer. For example, erase operations are quite time-consuming and normally aren't needed on the printer.

- Don't use clipping to select text to be printed. There are a number of subtle differences between how text appears on the screen and how it appears on the printer; you can't count on knowing the exact dimensions of the rectangle occupied by the text.

- Don't use fixed-width fonts to align columns. Since spacing gets adjusted on the printer, you should explicitly move the pen to where you want it.

For printing to the LaserWriter, you'll need to observe the following limitations:

- Regions aren't supported; try to simulate them with polygons.

- Clipping regions should be limited to rectangles.

- "Invert" routines aren't supported.

- Copy is the *only* transfer mode supported for all objects except text and bit images. For text, Bic is also supported. For bit images, the only transfer mode *not* supported is Xor.

- Don't change the grafPort's local coordinate system (with SetOrigin) within the printing loop (between PrOpenPage and PrClosePage).

For more information about optimizing your printing code for the LaserWriter, see the *Inside LaserWriter* manual.

Printing From the Finder

The Macintosh user can choose to print from the Finder as well as from an application. Your application should support both alternatives.

To print a document from the Finder, the user selects the document's icon and chooses the Print command from the File menu. Note that the user can select more than one document, or even a document and an application, which means that the application must verify that it can print the document before proceeding. When the Print command is chosen, the Finder starts up the application, and passes information to it indicating that the document is to be printed rather than opened (see chapter 2). Your application should then do the following, preferably without going through its entire startup sequence:

1. Call PrJobDialog. (If the user selected more than one document, you can use PrJobMerge to apply one job dialog to all of the documents.)

2. Print the document(s).

PRINTING MANAGER ROUTINES

This section describes the high-level Printing Manager routines; low-level routines are described below in the section "The Printer Driver".

Assembly-language note: There are no trap macros for these routines. To print from assembly language, call these Pascal routines from your program.

Initialization and Termination

```
PROCEDURE PrOpen;    [Not in ROM]
```

PrOpen prepares the Printing Manager for use. It opens the Printer Driver and the printer resource file. If either of these is missing, or if the printer resource file isn't properly formed, PrOpen will do nothing, and PrError will return a Resource Manager result code.

```
PROCEDURE PrClose;    [Not in ROM]
```

PrClose releases the memory used by the Printing Manager. It closes the printer resource file, allowing the file's resource map to be removed from memory. It doesn't close the Printer Driver.

Note: To close the Printer Driver, call the low-level routine PrDrvrClose, described in the section "The Printer Driver".

Print Records and Dialogs

PROCEDURE PrintDefault (hPrint: THPrint);   [Not in ROM]

PrintDefault fills the fields of the specified print record with default values that are stored in the printer resource file. HPrint is a handle to the record, which may be a new print record that you've just allocated with NewHandle or an existing one (from a document, for example).

FUNCTION PrValidate (hPrint: THPrint) : BOOLEAN;   [Not in ROM]

PrValidate checks the contents of the specified print record for compatibility with the current version of the Printing Manager and with the currently installed printer. If the record is valid, the function returns FALSE (no change); if invalid, the record is adjusted to the default values stored in the printer resource file, and the function returns TRUE.

PrValidate also makes sure all the information in the print record is internally self-consistent and updates the print record as necessary. These changes do *not* affect the function's Boolean result.

> **Warning:** You should never call PrValidate (or PrStlDialog or PrJobDialog, which call it) between pages of a document.

FUNCTION PrStlDialog (hPrint: THPrint) : BOOLEAN;   [Not in ROM]

PrStlDialog conducts a style dialog with the user to determine the page dimensions and other information needed for page setup. The initial settings displayed in the dialog box are taken from the most recent print record. If the user confirms the dialog, the results of the dialog are saved in the specified print record, PrValidate is called, and the function returns TRUE. Otherwise, the print record is left unchanged and the function returns FALSE.

> **Note:** If the print record was taken from a document, you should update its contents in the document's resource file if PrStlDialog returns TRUE. This makes the results of the style dialog "stick" to the document.

FUNCTION PrJobDialog (hPrint: THPrint) : BOOLEAN;   [Not in ROM]

PrJobDialog conducts a job dialog with the user to determine the print quality, range of pages to print, and so on. The initial settings displayed in the dialog box are taken from the printer resource file, where they were remembered from the previous job (with the exception of the page range, set to all, and the copies, set to 1).

If the user confirms the dialog, both the print record and the printer resource file are updated, PrValidate is called, and the function returns TRUE. Otherwise, the print record and printer resource file are left unchanged and the function returns FALSE.

> **Note:** Since the job dialog is associated with the Print command, you should proceed with the requested printing operation if PrJobDialog returns TRUE.

```
PROCEDURE PrJobMerge (hPrintSrc,hPrintDst: THPrint);   [Not in ROM]
```

PrJobMerge first calls PrValidate for each of the given print records. It then copies all of the information set as a result of a job dialog from hPrintSrc to hPrintDst. Finally, it makes sure that all the fields of hPrintDst are internally self-consistent.

PrJobMerge allows you to conduct a job dialog just once and then copy the job information to several print records, which means that you can print several documents with one dialog. This is useful when printing from the Finder.

Printing

```
FUNCTION PrOpenDoc (hPrint: THPrint; pPrPort: TPPrPort; pIOBuf:
         Ptr) : TPPrPort;   [Not in ROM]
```

PrOpenDoc initializes a printing grafPort for use in printing a document, makes it the current port, and returns a pointer to it.

HPrint is a handle to the print record for this printing operation; you should already have validated this print record.

Depending on the setting of the bJDocLoop field in the job subrecord, the printing grafPort will be set up for draft or spool printing. For spool printing, the spool file's name, volume reference number, and version number are taken from the job subrecord.

PPrPort and pIOBuf are normally NIL. PPrPort is a pointer to the printing grafPort; if it's NIL, PrOpenDoc allocates a new printing grafPort in the heap. Similarly, pIOBuf points to an area of memory to be used as an input/output buffer; if it's NIL, PrOpenDoc uses the volume buffer for the spool file's volume. If you allocate your own buffer, it must be 522 bytes long.

Note: These parameters are provided because the printing grafPort and input/output buffer are both nonrelocatable objects; to avoid fragmenting the heap, you may want to allocate them yourself.

You must balance every call to PrOpenDoc with a call to PrCloseDoc.

```
PROCEDURE PrOpenPage (pPrPort: TPPrPort; pPageFrame: TPRect);
         [Not in ROM]
```

PrOpenPage begins a new page. The page is printed only if it falls within the page range given in the job subrecord.

For spool printing, the pPageFrame parameter is used for scaling. It points to a rectangle to be used as the QuickDraw picture frame for this page:

```
TYPE TPRect = ^Rect;
```

When you print the spooled document, this rectangle will be scaled (with the QuickDraw procedure DrawPicture) to coincide with the rPage rectangle in the printer information subrecord. Unless you want the printout to be scaled, you should set pPageFrame to NIL—this uses the rPage rectangle as the picture frame, so that the page will be printed with no scaling.

Warning: Don't call the QuickDraw function OpenPicture while a page is open (after a call to PrOpenPage and before the following PrClosePage). You can, however, call DrawPicture at any time.

Warning: The printing grafPort is completely reinitialized by PrOpenPage. Therefore, you must set grafPort features such as the font and font size for every page that you draw.

You must balance every call to PrOpenPage with a call to PrClosePage.

```
PROCEDURE PrClosePage (pPrPort: TPPrPort);   [Not in ROM]
```

PrClosePage finishes the printing of the current page. It lets the Printing Manager know that you're finished with this page, so that it can do whatever is required for the current printer and printing method.

```
PROCEDURE PrCloseDoc (pPrPort: TPPrPort);   [Not in ROM]
```

PrCloseDoc closes the printing grafPort. For draft printing, PrCloseDoc ends the printing job. For spool printing, PrCloseDoc ends the spooling process: The spooled document must now be printed. Before printing it, call PrError to find out whether spooling succeeded; if it did, you should swap out as much code as possible and then call PrPicFile.

```
PROCEDURE PrPicFile (hPrint: THPrint; pPrPort: TPPrPort; pIOBuf:
         Ptr; pDevBuf: Ptr; VAR prStatus: TPrStatus);   [Not in
         ROM]
```

PrPicFile prints a spooled document. If spool printing is being used, your application should normally call PrPicFile after PrCloseDoc.

HPrint is a handle to the print record for this printing job. The spool file's name, volume reference number, and version number are taken from the job subrecord of this print record. After printing is successfully completed, the Printing Manager deletes the spool file from the disk.

You'll normally pass NIL for pPrPort, pIOBuf, and pDevBuf. PPrPort is a pointer to the printing grafPort for this operation; if it's NIL, PrPicFile allocates a new printing grafPort in the heap. Similarly, pIOBuf points to an area of memory to be used as an input /output buffer for reading the spool file; if it's NIL, PrPicFile uses the volume buffer for the spool file's volume. PDevBuf points to a device-dependent buffer; if NIL, PrPicFile allocates a buffer in the heap.

Note: If you provide your own storage for pDevBuf, it has to be big enough to hold the number of bytes indicated by the iDevBytes field of the PrXInfo subrecord.

Warning: Be sure not to pass, in pPrPort, a pointer to the same printing grafPort you received from PrOpenDoc. If that port was allocated by PrOpenDoc itself (that is, if the pPrPort parameter to PrOpenDoc was NIL), then PrCloseDoc will have disposed of the port, making your pointer to it invalid. Of course, if you earlier provided your own storage to PrOpenDoc, there's no reason you can't use the same storage again for PrPicFile.

The prStatus parameter is a printer status record that PrPicFile will use to report on its progress:

```
TYPE TPrStatus = RECORD
                    iTotPages:   INTEGER;   {number of pages in spool file}
                    iCurPage:    INTEGER;   {page being printed}
                    iTotCopies:  INTEGER;   {number of copies requested}
                    iCurCopy:    INTEGER;   {copy being printed}
                    iTotBands:   INTEGER;   {used internally}
                    iCurBand:    INTEGER;   {used internally}
                    fPgDirty:    BOOLEAN;   {TRUE if started printing page}
                    fImaging:    BOOLEAN;   {used internally}
                    hPrint:      THPrint;   {print record}
                    pPrPort:     TPPrPort;  {printing grafPort}
                    hPic:        PicHandle  {used internally}
                 END;
```

The fPgDirty field is TRUE if anything has already been printed on the current page, FALSE if not.

Your background procedure (if any) can use this record to monitor the state of the printing operation.

Error Handling

```
FUNCTION PrError : INTEGER;   [Not in ROM]
```

PrError returns the result code left by the last Printing Manager routine. Some possible result codes are:

```
CONST noErr       =  0;    {no error}
      iPrSavPFil  = -1;    {saving print file}
      controlErr  = -17;   {unimplemented control instruction}
      iIOAbort    = -27;   {I/O error}
      iMemFullErr = -108;  {not enough room in heap zone}
      iPrAbort    = 128;   {application or user requested abort}
```

ControlErr is returned by the Device Manager. Other Operating System or Toolbox result codes may also be returned; a list of all result codes is given in Appendix A (Volume III).

Assembly-language note: The current result code is contained in the global variable PrintErr.

```
PROCEDURE PrSetError (iErr: INTEGER);   [Not in ROM]
```

PrSetError stores the specified value into the global variable where the Printing Manager keeps its result code. This procedure is used for canceling a printing operation in progress. To do this, call:

```
IF PrError <> noErr THEN PrSetError(iPrAbort)
```

Assembly-language note: You can achieve the same effect as PrSetError by storing directly into the global variable PrintErr. You shouldn't, however, store into this variable if it already contains a nonzero value.

THE PRINTER DRIVER

The Printing Manager provides a high-level interface that interprets QuickDraw commands for printing; it also provides a low-level interface that lets you directly access the Printer Driver.

Note: You should not use the high-level and low-level calls together.

The Printer Driver is the device driver that communicates with a printer. You only need to read this section if you're interested in low-level printing or writing your own device driver. For more information, see chapter 6.

The printer resource file for each type of printer includes a device driver for that printer. When the user chooses a printer, the printer's device driver becomes the active Printer Driver.

You can communicate with the Printer Driver via the following low-level routines:

- PrDrvrOpen opens the Printer Driver; it remains open until you call PrDrvrClose.

- PrCtlCall enables you to perform low-level printing operations such as bit map printing and direct streaming of text to the printer.

- PrDrvrVers tells you the version number of the Printer Driver.

- PrDrvrDCE gets a handle to the driver's device control entry.

Note: Advanced programmers: You can also communicate with the Printer Driver through the standard Device Manager calls OpenDriver, CloseDriver, and Control. The driver name and driver reference number are available as predefined constants:

```
CONST sPrDrvr   = '.Print';   {Printer Driver resource name}
      iPrDrvrRef = -3;        {Printer Driver reference number}
```

Note also that when you make direct Device Manager calls, the driver I/O queue entries should be initialized to all zeroes.

Low-Level Driver Access Routines

The routines in this section are used for communicating directly with the Printer Driver.

Assembly-language note: See chapter 6 for information about how to make the Device Manager calls corresponding to these routines.

```
PROCEDURE PrDrvrOpen;    [Not in ROM]
```

PrDrvrOpen opens the Printer Driver, reading it into memory if necessary.

```
PROCEDURE PrDrvrClose;    [Not in ROM]
```

PrDrvrClose closes the Printer Driver, releasing the memory it occupies. (Notice that PrClose doesn't close the Printer Driver.)

```
PROCEDURE PrCtlCall (iWhichCtl: INTEGER; lParam1,lParam2,lParam3:
           LONGINT);    [Not in ROM]
```

PrCtlCall calls the Printer Driver's control routine. The iWhichCtl parameter identifies the operation to perform. The following values are predefined:

```
CONST  iPrBitsCtl = 4;    {bit map printing}
       iPrIOCtl   = 5;    {text streaming}
       iPrDevCtl  = 7;    {printer control}
```

These operations are described in detail in the following sections of this chapter. The meanings of the lParam1, lParam2, and lParam3 parameters depend on the operation.

Note: Advanced programmers: If you're making a direct Device Manager Control call, iWhichCtl will be the csCode parameter, and lParam1, lParam2, and lParam3 will be csParam, csParam+4, and csParam+8.

```
FUNCTION PrDrvrDCE : Handle;    [Not in ROM]
```

PrDrvrDCE returns a handle to the Printer Driver's device control entry.

```
FUNCTION PrDrvrVers : INTEGER;    [Not in ROM]
```

PrDrvrVers returns the version number of the Printer Driver in the system resource file.

The version number of the Printing Manager is available as the predefined constant iPrRelease. You may want to compare the result of PrDrvrVers with iPrRelease to see if the Printer Driver in the resource file is the most recent version.

Printer Control

The iPrDevCtl parameter to PrCtlCall is used for several printer control operations. The high-order word of the lParam1 parameter specifies the operation to perform:

```
CONST  lPrReset    = $00010000;    {reset printer}
       lPrLineFeed = $00030000;    {carriage return only}
       lPrLFSixth  = $0003FFFF;    {standard 1/6-inch line feed}
       lPrPageEnd  = $00020000;    {end page}
```

The low-order word of lParam1 may specify additional information. The lParam2 and lParam3 parameters should always be 0.

Before starting to print, use

```
PrCtlCall(iPrDevCtl,lPrReset,0,0)
```

to reset the printer to its standard initial state. This call should be made only once per document. You can also specify the number of copies to make in the low-order byte of this parameter; for example, a value of $00010002 specifies two copies.

The lPrLineFeed and lPrLFSixth parameters allow you to achieve the effect of carriage returns and line feeds in a printer-independent way:

- LPrLineFeed specifies a carriage return only (with a line feed of 0).

- LPrLFSixth causes a carriage return and advances the paper by 1/6 inch (the standard "CR LF" sequence).

You can also specify the exact number of dots the paper advances in the low-order word of the lParam1 parameter. For example, a value of $00030008 for lParam1 causes a carriage return and advances the paper eight dots.

You should use these methods instead of sending carriage returns and line feeds directly to the printer.

The call

```
PrCtlCall(iPrDevCtl,lPrPageEnd,0,0)
```

does whatever is appropriate for the given printer at the end of each page, such as sending a form feed character and advancing past the paper fold. You should use this call instead of just sending a form feed yourself.

Bit Map Printing

To send all or part of a QuickDraw bit map directly to the printer, use

```
PrCtlCall(iPrBitsCtl,pBitMap,pPortRect,lControl)
```

The pBitMap parameter is a pointer to a QuickDraw bit map; pPortRect is a pointer to the rectangle to be printed, in the coordinates of the printing grafPort.

LControl should be one of the following predefined constants:

```
CONST lScreenBits = 0;    {default for printer}
      lPaintBits  = 1;    {square dots (72 by 72)}
```

The Imagewriter, in standard resolution, normally prints rectangular dots that are taller than they are wide (80 dots per inch horizontally by 72 vertically). Since the Macintosh 128K and 512K screen has square pixels (approximately 72 per inch both horizontally and vertically), lPaintBits gives a truer reproduction of the screen, although printing is somewhat slower.

On the LaserWriter, lControl should always be set to lPaintBits.

Putting all this together, you can print the entire screen at the default setting with

```
PrCtlCall(iPrBitsCtl,ORD(@screenBits),
                        ORD(@screenBits.bounds),lScreenBits)
```

To print the contents of a single window in square dots, use

```
PrCtlCall(iPrBitsCtl,ORD(@theWindow^.portBits),
                        ORD(@theWindow^.portRect),lPaintBits)
```

Text Streaming

Text streaming is useful for fast printing of text when speed is more important than fancy formatting or visual fidelity. It gives you full access to the printer's native text facilities (such as control or escape sequences for boldface, italic, underlining, or condensed or extended type), but makes no use of QuickDraw.

You can send a stream of characters (including control and escape sequences) directly to the printer with

```
PrCtlCall(iPrIOCtl,pBuf,lBufCount,0)
```

The pBuf parameter is a pointer to the beginning of the text. The low-order word of lBufCount is the number of bytes to transfer; the high-order word must be 0.

Warning: Relying on specific printer capabilities and control sequences will make your application printer-dependent. You can use iPrDevCtl to perform form feeds and line feeds in a printer-independent way.

Note: Advanced programmers who need more information about sending commands directly to the LaserWriter should see the *Inside LaserWriter* manual.

SUMMARY OF THE PRINTING MANAGER

Constants

```
CONST  { Printing methods }

       bDraftLoop = 0;     {draft printing}
       bSpoolLoop = 1;     {spool printing}

       { Printer specification in prStl field of print record }

       bDevCItoh = 1;      {Imagewriter printer}
       bDevLaser = 3;      {LaserWriter printer}

       { Maximum number of pages in a spool file }

       iPFMaxPgs = 128;

       { Result codes }

       noErr       =   0;      {no error}
       iPrSavPFil  =  -1;      {saving spool file}
       controlErr  = -17;      {unimplemented control instruction}
       iIOAbort    = -27;      {I/O abort error}
       iMemFullErr = -108;     {not enough room in heap zone}
       iPrAbort    = 128;      {application or user requested abort}

       { PrCtlCall parameters }

       iPrDevCtl   = 7;           {printer control}
       lPrReset    = $00010000;   {reset printer}
       lPrLineFeed = $00030000;   {carriage return only}
       lPrLFSixth  = $0003FFFF;   {standard 1/6-inch line feed}
       lPrPageEnd  = $00020000;   {end page}
       iPrBitsCtl  = 4;           {bit map printing}
       lScreenBits = 0;           {default for printer}
       lPaintBits  = 1;           {square dots (72 by 72)}
       iPrIOCtl    = 5;           {text streaming}

       { Printer Driver information }

       sPrDrvr     = '.Print';    {Printer Driver resource name}
       iPrDrvrRef  = -3;          {Printer Driver reference number}
```

Data Types

```
TYPE TPPrPort = ^TPrPort;
     TPrPort  = RECORD
                    gPort: GrafPort;  {grafPort to draw in}
                    {more fields for internal use}
                END;

     THPrint = ^TPPrint;
     TPPrint = ^TPrint;
     TPrint  = RECORD
                    iPrVersion: INTEGER;   {Printing Manager version}
                    prInfo:     TPrInfo;   {printer information subrecord}
                    rPaper:     Rect;      {paper rectangle}
                    prStl:      TPrStl;    {additional device information}
                    prInfoPT:   TPrInfo;   {used internally}
                    prXInfo:    TPrXInfo;  {additional device information}
                    prJob:      TPrJob;    {job subrecord}
                    printX:     ARRAY[1..19] OF INTEGER  {not used}
                END;

     TPrInfo = RECORD
                   iDev:  INTEGER;  {used internally}
                   iVRes: INTEGER;  {vertical resolution of printer}
                   iHRes: INTEGER;  {horizontal resolution of printer}
                   rPage: Rect      {page rectangle}
               END;

     TPrJob =
         RECORD
             iFstPage:  INTEGER;     {first page to print}
             iLstPage:  INTEGER;     {last page to print}
             iCopies:   INTEGER;     {number of copies}
             bJDocLoop: SignedByte;  {printing method}
             fFromUsr:  BOOLEAN;     {used internally}
             pIdleProc: ProcPtr;     {background procedure}
             pFileName: StringPtr;   {spool file name}
             iFileVol:  INTEGER;     {spool file volume reference number}
             bFileVers: SignedByte;  {spool file version number}
             bJobX:     SignedByte   {used internally}
         END;

     TPrStl = RECORD
                  wDev: INTEGER;   {high byte specifies device}
                  {more fields for internal use}
              END;
```

```
TPrXInfo = RECORD
                iRowBytes: INTEGER;      {used internally}
                iBandV:    INTEGER;      {used internally}
                iBandH:    INTEGER;      {used internally}
                iDevBytes: INTEGER;      {size of buffer}
             {more fields for internal use}
           END;


TPRect = ^Rect;


TPrStatus = RECORD
                iTotPages:  INTEGER;     {number of pages in spool file}
                iCurPage:   INTEGER;     {page being printed}
                iTotCopies: INTEGER;     {number of copies requested}
                iCurCopy:   INTEGER;     {copy being printed}
                iTotBands:  INTEGER;     {used internally}
                iCurBand:   INTEGER;     {used internally}
                fPgDirty:   BOOLEAN;     {TRUE if started printing page}
                fImaging:   BOOLEAN;     {used internally}
                hPrint:     THPrint;     {print record}
                pPrPort:    TPPrPort;    {printing grafPort}
                hPic:       PicHandle    {used internally}
            END;
```

Routines [Not in ROM]

Initialization and Termination

```
PROCEDURE PrOpen;
PROCEDURE PrClose;
```

Print Records and Dialogs

```
PROCEDURE PrintDefault (hPrint: THPrint);
FUNCTION  PrValidate   (hPrint: THPrint) : BOOLEAN;
FUNCTION  PrStlDialog  (hPrint: THPrint) : BOOLEAN;
FUNCTION  PrJobDialog  (hPrint: THPrint) : BOOLEAN;
PROCEDURE PrJobMerge   (hPrintSrc,hPrintDst: THPrint);
```

Printing

```
FUNCTION  PrOpenDoc  (hPrint: THPrint; pPrPort: TPPrPort; pIOBuf: Ptr) :
                      TPPrPort;
PROCEDURE PrOpenPage (pPrPort: TPPrPort; pPageFrame: TPRect);
PROCEDURE PrClosePage (pPrPort: TPPrPort);
PROCEDURE PrCloseDoc  (pPrPort: TPPrPort);
PROCEDURE PrPicFile   (hPrint: THPrint; pPrPort: TPPrPort; pIOBuf: Ptr;
                       pDevBuf: Ptr; VAR prStatus: TPrStatus);
```

Error Handling

```
FUNCTION  PrError :     INTEGER;
PROCEDURE PrSetError (iErr: INTEGER);
```

Low-Level Driver Access

```
PROCEDURE PrDrvrOpen;
PROCEDURE PrDrvrClose;
PROCEDURE PrCtlCall      (iWhichCtl: INTEGER; lParam1,lParam2,lParam3:
                          LONGINT);
FUNCTION  PrDrvrDCE :    Handle;
FUNCTION  PrDrvrVers :   INTEGER;
```

Assembly-Language Information

Constants

```
; Printing methods

bDraftLoop    .EQU    0       ;draft printing
bSpoolLoop    .EQU    1       ;spool printing

; Result codes

noErr         .EQU     0      ;no error
iPrSavPFil    .EQU    -1      ;saving spool file
controlErr    .EQU    -17     ;unimplemented control instruction
iIOAbort      .EQU    -27     ;I/O abort error
iMemFullErr   .EQU    -108    ;not enough room in heap zone
iPrAbort      .EQU     128    ;application or user requested abort

; Printer Driver Control call parameters

iPrDevCtl     .EQU    7       ;printer control
lPrReset      .EQU    1       ; reset printer
iPrLineFeed   .EQU    3       ; carriage return/paper advance
iPrLFSixth    .EQU    3       ;standard 1/6-inch line feed
lPrPageEnd    .EQU    2       ; end page
iPrBitsCtl    .EQU    4       ;bit map printing
lScreenBits   .EQU    0       ; default for printer
lPaintBits    .EQU    1       ; square dots (72 by 72)
iPrIOCtl      .EQU    5       ;text streaming

; Printer Driver information

iPrDrvrRef    .EQU    -3      ;Printer Driver reference number
```

Printing GrafPort Data Structure

gPort	GrafPort to draw in (portRec bytes)
iPrPortSize	Size in bytes of printing grafPort

Print Record Data Structure

iPrVersion	Printing Manager version (word)
prInfo	Printer information subrecord (14 bytes)
rPaper	Paper rectangle (8 bytes)
prStl	Additional device information (8 bytes)
prXInfo	Additional device information (16 bytes)
prJob	Job subrecord (iPrJobSize bytes)
iPrintSize	Size in bytes of print record

Structure of Printer Information Subrecord

iVRes	Vertical resolution of printer (word)
iHRes	Horizontal resolution of printer (word)
rPage	Page rectangle (8 bytes)

Structure of Job Subrecord

iFstPage	First page to print (word)
iLstPage	Last page to print (word)
iCopies	Number of copies (word)
bJDocLoop	Printing method (byte)
pIdleProc	Address of background procedure
pFileName	Pointer to spool file name (preceded by length byte)
iFileVol	Spool file volume reference number (word)
bFileVers	Spool file version number (byte)
iPrJobSize	Size in bytes of job subrecord

Structure of PrXInfo Subrecord

iDevBytes	Size of buffer (word)

Structure of Printer Status Record

iTotPages	Number of pages in spool file (word)
iCurPage	Page being printed (word)
iTotCopies	Number of copies requested (word)
iCurCopy	Copy being printed (word)
fPgDirty	Nonzero if started printing page (byte)
hPrint	Handle to print record
pPrPort	Pointer to printing grafPort
iPrStatSize	Size in bytes of printer status record

Variables

PrintErr   Result code from last Printing Manager routine (word)

6 THE DEVICE MANAGER

6 Device Manager

ABOUT THIS CHAPTER

This chapter describes the Device Manager, the part of the Operating System that controls the exchange of information between a Macintosh application and devices. It gives general information about using and writing device drivers, and also discusses interrupts: how the Macintosh uses them and how you can use them if you're writing your own device driver.

Note: Specific information about the standard Macintosh drivers is contained in separate chapters.

You should already be familiar with resources, as discussed in chapter 5 of Volume I.

ABOUT THE DEVICE MANAGER

The Device Manager is the part of the Operating System that handles communication between applications and devices. A **device** is a part of the Macintosh, or a piece of external equipment, that can transfer information into or out of the Macintosh. Macintosh devices include disk drives, two serial communications ports, and printers.

Note: The display screen is *not* a device; drawing on the screen is handled by QuickDraw.

There are two kinds of devices: character devices and block devices. A **character device** reads or writes a stream of characters, or bytes, one at a time: It can neither skip bytes nor go back to a previous byte. A character device is used to get information from or send information to the world outside of the Operating System and memory: It can be an input device, an output device, or an input/output device. The serial ports and printers are all character devices.

A **block device** reads and writes blocks of bytes at a time; it can read or write any accessible block on demand. Block devices are usually used to store and retrieve information; for example, disk drives are block devices.

Applications communicate with devices through the Device Manager—either directly or indirectly (through another part of the Operating System or Toolbox). For example, an application can communicate with a disk drive directly via the Device Manager, or indirectly via the File Manager (which calls the Device Manager). The Device Manager doesn't manipulate devices directly; it calls **device drivers** that do (see Figure 1). Device drivers are programs that take data coming from the Device Manager and convert them into actions of devices, or convert device actions into data for the Device Manager to process.

The Operating System includes three standard device drivers in ROM: the Disk Driver, the Sound Driver, and the ROM Serial Driver. There are also a number of standard RAM drivers, including the Printer Driver, the RAM Serial Driver, the AppleTalk drivers, and desk accessories. RAM drivers are resources, and are read from the system resource file as needed.

You can add other drivers independently or build on top of the existing drivers (for example, the Printer Driver is built on top of the Serial Driver); the section "Writing Your Own Device Drivers" describes how to do this. Desk accessories are a special type of device driver, and are manipulated via the routines of the Desk Manager.

6 Device Manager

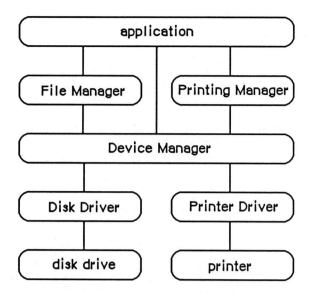

Figure 1. Communication with Devices

Warning: Information about desk accessories covered in chapter 14 of Volume I is not repeated here. Some information in this chapter may not apply to desk accessories.

A device driver can be either **open** or **closed**. The Sound Driver and Disk Driver are opened when the system starts up; the rest of the drivers are opened at the specific request of an application. After a driver has been opened, an application can read data from and write data to it. You can close device drivers that are no longer in use, and recover the memory used by them. Up to 32 device drivers may be open at any one time.

Before it's opened, you identify a device driver by its driver name; after it's opened, you identify it by its reference number. A **driver name** consists of a period (.) followed by any sequence of 1 to 254 printing characters. A RAM driver's name is the same as its resource name. You can use uppercase and lowercase letters when naming drivers, but the Device Manager ignores case when comparing names (it doesn't ignore diacritical marks).

Note: Although device driver names can be quite long, there's little reason for them to be more than a few characters in length.

The Device Manager assigns each open device driver a **driver reference number**, from –1 to –32, that's used instead of its driver name to refer to it.

Most communication between an application and an open device driver occurs by reading and writing data. Data read from a driver is placed in the application's **data buffer**, and data written to a driver is taken from the application's data buffer. A data buffer is memory allocated by the application for communication with drivers.

In addition to data that's read from or written to device drivers, drivers may require or provide other information. Information transmitted to a driver by an application is called **control information**; information provided by a driver is called **status information**. Control information may select modes of operation, start or stop processes, enable buffers, choose protocols, and so on. Status information may indicate the current mode of operation, the readiness of the device, the occurrence of errors, and so on. Each device driver may respond to a number of different types of control information and may provide a number of different types of status information.

Each of the standard Macintosh drivers includes predefined calls for transmitting control information and receiving status information. Explanations of these calls can be found in the chapters describing the drivers.

USING THE DEVICE MANAGER

You can call Device Manager routines via three different methods: high-level Pascal calls, low-level Pascal calls, and assembly language. The high-level Pascal calls are designed for Pascal programmers interested in using the Device Manager in a simple manner; they provide adequate device I/O and don't require much special knowledge to use. The low-level Pascal and assembly-language calls are designed for advanced Pascal programmers and assembly-language programmers interested in using the Device Manager to its fullest capacity; they require some special knowledge to be used most effectively.

> **Note:** The names used to refer to routines here are actually assembly-language macro names for the low-level routines, but the Pascal routine names are very similar.

The Device Manager is automatically initialized each time the system starts up.

Before an application can exchange information with a device driver, the driver must be opened. The Sound Driver and Disk Driver are opened when the system starts up; for other drivers, the application must call Open. The Open routine will return the driver reference number that you'll use every time you want to refer to that device driver.

An application can send data from its data buffer to an open driver with a Write call, and transfer data from an open driver to its data buffer with Read. An application passes control information to a device driver by calling Control, and receives status information from a driver by calling Status.

Whenever you want to stop a device driver from completing I/O initiated by a Read, Write, Control, or Status call, call KillIO. KillIO halts any current I/O and deletes any pending I/O.

When you're through using a driver, call Close. Close forces the device driver to complete any pending I/O, and then releases all the memory used by the driver.

DEVICE MANAGER ROUTINES

This section describes the Device Manager routines used to call drivers. It's divided into two parts: The first describes all the high-level Pascal routines of the Device Manager, and the second presents information about calling the low-level Pascal and assembly-language routines.

All the Device Manager routines in this section return an integer result code of type OSErr. Each routine description lists all of the applicable result codes, along with a short description of what the result code means. Lengthier explanations of all the result codes can be found in the summary at the end of this chapter.

High-Level Device Manager Routines

Note: As described in chapter 4, the FSRead and FSWrite routines are also used to read from and write to files.

FUNCTION OpenDriver (name: Str255; VAR refNum: INTEGER) : OSErr;
        [Not in ROM]

OpenDriver opens the device driver specified by name and returns its reference number in refNum.

Result codes	noErr	No error
	badUnitErr	Bad reference number
	dInstErr	Couldn't find driver in resource file
	openErr	Driver can't perform the requested reading or writing
	unitEmptyErr	Bad reference number

FUNCTION CloseDriver (refNum: INTEGER) : OSErr;   [Not in ROM]

CloseDriver closes the device driver having the reference number refNum. Any pending I/O is completed, and the memory used by the driver is released.

Warning: Before using this command to close a particular driver, refer to the chapter describing the driver for the consequences of closing it.

Result codes	noErr	No error
	badUnitErr	Bad reference number
	dRemoveErr	Attempt to remove an open driver
	unitEmptyErr	Bad reference number

FUNCTION FSRead (refNum: INTEGER; VAR count: LONGINT; buffPtr:
        Ptr) : OSErr;   [Not in ROM]

FSRead attempts to read the number of bytes specified by the count parameter from the open device driver having the reference number refNum, and transfer them to the data buffer pointed to by buffPtr. After the read operation is completed, the number of bytes actually read is returned in the count parameter.

Result codes	noErr	No error
	badUnitErr	Bad reference number
	notOpenErr	Driver isn't open
	unitEmptyErr	Bad reference number
	readErr	Driver can't respond to Read calls

```
FUNCTION FSWrite (refNum: INTEGER; VAR count: LONGINT; buffPtr:
        Ptr) : OSErr;   [Not in ROM]
```

FSWrite takes the number of bytes specified by the count parameter from the buffer pointed to by buffPtr and attempts to write them to the open device driver having the reference number refNum. After the write operation is completed, the number of bytes actually written is returned in the count parameter.

Result codes	noErr	No error
	badUnitErr	Bad reference number
	notOpenErr	Driver isn't open
	unitEmptyErr	Bad reference number
	writErr	Driver can't respond to Write calls

```
FUNCTION Control (refNum: INTEGER; csCode: INTEGER; csParamPtr:
        Ptr) : OSErr;   [Not in ROM]
```

Control sends control information to the device driver having the reference number refNum. The type of information sent is specified by csCode, and the information itself is pointed to by csParamPtr. The values passed in csCode and pointed to by csParamPtr depend on the driver being called.

Result codes	noErr	No error
	badUnitErr	Bad reference number
	notOpenErr	Driver isn't open
	unitEmptyErr	Bad reference number
	controlErr	Driver can't respond to this Control call

```
FUNCTION Status (refNum: INTEGER; csCode: INTEGER; csParamPtr:
        Ptr) : OSErr;   [Not in ROM]
```

Status returns status information about the device driver having the reference number refNum. The type of information returned is specified by csCode, and the information itself is pointed to by csParamPtr. The values passed in csCode and pointed to by csParamPtr depend on the driver being called.

Result codes	noErr	No error
	badUnitErr	Bad reference number
	notOpenErr	Driver isn't open
	unitEmptyErr	Bad reference number
	statusErr	Driver can't respond to this Status call

```
FUNCTION KillIO (refNum: INTEGER) : OSErr;   [Not in ROM]
```

KillIO terminates all current and pending I/O with the device driver having the reference number refNum.

6 Device Manager

Result codes	noErr	No error
	badUnitErr	Bad reference number
	unitEmptyErr	Bad reference number

Low-Level Device Manager Routines

This section contains special information for programmers using the low-level Pascal or assembly-language routines of the Device Manager, and describes them in detail.

Note: The Device Manager routines for writing device drivers are described in the section "Writing Your Own Device Drivers".

All low-level Device Manager routines can be executed either **synchronously** (meaning that the application can't continue until the routine is completed) or **asynchronously** (meaning that the application is free to perform other tasks while the routine is executing). Some cannot be executed asynchronously, because they use the Memory Manager to allocate and release memory.

When an application calls a Device Manager routine asynchronously, an **I/O request** is placed in the **driver I/O queue**, and control returns to the calling program—possibly even before the actual I/O is completed. Requests are taken from the queue one at a time, and processed; meanwhile, the calling program is free to work on other things.

The calling program may specify **a completion routine** to be executed at the end of an asynchronous operation.

Routine parameters passed by an application to the Device Manager and returned by the Device Manager to an application are contained in a **parameter block**, which is a data structure in the heap or stack. All low-level Pascal calls to the Device Manager are of the form

```
FUNCTION PBCallName (paramBlock: ParmBlkPtr; async: BOOLEAN) : OSErr;
```

PBCallName is the name of the routine. ParamBlock points to the parameter block containing the parameters for the routine. If async is TRUE, the call is executed asynchronously; otherwise the call is executed synchronously. Each call returns an integer result code of type OSErr.

Assembly-language note: When you call a Device Manager routine, A0 must point to a parameter block containing the parameters for the routine. If you want the routine to be executed asynchronously, set bit 10 of the routine trap word. You can do this by supplying the word ASYNC as the second argument to the routine macro. For example:

```
_Read  ,ASYNC
```

You can set or test bit 10 of a trap word by using the global constant asyncTrpBit.

If you want a routine to be executed immediately (bypassing the driver I/O queue), set bit 9 of the routine trap word. This can be accomplished by supplying the word IMMED as the second argument to the routine macro. (The driver must be able to handle immediate calls for this to work.) For example:

```
_Write  ,IMMED
```

You can set or test bit 9 of a trap word by using the global constant noQueueBit. You can specify either ASYNC or IMMED, but not both. (The syntax shown above applies to the Lisa Workshop Assembler; programmers using another development system should consult its documentation for the proper syntax.)

All routines return a result code in D0.

Routine Parameters

There are two different kinds of parameter blocks you'll pass to Device Manager routines: one for I/O routines and another for Control and Status calls.

The lengthy, variable-length data structure of a parameter block is given below. The Device Manager and File Manager use this same data structure, but only the parts relevant to the Device Manager are discussed here. Each kind of parameter block contains eight fields of standard information and three to nine fields of additional information:

```
TYPE  ParamBlkType   = (ioParam,fileParam,volumeParam,cntrlParam);

      ParamBlockRec  =
          RECORD
              qLink:        QElemPtr;    {next queue entry}
              qType:        INTEGER;     {queue type}
              ioTrap:       INTEGER;     {routine trap}
              ioCmdAddr:    Ptr;         {routine address}
              ioCompletion: ProcPtr;     {completion routine}
              ioResult:     OSErr;       {result code}
              ioNamePtr:    StringPtr;   {driver name}
              ioVRefNum:    INTEGER;     {volume reference or drive number}
              CASE ParamBlkType OF
                  ioParam:
                    . . . {I/O routine parameters}
                  fileParam:
                    . . . {used by the File Manager}
                  volumeParam:
                    . . . {used by the File Manager}
                  cntrlParam:
                    . . . {Control and Status call parameters}
          END;

      ParmBlkPtr = ^ParamBlockRec;
```

The first four fields in each parameter block are handled entirely by the Device Manager, and most programmers needn't be concerned with them; programmers who are interested in them should see the section "The Structure of a Device Driver".

IOCompletion contains a pointer to a completion routine to be executed at the end of an asynchronous call; it should be NIL for asynchronous calls with no completion routine, and is automatically set to NIL for all synchronous calls.

> **Warning:** Completion routines are executed at the interrupt level and must preserve all registers other than A0, A1, and D0-D2. Your completion routine must not make any calls

6 Device Manager

to the Memory Manager, directly or indirectly, and can't depend on handles to unlocked blocks being valid. If it uses application globals, it must also ensure that register A5 contains the address of the boundary between the application globals and the application parameters; for details, see SetUpA5 and RestoreA5 in chapter 13.

Assembly-language note: When your completion routine is called, register A0 points to the parameter block of the asynchronous call and register D0 contains the result code.

Routines that are executed asynchronously return control to the calling program with the result code noErr as soon as the call is placed in the driver I/O queue. This isn't an indication of successful call completion, but simply indicates that the call was successfully queued. To determine when the call is actually completed, you can poll the ioResult field; this field is set to 1 when the call is made, and receives the actual result code upon completion of the call. Completion routines are executed after the result code is placed in ioResult.

IONamePtr is a pointer to the name of a driver and is used only for calls to the Open function. IOVRefNum is used by the Disk Driver to identify drives.

I/O routines use the following additional fields:

```
ioParam:
   (ioRefNum:    INTEGER;        {driver reference number}
    ioVersNum:   SignedByte;     {not used}
    ioPermssn:   SignedByte;     {read/write permission}
    ioMisc:      Ptr;            {not used}
    ioBuffer:    Ptr;            {pointer to data buffer}
    ioReqCount:  LONGINT;        {requested number of bytes}
    ioActCount:  LONGINT;        {actual number of bytes}
    ioPosMode:   INTEGER;        {positioning mode}
    ioPosOffset: LONGINT);       {positioning offset}
```

IOPermssn requests permission to read from or write to a driver when the driver is opened, and must contain one of the following values:

```
CONST fsCurPerm   = 0;     {whatever is currently allowed}
      fsRdPerm    = 1;     {request to read only}
      fsWrPerm    = 2;     {request to write only}
      fsRdWrPerm  = 3;     {request to read and write}
```

This request is compared with the capabilities of the driver (some drivers are read-only, some are write-only). If the driver is incapable of performing as requested, a result code indicating the error is returned.

IOBuffer points to a data buffer into which data is written by Read calls and from which data is read by Write calls. IOReqCount specifies the requested number of bytes to be read or written. IOActCount contains the number of bytes actually read or written.

IOPosMode and ioPosOffset contain positioning information used for Read and Write calls by drivers of block devices. IOPosMode contains the positioning mode; bits 0 and 1 indicate where an operation should begin relative to the physical beginning of the block-formatted medium (such as a disk). You can use the following predefined constants to test or set the value of these bits:

```
CONST fsAtMark   = 0;   {at current position}
      fsFromStar = 1;   {offset relative to beginning of medium}
      fsFromMark = 3;   {offset relative to current position}
```

IOPosOffset specifies the byte offset (either positive or negative), relative to the position specified by the positioning mode, where the operation will be performed (except when the positioning mode is fsAtMark, in which case ioPosOffset is ignored). IOPosOffset must be a 512-byte multiple.

To verify that data written to a block device matches the data in memory, make a Read call right after the Write call. The parameters for a read-verify operation are the same as for a standard Read call, except that the following constant must be added to the positioning mode:

```
CONST rdVerify = 64;   {read-verify mode}
```

The result code ioErr is returned if any of the data doesn't match.

Control and Status calls use three additional fields:

```
cntrlParam:
  (ioCRefNum: INTEGER;    {driver reference number}
   csCode:    INTEGER;    {type of Control or Status call}
   csParam:   ARRAY[0..10] OF INTEGER); {control or status information}
```

IOCRefNum contains the reference number of the device driver. The csCode field contains a number identifying the type of call; this number may be interpreted differently by each driver. The csParam field contains the control or status information for the call; it's declared as up to 22 bytes of information because its exact contents will vary from one Control or Status call to the next. To store information in this field, you must perform the proper type coercion.

Routine Descriptions

This section describes the procedures and functions. Each routine description includes the low-level Pascal form of the call and the routine's assembly-language macro. A list of the fields in the parameter block affected by the call is also given.

Assembly-language note: The field names given in these descriptions are those of the ParamBlockRec data type; see the summary at the end of this chapter for the names of the corresponding assembly-language offsets. (The names for some offsets differ from their Pascal equivalents, and in certain cases more than one name for the same offset is provided.)

The number next to each parameter name indicates the byte offset of the parameter from the start of the parameter block pointed to by register A0; only assembly-language programmers need be concerned with it. An arrow next to each parameter name indicates whether it's an input, output, or input/output parameter:

Arrow	Meaning
→	Parameter is passed to the routine
←	Parameter is returned by the routine
↔	Parameter is passed to and returned by the routine

Note: As described in chapter 4, the Open and Close functions are also used to open and close files.

```
FUNCTION PBOpen (paramBlock: ParmBlkPtr; async: BOOLEAN) : OSErr;
```

Trap macro   _Open

Parameter block

→	12	ioCompletion	pointer
←	16	ioResult	word
→	18	ioNamePtr	pointer
←	24	ioRefNum	word
→	27	ioPermssn	byte

PBOpen opens the device driver specified by ioNamePtr, reading it into memory if necessary, and returns its reference number in ioRefNum. IOPermssn specifies the requested read/write permission.

Result codes	noErr	No error
	badUnitErr	Bad reference number
	dInstErr	Couldn't find driver in resource file
	openErr	Driver can't perform the requested reading or writing
	unitEmptyErr	Bad reference number

```
FUNCTION PBClose (paramBlock: ParmBlkPtr; async: BOOLEAN) : OSErr;
```

Trap macro   _Close

Parameter block

→	12	ioCompletion	pointer
←	16	ioResult	word
→	24	ioRefNum	word

PBClose closes the device driver having the reference number ioRefNum. Any pending I/O is completed, and the memory used by the driver is released.

Result codes	noErr	No error
	badUnitErr	Bad reference number
	dRemovErr	Attempt to remove an open driver
	unitEmptyErr	Bad reference number

```
FUNCTION PBRead (paramBlock: ParmBlkPtr; async: BOOLEAN) : OSErr;
```

Trap macro   _Read

Parameter block

→	12	ioCompletion	pointer
←	16	ioResult	word
→	22	ioVRefNum	word
→	24	ioRefNum	word
→	32	ioBuffer	pointer
→	36	ioReqCount	long word
←	40	ioActCount	long word
→	44	ioPosMode	word
↔	46	ioPosOffset	long word

PBRead attempts to read ioReqCount bytes from the device driver having the reference number ioRefNum, and transfer them to the data buffer pointed to by ioBuffer. The drive number, if any, of the device to be read from is specified by ioVRefNum. After the read is completed, the position is returned in ioPosOffset and the number of bytes actually read is returned in ioActCount.

Result codes	noErr	No error
	badUnitErr	Bad reference number
	notOpenErr	Driver isn't open
	unitEmptyErr	Bad reference number
	readErr	Driver can't respond to Read calls

```
FUNCTION PBWrite (paramBlock: ParmBlkPtr; async: BOOLEAN) :
         OSErr;
```

Trap macro   _Write

Parameter block

→	12	ioCompletion	pointer
←	16	ioResult	word
→	22	ioVRefNum	word
→	24	ioRefNum	word
→	32	ioBuffer	pointer
→	36	ioReqCount	long word
←	40	ioActCount	long word
→	44	ioPosMode	word
↔	46	ioPosOffset	long word

PBWrite takes ioReqCount bytes from the buffer pointed to by ioBuffer and attempts to write them to the device driver having the reference number ioRefNum. The drive number, if any, of the device to be written to is specified by ioVRefNum. After the write is completed, the position is returned in ioPosOffset and the number of bytes actually written is returned in ioActCount.

Result codes	noErr	No error
	badUnitErr	Bad reference number
	notOpenErr	Driver isn't open
	unitEmptyErr	Bad reference number
	writErr	Driver can't respond to Write calls

```
FUNCTION PBControl (paramBlock: ParmBlkPtr; async: BOOLEAN) :
            OSErr;
```

Trap macro   _Control

Parameter block

→	12	ioCompletion	pointer
←	16	ioResult	word
→	22	ioVRefNum	word
→	24	ioRefNum	word
→	26	csCode	word
→	28	csParam	record

PBControl sends control information to the device driver having the reference number ioRefNum; the drive number, if any, is specified by ioVRefNum. The type of information sent is specified by csCode, and the information itself begins at csParam. The values passed in csCode and csParam depend on the driver being called.

Result codes	noErr	No error
	badUnitErr	Bad reference number
	notOpenErr	Driver isn't open
	unitEmptyErr	Bad reference number
	controlErr	Driver can't respond to this Control call

```
FUNCTION PBStatus (paramBlock: ParmBlkPtr; async: BOOLEAN) :
            OSErr;
```

Trap macro   _Status

Parameter block

→	12	ioCompletion	pointer
←	16	ioResult	word
→	22	ioVRefNum	word
→	24	ioRefNum	word
→	26	csCode	word
←	28	csParam	record

PBStatus returns status information about the device driver having the reference number ioRefNum; the drive number, if any, is specified by ioVRefNum. The type of information returned is specified by csCode, and the information itself begins at csParam. The values passed in csCode and csParam depend on the driver being called.

Result codes	noErr	No error
	badUnitErr	Bad reference number
	notOpenErr	Driver isn't open
	unitEmptyErr	Bad reference number
	statusErr	Driver can't respond to this Status call

```
FUNCTION PBKillIO (paramBlock: ParmBlkPtr; async: BOOLEAN) :
         OSErr;
```

Trap macro   _KillIO

Parameter block

→	12	ioCompletion	pointer
←	16	ioResult	word
→	24	ioRefNum	word

PBKillIO stops any current I/O request being processed, and removes all pending I/O requests from the I/O queue of the device driver having the reference number ioRefNum. The completion routine of each pending I/O request is called, with the ioResult field of each request equal to the result code abortErr.

Result codes	noErr	No error
	badUnitErr	Bad reference number
	unitEmptyErr	Bad reference number

THE STRUCTURE OF A DEVICE DRIVER

This section describes the structure of device drivers for programmers interested in writing their own driver or manipulating existing drivers. Some of the information presented here is accessible only through assembly language.

RAM drivers are stored in resource files. The resource type for drivers is 'DRVR'. The resource name is the driver name. The resource ID for a driver is its unit number (explained below) and must be between 0 and 31 inclusive.

Warning: Don't use the unit number of an existing driver unless you want the existing driver to be replaced.

As shown in Figure 2, a driver begins with a few words of flags and other data, followed by offsets to the routines that do the work of the driver, an optional title, and finally the routines themselves.

Every driver contains a routine to handle Open and Close calls, and may contain routines to handle Read, Write, Control, Status, and KillIO calls. The driver routines that handle Device Manager calls are as follows:

Device Manager call	Driver routine
Open	Open
Read	Prime
Write	Prime
Control	Control
KillIO	Control
Status	Status
Close	Close

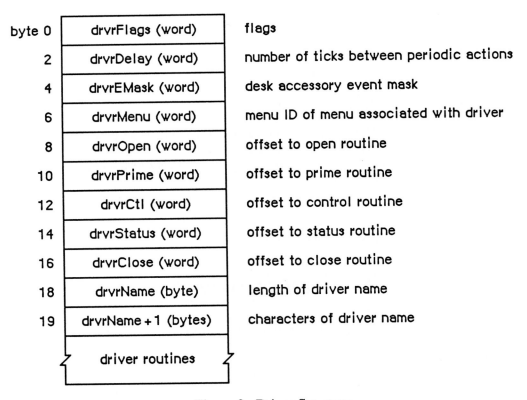

byte 0	drvrFlags (word)	flags
2	drvrDelay (word)	number of ticks between periodic actions
4	drvrEMask (word)	desk accessory event mask
6	drvrMenu (word)	menu ID of menu associated with driver
8	drvrOpen (word)	offset to open routine
10	drvrPrime (word)	offset to prime routine
12	drvrCtl (word)	offset to control routine
14	drvrStatus (word)	offset to status routine
16	drvrClose (word)	offset to close routine
18	drvrName (byte)	length of driver name
19	drvrName + 1 (bytes)	characters of driver name
	driver routines	

Figure 2. Driver Structure

For example, when a KillIO call is made to a driver, the driver's control routine must implement the call.

Each bit of the *high-order* byte of the drvrFlags word contains a flag:

```
dReadEnable     .EQU    0   ;set if driver can respond to Read calls
dWritEnable     .EQU    1   ;set if driver can respond to Write calls
dCtlEnable      .EQU    2   ;set if driver can respond to Control calls
dStatEnable     .EQU    3   ;set if driver can respond to Status calls
dNeedGoodBye    .EQU    4   ;set if driver needs to be called before the
                            ; application heap is reinitialized
dNeedTime       .EQU    5   ;set if driver needs time for performing a
                            ; periodic action
dNeedLock       .EQU    6   ;set if driver will be locked in memory as
                            ; soon as it's opened (always set for ROM
                            ; drivers)
```

Bits 8-11 (bits 0-3 of the high-order byte) indicate which Device Manager calls the driver's routines can respond to.

Unlocked RAM drivers in the application heap will be lost every time the heap is reinitialized (when an application starts up, for example). If dNeedGoodBye is set, the control routine of the device driver will be called before the heap is reinitialized, and the driver can perform any "clean-up" actions it needs to. The driver's control routine identifies this "good-bye" call by checking the csCode parameter—it will be the global constant

```
goodBye    .EQU  -1    ;heap will be reinitialized, clean up if necessary
```

Device drivers may need to perform predefined actions periodically. For example, a network driver may want to poll its input buffer every ten seconds to see if it has received any messages. If the dNeedTime flag is set, the driver *does* need to perform a periodic action, and the drvrDelay word contains a tick count indicating how often the periodic action should occur. A tick count of 0 means it should happen as often as possible, 1 means it should happen at most every sixtieth of a second, 2 means at most every thirtieth of a second, and so on. Whether the action actually occurs this frequently depends on how often the application calls the Desk Manager procedure SystemTask. SystemTask calls the driver's control routine (if the time indicated by drvrDelay has elapsed), and the control routine must perform whatever predefined action is desired. The driver's control routine identifies the SystemTask call by checking the csCode parameter—it will be the global constant

```
accRun    .EQU  65    ;take the periodic action, if any, for this driver
```

Note: Some drivers may not want to rely on the application to call SystemTask. They can instead install a task to be executed during the vertical retrace interrupt. There are, however, certain restrictions on tasks performed during interrupts, such as not being able to make calls to the Memory Manager. For more information on these restrictions, see chapter 11. Periodic actions performed in response to SystemTask calls are not performed via an interrupt and so don't have these restrictions.

DrvrEMask and drvrMenu are used only for desk accessories and are discussed in chapter 14 of Volume I.

Following drvrMenu are the offsets to the driver routines, a title for the driver (preceded by its length in bytes), and the routines that do the work of the driver.

Note: Each of the driver routines must be aligned on a word boundary.

Device Control Entry

The first time a driver is opened, information about it is read into a structure in memory called a **device control entry**. A device control entry contains the header of the driver's I/O queue, the location of the driver's routines, and other information. A device control entry is a 40-byte relocatable block located in the system heap. It's locked while the driver is open, and unlocked while the driver is closed.

Most of the data in the device control entry is stored and accessed only by the Device Manager, but in some cases the driver itself must store into it. The structure of a device control entry is shown below; note that the first four words of the driver are copied into the dCtlFlags, dCtlDelay, dCtlEMask, and dCtlMenu fields.

```
TYPE DCtlEntry =
  RECORD
    dCtlDriver:    Ptr;         {pointer to ROM driver or handle to RAM driver}
    dCtlFlags:     INTEGER;     {flags}
    dCtlQHdr:      QHdr;        {driver I/O queue header}
    dCtlPosition:  LONGINT;     {byte position used by Read and Write calls}
    dCtlStorage:   Handle;      {handle to RAM driver's private storage}
    dCtlRefNum:    INTEGER;     {driver reference number}
    dCtlCurTicks:  LONGINT;     {used internally}
    dCtlWindow:    WindowPtr;   {pointer to driver's window}
    dCtlDelay:     INTEGER;     {number of ticks between periodic actions}
    dCtlEMask:     INTEGER;     {desk accessory event mask}
    dCtlMenu:      INTEGER      {menu ID of menu associated with driver}
  END;

    DCtlPtr    = ^DCtlEntry;
    DCtlHandle = ^DCtlPtr;
```

The low-order byte of the dCtlFlags word contains the following flags:

Bit number	Meaning
5	Set if driver is open
6	Set if driver is RAM-based
7	Set if driver is currently executing

Assembly-language note: These flags can be accessed with the global constants dOpened, dRAMBased, and drvrActive.

The high-order byte of the dCtlFlags word contains flags copied from the drvrFlags word of the driver, as described above.

DCtlQHdr contains the header of the driver's I/O queue (described below). DCtlPosition is used only by drivers of block devices, and indicates the current source or destination position of a Read or Write call. The position is given as a number of bytes beyond the physical beginning of the medium used by the device. For example, if one logical block of data has just been read from a 3 1/2-inch disk via the Disk Driver, dCtlPosition will be 512.

ROM drivers generally use locations in low memory for their local storage. RAM drivers may reserve memory within their code space, or allocate a relocatable block and keep a handle to it in dCtlStorage (if the block resides in the application heap, its handle will be set to NIL when the heap is reinitialized).

You can get a handle to a driver's device control entry by calling the Device Manager function GetDCtlEntry.

```
FUNCTION GetDCtlEntry (refNum: INTEGER) : DCtlHandle;   [Not in ROM]
```

GetDCtlEntry returns a handle to the device control entry of the device driver having the reference number refNum.

Assembly-language note: You can get a handle to a driver's device control entry from the unit table, as described below.

The Driver I/O Queue

Each device driver has a driver I/O queue; this is a standard Operating System queue (described in chapter 13) that contains the parameter blocks for all asynchronous routines awaiting execution. Each time a routine is called, the driver places an entry in the queue; each time a routine is completed, its entry is removed from the queue. The queue's header is located in the dCtlQHdr field of the driver's device control entry. The low-order byte of the queue flags field in the queue header contains the version number of the driver, and can be used for distinguishing between different versions of the same driver.

Each entry in the driver I/O queue consists of a parameter block for the routine that was called. Most of the fields of this parameter block contain information needed by the specific Device Manager routines; these fields are explained above in the section "Low-Level Device Manager Routines". The first four fields of this parameter block, shown below, are used by the Device Manager in processing the I/O requests in the queue.

```
TYPE ParamBlockRec = RECORD
                    qLink:     QElemPtr;    {next queue entry}
                    qType:     INTEGER;     {queue type}
                    ioTrap:    INTEGER;     {routine trap}
                    ioCmdAddr: Ptr;         {routine address}
                    . . .                   {rest of block}
                  END;
```

QLink points to the next entry in the queue, and qType indicates the queue type, which must always be ORD(ioQType). IOTrap and ioCmdAddr contain the trap and address of the Device Manager routine that was called.

The Unit Table

The location of each device control entry is maintained in a list called the **unit table**. The unit table is a 128-byte nonrelocatable block containing 32 four-byte entries. Each entry has a number, from 0 to 31, called the **unit number**, and contains a handle to the device control entry for a driver. The unit number can be used as an index into the unit table to locate the handle to a specific driver's device control entry; it's equal to

$$-1 * (\text{refNum} + 1)$$

where refNum is the driver reference number. For example, the Sound Driver's reference number is −4 and its unit number is 3.

Figure 3 shows the layout of the unit table with the standard drivers and desk accessories installed.

6 Device Manager

byte 0	reserved	unit number 0
4	hard disk driver (XL only)	1
8	Printer Driver	2
12	Sound Driver	3
16	Disk Driver	4
20	Serial Driver port A input	5
24	Serial Driver port A output	6
28	Serial Driver port B input	7
32	Serial Driver port B output	8
36	AppleTalk .MPP Driver	9
40	AppleTalk .ATP Driver	10
44	reserved	11
48	Calculator	12
52	Alarm Clock	13
56	Key Caps	14·
60	Puzzle	15
64	Note Pad	16
68	Scrapbook	17
72	Control Panel	18
	not used	
124	not used	31

Figure 3. The Unit Table

Warning: Any new drivers contained in resource files should have resource IDs that don't conflict with the unit numbers of existing drivers—unless you want an existing driver to be replaced. Be sure to check the unit table before installing a new driver; the base address of the unit table is stored in the global variable UTableBase.

WRITING YOUR OWN DEVICE DRIVERS

Drivers are usually written in assembly language. The structure of your driver must match that shown in the previous section. The routines that do the work of the driver should be written to operate the device in whatever way you require. Your driver must contain routines to handle Open and Close calls, and may choose to handle Read, Write, Control, Status, and KillIO calls as well.

> **Warning:** A device driver doesn't "own" the hardware it operates, and has no way of determining whether another driver is attempting to use that hardware at the same time. There's a possiblity of conflict in situations where two drivers that operate the same device are installed concurrently.

When the Device Manager executes a driver routine to handle an application call, it passes a pointer to the call's parameter block in register A0 and a pointer to the driver's device control entry in register A1. From this information, the driver can determine exactly what operations are required to fulfill the call's requests, and do them.

Open and close routines must execute synchronously and return via an RTS instruction. They needn't preserve any registers that they use. Close routines should put a result code in register D0. Since the Device Manager sets D0 to 0 upon return from an Open call, open routines should instead place the result code in the ioResult field of the parameter block.

The **open routine** must allocate any private storage required by the driver, store a handle to it in the device control entry (in the dCtlStorage field), initialize any local variables, and then be ready to receive a Read, Write, Status, Control, or KillIO call. It might also install interrupt handlers, change interrupt vectors, and store a pointer to the device control entry somewhere in its local storage for its interrupt handlers to use. The **close routine** must reverse the effects of the open routine, by releasing all used memory, removing interrupt handlers, and replacing changed interrupt vectors. If anything about the operational state of the driver should be saved until the next time the driver is opened, it should be kept in the relocatable block of memory pointed to by dCtlStorage.

Prime, control, and status routines must be able to respond to queued calls and asynchronous calls, and should be interrupt-driven. Asynchronous portions of the routines can use registers A0-A3 and D0-D3, but must preserve any other registers used; synchronous portions can use all registers. Prime, control, and status routines should return a result code in D0. They must return via an RTS if called immediately (with noQueueBit set in the ioTrap field) or if the device couldn't complete the I/O request right away, or via a JMP to the IODone routine (explained below) if not called immediately and if the device completed the request.

> **Warning:** If the prime, control, and status routines can be called as the result of an interrupt, they must preserve all registers other than A0, A1, and D0-D2. They can't make any calls to the Memory Manager and cannot depend on unlocked handles being valid. If they use application globals, they must also ensure that register A5 contains the address of the boundary between the application globals and the application parameters; for details, see SetUpA5 and RestoreA5 in chapter 13.

The **prime routine** implements Read and Write calls made to the driver. It can distinguish between Read and Write calls by comparing the low-order byte of the ioTrap field with the following predefined constants:

```
aRdCmd      .EQU    2      ;Read call
aWrCmd      .EQU    3      ;Write call
```

You may want to use the Fetch and Stash routines (described below) to read and write characters. If the driver is for a block device, it should update the dCtlPosition field of the device control entry after each read or write.

The **control routine** accepts the control information passed to it, and manipulates the device as requested. The **status routine** returns requested status information. Since both the control and status routines may be subjected to Control and Status calls sending and requesting a variety of information, they must be prepared to respond correctly to all types. The control routine must handle KillIO calls. The driver identifies KillIO calls by checking the csCode parameter—it will be the global constant

```
killCode    .EQU    1      ;handle the KillIO call
```

Warning: KillIO calls must return via an RTS, and shouldn't jump (via JMP) to the IODone routine.

Routines for Writing Drivers

The Device Manager includes three routines—Fetch, Stash, and IODone—that provide low-level support for driver routines. These routines can be used only with a pending, asynchronous request; include them in the code of your device driver if they're useful to you. A pointer to the device control entry is passed to each of these routines in register A1. The device control entry contains the driver I/O queue header, which is used to locate the pending request. If there are no pending requests, these routines generate the system error dsIOCoreErr (see chapter 12 for more information).

Fetch, Stash, and IODone are invoked via "jump vectors" (stored in the global variables JFetch, JStash, and JIODone) rather than macros, in the interest of speed. You use a jump vector by moving its address onto the stack. For example:

```
MOVE.L          JIODone,-(SP)
RTS
```

Fetch and Stash don't return a result code; if an error occurs, the System Error Handler is invoked. IODone may return a result code.

Fetch function

Jump vector	JFetch
On entry	A1: pointer to device control entry
On exit	D0: character fetched; bit 15=1 if it's the last character in data buffer

Fetch gets the next character from the data buffer pointed to by ioBuffer and places it in D0. IOActCount is incremented by 1. If ioActCount equals ioReqCount, bit 15 of D0 is set. After receiving the last byte requested, the driver should call IODone.

Stash function

Jump vector	JStash
On entry	A1: pointer to device control entry
	D0: character to stash
On exit	D0: bit 15=1 if it's the last character requested

Stash places the character in D0 into the data buffer pointed to by ioBuffer, and increments ioActCount by 1. If ioActCount equals ioReqCount, bit 15 of D0 is set. After stashing the last byte requested, the driver should call IODone.

IODone function

Jump vector	JIODone
On entry	A1: pointer to device control entry
	D0: result code (word)

IODone removes the current I/O request from the driver I/O queue, marks the driver inactive, unlocks the driver and its device control entry (if it's allowed to by the dNeedLock bit of the dCtlFlags word), and executes the completion routine (if there is one). Then it begins executing the next I/O request in the driver I/O queue.

Warning: Due to the way the File Manager does directory lookups, block device drivers should take care to support asynchronous I/O operations. If the driver's prime routine has completed an asynchronous Read or Write call just prior to calling IODone *and* its completion routine starts an additional Read or Write, large amounts of the stack may be used (potentially causing the stack to expand into the heap). To avoid this problem, the prime routine should exit via an RTS instruction and then jump to IODone via an interrupt.

INTERRUPTS

This section discusses how **interrupts** are used on the Macintosh 128K and 512K; only programmers who want to write interrupt-driven device drivers need read this section.

Warning: Only the Macintosh 128K and 512K are covered in this section. Much of the information presented here is hardware-dependent; programmers are encouraged to write code that's hardware-independent to ensure compatibility with future versions of the Macintosh.

An interrupt is a form of **exception**: an error or abnormal condition detected by the processor in the course of program execution. Specifically, an interrupt is an exception that's signaled to the processor by a device, as distinct from a trap, which arises directly from the execution of an instruction. Interrupts are used by devices to notify the processor of a change in condition of the device, such as the completion of an I/O request. An interrupt causes the processor to suspend normal execution, save the address of the next instruction and the processor's internal status on the stack, and execute an **interrupt handler**.

The MC68000 recognizes seven different levels of interrupt, each with its own interrupt handler. The addresses of the various handlers, called **interrupt vectors**, are kept in a **vector table** in low memory. Each level of interrupt has its own vector located in the vector table. When an interrupt occurs, the processor fetches the proper vector from the table, uses it to locate the interrupt handler for that level of interrupt, and jumps to the handler. On completion, the handler restores the internal status of the processor from the stack and resumes normal execution from the point of suspension.

There are three devices that can create interrupts: the Synertek SY6522 Versatile Interface Adapter (VIA), the Zilog Z8530 Serial Communications Controller (SCC), and the debugging switch. They send a three-bit number called the **interrupt priority level** to the processor. This number indicates which device is interrupting, and which interrupt handler should be executed:

Level	Interrupting device
0	None
1	VIA
2	SCC
3	VIA and SCC
4-7	Debugging switch

A level-3 interrupt occurs when both the VIA and the SCC interrupt at the same instant; the interrupt handler for a level-3 interrupt is simply an RTE instruction. Debugging interrupts shouldn't occur during the normal execution of an application.

The interrupt priority level is compared with the **processor priority** in bits 8-10 of the status register. If the interrupt priority level is greater than the processor priority, the MC68000 acknowledges the interrupt and initiates interrupt processing. The processor priority determines which interrupting devices are ignored, and which are serviced:

Level	Services
0	All interrupts
1	SCC and debugging interrupts only
2-6	Debugging interrupts only
7	No interrupts

When an interrupt is acknowledged, the processor priority is set to the interrupt priority level, to prevent additional interrupts of equal or lower priority, until the interrupt handler has finished servicing the interrupt.

The interrupt priority level is used as an index into the primary interrupt vector table. This table contains seven long words beginning at address $64. Each long word contains the starting address of an interrupt handler (see Figure 4).

Execution jumps to the interrupt handler at the address specified in the table. The interrupt handler must identify and service the interrupt. Then it must restore the processor priority, status register, and program counter to the values they contained before the interrupt occurred.

$64	autoInt1	vector to level-1 interrupt handler
$68	autoInt2	vector to level-2 interrupt handler
$6C	autoInt3	vector to level-3 interrupt handler
$70	autoInt4	vector to level-4 interrupt handler
$74	autoInt5	vector to level-5 interrupt handler
$78	autoInt6	vector to level-6 interrupt handler
$7C	autoInt7	vector to level-7 interrupt handler

Figure 4. Primary Interrupt Vector Table

Level-1 (VIA) Interrupts

Level-1 interrupts are generated by the VIA. You'll need to read the Synertek manual describing the VIA to use most of the information provided in this section. The level-1 interrupt handler determines the source of the interrupt (via the VIA's interrupt flag register and interrupt enable register) and then uses a table of secondary vectors in low memory to determine which interrupt handler to call (see Figure 5).

byte 0	one-second interrupt	VIA's CA2 control line
4	vertical retrace interrupt	VIA's CA1 control line
8	shift-register interrupt	VIA's shift register
12	not used	
16	not used	
20	T2 timer: Disk Driver	VIA's timer 2
24	T1 timer: Sound Driver	VIA's timer 1
28	not used	

Figure 5. Level-1 Secondary Interrupt Vector Table

The level-1 secondary interrupt vector table is stored in the global variable Lvl1DT. Each vector in the table points to the interrupt handler for a different source of interrupt. The interrupts are handled in order of their entry in the table, and only one interrupt handler is called per level-1 interrupt (even if two or more sources are interrupting). This allows the level-1 interrupt handler to be reentrant; interrupt handlers should lower the processor priority as soon as possible in order to enable other pending interrupts to be processed.

The one-second interrupt updates the global variable Time (explained in chapter 13); it's also used for inverting ("blinking") the apple symbol in the menu bar when the alarm goes off. Vertical retrace interrupts are generated once every vertical retrace interval; control is passed to the Vertical Retrace Manager, which performs recurrent system tasks (such as updating the global variable Ticks) and executes tasks installed by the application. (For more information, see chapter 11.)

If the cumulative elapsed time for all tasks during a vertical retrace interrupt exceeds about 16 milliseconds (one video frame), the vertical retrace interrupt may itself be interrupted by another vertical retrace interrupt. In this case, tasks to be performed during the second vertical retrace interrupt are ignored, with one exception: The global variable Ticks will still be updated.

The shift-register interrupt is used by the keyboard and mouse interrupt handlers. Whenever the Disk Driver or Sound Driver isn't being used, you can use the T1 and T2 timers for your own needs; there's no way to tell, however, when they'll be needed again by the Disk Driver or Sound Driver.

The base address of the VIA (stored in the global variable VIA) is passed to each interrupt handler in register A1.

Level-2 (SCC) Interrupts

Level-2 interrupts are generated by the SCC. You'll need to read the Zilog manual describing the SCC to effectively use the information provided in this section. The level-2 interrupt handler determines the source of the interrupt, and then uses a table of secondary vectors in low memory to determine which interrupt handler to call (see Figure 6).

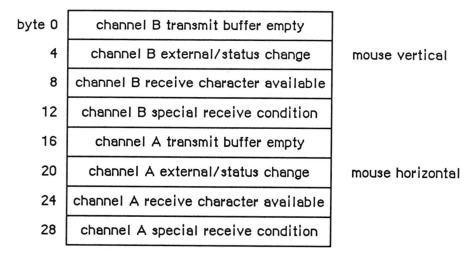

Figure 6. Level-2 Secondary Interrupt Vector Table

The level-2 secondary interrupt vector table is stored in the global variable Lvl2DT. Each vector in the table points to the interrupt handler for a different source of interrupt. The interrupts are handled according to the following fixed priority:

    channel A receive character available and special receive
    channel A transmit buffer empty
    channel A external/status change
    channel B receive character available and special receive
    channel B transmit buffer empty
    channel B external/status change

Only one interrupt handler is called per level-2 interrupt (even if two or more sources are interrupting). This allows the level-2 interrupt handler to be reentrant; interrupt handlers should lower the processor priority as soon as possible in order to enable other pending interrupts to be processed.

External/status interrupts pass through a tertiary vector table in low memory to determine which interrupt handler to call (see Figure 7).

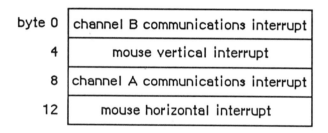

Figure 7. Level-2 External/Status Interrupt Vector Table

The external/status interrupt vector table is stored in the global variable ExtStsDT. Each vector in the table points to the interrupt handler for a different source of interrupt. Communications interrupts (break/abort, for example) are always handled before mouse interrupts.

When a level-2 interrupt handler is called, D0 contains the address of the SCC read register 0 (external/status interrupts only), and D1 contains the bits of read register 0 that have changed since the last external/status interrupt. A0 points to the SCC channel A or channel B control read address and A1 points to SCC channel A or channel B control write address, depending on which channel is interrupting. The SCC's data read address and data write address are located four bytes beyond A0 and A1, respectively; they're also contained in the global variables SCCWr and

SCCRd. You can use the following predefined constants as offsets from these base addresses to locate the SCC control and data lines:

```
aData      .EQU      6       ;channel A data in or out
aCtl       .EQU      2       ;channel A control
bData      .EQU      4       ;channel B data in or out
bCtl       .EQU      0       ;channel B control
```

6 Device Manager

Writing Your Own Interrupt Handlers

You can write your own interrupt handlers to replace any of the standard interrupt handlers just described. Be sure to place a vector that points to your interrupt handler in one of the vector tables.

Both the level-1 and level-2 interrupt handlers preserve registers A0-A3 and D0-D3. Every interrupt handler (except for external/status interrupt handlers) is responsible for clearing the source of the interrupt, and for saving and restoring any additional registers used. Interrupt handlers should return directly via an RTS instruction, unless the interrupt is completing an asynchronous call, in which case they should jump (via JMP) to the IODone routine.

SUMMARY OF THE DEVICE MANAGER

Constants

```
CONST { Values for requesting read/write access }

        fsCurPerm    = 0;     {whatever is currently allowed}
        fsRdPerm     = 1;     {request to read only}
        fsWrPerm     = 2;     {request to write only}
        fsRdWrPerm   = 3;     {request to read and write}


        { Positioning modes }

        fsAtMark     = 0;     {at current position}
        fsFromStart  = 1;     {offset relative to beginning of medium}
        fsFromMark   = 3;     {offset relative to current position}
        rdVerify     = 64;    {add to above for read-verify}
```

Data Types

```
TYPE  ParamBlkType   = (ioParam,fileParam,volumeParam,cntrlParam);

      ParmBlkPtr      = ^ParamBlockRec;
      ParamBlockRec  = RECORD
          qLink:          QElemPtr;      {next queue entry}
          qType:          INTEGER;       {queue type}
          ioTrap:         INTEGER;       {routine trap}
          ioCmdAddr:      Ptr;           {routine address}
          ioCompletion:   ProcPtr;       {completion routine}
          ioResult:       OSErr;         {result code}
          ioNamePtr:      StringPtr;     {driver name}
          ioVRefNum:      INTEGER;       {volume reference or drive number}
        CASE ParamBlkType OF
          ioParam:
          (ioRefNum:      INTEGER;       {driver reference number}
           ioVersNum:     SignedByte;    {not used}
           ioPermssn:     SignedByte;    {read/write permission}
           ioMisc:        Ptr;           {not used}
           ioBuffer:      Ptr;           {pointer to data buffer}
           ioReqCount:    LONGINT;       {requested number of bytes}
           ioActCount:    LONGINT;       {actual number of bytes}
           ioPosMode:     INTEGER;       {positioning mode}
           ioPosOffset:   LONGINT);      {positioning offset}
          fileParam:
          . . . {used by File Manager}
          volumeParam:
          . . . {used by File Manager}
```

```
        cntrlParam:
          (ioCRefNum: INTEGER;   {driver reference number}
           csCode:    INTEGER;   {type of Control or Status call}
           csParam:   ARRAY[0..10] OF INTEGER) {control or status information}
        END;

        DCtlHandle  = ^DCtlPtr;
        DCtlPtr     = ^DCtlEntry;
        DCtlEntry   =
          RECORD
            dCtlDriver:   Ptr;        {pointer to ROM driver or handle to }
                                      { RAM driver}
            dCtlFlags:    INTEGER;    {flags}
            dCtlQHdr:     QHdr;       {driver I/O queue header}
            dCtlPosition: LONGINT;    {byte position used by Read and }
                                      { Write calls}
            dCtlStorage:  Handle;     {handle to RAM driver's private }
                                      { storage}
            dCtlRefNum:   INTEGER;    {driver reference number}
            dCtlCurTicks: LONGINT;    {used internally}
            dCtlWindow:   WindowPtr;  {pointer to driver's window}
            dCtlDelay:    INTEGER;    {number of ticks between periodic }
                                      { actions}
            dCtlEMask:    INTEGER;    {desk accessory event mask}
            dCtlMenu:     INTEGER     {menu ID of menu associated with }
                                      { driver}
          END;
```

High-Level Routines [Not in ROM]

```
FUNCTION OpenDriver   (name: Str255; VAR refNum: INTEGER) : OSErr;
FUNCTION CloseDriver  (refNum: INTEGER) : OSErr;
FUNCTION FSRead       (refNum: INTEGER; VAR count: LONGINT; buffPtr: Ptr)
                        : OSErr;
FUNCTION FSWrite      (refNum: INTEGER; VAR count: LONGINT; buffPtr: Ptr)
                        : OSErr;
FUNCTION Control      (refNum: INTEGER; csCode: INTEGER; csParamPtr: Ptr)
                        : OSErr;
FUNCTION Status       (refNum: INTEGER; csCode: INTEGER; csParamPtr: Ptr)
                        : OSErr;
FUNCTION KillIO       (refNum: INTEGER) : OSErr;
```

Low-Level Routines

```
FUNCTION PBOpen (paramBlock: ParmBlkPtr; async: BOOLEAN) : OSErr;
    →   12      ioCompletion        pointer
    ←   16      ioResult            word
    →   18      ioNamePtr           pointer
    ←   24      ioRefNum            word
    →   27      ioPermssn           byte
```

```
FUNCTION PBClose (paramBlock: ParmBlkPtr; async: BOOLEAN) : OSErr;
```
→	12	ioCompletion	pointer
←	16	ioResult	word
→	24	ioRefNum	word

```
FUNCTION PBRead (paramBlock: ParmBlkPtr; async: BOOLEAN) : OSErr;
```
→	12	ioCompletion	pointer
←	16	ioResult	word
→	22	ioVRefNum	word
→	24	ioRefNum	word
→	32	ioBuffer	pointer
→	36	ioReqCount	long word
←	40	ioActCount	long word
→	44	ioPosMode	word
↔	46	ioPosOffset	long word

```
FUNCTION PBWrite (paramBlock: ParmBlkPtr; async: BOOLEAN) : OSErr;
```
→	12	ioCompletion	pointer
←	16	ioResult	word
→	22	ioVRefNum	word
→	24	ioRefNum	word
→	32	ioBuffer	pointer
→	36	ioReqCount	long word
←	40	ioActCount	long word
→	44	ioPosMode	word
↔	46	ioPosOffset	long word

```
FUNCTION PBControl (paramBlock: ParmBlkPtr; async: BOOLEAN) : OSErr;
```
→	12	ioCompletion	pointer
←	16	ioResult	word
→	22	ioVRefNum	word
→	24	ioRefNum	word
→	26	csCode	word
→	28	csParam	record

```
FUNCTION PBStatus (paramBlock: ParmBlkPtr; async: BOOLEAN) : OSErr;
```
→	12	ioCompletion	pointer
←	16	ioResult	word
→	22	ioVRefNum	word
→	24	ioRefNum	word
→	26	csCode	word
←	28	csParam	record

```
FUNCTION PBKillIO (paramBlock: ParmBlkPtr; async: BOOLEAN) : OSErr;
```
→	12	ioCompletion	pointer
←	16	ioResult	word
→	24	ioRefNum	word

6 Device Manager

Accessing a Driver's Device Control Entry

```
FUNCTION GetDCtlEntry (refNum: INTEGER) : DCtlHandle;   [Not in ROM]
```

Result Codes

Name	Value	Meaning
abortErr	−27	I/O request aborted by KillIO
badUnitErr	−21	Driver reference number doesn't match unit table
controlErr	−17	Driver can't respond to this Control call
dInstErr	−26	Couldn't find driver in resource file
dRemovErr	−25	Attempt to remove an open driver
noErr	0	No error
notOpenErr	−28	Driver isn't open
openErr	−23	Requested read/write permission doesn't match driver's open permission
readErr	−19	Driver can't respond to Read calls
statusErr	−18	Driver can't respond to this Status call
unitEmptyErr	−22	Driver reference number specifies NIL handle in unit table
writErr	−20	Driver can't respond to Write calls

Assembly-Language Information

Constants

```
; Flags in trap words

asnycTrpBit     .EQU     10      ;set for an asynchronous call
noQueueBit      .EQU     9       ;set for immediate execution

; Values for requesting read/write access

fsCurPerm       .EQU     0       ;whatever is currently allowed
fsRdPerm        .EQU     1       ;request to read only
fsWrPerm        .EQU     2       ;request to write only
fsRdWrPerm      .EQU     3       ;request to read and write

; Positioning modes

fsAtMark        .EQU     0       ;at current position
fsFromStart     .EQU     1       ;offset relative to beginning of medium
fsFromMark      .EQU     3       ;offset relative to current position
rdVerify        .EQU     64      ;add to above for read-verify
```

```
; Driver flags

dReadEnable     .EQU     0    ;set if driver can respond to Read calls
dWritEnable     .EQU     1    ;set if driver can respond to Write calls
dCtlEnable      .EQU     2    ;set if driver can respond to Control calls
dStatEnable     .EQU     3    ;set if driver can respond to Status calls
dNeedGoodBye    .EQU     4    ;set if driver needs to be called before the
                              ; application heap is reinitialized
dNeedTime       .EQU     5    ;set if driver needs time for performing a
                              ; periodic action
dNeedLock       .EQU     6    ;set if driver will be locked in memory as
                              ; soon as it's opened (always set for ROM
                              ; drivers)

; Device control entry flags

dOpened         .EQU     5    ;set if driver is open
dRAMBased       .EQU     6    ;set if driver is RAM-based
drvrActive      .EQU     7    ;set if driver is currently executing

; csCode values for driver control routine

accRun          .EQU     65   ;take the periodic action, if any, for this
                              ; driver
goodBye         .EQU     -1   ;heap will be reinitialized, clean up if
                              ; necessary
killCode        .EQU     1    ;handle the KillIO call

; Low-order byte of Device Manager traps

aRdCmd          .EQU     2    ;Read call (trap $A002)
aWrCmd          .EQU     3    ;Write call (trap $A003)

; Offsets from SCC base addresses

aData           .EQU     6    ;channel A data in or out
aCtl            .EQU     2    ;channel A control
bData           .EQU     4    ;channel B data in or out
bCtl            .EQU     0    ;channel B control
```

Standard Parameter Block Data Structure

qLink	Pointer to next queue entry
qType	Queue type (word)
ioTrap	Routine trap (word)
ioCmdAddr	Routine address
ioCompletion	Address of completion routine
ioResult	Result code (word)
ioVNPtr	Pointer to driver name (preceded by length byte)
ioVRefNum	Volume reference number (word)
ioDrvNum	Drive number (word)

6 Device Manager

Control and Status Parameter Block Data Structure

ioRefNum	Driver reference number (word)
csCode	Type of Control or Status call (word)
csParam	Parameters for Control or Status call (22 bytes)

I/O Parameter Block Data Structure

ioRefNum	Driver reference number (word)
ioPermssn	Open permission (byte)
ioBuffer	Pointer to data buffer
ioReqCount	Requested number of bytes (long)
ioActCount	Actual number of bytes (long)
ioPosMode	Positioning mode (word)
ioPosOffset	Positioning offset (long)

Device Driver Data Structure

drvrFlags	Flags (word)
drvrDelay	Number of ticks between periodic actions (word)
drvrEMask	Desk accessory event mask (word)
drvrMenu	Menu ID of menu associated with driver (word)
drvrOpen	Offset to open routine (word)
drvrPrime	Offset to prime routine (word)
drvrCtl	Offset to control routine (word)
drvrStatus	Offset to status routine (word)
drvrClose	Offset to close routine (word)
drvrName	Driver name (preceded by length byte)

Device Control Entry Data Structure

dCtlDriver	Pointer to ROM driver or handle to RAM driver
dCtlFlags	Flags (word)
dCtlQueue	Queue flags: low-order byte is driver's version number (word)
dCtlQHead	Pointer to first entry in driver's I/O queue
dCtlQTail	Pointer to last entry in driver's I/O queue
dCtlPosition	Byte position used by Read and Write calls (long)
dCtlStorage	Handle to RAM driver's private storage
dCtlRefNum	Driver's reference number (word)
dCtlWindow	Pointer to driver's window
dCtlDelay	Number of ticks between periodic actions (word)
dCtlEMask	Desk accessory event mask (word)
dCtlMenu	Menu ID of menu associated with driver (word)

Structure of Primary Interrupt Vector Table

autoInt1	Vector to level-1 interrupt handler
autoInt2	Vector to level-2 interrupt handler

autoInt3   Vector to level-3 interrupt handler
autoInt4   Vector to level-4 interrupt handler
autoInt5   Vector to level-5 interrupt handler
autoInt6   Vector to level-6 interrupt handler
autoInt7   Vector to level-7 interrupt handler

Macro Names

Pascal name	Macro name
PBRead	_Read
PBWrite	_Write
PBControl	_Control
PBStatus	_Status
PBKillIO	_KillIO

Routines for Writing Drivers

Routine	Jump vector	On entry		On exit	
Fetch	JFetch	A1:	ptr to device control entry	D0:	character fetched; bit 15=1 if last character in buffer
Stash	JStash	A1:	ptr to device control entry	D0:	bit 15=1 if last character requested
		D0:	character to stash		
IODone	JIODone	A1:	ptr to device control entry		
		D0:	result code (word)		

Variables

UTableBase   Base address of unit table
JFetch   Jump vector for Fetch function
JStash   Jump vector for Stash function
JIODone   Jump vector for IODone function
Lvl1DT   Level-1 secondary interrupt vector table (32 bytes)
Lvl2DT   Level-2 secondary interrupt vector table (32 bytes)
VIA   VIA base address
ExtStsDT   External/status interrupt vector table (16 bytes)
SCCWr   SCC write base address
SCCRd   SCC read base address

7 THE DISK DRIVER

7 Disk Driver

ABOUT THIS CHAPTER

The Disk Driver is a Macintosh device driver used for storing and retrieving information on Macintosh 3 1/2-inch disk drives. This chapter describes the Disk Driver in detail. It's intended for programmers who want to access Macintosh drives directly, bypassing the File Manager.

You should already be familiar with:

- events, as discussed in chapter 8 of Volume I and in chapter 3 of this volume

- files and disk drives, as described in chapter 4

- interrupts and the use of devices and device drivers, as described in chapter 6

ABOUT THE DISK DRIVER

The Disk Driver is a standard Macintosh device driver in ROM. It allows Macintosh applications to read from disks, write to disks, and eject disks.

> **Note:** The Disk Driver cannot format disks; this task is accomplished by the Disk Initialization Package.

Information on disks is stored in 512-byte **sectors**. There are 800 sectors on one 400K-byte Macintosh disk. Each sector consists of an **address mark** that contains information used by the Disk Driver to determine the position of the sector on the disk, and a **data mark** that primarily contains data stored in that sector.

Consecutive sectors on a disk are grouped into **tracks**. There are 80 tracks on one 400K-byte Macintosh disk. Track 0 is the outermost and track 79 is the innermost. Each track corresponds to a ring of constant radius around the disk.

Macintosh disks are formatted in a manner that allows a more efficient use of disk space than most microcomputer formatting schemes: The tracks are divided into five groups of 16 tracks each, and each group of tracks is accessed at a different rotational speed from the other groups. (Those at the edge of the disk are accessed at slower speeds than those toward the center.)

Each group of tracks contains a different number of sectors:

Tracks	Sectors per track	Sectors
0-15	12	0-191
16-31	11	192-367
32-47	10	368-527
48-63	9	528-671
64-79	8	672-799

An application can read or write data in *whole* disk sectors only. The application must specify the data to be read or written in 512-byte multiples, and the Disk Driver automatically calculates which sector to access. The application specifies where on the disk the data should be read or

7 Disk Driver

written by providing a positioning mode and a positioning offset. Data can be read from or written to the disk:

- at the current sector on the disk (the sector following the last sector read or written)

- from a position relative to the current sector on the disk

- from a position relative to the beginning of first sector on the disk

The following constants are used to specify the positioning mode:

```
CONST fsAtMark    = 0;   {at current sector}
      fsFromStart = 1;   {relative to first sector}
      fsFromMark  = 3;   {relative to current sector}
```

If the positioning mode is relative to a sector (fsFromStart or fsFromMark), the relative offset from that sector must be given as a 512-byte multiple.

In addition to the 512 bytes of standard information, each sector contains 12 bytes of **file tags**. The file tags are designed to allow easy reconstruction of files from a volume whose directory or other file-access information has been destroyed. Whenever the Disk Driver reads a sector from a disk, it places the sector's file tags at a special location in low memory called the **file tags buffer** (the remaining 512 bytes in the sector are passed on to the File Manager). Each time one sector's file tags are written there, the previous file tags are overwritten. Conversely, whenever the Disk Driver writes a sector on a disk, it takes the 12 bytes in the file tags buffer and writes them on the disk.

Assembly-language note: The information in the file tags buffer can be accessed through the following global variables:

Name	Contents
BufTgFNum	File number (long)
BufTgFFlag	Flags (word: bit 1=1 if resource fork)
BufTgFBkNum	Logical block number (word)
BufTgDate	Date and time of last modification (long)

The logical block number indicates which relative portion of a file the block contains—the first logical block of a file is numbered 0, the second is numbered 1, and so on.

The Disk Driver disables interrupts during disk accesses. While interrupts are disabled, it stores any serial data received via the modem port and later passes the data to the Serial Driver. This allows the modem port to be used simultaneously with disk accesses without fear of hardware overrun errors. (For more information, see chapter 9.)

USING THE DISK DRIVER

The Disk Driver is opened automatically when the system starts up. It allocates space in the system heap for variables, installs entries in the drive queue for each drive that's attached to the

Macintosh, and installs a task into the vertical retrace queue. The Disk Driver's name is '.Sony', and its reference number is –5.

To write data onto a disk, make a Device Manager Write call. You must pass the following parameters:

■ the driver reference number –5

■ the drive number 1 (internal drive) or 2 (external drive)

■ a positioning mode indicating where on the disk the information should be written

■ a positioning offset that's a multiple of 512 bytes

■ a buffer that contains the data you want to write

■ the number of bytes (in multiples of 512) that you want to write

The Disk Driver's prime routine returns one of the following result codes to the Write function:

noErr	No error
nsDrvErr	No such drive
paramErr	Bad positioning information
wPrErr	Volume is locked by a hardware setting
firstDskErr	Low-level disk error
through lastDskErr	

To read data from a disk, make a Device Manager Read call. You must pass the following parameters:

■ the driver reference number –5

■ the drive number 1 (internal drive) or 2 (external drive)

■ a positioning mode indicating where on the disk the information should be read from

■ a positioning offset that's a multiple of 512 bytes

■ a buffer to receive the data that's read

■ the number of bytes (in multiples of 512) that you want to read

The Disk Driver's prime routine returns one of the following result codes to the Read function:

noErr	No error
nsDrvErr	No such drive
paramErr	Bad positioning information
firstDskErr	Low-level disk error
through lastDskErr	

To verify that data written to a disk exactly matches the data in memory, make a Device Manager Read call right after the Write call. The parameters for a read-verify operation are the same as for a standard Read call, except that the following constant must be added to the positioning mode:

```
CONST rdVerify = 64;   {read-verify mode}
```

The result code dataVerErr will be returned if any of the data doesn't match.

The Disk Driver can read and write sectors in any order, and therefore operates faster on one large data request than it would on a series of equivalent but smaller data requests.

There are three different calls you can make to the Disk Driver's control routine:

- KillIO causes all current I/O requests to be aborted. KillIO is a Device Manager call.
- SetTagBuffer specifies the information to be used in the file tags buffer.
- DiskEject ejects a disk from a drive.

An application using the File Manager should always unmount the volume in a drive before ejecting the disk.

You can make one call, DriveStatus, to the Disk Driver's status routine, to learn about the state of the driver.

An application can bypass the implicit mounting of volumes done by the File Manager by calling the Operating System Event Manager function GetOSEvent and looking for disk-inserted events. Once the volume has been inserted in the drive, it can be read from normally.

DISK DRIVER ROUTINES

The Disk Driver routines return an integer result code of type OSErr; each routine description lists all of the applicable result codes.

```
FUNCTION DiskEject (drvNum: INTEGER) : OSErr;    [Not in ROM]
```

Assembly-language note: DiskEject is equivalent to a Control call with csCode equal to the global constant ejectCode.

DiskEject ejects the disk from the internal drive if drvNum is 1, or from the external drive if drvNum is 2.

Result codes   noErr   No error
                 nsDrvErr   No such drive

```
FUNCTION SetTagBuffer (buffPtr: Ptr) : OSErr;    [Not in ROM]
```

Assembly-language note: SetTagBuffer is equivalent to a Control call with csCode equal to the global constant tgBuffCode.

An application can change the information used in the file tags buffer by calling SetTagBuffer. The buffPtr parameter points to a buffer that contains the information to be used. If buffPtr is NIL, the information in the file tags buffer isn't changed.

If buffPtr isn't NIL, every time the Disk Driver reads a sector from the disk, it stores the file tags in the file tags buffer and in the buffer pointed to by buffPtr. Every time the Disk Driver writes a sector onto the disk, it reads 12 bytes from the buffer pointed to by buffPtr, places them in the file tags buffer, and then writes them onto the disk.

The contents of the buffer pointed to by buffPtr are overwritten at the end of every read request (which can be composed of a number of sectors) instead of at the end of every sector. Each read request places 12 bytes in the buffer for *each* sector, always beginning at the start of the buffer. This way an application can examine the file tags for a number of sequentially read sectors. If a read request is composed of a number of sectors, the Disk Driver places 12 bytes in the buffer for each sector. For example, for a read request of five sectors, the Disk Driver will place 60 bytes in the buffer.

Result codes   noErr   No error

```
FUNCTION DriveStatus (drvNum: INTEGER; VAR status: DrvSts) :
        OSErr;    [Not in ROM]
```

Assembly-language note: DriveStatus is equivalent to a Status call with csCode equal to the global constant drvStsCode; status is returned in csParam through csParam+21.

DriveStatus returns information about the internal drive if drvNum is 1, or about the external drive if drvNum is 2. The information is returned in a record of type DrvSts:

```
TYPE DrvSts  = RECORD
                track:        INTEGER;       {current track}
                writeProt:    SignedByte;    {bit 7=1 if volume is locked}
                diskInPlace:  SignedByte;    {disk in place}
                installed:    SignedByte;    {drive installed}
                sides:        SignedByte;    {bit 7=0 if single-side drive}
                qLink:        QElemPtr;      {next queue entry}
                qType:        INTEGER;       {reserved for future use}
                dQDrive:      INTEGER;       {drive number}
                dQRefNum:     INTEGER;       {driver reference number}
                dQFSID:       INTEGER;       {file-system identifier}
                twoSideFmt:   SignedByte;    {-1 if two-sided disk}
                needsFlush:   SignedByte;    {reserved for future use}
                diskErrs:     INTEGER        {error count}
              END;
```

The diskInPlace field is 0 if there's no disk in the drive, 1 or 2 if there is a disk in the drive, or –4 to –1 if the disk was ejected in the last 1.5 seconds. The installed field is 1 if the drive is connected to the Macintosh, 0 if the drive might be connected to the Macintosh, and –1 if the drive isn't installed. The value of twoSideFmt is valid only when diskInPlace=2. The value of diskErrs is incremented every time an error occurs internally within the Disk Driver.

Result codes   noErr   No error
                nsDrvErr   No such drive

7 Disk Driver

ASSEMBLY-LANGUAGE EXAMPLE

The following assembly-language example ejects the disk in drive 1:

```
MyEject   MOVEQ     #<ioVQElSize/2>-1,D0        ;prepare an I/O
@1        CLR.W     -(SP)                        ; parameter block
          DBRA      D0,@1                        ; on the stack
          MOVE.L    SP,A0                        ;A0 points to it
          MOVE.W    #-5,ioRefNum(A0)             ;driver refNum
          MOVE.W    #1,ioDrvNum(A0)              ;internal drive
          MOVE.W    #ejectCode,csCode(A0)        ;eject control code
          _Eject                                 ;synchronous call
          ADD       #ioVQElSize,SP               ;clean up stack
```

To asynchronously read sector 4 from the disk in drive 1, you would do the following:

```
MyRead    MOVEQ     #<ioQElSize/2>-1,D0          ;prepare an I/O
@1        CLR.W     -(SP)                        ; parameter block
          DBRA      D0,@1                        ; on the stack
          MOVE.L    SP,A0                        ;A0 points to it
          MOVE.W    #-5,ioRefNum(A0)             ;driver refNum
          MOVE.W    #1,ioDrvNum(A0)              ;internal drive
          MOVE.W    #1,ioPosMode(A0)             ;absolute positioning
          MOVE.L    #<512*4>,ioPosOffset(A0)     ;sector 4

          MOVE.L    #512,ioReqCount(A0)          ;read one sector
          LEA       myBuffer,A1
          MOVE.L    A1,ioBuffer(A0)              ;buffer address
          _Read     ,ASYNC                       ;read data

; Do any other processing here.  Then, when the sector is needed:

@2        MOVE.W    ioResult(A0),D0              ;wait for completion
          BGT.S     @2
          ADD       #ioQElSize,SP                ;clean up stack


myBuffer  .BLOCK    512,0
```

SUMMARY OF THE DISK DRIVER

Constants

```
CONST { Positioning modes }

        fsAtMark      = 0;    {at current sector}
        fsFromStart   = 1;    {relative to first sector}
        fsFromMark    = 3;    {relative to current sector}
        rdVerify      = 64;   {add to above for read-verify}
```

Data Types

```
TYPE DrvSts = RECORD
                track:       INTEGER;      {current track}
                writeProt:   SignedByte;   {bit 7=1 if volume is locked}
                diskInPlace: SignedByte;   {disk in place}
                installed:   SignedByte;   {drive installed}
                sides:       SignedByte;   {bit 7=0 if single-sided drive}
                qLink:       QElemPtr;     {next queue entry}
                qType:       INTEGER;      {reserved for future use}
                dQDrive:     INTEGER;      {drive number}
                dQRefNum:    INTEGER;      {driver reference number}
                dQFSID:      INTEGER;      {file-system identifier}
                twoSideFmt:  SignedByte;   {-1 if two-sided disk}
                needsFlush:  SignedByte;   {reserved for future use}
                diskErrs:    INTEGER       {error count}
              END;
```

Routines [Not in ROM]

```
FUNCTION DiskEject    (drvNum: INTEGER) : OSErr;
FUNCTION SetTagBuffer (buffPtr: Ptr) : OSErr;
FUNCTION DriveStatus  (drvNum: INTEGER; VAR status: DrvSts) : OSErr;
```

Result Codes

Name	Value	Meaning
noErr	0	No error
nsDrvErr	−56	No such drive
paramErr	−50	Bad positioning information
wPrErr	−44	Volume is locked by a hardware setting

Name	Value	Meaning
firstDskErr	–84	First of the range of low-level disk errors
sectNFErr	–81	Can't find sector
seekErr	–80	Drive error
spdAdjErr	–79	Can't correctly adjust disk speed
twoSideErr	–78	Tried to read side 2 of a disk in a single-sided drive
initIWMErr	–77	Can't initialize disk controller chip
tk0BadErr	–76	Can't find track 0
cantStepErr	–75	Drive error
wrUnderrun	–74	Write underrun occurred
badDBtSlp	–73	Bad data mark
badDCksum	–72	Bad data mark
noDtaMkErr	–71	Can't find data mark
badBtSlpErr	–70	Bad address mark
badCksmErr	–69	Bad address mark
dataVerErr	–68	Read-verify failed
noAdrMkErr	–67	Can't find an address mark
noNybErr	–66	Disk is probably blank
offLinErr	–65	No disk in drive
noDriveErr	–64	Drive isn't connected
lastDskErr	–64	Last of the range of low-level disk errors

Assembly-Language Information

Constants

```
; Positioning modes


fsAtMark      .EQU    0     ;at current sector
fsFromStart   .EQU    1     ;relative to first sector
fsFromMark    .EQU    3     ;relative to current sector
rdVerify      .EQU   64     ;add to above for read-verify


; csCode values for Control/Status calls


ejectCode     .EQU    7     ;Control call, DiskEject
tgBuffCode    .EQU    8     ;Control call, SetTagBuffer
drvStsCode    .EQU    8     ;Status call, DriveStatus
```

Structure of Status Information

dsTrack	Current track (word)
dsWriteProt	Bit 7=1 if volume is locked (byte)
dsDiskInPlace	Disk in place (byte)
dsInstalled	Drive installed (byte)
dsSides	Bit 7=0 if single-sided drive (byte)
dsQLink	Pointer to next queue entry
dsDQDrive	Drive number (word)

dsDQRefNum	Driver reference number (word)
dsDQFSID	File-system identifier (word)
dsTwoSideFmt	−1 if two-sided disk (byte)
dsDiskErrs	Error count (word)

Equivalent Device Manager Calls

Pascal routine	Call
DiskEject	Control with csCode=ejectCode
SetTagBuffer	Control with csCode=tgBuffCode
DriveStatus	Status with csCode=drvStsCode, status returned in csParam through csParam+21

Variables

BufTgFNum	File tags buffer: file number (long)
BufTgFFlag	File tags buffer: flags (word: bit 1=1 if resource fork)
BufTgFBkNum	File tags buffer: logical block number (word)
BufTgDate	File tags buffer: date and time of last modification (long)

7 Disk Driver

8 THE SOUND DRIVER

8 Sound Driver

ABOUT THIS CHAPTER

The Sound Driver is a Macintosh device driver for handling sound and music generation in a Macintosh application. This chapter describes the Sound Driver in detail.

You should already be familiar with:

■ events, as discussed in chapter 8 of Volume I

■ the Memory Manager

■ the use of devices and device drivers, as described in chapter 6

ABOUT THE SOUND DRIVER

The Sound Driver is a standard Macintosh device driver in ROM that's used to synthesize sound. You can generate sound characterized by any kind of waveform by using the three different sound synthesizers in the Sound Driver:

■ The **four-tone synthesizer** is used to make simple harmonic tones, with up to four "voices" producing sound simultaneously; it requires about 50% of the microprocessor's attention during any given time interval.

■ The **square-wave synthesizer** is used to produce less harmonic sounds such as beeps, and requires about 2% of the processor's time.

■ The **free-form synthesizer** is used to make complex music and speech; it requires about 20% of the processor's time.

The Macintosh XL is equipped only with a square-wave synthesizer; all information in this chapter about four-tone and free-form sound applies only to the Macintosh 128K and 512K.

Figure 1 depicts the **waveform** of a typical sound wave, and the terms used to describe it. The **magnitude** is the vertical distance between any given point on the wave and the horizontal line about which the wave oscillates; you can think of the magnitude as the volume level. The **amplitude** is the maximum magnitude of a periodic wave. The **wavelength** is the horizontal extent of one complete cycle of the wave. Magnitude and wavelength can be measured in any unit of distance. The **period** is the time elapsed during one complete cycle of a wave. The **frequency** is the reciprocal of the period, or the number of cycles per second—also called hertz (Hz). The **phase** is some fraction of a wave cycle (measured from a fixed point on the wave).

There are many different types of waveforms, three of which are depicted in Figure 2. Sine waves are generated by objects that oscillate periodically at a single frequency (such as a tuning fork). Square waves are generated by objects that toggle instantly between two states at a single frequency (such as an electronic "beep"). Free-form waves are the most common of all, and are generated by objects that vibrate at rapidly changing frequencies with rapidly changing magnitudes (such as your vocal cords).

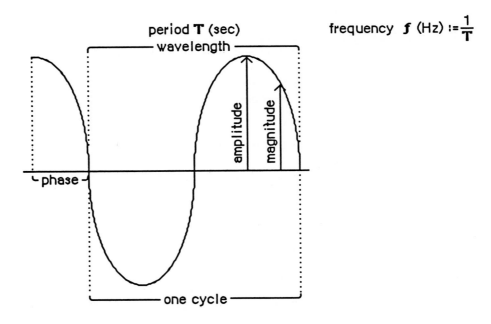

Figure 1. Waveform

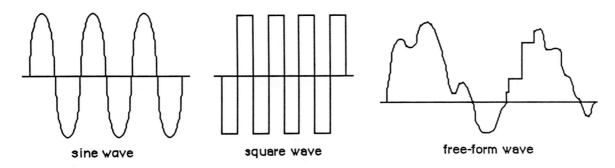

Figure 2. Types of Waveforms

Figure 3 shows analog and digital representations of a waveform. The Sound Driver represents waveforms digitally, so all waveforms must be converted from their analog representation to a digital representation. The rows of numbers at the bottom of the figure are digital representations of the waveform. The numbers in the upper row are the magnitudes relative to the horizontal zero-magnitude line. The numbers in the lower row all represent the same relative magnitudes, but have been normalized to positive numbers; you'll use numbers like these when calling the Sound Driver.

A digital representation of a waveform is simply a sequence of wave magnitudes measured at fixed intervals. This sequence of magnitudes is stored in the Sound Driver as a sequence of bytes, each one of which specifies an instantaneous voltage to be sent to the speaker. The bytes are stored in a data structure called a **waveform description**. Since a sequence of bytes can only represent a group of numbers whose maximum and minimum values differ by less than 256, the magnitudes of your waveforms must be constrained to these same limits.

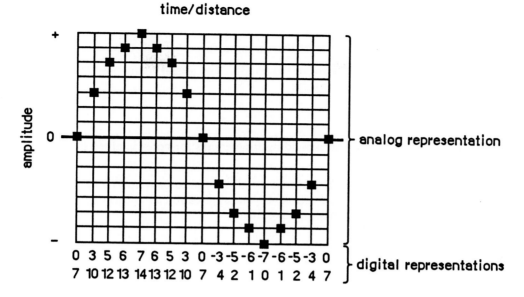

Figure 3. Analog and Digital Representations of a Waveform

SOUND DRIVER SYNTHESIZERS

A description of the sound to be generated by a synthesizer is contained in a data structure called a **synthesizer buffer**. A synthesizer buffer contains the duration, pitch, phase, and waveform of the sound the synthesizer will generate. The exact structure of a synthesizer buffer differs for each type of synthesizer being used. The first word in every synthesizer buffer is an integer that identifies the synthesizer, and must be one of the following predefined constants:

```
CONST swMode = -1;  {square-wave synthesizer}
      ftMode =  1;  {four-tone synthesizer}
      ffMode =  0;  {free-form synthesizer}
```

Square-Wave Synthesizer

The square-wave synthesizer is used to make sounds such as beeps. A square-wave synthesizer buffer has the following structure:

```
TYPE  SWSynthRec = RECORD
                     mode:     INTEGER;  {always swMode}
                     triplets: Tones     {sounds}
                   END;

      SWSynthPtr = ^SWSynthRec;

      Tones = ARRAY[0..5000] OF Tone;
      Tone  = RECORD
                count:     INTEGER;  {frequency}
                amplitude: INTEGER;  {amplitude, 0-255}
                duration:  INTEGER   {duration in ticks}
              END;
```

Each tone triplet contains the count, amplitude, and duration of a different sound. You can store as many triplets in a synthesizer buffer as there's room for.

The count integer can range in value from 0 to 65535. The actual frequency the count corresponds to is given by the relationship:

$$\text{frequency (Hz)} = 783360 \,/\, \text{count}$$

A partial list of count values and corresponding frequencies for notes is given in the summary at the end of this chapter.

The type Tones is declared with 5001 elements to allow you to pass up to 5000 sounds (the last element must contain 0). To be space-efficient, your application shouldn't declare a variable of type Tones; instead, you can do something like this:

```
VAR myPtr: Ptr;
    myHandle: Handle;
    mySWPtr: SWSynthPtr;
    . . .

myHandle := NewHandle(buffSize);          {allocate space for the buffer}
HLock(myHandle);                          {lock the buffer}
myPtr := myHandle^;                       {dereference the handle}
mySWPtr := SWSynthPtr(myPtr);             {coerce type to SWSynthPtr}
mySWPtr^.mode := swMode;                  {identify the synthesizer}
mySWPtr^.triplets[0].count := 2;          {fill the buffer with values }
    . . .                                 { describing the sound}
StartSound(myPtr,buffSize,POINTER(-1));   {produce the sound}
HUnlock(myHandle)                         {unlock the buffer}
```

where buffSize contains the number of bytes in the synthesizer buffer. This example dereferences handles instead of using pointers directly, to minimize the number of nonrelocatable objects in the heap.

Assembly-language note: The global variable CurPitch contains the current value of the count field.

The amplitude can range from 0 to 255. The duration specifies the number of ticks that the sound will be generated.

The list of tones ends with a triplet in which all fields are set to 0. When the square-wave synthesizer is used, the sound specified by each triplet is generated once, and then the synthesizer stops.

Four-Tone Synthesizer

The four-tone synthesizer is used to produce harmonic sounds such as music. It can simultaneously generate four different sounds, each with its own frequency, phase, and waveform.

A four-tone synthesizer buffer has the following structure:

```
TYPE  FTSynthRec  =  RECORD
                        mode:    INTEGER;        {always ftMode}
                        sndRec:  FTSndRecPtr     {tones to play}
                     END;


      FTSynthPtr = ^FTSynthRec;
```

The sndRec field points to a **four-tone record,** which describes the four tones:

```
TYPE  FTSoundRec  =  RECORD
                        duration:     INTEGER;    {duration in ticks}
                        sound1Rate:   Fixed;      {tone 1 cycle rate}
                        sound1Phase:  LONGINT;    {tone 1 byte offset}
                        sound2Rate:   Fixed;      {tone 2 cycle rate}
                        sound2Phase:  LONGINT;    {tone 2 byte offset}
                        sound3Rate:   Fixed;      {tone 3 cycle rate}
                        sound3Phase:  LONGINT;    {tone 3 byte offset}
                        sound4Rate:   Fixed;      {tone 4 cycle rate}
                        sound4Phase:  LONGINT;    {tone 4 byte offset}
                        sound1Wave:   WavePtr;    {tone 1 waveform}
                        sound2Wave:   WavePtr;    {tone 2 waveform}
                        sound3Wave:   WavePtr;    {tone 3 waveform}
                        sound4Wave:   WavePtr     {tone 4 waveform}
                     END;


      FTSndRecPtr = ^FTSoundRec:

      Wave      = PACKED ARRAY[0..255] OF Byte;
      WavePtr   = ^Wave;
```

Assembly-language note: The address of the four-tone record currently in use is stored in the global variable SoundPtr.

The duration integer indicates the number of ticks that the sound will be generated. Each phase long integer indicates the byte within the waveform description at which the synthesizer should begin producing sound (the first byte is byte number 0). Each rate value determines the speed at which the synthesizer cycles through the waveform, from 0 to 255.

The four-tone synthesizer creates sound by starting at the byte in the waveform description specified by the phase, and skipping ahead the number of bytes specified by the rate field every 44.93 microseconds; when the time specified by the duration has elapsed, the synthesizer stops. The rate field determines how the waveform will be "sampled", as shown in Figure 4. For nonperiodic waveforms, this is best illustrated by example: If the rate field is 1, each byte value in the waveform will be used, each producing sound for 44.93 microseconds. If the rate field is 0.1, each byte will be used 10 times, each therefore producing sound for a total of 449.3 microseconds. If the rate field is 5, only every fifth byte in the waveform will be sampled, each producing sound for 44.93 microseconds.

If the waveform contains one wavelength, the frequency that the rate corresponds to is given by:

frequency (Hz) = 1000000 / (44.93 / (rate/256))

You can use the Toolbox Utility routines FixMul and FixRatio to calculate this, as follows:

```
frequency := FixMul(rate,FixRatio(22257,256))
```

The maximum rate of 256 corresponds to approximately 22.3 kilohertz if the waveform contains one wavelength, and a rate of 0 produces no sound. A partial list of rate values and corresponding frequencies for notes is given in the summary at the end of this chapter.

Free-Form Synthesizer

The free-form synthesizer is used to synthesize complex music and speech. The sound to be produced is represented as a waveform whose complexity and length are limited only by available memory.

A free-form synthesizer buffer has the following structure:

```
TYPE  FFSynthRec = RECORD
                      mode:      INTEGER;    {always ffMode}
                      count:     Fixed;      {"sampling" factor}
                      waveBytes: FreeWave    {waveform description}
                   END;

      FFSynthPtr = ^FFSynthRec;

      FreeWave   = PACKED ARRAY[0..30000] OF Byte;
```

The type FreeWave is declared with 30001 elements to allow you to pass a very long waveform. To be space-efficient, your application shouldn't declare a variable of type FreeWave; instead, you can do something like this:

```
VAR  myPtr: Ptr;
     myHandle: Handle;
     myFFPtr: FFSynthPtr;
     . . .

myHandle := NewHandle(buffSize);      {allocate space for the buffer}
HLock(myHandle);                      {lock the buffer}
myPtr := myHandle^;                   {dereference the handle}
myFFPtr := FFSynthPtr(myPtr);         {coerce type to FFSynthPtr}
myFFPtr^.mode := ffMode;              {identify the synthesizer}
myFFPtr^.count := FixRatio(1,1);      {fill the buffer with values }
myFFPtr^.waveBytes[0] := 0;           { describing the sound}
. . .
StartSound(myPtr,buffSize,POINTER(-1));   {produce the sound}
HUnlock(myHandle)                         {unlock the buffer}
```

where buffSize contains the number of bytes in the synthesizer buffer. This example dereferences handles instead of using pointers directly, to minimize the number of nonrelocatable objects in the heap.

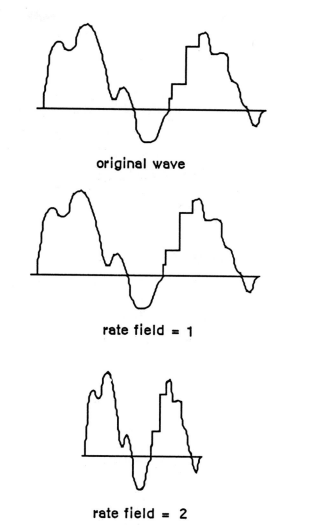

original wave

rate field = 1

rate field = 2

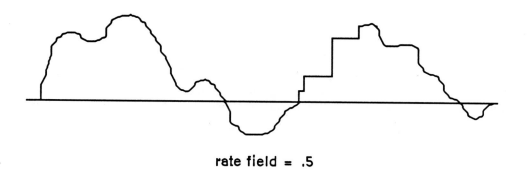

rate field = .5

Figure 4. Effect of the Rate Field

8 Sound Driver

The free-form synthesizer creates sound by starting at the first byte in the waveform and skipping ahead the number of bytes specified by count every 44.93 microseconds. The count field determines how the waveform will be "sampled"; it's analogous to the rate field of the four-tone synthesizer (see Figure 4 above). When the end of the waveform is reached, the synthesizer will stop.

For periodic waveforms, you can determine the frequency of the wave cycle by using the following relationship:

frequency (Hz) = 1000000 / (44.93 * (wavelength/count))

You can calculate this with Toolbox Utility routines as follows:

```
frequency := FixMul(count,FixRatio(22257,wavelength))
```

The wavelength is given in bytes. For example, the frequency of a wave with a 100-byte wavelength played at a count value of 2 would be approximately 445 Hz.

USING THE SOUND DRIVER

The Sound Driver is opened automatically when the system starts up. Its driver name is '.Sound', and its driver reference number is –4. To close or open the Sound Driver, you can use the Device Manager Close and Open functions. Because the driver is in ROM, there's really no reason to close it.

To use one of the three types of synthesizers to generate sound, you can do the following: Use the Memory Manager function NewHandle to allocate heap space for a synthesizer buffer; then lock the buffer, fill it with values describing the sound, and make a StartSound call to the Sound Driver. StartSound can be called either synchronously or asynchronously (with an optional completion routine). When called synchronously, control returns to your application after the sound is completed. When called asynchronously, control returns to your application immediately, and your application is free to perform other tasks while the sound is produced.

To produce continuous, unbroken sounds, it's sometimes advantageous to preallocate space for all the synthesizer buffers you require before you make the first StartSound call. Then, while one asynchronous StartSound call is being completed, you can calculate the waveform values for the next call.

To avoid the click that may occur between StartSound calls when using the four-tone synthesizer, set the duration field to a large value and just change the value of one of the rate fields to start a new sound. To avoid the clicks that may occur during four-tone and free-form sound generation, fill the waveform description with multiples of 740 bytes.

> **Warning:** The Sound Driver uses interrupts to produce sound. If other device drivers are in use, they may turn off interrupts, making sound production unreliable. For instance, if the Disk Driver is accessing a disk during sound generation, a "crackling" sound may be produced.

To determine when the sound initiated by a StartSound call has been completed, you can poll the SoundDone function. You can cancel any current StartSound call and any pending asynchronous StartSound calls by calling StopSound. By calling GetSoundVol and SetSoundVol, you can get and set the current speaker volume level.

SOUND DRIVER ROUTINES

```
PROCEDURE StartSound (synthRec: Ptr; numBytes: LONGINT;
        completionRtn: ProcPtr);    [Not in ROM]
```

Assembly-language note: StartSound is equivalent to a Device Manager Write call with ioRefNum=–4, ioBuffer=synthRec, and ioReqCount=numBytes.

StartSound begins producing the sound described by the synthesizer buffer pointed to by synthRec. NumBytes indicates the size of the synthesizer buffer (in bytes), and completionRtn points to a completion routine to be executed when the sound finishes:

■ If completionRtn is POINTER(–1), the sound will be produced synchronously.

■ If completionRtn is NIL, the sound will be produced asynchronously, but no completion routine will be executed.

■ Otherwise, the sound will be produced asynchronously and the routine pointed to by completionRtn will be executed when the sound finishes.

Warning: You may want the completion routine to start the next sound when one sound finishes, but beware: Completion routines are executed at the interrupt level and must preserve all registers other than A0, A1, and D0-D2. They must not make any calls to the Memory Manager, directly or indirectly, and can't depend on handles to unlocked blocks being valid; be sure to preallocate all the space you'll need. Or, instead of starting the next sound itself, the completion routine can post an application-defined event and your application's main event loop can start the next sound when it gets the event.

Because the type of pointer for each type of synthesizer buffer is different and the type of the synthRec parameter is Ptr, you'll need to do something like the following example (which applies to the free-form synthesizer):

```
VAR myPtr: Ptr;
    myHandle: Handle;
    myFFPtr: FFSynthPtr;
    . . .

myHandle := NewHandle(buffSize);        {allocate space for the buffer}
HLock(myHandle);                         {lock the buffer}
myPtr := myHandle^;                       {dereference the handle}
myFFPtr := FFSynthPtr(myPtr);            {coerce type to FFSynthPtr}
myFFPtr^.mode := ffMode;                 {identify the synthesizer}
. . .                                     {fill the buffer with values }
                                          { describing the sound}
StartSound(myPtr,buffSize,POINTER(-1));    {produce the sound}
HUnlock(myHandle)                         {unlock the buffer}
```

where buffSize is the number of bytes in the synthesizer buffer.

8 Sound Driver

The sounds are generated as follows:

- Free-form synthesizer: The magnitudes described by each byte in the waveform description are generated sequentially until the number of bytes specified by the numBytes parameter have been written.

- Square-wave synthesizer: The sounds described by each sound triplet are generated sequentially until either the end of the buffer has been reached (indicated by a count, amplitude, and duration of 0 in the square-wave buffer), or the number of bytes specified by the numBytes parameter have been written.

- Four-tone synthesizer: All four sounds are generated for the length of time specified by the duration integer in the four-tone record.

PROCEDURE StopSound;   [Not in ROM]

StopSound immediately stops the current StartSound call (if any), executes the current StartSound call's completion routine (if any), and cancels any pending asynchronous StartSound calls.

Assembly-language note: To stop sound from assembly language, you can make a Device Manager KillIO call (and, when using the square-wave synthesizer, set the global variable CurPitch to 0). Although StopSound executes the completion routine of only the current StartSound call, KillIO executes the completion routine of every pending asynchronous call.

FUNCTION SoundDone : BOOLEAN;   [Not in ROM]

SoundDone returns TRUE if the Sound Driver isn't currently producing sound and there are no asynchronous StartSound calls pending; otherwise it returns FALSE.

Assembly-language note: Assembly-language programmers can poll the ioResult field of the most recent Device Manager Write call's parameter block to determine when the Write call finishes.

PROCEDURE GetSoundVol (VAR level: INTEGER);   [Not in ROM]

GetSoundVol returns the current speaker volume, from 0 (silent) to 7 (loudest).

Assembly-language note: Assembly-language programmers can get the speaker volume level from the low-order three bits of the global variable SdVolume.

```
PROCEDURE SetSoundVol (level: INTEGER);    [Not in ROM]
```

SetSoundVol immediately sets the speaker volume to the specified level, from 0 (silent) to 7 (loudest); it doesn't, however, change the volume setting that's under user control via the Control Panel desk accessory. If your application calls SetSoundVol, it should save the current volume (using GetSoundVol) when it starts up and restore it (with SetSoundVol) upon exit; this resets the actual speaker volume to match the Control Panel setting.

Assembly-language note: To set the speaker volume level from assembly language, call this Pascal procedure from your program. As a side effect, it will set the low-order three bits of the global variable SdVolume to the specified level.

Note: The Control Panel volume setting is stored in parameter RAM; if you're writing a similar desk accessory and want to change this setting, see the discussion of parameter RAM in chapter 13.

SOUND DRIVER HARDWARE

The information in this section applies to the Macintosh 128K and 512K, but not the Macintosh XL.

This section briefly describes how the Sound Driver uses the Macintosh hardware to produce sound, and how assembly-language programmers can intervene in this process to control the square-wave synthesizer. You can skip this section if it doesn't interest you, and you'll still be able to use the Sound Driver as described.

Note: For more information about the hardware used by the Sound Driver, see chapter 2 of Volume III.

The Sound Driver and disk speed-control circuitry share a special 740-byte buffer in memory, of which the Sound Driver uses the 370 even-numbered bytes to generate sound. Every horizontal blanking interval (every 44.93 microseconds—when the beam of the display tube moves from the right edge of the screen to the left), the MC68000 automatically fetches two bytes from this buffer and sends the high-order byte to the speaker.

Note: The period of any four-tone or free-form sound generated by the Sound Driver is a multiple of this 44.93-microsecond interval; the highest frequency is 11128 Hz, which corresponds to twice this interval.

Every vertical blanking interval (every 16.6 milliseconds—when the beam of the display tube moves from the bottom of the screen to the top), the Sound Driver fills its half of the 740-byte buffer with the next set of values. For square-wave sound, the buffer is filled with a constant value; for more complex sound, it's filled with many values.

From assembly language, you can cause the square-wave synthesizer to start generating sound, and then change the amplitude of the sound being generated any time you wish:

1. Make an asynchronous Device Manager Write call to the Sound Driver specifying the count, amplitude, and duration of the sound you want. The amplitude you specify will be placed in the 740-byte buffer, and the Sound Driver will begin producing sound.

2. Whenever you want to change the sound being generated, make an *immediate* Control call to the Sound Driver with the following parameters: ioRefNum must be –4, csCode must be 3, and csParam must provide the new amplitude level. The amplitude you specify will be placed in the 740-byte buffer, and the sound will change. You can continue to change the sound until the time specified by the duration has elapsed.

When the immediate Control call is completed, the Device Manager will execute the completion routine (if any) of the currently executing Write call. For this reason, the Write call shouldn't have a completion routine.

Note: You can determine the amplitude placed in the 740-byte buffer from the global variable SoundLevel.

SUMMARY OF THE SOUND DRIVER

Constants

```
CONST { Mode values for synthesizers }

    swMode = -1;    {square-wave synthesizer}
    ftMode = 1;     {four-tone synthesizer}
    ffMode = 0;     {free-form synthesizer}
```

Data Types

```
TYPE  { Free-form synthesizer }

    FFSynthPtr =  ^FFSynthRec;
    FFSynthRec = RECORD
                    mode:      INTEGER;    {always ffMode}
                    count:     Fixed;      {"sampling" factor}
                    waveBytes: FreeWave    {waveform description}
                 END;

    FreeWave   = PACKED ARRAY[0..30000] OF Byte;

    { Square-wave synthesizer }

    SWSynthPtr = ^SWSynthRec;
    SWSynthRec = RECORD
                    mode:      INTEGER;    {always swMode}
                    triplets:  Tones       {sounds}
                 END;

    Tones = ARRAY[0..5000] OF Tone;
    Tone  = RECORD
                count:      INTEGER;  {frequency}
                amplitude:  INTEGER;  {amplitude, 0-255}
                duration:   INTEGER   {duration in ticks}
            END;

    { Four-tone synthesizer }

    FTSynthPtr  = ^FTSynthRec;
    FTSynthRec  = RECORD
                    mode:    INTEGER;      {always ftMode}
                    sndRec:  FTSndRecPtr   {tones to play}
                  END;
```

```
FTSndRecPtr = ^FTSoundRec;
FTSoundRec  = RECORD
                duration:    INTEGER;  {duration in ticks}
                sound1Rate:  Fixed;    {tone 1 cycle rate}
                sound1Phase: LONGINT;  {tone 1 byte offset}
                sound2Rate:  Fixed;    {tone 2 cycle rate}
                sound2Phase: LONGINT;  {tone 2 byte offset}
                sound3Rate:  Fixed;    {tone 3 cycle rate}
                sound3Phase: LONGINT;  {tone 3 byte offset}
                sound4Rate:  Fixed;    {tone 4 cycle rate}
                sound4Phase: LONGINT;  {tone 4 byte offset}
                sound1Wave:  WavePtr;  {tone 1 waveform}
                sound2Wave:  WavePtr;  {tone 2 waveform}
                sound3Wave:  WavePtr;  {tone 3 waveform}
                sound4Wave:  WavePtr   {tone 4 waveform}
              END;

WavePtr = ^Wave;
Wave    = PACKED ARRAY[0..255] OF Byte;
```

Routines [Not in ROM]

```
PROCEDURE StartSound  (synthRec: Ptr; numBytes: LONGINT; completionRtn:
                         ProcPtr);
PROCEDURE StopSound;
FUNCTION  SoundDone :  BOOLEAN;
PROCEDURE GetSoundVol (VAR level: INTEGER);
PROCEDURE SetSoundVol (level: INTEGER);
```

Assembly-Language Information

Routines

Pascal name	Equivalent for assembly language
StartSound	Call Write with ioRefNum=–4, ioBuffer=synthRec, ioReqCount=numBytes
StopSound	Call KillIO and (for square-wave) set CurPitch to 0
SoundDone	Poll ioResult field of most recent Write call's parameter block
GetSoundVol	Get low-order three bits of variable SdVolume
SetSoundVol	Call this Pascal procedure from your program

Variables

SdVolume	Speaker volume (byte: low-order three bits only)
SoundPtr	Pointer to four-tone record
SoundLevel	Amplitude in 740-byte buffer (byte)
CurPitch	Value of count in square-wave synthesizer buffer (word)

Sound Driver Values for Notes

The following table contains values for the rate field of a four-tone synthesizer and the count field of a square-wave synthesizer. A just-tempered scale—in the key of C, as an example—is given in the first four columns; you can use a just-tempered scale for perfect tuning in a particular key. The last four columns give an equal-tempered scale, for applications that may use any key; this scale is appropriate for most Macintosh sound applications. Following this table is a list of the ratios used in calculating these values, and instructions on how to calculate them for a just-tempered scale in any key.

| | Just-Tempered Scale | | | | Equal-Tempered Scale | | | |
| | Rate for Four-Tone | | Count for Square-Wave | | Rate for Four-Tone | | Count for Square-Wave | |
Note	Long	Fixed	Word	Integer	Long	Fixed	Word	Integer
3 octaves below middle C								
C	612B	0.37956	5CBA	23738	604C	0.37616	5D92	23954
C#	667C	0.40033	57EB	22507	6606	0.39853	5851	22609
Db	67A6	0.40488	56EF	22255				
D	6D51	0.42702	526D	21101	6C17	0.42223	535C	21340
Ebb	6E8F	0.43187	5180	20864				
D#	71DF	0.44481	4F21	20257	7284	0.44733	4EAF	20143
Eb	749A	0.45547	4D46	19782				
E	7976	0.47446	4A2F	18991	7953	0.47392	4A44	19012
F	818F	0.50609	458C	17804	808A	0.50211	4619	17945
F#	88A5	0.53377	41F0	16880	882F	0.53197	422A	16938
Gb	8A32	0.53983	4133	16691				
G	91C1	0.56935	3DD1	15825	9048	0.56360	3E73	15987
G#	97D4	0.59308	3B58	15192	98DC	0.59711	3AF2	15090
Ab	9B79	0.60732	39F4	14836				
A	A1F3	0.63261	37A3	14243	A1F3	0.63261	37A3	14243
Bbb	A3CA	0.63980	3703	14083				
A#	AA0C	0.66425	34FD	13565	AB94	0.67023	3484	13444
Bb	ACBF	0.67479	3429	13353				
B	B631	0.71169	3174	12660	B5C8	0.71008	3191	12689
2 octaves below middle C								
C	C257	0.75914	2E5D	11869	C097	0.75230	2EC9	11977
C#	CCF8	0.80066	2BF6	11254	CC0B	0.79704	2C29	11305
Db	CF4C	0.80975	2B77	11127				
D	DAA2	0.85403	2936	10550	D82D	0.84444	29AE	10670
Ebb	DD1D	0.86372	28C0	10432				
D#	E3BE	0.88962	2790	10128	E508	0.89465	2757	10071
Eb	E935	0.91096	26A3	9891				
E	F2ED	0.94893	2517	9495	F2A6	0.94785	2522	9506
F	1031E	1.01218	22C6	8902	10114	1.00421	230C	8972
F#	1114A	1.06754	20F8	8440	1105D	1.06392	2115	8469
Gb	11465	1.07967	2099	8345				
G	12382	1.13870	1EE9	7913	12090	1.12720	1F3A	7994

Note	Long	Fixed	Word	Integer	Long	Fixed	Word	Integer
2 octaves below middle C								
G#	12FA8	1.18616	1DAC	7596	131B8	1.19421	1D79	7545
Ab	136F1	1.21461	1CFA	7418				
A	143E6	1.26523	1BD1	7121	143E6	1.26523	1BD1	7121
Bbb	14794	1.27960	1B81	7041				
A#	15418	1.32849	1A7E	6782	15729	1.34047	1A42	6722
Bb	1597E	1.34958	1A14	6676				
B	16C63	1.42339	18BA	6330	16B90	1.42017	18C8	6344
1 octave below middle C								
C	184AE	1.51828	172F	5935	1812F	1.50462	1764	5988
C#	199EF	1.60130	15FB	5627	19816	1.59409	1614	5652
Db	19E97	1.61949	15BC	5564				
D	1B543	1.70805	149B	5275	1B05A	1.68887	14D7	5335
Ebb	1BA3B	1.72746	1460	5216				
D#	1C77B	1.77922	13C8	5064	1CA10	1.78931	13AC	5036
Eb	1D26A	1.82193	1351	4945				
E	1E5D9	1.89784	128C	4748	1E54D	1.89571	1291	4753
F	2063D	2.02437	1163	4451	20228	2.00842	1186	4486
F#	22294	2.13507	107C	4220	220BB	2.12785	108A	4234
Gb	228C9	2.15932	104D	4173				
G	24704	2.27740	F74	3956	2411F	2.25438	F9D	3997
G#	25F4F	2.37230	ED6	3798	26370	2.38843	EBC	3772
Ab	26DE3	2.42924	E7D	3709				
A	287CC	2.53046	DE9	3561	287CC	2.53046	DE9	3561
Bbb	28F28	2.55920	DC1	3521				
A#	2A830	2.65698	D3F	3391	2AE51	2.68092	D21	3361
Bb	2B2FC	2.69916	D0A	3338				
B	2D8C6	2.84677	C5D	3165	2D721	2.84035	C64	3172
Middle C								
C	3095B	3.03654	B97	2967	3025D	3.00923	BB2	2994
C#	333DE	3.20261	AFD	2813	3302C	3.18817	B0A	2826
Db	33D2E	3.23898	ADE	2782				
D	36A87	3.41612	A4E	2638	360B5	3.37776	A6C	2668
Ebb	37476	3.45493	A30	2608				
D#	38EF7	3.55846	9E4	2532	39420	3.57861	9D6	2518
Eb	3A4D4	3.64386	9A9	2473				
E	3CBB2	3.79568	946	2374	3CA99	3.79140	949	2377
F	40C7A	4.04874	8B1	2225	40450	4.01685	8C3	2243
F#	44528	4.27014	83E	2110	44176	4.25571	845	2117
Gb	45193	4.31865	826	2086				
G	48E09	4.55482	7BA	1978	4823E	4.50876	7CE	1998
G#	4BE9F	4.74461	76B	1899	4C6E1	4.77687	75E	1886
Ab	4DBC5	4.85847	73F	1855				
A	50F98	5.06091	6F4	1780	50F98	5.06091	6F4	1780

Note	Long	Fixed	Word	Integer	Long	Fixed	Word	Integer
Middle C								
Bbb	51E4F	5.11839	6E0	1760				
A#	55060	5.31396	6A0	1696	55CA2	5.36185	690	1680
Bb	565F8	5.39832	685	1669				
B	5B18B	5.69353	62F	1583	5AE41	5.68068	632	1586
1 octave above middle C								
C	612B7	6.07310	5CC	1484	604BB	6.01848	5D9	1497
C#	667BD	6.40523	57F	1407	66059	6.37636	585	1413
Db	67A5C	6.47797	56F	1391				
D	6D50D	6.83223	527	1319	6C169	6.75551	536	1334
Ebb	6E8EB	6.90984	518	1304				
D#	71DEE	7.11691	4F2	1266	7283F	7.15721	4EB	1259
Eb	749A8	7.28772	4D4	1236				
E	79764	7.59137	4A3	1187	79533	7.58281	4A4	1188
F	818F3	8.09746	459	1113	808A1	8.03371	462	1122
F#	88A51	8.54030	41F	1055	882EC	8.51141	423	1059
Gb	8A326	8.63730	413	1043				
G	91C12	9.10965	3DD	989	9047D	9.01753	3E7	999
G#	97D3D	9.48921	3B6	950	98DC2	9.55374	3AF	943
Ab	9B78B	9.71696	39F	927				
A	A1F30	10.12183	37A	890	A1F30	10.12183	37A	890
Bbb	A3C9F	10.23680	370	880				
A#	AA0BF	10.62791	350	848	AB945	10.72371	348	840
Bb	ACBEF	10.79662	343	835				
B	B6316	11.38705	317	791	B5C83	11.36137	319	793
2 octaves above middle C								
C	C256D	12.14619	2E6	742	C0976	12.03696	2ED	749
C#	CCF79	12.81044	2BF	703	CC0B1	12.75270	2C3	707
Db	CF4B9	12.95595	2B7	695				
D	DAA1B	13.66447	293	659	D82D2	13.51102	29B	667
Ebb	DD1D6	13.81967	28C	652				
D#	E3BDC	14.23383	279	633	E507E	14.31442	275	629
Eb	E9350	14.57544	26A	618				
E	F2EC8	15.18274	251	593	F2A65	15.16560	252	594
F	1031E7	16.19493	22C	556	101141	16.06740	231	561
F#	1114A1	17.08058	210	528	1105D8	17.02283	211	529
Gb	11464C	17.27460	20A	522				
G	123824	18.21930	1EF	495	1208F9	18.03505	1F4	500
G#	12FA7B	18.97844	1DB	475	131B83	19.10747	1D8	472
Ab	136F15	19.43391	1D0	464				
A	143E61	20.24367	1BD	445	143E61	20.24367	1BD	445
Bbb	14793D	20.47359	1B8	440				
A#	15417F	21.25584	1A8	424	15728A	21.44742	1A4	420
Bb	1597DE	21.59323	1A1	417				
B	16C62D	22.77412	18C	396	16B906	22.72275	18D	397

8 Sound Driver

Note	Long	Fixed	Word	Integer	Long	Fixed	Word	Integer

3 octaves above middle C

Note	Long	Fixed	Word	Integer	Long	Fixed	Word	Integer
C	184ADA	24.29239	173	371	1812EB	24.07390	176	374
C#	199EF2	25.62088	160	352	198163	25.50542	161	353
Db	19E971	25.91188	15C	348				
D	1B5436	27.32895	14A	330	1B05A5	27.02205	14D	333
Ebb	1BA3AC	27.63934	146	326				
D#	1C77B8	28.46765	13D	317	1CA0FD	28.62886	13B	315
Eb	1D26A0	29.15088	135	309				
E	1E5D91	30.36549	129	297	1E54CB	30.33122	129	297
F	2063CE	32.38986	116	278	202283	32.13481	118	280
F#	222943	34.16118	108	264	220BAF	34.04564	109	265
Gb	228C97	34.54918	105	261				
G	247047	36.43858	F7	247	2411F2	36.07010	FA	250
G#	25F4F5	37.95686	ED	237	263706	38.21494	EC	236
Ab	26DE2A	38.86783	E8	232				
A	287CC1	40.48732	DF	223	287CC1	40.48732	DF	223
Bbb	28F27A	40.94717	DC	220				
A#	2A82FE	42.51169	D4	212	2AE513	42.89482	D2	210
Bb	2B2FBD	43.18648	D1	209				
B	2D8C59	45.54823	C6	198	2D720B	45.44548	C6	198

The following table gives the ratios used in calculating the above values. It shows the relationship between the notes making up the just-tempered scale in the key of C; should you need to implement a just-tempered scale in some other key, you can do so as follows: First get the value of the root note in the proper octave in the equal-tempered scale (from the above table). Then use the following table to determine the values of the intervals for the other notes in the key by multiplying the ratio by the root note.

Chromatic interval	Note	Just-tempered frequency ratio	Equal-tempered frequency ratio	Interval type
0	C	1.00000	1.00000	Unison
1	C#	1.05469	1.05946	Minor second as chromatic semitone
	Db	1.06667		Minor second as diatonic semitone
2	D	1.11111	1.12246	Major second as minor tone
	D	1.12500		Major second as major tone
	Ebb	1.13778		Diminished third
3	D#	1.17188	1.18921	Augmented second
	Eb	1.20000		Minor third
4	E	1.25000	1.25992	Major third
5	F	1.33333	1.33484	Fourth
6	F#	1.40625	1.41421	Tritone as augmented fourth
	Gb	1.42222		Tritone as diminished fifth
7	G	1.50000	1.49831	Fifth

Chromatic interval	Note	Just-tempered frequency ratio	Equal-tempered frequency ratio	Interval type
8	G#	1.56250	1.58740	Augmented fifth
	Ab	1.60000		Minor sixth
9	A	1.66667	1.68179	Major sixth
	Bbb	1.68560		Diminished seventh
10	A#	1.75000	1.78180	Augmented sixth
	Bb	1.77778		Minor seventh
11	B	1.87500	1.88775	Major seventh
12	C	2.00000	2.00000	Octave

8 Sound Driver

9 THE SERIAL DRIVERS

9 Serial Drivers

ABOUT THIS CHAPTER

The Macintosh RAM Serial Driver and ROM Serial Driver are Macintosh device drivers for handling asynchronous serial communication between a Macintosh application and serial devices. This chapter describes the Serial Drivers in detail.

You should already be familiar with:

- resources, as discussed in chapter 5 of Volume I
- events, as discussed in chapter 8 of Volume I
- the Memory Manager
- interrupts and the use of devices and device drivers, as described in chapter 6
- asynchronous serial data communication

SERIAL COMMUNICATION

The Serial Drivers support full-duplex asynchronous serial communication. **Serial data** is transmitted over a single-path communication line, one bit at a time (as opposed to parallel data, which is transmitted over a multiple-path communication line, multiple bits at a time). **Full-duplex** means that the Macintosh and another serial device connected to it can transmit data simultaneously (as opposed to half-duplex operation, in which data can be transmitted by only one device at a time). **Asynchronous communication** means that the Macintosh and other serial devices communicating with it don't share a common timer, and no timing data is transmitted. The time interval between characters transmitted asynchronously can be of any length. The format of asynchronous serial data communication used by the Serial Drivers is shown in Figure 1.

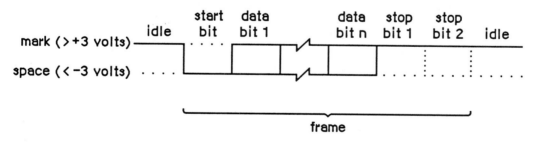

Figure 1. Asynchronous Data Transmission

When a transmitting serial device is idle (not sending data), it maintains the transmission line in a continuous state ("mark" in Figure 1). The transmitting device may begin sending a character at any time by sending a **start bit**. The start bit tells the receiving device to prepare to receive a character. The transmitting device then transmits 5, 6, 7, or 8 **data bits**, optionally followed by a **parity bit**. The value of the parity bit is chosen such that the number of 1's among the data and parity bits is even or odd, depending on whether the parity is even or odd, respectively. Finally, the transmitting device sends 1, 1.5, or 2 **stop bits**, indicating the end of the character. The measure of the total number of bits sent over the transmission line per second is called the **baud rate**.

If a parity bit is set incorrectly, the receiving device will note a **parity error**. The time elapsed from the start bit to the last stop bit is called a **frame**. If the receiving device doesn't get a stop bit after the data and parity bits, it will note a **framing error**. After the stop bits, the transmitting device may send another character or maintain the line in the mark state. If the line is held in the "space" state (Figure 1) for one frame or longer, a **break** occurs. Breaks are used to interrupt data transmission.

ABOUT THE SERIAL DRIVERS

There are two Macintosh device drivers for serial communication: the RAM Serial Driver and the ROM Serial Driver. The two drivers are nearly identical, although the RAM driver has a few features the ROM driver doesn't. Both allow Macintosh applications to communicate with serial devices via the two serial ports on the back of the Macintosh.

> **Note:** There are actually two versions of the RAM Serial Driver; one is for the Macintosh 128K and 512K, the other is for the Macintosh XL. If you want your application to run on all versions of the Macintosh, you should install both drivers in your application resource file, as resources of type 'SERD'. The resource ID should be 1 for the Macintosh 128K and 512K driver, and 2 for the Macintosh XL driver.

Each Serial Driver actually consists of four drivers: one input driver and one output driver for the modem port, and one input driver and one output driver for the printer port (Figure 2). Each **input driver** receives data via a serial port and transfers it to the application. Each **output driver** takes data from the application and sends it out through a serial port. The input and output drivers for a port are closely related, and share some of the same routines. Each driver does, however, have a separate device control entry, which allows the Serial Drivers to support full-duplex communication. An individual port can both transmit and receive data at the same time. The serial ports are controlled by the Macintosh's Zilog Z8530 Serial Communications Controller (SCC). Channel A of the SCC controls the modem port, and channel B controls the printer port.

Data received via a serial port passes through a three-character buffer in the SCC and then into a buffer in the input driver for the port. Characters are removed from the input driver's buffer each time an application issues a Read call to the driver. Each input driver's buffer can initially hold up to 64 characters, but your application can specify a larger buffer if necessary. The following errors may occur:

- If the SCC buffer ever overflows (because the input driver doesn't read it often enough), a **hardware overrun error** occurs.

- If an input driver's buffer ever overflows (because the application doesn't issue Read calls to the driver often enough), a **software overrun error** occurs.

The printer port should be used for output-only connections to devices such as printers, or at low baud rates (300 baud or less). The modem port has no such restrictions. It may be used simultaneously with disk accesses without fear of hardware overrun errors, because whenever the Disk Driver must turn off interrupts for longer than 100 microseconds, it stores any data received via the modem port and later passes the data to the modem port's input driver.

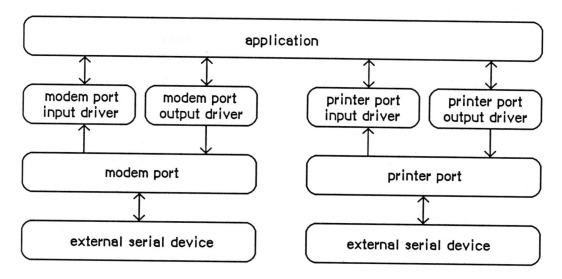

Figure 2. Input and Output Drivers of a Serial Driver

All four drivers default to 9600 baud, eight data bits per character, no parity bit, and two stop bits. You can change any of these options. The Serial Drivers support Clear To Send (CTS) hardware handshake and XOn/XOff software flow control.

Note: The ROM Serial Driver defaults to hardware handshake only; it doesn't support XOn/XOff input flow control—only output flow control. Use the RAM Serial Driver if you want XOn/XOff input flow control. The RAM Serial Driver defaults to no hardware handshake and no software flow control.

Whenever an input driver receives a break, it terminates any pending Read requests, but not Write requests. You can choose to have the input drivers terminate Read requests whenever a parity, overrun, or framing error occurs.

Note: The ROM Serial Driver always terminates input requests when an error occurs. Use the RAM Serial Driver if you don't want input requests to be terminated by errors.

You can request the Serial Drivers to post device driver events whenever a change in the hardware handshake status or a break occurs, if you want your application to take some specific action upon these occurrences.

USING THE SERIAL DRIVERS

This section introduces you to the Serial Driver routines described in detail in the next section, and discusses other calls you can make to communicate with the Serial Drivers.

Drivers are referred to by name and reference number:

9 Serial Drivers

Driver	Driver name	Reference number
Modem port input	.AIn	–6
Modem port output	.AOut	–7
Printer port input	.BIn	–8
Printer port output	.BOut	–9

Before you can receive data through a port, both the input and output drivers for the port must be opened. Before you can send data through a port, the output driver for the port must be opened. To open the ROM input and output drivers, call the Device Manager Open function; to open the RAM input and output drivers, call the Serial Driver function RAMSDOpen. The RAM drivers occupy less than 2K bytes of memory in the application heap.

When you open an output driver, the Serial Driver initializes local variables for the output driver and the associated input driver, allocates and locks buffer storage for both drivers, installs interrupt handlers for both drivers, and initializes the correct SCC channel (ROM Serial Driver only). When you open an input driver, the Serial Driver only notes the location of its device control entry.

You shouldn't ever close the ROM Serial Driver with a Device Manager Close call. If you wish to replace it with a RAM Serial Driver, the RAMSDOpen call will automatically close the ROM driver for you. You must close the RAM Serial Driver with a call to RAMSDClose before your application terminates; this will also release the memory occupied by the driver itself. When you close an output driver, the Serial Driver resets the appropriate SCC channel, releases all local variable and buffer storage space, and restores any changed interrupt vectors.

To transmit serial data out through a port, make a Device Manager Write call to the output driver for the port. You must pass the following parameters:

■ the driver reference number –7 or –9, depending on whether you're using the modem port or the printer port

■ a buffer that contains the data you want to transmit

■ the number of bytes you want to transmit

To receive serial data from a port, make a Device Manager Read call to the input driver for the port. You must pass the following parameters:

■ the driver reference number –6 or –8, depending on whether you're using the modem port or the printer port

■ a buffer to receive the data

■ the number of bytes you want to receive

There are six different calls you can make to the Serial Driver's control routine:

■ KillIO causes all current I/O requests to be aborted and any bytes remaining in both input buffers to be discarded. KillIO is a Device Manager call.

■ SerReset resets and reinitializes a driver with new data bits, stop bits, parity bit, and baud rate information.

■ SerSetBuf allows you to specify a new input buffer, replacing the driver's 64-character default buffer.

■ SerHShake allows you to specify handshake options.

- SerSetBrk sets break mode.

- SerClrBrk clears break mode.

Advanced programmers can make nine additional calls to the RAM Serial Driver's control routine; see the "Advanced Control Calls" section.

There are two different calls you can make to the Serial Driver's status routine:

- SerGetBuf returns the number of bytes in the buffer of an input driver.

- SerStatus returns information about errors, I/O requests, and handshake.

Assembly-language note: Control and Status calls to the RAM Serial Driver may be immediate (use IMMED as the second argument to the routine macro).

SERIAL DRIVER ROUTINES

Most of the Serial Driver routines return an integer result code of type OSErr; each routine description lists all of the applicable result codes.

Opening and Closing the RAM Serial Driver

```
FUNCTION RAMSDOpen (whichPort: SPortSel) : OSErr;    [Not in ROM]
```

RAMSDOpen closes the ROM Serial Driver and opens the RAM input and output drivers for the port identified by the whichPort parameter, which must be a member of the SPortSel set:

```
TYPE SPortSel =  (sPortA, {modem port}
                  sPortB  {printer port});
```

RAMSDOpen determines what type of Macintosh is in use and chooses the RAM Serial Driver appropriate to that machine.

Assembly-language note: To open the RAM input and output drivers from assembly language, call this Pascal procedure from your program.

Result codes   noErr   No error
                      openErr   Can't open driver

```
PROCEDURE RAMSDClose (whichPort: SPortSel);    [Not in ROM]
```

RAMSDClose closes the RAM input and output drivers for the port identified by the whichPort parameter, which must be a member of the SPortSel set (defined in the description of RAMSDOpen above).

> **Warning:** The RAM Serial Driver *must* be closed with a call to RAMSDClose before your application terminates.

> **Assembly-language note:** To close the RAM input and output drivers from assembly language, call this Pascal procedure from your program.

Changing Serial Driver Information

```
FUNCTION SerReset (refNum: INTEGER; serConfig: INTEGER) : OSErr;
          [Not in ROM]
```

> **Assembly-language note:** SerReset is equivalent to a Control call with csCode=8 and csParam=serConfig.

SerReset resets and reinitializes the input or output driver having the reference number refNum according to the information in serConfig. Figure 3 shows the format of serConfig.

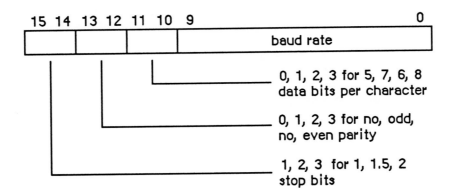

Figure 3. Driver Reset Information

You can use the following predefined constants to set the values of various bits of serConfig:

```
CONST baud300    =  380;    {300 baud}
      baud600    =  189;    {600 baud}
      baud1200   =   94;    {1200 baud}
      baud1800   =   62;    {1800 baud}
      baud2400   =   46;    {2400 baud}
```

```
baud3600    =    30;      {3600 baud}
baud4800    =    22;      {4800 baud}
baud7200    =    14;      {7200 baud}
baud9600    =    10;      {9600 baud}
baud19200   =    4;       {19200 baud}
baud57600   =    0;       {57600 baud}
stop10      =    16384;   {1 stop bit}
stop15      =   -32768;   {1.5 stop bits}
stop20      =   -16384;   {2 stop bits}
noParity    =    0;       {no parity}
oddParity   =    4096;    {odd parity}
evenParity  =    12288;   {even parity}
data5       =    0;       {5 data bits}
data6       =    2048;    {6 data bits}
data7       =    1024;    {7 data bits}
data8       =    3072;    {8 data bits}
```

For example, the default setting of 9600 baud, eight data bits, two stop bits, and no parity bit is equivalent to passing the following value in serConfig: baud9600 + data8 + stop20 + noParity.

Result codes   noErr   No error

```
FUNCTION SerSetBuf (refNum: INTEGER; serBPtr: Ptr; serBLen:
        INTEGER) : OSErr;    [Not in ROM]
```

Assembly-language note: SerSetBuf is equivalent to a Control call with csCode=9, csParam=serBPtr, and csParam+4=serBLen.

SerSetBuf specifies a new input buffer for the input driver having the reference number refNum. SerBPtr points to the buffer, and serBLen specifies the number of bytes in the buffer. To restore the driver's default buffer, call SerSetBuf with serBLen set to 0.

Warning: You must lock a new input buffer while it's in use.

Result codes   noErr   No error

```
FUNCTION SerHShake (refNum: INTEGER; flags: SerShk) : OSErr;    [Not
        in ROM]
```

Assembly-language note: SerHShake is equivalent to a Control call with csCode=10 and csParam through csParam+6 flags.

SerHShake sets handshake options and other control information, as specified by the flags parameter, for the input or output driver having the reference number refNum. The flags parameter has the following data structure:

```
TYPE SerShk =   PACKED RECORD
                fXOn: Byte;   {XOn/XOff output flow control flag}
                fCTS: Byte;   {CTS hardware handshake flag}
                xOn:  CHAR;   {XOn character}
                xOff: CHAR;   {XOff character}
                errs: Byte;   {errors that cause abort}
                evts: Byte;   {status changes that cause events}
                fInX: Byte;   {XOn/XOff input flow control flag}
                null: Byte    {not used}
              END;
```

If fXOn is nonzero, XOn/XOff output flow control is enabled; if fInX is nonzero, XOn/XOff input flow control is enabled. XOn and xOff specify the XOn character and XOff character used for XOn/XOff flow control. If fCTS is nonzero, CTS hardware handshake is enabled. The errs field indicates which errors will cause input requests to be aborted; for each type of error, there's a predefined constant in which the corresponding bit is set:

```
CONST parityErr     = 16;   {set if parity error}
      hwOverrunErr  = 32;   {set if hardware overrun error}
      framingErr    = 64;   {set if framing error}
```

Note: The ROM Serial Driver doesn't support XOn/XOff input flow control or aborts caused by error conditions.

The evts field indicates whether changes in the CTS or break status will cause the Serial Driver to post device driver events. You can use the following predefined constants to set or test the value of evts:

```
CONST ctsEvent    = 32;    {set if CTS change will cause event to be }
                           { posted}
      breakEvent = 128;    {set if break status change will cause event }
                           { to be posted}
```

Warning: Use of this option is discouraged because of the long time that interrupts are disabled while such an event is posted.

Result codes   noErr   No error

```
FUNCTION SerSetBrk (refNum: INTEGER) : OSErr;   [Not in ROM]
```

Assembly-language note: SerSetBrk is equivalent to a Control call with csCode=12.

SerSetBrk sets break mode in the input or output driver having the reference number refNum.

Result codes   noErr   No error

```
FUNCTION SerClrBrk (refNum: INTEGER) : OSErr;   [Not in ROM]
```

Assembly-language note: SerClrBrk is equivalent to a Control call with csCode=11.

SerClrBrk clears break mode in the input or output driver having the reference number refNum.

Result codes   noErr   No error

Getting Serial Driver Information

```
FUNCTION SerGetBuf (refNum: INTEGER; VAR count: LONGINT) : OSErr;
        [Not in ROM]
```

Assembly-language note: SerGetBuf is equivalent to a Status call with csCode=2; count is returned in csParam as a long word.

SerGetBuf returns, in the count parameter, the number of bytes in the buffer of the input driver having the reference number refNum.

Result codes   noErr   No error

```
FUNCTION SerStatus (refNum: INTEGER; VAR serSta: SerStaRec) :
        OSErr;   [Not in ROM]
```

Assembly-language note: SerStatus is equivalent to a Status call with csCode=8; serSta is returned in csParam through csParam+5.

SerStatus returns in serSta three words of status information for the input or output driver having the reference number refNum. SerSta has the following data structure:

```
TYPE SerStaRec =  PACKED RECORD
                    cumErrs:  Byte;   {cumulative errors}
                    xOffSent: Byte;   {XOff sent as input flow control}
                    rdPend:   Byte;   {read pending flag}
                    wrPend:   Byte;   {write pending flag}
                    ctsHold:  Byte;   {CTS flow control hold flag}
                    xOffHold: Byte    {XOff flow control hold flag}
                  END;
```

CumErrs indicates which errors have occurred since the last time SerStatus was called:

```
CONST swOverrunErr = 1;    {set if software overrun error}
      parityErr    = 16;   {set if parity error}
      hwOverrunErr = 32;   {set if hardware overrun error}
      framingErr   = 64;   {set if framing error}
```

If the driver has sent an XOff character, xOffSent will be equal to the following predefined constant:

```
CONST xOffWasSent = $80;   {XOff character was sent}
```

If the driver has a Read or Write call pending, rdPend or wrPend, respectively, will be nonzero. If output has been suspended because the hardware handshake was disabled, ctsHold will be nonzero. If output has been suspended because an XOff character was received, xOffHold will be nonzero.

Result codes   noErr   No error

ADVANCED CONTROL CALLS

This section describes the calls that advanced programmers can make to the RAM Serial Driver's control routine via a Device Manager Control call.

csCode = 13   csParam = baudRate

This call provides an additional way (besides SerReset) to set the baud rate. CsParam specifies the actual baud rate as an integer (for instance, 9600). The closest baud rate that the Serial Driver will generate is returned in csParam.

csCode = 19   csParam = char

After this call is made, all incoming characters with parity errors will be replaced by the character specified by the ASCII code in csParam. If csParam is 0, no character replacement will be done.

csCode = 21

This call unconditionally sets XOff for output flow control. It's equivalent to receiving an XOff character. Data transmission is halted until an XOn is received or a Control call with csCode=24 is made.

csCode = 22

This call unconditionally clears XOff for output flow control. It's equivalent to receiving an XOn character.

csCode = 23

This call sends an XOn character for input flow control if the last input flow control character sent was XOff.

csCode = 24

This call unconditionally sends an XOn character for input flow control, regardless of the current state of input flow control.

csCode = 25

This call sends an XOff character for input flow control if the last input flow control character sent was XOn.

csCode = 26

This call unconditionally sends an XOff character for input flow control, regardless of the current state of input flow control.

csCode = 27

This call lets you reset the SCC channel belonging to the driver specified by ioRefNum before calling RAMSDClose or SerReset.

SUMMARY OF THE SERIAL DRIVERS

Constants

```
CONST  { Driver reset information }

       baud300     =  380;      {300 baud}
       baud600     =  189;      {600 baud}
       baud1200    =  94;       {1200 baud}
       baud1800    =  62;       {1800 baud}
       baud2400    =  46;       {2400 baud}
       baud3600    =  30;       {3600 baud}
       baud4800    =  22;       {4800 baud}
       baud7200    =  14;       {7200 baud}
       baud9600    =  10;       {9600 baud}
       baud19200   =  4;        {19200 baud}
       baud57600   =  0;        {57600 baud}
       stop10      =  16384;    {1 stop bit}
       stop15      = -32768;    {1.5 stop bits}
       stop20      = -16384;    {2 stop bits}
       noParity    =  0;        {no parity}
       oddParity   =  4096;     {odd parity}
       evenParity  =  12288;    {even parity}
       data5       =  0;        {5 data bits}
       data6       =  2048;     {6 data bits}
       data7       =  1024;     {7 data bits}
       data8       =  3072;     {8 data bits}

       { Masks for errors }

       swOverrunErr = 1;   {set if software overrun error}
       parityErr    = 16;  {set if parity error}
       hwOverrunErr = 32;  {set if hardware overrun error}
       framingErr   = 64;  {set if framing error}

       { Masks for changes that cause events to be posted }

       ctsEvent    = 32;   {set if CTS change will cause event to be }
                           { posted}
       breakEvent  = 128;  {set if break status change will cause event }
                           { to be posted}

       { Indication that an XOff character was sent }

       xOffWasSent = $80;

       { Result codes }

       noErr   =  0;    {no error}
       openErr = -23;   {attempt to open RAM Serial Driver failed}
```

Data Types

```
TYPE SPortSel = (sPortA,  {modem port}
                 sPortB   {printer port});

     SerShk =  PACKED RECORD
                 fXOn: Byte;  {XOn/XOff output flow control flag}
                 fCTS: Byte;  {CTS hardware handshake flag}
                 xOn:  CHAR;  {XOn character}
                 xOff: CHAR;  {XOff character}
                 errs: Byte;  {errors that cause abort}
                 evts: Byte;  {status changes that cause events}
                 fInX: Byte;  {XOn/XOff input flow control flag}
                 null: Byte   {not used}
               END;

     SerStaRec =  PACKED RECORD
                 cumErrs:  Byte;  {cumulative errors}
                 xOffSent: Byte;  {XOff sent as input flow control}
                 rdPend:   Byte;  {read pending flag}
                 wrPend:   Byte;  {write pending flag}
                 ctsHold:  Byte;  {CTS flow control hold flag}
                 xOffHold: Byte   {XOff flow control hold flag}
               END;
```

Routines [Not in ROM]

Opening and Closing the RAM Serial Driver

```
FUNCTION  RAMSDOpen  (whichPort: SPortSel) : OSErr;
PROCEDURE RAMSDClose (whichPort: SPortSel);
```

Changing Serial Driver Information

```
FUNCTION SerReset  (refNum: INTEGER; serConfig: INTEGER) : OSErr;
FUNCTION SerSetBuf (refNum: INTEGER; serBPtr: Ptr; serBLen: INTEGER) :
                    OSErr;
FUNCTION SerHShake (refNum: INTEGER; flags: SerShk) : OSErr;
FUNCTION SerSetBrk (refNum: INTEGER) : OSErr;
FUNCTION SerClrBrk (refNum: INTEGER) : OSErr;
```

Getting Serial Driver Information

```
FUNCTION SerGetBuf (refNum: INTEGER; VAR count: LONGINT) : OSErr;
FUNCTION SerStatus (refNum: INTEGER; VAR serSta: SerStaRec) : OSErr;
```

Advanced Control Calls (RAM Serial Driver)

csCode	csParam	Effect
13	baudRate	Set baud rate (actual rate, as an integer)
19	char	Replace parity errors
21		Unconditionally set XOff for output flow control
22		Unconditionally clear XOff for input flow control
23		Send XOn for input flow control if XOff was sent last
24		Unconditionally send XOn for input flow control
25		Send XOff for input flow control if XOn was sent last
26		Unconditionally send XOff for input flow control
27		Reset SCC channel

Driver Names and Reference Numbers

Driver	Driver name	Reference number
Modem port input	.AIn	–6
Modem port output	.AOut	–7
Printer port input	.BIn	–8
Printer port output	.BOut	–9

Assembly-Language Information

Constants

```
; Result codes

noErr       .EQU    0       ;no error
openErr     .EQU    -23     ;attempt to open RAM Serial Driver failed
```

Structure of Control Information for SerHShake

shFXOn	XOn/XOff output flow control flag (byte)
shFCTS	CTS hardware handshake flag (byte)
shXOn	XOn character (byte)
shXOff	XOff character (byte)
shErrs	Errors that cause abort (byte)
shEvts	Status changes that cause events (byte)
shFInX	XOn/XOff input flow control flag (byte)

Structure of Status Information for SerStatus

ssCumErrs	Cumulative errors (byte)
ssXOffSent	XOff sent as input flow control (byte)
ssRdPend	Read pending flag (byte)
ssWrPend	Write pending flag (byte)
ssCTSHold	CTS flow control hold flag (byte)
ssXOffHold	XOff flow control hold flag (byte)

Equivalent Device Manager Calls

Pascal routine	Call
SerReset	Control with csCode=8, csParam=serConfig
SerSetBuf	Control with csCode=8, csParam=serBPtr, csParam+4=serBLen
SerHShake	Control with csCode=10, csParam through csParam+6=flags
SerSetBrk	Control with csCode=12
SerClrBrk	Control with csCode=11
SerGetBuf	Status with csCode=2; count returned in csParam
SerStatus	Status with csCode=8; serSta returned in csParam through csParam+5

9 Serial Drivers

10   THE APPLETALK MANAGER

ABOUT THIS CHAPTER

The AppleTalk Manager is an interface to a pair of RAM device drivers that allow Macintosh programs to send and receive information via an AppleTalk network. This chapter describes the AppleTalk Manager in detail.

You should already be familiar with:

- events, as discussed in chapter 8 of Volume I

- interrupts and the use of devices and device drivers, as described in chapter 6, if you want to write your own assembly-language additions to the AppleTalk Manager

- the *Inside AppleTalk* manual, if you want to understand AppleTalk protocols in detail

APPLETALK PROTOCOLS

The AppleTalk Manager provides a variety of services that allow Macintosh programs to interact with programs in devices connected to an AppleTalk network. This interaction, achieved through the exchange of variable-length blocks of data (known as packets) over AppleTalk, follows well-defined sets of rules known as **protocols**.

Although most programmers using AppleTalk needn't understand the details of these protocols, they should understand the information in this section—what the services provided by the different protocols are, and how the protocols are interrelated. Detailed information about AppleTalk protocols is available in *Inside AppleTalk*.

The AppleTalk system architecture consists of a number of protocols arranged in layers. Each protocol in a specific layer provides services to higher-level layers (known as the protocol's clients) by building on the services provided by lower-level layers. A Macintosh program can use services provided by any of the layers in order to construct more sophisticated or more specialized services.

The AppleTalk Manager contains the following protocols:

- AppleTalk Link Access Protocol

- Datagram Delivery Protocol

- Routing Table Maintenance Protocol

- Name-Binding Protocol

- AppleTalk Transaction Protocol

Figure 1 illustrates the layered structure of the protocols in the AppleTalk Manager; the heavy connecting lines indicate paths of interaction. Note that the Routing Table Maintenance Protocol isn't directly accessible to Macintosh programs.

The **AppleTalk Link Access Protocol** (ALAP) provides the lowest-level services of the AppleTalk system. Its main function is to control access to the AppleTalk network among various competing devices. Each device connected to an AppleTalk network, known as a **node**, is assigned an eight-bit **node ID** number that identifies the node. ALAP ensures that each node

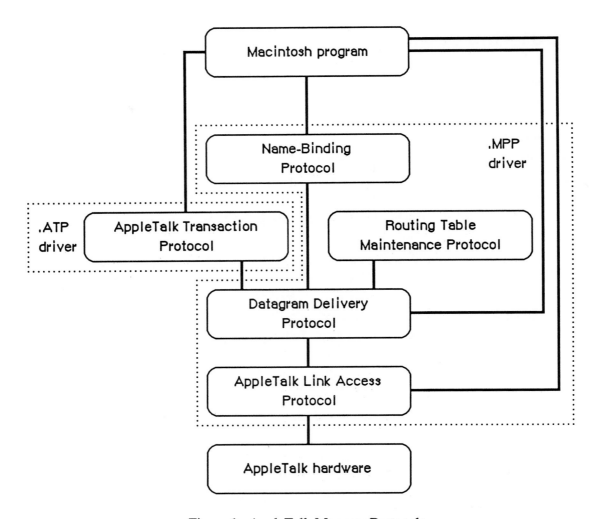

Figure 1. AppleTalk Manager Protocols

on an AppleTalk network has a unique node ID, assigned dynamically when the node is started up.

ALAP provides its clients with node-to-node delivery of data frames on a *single* AppleTalk network. An **ALAP frame** is a variable-length packet of data preceded and followed by control information referred to as the ALAP **frame header** and **frame trailer**, respectively. The ALAP frame header includes the node IDs of the frame's destination and source nodes. The AppleTalk hardware uses the destination node ID to deliver the frame. The frame's source node ID allows a program in the receiving node to determine the identity of the source. A sending node can ask ALAP to send a frame to all nodes on the AppleTalk network; this **broadcast service** is obtained by specifying a destination node ID of 255.

ALAP can have multiple clients in a single node. When a frame arrives at a node, ALAP determines which client it should be delivered to by reading the frame's **ALAP protocol type**. The ALAP protocol type is an eight-bit quantity, contained in the frame's header, that identifies the ALAP client to whom the frame will be sent. ALAP calls the client's **protocol handler**, which is a software process in the node that reads in and then services the frames. The protocol handlers for a node are listed in a **protocol handler table**.

An ALAP frame trailer contains a 16-bit **frame check sequence** generated by the AppleTalk hardware. The receiving node uses the frame check sequence to detect transmission errors, and discards frames with errors. In effect, a frame with an error is "lost" in the AppleTalk network, because ALAP doesn't attempt to recover from errors by requesting the sending node to retransmit such frames. Thus ALAP is said to make a "best effort" to deliver frames, without any guarantee of delivery.

An ALAP frame can contain up to 600 bytes of client data. The first two bytes must be an integer equal to the length of the client data (including the length bytes themselves).

Datagram Delivery Protocol (DDP) provides the next-higher level protocol in the AppleTalk architecture, managing socket-to-socket delivery of datagrams over AppleTalk internets. DDP is an ALAP client, and uses the node-to-node delivery service provided by ALAP to send and receive datagrams. **Datagrams** are packets of data transmitted by DDP. A DDP datagram can contain up to 586 bytes of client data. **Sockets** are logical entities within the nodes of a network; each socket within a given node has a unique eight-bit **socket number**.

On a single AppleTalk network, a socket is uniquely identified by its **AppleTalk address**—its socket number together with its node ID. To identify a socket in the scope of an AppleTalk internet, the socket's AppleTalk address and **network number** are needed. **Internets** are formed by interconnecting AppleTalk networks via intelligent nodes called **bridges**. A network number is a 16-bit number that uniquely identifies a network in an internet. A socket's AppleTalk address together with its network number provide an internet-wide unique socket identifier called an **internet address**.

Sockets are owned by **socket clients**, which typically are software processes in the node. Socket clients include code called the **socket listener**, which receives and services datagrams addressed to that socket. Socket clients must open a socket before datagrams can be sent or received through it. Each node contains a **socket table** that lists the listener for each open socket.

A datagram is sent from its source socket through a series of AppleTalk networks, being passed on from bridge to bridge, until it reaches its destination network. The ALAP in the destination network then delivers the datagram to the node containing the destination socket. Within that node the datagram is received by ALAP calling the DDP protocol handler, and by the DDP protocol handler in turn calling the destination socket listener, which for most applications will be a higher-level protocol such as the AppleTalk Transaction Protocol. You can't send a datagram between two sockets in the same node.

Bridges on AppleTalk internets use the **Routing Table Maintenance Protocol** (RTMP) to maintain **routing tables** for routing datagrams through the internet. In addition, nonbridge nodes use RTMP to determine the number of the network to which they're connected and the node ID of one bridge on their network. The RTMP code in nonbridge nodes contains only a subset of RTMP (the **RTMP stub**), and is a DDP client owning socket number 1 (the **RTMP socket**).

Socket clients are also known as **network-visible entities**, because they're the primary accessible entities on an internet. Network-visible entities can choose to identify themselves by an **entity name**, an identifier of the form

object:type@zone

Each of the three fields of this name is an alphanumeric string of up to 32 characters. The object and type fields are arbitrary identifiers assigned by a socket client, to provide itself with a name and type descriptor (for example, abs:Mailbox). The zone field identifies the zone in which the socket client is located; a **zone** is an arbitrary subset of AppleTalk networks in an internet. A socket client can identify itself by as many different names as it chooses. These **aliases** are all treated as independent identifiers for the same socket client.

The **Name-Binding Protocol** (NBP) maintains a **names table** in each node that contains the name and internet address of each entity in *that* node. These name-address pairs are called **NBP tuples**. The collection of names tables in an internet is known as the **names directory**.

NBP allows its clients to add or delete their name-address tuples from the node's names table. It also allows its clients to obtain the internet addresses of entities from their names. This latter operation, known as **name lookup** (in the names directory), requires that NBP install itself as a DDP client and broadcast special name-lookup packets to the nodes in a specified zone. These datagrams are sent by NBP to the **names information socket**—socket number 2 in every node using NBP.

NBP clients can use special meta-characters in place of one or more of the three fields of the name of an entity it wishes to look up. The character "=" in the object or type field signifies "all possible values". The zone field can be replaced by "*", which signifies "this zone"—the zone in which the NBP client's node is located. For example, an NBP client performing a lookup with the name

```
=:Mailbox@*
```

will obtain in return the entity names and internet addresses of all mailboxes in the client's zone (excluding the client's own names and addresses). The client can specify whether one or all of the matching names should be returned.

NBP clients specify how thorough a name lookup should be by providing NBP with the number of times (**retry count**) that NBP should broadcast the lookup packets and the time interval (**retry interval**) between these retries.

As noted above, ALAP and DDP provide "best effort" delivery services with no recovery mechanism when packets are lost or discarded because of errors. Although for many situations such a service suffices, the **AppleTalk Transaction Protocol** (ATP) provides a reliable loss-free transport service. ATP uses **transactions**, consisting of a **transaction request** and a **transaction response**, to deliver data reliably. Each transaction is assigned a 16-bit **transaction ID** number to distinguish it from other transactions. A transaction request is retransmitted by ATP until a complete response has been received, thus allowing for recovery from packet-loss situations. The retry interval and retry count are specified by the ATP client sending the request.

Although transaction requests must be contained in a single datagram, transaction responses can consist of as many as eight datagrams. Each datagram in a response is assigned a **sequence number** from 0 to 7, to indicate its ordering within the response.

ATP is a DDP client, and uses the services provided by DDP to transmit requests and responses. ATP supports both **at-least-once** and **exactly-once** transactions. Four of the bytes in an ATP header, called the **user bytes**, are provided for use by ATP's clients—they're ignored by ATP.

ATP's transaction model and means of recovering from datagram loss are covered in detail below.

APPLETALK TRANSACTION PROTOCOL

This section covers ATP in greater depth, providing more detail about three of its fundamental concepts: transactions, buffer allocation, and recovery of lost datagrams.

Transactions

A transaction is a interaction between two ATP clients, known as the requester and the responder. The requester calls the .ATP driver in its node to send a transaction request (TReq) to the responder, and then awaits a response. The TReq is received by the .ATP driver in the responder's node and is delivered to the responder. The responder then calls its .ATP driver to send back a transaction response (TResp), which is received by the requester's .ATP driver and delivered to the requester. Figure 2 illustrates this process.

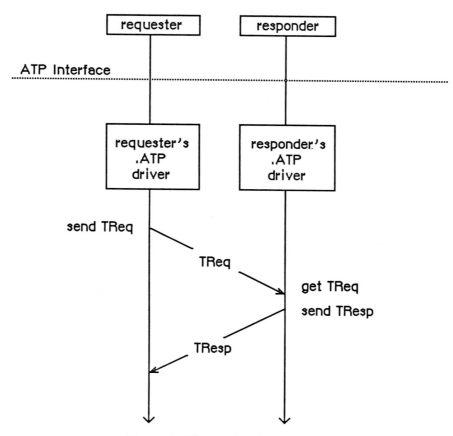

Figure 2. Transaction Process

Simple examples of transactions are:

- read a counter, reset it and send back the value read

- read six sectors of a disk and send back the data read

- write the data sent in the TReq to a printer

A basic assumption of the transaction model is that the amount of ATP data sent in the TReq specifying the operation to be performed is small enough to fit in a single datagram. A TResp, on the other hand, may span several datagrams, as in the second example. Thus, a TReq is a single datagram, while a TResp consists of up to eight datagrams, each of which is assigned a sequence number from 0 to 7 to indicate its position in the response.

The requester must, before calling for a TReq to be sent, set aside enough buffer space to receive the datagram(s) of the TResp. The number of buffers allocated (in other words, the maximum number of datagrams that the responder can send) is indicated in the TReq by an eight-bit bit map. The bits of this bit map are numbered 0 to 7 (the least significant bit being number 0); each bit corresponds to the response datagram with the respective sequence number.

Datagram Loss Recovery

The way that ATP recovers from datagram loss situations is best explained by an example; see Figure 3. Assume that the requester wants to read six sectors of 512 bytes each from the responder's disk. The requester puts aside six 512-byte buffers (which may or may not be contiguous) for the response datagrams, and calls ATP to send a TReq. In this TReq the bit map is set to binary 00111111 or decimal 63. The TReq carries a 16-bit transaction ID, generated by the requester's .ATP driver before sending it. (This example assumes that the requester and responder have already agreed that each buffer can hold 512 bytes.) The TReq is delivered to the responder, which reads the six disk sectors and sends them back, through ATP, in TResp datagrams bearing sequence numbers 0 through 5. Each TResp datagram also carries exactly the same transaction ID as the TReq to which they're responding.

There are several ways that datagrams may be lost in this case. The original TReq could be lost for one of many reasons. The responding node might be too busy to receive the TReq or might be out of buffers for receiving it, there could be an undetected collision on the network, a bit error in the transmission line, and so on. To recover from such errors, the requester's .ATP driver maintains an ATP retry timer for each transaction sent. If this timer expires and the complete TResp has not been received, the TReq is retransmitted and the retry timer is restarted.

A second error situation occurs when one or more of the TResp datagrams isn't received correctly by the requester's .ATP driver (datagram 1 in Figure 3). Again, the retry timer will expire and the complete TResp will not have been received; this will result in a retransmission of the TReq. However, to avoid unnecessary retransmission of the TResp datagrams already properly received, the bit map of this retransmitted TReq is modified to reflect only those datagrams not yet received. Upon receiving this TReq, the responder retransmits only the missing response datagrams.

Another possible failure is that the responder's .ATP driver goes down or the responder becomes unreachable through the underlying network system. In this case, retransmission of the TReq could continue indefinitely. To avoid this situation, the requester provides a maximum retry count; if this count is exceeded, the requester's .ATP driver returns an appropriate error message to the requester.

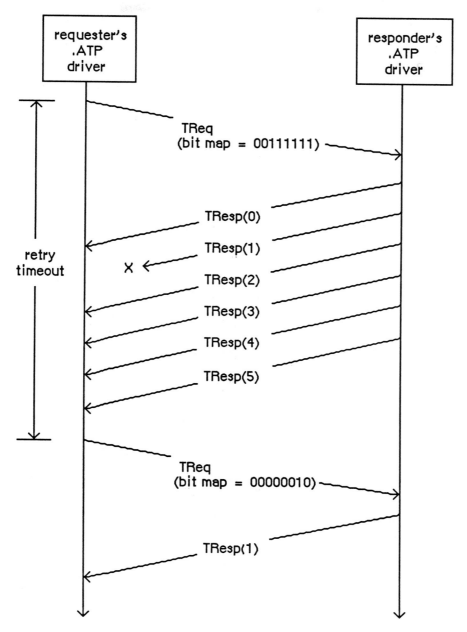

Figure 3. Datagram Loss Recovery

Note: There may be situations where, due to an anticipated delay, you'll want a request to be retransmitted more than 255 times; specifying a retry count of 255 indicates "infinite retries" to ATP and will cause a message to be retransmitted until the request has either been serviced, or been cancelled through a specific call.

Finally, in our example, what if the responder is able to provide only four disk sectors (having reached the end of the disk) instead of the six requested? To handle this situation, there's an end-of-message (EOM) flag in each TResp datagram. In this case, the TResp datagram numbered 3 would come with this flag set. The reception of this datagram informs the requester's .ATP driver that TResps numbered 4 and 5 will not be sent and should not be expected.

When the transaction completes successfully (all expected TResp datagrams are received or TResp datagrams numbered 0 to n are received with datagram n's EOM flag set), the requester is informed and can then use the data received in the TResp.

ATP provides two classes of service: at-least-once (ALO) and exactly-once (XO). The TReq datagram contains an XO flag that's set if XO service is required and cleared if ALO service is adequate. The main difference between the two is in the sequence of events that occurs when the TReq is received by the responder's .ATP driver.

In the case of ALO service, each time a TReq is received (with the XO flag cleared), it's delivered to the responder by its .ATP driver; this is true even for retransmitted TReqs of the same transaction. Each time the TReq is delivered, the responder performs the requested operation and sends the necessary TResp datagrams. Thus, the requested operation is performed at least once, and perhaps several times, until the transaction is completed at the requester's end.

The at-least-once service is satisfactory in a variety of situations—for instance, if the requester wishes to read a clock or a counter being maintained at the responder's end. However, in other circumstances, repeated execution of the requested operation is unacceptable. This is the case, for instance, if the requester is sending data to be printed at the responding end; exactly-once service is designed for such situations.

The responder's .ATP driver maintains a transactions list of recently received XO TReqs. Whenever a TReq is received with its XO flag set, the driver goes through this list to see if this is a retransmitted TReq. If it's the first TReq of a transaction, it's entered into the list and delivered to the responder. The responder executes the requested operation and calls its driver to send a TResp. Before sending it out, the .ATP driver *saves* the TResp in the list.

When a retransmitted TReq for the same XO transaction is received, the responder's .ATP driver will find a corresponding entry in the list. The retransmitted TReq is *not* delivered to the responder; instead, the driver automatically retransmits the response datagrams that were saved in the list. In this way, the responder never sees the retransmitted TReqs and the requested operation is performed only once.

ATP must include a mechanism for eventually removing XO entries from the responding end's transaction list; two provisions are made for this. When the requester's .ATP driver has received all the TResp datagrams of a particular transaction, it sends a datagram known as a transaction release (TRel); this tells the responder's .ATP driver to remove the transaction from the list. However, the TRel could be lost in the network (or the responding end may die, and so on), leaving the entry in the list forever. To account for this situation, the responder's .ATP driver maintains a **release timer** for each transaction. If this timer expires and no activity has occurred for the transaction, its entry is removed from the transactions list.

ABOUT THE APPLETALK MANAGER

The AppleTalk Manager is divided into three parts (see Figure 4):

- A lower-level driver called ".MPP" that contains code to implement ALAP, DDP, NBP, and the RTMP stub; this includes separate code resources loaded in when an NBP name is registered or looked up.

- A higher-level driver called ".ATP" that implements ATP.

- A Pascal interface to these two drivers, which is a set of Pascal data types and routines to aid Pascal programmers in calling the AppleTalk Manager.

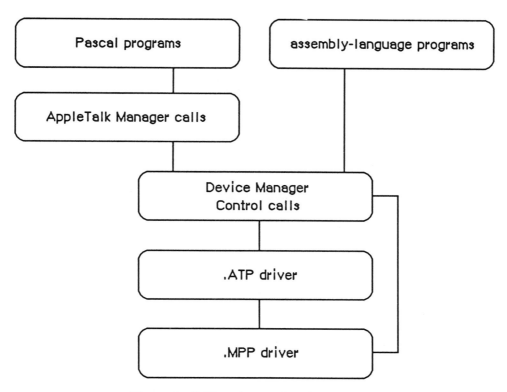

Figure 4. Calling the AppleTalk Manager

The two drivers and the interface to them are not in ROM; your application must link to the appropriate object files.

Pascal programmers make calls to the AppleTalk Manager's Pascal interface, which in turn makes Device Manager Control calls to the two drivers. Assembly-language programmers make Device Manager Control calls directly to the drivers.

Note: Pascal programmers can, of course, make PBControl calls directly if they wish.

The AppleTalk Manager provides ALAP routines that allow a program to:

■ send a frame to another node

■ receive a frame from another node

■ add a protocol handler to the protocol handler table

■ remove a protocol handler from the protocol handler table

Each node may have up to four protocol handlers in its protocol handler table, two of which are currently used by DDP.

By calling DDP, socket clients can:

■ send a datagram via a socket

■ receive a datagram via a socket

■ open a socket and add a socket listener to the socket table

■ close a socket and remove a socket listener from the socket table

Each node may have up to 12 open sockets in its socket table.

Programs cannot access RTMP directly via the AppleTalk Manager; RTMP exists solely for the purpose of providing DDP with routing information.

The NBP code allows a socket client to:

■ register the name and socket number of an entity in the node's names table

■ determine the address (and confirm the existence) of an entity

■ delete the name of an entity from the node's names table

The AppleTalk Manager's .ATP driver allows a socket client to do the following:

■ open a responding socket to receive requests

■ send a request to another socket and get back a response

■ receive a request via a responding socket

■ send a response via a responding socket

■ close a responding socket

Note: Although the AppleTalk Manager provides four different protocols for your use, you're not bound to use all of them. In fact, most programmers will use only the NBP and ATP protocols.

AppleTalk communicates via channel B of the Serial Communications Controller (SCC). When the Macintosh is started up with a disk containing the AppleTalk code, the status of serial port B is checked. If port B isn't being used by another device driver, and is available for use by AppleTalk, the .MPP driver is loaded into the system heap. On a Macintosh 128K, only the MPP code is loaded at system startup; the .ATP driver and NBP code are read into the application heap when the appropriate commands are issued. On a Macintosh 512K or XL, all AppleTalk code is loaded into the system heap at system startup.

After loading the AppleTalk code, the .MPP driver installs its own interrupt handlers, installs a task into the vertical retrace queue, and prepares the SCC for use. It then chooses a node ID for the Macintosh and confirms that the node ID isn't already being used by another node on the network.

> **Warning:** For this reason it's imperative that the Macintosh be connected to the AppleTalk network through serial port B (the printer port) *before* being switched on.

The AppleTalk Manager also provides Pascal routines for opening and closing the .MPP and .ATP drivers. The open calls allow a program to load AppleTalk code at times other than system startup. The close calls allow a program to remove the AppleTalk code from the Macintosh; the use of close calls is highly discouraged, since other co-resident programs are then "disconnected" from AppleTalk. Both sets of calls are described in detail under "Calling the AppleTalk Manager from Pascal".

> **Warning:** If, at system startup, serial port B isn't available for use by AppleTalk, the .MPP driver won't open. However, a driver doesn't return an error message when it fails to open. Pascal programmers must ensure the proper opening of AppleTalk by calling one of the two routines for opening the AppleTalk drivers (either MPPOpen or ATPLoad). If AppleTalk was successfully loaded at system startup, these calls will have no effect; otherwise they'll check the availability of port B, attempt to load the AppleTalk code, and return an appropriate result code.

Assembly-language note: Assembly-language programmers can use the Pascal routines for opening AppleTalk. They can also check the availability of port B themselves and then decide whether to open MPP or ATP. Detailed information on how to do this is provided in the section "Calling the AppleTalk Manager from Assembly Language".

CALLING THE APPLETALK MANAGER FROM PASCAL

This section discusses how to use the AppleTalk Manager from Pascal. Equivalent assembly-language information is given in the next section.

You can execute many AppleTalk Manager routines either **synchronously** (meaning that the application can't continue until the routine is completed) or **asynchronously** (meaning that the application is free to perform other tasks while the routine is being executed).

When an application calls an AppleTalk Manager routine asynchronously, an I/O request is placed in the appropriate driver's I/O queue, and control returns to the calling program—possibly even before the actual I/O is completed. Requests are taken from the queue one at a time, and processed; meanwhile, the calling program is free to work on other things.

The routines that can be executed asynchronously contain a Boolean parameter called async. If async is TRUE, the call is executed asynchronously; otherwise the call is executed synchronously. Every time an asynchronous routine call is completed, the AppleTalk Manager posts a network event. The message field of the event record will contain a handle to the parameter block that was used to make that call.

Most AppleTalk Manager routines return an integer result code of type OSErr. Each routine description lists all of the applicable result codes generated by the AppleTalk Manager, along with a short description of what the result code means. Lengthier explanations of all the result codes can be found in the summary at the end of the chapter. Result codes from other parts of the

Operating System may also be returned. (See Appendix A in Volume III for a list of all result codes.)

Many Pascal calls to the AppleTalk Manager require information passed in a parameter block of type ABusRecord. The exact content of an ABusRecord depends on the protocol being called:

```
TYPE ABProtoType = (lapProto,ddpProto,nbpProto,atpProto);

     ABusRecord = RECORD
                      abOpcode:       ABCallType; {type of call}
                      abResult:       INTEGER;    {result code}
                      abUserReference: LONGINT;   {for your use}
                      CASE ABProtoType OF
                        lapProto:
                          . . .  {ALAP parameters}
                        ddpProto:
                          . . .  {DDP parameters}
                        nbpProto:
                          . . .  {NBP parameters}
                        atpProto:
                          . . .  {ATP parameters}
                      END;
                  END;

     ABRecPtr    = ^ABusRecord;
     ABRecHandle = ^ABRecPtr;
```

The value of the abOpcode field is inserted by the AppleTalk Manager when the call is made, and is always a member of the following set:

```
TYPE ABCallType = (tLAPRead,tLAPWrite,tDDPRead,tDDPWrite,tNBPLookup,
                   tNBPConfirm,tNBPRegister,tATPSndRequest,
                   tATPGetRequest,tATPSdRsp,tATPAddRsp,tATPRequest,
                   tATPRespond);
```

The abUserReference field is available for use by the calling program in any way it wants. This field isn't used by the AppleTalk Manager routines or drivers.

The size of an ABusRecord data structure in bytes is given by one of the following constants:

```
CONST lapSize = 20;
      ddpSize = 26;
      nbpSize = 26;
      atpSize = 56;
```

Variables of type ABusRecord must be allocated in the heap with Memory Manager NewHandle calls. For example:

```
myABRecord := ABRecHandle(NewHandle(ddpSize))
```

Warning: These Memory Manager calls can't be made inside interrupts.

Routines that are executed asynchronously return control to the calling program with the result code noErr as soon as the call is placed in the driver's I/O queue. This isn't an indication of successful call completion; it simply indicates that the call was successfully queued to the appropriate driver. To determine when the call is actually completed, you can either check for a network event or poll the abResult field of the call's ABusRecord. The abResult field, set to 1 when the call is made, receives the actual result code upon completion of the call.

> **Warning:** A data structure of type ABusRecord is often used by the AppleTalk Manager during an asynchronous call, and so is locked by the AppleTalk Manager. Don't attempt to unlock or use such a variable.

Each routine description includes a list of the ABusRecord fields affected by the routine. The arrow next to each field name indicates whether it's an input, output, or input/output parameter:

Arrow	Meaning
→	Parameter is passed to the routine
←	Parameter is returned by the routine
↔	Parameter is passed to and returned by the routine

Opening and Closing AppleTalk

```
FUNCTION MPPOpen : OSErr;   [Not in ROM]
```

MPPOpen first checks whether the .MPP driver has already been loaded; if it has, MPPOpen does nothing and returns noErr. If MPP hasn't been loaded, MPPOpen attempts to load it into the system heap. If it succeeds, it then initializes the driver's variables and goes through the process of dynamically assigning a node ID to that Macintosh. On a Macintosh 512K or XL, it also loads the .ATP driver and NBP code into the system heap.

If serial port B isn't configured for AppleTalk, or is already in use, the .MPP driver isn't loaded and an appropriate result code is returned.

Result codes	noErr	No error
	portInUse	Port B is already in use
	portNotCf	Port B not configured for AppleTalk

```
FUNCTION MPPClose : OSErr;   [Not in ROM]
```

MPPClose removes the .MPP driver, and any data structures associated with it, from memory. If the .ATP driver or NBP code were also installed, they're removed as well. MPPClose also returns the use of port B to the Serial Driver.

> **Warning:** Since other co-resident programs may be using AppleTalk, it's strongly recommended that you never use this call. MPPClose will completely disable AppleTalk; the only way to restore AppleTalk is to call MPPOpen again.

AppleTalk Link Access Protocol

Data Structures

ALAP calls use the following ABusRecord fields:

```
lapProto:
   (lapAddress:   LAPAdrBlock; {destination or source node ID}
    lapReqCount:  INTEGER;     {length of frame data or buffer size in bytes}
    lapActCount:  INTEGER;     {number of frame data bytes actually received}
    lapDataPtr:   Ptr);        {pointer to frame data or pointer to buffer}
```

When an ALAP frame is sent, the lapAddress field indicates the ID of the destination node. When an ALAP frame is received, lapAddress returns the ID of the source node. The lapAddress field also indicates the ALAP protocol type of the frame:

```
TYPE LAPAdrBlock =  PACKED RECORD
                      dstNodeID:   Byte;      {destination node ID}
                      srcNodeID:   Byte;      {source node ID}
                      lapProtType: ABByte     {ALAP protocol type}
                    END;
```

When an ALAP frame is sent, lapReqCount indicates the size of the frame data in bytes and lapDataPtr points to a buffer containing the frame data to be sent. When an ALAP frame is received, lapDataPtr points to a buffer in which the incoming data can be stored and lapReqCount indicates the size of the buffer in bytes. The number of bytes actually sent or received is returned in the lapActCount field.

Each ALAP frame contains an eight-bit ALAP protocol type in the header. ALAP protocol types 128 through 255 are reserved for internal use by ALAP, hence the declaration:

```
TYPE ABByte = 1..127;   {ALAP protocol type}
```

Warning: Don't use ALAP protocol type values 1 and 2; they're reserved for use by DDP. Value 3 through 15 are reserved for internal use by Apple and also shouldn't be used.

Using ALAP

Most programs will never need to call ALAP, because higher-level protocols will automatically call it as necessary. If you do want to send a frame directly via ALAP, call the LAPWrite function. If you want to read ALAP frames, you have two choices:

■ Call LAPOpenProtocol with NIL for protoPtr (see below); this installs the default protocol handler provided by the AppleTalk Manager. Then call LAPRead to receive frames.

■ Write your own protocol handler, and call LAPOpenProtocol to add it to the node's protocol handler table. The ALAP code will examine every incoming frame and send all those with the correct ALAP protocol type to your protocol handler. See the section "Protocol Handlers and Socket Listeners" for information on how to write a protocol handler.

When your program no longer wants to receive frames with a particular ALAP protocol type value, it can call LAPCloseProtocol to remove the corresponding protocol handler from the protocol handler table.

ALAP Routines

```
FUNCTION LAPOpenProtocol (theLAPType: ABByte; protoPtr: Ptr) :
         OSErr;   [Not in ROM]
```

LAPOpenProtocol adds the ALAP protocol type specified by theLAPType to the node's protocol table. If you provide a pointer to a protocol handler in protoPtr, ALAP will send each frame with an ALAP protocol type of theLAPType to that protocol handler.

If protoPtr is NIL, the default protocol handler will be used for receiving frames with an ALAP protocol type of theLAPType. In this case, to receive a frame you must call LAPRead to provide the default protocol handler with a buffer for placing the data. If, however, you've written your own protocol handler and protoPtr points to it, your protocol handler will have the responsibility for receiving the frame and it's not necessary to call LAPRead.

Result codes	noErr	No error
	lapProtErr	Error attaching protocol type

```
FUNCTION LAPCloseProtocol (theLAPType: ABByte) : OSErr;   [Not in
         ROM]
```

LAPCloseProtocol removes from the node's protocol table the specified ALAP protocol type, as well as its protocol handler.

Warning: Don't close ALAP protocol type values 1 or 2. If you close these protocol types, DDP will be disabled; once disabled, the only way to restore DDP is to restart the system, or to close and then reopen AppleTalk.

Result codes	noErr	No error
	lapProtErr	Error detaching protocol type

```
FUNCTION LAPWrite (abRecord: ABRecHandle; async: BOOLEAN) :
         OSErr;   [Not in ROM]
```

ABusRecord

←	abOpcode	{always tLAPWrite}
←	abResult	{result code}
→	abUserReference	{for your use}
→	lapAddress.dstNodeID	{destination node ID}
→	lapAddress.lapProtType	{ALAP protocol type}
→	lapReqCount	{length of frame data}
→	lapDataPtr	{pointer to frame data}

LAPWrite sends a frame to another node. LAPReqCount and lapDataPtr specify the length and location of the data to send. The lapAddress.lapProtType field indicates the ALAP protocol type of the frame and the lapAddress.dstNodeID indicates the node ID of the node to which the frame should be sent.

Note: The first two bytes of an ALAP frame's data must contain the length in bytes of that data, including the length bytes themselves.

Result codes	noErr	No error
	excessCollsns	Unable to contact destination node; packet not sent
	ddpLenErr	ALAP data length too big
	lapProtErr	Invalid ALAP protocol type

```
FUNCTION LAPRead (abRecord: ABRecHandle; async: BOOLEAN) : OSErr;
        [Not in ROM]
```

ABusRecord

←	abOpcode	{always tLAPRead}
←	abResult	{result code}
→	abUserReference	{for your use}
←	lapAddress.dstNodeID	{destination node ID}
←	lapAddress.srcNodeID	{source node ID}
→	lapAddress.lapProtType	{ALAP protocol type}
→	lapReqCount	{buffer size in bytes}
←	lapActCount	{number of frame data bytes actually received}
→	lapDataPtr	{pointer to buffer}

LAPRead receives a frame from another node. LAPReqCount and lapDataPtr specify the size and location of the buffer that will receive the frame data. If the buffer isn't large enough to hold all of the incoming frame data, the extra bytes will be discarded and buf2SmallErr will be returned. The number of bytes actually received is returned in lapActCount. Only frames with ALAP protocol type equal to lapAddress.lapProtType will be received. The node IDs of the frame's source and destination nodes are returned in lapAddress.srcNodeID and lapAddress.dstNodeID. You can determine whether the packet was broadcast to you by examining the value of lapAddress.dstNodeID—if the packet was broadcast it's equal to 255, otherwise it's equal to your node ID.

Note: You should issue LAPRead calls only for ALAP protocol types that were opened (via LAPOpenProtocol) to use the default protocol handler.

Warning: If you close a protocol type for which there are still LAPRead calls pending, the calls will be canceled but the memory occupied by their ABusRecords will not be released. For this reason, before closing a protocol type, call LAPRdCancel to cancel any pending LAPRead calls associated with that protocol type.

Result codes	noErr	No error
	buf2SmallErr	Frame too large for buffer
	readQErr	Invalid protocol type or protocol type not found in table

```
FUNCTION LAPRdCancel (abRecord: ABRecHandle) : OSErr;    [Not in ROM]
```

Given the handle to the ABusRecord of a previously made LAPRead call, LAPRdCancel dequeues the LAPRead call, provided that a packet satisfying the LAPRead has not already arrived. LAPRdCancel returns noErr if the LAPRead call is successfully removed from the queue. If LAPRdCancel returns recNotFnd, check the abResult field to verify that the LAPRead has been completed and determine its outcome.

Result codes		
noErr	No error	
readQErr	Invalid protocol type or protocol type not found in table	
recNotFnd	ABRecord not found in queue	

Example

This example sends an ALAP packet synchronously and waits asynchronously for a response. Assume that both nodes are using a known protocol type (in this case, 73) to receive packets, and that the destination node has a node ID of 4.

```
VAR  myABRecord: ABRecHandle;
     myBuffer: PACKED ARRAY[0..599] OF CHAR; {buffer for both send and }
                                             { receive}

     myLAPType: Byte;
     errCode,index,dataLen: INTEGER;
     someText: Str255;
     async: BOOLEAN;

BEGIN
errCode := MPPOpen;
IF errCode <> noErr
  THEN
     WRITELN('Error in opening AppleTalk')
     {Maybe serial port B isn't available for use by AppleTalk}
  ELSE
     BEGIN
     {Call Memory Manager to allocate ABusRecord}
     myABRecord := ABRecHandle(NewHandle(lapSize));
     myLAPType := 73;
     {Enter myLAPType into protocol handler table and install default }
     { handler to service frames of that ALAP type.  No packets of }
     { that ALAP type will be received until we call LAPRead.}
     errCode := LAPOpenProtocol(myLAPType,NIL);
     IF errCode <> noErr
       THEN
         WRITELN('Error while opening the protocol type')
         {Have we opened too many protocol types?  Remember that DDP }
         { uses two of them.}
       ELSE
         BEGIN
         {Prepare data to be sent}
         someText := 'This data will be in the ALAP data area';
```

```
{The .MPP implementation requires that the first two bytes }
{ of the ALAP data field contain the length of the data, }
{ including the length bytes themselves.}
dataLen := LENGTH(someText)+2;
buffer[0] := CHR(dataLen DIV 256); {high byte of data length}
buffer[1] := CHR(dataLen MOD 256); {low byte of data length}
FOR index := 1 TO dataLen-2 DO {stuff buffer with packet data}
  buffer[index+1] := someText[index];
async := FALSE;
WITH myABRecord^^ DO    {fill parameters in the ABusRecord}
  BEGIN
  lapAddress.lapProtType := myLAPType;
  lapAddress.dstNodeID := 4;
  lapReqCount := dataLen;
  lapDataPtr := @buffer;
  END;
{Send the frame}
errCode := LAPWrite(myABRecord,async);
{In the case of a sync call, errCode and the abResult field of }
{ the myABRecord will contain the same result code.  We can also }
{ reuse myABRecord, since we know whether the call has completed.}
IF errCode <> noErr
  THEN
    WRITELN('Error while writing out the packet')
    {Maybe the receiving node wasn't on-line}
  ELSE
    BEGIN
    {We have sent out the packet and are now waiting for a }
    { response.  We issue an async LAPRead call so that we don't }
    { "hang" waiting for a response that may not come.}
    async := TRUE;
    WITH myABRecord^^ DO
      BEGIN
      lapAddress.lapProtType := myLAPType; {ALAP type we want }
                                          { to receive}
      lapReqCount := 600;  {our buffer is maximum size}
      lapDataPtr := @buffer;
      END;
    errCode := LAPRead(myABRecord,async);    {wait for a packet}
    IF errCode <> noErr
      THEN
        WRITELN('Error while trying to queue up a LAPRead')
        {Was the protocol handler installed correctly?}
      ELSE
        BEGIN
        {We can either sit here in a loop and poll the abResult }
        { field or just exit our code and use the event }
        { mechanism to flag us when the packet arrives.}
        CheckForMyEvent;    {your procedure for checking for a }
                            { network event}
        errCode := LAPCloseProtocol(myLAPType);
```

```
                    IF errCode <> noErr
                        THEN
                            WRITELN('Error while closing the protocol type');
                    END;
                END;
            END;
        END;
    END.
```

Datagram Delivery Protocol

Data Structures

DDP calls use the following ABusRecord fields:

```
ddpProto:
    (ddpType:      Byte;         {DDP protocol type}
     ddpSocket:    Byte;         {source or listening socket number}
     ddpAddress:   AddrBlock;    {destination or source socket address}
     ddpReqCount:  INTEGER;      {length of datagram data or buffer size }
                                 { in bytes}
     ddpActCount:  INTEGER;      {number of bytes actually received}
     ddpDataPtr:   Ptr;          {pointer to buffer}
     ddpNodeID:    Byte);        {original destination node ID}
```

When a DDP datagram is sent, ddpReqCount indicates the size of the datagram data in bytes and ddpDataPtr points to a buffer containing the datagram data. DDPSocket specifies the socket from which the datagram should be sent. DDPAddress is the internet address of the socket to which the datagram should be sent:

```
TYPE AddrBlock =   PACKED RECORD
                    aNet:     INTEGER;      {network number}
                    aNode:    Byte;         {node ID}
                    aSocket:  Byte          {socket number}
                END;
```

Note: The network number you specify in ddpAddress.aNet tells MPP whether to create a long header (for an internet) or a short header (for a local network only). A short DDP header will be sent if ddpAddress.aNet is 0 or equal to the network number of the local network.

When a DDP datagram is received, ddpDataPtr points to a buffer in which the incoming data can be stored and ddpReqCount indicates the size of the buffer in bytes. The number of bytes actually sent or received is returned in the ddpActCount field. DDPAddress is the internet address of the socket from which the datagram was sent.

DDPType is the DDP protocol type of the datagram, and ddpSocket specifies the socket that will receive the datagram.

Warning: DDP protocol types 1 through 15 and DDP socket numbers 1 through 63 are reserved by Apple for internal use. Socket numbers 64 through 127 are available for experimental use. Use of these experimental sockets isn't recommended for commercial products, since there's no mechanism for eliminating conflicting usage by different developers.

Using DDP

Before it can use a socket, the program must call DDPOpenSocket, which adds a socket and its socket listener to the socket table. When a program is finished using a socket, call DDPCloseSocket, which removes the socket's entry from the socket table. To send a datagram via DDP, call DDPWrite. To receive datagrams, you have two choices:

■ Call DDPOpenSocket with NIL for sktListener (see below); this installs the default socket listener provided by the AppleTalk Manager. Then call DDPRead to receive datagrams.

■ Write your own socket listener and call DDPOpenSocket to install it. DDP will call your socket listener for every incoming datagram for that socket; in this case, you shouldn't call DDPRead. For information on how to write a socket listener, see the section "Protocol Handlers and Socket Listeners".

To cancel a previously issued DDPRead call (provided it's still in the queue), call DDPRdCancel.

DDP Routines

```
FUNCTION DDPOpenSocket (VAR theSocket: Byte; sktListener: Ptr) :
            OSErr;   [Not in ROM]
```

DDPOpenSocket adds a socket and its socket listener to the socket table. If theSocket is nonzero, it must be in the range 64 to 127, and it specifies the socket's number; if theSocket is 0, DDPOpenSocket dynamically assigns a socket number in the range 128 to 254, and returns it in theSocket. SktListener contains a pointer to the socket listener; if it's NIL, the default listener will be used.

If you're using the default socket listener, you must then call DDPRead to receive a datagram (in order to specify buffer space for the default socket listener). If, however, you've written your own socket listener and sktListener points to it, your listener will provide buffers for receiving datagrams and you shouldn't use DDPRead calls.

DDPOpenSocket will return ddpSktErr if you pass the number of an already opened socket, if you pass a socket number greater than 127, or if the socket table is full.

> **Note:** The range of static socket numbers 1 through 63 is reserved by Apple for internal use. Socket numbers 64 through 127 are available for unrestricted experimental use.

Result codes   noErr   No error
                        ddpSktErr   Socket error

```
FUNCTION DDPCloseSocket (theSocket: Byte) : OSErr;   [Not in ROM]
```

DDPCloseSocket removes the entry of the specified socket from the socket table and cancels all pending DDPRead calls that have been made for that socket. If you pass a socket number of 0, or if you attempt to close a socket that isn't open, DDPCloseSocket will return ddpSktErr.

Result codes   noErr   No error
                ddpSktErr   Socket error

```
FUNCTION DDPWrite (abRecord: ABRecHandle; doChecksum: BOOLEAN;
        async: BOOLEAN) : OSErr;  [Not in ROM]
```

ABusRecord

←	abOpcode	{always tDDPWrite}
←	abResult	{result code}
→	abUserReference	{for your use}
→	ddpType	{DDP protocol type}
→	ddpSocket	{source socket number}
→	ddpAddress	{destination socket address}
→	ddpReqCount	{length of datagram data}
→	ddpDataPtr	{pointer to buffer}

DDPWrite sends a datagram to another socket. DDPReqCount and ddpDataPtr specify the length and location of the data to send. The ddpType field indicates the DDP protocol type of the frame, and ddpAddress is the complete internet address of the socket to which the datagram should be sent. DDPSocket specifies the socket from which the datagram should be sent. Datagrams sent over the internet to a node on an AppleTalk network different from the sending node's network have an optional software checksum to detect errors that might occur inside the intermediate bridges. If doChecksum is TRUE, DDPWrite will compute this checksum; if it's FALSE, this software checksum feature is ignored.

Note: The destination socket can't be in the same node as the program making the DDPWrite call.

Result codes   noErr   No error
                ddpLenErr   Datagram length too big
                ddpSktErr   Source socket not open
                noBridgeErr No bridge found

```
FUNCTION DDPRead (abRecord: ABRecHandle; retCksumErrs: BOOLEAN;
        async: BOOLEAN) : OSErr;  [Not in ROM]
```

ABusRecord

←	abOpcode	{always tDDPRead}
←	abResult	{result code}
→	abUserReference	{for your use}
←	ddpType	{DDP protocol type}
→	ddpSocket	{listening socket number}
←	ddpAddress	{source socket address}
→	ddpReqCount	{buffer size in bytes}
←	ddpActCount	{number of bytes actually received}
→	ddpDataPtr	{pointer to buffer}
←	ddpNodeID	{original destination node ID}

DDPRead receives a datagram from another socket. The size and location of the buffer that will receive the data are specified by ddpReqCount and ddpDataPtr. If the buffer isn't large enough to hold all of the incoming frame data, the extra bytes will be discarded and buf2SmallErr will be returned. The number of bytes actually received is returned in ddpActCount. DDPSocket specifies the socket to receive the datagram (the "listening" socket). The node to which the packet was sent is returned in ddpNodeID; if the packet was broadcast ddpNodeID will contain 255. The address of the socket that sent the packet is returned in ddpAddress. If retCksumErrs is FALSE, DDPRead will discard any packets received with an invalid checksum and inform the caller of the error. If retCksumErrs is TRUE, DDPRead will deliver all packets, whether or not the checksum is valid; it will also notify the caller when there's a checksum error.

> **Note:** The sender of the datagram must be in a different node from the receiver. You should issue DDPRead calls only for receiving datagrams for sockets opened with the default socket listener; see the description of DDPOpenSocket.

> **Note:** If the buffer provided isn't large enough to hold all of the incoming frame data (buf2SmallErr), the checksum can't be calculated; in this case, DDPRead will deliver packets even if retCksumErrs is FALSE.

Result codes		
	noErr	No error
	buf2SmallErr	Datagram too large for buffer
	cksumErr	Checksum error
	ddpLenErr	Datagram length too big
	ddpSktErr	Socket error
	readQErr	Invalid socket or socket not found in table

```
FUNCTION DDPRdCancel (abRecord: ABRecHandle) : OSErr;   [Not in ROM]
```

Given the handle to the ABusRecord of a previously made DDPRead call, DDPRdCancel dequeues the DDPRead call, provided that a packet satisfying the DDPRead hasn't already arrived. DDPRdCancel returns noErr if the DDPRead call is successfully removed from the queue. If DDPRdCancel returns recNotFnd, check the abResult field of abRecord to verify that the DDPRead has been completed and determine its outcome.

Result codes		
	noErr	No error
	readQErr	Invalid socket or socket not found in table
	recNotFnd	ABRecord not found in queue

Example

This example sends a DDP packet synchronously and waits asynchronously for a response. Assume that both nodes are using a known socket number (in this case, 30) to receive packets. Normally, you would want to use NBP to look up your destination's socket address.

```
    VAR myABRecord: ABRecHandle;
        myBuffer: PACKED ARRAY[0..599] OF CHAR;        {buffer for both send and }
                                                       { receive}
        mySocket: Byte;
        errCode,index,dataLen: INTEGER;
        someText: Str255;
        async,retCksumErrs,doChecksum: BOOLEAN;

BEGIN
errCode := MPPOpen;
IF errCode <> noErr
  THEN
      WRITELN('Error in opening AppleTalk')
      {Maybe serial port B isn't available for use by AppleTalk}
  ELSE
      BEGIN
      {Call Memory Manager to allocate ABusRecord}
      myABRecord := ABRecHandle(NewHandle(ddpSize));
      mySocket := 30;
      {Add mySocket to socket table and install default socket listener }
      { to service datagrams addressed to that socket.  No packets }
      { addressed to mySocket will be received until we call DDPRead.}
      errCode := DDPOpenSocket(mySocket,NIL);
IF errCode <> noErr
  THEN
      WRITELN('Error while opening the socket')
      {Have we opened too many socket listeners?  Remember that DDP }
      { uses two of them.}
  ELSE
      BEGIN
      {Prepare data to be sent}
      someText := 'This is a sample datagram';
      dataLen := LENGTH(someText);
      FOR index := 0 TO dataLen-1 DO  {stuff buffer with packet data}
          myBuffer[index] := someText[index+1];
      async := FALSE;
      WITH myABRecord^^ DO  {fill the parameters in the ABusRecord}
          BEGIN
          ddpType := 5;
          ddpAddress.aNet := 0;  {send on "our" network}
          ddpAddress.aNode := 34;
          ddpAddress.aSocket := mySocket;
          ddpReqCount := dataLen;
          ddpDataPtr := @myBuffer;
          END;
      doChecksum := FALSE;
      {If packet contains a DDP long header, compute checksum and insert }
      { it into the header.}
      errCode := DDPWrite(myABRecord,doChecksum,async); {send packet}
      {In the case of a sync call, errCode and the abResult field of }
      { myABRecord will contain the same result code.  We can also reuse }
      { myABRecord, since we know whether the call has completed.}
```

```
    IF errCode <> noErr
        THEN
            WRITELN('Error while writing out the packet')
            {Maybe the receiving node wasn't on-line}
        ELSE
            BEGIN
            {We have sent out the packet and are now waiting for a }
            { response.  We issue an async DDPRead call so that we }
            { don't "hang" waiting for a response that may not come. }
            { To cancel the async read call, we must close the socket }
            { associated with the call or call DDPRdCancel.}
            async := TRUE;
            retCksumErrs := TRUE;   {return packets even if they have a }
                                    { checksum error}
            WITH myABRecord^^ DO
                BEGIN
                ddpSocket := mySocket;
                ddpReqCount := 600; {our reception buffer is max size}
                ddpDataPtr := @myBuffer;
                END;
            {Wait for a packet asynchronously}
            errCode := DDPRead(myABRecord,retCksumErrs,async);
            IF errCode <> noErr
                THEN
                    WRITELN('Error while trying to queue up a DDPRead')
                    {Was the socket listener installed correctly?}
                ELSE
                    BEGIN
                    {We can either sit here in a loop and poll the }
                    { abResult field or just exit our code and use the }
                    { event mechanism to flag us when the packet arrives.}
                    CheckForMyEvent;  {your procedure for checking for a }
                                      { network event}
                    {If there were no errors, a packet is inside the array }
                    { mybuffer, the length is in ddpActCount, and the }
                    { address of the sending socket is in ddpAddress. }
                    { Process the packet received here and report any errors.}
                    errCode := DDPCloseSocket(mySocket); {we're done with it}
                    IF errCode <> noErr
                        THEN
                            WRITELN('Error while closing the socket');
                    END;
                END;
            END;
        END;
END.
```

AppleTalk Transaction Protocol

Data Structures

ATP calls use the following ABusRecord fields:

```
atpProto:
  (atpSocket:      Byte;          {listening or responding socket number}
   atpAddress:     AddrBlock;     {destination or source socket address}
   atpReqCount:    INTEGER;       {request size or buffer size}
   atpDataPtr:     Ptr;           {pointer to buffer}
   atpRspBDSPtr:   BDSPtr;        {pointer to response BDS}
   atpBitMap:      BitMapType;    {transaction bit map}
   atpTransID:     INTEGER;       {transaction ID}
   atpActCount:    INTEGER;       {number of bytes actually received}
   atpUserData:    LONGINT;       {user bytes}
   atpXO:          BOOLEAN;       {exactly-once flag}
   atpEOM:         BOOLEAN;       {end-of-message flag}
   atpTimeOut:     Byte;          {retry timeout interval in seconds}
   atpRetries:     Byte;          {maximum number of retries}
   atpNumBufs:     Byte;          {number of elements in response BDS or }
                                  { number of response packets sent}
   atpNumRsp:      Byte;          {number of response packets received or }
                                  { sequence number}
   atpBDSSize:     Byte;          {number of elements in response BDS}
   atpRspUData:    LONGINT;       {user bytes sent or received in transaction }
                                  { response}
   atpRspBuf:      Ptr;           {pointer to response message buffer}
   atpRspSize:     INTEGER);      {size of response message buffer}
```

The socket receiving the request or sending the response is identified by atpSocket. ATPAddress is the address of either the destination or the source socket of a transaction, depending on whether the call is sending or receiving data, respectively. ATPDataPtr and atpReqCount specify the location and size (in bytes) of a buffer that either contains a request or will receive a request. The number of bytes actually received in a request is returned in atpActCount. ATPTransID specifies the transaction ID. The transaction bit map is contained in atpBitMap, in the form:

```
TYPE BitMapType = PACKED ARRAY[0..7] OF BOOLEAN;
```

Each bit in the bit map corresponds to one of the eight possible packets in a response. For example, when a request is made for which five response packets are expected, the bit map sent is binary 00011111 or decimal 31. If the second packet in the response is lost, the requesting socket will retransmit the request with a bit map of binary 00000010 or decimal 2.

ATPUserData contains the user bytes of an ATP header. ATPXO is TRUE if the transaction is to be made with exactly-once service. ATPEOM is TRUE if the response packet is the last packet of a transaction. If the number of responses is less than the number that were requested, then ATPEOM must also be TRUE. ATPNumRsp contains either the number of responses received or the sequence number of a response.

The timeout interval in seconds and the maximum number of times that a request should be made are indicated by atpTimeOut and atpRetries, respectively.

Note: Setting atpRetries to 255 will cause the request to be retransmitted indefinitely, until a full response is received or the call is canceled.

ATP provides a data structure, known as a response buffer data structure (**response BDS**), for allocating buffer space to receive the datagram(s) of the response. A response BDS is an array of one to eight elements. Each BDS element defines the size and location of a buffer for receiving one response datagram; they're numbered 0 to 7 to correspond to the sequence numbers of the response datagrams.

ATP needs a separate buffer for each response datagram expected, since packets may not arrive in the proper sequence. It does not, however, require you to set up and use the BDS data structure to describe the response buffers; if you don't, ATP will do it for you. Two sets of calls are provided for both requests and responses; one set requires you to allocate a response BDS and the other doesn't.

Assembly-language note: The two calls that don't require you to define a BDS data structure (ATPRequest and ATPResponse) are available in Pascal only.

The number of BDS elements allocated (in other words, the maximum number of datagrams that the responder can send) is indicated in the TReq by an eight-bit bit map. The bits of this bit map are numbered 0 to 7 (the least significant bit being number 0); each bit corresponds to the response datagram with the respective sequence number.

ATPRspBDSPtr and atpBDSSize indicate the location and number of elements in the response BDS, which has the following structure:

```
TYPE  BDSElement =
          RECORD
              buffSize:  INTEGER;    {buffer size in bytes}
              buffPtr:   Ptr;        {pointer to buffer}
              dataSize:  INTEGER;    {number of bytes actually received}
              userBytes: LONGINT     {user bytes}
          END;

      BDSType = ARRAY[0..7] OF BDSElement; {response BDS}
      BDSPtr  = ^BDSType;
```

ATPNumBufs indicates the number of elements in the response BDS that contain information. In most cases, you can allocate space for your variables of BDSType statically with a VAR declaration. However, you can allocate only the minimum space required by your ATP calls by doing the following:

```
VAR myBDSPtr: BDSPtr;

   . . .

numOfBDS := 3; {number of elements needed}
myBDSPtr := BDSPtr(NewPtr(SIZEOF(BDSElement) * numOfBDS));
```

Note: The userBytes field of the BDSElement and the atpUserData field of the ABusRecord represent the same information in the datagram. Depending on the ATP call made, one or both of these fields will be used.

Using ATP

Before you can use ATP on a Macintosh 128K, the .ATP driver must be read from the system resource file via an ATPLoad call. The .ATP driver loads itself into the application heap and installs a task into the vertical retrace queue.

Warning: When another application starts up, the application heap is reinitialized; on a Macintosh 128K, this means that the ATP code is lost (and must be reloaded by the next application).

When you're through using ATP on a Macintosh 128K, call ATPUnload—the system will be returned to the state it was in before the .ATP driver was opened.

On a Macintosh 512K or XL, the .ATP driver will have been loaded into the system heap either at system startup or upon execution of MPPOpen or ATPLoad. ATPUnload has no effect on a Macintosh 512K or XL.

To send a transaction request, call ATPSndRequest or ATPRequest. The .ATP driver will automatically select and open a socket through which the request datagram will be sent, and through which the response datagrams will be received. The transaction requester can't specify the number of this socket. However, the requester must specify the full network address (network number, node ID, and socket number) of the socket to which the request is to be sent. This socket is known as the responding socket, and its address must be known in advance by the requester.

Note: The requesting and responding sockets can't be in the same node.

At the responder's end, before a transaction request can be received, a responding socket must be opened, and the appropriate calls be made, to receive a request. To do this, the responder first makes an ATPOpenSocket call which allows the responder to specify the address (or part of it) of the requesters from whom it's willing to accept transaction requests. Then it issues an ATPGetRequest call to provide ATP with a buffer for receiving a request; when a request is received, ATPGetRequest is completed. The responder can queue up several ATPGetRequest calls, each of which will be completed as requests are received.

Upon receiving a request, the responder performs the requested operation, and then prepares the information to be returned to the requester. It then calls ATPSndRsp (or ATPResponse) to send the response. Actually, the responder can issue the ATPSndRsp call with only part (or none) of the response specified. Additional portions of the response can be sent later by calling ATPAddRsp.

The ATPSndRsp and ATPAddRsp calls provide flexibility in the design (and range of types) of transaction responders. For instance, the responder may, for some reason, be forced to send the responses out of sequence. Also, there might be memory constraints that force sending the complete transaction response in parts. Even though eight response datagrams might need to be sent, the responder might have only enough memory to build one datagram at a time. In this case, it would build the first response datagram and call ATPSndRsp to send it. It would then build the second response datagram in the same buffer and call ATPAddRsp to send it; and so on, for the third through eighth response datagrams.

A responder can close a responding socket by calling ATPCloseSocket. This call cancels all pending ATP calls for that socket, such as ATPGetRequest, ATPSndRsp, and ATPResponse.

For exactly-once transactions, the ATPSndRsp and ATPAddRsp calls don't terminate until the entire transaction has completed (that is, the responding end receives a release packet, or the release timer has expired).

To cancel a pending, asynchronous ATPSndRequest or ATPRequest call, call ATPReqCancel. To cancel a pending, asynchronous ATPSndRsp or ATPResponse call, call ATPRspCancel. Pending asynchronous ATPGetRequest calls can be canceled only by issuing the ATPCloseSocket call, but that will cancel all outstanding calls for that socket.

> **Warning:** You cannot reuse a variable of type ABusRecord passed to an ATP routine until the entire transaction has either been completed or canceled.

ATP Routines

FUNCTION ATPLoad : OSErr;   [Not in ROM]

ATPLoad first verifies that the .MPP driver is loaded and running. If it isn't, ATPLoad verifies that port B is configured for AppleTalk and isn't in use, and then loads MPP into the system heap.

ATPLoad then loads the .ATP driver, unless it's already in memory. On a Macintosh 128K, ATPLoad reads the .ATP driver from the system resource file into the application heap; on a Macintosh 512K or XL, ATP is read into the system heap.

> **Note:** On a Macintosh 512K or XL, ATPLoad and MPPOpen perform essentially the same function.

Result codes   noErr   No error
                  portInUse   Port B is already in use
                  portNotCf   Port B not configured for AppleTalk

FUNCTION ATPUnload : OSErr;   [Not in ROM]

ATPUnload makes the .ATP driver purgeable; the space isn't actually released by the Memory Manager until necessary.

> **Note:** This call applies only to a Macintosh 128K; on a Macintosh 512K or Macintosh XL, ATPUnload has no effect.

Result codes   noErr   No error

FUNCTION ATPOpenSocket (addrRcvd: AddrBlock; VAR atpSocket: Byte)
         : OSErr;   [Not in ROM]

ATPOpenSocket opens a socket for the purpose of receiving requests. ATPSocket contains the socket number of the socket to open; if it's 0, a number is dynamically assigned and returned in atpSocket. AddrRcvd contains a filter of the sockets from which requests will be accepted. A 0 in the network number, node ID, or socket number field of the addrRcvd record acts as a "wild card"; for instance, a 0 in the socket number field means that requests will be accepted from all sockets in the node(s) specified by the network and node fields.

Result codes   noErr   No error
    tooManySkts   Socket table full
    noDataArea   Too many outstanding ATP calls

Note: If you're only going to send requests and receive responses to these requests, you don't need to open an ATP socket. When you make the ATPSndRequest or ATPRequest call, ATP automatically opens a dynamically assigned socket for that purpose.

```
FUNCTION ATPCloseSocket (atpSocket: Byte) : OSErr;   [Not in ROM]
```

ATPCloseSocket closes the responding socket whose number is specified by atpSocket. It releases the data structures associated with all pending, asynchronous calls involving that socket; these pending calls are completed immediately and return the result code sktClosed.

Result codes   noErr   No error
    noDataArea Too many outstanding ATP calls

```
FUNCTION ATPSndRequest (abRecord: ABRecHandle; async: BOOLEAN) :
              OSErr;   [Not in ROM]
```

ABusRecord

←	abOpcode	{always tATPSndRequest}
←	abResult	{result code}
→	abUserReference	{for your use}
→	atpAddress	{destination socket address}
→	atpReqCount	{request size in bytes}
→	atpDataPtr	{pointer to buffer}
→	atpRspBDSPtr	{pointer to response BDS}
→	atpUserData	{user bytes}
→	atpXO	{exactly-once flag}
←	atpEOM	{end-of-message flag}
→	atpTimeOut	{retry timeout interval in seconds}
→	atpRetries	{maximum number of retries}
→	atpNumBufs	{number of elements in response BDS}
←	atpNumRsp	{number of response packets actually received}

ATPSndRequest sends a request to another socket. ATPAddress is the internet address of the socket to which the request should be sent. ATPDataPtr and atpReqCount specify the location and size of a buffer that contains the request information to be sent. ATPUserData contains the user bytes for the ATP header.

ATPSndRequest requires you to allocate a response BDS. ATPRspBDSPtr is a pointer to the response BDS; atpNumBufs indicates the number of elements in the BDS (this is also the maximum number of response datagrams that will be accepted). The number of response datagrams actually received is returned in atpNumRsp; if a nonzero value is returned, you can examine the response BDS to determine which packets of the transaction were actually received. If the number returned is less than requested, one of the following is true:

■ Some of the packets have been lost and the retry count has been exceeded.

■ ATPEOM is TRUE; this means that the response consisted of fewer packets than were expected, but that all packets sent were received (the last packet came with the atpEOM flag set).

ATPTimeOut indicates the length of time that ATPSndRequest should wait for a response before retransmitting the request. ATPRetries indicates the maximum number of retries ATPSndRequest should attempt. ATPXO should be TRUE if you want the request to be part of an exactly-once transaction.

ATPSndRequest completes when either the transaction is completed or the retry count is exceeded.

Result codes	noErr	No error
	reqFailed	Retry count exceeded
	tooManyReqs	Too many concurrent requests
	noDataArea	Too many outstanding ATP calls

```
FUNCTION ATPRequest (abRecord: ABRecHandle; async: BOOLEAN) :
          OSErr;    [Not in ROM]
```

ABusRecord

←	abOpcode	{always tATPRequest}
←	abResult	{result code}
→	abUserReference	{for your use}
→	atpAddress	{destination socket address}
→	atpReqCount	{request size in bytes}
→	atpDataPtr	{pointer to buffer}
←	atpActCount	{number of bytes actually received}
→	atpUserData	{user bytes}
→	atpXO	{exactly-once flag}
←	atpEOM	{end-of-message flag}
→	atpTimeOut	{retry timeout interval in seconds}
→	atpRetries	{maximum number of retries}
←	atpRspUData	{user bytes received in transaction response}
→	atpRspBuf	{pointer to response message buffer}
→	atpRspSize	{size of response message buffer}

ATPRequest is functionally analogous to ATPSndRequest. It sends a request to another socket, but doesn't require the caller to set up and use the BDS data structure to describe the response buffers. ATPAddress indicates the socket to which the request should be sent. ATPDataPtr and atpReqCount specify the location and size of a buffer that contains the request information to be sent. ATPUserData contains the user bytes to be sent in the request's ATP header. ATPTimeOut indicates the length of time that ATPRequest should wait for a response before retransmitting the request. ATPRetries indicates the maximum number of retries ATPRequest should attempt.

To use this call, you must have an area of contiguous buffer space that's large enough to receive all expected datagrams. The various datagrams will be assembled in this buffer and returned to you as a complete message upon completion of the transaction. The location and size of this buffer are passed in atpRspBuf and atpRspSize. Upon completion of the call, the size of the received response message is returned in atpActCount. The user bytes received in the ATP header of the first response packet are returned in atpRspUData. ATPXO should be TRUE if you want the request to be part of an exactly-once transaction.

Although you don't provide a BDS, ATPRequest in fact creates one and calls the .ATP driver (as in an ATPSndRequest call). For this reason, the abRecord fields atpRspBDSPtr and atpNumBufs are used by ATPRequest; you should not expect these fields to remain unaltered during or after the function's execution.

For ATPRequest to receive and correctly deliver the response as a single message, the responding end must, upon receiving the request (with an ATPGetRequest call), generate the complete response as a message in a single buffer and then call ATPResponse.

> **Note:** The responding end could also use ATPSndRsp and ATPAddRsp provided that each response packet (except the last one) contains exactly 578 ATP data bytes; the last packet in the response can contain less than 578 ATP data bytes. Also, if this method is used, only the ATP user bytes of the first response packet will be delivered to the requester; any information in the user bytes of the remaining response packets will not be delivered.

ATPRequest completes when either the transaction is completed or the retry count is exceeded.

Result codes	noErr	No error
	reqFailed	Retry count exceeded
	tooManyReqs	Too many concurrent requests
	sktClosed	Socket closed by a cancel call
	noDataArea	Too many outstanding ATP calls

```
FUNCTION ATPReqCancel (abRecord: ABRecHandle; async: BOOLEAN) :
        OSErr;   [Not in ROM]
```

Given the handle to the ABusRecord of a previously made ATPSndRequest or ATPRequest call, ATPReqCancel dequeues the ATPSndRequest or ATPRequest call, provided that the call hasn't already completed. ATPReqCancel returns noErr if the ATPSndRequest or ATPRequest call is successfully removed from the queue. If it returns cbNotFound, check the abResult field of abRecord to verify that the ATPSndRequest or ATPRequest call has completed and determine its outcome.

Result codes	noErr	No error
	cbNotFound	ATP control block not found

```
FUNCTION ATPGetRequest (abRecord: ABRecHandle; async: BOOLEAN) :
        OSErr;   [Not in ROM]
```

ABusRecord

←	abOpcode	{always tATPGetRequest}
←	abResult	{result code}
→	abUserReference	{for your use}
→	atpSocket	{listening socket number}
←	atpAddress	{source socket address}
→	atpReqCount	{buffer size in bytes}
→	atpDataPtr	{pointer to buffer}
←	atpBitMap	{transaction bit map}
←	atpTransID	{transaction ID}

←	atpActCount	{number of bytes actually received}
←	atpUserData	{user bytes}
←	atpXO	{exactly-once flag}

ATPGetRequest sets up the mechanism to receive a request sent by either an ATPSndRequest or an ATPRequest call. ATPSocket contains the socket number of the socket that should listen for a request; this socket must already have been opened by calling ATPOpenSocket. The address of the socket from which the request was sent is returned in atpAddress. ATPDataPtr specifies a buffer to store the incoming request; atpReqCount indicates the size of the buffer in bytes. The number of bytes actually received in the request is returned in atpActCount. ATPUserData contains the user bytes from the ATP header. The transaction bit map is returned in atpBitMap. The transaction ID is returned in atpTransID. ATPXO will be TRUE if the request is part of an exactly-once transaction.

ATPGetRequest completes when a request is received. To cancel an asynchronous ATPGetRequest call, you must call ATPCloseSocket, but this cancels all pending calls involving that socket.

Result codes	noErr	No error
	badATPSkt	Bad responding socket
	sktClosed	Socket closed by a cancel call

```
FUNCTION ATPSndRsp (abRecord: ABRecHandle; async: BOOLEAN) :
         OSErr;    [Not in ROM]
```

ABusRecord

←	abOpcode	{always tATPSdRsp}
←	abResult	{result code}
→	abUserReference	{for your use}
→	atpSocket	{responding socket number}
→	atpAddress	{destination socket address}
→	atpRspBDSPtr	{pointer to response BDS}
→	atpTransID	{transaction ID}
→	atpEOM	{end-of-message flag}
→	atpNumBufs	{number of response packets being sent}
→	atpBDSSize	{number of elements in response BDS}

ATPSndRsp sends a response to another socket. ATPSocket contains the socket number from which the response should be sent and atpAddress contains the internet address of the socket to which the response should be sent. ATPTransID must contain the transaction ID. ATPEOM is TRUE if the response BDS contains the final packet in a transaction composed of a group of packets and the number of packets in the response is less than expected. ATPRspBDSPtr points to the buffer data structure containing the responses to be sent. ATPBDSSize indicates the number of elements in the response BDS, and must be in the range 1 to 8. ATPNumBufs indicates the number of response packets being sent with this call, and must be in the range 0 to 8.

Note: In some situations, you may want to send only part (or possibly none) of your response message back immediately. For instance, you might be requested to send back seven disk blocks, but have only enough internal memory to store one block. In this case, set atpBDSSize to 7 (total number of response packets), atpNumBufs to 0 (number of response packets currently being sent), and call ATPSndRsp. Then as you read in one block at a time, call ATPAddRsp until all seven response datagrams have been sent.

During exactly-once transactions, ATPSndRsp won't complete until the release packet is received or the release timer expires.

Result codes	noErr	No error
	badATPSkt	Bad responding socket
	noRelErr	No release received
	sktClosed	Socket closed by a cancel call
	noDataArea	Too many outstanding ATP calls
	badBuffNum	Bad sequence number

FUNCTION ATPAddRsp (abRecord: ABRecHandle) : OSErr;   [Not in ROM]

ABusRecord

←	abOpcode	{always tATPAddRsp}
←	abResult	{result code}
→	abUserReference	{for your use}
→	atpSocket	{responding socket number}
→	atpAddress	{destination socket address}
→	atpReqCount	{buffer size in bytes}
→	atpDataPtr	{pointer to buffer}
→	atpTransID	{transaction ID}
→	atpUserData	{user bytes}
→	atpEOM	{end-of-message flag}
→	atpNumRsp	{sequence number}

ATPAddRsp sends one additional response packet to a socket that has already been sent the initial part of a response via ATPSndRsp. ATPSocket contains the socket number from which the response should be sent and atpAddress contains the internet address of the socket to which the response should be sent. ATPTransID must contain the transaction ID. ATPDataPtr and atpReqCount specify the location and size of a buffer that contains the information to send; atpNumRsp is the sequence number of the response. ATPEOM is TRUE if this response datagram is the final packet in a transaction composed of a group of packets. ATPUserData contains the user bytes to be sent in this response datagram's ATP header.

Note: No BDS is needed with ATPAddRsp because all pertinent information is passed within the record.

Result codes	noErr	No error
	badATPSkt	Bad responding socket
	badBuffNum	Bad sequence number
	noSendResp	ATPAddRsp issued before ATPSndRsp
	noDataArea	Too many outstanding ATP calls

```
FUNCTION ATPResponse (abRecord: ABRecHandle; async: BOOLEAN) :
          OSErr;   [Not in ROM]
```

ABusRecord

←	abOpcode	{always tATPResponse}
←	abResult	{result code}
→	abUserReference	{for your use}
→	atpSocket	{responding socket number}
→	atpAddress	{destination socket address}
→	atpTransID	{transaction ID)
→	atpRspUData	{user bytes sent in transaction response}
→	atpRspBuf	{pointer to response message buffer}
→	atpRspSize	{size of response message buffer}

ATPResponse is functionally analogous to ATPSndRsp. It sends a response to another socket, but doesn't require the caller to provide a BDS. ATPAddress must contain the complete network address of the socket to which the response should be sent (taken from the data provided by an ATPGetRequest call). ATPTransID must contain the transaction ID. ATPSocket indicates the socket from which the response should be sent (the socket on which the corresponding ATPGetRequest was issued). ATPRspBuf points to the buffer containing the response message; the size of this buffer must be passed in atpRspSize. The four user bytes to be sent in the ATP header of the first response packet are passed in atpRspUData. The last packet of the transaction response is sent with the EOM flag set.

Although you don't provide a BDS, ATPResponse in fact creates one and calls the .ATP driver (as in an ATPSndRsp call). For this reason, the abRecord fields atpRspBDSPtr and atpNumBufs are used by ATPResponse; you should not expect these fields to remain unaltered during or after the function's execution.

During exactly-once transactions ATPResponse won't complete until the release packet is received or the release timer expires.

Warning: The maximum permissible size of the response message is 4624 bytes.

Result codes	noErr	No error
	badATPSkt	Bad responding socket
	noRelErr	No release received
	atpLenErr	Response too big
	sktClosed	Socket closed by a cancel call
	noDataArea	Too many outstanding ATP calls

```
FUNCTION ATPRspCancel (abRecord: ABRecHandle; async: BOOLEAN) :
          OSErr;   [Not in ROM]
```

Given the handle to the ABusRecord of a previously made ATPSndRsp or ATPResponse call, ATPRspCancel dequeues the ATPSndRsp or ATPResponse call, provided that the call hasn't already completed. ATPRspCancel returns noErr if the ATPSndRsp or ATPResponse call is successfully removed from the queue. If it returns cbNotFound, check the abResult field of abRecord to verify that the ATPSndRsp or ATPResponse call has completed and determine its outcome.

Result codes   noErr   No error
                   cbNotFound   ATP control block not found

Example

This example shows the requesting side of an ATP transaction that asks for a 512-byte disk block from the responding end. The block number of the file is a byte and is contained in myBuffer[0].

```
VAR  myABRecord: ABRecHandle;
     myBDSPtr: BDSPtr;
     myBuffer: PACKED ARRAY[0..511] OF CHAR;
     errCode: INTEGER;
     async: BOOLEAN;

BEGIN
errCode := ATPLoad;
IF errCode <> noErr
  THEN
     WRITELN('Error in opening AppleTalk')
     {Maybe serial port B isn't available for use by AppleTalk}
  ELSE
     BEGIN
     {Prepare the BDS; allocate space for a one-element BDS}
     myBDSPtr := BDSPtr(NewPtr(SIZEOF(BDSElement)));
     WITH myBDSPtr^[0] DO
       BEGIN
       buffSize := 512;        {size of our buffer used in reception}
       buffPtr := @myBuffer;   {pointer to the buffer}
       END;
     {Prepare the ABusRecord}
     myBuffer[0] := CHR(1);    {requesting disk block number 1}
     myABRecord := ABRecHandle(NewHandle(atpSize));
     WITH myABRecord^^ DO
       BEGIN
       atpAddress.aNet := 0;
       atpAddress.aNode := 30;     {we probably got this from an NBP call}
       atpAddress.aSocket := 15;   {socket to send request to}
       atpReqCount := 1;           {size of request data field (disk block #)}
       atpDataPtr := @myBuffer;    {ptr to request to be sent}
       atpRspBDSPtr := @myBDSPtr;
       atpUserData := 0;     {for your use}
       atpXO := FALSE;       {at-least-once service}
       atpTimeOut := 5;      {5-second timeout}
       atpRetries := 3;      {3 retries; request will be sent 4 times max}
       atpNumBufs := 1;      {we're only expecting 1 block to be returned}
       END;
     async := FALSE;
     {Send the request and wait for the response}
     errCode := ATPSndRequest(myABRecord,async);
```

```
      IF errCode <> noErr
        THEN
          WRITELN('An error occurred in the ATPSndRequest call')
        ELSE
          BEGIN
          {The disk block requested is now in myBuffer.  We can verify }
          { that atpNumRsp contains 1, meaning one response received.}
          . . .
          END;
      END;
  END.
```

Name-Binding Protocol

Data Structures

NBP calls use the following fields:

```
nbpProto:
(nbpEntityPtr:       EntityPtr;    {pointer to entity name}
 nbpBufPtr:          Ptr;          {pointer to buffer}
 nbpBufSize:         INTEGER;      {buffer size in bytes}
 nbpDataField:       INTEGER;      {number of addresses or socket }
                                   { number}
 nbpAddress:         AddrBlock;    {socket address}
 nbpRetransmitInfo: RetransType); {retransmission information}
```

When data is sent via NBP, nbpBufSize indicates the size of the data in bytes and nbpBufPtr points to a buffer containing the data. When data is received via NBP, nbpBufPtr points to a buffer in which the incoming data can be stored and nbpBufSize indicates the size of the buffer in bytes. NBPAddress is used in some calls to give the internet address of a named entity. The AddrBlock data type is described above under "Datagram Delivery Protocol".

NBPEntityPtr points to a variable of type EntityName, which has the following data structure:

```
TYPE EntityName = RECORD
                    objStr: Str32;  {object}
                    typeStr: Str32; {type}
                    zoneStr: Str32  {zone}
                  END;

     EntityPtr = ^EntityName;

     Str32 = STRING[32];
```

NBPRetransmitInfo contains information about the number of times a packet should be transmitted and the interval between retransmissions:

```
TYPE RetransType =
       PACKED RECORD
          retransInterval: Byte; {retransmit interval in 8-tick units}
          retransCount:    Byte  {total number of attempts}
       END;
```

RetransCount contains the *total* number of times a packet should be transmitted, including the first transmission. If retransCount is 0, the packet will be transmitted a total of 255 times.

Using NBP

On a Macintosh 128K, the AppleTalk Manager's NBP code is read into the application heap when any one of the NBP (Pascal) routines is called; you can call the NBPLoad function yourself if you want to load the NBP code explicitly. When you're finished with the NBP code and want to reclaim the space it occupies, call NBPUnload. On a Macintosh 512K or XL, the NBP code is read in when the .MPP driver is loaded.

Note: When another application starts up, the application heap is reinitialized; on a Macintosh 128K, this means that the NBP code is lost (and must be reloaded by the next application).

When an entity wants to communicate via an AppleTalk network, it should call NBPRegister to place its name and internet address in the names table. When an entity no longer wants to communicate on the network, or is being shut down, it should call NBPRemove to remove its entry from the names table.

To determine the address of an entity you know only by name, call NBPLookup, which returns a list of all entities with the name you specify. Call NBPExtract to extract entity names from the list.

If you already know the address of an entity, and want only to confirm that it still exists, call NBPConfirm. NBPConfirm is more efficient than NBPLookup in terms of network traffic.

NBP Routines

```
FUNCTION NBPRegister (abRecord: ABRecHandle; async: BOOLEAN) :
          OSErr;   [Not in ROM]
```

ABusRecord

←	abOpcode	{always tNBPRegister}
←	abResult	{result code}
→	abUserReference	{for your use}
→	nbpEntityPtr	{pointer to entity name}
→	nbpBufPtr	{pointer to buffer}
→	nbpBufSize	{buffer size in bytes}
→	nbpAddress.aSocket	{socket address}
→	nbpRetransmitInfo	{retransmission information}

NBPRegister adds the name and address of an entity to the node's names table. NBPEntityPtr points to a variable of type EntityName containing the entity's name. If the name is already registered, NBPRegister returns the result code nbpDuplicate. NBPAddress indicates the socket for which the name should be registered. NBPBufPtr and nbpBufSize specify the location and size of a buffer for NBP to use internally.

While the variable of type EntityName is declared as three 32-byte strings, only the actual characters of the name are placed in the buffer pointed to by nbpBufPtr. For this reason, nbpBufSize needs only to be equal to the actual length of the name, plus an additional 12 bytes for use by NBP.

Warning: This buffer must not be altered or released until the name is removed from the names table via an NBPRemove call. If you allocate the buffer through a NewHandle call, you must lock it as long as the name is registered.

Warning: The zone field of the entity name must be set to the meta-character "*".

Result codes   noErr   No error
                       nbpDuplicate   Duplicate name already exists

```
FUNCTION NBPLookup (abRecord: ABRecHandle; async: BOOLEAN) :
          OSErr;   [Not in ROM]
```

ABusRecord

←	abOpcode	{always tNBPLookup}
←	abResult	{result code}
→	abUserReference	{for your use}
→	nbpEntityPtr	{pointer to entity name}
→	nbpBufPtr	{pointer to buffer}
→	nbpBufSize	{buffer size in bytes}
↔	nbpDataField	{number of addresses received}
→	nbpRetransmitInfo	{retransmission information}

NBPLookup returns the addresses of all entities with a specified name. NBPEntityPtr points to a variable of type EntityName containing the name of the entity whose address should be returned. (Meta-characters are allowed in the entity name.) NBPBufPtr and nbpBufSize contain the location and size of an area of memory in which the entity names and their corresponding addresses should be returned. NBPDataField indicates the maximum number of matching names to find addresses for; the actual number of addresses found is returned in nbpDataField. NBPRetransmitInfo contains the retry interval and the retry count.

When specifying nbpBufSize, for each NBP tuple expected, allow space for the actual characters of the name, the address, and four bytes for use by NBP.

Result codes   noErr   No error
                       nbpBuffOvr   Buffer overflow

```
FUNCTION NBPExtract (theBuffer: Ptr; numInBuf: INTEGER; whichOne:
          INTEGER; VAR abEntity: EntityName; VAR address:
          AddrBlock) : OSErr;   [Not in ROM]
```

NBPExtract returns one address from the list of addresses returned by NBPLookup. TheBuffer and numInBuf indicate the location and number of tuples in the buffer. WhichOne specifies which one of the tuples in the buffer should be returned in the abEntity and address parameters.

Result codes   noErr   No error
                       extractErr   Can't find tuple in buffer

```
FUNCTION NBPConfirm (abRecord: ABRecHandle; async: BOOLEAN) :
         OSErr;   [Not in ROM]
```

ABusRecord

←	abOpcode	{always tNBPConfirm}
←	abResult	{result code}
→	abUserReference	{for your use}
→	nbpEntityPtr	{pointer to entity name}
←	nbpDataField	{socket number}
→	nbpAddress	{socket address}
→	nbpRetransmitInfo	{retransmission information}

NBPConfirm confirms that an entity known by name and address still exists (is still entered in the names directory). NBPEntityPtr points to a variable of type EntityName that contains the name to confirm, and nbpAddress specifies the address to be confirmed. (No meta-characters are allowed in the entity name.) NBPRetransmitInfo contains the retry interval and the retry count. The socket number of the entity is returned in nbpDataField. NBPConfirm is more efficient than NBPLookup in terms of network traffic.

Result codes	noErr	No error
	nbpConfDiff	Name confirmed for different socket
	nbpNoConfirm	Name not confirmed

```
FUNCTION NBPRemove (abEntity: EntityPtr) : OSErr;   [Not in ROM]
```

NBPRemove removes an entity name from the names table of the given entity's node.

Result codes	noErr	No error
	nbpNotFound	Name not found

```
FUNCTION NBPLoad : OSErr;   [Not in ROM]
```

On a Macintosh 128K, NBPLoad reads the NBP code from the system resource file into the application heap. On a Macintosh 512K or XL, NBPLoad has no effect since the NBP code should have already been loaded when the .MPP driver was opened. Normally you'll never need to call NBPLoad, because the AppleTalk Manager calls it when necessary.

Result codes	noErr	No error

```
FUNCTION NBPUnload : OSErr;   [Not in ROM]
```

On a Macintosh 128K, NBPUnload makes the NBP code purgeable; the space isn't actually released by the Memory Manager until necessary. On a Macintosh 512K or Macintosh XL, NBPUnload has no effect.

Result codes	noErr	No error

Example

This example of NBP registers our node as a print spooler, searches for any print spoolers registered on the network, and then extracts the information for the first one found.

```
CONST mySocket = 20;

VAR  myABRecord: ABRecHandle;
     myEntity: EntityName;
     entityAddr: AddrBlock;
     nbpNamePtr: Ptr;
     myBuffer: PACKED ARRAY[0..999] OF CHAR;
     errCode: INTEGER;
     async: BOOLEAN;

BEGIN
errCode := MPPOpen;
IF errCode <> noErr
  THEN
    WRITELN('Error in opening AppleTalk')
    {Maybe serial port B isn't available for use by AppleTalk}
  ELSE
    BEGIN
    {Call Memory Manager to allocate ABusRecord}
    myABRecord := ABRecHandle(NewHandle(nbpSize));
    {Set up our entity name to register}
    WITH myEntity DO
      BEGIN
      objStr := 'Gene Station';    {we are called 'Gene Station' }
      typeStr := 'PrintSpooler';   { and are of type 'PrintSpooler'}
      zoneStr := '*';
      {Allocate data space for the entity name (used by NBP)}
      nbpNamePtr := NewPtr(LENGTH(objStr)+LENGTH(typeStr)+
                                          LENGTH(zoneStr)+12);
      END;
    {Set up the ABusRecord for the NBPRegister call}
    WITH myABRecord^^ DO
      BEGIN
      nbpEntityPtr := @myEntity;
      nbpBufPtr := nbpNamePtr;      {buffer used by NBP internally}
      nbpBufSize := nbpNameBufSize;
      nbpAddress.aSocket := mySocket; {socket to register us on}
      nbpRetransmitInfo.retransInterval := 8; {retransmit every 64 }
      nbpRetransmitInfo.retransCount := 3;    { ticks and try 3 times}
      END;
    async := FALSE;
    errCode := NBPRegister(myABRecord,async);
    IF errCode <> noErr
      THEN
        WRITELN('Error occurred in the NBPRegister call')
        {Maybe the name is already registered somewhere else on the }
        { network.}
```

```
      ELSE
        BEGIN
        {Now that we've registered our name, find others of type }
        { 'PrintSpooler'.}
        WITH myEntity DO
          BEGIN
          objStr := '=';              {any one of type }
          typeStr := 'PrintSpooler';  { "PrintSpooler" }
          zoneStr := '*';             { in our zone}
          END;
        WITH myABRecord^^ DO
          BEGIN
          nbpEntityPtr := @myEntity;
          nbpBufPtr := @myBuffer;   {buffer to place responses in}
          nbpBufSize := SIZEOF(myBuffer);
          {The field nbpDataField, before the NBPLookup call, }
          { represents an approximate number of responses.  After the }
          { call, nbpDataField contains the actual number of responses }
          { received.}
          nbpDataField := 100;   {we want about 100 responses back}
          END;
        errCode := NBPLookup(myABRecord,async);     {make sync call}
        IF errCode <> noErr
          THEN
            WRITELN('An error occurred in the NBPLookup')
            {Did the buffer overflow?}
          ELSE
            BEGIN
            {Get the first reply}
            errCode := NBPExtract(@mybuffer,myABRecord^^.nbpDataField,1,
                                  myEntity,entityAddr);
            {The socket address and name of the entity are returned here. }
            { If we want all of them, we'll have to loop for each one in }
            { the buffer.}
            IF errCode <> noErr
              THEN
                WRITELN('Error in NBPExtract');
                {Maybe the one we wanted wasn't in the buffer}
            END;
        END;
      END;
  END.
```

Miscellaneous Routines

```
FUNCTION GetNodeAddress (VAR myNode,myNet: INTEGER) : OSErr;
                [Not in ROM]
```

GetNodeAddress returns the current node ID and network number of the caller. If the .MPP driver isn't installed, it returns noMPPErr. If myNet contains 0, this means that a bridge hasn't yet been found.

Result codes   noErr   No error
                             noMPPErr   MPP driver not installed

```
FUNCTION IsMPPOpen : BOOLEAN;   [Not in ROM]
```

IsMPPOpen returns TRUE if the .MPP driver is loaded and running.

```
FUNCTION IsATPOpen : BOOLEAN;   [Not in ROM]
```

IsATPOpen returns TRUE if the .ATP driver is loaded and running.

CALLING THE APPLETALK MANAGER FROM ASSEMBLY LANGUAGE

This section discusses how to use the AppleTalk Manager from assembly language. Equivalent Pascal information is given in the preceding section.

All routines make Device Manager Control calls. The description of each routine includes a list of the fields needed. Some of these fields are part of the parameter block described in chapter 6; additional fields are provided for the AppleTalk Manager.

The number next to each field name indicates the byte offset of the field from the start of the parameter block pointed to by A0. An arrow next to each parameter name indicates whether it's an input, output, or input/output parameter:

Arrow	Meaning
→	Parameter is passed to the routine
←	Parameter is returned by the routine
↔	Parameter is passed to and returned by the routine

All Device Manager Control calls return an integer result code of type OSErr in the ioResult field. Each routine description lists all of the applicable result codes generated by the AppleTalk Manager, along with a short description of what the result code means. Lengthier explanations of all the result codes can be found in the summary at the end of this chapter. Result codes from other parts of the Operating System may also be returned. (See Appendix A in Volume III for a list of all result codes.)

Opening AppleTalk

Two tests are made at system startup to determine whether the .MPP driver should be opened at that time. If port B is already in use, or isn't configured for AppleTalk, .MPP isn't opened until explicitly requested by an application; otherwise it's opened at system startup.

It's the application's responsibility to test the availability of port B before opening AppleTalk. Assembly-language programmers can use the Pascal calls MPPOpen and ATPLoad to open the .MPP and .ATP drivers.

The global variable SPConfig is used for configuring the serial ports; it's copied from a byte in parameter RAM (which is discussed in chapter 13). The low-order four bits of this variable contain the current configuration of port B. The following use types are provided as global constants for testing or setting the configuration of port B:

```
useFree          .EQU    0      ;unconfigured
useATalk         .EQU    1      ;configured for AppleTalk
useAsync         .EQU    2      ;configured for the Serial Driver
```

The application shouldn't attempt to open AppleTalk unless SPConfig is equal to either useFree or useATalk.

A second test involves the global variable PortBUse; the low-order four bits of this byte are used to monitor the current use of port B. If PortBUse is negative, the program is free to open AppleTalk. If PortBUse is positive, the program should test to see whether port B is already being used by AppleTalk; if it is, the low-order four bits of PortBUse will be equal to the use type useATalk.

The .MPP driver sets PortBUse to the correct value (useATalk) when it's opened and resets it to $FF when it's closed. Bits 4-6 of this byte are used for driver-specific information; ATP uses bit 4 to indicate whether it's currently opened:

```
atpLoadedBit     .EQU    4      ;set if ATP is opened
```

Example

The following code illustrates the use of the SPConfig and PortBUse variables.

```
          MOVE     #-<atpUnitNum+1>,atpRefNum(A0)   ;save known ATP refNum
                                                    ; in case ATP not opened
OpenAbus  SUB      #ioQElSize,SP         ;allocate queue entry
          MOVE.L   SP,A0                 ;A0 -> queue entry
          CLR.B    ioPermssn(A0)         ;make sure permission's clear
          MOVE.B   PortBUse,D1           ;is port B in use?
          BPL.S    @10                   ;if so, make sure by AppleTalk
          MOVEQ    #portNotCf,D0         ;assume port not configured for
                                         ; AppleTalk
          MOVE.B   SPConfig,D1           ;get configuration data
          AND.B    #$0F,D1               ;mask it to low 4 bits
          SUBQ.B   #useATalk,D1          ;unconfigured or configured for
                                         ; AppleTalk
          BGT.S    @30                   ;if not, return error
          LEA      mppName,A1            ;A1 = address of driver name
          MOVE.L   A1,ioFileName(A0)     ;set in queue entry
          _Open                          ;open MPP
          BNE.S    @30                   ;return error, if it can't load it
          BRA.S    @20                   ;otherwise, go check ATP
@10       MOVEQ    #portInUse,D0         ;assume port in use error
          AND.B    #$0F,D1               ;clear all but use bits
          SUBQ.B   #useATalk,D1          ;is AppleTalk using it?
          BNE.S    @30                   ;if not, then error
@20       MOVEQ    #0,D0                 ;assume no error
          BTST     #atpLoadedBit,PortBUse   ;ATP already open?
          BNE.S    @30                   ;just return if so
          LEA      atpName,A1            ;A1 = address of driver name
```

```
        MOVE.L    A1,ioFileName(A0)   ;set in queue entry
        _Open                         ;open ATP
@30     ADD       #ioQElSize,SP       ;deallocate queue entry
        RTS                           ;and return
mppName .BYTE     4                   ;length of .MPP driver name
        .ASCII    '.MPP'              ;name of .MPP driver
atpName .BYTE     4                   ;length of .ATP driver name
        .ASCII    '.ATP'              ;name of .ATP driver
```

AppleTalk Link Access Protocol

Data Structures

An ALAP frame is composed of a three-byte header, up to 600 bytes of data, and a two-byte frame check sequence (Figure 5). You can use the following global constants to access the contents of an ALAP header:

```
    lapDstAdr    .EQU    0      ;destination node ID
    lapSrcAdr    .EQU    1      ;source node ID
    lapType      .EQU    2      ;ALAP protocol type
    lapHdSz      .EQU    3      ;ALAP header size
```

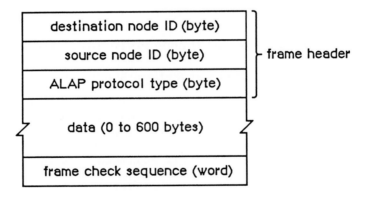

Figure 5. ALAP Frame

Two of the protocol handlers in every node are used by DDP. These protocol handlers service frames with ALAP protocol types equal to the following global constants:

```
    shortDDP    .EQU    1      ;short DDP header
    longDDP     .EQU    2      ;long DDP header
```

When you call ALAP to send a frame, you pass it information about the frame in a **write data structure**, which has the format shown in Figure 6.

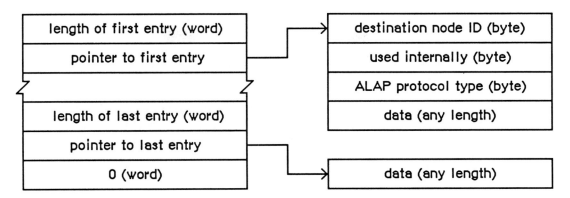

Figure 6. Write Data Structure for ALAP

Using ALAP

Most programs will never need to call ALAP, because higher-level protocols will automatically call ALAP as necessary. If you do want to send a frame directly via an ALAP, call the WriteLAP function. There's no ReadLAP function in assembly language; if you want to read ALAP frames, you must call AttachPH to add your protocol handler to the node's protocol handler table. The ALAP module will examine every incoming frame and call your protocol handler for each frame received with the correct ALAP protocol. When your program no longer wants to receive frames with a particular ALAP protocol type value, it can call DetachPH to remove the corresponding protocol handler from the protocol handler table.

See the "Protocol Handlers and Socket Listeners" section for information on how to write a protocol handler.

ALAP Routines

WriteLAP function

Parameter block

→	26	csCode	word	;always writeLAP
→	30	wdsPointer	pointer	;write data structure

WriteLAP sends a frame to another node. The frame data and destination of the frame are described by the write data structure pointed to by wdsPointer. The first two data bytes of an ALAP frame sent to another computer using the AppleTalk Manager must indicate the length of the frame in bytes. The ALAP protocol type byte must be in the range 1 to 127.

Result codes	noErr	No error
	excessCollsns	No CTS received after 32 RTS's
	ddpLengthErr	Packet length exceeds maximum
	lapProtErr	Invalid ALAP protocol type

AttachPH function

Parameter block

→	26	csCode	word	;always attachPH
→	28	protType	byte	;ALAP protocol type
→	30	handler	pointer	;protocol handler

AttachPH adds the protocol handler pointed to by handler to the node's protocol table. ProtType specifies what kind of frame the protocol handler can service. After AttachPH is called, the protocol handler is called for each incoming frame whose ALAP protocol type equals protType.

Result codes	noErr	No error
	lapProtErr	Error attaching protocol type

DetachPH function

Parameter block

→	26	csCode	word	;always detachPH
→	28	protType	byte	;ALAP protocol type

DetachPH removes from the node's protocol table the specified ALAP protocol type and corresponding protocol handler.

Result codes	noErr	No error
	lapProtErr	Error detaching protocol type

Datagram Delivery Protocol

Data Structures

A DDP datagram consists of a header followed by up to 586 bytes of actual data (Figure 7). The headers can be of two different lengths; they're identified by the following ALAP protocol types:

```
shortDDP   .EQU    1       ;short DDP header
longDDP    .EQU    2       ;long DDP header
```

Long DDP headers (13 bytes) are used for sending datagrams between two or more different AppleTalk networks. You can use the following global constants to access the contents of a long DDP header:

```
ddpHopCnt    .EQU    0       ;count of bridges passed (4 bits)
ddpLength    .EQU    0       ;datagram length (10 bits)
ddpChecksum  .EQU    2       ;checksum
ddpDstNet    .EQU    4       ;destination network number
ddpSrcNet    .EQU    6       ;source network number
ddpDstNode   .EQU    8       ;destination node ID
ddpSrcNode   .EQU    9       ;source node ID
```

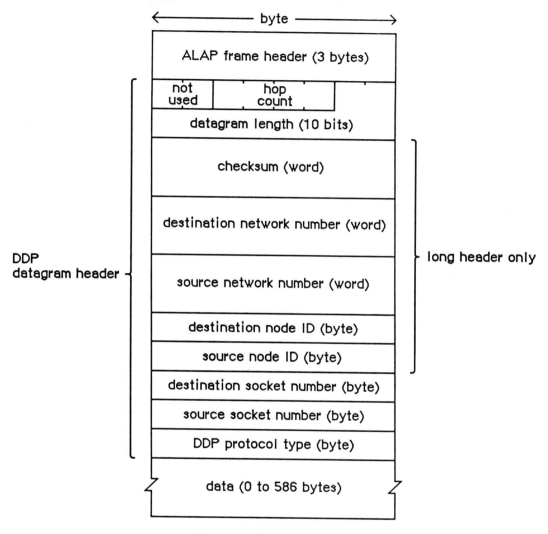

Figure 7. DDP Datagram

```
ddpDstSkt      .EQU      10      ;destination socket number
ddpSrcSkt      .EQU      11      ;source socket number
ddpType        .EQU      12      ;DDP protocol type
```

The size of a DDP long header is given by the following constant:

```
ddpHSzLong     .EQU      ddpType+1
```

The short headers (five bytes) are used for datagrams sent to sockets within the same network as the source socket. You can use the following global constants to access the contents of a short DDP header:

```
ddpLength     .EQU     0              ;datagram length
sDDPDstSkt    .EQU     ddpChecksum    ;destination socket number
sDDPSrcSkt    .EQU     sDDPDstSkt+1   ;source socket number
sDDPType      .EQU     sDDPSrcSkt+1   ;DDP protocol type
```

The size of a DDP short header is given by the following constant:

```
ddpHSzShort   .EQU     sDDPType+1
```

The datagram length is a ten-bit field. You can use the following global constant as a mask for these bits:

```
ddpLenMask    .EQU     $03FF
```

The following constant indicates the maximum length of a DDP datagram:

```
ddpMaxData    .EQU     586
```

When you call DDP to send a datagram, you pass it information about the datagram in a write data structure with the format shown in Figure 8.

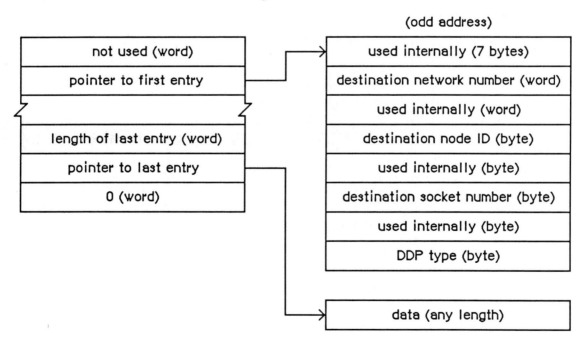

Figure 8. Write Data Structure for DDP

The first seven bytes are used internally for the ALAP header and the DDP datagram length and checksum. The other bytes used internally store the network number, node ID, and socket number of the socket client sending the datagram.

Warning: The first entry in a DDP write data structure must begin at an odd address.

If you specify a node ID of 255, the datagram will be broadcast to all nodes within the destination network. A network number of 0 means the local network to which the node is connected.

Warning: DDP always destroys the high-order byte of the destination network number when it sends a datagram with a short header. Therefore, if you want to reuse the first entry of a DDP write data structure entry, you must restore the destination network number.

Using DDP

Before it can use a socket, the program must call OpenSkt, which adds a socket and its socket listener to the socket table. When a client is finished using a socket, call CloseSkt, which removes the socket's entry from the socket table. To send a datagram via DDP, call WriteDDP. If you want to read DDP datagrams, you must write your own socket listener. DDP will send every incoming datagram for that socket to your socket listener.

See the "Protocol Handlers and Socket Listeners" section for information on how to write a socket listener.

DDP Routines

OpenSkt function

Parameter block

→	26	csCode	word	;always openSkt
↔	28	socket	byte	;socket number
→	30	listener	pointer	;socket listener

OpenSkt adds a socket and its socket listener to the socket table. If the socket parameter is nonzero, it must be in the range 64 to 127, and it specifies the socket's number; if socket is 0, OpenSkt opens a socket with a socket number in the range 128 to 254, and returns it in the socket parameter. Listener contains a pointer to the socket listener.

OpenSkt will return ddpSktErr if you pass the number of an already opened socket, if you pass a socket number greater than 127, or if the socket table is full (the socket table can hold a maximum of 12 sockets).

Result codes	noErr	No error
	ddpSktErr	Socket error

CloseSkt function

Parameter block

→	26	csCode	word	;always closeSkt
→	28	socket	byte	;socket number

CloseSkt removes the entry of the specified socket from the socket table. If you pass a socket number of 0, or if you attempt to close a socket that isn't open, CloseSkt will return ddpSktErr.

Result codes	noErr	No error
	ddpSktErr	Socket error

WriteDDP function

Parameter block

→	26	csCode	word	;always writeDDP
→	28	socket	byte	;socket number
→	29	checksumFlag	byte	;checksum flag
→	30	wdsPointer	pointer	;write data structure

WriteDDP sends a datagram to another socket. WDSPointer points to a write data structure containing the datagram and the address of the destination socket. If checksumFlag is TRUE, WriteDDP will compute the checksum for all datagrams requiring long headers.

Result codes	noErr	No error
	ddpLenErr	Datagram length too big
	ddpSktErr	Socket error
	noBridgeErr	No bridge found

AppleTalk Transaction Protocol

Data Structures

An ATP packet consists of an ALAP header, DDP header, and ATP header, followed by actual data (Figure 9). You can use the following global constants to access the contents of an ATP header:

```
atpControl     .EQU     0      ;control information
atpBitMap      .EQU     1      ;bit map
atpRespNo      .EQU     1      ;sequence number
atpTransID     .EQU     2      ;transaction ID
atpUserData    .EQU     4      ;user bytes
```

The size of an ATP header is given by the following constant:

```
atpHdSz        .EQU     8
```

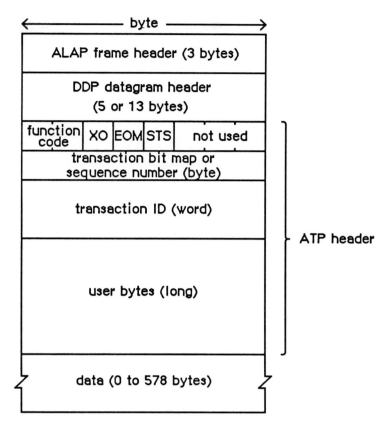

Figure 9. ATP Packet

ATP packets are identified by the following DDP protocol type:

```
atp             .EQU    3
```

The control information contains a function code and various control bits. The function code
identifies either a TReq, TResp, or TRel packet with one of the following global constants:

```
atpReqCode      .EQU    $40     ;TReq packet
atpRspCode      .EQU    $80     ;TResp packet
atpRelCode      .EQU    $C0     ;TRel packet
```

The send-transmission-status, end-of-message, and exactly-once bits in the control information
are accessed via the following global constants:

```
atpSTSBit       .EQU    3       ;send-transmission-status bit
atpEOMBit       .EQU    4       ;end-of-message bit
atpXOBit        .EQU    5       ;exactly-once bit
```

Many ATP calls require a field called atpFlags (Figure 10), which contains the above three bits plus the following two bits:

```
sendChk      .EQU    0       ;send-checksum bit
tidValid     .EQU    1       ;transaction ID validity bit
```

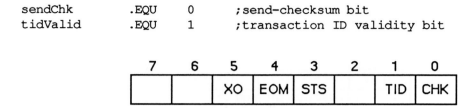

Figure 10. ATPFlags Field

The maximum number of response packets in an ATP transaction is given by the following global constant:

```
atpMaxNum    .EQU    8
```

When you call ATP to send responses, you pass the responses in a response BDS, which is a list of up to eight elements, each of which contains the following:

```
bdsBuffSz    .EQU    0       ;size of data to send
bdsBuffAddr  .EQU    2       ;pointer to data
bdsUserData  .EQU    8       ;user bytes
```

When you call ATP to receive responses, you pass it a response BDS with up to eight elements, each in the following format:

```
bdsBuffSz    .EQU    0       ;buffer size in bytes
bdsBuffAddr  .EQU    2       ;pointer to buffer
bdsDataSz    .EQU    6       ;number of bytes actually received
bdsUserData  .EQU    8       ;user bytes
```

The size of a BDS element is given by the following constant:

```
bdsEntrySz   .EQU    12
```

ATP clients are identified by internet addresses in the form shown in Figure 11.

network number (word)
node ID (byte)
socket number (byte)

Figure 11. Internet Address

Using ATP

Before you can use ATP on a Macintosh 128K, the .ATP driver must be read from the system resource file via a Device Manager Open call. The name of the .ATP driver is '.ATP' and its reference number is −11. When the .ATP driver is opened, it reads its ATP code into the application heap and installs a task into the vertical retrace queue.

> **Warning:** When another application starts up, the application heap is reinitialized; on a Macintosh 128K, this means that the ATP code is lost (and must be reloaded by the next application).

When you're through using ATP on a Macintosh 128K, call the Device Manager Close routine—the system will be returned to the state it was in before the .ATP driver was opened.

On a Macintosh 512K or XL, the .ATP driver will have been loaded into the system heap either at system startup or upon execution of a Device Manager Open call loading MPP. You shouldn't close the .ATP driver on a Macintosh 512K or XL; AppleTalk expects it to remain open on these systems.

To send a request to another socket and get a response, call SendRequest. The call terminates when either an entire response is received or a specified retry timeout interval elapses. To open a socket for the purpose of responding to requests, call OpenATPSkt. Then call GetRequest to receive a request; when a request is received, the call is completed. After receiving and servicing a request, call SendResponse to return response information. If you cannot or do not want to send the entire response all at once, make a SendResponse call to send some of the response, and then call AddResponse later to send the remainder of the response. To close a socket opened for the purpose of sending responses, call CloseATPSkt.

During exactly-once transactions, SendResponse doesn't terminate until the transaction is completed via a TRel packet, or the retry count is exceeded.

> **Warning:** Don't modify the parameter block passed to an ATP call until the call is completed.

ATP Routines

OpenATPSkt function

Parameter block

→	26	csCode	word	;always openATPSkt
↔	28	atpSocket	byte	;socket number
→	30	addrBlock	long word	;socket request specification

OpenATPSkt opens a socket for the purpose of receiving requests. ATPSocket contains the socket number of the socket to open. If it's 0, a number is dynamically assigned and returned in atpSocket. AddrBlock contains a specification of the socket addresses from which requests will be accepted. A 0 in the network number, node ID, or socket number field of addrBlock means that requests will be accepted from every network, node, or socket, respectively.

Result codes	noErr	No error
	tooManySkts	Too many responding sockets
	noDataArea	Too many outstanding ATP calls

CloseATPSkt function

Parameter block

→	26	csCode	word	;always closeATPSkt
→	28	atpSocket	byte	;socket number

CloseATPSkt closes the socket whose number is specified by atpSocket, for the purpose of receiving requests.

Result codes	noErr	No error
	noDataArea	Too many outstanding ATP calls

SendRequest function

Parameter block

→	18	userData	long word	;user bytes
←	22	reqTID	word	;transaction ID used in request
→	26	csCode	word	;always sendRequest
←	28	currBitMap	byte	;bit map
↔	29	atpFlags	byte	;control information
→	30	addrBlock	long word	;destination socket address
→	34	reqLength	word	;request size in bytes
→	36	reqPointer	pointer	;pointer to request data
→	40	bdsPointer	pointer	;pointer to response BDS
→	44	numOfBuffs	byte	;number of responses expected
→	45	timeOutVal	byte	;timeout interval
←	46	numOfResps	byte	;number of responses received
↔	47	retryCount	byte	;number of retries

SendRequest sends a request to another socket and waits for a response. UserData contains the four user bytes. AddrBlock indicates the socket to which the request should be sent. ReqLength and reqPointer contain the size and location of the request to send. BDSPointer points to a response BDS where the responses are to be returned; numOfBuffs indicates the number of responses requested. The number of responses received is returned in numOfResps. If a nonzero value is returned in numOfResps, you can examine currBitMap to determine which packets of the transaction were actually received and to detect pieces for higher-level recovery, if desired.

TimeOutVal indicates the number of seconds that SendRequest should wait for a response before resending the request. RetryCount indicates the maximum number of retries SendRequest should attempt. The end-of-message flag of atpFlags will be set if the EOM bit is set in the last packet received in a valid response sequence. The exactly-once flag should be set if you want the request to be part of an exactly-once transaction.

To cancel a SendRequest call, you need the transaction ID; it's returned in reqTID. You can examine reqTID before the completion of the call, but its contents are valid only after the tidValid bit of atpFlags has been set.

SendRequest completes when either an entire response is received or the retry count is exceeded.

Note: The value provided in retryCount will be modified during SendRequest if any retries are made. This field is used to monitor the number of retries; for each retry, it's decremented by 1.

Result codes	noErr	No error
reqFailed	Retry count exceeded
tooManyReqs	Too many concurrent requests
noDataArea	Too many outstanding ATP calls
reqAborted	Request canceled by user

GetRequest function

Parameter block

←	18	userData	long word	;user bytes
→	26	csCode	word	;always getRequest
→	28	atpSocket	byte	;socket number
←	29	atpFlags	byte	;control information
←	30	addrBlock	long word	;source of request
↔	34	reqLength	word	;request buffer size
→	36	reqPointer	pointer	;pointer to request buffer
←	44	bitMap	byte	;bit map
←	46	transID	word	;transaction ID

GetRequest sets up the mechanism to receive a request sent by a SendRequest call. UserData returns the four user bytes from the request. ATPSocket contains the socket number of the socket that should listen for a request. The internet address of the socket from which the request was sent is returned in addrBlock. ReqLength and reqPointer indicate the size (in bytes) and location of a buffer to store the incoming request. The actual size of the request is returned in reqLength. The transaction bit map and transaction ID will be returned in bitMap and transID. The exactly-once flag in atpFlags will be set if the request is part of an exactly-once transaction.

GetRequest completes when a request is received.

Result codes	noErr	No error
badATPSkt	Bad responding socket

SendResponse function

Parameter block

←	18	userData	long word	;user bytes from TRel
→	26	csCode	word	;always sendResponse
→	28	atpSocket	byte	;socket number
→	29	atpFlags	byte	;control information
→	30	addrBlock	long word	;response destination
→	40	bdsPointer	pointer	;pointer to response BDS
→	44	numOfBuffs	byte	;number of response packets being sent
→	45	bdsSize	byte	;BDS size in elements
→	46	transID	word	;transaction ID

SendResponse sends a response to a socket. If the response was part of an exactly-once transaction, userData will contain the user bytes from the TRel packet. ATPSocket contains the socket number from which the response should be sent. The end-of-message flag in atpFlags should be set if the response contains the final packet in a transaction composed of a group of packets and the number of responses is less than requested. AddrBlock indicates the address of the socket to which the response should be sent. BDSPointer points to a response BDS containing room for the maximum number of responses to be sent; bdsSize contains this maximum number. NumOfBuffs contains the number of response packets to be sent in this call; you may wish to make AddResponse calls to complete the response. TransID indicates the transaction ID of the associated request.

During exactly-once transactions, SendResponse doesn't complete until either a TRel packet is received from the socket that made the request, or the retry count is exceeded.

Result codes	noErr	No error
	badATPSkt	Bad responding socket
	noRelErr	No release received
	noDataArea	Too many outstanding ATP calls
	badBuffNum	Sequence number out of range

AddResponse function

Parameter block

→	18	userData	long word	;user bytes
→	26	csCode	word	;always addResponse
→	28	atpSocket	byte	;socket number
→	29	atpFlags	byte	;control information
→	30	addrBlock	long word	;response destination
→	34	reqLength	word	;response size
→	36	reqPointer	pointer	;pointer to response
→	44	rspNum	byte	;sequence number
→	46	transID	word	;transaction ID

AddResponse sends an additional response packet to a socket that has already been sent the initial part of a response via SendResponse. UserData contains the four user bytes. ATPSocket contains the socket number from which the response should be sent. The end-of-message flag in atpFlags should be set if this response packet is the final packet in a transaction composed of a group of packets and the number of responses is less than requested. AddrBlock indicates the socket to which the response should be sent. ReqLength and reqPointer contain the size (in bytes) and location of the response to send; rspNum indicates the sequence number of the response (in the range 0 to 7). TransID must contain the transaction ID.

Warning: If the transaction is part of an exactly-once transaction, the buffer used in the AddResponse call must not be altered or released until the corresponding SendResponse call has completed.

Result codes	noErr	No error
	badATPSkt	Bad responding socket
	noSendResp	AddResponse issued before SendResponse
	badBuffNum	Sequence number out of range
	noDataArea	Too many outstanding ATP calls

RelTCB function

Parameter block

→	26	csCode	word	;always relTCB
→	30	addrBlock	long word	;destination of request
→	46	transID	word	;transaction ID of request

RelTCB dequeues the specified SendRequest call and returns the result code reqAborted for the aborted call. The transaction ID can be obtained from the reqTID field of the SendRequest queue entry; see the description of SendRequest for details.

Result codes	noErr	No error
	cbNotFound	ATP control block not found
	noDataArea	Too many outstanding ATP calls

RelRspCB function

Parameter block

→	26	csCode	word	;always relRspCB
→	28	atpSocket	byte	;socket number that request was received on
→	30	addrBlock	long word	;source of request
→	46	transID	word	;transaction ID of request

In an exactly-once transaction, RelRspCB cancels the specified SendResponse, without waiting for the release timer to expire or a TRel packet to be received. No error is returned for the SendResponse call. Whan called to cancel a transaction that isn't using exactly-once service, RelRspCB returns cbNotFound. The transaction ID can be obtained from the reqTID field of the SendResponse queue entry; see the description of SendResponse for details.

Result codes	noErr	No error
	cbNotFound	ATP control block not found

Name-Binding Protocol

Data Structures

The first two bytes in the NBP header (Figure 12) indicate the type of the packet, the number of tuples in the packet, and an NBP packet identifier. You can use the following global constants to access these bytes:

```
nbpControl      .EQU      0     ;packet type
nbpTCount       .EQU      0     ;tuple count
nbpID           .EQU      1     ;packet identifier
nbpTuple        .EQU      2     ;start of first tuple
```

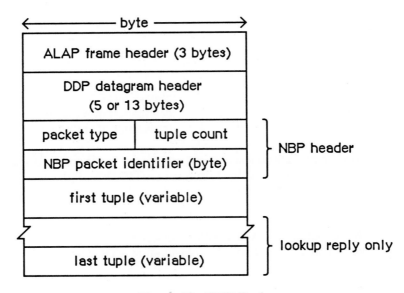

Figure 12. NBP Packet

NBP packets are identified by the following DDP protocol type:

```
nbp             .EQU      2
```

NBP uses the following global constants in the nbpControl field to identify NBP packets:

```
brRq            .EQU      1     ;broadcast request
lkUp            .EQU      2     ;lookup request
lkUpReply       .EQU      3     ;lookup reply
```

NBP entities are identified by internet address in the form shown in Figure 13 below. Entities are also identified by tuples, which include both an internet address and an entity name. You can use the following global constants to access information in tuples:

```
tupleNet        .EQU      0     ;network number
tupleNode       .EQU      2     ;node ID
tupleSkt        .EQU      3     ;socket number
tupleEnum       .EQU      4     ;used internally
tupleName       .EQU      5     ;entity name
```

The meta-characters in an entity name can be identified with the following global constants:

```
equals          .EQU      '='   ;"wild-card" meta-character
star            .EQU      '*'   ;"this zone" meta-character
```

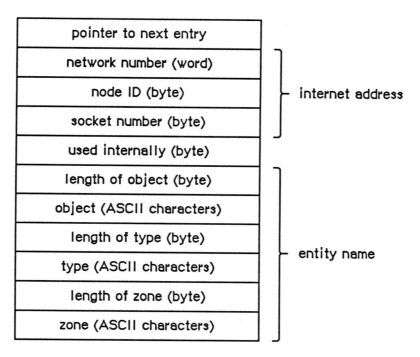

Figure 13. Names Table Entry

The maximum number of tuples in an NBP packet is given by the following global constant:

```
tupleMax        .EQU        15
```

Entity names are mapped to sockets via the names table. Each entry in the names table has the structure shown in Figure 13.

You can use the following global constants to access some of the elements of a names table entry:

```
ntLink          .EQU        0       ;pointer to next entry
ntTuple         .EQU        4       ;tuple
ntSocket        .EQU        7       ;socket number
ntEntity        .EQU        9       ;entity name
```

The socket number of the names information socket is given by the following global constant:

```
nis             .EQU        2
```

Using NBP

On a Macintosh 128K, before calling any other NBP routines, call the LoadNBP function, which reads the NBP code from the system resource file into the application heap. (The NBP code is part of the .MPP driver, which has a driver reference number of –10.) When you're finished with NBP and want to reclaim the space its code occupies, call UnloadNBP. On a Macintosh 512K or XL, the NBP code is read in when the .MPP driver is loaded.

Warning: When an application starts up, the application heap is reinitialized; on a Macintosh 128K, this means that the NBP code is lost (and must be reloaded by the next application).

When an entity wants to communicate via an AppleTalk network, it should call RegisterName to place its name and internet address in the names table. When an entity no longer wants to communicate on the network, or is being shut down, it should call RemoveName to remove its entry from the names table.

To determine the address of an entity you know only by name, call LookupName, which returns a list of all entities with the name you specify. If you already know the address of an entity, and want only to confirm that it still exists, call ConfirmName. ConfirmName is more efficient than LookupName in terms of network traffic.

NBP Routines

RegisterName function

Parameter block

→	26	csCode	word	;always registerName
→	28	interval	byte	;retry interval
↔	29	count	byte	;retry count
→	30	ntQElPtr	pointer	;names table element pointer
→	34	verifyFlag	byte	;set if verify needed

RegisterName adds the name and address of an entity to the node's names table. NTQElPtr points to a names table entry containing the entity's name and internet address (in the form shown in Figure 13 above). Meta-characters aren't allowed in the object and type fields of the entity name; the zone field, however, *must* contain the meta-character "*". If verifyFlag is TRUE, RegisterName checks on the network to see if the name is already in use, and returns a result code of nbpDuplicate if so. Interval and count contain the retry interval in eight-tick units and the retry count. When a retry is made, the count field is modified.

Warning: The names table entry passed to RegisterName remains the property of NBP until removed from the names table. Don't attempt to remove or modify it. If you've allocated memory using a NewHandle call, you must lock it as long as the name is registered.

Warning: VerifyFlag should normally be set before calling RegisterName.

Result codes	noErr	No error
	nbpDuplicate	Duplicate name already exists
	nbpNISErr	Error opening names information socket

LookupName function

Parameter block

→	26	csCode	word	;always lookupName
→	28	interval	byte	;retry interval
↔	29	count	byte	;retry count
→	30	entityPtr	pointer	;pointer to entity name
→	34	retBuffPtr	pointer	;pointer to buffer
→	38	retBuffSize	word	;buffer size in bytes
→	40	maxToGet	word	;matches to get
←	42	numGotten	word	;matches found

LookupName returns the addresses of all entities with a specified name. EntityPtr points to the entity's name (in the form shown in Figure 13 above). Meta-characters are allowed in the entity name. RetBuffPtr and retBuffSize contain the location and size of an area of memory in which the tuples describing the entity names and their corresponding addresses should be returned. MaxToGet indicates the maximum number of matching names to find addresses for; the actual number of addresses found is returned in numGotten. Interval and count contain the retry interval and the retry count. LookupName completes when either the number of matches is equal to or greater than maxToGet, or the retry count has been exceeded. The count field is decremented for each retransmission.

Note: NumGotten is first set to 0 and then incremented with each match found. You can test the value in this field, and can start examining the received addresses in the buffer while the lookup continues.

Result codes	noErr	No error
	nbpBuffOvr	Buffer overflow

ConfirmName function

Parameter block

→	26	csCode	word	;always confirmName
→	28	interval	byte	;retry interval
↔	29	count	byte	;retry count
→	30	entityPtr	pointer	;pointer to entity name
→	34	confirmAddr	pointer	;entity address
←	38	newSocket	byte	;socket number

ConfirmName confirms that an entity known by name and address still exists (is still entered in the names directory). EntityPtr points to the entity's name (in the form shown in Figure 13 above). ConfirmAddr specifies the address to confirmed. No meta-characters are allowed in the entity name. Interval and count contain the retry interval and the retry count. The socket number of the entity is returned in newSocket. ConfirmName is more efficient than LookupName in terms of network traffic.

Result codes	noErr	No error
	nbpConfDiff	Name confirmed for different socket
	nbpNoConfirm	Name not confirmed

RemoveName function

Parameter block

→	26	csCode	word	;always removeName
→	30	entityPtr	pointer	;pointer to entity name

RemoveName removes an entity name from the names table of the given entity's node.

Result codes	noErr	No error
	nbpNotFound	Name not found

LoadNBP function

Parameter block

→	26	csCode	word	;always loadNBP

On a Macintosh 128K, LoadNBP reads the NBP code from the system resource file into the application heap; on a Macintosh 512K or XL it has no effect.

Result codes	noErr	No error

UnloadNBP function

Parameter block

→	26	csCode	word	;always unloadNBP

On a Macintosh 128K, UnloadNBP makes the NBP code purgeable; the space isn't actually released by the Memory Manager until necessary. On a Macintosh 512K or XL, UnloadNBP has no effect.

Result codes	noErr	No error

PROTOCOL HANDLERS AND SOCKET LISTENERS

This section describes how to write your own protocol handlers and socket listeners. If you're only interested in using the default protocol handlers and socket listeners provided by the Pascal interface, you can skip this section. Protocol handlers and socket listeners must be written in assembly language because they'll be called by the .MPP driver with parameters in various registers not directly accessible from Pascal.

The .MPP and .ATP drivers have been designed to maximize overall throughput while minimizing code size. Two principal sources of loss of throughput are unnecessary buffer copying and inefficient mechanisms for dispatching (routing) packets between the various layers of the network protocol architecture. The AppleTalk Manager completely eliminates buffer copying by using simple, efficient dispatching mechanisms at two important points of the data reception path: protocol handlers and socket listeners. To write your own, you should understand the flow of control in this path.

Data Reception in the AppleTalk Manager

When the SCC detects an ALAP frame addressed to the particular node (or a broadcast frame), it interrupts the Macintosh's MC68000. An interrupt handler built into the .MPP driver gets control and begins servicing the interrupt. Meanwhile, the frame's ALAP header bytes are coming into the SCC's data reception buffer; this is a three-byte FIFO buffer. The interrupt handler must remove these bytes from the SCC's buffer to make room for the bytes right behind; for this purpose, MPP has an internal buffer, known as the Read Header Area (RHA), into which it places these three bytes.

The third byte of the frame contains the ALAP protocol type field. If the most significant bit of this field is set (that is, ALAP protocol types 128 to 255), the frame is an ALAP control frame. Since ALAP control frames are only three bytes long (plus two CRC bytes), for such frames the interrupt handler simply confirms that the CRC bytes indicate an error-free frame and then performs the specified action.

If, however, the frame being received is a data frame (that is, ALAP protocol types 1 to 127), intended for a higher layer of the protocol architecture implemented on that Macintosh, this means that additional data bytes are coming right behind. The interrupt handler must immediately pass control to the protocol handler corresponding to the protocol type specified in the third byte of the ALAP frame for continued reception of the frame. To allow for such a dispatching mechanism, the ALAP code in MPP maintains a protocol table. This consists of a list of currently used ALAP protocol types with the memory addresses of their corresponding protocol handlers. To allow MPP to transfer control to a protocol handler you've written, you must make an appropriate entry in the protocol table with a valid ALAP protocol type and the memory address of your code module.

To enter your protocol handler into the protocol table, issue the LAPOpenProtocol call from Pascal or an AttachPH call from assembly language. Thereafter, whenever an ALAP header with your ALAP protocol type is received, MPP will call your protocol handler. When you no longer wish to receive packets of that ALAP protocol type, call LAPCloseProtocol from Pascal or DetachPH from assembly language.

> **Warning:** Remember that ALAP protocol types 1 and 2 are reserved by DDP for the default protocol handler and that types 128 to 255 are used by ALAP for its control frames.

A protocol handler is a piece of assembly-language code that controls the reception of AppleTalk packets of a given ALAP protocol type. More specifically, a protocol handler must carry out the reception of the rest of the frame following the ALAP header. The nature of a particular protocol handler depends on the characteristics of the protocol for which it was written. In the simplest case, the protocol handler simply reads the entire packet into an internal buffer. A more sophisticated protocol handler might read in the header of its protocol, and on the basis of information contained in it, decide where to put the rest of the packet's data. In certain cases, the protocol handler might, after examining the header corresponding to its own protocol, in turn transfer control to a similar piece of code at the next-higher level of the protocol architecture (for example, in the case of DDP, its protocol handler must call the socket listener of the datagram's destination socket).

In this way, protocol handlers are used to allow "on the fly" decisions regarding the intended recipient of the packets's data, and thus avoid buffer copying. By using protocol handlers and their counterparts in higher layers (for instance, socket listeners), data sent over the AppleTalk network is read directly from the network into the destination's buffer.

Writing Protocol Handlers

When the .MPP driver calls your protocol handler, it has already read the first five bytes of the packet into the RHA. These are the three-byte ALAP header and the next two bytes of the packet. The two bytes following the header must contain the length in bytes of the data in the packet, including these two bytes themselves, but excluding the ALAP header.

> **Note:** Since ALAP packets can have at most 600 data bytes, only the lower ten bits of this length value are significant.

After determining how many bytes to read and where to put them, the protocol handler must call one or both of two functions that perform all the low-level manipulation of the SCC required to read bytes from the network. ReadPacket can be called repeatedly to read in the packet piecemeal or ReadRest can be called to read the rest of the packet. Any number of ReadPacket calls can be used, as long as a ReadRest call is made to read the final piece of the packet. This is necessary because ReadRest restores state information and verifies that the hardware-generated CRC is correct. An error will be returned if the protocol handler attempts to use ReadPacket to read more bytes than remain in the packet.

When MPP passes control to your protocol handler, it passes various parameters and pointers in the processor's registers:

Register(s)	Contents
A0-A1	SCC addresses used by MPP
A2	Pointer to MPP's local variables (discussed below)
A3	Pointer to next free byte in RHA
A4	Pointer to ReadPacket and ReadRest jump table
D1 (word)	Number of bytes left to read in packet

These registers, with the exception of A3, must be preserved until ReadRest is called. A3 is used as an input parameter to ReadPacket and ReadRest, so its contents may be changed. D0, D2, and D3 are free for your use. In addition, register A5 has been saved by MPP and may be used by the protocol handler until ReadRest is called. When control returns to the protocol handler from ReadRest, MPP no longer needs the data in these registers. At that point, standard interrupt routine conventions apply and the protocol handler can freely use A0-A3 and D0-D3 (they're restored by the interrupt handler).

D1 contains the number of bytes left to be read in the packet as derived from the packet's length field. A transmission error could corrupt the length field or some bytes in the packet might be lost, but this won't be discovered until the end of the packet is reached and the CRC checked.

When the protocol handler is first called, the first five bytes of the packet (ALAP destination node ID, source node ID, ALAP protocol type, and length) can be read from the RHA. Since A3 is pointing to the next free position in the RHA, these bytes can be read using negative offsets from A3. For instance, the ALAP source node ID is at –4(A3), the packet's data length (given in D1) is also pointed to by –2(A3), and so on. Alternatively, they can be accessed as positive offsets from the top of the RHA. The effective address of the top of the RHA is toRHA(A2), so the following code could be used to obtain the ALAP type field:

```
LEA       toRHA(A2),A5      ;A5 points to top of RHA
MOVE.B    lapType(A5),D2    ;load D2 with type field
```

These methods are valid only as long as SCC interrupts remain locked out (which they are when the protocol handler is first called). If the protocol handler lowers the interrupt level, another packet could arrive over the network and invalidate the contents of the RHA.

You can call ReadPacket by jumping through the jump table in the following way:

```
JSR    (A4)
```

On entry	D3:	number of bytes to be read (word)
	A3:	pointer to a buffer to hold the bytes
On exit	D0:	modified
	D1:	number of bytes left to read in packet (word)
	D2:	preserved
	D3:	= 0 if requested number of bytes were read
		<> 0 if error
	A0-A2:	preserved
	A3:	pointer to one byte past the last byte read

ReadPacket reads the number of bytes specified in D3 into the buffer pointed to by A3. The number of bytes remaining to be read in the packet is returned in D1. A3 points to the byte following the last byte read.

You can call ReadRest by jumping through the jump table in the following way:

```
JSR    2(A4)
```

On entry	A3:	pointer to a buffer to hold the bytes
	D3:	size of the buffer (word)
On exit	D0-D1:	modified
	D2:	preserved
	D3:	= 0 if packet was exactly the size of the buffer
		< 0 if packet was (–D3) bytes too large to fit in buffer and was truncated
		> 0 if D3 bytes weren't read (packet is smaller than buffer)
	A0-A2:	preserved
	A3:	pointer to one byte past the last byte read

ReadRest reads the remaining bytes of the packet into the buffer whose size is given in D3 and whose location is pointed to by A3. The result of the operation is returned in D3.

ReadRest can be called with D3 set to a buffer size greater than the packet size; ReadPacket cannot (it will return an error).

Warning: Remember to always call ReadRest to read the last part of a packet; otherwise the system will eventually crash.

If at any point before it has read the last byte of a packet, the protocol handler wants to discard the remaining data, it should terminate by calling ReadRest as follows:

```
        MOVEQ    #0,D3        ;byte count of 0
        JSR      2(A4)        ;call ReadRest
        RTS
```

Or, equivalently:

```
        MOVEQ    #0,D3        ;byte count of 0
        JMP      2(A4)        ;JMP to ReadRest, not JSR
```

In all other cases, the protocol handler should end with an RTS, even if errors were detected. If MPP returns an error from a ReadPacket call, the protocol handler must quit via an RTS without calling ReadRest at all (in this case it has already been called by MPP).

The Z (Zero) condition code is set upon return from these routines to indicate the presence of errors (CRC, overrun, and so on). Zero bit set means no error was detected; a nonzero condition code implies an error of some kind.

Up to 24 bytes of temporary storage are available in MPP's RHA. When the protocol handler is called, 19 of these bytes are free for its use. It may read several bytes (at least four are suggested) into this area to empty the SCC's buffer and buy some time for further processing.

MPP's globals include some variables that you may find useful. They're allocated as a block of memory pointed to by the contents of the global variable ABusVars, but a protocol handler can access them by offsets from A2:

Name	Contents
sysLAPAddr	This node's node ID (byte)
toRHA	Top of the Read Header Area (24 bytes)
sysABridge	Node ID of a bridge (byte)
sysNetNum	This node's network number (word)
vSCCEnable	Status Register (SR) value to re-enable SCC interrupts (word)

Warning: Under no circumstances should your protocol handler modify these variables. It can read them to find the node's ID, its network number, and the node ID of a bridge on the AppleTalk internet.

If, after reading the entire packet from the network and using the data in the RHA, the protocol handler needs to do extensive post-processing, it can load the value in vSCCEnable into the SR to enable interrupts. To allow your programs to run transparently on any Macintosh, use the value in vSCCEnable rather than directly manipulating the interrupt level by changing specific bits in the SR.

Additional information, such as the driver's version number or reference number and a pointer (or handle) to the driver itself, may be obtained from MPP's device control entry. This can be found by dereferencing the handle in the unit table's entry corresponding to unit number 9; for more information, see the section "The Structure of a Device Driver" in chapter 6.

Timing Considerations

Once it's been called by MPP, your protocol handler has complete responsibility for receiving the rest of the packet. The operation of your protocol handler is time-critical. Since it's called just after MPP has emptied the SCC's three-byte buffer, the protocol handler has approximately 95 microseconds (best case) before it must call ReadPacket or ReadRest. Failure to do so will result in an overrun of the SCC's buffer and loss of packet information. If, within that time, the protocol handler can't determine where to put the entire incoming packet, it should call ReadPacket to read at least four bytes into some private buffer (possibly the RHA). Doing this will again empty the SCC's buffer and buy another 95 microseconds. You can do this as often as necessary, as long as the processing time between successive calls to ReadPacket doesn't exceed 95 microseconds.

Writing Socket Listeners

A socket listener is a piece of assembly-language code that receives datagrams delivered by the DDP built-in protocol handler and delivers them to the client owning that socket.

When a datagram (a packet with ALAP protocol type 1 or 2) is received by the ALAP, DDP's built-in protocol handler is called. This handler reads the DDP header into the RHA, examines the destination socket number, and determines whether this socket is open by searching DDP's socket table. This table lists the socket number and corresponding socket listener address for each open socket. If an entry is found matching the destination socket, the protocol handler immediately transfers control to the appropriate socket listener. (To allow DDP to recognize and branch to a socket listener you've written, call DDPOpenSocket from Pascal or OpenSkt from assembly language.)

At this point, the registers are set up as follows:

Register(s)	Contents
A0-A1	SCC addresses used by MPP
A2	Pointer to MPP's local variables (discussed above)
A3	Pointer to next free byte in RHA
A4	Pointer to ReadPacket and ReadRest jump table
D0	This packet's destination socket number (byte)
D1	Number of bytes left to read in packet (word)

The entire ALAP and DDP headers are in the RHA; these are the only bytes of the packet that have been read in from the SCC's buffer. The socket listener can get the destination socket number from D0 to select a buffer into which the packet can be read. The listener then calls ReadPacket and ReadRest as described under "Writing Protocol Handlers" above. The timing considerations discussed in that section apply as well, as do the issues related to accessing the MPP local variables.

The socket listener may examine the ALAP and DDP headers to extract the various fields relevant to its particular client's needs. To do so, it must first examine the ALAP protocol type field (three bytes from the beginning of the RHA) to decide whether a short (ALAP protocol type=1) or long (ALAP protocol type=2) header has been received.

A long DDP header containing a nonzero checksum field implies that the datagram was
checksummed at the source. In this case, the listener can recalculate the checksum using the
received datagram, and compare it with the checksum value. The following subroutine can be
used for this purpose:

```
DoChksum    ;
            ; D1 (word) = number of bytes to checksum
            ; D3 (word) = current checksum
            ; A1 points to the bytes to checksum
            ;
            CLR.W     D0          ;clear high byte
            SUBQ.W    #1,D1       ;decrement count for DBRA
Loop        MOVE.B    (A1)+,D0    ;read a byte into D0
            ADD.W     D0,D3       ;accumulate checksum
            ROL.W     #1,D3       ;rotate left one bit
            DBRA      D1,Loop     ;loop if more bytes
            RTS
```

Note: D0 is modified by DoChksum.

The checksum must be computed for all bytes starting with the DDP header byte following the
checksum field up to the last data byte (not including the CRC bytes). The socket listener must
start by first computing the checksum for the DDP header fields in the RHA. This is done as
follows:

```
            CLR.W     D3          ;set checksum to 0
            MOVEQ     #ddpHSzLong-ddpDstNet,D1
                                  ;length of header part to checksum
            LEA       toRHA+lapHdSz+ddpDstNet(A2),A1
                                  ;point to destination network number
            JSR       DoChksum
            ; D3 = accumulated checksum of DDP header part
```

The socket listener must now continue to set up D1 and A1 for each subsequent portion of the
datagram, and call DoChksum for each. It must not alter the value in D3.

The situation of the calculated checksum being equal to 0 requires special attention. For such
packets, the source sends a value of −1 to distinguish them from unchecksummed packets. At the
end of its checksum computation, the socket listener must examine the value in D3 to see if it's 0.
If so, it's converted to −1 and compared with the received checksum to determine whether there
was a checksum error:

```
            TST.W     D3          ;is calculated value 0?
            BNE.S     @1          ;no -- go and use it
            SUBQ.W    #1,D3       ;it is 0; make it -1
@1          CMP.W     toRHA+lapHdSz+ddpChecksum(A2),D3
            BNE       ChksumError
```

SUMMARY OF THE APPLETALK MANAGER

Constants

```
CONST lapSize = 20;     {ABusRecord size for ALAP}
      ddpSize = 26;     {ABusRecord size for DDP}
      nbpSize = 26;     {ABusRecord size for NBP}
      atpSize = 56;     {ABusRecord size for ATP}
```

Data Types

```
TYPE ABProtoType = (lapProto,ddpProto,nbpProto,atpProto);

     ABRecHandle = ^ABRecPtr;
     ABRecPtr    = ^ABusRecord;
     ABusRecord  =
       RECORD
          abOpcode:        ABCallType;   {type of call}
          abResult:        INTEGER;      {result code}
          abUserReference: LONGINT;      {for your use}
          CASE ABProtoType OF
           lapProto:
            (lapAddress:   LAPAdrBlock;  {destination or source node ID}
             lapReqCount:  INTEGER;      {length of frame data or buffer }
                                         { size in bytes}
             lapActCount   INTEGER;      {number of frame data bytes }
                                         { actually received}
             lapDataPtr:   Ptr);         {pointer to frame data or pointer }
                                         { to buffer}
           ddpProto:
            (ddpType:      Byte;         {DDP protocol type}
             ddpSocket:    Byte;         {source or listening socket number}
             ddpAddress:   AddrBlock;    {destination or source socket address}
             ddpReqCount:  INTEGER;      {length of datagram data or buffer }
                                         { size in bytes}
             ddpActCount:  INTEGER;      {number of bytes actually received}
             ddpDataPtr:   Ptr;          {pointer to buffer}
             ddpNodeID:    Byte);        {original destination node ID}
           nbpProto:
            (nbpEntityPtr:        EntityPtr;   {pointer to entity name}
             nbpBufPtr:           Ptr;         {pointer to buffer}
             nbpBufSize:          INTEGER;     {buffer size in bytes}
             nbpDataField:        INTEGER;     {number of addresses or }
                                               { socket number}
             nbpAddress:          AddrBlock;   {socket address}
             nbpRetransmitInfo: RetransType);  {retransmission information}
```

```
            atpProto:
                (atpSocket:     Byte;        {listening or responding socket }
                                             { number}
                 atpAddress:    AddrBlock;   {destination or source socket }
                                             { address}
                 atpReqCount:   INTEGER;     {request size or buffer size}
                 atpDataPtr     Ptr;         {pointer to buffer}
                 atpRspBDSPtr:  BDSPtr;      {pointer to response BDS}
                 atpBitMap:     BitMapType;  {transaction bit map}
                 atpTransID:    INTEGER;     {transaction ID}
                 atpActCount:   INTEGER;     {number of bytes actually received}
                 atpUserData:   LONGINT;     {user bytes}
                 atpXO:         BOOLEAN;     {exactly-once flag}
                 atpEOM:        BOOLEAN;     {end-of-message flag}
                 atpTimeOut:    Byte;        {retry timeout interval in seconds}
                 atpRetries:    Byte;        {maximum number of retries}
                 atpNumBufs:    Byte;        {number of elements in response }
                                             { BDS or number of response }
                                             { packets sent}

                 atpNumRsp:     Byte;        {number of response packets }
                                             { received or sequence number}

                 atpBDSSize:    Byte;        {number of elements in response BDS}
                 atpRspUData:   LONGINT;     {user bytes sent or received in }
                                             { transaction response}

                 atpRspBuf:     Ptr;         {pointer to response message buffer}
                 atpRspSize:    INTEGER);    {size of response message buffer}
            END;

    ABCallType = (tLAPRead,tLAPWrite,tDDPRead,tDDPWrite,tNBPLookup,
                  tNBPConfirm,tNBPRegister,tATPSndRequest,
                  tATPGetRequest,tATPSdRsp,tATPAddRsp,tATPRequest,
                  tATPResponse);

    LAPAdrBlock = PACKED RECORD
                     dstNodeID:   Byte;     {destination node ID}
                     srcNodeID:   Byte;     {source node ID}
                     lapProtType: ABByte    {ALAP protocol type}
                  END;

    ABByte = 1..127; {ALAP protocol type}

    AddrBlock = PACKED RECORD
                     aNet:    INTEGER; {network number}
                     aNode:   Byte;    {node ID}
                     aSocket: Byte     {socket number}
                  END;

    BDSPtr    = ^BDSType;
    BDSType   = ARRAY[0..7] OF BDSElement; {response BDS}
```

```
BDSElement = RECORD
                buffSize:  INTEGER;  {buffer size in bytes}
                buffPtr:   Ptr;      {pointer to buffer}
                dataSize:  INTEGER;  {number of bytes actually received}
                userBytes: LONGINT   {user bytes}
             END;

BitMapType = PACKED ARRAY[0..7] OF BOOLEAN;

EntityPtr  = ^EntityName;
EntityName = RECORD
                objStr:   Str32;  {object}
                typeStr:  Str32;  {type}
                zoneStr:  Str32   {zone}
             END;

Str32 = STRING[32];

RetransType =
     PACKED RECORD
        retransInterval: Byte;  {retransmit interval in 8-tick units}
        retransCount:    Byte   {total number of attempts}
     END;
```

Routines [Not in ROM]

Opening and Closing AppleTalk

```
FUNCTION MPPOpen  :  OSErr;
FUNCTION MPPClose :  OSErr;
```

AppleTalk Link Access Protocol

```
FUNCTION LAPOpenProtocol  (theLAPType: ABByte; protoPtr: Ptr) : OSErr;
FUNCTION LAPCloseProtocol (theLAPType: ABByte) : OSErr;

FUNCTION LAPWrite (abRecord: ABRecHandle; async: BOOLEAN) : OSErr;
```

←	abOpcode	{always tLAPWrite}
←	abResult	{result code}
→	abUserReference	{for your use}
→	lapAddress.dstNodeID	{destination node ID}
→	lapAddress.lapProtType	{ALAP protocol type}
→	lapReqCount	{length of frame data}
→	lapDataPtr	{pointer to frame data}

```
FUNCTION LAPRead (abRecord: ABRecHandle; async: BOOLEAN) : OSErr;
```
←	abOpcode	{always tLAPRead}
←	abResult	{result code}
→	abUserReference	{for your use}
←	lapAddress.dstNodeID	{destination node ID}
←	lapAddress.srcNodeID	{source node ID}
→	lapAddress.lapProtType	{ALAP protocol type}
→	lapReqCount	{buffer size in bytes}
←	lapActCount	{number of frame data bytes actually received}
→	lapDataPtr	{pointer to buffer}

```
FUNCTION LAPRdCancel (abRecord: ABRecHandle) : OSErr;
```

Datagram Delivery Protocol

```
FUNCTION DDPOpenSocket  (VAR theSocket: Byte; sktListener: Ptr) : OSErr;
FUNCTION DDPCloseSocket (theSocket: Byte) : OSErr;
```

```
FUNCTION DDPWrite (abRecord: ABRecHandle; doChecksum: BOOLEAN; async:
                BOOLEAN) : OSErr;
```
←	abOpcode	{always tDDPWrite}
←	abResult	{result code}
→	abUserReference	{for your use}
→	ddpType	{DDP protocol type}
→	ddpSocket	{source socket number}
→	ddpAddress	{destination socket address}
→	ddpReqCount	{length of datagram data}
→	ddpDataPtr	{pointer to buffer}

```
FUNCTION DDPRead (abRecord: ABRecHandle; retCksumErrs: BOOLEAN; async:
                BOOLEAN) : OSErr;
```
←	abOpcode	{always tDDPRead}
←	abResult	{result code}
→	abUserReference	{for your use}
←	ddpType	{DDP protocol type}
→	ddpSocket	{listening socket number}
←	ddpAddress	{source socket address}
→	ddpReqCount	{buffer size in bytes}
←	ddpActCount	{number of bytes actually received}
→	ddpDataPtr	{pointer to buffer}
←	ddpNodeID	{original destination node ID}

```
FUNCTION DDPRdCancel (abRecord: ABRecHandle) : OSErr;
```

AppleTalk Transaction Protocol

```
FUNCTION ATPLoad :        OSErr;
FUNCTION ATPUnload :      OSErr;
FUNCTION ATPOpenSocket (addrRcvd: AddrBlock; VAR atpSocket: Byte) : OSErr;
FUNCTION ATPCloseSocket (atpSocket: Byte) : OSErr;
```

```
FUNCTION ATPSndRequest (abRecord: ABRecHandle; async: BOOLEAN) : OSErr;
```

←	abOpcode	{always tATPSndRequest}
←	abResult	{result code}
→	abUserReference	{for your use}
→	atpAddress	{destination socket address}
→	atpReqCount	{request size in bytes}
→	atpDataPtr	{pointer to buffer}
→	atpRspBDSPtr	{pointer to response BDS}
→	atpUserData	{user bytes}
→	atpXO	{exactly-once flag}
←	atpEOM	{end-of-message flag}
→	atpTimeOut	{retry timeout interval in seconds}
→	atpRetries	{maximum number of retries}
→	atpNumBufs	{number of elements in response BDS}
←	atpNumRsp	{number of response packets actually received}

```
FUNCTION ATPRequest (abRecord: ABRecHandle; async: BOOLEAN) : OSErr;
```

←	abOpcode	{always tATPRequest}
←	abResult	{result code}
→	abUserReference	{for your use}
→	atpAddress	{destination socket address}
→	atpReqCount	{request size in bytes}
→	atpDataPtr	{pointer to buffer}
←	atpActCount	{number of bytes actually received}
→	atpUserData	{user bytes}
→	atpXO	{exactly-once flag}
←	atpEOM	{end-of-message flag}
→	atpTimeOut	{retry timeout interval in seconds}
→	atpRetries	{maximum number of retries}
←	atpRspUData	{user bytes received in transaction response}
→	atpRspBuf	{pointer to response message buffer}
→	atpRspSize	{size of response message buffer}

```
FUNCTION ATPReqCancel (abRecord: ABRecHandle; async: BOOLEAN) : OSErr;
```

```
FUNCTION ATPGetRequest (abRecord: ABRecHandle; async: BOOLEAN) : OSErr;
```

←	abOpcode	{always tATPGetRequest}
←	abResult	{result code}
→	abUserReference	{for your use}
→	atpSocket	{listening socket number}
←	atpAddress	{source socket address}
→	atpReqCount	{buffer size in bytes}
→	atpDataPtr	{pointer to buffer}
←	atpBitMap	{transaction bit map}
←	atpTransID	{transaction ID}
←	atpActCount	{number of bytes actually received}
←	atpUserData	{user bytes}
←	atpXO	{exactly-once flag}

```
FUNCTION ATPSndRsp (abRecord: ABRecHandle; async: BOOLEAN) : OSErr;
```

←	abOpcode	{always tATPSdRsp}
←	abResult	{result code}
→	abUserReference	{for your use}
→	atpSocket	{responding socket number}
→	atpAddress	{destination socket address}
→	atpRspBDSPtr	{pointer to response BDS}
→	atpTransID	{transaction ID}
→	atpEOM	{end-of-message flag}
→	atpNumBufs	{number of response packets being sent}
→	atpBDSSize	{number of elements in response BDS}

```
FUNCTION ATPAddRsp (abRecord: ABRecHandle) : OSErr;
```

←	abOpcode	{always tATPAddRsp}
←	abResult	{result code}
→	abUserReference	{for your use}
→	atpSocket	{responding socket number}
→	atpAddress	{destination socket address}
→	atpReqCount	{buffer size in bytes}
→	atpDataPtr	{pointer to buffer}
→	atpTransID	{transaction ID}
→	atpUserData	{user bytes}
→	atpEOM	{end-of-message flag}
→	atpNumRsp	{sequence number}

```
FUNCTION ATPResponse (abRecord: ABRecHandle; async: BOOLEAN) : OSErr;
```

←	abOpcode	{always tATPResponse}
←	abResult	{result code}
→	abUserReference	{for your use}
→	atpSocket	{responding socket number}
→	atpAddress	{destination socket address}
→	atpTransID	{transaction ID)
→	atpRspUData	{user bytes sent in transaction response}
→	atpRspBuf	{pointer to response message buffer}
→	atpRspSize	{size of response message buffer}

```
FUNCTION ATPRspCancel (abRecord: ABRecHandle; async: BOOLEAN) : OSErr;
```

Name-Binding Protocol

```
FUNCTION NBPRegister (abRecord: ABRecHandle; async: BOOLEAN) : OSErr;
```

←	abOpcode	{always tNBPRegister}
←	abResult	{result code}
→	abUserReference	{for your use}
→	nbpEntityPtr	{pointer to entity name}
→	nbpBufPtr	{pointer to buffer}
→	nbpBufSize	{buffer size in bytes}
→	nbpAddress.aSocket	{socket address}
→	nbpRetransmitInfo	{retransmission information}

```
FUNCTION NBPLookup (abRecord: ABRecHandle; async: BOOLEAN) : OSErr;
```
←	abOpcode	{always tNBPLookup}
←	abResult	{result code}
→	abUserReference	{for your use}
→	nbpEntityPtr	{pointer to entity name}
→	nbpBufPtr	{pointer to buffer}
→	nbpBufSize	{buffer size in bytes}
↔	nbpDataField	{number of addresses received}
→	nbpRetransmitInfo	{retransmission information}

```
FUNCTION NBPExtract (theBuffer: Ptr; numInBuf: INTEGER; whichOne:
                     INTEGER; VAR abEntity: EntityName; VAR address:
                     AddrBlock) : OSErr;
```

```
FUNCTION NBPConfirm (abRecord: ABRecHandle; async: BOOLEAN) : OSErr;
```
←	abOpcode	{always tNBPConfirm}
←	abResult	{result code}
→	abUserReference	{for your use}
→	nbpEntityPtr	{pointer to entity name}
←	nbpDataField	{socket number}
→	nbpAddress	{socket address}
→	nbpRetransmitInfo	{retransmission information}

```
FUNCTION NBPRemove  (abEntity: EntityPtr) : OSErr;
FUNCTION NBPLoad :   OSErr;
FUNCTION NBPUnload : OSErr;
```

Miscellaneous Routines

```
FUNCTION GetNodeAddress (VAR myNode,myNet: INTEGER) : OSErr;
FUNCTION IsMPPOpen :        BOOLEAN;
FUNCTION IsATPOpen :        BOOLEAN;
```

Result Codes

Name	Value	Meaning
atpBadRsp	−3107	Bad response from ATPRequest
atpLenErr	−3106	ATP response message too large
badATPSkt	−1099	ATP bad responding socket
badBuffNum	−1100	ATP bad sequence number
buf2SmallErr	−3101	ALAP frame too large for buffer DDP datagram too large for buffer
cbNotFound	−1102	ATP control block not found
cksumErr	−3103	DDP bad checksum
ddpLenErr	−92	DDP datagram or ALAP data length too big

Name	Value	Meaning
ddpSktErr	−91	DDP socket error: socket already active; not a well-known socket; socket table full; all dynamic socket numbers in use
excessCollsns	−95	ALAP no CTS received after 32 RTS's, or line sensed in use 32 times (not necessarily caused by collisions)
extractErr	−3104	NBP can't find tuple in buffer
lapProtErr	−94	ALAP error attaching/detaching ALAP protocol type: attach error when ALAP protocol type is negative, not in range, already in table, or when table is full; detach error when ALAP protocol type isn't in table
nbpBuffOvr	−1024	NBP buffer overflow
nbpConfDiff	−1026	NBP name confirmed for different socket
nbpDuplicate	−1027	NBP duplicate name already exists
nbpNISErr	−1029	NBP names information socket error
nbpNoConfirm	−1025	NBP name not confirmed
nbpNotFound	−1028	NBP name not found
noBridgeErr	−93	No bridge found
noDataArea	−1104	Too many outstanding ATP calls
noErr	0	No error
noMPPError	−3102	MPP driver not installed
noRelErr	−1101	ATP no release received
noSendResp	−1103	ATPAddRsp issued before ATPSndRsp
portInUse	−97	Driver Open error, port already in use
portNotCf	−98	Driver Open error, port not configured for this connection
readQErr	−3105	Socket or protocol type invalid or not found in table
recNotFnd	−3108	ABRecord not found
reqAborted	−1105	Request aborted
reqFailed	−1096	ATPSndRequest failed: retry count exceeded
sktClosedErr	−3109	Asynchronous call aborted because socket was closed before call was completed
tooManyReqs	−1097	ATP too many concurrent requests
tooManySkts	−1098	ATP too many responding sockets

Assembly-Language Information

Constants

```
; Serial port use types

useFree         .EQU    0       ;unconfigured
useATalk        .EQU    1       ;configured for AppleTalk
useASync        .EQU    2       ;configured for the Serial Driver

; Bit in PortBUse for .ATP driver status

atpLoadedBit    .EQU    4       ;set if .ATP driver is opened

; Unit numbers for AppleTalk drivers

mppUnitNum      .EQU    9       ;.MPP driver
atpUnitNum      .EQU    10      ;.ATP driver

; csCode values for Control calls (MPP)

writeLAP        .EQU    243
detachPH        .EQU    244
attachPH        .EQU    245
writeDDP        .EQU    246
closeSkt        .EQU    247
openSkt         .EQU    248
loadNBP         .EQU    249
confirmName     .EQU    250
lookupName      .EQU    251
removeName      .EQU    252
registerName    .EQU    253
killNBP         .EQU    254
unloadNBP       .EQU    255

; csCode values for Control calls (ATP)

relRspCB        .EQU    249
closeATPSkt     .EQU    250
addResponse     .EQU    251
sendResponse    .EQU    252
getRequest      .EQU    253
openATPSkt      .EQU    254
sendRequest     .EQU    255
relTCB          .EQU    256

; ALAP header

lapDstAdr       .EQU    0       ;destination node ID
lapSrcAdr       .EQU    1       ;source node ID
lapType         .EQU    2       ;ALAP protocol type
```

```
; ALAP header size

lapHdSz         .EQU    3

; ALAP protocol type values

shortDDP        .EQU    1       ;short DDP header
longDDP         .EQU    2       ;long DDP header

; Long DDP header

ddpHopCnt       .EQU    0       ;count of bridges passed (4 bits)
ddpLength       .EQU    0       ;datagram length (10 bits)
ddpChecksum     .EQU    2       ;checksum
ddpDstNet       .EQU    4       ;destination network number
ddpSrcNet       .EQU    6       ;source network number
ddpDstNode      .EQU    8       ;destination node ID
ddpSrcNode      .EQU    9       ;source node ID
ddpDstSkt       .EQU    10      ;destination socket number
ddpSrcSkt       .EQU    11      ;source socket number
ddpType         .EQU    12      ;DDP protocol type

; DDP long header size

ddpHSzLong      .EQU    ddpType+1

; Short DDP header

ddpLength       .EQU    0                   ;datagram length
sDDPDstSkt      .EQU    ddpChecksum         ;destination socket number
sDDPSrcSkt      .EQU    sDDPDstSkt+1        ;source socket number
sDDPType        .EQU    sDDPSrcSkt+1        ;DDP protocol type

; DDP short header size

ddpHSzShort     .EQU    sDDPType+1

; Mask for datagram length

ddpLenMask      .EQU    $03FF

; Maximum size of DDP data

ddpMaxData      .EQU    586

; ATP header

atpControl      .EQU    0       ;control information
atpBitMap       .EQU    1       ;bit map
atpRespNo       .EQU    1       ;sequence number
atpTransID      .EQU    2       ;transaction ID
atpUserData     .EQU    4       ;user bytes
```

```
; ATP header size

atpHdSz          .EQU     8

; DDP protocol type for ATP packets

atp              .EQU     3

; ATP function code

atpReqCode       .EQU     $40      ;TReq packet
atpRspCode       .EQU     $80      ;TResp packet
atpRelCode       .EQU     $C0      ;TRel packet

; ATPFlags control information bits

sendChk          .EQU     0        ;send-checksum bit
tidValid         .EQU     1        ;transaction ID validity bit
atpSTSBit        .EQU     3        ;send-transmission-status bit
atpEOMBit        .EQU     4        ;end-of-message bit
atpXOBit         .EQU     5        ;exactly-once bit

; Maximum number of ATP request packets

atpMaxNum        .EQU     8

; ATP buffer data structure

bdsBuffSz        .EQU     0        ;size of data to send or buffer size
bdsBuffAddr      .EQU     2        ;pointer to data or buffer
bdsDataSz        .EQU     6        ;number of bytes actually received
bdsUserData      .EQU     8        ;user bytes

; BDS element size

bdsEntrySz       .EQU     12

; NBP packet

nbpControl       .EQU     0        ;packet type
nbpTCount        .EQU     0        ;tuple count
nbpID            .EQU     1        ;packet identifier
nbpTuple         .EQU     2        ;start of first tuple

; DDP protocol type for NBP packets

nbp              .EQU     2
```

```
; NBP packet types

brRq            .EQU    1       ;broadcast request
lkUp            .EQU    2       ;lookup request
lkUpReply       .EQU    3       ;lookup reply

; NBP tuple

tupleNet        .EQU    0       ;network number
tupleNode       .EQU    2       ;node ID
tupleSkt        .EQU    3       ;socket number
tupleEnum       .EQU    4       ;used internally
tupleName       .EQU    5       ;entity name

; Maximum number of tuples in NBP packet

tupleMax        .EQU    15

; NBP meta-characters

equals          .EQU    '='     ;"wild-card" meta-character
star            .EQU    '*'     ;"this zone" meta-character

; NBP names table entry

ntLink          .EQU    0       ;pointer to next entry
ntTuple         .EQU    4       ;tuple
ntSocket        .EQU    7       ;socket number
ntEntity        .EQU    9       ;entity name

; NBP names information socket number

nis             .EQU    2
```

Routines

Link Access Protocol

WriteLAP function

→	26	csCode	word	;always writeLAP
→	30	wdsPointer	pointer	;write data structure

AttachPH function

→	26	csCode	word	;always attachPH
→	28	protType	byte	;ALAP protocol type
→	30	handler	pointer	;protocol handler

DetachPH function

→	26	csCode	word	;always detachPH
→	28	protType	byte	;ALAP protocol type

Datagram Delivery Protocol

OpenSkt function

→	26	csCode	word	;always openSkt
↔	28	socket	byte	;socket number
→	30	listener	pointer	;socket listener

CloseSkt function

→	26	csCode	word	;always closeSkt
→	28	socket	byte	;socket number

WriteDDP function

→	26	csCode	word	;always writeDDP
→	28	socket	byte	;socket number
→	29	checksumFlag	byte	;checksum flag
→	30	wdsPointer	pointer	;write data structure

AppleTalk Transaction Protocol

OpenATPSkt function

→	26	csCode	word	;always openATPSkt
↔	28	atpSocket	byte	;socket number
→	30	addrBlock	long word	;socket request specification

CloseATPSkt function

→	26	csCode	word	;always closeATPSkt
→	28	atpSocket	byte	;socket number

SendRequest function

→	18	userData	long word	;user bytes
←	22	reqTID	word	;transaction ID used in request
→	26	csCode	word	;always sendRequest
←	28	currBitMap	byte	;bit map
↔	29	atpFlags	byte	;control information
→	30	addrBlock	long word	;destination socket address
→	34	reqLength	word	;request size in bytes
→	36	reqPointer	pointer	;pointer to request data
→	40	bdsPointer	pointer	;pointer to response BDS
→	44	numOfBuffs	byte	;number of responses expected
→	45	timeOutVal	byte	;timeout interval
←	46	numOfResps	byte	;number of responses received
↔	47	retryCount	byte	;number of retries

GetRequest function

←	18	userData	long word	;user bytes
→	26	csCode	word	;always getRequest
→	28	atpSocket	byte	;socket number
←	29	atpFlags	byte	;control information
←	30	addrBlock	long word	;source of request
↔	34	reqLength	word	;request buffer size
→	36	reqPointer	pointer	;pointer to request buffer
←	44	bitMap	byte	;bit map
←	46	transID	word	;transaction ID

SendResponse function

←	18	userData	long word	;user bytes from TRel
→	26	csCode	word	;always sendResponse
→	28	atpSocket	byte	;socket number
→	29	atpFlags	byte	;control information
→	30	addrBlock	long word	;response destination
→	40	bdsPointer	pointer	;pointer to response BDS
→	44	numOfBuffs	byte	;number of response packets being sent
→	45	bdsSize	byte	;BDS size in elements
→	46	transID	word	;transaction ID

AddResponse function

→	18	userData	long word	;user bytes
→	26	csCode	word	;always addResponse
→	28	atpSocket	byte	;socket number
→	29	atpFlags	byte	;control information
→	30	addrBlock	long word	;response destination
→	34	reqLength	word	;response size
→	36	reqPointer	pointer	;pointer to response
→	44	rspNum	byte	;sequence number
→	46	transID	word	;transaction ID

RelTCB function

→	26	csCode	word	;always relTCB
→	30	addrBlock	long word	;destination of request
→	46	transID	word	;transaction ID of request

RelRspCB function

→	26	csCode	word	;always relRspCB
→	28	atpSocket	byte	;socket number that request was received on
→	30	addrBlock	long word	;source of request
→	46	transID	word	;transaction ID of request

Name-Binding Protocol

RegisterName function

→	26	csCode	word	;always registerName
→	28	interval	byte	;retry interval
↔	29	count	byte	;retry count
→	30	ntQElPtr	pointer	;names table element pointer
→	34	verifyFlag	byte	;set if verify needed

LookupName function

→	26	csCode	word	;always lookupName
→	28	interval	byte	;retry interval
↔	29	count	byte	;retry count
→	30	entityPtr	pointer	;pointer to entity name
→	34	retBuffPtr	pointer	;pointer to buffer
→	38	retBuffSize	word	;buffer size in bytes
→	40	maxToGet	word	;matches to get
←	42	numGotten	word	;matches found

ConfirmName function

→	26	csCode	word	;always confirmName
→	28	interval	byte	;retry interval
↔	29	count	byte	;retry count
→	30	entityPtr	pointer	;pointer to entity name
→	34	confirmAddr	pointer	;entity address
←	38	newSocket	byte	;socket number

RemoveName function

→	26	csCode	word	;always removeName
→	30	entityPtr	pointer	;pointer to entity name

LoadNBP function

→	26	csCode	word	;always loadNBP

UnloadNBP function

→	26	csCode	word	;always unloadNBP

Variables

SPConfig	Use types for serial ports (byte) (bits 0-3: current configuration of serial port B bits 4-6: current configuration of serial port A)
PortBUse	Current availability of serial port B (byte) (bit 7: 1 = not in use, 0 = in use bits 0-3: current use of port bits bits 4-6: driver-specific)
ABusVars	Pointer to AppleTalk variables

11 THE VERTICAL RETRACE MANAGER

ABOUT THIS CHAPTER

This chapter describes the Vertical Retrace Manager, the part of the Operating System that schedules and performs recurrent tasks during vertical retrace interrupts. It describes how your application can install and remove its own recurrent tasks.

You should already be familiar with:

- events, as discussed in chapter 8 of Volume I
- interrupts, as described in chapter 6

ABOUT THE VERTICAL RETRACE MANAGER

The Macintosh video circuitry generates a **vertical retrace interrupt**, also known as the **vertical blanking** (or VBL) **interrupt**, 60 times a second while the beam of the display tube returns from the bottom of the screen to the top to display the next frame. This interrupt is used as a convenient time for performing the following sequence of recurrent system tasks:

1. Increment the number of ticks since system startup (every interrupt). You can get this number by calling the Toolbox Event Manager function TickCount.

2. Check whether the stack has expanded into the heap; if so, it calls the System Error Handler (every interrupt).

3. Handle cursor movement (every interrupt).

4. Post a mouse event if the state of the mouse button changed from its previous state and then remained unchanged for four interrupts (every other interrupt).

5. Reset the keyboard if it's been reattached after having been detached (every 32 interrupts).

6. Post a disk-inserted event if the user has inserted a disk or taken any other action that requires a volume to be mounted (every 30 interrupts).

These tasks must execute at regular intervals based on the "heartbeat" of the Macintosh, and shouldn't be changed.

Tasks performed during the vertical retrace interrupt are known as **VBL tasks**. An application can add any number of its own VBL tasks for the Vertical Retrace Manager to execute. VBL tasks can be set to execute at any frequency (up to once per vertical retrace interrupt). For example, an electronic mail application might add a VBL task that checks every tenth of a second (every six interrupts) to see if it has received any messages. These tasks can perform any desired action as long as they don't make any calls to the Memory Manager, directly or indirectly, and don't depend on handles to unlocked blocks being valid. They must preserve all registers other than A0-A3 and D0-D3. If they use application globals, they must also ensure that register A5 contains the address of the boundary between the application globals and the application parameters; for details, see SetUpA5 and RestoreA5 in chapter 13.

Warning: When interrupts are disabled (such as during a disk access), or when VBL tasks take longer than about a sixtieth of a second to perform, one or more vertical retrace interrupts may be missed, thereby affecting the performance of certain VBL tasks. For instance, while a disk is being accessed, the updating of the cursor movement may be irregular.

Note: To perform periodic actions that do allocate and release memory, you can use the Desk Manager procedure SystemTask. Or, since the first thing the Vertical Retrace Manager does during a vertical retrace interrupt is increment the tick count, you can call TickCount repeatedly and perform periodic actions whenever a specific number of ticks have elapsed.

Information describing each VBL task is contained in the **vertical retrace queue**. The vertical retrace queue is a standard Macintosh Operating System queue, as described in chapter 13. Each entry in the vertical retrace queue has the following structure:

```
TYPE VBLTask =  RECORD
                  qLink:    QElemPtr;  {next queue entry}
                  qType:    INTEGER;   {queue type}
                  vblAddr:  ProcPtr;   {pointer to task}
                  vblCount: INTEGER;   {task frequency}
                  vblPhase: INTEGER    {task phase}
                END;
```

QLink points to the next entry in the queue, and qType indicates the queue type, which must be ORD(vType).

VBLAddr contains a pointer to the task. VBLCount specifies the number of ticks between successive calls to the task. This value is decremented each sixtieth of a second until it reaches 0, at which point the task is called. The task must then reset vblCount, or its entry will be removed from the queue after it has been executed. VBLPhase contains an integer (smaller than vblCount) used to modify vblCount when the task is first added to the queue. This ensures that two or more tasks added to the queue at the same time with the same vblCount value will be out of phase with each other, and won't be called during the same interrupt. Unless there are many tasks to be added to the queue at the same time, vblPhase can usually be set to 0.

The Vertical Retrace Manager uses bit 6 of the queue flags field in the queue header to indicate when a task is being executed:

Bit	Meaning
6	Set if a task is being executed

Assembly-language note: Assembly-programmers can use the global constant inVBL to test this bit.

USING THE VERTICAL RETRACE MANAGER

The Vertical Retrace Manager is automatically initialized each time the system starts up. To add a VBL task to the vertical retrace queue, call VInstall. When your application no longer wants a task to be executed, it can remove the task from the vertical retrace queue by calling VRemove. A VBL task shouldn't call VRemove to remove its entry from the queue—either the application should call VRemove, or the task should simply not reset the vblCount field of the queue entry.

Assembly-language note: VBL tasks may use registers A0-A3 and D0-D3, and must save and restore any additional registers used. They must exit with an RTS instruction.

If you'd like to manipulate the contents of the vertical retrace queue directly, you can get a pointer to the header of the vertical retrace queue by calling GetVBLQHdr.

VERTICAL RETRACE MANAGER ROUTINES

FUNCTION VInstall (vblTaskPtr: QElemPtr) : OSErr;

Trap macro	_VInstall
On entry	A0: vblTaskPtr (pointer)
On exit	D0: result code (word)

VInstall adds the VBL task specified by vblTaskPtr to the vertical retrace queue. Your application must fill in all fields of the task except qLink. VInstall returns one of the result codes listed below.

Result codes	noErr	No error
	vTypErr	QType field isn't ORD(vType)

FUNCTION VRemove (vblTaskPtr: QElemPtr) : OSErr;

Trap macro	_VRemove
On entry	A0: vblTaskPtr (pointer)
On exit	D0: result code (word)

VRemove removes the VBL task specified by vblTaskPtr from the vertical retrace queue. It returns one of the result codes listed below.

Result codes   noErr   No error
                          vTypErr   QType field isn't ORD(vType)
                          qErr   Task entry isn't in the queue

```
FUNCTION GetVBLQHdr : QHdrPtr;    [Not in ROM]
```

GetVBLQHdr returns a pointer to the header of the vertical retrace queue.

Assembly-language note: The global variable VBLQueue contains the header of the vertical retrace queue.

SUMMARY OF THE VERTICAL RETRACE MANAGER

Constants

```
CONST  { Result codes }

      noErr   =  0;    {no error}
      qErr    = -1;    {task entry isn't in the queue}
      vTypErr = -2;    {qType field isn't ORD(vType)}
```

Data Types

```
TYPE VBLTask = RECORD
                qLink:    QElemPtr;   {next queue entry}
                qType:    INTEGER;    {queue type}
                vblAddr:  ProcPtr;    {pointer to task}
                vblCount: INTEGER;    {task frequency}
                vblPhase: INTEGER     {task phase}
              END;
```

Routines

```
FUNCTION VInstall    (vblTaskPtr: QElemPtr) : OSErr;
FUNCTION VRemove     (vblTaskPtr: QElemPtr) : OSErr;
FUNCTION GetVBLQHdr : QHdrPtr;   [Not in ROM]
```

Assembly-Language Information

Constants

```
inVBL    .EQU   6    ;set if Vertical Retrace Manager is executing a task

; Result codes

noErr    .EQU    0   ;no error
qErr     .EQU   -1   ;task entry isn't in the queue
vTypErr  .EQU   -2   ;qType field isn't vType
```

Structure of Vertical Retrace Queue Entry

qLink	Pointer to next queue entry
qType	Queue type (word)
vblAddr	Address of task
vblCount	Task frequency (word)
vblPhase	Task phase (word)

Routines

Trap macro	On entry	On exit
_VInstall	A0: vblTaskPtr (ptr)	D0: result code (word)
_VRemove	A0: vblTaskPtr (ptr)	D0: result code (word)

Variables

VBLQueue   Vertical retrace queue header (10 bytes)

12 THE SYSTEM ERROR HANDLER

12 System Error

ABOUT THIS CHAPTER

The System Error Handler is the part of the Operating System that assumes control when a fatal system error occurs. This chapter introduces you to the System Error Handler and describes how your application can recover from system errors.

You'll already need to be somewhat familiar with most of the User Interface Toolbox and the rest of the Operating System.

ABOUT THE SYSTEM ERROR HANDLER

The System Error Handler assumes control when a fatal system error occurs. Its main function is to display an alert box with an error message (called a **system error alert**) and provide a mechanism for the application to resume execution.

> **Note:** The system error alerts simply identify the type of problem encountered and, in some cases, the part of the Toolbox or Operating System involved. They don't, however, tell you where in your application code the failure occurred.

Because a system error usually indicates that a very low-level part of the system has failed, the System Error Handler performs its duties by using as little of the system as possible. It requires only the following:

- The trap dispatcher is operative.

- The Font Manager procedure InitFonts has been called (it's called when the system starts up).

- Register A7 points to a reasonable place in memory (for example, not to the main screen buffer).

- A few important system data structures aren't too badly damaged.

The System Error Handler doesn't require the Memory Manager to be operative.

The content of the alert box displayed is determined by a **system error alert table,** a resource stored in the system resource file. There are two different system error alert tables: a system startup alert table used when the system starts up, and a user alert table for informing the user of system errors.

The system startup alerts are used to display messages at system startup such as the "Welcome to Macintosh" message (Figure 1). They're displayed by the System Error Handler instead of the Dialog Manager because the System Error Handler needs very little of the system to operate.

The user alerts (Figure 2) notify the user of system errors. The bottom right corner of a user alert contains a **system error ID** that identifies the error. Usually the message "Sorry, a system error occurred", a Restart button, and a Resume button are also shown. If the Finder can't be found on a disk, the message "Can't load the finder" and a Restart button will be shown. The Macintosh will attempt to restart if the user clicks the Restart button, and the application will attempt to resume execution if the user clicks the Resume button.

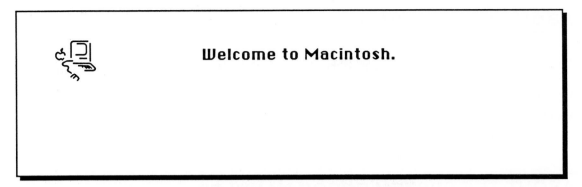

Figure 1. System Startup Alert

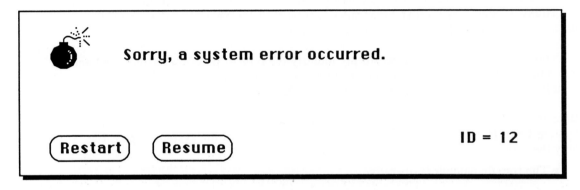

Figure 2. User Alert

The "Please insert the disk:" message displayed by the File Manager is also a user alert; however, unlike the other alerts, it's displayed in a dialog box.

The summary at the end of this chapter lists the system error IDs for the various user alerts, as well as the system startup alert messages.

RECOVERING FROM SYSTEM ERRORS

An application recovers from a system error by means of a **resume procedure**. You pass a pointer to your resume procedure when you call the Dialog Manager procedure InitDialogs. When the user clicks the Resume button in a system error alert, the System Error Handler attempts to restore the state of the system and then calls your resume procedure.

Assembly-language note: The System Error Handler actually restores the value of register A5 to what it was before the system error occurred, sets the stack pointer to the address stored in the global variable CurStackBase (throwing away the stack), and then jumps to your resume procedure.

If you don't have a resume procedure, you'll pass NIL to InitDialogs (and the Resume button in the system error alert will be dimmed).

SYSTEM ERROR ALERT TABLES

This section describes the data structures that define the alert boxes displayed by the System Error Handler; this information is provided mainly to allow you to edit and translate the messages displayed in the alerts. Rearranging the alert tables or creating new ones is discouraged because the Operating System depends on having the alert information stored in a very specific and constant way.

In the system resource file, the system error alerts have the following resource types and IDs:

Table	Resource type	Resource ID
System startup alert table	'DSAT'	0
User alert table	'INIT'	2

Assembly-language note: The global variable DSAlertTab contains a pointer to the current system error alert table. DSAlertTab points to the system startup alert table when the system is starting up; then it's changed to point to the user alert table.

A system error alert table consists of a word indicating the number of entries in the table, followed by alert, text, icon, button, and procedure definitions, all of which are explained below. The first definition in a system error alert table is an alert definition that applies to *all* system errors that don't have their own alert definition. The rest of the definitions within the alert table needn't be in any particular order, nor do the definitions of one type need to be grouped together. The first two words in every definition are used for the same purpose: The first word contains an ID number identifying the definition, and the second specifies the length of the rest of the definition in bytes.

An alert definition specifies the IDs of the text, icon, button, and procedure definitions that together determine the appearance and operation of the alert box that will be drawn (Figure 3). The ID of an alert definition is the system error ID that the alert pertains to. The System Error Handler uses the system error ID to locate the alert definition. The alert definition specifies the IDs of the other definitions needed to create the alert; 0 is specified if the alert doesn't include any items of that type.

A text definition specifies the text that will be drawn in the system error alert (Figure 4). Each alert definition refers to two text definitions; the secondary text definition allows a second line of text to be added to the alert message. (No more than two lines of text may be displayed.) The pen location at which QuickDraw will begin drawing the text is given as a point in global coordinates. The actual characters that comprise the text are suffixed by one NUL character (ASCII code 0).

Warning: The slash character (/) can't be used in the text.

system error ID (word)
length of rest of definition (word)
primary text definition ID (word)
secondary text definition ID (word)
icon definition ID (word)
procedure definition ID (word)
button definition ID (word)

Figure 3. Alert Definition

text definition ID (word)
length of rest of definition (word)
location (point)
text (ASCII characters)
NUL character (byte)

Figure 4. Text Definition

An icon definition specifies the icon that will be drawn in the system error alert (Figure 5). The location of the icon is given as a rectangle in global coordinates. The 128 bytes that comprise the icon complete the definition.

icon definition ID (word)
length of rest of definition (word)
location (rectangle)
icon data (128 bytes)

Figure 5. Icon Definition

A procedure definition specifies a procedure that will be executed whenever the system error alert is drawn (Figure 6). Procedure definitions are also used to specify the action to be taken when a particular button is pressed, as described below. Most of a procedure definition is simply the code comprising the procedure.

procedure definition ID (word)
length of rest of definition (word)
procedure code

Figure 6. Procedure Definition

A button definition specifies the button(s) that will be drawn in the system error alert (Figure 7). It indicates the number of buttons that will be drawn, followed by that many six-word groups, each specifying the text, location, and operation of a button.

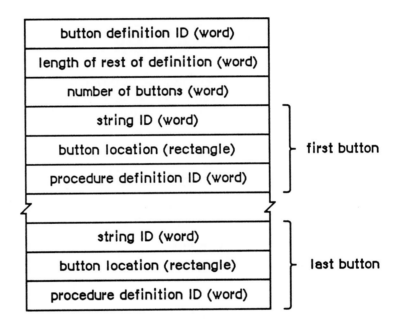

Figure 7. Button Definition

The first word of each six-word group contains a string ID (explained below) specifying the text that will be drawn inside the button. The button's location is given as a rectangle in global coordinates. The last word contains a procedure definition ID identifying the code to be executed when the button is clicked.

The text that will be drawn inside each button is specified by the data structure shown in Figure 8. The first word contains a string ID identifying the string and the second indicates the length of the string in bytes. The actual characters of the string follow.

Each alert has two button definitions; these definitions have sequential button definition IDs (such as 60 and 61). The button definition ID of the first definition is placed in the alert definition. This definition is used if no resume procedure has been specified (with a call to the Dialog Manager's InitDialogs procedure). If a resume procedure has been specified, the System Error Handler adds 1 to the button definition ID specified in the alert definition and so uses the second

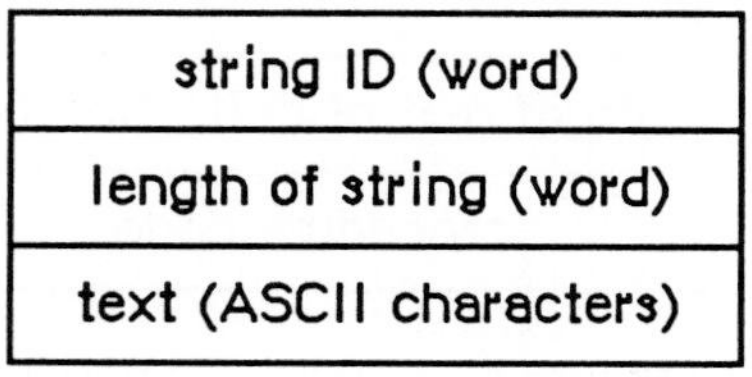

```
+------------------------------+
|      string ID (word)        |
+------------------------------+
|    length of string (word)   |
+------------------------------+
|     text (ASCII characters)  |
+------------------------------+
```

Figure 8. Strings Drawn in Buttons

button definition. In this definition, the procedure for the Resume button attempts to restore the state of the system and calls the resume procedure that was specified with InitDialogs.

SYSTEM ERROR HANDLER ROUTINE

The System Error Handler has only one routine, SysError, described below. Most application programs won't have any reason to call it. The system itself calls SysError whenever a system error occurs, and most applications need only be concerned with recovering from the error and resuming execution.

```
PROCEDURE SysError (errorCode: INTEGER);
```

Trap macro	_SysError
On entry	D0: errorCode (word)
On exit	All registers changed

SysError generates a system error with the ID specified by the errorCode parameter.

It takes the following precise steps:

1. It saves all registers and the stack pointer.

2. It stores the system error ID in a global variable (named DSErrCode).

3. It checks to see whether there's a system error alert table in memory (by testing whether the global variable DSAlertTab is 0); if there isn't, it draws the "sad Macintosh" icon.

4. It allocates memory for QuickDraw globals on the stack, initializes QuickDraw, and initializes a grafPort in which the alert box will be drawn.

5. It checks the system error ID. If the system error ID is negative, the alert box isn't redrawn (this is used for system startup alerts, which can display a sequence of consecutive messages in the same box). If the system error ID doesn't correspond to an entry in the system error alert table, the default alert definition at the start of the table will be used, displaying the message "Sorry, a system error occurred".

6. It draws an alert box (in the rectangle specified by the global variable DSAlertRect).

7. If the text definition IDs in the alert definition for this alert aren't 0, it draws both strings.

8. If the icon definition ID in the alert definition isn't 0, it draws the icon.

9. If the procedure definition ID in the alert definition isn't 0, it invokes the procedure with the specified ID.

10. If the button definition ID in the alert definition is 0, it returns control to the procedure that called it (this is used during the disk-switch alert to return control to the File Manager after the "Please insert the disk:" message has been displayed).

11. If there's a resume procedure, it increments the button definition ID by 1.

12. It draws the buttons.

13. It hit-tests the buttons and calls the corresponding procedure code when a button is pressed. If there's no procedure code, it returns to the procedure that called it.

SUMMARY OF THE SYSTEM ERROR HANDLER

Routines

```
PROCEDURE SysError (errorCode: INTEGER);
```

User Alerts

ID	Explanation
1	Bus error: Invalid memory reference; happens only on a Macintosh XL
2	Address error: Word or long-word reference made to an odd address
3	Illegal instruction: The MC68000 received an instruction it didn't recognize.
4	Zero divide: Signed Divide (DIVS) or Unsigned Divide (DIVU) instruction with a divisor of 0 was executed.
5	Check exception: Check Register Against Bounds (CHK) instruction was executed and failed. Pascal "value out of range" errors are usually reported in this way.
6	TrapV exception: Trap On Overflow (TRAPV) instruction was executed and failed.
7	Privilege violation: Macintosh always runs in supervisor mode; perhaps an erroneous Return From Execution (RTE) instruction was executed.
8	Trace exception: The trace bit in the status register is set.
9	Line 1010 exception: The 1010 trap dispatcher has failed.
10	Line 1111 exception: Unimplemented instruction
11	Miscellaneous exception: All other MC68000 exceptions
12	Unimplemented core routine: An unimplemented trap number was encountered.
13	Spurious interrupt: The interrupt vector table entry for a particular level of interrupt is NIL; usually occurs with level 4, 5, 6, or 7 interrupts.
14	I/O system error: The File Manager is attempting to dequeue an entry from an I/O request queue that has a bad queue type field; perhaps the queue entry is unlocked. Or, the dCtlQHead field was NIL during a Fetch or Stash call. Or, a needed device control entry has been purged.
15	Segment Loader error: A GetResource call to read a segment into memory failed.
16	Floating point error: The halt bit in the floating-point environment word was set.
17-24	Can't load package: A GetResource call to read a package into memory failed.
25	Can't allocate requested memory block in the heap
26	Segment Loader error: A GetResource call to read 'CODE' resource 0 into memory failed; usually indicates a nonexecutable file.

27   File map destroyed: A logical block number was found that's greater than the number of the last logical block on the volume or less than the logical block number of the first allocation block on the volume.

28   Stack overflow error: The stack has expanded into the heap.

30   "Please insert the disk:" File Manager alert

41   The file named "Finder" can't be found on the disk.

100   Can't mount system startup volume. The system couldn't read the system resource file into memory.

32767   "Sorry, a system error occurred": Default alert message

System Startup Alerts

"Welcome to Macintosh"
"Disassembler installed"
"MacsBug installed"
"Warning—this startup disk is not usable"

Assembly-Language Information

Constants

```
; System error IDs

dsBusError      .EQU   1      ;bus error
dsAddressErr    .EQU   2      ;address error
dsIllInstErr    .EQU   3      ;illegal instruction
dsZeroDivErr    .EQU   4      ;zero divide
dsChkErr        .EQU   5      ;check exception
dsOvflowErr     .EQU   6      ;trapV exception
dsPrivErr       .EQU   7      ;privilege violation
dsTraceErr      .EQU   8      ;trace exception
dsLineAErr      .EQU   9      ;line 1010 exception
dsLineFErr      .EQU   10     ;line 1111 exception
dsMiscErr       .EQU   11     ;miscellaneous exception
dsCoreErr       .EQU   12     ;unimplemented core routine
dsIrqErr        .EQU   13     ;spurious interrupt
dsIOCoreErr     .EQU   14     ;I/O system error
dsLoadErr       .EQU   15     ;Segment Loader error
dsFPErr         .EQU   16     ;floating point error
dsNoPackErr     .EQU   17     ;can't load package 0
dsNoPk1         .EQU   18     ;can't load package 1
dsNoPk2         .EQU   19     ;can't load package 2
dsNoPk3         .EQU   20     ;can't load package 3
dsNoPk4         .EQU   21     ;can't load package 4
dsNoPk5         .EQU   22     ;can't load package 5
dsNoPk6         .EQU   23     ;can't load package 6
```

```
dsNoPk7          .EQU     24        ;can't load package 7
dsMemFullErr     .EQU     25        ;can't allocate requested block
dsBadLaunch      .EQU     26        ;Segment Loader error
dsFSErr          .EQU     27        ;file map destroyed
dsStkNHeap       .EQU     28        ;stack overflow error
dsReinsert       .EQU     30        ;"Please insert the disk:"
dsSysErr         .EQU     32767     ;undifferentiated system error
```

Routines

Trap macro	On entry	On exit
_SysError	D0: errorCode (word)	All registers changed

Variables

DSErrCode	Current system error ID (word)
DSAlertTab	Pointer to system error alert table in use
DSAlertRect	Rectangle enclosing system error alert (8 bytes)

13 THE OPERATING SYSTEM UTILITIES

13 OS Utilities

ABOUT THIS CHAPTER

This chapter describes the Operating System Utilities, a set of routines and data types in the Operating System that perform generally useful operations such as manipulating pointers and handles, comparing strings, and reading the date and time.

Depending on which Operating System Utilities you're interested in using, you may need to be familiar with other parts of the Toolbox or Operating System; where that's necessary, you're referred to the appropriate chapters.

PARAMETER RAM

Various settings, such as those specified by the user by means of the Control Panel desk accessory, need to be preserved when the Macintosh is off so they will still be present at the next system startup. This information is kept in **parameter RAM**, 20 bytes that are stored in the **clock chip** together with the current date and time setting. The clock chip is powered by a battery when the system is off, thereby preserving all the settings stored in it.

You may find it necessary to read the values in parameter RAM or even change them (for example, if you create a desk accessory like the Control Panel). Since the clock chip itself is difficult to access, its contents are copied into low memory at system startup. You read and change parameter RAM through this low-memory copy.

> **Note:** Certain values from parameter RAM are used so frequently that special routines have been designed to return them (for example, the Toolbox Event Manager function GetDblTime). These routines are discussed in other chapters where appropriate.

> **Assembly-language note:** The low-memory copy of parameter RAM begins at the address SysParam; the various portions of the copy can be accessed through individual global variables, listed in the summary at the end of this chapter. Some of these are copied into other global variables at system startup for even easier access; for example, the auto-key threshold and rate, which are contained in the variable SPKbd in the copy of parameter RAM, are copied into the variables KeyThresh and KeyRepThresh. Each such variable is discussed in the appropriate chapter.

The date and time setting is also copied at system startup from the clock chip into its own low-memory location. It's stored as a number of seconds since midnight, January 1, 1904, and is updated every second. The maximum value, $FFFFFFFF, corresponds to 6:28:15 AM, February 6, 2040; after that, it wraps around to midnight, January 1, 1904.

> **Assembly-language note:** The low-memory location containing the date and time is the global variable Time.

The structure of parameter RAM is represented by the following data type:

```
TYPE SysParmType =
    RECORD
        valid:     Byte;     {validity status}
        aTalkA:    Byte;     {AppleTalk node ID hint for modem port}
        aTalkB:    Byte;     {AppleTalk node ID hint for printer port}
        config:    Byte;     {use types for serial ports}
        portA:     INTEGER;  {modem port configuration}
        portB:     INTEGER;  {printer port configuration}
        alarm:     LONGINT;  {alarm setting}
        font:      INTEGER;  {application font number minus 1}
        kbdPrint:  INTEGER;  {auto-key settings, printer connection}
        volClik:   INTEGER;  {speaker volume, double-click, caret blink}
        misc:      INTEGER   {mouse scaling, startup disk, menu blink}
    END;

    SysPPtr = ^SysParmType;
```

The valid field contains the **validity status** of the clock chip: Whenever you successfully write to the clock chip, $A8 is stored in this byte. The validity status is examined when the clock chip is read at system startup. It won't be $A8 if a hardware problem prevented the values from being written; in this case, the low-memory copy of parameter RAM is set to the default values shown in the table below, and these values are then written to the clock chip itself. (The meanings of the parameters are explained below in the descriptions of the various fields.)

Parameter	Default value
Validity status	$A8
Node ID hint for modem port	0
Node ID hint for printer port	0
Use types for serial ports	0 (both ports)
Modem port configuration	9600 baud, 8 data bits, 2 stop bits, no parity
Printer port configuration	Same as for modem port
Alarm setting	0 (midnight, January 1, 1904)
Application font number minus 1	2 (Geneva)
Auto-key threshold	6 (24 ticks)
Auto-key rate	3 (6 ticks)
Printer connection	0 (printer port)
Speaker volume	3 (medium)
Double-click time	8 (32 ticks)
Caret-blink time	8 (32 ticks)
Mouse scaling	1 (on)
Preferred system startup disk	0 (internal drive)
Menu blink	3

Warning: Your program must not use bits indicated below as "reserved for future use" in parameter RAM, since future Macintosh software features will use them.

The aTalkA and aTalkB fields are used by the AppleTalk Manager; they're described in the manual *Inside AppleTalk*.

The config field indicates which device or devices may use each of the serial ports; for details, see the section "Calling the AppleTalk Manager from Assembly Language" in chapter 10.

The portA and portB fields contain the baud rates, data bits, stop bits, and parity for the device drivers using the modem port ("port A") and printer port ("port B"). An explanation of these terms and the exact format of the information are given in chapter 9.

The alarm field contains the alarm setting in seconds since midnight, January 1, 1904.

The font field contains 1 less than the number of the application font. See chapter 7 of Volume I for a list of font numbers.

Bit 0 of the kbdPrint field (Figure 1) designates whether the printer (if any) is connected to the printer port (0) or the modem port (1). Bits 8-11 of this field contain the **auto-key rate,** the rate of the repeat when a character key is held down; this value is stored in two-tick units. Bits 12-15 contain the **auto-key threshold,** the length of time the key must be held down before it begins to repeat; it's stored in four-tick units.

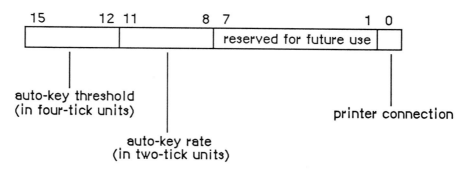

Figure 1. The KbdPrint Field

Bits 0-3 of the volClik field (Figure 2) contain the **caret-blink time,** and bits 4-7 contain the **double-click time;** both values are stored in four-tick units. The caret-blink time is the interval between blinks of the caret that marks the insertion point in text. The double-click time is the greatest interval between a mouse-up and mouse-down event that would qualify two mouse clicks as a double-click. Bits 8-10 of the volClik field contain the speaker volume setting, which ranges from silent (0) to loud (7).

Note: The Sound Driver procedure SetSoundVol changes the speaker volume without changing the setting in parameter RAM, so it's possible for the actual volume to be different from this setting.

Bits 2 and 3 of the misc field (Figure 3) contain a value from 0 to 3 designating how many times a menu item will blink when it's chosen. Bit 4 of this field indicates whether the preferred disk to use to start up the system is in the internal (0) or the external (1) drive; if there's any problem using the disk in the specified drive, the other drive will be used.

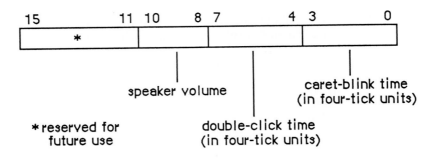

Figure 2. The VolClik Field

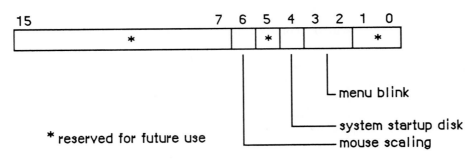

Figure 3. The Misc Field

Finally, bit 6 of the misc field designates whether **mouse scaling** is on (1) or off (0). If mouse scaling is on, the system looks every sixtieth of a second at whether the mouse has moved; if in that time the sum of the mouse's horizontal and vertical changes in position is greater than the **mouse-scaling threshold** (normally six pixels), then the cursor will move twice as far horizontally and vertically as it would if mouse scaling were off.

Assembly-language note: The mouse-scaling threshold is contained in the global variable CrsrThresh.

OPERATING SYSTEM QUEUES

Some of the information used by the Operating System is stored in data structures called **queues**. A queue is a list of identically structured entries linked together by pointers. Queues are used to keep track of VBL tasks, I/O requests, events, mounted volumes, and disk drives (or other block-formatted devices).

A standard Operating System queue has a header with the following structure:

```
TYPE QHdr  = RECORD
              qFlags: INTEGER;     {queue flags}
              qHead: QElemPtr;     {first queue entry}
              qTail: QElemPtr      {last queue entry}
            END;
```

13 OS Utilities

```
QHdrPtr = ^QHdr;
```

QFlags contains information (usually flags) that's different for each queue type. QHead points to the first entry in the queue, and qTail points to the last entry in the queue. The entries within each type of queue are different; the Operating System uses the following variant record to access them:

```
TYPE QTypes    = (dummyType,
                  vType,        {vertical retrace queue type}
                  ioQType,      {file I/O or driver I/O queue type}
                  drvQType,     {drive queue type}
                  evType,       {event queue type}
                  fsQType);     {volume-control-block queue type}

     QElem     = RECORD
                   CASE QTypes OF
                     vType:    (vblQElem: VBLTask);
                     ioQType:  (ioQElem:  ParamBlockRec);
                     drvQType: (drvQElem: DrvQEl);
                     evType:   (evQElem:  EvQEl);
                     fsQType:  (vcbQElem: VCB)
                   END;

     QElemPtr  = ^QElem;
```

All entries in queues, regardless of the queue type, begin with four bytes of flags followed by a pointer to the next queue entry. The entries are linked through these pointers; each one points to the pointer field in the next entry. In Pascal, the data type of the pointer is QElemPtr, and the data type of the entry begins with the pointer field. Consequently, the flag bytes are inaccessible from Pascal.

Following the pointer to the next entry, each entry contains an integer designating the queue type (for example, ORD(evType) for the event queue). The exact structure of the rest of the entry depends on the type of queue; for more information, see the chapter that discusses that queue in detail.

GENERAL OPERATING SYSTEM DATA TYPES

This section describes two data types of general interest to users of the Operating System.

There are several places in the Operating System where you specify a four-character sequence for something, such as for file types and application signatures (described in chapter 1 of Volume III). The Pascal data type for such sequences is

```
TYPE OSType = PACKED ARRAY[1..4] OF CHAR;
```

Another data type that's used frequently in the Operating System is

```
TYPE OSErr = INTEGER;
```

This is the data type for a **result code**, which many Operating System routines (including those described in this chapter) return in addition to their normal results. A result code is an integer indicating whether the routine completed its task successfully or was prevented by some error condition (or other special condition, such as reaching the end of a file). In the normal case that no error is detected, the result code is

```
CONST noErr = 0;  {no error}
```

A nonzero result code (usually negative) signals an error. A list of all result codes is provided in Appendix A (Volume III).

OPERATING SYSTEM UTILITY ROUTINES

Pointer and Handle Manipulation

These functions would be easy to duplicate with Memory Manager calls; they're included in the Operating System Utilities as a convenience because the operations they perform are so common.

```
FUNCTION HandToHand (VAR theHndl: Handle) : OSErr;
```

Trap macro	_HandToHand
On entry	A0: theHndl (handle)
On exit	A0: theHndl (handle)
	D0: result code (word)

HandToHand copies the information to which theHndl is a handle and returns a new handle to the copy in theHndl. Since HandToHand replaces the input parameter with a new handle, you should retain the original value of the input parameter somewhere else, or you won't be able to access it. For example:

```
VAR x,y: Handle;
    err: OSErr;

y := x;
err := HandToHand(y)
```

The original handle remains in x while y becomes a different handle to an identical copy of the data.

Result codes	noErr	No error
	memFullErr	Not enough room in heap zone
	nilHandleErr	NIL master pointer
	memWZErr	Attempt to operate on a free block

```
FUNCTION PtrToHand (srcPtr: Ptr; VAR dstHndl: Handle; size:
          LONGINT) : OSErr;
```

Trap macro	_PtrToHand
On entry	A0: srcPtr (pointer)
	D0: size (long word)
On exit	A0: dstHndl (handle)
	D0: result code (word)

PtrToHand returns in dstHndl a newly created handle to a copy of the number of bytes specified by the size parameter, beginning at the location specified by srcPtr.

Result codes	noErr	No error
	memFullErr	Not enough room in heap zone

```
FUNCTION PtrToXHand (srcPtr: Ptr; dstHndl: Handle; size: LONGINT)
          : OSErr;
```

Trap macro	_PtrToXHand
On entry	A0: srcPtr (pointer)
	A1: dstHndl (handle)
	D0: size (long word)
On exit	A0: dstHndl (handle)
	D0: result code (word)

PtrToXHand takes the existing handle specified by dstHndl and makes it a handle to a copy of the number of bytes specified by the size parameter, beginning at the location specified by srcPtr.

Result codes	noErr	No error
	memFullErr	Not enough room in heap zone
	nilHandleErr	NIL master pointer
	memWZErr	Attempt to operate on a free block

```
FUNCTION HandAndHand (aHndl,bHndl: Handle) : OSErr;
```

Trap macro	_HandAndHand
On entry	A0: aHndl (handle)
	A1: bHndl (handle)
On exit	A0: bHndl (handle)
	D0: result code (word)

HandAndHand concatenates the information to which aHndl is a handle onto the end of the information to which bHndl is a handle.

> **Warning:** HandAndHand dereferences aHndl, so be sure to call the Memory Manager procedure HLock to lock the block before calling HandAndHand.

Result codes	noErr	No error
	memFullErr	Not enough room in heap zone
	nilHandleErr	NIL master pointer
	memWZErr	Attempt to operate on a free block

```
FUNCTION PtrAndHand (pntr: Ptr; hndl: Handle; size: LONGINT) :
        OSErr;
```

Trap macro	_PtrAndHand
On entry	A0: pntr (pointer)
	A1: hndl (handle)
	D0: size (long word)
On exit	A0: hndl (handle)
	D0: result code (word)

PtrAndHand takes the number of bytes specified by the size parameter, beginning at the location specified by pntr, and concatenates them onto the end of the information to which hndl is a handle.

Result codes	noErr	No error
	memFullErr	Not enough room in heap zone
	nilHandleErr	NIL master pointer
	memWZErr	Attempt to operate on a free block

String Comparison

Assembly-language note: The trap macros for these utility routines have optional arguments corresponding to the Pascal flags passed to the routines. When present, such an argument sets a certain bit of the routine trap word; this is equivalent to setting the corresponding Pascal flag to either TRUE or FALSE, depending on the flag. The trap macros for these routines are listed with all the possible permutations of arguments. Whichever permutation you use, you must type it exactly as shown. (The syntax shown applies to the Lisa Workshop Assembler; programmers using another development system should consult its documentation for the proper syntax.)

```
FUNCTION EqualString (aStr,bStr: Str255; caseSens,diacSens:
          BOOLEAN) :  BOOLEAN;
```

Trap macro	_CmpString	
	_CmpString ,MARKS	(sets bit 9, for diacSens=FALSE)
	_CmpString ,CASE	(sets bit 10, for caseSens=TRUE)
	_CmpString ,MARKS,CASE	(sets bits 9 and 10)
On entry	A0: pointer to first character of first string	
	A1: pointer to first character of second string	
	D0: high-order word: length of first string	
	low-order word: length of second string	
On exit	D0: 0 if strings equal, 1 if strings not equal (long word)	

EqualString compares the two given strings for equality on the basis of their ASCII values. If caseSens is TRUE, uppercase characters are distinguished from the corresponding lowercase characters. If diacSens is FALSE, diacritical marks are ignored during the comparison. The function returns TRUE if the strings are equal.

Note: See also the International Utilities Package function IUEqualString.

```
PROCEDURE UprString (VAR theString: Str255; diacSens: BOOLEAN);
```

Trap macro	_UprString	
	_UprString ,MARKS	(sets bit 9, for diacSens=FALSE)
On entry	A0: pointer to first character of string	
	D0: length of string (word)	
On exit	A0: pointer to first character of string	

UprString converts any lowercase letters in the given string to uppercase, returning the converted string in theString. In addition, diacritical marks are stripped from the string if diacSens is FALSE.

Date and Time Operations

The following utilities are for reading and setting the date and time stored in the clock chip. Reading the date and time is a fairly common operation; setting it is somewhat rarer, but could be necessary for implementing a desk accessory like the Control Panel.

The date and time setting is stored as an unsigned number of seconds since midnight, January 1, 1904; you can use a utility routine to convert this to a **date/time record**. Date/time records are defined as follows:

```
TYPE DateTimeRec =
        RECORD
          year:      INTEGER;  {1904 to 2040}
          month:     INTEGER;  {1 to 12 for January to December}
          day:       INTEGER;  {1 to 31}
          hour:      INTEGER;  {0 to 23}
          minute:    INTEGER;  {0 to 59}
          second:    INTEGER;  {0 to 59}
          dayOfWeek: INTEGER   {1 to 7 for Sunday to Saturday}
        END;
```

```
FUNCTION ReadDateTime (VAR secs: LONGINT) : OSErr;
```

Trap macro	_ReadDateTime
On entry	A0: pointer to long word secs
On exit	A0: pointer to long word secs
	D0: result code (word)

ReadDateTime copies the date and time stored in the clock chip to a low-memory location and returns it in the secs parameter. This routine is called at system startup; you'll probably never need to call it yourself. Instead you'll call GetDateTime (see below).

Assembly-language note: The low-memory location to which ReadDateTime copies the date and time is the global variable Time.

Result codes	noErr	No error
	clkRdErr	Unable to read clock

```
PROCEDURE GetDateTime (VAR secs: LONGINT);   [Not in ROM]
```

GetDateTime returns in the secs parameter the contents of the low-memory location in which the date and time setting is stored; if this setting reflects the actual current date and time, secs will contain the number of seconds between midnight, January 1, 1904 and the time that the function was called.

Note: If your application disables interrupts for longer than a second, the number of seconds returned will not be exact.

Assembly-language note: Assembly-language programmers can just access the global variable Time.

If you wish, you can convert the value returned by GetDateTime to a date/time record by calling the Secs2Date procedure.

Note: Passing the value returned by GetDateTime to the International Utilities Package procedure IUDateString or IUTimeString will yield a string representing the corresponding date or time of day, respectively.

```
FUNCTION SetDateTime (secs: LONGINT) : OSErr;
```

Trap macro	_SetDateTime
On entry	D0: secs (long word)
On exit	D0: result code (word)

SetDateTime takes a number of seconds since midnight, January 1, 1904, as specified by the secs parameter, and writes it to the clock chip as the current date and time. It then attempts to read the value just written and verify it by comparing it to the secs parameter.

Assembly-language note: SetDateTime updates the global variable Time to the value of the secs parameter.

Result codes	noErr	No error
	clkWrErr	Time written did not verify
	clkRdErr	Unable to read clock

```
PROCEDURE Date2Secs (date: DateTimeRec; VAR secs: LONGINT);
```

Trap macro	_Date2Secs
On entry	A0: pointer to date/time record
On exit	D0: secs (long word)

Date2Secs takes the given date/time record, converts it to the corresponding number of seconds elapsed since midnight, January 1, 1904, and returns the result in the secs parameter. The dayOfWeek field of the date/time record is ignored. The values passed in the year and month fields should be within their allowable ranges, or unpredictable results will occur. The remaining four fields of the date/time record may contain any value. For example, September 34 will be interpreted as October 4, and you could specify the 300th day of the year as January 300.

```
PROCEDURE Secs2Date (secs: LONGINT; VAR date: DateTimeRec);
```

Trap macro	_Secs2Date
On entry	D0: secs (long word)
On exit	A0: pointer to date/time record

Secs2Date takes a number of seconds elapsed since midnight, January 1, 1904 as specified by the secs parameter, converts it to the corresponding date and time, and returns the corresponding date/time record in the date parameter.

```
PROCEDURE GetTime (VAR date: DateTimeRec);   [Not in ROM]
```

GetTime takes the number of seconds elapsed since midnight, January 1, 1904 (obtained by calling GetDateTime), converts that value into a date and time (by calling Secs2Date), and returns the result in the date parameter.

Assembly-language note: From assembly language, you can pass the value of the global variable Time to Secs2Date.

```
PROCEDURE SetTime (date: DateTimeRec);   [Not in ROM]
```

SetTime takes the date and time specified by the date parameter, converts it into the corresponding number of seconds elapsed since midnight, January 1, 1904 (by calling Date2Secs), and then writes that value to the clock chip as the current date and time (by calling SetDateTime).

Assembly-language note: From assembly language, you can just call Date2Secs and SetDateTime directly.

Parameter RAM Operations

The following three utilities are used for reading from and writing to parameter RAM. Figure 4 illustrates the function of these three utilities; further details are given below and in the "Parameter RAM" section.

```
FUNCTION InitUtil : OSErr;
```

Trap macro	_InitUtil
On exit	D0: result code (word)

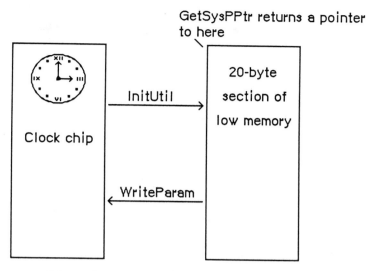

Figure 4. Parameter RAM Routines

InitUtil copies the contents of parameter RAM into 20 bytes of low memory and copies the date and time from the clock chip into its own low-memory location. This routine is called at system startup; you'll probably never need to call it yourself.

Assembly-language note: InitUtil copies parameter RAM into 20 bytes starting at the address SysParam and copies the date and time into the global variable Time.

If the validity status in parameter RAM is not $A8 when InitUtil is called, an error is returned as the result code, and the default values (given in the "Parameter RAM" section) are read into the low-memory copy of parameter RAM; these values are then written to the clock chip itself.

Result codes	noErr	No error
	prInitErr	Validity status not $A8

```
FUNCTION GetSysPPtr : SysPPtr;   [Not in ROM]
```

GetSysPPtr returns a pointer to the low-memory copy of parameter RAM. You can examine the values stored in its various fields, or change them before calling WriteParam (below).

Assembly-language note: Assembly-language programmers can simply access the global variables corresponding to the low-memory copy of parameter RAM. These variables, which begin at the address SysParam, are listed in the summary.

```
FUNCTION WriteParam : OSErr;
```

Trap macro	_WriteParam
On entry	A0: SysParam (pointer)
	D0: MinusOne (long word)
	(You have to pass the values of these global variables for historical reasons.)
On exit	D0: result code (word)

WriteParam writes the low-memory copy of parameter RAM to the clock chip. You should previously have called GetSysPPtr and changed selected values as desired.

WriteParam also attempts to verify the values written by reading them back in and comparing them to the values in the low-memory copy.

Note: If you've accidentally written incorrect values into parameter RAM, the system may not be able to start up. If this happens, you can reset parameter RAM by removing the battery, letting the Macintosh sit turned off for about five minutes, and then putting the battery back in.

Result codes	noErr	No error
	prWrErr	Parameter RAM written did not verify

Queue Manipulation

This section describes utilities that advanced programmers may want to use for adding entries to or deleting entries from an Operating System queue. Normally you won't need to use these utilities, since queues are manipulated for you as necessary by routines that need to deal with them.

```
PROCEDURE Enqueue (qEntry: QElemPtr; theQueue: QHdrPtr);
```

Trap macro	_Enqueue
On entry	A0: qEntry (pointer)
	A1: theQueue (pointer)
On exit	A1: theQueue (pointer)

Enqueue adds the queue entry pointed to by qEntry to the end of the queue specified by theQueue.

Note: Interrupts are disabled for a short time while the queue is updated.

```
FUNCTION Dequeue (qEntry: QElemPtr; theQueue: QHdrPtr) : OSErr;
```

Trap macro	_Dequeue
On entry	A0: qEntry (pointer)
	A1: theQueue (pointer)
On exit	A1: theQueue (pointer)
	D0: result code (word)

Dequeue removes the queue entry pointed to by qEntry from the queue specified by theQueue (without deallocating the entry) and adjusts other entries in the queue accordingly.

Note: The note under Enqueue above also applies here. In this case, the amount of time interrupts are disabled depends on the length of the queue and the position of the entry in the queue.

Note: To remove all entries from a queue, you can just clear all the fields of the queue's header.

Result codes	noErr	No error
	qErr	Entry not in specified queue

Trap Dispatch Table Utilities

The Operating System Utilities include two routines for manipulating the trap dispatch table, which is described in detail in chapter 4 of Volume I. Using these routines, you can intercept calls to an Operating System or Toolbox routine and do some pre- or post-processing of your own: Call GetTrapAddress to get the address of the original routine, save that address for later use, and call SetTrapAddress to install your own version of the routine in the dispatch table. Before or after its own processing, the new version of the routine can use the saved address to call the original version.

Warning: You can replace as well as intercept existing routines; in any case, you should be absolutely sure you know what you're doing. Remember that some calls that aren't in ROM do some processing of their own before invoking a trap macro (for example, FSOpen eventually invokes _Open, and IUCompString invokes the macro for IUMagString). Also, a number of ROM routines have been patched with corrected versions in RAM; if you intercept a patched routine, you must not do any processing *after* the existing patch, and you must be sure to preserve the registers and the stack (or the system won't work properly).

Assembly-language note: You can tell whether a routine is patched by comparing its address to the global variable ROMBase; if the address is less than ROMBase, the routine is patched.

In addition, you can use GetTrapAddress to save time in critical sections of your program by calling an Operating System or Toolbox routine directly, avoiding the overhead of a normal trap dispatch.

```
FUNCTION GetTrapAddress (trapNum: INTEGER) : LONGINT;
```

Trap macro	_GetTrapAddress
On entry	D0: trapNum (word)
On exit	A0: address of routine

GetTrapAddress returns the address of a routine currently installed in the trap dispatch table under the trap number designated by trapNum. To find out the trap number for a particular routine, see Appendix C (Volume III).

Assembly-language note: When you use this technique to bypass the trap dispatcher, you don't get the extra level of register saving. The routine itself will preserve A2-A6 and D3-D7, but if you want any other registers preserved across the call you have to save and restore them yourself.

```
PROCEDURE SetTrapAddress (trapAddr: LONGINT; trapNum: INTEGER);
```

Trap macro	_SetTrapAddress
On entry	A0: trapAddr (address)
	D0: trapNum (word)

SetTrapAddress installs in the trap dispatch table a routine whose address is trapAddr; this routine is installed under the trap number designated by trapNum.

Warning: Since the trap dispatch table can address locations within a range of only 64K bytes from the beginning of the system heap, the routine you install should be in the system heap.

Miscellaneous Utilities

```
PROCEDURE Delay (numTicks: LONGINT; VAR finalTicks: LONGINT);
```

Trap macro	_Delay
On entry	A0: numTicks (long word)
On exit	D0: finalTicks (long word)

Delay causes the system to wait for the number of ticks (sixtieths of a second) specified by numTicks, and returns in finalTicks the total number of ticks from system startup to the end of the delay.

> **Warning:** Don't rely on the duration of the delay being exact; it will usually be accurate to within one tick, but may be off by more than that. The Delay procedure enables all interrupts and checks the tick count that's incremented during the vertical retrace interrupt; however, it's possible for this interrupt to be disabled by other interrupts, in which case the duration of the delay will not be exactly what you requested.

> **Assembly-language note:** On exit from this procedure, register D0 contains the value of the global variable Ticks as measured at the end of the delay.

```
PROCEDURE SysBeep (duration: INTEGER);
```

SysBeep causes the system to beep for approximately the number of ticks specified by the duration parameter. The sound decays from loud to soft; after about five seconds it's inaudible. The initial volume of the beep depends on the current speaker volume setting, which the user can adjust with the Control Panel desk accessory. If the speaker volume has been set to 0 (silent), SysBeep instead causes the menu bar to blink once.

> **Assembly-language note:** Unlike all other Operating System Utilities, this procedure is stack-based.

```
PROCEDURE Environs (VAR rom,machine: INTEGER);   [Not in ROM]
```

In the rom parameter, Environs returns the current ROM version number (for a Macintosh XL, the version number of the ROM image installed by MacWorks). In the machine parameter, it returns an indication of which machine is in use, as follows:

```
CONST macXLMachine = 0;   {Macintosh XL}
      macMachine    = 1;   {Macintosh 128K or 512K}
```

> **Assembly-language note:** From assembly language, you can get this information from the word that's at an offset of 8 from the beginning of ROM (which is stored in the global variable ROMBase). The format of this word is $00xx for the Macintosh 128K or 512K and $xxFF for the Macintosh XL, where xx is the ROM version number. (The ROM version number will always be between 1 and $FE.)

```
PROCEDURE Restart;   [Not in ROM]
```

This procedure restarts the system.

Assembly-language note: From assembly language, you can give the following
instructions to restart the system:

```
MOVE   ROMBase,A0
JMP    $0A(A0)
```

PROCEDURE SetUpA5;   [Not in ROM]

SetUpA5 saves the current value of register A5 (for restoring later with RestoreA5, described
below) and then resets A5 to point to the boundary between the application globals and the
application parameters. This procedure is useful only within the interrupt environment, where the
state of A5 is unpredictable; for instance, in a completion routine or a VBL task, calling SetUpA5
will ensure that A5 contains the proper value, allowing the routine or task to access the
application globals.

Assembly-language note: You can get the boundary between the application globals
and the application parameters from the global variable CurrentA5.

PROCEDURE RestoreA5;   [Not in ROM]

Call RestoreA5 at the conclusion of a routine or task that required a call to SetUpA5 (above); it
restores register A5 to whatever its value was when SetUpA5 was called.

SUMMARY OF THE OPERATING SYSTEM UTILITIES

Constants

```
CONST  { Values returned by Environs procedure }

    macXLMachine  = 0;      {Macintosh XL}
    macMachine    = 1;      {Macintosh 128K or 512K}

    { Result codes }

    clkRdErr      = -85;    {unable to read clock}
    clkWrErr      = -86;    {time written did not verify}
    memFullErr    = -108;   {not enough room in heap zone}
    memWZErr      = -111;   {attempt to operate on a free block}
    nilHandleErr  = -109;   {NIL master pointer}
    noErr         =  0;     {no error}
    prInitErr     = -88;    {validity status is not $A8}
    prWrErr       = -87;    {parameter RAM written did not verify}
    qErr          = -1;     {entry not in specified queue}
```

Data Types

```
TYPE  OSType = PACKED ARRAY[1..4] OF CHAR;

    OSErr = INTEGER;

    SysPPtr     = ^SysParmType;
    SysParmType =
      RECORD
        valid:    Byte;     {validity status}
        aTalkA:   Byte;     {AppleTalk node ID hint for modem port}
        aTalkB:   Byte;     {AppleTalk node ID hint for printer port}
        config:   Byte;     {use types for serial ports}
        portA:    INTEGER;  {modem port configuration}
        portB:    INTEGER;  {printer port configuration}
        alarm:    LONGINT;  {alarm setting}
        font:     INTEGER;  {application font number minus 1}
        kbdPrint: INTEGER;  {auto-key settings, printer connection}
        volClik:  INTEGER;  {speaker volume, double-click, caret blink}
        misc:     INTEGER   {mouse scaling, startup disk, menu blink}
      END;

    QHdrPtr  = ^QHdr;
    QHdr     = RECORD
                 qFlags:  INTEGER;    {queue flags}
                 qHead:   QElemPtr;   {first queue entry}
                 qTail:   QElemPtr;   {last queue entry}
               END;
```

```
QTypes = (dummyType,
          vType,          {vertical retrace queue type}
          ioQType,        {file I/O or driver I/O queue type}
          drvQType,       {drive queue type}
          evType,         {event queue type}
          fsQType);       {volume-control-block queue type}

QElemPtr = ^QElem;
QElem    = RECORD
             CASE QTypes OF
               vType:    (vblQElem: VBLTask);
               ioQType:  (ioQElem:  ParamBlockRec);
               drvQType: (drvQElem: DrvQEl);
               evType:   (evQElem:  EvQEl);
               fsQType:  (vcbQElem: VCB)
             END;

DateTimeRec =
        RECORD
          year:      INTEGER;  {1904 to 2040}
          month:     INTEGER;  {1 to 12 for January to December}
          day:       INTEGER;  {1 to 31}
          hour:      INTEGER;  {0 to 23}
          minute:    INTEGER;  {0 to 59}
          second:    INTEGER;  {0 to 59}
          dayOfWeek: INTEGER   {1 to 7 for Sunday to Saturday}
        END;
```

Routines

Pointer and Handle Manipulation

```
FUNCTION HandToHand  (VAR theHndl: Handle) : OSErr;
FUNCTION PtrToHand   (srcPtr: Ptr; VAR dstHndl: Handle; size: LONGINT) :
                      OSErr;
FUNCTION PtrToXHand  (srcPtr: Ptr; dstHndl: Handle; size: LONGINT) :
                      OSErr;
FUNCTION HandAndHand (aHndl,bHndl: Handle) : OSErr;
FUNCTION PtrAndHand  (pntr: Ptr; hndl: Handle; size: LONGINT) : OSErr;
```

String Comparison

```
FUNCTION  EqualString (aStr,bStr: Str255; caseSens,diacSens: BOOLEAN) :
                       BOOLEAN;
PROCEDURE UprString   (VAR theString: Str255; diacSens: BOOLEAN);
```

Date and Time Operations

```
FUNCTION  ReadDateTime    (VAR secs: LONGINT) : OSErr;
PROCEDURE GetDateTime     (VAR secs: LONGINT);  [Not in ROM]
FUNCTION  SetDateTime     (secs: LONGINT) : OSErr;
PROCEDURE Date2Secs       (date: DateTimeRec; VAR secs: LONGINT);
PROCEDURE Secs2Date       (secs: LONGINT; VAR date: DateTimeRec);
PROCEDURE GetTime         (VAR date: DateTimeRec);   [Not in ROM]
PROCEDURE SetTime         (date: DateTimeRec);   [Not in ROM]
```

Parameter RAM Operations

```
FUNCTION  InitUtil :    OSErr;
FUNCTION  GetSysPPtr :  SysPPtr;   [Not in ROM]
FUNCTION  WriteParam :  OSErr;
```

Queue Manipulation

```
PROCEDURE Enqueue (qEntry: QElemPtr; theQueue: QHdrPtr);
FUNCTION  Dequeue (qEntry: QElemPtr; theQueue: QHdrPtr) : OSErr;
```

Trap Dispatch Table Utilities

```
PROCEDURE SetTrapAddress (trapAddr: LONGINT; trapNum: INTEGER);
FUNCTION  GetTrapAddress (trapNum: INTEGER) : LONGINT;
```

Miscellaneous Utilities

```
PROCEDURE Delay     (numTicks: LONGINT; VAR finalTicks: LONGINT);
PROCEDURE SysBeep   (duration: INTEGER);
PROCEDURE Environs  (VAR rom,machine: INTEGER);   [Not in ROM]
PROCEDURE Restart;      [Not in ROM]
PROCEDURE SetUpA5;      [Not in ROM]
PROCEDURE RestoreA5;    [Not in ROM]
```

Default Parameter RAM Values

Parameter	Default value
Validity status	$A8
Node ID hint for modem port	0
Node ID hint for printer port	0
Use types for serial ports	0 (both ports)
Modem port configuration	9600 baud, 8 data bits, 2 stop bits, no parity

Parameter	Default value
Printer port configuration	Same as for modem port
Alarm setting	0 (midnight, January 1, 1904)
Application font number minus 1	2 (Geneva)
Auto-key threshold	6 (24 ticks)
Auto-key rate	3 (6 ticks)
Printer connection	0 (printer port)
Speaker volume	3 (medium)
Double-click time	8 (32 ticks)
Caret-blink time	8 (32 ticks)
Mouse scaling	1 (on)
Preferred system startup disk	0 (internal drive)
Menu blink	3

Assembly-Language Information

Constants

```
; Result codes

clkRdErr      .EQU    -85     ;unable to read clock
clkWrErr      .EQU    -86     ;time written did not verify
memFullErr    .EQU    -108    ;not enough room in heap zone
memWZErr      .EQU    -111    ;attempt to operate on a free block
nilHandleErr  .EQU    -109    ;NIL master pointer
noErr         .EQU    0       ;no error
prInitErr     .EQU    -88     ;validity status is not $A8
prWrErr       .EQU    -87     ;parameter RAM written did not verify
qErr          .EQU    -1      ;entry not in specified queue

; Queue types

vType         .EQU    1       ;vertical retrace queue type
ioQType       .EQU    2       ;file I/O or driver I/O queue type
drvQType      .EQU    3       ;drive queue type
evType        .EQU    4       ;event queue type
fsQType       .EQU    5       ;volume-control-block queue type
```

Queue Data Structure

qFlags	Queue flags (word)
qHead	Pointer to first queue entry
qTail	Pointer to last queue entry

Date/Time Record Data Structure

dtYear	1904 to 2040 (word)
dtMonth	1 to 12 for January to December (word)
dtDay	1 to 31 (word)
dtHour	0 to 23 (word)
dtMinute	0 to 59 (word)
dtSecond	0 to 59 (word)
dtDayOfWeek	1 to 7 for Sunday to Saturday (word)

Routines

Trap macro	On entry	On exit
_HandToHand	A0: theHndl (handle)	A0: theHndl (handle)
		D0: result code(word)
_PtrToHand	A0: srcPtr (ptr)	A0: dstHndl (handle)
	D0: size (long)	D0: result code (word)
_PtrToXHand	A0: srcPtr (ptr)	A0: dstHndl (handle)
	A1: dstHndl (handle)	D0: result code (word)
	D0: size (long)	
_HandAndHand	A0: aHndl (handle)	A0: bHndl (handle)
	A1: bHndl (handle)	D0: result code (word)
_PtrAndHand	A0: pntr (ptr)	A0: hndl (handle)
	A1: hndl (handle)	D0: result code (word)
	D0: size (long)	
_CmpString	_CmpString ,MARKS sets bit 9, for diacSens=FALSE	
	_CmpString ,CASE sets bit 10, for caseSens=TRUE	
	_CmpString ,MARKS,CASE sets bits 9 and 10	
	A0: ptr to first string	D0: 0 if equal, 1 if
	A1: ptr to second string	not equal (long)
	D0: high word: length of	
	first string	
	low word: length of	
	second string	
_UprString	_UprString ,MARKS sets bit 9, for diacSens=FALSE	
	A0: ptr to string	A0: ptr to string
	D0: length of string (word)	
_ReadDateTime	A0: ptr to long word secs	A0: ptr to long word secs
		D0: result code (word)
_SetDateTime	D0: secs (long)	D0: result code (word)
_Date2Secs	A0: ptr to date/time record	D0: secs (long)
_Secs2Date	D0: secs (long)	A0: ptr to date/time record
_InitUtil		D0: result code (word)
_WriteParam	A0: SysParam (ptr)	D0: result code (word)
	D0: MinusOne (long)	

Trap macro	On entry	On exit
_Enqueue	A0: qEntry (ptr) A1: theQueue (ptr)	A1: theQueue (ptr)
_Dequeue	A0: qEntry (ptr) A1: theQueue (ptr)	A1: theQueue (ptr) D0: result code (word)
_GetTrapAddress	D0: trapNum (word)	A0: address of routine
_SetTrapAddress	A0: trapAddr (address) D0: trapNum (word)	
_Delay	A0: numTicks (long)	D0: finalTicks (long)
_SysBeep	stack: duration (word)	

Variables

SysParam	Low-memory copy of parameter RAM (20 bytes)
SPValid	Validity status (byte)
SPATalkA	AppleTalk node ID hint for modem port (byte)
SPATalkB	AppleTalk node ID hint for printer port (byte)
SPConfig	Use types for serial ports (byte)
SPPortA	Modem port configuration (word)
SPPortB	Printer port configuration (word)
SPAlarm	Alarm setting (long)
SPFont	Application font number minus 1 (word)
SPKbd	Auto-key threshold and rate (byte)
SPPrint	Printer connection (byte)
SPVolCtl	Speaker volume (byte)
SPClikCaret	Double-click and caret-blink times (byte)
SPMisc2	Mouse scaling, system startup disk, menu blink (byte)
CrsrThresh	Mouse-scaling threshold (word)
Time	Seconds since midnight, January 1, 1904 (long)

14 THE DISK INITIALIZATION PACKAGE

14 Disk Initialization

ABOUT THIS CHAPTER

This chapter describes the Disk Initialization Package, which provides routines for initializing disks to be accessed with the File Manager and Disk Driver. A single routine lets you easily present the standard user interface for initializing and naming a disk; the Standard File Package calls this routine when the user inserts an uninitialized disk. You can also use the Disk Initialization Package to perform each of the three steps of initializing a disk separately if desired.

You should already be familiar with:

- the basic concepts and structures behind QuickDraw, particularly points
- the Toolbox Event Manager
- the File Manager
- packages in general, as discussed in chapter 17 of Volume I

USING THE DISK INITIALIZATION PACKAGE

The Disk Initialization Package and the resources it uses are automatically read into memory from the system resource file when one of the routines in the package is called. Together, the package and its resources occupy about 2.5K bytes. If the disk containing the system resource file isn't currently in a Macintosh disk drive, the user will be asked to switch disks and so may have to remove the one to be initialized. To avoid this, you can use the DILoad procedure, which explicitly reads the necessary resources into memory and makes them unpurgeable. You would need to call DILoad before explicitly ejecting the system disk or before any situations where it may be switched with another disk (except for situations handled by the Standard File Package, which calls DILoad itself).

Note: The resources used by the Disk Initialization Package consist of a single dialog and its associated items, even though the package may present what seem to be a number of different dialogs. A special technique is used to allow the single dialog to contain all possible dialog items with only some of them visible at one time.

When you no longer need to have the Disk Initialization Package in memory, call DIUnload. The Standard File Package calls DIUnload before returning.

When a disk-inserted event occurs, the system attempts to mount the volume (by calling the File Manager function MountVol) and returns MountVol's result code in the high-order word of the event message. In response to such an event, your application can examine the result code in the event message and call DIBadMount if an error occurred (that is, if the volume could not be mounted). If the error is one that can be corrected by initializing the disk, DIBadMount presents the standard user interface for initializing and naming the disk, and then mounts the volume itself. For other errors, it justs ejects the disk; these errors are rare, and may reflect a problem in your program.

Note: Disk-inserted events during standard file saving and opening are handled by the Standard File Package. You'll call DIBadMount only in other, less common situations (for example, if your program explicitly ejects disks, or if you want to respond to the user's inserting an uninitialized disk when not expected).

Disk initialization consists of three steps, each of which can be performed separately by the functions DIFormat, DIVerify, and DIZero. Normally you won't call these in a standard application, but they may be useful in special utility programs that have a nonstandard interface.

DISK INITIALIZATION PACKAGE ROUTINES

Assembly-language note: The trap macro for the Disk Initialization Package is _Pack2. The routine selectors are as follows:

```
diBadMount   .EQU   0
diLoad       .EQU   2
diUnload     .EQU   4
diFormat     .EQU   6
diVerify     .EQU   8
diZero       .EQU   10
```

PROCEDURE DILoad;

DILoad reads the Disk Initialization Package, and its associated dialog and dialog items, from the system resource file into memory and makes them unpurgeable.

Note: DIFormat, DIVerify, and DIZero don't need the dialog, so if you use only these routines you can call the Resource Manager function GetResource to read just the package resource into memory (and the Memory Manager procedure HNoPurge to make it unpurgeable).

PROCEDURE DIUnload;

DIUnload makes the Disk Initialization Package (and its associated dialog and dialog items) purgeable.

FUNCTION DIBadMount (where: Point; evtMessage: LONGINT) : INTEGER;

Call DIBadMount when a disk-inserted event occurs if the result code in the high-order word of the associated event message indicates an error (that is, the result code is other than noErr). Given the event message in evtMessage, DIBadMount evaluates the result code and either ejects the disk or lets the user initialize and name it. The low-order word of the event message contains the drive number. The where parameter specifies the location (in global coordinates) of the top left corner of the dialog box displayed by DIBadMount.

If the result code passed is extFSErr, memFullErr, nsDrvErr, paramErr, or volOnLinErr, DIBadMount simply ejects the disk from the drive and returns the result code. If the result code ioErr, badMDBErr, or noMacDskErr is passed, the error can be corrected by initializing the disk; DIBadMount displays a dialog box that describes the problem and asks whether the user wants to initialize the disk. For the result code ioErr, the dialog box shown in Figure 1 is displayed. (This happens if the disk is brand new.) For badMDBErr and noMacDskErr, DIBadMount displays a similar dialog box in which the description of the problem is "This disk is damaged" and "This is not a Macintosh disk", respectively.

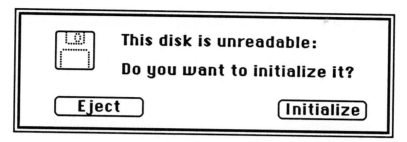

Figure 1. Disk Initialization Dialog for IOErr

Note: Before presenting the disk initialization dialog, DIBadMount checks whether the drive contains an already mounted volume; if so, it ejects the disk and returns 2 as its result. This will happen rarely and may reflect an error in your program (for example, you forgot to call DILoad and the user had to switch to the disk containing the system resource file).

If the user responds to the disk initialization dialog by clicking the Eject button, DIBadMount ejects the disk and returns 1 as its result. If the Initialize button is clicked, a box displaying the message "Initializing disk..." appears, and DIBadMount attempts to initialize the disk. If initialization fails, the disk is ejected and the user is informed as shown in Figure 2; after the user clicks OK, DIBadMount returns a negative result code ranging from firstDskErr to lastDskErr, indicating that a low-level disk error occurred.

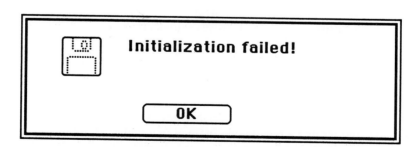

Figure 2. Initialization Failure Dialog

If the disk is successfully initialized, the dialog box in Figure 3 appears. After the user names the disk and clicks OK, DIBadMount mounts the volume by calling the File Manager function MountVol and returns MountVol's result code (noErr if no error occurs).

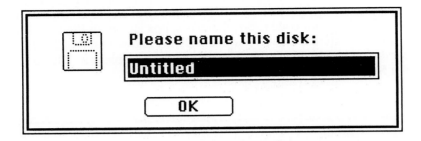

Figure 3. Dialog for Naming a Disk

Result codes   noErr   No error
               extFSErr   External file system
               memFullErr   Not enough room in heap zone
               nsDrvErr   No such drive
               paramErr   Bad drive number
               volOnLinErr   Volume already on-line
               firstDskErr   Low-level disk error
               through lastDskErr

Other results 1   User clicked Eject
               2   Mounted volume in drive

```
FUNCTION DIFormat (drvNum: INTEGER) : OSErr;
```

DIFormat formats the disk in the drive specified by the given drive number and returns a result code indicating whether the formatting was completed successfully or failed. Formatting a disk consists of writing special information onto it so that the Disk Driver can read from and write to the disk.

Result codes   noErr   No error
               firstDskErr   Low-level disk error
               through lastDskErr

```
FUNCTION DIVerify (drvNum: INTEGER) : OSErr;
```

DIVerify verifies the format of the disk in the drive specified by the given drive number; it reads each bit from the disk and returns a result code indicating whether all bits were read successfully or not. DIVerify doesn't affect the contents of the disk itself.

Result codes   noErr   No error
               firstDskErr   Low-level disk error
               through lastDskErr

```
FUNCTION DIZero (drvNum: INTEGER; volName: Str255) : OSErr;
```

On the unmounted volume in the drive specified by the given drive number, DIZero writes the volume information, a block map, and a file directory as for a volume with no files; the volName parameter specifies the volume name to be included in the volume information. This is the last step in initialization (after formatting and verifying) and makes any files that are already on the volume permanently inaccessible. If the operation fails, DIZero returns a result code indicating that a low-level disk error occurred; otherwise, it mounts the volume by calling the File Manager function MountVol and returns MountVol's result code (noErr if no error occurs).

Result codes	noErr	No error
	badMDBErr	Bad master directory block
	extFSErr	External file system
	ioErr	I/O error
	memFullErr	Not enough room in heap zone
	noMacDskErr	Not a Macintosh disk
	nsDrvErr	No such drive
	paramErr	Bad drive number
	volOnLinErr	Volume already on-line
	firstDskErr	Low-level disk error
	through lastDskErr	

14 Disk Initialization

SUMMARY OF THE DISK INITIALIZATION PACKAGE

Routines

```
PROCEDURE DILoad;
PROCEDURE DIUnload;
FUNCTION  DIBadMount (where: Point; evtMessage: LONGINT) : INTEGER;
FUNCTION  DIFormat   (drvNum: INTEGER) : OSErr;
FUNCTION  DIVerify   (drvNum: INTEGER) : OSErr;
FUNCTION  DIZero     (drvNum: INTEGER; volName: Str255) : OSErr;
```

Result Codes

Name	Value	Meaning
badMDBErr	–60	Bad master directory block
extFSErr	–58	External file system
firstDskErr	–84	First of the range of low-level disk errors
ioErr	–36	I/O error
lastDskErr	–64	Last of the range of low-level disk errors
memFullErr	–108	Not enough room in heap zone
noErr	0	No error
noMacDskErr	–57	Not a Macintosh disk
nsDrvErr	–56	No such drive
paramErr	–50	Bad drive number
volOnLinErr	–55	Volume already on-line

Assembly-Language Information

Constants

```
; Routine selectors

diBadMount    .EQU    0
diLoad        .EQU    2
diUnload      .EQU    4
diFormat      .EQU    6
diVerify      .EQU    8
diZero        .EQU    10
```

Trap Macro Name

_Pack2

15 THE FLOATING-POINT ARITHMETIC AND TRANSCENDENTAL FUNCTIONS PACKAGES

15 Floating Point

ABOUT THIS CHAPTER

This chapter discusses the Floating-Point Arithmetic Package and the Transcendental Functions Package, which provide facilities for extended-precision floating-point arithmetic and advanced numerical applications programming. These two packages support the Standard Apple Numeric Environment (SANE), which is designed in strict accordance with IEEE Standard 754 for Binary Floating-Point Arithmetic.

You should already be familiar with packages in general, as discussed in chapter 17 of Volume I.

ABOUT THE PACKAGES

Pascal programmers will rarely, if ever, need to call the Floating-Point Arithmetic or Transcendental Functions packages explicitly. These facilities are built into post-3.0 versions of Lisa Pascal (as well as most Macintosh high-level languages); that is, the compiler recognizes SANE data types, and automatically calls the packages to perform the standard arithmetic operations (+, -, *, /) as well as data type conversion. Mathematical functions that aren't built in are accessible through a run-time library—see your language manual for details.

If you're using assembly language or a language without built-in support for SANE, you'll need to be familiar with the *Apple Numerics Manual*. This is the standard reference guide to SANE, and describes in detail how to call the Floating-Point Arithmetic and Transcendental Functions routines from assembly language. Some general information about the packages is given below.

THE FLOATING-POINT ARITHMETIC PACKAGE

The Floating-Point Arithmetic Package contains routines for performing the following operations:

Arithmetic and Auxiliary Routines
Add
Subtract
Multiply
Divide
Square Root
Round to Integral Value
Truncate to Integral Value
Remainder
Binary Log
Binary Scale
Negate
Absolute Value
Copy Sign
Next-After

Converting Between Data Types

Binary to Binary
Binary to Decimal Record (see note below)
Decimal Record to Binary

Comparing and Classifying

Compare
Compare, Signaling Invalid if Unordered
Classify

Controlling the Floating-Point Environment

Get Environment
Set Environment
Test Exception
Set Exception
Procedure Entry Protocol
Procedure Exit Protocol

Halt Control

Set Halt Vector
Get Halt Vector

Note: Don't confuse the floating-point binary-decimal conversions with the integer routines provided by the Binary-Decimal Conversion Package.

The following data types are provided:

- Single (32-bit floating-point format)

- Double (64-bit floating-point format)

- Comp (64-bit integer format for accounting-type applications)

- Extended (80-bit floating-point format)

The Floating-Point Arithmetic Package is automatically read into memory from the system resource file when one of its routines is called. It occupies about 4.4K bytes.

Assembly-language note: The macros for calling the Floating-Point routines push a two-byte opword onto the stack and then invoke _FP68K (same as _Pack4). These macros are fully documented in the *Apple Numerics Manual*.

The package uses at most 200 bytes of stack space. It preserves all MC68000 registers across invocations (except that the remainder operation modifies D0), but modifies the MC68000 CCR flags.

THE TRANSCENDENTAL FUNCTIONS PACKAGE

The Transcendental Functions Package contains the following mathematical functions:

Logarithmic Functions

Base-e logarithm	ln(x)
Base-2 logarithm	log(x) base 2
Base-e logarithm of 1 plus argument	ln(1+x)
Base-2 logarithm of 1 plus argument	log(1+x) base 2

Exponential Functions

Base-e exponential	e^x
Base-2 exponential	2^x
Base-e exponential minus 1	(e^x)–1
Base-2 exponential minus 1	(2^x)–1
Integer exponential	x^i
General exponential	x^y

Financial Functions

Compound Interest	(1+x)^y
Annuity Factor	(1–(1+x)^–y)/y

Trigonometric Functions

Sine
Cosine
Tangent
Arctangent

Random Number Generator

Note: The functions in this package are also called elementary functions.

The Transcendental Functions Package is automatically read into memory when one of its routines is called. It in turn calls the Floating-Point Arithmetic Package to perform the basic arithmetic. Together they occupy about 8.5K bytes.

Assembly-language note: The macros for calling the transcendental functions push a two-byte opword onto the stack and then invoke _Elems68K (same as _Pack5). These macros are fully documented in the *Apple Numerics Manual*.

The package uses at most 200 bytes of stack space. It preserves all MC68000 registers across invocations, but modifies the CCR flags.

Note: Early versions of the Transcendental Functions Package lock themselves when read into memory and remain locked unless explicitly unlocked. Apple high-level languages that access the package through a SANE library avoid this problem by preserving the state of the lock bit across calls to the package. However, pre-3.1 versions of Lisa Pascal

15 Floating Point

require that you explicitly unlock the package with the Memory Manager function HUnlock, as follows:

```
HUnlock(GetResource('PACK',5))
```

Assembly-language note: In assembly language, you can unlock the package as follows:

```
        CLR.L           -(SP)           ;slot for handle
        MOVE.L          #'PACK',-(SP)   ;resource type
        MOVE.W          #5,-(SP)        ;resource ID
        _GetResource
        MOVE.L          (SP)+,A0        ;store handle in A0
        _HUnlock
```

Inside Macintosh
Volume III

Contents

PREFACE

ABOUT INSIDE MACINTOSH

Inside Macintosh is a three-volume set of manuals that tells you what you need to know to write software for the Apple® Macintosh™ 128K, 512K, or XL (or a Lisa® running MacWorks™ XL). Although directed mainly toward programmers writing standard Macintosh applications, *Inside Macintosh* also contains the information needed to write simple utility programs, desk accessories, device drivers, or any other Macintosh software. It includes:

■ the user interface guidelines for applications on the Macintosh

■ a complete description of the routines available for your program to call (both those built into the Macintosh and others on disk), along with related concepts and background information

■ a description of the Macintosh 128K and 512K hardware

It does *not* include information about:

■ Programming in general.

■ Getting started as a developer. For this, write to:

> Developer Relations
> Mail Stop 27-S
> Apple Computer, Inc.
> 20525 Mariani Avenue
> Cupertino, CA 95014

■ Any specific development system, except where indicated. You'll need to have additional documentation for the development system you're using.

■ The Standard Apple Numeric Environment (SANE), which your program can access to perform extended-precision floating-point arithmetic and transcendental functions. This environment is described in the *Apple Numerics Manual*.

You should already be familiar with the basic information that's in *Macintosh*, the owner's guide, and have some experience using a standard Macintosh application (such as MacWrite™).

The Language

The routines you'll need to call are written in assembly language, but (with a few exceptions) they're also accessible from high-level languages, such as Pascal on the Lisa Workshop development system. *Inside Macintosh* documents the Lisa Pascal interfaces to the routines and the symbolic names defined for assembly-language programmers using the Lisa Workshop; if you're using a different development system, its documentation should tell you how to apply the information presented here to that system.

Inside Macintosh is intended to serve the needs of both high-level language and assembly-language programmers. Every routine is shown in its Pascal form (if it has one), but assembly-language programmers are told how they can access the routines. Information of interest only to assembly-language programmers is isolated and labeled so that other programmers can conveniently skip it.

Familiarity with Lisa Pascal (or a similar high-level language) is recommended for all readers, since it's used for most examples. Lisa Pascal is described in the documentation for the Lisa Pascal Workshop.

What's in Each Volume

Inside Macintosh consists of three volumes. Volume I begins with the following information of general interest:

- a "road map" to the software and the rest of the documentation

- the user interface guidelines

- an introduction to memory management (the least you need to know, with a complete discussion following in Volume II)

- some general information for assembly-language programmers

It then describes the various parts of the **User Interface Toolbox**, the software in ROM that helps you implement the standard Macintosh user interface in your application. This is followed by descriptions of other, RAM-based software that's similar in function to the User Interface Toolbox. (The software overview in the Road Map chapter gives further details.)

Volume II describes the **Operating System**, the software in ROM that does basic tasks such as input and output, memory management, and interrupt handling. As in Volume I, some functionally similar RAM-based software is then described.

Volume III discusses your program's interface with the Finder and then describes the Macintosh 128K and 512K hardware. A comprehensive summary of all the software is provided, followed by some useful appendices and a glossary of all terms defined in *Inside Macintosh*.

Version Numbers

This edition of *Inside Macintosh* describes the following versions of the software:

- version 105 of the ROM in the Macintosh 128K or 512K

- version 112 of the ROM image installed by MacWorks in the Macintosh XL

- version 1.1 of the Lisa Pascal interfaces and the assembly-language definitions

Some of the RAM-based software is read from the file named System (usually kept in the System Folder). This manual describes the software in the System file whose creation date is May 2, 1984.

A HORSE OF A DIFFERENT COLOR

On an innovative system like the Macintosh, programs don't look quite the way they do on other systems. For example, instead of carrying out a sequence of steps in a predetermined order, your program is driven primarily by user actions (such as clicking and typing) whose order cannot be predicted.

You'll probably find that many of your preconceptions about how to write applications don't apply here. Because of this, and because of the sheer volume of information in *Inside Macintosh*, it's essential that you read the Road Map chapter. It will help you get oriented and figure out where to go next.

THE STRUCTURE OF A TYPICAL CHAPTER

Most chapters of *Inside Macintosh* have the same structure, as described below. Reading through this now will save you a lot of time and effort later on. It contains important hints on how to find what you're looking for within this vast amount of technical documentation.

Every chapter begins with a very brief description of its subject and a list of what you should already know before reading that chapter. Then there's a section called, for example, "About the Window Manager", which gives you more information about the subject, telling you what you can do with it in general, elaborating on related user interface guidelines, and introducing terminology that will be used in the chapter. This is followed by a series of sections describing important related concepts and background information; unless they're noted to be for advanced programmers only, you'll have to read them in order to understand how to use the routines described later.

Before the routine descriptions themselves, there's a section called, for example, "Using the Window Manager". It introduces you to the routines, telling you how they fit into the general flow of an application program and, most important, giving you an idea of which ones you'll need to use. Often you'll need only a few routines out of many to do basic operations; by reading this section, you can save yourself the trouble of learning routines you'll never use.

Then, for the details about the routines, read on to the next section. It gives the calling sequence for each routine and describes all the parameters, effects, side effects, and so on.

Following the routine descriptions, there may be some sections that won't be of interest to all readers. Usually these contain information about advanced techniques, or behind the scenes details for the curious.

For review and quick reference, each chapter ends with a summary of the subject matter, including the entire Pascal interface and a separate section for assembly-language programmers.

CONVENTIONS

The following notations are used in *Inside Macintosh* to draw your attention to particular items of information:

  Note: A note that may be interesting or useful

  Warning: A point you need to be cautious about

  Assembly-language note: A note of interest to assembly-language programmers only

[Not in ROM]

Routines marked with this notation are not part of the Macintosh ROM. Depending on how the interfaces have been set up on the development system you're using, these routines may or may not be available. They're available to users of Lisa Pascal; other users should check the documentation for their development system for more information. (For related information of interest to assembly-language programmers, see chapter 4 of Volume I.)

1 THE FINDER INTERFACE

ABOUT THIS CHAPTER

This chapter describes the interface between a Macintosh application program and the Finder.

You should already be familiar with the details of the User Interface Toolbox and the Operating System.

SIGNATURES AND FILE TYPES

Every application must have a unique **signature** by which the Finder can identify it. The signature can be any four-character sequence not being used for another application on any currently mounted volume (except that it can't be one of the standard resource types). To ensure uniqueness on all volumes, you must register your application's signature by writing to:

> Macintosh Technical Support
> Mail Stop 3-T
> Apple Computer, Inc.
> 20525 Mariani Avenue
> Cupertino, CA 95014

> **Note:** There's no need to register your own resource types, since they'll usually exist only in your own applications or documents.

Signatures work together with **file types** to enable the user to open or print a document (any file created by an application) from the Finder. When the application creates a file, it sets the file's creator and file type. Normally it sets the creator to its signature and the file type to a four-character sequence that identifies files of that type. When the user asks the Finder to open or print the file, the Finder starts up the application whose signature is the file's creator and passes the file type to the application along with other identifying information, such as the file name. (More information about this process is given in chapter 2 of Volume II.)

An application may create its own special type or types of files. Like signatures, file types must be registered with Macintosh Technical Support to ensure uniqueness. When the user chooses Open from an application's File menu, the application will display (via the Standard File Package) the names of all files of a given type or types, regardless of which application created the files. Having a unique file type for your application's special files ensures that only the names of those files will be displayed for opening.

> **Note:** Signatures and file types may be strange, unreadable combinations of characters; they're never seen by end users of Macintosh.

Applications may also create existing types of files. There might, for example, be an application that merges two MacWrite documents into a single document. In such cases, the application should use the same file type as the original application uses for those files. It should also specify the original application's signature as the file's creator; that way, when the user asks the Finder to open or print the file, the Finder will call on the original application to perform the operation. To learn the signature and file types used by an existing application, check with the application's manufacturer.

Files that consist only of text—a stream of characters, with Return characters at the ends of paragraphs or short lines—should be given the standard file type 'TEXT'. This is the type that MacWrite gives to text only files it creates, for example. If your application uses this file type, its files will be accepted by MacWrite and it in turn will accept MacWrite text-only files (likewise for any other application that deals with 'TEXT' files, such as MacTerminal). Your application can give its own signature as the file's creator if it wants to be called to open or print the file when the user requests this from the Finder.

For files that aren't to be opened or printed from the Finder, as may be the case for certain data files created by the application, the creator should be set to '????' (and the file type to whatever is appropriate).

FINDER-RELATED RESOURCES

To establish the proper interface with the Finder, every application's resource file must specify the signature of the application along with data that provides version information. In addition, there may be resources that provide information about icons and files related to the application. All of these Finder-related resources are described below, followed by a comprehensive example and (for interested programmers) the exact formats of the resources.

Version Data

Your application's resource file must contain a special resource that has the signature of the application as its resource type. This resource is called the **version data** of the application. The version data is typically a string that gives the name, version number, and date of the application, but it can in fact be any data at all. The resource ID of the version data is 0 by convention.

Part of the process of installing an application on the Macintosh is to set the creator of the file that contains the application. You set the creator to the application's signature, and the Finder copies the corresponding version data into a resource file named **Desktop**. (The Finder doesn't display this file on the Macintosh desktop, to ensure that the user won't tamper with it.)

> **Note:** Additional, related resources may be copied into the Desktop file; see "Bundles" below for more information.

Icons and File References

For each application, the Finder needs to know:

- the icon to be displayed for the application on the desktop, if different from the Finder's default icon for applications (see Figure 1)

- if the application creates any files, the icon to be displayed for each type of file it creates, if different from the Finder's default icon for documents

The Finder learns this information from resources called **file references** in the application's resource file. Each file reference contains a file type and an ID number, called a **local ID**, that identifies the icon to be displayed for that type of file. (The local ID is mapped to an actual resource ID as described under "Bundles" below.)

Figure 1. The Finder's Default Icons

The file type for the application itself is 'APPL'. This is the file type in the file reference that designates the application's icon. You also specify it as the application's file type at the same time that you specify its creator—when you install the application on the Macintosh.

The ID number in a file reference corresponds not to a single icon but to an **icon list** in the application's resource file. The icon list consists of two icons: the actual icon to be displayed on the desktop, and a mask consisting of that icon's outline filled with black (see Figure 2).

Figure 2. Icon and Mask

Bundles

A bundle in the application's resource file groups together all the Finder-related resources. It specifies the following:

- the application's signature and the resource ID of its version data

- a mapping between the local IDs for icon lists (as specified in file references) and the actual resource IDs of the icon lists in the resource file

- local IDs for the file references themselves and a mapping to their actual resource IDs

When you install the application on the Macintosh, you set its "bundle bit"; the first time the Finder sees this, it copies the version data, bundle, icon lists, and file references from the application's resource file into the Desktop file. If there are any resource ID conflicts between the icon lists and file references in the application's resource file and those in Desktop, the Finder will change those resource IDs in Desktop. The Finder does this same resource copying and ID conflict resolution when you transfer an application to another volume.

Note: The local IDs are needed only for use by the Finder.

An Example

Suppose you've written an application named SampWriter. The user can create a unique type of document from it, and you want a distinctive icon for both the application and its documents. The application's signature, as recorded with Macintosh Technical Support, is 'SAMP'; the file type assigned for its documents is 'SAMF'. You would include the following resources in the application's resource file:

Resource	Resource ID	Description
Version data with resource type 'SAMP'	0	The string 'SampWriter Version 1--2/1/85'
Icon list	128	The icon for the application The icon's mask
Icon list	129	The icon for documents The icon's mask
File reference	130	File type 'APPL' Local ID 0 for the icon list
File reference	131	File type 'SAMF' Local ID 1 for the icon list
Bundle	132	Signature 'SAMP' Resource ID 0 for the version data

For icon lists, the mapping:

local ID 0 → resource ID 128
local ID 1 → resource ID 129

For file references, the mapping:

local ID 2 → resource ID 130
local ID 3 → resource ID 131

Note: See the documentation for the development system you're using for information about how to include these resources in a resource file.

Formats of Finder-Related Resources

The resource type for an application's version data is the signature of the application, and the resource ID is 0 by convention. The resource data can be anything at all; typically it's a string giving the name, version number, and date of the application.

The resource type for an icon list is 'ICN#'. The resource data simply consists of the icons, 128 bytes each.

The resource type for a file reference is 'FREF'. The resource data has the format shown below.

Number of bytes	Contents
4 bytes	File type
2 bytes	Local ID for icon list

The resource type for a bundle is 'BNDL'. The resource data has the format shown below. The format is more general than needed for Finder-related purposes because bundles will be used in other ways in the future.

Number of bytes	Contents
4 bytes	Signature of the application
2 bytes	Resource ID of version data
2 bytes	Number of resource types in bundle minus 1

For each resource type:

4 bytes	Resource type
2 bytes	Number of resources of this type minus 1

For each resource:

2 bytes	Local ID
2 bytes	Actual resource ID

A bundle used for establishing the Finder interface contains the two resource types 'ICN#' and 'FREF'.

2 THE MACINTOSH HARDWARE

ABOUT THIS CHAPTER

This chapter provides a basic description of the hardware of the Macintosh 128K and 512K computers. It gives you information that you'll need to connect other devices to the Macintosh and to write device drivers or other low-level programs. It will help you figure out which technical documents you'll need to design peripherals; in some cases, you'll have to obtain detailed specifications from the manufacturers of the various interface chips.

This chapter is oriented toward assembly-language programmers. It assumes you're familiar with the basic operation of microprocessor-based devices. Knowledge of the Macintosh Operating System will also be helpful.

Warning: Only the Macintosh 128K and 512K are covered in this chapter. In particular, note that the memory addresses and screen size are different on the Macintosh XL (and may be different in future versions of the Macintosh). To maintain software compatibility across the Macintosh line, and to allow for future changes to the hardware, you're *strongly advised* to use the Toolbox and Operating System routines wherever possible.

To learn how your program can determine which hardware environment it's operating in, see the description of the Environs procedure in chapter 13 of Volume II.

OVERVIEW OF THE HARDWARE

The Macintosh computer contains a Motorola MC68000 microprocessor clocked at 7.8336 megahertz, random access memory (RAM), read-only memory (ROM), and several chips that enable it to communicate with external devices. There are five I/O devices: the video display; the sound generator; a Synertek SY6522 Versatile Interface Adapter (VIA) for the mouse and keyboard; a Zilog Z8530 Serial Communications Controller (SCC) for serial communication; and an Apple custom chip, called the **IWM** ("Integrated Woz Machine") for disk control.

The Macintosh uses memory-mapped I/O, which means that each device in the system is accessed by reading or writing to specific locations in the address space of the computer. Each device contains logic that recognizes when it's being accessed and responds in the appropriate manner.

The MC68000 can directly access 16 megabytes (Mb) of address space. In the Macintosh, this is divided into four equal sections. The first four Mb are for RAM, the second four Mb are for ROM, the third are for the SCC, and the last four are for the IWM and the VIA. Since each of the devices within the blocks has far fewer than four Mb of individually addressable locations or registers, the addresses within each block "wrap around" and are repeated several times within the block.

RAM is the "working memory" of the system. Its base address is address 0. The first 256 bytes of RAM (addresses 0 through $FF) are used by the MC68000 as **exception vectors**; these are the addresses of the routines that gain control whenever an exception such as an interrupt or a trap occurs. (The summary at the end of this chapter includes a list of all the exception vectors.) RAM also contains the system and application heaps, the stack, and other information used by applications. In addition, the following hardware devices share the use of RAM with the MC68000:

■ the video display, which reads the information for the display from one of two **screen buffers**

■ the sound generator, which reads its information from one of two **sound buffers**

■ the disk speed controller, which shares its data space with the sound buffers

The MC68000 accesses to RAM are interleaved (alternated) with the video display's accesses during the active portion of a screen scan line (video scanning is described in the next section). The sound generator and disk speed controller are given the first access after each scan line. At all other times, the MC68000 has uninterrupted access to RAM, increasing the average RAM access rate to about 6 megahertz (MHz).

ROM is the system's permanent read-only memory. Its base address, $400000, is available as the constant romStart and is also stored in the global variable ROMBase. ROM contains the routines for the Toolbox and Operating System, and the various system traps. Since the ROM is used exclusively by the MC68000, it's always accessed at the full processor rate of 7.83 MHz.

The address space reserved for the device I/O contains blocks devoted to each of the devices within the computer. This region begins at address $800000 and continues to the highest address at $FFFFFF.

Note: Since the VIA is involved in some way in almost every operation of the Macintosh, the following sections frequently refer to the VIA and VIA-related constants. The VIA itself is described later, and all the constants are listed in the summary at the end of this chapter.

THE VIDEO INTERFACE

The video display is created by a moving electron beam that scans across the screen, turning on and off as it scans in order to create black and white pixels. Each pixel is a square, approximately 1/74 inch on a side.

To create a screen image, the electron beam starts at the top left corner of the screen (see Figure 1). The beam scans horizontally across the screen from left to right, creating the top line of graphics. When it reaches the last pixel on the right end of the top line it turns off, and continues past the last pixel to the physical right edge of the screen. Then it flicks invisibly back to the left edge and moves down one scan line. After tracing across the black border, it begins displaying the data in the second scan line. The time between the display of the rightmost pixel on one line and the leftmost pixel on the next is called the **horizontal blanking interval**. When the electron beam reaches the last pixel of the last (342nd) line on the screen, it traces out to the right edge and then flicks up to the top left corner, where it traces the left border and then begins once again to display the top line. The time between the last pixel on the bottom line and the first one on the top line is called the **vertical blanking interval**. At the beginning of the vertical blanking interval, the VIA generates a **vertical blanking interrupt**.

The pixel clock rate (the frequency at which pixels are displayed) is 15.6672 MHz, or about .064 microseconds (μsec) per pixel. For each scan line, 512 pixels are drawn on the screen, requiring 32.68 μsec. The horizontal blanking interval takes the time of an additional 192 pixels, or 12.25 μsec. Thus, each full scan line takes 44.93 μsec, which means the horizontal scan rate is 22.25 kilohertz.

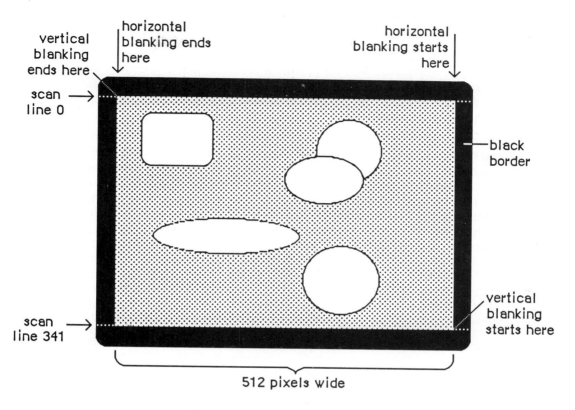

Figure 1. Video Scanning Pattern

A full screen display consists of 342 horizontal scan lines, occupying 15367.65 μsec, or about 15.37 milliseconds (msec). The vertical blanking interval takes the time of an additional 28 scan lines—1258.17 μsec, or about 1.26 msec. This means the full screen is redisplayed once every 16625.8 μsec. That's about 16.6 msec per frame, which means the vertical scan rate (the full screen display frequency) is 60.15 hertz.

The video generator uses 21,888 bytes of RAM to compose a bit-mapped video image 512 pixels wide by 342 pixels tall. Each bit in this range controls a single pixel in the image: A 0 bit is white, and a 1 bit is black.

There are two screen buffers (areas of memory from which the video circuitry can read information to create a screen display): the main buffer and the alternate buffer. The starting addresses of the screen buffers depend on how much memory you have in your Macintosh. In a Macintosh 128K, the main screen buffer starts at $1A700 and the alternate buffer starts at $12700; for a 512K Macintosh, add $60000 to these numbers.

> **Warning:** To be sure you don't use the wrong area of memory and to maintain compatibility with future Macintosh systems, you should get the video base address and bit map dimensions from screenBits (see chapter 6 of Volume I).

Each scan line of the screen displays the contents of 32 consecutive words of memory, each word controlling 16 horizontally adjacent pixels. In each word, the high-order bit (bit 15) controls the leftmost pixel and the low-order bit (bit 0) controls the rightmost pixel. The first word in each scan line follows the last word on the line above it. The starting address of the screen is thus in the top left corner, and the addresses progress from there to the right and down, to the last byte in the extreme bottom right corner.

Normally, the video display doesn't flicker when you read from or write to it, because the video memory accesses are interleaved with the processor accesses. But if you're creating an animated image by repeatedly drawing the graphics in quick succession, it may appear to flicker if the electron beam displays it when your program hasn't finished updating it, showing some of the new image and some of the old in the same frame.

One way to prevent flickering when you're updating the screen continuously is to use the vertical and horizontal blanking signals to synchronize your updates to the scanning of video memory. Small changes to your screen can be completed entirely during the interval between frames (the first 1.26 msec following a vertical blanking interrupt), when nothing is being displayed on the screen. When making larger changes, the trick is to keep your changes happening always ahead of the spot being displayed by the electron beam, as it scans byte by byte through the video memory. Changes you make in the memory already passed over by the scan spot won't appear until the *next* frame. If you start changing your image when the vertical blanking interrupt occurs, you have 1.26 msec of unrestricted access to the image. After that, you can change progressively less and less of your image as it's scanned onto the screen, starting from the top (the lowest video memory address). From vertical blanking interrupt, you have only 1.26 msec in which to change the first (lowest address) screen location, but you have almost 16.6 msec to change the last (highest address) screen location.

Another way to create smooth, flicker-free graphics, especially useful with changes that may take more 16.6 msec, is to use the two screen buffers as alternate displays. If you draw into the one that's currently *not* being displayed, and then switch the buffers during the next vertical blanking, your graphics will change all at once, producing a clean animation. (See chapter 11 of Volume II to find out how to specify tasks to be performed during vertical blanking.)

If you want to use the alternate screen buffer, you'll have to specify this to the Segment Loader (see chapter 2 of Volume II for details). To switch to the alternate screen buffer, clear the following bit of VIA data register A (vBase+vBufA):

```
vPage2      .EQU        6       ;0 = alternate screen buffer
```

For example:

```
        BCLR        #vPage2,vBase+vBufA
```

To switch back to the main buffer, set the same bit.

> **Warning:** Whenever you change a bit in a VIA data register, be sure to leave the other bits in the register unchanged.

> **Warning:** The alternate screen buffer may not be supported in future versions of the Macintosh.

THE SOUND GENERATOR

The Macintosh sound circuitry uses a series of values taken from an area of RAM to create a changing waveform in the output signal. This signal drives a small speaker inside the Macintosh and is connected to the external sound jack on the back of the computer. If a plug is inserted into the external sound jack, the internal speaker is disabled. The external sound line can drive a load of 600 or more ohms, such as the input of almost any audio amplifier, but not a directly connected external speaker.

The sound generator may be turned on or off by writing 1 (off) or 0 (on) to the following bit of VIA data register B (vBase+vBufB):

```
vSndEnb        .EQU          7         ;0 = sound enabled, 1 = disabled
```

For example:

```
        BSET       #vSndEnb,vBase+vBufB    ;turn off sound
```

By storing a range of values in the sound buffer, you can create the corresponding waveform in the sound channel. The sound generator uses a form of pulse-width encoding to create sounds. The sound circuitry reads one word in the sound buffer during each horizontal blanking interval (including the "virtual" intervals during vertical blanking) and uses the high-order byte of the word to generate a pulse of electricity whose duration (width) is proportional to the value in the byte. Another circuit converts this pulse into a voltage that's attenuated (reduced) by a three-bit value from the VIA. This reduction corresponds to the current setting of the volume level. To set the volume directly, store a three-bit number in the low-order bits of VIA data register A (vBase+vBufA). You can use the following constant to isolate the bits involved:

```
vSound         .EQU          7         ;sound volume bits
```

Here's an example of how to set the sound level:

```
        MOVE.B     vBase+vBufA,D0     ;get current value of register A
        ANDI.B     #255-vSound,D0     ;clear the sound bits
        ORI.B      #3,D0              ;set medium sound level
        MOVE.B     D0,vBase+vBufA     ;put the data back
```

After attenuation, the sound signal is passed to the audio output line.

The sound circuitry scans the sound buffer at a fixed rate of 370 words per video frame, repeating the full cycle 60.15 times per second. To create sounds with frequencies other than multiples of the basic scan rate, you must store phase-shifted patterns into the sound buffer between each scan. You can use the vertical and horizontal blanking signals (available in the VIA) to synchronize your sound buffer updates to the buffer scan. You may find that it's much easier to use the routines in the Sound Driver to do these functions.

> **Warning:** The low-order byte of each word in the sound buffer is used to control the speed of the motor in the disk drive. Don't store any information there, or you'll interfere with the disk I/O.

There are two sound buffers, just as there are two screen buffers. The address of the main sound buffer is stored in the global variable SoundBase and is also available as the constant soundLow. The main sound buffer is at $1FD00 in a 128K Macintosh, and the alternate buffer is at $1A100; for a 512K Macintosh, add $60000 to these values. Each sound buffer contains 370 words of data. As when you want to use the alternate screen buffer, you'll have to specify to the Segment Loader that you want the alternate buffer (see chapter 2 of Volume II for details). To select the alternate sound buffer for output, clear the following bit of VIA data register A (vBase+vBufA):

```
vSndPg2       .EQU         3       ;0 = alternate sound buffer
```

To return to the main buffer, set the same bit.

> **Warning:** Be sure to switch back to the main sound buffer before doing a disk access, or the disk won't work properly.

> **Warning:** The alternate sound buffer may not be supported in future versions of the Macintosh.

There's another way to generate a simple, square-wave tone of any frequency, using almost no processor intervention. To do this, first load a constant value into all 370 sound buffer locations (use $00's for minumum volume, $FF's for maximum volume). Next, load a value into the VIA's timer 1 latches, and set the high-order two bits of the VIA's auxiliary control register (vBase+vACR) for "square wave output" from timer 1. The timer will then count down from the latched value at 1.2766 µsec/count, over and over, inverting the vSndEnb bit of VIA register B (vBase+vBufB) after each count down. This takes the constant voltage being generated from the sound buffer and turns it on and off, creating a square-wave sound whose period is

2 * 1.2766 µsec * timer 1's latched value

> **Note:** You may want to disable timer 1 interrupts during this process (bit 6 in the VIA's interrupt enable register, which is at vBase+vIER).

To stop the square-wave sound, reset the high-order two bits of the auxiliary control register.

> **Note:** See the SY6522 technical specifications for details of the VIA registers. See also "Sound Driver Hardware" in chapter 8 of Volume II.

Diagram

Figure 2 shows a block diagram for the sound port.

THE SCC

The two serial ports are controlled by a Zilog Z8530 **Serial Communications Controller** (SCC). The port known as SCC port A is the one with the modem icon on the back of the Macintosh. SCC port B is the one with the printer icon.

Macintosh serial ports conform to the EIA standard RS422, which differs from the more common RS232C standard. While RS232C modulates a signal with respect to a common ground ("single-ended" transmission), RS422 modulates two signals against each other ("differential" transmission). The RS232C receiver senses whether the received signal is sufficiently negative with respect to ground to be a logic "1", whereas the RS422 receiver simply senses which line is more negative than the other. This makes RS422 more immune to noise and interference, and more versatile over longer distances. If you ground the positive side of each RS422 receiver and leave unconnected the positive side of each transmitter, you've converted to EIA standard RS423, which can be used to communicate with most RS232C devices over distances up to fifty feet or so.

2 Hardware

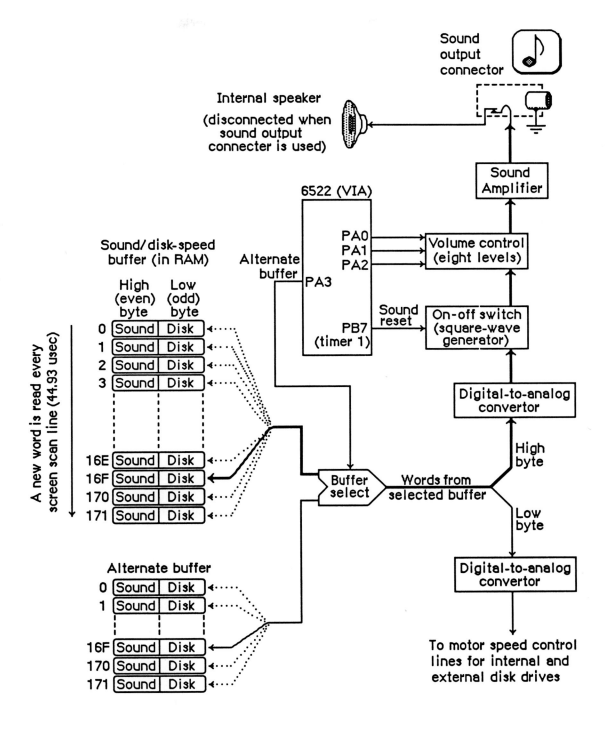

Figure 2. Diagram of Sound Port

The serial inputs and outputs of the SCC are connected to the ports through differential line drivers (26LS30) and receivers (26LS32). The line drivers can be put in high-impedance mode between transmissions, to allow other devices to transmit over those lines. A driver is activated by lowering the SCC's Request To Send (RTS) output for that port. Port A and port B are identical except that port A (the modem port) has a higher interrupt priority, making it more suitable for high-speed communication.

Figure 3 shows the DB-9 pinout for the SCC output jacks.

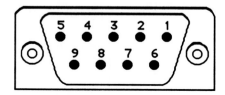

1	Ground
2	+5 volts
3	Ground
4	Transmit data +
5	Transmit data -
6	+12 volts
7	Handshake/external clock
8	Receive data +
9	Receive data -

Figure 3. Pinout for SCC Output Jacks

Warning: Do not draw more than 100 milliamps at +12 volts, and 200 milliamps at +5 volts from all connectors combined.

Each port's input-only handshake line (pin 7) is connected to the SCC's Clear To Send (CTS) input for that port, and is designed to accept an external device's Data Terminal Ready (DTR) handshake signal. This line is also connected to the SCC's external synchronous clock (TRxC) input for that port, so that an external device can perform high-speed synchronous data exchange. Note that you can't use the line for receiving DTR if you're using it to receive a high-speed data clock.

The handshake line is sensed by the Macintosh using the positive (noninverting) input of one of the standard RS422 receivers (26LS32 chip), with the negative input grounded. The positive input was chosen because this configuration is more immune to noise when no active device is connected to pin 7.

Note: Because this is a differential receiver, any handshake or clock signal driving it must be "bi-polar", alternating between a positive voltage and a negative voltage, with respect to the internally grounded negative input. If a device tries to use ground (0 volts) as one of its handshake logic levels, the Macintosh will receive that level as an indeterminate state, with unpredictable results.

The SCC itself (at its PCLK pin) is clocked at 3.672 megahertz. The internal synchronous clock (RTxC) pins for both ports are also connected to this 3.672 MHz clock. This is the clock that, after dividing by 16, is normally fed to the SCC's internal baud-rate generator.

The SCC chip generates level-1 processor interrupts during I/O over the serial lines. For more information about SCC interrupts, see chapter 6 of Volume II.

The locations of the SCC control and data lines are given in the following table as offsets from the constant sccWBase for writes, or sccRBase for reads. These base addresses are also available in the global variables SCCWr and SCCRd. The SCC is on the upper byte of the data bus, so you must use only even-addressed byte reads (a byte read of an odd SCC read address tries to reset the entire SCC). When writing, however, you must use only *odd*-addressed byte writes (the MC68000 puts your data on both bytes of the bus, so it works correctly). A word access to any SCC address will shift the phase of the computer's high-frequency timing by 128 nanoseconds (system software adjusts it correctly during the system startup process).

Location	Contents
sccWBase+aData	Write data register A
sccRBase+aData	Read data register A
sccWBase+bData	Write data register B
sccRBase+bData	Read data register B
sccWBase+aCtl	Write control register A
sccRBase+aCtl	Read control register A
sccWBase+bCtl	Write control register B
sccRBase+bCtl	Read control register B

Warning: Don't access the SCC chip more often than once every 2.2 μsec. The SCC requires that much time to let its internal lines stabilize.

Refer to the technical specifications of the Zilog Z8530 for the detailed bit maps and control methods (baud rates, protocols, and so on) of the SCC.

Diagram

Figure 4 shows a circuit diagram for the serial ports.

THE MOUSE

The DB-9 connector labeled with the mouse icon connects to the Apple mouse (Apple II, Apple III, Lisa, and Macintosh mice are electrically identical). The mouse generates four square-wave signals that describe the amount and direction of the mouse's travel. Interrupt-driven routines in the Macintosh ROM convert this information into the corresponding motion of the pointer on the screen. By turning an option called **mouse scaling** on or off in the Control Panel desk accessory, the user can change the amount of screen pointer motion that corresponds to a

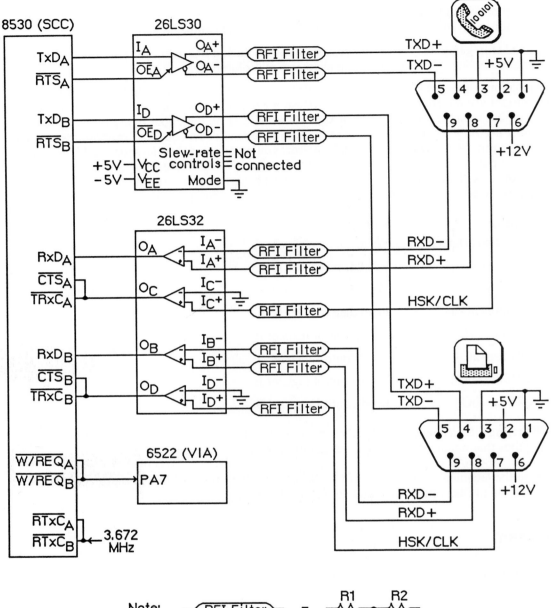

Figure 4. Diagram of Serial Ports

given mouse motion, depending on how fast the mouse is moved; for more information about mouse scaling, see the discussion of parameter RAM in chapter 13 of Volume II.

Note: The mouse is a relative-motion device; that is, it doesn't report where it is, only how far and in which direction it's moving. So if you want to connect graphics tablets, touch screens, light pens, or other absolute-position devices to the mouse port, you must either convert their coordinates into motion information or install your own device-handling routines.

The mouse operates by sending square-wave trains of information to the Macintosh that change as the velocity and direction of motion change. The rubber-coated steel ball in the mouse contacts two capstans, each connected to an interrupter wheel: Motion along the mouse's X axis rotates one of the wheels and motion along the Y axis rotates the other wheel.

The Macintosh uses a scheme known as quadrature to detect which direction the mouse is moving along each axis. There's a row of slots on an interrupter wheel, and two beams of infrared light shine through the slots, each one aimed at a phototransistor detector. The detectors are offset just enough so that, as the wheel turns, they produce two square-wave signals (called the interrupt signal and the quadrature signal) 90 degrees out of phase. The quadrature signal precedes the interrupt signal by 90 degrees when the wheel turns one way, and trails it when the wheel turns the other way.

The interrupt signals, X1 and Y1, are connected to the SCC's DCDA and DCDB inputs, respectively, while the quadrature signals, X2 and Y2, go to inputs of the VIA's data register B. When the Macintosh is interrupted (from the SCC) by the rising edge of a mouse interrupt signal, it checks the VIA for the state of the quadrature signal for that axis: If it's low, the mouse is moving to the left (or down), and if it's high, the mouse is moving to the right (or up). When the SCC interrupts on the falling edge, a high quadrature level indicates motion to the left (or down) and a low quadrature level indicates motion to the right (or up):

SCC	VIA	Mouse
Mouse interrupt X1 (or Y1)	Mouse quadrature X2 (or Y2)	Motion direction in X (or Y) axis
Positive edge	Low	Left (or down)
	High	Right (or up)
Negative edge	Low	Right (or up)
	High	Left (or down)

Figure 5 shows the interrupt (Y1) and quadrature (Y2) signals when the mouse is moved downwards.

The switch on the mouse is a pushbutton that grounds pin 7 on the mouse connector when pressed. The state of the button is checked by software during each vertical blanking interrupt. The small delay between each check is sufficient to debounce the button. You can look directly at the mouse button's state by examining the following bit of VIA data register B (vBase+vBufB):

```
vSW          .EQU          3        ;0 = mouse button is down
```

If the bit is clear, the mouse button is down. However, it's recommended that you let the Operating System handle this for you through the event mechanism.

Figure 6 shows the DB-9 pinout for the mouse jack at the back of the Macintosh.

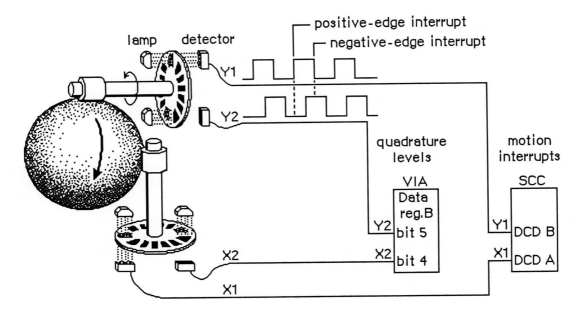

Figure 5. Mouse Mechanism

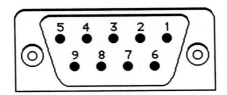

1   Ground
2   +5 volts
3   Ground
4   Mouse X2 (VIA quadrature signal)
5   Mouse X1 (SCC interrupt signal)
6   (not connected)
7   Mouse switch
8   Mouse Y2 (VIA quadrature signal)
9   Mouse Y1 (SCC interrupt signal)

Figure 6. Pinout for Mouse Jack

Warning: Do not draw more than 200 milliamps at +5 volts from all connectors combined.

Diagram

Figure 7 shows a circuit diagram for the mouse port.

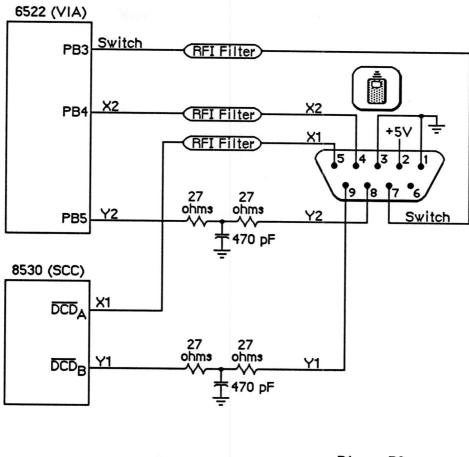

Figure 7. Diagram of Mouse Port

THE KEYBOARD AND KEYPAD

The Macintosh keyboard and numeric keypad each contain an Intel 8021 microprocessor that scans the keys. The 8021 contains ROM and RAM, and is programmed to conform to the interface protocol described below.

The keyboard plugs into the Macintosh through a four-wire RJ-11 telephone-style jack. If a numeric keypad is installed in the system, the keyboard plugs into it and it in turn plugs into the

Macintosh. Figure 8 shows the pinout for the keyboard jack on the Macintosh, on the keyboard itself, and on the numeric keypad.

1	Ground
2	Clock
3	Data
4	+5 volts

Figure 8. Pinout for Keyboard Jack

Warning: Do not draw more than 200 milliamps at +5 volts from all connectors combined.

Keyboard Communication Protocol

The keyboard data line is bidirectional and is driven by whatever device is sending data. The keyboard clock line is driven by the keyboard only. All data transfers are synchronous with the keyboard clock. Each transmission consists of eight bits, with the highest-order bits first.

When sending data to the Macintosh, the keyboard clock transmits eight 330-µsec cycles (160 µsec low, 170 µsec high) on the normally high clock line. It places the data bit on the data line 40 µsec before the falling edge of the clock line and maintains it for 330 µsec. The data bit is clocked into the Macintosh's VIA shift register on the rising edge of the keyboard clock cycle.

When the Macintosh sends data to the keyboard, the keyboard clock transmits eight 400-µsec cycles (180 µsec low, 220 µsec high) on the clock line. On the falling edge of the keyboard clock cycle, the Macintosh places the data bit on the data line and holds it there for 400 µsec. The keyboard reads the data bit 80 µsec after the rising edge of the keyboard clock cycle.

Only the Macintosh can initiate communication over the keyboard lines. On power-up of either the Macintosh or the keyboard, the Macintosh is in charge, and the external device is passive. The Macintosh signals that it's ready to begin communication by pulling the keyboard data line low. Upon detecting this, the keyboard starts clocking and the Macintosh sends a command. The last bit of the command leaves the keyboard data line low; the Macintosh then indicates it's ready to receive the keyboard's response by setting the data line high.

The first command the Macintosh sends out is the Model Number command. The keyboard's response to this command is to reset itself and send back its model number to the Macintosh. If no response is received for 1/2 second, the Macintosh tries the Model Number command again. Once the Macintosh has successfully received a model number from the keyboard, normal operation can begin. The Macintosh sends the Inquiry command; the keyboard sends back a Key Transition response if a key has been pressed or released. If no key transition has occurred after 1/4 second, the keyboard sends back a Null response to let the Macintosh know it's still there. The Macintosh then sends the Inquiry command again. In normal operation, the Macintosh sends out an Inquiry command every 1/4 second. If it receives no response within 1/2 second, it assumes the keyboard is missing or needs resetting, so it begins again with the Model Number command.

There are two other commands the Macintosh can send: the Instant command, which gets an instant keyboard status without the 1/4-second timeout, and the Test command, to perform a keyboard self-test. Here's a list of the commands that can be sent from the Macintosh to the keyboard:

Command name	Value	Keyboard response
Inquiry	$10	Key Transition code or Null ($7B)
Instant	$14	Key Transition code or Null ($7B)
Model Number	$16	Bit 0: 1 Bits 1-3: keyboard model number, 1-8 Bits 4-6: next device number, 1-8 Bit 7: 1 if another device connected
Test	$36	ACK ($7D) or NAK ($77)

The Key Transition responses are sent out by the keyboard as a single byte: Bit 7 high means a key-up transition, and bit 7 low means a key-down. Bit 0 is always high. The Key Transition responses for key-down transitions on the keyboard are shown (in hexadecimal) in Figure 9. Note that these response codes are different from the key codes returned by the keyboard driver software. The keyboard driver strips off bit 7 of the response and shifts the result one bit to the right, removing bit 0. For example, response code $33 becomes $19, and $2B becomes $15.

Keypad Communication Protocol

When a numeric keypad is used, it must be inserted *between* the keyboard and the Macintosh; that is, the keypad cable plugs into the jack on the front of the Macintosh, and the keyboard cable plugs into a jack on the numeric keypad. In this configuration, the timings and protocol for the clock and data lines work a little differently: The keypad acts like a keyboard when communicating with the Macintosh, and acts like a Macintosh when communicating over the separate clock and data lines going to the keyboard. All commands from the Macintosh are now received by the keypad instead of the keyboard, and only the keypad can communicate directly with the keyboard.

When the Macintosh sends out an Inquiry command, one of two things may happen, depending on the state of the keypad. If no key transitions have occurred on the keypad since the last Inquiry, the keypad sends an Inquiry command to the keyboard and, later, retransmits the keyboard's response back to the Macintosh. But if a key transition has occurred on the keypad, the keypad responds to an Inquiry by sending back the Keypad response ($79) to the Macintosh. In that case, the Macintosh immediately sends an Instant command, and this time the keypad sends back its own Key Transition response. As with the keyboard, bit 7 high means key-up and bit 7 low means key-down.

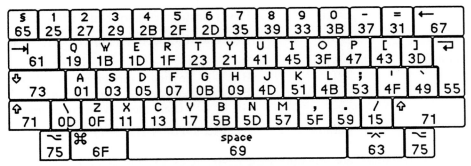

U.S. keyboard

International keyboard (Great Britain key caps shown)

Keypad (U.S. key caps shown)

Figure 9. Key-Down Transitions

The Key Transition responses for key-down transitions on the keypad are shown in Figure 9. Again, note that these response codes are different from the key codes returned by the keyboard driver software. The keyboard driver strips off bit 7 of the response and shifts the result one bit to the right, removing bit 0.

THE DISK INTERFACE

The Macintosh disk interface uses a design similar to that used on the Apple II and Apple III computers, employing the Apple custom IWM chip. Another custom chip called the Analog Signal Generator (ASG) reads the disk speed buffer in RAM and generates voltages that control the disk speed. Together with the VIA, the IWM and the ASG generate all the signals necessary to read, write, format, and eject the 3 1/2-inch disks used by the Macintosh.

The IWM controls four of the disk state-control lines (called CA0, CA1, CA2, and LSTRB), chooses which drive (internal or external) to enable, and processes the disk's read-data and write-data signals. The VIA provides another disk state-control line called SEL.

A buffer in RAM (actually the low-order bytes of words in the sound buffer) is read by the ASG to generate a pulse-width modulated signal that's used to control the speed of the disk motor. The Macintosh Operating System uses this speed control to allow it to store more sectors of information in the tracks closer to the edge of the disk by running the disk motor at slower speeds.

Figure 10 shows the DB-19 pinout for the external disk jack at the back of the Macintosh.

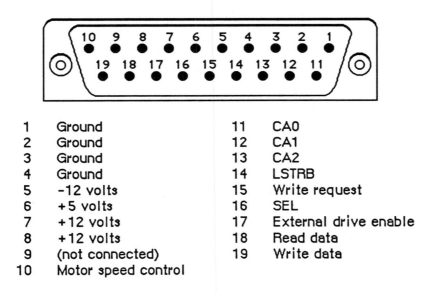

1	Ground	11	CA0
2	Ground	12	CA1
3	Ground	13	CA2
4	Ground	14	LSTRB
5	-12 volts	15	Write request
6	+5 volts	16	SEL
7	+12 volts	17	External drive enable
8	+12 volts	18	Read data
9	(not connected)	19	Write data
10	Motor speed control		

Figure 10. Pinout for Disk Jack

Warning: This connector was designed for a Macintosh 3 1/2-inch disk drive, which represents a load of 500 milliamps at +12 volts, 500 milliamps at +5 volts, and 0 milliamps at −12 volts. If any other device uses this connector, it must not exceed these loads by more than 100 milliamps at +12 volts, 200 milliamps at +5 volts, and 10 milliamps at −12 volts, including loads from all other connectors combined.

Controlling the Disk State-Control Lines

The IWM contains registers that can be used by the software to control the state-control lines leading out to the disk. By reading or writing certain memory locations, you can turn these state-control lines on or off. Other locations set various IWM internal states. The locations are given in the following table as offsets from the constant dBase, the base address of the IWM; this base address is also available in a global variable named IWM. The IWM is on the lower byte of the data bus, so use odd-addressed byte accesses only.

IWM line	Location to turn line on	Location to turn line off
Disk state-control lines:		
CA0	dBase+ph0H	dBase+ph0L
CA1	dBase+ph1H	dBase+ph1L
CA2	dBase+ph2H	dBase+ph2L
LSTRB	dBase+ph3H	dBase+ph3L
Disk enable line:		
ENABLE	dBase+motorOn	dBase+motorOff
IWM internal states:		
SELECT	dBase+extDrive	dBase+intDrive
Q6	dBase+q6H	dBase+q6L
Q7	dBase+q7H	dBase+q7L

To turn one of the lines on or off, do any kind of memory byte access (read or write) to the respective location.

The CA0, CA1, and CA2 lines are used along with the SEL line from the VIA to select from among the registers and data signals in the disk drive. The LSTRB line is used when writing control information to the disk registers (as described below), and the ENABLE line enables the selected disk drive. SELECT is an IWM internal line that chooses which disk drive can be enabled: On selects the external drive, and off selects the internal drive. The Q6 and Q7 lines are used to set up the internal state of the IWM for reading disk register information, as well as for reading or writing actual disk-storage data.

You can read information from several registers in the disk drive to find out whether the disk is locked, whether a disk is in the drive, whether the head is at track 0, how many heads the drive has, and whether there's a drive connected at all. In turn, you can write to some of these registers to step the head, turn the motor on or off, and eject the disk.

Reading from the Disk Registers

Before you can read from any of the disk registers, you must set up the state of the IWM so that it can pass the data through to the MC68000's memory space where you'll be able to read it. To do that, you must first turn off Q7 by reading or writing dBase+q7L. Then turn on Q6 by accessing dBase+q6H. After that, the IWM will be able to pass data from the disk's RD/SENSE line through to you.

Once you've set up the IWM for disk register access, you must next select which register you want to read. To read one of the disk registers, first enable the drive you want to use (by accessing dBase+intDrive or dBase+extDrive and then dBase+motorOn) and make sure LSTRB is low. Then set CA0, CA1, CA2, and SEL to address the register you want. Once this is done, you can read the disk register data bit in the high-order bit of dBase+q7L. After you've read the data, you may read another disk register by again setting the proper values in CA0, CA1, CA2, and SEL, and then reading dBase+q7L.

Warning: When you're finished reading data from the disk registers, it's important to leave the IWM in a state that the Disk Driver will recognize. To be sure it's in a valid logic state, always turn Q6 back off (by accessing dBase+q6L) after you've finished reading the disk registers.

The following table shows how you must set the disk state-control lines to read from the various disk registers and data signals:

| State-control lines | | | | Register | |
CA2	CA1	CA0	SEL	addressed	Information in register
0	0	0	0	DIRTN	Head step direction
0	0	0	1	CSTIN	Disk in place
0	0	1	0	STEP	Disk head stepping
0	0	1	1	WRTPRT	Disk locked
0	1	0	0	MOTORON	Disk motor running
0	1	0	1	TK0	Head at track 0
0	1	1	1	TACH	Tachometer
1	0	0	0	RDDATA0	Read data, lower head
1	0	0	1	RDDATA1	Read data, upper head
1	1	0	0	SIDES	Single- or double-sided drive
1	1	1	1	DRVIN	Drive installed

Writing to the Disk Registers

To write to a disk register, first be sure that LSTRB is off, then turn on CA0 and CA1. Next, set SEL to 0. Set CA0 and CA1 to the proper values from the table below, then set CA2 to the value you want to write to the disk register. Hold LSTRB high for at least one µsec but not more than one msec (unless you're ejecting a disk) and bring it low again. Be sure that you don't change CA0-CA2 or SEL while LSTRB is high, and that CA0 and CA1 are set high before changing SEL.

The following table shows how you must set the disk state-control lines to write to the various disk registers:

| Control lines | | | Register | |
CA1	CA0	SEL	addressed	Register function
0	0	0	DIRTN	Set stepping direction
0	1	0	STEP	Step disk head one track
1	0	0	MOTORON	Turn on/off disk motor
1	1	0	EJECT	Eject the disk

Explanations of the Disk Registers

The information written to or read from the various disk registers can be interpreted as follows:

- The DIRTN signal sets the direction of subsequent head stepping: 0 causes steps to go toward the inside track (track 79), 1 causes them to go toward the outside track (track 0).

- CSTIN is 0 only when a disk is in the drive.

- Setting STEP to 0 steps the head one full track in the direction last set by DIRTN. When the step is complete (about 12 msec), the disk drive sets STEP back to 1, and then you can step again.

- WRTPRT is 0 whenever the disk is locked. Do not write to a disk unless WRTPRT is 1.

- MOTORON controls the state of the disk motor: 0 turns on the motor, and 1 turns it off. The motor will run only if the drive is enabled and a disk is in place; otherwise, writing to this line will have no effect.

- TKO goes to 0 only if the head is at track 0. This is valid beginning 12 msec after the step that puts it at track 0.

- Writing 1 to EJECT ejects the disk from the drive. To eject a disk, you must hold LSTRB high for at least 1/2 second.

- The current disk speed is available as a pulse train on TACH. The TACH line produces 60 pulses for each rotation of the drive motor. The disk motor speed is controlled by the ASG as it reads the disk speed RAM buffer.

- RDDATA0 and RDDATA1 carry the instantaneous data from the disk head.

- SIDES is always 0 on single-sided drives and 1 on double-sided drives.

- DRVIN is always 0 if the selected disk drive is physically connected to the Macintosh, otherwise it floats to 1.

THE REAL-TIME CLOCK

The Macintosh real-time clock is a custom chip whose interface lines are available through the VIA. The clock contains a four-byte counter that's incremented once each second, as well as a line that can be used by the VIA to generate an interrupt once each second. It also contains 20 bytes of RAM that are powered by a battery when the Macintosh is turned off. These RAM bytes, called **parameter RAM**, contain important data that needs to be preserved even when the system power is not available. The Operating System maintains a copy of parameter RAM that you can access in low memory. To find out how to use the values in parameter RAM, see chapter 13 of Volume II.

Accessing the Clock Chip

The clock is accessed through the following bits of VIA data register B (vBase+vBufB):

```
rTCData      .EQU     0        ;real-time clock serial data line
rTCClk       .EQU     1        ;real-time clock data-clock line
rTCEnb       .EQU     2        ;real-time clock serial enable
```

These three bits constitute a simple serial interface. The rTCData bit is a bidirectional serial data line used to send command and data bytes back and forth. The rTCClk bit is a data-clock line, always driven by the processor (you set it high or low yourself) that regulates the transmission of the data and command bits. The rTCEnb bit is the serial enable line, which signals the real-time clock that the processor is about to send it serial commands and data.

To access the clock chip, you must first enable its serial function. To do this, set the serial enable line (rTCEnb) to 0. Keep the serial enable line low during the entire transaction; if you set it to 1, you'll abort the transfer.

> **Warning:** Be sure you don't alter any of bits 3-7 of VIA data register B during clock serial access.

A command can be either a write request or a read request. After the eight bits of a write request, the clock will expect the next eight bits across the serial data line to be your data for storage into one of the internal registers of the clock. After receiving the eight bits of a read request, the clock will respond by putting eight bits of its data on the serial data line. Commands and data are transferred serially in eight-bit groups over the serial data line, with the high-order bit first and the low-order bit last.

To send a command to the clock, first set the rTCData bit of VIA data direction register B (vBase+vDirB) so that the real-time clock's serial data line will be used for output to the clock. Next, set the rTCClk bit of vBase+vBufB to 0, then set the rTCData bit to the value of the first (high-order) bit of your data byte. Then raise (set to 1) the data-clock bit (rTCClk). Then lower the data-clock, set the serial data line to the next bit, and raise the data-clock line again. After the last bit of your command has been sent in this way, you can either continue by sending your data byte in the same way (if your command was a write request) or switch to receiving a data byte from the clock (if your command was a read request).

To receive a byte of data from the clock, you must first send a command that's a read request. After you've clocked out the last bit of the command, clear the rTCData bit of the data direction register so that the real-time clock's serial data line can be used for input from the clock; then lower the data-clock bit (rTCClk) and read the first (high-order) bit of the clock's data byte on the serial data line. Then raise the data-clock, lower it again, and read the next bit of data. Continue this until all eight bits are read, then raise the serial enable line (rTCEnb), disabling the data transfer.

The following table lists the commands you can send to the clock. A 1 in the high-order bit makes your command a read request; a 0 in the high-order bit makes your command a write request. (In this table, "z" is the bit that determines read or write status, and bits marked "a" are bits whose values depend on what parameter RAM byte you want to address.)

Command byte	Register addressed by the command
z0000001	Seconds register 0 (lowest-order byte)
z0000101	Seconds register 1
z0001001	Seconds register 2
z0001101	Seconds register 3 (highest-order byte)
00110001	Test register (write only)
00110101	Write-protect register (write only)
z010aa01	RAM address 100aa ($10-$13)
z1aaaa01	RAM address 0aaaa ($00-$0F)

Note that the last two bits of a command byte must always be 01.

If the high-order bit (bit 7) of the write-protect register is set, this prevents writing into any other register on the clock chip (including parameter RAM). Clearing the bit allows you to change any values in any registers on the chip. Don't try to read from this register; it's a write-only register.

The two highest-order bits (bits 7 and 6) of the test register are used as device control bits during testing, and should always be set to 0 during normal operation. Setting them to anything else will interfere with normal clock counting. Like the write-protect register, this is a write-only register; don't try to read from it.

All clock data must be sent as full eight-bit bytes, even if only one or two bits are of interest. The rest of the bits may not matter, but you must send them to the clock or the write will be aborted when you raise the serial enable line.

It's important to use the proper sequence if you're writing to the clock's seconds registers. If you write to a given seconds register, there's a chance that the clock may increment the data in the next higher-order register during the write, causing unpredictable results. To avoid this possibility, always write to the registers in low-to-high order. Similarly, the clock data may increment during a read of all four time bytes, which could cause invalid data to be read. To avoid this, always read the time twice (or until you get the same value twice).

Warning: When you've finished reading from the clock registers, always end by doing a final write such as setting the write-protect bit. Failure to do this may leave the clock in a state that will run down the battery more quickly than necessary.

The One-Second Interrupt

The clock also generates a VIA interrupt once each second (if this interrupt is enabled). The enable status for this interrupt can be read from or written to bit 0 of the VIA's interrupt enable register (vBase+vIER). When reading the enable register, a 1 bit indicates the interrupt is enabled, and 0 means it's disabled. Writing $01 to the enable register disables the clock's one-second interrupt (without affecting any other interrupts), while writing $81 enables it again. See chapter 6 of Volume II for more information about writing your own interrupt handlers.

Warning: Be sure when you write to bit 0 of the VIA's interrupt enable register that you don't change any of the other bits.

THE VIA

The Synertek SY6522 **Versatile Interface Adapter** (VIA) controls the keyboard, internal real-time clock, parts of the disk, sound, and mouse interfaces, and various internal Macintosh signals. Its base address is available as the constant vBase and is also stored in a global variable named VIA. The VIA is on the upper byte of the data bus, so use even-addressed byte accesses only.

There are two parallel data registers within the VIA, called A and B, each with a data direction register. There are also several event timers, a clocked shift register, and an interrupt flag register with an interrupt enable register.

Normally you won't have to touch the direction registers, since the Operating System sets them up for you at system startup. A 1 bit in a data direction register means the corresponding bit of the respective data register will be used for output, while a 0 bit means it will be used for input.

Note: For more information on the registers and control structure of the VIA, consult the technical specifications for the SY6522 chip.

VIA Register A

VIA data register A is at vBase+vBufA. The corresponding data direction register is at vBase+vDirA.

Bit(s)	Name	Description
7	vSCCWReq	SCC wait/request
6	vPage2	Alternate screen buffer
5	vHeadSel	Disk SEL line
4	vOverlay	ROM low-memory overlay
3	vSndPg2	Alternate sound buffer
0-2	vSound (mask)	Sound volume

The vSCCWReq bit can signal that the SCC has received a character (used to maintain serial communications during disk accesses, when the CPU's interrupts from the SCC are disabled). The vPage2 bit controls which screen buffer is being displayed, and the vHeadSel bit is the SEL control line used by the disk interface. The vOverlay bit (used only during system startup) can be used to place another image of ROM at the bottom of memory, where RAM usually is (RAM moves to $600000). The sound buffer is selected by the vSndPg2 bit. Finally, the vSound bits control the sound volume.

VIA Register B

VIA data register B is at vBase+vBufB. The corresponding data direction register is at vBase+vDirB.

Bit	Name	Description
7	vSndEnb	Sound enable/disable
6	vH4	Horizontal blanking
5	vY2	Mouse Y2
4	vX2	Mouse X2
3	vSW	Mouse switch
2	rTCEnb	Real-time clock serial enable
1	rTCClk	Real-time clock data-clock line
0	rTCData	Real-time clock serial data

The vSndEnb bit turns the sound generator on or off, and the vH4 bit is set when the video beam is in its horizontal blanking period. The vY2 and vX2 bits read the quadrature signals from the Y (vertical) and X (horizontal) directions, respectively, of the mouse's motion lines. The vSW bit reads the mouse switch. The rTCEnb, rTCClk, and rTCData bits control and read the real-time clock.

The VIA Peripheral Control Register

The VIA's peripheral control register, at vBase+vPCR, allows you to set some very low-level parameters (such as positive-edge or negative-edge triggering) dealing with the keyboard data and clock interrupts, the one-second real-time clock interrupt line, and the vertical blanking interrupt.

Bit(s)	Description
5-7	Keyboard data interrupt control
4	Keyboard clock interrupt control
1-3	One-second interrupt control
0	Vertical blanking interrupt control

The VIA Timers

The timers controlled by the VIA are called timer 1 and timer 2. Timer 1 is used to time various events having to do with the Macintosh sound generator. Timer 2 is used by the Disk Driver to time disk I/O events. If either timer isn't being used by the Operating System, you're free to use it for your own purposes. When a timer counts down to 0, an interrupt will be generated if the proper interrupt enable has been set. See chapter 6 of Volume II for information about writing your own interrupt handlers.

To start one of the timers, store the appropriate values in the high- and low-order bytes of the timer counter (or the timer 1 latches, for multiple use of the value). The counters and latches are at the following locations:

Location	Contents
vBase+vT1C	Timer 1 counter (low-order byte)
vBase+vT1CH	Timer 1 counter (high-order byte)
vBase+vT1L	Timer 1 latch (low-order byte)
vBase+vT1LH	Timer 1 latch (high-order byte)
vBase+vT2C	Timer 2 counter (low-order byte)
vBase+vT2CH	Timer 2 counter (high-order byte)

Note: When setting a timer, it's not enough to simply store a full word to the high-order address, because the high- and low-order bytes of the counters are not adjacent. You must explicitly do *two* stores, one for the high-order byte and one for the low-order byte.

VIA Interrupts

The VIA (through its IRQ line) can cause a level-0 processor interrupt whenever one of the following occurs: Timer 1 or timer 2 times out; the keyboard is clocking a bit in through its serial port; the shift register for the keyboard serial interface has finished shifting in or out; the vertical blanking interval is beginning; or the one-second clock has ticked. For more information on how to use these interrupts, see chapter 6 of Volume II.

The interrupt flag register at vBase+vIFR contains flag bits that are set whenever the interrupt corresponding to that bit has occurred. The Operating System uses these flags to determine which device has caused an interrupt. Bit 7 of the interrupt flag register is not really a flag: It remains set (and the IRQ line to the processor is held low) as long as any enabled VIA interrupt is occurring.

Bit	Interrupting device
7	IRQ (all enabled VIA interrupts)
6	Timer 1
5	Timer 2
4	Keyboard clock
3	Keyboard data bit
2	Keyboard data ready
1	Vertical blanking interrupt
0	One-second interrupt

The interrupt enable register, at vBase+vIER, lets you enable or disable any of these interrupts. If an interrupt is disabled, its bit in the interrupt flag register will continue to be set whenever that interrupt occurs, but it won't affect the IRQ flag, nor will it interrupt the processor.

The bits in the interrupt enable register are arranged just like those in the interrupt flag register, except for bit 7. When you write to the interrupt enable register, bit 7 is "enable/disable": If bit 7 is a 1, each 1 in bits 0-6 enables the corresponding interrupt; if bit 7 is a 0, each 1 in bits 0-6 disables that interrupt. In either case, 0's in bits 0-6 do not change the status of those interrupts. Bit 7 is always read as a 1.

Other VIA Registers

The shift register, at vBase+vSR, contains the eight bits of data that have been shifted in or that will be shifted out over the keyboard data line.

The auxiliary control register, at vBase+vACR, is described in the SY6522 documentation. It controls various parameters having to do with the timers and the shift register.

SYSTEM STARTUP

When power is first supplied to the Macintosh, a carefully orchestrated sequence of events takes place.

First, the processor is held in a wait state while a series of circuits gets the system ready for operation. The VIA and IWM are initialized, and the mapping of ROM and RAM are altered temporarily by setting the overlay bit in VIA data register A. This places the ROM starting at the normal ROM location $400000, and a duplicate image of the same ROM starting at address 0 (where RAM normally is), while RAM is placed starting at $600000. Under this mapping, the Macintosh software executes out of the normal ROM locations above $400000, but the MC68000 can obtain some critical low-memory vectors from the ROM image it finds at address 0.

Next, a memory test and several other system tests take place. After the system is fully tested and initialized, the software clears the VIA's overlay bit, mapping the system RAM back where it belongs, starting at address 0. Then the disk startup process begins.

First the internal disk is checked: If there's a disk inserted, the system attempts to read it. If no disk is in the internal drive and there's an external drive with an inserted disk, the system will try to read that one. Otherwise, the question-mark disk icon is displayed until a disk is inserted. If the disk startup fails for some reason, the "sad Macintosh" icon is displayed and the Macintosh goes into an endless loop until it's turned off again.

Once a readable disk has been inserted, the first two sectors (containing the system startup blocks) are read in and the normal disk load begins.

SUMMARY

Warning: This information applies only to the Macintosh 128K and 512K, not to the Macintosh XL.

Constants

```
; VIA base addresses

vBase      .EQU    $EFE1FE      ;main base for VIA chip (in variable VIA)
aVBufB     .EQU    vBase        ;register B base
aVBufA     .EQU    $EFFFFE      ;register A base
aVBufM     .EQU    aVBufB       ;register containing mouse signals
aVIFR      .EQU    $EFFBFE      ;interrupt flag register
aVIER      .EQU    $EFFDFE      ;interrupt enable register

; Offsets from vBase

vBufB      .EQU    512*0        ;register B (zero offset)
vDirB      .EQU    512*2        ;register B direction register
vDirA      .EQU    512*3        ;register A direction register
vT1C       .EQU    512*4        ;timer 1 counter (low-order byte)
vT1CH      .EQU    512*5        ;timer 1 counter (high-order byte)
vT1L       .EQU    512*6        ;timer 1 latch (low-order byte)
vT1LH      .EQU    512*7        ;timer 1 latch (high-order byte)
vT2C       .EQU    512*8        ;timer 2 counter (low-order byte)
vT2CH      .EQU    512*9        ;timer 2 counter (high-order byte)
vSR        .EQU    512*10       ;shift register (keyboard)
vACR       .EQU    512*11       ;auxiliary control register
vPCR       .EQU    512*12       ;peripheral control register
vIFR       .EQU    512*13       ;interrupt flag register
vIER       .EQU    512*14       ;interrupt enable register
vBufA      .EQU    512*15       ;register A

; VIA register A constants

vAOut      .EQU    $7F          ;direction register A:  1 bits = outputs
vAInit     .EQU    $7B          ;initial value for vBufA (medium volume)
vSound     .EQU    7            ;sound volume bits

; VIA register A bit numbers

vSndPg2    .EQU    3            ;0 = alternate sound buffer
vOverlay   .EQU    4            ;1 = ROM overlay (system startup only)
vHeadSel   .EQU    5            ;disk SEL control line
vPage2     .EQU    6            ;0 = alternate screen buffer
vSCCWReq   .EQU    7            ;SCC wait/request line
```

```
; VIA register B constants

vBOut       .EQU    $87         ;direction register B:  1 bits = outputs
vBInit      .EQU    $07         ;initial value for vBufB

; VIA register B bit numbers

rTCData     .EQU    0           ;real-time clock serial data line
rTCClk      .EQU    1           ;real-time clock data-clock line
rTCEnb      .EQU    2           ;real-time clock serial enable
vSW         .EQU    3           ;0 = mouse button is down
vX2         .EQU    4           ;mouse X quadrature level
vY2         .EQU    5           ;mouse Y quadrature level
vH4         .EQU    6           ;1 = horizontal blanking
vSndEnb     .EQU    7           ;0 = sound enabled, 1 = disabled

; SCC base addresses

sccRBase    .EQU    $9FFFF8     ;SCC base read address (in variable SCCRd)
sccWBase    .EQU    $BFFFF9     ;SCC base write address (in variable SCCWr)

; Offsets from SCC base addresses

aData       .EQU    6           ;channel A data in or out
aCtl        .EQU    2           ;channel A control
bData       .EQU    4           ;channel B data in or out
bCtl        .EQU    0           ;channel B control

; Bit numbers for control register RR0

rxBF        .EQU    0           ;1 = SCC receive buffer full
txBE        .EQU    2           ;1 = SCC send buffer empty

; IWM base address

dBase       .EQU    $DFE1FF     ;IWM base address (in variable IWM)

; Offsets from dBase

ph0L        .EQU    512*0       ;CA0 off (0)
ph0H        .EQU    512*1       ;CA0 on (1)
ph1L        .EQU    512*2       ;CA1 off (0)
ph1H        .EQU    512*3       ;CA1 on (1)
ph2L        .EQU    512*4       ;CA2 off (0)
ph2H        .EQU    512*5       ;CA2 on (1)
ph3L        .EQU    512*6       ;LSTRB off (low)
ph3H        .EQU    512*7       ;LSTRB on (high)
mtrOff      .EQU    512*8       ;disk enable off
mtrOn       .EQU    512*9       ;disk enable on
intDrive    .EQU    512*10      ;select internal drive
extDrive    .EQU    512*11      ;select external drive
q6L         .EQU    512*12      ;Q6 off
```

```
q6H          .EQU     512*13      ;Q6 on
q7L          .EQU     512*14      ;Q7 off
q7H          .EQU     512*15      ;Q7 on

; Screen and sound addresses for 512K Macintosh (will also work for
; 128K, since addresses wrap)

screenLow    .EQU     $7A700      ;top left corner of main screen buffer
soundLow     .EQU     $7FD00      ;main sound buffer (in variable SoundBase)
pwmBuffer    .EQU     $7FD01      ;main disk speed buffer
ovlyRAM      .EQU     $600000     ;RAM start address when overlay is set
ovlyScreen   .EQU     $67A700     ;screen start with overlay set
romStart     .EQU     $400000     ;ROM start address (in variable ROMBase)
```

Variables

ROMBase	Base address of ROM
SoundBase	Address of main sound buffer
SCCRd	SCC read base address
SCCWr	SCC write base address
IWM	IWM base address
VIA	VIA base address

Exception Vectors

Location	Purpose
$00	Reset: initial stack pointer (not a vector)
$04	Reset: initial vector
$08	Bus error
$0C	Address error
$10	Illegal instruction
$14	Divide by zero
$18	CHK instruction
$1C	TRAPV instruction
$20	Privilege violation
$24	Trace interrupt
$28	Line 1010 emulator
$2C	Line 1111 emulator
$30-$3B	Unassigned (reserved)
$3C	Uninitialized interrupt
$40-$5F	Unassigned (reserved)

Location	Purpose
$60	Spurious interrupt
$64	VIA interrupt
$68	SCC interrupt
$6C	VIA+SCC vector (temporary)
$70	Interrupt switch
$74	Interrupt switch + VIA
$78	Interrupt switch + SCC
$7C	Interrupt switch + VIA + SCC
$80-$BF	TRAP instructions
$C0-$FF	Unassigned (reserved)

3 SUMMARY

3 Summary

ABOUT THIS CHAPTER

This chapter includes all the summaries that appear at the end of other chapters of *Inside Macintosh*. The summaries are arranged in alphabetical order of the part of the Toolbox or Operating System being summarized.

Note: The summaries of the Event Managers are listed under "Event Manager, Operating System" and "Event Manager, Toolbox". The Toolbox and Operating System Utilities are listed similarly.

The last section of this chapter, "Assembly Language", contains information for assembly-language programmers only. It lists some miscellaneous global variables along with hardware-related definitions for the Macintosh 128K and 512K.

APPLETALK MANAGER

Constants

```
CONST lapSize = 20;     {ABusRecord size for ALAP}
      ddpSize = 26;     {ABusRecord size for DDP}
      nbpSize = 26;     {ABusRecord size for NBP}
      atpSize = 56;     {ABusRecord size for ATP}
```

Data Types

```
TYPE  ABProtoType  = (lapProto,ddpProto,nbpProto,atpProto);

      ABRecHandle = ^ABRecPtr;
      ABRecPtr    = ^ABusRecord;
      ABusRecord  =
        RECORD
            abOpcode:       ABCallType;   {type of call}
            abResult:       INTEGER;      {result code}
            abUserReference: LONGINT;     {for your use}
            CASE ABProtoType OF
              lapProto:
                (lapAddress:  LAPAdrBlock; {destination or source node ID}
                 lapReqCount: INTEGER;    {length of frame data or buffer }
                                          { size in bytes}
                 lapActCount  INTEGER;    {number of frame data bytes }
                                          { actually received}
                 lapDataPtr:  Ptr);       {pointer to frame data or pointer }
                                          { to buffer}

              ddpProto:
                (ddpType:     Byte;       {DDP protocol type}
                 ddpSocket:   Byte;       {source or listening socket number}
                 ddpAddress:  AddrBlock;  {destination or source socket address}
                 ddpReqCount: INTEGER;    {length of datagram data or buffer }
                                          { size in bytes}
                 ddpActCount: INTEGER;    {number of bytes actually received}
                 ddpDataPtr:  Ptr;        {pointer to buffer}
                 ddpNodeID:   Byte);      {original destination node ID}
              nbpProto:
                (nbpEntityPtr:      EntityPtr;   {pointer to entity name}
                 nbpBufPtr:         Ptr;         {pointer to buffer}
                 nbpBufSize:        INTEGER;     {buffer size in bytes}
                 nbpDataField:      INTEGER;     {number of addresses or }
                                                 { socket number}
                 nbpAddress:        AddrBlock;   {socket address}
                 nbpRetransmitInfo: RetransType); {retransmission information}
```

```
        atpProto:
           (atpSocket:        Byte;          {listening or responding socket }
                                             { number}
             atpAddress:      AddrBlock;     {destination or source socket }
                                             { address}
             atpReqCount:     INTEGER;       {request size or buffer size}
             atpDataPtr       Ptr;           {pointer to buffer}
             atpRspBDSPtr:    BDSPtr;        {pointer to response BDS}
             atpBitMap:       BitMapType;    {transaction bit map}
             atpTransID:      INTEGER;       {transaction ID}
             atpActCount:     INTEGER;       {number of bytes actually received}
             atpUserData:     LONGINT;       {user bytes}
             atpXO:           BOOLEAN;       {exactly-once flag}
             atpEOM:          BOOLFAN;       {end-of-message flag}
             atpTimeOut:      Byte;          {retry timeout interval in seconds}
             atpRetries:      Byte;          {maximum number of retries}
             atpNumBufs:      Byte;          {number of elements in response }
                                             { BDS or number of response }
                                             { packets sent}
             atpNumRsp:       Byte;          {number of response packets }
                                             { received or sequence number}
             atpBDSSize:      Byte;          {number of elements in response BDS}
             atpRspUData:     LONGINT;       {user bytes sent or received in }
                                             { transaction response}
             atpRspBuf:       Ptr;           {pointer to response message buffer}
             atpRspSize:      INTEGER);      {size of response message buffer}
        END;


ABCallType =   (tLAPRead,tLAPWrite,tDDPRead,tDDPWrite,tNBPLookup,
                tNBPConfirm,tNBPRegister,tATPSndRequest,
                tATPGetRequest,tATPSdRsp,tATPAddRsp,tATPRequest,
                tATPResponse);


LAPAdrBlock =   PACKED RECORD
                    dstNodeID:     Byte;      {destination node ID}
                    srcNodeID:     Byte;      {source node ID}
                    lapProtType:   ABByte     {ALAP protocol type}
                END;


ABByte = 1..127; {ALAP protocol type}


AddrBlock =   PACKED RECORD
                  aNet:      INTEGER;   {network number}
                  aNode:     Byte;      {node ID}
                  aSocket:   Byte       {socket number}
              END;


BDSPtr      =   ^BDSType;
BDSType     =   ARRAY[0..7] OF BDSElement; {response BDS}
```

```
BDSElement = RECORD
                buffSize:  INTEGER;  {buffer size in bytes}
                buffPtr:   Ptr;      {pointer to buffer}
                dataSize:  INTEGER;  {number of bytes actually received}
                userBytes: LONGINT   {user bytes}
             END;


BitMapType = PACKED ARRAY[0..7] OF BOOLEAN;


EntityPtr  = ^EntityName;
EntityName = RECORD
                objStr:   Str32;  {object}
                typeStr:  Str32;  {type}
                zoneStr:  Str32   {zone}
             END;


Str32 = STRING[32];


RetransType =
     PACKED RECORD
        retransInterval: Byte;  {retransmit interval in 8-tick units}
        retransCount:    Byte   {total number of attempts}
     END;
```

Routines [Not in ROM]

Opening and Closing AppleTalk

```
FUNCTION MPPOpen :  OSErr;
FUNCTION MPPClose :  OSErr;
```

AppleTalk Link Access Protocol

```
FUNCTION LAPOpenProtocol  (theLAPType: ABByte; protoPtr: Ptr) : OSErr;
FUNCTION LAPCloseProtocol (theLAPType: ABByte) : OSErr;

FUNCTION LAPWrite (abRecord: ABRecHandle; async: BOOLEAN) : OSErr;
```

←	abOpcode	{always tLAPWrite}
←	abResult	{result code}
→	abUserReference	{for your use}
→	lapAddress.dstNodeID	{destination node ID}
→	lapAddress.lapProtType	{ALAP protocol type}
→	lapReqCount	{length of frame data}
→	lapDataPtr	{pointer to frame data}

```
FUNCTION LAPRead (abRecord: ABRecHandle; async: BOOLEAN) : OSErr;
```
←	abOpcode	{always tLAPRead}
←	abResult	{result code}
→	abUserReference	{for your use}
←	lapAddress.dstNodeID	{destination node ID}
←	lapAddress.srcNodeID	{source node ID}
→	lapAddress.lapProtType	{ALAP protocol type}
→	lapReqCount	{buffer size in bytes}
←	lapActCount	{number of frame data bytes actually received}
→	lapDataPtr	{pointer to buffer}

```
FUNCTION LAPRdCancel (abRecord: ABRecHandle) : OSErr;
```

Datagram Delivery Protocol

```
FUNCTION DDPOpenSocket  (VAR theSocket: Byte; sktListener: Ptr) : OSErr;
FUNCTION DDPCloseSocket (theSocket: Byte) : OSErr;

FUNCTION DDPWrite (abRecord: ABRecHandle; doChecksum: BOOLEAN; async:
                   BOOLEAN) : OSErr;
```
←	abOpcode	{always tDDPWrite}
←	abResult	{result code}
→	abUserReference	{for your use}
→	ddpType	{DDP protocol type}
→	ddpSocket	{source socket number}
→	ddpAddress	{destination socket address}
→	ddpReqCount	{length of datagram data}
→	ddpDataPtr	{pointer to buffer}

```
FUNCTION DDPRead (abRecord: ABRecHandle; retCksumErrs: BOOLEAN; async:
                  BOOLEAN) : OSErr;
```
←	abOpcode	{always tDDPRead}
←	abResult	{result code}
→	abUserReference	{for your use}
←	ddpType	{DDP protocol type}
→	ddpSocket	{listening socket number}
←	ddpAddress	{source socket address}
→	ddpReqCount	{buffer size in bytes}
←	ddpActCount	{number of bytes actually received}
→	ddpDataPtr	{pointer to buffer}
←	ddpNodeID	{original destination node ID}

```
FUNCTION DDPRdCancel (abRecord: ABRecHandle) : OSErr;
```

AppleTalk Transaction Protocol

```
FUNCTION ATPLoad :        OSErr;
FUNCTION ATPUnload :      OSErr;
FUNCTION ATPOpenSocket  (addrRcvd: AddrBlock; VAR atpSocket: Byte) : OSErr;
FUNCTION ATPCloseSocket (atpSocket: Byte) : OSErr;
```

```
FUNCTION ATPSndRequest (abRecord: ABRecHandle; async: BOOLEAN) : OSErr;
```

←	abOpcode	{always tATPSndRequest}
←	abResult	{result code}
→	abUserReference	{for your use}
→	atpAddress	{destination socket address}
→	atpReqCount	{request size in bytes}
→	atpDataPtr	{pointer to buffer}
→	atpRspBDSPtr	{pointer to response BDS}
→	atpUserData	{user bytes}
→	atpXO	{exactly-once flag}
←	atpEOM	{end-of-message flag}
→	atpTimeOut	{retry timeout interval in seconds}
→	atpRetries	{maximum number of retries}
→	atpNumBufs	{number of elements in response BDS}
←	atpNumRsp	{number of response packets actually received}

```
FUNCTION ATPRequest (abRecord: ABRecHandle; async: BOOLEAN) : OSErr;
```

←	abOpcode	{always tATPRequest}
←	abResult	{result code}
→	abUserReference	{for your use}
→	atpAddress	{destination socket address}
→	atpReqCount	{request size in bytes}
→	atpDataPtr	{pointer to buffer}
←	atpActCount	{number of bytes actually received}
→	atpUserData	{user bytes}
→	atpXO	{exactly-once flag}
←	atpEOM	{end-of-message flag}
→	atpTimeOut	{retry timeout interval in seconds}
→	atpRetries	{maximum number of retries}
←	atpRspUData	{user bytes received in transaction response}
→	atpRspBuf	{pointer to response message buffer}
→	atpRspSize	{size of response message buffer}

```
FUNCTION ATPReqCancel (abRecord: ABRecHandle; async: BOOLEAN) : OSErr;

FUNCTION ATPGetRequest (abRecord: ABRecHandle; async: BOOLEAN) : OSErr;
```

←	abOpcode	{always tATPGetRequest}
←	abResult	{result code}
→	abUserReference	{for your use}
→	atpSocket	{listening socket number}
←	atpAddress	{source socket address}
→	atpReqCount	{buffer size in bytes}
→	atpDataPtr	{pointer to buffer}
←	atpBitMap	{transaction bit map}
←	atpTransID	{transaction ID}
←	atpActCount	{number of bytes actually received}
←	atpUserData	{user bytes}
←	atpXO	{exactly-once flag}

```
FUNCTION ATPSndRsp (abRecord: ABRecHandle; async: BOOLEAN) : OSErr;
```
←	abOpcode	{always tATPSdRsp}
←	abResult	{result code}
→	abUserReference	{for your use}
→	atpSocket	{responding socket number}
→	atpAddress	{destination socket address}
→	atpRspBDSPtr	{pointer to response BDS}
→	atpTransID	{transaction ID}
→	atpEOM	{end-of-message flag}
→	atpNumBufs	{number of response packets being sent}
→	atpBDSSize	{number of elements in response BDS}

```
FUNCTION ATPAddRsp (abRecord: ABRecHandle) : OSErr;
```
←	abOpcode	{always tATPAddRsp}
←	abResult	{result code}
→	abUserReference	{for your use}
→	atpSocket	{responding socket number}
→	atpAddress	{destination socket address}
→	atpReqCount	{buffer size in bytes}
→	atpDataPtr	{pointer to buffer}
→	atpTransID	{transaction ID}
→	atpUserData	{user bytes}
→	atpEOM	{end-of-message flag}
→	atpNumRsp	{sequence number}

```
FUNCTION ATPResponse (abRecord: ABRecHandle; async: BOOLEAN) : OSErr;
```
←	abOpcode	{always tATPResponse}
←	abResult	{result code}
→	abUserReference	{for your use}
→	atpSocket	{responding socket number}
→	atpAddress	{destination socket address}
→	atpTransID	{transaction ID)
→	atpRspUData	{user bytes sent in transaction response}
→	atpRspBuf	{pointer to response message buffer}
→	atpRspSize	{size of response message buffer}

```
FUNCTION ATPRspCancel (abRecord: ABRecHandle; async: BOOLEAN) : OSErr;
```

Name-Binding Protocol

```
FUNCTION NBPRegister (abRecord: ABRecHandle; async: BOOLEAN) : OSErr;
```
←	abOpcode	{always tNBPRegister}
←	abResult	{result code}
→	abUserReference	{for your use}
→	nbpEntityPtr	{pointer to entity name}
→	nbpBufPtr	{pointer to buffer}
→	nbpBufSize	{buffer size in bytes}
→	nbpAddress.aSocket	{socket address}
→	nbpRetransmitInfo	{retransmission information}

```
FUNCTION NBPLookup (abRecord: ABRecHandle; async: BOOLEAN) : OSErr;
```
←	abOpcode	{always tNBPLookup}
←	abResult	{result code}
→	abUserReference	{for your use}
→	nbpEntityPtr	{pointer to entity name}
→	nbpBufPtr	{pointer to buffer}
→	nbpBufSize	{buffer size in bytes}
↔	nbpDataField	{number of addresses received}
→	nbpRetransmitInfo	{retransmission information}

```
FUNCTION NBPExtract (theBuffer: Ptr; numInBuf: INTEGER; whichOne:
                     INTEGER; VAR abEntity: EntityName; VAR address:
                     AddrBlock) : OSErr;
```

```
FUNCTION NBPConfirm (abRecord: ABRecHandle; async: BOOLEAN) : OSErr;
```
←	abOpcode	{always tNBPConfirm}
←	abResult	{result code}
→	abUserReference	{for your use}
→	nbpEntityPtr	{pointer to entity name}
←	nbpDataField	{socket number}
→	nbpAddress	{socket address}
→	nbpRetransmitInfo	{retransmission information}

```
FUNCTION NBPRemove (abEntity: EntityPtr) : OSErr;
FUNCTION NBPLoad :    OSErr;
FUNCTION NBPUnload : OSErr;
```

Miscellaneous Routines

```
FUNCTION GetNodeAddress (VAR myNode,myNet: INTEGER) : OSErr;
FUNCTION IsMPPOpen :     BOOLEAN;
FUNCTION IsATPOpen :     BOOLEAN;
```

Result Codes

Name	Value	Meaning
atpBadRsp	−3107	Bad response from ATPRequest
atpLenErr	−3106	ATP response message too large
badATPSkt	−1099	ATP bad responding socket
badBuffNum	−1100	ATP bad sequence number
buf2SmallErr	−3101	ALAP frame too large for buffer DDP datagram too large for buffer
cbNotFound	−1102	ATP control block not found
cksumErr	−3103	DDP bad checksum
ddpLenErr	−92	DDP datagram or ALAP data length too big

Name	Value	Meaning
ddpSktErr	−91	DDP socket error: socket already active; not a well-known socket; socket table full; all dynamic socket numbers in use
excessCollsns	−95	ALAP no CTS received after 32 RTS's, or line sensed in use 32 times (not necessarily caused by collisions)
extractErr	−3104	NBP can't find tuple in buffer
lapProtErr	−94	ALAP error attaching/detaching ALAP protocol type: attach error when ALAP protocol type is negative, not in range, already in table, or when table is full; detach error when ALAP protocol type isn't in table
nbpBuffOvr	−1024	NBP buffer overflow
nbpConfDiff	−1026	NBP name confirmed for different socket
nbpDuplicate	−1027	NBP duplicate name already exists
nbpNISErr	−1029	NBP names information socket error
nbpNoConfirm	−1025	NBP name not confirmed
nbpNotFound	−1028	NBP name not found
noBridgeErr	−93	No bridge found
noDataArea	−1104	Too many outstanding ATP calls
noErr	0	No error
noMPPError	−3102	MPP driver not installed
noRelErr	−1101	ATP no release received
noSendResp	−1103	ATPAddRsp issued before ATPSndRsp
portInUse	−97	Driver Open error, port already in use
portNotCf	−98	Driver Open error, port not configured for this connection
readQErr	−3105	Socket or protocol type invalid or not found in table
recNotFnd	−3108	ABRecord not found
reqAborted	−1105	Request aborted
reqFailed	−1096	ATPSndRequest failed: retry count exceeded
sktClosedErr	−3109	Asynchronous call aborted because socket was closed before call was completed
tooManyReqs	−1097	ATP too many concurrent requests
tooManySkts	−1098	ATP too many responding sockets

3 Summary

Assembly-Language Information

Constants

```
; Serial port use types

useFree         .EQU    0       ;unconfigured
useATalk        .EQU    1       ;configured for AppleTalk
useASync        .EQU    2       ;configured for the Serial Driver

; Bit in PortBUse for .ATP driver status

atpLoadedBit    .EQU    4       ;set if .ATP driver is opened

; Unit numbers for AppleTalk drivers

mppUnitNum      .EQU    9       ;.MPP driver
atpUnitNum      .EQU    10      ;.ATP driver

; csCode values for Control calls (MPP)

writeLAP        .EQU    243
detachPH        .EQU    244
attachPH        .EQU    245
writeDDP        .EQU    246
closeSkt        .EQU    247
openSkt         .EQU    248
loadNBP         .EQU    249
confirmName     .EQU    250
lookupName      .EQU    251
removeName      .EQU    252
registerName    .EQU    253
killNBP         .EQU    254
unloadNBP       .EQU    255

; csCode values for Control calls (ATP)

relRspCB        .EQU    249
closeATPSkt     .EQU    250
addResponse     .EQU    251
sendResponse    .EQU    252
getRequest      .EQU    253
openATPSkt      .EQU    254
sendRequest     .EQU    255
relTCB          .EQU    256

; ALAP header

lapDstAdr       .EQU    0       ;destination node ID
lapSrcAdr       .EQU    1       ;source node ID
lapType         .EQU    2       ;ALAP protocol type
```

```
; ALAP header size

lapHdSz          .EQU     3

; ALAP protocol type values

shortDDP         .EQU     1         ;short DDP header
longDDP          .EQU     2         ;long DDP header

; Long DDP header

ddpHopCnt        .EQU     0         ;count of bridges passed (4 bits)
ddpLength        .EQU     0         ;datagram length (10 bits)
ddpChecksum      .EQU     2         ;checksum
ddpDstNet        .EQU     4         ;destination network number
ddpSrcNet        .EQU     6         ;source network number
ddpDstNode       .EQU     8         ;destination node ID
ddpSrcNode       .EQU     9         ;source node ID
ddpDstSkt        .EQU     10        ;destination socket number
ddpSrcSkt        .EQU     11        ;source socket number
ddpType          .EQU     12        ;DDP protocol type

; DDP long header size

ddpHSzLong       .EQU     ddpType+1

; Short DDP header

ddpLength        .EQU     0                     ;datagram length
sDDPDstSkt       .EQU     ddpChecksum           ;destination socket number
sDDPSrcSkt       .EQU     sDDPDstSkt+1          ;source socket number
sDDPType         .EQU     sDDPSrcSkt+1          ;DDP protocol type

; DDP short header size

ddpHSzShort      .EQU     sDDPType+1

; Mask for datagram length

ddpLenMask       .EQU     $03FF

; Maximum size of DDP data

ddpMaxData       .EQU     586

; ATP header

atpControl       .EQU     0         ;control information
atpBitMap        .EQU     1         ;bit map
atpRespNo        .EQU     1         ;sequence number
atpTransID       .EQU     2         ;transaction ID
atpUserData      .EQU     4         ;user bytes
```

3 Summary

```
; ATP header size

atpHdSz          .EQU    8

; DDP protocol type for ATP packets

atp              .EQU    3

; ATP function code

atpReqCode       .EQU    $40     ;TReq packet
atpRspCode       .EQU    $80     ;TResp packet
atpRelCode       .EQU    $C0     ;TRel packet

; ATPFlags control information bits

sendChk          .EQU    0       ;send-checksum bit
tidValid         .EQU    1       ;transaction ID validity bit
atpSTSBit        .EQU    3       ;send-transmission-status bit
atpEOMBit        .EQU    4       ;end-of-message bit
atpXOBit         .EQU    5       ;exactly-once bit

; Maximum number of ATP request packets

atpMaxNum        .EQU    8

; ATP buffer data structure

bdsBuffSz        .EQU    0       ;size of data to send or buffer size
bdsBuffAddr      .EQU    2       ;pointer to data or buffer
bdsDataSz        .EQU    6       ;number of bytes actually received
bdsUserData      .EQU    8       ;user bytes

; BDS element size

bdsEntrySz       .EQU    12

; NBP packet

nbpControl       .EQU    0       ;packet type
nbpTCount        .EQU    0       ;tuple count
nbpID            .EQU    1       ;packet identifier
nbpTuple         .EQU    2       ;start of first tuple

; DDP protocol type for NBP packets

nbp              .EQU    2
```

```
; NBP packet types

brRq            .EQU    1       ;broadcast request
lkUp            .EQU    2       ;lookup request
lkUpReply       .EQU    3       ;lookup reply

; NBP tuple

tupleNet        .EQU    0       ;network number
tupleNode       .EQU    2       ;node ID
tupleSkt        .EQU    3       ;socket number
tupleEnum       .EQU    4       ;used internally
tupleName       .EQU    5       ;entity name

; Maximum number of tuples in NBP packet

tupleMax        .EQU    15

; NBP meta-characters

equals          .EQU    '='     ;"wild-card" meta-character
star            .EQU    '*'     ;"this zone" meta-character

; NBP names table entry

ntLink          .EQU    0       ;pointer to next entry
ntTuple         .EQU    4       ;tuple
ntSocket        .EQU    7       ;socket number
ntEntity        .EQU    9       ;entity name

; NBP names information socket number

nis             .EQU    2
```

Routines

Link Access Protocol

WriteLAP function

→	26	csCode	word	;always writeLAP
→	30	wdsPointer	pointer	;write data structure

AttachPH function

→	26	csCode	word	;always attachPH
→	28	protType	byte	;ALAP protocol type
→	30	handler	pointer	;protocol handler

DetachPH function

→	26	csCode	word	;always detachPH
→	28	protType	byte	;ALAP protocol type

Datagram Delivery Protocol

OpenSkt function

→	26	csCode	word	;always openSkt
↔	28	socket	byte	;socket number
→	30	listener	pointer	;socket listener

CloseSkt function

→	26	csCode	word	;always closeSkt
→	28	socket	byte	;socket number

WriteDDP function

→	26	csCode	word	;always writeDDP
→	28	socket	byte	;socket number
→	29	checksumFlag	byte	;checksum flag
→	30	wdsPointer	pointer	;write data structure

AppleTalk Transaction Protocol

OpenATPSkt function

→	26	csCode	word	;always openATPSkt
↔	28	atpSocket	byte	;socket number
→	30	addrBlock	long word	;socket request specification

CloseATPSkt function

→	26	csCode	word	;always closeATPSkt
→	28	atpSocket	byte	;socket number

SendRequest function

→	18	userData	long word	;user bytes
←	22	reqTID	word	;transaction ID used in request
→	26	csCode	word	;always sendRequest
←	28	currBitMap	byte	;bit map
↔	29	atpFlags	byte	;control information
→	30	addrBlock	long word	;destination socket address
→	34	reqLength	word	;request size in bytes
→	36	reqPointer	pointer	;pointer to request data
→	40	bdsPointer	pointer	;pointer to response BDS
→	44	numOfBuffs	byte	;number of responses expected
→	45	timeOutVal	byte	;timeout interval
←	46	numOfResps	byte	;number of responses received
↔	47	retryCount	byte	;number of retries

GetRequest function

←	18	userData	long word	;user bytes
→	26	csCode	word	;always getRequest
→	28	atpSocket	byte	;socket number

GetRequest function

←	18	userData	long word	;user bytes
→	26	csCode	word	;always getRequest
→	28	atpSocket	byte	;socket number
←	29	atpFlags	byte	;control information
←	30	addrBlock	long word	;source of request
↔	34	reqLength	word	;request buffer size
→	36	reqPointer	pointer	;pointer to request buffer
←	44	bitMap	byte	;bit map
←	46	transID	word	;transaction ID

SendResponse function

←	18	userData	long word	;user bytes from TRel
→	26	csCode	word	;always sendResponse
→	28	atpSocket	byte	;socket number
→	29	atpFlags	byte	;control information
→	30	addrBlock	long word	;response destination
→	40	bdsPointer	pointer	;pointer to response BDS
→	44	numOfBuffs	byte	;number of response packets being sent
→	45	bdsSize	byte	;BDS size in elements
→	46	transID	word	;transaction ID

AddResponse function

→	18	userData	long word	;user bytes
→	26	csCode	word	;always addResponse
→	28	atpSocket	byte	;socket number
→	29	atpFlags	byte	;control information
→	30	addrBlock	long word	;response destination
→	34	reqLength	word	;response size
→	36	reqPointer	pointer	;pointer to response
→	44	rspNum	byte	;sequence number
→	46	transID	word	;transaction ID

RelTCB function

→	26	csCode	word	;always relTCB
→	30	addrBlock	long word	;destination of request
→	46	transID	word	;transaction ID of request

RelRspCB function

→	26	csCode	word	;always relRspCB
→	28	atpSocket	byte	;socket number that request was received on
→	30	addrBlock	long word	;source of request
→	46	transID	word	;transaction ID of request

Name-Binding Protocol

RegisterName function

→	26	csCode	word	;always registerName
→	28	interval	byte	;retry interval
↔	29	count	byte	;retry count
→	30	ntQElPtr	pointer	;names table element pointer
→	34	verifyFlag	byte	;set if verify needed

LookupName function

→	26	csCode	word	;always lookupName
→	28	interval	byte	;retry interval
↔	29	count	byte	;retry count
→	30	entityPtr	pointer	;pointer to entity name
→	34	retBuffPtr	pointer	;pointer to buffer
→	38	retBuffSize	word	;buffer size in bytes
→	40	maxToGet	word	;matches to get
←	42	numGotten	word	;matches found

ConfirmName function

→	26	csCode	word	;always confirmName
→	28	interval	byte	;retry interval
↔	29	count	byte	;retry count
→	30	entityPtr	pointer	;pointer to entity name
→	34	confirmAddr	pointer	;entity address
←	38	newSocket	byte	;socket number

RemoveName function

→	26	csCode	word	;always removeName
→	30	entityPtr	pointer	;pointer to entity name

LoadNBP function

→	26	csCode	word	;always loadNBP

UnloadNBP function

→	26	csCode	word	;always unloadNBP

Variables

SPConfig   Use types for serial ports (byte)
                     (bits 0-3: current configuration of serial port B
                      bits 4-6: current configuration of serial port A)

PortBUse   Current availability of serial port B (byte)
                     (bit 7: 1 = not in use, 0 = in use
                      bits 0-3: current use of port bits
                      bits 4-6: driver-specific)

ABusVars   Pointer to AppleTalk variables

BINARY-DECIMAL CONVERSION PACKAGE

Routines

```
PROCEDURE NumToString (theNum: LONGINT; VAR theString: Str255);
PROCEDURE StringToNum (theString: Str255; VAR theNum: LONGINT);
```

Assembly-Language Information

Constants

```
; Routine selectors

numToString     .EQU     0
stringToNum     .EQU     1
```

Routines

Name	On entry	On exit
NumToString	A0: ptr to theString (preceded by length byte) D0: theNum (long)	A0: ptr to theString
StringToNum	A0: ptr to theString (preceded by length byte)	D0: theNum (long)

Trap Macro Name

_Pack7

CONTROL MANAGER

Constants

```
CONST  { Control definition IDs }

       pushButProc    = 0;   {simple button}
       checkBoxProc   = 1;   {check box}
       radioButProc   = 2;   {radio button}
       useWFont       = 8;   {add to above to use window's font}
       scrollBarProc  = 16;  {scroll bar}

       { Part codes }

       inButton     = 10;  {simple button}
       inCheckBox   = 11;  {check box or radio button}
       inUpButton   = 20;  {up arrow of a scroll bar}
       inDownButton = 21;  {down arrow of a scroll bar}
       inPageUp     = 22;  {"page up" region of a scroll bar}
       inPageDown   = 23;  {"page down" region of a scroll bar}
       inThumb      = 129; {thumb of a scroll bar}

       { Axis constraints for DragControl }

       noConstraint = 0;  {no constraint}
       hAxisOnly    = 1;  {horizontal axis only}
       vAxisOnly    = 2;  {vertical axis only}

       { Messages to control definition function }

       drawCntl  = 0; {draw the control (or control part)}
       testCntl  = 1; {test where mouse button was pressed}
       calcCRgns = 2; {calculate control's region (or indicator's)}
       initCntl  = 3; {do any additional control initialization}
       dispCntl  = 4; {take any additional disposal actions}
       posCntl   = 5; {reposition control's indicator and update it}
       thumbCntl = 6; {calculate parameters for dragging indicator}
       dragCntl  = 7; {drag control (or its indicator)}
       autoTrack = 8; {execute control's action procedure}
```

Data Types

```
TYPE ControlHandle = ^ControlPtr;
     ControlPtr    = ^ControlRecord;
```

```
ControlRecord =
    PACKED RECORD
        nextControl:   ControlHandle;    {next control}
        contrlOwner:   WindowPtr;        {control's window}
        contrlRect:    Rect;             {enclosing rectangle}
        contrlVis:     Byte;             {255 if visible}
        contrlHilite:  Byte;             {highlight state}
        contrlValue:   INTEGER;          {control's current setting}
        contrlMin:     INTEGER;          {control's minimum setting}
        contrlMax:     INTEGER;          {control's maximum setting}
        contrlDefProc: Handle;           {control definition function}
        contrlData:    Handle;           {data used by contrlDefProc}
        contrlAction:  ProcPtr;          {default action procedure}
        contrlRfCon:   LONGINT;          {control's reference value}
        contrlTitle:   Str255            {control's title}
    END;
```

Routines

Initialization and Allocation

```
FUNCTION   NewControl      (theWindow: WindowPtr; boundsRect: Rect; title:
                            Str255; visible: BOOLEAN; value: INTEGER;
                            min,max: INTEGER; procID: INTEGER; refCon:
                            LONGINT) : ControlHandle;
FUNCTION   GetNewControl   (controlID: INTEGER; theWindow: WindowPtr) :
                            ControlHandle;
PROCEDURE  DisposeControl  (theControl: ControlHandle);
PROCEDURE  KillControls    (theWindow: WindowPtr);
```

Control Display

```
PROCEDURE  SetCTitle       (theControl: ControlHandle; title: Str255);
PROCEDURE  GetCTitle       (theControl: ControlHandle; VAR title: Str255);
PROCEDURE  HideControl     (theControl: ControlHandle);
PROCEDURE  ShowControl     (theControl: ControlHandle);
PROCEDURE  DrawControls    (theWindow: WindowPtr);
PROCEDURE  HiliteControl   (theControl: ControlHandle; hiliteState:
                            INTEGER);
```

Mouse Location

```
FUNCTION   FindControl     (thePoint: Point; theWindow: WindowPtr; VAR
                            whichControl: ControlHandle) : INTEGER;
FUNCTION   TrackControl    (theControl: ControlHandle; startPt: Point;
                            actionProc: ProcPtr) : INTEGER;
FUNCTION   TestControl     (theControl: ControlHandle; thePoint: Point) :
                            INTEGER;
```

Control Movement and Sizing

```
PROCEDURE MoveControl    (theControl: ControlHandle; h,v: INTEGER);
PROCEDURE DragControl    (theControl: ControlHandle; startPt: Point;
                            limitRect,slopRect: Rect; axis: INTEGER);
PROCEDURE SizeControl    (theControl: ControlHandle; w,h: INTEGER);
```

Control Setting and Range

```
PROCEDURE SetCtlValue    (theControl: ControlHandle; theValue: INTEGER);
FUNCTION  GetCtlValue    (theControl: ControlHandle) : INTEGER;
PROCEDURE SetCtlMin      (theControl: ControlHandle; minValue: INTEGER);
FUNCTION  GetCtlMin      (theControl: ControlHandle) : INTEGER;
PROCEDURE SetCtlMax      (theControl: ControlHandle; maxValue INTEGER);
FUNCTION  GetCtlMax      (theControl: ControlHandle) : INTEGER;
```

Miscellaneous Routines

```
PROCEDURE SetCRefCon     (theControl: ControlHandle; data: LONGINT);
FUNCTION  GetCRefCon     (theControl: ControlHandle) : LONGINT;
PROCEDURE SetCtlAction   (theControl: ControlHandle; actionProc ProcPtr);
FUNCTION  GetCtlAction   (theControl: ControlHandle) : ProcPtr;
```

Action Procedure for TrackControl

```
If an indicator:        PROCEDURE MyAction;
If not an indicator:    PROCEDURE MyAction (theControl: ControlHandle;
                                              partCode: INTEGER);
```

Control Definition Function

```
FUNCTION MyControl  (varCode: INTEGER; theControl: ControlHandle;
                       message: INTEGER; param: LONGINT) : LONGINT;
```

Assembly-Language Information

Constants

```
; Control definition IDs

pushButProc     .EQU  0    ;simple button
checkBoxProc    .EQU  1    ;check box
radioButProc    .EQU  2    ;radio button
useWFont        .EQU  8    ;add to above to use window's font
scrollBarProc   .EQU  16   ;scroll bar
```

; Part codes

```
inButton          .EQU   10    ;simple button
inCheckBox        .EQU   11    ;check box or radio button
inUpButton        .EQU   20    ;up arrow of a scroll bar
inDownButton      .EQU   21    ;down arrow of a scroll bar
inPageUp          .EQU   22    ;"page up" region of a scroll bar
inPageDown        .EQU   23    ;"page down" region of a scroll bar
inThumb           .EQU   129   ;thumb of a scroll bar
```

; Axis constraints for DragControl

```
noConstraint      .EQU   0     ;no constraint
hAxisOnly         .EQU   1     ;horizontal axis only
vAxisOnly         .EQU   2     ;vertical axis only
```

; Messages to control definition function

```
drawCtlMsg        .EQU   0     ;draw the control (or control part)
hitCtlMsg         .EQU   1     ;test where mouse button was pressed
calcCtlMsg        .EQU   2     ;calculate control's region (or indicator's)
newCtlMsg         .EQU   3     ;do any additional control initialization
dispCtlMsg        .EQU   4     ;take any additional disposal actions
posCtlMsg         .EQU   5     ;reposition control's indicator and update it
thumbCtlMsg       .EQU   6     ;calculate parameters for dragging indicator
dragCtlMsg        .EQU   7     ;drag control (or its indicator)
trackCtlMsg       .EQU   8     ;execute control's action procedure
```

Control Record Data Structure

nextControl	Handle to next control in control list
contrlOwner	Pointer to this control's window
contrlRect	Control's enclosing rectangle (8 bytes)
contrlVis	255 if control is visible (byte)
contrlHilite	Highlight state (byte)
contrlValue	Control's current setting (word)
contrlMin	Control's minimum setting (word)
contrlMax	Control's maximum setting (word)
contrlDefHandle	Handle to control definition function
contrlData	Data used by control definition function (long)
contrlAction	Address of default action procedure
contrlRfCon	Control's reference value (long)
contrlTitle	Handle to control's title (preceded by length byte)
contrlSize	Size in bytes of control record except contrlTitle field

Special Macro Names

Pascal name	Macro name
DisposeControl	_DisposControl
GetCtlMax	_GetMaxCtl
GetCtlMin	_GetMinCtl
SetCtlMax	_SetMaxCtl
SetCtlMin	_SetMinCtl

Variables

DragHook   Address of procedure to execute during TrackControl and DragControl
DragPattern Pattern of dragged region's outline (8 bytes)

DESK MANAGER

Routines

Opening and Closing Desk Accessories

```
FUNCTION  OpenDeskAcc  (theAcc: Str255) : INTEGER;
PROCEDURE CloseDeskAcc (refNum: INTEGER);
```

Handling Events in Desk Accessories

```
PROCEDURE SystemClick (theEvent: EventRecord; theWindow: WindowPtr);
FUNCTION  SystemEdit  (editCmd: INTEGER) : BOOLEAN;
```

Performing Periodic Actions

```
PROCEDURE SystemTask;
```

Advanced Routines

```
FUNCTION  SystemEvent (theEvent: EventRecord) : BOOLEAN;
PROCEDURE SystemMenu  (menuResult: LONGINT);
```

Assembly-Language Information

Constants

```
; Desk accessory flag

dNeedTime      .EQU      5        ;set if driver needs time for performing a
                                  ; periodic action

; Control routine messages

accEvent       .EQU      64       ;handle a given event
accRun         .EQU      65       ;take the periodic action, if any, for
                                  ; this desk accessory
accCursor      .EQU      66       ;change cursor shape if appropriate;
                                  ; generate null event if window was
                                  ; created by Dialog Manager
accMenu        .EQU      67       ;handle a given menu item
accUndo        .EQU      68       ;handle the Undo command
```

```
accCut        .EQU      70      ;handle the Cut command
accCopy       .EQU      71      ;handle the Copy command
accPaste      .EQU      72      ;handle the Paste command
accClear      .EQU      73      ;handle the Clear command
```

Special Macro Names

Pascal name	Macro name
SystemEdit	_SysEdit

Variables

MBarEnable	Unique menu ID for active desk accessory, when menu bar belongs to the accessory (word)
SEvtEnb	0 if SystemEvent should return FALSE (byte)

DEVICE MANAGER

Constants

```
CONST { Values for requesting read/write access }

      fsCurPerm   = 0;    {whatever is currently allowed}
      fsRdPerm    = 1;    {request to read only}
      fsWrPerm    = 2;    {request to write only}
      fsRdWrPerm  = 3;    {request to read and write}


      { Positioning modes }

      fsAtMark    = 0;    {at current position}
      fsFromStart = 1;    {offset relative to beginning of medium}
      fsFromMark  = 3;    {offset relative to current position}
      rdVerify    = 64;   {add to above for read-verify}
```

Data Types

```
TYPE  ParamBlkType   = (ioParam, fileParam, volumeParam, cntrlParam);

      ParmBlkPtr    = ^ParamBlockRec;
      ParamBlockRec = RECORD
          qLink:          QElemPtr;      {next queue entry}
          qType:          INTEGER;       {queue type}
          ioTrap:         INTEGER;       {routine trap}
          ioCmdAddr:      Ptr;           {routine address}
          ioCompletion:   ProcPtr;       {completion routine}
          ioResult:       OSErr;         {result code}
          ioNamePtr:      StringPtr;     {driver name}
          ioVRefNum:      INTEGER;       {volume reference or drive number}
        CASE ParamBlkType OF
          ioParam:
          (ioRefNum:      INTEGER;       {driver reference number}
           ioVersNum:     SignedByte;    {not used}
           ioPermssn:     SignedByte;    {read/write permission}
           ioMisc:        Ptr;           {not used}
           ioBuffer:      Ptr;           {pointer to data buffer}
           ioReqCount:    LONGINT;       {requested number of bytes}
           ioActCount:    LONGINT;       {actual number of bytes}
           ioPosMode:     INTEGER;       {positioning mode}
           ioPosOffset:   LONGINT);      {positioning offset}
          fileParam:
          . . . {used by File Manager}
          volumeParam:
          . . . {used by File Manager}
```

```
cntrlParam:
  (ioCRefNum: INTEGER;   {driver reference number}
   csCode:    INTEGER;   {type of Control or Status call}
   csParam:   ARRAY[0..10] OF INTEGER) {control or status information}
END;

DCtlHandle  = ^DCtlPtr;
DCtlPtr     = ^DCtlEntry;
DCtlEntry   =
  RECORD
    dCtlDriver:   Ptr;        {pointer to ROM driver or handle to }
                             { RAM driver}
    dCtlFlags:    INTEGER;    {flags}
    dCtlQHdr:     QHdr;       {driver I/O queue header}
    dCtlPosition: LONGINT;    {byte position used by Read and }
                             { Write calls}
    dCtlStorage:  Handle;     {handle to RAM driver's private }
                             { storage}
    dCtlRefNum:   INTEGER;    {driver reference number}
    dCtlCurTicks: LONGINT;    {used internally}
    dCtlWindow:   WindowPtr;  {pointer to driver's window}
    dCtlDelay:    INTEGER;    {number of ticks between periodic }
                             { actions}
    dCtlEMask:    INTEGER;    {desk accessory event mask}
    dCtlMenu:     INTEGER     {menu ID of menu associated with }
                             { driver}
  END;
```

High-Level Routines [Not in ROM]

```
FUNCTION OpenDriver   (name: Str255; VAR refNum: INTEGER) : OSErr;
FUNCTION CloseDriver  (refNum: INTEGER) : OSErr;
FUNCTION FSRead       (refNum: INTEGER; VAR count: LONGINT; buffPtr: Ptr)
                       : OSErr;
FUNCTION FSWrite      (refNum: INTEGER; VAR count: LONGINT; buffPtr: Ptr)
                       : OSErr;
FUNCTION Control      (refNum: INTEGER; csCode: INTEGER; csParamPtr: Ptr)
                       : OSErr;
FUNCTION Status       (refNum: INTEGER; csCode: INTEGER; csParamPtr: Ptr)
                       : OSErr;
FUNCTION KillIO       (refNum: INTEGER) : OSErr;
```

Low-Level Routines

```
FUNCTION PBOpen (paramBlock: ParmBlkPtr; async: BOOLEAN) : OSErr;
    →   12      ioCompletion        pointer
    ←   16      ioResult            word
    →   18      ioNamePtr           pointer
    ←   24      ioRefNum            word
    →   27      ioPermssn           byte
```

```
FUNCTION PBClose (paramBlock: ParmBlkPtr; async: BOOLEAN) : OSErr;
    →   12          ioCompletion        pointer
    ←   16          ioResult            word
    →   24          ioRefNum            word


FUNCTION PBRead (paramBlock: ParmBlkPtr; async: BOOLEAN) : OSErr;
    →   12          ioCompletion        pointer
    ←   16          ioResult            word
    →   22          ioVRefNum           word
    →   24          ioRefNum            word
    →   32          ioBuffer            pointer
    →   36          ioReqCount          long word
    ←   40          ioActCount          long word
    →   44          ioPosMode           word
    ↔   46          ioPosOffset         long word


FUNCTION PBWrite (paramBlock: ParmBlkPtr; async: BOOLEAN) : OSErr;
    →   12          ioCompletion        pointer
    ←   16          ioResult            word
    →   22          ioVRefNum           word
    →   24          ioRefNum            word
    →   32          ioBuffer            pointer
    →   36          ioReqCount          long word
    ←   40          ioActCount          long word
    →   44          ioPosMode           word
    ↔   46          ioPosOffset         long word


FUNCTION PBControl (paramBlock: ParmBlkPtr; async: BOOLEAN) : OSErr;
    →   12          ioCompletion        pointer
    ←   16          ioResult            word
    →   22          ioVRefNum           word
    →   24          ioRefNum            word
    →   26          csCode              word
    →   28          csParam             record


FUNCTION PBStatus (paramBlock: ParmBlkPtr; async: BOOLEAN) : OSErr;
    →   12          ioCompletion        pointer
    ←   16          ioResult            word
    →   22          ioVRefNum           word
    →   24          ioRefNum            word
    →   26          csCode              word
    ←   28          csParam             record


FUNCTION PBKillIO (paramBlock: ParmBlkPtr; async: BOOLEAN) : OSErr;
    →   12          ioCompletion        pointer
    ←   16          ioResult            word
    →   24          ioRefNum            word
```

Accessing a Driver's Device Control Entry

```
FUNCTION GetDCtlEntry (refNum: INTEGER) : DCtlHandle;   [Not in ROM]
```

Result Codes

Name	Value	Meaning
abortErr	−27	I/O request aborted by KillIO
badUnitErr	−21	Driver reference number doesn't match unit table
controlErr	−17	Driver can't respond to this Control call
dInstErr	−26	Couldn't find driver in resource file
dRemovErr	−25	Attempt to remove an open driver
noErr	0	No error
notOpenErr	−28	Driver isn't open
openErr	−23	Requested read/write permission doesn't match driver's open permission
readErr	−19	Driver can't respond to Read calls
statusErr	−18	Driver can't respond to this Status call
unitEmptyErr	−22	Driver reference number specifies NIL handle in unit table
writErr	−20	Driver can't respond to Write calls

Assembly-Language Information

Constants

```
; Flags in trap words

asnycTrpBit     .EQU     10       ;set for an asynchronous call
noQueueBit      .EQU     9        ;set for immediate execution

; Values for requesting read/write access

fsCurPerm       .EQU     0        ;whatever is currently allowed
fsRdPerm        .EQU     1        ;request to read only
fsWrPerm        .EQU     2        ;request to write only
fsRdWrPerm      .EQU     3        ;request to read and write

; Positioning modes

fsAtMark        .EQU     0        ;at current position
fsFromStart     .EQU     1        ;offset relative to beginning of medium
fsFromMark      .EQU     3        ;offset relative to current position
rdVerify        .EQU     64       ;add to above for read-verify
```

```
; Driver flags

dReadEnable     .EQU     0     ;set if driver can respond to Read calls
dWritEnable     .EQU     1     ;set if driver can respond to Write calls
dCtlEnable      .EQU     2     ;set if driver can respond to Control calls
dStatEnable     .EQU     3     ;set if driver can respond to Status calls
dNeedGoodBye    .EQU     4     ;set if driver needs to be called before the
                               ; application heap is reinitialized
dNeedTime       .EQU     5     ;set if driver needs time for performing a
                               ; periodic action
dNeedLock       .EQU     6     ;set if driver will be locked in memory as
                               ; soon as it's opened (always set for ROM
                               ; drivers)

; Device control entry flags

dOpened         .EQU     5     ;set if driver is open
dRAMBased       .EQU     6     ;set if driver is RAM-based
drvrActive      .EQU     7     ;set if driver is currently executing

; csCode values for driver control routine

accRun          .EQU    65     ;take the periodic action, if any, for this
                               ; driver
goodBye         .EQU    -1     ;heap will be reinitialized, clean up if
                               ; necessary
killCode        .EQU     1     ;handle the KillIO call

; Low-order byte of Device Manager traps

aRdCmd          .EQU     2     ;Read call (trap $A002)
aWrCmd          .EQU     3     ;Write call (trap $A003)

; Offsets from SCC base addresses

aData           .EQU     6     ;channel A data in or out
aCtl            .EQU     2     ;channel A control
bData           .EQU     4     ;channel B data in or out
bCtl            .EQU     0     ;channel B control
```

Standard Parameter Block Data Structure

qLink	Pointer to next queue entry
qType	Queue type (word)
ioTrap	Routine trap (word)
ioCmdAddr	Routine address
ioCompletion	Address of completion routine
ioResult	Result code (word)
ioVNPtr	Pointer to driver name (preceded by length byte)
ioVRefNum	Volume reference number (word)
ioDrvNum	Drive number (word)

Control and Status Parameter Block Data Structure

ioRefNum	Driver reference number (word)
csCode	Type of Control or Status call (word)
csParam	Parameters for Control or Status call (22 bytes)

I/O Parameter Block Data Structure

ioRefNum	Driver reference number (word)
ioPermssn	Open permission (byte)
ioBuffer	Pointer to data buffer
ioReqCount	Requested number of bytes (long)
ioActCount	Actual number of bytes (long)
ioPosMode	Positioning mode (word)
ioPosOffset	Positioning offset (long)

Device Driver Data Structure

drvrFlags	Flags (word)
drvrDelay	Number of ticks between periodic actions (word)
drvrEMask	Desk accessory event mask (word)
drvrMenu	Menu ID of menu associated with driver (word)
drvrOpen	Offset to open routine (word)
drvrPrime	Offset to prime routine (word)
drvrCtl	Offset to control routine (word)
drvrStatus	Offset to status routine (word)
drvrClose	Offset to close routine (word)
drvrName	Driver name (preceded by length byte)

Device Control Entry Data Structure

dCtlDriver	Pointer to ROM driver or handle to RAM driver
dCtlFlags	Flags (word)
dCtlQueue	Queue flags: low-order byte is driver's version number (word)
dCtlQHead	Pointer to first entry in driver's I/O queue
dCtlQTail	Pointer to last entry in driver's I/O queue
dCtlPosition	Byte position used by Read and Write calls (long)
dCtlStorage	Handle to RAM driver's private storage
dCtlRefNum	Driver's reference number (word)
dCtlWindow	Pointer to driver's window
dCtlDelay	Number of ticks between periodic actions (word)
dCtlEMask	Desk accessory event mask (word)
dCtlMenu	Menu ID of menu associated with driver (word)

Structure of Primary Interrupt Vector Table

autoInt1	Vector to level-1 interrupt handler
autoInt2	Vector to level-2 interrupt handler

autoInt3	Vector to level-3 interrupt handler
autoInt4	Vector to level-4 interrupt handler
autoInt5	Vector to level-5 interrupt handler
autoInt6	Vector to level-6 interrupt handler
autoInt7	Vector to level-7 interrupt handler

Macro Names

Pascal name	Macro name
PBRead	_Read
PBWrite	_Write
PBControl	_Control
PBStatus	_Status
PBKillIO	_KillIO

Routines for Writing Drivers

Routine	Jump vector	On entry	On exit
Fetch	JFetch	A1: ptr to device control entry	D0: character fetched; bit 15=1 if last character in buffer
Stash	JStash	A1: ptr to device control entry D0: character to stash	D0: bit 15=1 if last character requested
IODone	JIODone	A1: ptr to device control entry D0: result code (word)	

Variables

UTableBase	Base address of unit table
JFetch	Jump vector for Fetch function
JStash	Jump vector for Stash function
JIODone	Jump vector for IODone function
Lvl1DT	Level-1 secondary interrupt vector table (32 bytes)
Lvl2DT	Level-2 secondary interrupt vector table (32 bytes)
VIA	VIA base address
ExtStsDT	External/status interrupt vector table (16 bytes)
SCCWr	SCC write base address
SCCRd	SCC read base address

DIALOG MANAGER

Constants

```
CONST  { Item types }

       ctrlItem     = 4;    {add to following four constants}
       btnCtrl      = 0;    {standard button control}
       chkCtrl      = 1;    {standard check box control}
       radCtrl      = 2;    {standard radio button control}
       resCtrl      = 3;    {control defined in control template}
       statText     = 8;    {static text}
       editText     = 16;   {editable text (dialog only)}
       iconItem     = 32;   {icon}
       picItem      = 64;   {QuickDraw picture}
       userItem     = 0;    {application-defined item (dialog only)}
       itemDisable  = 128;  {add to any of above to disable}

       { Item numbers of OK and Cancel buttons }

       ok     = 1;
       cancel = 2;

       { Resource IDs of alert icons }

       stopIcon     = 0;
       noteIcon     = 1;
       cautionIcon  = 2;
```

Data Types

```
TYPE DialogPtr  = WindowPt.r;
     DialogPeek = ^DialogRecord;

     DialogRecord =
          RECORD
               window:     WindowRecord;  {dialog window}
               items:      Handle;        {item list}
               textH:      TEHandle;      {current editText item}
               editField:  INTEGER;       {editText item number minus 1}
               editOpen:   INTEGER;       {used internally}
               aDefItem:   INTEGER        {default button item number}
          END;

     DialogTHndl = ^DialogTPtr;
     DialogTPtr  = ^DialogTemplate;
```

```
DialogTemplate  =
        RECORD
            boundsRect: Rect;        {becomes window's portRect}
            procID:     INTEGER;     {window definition ID}
            visible:    BOOLEAN;     {TRUE if visible}
            filler1:    BOOLEAN;     {not used}
            goAwayFlag: BOOLEAN;     {TRUE if has go-away region}
            filler2:    BOOLEAN;     {not used}
            refCon:     LONGINT;     {window's reference value}
            itemsID:    INTEGER;     {resource ID of item list}
            title:      Str255       {window's title}
        END;

AlertTHndl    = ^AlertTPtr;
AlertTPtr     = ^AlertTemplate;
AlertTemplate = RECORD
                    boundsRect: Rect;       {becomes window's portRect}
                    itemsID:    INTEGER;    {resource ID of item list}
                    stages:     StageList   {alert stage information}
                END:

StageList =  PACKED RECORD
                 boldItm4: 0..1;    {default button item number minus 1}
                 boxDrwn4: BOOLEAN; {TRUE if alert box to be drawn}
                 sound4:   0..3     {sound number}
                 boldItm3: 0..1;
                 boxDrwn3: BOOLEAN;
                 sound3:   0..3;
                 boldItm2: 0..1;
                 boxDrwn2: BOOLEAN;
                 sound2:   0..3;
                 boldItm1: 0..1;
                 boxDrwn1: BOOLEAN;
                 sound1:   0..3
             END;
```

Routines

Initialization

```
PROCEDURE InitDialogs  (resumeProc: ProcPtr);
PROCEDURE ErrorSound   (soundProc: ProcPtr);
PROCEDURE SetDAFont    (fontNum: INTEGER);   [Not in ROM]
```

Creating and Disposing of Dialogs

```
FUNCTION  NewDialog    (dStorage: Ptr; boundsRect: Rect; title: Str255;
                        visible: BOOLEAN; procID: INTEGER; behind:
                        WindowPtr; goAwayFlag: BOOLEAN; refCon: LONGINT;
                        items: Handle) : DialogPtr;
```

```
FUNCTION    GetNewDialog  (dialogID: INTEGER; dStorage: Ptr; behind:
                           WindowPtr) : DialogPtr;
PROCEDURE   CloseDialog   (theDialog: DialogPtr);
PROCEDURE   DisposDialog  (theDialog: DialogPtr);
PROCEDURE   CouldDialog   (dialogID: INTEGER);
PROCEDURE   FreeDialog    (dialogID: INTEGER);
```

Handling Dialog Events

```
PROCEDURE   ModalDialog   (filterProc: ProcPtr; VAR itemHit: INTEGER);
FUNCTION    IsDialogEvent (theEvent: EventRecord) : BOOLEAN;
FUNCTION    DialogSelect  (theEvent: EventRecord; VAR theDialog:
                           DialogPtr; VAR itemHit: INTEGER) : BOOLEAN;
PROCEDURE   DlgCut        (theDialog: DialogPtr);    [Not in ROM]
PROCEDURE   DlgCopy       (theDialog: DialogPtr);    [Not in ROM]
PROCEDURE   DlgPaste      (theDialog: DialogPtr);    [Not in ROM]
PROCEDURE   DlgDelete     (theDialog: DialogPtr);    [Not in ROM]
PROCEDURE   DrawDialog    (theDialog: DialogPtr);
```

Invoking Alerts

```
FUNCTION    Alert         (alertID: INTEGER; filterProc: ProcPtr) : INTEGER;
FUNCTION    StopAlert     (alertID: INTEGER; filterProc: ProcPtr) : INTEGER;
FUNCTION    NoteAlert     (alertID: INTEGER; filterProc: ProcPtr) : INTEGER;
FUNCTION    CautionAlert  (alertID: INTEGER; filterProc: ProcPtr) : INTEGER;
PROCEDURE   CouldAlert    (alertID: INTEGER);
PROCEDURE   FreeAlert     (alertID: INTEGER);
```

Manipulating Items in Dialogs and Alerts

```
PROCEDURE   ParamText     (param0,param1,param2,param3: Str255);
PROCEDURE   GetDItem      (theDialog: DialogPtr; itemNo: INTEGER; VAR
                           itemType: INTEGER; VAR item: Handle; VAR box:
                           Rect);
PROCEDURE   SetDItem      (theDialog: DialogPtr; itemNo: INTEGER;
                           itemType: INTEGER; item: Handle; box: Rect);
PROCEDURE   GetIText      (item: Handle; VAR text: Str255);
PROCEDURE   SetIText      (item: Handle; text: Str255);
PROCEDURE   SelIText      (theDialog: DialogPtr; itemNo: INTEGER;
                           strtSel,endSel: INTEGER);
FUNCTION    GetAlrtStage :  INTEGER;      [Not in ROM]
PROCEDURE   ResetAlrtStage;    [Not in ROM]
```

UserItem Procedure

```
PROCEDURE   MyItem (theWindow: WindowPtr; itemNo: INTEGER);
```

Sound Procedure

```
PROCEDURE MySound (soundNo: INTEGER);
```

FilterProc Function for Modal Dialogs and Alerts

```
FUNCTION MyFilter (theDialog: DialogPtr; VAR theEvent: EventRecord;
                   VAR itemHit: INTEGER) : BOOLEAN;
```

Assembly-Language Information

Constants

```
; Item types

ctrlItem      .EQU    4       ;add to following four constants
btnCtrl       .EQU    0       ;standard button control
chkCtrl       .EQU    1       ;standard check box control
radCtrl       .EQU    2       ;standard radio button control
resCtrl       .EQU    3       ;control defined in control template
statText      .EQU    8       ;static text
editText      .EQU    16      ;editable text (dialog only)
iconItem      .EQU    32      ;icon
picItem       .EQU    64      ;QuickDraw picture
userItem      .EQU    0       ;application-defined item (dialog only)
itemDisable   .EQU    128     ;add to any of above to disable

; Item numbers of OK and Cancel buttons

okButton      .EQU    1
cancelButton .EQU     2

; Resource IDs of alert icons

stopIcon      .EQU    0
noteIcon      .EQU    1
cautionIcon   .EQU    2

; Masks for stages word in alert template

volBits       .EQU    3       ;sound number
alBit         .EQU    4       ;whether to draw box
okDismissal   .EQU    8       ;item number of default button minus 1
```

Dialog Record Data Structure

dWindow	Dialog window
items	Handle to dialog's item list
teHandle	Handle to current editText item
editField	Item number of editText item minus 1 (word)
aDefItem	Item number of default button (word)
dWindLen	Size in bytes of dialog record

Dialog Template Data Structure

dBounds	Rectangle that becomes portRect of dialog window's grafPort (8 bytes)
dWindProc	Window definition ID (word)
dVisible	Nonzero if dialog window is visible (word)
dGoAway	Nonzero if dialog window has a go-away region (word)
dRefCon	Dialog window's reference value (long)
dItems	Resource ID of dialog's item list (word)
dTitle	Dialog window's title (preceded by length byte)

Alert Template Data Structure

aBounds	Rectangle that becomes portRect of alert window's grafPort (8 bytes)
aItems	Resource ID of alert's item list (word)
aStages	Stages word; information for alert stages

Item List Data Structure

dlgMaxIndex	Number of items minus 1 (word)
itmHndl	Handle or procedure pointer for this item
itmRect	Display rectangle for this item (8 bytes)
itmType	Item type for this item (byte)
itmData	Length byte followed by data for this item (data must be even number of bytes)

Variables

ResumeProc	Address of resume procedure
DAStrings	Handles to ParamText strings (16 bytes)
DABeeper	Address of current sound procedure
DlgFont	Font number for dialogs and alerts (word)
ACount	Stage number (0 through 3) of last alert (word)
ANumber	Resource ID of last alert (word)

DISK DRIVER

Constants

```
CONST  { Positioning modes }

      fsAtMark     = 0;      {at current sector}
      fsFromStart  = 1;      {relative to first sector}
      fsFromMark   = 3;      {relative to current sector}
      rdVerify     = 64;     {add to above for read-verify}
```

Data Types

```
TYPE DrvSts = RECORD
                track:        INTEGER;      {current track}
                writeProt:    SignedByte;   {bit 7=1 if volume is locked}
                diskInPlace:  SignedByte;   {disk in place}
                installed:    SignedByte;   {drive installed}
                sides:        SignedByte;   {bit 7=0 if single-sided drive}
                qLink:        QElemPtr;     {next queue entry}
                qType:        INTEGER;      {reserved for future use}
                dQDrive:      INTEGER;      {drive number}
                dQRefNum:     INTEGER;      {driver reference number}
                dQFSID:       INTEGER;      {file-system identifier}
                twoSideFmt:   SignedByte;   {-1 if two-sided disk}
                needsFlush:   SignedByte;   {reserved for future use}
                diskErrs:     INTEGER       {error count}
              END;
```

Routines   [Not in ROM]

```
FUNCTION DiskEject    (drvNum: INTEGER) : OSErr;
FUNCTION SetTagBuffer (buffPtr: Ptr) : OSErr;
FUNCTION DriveStatus  (drvNum: INTEGER; VAR status: DrvSts) : OSErr;
```

Result Codes

Name	Value	Meaning
noErr	0	No error
nsDrvErr	−56	No such drive
paramErr	−50	Bad positioning information
wPrErr	−44	Volume is locked by a hardware setting

Name	Value	Meaning
firstDskErr	−84	First of the range of low-level disk errors
sectNFErr	−81	Can't find sector
seekErr	−80	Drive error
spdAdjErr	−79	Can't correctly adjust disk speed
twoSideErr	−78	Tried to read side 2 of a disk in a single-sided drive
initIWMErr	−77	Can't initialize disk controller chip
tk0BadErr	−76	Can't find track 0
cantStepErr	−75	Drive error
wrUnderrun	−74	Write underrun occurred
badDBtSlp	−73	Bad data mark
badDCksum	−72	Bad data mark
noDtaMkErr	−71	Can't find data mark
badBtSlpErr	−70	Bad address mark
badCksmErr	−69	Bad address mark
dataVerErr	−68	Read-verify failed
noAdrMkErr	−67	Can't find an address mark
noNybErr	−66	Disk is probably blank
offLinErr	−65	No disk in drive
noDriveErr	−64	Drive isn't connected
lastDskErr	−64	Last of the range of low-level disk errors

Assembly-Language Information

Constants

```
; Positioning modes

fsAtMark        .EQU    0       ;at current sector
fsFromStart     .EQU    1       ;relative to first sector
fsFromMark      .EQU    3       ;relative to current sector
rdVerify        .EQU    64      ;add to above for read-verify

; csCode values for Control/Status calls

ejectCode       .EQU    7       ;Control call, DiskEject
tgBuffCode      .EQU    8       ;Control call, SetTagBuffer
drvStsCode      .EQU    8       ;Status call, DriveStatus
```

Structure of Status Information

dsTrack	Current track (word)
dsWriteProt	Bit 7=1 if volume is locked (byte)
dsDiskInPlace	Disk in place (byte)
dsInstalled	Drive installed (byte)
dsSides	Bit 7=0 if single-sided drive (byte)
dsQLink	Pointer to next queue entry
dsDQDrive	Drive number (word)

dsDQRefNum	Driver reference number (word)
dsDQFSID	File-system identifier (word)
dsTwoSideFmt	−1 if two-sided disk (byte)
dsDiskErrs	Error count (word)

Equivalent Device Manager Calls

Pascal routine	Call
DiskEject	Control with csCode=ejectCode
SetTagBuffer	Control with csCode=tgBuffCode
DriveStatus	Status with csCode=drvStsCode, status returned in csParam through csParam+21

Variables

BufTgFNum	File tags buffer: file number (long)
BufTgFFlag	File tags buffer: flags (word: bit 1=1 if resource fork)
BufTgFBkNum	File tags buffer: logical block number (word)
BufTgDate	File tags buffer: date and time of last modification (long)

DISK INITIALIZATION PACKAGE

Routines

```
PROCEDURE DILoad;
PROCEDURE DIUnload;
FUNCTION  DIBadMount (where: Point; evtMessage: LONGINT) : INTEGER;
FUNCTION  DIFormat   (drvNum: INTEGER) : OSErr;
FUNCTION  DIVerify   (drvNum: INTEGER) : OSErr;
FUNCTION  DIZero     (drvNum: INTEGER; volName: Str255) : OSErr;
```

Result Codes

Name	Value	Meaning
badMDBErr	–60	Bad master directory block
extFSErr	–58	External file system
firstDskErr	–84	First of the range of low-level disk errors
ioErr	–36	I/O error
lastDskErr	–64	Last of the range of low-level disk errors
memFullErr	–108	Not enough room in heap zone
noErr	0	No error
noMacDskErr	–57	Not a Macintosh disk
nsDrvErr	–56	No such drive
paramErr	–50	Bad drive number
volOnLinErr	–55	Volume already on-line

Assembly-Language Information

Constants

```
; Routine selectors

diBadMount    .EQU    0
diLoad        .EQU    2
diUnload      .EQU    4
diFormat      .EQU    6
diVerify      .EQU    8
diZero        .EQU    10
```

Trap Macro Name

_Pack2

EVENT MANAGER, OPERATING SYSTEM

Constants

```
CONST { Event codes }

      nullEvent   = 0;      {null}
      mouseDown   = 1;      {mouse-down}
      mouseUp     = 2;      {mouse-up}
      keyDown     = 3;      {key-down}
      keyUp       = 4;      {key-up}
      autoKey     = 5;      {auto-key}
      updateEvt   = 6;      {update; Toolbox only}
      diskEvt     = 7;      {disk-inserted}
      activateEvt = 8;      {activate; Toolbox only}
      networkEvt  = 10;     {network}
      driverEvt   = 11;     {device driver}
      app1Evt     = 12;     {application-defined}
      app2Evt     = 13;     {application-defined}
      app3Evt     = 14;     {application-defined}
      app4Evt     = 15;     {application-defined}

      { Masks for keyboard event message }

      charCodeMask = $000000FF;    {character code}
      keyCodeMask  = $0000FF00;    {key code}

      { Masks for forming event mask }

      mDownMask    = 2;      {mouse-down}
      mUpMask      = 4;      {mouse-up}
      keyDownMask  = 8;      {key-down}
      keyUpMask    = 16;     {key-up}
      autoKeyMask  = 32;     {auto-key}
      updateMask   = 64;     {update}
      diskMask     = 128;    {disk-inserted}
      activMask    = 256;    {activate}
      networkMask  = 1024;   {network}
      driverMask   = 2048;   {device driver}
      app1Mask     = 4096;   {application-defined}
      app2Mask     = 8192;   {application-defined}
      app3Mask     = 16384;  {application-defined}
      app4Mask     = -32768; {application-defined}
      everyEvent   = -1;     {all event types}
```

```
{ Modifier flags in event record }

activeFlag = 1;        {set if window being activated}
btnState   = 128;      {set if mouse button up}
cmdKey     = 256;      {set if Command key down}
shiftKey   = 512;      {set if Shift key down}
alphaLock  = 1024;     {set if Caps Lock key down}
optionKey  = 2048;     {set if Option key down}

{ Result codes returned by PostEvent }

noErr      = 0;  {no error (event posted)}
evtNotEnb  = 1;  {event type not designated in system event mask}
```

Data Types

```
TYPE EventRecord = RECORD
                what:       INTEGER;   {event code}
                message:    LONGINT;   {event message}
                when:       LONGINT;   {ticks since startup}
                where:      Point;     {mouse location}
                modifiers:  INTEGER    {modifier flags}
            END;

     EvQEl = RECORD
             qLink:          QElemPtr; {next queue entry}
             qType:          INTEGER;  {queue type}
             evtQWhat:       INTEGER;  {event code}
             evtQMessage:    LONGINT;  {event message}
             evtQWhen:       LONGINT;  {ticks since startup}
             evtQWhere:      Point;    {mouse location}
             evtQModifiers:  INTEGER   {modifier flags}
         END;
```

Routines

Posting and Removing Events

```
FUNCTION  PostEvent   (eventCode: INTEGER; eventMsg: LONGINT) : OSErr;
PROCEDURE FlushEvents (eventMask,stopMask: INTEGER);
```

Accessing Events

```
FUNCTION GetOSEvent    (eventMask: INTEGER; VAR theEvent: EventRecord) :
                        BOOLEAN;
FUNCTION OSEventAvail  (eventMask: INTEGER; VAR theEvent: EventRecord) :
                        BOOLEAN;
```

Setting the System Event Mask

```
PROCEDURE SetEventMask (theMask: INTEGER);    [Not in ROM]
```

Directly Accessing the Event Queue

```
FUNCTION GetEvQHdr : QHdrPtr;    [Not in ROM]
```

Assembly-Language Information

Constants

```
; Event codes

nullEvt           .EQU      0      ;null
mButDwnEvt        .EQU      1      ;mouse-down
mButUpEvt         .EQU      2      ;mouse-up
keyDwnEvt         .EQU      3      ;key-down
keyUpEvt          .EQU      4      ;key-up
autoKeyEvt        .EQU      5      ;auto-key
updatEvt          .EQU      6      ;update; Toolbox only
diskInsertEvt     .EQU      7      ;disk-inserted
activateEvt       .EQU      8      ;activate; Toolbox only
networkEvt        .EQU      10     ;network
ioDrvrEvt         .EQU      11     ;device driver
app1Evt           .EQU      12     ;application-defined
app2Evt           .EQU      13     ;application-defined
app3Evt           .EQU      14     ;application-defined
app4Evt           .EQU      15     ;application-defined


; Modifier flags in event record

activeFlag        .EQU      0      ;set if window being activated
btnState          .EQU      2      ;set if mouse button up
cmdKey            .EQU      3      ;set if Command key down
shiftKey          .EQU      4      ;set if Shift key down
alphaLock         .EQU      5      ;set if Caps Lock key down
optionKey         .EQU      6      ;set if Option key down


; Result codes returned by PostEvent

noErr             .EQU      0      ;no error (event posted)
evtNotEnb         .EQU      1      ;event type not designated in system
                                   ; event mask
```

Event Record Data Structure

evtNum	Event code (word)
evtMessage	Event message (long)
evtTicks	Ticks since startup (long)
evtMouse	Mouse location (point; long)
evtMeta	State of modifier keys (byte)
evtMBut	State of mouse button (byte)
evtBlkSize	Size in bytes of event record

Event Queue Entry Data Structure

qLink	Pointer to next queue entry
qType	Queue type (word)
evtQWhat	Event code (word)
evtQMessage	Event message (long)
evtQWhen	Ticks since startup (long)
evtQWhere	Mouse location (point; long)
evtQMeta	State of modifier keys (byte)
evtQMBut	State of mouse button (byte)
evtQBlkSize	Size in bytes of event queue entry

Routines

Trap macro	On entry	On exit
_PostEvent	A0: eventCode (word) D0: eventMsg (long)	D0: result code (word)
_FlushEvents	D0: low word: eventMask high word: stopMask	D0: 0 or event code (word)
_GetOSEvent and _OSEventAvail	A0: ptr to event record theEvent D0: eventMask (word)	D0: 0 if non-null event, −1 if null event (byte)

Variables

SysEvtMask	System event mask (word)
EventQueue	Event queue header (10 bytes)

EVENT MANAGER, TOOLBOX

Constants

```
CONST { Event codes }
        nullEvent   = 0;      {null}
        mouseDown   = 1;      {mouse down}
        mouseUp     = 2;      {mouse up}
        keyDown     = 3;      {key-down}
        keyUp       = 4;      {key-up}
        autoKey     = 5;      {auto-key}
        updateEvt   = 6;      {update}
        diskEvt     = 7;      {disk-inserted}
        activateEvt = 8;      {activate}
        networkEvt  = 10;     {network}
        driverEvt   = 11;     {device driver}
        app1Evt     = 12;     {application-defined}
        app2Evt     = 13;     {application-defined}
        app3Evt     = 14;     {application-defined}
        app4Evt     = 15;     {application-defined}

        { Masks for keyboard event message }

        charCodeMask = $000000FF; {character code}
        keyCodeMask  = $0000FF00; {key code}


        { Masks for forming event mask }

        mDownMask    =  2;      {mouse down}
        mUpMask      =  4;      {mouse up}
        keyDownMask  =  8;      {key-down}
        keyUpMask    =  16;     {key-up}
        autoKeyMask  =  32;     {auto-key}
        updateMask   =  64;     {update}
        diskMask     =  128;    {disk-inserted}
        activMask    =  256;    {activate}
        networkMask  =  1024;   {network}
        driverMask   =  2048;   {device driver}
        app1Mask     =  4096;   {application-defined}
        app2Mask     =  8192;   {application-defined}
        app3Mask     =  16384;  {application-defined}
        app4Mask     = -32768;  {application-defined}
        everyEvent   = -1;      {all event types}
```

```
{ Modifier flags in event record }

activeFlag  = 1;     {set if window being activated}
btnState    = 128;   {set if mouse button up}
cmdKey      = 256;   {set if Command key down}
shiftKey    = 512;   {set if Shift key down}
alphaLock   = 1024;  {set if Caps Lock key down}
optionKey   = 2048;  {set if Option key down}
```

Data Types

```
TYPE EventRecord = RECORD
                what:       INTEGER;  {event code}
                message:    LONGINT;  {event message}
                when:       LONGINT;  {ticks since startup}
                where:      Point;    {mouse location}
                modifiers:  INTEGER   {modifier flags}
            END;

     KeyMap = PACKED ARRAY[0..127] OF BOOLEAN;
```

Routines

Accessing Events

```
FUNCTION GetNextEvent (eventMask: INTEGER; VAR theEvent:
                    EventRecord) : BOOLEAN;
FUNCTION EventAvail   (eventMask: INTEGER; VAR theEvent:
                    EventRecord) : BOOLEAN;
```

Reading the Mouse

```
PROCEDURE  GetMouse       (VAR mouseLoc: Point);
FUNCTION   Button :       BOOLEAN;
FUNCTION   StillDown :    BOOLEAN;
FUNCTION   WaitMouseUp : BOOLEAN;
```

Reading the Keyboard and Keypad

```
PROCEDURE GetKeys (VAR theKeys: KeyMap);
```

Miscellaneous Routines

```
FUNCTION TickCount    : LONGINT;
FUNCTION GetDblTime   : LONGINT;   [Not in ROM]
FUNCTION GetCaretTime : LONGINT;   [Not in ROM]
```

Event Message in Event Record

Event type	Event message
Keyboard	Character code and key code in low-order word
Activate, update	Pointer to window
Disk-inserted	Drive number in low-order word, File Manager result code in high-order word
Mouse-down, mouse-up, null	Undefined
Network	Handle to parameter block
Device driver	See chapter describing driver
Application-defined	Whatever you wish

Assembly-Language Information

Constants

```
; Event codes

nullEvt          .EQU   0    ;null
mButDwnEvt       .EQU   1    ;mouse-down
mButUpEvt        .EQU   2    ;mouse-up
keyDwnEvt        .EQU   3    ;key-down
keyUpEvt         .EQU   4    ;key-up
autoKeyEvt       .EQU   5    ;auto-key
updatEvt         .EQU   6    ;update
diskInsertEvt    .EQU   7    ;disk-inserted
activateEvt      .EQU   8    ;activate
networkEvt       .EQU   10   ;network
ioDrvrEvt        .EQU   11   ;device driver
app1Evt          .EQU   12   ;application-defined
app2Evt          .EQU   13   ;application-defined
app3Evt          .EQU   14   ;application-defined
app4Evt          .EQU   15   ;application-defined

; Modifier flags in event record

activeFlag       .EQU   0    ;set if window being activated
btnState         .EQU   2    ;set if mouse button up
cmdKey           .EQU   3    ;set if Command key down
shiftKey         .EQU   4    ;set if Shift key down
alphaLock        .EQU   5    ;set if Caps Lock key down
optionKey        .EQU   6    ;set if Option key down
```

```
; Journaling mechanism Control call

jPlayCtl        .EQU    16      ;journal in playback mode
jRecordCtl      .EQU    17      ;journal in recording mode
jcTickCount     .EQU    0       ;journal code for TickCount
jcGetMouse      .EQU    1       ;journal code for GetMouse
jcButton        .EQU    2       ;journal code for Button
jcGetKeys       .EQU    3       ;journal code for GetKeys
jcEvent         .EQU    4       ;journal code for GetNextEvent and EventAvail
```

Event Record Data Structure

evtNum	Event code (word)
evtMessage	Event message (long)
evtTicks	Ticks since startup (long)
evtMouse	Mouse location (point; long)
evtMeta	State of modifier keys (byte)
evtMBut	State of mouse button (byte)
evtBlkSize	Size in bytes of event record

Variables

KeyThresh	Auto-key threshold (word)
KeyRepThresh	Auto-key rate (word)
WindowList	0 if using events but not windows (long)
ScrDmpEnb	0 if GetNextEvent shouldn't process Command-Shift-number combinations (byte)
Ticks	Current number of ticks since system startup (long)
DoubleTime	Double-click interval in ticks (long)
CaretTime	Caret-blink interval in ticks (long)
JournalRef	Reference number of journaling device driver (word)
JournalFlag	Journaling mode (word)

FILE MANAGER

Constants

```
CONST { Flags in file information used by the Finder }

        fHasBundle =  8192;  {set if file has a bundle}
        fInvisible = 16384;  {set if file's icon is invisible}
        fTrash     = -3;     {file is in Trash window}
        fDesktop   = -2;     {file is on desktop}
        fDisk      =  0;     {file is in disk window}

        { Values for requesting read/write access }

        fsCurPerm   = 0;  {whatever is currently allowed}
        fsRdPerm    = 1;  {request to read only}
        fsWrPerm    = 2;  {request to write only}
        fsRdWrPerm  = 3;  {request to read and write}

        { Positioning modes }

        fsAtMark    = 0;  {at current mark}
        fsFromStart = 1;  {offset relative to beginning of file}
        fsFromLEOF  = 2;  {offset relative to logical end-of-file}
        fsFromMark  = 3;  {offset relative to current mark}
        rdVerify    = 64; {add to above for read-verify}
```

Data Types

```
TYPE FInfo = RECORD
                fdType:     OSType;  {file type}
                fdCreator:  OSType;  {file's creator}
                fdFlags:    INTEGER; {flags}
                fdLocation: Point;   {file's location}
                fdFldr:     INTEGER  {file's window}
             END;

     ParamBlkType  = (ioParam,fileParam,volumeParam,cntrlParam);

     ParmBlkPtr    = ^ParamBlockRec;
     ParamBlockRec = RECORD
        qLink:         QElemPtr;  {next queue entry}
        qType:         INTEGER;   {queue type}
        ioTrap:        INTEGER;   {routine trap}
        ioCmdAddr:     Ptr;       {routine address}
        ioCompletion:  ProcPtr;   {completion routine}
        ioResult:      OSErr;     {result code}
        ioNamePtr:     StringPtr; {volume or file name}
        ioVRefNum:     INTEGER;   {volume reference or drive number}
```

3 Summary

```
CASE ParamBlkType OF
  ioParam:
    (ioRefNum:    INTEGER;    {path reference number}
     ioVersNum:   SignedByte; {version number}
     ioPermssn:   SignedByte; {read/write permission}
     ioMisc:      Ptr;        {miscellaneous}
     ioBuffer:    Ptr;        {data buffer}
     ioReqCount:  LONGINT;    {requested number of bytes}
     ioActCount:  LONGINT;    {actual number of bytes}
     ioPosMode:   INTEGER;    {positioning mode and newline character}
     ioPosOffset: LONGINT);   {positioning offset}
  fileParam:
    (ioFRefNum:   INTEGER;    {path reference number}
     ioFVersNum:  SignedByte; {version number}
     filler1:     SignedByte; {not used}
     ioFDirIndex: INTEGER;    {sequence number of file}
     ioFlAttrib:  SignedByte; {file attributes}
     ioFlVersNum: SignedByte  {version number}
     ioFlFndrInfo: FInfo;     {information used by the Finder}
     ioFlNum:     LONGINT;    {file number}
     ioFlStBlk:   INTEGER;    {first allocation block of data fork}
     ioFlLgLen:   LONGINT;    {logical end-of-file of data fork}
     ioFlPyLen:   LONGINT;    {physical end-of-file of data fork}
     ioFlRStBlk:  INTEGER;    {first allocation block of resource }
                              { fork}
     ioFlRLgLen:  LONGINT;    {logical end-of-file of resource fork}
     ioFlRPyLen:  LONGINT;    {physical end-of-file of resource }
                              { fork}
     ioFlCrDat:   LONGINT;    {date and time of creation}
     ioFlMdDat:   LONGINT);   {date and time of last modification}
  volumeParam:
    (filler2:     LONGINT;    {not used}
     ioVolIndex:  INTEGER;    {volume index}
     ioVCrDate:   LONGINT;    {date and time of initialization}
     ioVLsBkUp:   LONGINT;    {date and time of last backup}
     ioVAtrb:     INTEGER;    {bit 15=1 if volume locked}
     ioVNmFls:    INTEGER;    {number of files in directory}
     ioVDirSt:    INTEGER;    {first block of directory}
     ioVBlLn:     INTEGER;    {length of directory in blocks}
     ioVNmAlBlks: INTEGER;    {number of allocation blocks}
     ioVAlBlkSiz: LONGINT;    {size of allocation blocks}
     ioVClpSiz:   LONGINT;    {number of bytes to allocate}
     ioAlBlSt:    INTEGER;    {first allocation block in block map}
     ioVNxtFNum:  LONGINT;    {next unused file number}
     ioVFrBlk:    INTEGER);   {number of unused allocation blocks}
  cntrlParam:
    . . . {used by Device Manager}
END;
```

```
VCB = RECORD
        qLink:       QElemPtr;   {next queue entry}
        qType:       INTEGER;    {queue type}
        vcbFlags:    INTEGER;    {bit 15=1 if dirty}
        vcbSigWord:  INTEGER;    {always $D2D7}
        vcbCrDate:   LONGINT;    {date and time of initialization}
        vcbLsBkUp:   LONGINT;    {date and time of last backup}
        vcbAtrb:     INTEGER;    {volume attributes}
        vcbNmFls:    INTEGER;    {number of files in directory}
        vcbDirSt:    INTEGER;    {first block of directory}
        vcbBlLn:     INTEGER;    {length of directory in blocks}
        vcbNmBlks:   INTEGER;    {number of allocation blocks}
        vcbAlBlkSiz: LONGINT;    {size of allocation blocks}
        vcbClpSiz:   LONGINT;    {number of bytes to allocate}
        vcbAlBlSt:   INTEGER;    {first allocation block in block map}
        vcbNxtFNum:  LONGINT;    {next unused file number}
        vcbFreeBks:  INTEGER;    {number of unused allocation blocks}
        vcbVN:       STRING[27]; {volume name}
        vcbDrvNum    INTEGER;    {drive number}
        vcbDRefNum:  INTEGER;    {driver reference number}
        vcbFSID:     INTEGER;    {file-system identifier}
        vcbVRefNum:  INTEGER;    {volume reference number}
        vcbMAdr:     Ptr;        {pointer to block map}
        vcbBufAdr:   Ptr;        {pointer to volume buffer}
        vcbMLen:     INTEGER;    {number of bytes in block map}
        vcbDirIndex: INTEGER;    {used internally}
        vcbDirBlk:   INTEGER     {used internally}
      END;

DrvQEl = RECORD
        qLink:       QElemPtr;   {next queue entry}
        qType:       INTEGER;    {queue type}
        dQDrive:     INTEGER;    {drive number}
        dQRefNum:    INTEGER;    {driver reference number}
        dQFSID:      INTEGER;    {file-system identifier}
        dQDrvSize:   INTEGER     {number of logical blocks}
      END;
```

High-Level Routines [Not in ROM]

Accessing Volumes

```
FUNCTION GetVInfo     (drvNum: INTEGER; volName: StringPtr; VAR vRefNum:
                       INTEGER; VAR freeBytes: LONGINT) : OSErr;
FUNCTION GetVRefNum   (pathRefNum: INTEGER; VAR vRefNum: INTEGER) : OSErr;
FUNCTION GetVol       (volName: StringPtr; VAR vRefNum: INTEGER) : OSErr;
FUNCTION SetVol       (volName: StringPtr; vRefNum: INTEGER) : OSErr;
FUNCTION FlushVol     (volName: StringPtr; vRefNum: INTEGER) : OSErr;
FUNCTION UnmountVol   (volName: StringPtr; vRefNum: INTEGER) : OSErr;
FUNCTION Eject        (volName: StringPtr; vRefNum: INTEGER) : OSErr;
```

Accessing Files

```
FUNCTION Create    (fileName: Str255; vRefNum: INTEGER; creator: OSType;
                     fileType: OSType) : OSErr;
FUNCTION FSOpen    (fileName: Str255; vRefNum: INTEGER; VAR refNum:
                     INTEGER) : OSErr;
FUNCTION OpenRF    (fileName: Str255; vRefNum: INTEGER; VAR refNum:
                     INTEGER) : OSErr;
FUNCTION FSRead    (refNum: INTEGER; VAR count: LONGINT; buffPtr: Ptr) :
                     OSErr;
FUNCTION FSWrite   (refNum: INTEGER; VAR count: LONGINT; buffPtr: Ptr) :
                     OSErr;
FUNCTION GetFPos   (refNum: INTEGER; VAR filePos: LONGINT) : OSErr;
FUNCTION SetFPos   (refNum: INTEGER; posMode: INTEGER; posOff: LONGINT) :
                     OSErr;
FUNCTION GetEOF    (refNum: INTEGER; VAR logEOF: LONGINT) : OSErr;
FUNCTION SetEOF    (refNum: INTEGER; logEOF: LONGINT) : OSErr;
FUNCTION Allocate  (refNum: INTEGER; VAR count: LONGINT) : OSErr;
FUNCTION FSClose   (refNum: INTEGER) : OSErr;
```

Changing Information About Files

```
FUNCTION GetFInfo (fileName: Str255; vRefNum: INTEGER; VAR fndrInfo:
                    FInfo) : OSErr;
FUNCTION SetFInfo (fileName: Str255; vRefNum: INTEGER; fndrInfo: FInfo):
                    OSErr;
FUNCTION SetFLock (fileName: Str255; vRefNum: INTEGER) : OSErr;
FUNCTION RstFLock (fileName: Str255; vRefNum: INTEGER) : OSErr;
FUNCTION Rename   (oldName: Str255; vRefNum: INTEGER; newName: Str255) :
                    OSErr;
FUNCTION FSDelete (fileName: Str255; vRefNum: INTEGER) : OSErr;
```

Low-Level Routines

Initializing the File I/O Queue

```
PROCEDURE FInitQueue;
```

Accessing Volumes

```
FUNCTION PBMountVol (paramBlock: ParmBlkPtr) : OSErr;
    ←   16    ioResult         word
    ↔   22    ioVRefNum        word
```

```
FUNCTION PBGetVInfo (paramBlock: ParmBlkPtr; async: BOOLEAN) : OSErr;
    →   12      ioCompletion        pointer
    ←   16      ioResult            word
    ↔   18      ioNamePtr           pointer
    ↔   22      ioVRefNum           word
    →   28      ioVolIndex          word
    ←   30      ioVCrDate           long word
    ←   34      ioVLsBkUp           long word
    ←   38      ioVAtrb             word
    ←   40      ioVNmFls            word
    ←   42      ioVDirSt            word
    ←   44      ioVBlLn             word
    ←   46      ioVNmAlBlks         word
    ←   48      ioVAlBlkSiz         long word
    ←   52      ioVClpSiz           long word
    ←   56      ioAlBlSt            word
    ←   58      ioVNxtFNum          long word
    ←   62      ioVFrBlk            word


FUNCTION PBGetVol (paramBlock: ParmBlkPtr; async: BOOLEAN) : OSErr;
    →   12      ioCompletion        pointer
    ←   16      ioResult            word
    ←   18      ioNamePtr           pointer
    ←   22      ioVRefNum           word


FUNCTION PBSetVol (paramBlock: ParmBlkPtr; async: BOOLEAN) : OSErr;
    →   12      ioCompletion        pointer
    ←   16      ioResult            word
    →   18      ioNamePtr           pointer
    →   22      ioVRefNum           word


FUNCTION PBFlushVol (paramBlock: ParmBlkPtr; async: BOOLEAN) : OSErr;
    →   12      ioCompletion        pointer
    ←   16      ioResult            word
    →   18      ioNamePtr           pointer
    →   22      ioVRefNum           word


FUNCTION PBUnmountVol (paramBlock: ParmBlkPtr) : OSErr;
    ←   16      ioResult            word
    →   18      ioNamePtr           pointer
    →   22      ioVRefNum           word


FUNCTION PBOffLine (paramBlock: ParmBlkPtr) : OSErr;
    →   12      ioCompletion        pointer
    ←   16      ioResult            word
    →   18      ioNamePtr           pointer
    →   22      ioVRefNum           word
```

```
FUNCTION PBEject (paramBlock: ParmBlkPtr) : OSErr;
    →   12      ioCompletion        pointer
    ←   16      ioResult            word
    →   18      ioNamePt            pointer
    →   22      ioVRefNum           word
```

Accessing Files

```
FUNCTION PBCreate (paramBlock: ParmBlkPtr; async: BOOLEAN) : OSErr;
    →   12      ioCompletion        pointer
    ←   16      ioResult            word
    →   18      ioNamePtr           pointer
    →   22      ioVRefNum           word
    →   26      ioFVersNum          byte
```

```
FUNCTION PBOpen (paramBlock: ParmBlkPtr; async: BOOLEAN) : OSErr;
    →   12      ioCompletion        pointer
    ←   16      ioResult            word
    →   18      ioNamePtr           pointer
    →   22      ioVRefNum           word
    ←   24      ioRefNum            word
    →   26      ioVersNum           byte
    →   27      ioPermssn           byte
    →   28      ioMisc              pointer
```

```
FUNCTION PBOpenRF (paramBlock: ParmBlkPtr; async: BOOLEAN) : OSErr;
    →   12      ioCompletion        pointer
    ←   16      ioResult            word
    →   18      ioNamePtr           pointer
    →   22      ioVRefNum           word
    ←   24      ioRefNum            word
    →   26      ioVersNum           byte
    →   27      ioPermssn           byte
    →   28      ioMisc              pointer
```

```
FUNCTION PBRead (paramBlock: ParmBlkPtr; async: BOOLEAN) : OSErr;
    →   12      ioCompletion        pointer
    ←   16      ioResult            word
    →   24      ioRefNum            word
    →   32      ioBuffer            pointer
    →   36      ioReqCount          long word
    ←   40      ioActCount          long word
    →   44      ioPosMode           word
    ↔   46      ioPosOffset         long word
```

```
FUNCTION PBWrite (paramBlock: ParmBlkPtr; async: BOOLEAN) : OSErr;
    →   12    ioCompletion      pointer
    ←   16    ioResult          word
    →   24    ioRefNum          word
    →   32    ioBuffer          pointer
    →   36    ioReqCount        long word
    ←   40    ioActCount        long word
    →   44    ioPosMode         word
    ↔   46    ioPosOffset       long word


FUNCTION PBGetFPos (paramBlock: ParmBlkPtr; async: BOOLEAN) : OSErr;
    →   12    ioCompletion      pointer
    ←   16    ioResult          word
    →   24    ioRefNum          word
    ←   36    ioReqCount        long word
    ←   40    ioActCount        long word
    ←   44    ioPosMode         word
    ←   46    ioPosOffset       long word


FUNCTION PBSetFPos (paramBlock: ParmBlkPtr; async: BOOLEAN) : OSErr;
    →   12    ioCompletion      pointer
    ←   16    ioResult          word
    →   24    ioRefNum          word
    →   44    ioPosMode         word
    ↔   46    ioPosOffset       long word


FUNCTION PBGetEOF (paramBlock: ParmBlkPtr; async: BOOLEAN) : OSErr;
    →   12    ioCompletion      pointer
    ←   16    ioResult          word
    →   24    ioRefNum          word
    ←   28    ioMisc            long word


FUNCTION PBSetEOF (paramBlock: ParmBlkPtr; async: BOOLEAN) : OSErr;
    →   12    ioCompletion      pointer
    ←   16    ioResult          word
    →   24    ioRefNum          word
    →   28    ioMisc            long word


FUNCTION PBAllocate (paramBlock: ParmBlkPtr; async: BOOLEAN) : OSErr;
    →   12    ioCompletion      pointer
    ←   16    ioResult          word
    →   24    ioRefNum          word
    →   36    ioReqCount        long word
    ←   40    ioActCount        long word


FUNCTION PBFlushFile (paramBlock: ParmBlkPtr; async: BOOLEAN) : OSErr;
    →   12    ioCompletion      pointer
    ←   16    ioResult          word
    →   24    ioRefNum          word
```

```
FUNCTION PBClose (paramBlock: ParmBlkPtr; async: BOOLEAN) : OSErr;
```
→	12	ioCompletion	pointer
←	16	ioResult	word
→	24	ioRefNum	word

Changing Information About Files

```
FUNCTION PBGetFInfo (paramBlock: ParmBlkPtr; async: BOOLEAN) : OSErr;
```
→	12	ioCompletion	pointer
←	16	ioResult	word
↔	18	ioNamePtr	pointer
→	22	ioVRefNum	word
←	24	ioFRefNum	word
→	26	ioFVersNum	byte
→	28	ioFDirIndex	word
←	30	ioFlAttrib	byte
←	31	ioFlVersNum	byte
←	32	ioFlFndrInfo	16 bytes
←	48	ioFlNum	long word
←	52	ioFlStBlk	word
←	54	ioFlLgLen	long word
←	58	ioFlPyLen	long word
←	62	ioFlRStBlk	word
←	64	ioFlRLgLen	long word
←	68	ioFlRPyLen	long word
←	72	ioFlCrDat	long word
←	76	ioFlMdDat	long word

```
FUNCTION PBSetFInfo (paramBlock: ParmBlkPtr; async: BOOLEAN) : OSErr;
```
→	12	ioCompletion	pointer
←	16	ioResult	word
→	18	ioNamePtr	pointer
→	22	ioVRefNum	word
→	26	ioFVersNum	byte
→	32	ioFlFndrInfo	16 bytes
→	72	ioFlCrDat	long word
→	76	ioFlMdDat	long word

```
FUNCTION PBSetFLock (paramBlock: ParmBlkPtr; async: BOOLEAN) : OSErr;
```
→	12	ioCompletion	pointer
←	16	ioResult	word
→	18	ioNamePtr	pointer
→	22	ioVRefNum	word
→	26	ioFVersNum	byte

```
FUNCTION PBRstFLock (paramBlock: ParmBlkPtr; async: BOOLEAN) : OSErr;
```
→	12	ioCompletion	pointer
←	16	ioResult	word
→	18	ioNamePtr	pointer
→	22	ioVRefNum	word
→	26	ioFVersNum	byte

```
FUNCTION PBSetFVers (paramBlock: ParmBlkPtr; async: BOOLEAN) : OSErr;
    →  12      ioCompletion        pointer
    ←  16      ioResult            word
    →  18      ioNamePtr           pointer
    →  22      ioVRefNum           word
    →  26      ioVersNum           byte
    →  28      ioMisc              byte

FUNCTION PBRename (paramBlock: ParmBlkPtr; async: BOOLEAN) : OSErr;
    →  12      ioCompletion        pointer
    ←  16      ioResult            word
    →  18      ioNamePtr           pointer
    →  22      ioVRefNum           word
    →  26      ioVersNum           byte
    →  28      ioMisc              pointer

FUNCTION PBDelete (paramBlock: ParmBlkPtr; async: BOOLEAN) : OSErr;
    →  12      ioCompletion        pointer
    ←  16      ioResult            word
    →  18      ioNamePtr           pointer
    →  22      ioVRefNum           word
    →  26      ioFVersNum          byte
```

Accessing Queues [Not in ROM]

```
FUNCTION GetFSQHdr  : QHdrPtr;
FUNCTION GetVCBQHdr : QHdrPtr;
FUNCTION GetDrvQHdr : QHdrPtr;
```

Result Codes

Name	Value	Meaning
badMDBErr	−60	Master directory block is bad; must reinitialize volume
bdNamErr	−37	Bad file name or volume name (perhaps zero-length)
dirFulErr	−33	File directory full
dskFulErr	−34	All allocation blocks on the volume are full
dupFNErr	−48	A file with the specified name and version number already exists
eofErr	−39	Logical end-of-file reached during read operation
extFSErr	−58	External file system; file-system identifier is nonzero, or path reference number is greater than 1024
fBsyErr	−47	One or more files are open
fLckdErr	−45	File locked
fnfErr	−43	File not found
fnOpnErr	−38	File not open

Name	Value	Meaning
fsRnErr	−59	Problem during rename
gfpErr	−52	Error during GetFPos
ioErr	−36	I/O error
memFullErr	−108	Not enough room in heap zone
noErr	0	No error
noMacDskErr	−57	Volume lacks Macintosh-format directory
nsDrvErr	−56	Specified drive number doesn't match any number in the drive queue
nsvErr	−35	Specified volume doesn't exist
opWrErr	−49	The read/write permission of only one access path to a file can allow writing
paramErr	−50	Parameters don't specify an existing volume, and there's no default volume
permErr	−54	Attempt to open locked file for writing
posErr	−40	Attempt to position before start of file
rfNumErr	−51	Reference number specifies nonexistent access path
tmfoErr	−42	Too many files open
volOffLinErr	−53	Volume not on-line
volOnLinErr	−55	Specified volume is already mounted and on-line
vLckdErr	−46	Volume is locked by a software flag
wrPermErr	−61	Read/write permission doesn't allow writing
wPrErr	−44	Volume is locked by a hardware setting

Assembly-Language Information

Constants

```
; Flags in file information used by the Finder

fHasBundle      .EQU     13      ;set if file has a bundle
fInvisible      .EQU     14      ;set if file's icon is invisible

; Flags in trap words

asnycTrpBit     .EQU     10      ;set for an asynchronous call
noQueueBit      .EQU     9       ;set for immediate execution
```

```
; Values for requesting read/write access

fsCurPerm        .EQU    0    ;whatever is currently allowed
fsRdPerm         .EQU    1    ;request to read only
fsWrPerm         .EQU    2    ;request to write only
fsRdWrPerm       .EQU    3    ;request to read and write

; Positioning modes

fsAtMark         .EQU    0    ;at current mark
fsFromStart      .EQU    1    ;offset relative to beginning of file
fsFromLEOF       .EQU    2    ;offset relative to logical end-of-file
fsFromMark       .EQU    3    ;offset relative to current mark
rdVerify         .EQU    64   ;add to above for read-verify
```

Structure of File Information Used by the Finder

fdType	File type (long)
fdCreator	File's creator (long)
fdFlags	Flags (word)
fdLocation	File's location (point; long)
fdFldr	File's window (word)

Standard Parameter Block Data Structure

qLink	Pointer to next queue entry
qType	Queue type (word)
ioTrap	Routine trap (word)
ioCmdAddr	Routine address
ioCompletion	Address of completion routine
ioResult	Result code (word)
ioFileName	Pointer to file name (preceded by length byte)
ioVNPtr	Pointer to volume name (preceded by length byte)
ioVRefNum	Volume reference number (word)
ioDrvNum	Drive number (word)

I/O Parameter Block Data Structure

ioRefNum	Path reference number (word)
ioFileType	Version number (byte)
ioPermssn	Read/write permission (byte)
ioNewName	Pointer to new file or volume name for Rename
ioLEOF	Logical end-of-file for SetEOF (long)
ioOwnBuf	Pointer to access path buffer
ioNewType	New version number for SetFilType (byte)
ioBuffer	Pointer to data buffer
ioReqCount	Requested number of bytes (long)
ioActCount	Actual number of bytes (long)
ioPosMode	Positioning mode and newline character (word)

| ioPosOffset | Positioning offset (long) |
| ioQElSize | Size in bytes of I/O parameter block |

Structure of File Information Parameter Block

ioRefNum	Path reference number (word)
ioFileType	Version number (byte)
ioFDirIndex	Sequence number of file (word)
ioFlAttrib	File attributes (byte)
ioFFlType	Version number (byte)
ioFlUsrWds	Information used by the Finder (16 bytes)
ioFFlNum	File number (long)
ioFlStBlk	First allocation block of data fork (word)
ioFlLgLen	Logical end-of-file of data fork (long)
ioFlPyLen	Physical end-of-file of data fork (long)
ioFlRStBlk	First allocation block of resource fork (word)
ioFlRLgLen	Logical end-of-file of resource fork (long)
ioFlRPyLen	Physical end-of-file of resource fork (long)
ioFlCrDat	Date and time of creation (long)
ioFlMdDat	Date and time of last modification (long)
ioFQElSize	Size in bytes of file information parameter block

Structure of Volume Information Parameter Block

ioVolIndex	Volume index (word)
ioVCrDate	Date and time of initialization (long)
ioVLsBkUp	Date and time of last backup (long)
ioVAtrb	Volume attributes (word)
ioVNmFls	Number of files in directory (word)
ioVDirSt	First block of directory (word)
ioVBlLn	Length of directory in blocks (word)
ioVNmAlBlks	Number of allocation blocks on volume (word)
ioVAlBlkSiz	Size of allocation blocks (long)
ioVClpSiz	Number of bytes to allocate (long)
ioAlBlSt	First allocation block in block map (word)
ioVNxtFNum	Next unused file number (long)
ioVFrBlk	Number of unused allocation blocks (word)
ioVQElSize	Size in bytes of volume information parameter block

Volume Information Data Structure

drSigWord	Always $D2D7 (word)
drCrDate	Date and time of initialization (long)
drLsBkUp	Date and time of last backup (long)
drAtrb	Volume attributes (word)
drNmFls	Number of files in directory (word)
drDirSt	First block of directory (word)
drBlLn	Length of directory in blocks (word)
drNmAlBlks	Number of allocation blocks on volume (word)
drAlBlkSiz	Size of allocation blocks (long)

drClpSiz	Number of bytes to allocate (long)
drAlBlSt	First allocation block in block map (word)
drNxtFNum	Next unused file number (long)
drFreeBks	Number of unused allocation blocks (word)
drVN	Volume name preceded by length byte (28 bytes)

File Directory Entry Data Structure

flFlags	Bit 7=1 if entry used; bit 0=1 if file locked (byte)
flTyp	Version number (byte)
flUsrWds	Information used by the Finder (16 bytes)
flFlNum	File number (long)
flStBlk	First allocation block of data fork (word)
flLgLen	Logical end-of-file of data fork (long)
flPyLen	Physical end-of-file of data fork (long)
flRStBlk	First allocation block of resource fork (word)
flRLgLen	Logical end-of-file of resource fork (long)
flRPyLen	Physical end-of-file of resource fork (long)
flCrDat	Date and time file of creation (long)
flMdDat	Date and time of last modification (long)
flNam	File name preceded by length byte

Volume Control Block Data Structure

qLink	Pointer to next queue entry
qType	Queue type (word)
vcbFlags	Bit 15=1 if volume control block is dirty (word)
vcbSigWord	Always $D2D7 (word)
vcbCrDate	Date and time of initialization (word)
vcbLsBkUp	Date and time of last backup (long)
vcbAtrb	Volume attributes (word)
vcbNmFls	Number of files in directory (word)
vcbDirSt	First block of directory (word)
vcbBlLn	Length of directory in blocks (word)
vcbNmBlks	Number of allocation blocks on volume (word)
vcbAlBlkSiz	Size of allocation blocks (long)
vcbClpSiz	Number of bytes to allocate (long)
vcbAlBlSt	First allocation block in block map (word)
vcbNxtFNum	Next unused file number (long)
vcbFreeBks	Number of unused allocation blocks (word)
vcbVN	Volume name preceded by length byte (28 bytes)
vcbDrvNum	Drive number of drive in which volume is mounted (word)
vcbDRefNum	Driver reference number of driver for drive in which volume is mounted (word)
vcbFSID	File-system identifier (word)
vcbVRefNum	Volume reference number (word)
vcbMAdr	Pointer to volume block map
vcbBufAdr	Pointer to volume buffer
vcbMLen	Number of bytes in volume block map (word)

File Control Block Data Structure

fcbFlNum	File number (long)
fcbMdRByt	Flags (byte)
fcbTypByt	Version number (byte)
fcbSBlk	First allocation block of file (word)
fcbEOF	Logical end-of-file (long)
fcbPLen	Physical end-of-file (long)
fcbCrPs	Mark (long)
fcbVPtr	Pointer to volume control block (long)
fcbBfAdr	Pointer to access path buffer (long)

Drive Queue Entry Data Structure

qLink	Pointer to next queue entry
qType	Queue type (word)
dQDrive	Drive number (word)
dQRefNum	Driver reference number (word)
dQFSID	File-system identifier (word)
dQDrvSize	Number of logical blocks (word)

Macro Names

Pascal name	Macro name
FInitQueue	_InitQueue
PBMountVol	_MountVol
PBGetVInfo	_GetVolInfo
PBGetVol	_GetVol
PBSetVol	_SetVol
PBFlushVol	_FlushVol
PBUnmountVol	_UnmountVol
PBOffLine	_OffLine
PBEject	_Eject
PBCreate	_Create
PBOpen	_Open
PBOpenRF	_OpenRF
PBRead	_Read
PBWrite	_Write
PBGetFPos	_GetFPos
PBSetFPos	_SetFPos
PBGetEOF	_GetEOF
PBSetEOF	_SetEOF
PBAllocate	_Allocate
PBFlushFile	_FlushFile
PBClose	_Close
PBGetFInfo	_GetFileInfo
PBSetFInfo	_SetFileInfo
PBSetFLock	_SetFilLock
PBRstFLock	_RstFilLock

PBSetFVers	_SetFilType
PBRename	_Rename
PBDelete	_Delete

Variables

FSQHdr	File I/O queue header (10 bytes)
VCBQHdr	Volume-control-block queue header (10 bytes)
DefVCBPtr	Pointer to default volume control block
FCBSPtr	Pointer to file-control-block buffer
DrvQHdr	Drive queue header (10 bytes)
ToExtFS	Pointer to external file system

FONT MANAGER

Constants

```
CONST  { Font numbers }

        systemFont  = 0;    {system font}
        applFont    = 1;    {application font}
        newYork     = 2;
        geneva      = 3;
        monaco      = 4;
        venice      = 5;
        london      = 6;
        athens      = 7;
        sanFran     = 8;
        toronto     = 9;
        cairo       = 11;
        losAngeles  = 12;
        times       = 20;
        helvetica   = 21;
        courier     = 22;
        symbol      = 23;
        taliesin    = 24;

        { Special characters }

        commandMark = $11;    {Command key symbol}
        checkMark   = $12;    {check mark}
        diamondMark = $13;    {diamond symbol}
        appleMark   = $14;    {apple symbol}

        { Font types }

        propFont    = $9000;  {proportional font}
        fixedFont   = $B000;  {fixed-width font}
        fontWid     = $ACB0;  {font width data}
```

Data Types

```
TYPE FMInput = PACKED RECORD
                family:    INTEGER;   {font number}
                size:      INTEGER;   {font size}
                face:      Style;     {character style}
                needBits:  BOOLEAN;   {TRUE if drawing}
                device:    INTEGER;   {device-specific information}
                numer:     Point;     {numerators of scaling factors}
                denom:     Point;     {denominators of scaling factors}
               END;
```

```
FMOutPtr = ^FMOutput;
FMOutput =
     PACKED RECORD
          errNum:      INTEGER;      {not used}
          fontHandle:  Handle;       {handle to font record}
          bold:        Byte;         {bold factor}
          italic:      Byte;         {italic factor}
          ulOffset:    Byte;         {underline offset}
          ulShadow:    Byte;         {underline shadow}
          ulThick:     Byte;         {underline thickness}
          shadow:      Byte;         {shadow factor}
          extra:       SignedByte;   {width of style}
          ascent:      Byte;         {ascent}
          descent:     Byte;         {descent}
          widMax:      Byte;         {maximum character width}
          leading:     SignedByte;   {leading}
          unused:      Byte;         {not used}
          numer:       Point;        {numerators of scaling factors}
          denom:       Point         {denominators of scaling factors}
     END;

FontRec =
     RECORD
          fontType:    INTEGER;      {font type}
          firstChar:   INTEGER;      {ASCII code of first character}
          lastChar:    INTEGER;      {ASCII code of last character}
          widMax:      INTEGER;      {maximum character width}
          kernMax:     INTEGER;      {negative of maximum character kern}
          nDescent:    INTEGER;      {negative of descent}
          fRectWidth:  INTEGER;      {width of font rectangle}
          fRectHeight: INTEGER;      {height of font rectangle}
          owTLoc:      INTEGER;      {offset to offset/width table}
          ascent:      INTEGER;      {ascent}
          descent:     INTEGER;      {descent}
          leading:     INTEGER;      {leading}
          rowWords:    INTEGER;      {row width of bit image / 2}
      { bitImage:      ARRAY[1..rowWords,1..fRectHeight] OF INTEGER; }
                                     {bit image}
      { locTable:      ARRAY[firstChar..lastChar+2] OF INTEGER; }
                                     {location table}
      { owTable:       ARRAY[firstChar..lastChar+2] OF INTEGER; }
                                     {offset/width table}
     END;
```

Routines

Initializing the Font Manager

```
PROCEDURE InitFonts;
```

Getting Font Information

```
PROCEDURE GetFontName (fontNum: INTEGER; VAR theName: Str255);
PROCEDURE GetFNum     (fontName: Str255; VAR theNum: INTEGER);
FUNCTION  RealFont    (fontNum: INTEGER; size: INTEGER) : BOOLEAN;
```

Keeping Fonts in Memory

```
PROCEDURE SetFontLock (lockFlag: BOOLEAN);
```

Advanced Routine

```
FUNCTION FMSwapFont (inRec: FMInput) : FMOutPtr;
```

Assembly-Language Information

Constants

```
; Font numbers

sysFont         .EQU    0       ;system font
applFont        .EQU    1       ;application font
newYork         .EQU    2
geneva          .EQU    3
monaco          .EQU    4
venice          .EQU    5
london          .EQU    6
athens          .EQU    7
sanFran         .EQU    8
toronto         .EQU    9
cairo           .EQU    11
losAngeles      .EQU    12
times           .EQU    20
helvetica       .EQU    21
courier         .EQU    22
symbol          .EQU    23
taliesin        .EQU    24

; Special characters

commandMark     .EQU    $11     ;Command key symbol
checkMark       .EQU    $12     ;check mark
diamondMark     .EQU    $13     ;diamond symbol
appleMark       .EQU    $14     ;apple symbol

; Font types

propFont        .EQU    $9000   ;proportional font
```

```
fixedFont      .EQU    $B000  ;fixed-width font
fontWid        .EQU    $ACB0  ;font width data

; Control and Status call code

fMgrCtl1       .EQU    8      ;code used to get and modify font
                             ; characterization table
```

Font Input Record Data Structure

fmInFamily	Font number (word)
fmInSize	Font size (word)
fmInFace	Character style (word)
fmInNeedBits	Nonzero if drawing (byte)
fmInDevice	Device-specific information (byte)
fmInNumer	Numerators of scaling factors (point; long)
fmInDenom	Denominators of scaling factors (point; long)

Font Output Record Data Structure

fmOutFontH	Handle to font record
fmOutBold	Bold factor (byte)
fmOutItalic	Italic factor (byte)
fmOutUlOffset	Underline offset (byte)
fmOutUlShadow	Underline shadow (byte)
fmOutUlThick	Underline thickness (byte)
fmOutShadow	Shadow factor (byte)
fmOutExtra	Width of style (byte)
fmOutAscent	Ascent (byte)
fmOutDescent	Descent (byte)
fmOutWidMax	Maximum character width (byte)
fmOutLeading	Leading (byte)
fmOutNumer	Numerators of scaling factors (point; long)
fmOutDenom	Denominators of scaling factors (point; long)

Font Record Data Structure

fFontType	Font type (word)
fFirstChar	ASCII code of first character (word)
fLastChar	ASCII code of last character (word)
fWidMax	Maximum character width (word)
fKernMax	Negative of maximum character kern (word)
fNDescent	Negative of descent (word)
fFRectWidth	Width of font rectangle (word)
fFRectHeight	Height of font rectangle (word)
fOWTLoc	Offset to offset/width table (word)
fAscent	Ascent (word)
fDescent	Descent (word)
fLeading	Leading (word)

fRowWords   Row width of bit image / 2 (word)

Special Macro Names

Pascal name   **Macro name**
GetFontName   _GetFName

Variables

ApFontID   Font number of application font (word)
FScaleDisable   Nonzero to disable scaling (byte)
ROMFont0   Handle to font record for system font

INTERNATIONAL UTILITIES PACKAGE

Constants

```
CONST { Masks for currency format }

      currSymLead    = 16;   {set if currency symbol leads}
      currNegSym     = 32;   {set if minus sign for negative}
      currTrailingZ  = 64;   {set if trailing decimal zeroes}
      currLeadingZ   = 128;  {set if leading integer zero}

      { Order of short date elements }

      mdy = 0;       {month day year}
      dmy = 1;       {day month year}
      ymd = 2;       {year month day}

      { Masks for short date format }

      dayLdingZ = 32;   {set if leading zero for day}
      mntLdingZ = 64;   {set if leading zero for month}
      century   = 128;  {set if century included}

      { Masks for time format }

      secLeadingZ = 32;   {set if leading zero for seconds}
      minLeadingZ = 64;   {set if leading zero for minutes}
      hrLeadingZ  = 128;  {set if leading zero for hours}

      { High-order byte of version information }

      verUS          = 0;
      verFrance      = 1;
      verBritain     = 2;
      verGermany     = 3;
      verItaly       = 4;
      verNetherlands = 5;
      verBelgiumLux  = 6;
      verSweden      = 7;
      verSpain       = 8;
      verDenmark     = 9;
      verPortugal    = 10;
      verFrCanada    = 11;
      verNorway      = 12;
      verIsrael      = 13;
      verJapan       = 14;
      verAustralia   = 15;
      verArabia      = 16;
      verFinland     = 17;
```

```
verFrSwiss        = 18;
verGrSwiss        = 19;
verGreece         = 20;
verIceland        = 21;
verMalta          = 22;
verCyprus         = 23;
verTurkey         = 24;
verYugoslavia     = 25;
```

Data Types

```
TYPE Intl0Hndl = ^Intl0Ptr;
     Intl0Ptr  = ^Intl0Rec;
     Intl0Rec  =
         PACKED RECORD
            decimalPt:   CHAR;   {decimal point character}
            thousSep:    CHAR;   {thousands separator}
            listSep:     CHAR;   {list separator}
            currSym1:    CHAR;   {currency symbol}
            currSym2:    CHAR;
            currSym3:    CHAR;
            currFmt:     Byte;   {currency format}
            dateOrder:   Byte;   {order of short date elements}
            shrtDateFmt: Byte;   {short date format}
            dateSep:     CHAR;   {date separator}
            timeCycle:   Byte;   {0 if 24-hour cycle, 255 if 12-hour}
            timeFmt:     Byte;   {time format}
            mornStr:     PACKED ARRAY[1..4] OF CHAR;
                                 {trailing string for first 12-hour cycle}
            eveStr:      PACKED ARRAY[1..4] OF CHAR;
                                 {trailing string for last 12-hour cycle}
            timeSep:     CHAR;   {time separator}
            time1Suff:   CHAR;   {trailing string for 24-hour cycle}
            time2Suff:   CHAR;
            time3Suff:   CHAR;
            time4Suff:   CHAR;
            time5Suff:   CHAR;
            time6Suff:   CHAR;
            time7Suff:   CHAR;
            time8Suff:   CHAR;
            metricSys:   Byte;   {255 if metric, 0 if not}
            intl0Vers:   INTEGER {version information}
         END;
```

```
Intl1Hndl = ^Intl1Ptr;
Intl1Ptr = ^Intl1Rec;
Intl1Rec =
         PACKED RECORD
            days:        ARRAY[1..7] OF STRING[15];   {day names}
            months:      ARRAY[1..12] OF STRING[15];  {month names}
            suppressDay: Byte;  {0 for day name, 255 for none}
            lngDateFmt:  Byte;  {order of long date elements}
            dayLeading0: Byte;  {255 for leading 0 in day number}
            abbrLen:     Byte;  {length for abbreviating names}
            st0:         PACKED ARRAY[1..4] OF CHAR;  {strings }
            st1:         PACKED ARRAY[1..4] OF CHAR;  { for }
            st2:         PACKED ARRAY[1..4] OF CHAR;  { long }
            st3:         PACKED ARRAY[1..4] OF CHAR;  { date }
            st4:         PACKED ARRAY[1..4] OF CHAR;  { format}
            intl1Vers:   INTEGER; {version information}
            localRtn:    INTEGER  {routine for localizing string }
                                  { comparison; actually may be }
                                  { longer than one integer}
         END;

   DateForm = (shortDate,longDate,abbrevDate);
```

Routines

```
PROCEDURE IUDateString (dateTime: LONGINT; form: DateForm; VAR result:
                        Str255);
PROCEDURE IUDatePString (dateTime: LONGINT; form: DateForm; VAR result:
                        Str255; intlParam: Handle);
PROCEDURE IUTimeString (dateTime: LONGINT; wantSeconds: BOOLEAN; VAR
                        result: Str255);
PROCEDURE IUTimePString (dateTime: LONGINT; wantSeconds: BOOLEAN; VAR
                        result: Str255; intlParam: Handle);
FUNCTION  IUMetric :    BOOLEAN;
FUNCTION  IUGetIntl    (theID: INTEGER) : Handle;
PROCEDURE IUSetIntl    (refNum: INTEGER; theID: INTEGER; intlParam:
                        Handle);
FUNCTION  IUCompString (aStr,bStr: Str255) : INTEGER;   [Not in ROM]
FUNCTION  IUMagString  (aPtr,bPtr: Ptr; aLen,bLen: INTEGER) : INTEGER;
FUNCTION  IUEqualString (aStr,bStr: Str255) : INTEGER;  [Not in ROM]
FUNCTION  IUMagIDString (aPtr,bPtr: Ptr; aLen,bLen: INTEGER) : INTEGER;
```

Assembly-Language Information

Constants

```
; Masks for currency format

currSymLead     .EQU    16      ;set if currency symbol leads
currNegSym      .EQU    32      ;set if minus sign for negative
currTrailingZ   .EQU    64      ;set if trailing decimal zeroes
currLeadingZ    .EQU    128     ;set if leading integer zero

; Order of short date elements

mdy             .EQU    0       ;month day year
dmy             .EQU    1       ;day month year
ymd             .EQU    2       ;year month day

; Masks for short date format

dayLdingZ       .EQU    32      ;set if leading zero for day
mntLdingZ       .EQU    64      ;set if leading zero for month
century         .EQU    128     ;set if century included

; Masks for time format

secLeadingZ     .EQU    32      ;set if leading zero for seconds
minLeadingZ     .EQU    64      ;set if leading zero for minutes
hrLeadingZ      .EQU    128     ;set if leading zero for hours

; High-order byte of version information

verUS           .EQU    0
verFrance       .EQU    1
verBritain      .EQU    2
verGermany      .EQU    3
verItaly        .EQU    4
verNetherlands  .EQU    5
verBelgiumLux   .EQU    6
verSweden       .EQU    7
verSpain        .EQU    8
verDenmark      .EQU    9
verPortugal     .EQU    10
verFrCanada     .EQU    11
verNorway       .EQU    12
verIsrael       .EQU    13
verJapan        .EQU    14
verAustralia    .EQU    15
verArabia       .EQU    16
verFinland      .EQU    17
verFrSwiss      .EQU    18
verGrSwiss      .EQU    19
```

```
verGreece          .EQU    20
verIceland         .EQU    21
verMalta           .EQU    22
verCyprus          .EQU    23
verTurkey          .EQU    24
verYugoslavia      .EQU    25


; Date form for IUDateString and IUDatePString

shortDate          .EQU    0       ;short form of date
longDate           .EQU    1       ;long form of date
abbrevDate         .EQU    2       ;abbreviated long form


; Routine selectors

iuDateString       .EQU    0
iuTimeString       .EQU    2
iuMetric           .EQU    4
iuGetIntl          .EQU    6
iuSetIntl          .EQU    8
iuMagString        .EQU    10
iuMagIDString      .EQU    12
iuDatePString      .EQU    14
iuTimePString      .EQU    16
```

International Resource 0 Data Structure

decimalPt	Decimal point character (byte)
thousSep	Thousands separator (byte)
listSep	List separator (byte)
currSym	Currency symbol (3 bytes)
currFmt	Currency format (byte)
dateOrder	Order of short date elements (byte)
shrtDateFmt	Short date format (byte)
dateSep	Date separator (byte)
timeCycle	0 if 24-hour cycle, 255 if 12-hour (byte)
timeFmt	Time format (byte)
mornStr	Trailing string for first 12-hour cycle (long)
eveStr	Trailing string for last 12-hour cycle (long)
timeSep	Time separator (byte)
timeSuff	Trailing string for 24-hour cycle (8 bytes)
metricSys	255 if metric, 0 if not (byte)
intl0Vers	Version information (word)

International Resource 1 Data Structure

days	Day names (112 bytes)
months	Month names (192 bytes)
suppressDay	0 for day name, 255 for none (byte)
lngDateFmt	Order of long date elements (byte)

dayLeading0	255 for leading 0 in day number (byte)
abbrLen	Length for abbreviating names (byte)
st0	Strings for long date format (longs)
st1	
st2	
st3	
st4	
intl1Vers	Version information (word)
localRtn	Comparison localization routine

Trap Macro Name

_Pack6

MEMORY MANAGER

Constants

CONST { Result codes }

```
    memFullErr    = -108;    {not enough room in heap zone}
    memLockedErr  = -117;    {block is locked}
    memPurErr     = -112;    {attempt to purge a locked block}
    memWZErr      = -111;    {attempt to operate on a free block}
    nilHandleErr  = -109;    {NIL master pointer}
    noErr         =   0;     {no error}
```

Data Types

```
TYPE SignedByte   = -128..127;
     Byte         = 0..255;
     Ptr          = ^SignedByte;
     Handle       = ^Ptr;

     Str255       = STRING[255];
     StringPtr    = ^Str255;
     StringHandle = ^StringPtr;

     ProcPtr = Ptr;

     Fixed = LONGINT;

     Size = LONGINT;

     THz  = ^Zone;
     Zone = RECORD
                bkLim:      Ptr;       {zone trailer block}
                purgePtr:   Ptr;       {used internally}
                hFstFree:   Ptr;       {first free master pointer}
                zcbFree:    LONGINT;   {number of free bytes}
                gzProc:     ProcPtr;   {grow zone function}
                moreMast:   INTEGER;   {master pointers to allocate}
                flags:      INTEGER;   {used internally}
                cntRel:     INTEGER;   {not used}
                maxRel:     INTEGER;   {not used}
                cntNRel:    INTEGER;   {not used}
                maxNRel:    INTEGER;   {not used}
                cntEmpty:   INTEGER;   {not used}
                cntHandles: INTEGER;   {not used}
                minCBFree:  LONGINT;   {not used}
                purgeProc:  ProcPtr;   {purge warning procedure}
                sparePtr:   Ptr;       {used internally}
                allocPtr:   Ptr;       {used internally}
                heapData:   INTEGER    {first usable byte in zone}
            END;
```

Routines

Initialization and Allocation

```
PROCEDURE  InitApplZone;
PROCEDURE  SetApplBase    (startPtr: Ptr);
PROCEDURE  InitZone       (pGrowZone: ProcPtr; cMoreMasters: INTEGER;
                           limitPtr,startPtr: Ptr);
FUNCTION   GetApplLimit :  Ptr;  [Not in ROM]
PROCEDURE  SetApplLimit   (zoneLimit: Ptr);
PROCEDURE  MaxApplZone;    [Not in ROM]
PROCEDURE  MoreMasters;
```

Heap Zone Access

```
FUNCTION   GetZone :    THz;
PROCEDURE  SetZone     (hz: THz);
FUNCTION   SystemZone : THz;   [Not in ROM]
FUNCTION   ApplicZone : THz;   [Not in ROM]
```

Allocating and Releasing Relocatable Blocks

```
FUNCTION   NewHandle     (logicalSize: Size) : Handle;
PROCEDURE  DisposHandle  (h: Handle);
FUNCTION   GetHandleSize (h: Handle) : Size;
PROCEDURE  SetHandleSize (h: Handle; newSize: Size);
FUNCTION   HandleZone    (h: Handle) : THz;
FUNCTION   RecoverHandle (p: Ptr) : Handle;
PROCEDURE  ReallocHandle (h: Handle; logicalSize: Size);
```

Allocating and Releasing Nonrelocatable Blocks

```
FUNCTION   NewPtr     (logicalSize: Size) : Ptr;
PROCEDURE  DisposPtr  (p: Ptr);
FUNCTION   GetPtrSize (p: Ptr) : Size;
PROCEDURE  SetPtrSize (p: Ptr; newSize: Size);
FUNCTION   PtrZone    (p: Ptr) : THz;
```

Freeing Space in the Heap

```
FUNCTION   FreeMem :    LONGINT;
FUNCTION   MaxMem      (VAR grow: Size) : Size;
FUNCTION   CompactMem  (cbNeeded: Size) : Size;
PROCEDURE  ResrvMem    (cbNeeded: Size);
PROCEDURE  PurgeMem    (cbNeeded: Size);
PROCEDURE  EmptyHandle (h: Handle);
```

Properties of Relocatable Blocks

```
PROCEDURE HLock    (h: Handle);
PROCEDURE HUnlock  (h: Handle);
PROCEDURE HPurge   (h: Handle);
PROCEDURE HNoPurge (h: Handle);
```

Grow Zone Operations

```
PROCEDURE SetGrowZone (growZone: ProcPtr);
FUNCTION  GZSaveHnd :  Handle;   [Not in ROM]
```

Miscellaneous Routines

```
PROCEDURE BlockMove (sourcePtr,destPtr: Ptr; byteCount: Size);
FUNCTION  TopMem :    Ptr;   [Not in ROM]
PROCEDURE MoveHHi    (h: Handle);   [Not in ROM]
FUNCTION  MemError :  OSErr;   [Not in ROM]
```

Grow Zone Function

```
FUNCTION MyGrowZone (cbNeeded: Size) : LONGINT;
```

Assembly-Language Information

Constants

```
; Values for tag byte of a block header

tyBkFree       .EQU    0       ;free block
tyBkNRel       .EQU    1       ;nonrelocatable block
tyBkRel        .EQU    2       ;relocatable block

; Flags for the high-order byte of a master pointer

lock           .EQU    7       ;lock bit
purge          .EQU    6       ;purge bit
resourc        .EQU    5       ;resource bit

; Result codes

memFullErr     .EQU    -108    ;not enough room in heap zone
memLockedErr   .EQU    -117    ;block is locked
memPurErr      .EQU    -112    ;attempt to purge a locked block
memWZErr       .EQU    -111    ;attempt to operate on a free block
nilHandleErr   .EQU    -109    ;NIL master pointer
noErr          .EQU    0       ;no error
```

Zone Record Data Structure

bkLim	Pointer to zone trailer block
hFstFree	Pointer to first free master pointer
zcbFree	Number of free bytes (long)
gzProc	Address of grow zone function
mAllocCnt	Master pointers to allocate (word)
purgeProc	Address of purge warning procedure
heapData	First usable byte in zone

Block Header Data Structure

tagBC	Tag byte and physical block size (long)
handle	Relocatable block: relative handle
	Nonrelocatable block: zone pointer
blkData	First byte of block contents

Parameter Block Structure for InitZone

startPtr	Pointer to first byte in zone
limitPtr	Pointer to first byte beyond end of zone
cMoreMasters	Number of master pointers for zone (word)
pGrowZone	Address of grow zone function

Routines

Trap macro	On entry	On exit
_InitApplZone		D0: result code (word)
_SetApplBase	A0: startPtr (ptr)	D0: result code (word)
_InitZone	A0: ptr to parameter block 0 startPtr (ptr) 4 limitPtr (ptr) 8 cMoreMasters (word) 10 pGrowZone (ptr)	D0: result code (word)
_SetApplLimit	A0: zoneLimit (ptr)	D0: result code (word)
_MoreMasters		
_GetZone		A0: function result (ptr) D0: result code (word)
_SetZone	A0: hz (ptr)	D0: result code (word)
_NewHandle	D0: logicalSize (long)	A0: function result (handle) D0: result code (word)
_DisposHandle	A0: h (handle)	D0: result code (word)

Trap macro	On entry	On exit
_GetHandleSize	A0: h (handle)	D0: if >=0, function result (long) if <0, result code (word)
_SetHandleSize	A0: h (handle) D0: newSize (long)	D0: result code (word)
_HandleZone	A0: h (handle)	A0: function result (ptr) D0: result code (word)
_RecoverHandle	A0: p (ptr)	A0: function result (handle) D0: unchanged
_ReallocHandle	A0: h (handle) D0: logicalSize (long)	D0: result code (word)
_NewPtr	D0: logicalSize (long)	A0: function result (ptr) D0: result code (word)
_DisposPtr	A0: p (ptr)	D0: result code (word)
_GetPtrSize	A0: p (ptr)	D0: if >=0, function result (long) if <0, result code (word)
_SetPtrSize	A0: p (ptr) D0: newSize (long)	D0: result code (word)
_PtrZone	A0: p (ptr)	A0: function result (ptr) D0: result code (word)
_FreeMem		D0: function result (long)
_MaxMem		D0: function result (long) A0: grow (long)
_CompactMem	D0: cbNeeded (long)	D0: function result (long)
_ResrvMem	D0: cbNeeded (long)	D0: result code (word)
_PurgeMem	D0: cbNeeded (long)	D0: result code (word)
_EmptyHandle	A0: h (handle)	A0: h (handle) D0: result code (word)
_HLock	A0: h (handle)	D0: result code (word)
_HUnlock	A0: h (handle)	D0: result code (word)
_HPurge	A0: h (handle)	D0: result code (word)
_HNoPurge	A0: h (handle)	D0: result code (word)
_SetGrowZone	A0: growZone (ptr)	D0: result code (word)
_BlockMove	A0: sourcePtr (ptr) A1: destPtr (ptr) D0: byteCount (long)	D0: result code (word)

Variables

DefltStack	Default space allotment for stack (long)
MinStack	Minimum space allotment for stack (long)
MemTop	Address of end of RAM (on Macintosh XL, end of RAM available to applications)
ScrnBase	Address of main screen buffer
BufPtr	Address of end of jump table
CurrentA5	Address of boundary between application globals and application parameters
CurStackBase	Address of base of stack; start of application globals
ApplLimit	Application heap limit
HeapEnd	Address of end of application heap zone
ApplZone	Address of application heap zone
SysZone	Address of system heap zone
TheZone	Address of current heap zone
GZRootHnd	Handle to relocatable block not to be moved by grow zone function

3 Summary

MENU MANAGER

Constants

```
CONST { Value indicating item has no mark }

      noMark = 0;

      { Messages to menu definition procedure }

      mDrawMsg    = 0;        {draw the menu}
      mChooseMsg  = 1;        {tell which item was chosen and highlight it}
      mSizeMsg    = 2;        {calculate the menu's dimensions}

      { Resource ID of standard menu definition procedure }

      textMenuProc = 0;
```

Data Types

```
TYPE MenuHandle = ^MenuPtr;
     MenuPtr    = ^MenuInfo;
     MenuInfo   = RECORD
                     menuID:       INTEGER;   {menu ID}
                     menuWidth:    INTEGER;   {menu width in pixels}
                     menuHeight:   INTEGER;   {menu height in pixels}
                     menuProc:     Handle;    {menu definition procedure}
                     enableFlags:  LONGINT;   {tells if menu or items are }
                                              { enabled}
                     menuData:     Str255     {menu title (and other data) }
                  END;
```

Routines

Initialization and Allocation

```
PROCEDURE  InitMenus;
FUNCTION   NewMenu      (menuID: INTEGER; menuTitle: Str255) : MenuHandle;
FUNCTION   GetMenu      (resourceID: INTEGER) : MenuHandle;
PROCEDURE  DisposeMenu  (theMenu: MenuHandle);
```

Forming the Menus

```
PROCEDURE  AppendMenu     (theMenu: MenuHandle; data: Str255);
PROCEDURE  AddResMenu     (theMenu: MenuHandle; theType: ResType);
PROCEDURE  InsertResMenu  (theMenu: MenuHandle; theType: ResType;
                           afterItem: INTEGER);
```

Forming the Menu Bar

```
PROCEDURE  InsertMenu  (theMenu: MenuHandle; beforeID: INTEGER);
PROCEDURE  DrawMenuBar;
PROCEDURE  DeleteMenu  (menuID: INTEGER);
PROCEDURE  ClearMenuBar;
FUNCTION   GetNewMBar  (menuBarID: INTEGER) : Handle;
FUNCTION   GetMenuBar  : Handle;
PROCEDURE  SetMenuBar  (menuList: Handle);
```

Choosing From a Menu

```
FUNCTION   MenuSelect  (startPt: Point) : LONGINT;
FUNCTION   MenuKey     (ch: CHAR) : LONGINT;
PROCEDURE  HiliteMenu  (menuID: INTEGER);
```

Controlling the Appearance of Items

```
PROCEDURE  SetItem      (theMenu: MenuHandle; item: INTEGER; itemString:
                         Str255);
PROCEDURE  GetItem      (theMenu: MenuHandle; item: INTEGER; VAR
                         itemString: Str255);
PROCEDURE  DisableItem  (theMenu: MenuHandle; item: INTEGER);
PROCEDURE  EnableItem   (theMenu: MenuHandle; item: INTEGER);
PROCEDURE  CheckItem    (theMenu: MenuHandle; item: INTEGER; checked:
                         BOOLEAN);
PROCEDURE  SetItemMark  (theMenu: MenuHandle; item: INTEGER; markChar:
                         CHAR);
PROCEDURE  GetItemMark  (theMenu: MenuHandle; item: INTEGER; VAR
                         markChar: CHAR);
PROCEDURE  SetItemIcon  (theMenu: MenuHandle; item: INTEGER; icon: Byte);
PROCEDURE  GetItemIcon  (theMenu: MenuHandle; item: INTEGER; VAR icon:
                         Byte);
PROCEDURE  SetItemStyle (theMenu: MenuHandle; item: INTEGER; chStyle:
                         Style);
PROCEDURE  GetItemStyle (theMenu: MenuHandle; item: INTEGER; VAR chStyle:
                         Style);
```

Miscellaneous Routines

```
PROCEDURE  CalcMenuSize (theMenu: MenuHandle);
FUNCTION   CountMItems  (theMenu: MenuHandle) : INTEGER;
FUNCTION   GetMHandle   (menuID: INTEGER) : MenuHandle;
PROCEDURE  FlashMenuBar (menuID: INTEGER);
PROCEDURE  SetMenuFlash (count: INTEGER);
```

Meta-Characters for AppendMenu

Meta-character	Usage
; or Return	Separates multiple items
^	Followed by an icon number, adds that icon to the item
!	Followed by a character, marks the item with that character
<	Followed by B, I, U, O, or S, sets the character style of the item
/	Followed by a character, associates a keyboard equivalent with the item
(	Disables the item

Menu Definition Procedure

```
PROCEDURE MyMenu (message: INTEGER; theMenu: MenuHandle; VAR menuRect:
                  Rect; hitPt: Point; VAR whichItem: INTEGER);
```

Assembly-Language Information

Constants

```
; Value indicating item has no mark

noMark         .EQU        0

; Messages to menu definition procedure

mDrawMsg       .EQU     0      ;draw the menu
mChooseMsg     .EQU     1      ;tell which item was chosen and highlight it
mSizeMsg       .EQU     2      ;calculate the menu's dimensions

; Resource ID of standard menu definition procedure

textMenuProc   .EQU        0
```

Menu Record Data Structure

menuID	Menu ID (word)
menuWidth	Menu width in pixels (word)
menuHeight	Menu height in pixels (word)
menuDefHandle	Handle to menu definition procedure
menuEnable	Enable flags (long)
menuData	Menu title (preceded by length byte) followed by data defining the items
menuBlkSize	Size in bytes of menu record except menuData field

Special Macro Names

Pascal name	Macro name
DisposeMenu	_DisposMenu
GetItemIcon	_GetItmIcon
GetItemMark	_GetItmMark
GetItemStyle	_GetItmStyle
GetMenu	_GetRMenu
SetItemIcon	_SetItmIcon
SetItemMark	_SetItmMark
SetItemStyle	_SetItmStyle
SetMenuFlash	_SetMFlash

Variables

MenuList	Handle to current menu list
MBarEnable	Nonzero if menu bar belongs to a desk accessory (word)
MenuHook	Address of routine called repeatedly during MenuSelect
MBarHook	Address of routine called by MenuSelect before menu is drawn (see below)
TheMenu	Menu ID of currently highlighted menu (word)
MenuFlash	Count for duration of menu item blinking (word)

MBarHook routine

On entry	stack: pointer to menu rectangle
On exit	D0: 0 to continue MenuSelect
	1 to abort MenuSelect

PACKAGE MANAGER

Constants

```
CONST { Resource IDs for packages }

        dskInit = 2;      {Disk Initialization}
        stdFile = 3;      {Standard File}
        flPoint = 4;      {Floating-Point Arithmetic}
        trFunc  = 5;      {Transcendental Functions}
        intUtil = 6;      {International Utilities}
        bdConv  = 7;      {Binary-Decimal Conversion}
```

Routines

```
PROCEDURE InitPack       (packID: INTEGER);
PROCEDURE InitAllPacks;
```

Assembly-Language Information

Constants

```
; Resource IDs for packages

dskInit     .EQU     2      ;Disk Initialization
stdFile     .EQU     3      ;Standard File
flPoint     .EQU     4      ;Floating-Point Arithmetic
trFunc      .EQU     5      ;Transcendental Functions
intUtil     .EQU     6      ;International Utilities
bdConv      .EQU     7      ;Binary-Decimal Conversion
```

Trap Macros for Packages

Disk Initialization	_Pack2	
Standard File	_Pack3	
Floating-Point Arithmetic	_Pack4	(synonym: _FP68K)
Transcendental Functions	_Pack5	(synonym: _Elems68K)
International Utilities	_Pack6	
Binary-Decimal Conversion	_Pack7	

PRINTING MANAGER

Constants

```
CONST  { Printing methods }

       bDraftLoop = 0;      {draft printing}
       bSpoolLoop = 1;      {spool printing}

       { Printer specification in prStl field of print record }

       bDevCItoh = 1;       {Imagewriter printer}
       bDevLaser = 3;       {LaserWriter printer}

       { Maximum number of pages in a spool file }

       iPFMaxPgs = 128;

       { Result codes }

       noErr       =   0;      {no error}
       iPrSavPFil  =  -1;      {saving spool file}
       controlErr  = -17;      {unimplemented control instruction}
       iIOAbort    = -27;      {I/O abort error}
       iMemFullErr = -108;     {not enough room in heap zone}
       iPrAbort    = 128;      {application or user requested abort}

       { PrCtlCall parameters }

       iPrDevCtl  = 7;           {printer control}
       lPrReset   = $00010000;   {reset printer}
       lPrLineFeed = $00030000;  {carriage return only}
       lPrLFSixth = $0003FFFF;   {standard 1/6-inch line feed}
       lPrPageEnd = $00020000;   {end page}
       iPrBitsCtl = 4;           {bit map printing}
       lScreenBits = 0;          {default for printer}
       lPaintBits = 1;           {square dots (72 by 72)}
       iPrIOCtl   = 5;           {text streaming}

       { Printer Driver information }

       sPrDrvr    = '.Print';   {Printer Driver resource name}
       iPrDrvrRef = -3;         {Printer Driver reference number}
```

Data Types

```
TYPE TPPrPort = ^TPrPort;
     TPrPort  = RECORD
                     gPort: GrafPort;   {grafPort to draw in}
                     {more fields for internal use}
                END;

     THPrint  = ^TPPrint;
     TPPrint  = ^TPrint;
     TPrint   = RECORD
                     iPrVersion: INTEGER;   {Printing Manager version}
                     prInfo:     TPrInfo;   {printer information subrecord}
                     rPaper:     Rect;      {paper rectangle}
                     prStl:      TPrStl;    {additional device information}
                     prInfoPT:   TPrInfo;   {used internally}
                     prXInfo:    TPrXInfo;  {additional device information}
                     prJob:      TPrJob;    {job subrecord}
                     printX:     ARRAY[1..19] OF INTEGER   {not used}
                END;

     TPrInfo = RECORD
                     iDev:  INTEGER;   {used internally}
                     iVRes: INTEGER;   {vertical resolution of printer}
                     iHRes: INTEGER;   {horizontal resolution of printer}
                     rPage: Rect       {page rectangle}
                END;

     TPrJob =
          RECORD
               iFstPage:  INTEGER;     {first page to print}
               iLstPage:  INTEGER;     {last page to print}
               iCopies:   INTEGER;     {number of copies}
               bJDocLoop: SignedByte;  {printing method}
               fFromUsr:  BOOLEAN;     {used internally}
               pIdleProc: ProcPtr;     {background procedure}
               pFileName: StringPtr;   {spool file name}
               iFileVol:  INTEGER;     {spool file volume reference number}
               bFileVers: SignedByte;  {spool file version number}
               bJobX:     SignedByte   {used internally}
          END;

     TPrStl = RECORD
                     wDev: INTEGER;    {high byte specifies device}
                     {more fields for internal use}
                END;
```

```
TPrXInfo = RECORD
            iRowBytes: INTEGER;      {used internally}
            iBandV:    INTEGER;      {used internally}
            iBandH:    INTEGER;      {used internally}
            iDevBytes: INTEGER;      {size of buffer}
            {more fields for internal use}
          END;


TPRect = ^Rect;


TPrStatus = RECORD
              iTotPages:  INTEGER;   {number of pages in spool file}
              iCurPage:   INTEGER;   {page being printed}
              iTotCopies: INTEGER;   {number of copies requested}
              iCurCopy:   INTEGER;   {copy being printed}
              iTotBands:  INTEGER;   {used internally}
              iCurBand:   INTEGER;   {used internally}
              fPgDirty:   BOOLEAN;   {TRUE if started printing page}
              fImaging:   BOOLEAN;   {used internally}
              hPrint:     THPrint;   {print record}
              pPrPort:    TPPrPort;  {printing grafPort}
              hPic:       PicHandle  {used internally}
            END;
```

Routines [Not in ROM]

Initialization and Termination

```
PROCEDURE PrOpen;
PROCEDURE PrClose;
```

Print Records and Dialogs

```
PROCEDURE PrintDefault (hPrint: THPrint);
FUNCTION  PrValidate   (hPrint: THPrint) : BOOLEAN;
FUNCTION  PrStlDialog  (hPrint: THPrint) : BOOLEAN;
FUNCTION  PrJobDialog  (hPrint: THPrint) : BOOLEAN;
PROCEDURE PrJobMerge   (hPrintSrc,hPrintDst: THPrint);
```

Printing

```
FUNCTION  PrOpenDoc   (hPrint: THPrint; pPrPort: TPPrPort; pIOBuf: Ptr) :
                       TPPrPort;
PROCEDURE PrOpenPage  (pPrPort: TPPrPort; pPageFrame: TPRect);
PROCEDURE PrClosePage (pPrPort: TPPrPort);
PROCEDURE PrCloseDoc  (pPrPort: TPPrPort);
PROCEDURE PrPicFile   (hPrint: THPrint; pPrPort: TPPrPort; pIOBuf: Ptr;
                       pDevBuf: Ptr; VAR prStatus: TPrStatus);
```

Error Handling

```
FUNCTION  PrError :    INTEGER;
PROCEDURE PrSetError (iErr: INTEGER);
```

Low-Level Driver Access

```
PROCEDURE PrDrvrOpen;
PROCEDURE PrDrvrClose;
PROCEDURE PrCtlCall     (iWhichCtl: INTEGER; lParam1,lParam2,lParam3:
                         LONGINT);
FUNCTION  PrDrvrDCE :    Handle;
FUNCTION  PrDrvrVers :   INTEGER;
```

<u>Assembly-Language Information</u>

Constants

```
; Printing methods

bDraftLoop    .EQU   0       ;draft printing
bSpoolLoop    .EQU   1       ;spool printing

; Result codes

noErr         .EQU    0       ;no error
iPrSavPFil    .EQU   -1       ;saving spool file
controlErr    .EQU   -17      ;unimplemented control instruction
iIOAbort      .EQU   -27      ;I/O abort error
iMemFullErr   .EQU   -108     ;not enough room in heap zone
iPrAbort      .EQU    128     ;application or user requested abort

; Printer Driver Control call parameters

iPrDevCtl     .EQU   7       ;printer control
lPrReset      .EQU   1       ; reset printer
iPrLineFeed   .EQU   3       ; carriage return/paper advance
iPrLFSixth    .EQU   3       ;standard 1/6-inch line feed
lPrPageEnd    .EQU   2       ; end page
iPrBitsCtl    .EQU   4       ;bit map printing
lScreenBits   .EQU   0       ; default for printer
lPaintBits    .EQU   1       ; square dots (72 by 72)
iPrIOCtl      .EQU   5       ;text streaming

; Printer Driver information

iPrDrvrRef    .EQU   -3      ;Printer Driver reference number
```

Printing GrafPort Data Structure

gPort   GrafPort to draw in (portRec bytes)
iPrPortSize   Size in bytes of printing grafPort

Print Record Data Structure

iPrVersion   Printing Manager version (word)
prInfo   Printer information subrecord (14 bytes)
rPaper   Paper rectangle (8 bytes)
prStl   Additional device information (8 bytes)
prXInfo   Additional device information (16 bytes)
prJob   Job subrecord (iPrJobSize bytes)
iPrintSize   Size in bytes of print record

Structure of Printer Information Subrecord

iVRes   Vertical resolution of printer (word)
iHRes   Horizontal resolution of printer (word)
rPage   Page rectangle (8 bytes)

Structure of Job Subrecord

iFstPage   First page to print (word)
iLstPage   Last page to print (word)
iCopies   Number of copies (word)
bJDocLoop   Printing method (byte)
pIdleProc   Address of background procedure
pFileName   Pointer to spool file name (preceded by length byte)
iFileVol   Spool file volume reference number (word)
bFileVers   Spool file version number (byte)
iPrJobSize   Size in bytes of job subrecord

Structure of PrXInfo Subrecord

iDevBytes   Size of buffer (word)

Structure of Printer Status Record

iTotPages   Number of pages in spool file (word)
iCurPage   Page being printed (word)
iTotCopies   Number of copies requested (word)
iCurCopy   Copy being printed (word)
fPgDirty   Nonzero if started printing page (byte)
hPrint   Handle to print record
pPrPort   Pointer to printing grafPort
iPrStatSize   Size in bytes of printer status record

Variables

PrintErr   Result code from last Printing Manager routine (word)

QUICKDRAW

Constants

```
CONST  { Source transfer modes }

       srcCopy    = 0;
       srcOr      = 1;
       srcXor     = 2;
       srcBic     = 3;
       notSrcCopy = 4;
       notSrcOr   = 5;
       notSrcXor  = 6;
       notSrcBic  = 7;


       { Pattern transfer modes }

       patCopy    = 8;
       patOr      = 9;
       patXor     = 10;
       patBic     = 11;
       notPatCopy = 12;
       notPatOr   = 13;
       notPatXor  = 14;
       notPatBic  = 15;


       { Standard colors for ForeColor and BackColor }

       blackColor   = 33;
       whiteColor   = 30;
       redColor     = 205;
       greenColor   = 341;
       blueColor    = 409;
       cyanColor    = 273;
       magentaColor = 137;
       yellowColor  = 69;


       { Standard picture comments }

       picLParen = 0;
       picRParen = 1;
```

Data Types

```
TYPE  StyleItem = (bold,italic,underline,outline,shadow,condense,extend);
      Style     = SET OF StyleItem;
```

```
VHSelect = (v,h);
Point    = RECORD CASE INTEGER OF

               0: (v: INTEGER;  {vertical coordinate}
                   h: INTEGER); {horizontal coordinate}

               1: (vh: ARRAY[VHSelect] OF INTEGER)

          END;


Rect = RECORD CASE INTEGER OF

            0: (top:    INTEGER;
                left:   INTEGER;
                bottom: INTEGER;
                right:  INTEGER);

            1: (topLeft:  Point;
                botRight: Point)

         END;


RgnHandle = ^RgnPtr;
RgnPtr    = ^Region;
Region    = RECORD
                rgnSize: INTEGER; {size in bytes}
                rgnBBox: Rect;    {enclosing rectangle}
                {more data if not rectangular}
            END;


BitMap = RECORD
            baseAddr: Ptr;     {pointer to bit image}
            rowBytes: INTEGER; {row width}
            bounds:   Rect     {boundary rectangle}
         END;


Pattern = PACKED ARRAY[0..7] OF 0..255;


Bits16 = ARRAY[0..15] OF INTEGER;


Cursor = RECORD
            data:    Bits16; {cursor image}
            mask:    Bits16; {cursor mask}
            hotSpot: Point   {point aligned with mouse}
         END;
```

```
QDProcsPtr = ^QDProcs;
QDProcs    = RECORD
                textProc:     Ptr;  {text drawing}
                lineProc:     Ptr;  {line drawing}
                rectProc:     Ptr;  {rectangle drawing}
                rRectProc:    Ptr;  {roundRect drawing}
                ovalProc:     Ptr;  {oval drawing}
                arcProc:      Ptr;  {arc/wedge drawing}
                rgnProc:      Ptr;  {region drawing}
                bitsProc:     Ptr;  {bit transfer}
                commentProc:  Ptr;  {picture comment processing}
                txMeasProc:   Ptr;  {text width measurement}
                getPicProc:   Ptr;  {picture retrieval}
                putPicProc:   Ptr   {picture saving}
            END;

GrafPtr  = ^GrafPort;
GrafPort = RECORD
                device:     INTEGER;    {device-specific information}
                portBits:   BitMap;     {grafPort's bit map}
                portRect:   Rect;       {grafPort's rectangle}
                visRgn:     RgnHandle;   {visible region}
                clipRgn:    RgnHandle;   {clipping region}
                bkPat:      Pattern;     {background pattern}
                fillPat:    Pattern;     {fill pattern}
                pnLoc:      Point;       {pen location}
                pnSize:     Point;       {pen size}
                pnMode:     INTEGER;     {pen's transfer mode}
                pnPat:      Pattern;     {pen pattern}
                pnVis:      INTEGER;     {pen visibility}
                txFont:     INTEGER;     {font number for text}
                txFace:     Style;       {text's character style}
                txMode:     INTEGER;     {text's transfer mode}
                txSize:     INTEGER;     {font size for text}
                spExtra:    Fixed;       {extra space}
                fgColor:    LONGINT;     {foreground color}
                bkColor:    LONGINT;     {background color}
                colrBit:    INTEGER;     {color bit}
                patStretch: INTEGER;     {used internally}
                picSave:    Handle;      {picture being saved}
                rgnSave:    Handle;      {region being saved}
                polySave:   Handle;      {polygon being saved}
                grafProcs:  QDProcsPtr   {low-level drawing routines}
            END;

PicHandle = ^PicPtr;
PicPtr    = ^Picture;
Picture   = RECORD
                picSize:    INTEGER;  {size in bytes}
                picFrame:   Rect;     {picture frame}
                {picture definition data}
            END;
```

```
PolyHandle = ^PolyPtr;
PolyPtr    = ^Polygon;
Polygon    = RECORD
                   polySize:   INTEGER;  {size in bytes}
                   polyBBox:   Rect;     {enclosing rectangle}
                   polyPoints: ARRAY[0..0] OF Point
             END;

PenState   = RECORD
                   pnLoc:  Point;    {pen location}
                   pnSize: Point;    {pen size}
                   pnMode: INTEGER;  {pen's transfer mode}
                   pnPat:  Pattern   {pen pattern}
             END;

FontInfo   = RECORD
                   ascent:   INTEGER;  {ascent}
                   descent:  INTEGER;  {descent}
                   widMax:   INTEGER;  {maximum character width}
                   leading:  INTEGER   {leading}
             END;

GrafVerb   = (frame,paint,erase,invert,fill);
```

Variables

```
VAR thePort:    GrafPtr;  {pointer to current grafPort}
    white:      Pattern;  {all-white pattern}
    black:      Pattern;  {all-black pattern}
    gray:       Pattern;  {50% gray pattern}
    ltGray:     Pattern;  {25% gray pattern}
    dkGray:     Pattern;  {75% gray pattern}
    arrow:      Cursor;   {standard arrow cursor}
    screenBits: BitMap;   {the entire screen}
    randSeed:   LONGINT;  {determines where Random sequence begins}
```

Routines

GrafPort Routines

```
PROCEDURE InitGraf     (globalPtr: Ptr);
PROCEDURE OpenPort     (port: GrafPtr);
PROCEDURE InitPort     (port: GrafPtr);
PROCEDURE ClosePort    (port: GrafPtr);
PROCEDURE SetPort      (port: GrafPtr);
PROCEDURE GetPort      (VAR port: GrafPtr);
PROCEDURE GrafDevice   (device: INTEGER);
PROCEDURE SetPortBits  (bm: BitMap);
PROCEDURE PortSize     (width,height: INTEGER);
```

```
PROCEDURE  MovePortTo    (leftGlobal,topGlobal: INTEGER);
PROCEDURE  SetOrigin     (h,v: INTEGER);
PROCEDURE  SetClip       (rgn: RgnHandle);
PROCEDURE  GetClip       (rgn: RgnHandle);
PROCEDURE  ClipRect      (r: Rect);
PROCEDURE  BackPat       (pat: Pattern);
```

Cursor Handling

```
PROCEDURE  InitCursor;
PROCEDURE  SetCursor (crsr: Cursor);
PROCEDURE  HideCursor;
PROCEDURE  ShowCursor;
PROCEDURE  ObscureCursor;
```

Pen and Line Drawing

```
PROCEDURE  HidePen;
PROCEDURE  ShowPen;
PROCEDURE  GetPen        (VAR pt: Point);
PROCEDURE  GetPenState   (VAR pnState: PenState);
PROCEDURE  SetPenState   (pnState: PenState);
PROCEDURE  PenSize       (width,height: INTEGER);
PROCEDURE  PenMode       (mode: INTEGER);
PROCEDURE  PenPat        (pat: Pattern);
PROCEDURE  PenNormal;
PROCEDURE  MoveTo        (h,v: INTEGER);
PROCEDURE  Move          (dh,dv: INTEGER);
PROCEDURE  LineTo        (h,v: INTEGER);
PROCEDURE  Line          (dh,dv: INTEGER);
```

Text Drawing

```
PROCEDURE  TextFont      (font: INTEGER);
PROCEDURE  TextFace      (face: Style);
PROCEDURE  TextMode      (mode: INTEGER);
PROCEDURE  TextSize      (size: INTEGER);
PROCEDURE  SpaceExtra    (extra: Fixed);
PROCEDURE  DrawChar      (ch: CHAR);
PROCEDURE  DrawString    (s: Str255);
PROCEDURE  DrawText      (textBuf: Ptr; firstByte,byteCount: INTEGER);
FUNCTION   CharWidth     (ch: CHAR) : INTEGER;
FUNCTION   StringWidth   (s: Str255) : INTEGER;
FUNCTION   TextWidth     (textBuf: Ptr; firstByte,byteCount: INTEGER) :
                          INTEGER;
PROCEDURE  GetFontInfo   (VAR info: FontInfo);
```

Drawing in Color

```
PROCEDURE ForeColor   (color: LONGINT);
PROCEDURE BackColor   (color: LONGINT);
PROCEDURE ColorBit    (whichBit: INTEGER);
```

Calculations with Rectangles

```
PROCEDURE SetRect      (VAR r: Rect; left,top,right,bottom: INTEGER);
PROCEDURE OffsetRect   (VAR r: Rect; dh,dv: INTEGER);
PROCEDURE InsetRect    (VAR r: Rect; dh,dv: INTEGER);
FUNCTION  SectRect     (src1,src2: Rect; VAR dstRect: Rect) : BOOLEAN;
PROCEDURE UnionRect    (src1,src2: Rect; VAR dstRect: Rect);
FUNCTION  PtInRect     (pt: Point; r: Rect) : BOOLEAN;
PROCEDURE Pt2Rect      (pt1,pt2: Point; VAR dstRect: Rect);
PROCEDURE PtToAngle    (r: Rect; pt: Point; VAR angle: INTEGER);
FUNCTION  EqualRect    (rect1,rect2: Rect) : BOOLEAN;
FUNCTION  EmptyRect    (r: Rect) : BOOLEAN;
```

Graphic Operations on Rectangles

```
PROCEDURE FrameRect    (r: Rect);
PROCEDURE PaintRect    (r: Rect);
PROCEDURE EraseRect    (r: Rect);
PROCEDURE InvertRect   (r: Rect);
PROCEDURE FillRect     (r: Rect; pat: Pattern);
```

Graphic Operations on Ovals

```
PROCEDURE FrameOval    (r: Rect);
PROCEDURE PaintOval    (r: Rect);
PROCEDURE EraseOval    (r: Rect);
PROCEDURE InvertOval   (r: Rect);
PROCEDURE FillOval     (r: Rect; pat: Pattern);
```

Graphic Operations on Rounded-Corner Rectangles

```
PROCEDURE FrameRoundRect    (r: Rect; ovalWidth,ovalHeight: INTEGER);
PROCEDURE PaintRoundRect    (r: Rect; ovalWidth,ovalHeight: INTEGER);
PROCEDURE EraseRoundRect    (r: Rect; ovalWidth,ovalHeight: INTEGER);
PROCEDURE InvertRoundRect   (r: Rect; ovalWidth,ovalHeight: INTEGER);
PROCEDURE FillRoundRect     (r: Rect; ovalWidth,ovalHeight: INTEGER; pat:
                            Pattern);
```

Graphic Operations on Arcs and Wedges

```
PROCEDURE  FrameArc   (r: Rect; startAngle,arcAngle: INTEGER);
PROCEDURE  PaintArc   (r: Rect; startAngle,arcAngle: INTEGER);
PROCEDURE  EraseArc   (r: Rect; startAngle,arcAngle: INTEGER);
PROCEDURE  InvertArc  (r: Rect; startAngle,arcAngle: INTEGER);
PROCEDURE  FillArc    (r: Rect; startAngle,arcAngle: INTEGER; pat:
                      Pattern);
```

Calculations with Regions

```
FUNCTION   NewRgn :      RgnHandle;
PROCEDURE  OpenRgn;
PROCEDURE  CloseRgn     (dstRgn: RgnHandle);
PROCEDURE  DisposeRgn   (rgn: RgnHandle);
PROCEDURE  CopyRgn      (srcRgn,dstRgn: RgnHandle);
PROCEDURE  SetEmptyRgn  (rgn: RgnHandle);
PROCEDURE  SetRectRgn   (rgn: RgnHandle; left,top,right,bottom: INTEGER);
PROCEDURE  RectRgn      (rgn: RgnHandle; r: Rect);
PROCEDURE  OffsetRgn    (rgn: RgnHandle; dh,dv: INTEGER);
PROCEDURE  InsetRgn     (rgn: RgnHandle; dh,dv: INTEGER);
PROCEDURE  SectRgn      (srcRgnA,srcRgnB,dstRgn: RgnHandle);
PROCEDURE  UnionRgn     (srcRgnA,srcRgnB,dstRgn: RgnHandle);
PROCEDURE  DiffRgn      (srcRgnA,srcRgnB,dstRgn: RgnHandle);
PROCEDURE  XorRgn       (srcRgnA,srcRgnB,dstRgn: RgnHandle);
FUNCTION   PtInRgn      (pt: Point; rgn: RgnHandle) : BOOLEAN;
FUNCTION   RectInRgn    (r: Rect; rgn: RgnHandle) : BOOLEAN;
FUNCTION   EqualRgn     (rgnA,rgnB: RgnHandle) : BOOLEAN;
FUNCTION   EmptyRgn     (rgn: RgnHandle) : BOOLEAN;
```

Graphic Operations on Regions

```
PROCEDURE  FrameRgn   (rgn: RgnHandle);
PROCEDURE  PaintRgn   (rgn: RgnHandle);
PROCEDURE  EraseRgn   (rgn: RgnHandle);
PROCEDURE  InvertRgn  (rgn: RgnHandle);
PROCEDURE  FillRgn    (rgn: RgnHandle; pat: Pattern);
```

Bit Transfer Operations

```
PROCEDURE  ScrollRect  (r: Rect; dh,dv: INTEGER; updateRgn: RgnHandle);
PROCEDURE  CopyBits    (srcBits,dstBits: BitMap; srcRect,dstRect: Rect;
                       mode: INTEGER; maskRgn: RgnHandle);
```

Pictures

```
FUNCTION   OpenPicture    (picFrame: Rect) : PicHandle;
PROCEDURE  PicComment     (kind,dataSize: INTEGER; dataHandle: Handle);
PROCEDURE  ClosePicture;
PROCEDURE  DrawPicture    (myPicture: PicHandle; dstRect: Rect);
PROCEDURE  KillPicture    (myPicture: PicHandle);
```

Calculations with Polygons

```
FUNCTION   OpenPoly :     PolyHandle;
PROCEDURE  ClosePoly;
PROCEDURE  KillPoly       (poly: PolyHandle);
PROCEDURE  OffsetPoly     (poly: PolyHandle; dh,dv: INTEGER);
```

Graphic Operations on Polygons

```
PROCEDURE  FramePoly      (poly: PolyHandle);
PROCEDURE  PaintPoly      (poly: PolyHandle);
PROCEDURE  ErasePoly      (poly: PolyHandle);
PROCEDURE  InvertPoly     (poly: PolyHandle);
PROCEDURE  FillPoly       (poly: PolyHandle; pat: Pattern);
```

Calculations with Points

```
PROCEDURE  AddPt          (srcPt: Point; VAR dstPt: Point);
PROCEDURE  SubPt          (srcPt: Point; VAR dstPt: Point);
PROCEDURE  SetPt          (VAR pt: Point; h,v: INTEGER);
FUNCTION   EqualPt        (pt1,pt2: Point) : BOOLEAN;
PROCEDURE  LocalToGlobal  (VAR pt: Point);
PROCEDURE  GlobalToLocal  (VAR pt: Point);
```

Miscellaneous Routines

```
FUNCTION   Random :    INTEGER;
FUNCTION   GetPixel   (h,v: INTEGER) : BOOLEAN;
PROCEDURE  StuffHex   (thingPtr: Ptr; s: Str255);
PROCEDURE  ScalePt    (VAR pt: Point; srcRect,dstRect: Rect);
PROCEDURE  MapPt      (VAR pt: Point; srcRect,dstRect: Rect);
PROCEDURE  MapRect    (VAR r: Rect; srcRect,dstRect: Rect);
PROCEDURE  MapRgn     (rgn: RgnHandle; srcRect,dstRect: Rect);
PROCEDURE  MapPoly    (poly: PolyHandle; srcRect,dstRect: Rect);
```

Customizing QuickDraw Operations

```
PROCEDURE SetStdProcs    (VAR procs: QDProcs);
PROCEDURE StdText        (byteCount: INTEGER; textBuf: Ptr; numer,denom:
                          Point);
PROCEDURE StdLine        (newPt: Point);
PROCEDURE StdRect        (verb: GrafVerb; r: Rect);
PROCEDURE StdRRect       (verb: GrafVerb; r: Rect; ovalwidth,ovalHeight:
                          INTEGER);
PROCEDURE StdOval        (verb: GrafVerb; r: Rect);
PROCEDURE StdArc         (verb: GrafVerb; r: Rect; startAngle,arcAngle:
                          INTEGER);
PROCEDURE StdPoly        (verb: GrafVerb; poly: PolyHandle);
PROCEDURE StdRgn         (verb: GrafVerb; rgn: RgnHandle);
PROCEDURE StdBits        (VAR srcBits: BitMap; VAR srcRect,dstRect: Rect;
                          mode: INTEGER; maskRgn: RgnHandle);
PROCEDURE StdComment     (kind,dataSize: INTEGER; dataHandle: Handle);
FUNCTION  StdTxMeas      (byteCount: INTEGER; textAddr: Ptr; VAR numer,
                          denom: Point; VAR info: FontInfo) : INTEGER;
PROCEDURE StdGetPic      (dataPtr: Ptr; byteCount: INTEGER);
PROCEDURE StdPutPic      (dataPtr: Ptr; byteCount: INTEGER);
```

Assembly-Language Information

Constants

```
; Size in bytes of QuickDraw global variables

grafSize        .EQU        206

; Source transfer modes

srcCopy         .EQU        0
srcOr           .EQU        1
srcXor          .EQU        2
srcBic          .EQU        3
notSrcCopy      .EQU        4
notSrcOr        .EQU        5
notSrcXor       .EQU        6
notSrcBic       .EQU        7

; Pattern transfer modes

patCopy         .EQU        8
patOr           .EQU        9
patXor          .EQU        10
patBic          .EQU        11
notPatCopy      .EQU        12
notPatOr        .EQU        13
notPatXor       .EQU        14
notPatBic       .EQU        15
```

```
; Standard colors for ForeColor and BackColor

blackColor      .EQU        33
whiteColor      .EQU        30
redColor        .EQU        205
greenColor      .EQU        341
blueColor       .EQU        409
cyanColor       .EQU        273
magentaColor    .EQU        137
yellowColor     .EQU        69


; Standard picture comments

picLParen       .EQU        0
picRParen       .EQU        1


; Character style

boldBit         .EQU        0
italicBit       .EQU        1
ulineBit        .EQU        2
outlineBit      .EQU        3
shadowBit       .EQU        4
condenseBit     .EQU        5
extendBit       .EQU        6


; Graphic operations

frame           .EQU        0
paint           .EQU        1
erase           .EQU        2
invert          .EQU        3
fill            .EQU        4
```

Point Data Structure

v	Vertical coordinate (word)
h	Horizontal coordinate (word)

Rectangle Data Structure

top	Vertical coordinate of top left corner (word)
left	Horizontal coordinate of top left corner (word)
bottom	Vertical coordinate of bottom right corner (word)
right	Horizontal coordinate of bottom right corner (word)
topLeft	Top left corner (point; long)
botRight	Bottom right corner (point; long)

Region Data Structure

rgnSize	Size in bytes (word)
rgnBBox	Enclosing rectangle (8 bytes)
rgnData	More data if not rectangular

Bit Map Data Structure

baseAddr	Pointer to bit image
rowBytes	Row width (word)
bounds	Boundary rectangle (8 bytes)
bitMapRec	Size in bytes of bit map data structure

Cursor Data Structure

data	Cursor image (32 bytes)
mask	Cursor mask (32 bytes)
hotSpot	Point aligned with mouse (long)
cursRec	Size in bytes of cursor data structure

Structure of QDProcs Record

textProc	Address of text-drawing routine
lineProc	Address of line-drawing routine
rectProc	Address of rectangle-drawing routine
rRectProc	Address of roundRect-drawing routine
ovalProc	Address of oval-drawing routine
arcProc	Address of arc/wedge-drawing routine
polyProc	Address of polygon-drawing routine
rgnProc	Address of region-drawing routine
bitsProc	Address of bit-transfer routine
commentProc	Address of routine for processing picture comments
txMeasProc	Address of routine for measuring text width
getPicProc	Address of picture-retrieval routine
putPicProc	Address of picture-saving routine
qdProcsRec	Size in bytes of QDProcs record

GrafPort Data Structure

device	Font-specific information (word)
portBits	GrafPort's bit map (bitMapRec bytes)
portBounds	Boundary rectangle of grafPort's bit map (8 bytes)
portRect	GrafPort's rectangle (8 bytes)
visRgn	Handle to visible region
clipRgn	Handle to clipping region
bkPat	Background pattern (8 bytes)
fillPat	Fill pattern (8 bytes)
pnLoc	Pen location (point; long)

pnSize   Pen size (point; long)
pnMode   Pen's transfer mode (word)
pnPat   Pen pattern (8 bytes)
pnVis   Pen visibility (word)
txFont   Font number for text (word)
txFace   Text's character style (word)
txMode   Text's transfer mode (word)
txSize   Font size for text (word)
spExtra   Extra space (long)
fgColor   Foreground color (long)
bkColor   Background color (long)
colrBit   Color bit (word)
picSave   Handle to picture being saved
rgnSave   Handle to region being saved
polySave   Handle to polygon being saved
grafProcs   Pointer to QDProcs record
portRec   Size in bytes of grafPort

Picture Data Structure

picSize   Size in bytes (word)
picFrame   Picture frame (rectangle; 8 bytes)
picData   Picture definition data

Polygon Data Structure

polySize   Size in bytes (word)
polyBBox   Enclosing rectangle (8 bytes)
polyPoints   Polygon points

Pen State Data Structure

psLoc   Pen location (point; long)
psSize   Pen size (point; long)
psMode   Pen's transfer mode (word)
psPat   Pen pattern (8 bytes)
psRec   Size in bytes of pen state data structure

Font Information Data Structure

ascent   Ascent (word)
descent   Descent (word)
widMax   Maximum character width (word)
leading   Leading (word)

Special Macro Names

Pascal name	Macro name
SetPortBits	_SetPBits
InvertRect	_InverRect
InvertRoundRect	_InverRoundRect
DisposeRgn	_DisposRgn
SetRectRgn	_SetRecRgn
OffsetRgn	_OfSetRgn
InvertRgn	_InverRgn
ClosePoly	_ClosePgon

Variables

RndSeed   Random number seed (long)

RESOURCE MANAGER

Constants

```
CONST   { Masks for resource attributes }

        resSysHeap    = 64;     {set if read into system heap}
        resPurgeable  = 32;     {set if purgeable}
        resLocked     = 16;     {set if locked}
        resProtected  = 8;      {set if protected}
        resPreload    = 4;      {set if to be preloaded}
        resChanged    = 2;      {set if to be written to resource file}

        { Resource Manager result codes }

        resNotFound   = -192;   {resource not found}
        resFNotFound  = -193;   {resource file not found}
        addResFailed  = -194;   {AddResource failed}
        rmvResFailed  = -196;   {RmveResource failed}

        { Masks for resource file attributes }

        mapReadOnly = 128;      {set if file is read-only}
        mapCompact  = 64;       {set to compact file on update}
        mapChanged  = 32;       {set to write map on update}
```

Data Types

```
TYPE ResType = PACKED ARRAY[1..4] OF CHAR;
```

Routines

Initialization

```
FUNCTION   InitResources : INTEGER;
PROCEDURE  RsrcZoneInit;
```

Opening and Closing Resource Files

```
PROCEDURE CreateResFile (fileName: Str255);
FUNCTION  OpenResFile   (fileName: Str255) : INTEGER;
PROCEDURE CloseResFile  (refNum: INTEGER);
```

Checking for Errors

```
FUNCTION ResError : INTEGER;
```

Setting the Current Resource File

```
FUNCTION   CurResFile : INTEGER;
FUNCTION   HomeResFile (theResource: Handle) : INTEGER;
PROCEDURE  UseResFile  (refNum: INTEGER);
```

Getting Resource Types

```
FUNCTION   CountTypes : INTEGER;
PROCEDURE  GetIndType  (VAR theType: ResType; index: INTEGER);
```

Getting and Disposing of Resources

```
PROCEDURE  SetResLoad      (load: BOOLEAN);
FUNCTION   CountResources  (theType: ResType) : INTEGER;
FUNCTION   GetIndResource  (theType: ResType; index: INTEGER) : Handle;
FUNCTION   GetResource     (theType: ResType; theID: INTEGER) : Handle;
FUNCTION   GetNamedResource (theType: ResType; name: Str255) : Handle;
PROCEDURE  LoadResource    (theResource: Handle);
PROCEDURE  ReleaseResource (theResource: Handle);
PROCEDURE  DetachResource  (theResource: Handle);
```

Getting Resource Information

```
FUNCTION   UniqueID    (theType: ResType) : INTEGER;
PROCEDURE  GetResInfo  (theResource: Handle; VAR theID: INTEGER; VAR
                        theType: ResType; VAR name: Str255);
FUNCTION   GetResAttrs  (theResource: Handle) : INTEGER;
FUNCTION   SizeResource (theResource: Handle) : LONGINT;
```

Modifying Resources

```
PROCEDURE  SetResInfo       (theResource: Handle; theID: INTEGER; name:
                            Str255);
PROCEDURE  SetResAttrs      (theResource: Handle; attrs: INTEGER);
PROCEDURE  ChangedResource  (theResource: Handle);
PROCEDURE  AddResource      (theData: Handle; theType: ResType; theID:
                            INTEGER; name: Str255);
PROCEDURE  RmveResource     (theResource: Handle);
PROCEDURE  UpdateResFile    (refNum: INTEGER);
PROCEDURE  WriteResource    (theResource: Handle);
PROCEDURE  SetResPurge      (install: BOOLEAN);
```

Advanced Routines

```
FUNCTION  GetResFileAttrs (refNum: INTEGER) : INTEGER;
PROCEDURE SetResFileAttrs (refNum: INTEGER; attrs: INTEGER);
```

Assembly-Language Information

Constants

```
; Resource attributes

resSysHeap      .EQU    6       ;set if read into system heap
resPurgeable    .EQU    5       ;set if purgeable
resLocked       .EQU    4       ;set if locked
resProtected    .EQU    3       ;set if protected
resPreload      .EQU    2       ;set if to be preloaded
resChanged      .EQU    1       ;set if to be written to resource file

; Resource Manager result codes

resNotFound     .EQU    -192    ;resource not found
resFNotFound    .EQU    -193    ;resource file not found
addResFailed    .EQU    -194    ;AddResource failed
rmvResFailed    .EQU    -196    ;RmveResource failed

; Resource file attributes

mapReadOnly     .EQU    7       ;set if file is read-only
mapCompact      .EQU    6       ;set to compact file on update
mapChanged      .EQU    5       ;set to write map on update
```

Special Macro Names

Pascal name	Macro name
SizeResource	_SizeRsrc

Variables

TopMapHndl	Handle to resource map of most recently opened resource file
SysMapHndl	Handle to map of system resource file
SysMap	Reference number of system resource file (word)
CurMap	Reference number of current resource file (word)
ResLoad	Current SetResLoad state (word)
ResErr	Current value of ResError (word)
ResErrProc	Address of resource error procedure
SysResName	Name of system resource file (length byte followed by up to 19 characters)

SCRAP MANAGER

Constants

```
CONST { Scrap Manager result codes }

    noScrapErr = -100;   {desk scrap isn't initialized}
    noTypeErr  = -102;   {no data of the requested type}
```

Data Types

```
TYPE PScrapStuff = ^ScrapStuff;
     ScrapStuff  = RECORD
                      scrapSize:   LONGINT;   {size of desk scrap}
                      scrapHandle: Handle;    {handle to desk scrap}
                      scrapCount:  INTEGER;   {count changed by ZeroScrap}
                      scrapState:  INTEGER;   {tells where desk scrap is}
                      scrapName:   StringPtr  {scrap file name}
                   END;
```

Routines

Getting Desk Scrap Information

```
FUNCTION InfoScrap : PScrapStuff;
```

Keeping the Desk Scrap on the Disk

```
FUNCTION UnloadScrap : LONGINT;
FUNCTION LoadScrap :   LONGINT;
```

Writing to the Desk Scrap

```
FUNCTION ZeroScrap : LONGINT;
FUNCTION PutScrap   (length: LONGINT; theType: ResType; source: Ptr) :
                    LONGINT;
```

Reading from the Desk Scrap

```
FUNCTION GetScrap (hDest: Handle; theType: ResType; VAR offset: LONGINT)
                : LONGINT;
```

Assembly-Language Information

Constants

```
; Scrap Manager result codes

noScrapErr      .EQU    -100    ;desk scrap isn't initialized
noTypeErr       .EQU    -102    ;no data of the requested type
```

Special Macro Names

Pascal name	Macro name
LoadScrap	_LodeScrap
UnloadScrap	_UnlodeScrap

Variables

ScrapSize	Size in bytes of desk scrap (long)
ScrapHandle	Handle to desk scrap in memory
ScrapCount	Count changed by ZeroScrap (word)
ScrapState	Tells where desk scrap is (word)
ScrapName	Pointer to scrap file name (preceded by length byte)

SEGMENT LOADER

Constants

```
CONST { Message returned by CountAppleFiles }

    appOpen  = 0;  {open the document(s)}
    appPrint = 1;  {print the document(s)}
```

Data Types

```
TYPE AppFile =  RECORD
                    vRefNum: INTEGER; {volume reference number}
                    fType:   OSType;  {file type}
                    versNum: INTEGER; {version number}
                    fName:   Str255   {file name}
                END;
```

Routines

```
PROCEDURE CountAppFiles (VAR message: INTEGER; VAR count: INTEGER);   [Not
                            in ROM]
PROCEDURE GetAppFiles   (index: INTEGER; VAR theFile: AppFile);   [Not in ROM]
PROCEDURE ClrAppFiles   (index: INTEGER);   [Not in ROM]
PROCEDURE GetAppParms   (VAR apName: Str255; VAR apRefNum: INTEGER; VAR
                            apParam: Handle);
PROCEDURE UnloadSeg     (routineAddr: Ptr);
PROCEDURE ExitToShell;
```

Assembly-Language Information

Advanced Routines

Trap macro	On entry
_Chain	(A0): pointer to application's file name (preceded by length byte)
	4(A0): configuration of sound and screen buffers (word)
_Launch	(A0): pointer to application's file name (preceded by length byte)
	4(A0): configuration of sound and screen buffers (word)
_LoadSeg	stack: segment number (word)

Variables

AppParmHandle	Handle to Finder information
CurApName	Name of current application (length byte followed by up to 31 characters)
CurApRefNum	Reference number of current application's resource file (word)
CurPageOption	Sound/screen buffer configuration passed to Chain or Launch (word)
CurJTOffset	Offset to jump table from location pointed to by A5 (word)
FinderName	Name of the Finder (length byte followed by up to 15 characters)

SERIAL DRIVERS

Constants

```
CONST { Driver reset information }

        baud300    =  380;      {300 baud}
        baud600    =  189;      {600 baud}
        baud1200   =  94;       {1200 baud}
        baud1800   =  62;       {1800 baud}
        baud2400   =  46;       {2400 baud}
        baud3600   =  30;       {3600 baud}
        baud4800   =  22;       {4800 baud}
        baud7200   =  14;       {7200 baud}
        baud9600   =  10;       {9600 baud}
        baud19200  =  4;        {19200 baud}
        baud57600  =  0;        {57600 baud}
        stop10     =  16384;    {1 stop bit}
        stop15     = -32768;    {1.5 stop bits}
        stop20     = -16384;    {2 stop bits}
        noParity   =  0;        {no parity}
        oddParity  =  4096;     {odd parity}
        evenParity =  12288;    {even parity}
        data5      =  0;        {5 data bits}
        data6      =  2048;     {6 data bits}
        data7      =  1024;     {7 data bits}
        data8      =  3072;     {8 data bits}

        { Masks for errors }

        swOverrunErr = 1;    {set if software overrun error}
        parityErr    = 16;   {set if parity error}
        hwOverrunErr = 32;   {set if hardware overrun error}
        framingErr   = 64;   {set if framing error}

        { Masks for changes that cause events to be posted }

        ctsEvent    = 32;    {set if CTS change will cause event to be }
                             { posted}
        breakEvent  = 128;   {set if break status change will cause event }
                             { to be posted}

        { Indication that an XOff character was sent }

        xOffWasSent = $80;

        { Result codes }

        noErr   =  0;    {no error}
        openErr = -23;   {attempt to open RAM Serial Driver failed}
```

Data Types

```
TYPE  SPortSel = (sPortA,  {modem port}
                  sPortB   {printer port});

      SerShk = PACKED RECORD
                  fXOn: Byte;  {XOn/XOff output flow control flag}
                  fCTS: Byte;  {CTS hardware handshake flag}
                  xOn:  CHAR;  {XOn character}
                  xOff: CHAR;  {XOff character}
                  errs: Byte;  {errors that cause abort}
                  evts: Byte;  {status changes that cause events}
                  fInX: Byte;  {XOn/XOff input flow control flag}
                  null: Byte   {not used}
               END;

      SerStaRec = PACKED RECORD
                     cumErrs:  Byte;  {cumulative errors}
                     xOffSent: Byte;  {XOff sent as input flow control}
                     rdPend:   Byte;  {read pending flag}
                     wrPend:   Byte;  {write pending flag}
                     ctsHold:  Byte;  {CTS flow control hold flag}
                     xOffHold: Byte   {XOff flow control hold flag}
                  END;
```

Routines [Not in ROM]

Opening and Closing the RAM Serial Driver

```
FUNCTION  RAMSDOpen  (whichPort: SPortSel) : OSErr;
PROCEDURE RAMSDClose (whichPort: SPortSel);
```

Changing Serial Driver Information

```
FUNCTION SerReset  (refNum: INTEGER; serConfig: INTEGER) : OSErr;
FUNCTION SerSetBuf (refNum: INTEGER; serBPtr: Ptr; serBLen: INTEGER) :
                   OSErr;
FUNCTION SerHShake (refNum: INTEGER; flags: SerShk) : OSErr;
FUNCTION SerSetBrk (refNum: INTEGER) : OSErr;
FUNCTION SerClrBrk (refNum: INTEGER) : OSErr;
```

Getting Serial Driver Information

```
FUNCTION SerGetBuf (refNum: INTEGER; VAR count: LONGINT) : OSErr;
FUNCTION SerStatus (refNum: INTEGER; VAR serSta: SerStaRec) : OSErr;
```

Advanced Control Calls (RAM Serial Driver)

csCode	csParam	Effect
13	baudRate	Set baud rate (actual rate, as an integer)
19	char	Replace parity errors
21		Unconditionally set XOff for output flow control
22		Unconditionally clear XOff for input flow control
23		Send XOn for input flow control if XOff was sent last
24		Unconditionally send XOn for input flow control
25		Send XOff for input flow control if XOn was sent last
26		Unconditionally send XOff for input flow control
27		Reset SCC channel

Driver Names and Reference Numbers

Driver	Driver name	Reference number
Modem port input	.AIn	–6
Modem port output	.AOut	–7
Printer port input	.BIn	–8
Printer port output	.BOut	–9

Assembly-Language Information

Constants

```
; Result codes

noErr      .EQU    0      ;no error
openErr    .EQU   -23     ;attempt to open RAM Serial Driver failed
```

Structure of Control Information for SerHShake

shFXOn	XOn/XOff output flow control flag (byte)
shFCTS	CTS hardware handshake flag (byte)
shXOn	XOn character (byte)
shXOff	XOff character (byte)
shErrs	Errors that cause abort (byte)
shEvts	Status changes that cause events (byte)
shFInX	XOn/XOff input flow control flag (byte)

Structure of Status Information for SerStatus

ssCumErrs	Cumulative errors (byte)
ssXOffSent	XOff sent as input flow control (byte)
ssRdPend	Read pending flag (byte)
ssWrPend	Write pending flag (byte)
ssCTSHold	CTS flow control hold flag (byte)
ssXOffHold	XOff flow control hold flag (byte)

Equivalent Device Manager Calls

Pascal routine	Call
SerReset	Control with csCode=8, csParam=serConfig
SerSetBuf	Control with csCode=8, csParam=serBPtr, csParam+4=serBLen
SerHShake	Control with csCode=10, csParam through csParam+6=flags
SerSetBrk	Control with csCode=12
SerClrBrk	Control with csCode=11
SerGetBuf	Status with csCode=2; count returned in csParam
SerStatus	Status with csCode=8; serSta returned in csParam through csParam+5

SOUND DRIVER

Constants

```
CONST { Mode values for synthesizers }

   swMode = -1;    {square-wave synthesizer}
   ftMode =  1;    {four-tone synthesizer}
   ffMode =  0;    {free-form synthesizer}
```

Data Types

```
TYPE  { Free-form synthesizer }

    FFSynthPtr = ^FFSynthRec;
    FFSynthRec = RECORD
                    mode:      INTEGER;   {always ffMode}
                    count:     Fixed;     {"sampling" factor}
                    waveBytes: FreeWave   {waveform description}
                 END;

    FreeWave    = PACKED ARRAY[0..30000] OF Byte;

    { Square-wave synthesizer }

    SWSynthPtr = ^SWSynthRec;
    SWSynthRec = RECORD
                    mode:      INTEGER;   {always swMode}
                    triplets:  Tones      {sounds}
                 END;

    Tones = ARRAY[0..5000] OF Tone;
    Tone  = RECORD
                    count:     INTEGER;   {frequency}
                    amplitude: INTEGER;   {amplitude, 0-255}
                    duration:  INTEGER    {duration in ticks}
                 END;

    { Four-tone synthesizer }

    FTSynthPtr  = ^FTSynthRec;
    FTSynthRec  = RECORD
                    mode:      INTEGER;     {always ftMode}
                    sndRec:    FTSndRecPtr  {tones to play}
                 END;
```

```
FTSndRecPtr = ^FTSoundRec;
FTSoundRec  = RECORD
                  duration:    INTEGER;     {duration in ticks}
                  sound1Rate:  Fixed;       {tone 1 cycle rate}
                  sound1Phase: LONGINT;     {tone 1 byte offset}
                  sound2Rate:  Fixed;       {tone 2 cycle rate}
                  sound2Phase: LONGINT;     {tone 2 byte offset}
                  sound3Rate:  Fixed;       {tone 3 cycle rate}
                  sound3Phase: LONGINT;     {tone 3 byte offset}
                  sound4Rate:  Fixed;       {tone 4 cycle rate}
                  sound4Phase: LONGINT;     {tone 4 byte offset}
                  sound1Wave:  WavePtr;     {tone 1 waveform}
                  sound2Wave:  WavePtr;     {tone 2 waveform}
                  sound3Wave:  WavePtr;     {tone 3 waveform}
                  sound4Wave:  WavePtr      {tone 4 waveform}
              END;

WavePtr = ^Wave;
Wave    = PACKED ARRAY[0..255] OF Byte;
```

Routines [Not in ROM]

```
PROCEDURE StartSound   (synthRec: Ptr; numBytes: LONGINT; completionRtn:
                          ProcPtr);
PROCEDURE StopSound;
FUNCTION  SoundDone :   BOOLEAN;
PROCEDURE GetSoundVol  (VAR level: INTEGER);
PROCEDURE SetSoundVol  (level: INTEGER);
```

Assembly-Language Information

Routines

Pascal name	Equivalent for assembly language
StartSound	Call Write with ioRefNum=–4, ioBuffer=synthRec, ioReqCount=numBytes
StopSound	Call KillIO and (for square-wave) set CurPitch to 0
SoundDone	Poll ioResult field of most recent Write call's parameter block
GetSoundVol	Get low-order three bits of variable SdVolume
SetSoundVol	Call this Pascal procedure from your program

Variables

SdVolume	Speaker volume (byte: low-order three bits only)
SoundPtr	Pointer to four-tone record
SoundLevel	Amplitude in 740-byte buffer (byte)
CurPitch	Value of count in square-wave synthesizer buffer (word)

Sound Driver Values for Notes

The following table contains values for the rate field of a four-tone synthesizer and the count field of a square-wave synthesizer. A just-tempered scale—in the key of C, as an example—is given in the first four columns; you can use a just-tempered scale for perfect tuning in a particular key. The last four columns give an equal-tempered scale, for applications that may use any key; this scale is appropriate for most Macintosh sound applications. Following this table is a list of the ratios used in calculating these values, and instructions on how to calculate them for a just-tempered scale in any key.

| | Just-Tempered Scale | | | | Equal-Tempered Scale | | | |
| | Rate for Four-Tone | | Count for Square-Wave | | Rate for Four-Tone | | Count for Square-Wave | |
Note	Long	Fixed	Word	Integer	Long	Fixed	Word	Integer
3 octaves below middle C								
C	612B	0.37956	5CBA	23738	604C	0.37616	5D92	23954
C#	667C	0.40033	57EB	22507	6606	0.39853	5851	22609
Db	67A6	0.40488	56EF	22255				
D	6D51	0.42702	526D	21101	6C17	0.42223	535C	21340
Ebb	6E8F	0.43187	5180	20864				
D#	71DF	0.44481	4F21	20257	7284	0.44733	4EAF	20143
Eb	749A	0.45547	4D46	19782				
E	7976	0.47446	4A2F	18991	7953	0.47392	4A44	19012
F	818F	0.50609	458C	17804	808A	0.50211	4619	17945
F#	88A5	0.53377	41F0	16880	882F	0.53197	422A	16938
Gb	8A32	0.53983	4133	16691				
G	91C1	0.56935	3DD1	15825	9048	0.56360	3E73	15987
G#	97D4	0.59308	3B58	15192	98DC	0.59711	3AF2	15090
Ab	9B79	0.60732	39F4	14836				
A	A1F3	0.63261	37A3	14243	A1F3	0.63261	37A3	14243
Bbb	A3CA	0.63980	3703	14083				
A#	AA0C	0.66425	34FD	13565	AB94	0.67023	3484	13444
Bb	ACBF	0.67479	3429	13353				
B	B631	0.71169	3174	12660	B5C8	0.71008	3191	12689
2 octaves below middle C								
C	C257	0.75914	2E5D	11869	C097	0.75230	2EC9	11977
C#	CCF8	0.80066	2BF6	11254	CC0B	0.79704	2C29	11305
Db	CF4C	0.80975	2B77	11127				
D	DAA2	0.85403	2936	10550	D82D	0.84444	29AE	10670
Ebb	DD1D	0.86372	28C0	10432				
D#	E3BE	0.88962	2790	10128	E508	0.89465	2757	10071
Eb	E935	0.91096	26A3	9891				
E	F2ED	0.94893	2517	9495	F2A6	0.94785	2522	9506
F	1031E	1.01218	22C6	8902	10114	1.00421	230C	8972
F#	1114A	1.06754	20F8	8440	1105D	1.06392	2115	8469
Gb	11465	1.07967	2099	8345				
G	12382	1.13870	1EE9	7913	12090	1.12720	1F3A	7994

Note	Long	Fixed	Word	Integer	Long	Fixed	Word	Integer
2 octaves below middle C								
G#	12FA8	1.18616	1DAC	7596	131B8	1.19421	1D79	7545
Ab	136F1	1.21461	1CFA	7418				
A	143E6	1.26523	1BD1	7121	143E6	1.26523	1BD1	7121
Bbb	14794	1.27960	1B81	7041				
A#	15418	1.32849	1A7E	6782	15729	1.34047	1A42	6722
Bb	1597E	1.34958	1A14	6676				
B	16C63	1.42339	18BA	6330	16B90	1.42017	18C8	6344
1 octave below middle C								
C	184AE	1.51828	172F	5935	1812F	1.50462	1764	5988
C#	199EF	1.60130	15FB	5627	19816	1.59409	1614	5652
Db	19E97	1.61949	15BC	5564				
D	1B543	1.70805	149B	5275	1B05A	1.68887	14D7	5335
Ebb	1BA3B	1.72746	1460	5216				
D#	1C77B	1.77922	13C8	5064	1CA10	1.78931	13AC	5036
Eb	1D26A	1.82193	1351	4945				
E	1E5D9	1.89784	128C	4748	1E54D	1.89571	1291	4753
F	2063D	2.02437	1163	4451	20228	2.00842	1186	4486
F#	22294	2.13507	107C	4220	220BB	2.12785	108A	4234
Gb	228C9	2.15932	104D	4173				
G	24704	2.27740	F74	3956	2411F	2.25438	F9D	3997
G#	25F4F	2.37230	ED6	3798	26370	2.38843	EBC	3772
Ab	26DE3	2.42924	E7D	3709				
A	287CC	2.53046	DE9	3561	287CC	2.53046	DE9	3561
Bbb	28F28	2.55920	DC1	3521				
A#	2A830	2.65698	D3F	3391	2AE51	2.68092	D21	3361
Bb	2B2FC	2.69916	D0A	3338				
B	2D8C6	2.84677	C5D	3165	2D721	2.84035	C64	3172
Middle C								
C	3095B	3.03654	B97	2967	3025D	3.00923	BB2	2994
C#	333DE	3.20261	AFD	2813	3302C	3.18817	B0A	2826
Db	33D2E	3.23898	ADE	2782				
D	36A87	3.41612	A4E	2638	360B5	3.37776	A6C	2668
Ebb	37476	3.45493	A30	2608				
D#	38EF7	3.55846	9E4	2532	39420	3.57861	9D6	2518
Eb	3A4D4	3.64386	9A9	2473				
E	3CBB2	3.79568	946	2374	3CA99	3.79140	949	2377
F	40C7A	4.04874	8B1	2225	40450	4.01685	8C3	2243
F#	44528	4.27014	83E	2110	44176	4.25571	845	2117
Gb	45193	4.31865	826	2086				
G	48E09	4.55482	7BA	1978	4823E	4.50876	7CE	1998
G#	4BE9F	4.74461	76B	1899	4C6E1	4.77687	75E	1886
Ab	4DBC5	4.85847	73F	1855				
A	50F98	5.06091	6F4	1780	50F98	5.06091	6F4	1780

Note	Long	Fixed	Word	Integer	Long	Fixed	Word	Integer
Middle C								
Bbb	51E4F	5.11839	6E0	1760				
A#	55060	5.31396	6A0	1696	55CA2	5.36185	690	1680
Bb	565F8	5.39832	685	1669				
B	5B18B	5.69353	62F	1583	5AE41	5.68068	632	1586
1 octave above middle C								
C	612B7	6.07310	5CC	1484	604BB	6.01848	5D9	1497
C#	667BD	6.40523	57F	1407	66059	6.37636	585	1413
Db	67A5C	6.47797	56F	1391				
D	6D50D	6.83223	527	1319	6C169	6.75551	536	1334
Ebb	6E8EB	6.90984	518	1304				
D#	71DEE	7.11691	4F2	1266	7283F	7.15721	4EB	1259
Eb	749A8	7.28772	4D4	1236				
E	79764	7.59137	4A3	1187	79533	7.58281	4A4	1188
F	818F3	8.09746	459	1113	808A1	8.03371	462	1122
F#	88A51	8.54030	41F	1055	882EC	8.51141	423	1059
Gb	8A326	8.63730	413	1043				
G	91C12	9.10965	3DD	989	9047D	9.01753	3E7	999
G#	97D3D	9.48921	3B6	950	98DC2	9.55374	3AF	943
Ab	9B78B	9.71696	39F	927				
A	A1F30	10.12183	37A	890	A1F30	10.12183	37A	890
Bbb	A3C9F	10.23680	370	880				
A#	AA0BF	10.62791	350	848	AB945	10.72371	348	840
Bb	ACBEF	10.79662	343	835				
B	B6316	11.38705	317	791	B5C83	11.36137	319	793
2 octaves above middle C								
C	C256D	12.14619	2E6	742	C0976	12.03696	2ED	749
C#	CCF79	12.81044	2BF	703	CC0B1	12.75270	2C3	707
Db	CF4B9	12.95595	2B7	695				
D	DAA1B	13.66447	293	659	D82D2	13.51102	29B	667
Ebb	DD1D6	13.81967	28C	652				
D#	E3BDC	14.23383	279	633	E507E	14.31442	275	629
Eb	E9350	14.57544	26A	618				
E	F2EC8	15.18274	251	593	F2A65	15.16560	252	594
F	1031E7	16.19493	22C	556	101141	16.06740	231	561
F#	1114A1	17.08058	210	528	1105D8	17.02283	211	529
Gb	11464C	17.27460	20A	522				
G	123824	18.21930	1EF	495	1208F9	18.03505	1F4	500
G#	12FA7B	18.97844	1DB	475	131B83	19.10747	1D8	472
Ab	136F15	19.43391	1D0	464				
A	143E61	20.24367	1BD	445	143E61	20.24367	1BD	445
Bbb	14793D	20.47359	1B8	440				
A#	15417F	21.25584	1A8	424	15728A	21.44742	1A4	420
Bb	1597DE	21.59323	1A1	417				
B	16C62D	22.77412	18C	396	16B906	22.72275	18D	397

Note	Long	Fixed	Word	Integer	Long	Fixed	Word	Integer

3 octaves above middle C

Note	Long	Fixed	Word	Integer	Long	Fixed	Word	Integer
C	184ADA	24.29239	173	371	1812EB	24.07390	176	374
C#	199EF2	25.62088	160	352	198163	25.50542	161	353
Db	19E971	25.91188	15C	348				
D	1B5436	27.32895	14A	330	1B05A5	27.02205	14D	333
Ebb	1BA3AC	27.63934	146	326				
D#	1C77B8	28.46765	13D	317	1CA0FD	28.62886	13B	315
Eb	1D26A0	29.15088	135	309				
E	1E5D91	30.36549	129	297	1E54CB	30.33122	129	297
F	2063CE	32.38986	116	278	202283	32.13481	118	280
F#	222943	34.16118	108	264	220BAF	34.04564	109	265
Gb	228C97	34.54918	105	261				
G	247047	36.43858	F7	247	2411F2	36.07010	FA	250
G#	25F4F5	37.95686	ED	237	263706	38.21494	EC	236
Ab	26DE2A	38.86783	E8	232				
A	287CC1	40.48732	DF	223	287CC1	40.48732	DF	223
Bbb	28F27A	40.94717	DC	220				
A#	2A82FE	42.51169	D4	212	2AE513	42.89482	D2	210
Bb	2B2FBD	43.18648	D1	209				
B	2D8C59	45.54823	C6	198	2D720B	45.44548	C6	198

The following table gives the ratios used in calculating the above values. It shows the relationship between the notes making up the just-tempered scale in the key of C; should you need to implement a just-tempered scale in some other key, you can do so as follows: First get the value of the root note in the proper octave in the equal-tempered scale (from the above table). Then use the following table to determine the values of the intervals for the other notes in the key by multiplying the ratio by the root note.

Chromatic interval	Note	Just-tempered frequency ratio	Equal-tempered frequency ratio	Interval type
0	C	1.00000	1.00000	Unison
1	C#	1.05469	1.05946	Minor second as chromatic semitone
	Db	1.06667		Minor second as diatonic semitone
2	D	1.11111	1.12246	Major second as minor tone
	D	1.12500		Major second as major tone
	Ebb	1.13778		Diminished third
3	D#	1.17188	1.18921	Augmented second
	Eb	1.20000		Minor third
4	E	1.25000	1.25992	Major third
5	F	1.33333	1.33484	Fourth
6	F#	1.40625	1.41421	Tritone as augmented fourth
	Gb	1.42222		Tritone as diminished fifth
7	G	1.50000	1.49831	Fifth

Chromatic interval	Note	Just-tempered frequency ratio	Equal-tempered frequency ratio	Interval type
8	G#	1.56250	1.58740	Augmented fifth
	Ab	1.60000		Minor sixth
9	A	1.66667	1.68179	Major sixth
	Bbb	1.68560		Diminished seventh
10	A#	1.75000	1.78180	Augmented sixth
	Bb	1.77778		Minor seventh
11	B	1.87500	1.88775	Major seventh
12	C	2.00000	2.00000	Octave

3 Summary

STANDARD FILE PACKAGE

Constants

```
CONST  { SFPutFile dialog template ID }

       putDlgID = -3999;

       { Item numbers of enabled items in SFPutFile dialog }

       putSave   = 1;    {Save button}
       putCancel = 2;    {Cancel button}
       putEject  = 5;    {Eject button}
       putDrive  = 6;    {Drive button}
       putName   = 7;    {editText item for file name}

       { SFGetFile dialog template ID }

       getDlgID = -4000;

       { Item numbers of enabled items in SFGetFile dialog }

       getOpen   = 1;    {Open button}
       getCancel = 3;    {Cancel button}
       getEject  = 5;    {Eject button}
       getDrive  = 6;    {Drive button}
       getNmList = 7;    {userItem for file name list}
       getScroll = 8;    {userItem for scroll bar}
```

Data Types

```
TYPE  SFReply = RECORD
                   good:    BOOLEAN;    {FALSE if ignore command}
                   copy:    BOOLEAN;    {not used}
                   fType:   OSType;     {file type or not used}
                   vRefNum: INTEGER;    {volume reference number}
                   version: INTEGER;    {file's version number}
                   fName:   STRING[63]  {file name}
                END;

      SFTypeList = ARRAY[0..3] OF OSType;
```

Routines

```
PROCEDURE SFPutFile    (where: Point; prompt: Str255; origName: Str255;
                        dlgHook: ProcPtr; VAR reply: SFReply);
PROCEDURE SFPPutFile   (where: Point; prompt: Str255; origName: Str255;
                        dlgHook: ProcPtr; VAR reply: SFReply; dlgID:
                        INTEGER; filterProc: ProcPtr);
PROCEDURE SFGetFile    (where: Point; prompt: Str255; fileFilter: ProcPtr;
                        numTypes: INTEGER; typeList: SFTypeList; dlgHook:
                        ProcPtr; VAR reply: SFReply);
PROCEDURE SFPGetFile   (where: Point; prompt: Str255; fileFilter: ProcPtr;
                        numTypes: INTEGER; typeList: SFTypeList; dlgHook:
                        ProcPtr; VAR reply: SFReply; dlgID: INTEGER;
                        filterProc: ProcPtr);
```

DlgHook Function

```
FUNCTION MyDlg (item: INTEGER; theDialog: DialogPtr) : INTEGER;
```

FileFilter Function

```
FUNCTION MyFileFilter (paramBlock: ParmBlkPtr) : BOOLEAN;
```

Standard SFPutFile Items

Item number	Item	Standard display rectangle
1	Save button	(12,74)(82,92)
2	Cancel button	(114,74)(184,92)
3	Prompt string (statText)	(12,12)(184,28)
4	UserItem for disk name	(209,16)(295,34)
5	Eject button	(217,43)(287,61)
6	Drive button	(217,74)(287,92)
7	EditText item for file name	(14,34)(182,50)
8	UserItem for dotted line	(200,16)(201,88)

Resource IDs of SFPutFile Alerts

Alert	Resource ID
Disk not found	–3994
System error	–3995
Existing file	–3996
Locked disk	–3997

Standard SFGetFile Items

Item number	Item	Standard display rectangle
1	Open button	(152,28)(232,46)
2	Invisible button	(1152,59)(1232,77)
3	Cancel button	(152,90)(232,108)
4	UserItem for disk name	(248,28)(344,46)
5	Eject button	(256,59)(336,77)
6	Drive button	(256,90)(336,108)
7	UserItem for file name list	(12,11)(125,125)
8	UserItem for scroll bar	(124,11)(140,125)
9	UserItem for dotted line	(244,20)(245,116)
10	Invisible text (statText)	(1044,20)(1145,116)

Assembly-Language Information

Constants

```
; SFPutFile dialog template ID

putDlgID    .EQU    -3999

; Item numbers of enabled items in SFPutFile dialog

putSave     .EQU    1    ;Save button
putCancel   .EQU    2    ;Cancel button
putEject    .EQU    5    ;Eject button
putDrive    .EQU    6    ;Drive button
putName     .EQU    7    ;editText item for file name

; SFGetFile dialog template ID

getDlgID    .EQU    -4000
```

```
; Item numbers of enabled items in SFGetFile dialog

getOpen      .EQU   1    ;Open button
getCancel    .EQU   3    ;Cancel button
getEject     .EQU   5    ;Eject button
getDrive     .EQU   6    ;Drive button
getNmList    .EQU   7    ;userItem for file name list
getScroll    .EQU   8    ;userItem for scroll bar

; Routine selectors

sfPutFile    .EQU   1
sfGetFile    .EQU   2
sfPPutFile   .EQU   3
sfPGetFile   .EQU   4
```

Reply Record Data Structure

rGood   0 if ignore command (byte)
rType   File type (long)
rVolume   Volume reference number (word)
rVersion   File's version number (word)
rName   File name (length byte followed by up to 63 characters)

Trap Macro Name

_Pack3

Variables

SFSaveDisk   Negative of volume reference number used by Standard File Package (word)

SYSTEM ERROR HANDLER

Routines

```
PROCEDURE SysError (errorCode: INTEGER);
```

User Alerts

ID   Explanation

1   Bus error: Invalid memory reference; happens only on a Macintosh XL

2   Address error: Word or long-word reference made to an odd address

3   Illegal instruction: The MC68000 received an instruction it didn't recognize.

4   Zero divide: Signed Divide (DIVS) or Unsigned Divide (DIVU) instruction with a divisor of 0 was executed.

5   Check exception: Check Register Against Bounds (CHK) instruction was executed and failed. Pascal "value out of range" errors are usually reported in this way.

6   TrapV exception: Trap On Overflow (TRAPV) instruction was executed and failed.

7   Privilege violation: Macintosh always runs in supervisor mode; perhaps an erroneous Return From Execution (RTE) instruction was executed.

8   Trace exception: The trace bit in the status register is set.

9   Line 1010 exception: The 1010 trap dispatcher has failed.

10   Line 1111 exception: Unimplemented instruction

11   Miscellaneous exception: All other MC68000 exceptions

12   Unimplemented core routine: An unimplemented trap number was encountered.

13   Spurious interrupt: The interrupt vector table entry for a particular level of interrupt is NIL; usually occurs with level 4, 5, 6, or 7 interrupts.

14   I/O system error: The File Manager is attempting to dequeue an entry from an I/O request queue that has a bad queue type field; perhaps the queue entry is unlocked. Or, the dCtlQHead field was NIL during a Fetch or Stash call. Or, a needed device control entry has been purged.

15   Segment Loader error: A GetResource call to read a segment into memory failed.

16   Floating point error: The halt bit in the floating-point environment word was set.

17-24   Can't load package: A GetResource call to read a package into memory failed.

25   Can't allocate requested memory block in the heap

26   Segment Loader error: A GetResource call to read 'CODE' resource 0 into memory failed; usually indicates a nonexecutable file.

27   File map destroyed: A logical block number was found that's greater than the number of the last logical block on the volume or less than the logical block number of the first allocation block on the volume.

28   Stack overflow error: The stack has expanded into the heap.

30   "Please insert the disk:" File Manager alert

41   The file named "Finder" can't be found on the disk.

100   Can't mount system startup volume. The system couldn't read the system resource file into memory.

32767 "Sorry, a system error occurred": Default alert message

System Startup Alerts

"Welcome to Macintosh"
"Disassembler installed"
"MacsBug installed"
"Warning—this startup disk is not usable"

Assembly-Language Information

Constants

```
; System error IDs

dsBusError      .EQU   1      ;bus error
dsAddressErr    .EQU   2      ;address error
dsIllInstErr    .EQU   3      ;illegal instruction
dsZeroDivErr    .EQU   4      ;zero divide
dsChkErr        .EQU   5      ;check exception
dsOvflowErr     .EQU   6      ;trapV exception
dsPrivErr       .EQU   7      ;privilege violation
dsTraceErr      .EQU   8      ;trace exception
dsLineAErr      .EQU   9      ;line 1010 exception
dsLineFErr      .EQU   10     ;line 1111 exception
dsMiscErr       .EQU   11     ;miscellaneous exception
dsCoreErr       .EQU   12     ;unimplemented core routine
dsIrqErr        .EQU   13     ;spurious interrupt
dsIOCoreErr     .EQU   14     ;I/O system error
dsLoadErr       .EQU   15     ;Segment Loader error
dsFPErr         .EQU   16     ;floating point error
dsNoPackErr     .EQU   17     ;can't load package 0
dsNoPk1         .EQU   18     ;can't load package 1
dsNoPk2         .EQU   19     ;can't load package 2
dsNoPk3         .EQU   20     ;can't load package 3
dsNoPk4         .EQU   21     ;can't load package 4
dsNoPk5         .EQU   22     ;can't load package 5
dsNoPk6         .EQU   23     ;can't load package 6
```

```
dsNoPk7          .EQU     24         ;can't load package 7
dsMemFullErr     .EQU     25         ;can't allocate requested block
dsBadLaunch      .EQU     26         ;Segment Loader error
dsFSErr          .EQU     27         ;file map destroyed
dsStkNHeap       .EQU     28         ;stack overflow error
dsReinsert       .EQU     30         ;"Please insert the disk:"
dsSysErr         .EQU     32767      ;undifferentiated system error
```

Routines

Trap macro	On entry	On exit
_SysError	D0: errorCode (word)	All registers changed

Variables

DSErrCode	Current system error ID (word)
DSAlertTab	Pointer to system error alert table in use
DSAlertRect	Rectangle enclosing system error alert (8 bytes)

TEXTEDIT

Constants

```
CONST { Text justification }

    teJustLeft   =  0;
    teJustCenter =  1;
    teJustRight  = -1;
```

Data Types

```
TYPE TEHandle = ^TEPtr;
     TEPtr    = ^TERec;
     TERec = RECORD
                destRect:   Rect;      {destination rectangle}
                viewRect:   Rect;      {view rectangle}
                selRect:    Rect;      {used from assembly language}
                lineHeight  INTEGER;   {for line spacing}
                fontAscent: INTEGER;   {caret/highlighting position}
                selPoint:   Point;     {used from assembly language}
                selStart:   INTEGER;   {start of selection range}
                selEnd:     INTEGER;   {end of selection range}
                active:     INTEGER;   {used internally}
                wordBreak:  ProcPtr;   {for word break routine}
                clikLoop:   ProcPtr;   {for click loop routine}
                clickTime:  LONGINT;   {used internally}
                clickLoc:   INTEGER;   {used internally}
                caretTime:  LONGINT;   {used internally}
                caretState: INTEGER;   {used internally}
                just:       INTEGER;   {justification of text}
                teLength:   INTEGER;   {length of text}
                hText:      Handle;    {text to be edited}
                recalBack:  INTEGER;   {used internally}
                recalLines: INTEGER;   {used internally}
                clikStuff:  INTEGER;   {used internally}
                crOnly:     INTEGER;   {if <0, new line at Return only}
                txFont:     INTEGER;   {text font}
                txFace:     Style;     {character style}
                txMode:     INTEGER;   {pen mode}
                txSize:     INTEGER;   {font size}
                inPort:     GrafPtr;   {grafPort}
                highHook:   ProcPtr;   {used from assembly language}
                caretHook:  ProcPtr;   {used from assembly language}
                nLines:     INTEGER;   {number of lines}
                lineStarts: ARRAY[0..16000] OF INTEGER
                                       {positions of line starts}
             END;
```

```
CharsHandle = ^CharsPtr;
CharsPtr    = ^Chars;
Chars       = PACKED ARRAY[0..32000] OF CHAR;
```

Routines

Initialization and Allocation

```
PROCEDURE TEInit;
FUNCTION  TENew      (destRect,viewRect: Rect) : TEHandle;
PROCEDURE TEDispose (hTE: TEHandle);
```

Accessing the Text of an Edit Record

```
PROCEDURE TESetText (text: Ptr; length: LONGINT; hTE: TEHandle);
FUNCTION  TEGetText (hTE: TEHandle) : CharsHandle;
```

Insertion Point and Selection Range

```
PROCEDURE TEIdle       (hTE: TEHandle);
PROCEDURE TEClick      (pt: Point; extend: BOOLEAN; hTE: TEHandle);
PROCEDURE TESetSelect  (selStart,selEnd: LONGINT; hTE: TEHandle);
PROCEDURE TEActivate   (hTE: TEHandle);
PROCEDURE TEDeactivate (hTE: TEHandle);
```

Editing

```
PROCEDURE TEKey    (key: CHAR; hTE: TEHandle);
PROCEDURE TECut    (hTE: TEHandle);
PROCEDURE TECopy   (hTE: TEHandle);
PROCEDURE TEPaste  (hTE: TEHandle);
PROCEDURE TEDelete (hTE: TEHandle);
PROCEDURE TEInsert (text: Ptr; length: LONGINT; hTE: TEHandle);
```

Text Display and Scrolling

```
PROCEDURE TESetJust (just: INTEGER; hTE: TEHandle);
PROCEDURE TEUpdate  (rUpdate: Rect; hTE: TEHandle);
PROCEDURE TextBox   (text: Ptr; length: LONGINT; box: Rect; just:
                     INTEGER);
PROCEDURE TEScroll  (dh,dv: INTEGER; hTE: TEHandle);
```

Scrap Handling [Not in ROM]

```
FUNCTION    TEFromScrap   :   OSErr;
FUNCTION    TEToScrap    :    OSErr;
FUNCTION    TEScrapHandle :   Handle;
FUNCTION    TEGetScrapLen :   LONGINT;
PROCEDURE   TESetScrapLen :   (length: LONGINT);
```

Advanced Routines

```
PROCEDURE   SetWordBreak (wBrkProc: ProcPtr; hTE: TEHandle);   [Not in ROM]
PROCEDURE   SetClikLoop  (clikProc: ProcPtr; hTE: TEHandle);   [Not in ROM]
PROCEDURE   TECalText     (hTE: TEHandle);
```

Word Break Routine

```
FUNCTION MyWordBreak (text: Ptr; charPos: INTEGER) : BOOLEAN;
```

Click Loop Routine

```
FUNCTION MyClikLoop : BOOLEAN;
```

Assembly-Language Information

Constants

```
; Text justification

teJustLeft      .EQU     0
teJustCenter    .EQU     1
teJustRight     .EQU    -1
```

Edit Record Data Structure

teDestRect	Destination rectangle (8 bytes)
teViewRect	View rectangle (8 bytes)
teSelRect	Selection rectangle (8 bytes)
teLineHite	For line spacing (word)
teAscent	Caret/highlighting position (word)
teSelPoint	Point selected with mouse (long)
teSelStart	Start of selection range (word)
teSelEnd	End of selection range (word)
teWordBreak	Address of word break routine (see below)
teClikProc	Address of click loop routine (see below)
teJust	Justification of text (word)

teLength	Length of text (word)
teTextH	Handle to text
teCROnly	If <0, new line at Return only (byte)
teFont	Text font (word)
teFace	Character style (word)
teMode	Pen mode (word)
teSize	Font size (word)
teGrafPort	Pointer to grafPort
teHiHook	Address of text highlighting routine (see below)
teCarHook	Address of routine to draw caret (see below)
teNLines	Number of lines (word)
teLines	Positions of line starts (teNLines*2 bytes)
teRecSize	Size in bytes of edit record except teLines field

Word break routine

On entry	A0:	pointer to text
	D0:	character position (word)
On exit	Z condition code:	0 to break at specified character
		1 not to break there

Click loop routine

On exit	D0:	1
	D2:	must be preserved

Text highlighting routine

On entry	A3:	pointer to locked edit record

Caret drawing routine

On entry	A3:	pointer to locked edit record

Variables

TEScrpHandle	Handle to TextEdit scrap
TEScrpLength	Size in bytes of TextEdit scrap (word)
TERecal	Address of routine to recalculate line starts (see below)
TEDoText	Address of multi-purpose routine (see below)

TERecal routine

On entry	A3:	pointer to locked edit record
	D7:	change in length of edit record (word)
On exit	D2:	line start of line containing first character to be redrawn (word)
	D3:	position of first character to be redrawn (word)
	D4:	position of last character to be redrawn (word)

TEDoText routine

On entry   A3:   pointer to locked edit record
   D3:   position of first character to be redrawn (word)
   D4:   position of last character to be redrawn (word)
   D7:   (word)   0 to hit-test a character
        1 to highlight selection range
        −1 to display text
        −2 to position pen to draw caret

On exit   A0:   pointer to current grafPort
   D0:   if hit-testing, character position or −1 for none (word)

UTILITIES, OPERATING SYSTEM

Constants

```
CONST  { Values returned by Environs procedure }

        macXLMachine  = 0;          {Macintosh XL}
        macMachine    = 1;          {Macintosh 128K or 512K}

        { Result codes }

        clkRdErr      = -85;        {unable to read clock}
        clkWrErr      = -86;        {time written did not verify}
        memFullErr    = -108;       {not enough room in heap zone}
        memWZErr      = -111;       {attempt to operate on a free block}
        nilHandleErr  = -109;       {NIL master pointer}
        noErr         =  0;         {no error}
        prInitErr     = -88;        {validity status is not $A8}
        prWrErr       = -87;        {parameter RAM written did not verify}
        qErr          = -1;         {entry not in specified queue}
```

Data Types

```
TYPE  OSType = PACKED ARRAY[1..4] OF CHAR;

      OSErr = INTEGER;

      SysPPtr      = ^SysParmType;
      SysParmType =
        RECORD
           valid:    Byte;       {validity status}
           aTalkA:   Byte;       {AppleTalk node ID hint for modem port}
           aTalkB:   Byte;       {AppleTalk node ID hint for printer port}
           config:   Byte;       {use types for serial ports}
           portA:    INTEGER;    {modem port configuration}
           portB:    INTEGER;    {printer port configuration}
           alarm:    LONGINT;    {alarm setting}
           font:     INTEGER;    {application font number minus 1}
           kbdPrint: INTEGER;    {auto-key settings, printer connection}
           volClik:  INTEGER;    {speaker volume, double-click, caret blink}
           misc:     INTEGER     {mouse scaling, startup disk, menu blink}
        END;

      QHdrPtr  = ^QHdr;
      QHdr     = RECORD
                    qFlags:  INTEGER;    {queue flags}
                    qHead:   QElemPtr;   {first queue entry}
                    qTail:   QElemPtr    {last queue entry}
                 END;
```

```
QTypes = (dummyType,
          vType,          {vertical retrace queue type}
          ioQType,        {file I/O or driver I/O queue type}
          drvQType,       {drive queue type}
          evType,         {event queue type}
          fsQType);       {volume-control-block queue type}

QElemPtr = ^QElem;
QElem    = RECORD
             CASE QTypes OF
               vType:     (vblQElem: VBLTask);
               ioQType:   (ioQElem:  ParamBlockRec);
               drvQType:  (drvQElem: DrvQEl);
               evType:    (evQElem:  EvQEl);
               fsQType:   (vcbQElem: VCB)
           END;

DateTimeRec =
           RECORD
             year:      INTEGER;  {1904 to 2040}
             month:     INTEGER;  {1 to 12 for January to December}
             day:       INTEGER;  {1 to 31}
             hour:      INTEGER;  {0 to 23}
             minute:    INTEGER;  {0 to 59}
             second:    INTEGER;  {0 to 59}
             dayOfWeek: INTEGER   {1 to 7 for Sunday to Saturday}
           END;
```

Routines

Pointer and Handle Manipulation

```
FUNCTION HandToHand  (VAR theHndl: Handle) : OSErr;
FUNCTION PtrToHand   (srcPtr: Ptr; VAR dstHndl: Handle; size: LONGINT) :
                      OSErr;
FUNCTION PtrToXHand  (srcPtr: Ptr; dstHndl: Handle; size: LONGINT) :
                      OSErr;
FUNCTION HandAndHand (aHndl,bHndl: Handle) : OSErr;
FUNCTION PtrAndHand  (pntr: Ptr; hndl: Handle; size: LONGINT) : OSErr;
```

String Comparison

```
FUNCTION  EqualString (aStr,bStr: Str255; caseSens,diacSens: BOOLEAN) :
                       BOOLEAN;
PROCEDURE UprString   (VAR theString: Str255; diacSens: BOOLEAN);
```

Date and Time Operations

```
FUNCTION   ReadDateTime  (VAR secs: LONGINT) : OSErr;
PROCEDURE  GetDateTime   (VAR secs: LONGINT);   [Not in ROM]
FUNCTION   SetDateTime   (secs: LONGINT) : OSErr;
PROCEDURE  Date2Secs     (date: DateTimeRec; VAR secs: LONGINT);
PROCEDURE  Secs2Date     (secs: LONGINT; VAR date: DateTimeRec);
PROCEDURE  GetTime       (VAR date: DateTimeRec);   [Not in ROM]
PROCEDURE  SetTime       (date: DateTimeRec);   [Not in ROM]
```

Parameter RAM Operations

```
FUNCTION   InitUtil :    OSErr;
FUNCTION   GetSysPPtr :  SysPPtr;   [Not in ROM]
FUNCTION   WriteParam :  OSErr;
```

Queue Manipulation

```
PROCEDURE  Enqueue (qEntry: QElemPtr; theQueue: QHdrPtr);
FUNCTION   Dequeue (qEntry: QElemPtr; theQueue: QHdrPtr) : OSErr;
```

Trap Dispatch Table Utilities

```
PROCEDURE  SetTrapAddress (trapAddr: LONGINT; trapNum: INTEGER);
FUNCTION   GetTrapAddress (trapNum: INTEGER) : LONGINT;
```

Miscellaneous Utilities

```
PROCEDURE  Delay      (numTicks: LONGINT; VAR finalTicks: LONGINT);
PROCEDURE  SysBeep    (duration: INTEGER);
PROCEDURE  Environs   (VAR rom,machine: INTEGER);   [Not in ROM]
PROCEDURE  Restart;      [Not in ROM]
PROCEDURE  SetUpA5;      [Not in ROM]
PROCEDURE  RestoreA5;    [Not in ROM]
```

Default Parameter RAM Values

Parameter	Default value
Validity status	$A8
Node ID hint for modem port	0
Node ID hint for printer port	0
Use types for serial ports	0 (both ports)
Modem port configuration	9600 baud, 8 data bits, 2 stop bits, no parity

Parameter	Default value
Printer port configuration	Same as for modem port
Alarm setting	0 (midnight, January 1, 1904)
Application font number minus 1	2 (Geneva)
Auto-key threshold	6 (24 ticks)
Auto-key rate	3 (6 ticks)
Printer connection	0 (printer port)
Speaker volume	3 (medium)
Double-click time	8 (32 ticks)
Caret-blink time	8 (32 ticks)
Mouse scaling	1 (on)
Preferred system startup disk	0 (internal drive)
Menu blink	3

Assembly-Language Information

Constants

```
; Result codes

clkRdErr      .EQU    -85      ;unable to read clock
clkWrErr      .EQU    -86      ;time written did not verify
memFullErr    .EQU    -108     ;not enough room in heap zone
memWZErr      .EQU    -111     ;attempt to operate on a free block
nilHandleErr  .EQU    -109     ;NIL master pointer
noErr         .EQU     0       ;no error
prInitErr     .EQU    -88      ;validity status is not $A8
prWrErr       .EQU    -87      ;parameter RAM written did not verify
qErr          .EQU    -1       ;entry not in specified queue

; Queue types

vType         .EQU     1       ;vertical retrace queue type
ioQType       .EQU     2       ;file I/O or driver I/O queue type
drvQType      .EQU     3       ;drive queue type
evType        .EQU     4       ;event queue type
fsQType       .EQU     5       ;volume-control-block queue type
```

Queue Data Structure

qFlags	Queue flags (word)
qHead	Pointer to first queue entry
qTail	Pointer to last queue entry

Date/Time Record Data Structure

dtYear	1904 to 2040 (word)
dtMonth	1 to 12 for January to December (word)
dtDay	1 to 31 (word)
dtHour	0 to 23 (word)
dtMinute	0 to 59 (word)
dtSecond	0 to 59 (word)
dtDayOfWeek	1 to 7 for Sunday to Saturday (word)

Routines

Trap macro	On entry	On exit
_HandToHand	A0: theHndl (handle)	A0: theHndl (handle) D0: result code(word)
_PtrToHand	A0: srcPtr (ptr) D0: size (long)	A0: dstHndl (handle) D0: result code (word)
_PtrToXHand	A0: srcPtr (ptr) A1: dstHndl (handle) D0: size (long)	A0: dstHndl (handle) D0: result code (word)
_HandAndHand	A0: aHndl (handle) A1: bHndl (handle)	A0: bHndl (handle) D0: result code (word)
_PtrAndHand	A0: pntr (ptr) A1: hndl (handle) D0: size (long)	A0: hndl (handle) D0: result code (word)
_CmpString	_CmpString ,MARKS sets bit 9, for diacSens=FALSE _CmpString ,CASE sets bit 10, for caseSens=TRUE _CmpString ,MARKS,CASE sets bits 9 and 10 A0: ptr to first string A1: ptr to second string D0: high word: length of first string low word: length of second string	D0: 0 if equal, 1 if not equal (long)
_UprString	_UprString ,MARKS sets bit 9, for diacSens=FALSE A0: ptr to string D0: length of string (word)	A0: ptr to string
_ReadDateTime	A0: ptr to long word secs	A0: ptr to long word secs D0: result code (word)
_SetDateTime	D0: secs (long)	D0: result code (word)
_Date2Secs	A0: ptr to date/time record	D0: secs (long)
_Secs2Date	D0: secs (long)	A0: ptr to date/time record
_InitUtil		D0: result code (word)
_WriteParam	A0: SysParam (ptr) D0: MinusOne (long)	D0: result code (word)

Trap macro	On entry	On exit
_Enqueue	A0: qEntry (ptr) A1: theQueue (ptr)	A1: theQueue (ptr)
_Dequeue	A0: qEntry (ptr) A1: theQueue (ptr)	A1: theQueue (ptr) D0: result code (word)
_GetTrapAddress	D0: trapNum (word)	A0: address of routine
_SetTrapAddress	A0: trapAddr (address) D0: trapNum (word)	
_Delay	A0: numTicks (long)	D0: finalTicks (long)
_SysBeep	stack: duration (word)	

Variables

SysParam	Low-memory copy of parameter RAM (20 bytes)
SPValid	Validity status (byte)
SPATalkA	AppleTalk node ID hint for modem port (byte)
SPATalkB	AppleTalk node ID hint for printer port (byte)
SPConfig	Use types for serial ports (byte)
SPPortA	Modem port configuration (word)
SPPortB	Printer port configuration (word)
SPAlarm	Alarm setting (long)
SPFont	Application font number minus 1 (word)
SPKbd	Auto-key threshold and rate (byte)
SPPrint	Printer connection (byte)
SPVolCtl	Speaker volume (byte)
SPClikCaret	Double-click and caret-blink times (byte)
SPMisc2	Mouse scaling, system startup disk, menu blink (byte)
CrsrThresh	Mouse-scaling threshold (word)
Time	Seconds since midnight, January 1, 1904 (long)

3 Summary

UTILITIES, TOOLBOX

Constants

```
CONST { Resource ID of standard pattern list }

        sysPatListID = 0;

        { Resource IDs of standard cursors }

        iBeamCursor = 1;   {to select text}
        crossCursor = 2;   {to draw graphics}
        plusCursor  = 3;   {to select cells in structured documents}
        watchCursor = 4;   {to indicate a long wait}
```

Data Types

```
TYPE Int64Bit =  RECORD
                    hiLong: LONGINT;
                    loLong: LONGINT
                 END;

    CursPtr    = ^Cursor;
    CursHandle = ^CursPtr;

    PatPtr    = ^Pattern;
    PatHandle = ^PatPtr;
```

Routines

Fixed-Point Arithmetic

```
FUNCTION FixRatio (numer,denom: INTEGER) : Fixed;
FUNCTION FixMul   (a,b: Fixed) : Fixed;
FUNCTION FixRound (x: Fixed) : INTEGER;
```

String Manipulation

```
FUNCTION  NewString     (theString: Str255) : StringHandle;
PROCEDURE SetString     (h: StringHandle; theString: Str255);
FUNCTION  GetString     (stringID: INTEGER) : StringHandle;
PROCEDURE GetIndString  (VAR theString: Str255; strListID: INTEGER;
                          index: INTEGER);   [Not in ROM]
```

Byte Manipulation

```
FUNCTION    Munger      (h: Handle; offset: LONGINT; ptr1: Ptr; len1:
                         LONGINT; ptr2: Ptr; len2: LONGINT) : LONGINT;
PROCEDURE PackBits      (VAR srcPtr,dstPtr: Ptr; srcBytes: INTEGER);
PROCEDURE UnpackBits    (VAR srcPtr,dstPtr: Ptr; dstBytes: INTEGER);
```

Bit Manipulation

```
FUNCTION    BitTst (bytePtr: Ptr; bitNum: LONGINT) : BOOLEAN;
PROCEDURE BitSet (bytePtr: Ptr; bitNum: LONGINT);
PROCEDURE BitClr (bytePtr: Ptr; bitNum: LONGINT);
```

Logical Operations

```
FUNCTION BitAnd    (value1,value2: LONGINT) : LONGINT;
FUNCTION BitOr     (value1,value2: LONGINT) : LONGINT;
FUNCTION BitXor    (value1,value2: LONGINT) : LONGINT;
FUNCTION BitNot    (value: LONGINT) : LONGINT;
FUNCTION BitShift (value: LONGINT; count: INTEGER) : LONGINT;
```

Other Operations on Long Integers

```
FUNCTION    HiWord  (x: LONGINT) : INTEGER;
FUNCTION    LoWord  (x: LONGINT) : INTEGER;
PROCEDURE LongMul (a,b: LONGINT; VAR dest: Int64Bit);
```

Graphics Utilities

```
PROCEDURE ScreenRes      (VAR scrnHRes,scrnVRes: INTEGER);   [Not in ROM]
FUNCTION    GetIcon       (iconID: INTEGER) : Handle;
PROCEDURE PlotIcon       (theRect: Rect; theIcon: Handle);
FUNCTION    GetPattern    (patID: INTEGER) : PatHandle;
PROCEDURE GetIndPattern (VAR thePattern: Pattern; patListID: INTEGER;
                          index: INTEGER);   [Not in ROM]
FUNCTION    GetCursor     (cursorID: INTEGER) : CursHandle;
PROCEDURE ShieldCursor   (shieldRect: Rect; offsetPt: Point);
FUNCTION    GetPicture    (picID: INTEGER) : PicHandle;
```

Miscellaneous Utilities

```
FUNCTION DeltaPoint      (ptA,ptB: Point) : LONGINT;
FUNCTION SlopeFromAngle (angle: INTEGER) : Fixed;
FUNCTION AngleFromSlope (slope: Fixed) : INTEGER;
```

Assembly-Language Information

Constants

```
; Resource ID of standard pattern list

sysPatListID    .EQU    0

; Resource IDs of standard cursors

iBeamCursor     .EQU    1       ;to select text
crossCursor     .EQU    2       ;to draw graphics
plusCursor      .EQU    3       ;to select cells in structured documents
watchCursor     .EQU    4       ;to indicate a long wait
```

Variables

ScrVRes   Pixels per inch vertically (word)
ScrHRes   Pixels per inch horizontally (word)

VERTICAL RETRACE MANAGER

Constants

```
CONST { Result codes }

      noErr   =  0;    {no error}
      qErr    = -1;    {task entry isn't in the queue}
      vTypErr = -2;    {qType field isn't ORD(vType)}
```

Data Types

```
TYPE VBLTask = RECORD
               qLink:    QElemPtr;    {next queue entry}
               qType:    INTEGER;     {queue type}
               vblAddr:  ProcPtr;     {pointer to task}
               vblCount: INTEGER;     {task frequency}
               vblPhase: INTEGER      {task phase}
             END;
```

Routines

```
FUNCTION VInstall    (vblTaskPtr: QElemPtr) : OSErr;
FUNCTION VRemove     (vblTaskPtr: QElemPtr) : OSErr;
FUNCTION GetVBLQHdr : QHdrPtr;  [Not in ROM]
```

Assembly-Language Information

Constants

```
inVBL   .EQU   6    ;set if Vertical Retrace Manager is executing a task

; Result codes

noErr   .EQU    0   ;no error
qErr    .EQU   -1   ;task entry isn't in the queue
vTypErr .EQU   -2   ;qType field isn't vType
```

Structure of Vertical Retrace Queue Entry

qLink	Pointer to next queue entry
qType	Queue type (word)
vblAddr	Address of task
vblCount	Task frequency (word)
vblPhase	Task phase (word)

3 Summary

Routines

Trap macro	On entry	On exit
_VInstall	A0: vblTaskPtr (ptr)	D0: result code (word)
_VRemove	A0: vblTaskPtr (ptr)	D0: result code (word)

Variables

VBLQueue	Vertical retrace queue header (10 bytes)

WINDOW MANAGER

Constants

```
CONST  { Window definition IDs }

       documentProc   = 0;    {standard document window}
       dBoxProc       = 1;    {alert box or modal dialog box}
       plainDBox      = 2;    {plain box}
       altDBoxProc    = 3;    {plain box with shadow}
       noGrowDocProc  = 4;    {document window without size box}
       rDocProc       = 16;   {rounded-corner window}

       { Window class, in windowKind field of window record }

       dialogKind     = 2;    {dialog or alert window}
       userKind       = 8;    {window created directly by the application}

       { Values returned by FindWindow }

       inDesk         = 0;    {none of the following}
       inMenuBar      = 1;    {in menu bar}
       inSysWindow    = 2;    {in system window}
       inContent      = 3;    {in content region (except grow, if active)}
       inDrag         = 4;    {in drag region}
       inGrow         = 5;    {in grow region (active window only)}
       inGoAway       = 6;    {in go-away region (active window only)}

       { Axis constraints for DragGrayRgn }

       noConstraint   = 0;    {no constraint}
       hAxisOnly      = 1;    {horizontal axis only}
       vAxisOnly      = 2;    {vertical axis only}

       { Messages to window definition function }

       wDraw          = 0;    {draw window frame}
       wHit           = 1;    {tell what region mouse button was pressed in}
       wCalcRgns      = 2;    {calculate strucRgn and contRgn}
       wNew           = 3;    {do any additional window initialization}
       wDispose       = 4;    {take any additional disposal actions}
       wGrow          = 5;    {draw window's grow image}
       wDrawGIcon     = 6;    {draw size box in content region}

       { Values returned by window definition function's hit routine }

       wNoHit         = 0;    {none of the following}
       wInContent     = 1;    {in content region (except grow, if active)}
       wInDrag        = 2;    {in drag region}
       wInGrow        = 3;    {in grow region (active window only)}
       wInGoAway      = 4;    {in go-away region (active window only)}
```

```
                { Resource ID of desktop pattern }

        deskPatID  = 16;
```

Data Types

```
TYPE WindowPtr  = GrafPtr;
     WindowPeek = ^WindowRecord;

     WindowRecord =
            RECORD
                port:           GrafPort;      {window's grafPort}
                windowKind:     INTEGER;       {window class}
                visible:        BOOLEAN;       {TRUE if visible}
                hilited:        BOOLEAN;       {TRUE if highlighted}
                goAwayFlag:     BOOLEAN;       {TRUE if has go-away region}
                spareFlag:      BOOLEAN;       {reserved for future use}
                strucRgn:       RgnHandle;     {structure region}
                contRgn:        RgnHandle;     {content region}
                updateRgn:      RgnHandle;     {update region}
                windowDefProc:  Handle;        {window definition function}
                dataHandle:     Handle;        {data used by windowDefProc}
                titleHandle:    StringHandle;  {window's title}
                titleWidth:     INTEGER;       {width of title in pixels}
                controlList:    ControlHandle; {window's control list}
                nextWindow:     WindowPeek;    {next window in window list}
                windowPic:      PicHandle;     {picture for drawing window}
                refCon:         LONGINT        {window's reference value}
            END;
```

Routines

Initialization and Allocation

```
PROCEDURE InitWindows;
PROCEDURE GetWMgrPort     (VAR wPort: GrafPtr);
FUNCTION  NewWindow       (wStorage: Ptr; boundsRect: Rect; title: Str255;
                           visible: BOOLEAN; procID: INTEGER; behind:
                           WindowPtr; goAwayFlag: BOOLEAN; refCon:
                           LONGINT) : WindowPtr;
FUNCTION  GetNewWindow    (windowID: INTEGER; wStorage: Ptr; behind:
                           WindowPtr) : WindowPtr;
PROCEDURE CloseWindow     (theWindow: WindowPtr);
PROCEDURE DisposeWindow   (theWindow: WindowPtr);
```

Window Display

```
PROCEDURE  SetWTitle      (theWindow: WindowPtr; title: Str255);
PROCEDURE  GetWTitle      (theWindow: WindowPtr; VAR title: Str255);
PROCEDURE  SelectWindow   (theWindow: WindowPtr);
PROCEDURE  HideWindow     (theWindow: WindowPtr);
PROCEDURE  ShowWindow     (theWindow: WindowPtr);
PROCEDURE  ShowHide       (theWindow: WindowPtr; showFlag: BOOLEAN);
PROCEDURE  HiliteWindow   (theWindow: WindowPtr; fHilite: BOOLEAN);
PROCEDURE  BringToFront   (theWindow: WindowPtr);
PROCEDURE  SendBehind     (theWindow,behindWindow: WindowPtr);
FUNCTION   FrontWindow :  WindowPtr;
PROCEDURE  DrawGrowIcon   (theWindow: WindowPtr);
```

Mouse Location

```
FUNCTION  FindWindow   (thePt: Point; VAR whichWindow: WindowPtr) :
                         INTEGER;
FUNCTION  TrackGoAway  (theWindow: WindowPtr; thePt: Point) : BOOLEAN;
```

Window Movement and Sizing

```
PROCEDURE  MoveWindow  (theWindow: WindowPtr; hGlobal,vGlobal: INTEGER;
                        front: BOOLEAN);
PROCEDURE  DragWindow  (theWindow: WindowPtr; startPt: Point; boundsRect:
                        Rect);
FUNCTION   GrowWindow  (theWindow: WindowPtr; startPt: Point; sizeRect:
                        Rect) : LONGINT;
PROCEDURE  SizeWindow  (theWindow: WindowPtr; w,h: INTEGER; fUpdate:
                        BOOLEAN);
```

Update Region Maintenance

```
PROCEDURE  InvalRect    (badRect: Rect);
PROCEDURE  InvalRgn     (badRgn: RgnHandle);
PROCEDURE  ValidRect    (goodRect: Rect);
PROCEDURE  ValidRgn     (goodRgn: RgnHandle);
PROCEDURE  BeginUpdate  (theWindow: WindowPtr);
PROCEDURE  EndUpdate    (theWindow: WindowPtr);
```

Miscellaneous Routines

```
PROCEDURE  SetWRefCon    (theWindow: WindowPtr; data: LONGINT);
FUNCTION   GetWRefCon    (theWindow: WindowPtr) : LONGINT;
PROCEDURE  SetWindowPic  (theWindow: WindowPtr; pic: PicHandle);
FUNCTION   GetWindowPic  (theWindow: WindowPtr) : PicHandle;
FUNCTION   PinRect       (theRect: Rect; thePt: Point) : LONGINT;
```

```
FUNCTION   DragGrayRgn    (theRgn: RgnHandle; startPt: Point; limitRect,
                          slopRect: Rect; axis: INTEGER; actionProc:
                          ProcPtr) : LONGINT;
```

Low-Level Routines

```
FUNCTION   CheckUpdate    (VAR theEvent: EventRecord) : BOOLEAN;
PROCEDURE  ClipAbove      (window: WindowPeek);
PROCEDURE  SaveOld        (window: WindowPeek);
PROCEDURE  DrawNew        (window: WindowPeek; update: BOOLEAN);
PROCEDURE  PaintOne       (window: WindowPeek; clobberedRgn: RgnHandle);
PROCEDURE  PaintBehind    (startWindow: WindowPeek; clobberedRgn:
                           RgnHandle);
PROCEDURE  CalcVis        (window: WindowPeek);
PROCEDURE  CalcVisBehind  (startWindow: WindowPeek; clobberedRgn:
                           RgnHandle);
```

Diameters of Curvature for Rounded-Corner Windows

Window definition ID	Diameters of curvature
rDocProc	16, 16
rDocProc + 1	4, 4
rDocProc + 2	6, 6
rDocProc + 3	8, 8
rDocProc + 4	10, 10
rDocProc + 5	12, 12
rDocProc + 6	20, 20
rDocProc + 7	24, 24

Window Definition Function

```
FUNCTION MyWindow (varCode: INTEGER; theWindow: WindowPtr; message:
                   INTEGER; param: LONGINT) : LONGINT;
```

Assembly-Language Information

Constants

```
; Window definition IDs

documentProc     .EQU  0   ;standard document window
dBoxProc         .EQU  1   ;alert box or modal dialog box
plainDBox        .EQU  2   ;plain box
```

```
altDBoxProc          .EQU   3   ;plain box with shadow
noGrowDocProc        .EQU   4   ;document window without size box
rDocProc             .EQU  16   ;rounded-corner window
```

; Window class, in windowKind field of window record

```
dialogKind           .EQU   2   ;dialog or alert window
userKind             .EQU   8   ;window created directly by the application
```

; Values returned by FindWindow

```
inDesk               .EQU   0   ;none of the following
inMenuBar            .EQU   1   ;in menu bar
inSysWindow          .EQU   2   ;in system window
inContent            .EQU   3   ;in content region (except grow, if active)
inDrag               .EQU   4   ;in drag region
inGrow               .EQU   5   ;in grow region (active window only)
inGoAway             .EQU   6   ;in go-away region (active window only)
```

; Axis constraints for DragGrayRgn

```
noConstraint         .EQU   0   ;no constraint
hAxisOnly            .EQU   1   ;horizontal axis only
vAxisOnly            .EQU   2   ;vertical axis only
```

; Messages to window definition function

```
wDrawMsg             .EQU   0   ;draw window frame
wHitMsg              .EQU   1   ;tell what region mouse button was pressed in
wCalcRgnMsg          .EQU   2   ;calculate strucRgn and contRgn
wInitMsg             .EQU   3   ;do any additional window initialization
wDisposeMsg          .EQU   4   ;take any additional disposal actions
wGrowMsg             .EQU   5   ;draw window's grow image
wGIconMsg            .EQU   6   ;draw size box in content region
```

; Value returned by window definition function's hit routine

```
wNoHit               .EQU   0   ;none of the following
wInContent           .EQU   1   ;in content region (except grow, if active)
wInDrag              .EQU   2   ;in drag region
wInGrow              .EQU   3   ;in grow region (active window only)
wInGoAway            .EQU   4   ;in go-away region (active window only)
```

; Resource ID of desktop pattern

```
deskPatID            .EQU  16
```

Window Record Data Structure

```
windowPort           Window's grafPort (portRec bytes)
windowKind           Window class (word)
wVisible             Nonzero if window is visible (byte)
wHilited             Nonzero if window is highlighted (byte)
```

wGoAway	Nonzero if window has go-away region (byte)
structRgn	Handle to structure region of window
contRgn	Handle to content region of window
updateRgn	Handle to update region of window
windowDef	Handle to window definition function
wDataHandle	Handle to data used by window definition function
wTitleHandle	Handle to window's title (preceded by length byte)
wTitleWidth	Width of title in pixels (word)
wControlList	Handle to window's control list
nextWindow	Pointer to next window in window list
windowPic	Picture handle for drawing window
wRefCon	Window's reference value (long)
windowSize	Size in bytes of window record

Special Macro Names

Pascal name	Macro name
CalcVisBehind	_CalcVBehind
DisposeWindow	_DisposWindow
DragGrayRgn	_DragGrayRgn or, after setting the global variable DragPattern, _DragTheRgn

Variables

WindowList	Pointer to first window in window list
SaveUpdate	Flag for whether to generate update events (word)
PaintWhite	Flag for whether to paint window white before update event (word)
CurActivate	Pointer to window to receive activate event
CurDeactive	Pointer to window to receive deactivate event
GrayRgn	Handle to region drawn as desktop
DeskPattern	Pattern with which desktop is painted (8 bytes)
DeskHook	Address of procedure for painting desktop or responding to clicks on desktop
WMgrPort	Pointer to Window Manager port
GhostWindow	Pointer to window never to be considered frontmost
DragHook	Address of procedure to execute during TrackGoAway, DragWindow, GrowWindow, and DragGrayRgn
DragPattern	Pattern of dragged region's outline (8 bytes)
OldStructure	Handle to saved structure region
OldContent	Handle to saved content region
SaveVisRgn	Handle to saved visRgn

ASSEMBLY LANGUAGE

Variables

OneOne	$00010001
MinusOne	$FFFFFFFF
Lo3Bytes	$00FFFFFF
Scratch20	20-byte scratch area
Scratch8	8-byte scratch area
ToolScratch	8-byte scratch area
ApplScratch	12-byte scratch area reserved for use by applications
ROMBase	Base address of ROM
RAMBase	Trap dispatch table's base address for routines in RAM
CurrentA5	Address of boundary between application globals and application parameters

Hardware

Warning: This information applies only to the Macintosh 128K and 512K, not to the Macintosh XL.

Constants

```
; VIA base addresses

vBase      .EQU    $EFE1FE      ;main base for VIA chip (in variable VIA)
aVBufB     .EQU    vBase        ;register B base
aVBufA     .EQU    $EFFFFE      ;register A base
aVBufM     .EQU    aVBufB       ;register containing mouse signals
aVIFR      .EQU    $EFFBFE      ;interrupt flag register
aVIER      .EQU    $EFFDFE      ;interrupt enable register


; Offsets from vBase

vBufB      .EQU    512*0        ;register B (zero offset)
vDirB      .EQU    512*2        ;register B direction register
vDirA      .EQU    512*3        ;register A direction register
vT1C       .EQU    512*4        ;timer 1 counter (low-order byte)
vT1CH      .EQU    512*5        ;timer 1 counter (high-order byte)
vT1L       .EQU    512*6        ;timer 1 latch (low-order byte)
vT1LH      .EQU    512*7        ;timer 1 latch (high-order byte)
vT2C       .EQU    512*8        ;timer 2 counter (low-order byte)
vT2CH      .EQU    512*9        ;timer 2 counter (high-order byte)
vSR        .EQU    512*10       ;shift register (keyboard)
vACR       .EQU    512*11       ;auxiliary control register
vPCR       .EQU    512*12       ;peripheral control register
vIFR       .EQU    512*13       ;interrupt flag register
```

```
vIER            .EQU    512*14        ;interrupt enable register
vBufA           .EQU    512*15        ;register A

; VIA register A constants

vAOut           .EQU    $7F           ;direction register A:  1 bits = outputs
vAInit          .EQU    $7B           ;initial value for vBufA (medium volume)
vSound          .EQU    7             ;sound volume bits

; VIA register A bit numbers

vSndPg2         .EQU    3             ;0 = alternate sound buffer
vOverlay        .EQU    4             ;1 = ROM overlay (system startup only)
vHeadSel        .EQU    5             ;disk SEL control line
vPage2          .EQU    6             ;0 = alternate screen buffer
vSCCWReq        .EQU    7             ;SCC wait/request line

; VIA register B constants

vBOut           .EQU    $87           ;direction register B:  1 bits = outputs
vBInit          .EQU    $07           ;initial value for vBufB

; VIA register B bit numbers

rTCData         .EQU    0             ;real-time clock serial data line
rTCClk          .EQU    1             ;real-time clock data-clock line
rTCEnb          .EQU    2             ;real-time clock serial enable
vSW             .EQU    3             ;0 = mouse button is down
vX2             .EQU    4             ;mouse X quadrature level
vY2             .EQU    5             ;mouse Y quadrature level
vH4             .EQU    6             ;1 = horizontal blanking
vSndEnb         .EQU    7             ;0 = sound enabled, 1 = disabled

; SCC base addresses

sccRBase        .EQU    $9FFFF8       ;SCC base read address (in variable SCCRd)
sccWBase        .EQU    $BFFFF9       ;SCC base write address (in variable SCCWr)

; Offsets from SCC base addresses

aData           .EQU    6             ;channel A data in or out
aCtl            .EQU    2             ;channel A control
bData           .EQU    4             ;channel B data in or out
bCtl            .EQU    0             ;channel B control

; Bit numbers for control register RR0

rxBF            .EQU    0             ;1 = SCC receive buffer full
txBE            .EQU    2             ;1 = SCC send buffer empty
```

```
; IWM base address

dBase        .EQU     $DFE1FF      ;IWM base address (in variable IWM)

; Offsets from dBase

ph0L         .EQU     512*0        ;CA0 off (0)
ph0H         .EQU     512*1        ;CA0 on (1)
ph1L         .EQU     512*2        ;CA1 off (0)
ph1H         .EQU     512*3        ;CA1 on (1)
ph2L         .EQU     512*4        ;CA2 off (0)
ph2H         .EQU     512*5        ;CA2 on (1)
ph3L         .EQU     512*6        ;LSTRB off (low)
ph3H         .EQU     512*7        ;LSTRB on (high)
mtrOff       .EQU     512*8        ;disk enable off
mtrOn        .EQU     512*9        ;disk enable on
intDrive     .EQU     512*10       ;select internal drive
extDrive     .EQU     512*11       ;select external drive
q6L          .EQU     512*12       ;Q6 off
q6H          .EQU     512*13       ;Q6 on
q7L          .EQU     512*14       ;Q7 off
q7H          .EQU     512*15       ;Q7 on

; Screen and sound addresses for 512K Macintosh (will also work for
; 128K, since addresses wrap)

screenLow    .EQU     $7A700       ;top left corner of main screen buffer
soundLow     .EQU     $7FD00       ;main sound buffer (in variable SoundBase)
pwmBuffer    .EQU     $7FD01       ;main disk speed buffer
ovlyRAM      .EQU     $600000      ;RAM start address when overlay is set
ovlyScreen   .EQU     $67A700      ;screen start with overlay set
romStart     .EQU     $400000      ;ROM start address (in variable ROMBase)
```

Variables

ROMBase	Base address of ROM
SoundBase	Address of main sound buffer
SCCRd	SCC read base address
SCCWr	SCC write base address
IWM	IWM base address
VIA	VIA base address

Exception Vectors

Location	Purpose
$00	Reset: initial stack pointer (not a vector)
$04	Reset: initial vector
$08	Bus error

Location	Purpose
$0C	Address error
$10	Illegal instruction
$14	Divide by zero
$18	CHK instruction
$1C	TRAPV instruction
$20	Privilege violation
$24	Trace interrupt
$28	Line 1010 emulator
$2C	Line 1111 emulator
$30-$3B	Unassigned (reserved)
$3C	Uninitialized interrupt
$40-$5F	Unassigned (reserved)
$60	Spurious interrupt
$64	VIA interrupt
$68	SCC interrupt
$6C	VIA+SCC vector (temporary)
$70	Interrupt switch
$74	Interrupt switch + VIA
$78	Interrupt switch + SCC
$7C	Interrupt switch + VIA + SCC
$80-$BF	TRAP instructions
$C0-$FF	Unassigned (reserved)

APPENDIX A: RESULT CODES

This appendix lists all the result codes returned by the Macintosh system software. They're ordered by value, for convenience when debugging; the names you should actually use in your program are also listed.

The result codes are grouped roughly according to the lowest level at which the error may occur. This doesn't mean that only routines at that level may cause those errors; higher-level software may yield the same result codes. For example, an Operating System Utility routine that calls the Memory Manager may return one of the Memory Manager result codes. Where a different or more specific meaning is appropriate in a different context, that meaning is also listed.

Value	Name	Meaning
0	noErr	No error

Operating System Event Manager Error

1	evtNotEnb	Event type not designated in system event mask

Printing Manager Errors

128	iPrAbort	Application or user requested abort
−1	iPrSavPFil	Saving spool file

Queuing Errors

−1	qErr	Entry not in queue
−2	vTypErr	QType field of entry in vertical retrace queue isn't vType (in Pascal, ORD(vType))

Device Manager Errors

−17	controlErr	Driver can't respond to this Control call Unimplemented control instruction (Printing Manager)
−18	statusErr	Driver can't respond to this Status call
−19	readErr	Driver can't respond to Read calls
−20	writErr	Driver can't respond to Write calls
−21	badUnitErr	Driver reference number doesn't match unit table
−22	unitEmptyErr	Driver reference number specifies NIL handle in unit table
−23	openErr	Requested read/write permission doesn't match driver's open permission Attempt to open RAM Serial Driver failed
−25	dRemovErr	Attempt to remove an open driver
−26	dInstErr	Couldn't find driver in resource file

−27	abortErr	I/O request aborted by KillIO
	iIOAbort	I/O abort error (Printing Manager)
−28	notOpenErr	Driver isn't open

File Manager Errors

−33	dirFulErr	File directory full
−34	dskFulErr	All allocation blocks on the volume are full
−35	nsvErr	Specified volume doesn't exist
−36	ioErr	I/O error
−37	bdNamErr	Bad file name or volume name (perhaps zero-length)
−38	fnOpnErr	File not open
−39	eofErr	Logical end-of-file reached during read operation
−40	posErr	Attempt to position before start of file
−42	tmfoErr	Too many files open
−43	fnfErr	File not found
−44	wPrErr	Volume is locked by a hardware setting
−45	fLckdErr	File is locked
−46	vLckdErr	Volume is locked by a software flag
−47	fBsyErr	File is busy; one or more files are open
−48	dupFNErr	File with specified name and version number already exists
−49	opWrErr	The read/write permission of only one access path to a file can allow writing
−50	paramErr	Error in parameter list Parameters don't specify an existing volume, and there's no default volume (File Manager) Bad positioning information (Disk Driver) Bad drive number (Disk Initialization Package)
−51	rfNumErr	Path reference number specifies nonexistent access path
−52	gfpErr	Error during GetFPos
−53	volOffLinErr	Volume not on-line
−54	permErr	Attempt to open locked file for writing
−55	volOnLinErr	Specified volume is already mounted and on-line
−56	nsDrvErr	No such drive; specified drive number doesn't match any number in the drive queue
−57	noMacDskErr	Not a Macintosh disk; volume lacks Macintosh-format directory
−58	extFSErr	External file system; file-system identifier is nonzero, or path reference number is greater than 1024

−59	fsRnErr	Problem during rename
−60	badMDBErr	Bad master directory block; must reinitialize volume
−61	wrPermErr	Read/write permission doesn't allow writing

Low-Level Disk Errors

−64	noDriveErr	Drive isn't connected
−65	offLinErr	No disk in drive
−66	noNybErr	Disk is probably blank
−67	noAdrMkErr	Can't find an address mark
−68	dataVerErr	Read-verify failed
−69	badCksmErr	Bad address mark
−70	badBtSlpErr	Bad address mark
−71	noDtaMkErr	Can't find a data mark
−72	badDCksum	Bad data mark
−73	badDBtSlp	Bad data mark
−74	wrUnderrun	Write underrun occurred
−75	cantStepErr	Drive error
−76	tk0BadErr	Can't find track 0
−77	initIWMErr	Can't initialize disk controller chip
−78	twoSideErr	Tried to read side 2 of a disk in a single-sided drive
−79	spdAdjErr	Can't correctly adjust disk speed
−80	seekErr	Drive error
−81	sectNFErr	Can't find sector

Also, to check for any low-level disk error:

| −84 | firstDskErr | First of the range of low-level disk errors |
| −64 | lastDskErr | Last of the range of low-level disk errors |

Clock Chip Errors

−85	clkRdErr	Unable to read clock
−86	clkWrErr	Time written did not verify
−87	prWrErr	Parameter RAM written did not verify
−88	prInitErr	Validity status is not $A8

Appendices

AppleTalk Manager Errors

−91	ddpSktErr	DDP socket error: socket already active; not a well-known socket; socket table full; all dynamic socket numbers in use
−92	ddpLenErr	DDP datagram or ALAP data length too big
−93	noBridgeErr	No bridge found
−94	lapProtErr	ALAP error attaching/detaching ALAP protocol type: attach error when ALAP protocol type is negative, not in range, or already in table, or when table is full; detach error when ALAP protocol type isn't in table
−95	excessCollsns	ALAP no CTS received after 32 RTS's, or line sensed in use 32 times (not necessarily caused by collisions)
−97	portInUse	Driver Open error, port already in use
−98	portNotCf	Driver Open error, port not configured for this connection

Scrap Manager Errors

−100	noScrapErr	Desk scrap isn't initialized
−102	noTypeErr	No data of the requested type

Memory Manager Errors

−108	memFullErr	Not enough room in heap zone
	iMemFullErr	Not enough room in heap zone (Printing Manager)
−109	nilHandleErr	NIL master pointer
−111	memWZErr	Attempt to operate on a free block
−112	memPurErr	Attempt to purge a locked block
−117	memLockedErr	Block is locked

Resource Manager Errors

−192	resNotFound	Resource not found
−193	resFNotFound	Resource file not found
−194	addResFailed	AddResource failed
−196	rmvResFailed	RmveResource failed

Additional AppleTalk Manager Errors

−1024	nbpBuffOvr	NBP buffer overflow
−1025	nbpNoConfirm	NBP name not confirmed
−1026	nbpConfDiff	NBP name confirmed for different socket
−1027	nbpDuplicate	NBP duplicate name already exists
−1028	nbpNotFound	NBP name not found

−1029	nbpNISErr	NBP names information socket error
−1096	reqFailed	ATPSndRequest failed: retry count exceeded
−1097	tooManyReqs	ATP too many concurrent requests
−1098	tooManySkts	ATP too many responding sockets
−1099	badATPSkt	ATP bad responding socket
−1100	badBuffNum	ATP bad sequence number
−1101	noRelErr	ATP no release received
−1102	cbNotFound	ATP control block not found
−1103	noSendResp	ATPAddRsp issued before ATPSndRsp
−1104	noDataArea	Too many outstanding ATP calls
−1105	reqAborted	Request aborted
−3101	buf2SmallErr	ALAP frame too large for buffer DDP datagram too large for buffer
−3102	noMPPError	MPP driver not installed
−3103	cksumErr	DDP bad checksum
−3104	extractErr	NBP can't find tuple in buffer
−3105	readQErr	Socket or protocol type invalid or not found in table
−3106	atpLenErr	ATP response message too large
−3107	atpBadRsp	Bad response from ATPRequest
−3108	recNotFnd	ABRecord not found
−3109	sktClosedErr	Asynchronous call aborted because socket was closed before call was completed

Appendices

APPENDIX B: ROUTINES THAT MAY MOVE OR PURGE MEMORY

This appendix lists all the routines that may move or purge blocks in the heap. As described in chapter 1 of Volume II, calling these routines may cause problems if a handle has been dereferenced. None of these routines may be called from within an interrupt, such as in a completion routine or a VBL task.

The Pascal name of each routine is shown, except for a few cases where there's no Pascal interface corresponding to a particular trap; in those cases, the trap macro name is shown instead (without its initial underscore character).

AddResMenu
Alert
AppendMenu
ATPAddRsp
ATPCloseSocket
ATPGetRequest
ATPLoad
ATPOpenSocket
ATPReqCancel
ATPRequest
ATPResponse
ATPRspCancel
ATPSndRequest
ATPSndRsp
ATPUnload
BeginUpdate
BringToFront
Button
CalcMenuSize
CalcVis
CalcVisBehind
CautionAlert
Chain
ChangedResource
CharWidth
CheckItem
CheckUpdate
ClipAbove
ClipRect
CloseDialog
ClosePicture
ClosePoly
ClosePort
CloseResFile
CloseRgn
CloseWindow
CompactMem
Control

CopyBits
CopyRgn
CouldAlert
CouldDialog
CreateResFile
DDPCloseSocket
DDPOpenSocket
DDPRdCancel
DDPRead
DDPWrite
DialogSelect
DIBadMount
DiffRgn
DIFormat
DILoad
DiskEject
DisposDialog
DisposeControl
DisposeMenu
DisposeRgn
DisposeWindow
DisposHandle
DisposPtr
DIUnload
DIVerify
DIZero
DlgCopy
DlgCut
DlgDelete
DlgPaste
DragControl
DragGrayRgn
DragWindow
DrawChar
DrawDialog
DrawGrowIcon
DrawMenuBar
DrawNew

DrawPicture
DrawString
DrawText
DriveStatus
DrvrInstall
DrvrRemove
Eject
EmptyHandle
EndUpdate
EraseArc
EraseOval
ErasePoly
EraseRect
EraseRgn
EraseRoundRect
EventAvail
ExitToShell
FillArc
FillOval
FillPoly
FillRect
FillRgn
FillRoundRect
FindControl
FlashMenuBar
FlushVol
FMSwapFont
FrameArc
FrameOval
FramePoly
FrameRect
FrameRgn
FrameRoundRect
FreeAlert
FreeDialog
FreeMem
GetClip
GetCursor

GetDCtlEntry	IUCompString	NumToString
GetDItem	IUDatePString	OpenDeskAcc
GetFNum	IUDateString	OpenPicture
GetFontInfo	IUEqualString	OpenPoly
GetFontName	IUGetIntl	OpenPort
GetIcon	IUMagIDString	OpenResFile
GetIndPattern	IUMagString	OpenRgn
GetIndResource	IUMetric	PaintArc
GetIndString	IUSetIntl	PaintBehind
GetKeys	IUTimePString	PaintOne
GetMenu	IUTimeString	PaintOval
GetMenuBar	KillControls	PaintPoly
GetMouse	KillPicture	PaintRect
GetNamedResource	KillPoly	PaintRgn
GetNewControl	LAPCloseProtocol	PaintRoundRect
GetNewDialog	LAPOpenProtocol	ParamText
GetNewMBar	LAPRdCancel	PBControl
GetNewWindow	LAPRead	PBEject
GetNextEvent	LAPWrite	PBFlushVol
GetPattern	Launch	PBMountVol
GetPicture	Line	PBOffLine
GetResource	LineTo	PBOpen
GetScrap	LoadResource	PBOpenRF
GetString	LoadScrap	PBStatus
GrowWindow	LoadSeg	PicComment
HandAndHand	MapRgn	PlotIcon
HandToHand	MenuKey	PrClose
HideControl	MenuSelect	PrCloseDoc
HideWindow	ModalDialog	PrClosePage
HiliteControl	MoreMasters	PrCtlCall
HiliteMenu	MoveControl	PrDrvrDCE
HiliteWindow	MoveHHi	PrDrvrVers
InitAllPacks	MoveWindow	PrintDefault
InitApplZone	MPPClose	PrJobDialog
InitFonts	MPPOpen	PrJobMerge
InitMenus	Munger	PrOpen
InitPack	NBPConfirm	PrOpenDoc
InitPort	NBPExtract	PrOpenPage
InitResources	NBPLoad	PrPicFile
InitWindows	NBPLookup	PrStlDialog
InitZone	NBPRegister	PrValidate
InsertMenu	NBPRemove	PtrAndHand
InsertResMenu	NBPUnload	PtrToHand
InsetRgn	NewControl	PtrToXHand
InvalRect	NewDialog	PurgeMem
InvalRgn	NewHandle	PutScrap
InvertArc	NewMenu	RAMSDClose
InvertOval	NewPtr	RAMSDOpen
InvertPoly	NewRgn	RealFont
InvertRect	NewString	ReallocHandle
InvertRgn	NewWindow	RecoverHandle
InvertRoundRect	NoteAlert	RectRgn

ReleaseResource	SetString	TEActivate
ResrvMem	SetTagBuffer	TECalText
Restart	SetWTitle	TEClick
RmveResource	SFGetFile	TECopy
RsrcZoneInit	SFPGetFile	TECut
SaveOld	SFPPutFile	TEDeactivate
ScrollRect	SFPutFile	TEDelete
SectRgn	ShowControl	TEDispose
SelectWindow	ShowHide	TEFromScrap
SelIText	ShowWindow	TEGetText
SendBehind	SizeControl	TEIdle
SerClrBrk	SizeWindow	TEInit
SerGetBrk	StartSound	TEInsert
SerHShake	Status	TEKey
SerReset	StdArc	TENew
SerSetBrk	StdBits	TEPaste
SerSetBuf	StdComment	TEScroll
SerStatus	StdLine	TESetJust
SetApplBase	StdOval	TESetSelect
SetClip	StdPoly	TESetText
SetCTitle	StdPutPic	TestControl
SetCtlMax	StdRect	TEToScrap
SetCtlMin	StdRgn	TEUpdate
SetCtlValue	StdRRect	TextBox
SetDItem	StdText	TextWidth
SetEmptyRgn	StdTxMeas	TickCount
SetFontLock	StillDown	TrackControl
SetHandleSize	StopAlert	TrackGoAway
SetItem	StopSound	UnionRgn
SetItemIcon	StringToNum	UnloadScrap
SetItemMark	StringWidth	UnloadSeg
SetItemStyle	SysBeep	ValidRect
SetIText	SysError	ValidRgn
SetPtrSize	SystemClick	WaitMouseUp
SetRectRgn	SystemEdit	XorRgn
SetResInfo	SystemMenu	ZeroScrap

Appendices

APPENDIX C: SYSTEM TRAPS

This appendix lists the trap macros for the Toolbox and Operating System routines and their corresponding trap word values in hexadecimal. The "Name" column gives the trap macro name (without its initial underscore character). In those cases where the name of the equivalent Pascal call is different, the Pascal name appears indented under the main entry. The routines in Macintosh packages are listed under the macros they invoke after pushing a routine selector onto the stack; the routine selector follows the Pascal routine name in parentheses.

There are two tables: The first is ordered alphabetically by name; the second is ordered numerically by trap number, for use when debugging. (The trap number is the last two digits of the trap word unless the trap word begins with A9, in which case the trap number is 1 followed by the last two digits of the trap word.)

Note: The Operating System Utility routines GetTrapAddress and SetTrapAddress take a trap number as a parameter, not a trap word.

Warning: Traps that aren't currently used by the system are reserved for future use.

Name	Trap word	Name	Trap word
AddDrive	A04E	ChangedResource	A9AA
(internal use only)		CharWidth	A88D
AddPt	A87E	CheckItem	A945
AddResMenu	A94D	CheckUpdate	A911
AddResource	A9AB	ClearMenuBar	A934
Alert	A985	ClipAbove	A90B
Allocate	A010	ClipRect	A87B
PBAllocate		Close	A001
AngleFromSlope	A8C4	PBClose	
AppendMenu	A933	CloseDeskAcc	A9B7
BackColor	A863	CloseDialog	A982
BackPat	A87C	ClosePgon	A8CC
BeginUpdate	A922	ClosePoly	
BitAnd	A858	ClosePicture	A8F4
BitClr	A85F	ClosePort	A87D
BitNot	A85A	CloseResFile	A99A
BitOr	A85B	CloseRgn	A8DB
BitSet	A85E	CloseWindow	A92D
BitShift	A85C	CmpString	A03C
BitTst	A85D	EqualString	
BitXor	A859	ColorBit	A864
BlockMove	A02E	CompactMem	A04C
BringToFront	A920	Control	A004
Button	A974	PBControl	
CalcMenuSize	A948	CopyBits	A8EC
CalcVBehind	A90A	CopyRgn	A8DC
CalcVisBehind		CouldAlert	A989
CalcVis	A909	CouldDialog	A979
CautionAlert	A988	CountMItems	A950
Chain	A9F3	CountResources	A99C

Name	Trap word	Name	Trap word
CountTypes	A99E	EndUpdate	A923
Create	A008	Enqueue	A96F
PBCreate		EqualPt	A881
CreateResFile	A9B1	EqualRect	A8A6
CurResFile	A994	EqualRgn	A8E3
Date2Secs	A9C7	EraseArc	A8C0
Delay	A03B	EraseOval	A8B9
Delete	A009	ErasePoly	A8C8
PBDelete		EraseRect	A8A3
DeleteMenu	A936	EraseRgn	A8D4
DeltaPoint	A94F	EraseRoundRect	A8B2
Dequeue	A96E	ErrorSound	A98C
DetachResource	A992	EventAvail	A971
DialogSelect	A980	ExitToShell	A9F4
DiffRgn	A8E6	FillArc	A8C2
DisableItem	A93A	FillOval	A8BB
DisposControl	A955	FillPoly	A8CA
DisposeControl		FillRect	A8A5
DisposDialog	A983	FillRgn	A8D6
DisposHandle	A023	FillRoundRect	A8B4
DisposMenu	A932	FindControl	A96C
DisposeMenu		FindWindow	A92C
DisposPtr	A01F	FixMul	A868
DisposRgn	A8D9	FixRatio	A869
DisposeRgn		FixRound	A86C
DisposWindow	A914	FlashMenuBar	A94C
DisposeWindow		FlushEvents	A032
DragControl	A967	FlushFile	A045
DragGrayRgn	A905	PBFlushFile	
DragTheRgn	A926	FlushVol	A013
DragWindow	A925	PBFlushVol	
DrawChar	A883	FMSwapFont	A901
DrawControls	A969	ForeColor	A862
DrawDialog	A981	FP68K	A9EB
DrawGrowIcon	A904	FrameArc	A8BE
DrawMenuBar	A937	FrameOval	A8B7
DrawNew	A90F	FramePoly	A8C6
DrawPicture	A8F6	FrameRect	A8A1
DrawString	A884	FrameRgn	A8D2
DrawText	A885	FrameRoundRect	A8B0
DrvrInstall	A03D	FreeAlert	A98A
(internal use only)		FreeDialog	A97A
DrvrRemove	A03E	FreeMem	A01C
(internal use only)		FrontWindow	A924
Eject	A017	GetAppParms	A9F5
PBEject		GetClip	A87A
Elems68K	A9EC	GetCRefCon	A95A
EmptyHandle	A02B	GetCTitle	A95E
EmptyRect	A8AE	GetCtlAction	A96A
EmptyRgn	A8E2	GetCtlValue	A960
EnableItem	A939	GetCursor	A9B9

Appendices

Name	Trap word
GetDItem	A98D
GetEOF	A011
PBGetEOF	
GetFileInfo	A00C
PBGetFInfo	
GetFName	A8FF
GetFontName	
GetFNum	A900
GetFontInfo	A88B
GetFPos	A018
PBGetFPos	
GetHandleSize	A025
GetIcon	A9BB
GetIndResource	A99D
GetIndType	A99F
GetItem	A946
GetIText	A990
GetItmIcon	A93F
GetItemIcon	
GetItmMark	A943
GetItemMark	
GetItmStyle	A941
GetItemStyle	
GetKeys	A976
GetMaxCtl	A962
GetCtlMax	
GetMenuBar	A93B
GetMHandle	A949
GetMinCtl	A961
GetCtlMin	
GetMouse	A972
GetNamedResource	A9A1
GetNewControl	A9BE
GetNewDialog	A97C
GetNewMBar	A9C0
GetNewWindow	A9BD
GetNextEvent	A970
GetOSEvent	A031
GetPattern	A9B8
GetPen	A89A
GetPenState	A898
GetPicture	A9BC
GetPixel	A865
GetPort	A874
GetPtrSize	A021
GetResAttrs	A9A6
GetResFileAttrs	A9F6
GetResInfo	A9A8
GetResource	A9A0
GetRMenu	A9BF
GetMenu	

Name	Trap word
GetScrap	A9FD
GetString	A9BA
GetTrapAddress	A146
GetVol	A014
PBGetVol	
GetVolInfo	A007
PBGetVInfo	
GetWindowPic	A92F
GetWMgrPort	A910
GetWRefCon	A917
GetWTitle	A919
GetZone	A11A
GlobalToLocal	A871
GrafDevice	A872
GrowWindow	A92B
HandAndHand	A9E4
HandleZone	A126
HandToHand	A9E1
HideControl	A958
HideCursor	A852
HidePen	A896
HideWindow	A916
HiliteControl	A95D
HiliteMenu	A938
HiliteWindow	A91C
HiWord	A86A
HLock	A029
HNoPurge	A04A
HomeResFile	A9A4
HPurge	A049
HUnlock	A02A
InfoScrap	A9F9
InitAllPacks	A9E6
InitApplZone	A02C
InitCursor	A850
InitDialogs	A97B
InitFonts	A8FE
InitGraf	A86E
InitMenus	A930
InitPack	A9E5
InitPort	A86D
InitQueue	A016
FInitQueue	
InitResources	A995
InitUtil	A03F
InitWindows	A912
InitZone	A019
InsertMenu	A935
InsertResMenu	A951
InsetRect	A8A9
InsetRgn	A8E1

Name	Trap word	Name	Trap word
InvalRect	A928	NewWindow	A913
InvalRgn	A927	NoteAlert	A987
InverRect	A8A4	ObscureCursor	A856
InvertRect		Offline	A035
InverRgn	A8D5	PBOffline	
InvertRgn		OffsetPoly	A8CE
InverRoundRect	A8B3	OffsetRect	A8A8
InvertRoundRect		OfsetRgn	A8E0
InvertArc	A8C1	OffsetRgn	
InvertOval	A8BA	Open	A000
InvertPoly	A8C9	PBOpen	
IsDialogEvent	A97F	OpenDeskAcc	A9B6
KillControls	A956	OpenPicture	A8F3
KillIO	A006	OpenPoly	A8CB
PBKillIO		OpenPort	A86F
KillPicture	A8F5	OpenResFile	A997
KillPoly	A8CD	OpenRF	A00A
Launch	A9F2	PBOpenRF	
Line	A892	OpenRgn	A8DA
LineTo	A891	OSEventAvail	A030
LoadResource	A9A2	Pack0	A9E7
LoadSeg	A9F0	(reserved for future use)	
LocalToGlobal	A870	Pack1	A9E8
LodeScrap	A9FB	(reserved for future use)	
LoadScrap		Pack2	A9E9
LongMul	A867	DIBadMount (0)	
LoWord	A86B	DIFormat (6)	
MapPoly	A8FC	DILoad (2)	
MapPt	A8F9	DIUnload (4)	
MapRect	A8FA	DIVerify (8)	
MapRgn	A8FB	DIZero (10)	
MaxMem	A11D	Pack3	A9EA
MenuKey	A93E	SFGetFile (2)	
MenuSelect	A93D	SFPGetFile (4)	
ModalDialog	A991	SFPPutFile (3)	
MoreMasters	A036	SFPutFile (1)	
MountVol	A00F	Pack4	A9EB
PBMountVol		Pack5	A9EC
Move	A894	Pack6	A9ED
MoveControl	A959	IUDatePString (14)	
MovePortTo	A877	IUDateString (0)	
MoveTo	A893	IUGetIntl (6)	
MoveWindow	A91B	IUMagIDString (12)	
Munger	A9E0	IUMagString (10)	
NewControl	A954	IUMetric (4)	
NewDialog	A97D	IUSetIntl (8)	
NewHandle	A122	IUTimePString (16)	
NewMenu	A931	IUTimeString (2)	
NewPtr	A11E	Pack7	A9EE
NewRgn	A8D8	NumToString (0)	
NewString	A906	StringToNum (1)	

Appendices

Name	Trap word	Name	Trap word
PackBits	A8CF	ScrollRect	A8EF
PaintArc	A8BF	Secs2Date	A9C6
PaintBehind	A90D	SectRect	A8AA
PaintOne	A90C	SectRgn	A8E4
PaintOval	A8B8	SelectWindow	A91F
PaintPoly	A8C7	SelIText	A97E
PaintRect	A8A2	SendBehind	A921
PaintRgn	A8D3	SetAppBase	A057
PaintRoundRect	A8B1	SetApplBase	
ParamText	A98B	SetApplLimit	A02D
PenMode	A89C	SetClip	A879
PenNormal	A89E	SetCRefCon	A95B
PenPat	A89D	SetCTitle	A95F
PenSize	A89B	SetCtlAction	A96B
PicComment	A8F2	SetCtlValue	A963
PinRect	A94E	SetCursor	A851
PlotIcon	A94B	SetDateTime	A03A
PortSize	A876	SetDItem	A98E
PostEvent	A02F	SetEmptyRgn	A8DD
Pt2Rect	A8AC	SetEOF	A012
PtInRect	A8AD	PBSetEOF	
PtInRgn	A8E8	SetFileInfo	A00D
PtrAndHand	A9EF	PBSetFInfo	
PtrToHand	A9E3	SetFilLock	A041
PtrToXHand	A9E2	PBSetFLock	
PtrZone	A148	SetFilType	A043
PtToAngle	A8C3	PBSetFVers	
PurgeMem	A04D	SetFontLock	A903
PutScrap	A9FE	SetFPos	A044
Random	A861	PBSetFPos	
RDrvrInstall	A04F	SetGrowZone	A04B
(internal use only)		SetHandleSize	A024
Read	A002	SetItem	A947
PBRead		SetIText	A98F
ReadDateTime	A039	SetItmIcon	A940
RealFont	A902	SetItemIcon	
ReallocHandle	A027	SetItmMark	A944
RecoverHandle	A128	SetItemMark	
RectInRgn	A8E9	SetItmStyle	A942
RectRgn	A8DF	SetItemStyle	
ReleaseResource	A9A3	SetMaxCtl	A965
Rename	A00B	SetCtlMax	
PBRename		SetMenuBar	A93C
ResError	A9AF	SetMFlash	A94A
ResrvMem	A040	SetMenuFlash	
RmveResource	A9AD	SetMinCtl	A964
RsrcZoneInit	A996	SetCtlMin	
RstFilLock	A042	SetOrigin	A878
PBRstFLock		SetPBits	A875
SaveOld	A90E	SetPortBits	
ScalePt	A8F8	SetPenState	A899

Name	Trap word	Name	Trap word
SetPort	A873	SubPt	A87F
SetPt	A880	SysBeep	A9C8
SetPtrSize	A020	SysEdit	A9C2
SetRecRgn	A8DE	SystemEdit	
SetRectRgn		SysError	A9C9
SetRect	A8A7	SystemClick	A9B3
SetResAttrs	A9A7	SystemEvent	A9B2
SetResFileAttrs	A9F7	SystemMenu	A9B5
SetResInfo	A9A9	SystemTask	A9B4
SetResLoad	A99B	TEActivate	A9D8
SetResPurge	A993	TECalText	A9D0
SetStdProcs	A8EA	TEClick	A9D4
SetString	A907	TECopy	A9D5
SetTrapAddress	A047	TECut	A9D6
SetVol	A015	TEDeactivate	A9D9
PBSetVol		TEDelete	A9D7
SetWindowPic	A92E	TEDispose	A9CD
SetWRefCon	A918	TEGetText	A9CB
SetWTitle	A91A	TEIdle	A9DA
SetZone	A01B	TEInit	A9CC
ShieldCursor	A855	TEInsert	A9DE
ShowControl	A957	TEKey	A9DC
ShowCursor	A853	TENew	A9D2
ShowHide	A908	TEPaste	A9DB
ShowPen	A897	TEScroll	A9DD
ShowWindow	A915	TESetJust	A9DF
SizeControl	A95C	TESetSelect	A9D1
SizeRsrc	A9A5	TESetText	A9CF
SizeResource		TestControl	A966
SizeWindow	A91D	TEUpdate	A9D3
SlopeFromAngle	A8BC	TextBox	A9CE
SpaceExtra	A88E	TextFace	A888
Status	A005	TextFont	A887
PBStatus		TextMode	A889
StdArc	A8BD	TextSize	A88A
StdBits	A8EB	TextWidth	A886
StdComment	A8F1	TickCount	A975
StdGetPic	A8EE	TrackControl	A968
StdLine	A890	TrackGoAway	A91E
StdOval	A8B6	UnionRect	A8AB
StdPoly	A8C5	UnionRgn	A8E5
StdPutPic	A8F0	UniqueID	A9C1
StdRect	A8A0	UnloadSeg	A9F1
StdRgn	A8D1	UnlodeScrap	A9FA
StdRRect	A8AF	UnloadScrap	
StdText	A882	UnmountVol	A00E
StdTxMeas	A8ED	PBUnmountVol	
StillDown	A973	UnpackBits	A8D0
StopAlert	A986	UpdateResFile	A999
StringWidth	A88C	UprString	A054
StuffHex	A866	UseResFile	A998

Name	Trap word	Name	Trap word
ValidRect	A92A	Write	A003
ValidRgn	A929	PBWrite	
VInstall	A033	WriteParam	A038
VRemove	A034	WriteResource	A9B0
WaitMouseUp	A977	XorRgn	A8E7
		ZeroScrap	A9FC

Trap word	Name	Trap word	Name
A000	Open	A014	GetVol
	PBOpen		PBGetVol
A001	Close	A015	SetVol
	PBClose		PBSetVol
A002	Read	A016	InitQueue
	PBRead	A017	Eject
A003	Write		PBEject
	PBWrite	A018	GetFPos
A004	Control		PBGetFPos
	PBControl	A019	InitZone
A005	Status	A11A	GetZone
	PBStatus	A01B	SetZone
A006	KillIO	A01C	FreeMem
	PBKillIO	A11D	MaxMem
A007	GetVolInfo	A11E	NewPtr
	PBGetVInfo	A01F	DisposPtr
A008	Create	A020	SetPtrSize
	PBCreate	A021	GetPtrSize
A009	Delete	A122	NewHandle
	PBDelete	A023	DisposHandle
A00A	OpenRF	A024	SetHandleSize
	PBOpenRF	A025	GetHandleSize
A00B	Rename	A126	HandleZone
	PBRename	A027	ReallocHandle
A00C	GetFileInfo	A128	RecoverHandle
	PBGetInfo	A029	HLock
A00D	SetFileInfo	A02A	HUnlock
	PBSetFInfo	A02B	EmptyHandle
A00E	UnmountVol	A02C	InitApplZone
	PBUnmountVol	A02D	SetApplLimit
A00F	MountVol	A02E	BlockMove
	PBMountVol	A02F	PostEvent
A010	Allocate	A030	OSEventAvail
	PBAllocate	A031	GetOSEvent
A011	GetEOF	A032	FlushEvents
	PBGetEOF	A033	VInstall
A012	SetEOF	A034	VRemove
	PBSetEOF	A035	Offline
A013	FlushVol		PBOffline
	PBFlushVol	A036	MoreMasters

Appendices

Trap word	Name	Trap word	Name
A038	WriteParam	A861	Random
A039	ReadDateTime	A862	ForeColor
A03A	SetDateTime	A863	BackColor
A03B	Delay	A864	ColorBit
A03C	CmpString	A865	GetPixel
	EqualString	A866	StuffHex
A03D	DrvrInstall	A867	LongMul
	(internal use only)	A868	FixMul
A03E	DrvrRemove	A869	FixRatio
	(internal use only)	A86A	HiWord
A03F	InitUtil	A86B	LoWord
A040	ResrvMem	A86C	FixRound
A041	SetFilLock	A86D	InitPort
	PBSetFLock	A86E	InitGraf
A042	RstFilLock	A86F	OpenPort
	PBRstFLock	A870	LocalToGlobal
A043	SetFilType	A871	GlobalToLocal
	PBSetFVers	A872	GrafDevice
A044	SetFPos	A873	SetPort
	PBSetFPos	A874	GetPort
A045	FlushFile	A875	SetPBits
	PBFlushFile		SetPortBits
A146	GetTrapAddress	A876	PortSize
A047	SetTrapAddress	A877	MovePortTo
A148	PtrZone	A878	SetOrigin
A049	HPurge	A879	SetClip
A04A	HNoPurge	A87A	GetClip
A04B	SetGrowZone	A87B	ClipRect
A04C	CompactMem	A87C	BackPat
A04D	PurgeMem	A87D	ClosePort
A04E	AddDrive	A87E	AddPt
	(internal use only)	A87F	SubPt
A04F	RDrvrInstall	A880	SetPt
	(internal use only)	A881	EqualPt
A850	InitCursor	A882	StdText
A851	SetCursor	A883	DrawChar
A852	HideCursor	A884	DrawString
A853	ShowCursor	A885	DrawText
A054	UprString	A886	TextWidth
A855	ShieldCursor	A887	TextFont
A856	ObscureCursor	A888	TextFace
A057	SetAppBase	A889	TextMode
	SetApplBase	A88A	TextSize
A858	BitAnd	A88B	GetFontInfo
A859	BitXor	A88C	StringWidth
A85A	BitNot	A88D	CharWidth
A85B	BitOr	A88E	SpaceExtra
A85C	BitShift	A890	StdLine
A85D	BitTst	A891	LineTo
A85E	BitSet	A892	Line
A85F	BitClr	A893	MoveTo

Trap word	Name	Trap word	Name
A894	Move	A8C8	ErasePoly
A896	HidePen	A8C9	InvertPoly
A897	ShowPen	A8CA	FillPoly
A898	GetPenState	A8CB	OpenPoly
A899	SetPenState	A8CC	ClosePgon
A89A	GetPen		ClosePoly
A89B	PenSize	A8CD	KillPoly
A89C	PenMode	A8CE	OffsetPoly
A89D	PenPat	A8CF	PackBits
A89E	PenNormal	A8D0	UnpackBits
A8A0	StdRect	A8D1	StdRgn
A8A1	FrameRect	A8D2	FrameRgn
A8A2	PaintRect	A8D3	PaintRgn
A8A3	EraseRect	A8D4	EraseRgn
A8A4	InverRect	A8D5	InverRgn
	InvertRect		InvertRgn
A8A5	FillRect	A8D6	FillRgn
A8A6	EqualRect	A8D8	NewRgn
A8A7	SetRect	A8D9	DisposRgn
A8A8	OffsetRect		DisposeRgn
A8A9	InsetRect	A8DA	OpenRgn
A8AA	SectRect	A8DB	CloseRgn
A8AB	UnionRect	A8DC	CopyRgn
A8AC	Pt2Rect	A8DD	SetEmptyRgn
A8AD	PtInRect	A8DE	SetRecRgn
A8AE	EmptyRect	A8DF	SetRectRgn
A8AF	StdRRect		RectRgn
A8B0	FrameRoundRect	A8E0	OfsetRgn
A8B1	PaintRoundRect		OffsetRgn
A8B2	EraseRoundRect	A8E1	InsetRgn
A8B3	InverRoundRect	A8E2	EmptyRgn
	InvertRoundRect	A8E3	EqualRgn
A8B4	FillRoundRect	A8E4	SectRgn
A8B6	StdOval	A8E5	UnionRgn
A8B7	FrameOval	A8E6	DiffRgn
A8B8	PaintOval	A8E7	XorRgn
A8B9	EraseOval	A8E8	PtInRgn
A8BA	InvertOval	A8E9	RectInRgn
A8BB	FillOval	A8EA	SetStdProcs
A8BC	SlopeFromAngle	A8EB	StdBits
A8BD	StdArc	A8EC	CopyBits
A8BE	FrameArc	A8ED	StdTxMeas
A8BF	PaintArc	A8EE	StdGetPic
A8C0	EraseArc	A8EF	ScrollRect
A8C1	InvertArc	A8F0	StdPutPic
A8C2	FillArc	A8F1	StdComment
A8C3	PtToAngle	A8F2	PicComment
A8C4	AngleFromSlope	A8F3	OpenPicture
A8C5	StdPoly	A8F4	ClosePicture
A8C6	FramePoly	A8F5	KillPicture
A8C7	PaintPoly	A8F6	DrawPicture

Appendices

Trap word	Name	Trap word	Name
A8F8	ScalePt	A929	ValidRgn
A8F9	MapPt	A92A	ValidRect
A8FA	MapRect	A92B	GrowWindow
A8FB	MapRgn	A92C	FindWindow
A8FC	MapPoly	A92D	CloseWindow
A8FE	InitFonts	A92E	SetWindowPic
A8FF	GetFName	A92F	GetWindowPic
	GetFontName	A930	InitMenus
A900	GetFNum	A931	NewMenu
A901	FMSwapFont	A932	DisposMenu
A902	RealFont		DisposeMenu
A903	SetFontLock	A933	AppendMenu
A904	DrawGrowIcon	A934	ClearMenuBar
A905	DragGrayRgn	A935	InsertMenu
A906	NewString	A936	DeleteMenu
A907	SetString	A937	DrawMenuBar
A908	ShowHide	A938	HiliteMenu
A909	CalcVis	A939	EnableItem
A90A	CalcVBehind	A93A	DisableItem
	CalcVisBehind	A93B	GetMenuBar
A90B	ClipAbove	A93C	SetMenuBar
A90C	PaintOne	A93D	MenuSelect
A90D	PaintBehind	A93E	MenuKey
A90E	SaveOld	A93F	GetItmIcon
A90F	DrawNew		GetItemIcon
A910	GetWMgrPort	A940	SetItmIcon
A911	CheckUpdate		SetItemIcon
A912	InitWindows	A941	GetItmStyle
A913	NewWindow		GetItemStyle
A914	DisposWindow	A942	SetItmStyle
	DisposeWindow		SetItemStyle
A915	ShowWindow	A943	GetItmMark
A916	HideWindow		GetItemMark
A917	GetWRefCon	A944	SetItmMark
A918	SetWRefCon		SetItemMark
A919	GetWTitle	A945	CheckItem
A91A	SetWTitle	A946	GetItem
A91B	MoveWindow	A947	SetItem
A91C	HiliteWindow	A948	CalcMenuSize
A91D	SizeWindow	A949	GetMHandle
A91E	TrackGoAway	A94A	SetMFlash
A91F	SelectWindow		SetMenuFlash
A920	BringToFront	A94B	PlotIcon
A921	SendBehind	A94C	FlashMenuBar
A922	BeginUpdate	A94D	AddResMenu
A923	EndUpdate	A94E	PinRect
A924	FrontWindow	A94F	DeltaPoint
A925	DragWindow	A950	CountMItems
A926	DragTheRgn	A951	InsertResMenu
A927	InvalRgn	A954	NewControl
A928	InvalRect		

Appendices

Trap word	Name	Trap word	Name
A955	DisposControl	A986	StopAlert
	DisposeControl	A987	NoteAlert
A956	KillControls	A988	CautionAlert
A957	ShowControl	A989	CouldAlert
A958	HideControl	A98A	FreeAlert
A959	MoveControl	A98B	ParamText
A95A	GetCRefCon	A98C	ErrorSound
A95B	SetCRefCon	A98D	GetDItem
A95C	SizeControl	A98E	SetDItem
A95D	HiliteControl	A98F	SetIText
A95E	GetCTitle	A990	GetIText
A95F	SetCTitle	A991	ModalDialog
A960	GetCtlValue	A992	DetachResource
A961	GetMinCtl	A993	SetResPurge
	GetCtlMin	A994	CurResFile
A962	GetMaxCtl	A995	InitResources
	GetCtlMax	A996	RsrcZoneInit
A963	SetCtlValue	A997	OpenResFile
A964	SetMinCtl	A998	UseResFile
	SetCtlMin	A999	UpdateResFile
A965	SetMaxCtl	A99A	CloseResFile
	SetCtlMax	A99B	SetResLoad
A966	TestControl	A99C	CountResources
A967	DragControl	A99D	GetIndResource
A968	TrackControl	A99E	CountTypes
A969	DrawControls	A99F	GetIndType
A96A	GetCtlAction	A9A0	GetResource
A96B	SetCtlAction	A9A1	GetNamedResource
A96C	FindControl	A9A2	LoadResource
A96E	Dequeue	A9A3	ReleaseResource
A96F	Enqueue	A9A4	HomeResFile
A970	GetNextEvent	A9A5	SizeRsrc
A971	EventAvail		SizeResource
A972	GetMouse	A9A6	GetResAttrs
A973	StillDown	A9A7	SetResAttrs
A974	Button	A9A8	GetResInfo
A975	TickCount	A9A9	SetResInfo
A976	GetKeys	A9AA	ChangedResource
A977	WaitMouseUp	A9AB	AddResource
A979	CouldDialog	A9AD	RmveResource
A97A	FreeDialog	A9AF	ResError
A97B	InitDialogs	A9B0	WriteResource
A97C	GetNewDialog	A9B1	CreateResFile
A97D	NewDialog	A9B2	SystemEvent
A97E	SelIText	A9B3	SystemClick
A97F	IsDialogEvent	A9B4	SystemTask
A980	DialogSelect	A9B5	SystemMenu
A981	DrawDialog	A9B6	OpenDeskAcc
A982	CloseDialog	A9B7	CloseDeskAcc
A983	DisposDialog	A9B8	GetPattern
A985	Alert	A9B9	GetCursor

Trap word	Name	Trap word	Name
A9BA	GetString	A9E9	Pack2
A9BB	GetIcon		DIBadMount (0)
A9BC	GetPicture		DILoad (2)
A9BD	GetNewWindow		DIUnload (4)
A9BE	GetNewControl		DIFormat (6)
A9BF	GetRMenu		DIVerify (8)
	GetMenu		DIZero (10)
A9C0	GetNewMBar	A9EA	Pack3
A9C1	UniqueID		SFPutFile (1)
A9C2	SysEdit		SFGetFile (2)
	SystemEdit		SFPPutFile (3)
A9C6	Secs2Date		SFPGetFile (4)
A9C7	Date2Secs	A9EB	Pack4
A9C8	SysBeep		(synonym: FP68K)
A9C9	SysError	A9EC	Pack5
A9CB	TEGetText		(synonym: Elems68K)
A9CC	TEInit	A9ED	Pack6
A9CD	TEDispose		IUDateString (0)
A9CE	TextBox		IUTimeString (2)
A9CF	TESetText		IUMetric (4)
A9D0	TECalText		IUDGetIntl (6)
A9D1	TESetSelect		IUSetIntl (8)
A9D2	TENew		IUMagString (10)
A9D3	TEUpdate		IUMagIDString (12)
A9D4	TEClick		IUDatePString (14)
A9D5	TECopy		IUTimePString (16)
A9D6	TECut	A9EE	Pack7
A9D7	TEDelete		NumToString (0)
A9D8	TEActivate		StringToNum (1)
A9D9	TEDeactivate	A9EF	PtrAndHand
A9DA	TEIdle	A9F0	LoadSeg
A9DB	TEPaste	A9F1	UnloadSeg
A9DC	TEKey	A9F2	Launch
A9DD	TEScroll	A9F3	Chain
A9DE	TEInsert	A9F4	ExitToShell
A9DF	TESetJust	A9F5	GetAppParms
A9E0	Munger	A9F6	GetResFileAttrs
A9E1	HandToHand	A9F7	SetResFileAttrs
A9E2	PtrToXHand	A9F9	InfoScrap
A9E3	PtrToHand	A9FA	UnlodeScrap
A9E4	HandAndHand		UnloadScrap
A9E5	InitPack	A9FB	LodeScrap
A9E6	InitAllPacks		LoadScrap
A9E7	Pack0	A9FC	ZeroScrap
	(reserved for future use)	A9FD	GetScrap
A9E8	Pack1	A9FE	PutScrap
	(reserved for future use)		

APPENDIX D: GLOBAL VARIABLES

This appendix gives an alphabetical list of all system global variables described in *Inside Macintosh*, along with their locations in memory.

Name	Location	Contents
ABusVars	$2D8	Pointer to AppleTalk variables
ACount	$A9A	Stage number (0 through 3) of last alert (word)
ANumber	$A98	Resource ID of last alert (word)
ApFontID	$984	Font number of application font (word)
ApplLimit	$130	Application heap limit
ApplScratch	$A78	12-byte scratch area reserved for use by applications
ApplZone	$2AA	Address of application heap zone
AppParmHandle	$AEC	Handle to Finder information
BufPtr	$10C	Address of end of jump table
BufTgDate	$304	File tags buffer: date and time of last modification (long)
BufTgFBkNum	$302	File tags buffer: logical block number (word)
BufTgFFlg	$300	File tags buffer: flags (word: bit 1=1 if resource fork)
BufTgFNum	$2FC	File tags buffer: file number (long)
CaretTime	$2F4	Caret-blink interval in ticks (long)
CrsrThresh	$8EC	Mouse-scaling threshold (word)
CurActivate	$A64	Pointer to window to receive activate event
CurApName	$910	Name of current application (length byte followed by up to 31 characters)
CurApRefNum	$900	Reference number of current application's resource file (word)
CurDeactive	$A68	Pointer to window to receive deactivate event
CurJTOffset	$934	Offset to jump table from location pointed to by A5 (word)
CurMap	$A5A	Reference number of current resource file (word)
CurPageOption	$936	Sound/screen buffer configuration passed to Chain or Launch (word)
CurPitch	$280	Value of count in square-wave synthesizer buffer (word)
CurrentA5	$904	Address of boundary between application globals and application parameters
CurStackBase	$908	Address of base of stack; start of application globals
DABeeper	$A9C	Address of current sound procedure
DAStrings	$AA0	Handles to ParamText strings (16 bytes)

Name	Location	Contents
DefltStack	$322	Default space allotment for stack (long)
DefVCBPtr	$352	Pointer to default volume control block
DeskHook	$A6C	Address of procedure for painting desktop or responding to clicks on desktop
DeskPattern	$A3C	Pattern with which desktop is painted (8 bytes)
DlgFont	$AFA	Font number for dialogs and alerts (word)
DoubleTime	$2F0	Double-click interval in ticks (long)
DragHook	$9F6	Address of procedure to execute during TrackGoAway, DragWindow, GrowWindow, DragGrayRgn, TrackControl, and DragControl
DragPattern	$A34	Pattern of dragged region's outline (8 bytes)
DrvQHdr	$308	Drive queue header (10 bytes)
DSAlertRect	$3F8	Rectangle enclosing system error alert (8 bytes)
DSAlertTab	$2BA	Pointer to system error alert table in use
DSErrCode	$AF0	Current system error ID (word)
EventQueue	$14A	Event queue header (10 bytes)
ExtStsDT	$2BE	External/status interrupt vector table (16 bytes)
FCBSPtr	$34E	Pointer to file-control-block buffer
FinderName	$2E0	Name of the Finder (length byte followed by up to 15 characters)
FScaleDisable	$A63	Nonzero to disable font scaling (byte)
FSQHdr	$360	File I/O queue header (10 bytes)
GhostWindow	$A84	Pointer to window never to be considered frontmost
GrayRgn	$9EE	Handle to region drawn as desktop
GZRootHnd	$328	Handle to relocatable block not to be moved by grow zone function
HeapEnd	$114	Address of end of application heap zone
JFetch	$8F4	Jump vector for Fetch function
JIODone	$8FC	Jump vector for IODone function
JournalFlag	$8DE	Journaling mode (word)
JournalRef	$8E8	Reference number of journaling device driver (word)
JStash	$8F8	Jump vector for Stash function
KeyRepThresh	$190	Auto-key rate (word)
KeyThresh	$18E	Auto-key threshold (word)
Lo3Bytes	$31A	$00FFFFFF
Lvl1DT	$192	Level-1 secondary interrupt vector table (32 bytes)

Name	Location	Contents
Lvl2DT	$1B2	Level-2 secondary interrupt vector table (32 bytes)
MBarEnable	$A20	Unique menu ID for active desk accessory, when menu bar belongs to the accessory (word)
MBarHook	$A2C	Address of routine called by MenuSelect before menu is drawn
MemTop	$108	Address of end of RAM (on Macintosh XL, end of RAM available to applications)
MenuFlash	$A24	Count for duration of menu item blinking (word)
MenuHook	$A30	Address of routine called during MenuSelect
MenuList	$A1C	Handle to current menu list
MinStack	$31E	Minimum space allotment for stack (long)
MinusOne	$A06	$FFFFFFFF
OldContent	$9EA	Handle to saved content region
OldStructure	$9E6	Handle to saved structure region
OneOne	$A02	$00010001
PaintWhite	$9DC	Flag for whether to paint window white before update event (word)
PortBUse	$291	Current availability of serial port B (byte)
PrintErr	$944	Result code from last Printing Manager routine (word)
RAMBase	$2B2	Trap dispatch table's base address for routines in RAM
ResErr	$A60	Current value of ResError (word)
ResErrProc	$AF2	Address of resource error procedure
ResLoad	$A5E	Current SetResLoad state (word)
ResumeProc	$A8C	Address of resume procedure
RndSeed	$156	Random number seed (long)
ROMBase	$2AE	Base address of ROM
ROMFont0	$980	Handle to font record for system font
SaveUpdate	$9DA	Flag for whether to generate update events (word)
SaveVisRgn	$9F2	Handle to saved visRgn
SCCRd	$1D8	SCC read base address
SCCWr	$1DC	SCC write base address
ScrapCount	$968	Count changed by ZeroScrap (word)
ScrapHandle	$964	Handle to desk scrap in memory
ScrapName	$96C	Pointer to scrap file name (preceded by length byte)
ScrapSize	$960	Size in bytes of desk scrap (long)
ScrapState	$96A	Tells where desk scrap is (word)

Appendices

Name	Location	Contents
Scratch8	$9FA	8-byte scratch area
Scratch20	$1E4	20-byte scratch area
ScrDmpEnb	$2F8	0 if GetNextEvent shouldn't process Command-Shift-number combinations (byte)
ScrHRes	$104	Pixels per inch horizontally (word)
ScrnBase	$824	Address of main screen buffer
ScrVRes	$102	Pixels per inch vertically (word)
SdVolume	$260	Current speaker volume (byte: low-order three bits only)
SEvtEnb	$15C	0 if SystemEvent should return FALSE (byte)
SFSaveDisk	$214	Negative of volume reference number used by Standard File Package (word)
SoundBase	$266	Pointer to free-form synthesizer buffer
SoundLevel	$27F	Amplitude in 740-byte buffer (byte)
SoundPtr	$262	Pointer to four-tone record
SPAlarm	$200	Alarm setting (long)
SPATalkA	$1F9	AppleTalk node ID hint for modem port (byte)
SPATalkB	$1FA	AppleTalk node ID hint for printer port (byte)
SPClikCaret	$209	Double-click and caret-blink times (byte)
SPConfig	$1FB	Use types for serial ports (byte)
SPFont	$204	Application font number minus 1 (word)
SPKbd	$206	Auto-key threshold and rate (byte)
SPMisc2	$20B	Mouse scaling, system startup disk, menu blink (byte)
SPPortA	$1FC	Modem port configuration (word)
SPPortB	$1FE	Printer port configuration (word)
SPPrint	$207	Printer connection (byte)
SPValid	$1F8	Validity status (byte)
SPVolCtl	$208	Speaker volume setting in parameter RAM (byte)
SysEvtMask	$144	System event mask (word)
SysMap	$A58	Reference number of system resource file (word)
SysMapHndl	$A54	Handle to map of system resource file
SysParam	$1F8	Low-memory copy of parameter RAM (20 bytes)
SysResName	$AD8	Name of system resource file (length byte followed by up to 19 characters)
SysZone	$2A6	Address of system heap zone
TEDoText	$A70	Address of TextEdit multi-purpose routine

Name	Location	Contents
TERecal	$A74	Address of routine to recalculate line starts for TextEdit
TEScrpHandle	$AB4	Handle to TextEdit scrap
TEScrpLength	$AB0	Size in bytes of TextEdit scrap (long)
TheMenu	$A26	Menu ID of currently highlighted menu (word)
TheZone	$118	Address of current heap zone
Ticks	$16A	Current number of ticks since system startup (long)
Time	$20C	Seconds since midnight, January 1, 1904 (long)
ToExtFS	$3F2	Pointer to external file system
ToolScratch	$9CE	8-byte scratch area
TopMapHndl	$A50	Handle to resource map of most recently opened resource file
UTableBase	$11C	Base address of unit table
VBLQueue	$160	Vertical retrace queue header (10 bytes)
VCBQHdr	$356	Volume-control-block queue header (10 bytes)
VIA	$1DA	VIA base address
WindowList	$9D6	Pointer to first window in window list; 0 if using events but not windows
WMgrPort	$9DE	Pointer to Window Manager port

GLOSSARY

access path: A description of the route that the File Manager follows to access a file; created when a file is opened.

access path buffer: Memory used by the File Manager to transfer data between an application and a file.

action procedure: A procedure, used by the Control Manager function TrackControl, that defines an action to be performed repeatedly for as long as the mouse button is held down.

activate event: An event generated by the Window Manager when a window changes from active to inactive or vice versa.

active control: A control that will respond to the user's actions with the mouse.

active window: The frontmost window on the desktop.

address mark: In a sector, information that's used internally by the Disk Driver, including information it uses to determine the position of the sector on the disk.

ALAP: See AppleTalk Link Access Protocol.

ALAP frame: A packet of data transmitted and received by ALAP.

ALAP protocol type: An identifier used to match particular kinds of packets with a particular protocol handler.

alert: A warning or report of an error, in the form of an alert box, sound from the Macintosh's speaker, or both.

alert box: A box that appears on the screen to give a warning or report an error during a Macintosh application.

alert template: A resource that contains information from which the Dialog Manager can create an alert.

alert window: The window in which an alert box is displayed.

alias: A different name for the same entity.

allocate: To reserve an area of memory for use.

allocation block: Volume space composed of an integral number of logical blocks.

amplitude: The maximum vertical distance of a periodic wave from the horizontal line about which the wave oscillates.

AppleTalk address: A socket's number and its node ID number.

AppleTalk Link Access Protocol (ALAP): The lowest-level protocol in the AppleTalk architecture, managing node-to-node delivery of frames on a single AppleTalk network.

AppleTalk Manager: An interface to a pair of RAM device drivers that enable programs to send and receive information via an AppleTalk network.

AppleTalk Transaction Protocol (ATP): An AppleTalk protocol that's a DDP client. It allows one ATP client to request another ATP client to perform some activity and report the activity's result as a response to the requesting socket with guaranteed delivery.

application font: The font your application will use unless you specify otherwise—Geneva, by default.

application heap: The portion of the heap available to the running application program and the Toolbox.

application heap limit: The boundary between the space available for the application heap and the space available for the stack.

application heap zone: The heap zone initially provided by the Memory Manager for use by the application program and the Toolbox; initially equivalent to the application heap, but may be subdivided into two or more independent heap zones.

application parameters: Thirty-two bytes of memory, located above the application globals, reserved for system use. The first application parameter is the address of the first QuickDraw global variable.

application space: Memory that's available for dynamic allocation by applications.

application window: A window created as the result of something done by the application, either directly or indirectly (as through the Dialog Manager).

ascent: The vertical distance from a font's base line to its ascent line.

ascent line: A horizontal line that coincides with the tops of the tallest characters in a font.

asynchronous communication: A method of data transmission where the receiving and sending devices don't share a common timer, and no timing data is transmitted.

asynchronous execution: After calling a routine asynchronously, an application is free to perform other tasks until the routine is completed.

at-least-once transaction: An ATP transaction in which the requested operation is performed at least once, and possibly several times.

ATP: See AppleTalk Transaction Protocol.

auto-key event: An event generated repeatedly when the user presses and holds down a character key on the keyboard or keypad.

auto-key rate: The rate at which a character key repeats after it's begun to do so.

auto-key threshold: The length of time a character key must be held down before it begins to repeat.

background procedure: A procedure passed to the Printing Manager to be run during idle times in the printing process.

base line: A horizontal line that coincides with the bottom of each character in a font, excluding descenders (such as the tail of a "p").

baud rate: The measure of the total number of bits sent over a transmission line per second.

Binary-Decimal Conversion Package: A Macintosh package for converting integers to decimal strings and vice versa.

bit image: A collection of bits in memory that have a rectilinear representation. The screen is a visible bit image.

bit map: A set of bits that represent the position and state of a corresponding set of items; in QuickDraw, a pointer to a bit image, the row width of that image, and its boundary rectangle.

block: A group regarded as a unit; usually refers to data or memory in which data is stored. See **allocation block** and **memory block**.

block contents: The area that's available for use in a memory block.

block device: A device that reads and writes blocks of bytes at a time. It can read or write any accessible block on demand.

block header: The internal "housekeeping" information maintained by the Memory Manager at the beginning of each block in a heap zone.

block map: Same as **volume allocation block map**.

boundary rectangle: A rectangle, defined as part of a QuickDraw bit map, that encloses the active area of the bit image and imposes a coordinate system on it. Its top left corner is always aligned around the first bit in the bit image.

break: The condition resulting when a device maintains its transmission line in the space state for at least one frame.

bridge: An intelligent link between two or more AppleTalk networks.

broadcast service: An ALAP service in which a frame is sent to all nodes on an AppleTalk network.

bundle: A resource that maps local IDs of resources to their actual resource IDs; used to provide mappings for file references and icon lists needed by the Finder.

button: A standard Macintosh control that causes some immediate or continuous action when clicked or pressed with the mouse. See also **radio button**.

caret: A generic term meaning a symbol that indicates where something should be inserted in text. The specific symbol used is a vertical bar (|).

caret-blink time: The interval between blinks of the caret that marks an insertion point.

character code: An integer representing the character that a key or combination of keys on the keyboard or keypad stands for.

character device: A device that reads or writes a stream of characters, one at a time. It can neither skip characters nor go back to a previous character.

character image: An arrangement of bits that defines a character in a font.

character key: A key that generates a keyboard event when pressed; any key except Shift, Caps Lock, Command, or Option.

character offset: The horizontal separation between a character rectangle and a font rectangle.

character origin: The point on a base line used as a reference location for drawing a character.

character position: An index into an array containing text, starting at 0 for the first character.

character rectangle: A rectangle enclosing an entire character image. Its sides are defined by the image width and the font height.

character style: A set of stylistic variations, such as bold, italic, and underline. The empty set indicates plain text (no stylistic variations).

character width: The distance to move the pen from one character's origin to the next character's origin.

check box: A standard Macintosh control that displays a setting, either checked (on) or unchecked (off). Clicking inside a check box reverses its setting.

clipping: Limiting drawing to within the bounds of a particular area.

clipping region: Same as clipRgn.

clipRgn: The region to which an application limits drawing in a grafPort.

clock chip: A special chip in which are stored parameter RAM and the current setting for the date and time. This chip is powered by a battery when the system is off, thus preserving the information.

close routine: The part of a device driver's code that implements Device Manager Close calls.

closed driver: A device driver that cannot be read from or written to.

closed file: A file without an access path. Closed files cannot be read from or written to.

compaction: The process of moving allocated blocks within a heap zone in order to collect the free space into a single block.

completion routine: Any application-defined code to be executed when an asynchronous call to a routine is completed.

content region: The area of a window that the application draws in.

control: An object in a window on the Macintosh screen with which the user, using the mouse, can cause instant action with visible results or change settings to modify a future action.

control definition function: A function called by the Control Manager when it needs to perform type-dependent operations on a particular type of control, such as drawing the control.

control definition ID: A number passed to control-creation routines to indicate the type of control. It consists of the control definition function's resource ID and a variation code.

control information: Information transmitted by an application to a device driver. It may select modes of operation, start or stop processes, enable buffers, choose protocols, and so on.

control list: A list of all the controls associated with a given window.

Control Manager: The part of the Toolbox that provides routines for creating and manipulating controls (such as buttons, check boxes, and scroll bars).

control record: The internal representation of a control, where the Control Manager stores all the information it needs for its operations on that control.

control routine: The part of a device driver's code that implements Device Manager Control and KillIO calls.

control template: A resource that contains information from which the Control Manager can create a control.

coordinate plane: A two-dimensional grid. In QuickDraw, the grid coordinates are integers ranging from –32767 to 32767, and all grid lines are infinitely thin.

current heap zone: The heap zone currently under attention, to which most Memory Manager operations implicitly apply.

current resource file: The last resource file opened, unless you specify otherwise with a Resource Manager routine.

cursor: A 16-by-16 bit image that appears on the screen and is controlled by the mouse; called the "pointer" in Macintosh user manuals.

cursor level: A value, initialized by InitCursor, that keeps track of the number of times the cursor has been hidden.

data bits: Data communications bits that encode transmitted characters.

data buffer: Heap space containing information to be written to a file or device driver from an application, or read from a file or device driver to an application.

data fork: The part of a file that contains data accessed via the File Manager.

data mark: In a sector, information that primarily contains data from an application.

datagram: A packet of data transmitted by DDP.

Datagram Delivery Protocol (DDP): An AppleTalk protocol that's an ALAP client, managing socket-to-socket delivery of datagrams over AppleTalk internets.

date/time record: An alternate representation of the date and time (which is stored on the clock chip in seconds since midnight, January 1, 1904).

DDP: See **Datagram Delivery Protocol**.

default button: In an alert box or modal dialog, the button whose effect will occur if the user presses Return or Enter. In an alert box, it's boldly outlined; in a modal dialog, it's boldly outlined or the OK button.

default volume: A volume that will receive I/O during a File Manager routine call, whenever no other volume is specified.

dereference: To refer to a block by its master pointer instead of its handle.

descent: The vertical distance from a font's base line to its descent line.

descent line: A horizontal line that coincides with the bottoms of the characters in a font that extend furthest below the base line.

desk accessory: A "mini-application", implemented as a device driver, that can be run at the same time as a Macintosh application.

Desk Manager: The part of the Toolbox that supports the use of desk accessories from an application.

desk scrap: The place where data is stored when it's cut (or copied) and pasted among applications and desk accessories.

desktop: The screen as a surface for doing work on the Macintosh.

Desktop file: A resource file in which the Finder stores the version data, bundle, icons, and file references for each application on the volume.

destination rectangle: In TextEdit, the rectangle in which the text is drawn.

device: A part of the Macintosh, or a piece of external equipment, that can transfer information into or out of the Macintosh.

device control entry: A 40-byte relocatable block of heap space that tells the Device Manager the location of a driver's routines, the location of a driver's I/O queue, and other information.

device driver: A program that controls the exchange of information between an application and a device.

device driver event: An event generated by one of the Macintosh's device drivers.

Device Manager: The part of the Operating System that supports device I/O.

dial: A control with a moving indicator that displays a quantitative setting or value. Depending on the type of dial, the user may be able to change the setting by dragging the indicator with the mouse.

dialog: Same as **dialog box**.

dialog box: A box that a Macintosh application displays to request information it needs to complete a command, or to report that it's waiting for a process to complete.

Dialog Manager: The part of the Toolbox that provides routines for implementing dialogs and alerts.

dialog record: The internal representation of a dialog, where the Dialog Manager stores all the information it needs for its operations on that dialog.

dialog template: A resource that contains information from which the Dialog Manager can create a dialog.

dialog window: The window in which a dialog box is displayed.

dimmed: Drawn in gray rather than black

disabled: A disabled menu item or menu is one that cannot be chosen; the menu item or menu title appears dimmed. A disabled item in a dialog or alert box has no effect when clicked.

Disk Driver: The device driver that controls data storage and retrieval on 3 1/2-inch disks.

Disk Initialization Package: A Macintosh package for initializing and naming new disks; called by the Standard File Package.

disk-inserted event: An event generated when the user inserts a disk in a disk drive or takes any other action that requires a volume to be mounted.

display rectangle: A rectangle that determines where an item is displayed within a dialog or alert box.

document window: The standard Macintosh window for presenting a document.

double-click time: The greatest interval between a mouse-up and mouse-down event that would qualify two mouse clicks as a double-click.

draft printing: Printing a document immediately as it's drawn in the printing grafPort.

drag region: A region in a window frame. Dragging inside this region moves the window to a new location and makes it the active window unless the Command key was down.

drive number: A number used to identify a disk drive. The internal drive is number 1, the external drive is number 2, and any additional drives will have larger numbers.

drive queue: A list of disk drives connected to the Macintosh.

driver name: A sequence of up to 255 printing characters used to refer to an open device driver. Driver names always begin with a period (.).

driver I/O queue: A queue containing the parameter blocks of all I/O requests for one device driver.

driver reference number: A number from −1 to −32 that uniquely identifies an individual device driver.

edit record: A complete editing environment in TextEdit, which includes the text to be edited, the grafPort and rectangle in which to display the text, the arrangement of the text within the rectangle, and other editing and display information.

empty handle: A handle that points to a NIL master pointer, signifying that the underlying relocatable block has been purged.

empty shape: A shape that contains no bits, such as one defined by only a single point.

end-of-file: See **logical end-of-file** or **physical end-of-file**.

entity name: An identifier for an entity, of the form object:type@zone.

event: A notification to an application of some occurrence that the application may want to respond to.

event code: An integer representing a particular type of event.

Event Manager: See **Toolbox Event Manager** or **Operating System Event Manager**.

event mask: A parameter passed to an Event Manager routine to specify which types of events the routine should apply to.

event message: A field of an event record containing information specific to the particular type of event.

event queue: The Operating System Event Manager's list of pending events.

event record: The internal representation of an event, through which your program learns all pertinent information about that event.

exactly-once transaction: An ATP transaction in which the requested operation is performed only once.

exception: An error or abnormal condition detected by the processor in the course of program execution; includes interrupts and traps.

exception vector: One of 64 vectors in low memory that point to the routines that are to get control in the event of an exception.

external reference: A reference to a routine or variable defined in a separate compilation or assembly.

file: A named, ordered sequence of bytes; a principal means by which data is stored and transmitted on the Macintosh.

file control block: A fixed-length data structure, contained in the file-control-block buffer, where information about an access path is stored.

file-control-block buffer: A nonrelocatable block in the system heap that contains one file control block for each access path.

file directory: The part of a volume that contains descriptions and locations of all the files on the volume.

file I/O queue: A queue containing parameter blocks for all I/O requests to the File Manager.

File Manager: The part of the Operating System that supports file I/O.

file name: A sequence of up to 255 printing characters, excluding colons (:), that identifies a file.

file number: A unique number assigned to a file, which the File Manager uses to distinguish it from other files on the volume. A file number specifies the file's entry in a file directory.

file reference: A resource that provides the Finder with file and icon information about an application.

file tags: Information associated with each logical block, designed to allow reconstruction of files on a volume whose directory or other file-access information has been destroyed.

file tags buffer: A location in memory where file tags are read from and written to.

file type: A four-character sequence, specified when a file is created, that identifies the type of file.

Finder information: Information that the Finder provides to an application upon starting it up, telling it which documents to open or print.

fixed-point number: A signed 32-bit quantity containing an integer part in the high-order word and a fractional part in the low-order word.

fixed-width font: A font whose characters all have the same width.

Floating-Point Arithmetic Package: A Macintosh package that supports extended-precision arithmetic according to IEEE Standard 754.

font: The complete set of characters of one typeface.

font characterization table: A table of parameters in a device driver that specifies how best to adapt fonts to that device.

font height: The vertical distance from a font's ascent line to its descent line.

Font Manager: The part of the Toolbox that supports the use of various character fonts for QuickDraw when it draws text.

font number: The number by which you identify a font to QuickDraw or the Font Manager.

font record: A data structure that contains all the information describing a font.

font rectangle: The smallest rectangle enclosing all the character images in a font, if the images were all superimposed over the same character origin.

font size: The size of a font in points; equivalent to the distance between the ascent line of one line of text and the ascent line of the next line of single-spaced text.

fork: One of the two parts of a file; see **data fork** and **resource fork**.

four-tone record: A data structure describing the tones produced by a four-tone synthesizer.

four-tone synthesizer: The part of the Sound Driver used to make simple harmonic tones, with up to four "voices" producing sound simultaneously.

frame: The time elapsed from the start bit to the last stop bit during serial communication.

frame check sequence: A 16-bit value generated by the AppleTalk hardware, used by the receiving node to detect transmission errors.

frame header: Information at the beginning of a packet.

frame pointer: A pointer to the end of the local variables within a routine's stack frame, held in an address register and manipulated with the LINK and UNLK instructions.

frame trailer: Information at the end of an ALAP frame.

framed shape: A shape that's drawn outlined and hollow.

framing error: The condition resulting when a device doesn't receive a stop bit when expected.

free block: A memory block containing space available for allocation.

free-form synthesizer: The part of the Sound Driver used to make complex music and speech.

frequency: The number of cycles per second (also called hertz) at which a wave oscillates.

full-duplex communication: A method of data transmission where two devices transmit data simultaneously.

global coordinate system: The coordinate system based on the top left corner of the bit image being at (0,0).

go-away region: A region in a window frame. Clicking inside this region of the active window makes the window close or disappear.

grafPort: A complete drawing environment, including such elements as a bit map, a subset of it in which to draw, a character font, patterns for drawing and erasing, and other pen characteristics.

grow image: The image pulled around when the user drags inside the grow region; whatever is appropriate to show that the window's size will change.

grow region: A window region, usually within the content region, where dragging changes the size of an active window.

grow zone function: A function supplied by the application program to help the Memory Manager create free space within a heap zone.

handle: A pointer to a master pointer, which designates a relocatable block in the heap by double indirection.

hardware overrun error: The condition that occurs when the SCC's buffer becomes full.

heap: The area of memory in which space is dynamically allocated and released on demand, using the Memory Manager.

heap zone: An area of memory initialized by the Memory Manager for heap allocation.

highlight: To display an object on the screen in a distinctive visual way, such as inverting it.

horizontal blanking interval: The time between the display of the rightmost pixel on one line and the leftmost pixel on the next line.

hotSpot: The point in a cursor that's aligned with the mouse location.

icon: A 32-by-32 bit image that graphically represents an object, concept, or message.

icon list: A resource consisting of a list of icons.

icon number: A digit from 1 to 255 to which the Menu Manager adds 256 to get the resource ID of an icon associated with a menu item.

image width: The width of a character image.

inactive control: A control that won't respond to the user's actions with the mouse. An inactive control is highlighted in some special way, such as dimmed.

inactive window: Any window that isn't the frontmost window on the desktop.

indicator: The moving part of a dial that displays its current setting.

input driver: A device driver that receives serial data via a serial port and transfers it to an application.

insertion point: An empty selection range; the character position where text will be inserted (usually marked with a blinking caret).

interface routine: A routine called from Pascal whose purpose is to trap to a certain Toolbox or Operating System routine.

International Utilities Package: A Macintosh package that gives you access to country-dependent information such as the formats for numbers, currency, dates, and times.

internet: An interconnected group of AppleTalk networks.

internet address: The AppleTalk address and network number of a socket.

interrupt: An exception that's signaled to the processor by a device, to notify the processor of a change in condition of the device, such as the completion of an I/O request.

interrupt handler: A routine that services interrupts.

interrupt priority level: A number identifying the importance of the interrupt. It indicates which device is interrupting, and which interrupt handler should be executed.

interrupt vector: A pointer to an interrupt handler.

invert: To highlight by changing white pixels to black and vice versa.

invisible control: A control that's not drawn in its window.

invisible window: A window that's not drawn in its plane on the desktop.

I/O queue: See **driver I/O queue** or **file I/O queue**.

I/O request: A request for input from or output to a file or device driver; caused by calling a File Manager or Device Manager routine asynchronously.

item: In dialog and alert boxes, a control, icon, picture, or piece of text, each displayed inside its own display rectangle. See also **menu item**.

item list: A list of information about all the items in a dialog or alert box.

item number: The index, starting from 1, of an item in an item list.

IWM: "Integrated Woz Machine"; the custom chip that controls the 3 1/2-inch disk drives.

job dialog: A dialog that sets information about one printing job; associated with the Print command.

journal code: A code passed by a Toolbox Event Manager routine in its Control call to the journaling device driver, to designate which routine is making the Control call.

journaling mechanism: A mechanism that allows you to feed the Toolbox Event Manager events from some source other than the user.

jump table: A table that contains one entry for every routine in an application and is the means by which the loading and unloading of segments is implemented.

justification: The horizontal placement of lines of text relative to the edges of the rectangle in which the text is drawn.

kern: To draw part of a character so that it overlaps an adjacent character.

key code: An integer representing a key on the keyboard or keypad, without reference to the character that the key stands for.

key-down event: An event generated when the user presses a character key on the keyboard or keypad.

key-up event: An event generated when the user releases a character key on the keyboard or keypad.

keyboard configuration: A resource that defines a particular keyboard layout by associating a character code with each key or combination of keys on the keyboard or keypad.

keyboard equivalent: The combination of the Command key and another key, used to invoke a menu item from the keyboard.

keyboard event: An event generated when the user presses, releases, or holds down a character key on the keyboard or keypad; any key-down, key-up, or auto-key event.

leading: The amount of blank vertical space between the descent line of one line of text and the ascent line of the next line of single-spaced text.

ligature: A character that combines two letters.

list separator: The character that separates numbers, as when a list of numbers is entered by the user.

local coordinate system: The coordinate system local to a grafPort, imposed by the boundary rectangle defined in its bit map.

local ID: A number that refers to an icon list or file reference in an application's resource file and is mapped to an actual resource ID by a bundle.

location table: An array of words (one for each character in a font) that specifies the location of each character's image in the font's bit image.

lock: To temporarily prevent a relocatable block from being moved during heap compaction.

lock bit: A bit in the master pointer to a relocatable block that indicates whether the block is currently locked.

locked file: A file whose data cannot be changed.

locked volume: A volume whose data cannot be changed. Volumes can be locked by either a software flag or a hardware setting.

logical block: Volume space composed of 512 consecutive bytes of standard information and an additional number of bytes of information specific to the Disk Driver.

logical end-of-file: The position of one byte past the last byte in a file; equal to the actual number of bytes in the file.

logical size: The number of bytes in a memory block's contents.

magnitude: The vertical distance between any given point on a wave and the horizontal line about which the wave oscillates.

main event loop: In a standard Macintosh application program, a loop that repeatedly calls the Toolbox Event Manager to get events and then responds to them as appropriate.

main segment: The segment containing the main program.

mark: The position of the next byte in a file that will be read or written.

mark state: The state of a transmission line indicating a binary 1.

master directory block: Part of the data structure of a volume; contains the volume information and the volume allocation block map.

master pointer: A single pointer to a relocatable block, maintained by the Memory Manager and updated whenever the block is moved, purged, or reallocated. All handles to a relocatable block refer to it by double indirection through the master pointer.

memory block: An area of contiguous memory within a heap zone.

Memory Manager: The part of the Operating System that dynamically allocates and releases memory space in the heap.

menu: A list of menu items that appears when the user points to a menu title in the menu bar and presses the mouse button. Dragging through the menu and releasing over an enabled menu item chooses that item.

menu bar: The horizontal strip at the top of the Macintosh screen that contains the menu titles of all menus in the menu list.

menu definition procedure: A procedure called by the Menu Manager when it needs to perform type-dependent operations on a particular type of menu, such as drawing the menu.

menu ID: A number in the menu record that identifies the menu.

menu item: A choice in a menu, usually a command to the current application.

menu item number: The index, starting from 1, of a menu item in a menu.

menu list: A list containing menu handles for all menus in the menu bar, along with information on the position of each menu.

Menu Manager: The part of the Toolbox that deals with setting up menus and letting the user choose from them.

menu record: The internal representation of a menu, where the Menu Manager stores all the information it needs for its operations on that menu.

menu title: A word or phrase in the menu bar that designates one menu.

missing symbol: A character to be drawn in case of a request to draw a character that's missing from a particular font.

modal dialog: A dialog that requires the user to respond before doing any other work on the desktop.

modeless dialog: A dialog that allows the user to work elsewhere on the desktop before responding.

modifier key: A key (Shift, Caps Lock, Option, or Command) that generates no keyboard events of its own, but changes the meaning of other keys or mouse actions.

mounted volume: A volume that previously was inserted into a disk drive and had descriptive information read from it by the File Manager.

mouse-down event: An event generated when the user presses the mouse button.

mouse scaling: A feature that causes the cursor to move twice as far during a mouse stroke than it would have otherwise, provided the change in the cursor's position exceeds the mouse-scaling threshold within one tick after the mouse is moved.

mouse-scaling threshold: A number of pixels which, if exceeded by the sum of the horizontal and vertical changes in the cursor position during one tick of mouse movement, causes mouse scaling to occur (if that feature is turned on); normally six pixels.

mouse-up event: An event generated when the user releases the mouse button.

Name-Binding Protocol (NBP): An AppleTalk protocol that's a DDP client, used to convert entity names to their internet socket addresses.

name lookup: An NBP operation that allows clients to obtain the internet addresses of entities from their names.

names directory: The union of all name tables in an internet.

names information socket: The socket in a node used to implement NBP (always socket number 2).

names table: A list of each entity's name and internet address in a node.

NBP: See **Name-Binding Protocol.**

NBP tuple: An entity name and an internet address.

network event: An event generated by the AppleTalk Manager.

network number: An identifier for an AppleTalk network.

network-visible entity: A named socket client on an internet.

newline character: Any character, but usually Return (ASCII code $0D), that indicates the end of a sequence of bytes.

newline mode: A mode of reading data where the end of the data is indicated by a newline character (and not by a specific byte count).

node: A device that's attached to and communicates via an AppleTalk network.

node ID: A number, dynamically assigned, that identifies a node.

nonbreaking space: The character with ASCII code $CA; drawn as a space the same width as a digit, but interpreted as a nonblank character for the purposes of word wraparound and selection.

nonrelocatable block: A block whose location in the heap is fixed and can't be moved during heap compaction.

null event: An event reported when there are no other events to report.

off-line volume: A mounted volume with all but 94 bytes of its descriptive information released.

offset/width table: An array of words that specifies the character offsets and character widths of all characters in a font.

on-line volume: A mounted volume with its volume buffer and descriptive information contained in memory.

open driver: A driver that can be read from and written to.

open file: A file with an access path. Open files can be read from and written to.

open permission: Information about a file that indicates whether the file can be read from, written to, or both.

open routine: The part of a device driver's code that implements Device Manager Open calls.

Operating System: The lowest-level software in the Macintosh. It does basic tasks such as I/O, memory management, and interrupt handling.

Operating System Event Manager: The part of the Operating System that reports hardware-related events such as mouse-button presses and keystrokes.

Operating System Utilities: Operating System routines that perform miscellaneous tasks such as getting the date and time, finding out the user's preferred speaker volume and other preferences, and doing simple string comparison.

output driver: A device driver that receives data via a serial port and transfers it to an application.

overrun error: See **hardware overrun error** and **software overrun error**.

package: A set of routines and data types that's stored as a resource and brought into memory only when needed.

Package Manager: The part of the Toolbox that lets you access Macintosh RAM-based packages.

page rectangle: The rectangle marking the boundaries of a printed page image. The boundary rectangle, portRect, and clipRgn of the printing grafPort are set to this rectangle.

palette: A collection of small symbols, usually enclosed in rectangles, that represent operations and can be selected by the user.

pane: An independently scrollable area of a window, for showing a different part of the same document.

panel: An area of a window that shows a different interpretation of the same part of a document.

paper rectangle: The rectangle marking the boundaries of the physical sheet of paper on which a page is printed.

parameter block: A data structure used to transfer information between applications and certain Operating System routines.

parameter RAM: In the clock chip, 20 bytes where settings such as those made with the Control Panel desk accessory are preserved.

parity bit: A data communications bit used to verify that data bits received by a device match the data bits transmitted by another device.

parity error: The condition resulting when the parity bit received by a device isn't what was expected.

part code: An integer between 1 and 253 that stands for a particular part of a control (possibly the entire control).

path reference number: A number that uniquely identifies an individual access path; assigned when the access path is created.

pattern: An 8-by-8 bit image, used to define a repeating design (such as stripes) or tone (such as gray).

pattern transfer mode: One of eight transfer modes for drawing lines or shapes with a pattern.

period: The time elapsed during one complete cycle of a wave.

phase: Some fraction of a wave cycle (measured from a fixed point on the wave).

physical end-of-file: The position of one byte past the last allocation block of a file; equal to 1 more than the maximum number of bytes the file can contain.

physical size: The actual number of bytes a memory block occupies within its heap zone.

picture: A saved sequence of QuickDraw drawing commands (and, optionally, picture comments) that you can play back later with a single procedure call; also, the image resulting from these commands.

picture comments: Data stored in the definition of a picture that doesn't affect the picture's appearance but may be used to provide additional information about the picture when it's played back.

picture frame: A rectangle, defined as part of a picture, that surrounds the picture and gives a frame of reference for scaling when the picture is played back.

pixel: The visual representation of a bit on the screen (white if the bit is 0, black if it's 1).

plane: The front-to-back position of a window on the desktop.

point: The intersection of a horizontal grid line and a vertical grid line on the coordinate plane, defined by a horizontal and a vertical coordinate; also, a typographical term meaning approximately 1/72 inch.

polygon: A sequence of connected lines, defined by QuickDraw line-drawing commands.

port: See **grafPort**.

portBits: The bit map of a grafPort.

portRect: A rectangle, defined as part of a grafPort, that encloses a subset of the bit map for use by the grafPort.

post: To place an event in the event queue for later processing.

prime routine: The part of a device driver's code that implements Device Manager Read and Write calls.

print record: A record containing all the information needed by the Printing Manager to perform a particular printing job.

Printer Driver: The device driver for the currently installed printer.

printer resource file: A file containing all the resources needed to run the Printing Manager with a particular printer.

printing grafPort: A special grafPort customized for printing instead of drawing on the screen.

Printing Manager: The routines and data types that enable applications to communicate with the Printer Driver to print on any variety of printer via the same interface.

processor priority: Bits 8-10 of the MC68000's status register, indicating which interrupts will be processed and which will be ignored.

proportional font: A font whose characters all have character widths that are proportional to their image width.

protocol: A well-defined set of communications rules.

protocol handler: A software process in a node that recognizes different kinds of frames by their ALAP type and services them.

protocol handler table: A list of the protocol handlers for a node.

purge: To remove a relocatable block from the heap, leaving its master pointer allocated but set to NIL.

purge bit: A bit in the master pointer to a relocatable block that indicates whether the block is currently purgeable.

purge warning procedure: A procedure associated with a particular heap zone that's called whenever a block is purged from that zone.

purgeable block: A relocatable block that can be purged from the heap.

queue: A list of identically structured entries linked together by pointers.

QuickDraw: The part of the Toolbox that performs all graphic operations on the Macintosh screen.

radio button: A standard Macintosh control that displays a setting, either on or off, and is part of a group in which only one button can be on at a time.

RAM: The Macintosh's random access memory, which contains exception vectors, buffers used by hardware devices, the system and application heaps, the stack, and other information used by applications.

read/write permission: Information associated with an access path that indicates whether the file can be read from, written to, both read from and written to, or whatever the file's open permission allows.

reallocate: To allocate new space in the heap for a purged block, updating its master pointer to point to its new location.

reference number: A number greater than 0, returned by the Resource Manager when a resource file is opened, by which you can refer to that file. In Resource Manager routines that expect a reference number, 0 represents the system resource file.

reference value: In a window record or control record, a 32-bit field that an application program may store into and access for any purpose.

region: An arbitrary area or set of areas on the QuickDraw coordinate plane. The outline of a region should be one or more closed loops.

register-based routine: A Toolbox or Operating System routine that receives its parameters and returns its results, if any, in registers.

relative handle: A handle to a relocatable block expressed as the offset of its master pointer within the heap zone, rather than as the absolute memory address of the master pointer.

release: To free an allocated area of memory, making it available for reuse.

release timer: A timer for determining when an exactly-once response buffer can be released.

relocatable block: A block that can be moved within the heap during compaction.

resource: Data or code stored in a resource file and managed by the Resource Manager.

resource attribute: One of several characteristics, specified by bits in a resource reference, that determine how the resource should be dealt with.

resource data: In a resource file, the data that comprises a resource.

resource file: The resource fork of a file.

resource fork: The part of a file that contains data used by an application (such as menus, fonts, and icons). The resource fork of an application file also contains the application code itself.

resource header: At the beginning of a resource file, data that gives the offsets to and lengths of the resource data and resource map.

resource ID: A number that, together with the resource type, identifies a resource in a resource file. Every resource has an ID number.

Resource Manager: The part of the Toolbox that reads and writes resources.

resource map: In a resource file, data that is read into memory when the file is opened and that, given a resource specification, leads to the corresponding resource data.

resource name: A string that, together with the resource type, identifies a resource in a resource file. A resource may or may not have a name.

resource reference: In a resource map, an entry that identifies a resource and contains either an offset to its resource data in the resource file or a handle to the data if it's already been read into memory.

resource specification: A resource type and either a resource ID or a resource name.

resource type: The type of a resource in a resource file, designated by a sequence of four characters (such as 'MENU' for a menu).

response BDS: A data structure used to pass response information to the ATP module.

result code: An integer indicating whether a routine completed its task successfully or was prevented by some error condition (or other special condition, such as reaching the end of a file).

resume procedure: A procedure within an application that allows the application to recover from system errors.

retry count: The maximum number of retransmissions for an NBP or ATP packet.

retry interval: The time between retransmissions of a packet by NBP or ATP.

ROM: The Macintosh's permanent read-only memory, which contains the routines for the Toolbox and Operating System, and the various system traps.

routine selector: An integer that's pushed onto the stack before the _PackN macro is invoked, to identify which routine to execute. (N is the resource ID of a package; all macros for calling routines in the package expand to invoke _PackN.)

routing table: A table in a bridge that contains routing information.

Routing Table Maintenance Protocol (RTMP): An AppleTalk protocol that's used internally by AppleTalk to maintain tables for routing datagrams through an internet.

row width: The number of bytes in each row of a bit image.

RTMP: See **Routing Table Maintenance Protocol**.

RTMP socket: The socket in a node used to implement RTMP.

RTMP stub: The RTMP code in a nonbridge node.

scaling factor: A value, given as a fraction, that specifies the amount a character should be stretched or shrunk before it's drawn.

SCC: See **Serial Communications Controller**.

scrap: A place where cut or copied data is stored.

scrap file: The file containing the desk scrap (usually named "Clipboard File").

Scrap Manager: The part of the Toolbox that enables cutting and pasting between applications, desk accessories, or an application and a desk accessory.

screen buffer: A block of memory from which the video display reads the information to be displayed.

sector: Disk space composed of 512 consecutive bytes of standard information and 12 bytes of file tags.

segment: One of several parts into which the code of an application may be divided. Not all segments need to be in memory at the same time.

Segment Loader: The part of the Operating System that loads the code of an application into memory, either as a single unit or divided into dynamically loaded segments.

selection range: The series of characters (inversely highlighted), or the character position (marked with a blinking caret), at which the next editing operation will occur.

sequence number: A number from 0 to 7, assigned to an ATP response datagram to indicate its ordering within the response.

Serial Communications Controller (SCC): The chip that handles serial I/O through the modem and printer ports.

serial data: Data communicated over a single-path communication line, one bit at a time.

Serial Driver: A device driver that controls communication, via serial ports, between applications and serial peripheral devices.

signature: A four-character sequence that uniquely identifies an application to the Finder.

socket: A logical entity within the node of a network.

socket client: A software process in a node that owns a socket.

socket listener: The portion of a socket client that receives and services datagrams addressed to that socket.

socket number: An identifier for a socket.

socket table: A listing of all the socket listeners for each active socket in a node.

software overrun error: The condition that occurs when an input driver's buffer becomes full.

solid shape: A shape that's filled in with any pattern.

sound buffer: A block of memory from which the sound generator reads the information to create an audio waveform.

Sound Driver: The device driver that controls sound generation in an application.

sound procedure: A procedure associated with an alert that will emit one of up to four sounds from the Macintosh's speaker. Its integer parameter ranges from 0 to 3 and specifies which sound.

source transfer mode: One of eight transfer modes for drawing text or transferring any bit image between two bit maps.

space state: The state of a transmission line indicating a binary 0.

spool printing: Writing a representation of a document's printed image to disk or to memory, and then printing it (as opposed to immediate draft printing).

square-wave synthesizer: The part of the Sound Driver used to produce less harmonic sounds than the four-tone synthesizer, such as beeps.

stack: The area of memory in which space is allocated and released in LIFO (last-in-first-out) order.

stack-based routine: A Toolbox or Operating System routine that receives its parameters and returns its results, if any, on the stack.

stack frame: The area of the stack used by a routine for its parameters, return address, local variables, and temporary storage.

stage: Every alert has four stages, corresponding to consecutive occurrences of the alert, and a different response may be specified for each stage.

Standard File Package: A Macintosh package for presenting the standard user interface when a file is to be saved or opened.

start bit: A serial data communications bit that signals that the next bits transmitted are data bits.

status information: Information transmitted to an application by a device driver. It may indicate the current mode of operation, the readiness of the device, the occurrence of errors, and so on.

status routine: The part of a device driver's code that implements Device Manager Status calls.

stop bit: A serial data communications bit that signals the end of data bits.

structure region: An entire window; its complete "structure".

style: See **character style**.

style dialog: A dialog that sets options affecting the page dimensions; associated with the Page Setup command.

synchronous execution: After calling a routine synchronously, an application cannot continue execution until the routine is completed.

synthesizer: See **free-form, four-tone,** or **square-wave synthesizer**.

synthesizer buffer: A description of the sound to be generated by a synthesizer.

system error alert: An alert box displayed by the System Error Handler.

system error alert table: A resource that determines the appearance and function of system error alerts.

System Error Handler: The part of the Operating System that assumes control when a fatal system error occurs.

system error ID: An ID number that appears in a system error alert to identify the error.

system event mask: A global event mask that controls which types of events get posted into the event queue.

system font: The font that the system uses (in menus, for example). Its name is Chicago.

system font size: The size of text drawn by the system in the system font; 12 points.

system heap: The portion of the heap reserved for use by the Operating System.

system heap zone: The heap zone provided by the Memory Manager for use by the Operating System; equivalent to the system heap.

system resource: A resource in the system resource file.

system resource file: A resource file containing standard resources, accessed if a requested resource wasn't found in any of the other resource files that were searched.

system startup information: Certain configurable system parameters that are stored in the first two logical blocks of a volume and read in at system startup.

system window: A window in which a desk accessory is displayed.

TextEdit: The part of the Toolbox that supports the basic text entry and editing capabilities of a standard Macintosh application.

TextEdit scrap: The place where certain TextEdit routines store the characters most recently cut or copied from text.

thousands separator: The character that separates every three digits to the left of the decimal point.

thumb: The Control Manager's term for the scroll box (the indicator of a scroll bar).

tick: A sixtieth of a second.

Toolbox: Same as **User Interface Toolbox**.

Toolbox Event Manager: The part of the Toolbox that allows your application program to monitor the user's actions with the mouse, keyboard, and keypad.

Toolbox Utilities: The part of the Toolbox that performs generally useful operations such as fixed-point arithmetic, string manipulation, and logical operations on bits.

track: Disk space composed of 8 to 12 consecutive sectors. A track corresponds to one ring of constant radius around the disk.

transaction: A request-response communication between two ATP clients. See **transaction request** and **transaction response**.

transaction ID: An identifier assigned to a transaction.

transaction request: The initial part of a transaction in which one socket client asks another to perform an operation and return a response.

transaction response: The concluding part of a transaction in which one socket client returns requested information or simply confirms that a requested operation was performed.

Transcendental Functions Package: A Macintosh package that contains trigonometric, logarithmic, exponential, and financial functions, as well as a random number generator.

transfer mode: A specification of which Boolean operation QuickDraw should perform when drawing or when transferring a bit image from one bit map to another.

trap dispatch table: A table in RAM containing the addresses of all Toolbox and Operating System routines in encoded form.

trap dispatcher: The part of the Operating System that examines a trap word to determine what operation it stands for, looks up the address of the corresponding routine in the trap dispatch table, and jumps to the routine.

trap macro: A macro that assembles into a trap word, used for calling a Toolbox or Operating System routine from assembly language.

trap number: The identifying number of a Toolbox or Operating System routine; an index into the trap dispatch table.

trap word: An unimplemented instruction representing a call to a Toolbox or Operating System routine.

unimplemented instruction: An instruction word that doesn't correspond to any valid machine-language instruction but instead causes a trap.

unit number: The number of each device driver's entry in the unit table.

unit table: A 128-byte nonrelocatable block containing a handle to the device control entry for each device driver.

unlock: To allow a relocatable block to be moved during heap compaction.

unmounted volume: A volume that hasn't been inserted into a disk drive and had descriptive information read from it, or a volume that previously was mounted and has since had the memory used by it released.

unpurgeable block: A relocatable block that can't be purged from the heap.

update event: An event generated by the Window Manager when a window's contents need to be redrawn.

update region: A window region consisting of all areas of the content region that have to be redrawn.

user bytes: Four bytes in an ATP header provided for use by ATP's clients.

User Interface Toolbox: The software in the Macintosh ROM that helps you implement the standard Macintosh user interface in your application.

validity status: A number stored in parameter RAM designating whether the last attempt to write there was successful. (The number is $A8 if so.)

variation code: The part of a window or control definition ID that distinguishes closely related types of windows or controls.

VBL task: A task performed during the vertical retrace interrupt.

vector table: A table of interrupt vectors in low memory.

version data: In an application's resource file, a resource that has the application's signature as its resource type; typically a string that gives the name, version number, and date of the application.

version number: A number from 0 to 255 used to distinguish between files with the same name.

Versatile Interface Adapter (VIA): The chip that handles most of the Macintosh's I/O and interrupts.

vertical blanking interrupt: See **vertical retrace interrupt**.

vertical blanking interval: The time between the display of the last pixel on the bottom line of the screen and the first one on the top line.

vertical retrace interrupt: An interrupt generated 60 times a second by the Macintosh video circuitry while the beam of the display tube returns from the bottom of the screen to the top; also known as vertical blanking interrupt.

Vertical Retrace Manager: The part of the Operating System that schedules and executes tasks during the vertical retrace interrupt.

vertical retrace queue: A list of the tasks to be executed during the vertical retrace interrupt.

VIA: See **Versatile Interface Adapter**.

view rectangle: In TextEdit, the rectangle in which the text is visible.

visible control: A control that's drawn in its window (but may be completely overlapped by another window or other object on the screen).

visible window: A window that's drawn in its plane on the desktop (but may be completely overlapped by another window or object on the screen).

visRgn: The region of a grafPort, manipulated by the Window Manager, that's actually visible on the screen.

volume: A piece of storage medium formatted to contain files; usually a disk or part of a disk. A 400K-byte 3 1/2-inch Macintosh disk is one volume.

volume allocation block map: A list of 12-bit entries, one for each allocation block, that indicate whether the block is currently allocated to a file, whether it's free for use, or which block is next in the file. Block maps exist both on volumes and in memory.

volume attributes: Information contained on volumes and in memory indicating whether the volume is locked, whether it's busy (in memory only), and whether the volume control block matches the volume information (in memory only).

volume buffer: Memory used initially to load the master directory block, and used thereafter for reading from files that are opened without an access path buffer.

volume control block: A nonrelocatable block that contains volume-specific information, including the volume information from the master directory block.

volume-control-block queue: A list of the volume control blocks for all mounted volumes.

volume index: A number identifying a mounted volume listed in the volume-control-block queue. The first volume in the queue has an index of 1, and so on.

volume information: Volume-specific information contained on a volume, including the volume name and the number of files on the volume.

volume name: A sequence of up to 27 printing characters that identifies a volume; followed by a colon (:) in File Manager routine calls, to distinguish it from a file name.

volume reference number: A unique number assigned to a volume as it's mounted, used to refer to the volume.

waveform: The physical shape of a wave.

waveform description: A sequence of bytes describing a waveform.

wavelength: The horizontal extent of one complete cycle of a wave.

window: An object on the desktop that presents information, such as a document or a message.

window class: In a window record, an indication of whether a window is a system window, a dialog or alert window, or a window created directly by the application.

window definition function: A function called by the Window Manager when it needs to perform certain type-dependent operations on a particular type of window, such as drawing the window frame.

window definition ID: A number passed to window-creation routines to indicate the type of window. It consists of the window definition function's resource ID and a variation code.

window frame: The structure region of a window minus its content region.

window list: A list of all windows ordered according to their front-to-back positions on the desktop.

Window Manager: The part of the Toolbox that provides routines for creating and manipulating windows.

Window Manager port: A grafPort that has the entire screen as its portRect and is used by the Window Manager to draw window frames.

window record: The internal representation of a window, where the Window Manager stores all the information it needs for its operations on that window.

window template: A resource that contains information from which the Window Manager can create a window.

word: In TextEdit, any series of printing characters, excluding spaces (ASCII code $20) but including nonbreaking spaces (ASCII code $CA).

word wraparound: Keeping words from being split between lines when text is drawn.

write data structure: A data structure used to pass information to the ALAP or DDP modules.

zone: An arbitrary subset of AppleTalk networks in an internet. See also **heap zone**.

zone header: The internal "housekeeping" information maintained by the Memory Manager at the beginning of each heap zone.

zone pointer: A pointer to a zone record.

zone record: A data structure representing a heap zone.

zone trailer: A minimum-size free block marking the end of a heap zone.

INDEX

Index

Index